EIGHTH EDITION

SOCIAL GERONTOLOGY

A MULTIDISCIPLINARY PERSPECTIVE

Nancy R. Hooyman
University of Washington

H. Asuman Kiyak
University of Washington

PEARSON

Boston New York San Francisco
Mexico City Montreal Toronto London Madrid Munich Paris
Hong Kong Singapore Tokyo Cape Town Sydney

Executive Editor: Jeff Lasser
Series Editorial Assistant: Lauren Houlihan
Associate Editor: Deb Hanlon
Senior Marketing Manager: Kelly May
Production Editor: Claudine Bellanton
Editorial Production Service: Nesbitt Graphics, Inc.
Composition Buyer: Linda Cox
Manufacturing Buyer: Debbie Rossi
Electronic Composition: Nesbitt Graphics, Inc.
Interior Design: Nesbitt Graphics, Inc.
Cover Administrator: Linda Knowles
Cover Designer: Susan Paradise

For related titles and support materials, visit our online catalog at www.ablongman.com.

Between the time website information is gathered and then published, it is not unusual for some sites to have closed. Also, the transcription of URLs can result in typographical errors. The publisher would appreciate notification where these errors occur so that they may be corrected in subsequent editions.

ISBN-13: 978-0-205-52561-4   ISBN-10: 0-205-52561-X

Library of Congress Cataloging-in-Publication Data

Hooyman, Nancy R.
    Social gerontology: a multidisciplinary perspective / Nancy R. Hooyman, H. Asuman Kiyak.—8th ed.
       p.   cm.
    Includes bibliographical references and index.
    ISBN-13: 978-0-205-52561-4
    ISBN-10: 0-205-52561-X
  1. Gerontology. 2. Aging. 3. Older people—United States. I. Kiyak, H. Asuman II. Title.
HQ1061.H583 2008
305.26—dc22

                                                                    2007015956

Printed in the United States of America

10 9 8 7 6 5 4 3   RRD-VA 11 10 09 08

*In dedication to students, faculty, and practitioners
who are committed to enhancing the quality of life of older
adults and their families.*

—NRH

*With love and gratitude to Joe for his support and
understanding; with love to Lara*

—HAK

*With hope that our daughters Mani and Lara will inherit
a world that supports active aging*

—NRH and HAK

CONTENTS

v

chapter 2 Aging in Other Countries and across Cultures in the United States   43

part two
The Biological and Physiological Context of Social Aging   67

chapter 3 The Social Consequences of Physical Aging   70

c h a p t e r   **4** Managing Chronic Diseases and Promoting
Well-Being in Old Age   **114**

chapter **7** Love, Intimacy, and Sexuality
in Old Age   **271**

p a r t four

The Social Context of Aging 301

c h a p t e r 8 Social Theories of Aging 305

c h a p t e r 9 The Importance of Social Supports: Family,
Friends, Neighbors, and Communities 333

chapter **10** Opportunities and Challenges
of Informal Caregiving   385

chapter **11** Living Arrangements and
Social Interactions   **429**

chapter **12** Productive Aging: Paid and Nonpaid
Roles and Activities 474

chapter **13** Death, Dying, Bereavement,
and Widowhood 539

c h a p t e r **14** The Resilience of Elders of Color   590

chapter **17** Health and Long-Term Care Policy and Programs   716

PREFACE

This edition of *Social Gerontology: A Multidisciplinary Perspective,* is in many ways a significant celebration for us. Its publication, 20 years after the first edition, celebrates a long collaborative relationship, many significant personal and professional events, and perhaps most importantly, a profound change in the way society views aging and older adults. We are moving from the widely held perspective that aging represents decline to the more optimistic viewpoint that people can influence their own future: Our lifestyles, to a large extent, during youth and middle age affect our health, cognition, and social lives in later years. This dramatic paradigm shift in the field of gerontology is attributable to two parallel and interactive processes. First, a growing body of research demonstrates the role of individual choices and behaviors in whether we age in a healthy, active manner, or with multiple chronic diseases and without supportive social networks. While genetic and societal factors, especially educational and economic opportunities, affect some aspects of aging, many recent studies provide evidence that even older adults with dementia, chronic systemic diseases, and living in poverty because of lifelong disadvantage nevertheless have resilience and can experience active aging in ways that were rarely recognized in the past. Another trend in the past 20 years has been society's recognition of the continuing contribution of older adults to our cultural, family, and work lives, as reflected in the increasing attention given to older adults' productivity and civic engagement. We are moving away from the perspective that aging means withdrawal from active participation in society to one where older adults remain an integral part of our communi-ties. These changes are reflected in this 20th anniversary revision of *Social Gerontology,* our 8th edition.

The subtitle of *Social Gerontology* reflects our focus on aging as a process with multiple facets—physiological, emotional, cognitive, economic, and interpersonal—all of which interact to influence our social functioning and well-being. It is a fascinating process because these changes occur differently in each one of us. There is considerable truth to the statement that, as we grow older, we become more *unlike* each other.

Aging is also a process that attracts the attention of the media, politicians, business and industry, and the general public, largely because of the visibility and influence of aging baby boomers. Changes in the numbers and proportion of older people in our population have numerous implications for societal structures, including the family, health and social services, long-term care, pension and retirement policies, political processes, recreational services, voluntarism, and housing. In addition, these changes are of growing concern because of the problems of poverty, inadequate housing, and chronic disease faced by some older people—particularly women, ethnic minorities, the oldest-old, and those living alone. Public officials as well as individuals in the private sector must address the challenge of planning for a not-so-distant future when there will be more people over age 65 than ever before.

These changes have also meant that a growing number of colleges and universities now offer courses in gerontology, the study of aging. The goal of many of these courses is to prepare students to understand the process of aging and the diversity among older people and to be able to work effectively with older adults and their families. These programs also attempt to enhance students' personal understanding of their own and others' aging. Frequently, students take such a course simply to meet a requirement, but they quickly learn how relevant the aging process is to their own lives. Thus, instructors are often faced with the need to help students see the connection between learning about aging and understanding their own behavior, the behavior of their parents, grandparents and other relatives, and eventually the behavior of their clients, consumers, or patients.

This book was first triggered by our experiences in teaching gerontology courses. In doing so, we were unable to locate a textbook that conveyed the excitement and relevance of understanding the aging process or one that adequately addressed the interaction between the biological, physiological, psychological, and social aspects of aging. We were frustrated by the lack of a text that was comprehensive, thorough, and current in its review of the rapidly growing research on older adults. As a sociologist/social worker and a psychologist, we have been committed to writing and continuously updating a text that can be useful to a wide range of disciplines, including nursing, social work, sociology, psychology, health education, and the allied health professions. We are pleased that we have created a text that both undergraduate and graduate students find helpful and even inspiring, both personally and professionally.

Aims and Focus

The primary focus of this book is on social gerontology. As the title implies, however, our goal is to present the diversities of the aging experience, the interaction between biological, psychological, and social forces on aging, and the older population in a multidisciplinary manner. As you will see throughout the 17 chapters, a careful examination of the social lives of older people requires a basic understanding of the historical, cultural, biological, physiological, psychological, and social contexts of aging across the life course. It is important to understand the changes that occur within the aging individual, how these changes influence interactions with social and physical environments, and how the older person is, in turn, affected by such interactions. Throughout this book, the impact of these dynamic interactions between older people and their environments on their quality of life is a unifying theme.

Social gerontology encompasses a wide range of topics with exciting research in so many domains. This book does not cover all these areas, but rather highlights major research findings that illuminate the complex processes of aging. Through such factual information, we intend to dispel some of the myths and negative attitudes about aging. We also hope to encourage the reader to pursue this field, both academically and for the personal rewards that come from gaining insight into older people's lives. Because the field is so complex and rapidly changing, more recent research findings may appear to contradict earlier studies as well as many of your own beliefs about aging and the older population. We have attempted to be thorough in presenting a multiplicity of theoretical perspectives and empirical data to ensure that the reader has as full and accurate a picture of the field as possible. We have tried to include up-to-date content throughout, but because the field—and especially social, health, and long-term care policies and programs—changes so rapidly, some current revisions will inevitably be out of date by the time the text is published. We encourage you to keep up with these changes by reading journals and periodicals that report on recent research findings and policies related to aging and older adults. Research Navigator, an important feature of this textbook introduced in the previous edition, provides up-to-date information on most of the issues covered in the book.

Features

This book begins by reviewing major demographic, societal, and cultural changes, and their implications for the development of the field of social gerontology, as well as methods used to study aging and older people. We then turn to the normal biological and physiological changes that affect older people's daily functioning, as well as their risk of chronic diseases, how they cope with these conditions, and their use of health and long-term care services. The third section considers normal age-related psychological changes in sensory functions, learning and memory, personality, cognitive ability and sexuality, as well as mental health issues affecting older adults. Given our emphasis on how such physical and psychological changes affect the social aspects of aging, the fourth section examines social theories of aging, the social context of the family, friends, and other multigenerational supports, current living arrangements and community-based innovations in long-term care, productivity and social and civic engagement in the later years, and the conditions under which people die. Throughout the book, the differential effects that these changes have on women and ethnic minorities are identified, with two chapters focusing specifically on such differences as well as the strength and resilience of these two rapidly growing populations. We conclude by turning to the larger context of social, health, and long-term care policies. To highlight the application of research findings to everyday situations, each chapter integrates discussions of policy and practice implications of the aging process, career opportunities, and some predictions regarding the experiences of future cohorts of elders. Vignettes of older people in different situations, Points to Ponder, and updated tables, figures, and boxes providing summaries or case examples attempt to bring to life many of the concepts discussed in these chapters.

New to This Edition

The positive responses of faculty and students to the first seven editions suggest that we have been successful in achieving our goals for this book. Based on feedback from faculty who have used the text in different colleges and universities nationally and internationally, the 8th edition builds on and expands many of the changes made in the previous edition. The book is designed to be completed in a 16-week semester, but readers can proceed at a faster pace through the chapters and select only the chapters most relevant to their focus of study. Themes that underlie each chapter are the importance of congruence between elders and their environment, and of the interaction between the biological, psychological, and social aspects of aging, all within a life course perspective that takes account of historical, economic, cultural, and structural contexts.

New research findings are presented on extending both years and quality of life, enhancing active aging, and maintaining productivity (i.e., contributing to society in a wide range of ways) through both paid and unpaid activities. These concepts are also critiqued. We have added new evidence-based findings on health and long-term care, including unpaid family caregivers and underpaid direct care workers, as well as public policies supporting them, such as consumer-directed care, integrated care systems, and Medicaid waivers for home and community-based care. Recent developments in the areas of preventing, diagnosing, and treating depression and dementias such as Alzheimer's disease are reviewed. The benefits of health promotion and of spirituality for achieving and maintaining active aging also has growing research support, as demonstrated in this edition. The chapters on informal supports and family caregiving recognize the growing number of grandparents as primary caregivers of grandchildren and the policy and programmatic barriers confronting them. The sections on technology, including growing computer use by elders, and universal design that help people "age in place" are expanded. At the same time, however, we recognize that some older adults face cognitive and physical declines that preclude their living autonomously. Research and interventions to change the culture of long-term care and to develop elder-friendly communities are described. The evolution of newer models of long-term care such as assisted living, adult family homes, and adult day health is discussed. The growing research on gay, lesbian, bisexual, and transsexual (GLBT) older adults and attendant policy and practice implications are incorporated in many chapters. Both the resilience of and the problems faced by older women and elders of color are emphasized. Given the dramatically changing political arena, the chapters on social, health, and long-term care policies reflect contemporary debates related to privatization, federal and state budget cuts, and the impact of the 2003 Medicare prescription drug law. Culturally competent methods to understand and meet the needs of an increasingly diverse older population are also identified throughout.

Each chapter begins with bulleted points to be covered. The glossary defines key terms, while more resources, especially Internet resources, are added at the end of each chapter.

Supplements

For Instructors

Instructor's Manual/Test Bank. The Instructor's Manual contains chapter summaries, chapter outlines, lists of key terms and people, discussion topics, classroom activities and projects, suggested films, and suggested websites. The Test Bank contains multiple choice, true-false, short answer, and essay questions.

Computerized Testing. The printed Test Bank is also available through Allyn and Bacon's computerized testing system, TestGen EQ. This fully networkable test-generating software is available on a multi-platform CD-ROM for Windows and Macintosh. The user-friendly interface allows you to view, edit, and add questions, transfer questions to tests, and print tests in a variety of fonts.

PowerPoint. The PowerPoint presentation contains a set of lecture outline slides for each chapter.

For Students

MySocKit for *Social Gerontology*, 8/e. MySocKit (www.mysockit) is a new online resource that contains chapter summaries, practice tests, flashcards, *New York Times* articles, audio and video activities, writing and research tutorials, access to scholarly literature on aging through Research Navigator, and materials for using the "Growing Old in a New Age" telecourse (formerly published in a print telecourse guide). MySocKit is available with *Social Gerontology*, 8/e when a MySocKit access code card is value-packed with the text.

A Note on Terminology

As with most other disciplines, the field of gerontology is constantly evolving and recognizing the problem of language that makes sweeping generalizations or has negative connotations. The commonly used terms *elderly, the aged,* and *seniors* have come to be associated with negative images of the older population. For this reason, we have chosen the terms *older adults, older persons,* and *elders* throughout this textbook. These terms parallel those of younger person/adult. The term *elder,* used widely among Native Americans, typically conveys respect and honor. Another change in terminology is our use of the word *Latino* in place of *Hispanic* wherever appropriate. This is because a growing number of scholars in this community have suggested that *Hispanic* has been associated with colonialism and the conquest of Spanish-speaking people in the Americas. Except where dictated by publications such as reports of the U.S. Census Bureau (where *Hispanic* is the standard term), we have chosen to refer to older adults from Spanish-speaking origins as *Latinos* and *Latinas*.

Acknowledgments

We are grateful to the many people who have contributed significantly to the successful completion of the 8th edition of *Social Gerontology*. In particular, we thank Andrea Panniero for her diligent literature and Web searches, and for updating our many charts and graphs. We thank Lisa Bancroft, Kevin Kawamoto, and Toni Moe for their help with literature searches and references. Their willingness to do whatever tasks necessary allowed us to concentrate on the big picture! We also thank our many colleagues around the United States who have given us valuable and candid feedback about the 7th edition that has helped us in preparing the 8th edition. They include: Boaz Kahuna, Cleveland State University; Jenni Fauchier, Metropolitan Community College; and Jacquelyn B. Frank, Illinois State University. It is feedback from faculty and students who value this text that motivates and sustains us through the long process of updating each edition. It means a great deal to both of us when a student or faculty member approaches us at a conference or meeting to convey how much they learned from the text. We hope this new edition excites a new generation of students about the possibilities of careers in gerontology.

Our families and good friends have been a mainstay of support throughout the preparation of all eight editions of this book, and we take this opportunity to express our gratitude to all of them.

ABOUT THE AUTHORS

Nancy R. Hooyman

Nancy R. Hooyman holds the Hooyman Professorship of Gerontology and is dean emeritus and co-Director of the Institute for Multigenerational Health, Development and Equality at the School of Social Work at the University of Washington. Her MSW and Ph.D. in sociology are from the University of Michigan. She is nationally recognized for her scholarship in aging and multigenerational policy and practice, gender inequities in family caregiving, and feminist gerontology. In addition to this textbook, Dr. Hooyman is the co-author of *Living through Loss: Interventions across the Life Span; Taking Care of Aging Family Members;* and *Feminist Perspectives on Family Care: Policies for Gender Justice.* She has published over 120 articles and chapters and is a frequent national and international presenter on issues related to gerontology, a multigenerational perspective, and women. She is Co-Principal Investigator of the Council on Social Work Education's National Center for Gerontological Social Work Education, funded by the John A. Hartford Foundation, and actively involved with the other Hartford Geriatric Social Work Initiatives. A Fellow in the Gerontological Society of America, Dr. Hooyman is currently chair of GSA's Social Research, Policy and Practice Section. She received the Career Achievement Award from the Association for Gerontology in Social Work Education.

H. Asuman Kiyak

H. Asuman Kiyak is Director of the Institute on Aging, professor in the School of Dentistry, and adjunct professor in the Departments of Architecture and Psychology at the University of Washington. She obtained her M.A. and Ph.D. in psychology at Wayne State University. Professor Kiyak has been the recipient of major research grants from NIH, CDC, AOA, the State of Washington, and private foundations in the areas of health promotion and health service utilization by older adults, and in person–environment adaptation to Alzheimer's disease by patients and their caregivers. She has published over 130 articles and 35 chapters in these areas and is known nationally and internationally for her research on geriatric dental care and the application of psychological theory to health promotion. In 2000 she received the Distinguished Scientist Award from the International Association for Dental Research, and has served as president of the Geriatric Oral Research, and the Behavioral Sciences and Health Services Research Groups of IADR. Dr. Kiyak was Principal Investigator of a recently completed clinical trial in geriatric dentistry funded by the National Institute of Dental and Craniofacial Research, and two studies of a community-based health promotion study funded by the CDC. She is collaborating with Intel to test new technologies to help older adults remain active and independent. In 2003 she was named Distinguished Professor of Geriatrics at UCLA, and received the Teaching Excellence Award from the University of Washington Educational Outreach division. Professor Kiyak is a Fellow in the Gerontological Society of America.

The Field of Social Gerontology

Toward Understanding Aging

From the perspective of youth and middle age, old age seems a remote and, to some, an undesirable period of life. Throughout history, humans have tried to prolong youth and to delay aging. The attempts to discover a substance to rejuvenate the body and mind have driven explorers to far corners of the globe and inspired alchemists and scientists to search for ways to restore youth and extend life. Indeed, the discovery of Florida by Ponce de Leon in 1513 was an accident, as he searched for a fountain in Bimini whose waters were rumored to bring back one's youth. Medieval Latin alchemists believed that eating gold could add years to life and spent many years trying to produce a digestible form of gold. In the seventeenth century, a popular belief was that smelling fresh earth each morning could prolong one's youth. The theme of prolonging or restoring youth is evident today in advertisements for skin creams, soaps, vitamins, and certain foods; in the popularity of cosmetic surgery; in books, movies, and T.V. shows that feature attractive, youthful-looking older characters; and even in medical research that is testing technological methods to replace depleted hormones in older people in an attempt to rejuvenate aging skin and physical and sexual functioning. One organization, by its name, reveals its bias that aging is a disease or process that can be fought or prevented. The International Academy of Anti-Aging Medicine actually promotes preventive and naturopathic medicine, but its name suggests a more negative view of aging than does its goal.

All these concerns point to underlying fears and denial of aging. Many of our concerns and fears arise from misconceptions about what happens to our bodies, our minds, our status in society, and our social lives as we reach our 70s, 80s, and beyond. They arise, in part, from negative attitudes toward older people within our own culture. These attitudes are sometimes identified as manifestations of **ageism,** a term that was coined by Robert Butler, the first Director of the National Institute on Aging, to describe

Most people are unprepared for the physical and cognitive signs of aging. As Leo Tolstoy noted, "Old age is the most unexpected of all things that happen to a man."

stereotypes about old age (1969). As is true for sexism and racism, ageism attributes certain characteristics to all members of a group solely because of a characteristic they share—in this case, their age. In fact, ageism is one prejudice that we are all likely to encounter if we live long enough, regardless of our gender, ethnic minority status, social class, or sexual orientation. A frequent result of ageism is discriminatory behavior against the target group (i.e., older persons). For example, some aging advocates argue that older, experienced workers are encouraged to retire early because of stereotypes about older people's abilities and productivity. Instead, advocates suggest that employers should consider each worker's skills and experience—not age—when organizational restructuring requires layoffs. Although attitudes toward older adults have improved in the past three decades, partially because of expanded education about the aging process,

"pockets" of negative attitudes persist, along with a "new ageism" that resents elders for their economic progress and tax burden (Palmore, 2004).

To distinguish the realities of aging from the social stereotypes surrounding this process requires an understanding of the "normal" changes that can be expected in the aging body, in mental and emotional functioning, and in social interactions and status. Aging can then be understood as a phase of growth and development—a universal biological phenomenon. Accordingly, the normal processes due to age alone need to be differentiated from pathological changes or disease. As life expectancy increases, as the older proportion of our population grows, and as more of us can look forward to becoming older ourselves, concerns and questions about the aging process continue to attract widespread public and professional attention.

The Growth of Social Gerontology

The Field of Gerontology

The growing interest in understanding the process of aging has given rise to the multidisciplinary field of **gerontology**, the study of the biological, psychological, and social aspects of aging. Gerontologists include researchers and practitioners in such diverse fields as biology, medicine, nursing, dentistry, social work, physical and occupational therapy, psychology, psychiatry, sociology, economics, political science, pharmacy, and anthropology. These individuals are concerned with many aspects of aging, from studying and describing the cellular processes involved to seeking ways to improve the quality of life for older people. **Geriatrics** focuses on how to prevent or manage the diseases of aging. Geriatrics has become a specialty in medicine, nursing, and dentistry, and is receiving more attention with the increase in the number of older people who have long-term health problems.

Gerontologists view aging in terms of four distinct processes that are examined throughout this book:

- *Chronological aging* is the definition of aging on the basis of a person's years from birth. Thus, a 75-year-old is chronologically older than a 45-year-old. Chronological age is not necessarily related to a person's biological or physical age, nor to his or her psychological or social age, as we will emphasize throughout this book. For example, we may remark that someone "looks younger (or older)" or "acts younger (or older)" than her or his age. This implies that the individual's *biological* or *psychological* or *social age* is incongruent with the person's *chronological age*.
- *Biological aging* refers to the physical changes that reduce the efficiency of organ systems, such as the lungs, heart, and circulatory system. A major cause of biological aging is the decline in the number of cell replications as an organism becomes chronologically older. Another factor is the loss of certain types of cells that do not replicate. This type of aging can be determined by measuring the efficiency and functional abilities of an individual's organ systems, as well as physical activity levels. Indeed, some have referred to this as *functional aging* (Hayflick, 1996).
- *Psychological aging* includes the changes that occur in sensory and perceptual processes, mental functioning (e.g., memory, learning, and intelligence), adaptive capacity, and personality. Thus, an individual who is intellectually active and adapts well to new situations can be considered psychologically young.
- *Social aging* refers to an individual's changing roles and relationships with family and friends, in both paid and unpaid productive roles, and within organizations such as religious and political groups. As people age chronologically, biologically, and psychologically, their social roles and relationships also alter. The social context, which can vary considerably

for different people, determines the meaning of aging for an individual and whether the aging experience will be primarily negative or positive.

Social gerontologists study the impact of these aging processes on both older people and social structures. They also study social attitudes toward aging and the effects of these attitudes on older adults and opportunities available to them. For example, as a society, we have tended to undervalue older people and to assume that most of them are less intelligent than younger people; that they are unemployable, nonproductive, uninterested in interacting with younger people, forgetful, and asexual. As a result, they have been limited in their access to activities such as jobs in high-tech fields. The research reviewed throughout this book demonstrates that these stereotypes are not true for the great majority of older adults and that most continue to participate actively in society.

With the rapid growth in the number and diversity of older persons, societal myths and stereotypes are increasingly being challenged. The public has become more aware of older citizens' strengths, contributions to society, and potential for civic engagement. Accordingly, the status of older people and the way they are viewed by other segments of the U.S. population are changing. Contemporary advertising, for example, reflects the changing status of older people from a group that is viewed as weak, ill, and poor to one perceived as politically and economically powerful and, therefore, a growing market.

The emergence of age-based advocacy groups and increased political activity of older adults in the past 50 years have changed not only public perceptions, but also policies and programs such as Social Security and Medicare. Organized groups of older people have influenced retirement and pension policies, housing options, health and long-term care policy, and other services, although they do not speak with a unified voice on all issues. As described in Chapter 6, with scarce public resources, age-based advocacy is being replaced by the need for cross-generational collaboration today.

Equally significant in this area of study are the social, economic, and health problems that continue to affect a large percentage of older people. Even though older adults today are financially better off than they were 50 years ago, slightly less than 10 percent still fall below the U.S. government's official poverty line. Poverty is an even greater problem for women, older people of color, those living alone, and the oldest of the old. Although less than 5 percent of the older population resides in nursing homes at any given time, the number who will require long-term care at some point in their lives is increasing. Growing percentages of older people in the community face chronic diseases that may limit their daily activities. At the same time, however, health and long-term care costs have escalated. In general, older people pay a higher proportion of their income for health and long-term care than they have at any time in the past, and often lack access to publicly supported home- and community-based services. Therefore, many gerontologists are also concerned with developing public policy and practice interventions to address these problems.

Social Gerontology

The purpose of this book is to introduce you to *social gerontology.* This term was first used by Clark Tibbitts in 1954 to describe the area of gerontology that is concerned with the impact of social and sociocultural conditions on the process of aging and with the social consequences of this process. This field has grown as the extent to which aging differs across cultures and societies has been recognized.

Social gerontologists are interested in how the older population and the diversity of aging experiences both affect and are affected by the social structure. As discussed later in this chapter, older people are now the fastest-growing population segment in the United States. This fact has far-reaching social implications for health and long-term care, the workplace, pension and retirement practices, community facilities, housing design, and patterns of government and private spending. Already, it has led to new specialties in health care and long-term care; the growth of specialized services such as assisted living and adult day health programs; and a leisure industry aimed at the older population. Changes in the sociopolitical structure, in turn, affect characteristics of the older population and civic engagement initiatives. For example, the greater availability of secondary and higher education, health promotion programs, and retirement planning offers hope that future generations of older people will be better educated, healthier, economically more secure and socially engaged than the current generation.

What Is Aging?

Contrary to the messages on birthday cards, aging does not start at age 40 or 65. Even though we are less conscious of age-related changes in earlier stages of our lives, we are all aging from the moment of birth. In fact, **aging** in general refers to changes that take place in the organism throughout the life span—good, bad and neutral. Younger stages are referred to as *development* or *maturation,* because the individual develops and matures, both socially and physically, from birth through adolescence. After age 30, additional changes occur that reflect normal declines in all organ systems. This is called **senescence.** Senescence happens gradually throughout the body, ultimately reducing the viability of different bodily systems and increasing their vulnerability to disease. This is the final stage in the development of an organism.

POINTS TO PONDER

For each age group below, list one activity or event that you think is typical for that age. These might include marriage, attending school, learning to ride a bike. Then think of an activity or event that is not so typical:

	TYPICAL	ATYPICAL
Toddler (ages 2–4)		
Child (ages 4–12)		
Young adult (ages 18–24)		
Old person (age 65+)		

Our place in the social structure also changes throughout our life span. Every society is *age-graded*; that is, it assigns different roles, expectations, opportunities, status, and constraints to people of different ages. For example, there are common societal expectations about the appropriate age to attend school, begin work, have children, and retire—even though many people deviate from these expectations, and some of these expectations are changing as people live longer. To call someone a *toddler, child, young adult,* or an *old person* is to imply a full range of social characteristics. As we age, we pass through a sequence of defined stages, each with its own social norms and characteristics. In sum, age is a social construct with social meanings and implications.

The specific effects of age grading, or age stratification, vary across different cultures and historical time periods. A primitive society, for instance, has very different expectations associated with stages of childhood, adolescence, and old age from our contemporary American cultures. Even within our society, those who are old today have different experiences of aging than previous or future groups of older people, and expectations about when to go to school, enter or leave the workforce, or start a family are changing dramatically. The term **cohort** is used to describe groups of people who were born at approximately the same time and therefore share many common experiences. For example, cohorts now in their late 70s experienced the Great Depression, World War II, and the Korean War. These experiences shaped their lives. Its members include large numbers of immigrants who came to the United States in the first third of the twentieth century, and many who have grown up in rural areas. Their average levels of education are lower than those of later generations. Such factors set today's oldest-old population apart from other cohorts and must be taken into account in any studies of the aging process.

The Older Population Is Diverse

Throughout this book, we will refer to the phenomenon of aging and the population of older people. These terms are based, to some extent, on chronological criteria, but, more importantly, on individual differences in functional age. In fact, each of us differs somewhat in the way we define old age. You may know an 80-year-old who seems youthful and a 50-year-old whom you consider old. Older people also define themselves differently. Some individuals, even in their 80s, do not want to associate with "those old people," whereas others readily join age-based organizations and are proud of the years they have lived. There are significant differences among the "young-old" (ages 65–74), the "old-old" (ages 75–84), and the "oldest-old" (ages 85 and over) (Riley and Riley, 1986). In addition, intragenerational diversity exists even within these divisions.

Older people vary greatly in their health status, their productive activities, and their family situations. Some are still employed full- or part-time; most are retired. Most are healthy; some

POINTS TO PONDER

Discuss with friends and family some common terms used to describe older adults, such as "elderly," "old folks," and "elders." What images of aging and older people do these terms convey?

are frail, confused, or homebound. Most still live in a house or apartment; a small percentage are in nursing homes. Some receive large incomes from pensions and investments; many depend primarily on Social Security and have little discretionary income. Most men over age 65 are married, whereas women are more likely to become widowed and live alone as they age. For all these reasons, we cannot consider the social aspects of aging without also assessing the impact of individual variables such as physiological changes, health status, psychological well-being, socioeconomic class, gender, sexual orientation, and ethnic minority status. Recognizing this, many chapters in this book focus on how these multiple factors intersect and influence elders' social functioning and current concepts of active aging and resilience.

It is likewise impossible to define aging only in chronological terms, since chronological age only partially reflects the biological, psychological, and sociological processes that define life stages. Although the terms *elders, elderly,* and *older persons* are often used to mean those over 65 years in chronological age, this book is based on the principle that aging is a complex process that involves many different factors and is unique to each individual. Rather than chronological age, the more important distinction may be functional ability—that is, the ability to perform activities of daily living that require cognitive and physical well-being. In addition, the authors deliberately use the term *older adults, older people,* or *elders* throughout the book. The reasons for this choice of more neutral terminology are:

1. There is no comparable term for "the elderly" among younger populations, while "older adults" or "older people" is similar to the concept of "young people."
2. Growing numbers of older adults do not like the term "seniors."
3. The word "elder" connotes respect in many cultures (Kaiser, 2006; Lesnoff-Caravaglia, 2002; Levy, 2001; Palmore, 2000).

An Active Aging Framework

The concept of **active aging** is an important and widely accepted perspective in gerontology. It is defined by the World Health Organization as "the process of optimizing opportunities for health, participation, and security in order to enhance quality of life as people age" (WHO, 2002, p. 2). This concept focuses on improving quality of life for all people, including those who are frail, disabled, or require assistance with daily activities. Active aging is consistent with the growing emphasis on autonomy and choice with aging, regardless of physical and mental decline, and benefits both the individual and society. Such a definition also shifts our thinking of old age as a time of passivity to one of continued participation in the family, community, workplace, and religious and political life. It serves as a useful framework for this textbook, since we address a growing number of studies that support the importance of active aging for physical, psychological, and social well-being in the later years.

Consistent with the life course approach underlying this book, the active aging perspective implies that aging is a lifelong process. As a result, people's lifestyles, socioeconomic status, health care, and educational and social activities in their childhood, youth and middle years determine the quality of their lives in their later years. This is also an important assumption of other models of active aging that we will introduce later in this book, including the concepts of "successful," "positive," "vital," "resilient," "robust," and "productive" aging. Accordingly, the determinants of active aging, as shown in Figure 1.1, include individual behaviors, personal characteristics, the physical and social environment (e.g., family, friends, and informal and formal support networks), economic security, and access to and use of health and social services across the life course. This model also places great importance on ethnicity and minority status variables that influence opportunities for active aging, such as access to education, employment, and health care

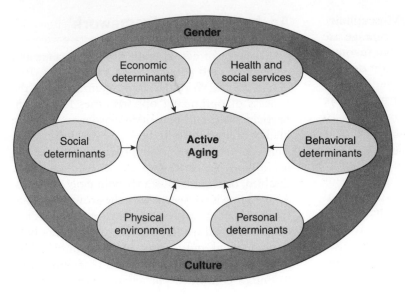

FIGURE 1.1   **The Determinants of Active Aging**

SOURCE: World Health Organization, *Active ageing: A policy framework* (WHO: 2002). Reprinted by permission of the World Health Organization.

beginning with childhood. A closely related concept is **resilience,** or individuals' ability to thrive despite adversity in their lives. We have all known older adults who have suffered multiple losses throughout their lives, but have turned those losses into opportunities for forgiveness and growth, in part because of the protective effects of family, community, and cultural and religious affiliation (Fredriksen-Goldsen, in press).

The concept of **life course** is also central to this model. A life course approach captures how earlier life experiences and decisions affect opportunities in later life and for future generations within and across cultures and time. By placing families and individuals in the larger context of historical, demographic, and social changes, the life course perspective differs from a life span approach that is focused on individual development. A life course perspective recognizes that gender or racial inequities that limit opportunities earlier in the life cycle are often intensified in old age, resulting in increased economic and health disparities and cumulative disadvantage for older women and persons of color (although these disparities tend to diminish among the oldest-old or survivors of historically underserved groups). Gender, ethnic minority status, sexual

orientation, childhood poverty, educational levels, and socioeconomic and generational differences have all been identified as associated with health disparities (Alwin and Wray, 2005; O'Rand and Hamil-Luker, 2005; Whitfield and Hayward, 2003; Williams, 2005). At the same time, however, many older adults, including those from historically disadvantaged groups, have demonstrated remarkable resilience and optimism, making the most of lifelong experiences despite cumulative adversity and set-backs throughout their lives. (Cohen, 2005). The terms *active aging, resilience,* and *health disparities across the life course* will be used throughout this text. Another perspective central to this text is "the person in the environment," discussed next.

A Person–Environment Perspective on Social Gerontology

Consistent with the framework of the interaction of physiological, psychological, and social changes with aging, this textbook will approach topics in social gerontology from a **person–environment perspective.** This model suggests that the environment is not a static backdrop, but changes continually as the older person takes from it what he or she needs, controls what can be modified, and adjusts to conditions that cannot be changed. Adaptation thus implies a dual process in which the individual adjusts to some characteristics of the social and physical environment (e.g., completing the numerous forms required by Medicare), and brings about changes in others (e.g., lobbying to expand Medicare benefits to cover prescription drugs).

Environmental Press

The **competence model** is one useful way to view the dynamic interactions between the person's physical and psychological characteristics and the social and physical environment (Lawton and Nahemow, 1973; Lawton, 1989; Parmelee and Lawton, 1990). *Environment* in this model, which is shown in Figure 1.2, may refer to the larger society, the community, the neighborhood, or the home. **Environmental press** is defined as the demands that social and physical environments make on the individual to adapt, respond, or change. The environmental press model can be approached from a variety of disciplinary perspectives. A concept fundamental to social work, for example, is that of human behavior and the environment, and the need to develop practice and policy interventions that achieve a better fit between the person and his or her social environment. Health care providers are increasingly aware of the necessity to take account of social

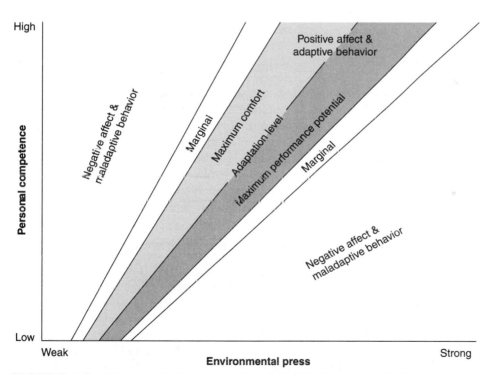

FIGURE 1.2 Diagrammatic Representation of the Behavioral and Affective Outcomes of Person–Environment Transactions

SOURCE: M. P. Lawton and L. Nahemow, Ecology and the aging process. In C. Eisdorfer and M. P. Lawton (Eds.), *Psychology of adult development and aging* (Washington, D.C.: American Psychological Association, 1973). p. 661. Copyright 1973 by the American Psychological Association. Reprinted by permission of the author and publisher.

and physical environmental factors (e.g., family caregivers and other informal supports as well as the elder's living situation) in their assessments of health problems.

Architects and advocates for persons with disabilities are developing ways to make physical environments more accessible. Psychologists are interested in how physical and social environments may be modified to maximize the older person's ability to learn new tasks and perform familiar ones such as driving, taking tests, and self-care. Sociologists study ways that the macro-environment (larger political and economic structures) affects and is affected by an individual's interactions with it. Because the concepts of this model are so basic to understanding the position of older people and to developing ways to improve the quality of their lives, such environmental interactions are referred to throughout this text.

Environmental press can range from minimal to quite high. For example, often very little environmental press is present in an institutional setting where an individual is not responsible for self-care, such as personal grooming and housekeeping, and may have few resources to stimulate the senses or challenge the mind. Other environments can create a great deal of press— for example, a multigenerational household in which the older person plays a pivotal role. An increase in the number of people sharing the living arrangement or a move to a new home increases the environmental demands. As the demands change, the individual must adapt in order to maintain one's sense of competence.

Individuals perform at their maximum level when the environmental press slightly exceeds the level at which they adapt. In other words, the environment challenges them to test their limits but does not overwhelm them. If the level of environmental demand becomes too high, the individual experiences excessive stress or overload. When the environmental press is far below the individual's adaptation level, sensory deprivation, boredom, learned helplessness, and

dependence on others may result. However, a situation of mild to moderate stress, just below the person's adaptation level, results in maximum comfort. It is important to challenge the individual in this situation as well, to prevent a decline to boredom and inadequate stimulation. In either situation—too much or too little environmental press—the person or the environment must change, if the individual's adaptive capacity is to be restored and quality of life enhanced.

As implied above, *individual competence* is another concept central to this model. This is defined by Lawton and Nahemow (1973) as the theoretical upper limit of an individual's abilities to function in the areas of health, social behavior, and cognition. Some of the capacities needed to adapt to environmental press include good health, effective problem-solving and learning skills, and the ability to manage the basic activities of daily living such as dressing, grooming, and cooking (Parmelee and Lawton, 1990). As suggested by the model in Figure 1.2, the higher a person's competence, the higher the levels of environmental press that can be tolerated. Thus, an older person with multiple physical disabilities and chronic illnesses has reduced physical competence, which may limit the level of physical demands with which he or she can cope. On the other hand, this individual may still maintain a high level of psychosocial competence, enjoy the company of others, and express life satisfaction.

Environmental Interventions

The competence model has numerous implications for identifying interventions to enhance the quality of older adults' lives. Most services for older people are oriented toward minimizing environmental demands and increasing supports. These services may focus on changing the physical or the social environment, or both. Physical environmental modifications, such as ramps and handrails, and community services, such as Meals-on-Wheels and escort vans, are relatively simple ways to reestablish the older person's level

POINTS TO PONDER

Think about your own home. In what ways would it create high environmental press for an older person with multiple health problems? How could you change it to make it more congruent with the older user's level of personal competence, in order to help him or her achieve positive affect and adaptive behavior?

of adaptation and to ease the burdens of daily coping. Such arrangements are undoubtedly essential to the well-being of some older people who require supports in the form of environmental adaptations or occasional assistance from family and paid caregivers to enhance their autonomy. For example, many older people with chronic conditions are able to remain in their own homes because of environmental modifications such as emergency systems that allow them to call for help, vans equipped for wheelchairs, computers that aid them with communication, and medication reminders. Other examples of both environmental and individual interventions to enhance older people's choices are considered throughout this text.

A fine line exists, however, between minimizing excessive environmental press and creating an environment that is not stimulating or is "too easy" to navigate. Well-intentioned families, for example, may do too much for an older person, assuming responsibility for daily activities, so that their older relative no longer has to exert any effort and may no longer feel he or she is a contributing family member. Likewise, professionals and family members may try to shield the older person from experiencing too many changes. For example, they may presume that an elder is too set in her or his ways to adjust to sharing a residence, thereby denying the person the opportunity to learn about and make an independent decision on home-sharing options. Well-intentioned nursing home staff may not challenge residents to perfom such daily tasks as getting out of bed or going to the dining hall. Protective efforts such as these can remove necessary levels of environmental press, with the result that the person's social, psychological, and physical levels of functioning may decline. Understimulating conditions, then, can be as negative in their effects on older people as those in which there is excessive environmental press.

Organization of the Text

This book is divided into five parts:

• Part One is a general introduction to the field of social gerontology and the demographics of an aging society, and includes a brief history of the field, the growth of the older population, a discussion of research methods and designs, descriptions of aging in other countries and cultures, and the lives of older immigrants to the United States.

• Part Two addresses the physiological changes that influence social aging. It begins with a review of normal age-related changes in the body's major organ systems, including modifications in the sensory system and their social/environmental effects. It also discusses the chronic diseases that occur most frequently among older people, how these diseases can be managed, factors that influence health care behavior (e.g., when and why older people are likely to seek professional care), and health promotion programs aimed at improving older adults' physical, psychological, and social functioning.

• In Part Three, we move to the psychological context of aging; this includes normal and disease-related changes in cognitive functioning (learning, intelligence, and memory), theories of personality development and coping styles, psychological and cognitive disorders in late life, the use of mental health services, as well as love, intimacy, and sexuality in the later years.

• Part Four explores the social issues of aging, beginning with a discussion of current social theories of aging, the importance of family, friends, and neighbors for elders, informal caregiving of older adults, and how the array of housing arrangements and long-term care options for older adults affects their social interactions and sense of competence. Issues related to productivity, employment, retirement, and income are next explored, followed by a review of unpaid productive roles and civic engagement in the community, educational and religious institutions, and politics. This part concludes with topics related to death, dying, and widowhood. The last two chapters of Part Four present both the challenges and strengths of older ethnic minorities and women.

• Part Five goes beyond the individual's social context to address societal perspectives, particularly social, health, and long-term care policy issues and contemporary policy debates.

Each part begins with an introduction to the key issues of aging that are discussed in that section. In order to emphasize the variations in physiological, psychological, social, and societal aspects of aging, vignettes of older people representing these differences are presented. Throughout each chapter, the diversity of the older population and of the aging process itself is highlighted in terms of chronological age, gender, culture, ethnic minority status, social class, functional ability, and sexual orientation. Where appropriate, the dynamic interaction between older people and their environment is emphasized. How age-related changes are measured and methods for improving measurement in this field are also discussed.

We encourage you to read the facts and examples in the boxed material, which illustrate some of the key concepts discussed in the chapters. At the end of each chapter, you will find a brief description of emerging trends, possible future directions relevant to that topic, and implications for careers in gerontology.

These projections are based on population trends and biological, social, and psychological research that allows us to glean some ideas of what aging will be like by the middle of the twenty-first century.

Why Study Aging?

As you begin this text, you may find it useful to think about your own motivations for learning about older adults and the aging process. You may be in a required course, questioning its relevance, and approaching this text as something you must read to satisfy requirements. Or you may have personal reasons for wishing to learn about aging. You may be concerned about your own age-related changes, wondering whether reduced energy or alterations in physical features are inevitable with age. After all, since middle and old age together encompass a longer time span than any other stage of our lives, it is important that we understand and prepare for these years. Perhaps you are looking forward to the freedom made possible by retirement and the "empty nest." Through increased knowledge about the aging process, you may be hoping to make decisions that can enhance your own positive adaptation to aging and old age. Or perhaps you are interested in assisting aging relatives, friends, and neighbors, wanting to know what can be done to help them maintain their autonomy, what housing options exist for them, and how you can improve your own caregiving abilities.

Learning about aging not only gives us insight into our own interpersonal relationships, self-esteem, competence, and meaningful activities as we grow older; it also helps us comprehend the aging process of our parents, grandparents, clients, patients, and friends. It is important to recognize that change and growth take place throughout the life course, and that the concerns of older people are not distinct from those of the young, but represent a continuation of earlier life periods. Such understanding can improve our effectiveness in communicating with relatives, friends, or professionals. In addition, such knowledge can help challenge any assumptions or stereotypes we may hold about behavior appropriate to various ages.

Perhaps you wish to work professionally with older people, but are unsure how your interests can fit in with the needs of the older population. The exciting and diverse range of career opportunities in both community and institutional settings and growing geriatric workforce needs are discussed throughout this book. If you are already working with older people, you may genuinely enjoy your work, but you may also be concerned about the social, economic, and health problems facing some older adults and thus feel a responsibility to change these negative social conditions. As a professional or future professional working with older people, you are probably eager to learn more about both policy and practice issues that can enhance their quality of life and life satisfaction.

Regardless of your motivations for reading this text, chances are that, like most Americans, you have some misconceptions about older people and the aging process. As products of our youth-oriented society, we have all sensed the pervasiveness of negative attitudes about aging, although our own personal experiences with older people may counter many stereotypes and myths. By studying aging and older people, you will not only become more aware of the older population's competence in many areas, but also be able to differentiate the normal changes that are associated with the aging process from pathological or disease-related changes. Such an understanding may serve to reduce some of your own fears about aging, as well as positively affect your professional and personal interactions with older people.

Our challenge as educators and authors is to present you with the facts and concepts that will give you a more accurate picture of the experience of aging. We also want to convey to you the excitement and importance of learning about the field of aging. We hope that by the time you have completed this text, you will have acquired information that strengthens positive attitudes toward living and working with older people and toward your own experience of aging. First, we will turn to the demographic changes that are resulting in the largest population of people age 65 and older in the history of the United States.

Growth of the Older Population

The increasing size of the older population is the single most important factor affecting current interest in the field of gerontology. In 1900, people over 65 accounted for approximately 4 percent of the United States population—less than 1 in 25. Today, slightly more than 100 years later, this segment of our population has grown to 36.8 million, or 12.4 percent of the United States (AOA, 2005). This represents a twelve-fold increase in the older population during this period, compared with a threefold increase in those under age 65. Population growth for this age group declined slightly between 1990 and 2005 because of the low birthrates experienced in the United States during the Great Depression (1929–1935). With the first baby boomers turning 60 in 2006, the population over 65 will again increase significantly after 2010. Thus, demographers predict that by 2030 the population age 65 and older may be as high as 72 million, representing a 100 percent increase over 30 years, compared with a 30 percent growth in the total population (U.S. Census Bureau, 2006c).

Changes in Life Expectancy

Why have these changes in the older population occurred? Chiefly because people are living longer. In 1900, the average **life expectancy** at birth in the United States (i.e., the average length of time one could expect to live if one were born that year) was 47 years. At that time, there were approximately 772,000 people between the ages of 75 and 84 in the United States, and only 123,000 age 85 and older. In 2005, there were over 5.1 million in the oldest group. The average life expectancy is now much longer, 77.9 years. About four out of five individuals can now expect to reach age 65, at which point there is a better than 50 percent chance of living past age 80 (NCHS, 2006).

According to the Census Bureau, life expectancy at birth is expected to increase from the current 77.9 years to 82.6 in 2050. Sex differences in life expectancy have declined since 1980, when females born that year could expect to live 7.4 years more than men; in 2005 the difference was only 5.2 years. Projections by the Census Bureau assume a fairly constant 5- to 6-year difference in life expectancy well into the future. Therefore, females born in 2005 are expected to reach age 80.4, whereas males in that birth cohort will reach age 75.2 (NCHS, 2006). Differences continue to be greater between African American females and males, with their current life expectancies at birth of 76.5 and 69.8, respectively. Even in the year 2050, however, male life expectancy will be less than 80 years, whereas women will achieve 84.3 years (NCHS, 2006; U.S. Census Bureau, 2000). Of course, these projections do not take into account potentially new diseases that could differentially increase mortality risks for men and women. On the other hand, death rates due to hypertension and stroke have already started to decline because of lifestyle changes. Since both conditions are somewhat more likely to affect men, these factors may narrow the sex differential and increase life expectancy more for men. Nevertheless, the trend illustrated in Figure 1.3, where women outnumber men at every age after 65, will continue at least to mid-century.

Most gains in life expectancy have occurred in the younger ages. For example, during the period from 1900 to 2005, the average life expectancy at birth increased from 47 years to 77.9 years. Although less dramatic, gains in life expectancy beyond age 65 during this same period also occurred, from about 12.3 to 18.4 years between 1900 and 2005. The gains that occurred in the early years of life are largely attributable to the eradication in the twentieth century of many diseases that caused high infant and childhood mortality. On the other hand, survival beyond age 65 may increase significantly in future cohorts, when heart disease and cancer become more chronic and less fatal diseases. Already there has been an acceleration of years gained. Between 1900 and 1960, only 2.4 years were gained beyond age 65, while the gain since 1960 has been 4 years.

This shift results mostly from advances in medicine. A hundred years ago, adults generally died from acute diseases, with influenza and pneumonia the principal killers. Few people survived these diseases long enough to need care for

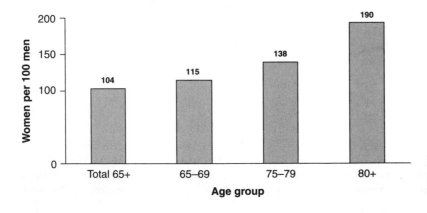

FIGURE 1.3   **Number of Women per 100 Men by Age: 2004**
SOURCE: U.S. Census Bureau, 2006a.

chronic or long-term conditions. Today, death from acute diseases is rare. Maternal, infant, and early childhood death rates have also declined considerably. The result is a growing number of people who survive to old age, often with one or more health problems requiring long-term care. The evidence from epidemiological studies suggests that older Americans are receiving better health care than their counterparts in other developed countries. As a result, white Americans at age 80 have a greater life expectancy (women = 9.1 years, men = 7 years) than 80-year-olds in Sweden, Japan, France, and England, even though life expectancy at birth is higher in Sweden and Japan (Manton and Vaupel, 1995).

Maximum Life Span

It is important to distinguish life expectancy from **maximum life span.** While life expectancy is a probability estimate based on environmental conditions such as disease and health care, as described previously, maximum life span is the maximum number of years a given species could expect to live if environmental hazards were

eliminated. There appears to be a maximum biologically determined life span for cells that comprise the organism, so that even with the elimination of all diseases, we could not expect to live much beyond 120 years. For these reasons, more and more persons will expect to live longer, but the maximum number of years they can expect to live will not be increased in the foreseeable future unless, of course, some extraordinary and unanticipated biological discoveries occur. Research on some biological factors that may increase longevity for future cohorts is discussed in Chapter 3.

Perhaps the most important goal of health planners and practitioners should be to approach a rectangular survival curve, that is, the "ideal curve." As seen in the survival curve in Figure 1.4, developments in medicine, public hygiene, and health have already increased the percentage of people surviving into the later years. The ideal situation is one where all people would survive to the maximum life span, creating a "rectangular curve." The survival curves of developed countries serve as a model for developing countries; that is, about 50 percent of all babies born today in developed countries will reach age 85, or more than

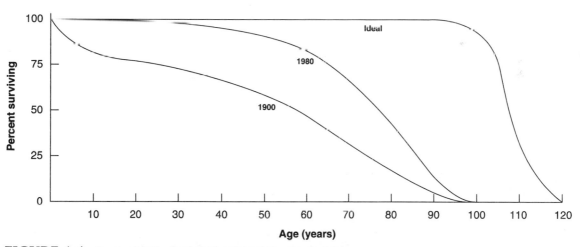

FIGURE 1.4 Increasing Rectangularization of the Survival Curve
SOURCE: Adapted from L. Hayflick, The cell biology of human aging. *Scientific American*, 1980, *242*, p. 60.
Copyright © 1980 by Scientific American, Inc. All rights reserved.

MORE FORMER U.S. PRESIDENTS AND FIRST LADIES ARE ALIVE TODAY

One example of the increasing likelihood of survival beyond age 65 is the current number of U.S. presidents who are still alive. In 2007, four were still alive, from George Bush and Jimmy Carter at age 82, Bill Clinton and George W. Bush at age 60. This was not the case at any other point in U.S. history. As an illustration of greater longevity among women beyond age 65, in 2007 there were seven current or former first ladies.

Picture taken during a dinner in honor of the 200th anniversary of the White House in 2000. Photo courtesy Associated Press (AP).

two-thirds of the maximum life span of 120 years (CDC, 2006). We are approaching this ideal curve, but it will not be achieved until the diseases of middle age—including cancer, heart disease, diabetes, and kidney diseases—can be totally prevented or at least effectively managed as chronic conditions.

The Oldest-Old

Ages 85 and Older

The population aged 85 and older, also referred to as the "oldest-old," has grown more rapidly than any other age group in our country. In 2005, of the 36.8 million persons aged 65 and over in the United States:

- Thirteen million, or 36 percent, were age 75 to 84.
- Almost 5 million, or 13 percent, were age 85 and over (AOA, 2005).

Since World War II, mortality rates in adulthood have declined significantly, resulting in an unprecedented number of people who are reaching advanced old age and who are most likely to require long-term care.

- The oldest-old population of Americans has increased by a factor of 23.
- The old-old (ages 75–84) have increased twelve-fold.
- The young-old (ages 65–74) increased eightfold.

TABLE 1.1   Population Increase per Age Group: United States (in millions)

	AGE		
YEAR	15–44	65＋	85+
1960		16.6	0.9
1990	118	31.1	3.02
2005	126	36.8	5.1
Increase (1990–2005)	6.8%	18.3%	68.9%

SOURCE: U.S. Administration on Aging, 2005.

vary, depending on assumptions about changes in chronic disease morbidity and mortality rates (AOA, 2005), as we will see in Chapter 4. The impact of such a surge in the oldest-old on the demand for health services, especially hospitals and long-term care settings, will be dramatic.

It is also important to consider the distribution of selected age groups now and in the future. The young-old (ages 65–74) currently represent 51 percent of the older population; those over 85 make up 13 percent. In contrast, the corresponding proportions in 2050 are projected to be 44 percent young-old and 24 percent oldest-old (see Figure 1.5).

Because they are more likely to have multiple health problems that often result in physical frailty, and because up to 50 percent of the oldest old may have some form of cognitive impairment, this group is disproportionately represented in institutional settings such as nursing homes, assisted living, adult family homes, and hospitals. Approximately 18 percent live in a long-term care setting, compared with 1.1 percent of those 65 to 74 (AOA, 2005; NCHS, 2005). However, the incidence of institutionalization among African Americans aged 85 and older is only about two-thirds this rate (12 percent). The oldest-old blacks are far more likely to be living with relatives other than a spouse or partner (40 percent). Only 27 percent of the oldest-old (regardless of ethnic minority status) live with a spouse,

Those over age 85 have increased by more than 500 percent from 1960 to 2005, to 5.1 million. As Table 1.1 illustrates, the oldest-old population has grown much more rapidly than other segments of the United States. In 15 years their numbers increased at a rate ten times that of 15- to 44-year-olds and almost four times that of the total population aged 65 and older. This does not mean that their absolute numbers are higher than the younger groups in Table 1.1, but that their rate of growth is much faster. Demographers project this age group to number 21 million by 2050, about four times their current number, and a 500 percent increase over 65 years. It is primarily attributable to the aging of baby boomers, who will start to turn 85 after 2030. The baby boom generation is generally defined as those born between 1946 and 1964, and currently numbers 69 million. However, these projections

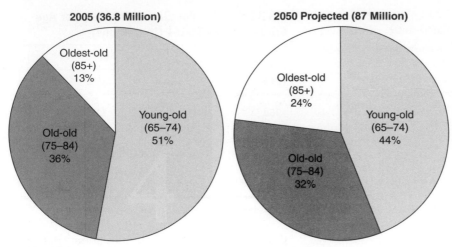

2005 (36.8 Million)

Oldest-old
(85+)
13%

Old-old
(75–84)
36%

Young-old
(65–74)
51%

2050 Projected (87 Million)

Oldest-old
(85+)
24%

Young-old
(65–74)
44%

Old-old
(75–84)
32%

FIGURE 1.5   Percentage of Older Americans by Age Group
SOURCE: U.S. Census Bureau, 2005, U.S. Administration on Aging, 2005.

compared with 63 percent of people age 65 to 74 (U.S. Census Bureau, 2005). Although functional health is more impaired in the oldest-old, a major study of Medicare expenditures during the last year of life showed that medical costs were not highest for this age group. The researchers compared Medicare expenditures during the last year of life for people aged 85 and over versus those who died at ages 65 to 74. They found that the charges to Medicare for the former group were 60 to 70 percent lower than the average charges for the latter group, regardless of gender and ethnicity. These findings reflect the shorter hospitalizations and less aggressive terminal health care received by the oldest-old (Hoover et al., 2002; Levinsky et al., 2001). These costs may be even lower for future cohorts of the oldest-old, who are likely to be healthier and more active than today's population.

Centenarians

Projections by the U.S. Census Bureau also suggest a substantial increase in the population of centenarians, people age 100 or older. In 2000, more than 50,000 Americans had reached this milestone, a 35 percent increase since 1990. Baby

boomers are expected to survive to age 100 at rates never before achieved; one in 26 Americans can expect to live to be 100 by 2025, compared with only 1 in 500 in 2000 (AOA, 2005).

LIVING AND DYING AT AGE 100

Bob Hope, labeled by the American media as "the quintessentially American entertainer" and the "greatest entertainer of the 20th century," turned 100 on May 29, 2003. He was honored by television, radio, and print stories for his contributions to the evolution of standup comedy, but more substantively for his dedication to America's armed forces through his USO-sponsored tours in World War II, Korea, Vietnam, and the 1991 Persian Gulf War. Because of his role as an American icon, 35 states declared his birthday "Bob Hope Day" and a famous street intersection in Los Angeles at Hollywood and Vine was named "Bob Hope Square." Only 2 months later, on July 28, 2003, Hope died of pneumonia. Although his eyesight and hearing had failed, his family reported that he was alert and aware of world events until his death. Comedian George Burns, a contemporary of Hope's, also died shortly after his 100th birthday, in 1996.

As more Americans become centenarians, there is growing interest in their genetics and the lifestyle that may have influenced their longevity. Data from the Georgia Centenarian Study support other findings of greater survival among women, as well as racial crossover effects in advanced old age (i.e. persons of color who live to age 85 are "hardier" than their Caucasian counterparts). In this follow-up of 137 people age 100 at entry into the study, African American women survived the longest beyond age 100. On average, they survived twice as many months as white men, who lived the shortest time beyond 100. White women had the next best survival rates, and lived slightly longer than African American men (Poon et al., 2000).

The New England Centenarian Study points to genetic factors that determine how well the older person copes with disease (Perls and Silver, 1999; Perls and Terry, 2003; Perls and Wood, 1996; Terry et al., 2004). As shown in Figure 1.6, the model proposed by this study suggests that the oldest-old are hardy because they have a higher threshold for disease and show slower rates of disease progression than

> ### A 105-YEAR-OLD-SHOT-PUTTER
>
> The obituary of a 108-year-old woman who died suddenly of congestive heart failure described her healthy lifestyle and enthusiasm for trying new activities. At age 103, she began to train as a shot-putter, and participated in two Senior Games in Washington. She lifted a 6.5 pound shot and flung it 7 feet, a record for these Senior Games.
>
> SOURCE: Krishman, K., *Seattle Times*, January 11, 2006, p. B5.

their peers who develop chronic diseases at a younger age and die earlier. Perls and colleagues illustrate this hypothesis with the case of a 103-year-old man who displayed few symptoms of Alzheimer's disease; however, at autopsy this man's brain had a high number of neuro-fibrillary tangles, which are a hallmark of this disease. The likelihood of a genetic advantage is also supported by the finding that male siblings of centenarians are 17 times as likely as the general population, and female siblings eight times as likely, to survive to age 100 (Perls et al., 1998; Willcox et al., 2006b).

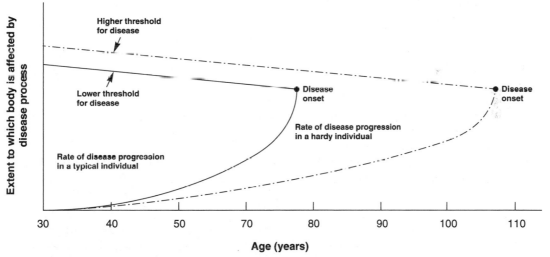

FIGURE 1.6   Response to Chronic Disease among Elders Who Survive to Age 100 versus Nonsurvivors
SOURCE: Adapted from "The Oldest Old" by Thomas T. Perls. Copyright © 1995 by Scientific American, Inc. All rights reserved.

Older men who survive to age 90, in particular, represent the hardiest segment of their birth cohort. Between ages 65 and 89, women score higher on tests of cognitive function. However, after age 90, men perform far better on these tests. Even at age 80, 44 percent of men were found to be robust and independent, compared with 28 percent of women. Contrary to the belief once prevalent in gerontology that dementia is a concomitant of advanced age, it appears that as many as 30 percent of centenarians have no memory problems, 20 percent have some, and 50 percent have serious problems. In one study of 69 centenarians who were tested for dementia, none of these robust elders showed significant levels of dementia, either in their neuropsychological testing or in the neuropathological studies of their brains (Samuelsson et al., 1997; Silver et al., 1998). Indeed, other researchers who have studied dementia in older adults have suggested that the genetic mutations most closely associated with Alzheimer's disease are not present in the oldest-old. Environmental factors that emerge much later in life appear to cause dementia in these survivors (Kaye, 1997).

The Okinawa Centenarian Study supports the importance of both genetic and environmental factors in explaining extreme longevity. Since 1976, researchers have examined more than 600 centenarians in this isolated prefecture of Japan. Most of these elders possess genetic patterns that place them at lower risk of autoimmune diseases, but even those without these patterns have lower rates of coronary heart disease, cancer, and stroke mortality than other Japanese. They have been found to have lower blood levels of cholesterol, homocysteine, and free radicals. Researchers attribute these biochemical advantages to a low-calorie diet with a high intake of folate, vitamins B6, B12, D, calcium, omega-3 fats, and high-fiber foods. The traditional Okinawan lifestyle includes high physical activity, social integration at all ages, a deep spirituality, adaptability, and optimistic attitudes. In fact, Okinawans who move from the island and abandon their traditional diet and lifestyle experience higher mortality rates from diseases that are rare among lifelong Okinawans (Bernstein et al., 2004; Suzuki, Willcox, and Willcox, 2001; Willcox et al., 2006a, 2006b).

Further evidence for the robustness of centenarians comes from the New England Centenarian Study and a similar assessment of centenarians in Sweden (Samuelsson et al., 1997). Of the 79 people who were age 100 or older in the former study, all had lived independently into their early 90s and, on average, took only one medication. In the Swedish Centenarian Study, among 143 respondents:

- Fifty-two percent were able to perform their activities of daily living with little or no assistance.
- Thirty-nine percent had a disorder of the circulatory system.
- Eighty percent had problems with vision and hearing.
- Twenty-seven percent had some signs of dementia and all performed worse on a test of cognitive function (memory and attention) than 70- to 80-year-olds.

Overall, centenarians appear to be healthy for a longer period of time, although almost 50 percent live in nursing homes, compared with 25 percent of all persons age 85 and older (U.S. Census Bureau, 1999).

Population Pyramids

The increase in longevity is partly responsible for an unusually rapid rise in the *median age* of the U.S. population—from 28 in 1970 to 36 in 2005—meaning that half the population was older than 36.5 and half younger in 2005. From a historical perspective, an 8-year increase in the median age over a 30-year period is a noteworthy demographic event. The other key factors contributing to this rise include a dramatic decline in the birth rate after the mid-1960s, high birthrates in the periods from 1890 to 1915 and just after World War II (these baby boomers are now all older than the median), and the large number of immigrants before the 1920s.

As stated earlier in this chapter, the baby boom generation (currently age 43 to 61) will dominate the age distribution in the next three decades. In fact, between 2010 and 2030, they will form the "senior boom" and swell the ranks of the 65-plus generation to the point that one in five Americans will be old. The projected growth in the older population will increase the median age of the U.S. population from 36 in 2005 to age 39 by 2030. If current fertility and immigration levels remain stable, the only age groups to experience significant growth will be those older than 55 (U.S. Census Bureau, 2006c).

One of the most dramatic examples of the changing age distribution of the American population is the shift in the proportion of older adults in relation to the proportion of young persons, as illustrated in Figure 1.7. In 1900, when approximately 4 percent of the population was age 65 and over, young persons aged 0 to 17 years made up 40 percent of the population. By 2005, reduced birthrates in the 1970s and 1980s had resulted in a decrease of young persons to 25 percent of the population. The U.S. Census Bureau predicts that, by 2030, the proportion of young and old persons will be almost equal, with those age 0 to 17 forming 23.5 percent of the population and older adults almost 20 percent.

After 2030 the death rate will be greater than the birthrate because baby boomers will be in the oldest cohorts.

The *population pyramid* is one way of illustrating the changing proportions of young and old persons in the population. Figure 1.8 contrasts the population pyramids for the years 2000, 2025, and 2050. Each horizontal bar in these pyramids represents a 10-year *birth cohort* (i.e., people born within the same 10-year period). By comparing these bars, we can determine the relative proportion of each birth cohort. As you can see in the first graph, the distribution of the population in 2000 had already moved from a true pyramid to one with a bulge in the 35- to 54-year-old group; this represents the population of baby boomers. This pyramid grows more column-like over the years, as shown in the other two graphs. These changes reflect the aging of the baby boomers (note the "pig in a python" phenomenon as this group moves up the age ladder), combined with declining birth rates and reduced death rates for older cohorts.

Support Ratios

One aspect of the changing age distribution in our population that has raised public concern is the so-called "old age support ratio." The way this ratio has generally been used is to indicate the relationship between the proportion of the

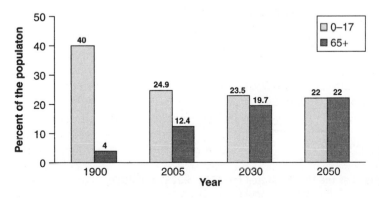

FIGURE 1.7   Actual and Projected Distribution of Children and Older Adults in the Population: 1900–2050
SOURCE: U.S. Census Bureau, Interim Population http://www.census.gov/population/project summaryTabC1.pdf.

(NP-P2) Projected Resident Population of the United States as of July 1, 2000, Middle Series

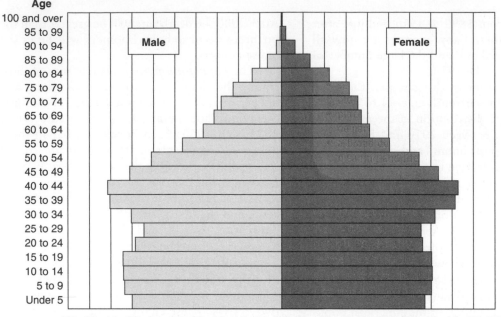

(NP-P3) Projected Resident Population of the United States as of July 1, 2025, Middle Series

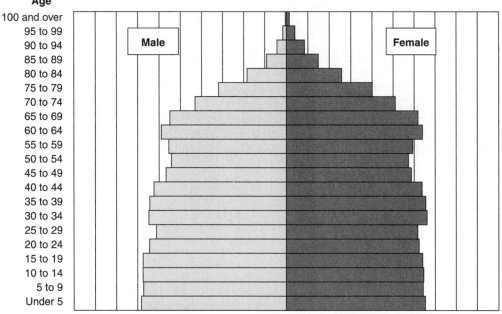

FIGURE 1.8 Projected Resident Populations of the United States for 2000, 2025, and 2050
SOURCE: National Projections Program, Population Division, U.S. Census Bureau, Washington, DC 20233.

(NP-P4) Projected Resident Population of the United States as of July 1, 2050, Middle Series

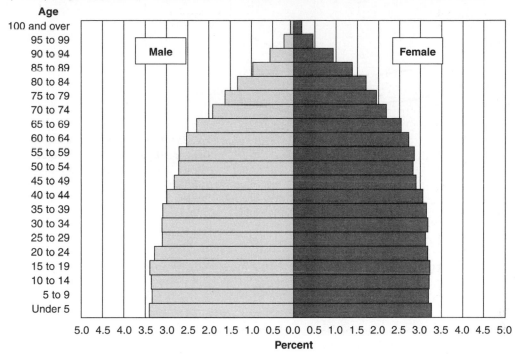

FIGURE 1.8   (Continued)

population that is employed (defined as "productive" members of society) and the proportion that is not in the workforce (and is thus viewed as "dependent" or as "requiring support"). This rough estimate is obtained by comparing the percent of the population age 20 to 64 (the working years) to the proportion age 19 and under (yielding the youth dependency ratio) and over 65 (yielding the old-age support ratio). This ratio has increased steadily, such that proportionately fewer employed persons appear to support retired older persons today. In 1910, the ratio was less than .10 (i.e., ten working people per retired older person), compared with .21 in 2000 (i.e., five working people per retired person). Assuming that the lower birth rate continues, this trend will be apparent in the early part of this century, as the baby boom cohort reaches old age. By the year 2030, a ratio of .36 (or fewer than three working people per retired person) is

expected (U.S. Census Bureau, 2006a). These changes since 1960, along with projections through 2030, are illustrated in Figure 1.9.

Such a crude measure of support ratios is problematic, however. Many younger and older persons are actually in the labor force and not dependent, while many people of labor-force age may not be employed. Another flaw is that support ratios do not take account of the labor-force participation rates of different groups; for example, the rates of employed women aged 16 and older are expected to increase in this century, while those of men are projected to remain steady. In addition, baby boomers are setting the trend toward starting new careers in middle age and continuing to work in their later years. When these variations are taken into account, the total support ratio in the year 2050 will remain lower than recent historical levels, even though it increases as the population ages.

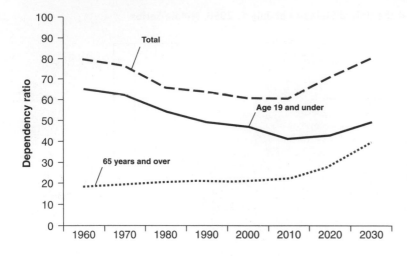

FIGURE 1.9   Number of Dependents per 100 Persons Aged 18–64 Years: Estimates and Projections 1960–2030
SOURCE: U.S. Census Bureau, International Data Base, Census 2000 Summary File 1.

Moreover, despite population aging, those under the age of 16 will continue to constitute the largest "dependent" group into this century. Therefore, we need to be cautious when policy makers predict "burdens" on the younger population and blame rising costs of public pension programs primarily on the changing support ratio (Reynolds, 2004).

Population Trends

In addition to the proportional growth of the older population in general, other demographic trends are of interest to gerontologists. These include statistics related to the social, ethnic, racial, gender, and geographic distribution of older populations. In this section, we will review some of these trends, beginning with the demographics of ethnic minorities in the United States.

Ethnic Minorities

Because of lifelong socioeconomic inequities in access to health care and preventive health services, elders of color have a lower life expectancy than whites. For example, in 2005, life expectancy at birth was 80.4 years for white females and 76.5 for African American females. White males could expect to live 75.2 years, compared with 69.8 years for their black counterparts. Nevertheless, the greatest improvement in life expectancy between 1990 and 2005 occurred for the latter group, an increase of 4.5 years. White males' life expectancy increased 2.6 years during that same period (NCHS, 2006).

Today, ethnic minorities comprise 17 percent of the population over age 65 (8.2 percent African American, 6.0 percent Latino, 2.9 percent Asian or Pacific Islander, and less than 1 percent American Indian or Native Alaskan); they include a smaller proportion of older people and a larger proportion of younger adults than the white population. In 2004, 15 percent of whites, but only 8.3 percent of African Americans and 5.2 percent of Latinos were age 65 and over. The difference results primarily from the higher fertility and mortality rates among the nonwhite population under age 65 than among the white population under 65. The Census Bureau estimates that the proportion of older persons will increase at a *higher* rate for the nonwhite population than for the white population. This is partly because of the large

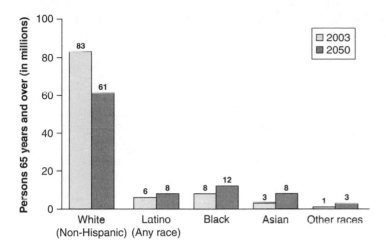

FIGURE 1.10   **Persons 65 Years and Over: 2003 and projected for 2050 (%) Hispanics are also included in racial group totals.**
SOURCE: U.S. Bureau of the Census, Middle Series Projections (1993).

percent of children in these groups, who, unlike their parents and especially their grandparents, are expected to reach old age (U.S. Census Bureau, 2006c). Figure 1.10 illustrates these differential patterns of growth. A more detailed discussion of ethnic minority elders is provided in Chapter 14.

Geographic Distribution

Demographic information on the location of older populations within the United States is important for a variety of reasons. For example, the differing needs of rural and urban older people may affect service delivery and local government policy decisions. Statistical information on older adults state-by-state is necessary in planning for the distribution of federal funds. The following are some of the most salient statistics on the geographic distribution of older adults today. The implications of these changes will be considered in later chapters, including their impact on living arrangements, social, health and long-term care policies, and cross-cultural issues.

Although older adults live in every state and region of the United States and represent 12.4

percent of the total population, they are not evenly distributed:

- The Northeast continues to be the region with the oldest population; those over age 65 represent 13.8 percent of its population.
- The western states have approximately 11 percent elders.
- In the Midwest and the South, the proportion of older adults declined between 1990 and 2000, from 13 percent to 12.8 percent, and from 12.6 percent to 12.4 percent, respectively (AOA, 2005).

POINTS TO PONDER

The majority of older people, 7.7 percent in 1998, lived in metropolitan areas. About 28 percent lived in cities, 49 percent in suburbs, and 23 percent in rural areas. Despite their low distribution in rural communities, older adults make up a greater percentage of rural populations than in the general population: 15 percent of all rural residents vs. 13 percent of the total U.S. population (AARP, 2000). What do you think accounts for this higher proportion of elders in rural communities?

About 52 percent of all persons 65 and older lived in nine states in 2004, with the highest number of older people in California:

- California (3.8 million older residents)
- Florida (2.9 million)
- New York (2.5 million)
- Texas (2.2 million)
- Pennsylvania (about 1.9 million)
- Ohio, Illinois, Michigan, and New Jersey (over 1 million each)

This does not necessarily mean that all these states have a higher *proportion* of older Americans than the national average, but their absolute numbers are large. Some states have a much higher proportion of residents over 65 than the national average. For example, in 2004 older people represented:

- 17 percent of the population in Florida.
- 15.3 percent in Pennsylvania and West Virginia.
- almost 15 percent in Iowa and North Dakota.

In contrast, elders comprised just 6.1 percent of the population of Alaska and 8.7 percent of the population of Utah (U.S. Census Bureau, 2006a).

Because of these disparate proportions of older adults in their states' population, it is not surprising that a northeastern state, Maine, has the highest median age (40.7 years), and Utah the lowest (28 years). In some cases, such as that of Florida, migration of retired persons to the state explains the increase, whereas in others, such as West Virginia and Maine, migration of younger persons out of the state leaves a greater proportion of older people. More than 20 percent of some rural counties in these states are over age 65. Other states may simply reflect the generalized "graying of America." These regional differences are expected to continue in this century, although there are some unexpected shifts, such as the greatest percentage increase (4.2 percent) of older adults in Nevada, followed by a 3.8 percent

growth in older residents in Alaska. Residential relocation is relatively rare for older people in the United States. In a typical year, less than 5 percent of people aged 65 and older move, compared with 14 percent of people under age 65 (AOA, 2005). The movement that occurs tends to be within the same region of the country and the same types of environment; that is, people over age 65 generally move from one metropolitan area to another or from one rural community to another. (AOA, 2005; U.S. Census Bureau, 2006a). These trends and their implications for person–environment fit in the later years are described further in Chapter 11.

Educational and Economic Status

In 1960, less than 20 percent of the population over age 65 had finished high school. By 2004, 73 percent of the new cohort age 65 and older had completed high school and 19 percent held a bachelor's degree or more, with only slight gender differences. However, racial and generational differences are striking. Among whites, 82 percent of men and women 65 to 69, and 72 percent of those 75 and older had at least a high school diploma. Corresponding rates are lower for older African Americans (58.5 percent and 48.6 percent, respectively) and for Latino elders (45.8 percent and 28.2 percent, respectively) (AOA, 2005). As a result of historical patterns of discrimination in educational opportunities, a disproportionate ratio of older persons of color today has less than a high school education. Since educational level is so closely associated with economic well-being, these ethnic differences have a major impact on poverty levels of persons of color across the life course and particularly in old age. Other implications of these gaps in educational attainment are discussed further in Chapter 14.

Not surprisingly, the baby boomers, as well as people age 65 to 69 currently, are more educated than the old-old and oldest-old. More than three-fourths (77 percent of the former versus 68 percent of those 75 years and older) have at least a high school education. For this reason, the median educational level today is 12.1 years for the young-old, 10.5 years for the old-old, and 8.6 years for the oldest-old. Because of cultural values and gender inequities in previous generations, fewer white women age 65 and older have college degrees than do white men. Among African Americans the pattern is mixed; for those 70 and older, more black women than men completed college while for the 65- to 69-year-olds, fewer women did so. It is noteworthy that an even greater proportion of people over 25 today (84.5 percent) have at least a high school education; 27.5 percent have a Bachelor's degree or more (He et al., 2005). This suggests that future generations of older people will be better educated—many with college degrees—than their grandparents are today. The implications of this shift for political activism, employment, and the nature of productive roles are explored in later chapters.

In recent years, the proportion of older people in the labor force has increased. Comprising 4.8 percent of the U.S. labor force, 19 percent of men and 11 percent of women age 65 and older reported working outside the home. The majority of these hold part-time jobs. Many older adults prefer to work part-time, but are unable to find such jobs. Among elders who work, more than 50 percent of women and more than 40 percent of men are employed in a part-time or temporary capacity (AOA, 2005; Bureau of Labor Statistics, 2004).

Social Security remains a source of income for 95 percent of older Americans. In 2004 only 18 percent said that they had earnings from current employment and about 36 percent reported income from private pensions. In fact, increases in Social Security benefits along with annual cost-of-living adjustments are major factors underlying the improved economic status of the older population. Currently, about 9.8 percent of older people subsist on incomes below the poverty level, compared to 35 percent in the late 1950s, and slightly lower than the 11.3 percent of Americans aged 18 to 64 who are poor.

Another 6.7 percent of older Americans are classified as "near-poor," with income levels between poverty and 125 percent of the poverty level (AOA, 2005). The improved economic status of the older population as a whole masks the growing rates of poverty among older women, elders of color, the oldest-old, and those living alone. Older women in 2004 were almost twice as likely to be poor as men (about 13 percent vs. 7.0 percent). Older African Americans and Latinos are far more likely to be poor than whites, although their situation has improved in recent years (25 and 19 percent, respectively vs. 7.5 percent for whites). Poverty is higher among elders in central cities (13 percent) and in rural communities (11 percent). The combination of ethnicity and marital status displays even more disparities; for example, in 2003 the median income for a non-Hispanic white household headed by someone 65 to 75 was $35,798, compared with $20,503 for older African American households and $19,962 for older Latino households (He et al., 2005). The current and projected economic status of the older population is discussed in detail in Chapters 12, 14, and 15.

Impact of Demographic Trends

As discussed later in this book, these trends have wide-ranging implications, especially in terms of federal and state spending. The growth in numbers and proportions of older people has already placed pressures on our health, long-term care, and social service systems, as discussed in Chapters 16 and 17. Although growing expenditures are directly related to the high cost of health care, the increase in life expectancy also has changed people's expectations about the quality of life in late adulthood. Increasingly, those facing retirement anticipate living 20 to 30 years in relatively good health, with adequate retirement incomes. When these expectations are not met, because of catastrophic medical costs, widowhood, or a retirement income eroded by inflation, downturns of the stock market, or elimination of employer-sponsored pensions, older adults may not be prepared to manage such changes in their lifestyles. For other segments of the older population, particularly women and elders of color, old age may represent a continuation of a lifetime of poverty or near-poverty. Fortunately, for most older people, the problems associated with old age, particularly chronic illness and the attendant costs, are forestalled until their 70s and 80s. Nevertheless, the rapid growth in numbers of frail elders, the majority of whom are women, may severely strain the health and income systems designed to provide resources in old age.

Longevity in Health or Disease?

Future cohorts of older people may be healthier and more independent well into their 80s and 90s. A strong argument was first put forth to this effect almost 30 years ago by Fries (1980, 1990), who suggested that more people will achieve the maximum life span in future years because of healthier lifestyles and better health care during their youth and middle years. Furthermore, Fries argued that future cohorts will have fewer debilitating illnesses and will, in fact, experience a phenomenon he labeled **compression of morbidity** (i.e., experiencing only a few years of major illness in very old age). The concept of "compressed morbidity" implies that premature death is minimized, because disease and functional decline are compressed into a brief period of 3 to 5 years before death. In fact, major chronic diseases like arthritis, arteriosclerosis, and respiratory problems now appear 10 to 25 years later than for past cohorts. As a result, people die a "natural death" from the failure of multiple organ systems, not because of disease per se (Hazzard, 2001). These older adults of the future may therefore expect to die a "natural death," or death due to the natural wearing out of all organ systems by approximately age 100. If this process does occur, it will have significant impacts on health and long-term care services needed by future generations of older

people, as well as their ability to experience active aging. Long-term care needs may be reduced, with more sub-acute care facilities and short-term home health services required.

Indeed, some evidence from a review of large national health surveys indicates that the older population today is generally healthier than previous cohorts. An analysis of two large longitudinal health surveys—the Longitudinal Study on Aging and the National Health Interview Survey (NHIS)—from 1982 through 1993 for respondents who were age 70 and older in each year, reveals that rates of disability are declining or stabilizing. At the same time, recovery from acute disabilities (e.g., due to falls) is improving. This may be due to more aggressive rehabilitation efforts for older adults in recent years and is consistent with the findings of another analysis of national health surveys. For example, in a comparison of responses to the National Long-Term Care Survey from 1982 through 1999, there was a notable decline in disability rates, from 26 percent in 1982 to less than 20 percent in 1999 (Manton and Gu, 2001). Rates of disability vary across ethnic groups:

- 19 percent for non-Hispanic white men and women.
- 27 percent for Latino men and 28 percent for Latino women.
- 29 percent for African American men and 28 percent for African American women (Reville and Schoeni, 2003–2004).

This means that future generations of the oldest-old may have lower health care expenditures and less reliance on acute care services, but may still need community-based services to support their autonomy.

The concept of **active versus dependent life expectancy** (Katz et al., 1983) is useful in this context. Katz and others distinguish between merely living a long life and living to a healthy old age. This is consistent with the concept of maintaining active aging. Instead of death, they define the endpoint of "active" life expectancy as the loss of independence or the need to rely on others for most activities of daily living. As life expectancy has increased beyond age 65, only about a quarter of these years are spent in a dependent state (Manton & Land, 2000; WHO, 2002). For example:

- A 65-year-old woman today has almost 20 years remaining, 15.7 in active life expectancy, 4 in dependency.
- A 65-year-old man can look forward to living 16.2 more years, with 13.7 of these years representing active life expectancy (Social Security Administration, 2006).

Not surprisingly, differences in life conditions of older persons with inadequate income and those above the median income have led to the conclusion that active life expectancy differs by 1 to 2.5 years between the poor and non-poor. This may result in a growing bimodal distribution of older people remaining healthier and free of disease (as predicted by Fries), and another, probably larger distribution of older adults surviving diseases that would have been fatal years ago, but living with "battle scars." This latter group may be the segment of the population that is distorting projections for compressed morbidity; as we have seen in the reviews of NHIS findings, this latter group also appears to be increasing in size. These are most likely the elders who will require long-term care services in the future. This group may become even larger as the growing trend toward obesity affects more people age 65 and older. Between 1980 and 2000, rates of obesity increased from 27 percent to 39 percent among older women, and from 24 percent to 33 percent among older men (U.S. Census Bureau, 2006b). This pattern may trigger an increase in obesity-related diseases such as heart disease and diabetes. On the other hand, the adoption of healthier lifestyles, such as physical exercise and maintaining a lean body weight, as well as advances in preventing and treating heart disease and stroke, may result in a longer active life expectancy (Freedman, Martin, and Schoeni, 2002; Manton and Gu, 2001).

How Aging and Older Adults Are Studied

You are undoubtedly aware that more researchers are studying older people and the process of aging now than in the past. Some of the concerns that have motivated this increasing professional interest in the field have probably influenced your own decision to study gerontology. In this section we turn to the question of how the older population is studied: What are the particular challenges of social gerontological research, and how are they addressed? Methods of conducting research in this field are described. The net effect of this information is to give you a basic orientation to the field of aging, how it has developed, and methods of studying the older population.

Development of the Field

Although the scientific study of social gerontology is relatively recent, it has its roots in biological studies of the aging processes and in the psychology of human development. Biologists have long explored the reasons for aging in living organisms. Several key publications and research studies are milestones in the history of the field.

One of the first textbooks on aging, *The History of Life and Death,* was written in the thirteenth century by Roger Bacon. With great foresight, Bacon suggested that life expectancy could be extended if health practices, such as personal and public hygiene, were improved. The first scientist to explain aging as a developmental process, rather than as stagnation or deterioration, was a nineteenth-century Belgian mathematician–statistician named Adolph Quetelet. His interest in age and creative achievement preceded the study of these issues by social scientists by 100 years. His training in the field of statistics also led him to consider the problems of **cross-sectional research**—that is, the collection of data on people of different ages at one time, instead of **longitudinal research,** the study of the same person over a period of months or years. These problems are examined in greater detail in the next section of this chapter. The first published reference to "gerontology" as a scientific concept is attributed to Elie Metchnikoff, a French researcher, whose book, *The Problem of Age, Growth, and Death,* was published in 1908.

One of the first laboratory studies of aging was undertaken in the 1920s by the Russian physiologist Ivan Pavlov. Pavlov is best known for his research with animals, which has provided the foundation for stimulus-response theories of behavior. Recognizing that the ability of older animals to learn and distinguish a response differed from that of younger animals, Pavlov explored the reasons for these differences in animal brains. The work of Raymond Pearl and colleagues in the 1920s established the insect *Drosophila* (or fruit fly) as an ideal animal model for studying biological aging and longevity. During this era, in 1922, American psychologist G. Stanley Hall published one of the first books on the social–psychological aspects of aging in the United States. Titled *Senescence, the Last Half of Life,* it remains a landmark text in social gerontology because it provided the experimental framework for examining changes in cognitive processes and social and personality functions.

Historical Forces of the Late Nineteenth and Early Twentieth Centuries

Two important forces led to the expansion of research in social gerontology in the late nineteenth and early twentieth centuries:

- the growth of the population over age 65 (as described earlier)
- the emergence of retirement policies

Changes in policies toward older adults were first evident in many European countries (e.g., Germany) where age-based social services and health insurance programs were developed. In contrast, these changes did not occur in the United States until the 1930s. In 1900, the focus on economic growth and the immediate problems of establishing workers' rights and child welfare laws took precedence over improving the welfare of older people. The prevailing belief in this country had been that families should be responsible for their aging members.

However, the Great Depression of the 1930s brought to policy makers the stark realization that families struck by unemployment and homelessness could not be responsible for their elders. The older segments of society suffered a disproportionate share of the economic blight of the Depression. New concern for the needs of the aging population was exemplified by the Social Security system, established in 1935 to help people maintain a minimal level of economic security after retirement. Early work in social gerontology dealt largely with social and economic problems of aging. For example, E. V. Cowdry's *Problems of Ageing,* published in 1939, focused on society's treatment of older people and their particular needs. It amazes us today that the second edition of Cowdry's book, published in 1942, contained all the research knowledge available on aging at that time!

Formal Development of the Field

As society grew more aware of issues facing the older population, the formal study of aging emerged in the 1940s. In 1945, the Gerontological Society of America (GSA) was founded, bringing together the small group of researchers and practitioners who were interested in gerontology and

---

THE GERONTOLOGICAL SOCIETY OF AMERICA

Today, the GSA has over 5000 members. It is the major professional association for people in diverse disciplines focused on research in aging. The GSA's mission is "to add life to years, not just years to life." This emphasizes the goal of most gerontologists—to enhance quality of life in the later years, not just to extend it.

geriatrics at that time. Gerontology became a division of the American Psychological Association in 1945 and, later, of the American Sociological Association.

The *Journal of Gerontology,* which the GSA began to publish in 1946, served as the first vehicle for transmitting new knowledge in this growing field. In 1988 it became two journals, *The Journals of Gerontology* composed of *Psychological Sciences and Social Sciences,* and *Biological Sciences and Medical Sciences,* which reflect the growth of gerontology. Today, the burgeoning periodicals in diverse disciplines focused on gerontology have resulted in an exponential growth of research publications in this field. An indicator of the knowledge explosion in the field is that the literature on aging published between 1950 and 1960 equaled that of the previous 115 years (Birren and Clayton, 1975). An effort to compile a bibliography of biomedical and social research from 1954 to 1974 produced 50,000 titles (Woodruff, 1975). Gerontology has also become increasingly more interdisciplinary; that is, specialists in diverse areas of the basic, clinical, behavioral, and social sciences, as well as engineering and design professions, are working together on research projects aimed at improving the aging process.

Major Research Centers Founded

Research in gerontology assumed greater significance after these developments, and an interest in the social factors associated with aging grew in the late 1950s and early 1960s. In 1946, a national gerontology research center, headed by the late Nathan Shock, a leader in geriatric medicine, was established at Baltimore City Hospital by the National Institutes of Health. This federally funded research center undertook several studies of physiological aspects of aging, using a cross-sectional approach.

In 1958, Dr. Shock and his colleagues began a longitudinal study of physiological changes in healthy, middle-aged and older men living in the community, by testing them every two years on numerous physiological parameters. They later started to examine the cognitive, personality, and social–psychological characteristics of these men. Much later, in 1978, older women were included in their samples. Known as the **Baltimore Longitudinal Studies of Aging,** these assessments of changes associated with healthy aging are still continuing, now under the direction of the National Institute on Aging. More than 2200 volunteers, men and women, aged 20 to 90, have participated, and today 1400 are continuing to participate in this study of the basic processes of aging. On average, these volunteers remain in the study for 13 years. More recently, ethnic minorities have been recruited as subjects; 13 percent are African Americans, mostly in the younger cohorts. The results of this ongoing research effort provide valuable information about normal age-related changes in physiological and psychological functions. As more persons of color in this longitudinal study grow older, they will provide valuable insights into the process of normal age-related changes versus disease in these populations.

Concurrently with the Baltimore Longitudinal Studies, several university-based centers were developed to study the aging process and the needs of older adults. One of the first, the Duke University Center on Aging, was founded in 1955 by one of the pioneers in gerontology, Ewald Busse. This center focused initially on physiological aging and on mental health, but has also examined many social aspects of aging.

The University of Chicago, under Robert Havighurst's direction, developed the first research center devoted exclusively to the social aspects of aging. The Kansas City studies of adult development, discussed in Chapter 8, represent the first major social–psychological studies of adult development, and were conducted by researchers from the Chicago center. Research and training centers on aging have since evolved at many other universities, generally stimulated by government sponsorship of gerontological research through the National Institute on Aging (established in 1974), the National Institute of Mental Health (which established its Center for Studies of the Mental Health of the Aging in 1976), and the Administration on Aging (established in 1965).

Research Methods

Before examining the issues and areas of special concern to social gerontologists, we first consider the ways in which such information about the aging process is gathered. The topic of research methodologies in gerontology may seem an advanced one to introduce in a basic text, but in fact, it is essential to understanding the meaning and validity of information presented throughout this book.

The study of aging presents particular conceptual and methodological difficulties. A major one is how research is designed and data interpreted regarding age changes. A point that complicates research in aging and also produces some misleading interpretations of data is how to distinguish *age changes* from *age differences*. This differentiation is necessary if we are to understand the processes of aging and the conditions under which age differences occur. If we wish to determine what changes or effects are experienced as an individual moves from middle age to old age and to advanced old age, we must examine the same individual over a period of years, or at least months. In order to understand age changes, longitudinal research is necessary—that is, the repeated measurement of the same person over a specified period of time.

Unfortunately, the time and cost of such studies prevent many researchers from undertaking longitudinal research. Instead, much of the research in this field focuses on age differences, by comparing people of different chronological ages at the same measurement period. These studies, cross-sectional in nature, are the most common ones in gerontology.

Many older adults participate in research that could benefit others.

The unique problems inherent in how gerontological research is designed and how data are interpreted are evident in the following question: Given that aging in humans is a complex process that proceeds quite differently among individuals in varied geographic, cultural, and historical settings, and that it occurs over a time span as long as 100 to 120 years, how does one study it? Obviously, scientists cannot follow successive generations—or even a single generation of subjects—throughout their life span. Nor can they be expected to address the entire range of variables that affect aging—including lifestyle, social class, cultural beliefs, gender, ethnic minority status, public policies, and so on—in a single study.

The Age/Period/Cohort Problem

The problem in each case is that of distinguishing *age differences* (ways that one generation differs from another) from *age changes* (ways that people normally change over time). This has been referred to as the "age/period/cohort" problem. (The word *cohort,* you will recall, refers to those people born at roughly the same time. *Period,* or time of measurement effect, refers to the impact of the specific historical period involved.) The concept of cohort is an important one in gerontology because historical events differentiate one generation from another in attitudes and behaviors. People in the same cohort are likely to be more similar to each other than to people in other cohorts because of comparable social forces acting on them during a given era. For example, the Depression era cohort has very different attitudes toward spending their savings than the Baby Boom cohort.

Cross-Sectional Studies

As noted earlier, the most common approach to studying aging is cross-sectional; that is, researchers compare a number of subjects of different ages on the same characteristics in order to determine age-related differences. One reason that cross-sectional studies are frequently used is that, compared to other designs, data can be readily gathered. Some examples might include a comparison of the lung capacity of men aged 30 with those who are aged 40, 50, 60, 70, and 80, or a study comparing church attendance by American adults under age 65 with those over age 65. The average differences among different age groups in each study might suggest conclusions about the changes that come with age.

The danger with such cross-sectional studies is that these differences might not be due to the process of aging, but rather to particular cultural and historical conditions that shaped each group of subjects being studied. For example, a higher rate of church attendance among today's older adults than among younger adults probably reflects a change in social attitudes toward attending church, as opposed to an increased need for spiritual and religious life as one grows older.

Even in studies of biological factors, such as lung capacity, many intervening variables may threaten the validity of comparative results. In this case, they include the effects of exercise, smoking, and other lifestyle factors, genetic inheritance, and exposure to pollution

(this, in turn, might be a product of work environments and social class) on relevant outcome variables.

The major limitation of cross-sectional studies occurs when differences among younger and older respondents are erroneously attributed to growing old; for example, some researchers have found that the older the respondent, the lower his or her score on intelligence tests. As a result, cognitive abilities have been misinterpreted as declining with age. In fact, such differences may be due to the lower educational levels and higher test anxiety of this cohort of older adults compared to younger adults, not to age. This is an example of *confounding*, or a joint effect of two variables on an outcome of interest. In this case, age effects are confounded by the impact of cohort differences. Because many issues in social gerontology center on distinguishing age from cohort effects, a number of research designs have emerged that attempt to do this. They include "longitudinal" and "sequential" designs.

Longitudinal Studies: Design and Limitations

Longitudinal designs permit inferences about *age changes*. They eliminate cohort effects by studying the same people over time. Each row in Table 1.2 represents a separate longitudinal study in which a given cohort (e.g., A, B, or C) is measured once every 10 years. Despite the advantages of longitudinal designs over the cross-sectional approach, they still have limitations. First, the longitudinal method does not allow a distinction between age and time of testing. Second, it cannot separate the effects of events extraneous to the study that influence people's responses in a particular measurement period.

Another problem with longitudinal studies is the potential for practice effects. This is a particular concern in studies that administer aptitude or knowledge tests, where repeated measurement with the same test improves the test-taker's performance because of familiarity or

TABLE 1.2   Alternative Research Designs in Aging

COHORT BORN IN	TIME OF MEASUREMENT			
	1970	1980	1990	2000
1920	A_1	A_2		
1930		B_1	B_2	
1940		C_1	C_2	C_3
1950				D_4

Cross-sectional: Cohorts A, B, and C are measured in 1980. *Longitudinal:* Cohort A is measured in 1970 and 1980; or Cohort B is measured in 1980 and 1990; or Cohort C is measured in 1980, 1990, and 2000. *Cohort-sequential:* Cohort A is measured in 1970 and 1980; Cohort B is measured in 1980 and 1990. *Time-sequential:* Cohort B and C are measured in 1980; Cohorts C and D are measured in 2000. *Cross-sequential:* Cohorts B and C are both measured in 1980 and 1990.

SOURCE: Adapted from K. W. Schaie (Ed.), *Longitudinal studies of adult psychological development* (New York: Guilford Press, 1983). Reprinted with permission from Guilford Press.

practice. For example, a psychologist who is interested in age-related changes in intelligence could expect to obtain improvements in people's scores if the same test is administered several times, with a brief interval (e.g., less than one year) between tests. In such cases, it is difficult to relate the changes to maturation unless the tests can be varied or parallel forms of the same tests can be used.

Longitudinal studies also present the problem of *attrition,* or dropout. Individuals in experimental studies and respondents in surveys that are administered repeatedly may drop out for many reasons—death, illness, loss of interest, or frustration with poor performance. To the extent that people who drop out are not different from the original sample in terms of demographic characteristics, health status, and intelligence, the researcher can still generalize from the results obtained with the remaining sample. However, more often it is the case that dropouts differ significantly from those who stay until the end. As we shall see in Chapter 5, those who drop out of longitudinal studies of intelligence are more likely:

- to be in poorer health,
- to score lower on intelligence tests, and
- to be more socially isolated.

In contrast, older participants who remain in a longitudinal study are generally:

- more educated,
- healthier, and
- more motivated.

AN EXAMPLE OF MISINTERPRETING LONGITUDINAL DATA

Imagine a study that attempted to determine attitudes about retirement. If a sample of 55-year-old workers had been interviewed in 1980, before mandatory retirement was changed to age 70, and again in 1990, after mandatory retirement was eliminated, it would be difficult to determine whether the changes in the workers' attitudes toward retirement occurred because of their increased age and proximity to retirement, or because of the modifications in retirement laws during this period.

EXAMPLE OF A COHORT-SEQUENTIAL DESIGN

An investigator may wish to compare changing attitudes toward federal aging policies among the cohort born in 1930 and the cohort born in 1940 and follow each one for 10 years, from 1980 to 1990 for the first cohort, and from 1990 to 2000 for the second. This approach is useful for many social gerontological studies in which age and cohort must be distinguished. However, it still does not separate the effects of cohort from historical effects or time of measurement. As a result, historical events that occurred just before one cohort entered a study (in this case, the Great Depression), but later than another cohort entered, may influence each cohort's attitude scores differently.

This is known as the problem of **selective dropout.** While many researchers have pointed to the potential bias introduced by selective dropout, others have suggested that the results of such longitudinal data provide a positive developmental image about aging (Cooney, Schaie, and Willis, 1988; Schaie, 1996).

Sequential Designs

Some alternative research designs have emerged in response to the problems of cross-sectional and longitudinal methods. One is the category of **sequential research designs** (Schaie, 1967, 1973, 1977, 1983). They combine the strengths of cross-sectional and longitudinal research designs. These include the cohort-sequential, time-sequential, and cross-sequential methods, which are illustrated in Table 1.2.

A *cohort-sequential* design is an extension of the longitudinal design, whereby two or more cohorts are followed for a period of time, so that measurements are taken of different cohorts at the same ages, but at different points in time.

The *time-sequential* design is useful for distinguishing between age and time of measurement or historical factors. It can be used to determine if changes obtained are due to aging or to historical factors. The researcher using this design would compare two or more cross-sectional samples at two or more measurement

> **EXAMPLE OF A TIME-SEQUENTIAL DESIGN**
>
> A group of 70-year-olds and a group of 60-year-olds might be compared on their attitudes toward religious activities in 1990. The latter group then could be compared with a new group of 60-year-olds in 2000. This would give some information on how people approaching old age at two different historical periods view the role of religion in their lives.

periods. Time-sequential designs do not prevent the confounding of age and cohort effects, but it is acceptable to use this method where one would not expect age differences to be confused with cohort differences.

The third technique that was first proposed by Schaie (1983) is the *cross-sequential* design, which combines cross-sectional and longitudinal designs. This approach is an improvement over both the traditional cross-sectional and longitudinal designs, but it still confounds age and time of measurement effects. These three sequential designs are becoming more widely used by gerontological researchers, especially in studies of intelligence. Table 1.3 summarizes potential confounding effects in each of these methods.

Despite the growth of new research methods, much of social gerontology is based on cross-sectional studies. For this reason, it is important to read carefully the description of a study and its

TABLE 1.3   Potential Confounding Effects in Developmental Studies

DESIGN	CONFOUNDING EFFECT		
	AGE × COHORT CONFOUNDED	AGE × TIME OF MEASUREMENT CONFOUNDED	COHORT × TIME OF MEASUREMENT CONFOUNDED
Cross-sectional	Yes	No	No
Longitudinal	No	Yes	No
Cohort-sequential	No	No	Yes
Time-sequential	Yes	No	No
Cross-sequential	No	Yes	No

SOURCE: Adapted from M. F. Elias, P. K. Elias, and J. W. Elias, *Basic processes in adult developmental psychology* (St. Louis: C. V. Mosby, 1977).

EXAMPLE OF A CROSS-SEQUENTIAL DESIGN

A researcher interested in examining the effects of cohort and historical factors on attitudes toward federal aging policy might compare two groups: people who were age 40 and 50 in 1990, and the same people in 2000 when they are age 50 and 60, respectively. This would permit the assessment of cohort and historical factors concurrently, with one providing information on changes from age 40 to 50, and the other representing changes from age 50 to 60.

results in order to make accurate inferences about age *changes* as opposed to age *differences*, and to determine whether the differences found between groups of different ages are due to cohort effects or to the true effects of aging.

Problems with Representative Samples of Older Persons in Research

Accurate sampling can be difficult with older populations. If the sample is not representative, the results are of questionable validity. However, comprehensive lists of older people are not readily available. Membership lists from organizations such as AARP tend to overrepresent those who are healthy, white, and financially secure. Studies in institutions, such as nursing homes and adult day centers, tend to overrepresent those with chronic impairments. Because whites represent almost 84 percent of the population over age 65 today, it is not surprising that they are more readily available for research.

Reaching older persons of color through organizational lists can be especially difficult. More effective means of recruiting these groups include the active participation of community leaders such as ministers and respected elders in churches attended by the population of interest. The problem of ensuring diverse samples of research participants is compounded by the mistrust toward research among many elders of color. Many African Americans, in particular, remember the

unethical practices of the Tuskegee Syphilis Study in the early twentieth century and are reluctant to participate in research today, despite significant improvements in the ethics of human research. Researchers must be sensitive to these issues when attempting to recruit elders of color into research projects. For example, older African Americans:

- prefer to participate in social science studies more than in clinical research.
- may need transportation to the research site.
- feel more comfortable when African Americans are represented on the research staff (Burnette, 1998).

Such disproportionate focus on whites and lack of data on ethnic minorities has slowed the development of gerontological theories that consider the impact of race, ethnicity, and culture on the aging process. Yet, even as researchers and funding agencies emphasize the need to include more people of color in all types of research, multiple confounding factors must be considered. For example, Latino elders represent U.S.-born as well as immigrant populations who have come here from countries as diverse as Mexico, Cuba, and Argentina. Therefore, any research that includes ethnic minorities must distinguish among subgroups by language, place of birth, and religion, not just the broader categories of Latino, African American, and Asian. It is not necessary to include all possible subgroups of a particular ethnic minority population in a given study.

POINTS TO PONDER

Think about some studies that are reported in newspapers, such as surveys of voter preferences. In the 2000 presidential election, several national polls reported the likelihood of "older voters" choosing one candidate or another. Did these surveys reflect the diversity among older voters, or put them into a monolithic block that distinguished them from another diverse group, "middle-class voters"?

However, it behooves the researcher to state clearly who is represented, in order to assure appropriate generalizability of the findings.

The problem of *measurement equivalence* in gerontological research is compounded when the sample includes elders of color. As will be discussed in Chapters 5 and 6, many tests of intelligence, memory, and personality traits were originally developed for testing younger populations. As a result, they may not be appropriate for older cohorts whose educational level is generally lower and whose educational and cultural experiences as children differed widely from newer cohorts. In order to achieve equivalence of tests and measures for diverse age groups, gerontologists have spent many years testing the *validity* of existing measures for this population—modifying them and developing new tests as needed. Similar work with elders of color has not been undertaken as extensively. Although there has been some work to assure linguistic equivalence, researchers have not spent as much time on testing the *conceptual equivalence* of these measures (i.e., that people of different ethnic backgrounds see the same meaning or concepts underlying a particular test). If we are to understand ethnic differences in aging, it is important to use valid measures that mean the same thing to all groups participating in research.

The problem of *selective survival* affects most studies of older people. Over time, the birth cohort loses members, so that those who remain are not necessarily representative of all members of the original group. Those who survive, for example, probably were healthiest at birth, and maintained their good health throughout their lives—all variables that tend to be associated with higher socioeconomic status.

Even when an adequate sample is located, older respondents may vary in their memories or attention spans; such variations can interfere with conducting interviews or tests. Ethical issues and unique difficulties arise in interviewing frail elders; yet there are no ethical guidelines specifically aimed at research with older adults.

The issue of informed consent becomes meaningless when dealing with a confused or a severely medically compromised older person. In such cases, family members or guardians must take an active role in judging the risks and benefits of research for frail older persons. An additional problem is that studies of the old-old may be influenced by *terminal drop,* a decline in some tests of intelligence shortly before death (Botwinick, 1984; White and Cunningham, 1988). Since death becomes increasingly likely with age, terminal drop will manifest as a gradual decline in performance test scores with age in cross-sectional designs. In longitudinal studies, this problem may result in an overestimation of performance abilities in the later years because those who survive are likely to represent the physically and cognitively most capable older individual (Schaie, 1996). This problem is explored further in Chapter 5.

Further refinement of research methodologies is a challenging task for social gerontologists. As progress is made in this area, the quality of data with which to study aging will continually improve.

Summary and Implications for the Future

A primary reason for the growing interest in gerontology is the dramatic increase in the population over age 65. This growth results from a reduction in infant and child mortality and improved treatment of acute diseases of childhood and adulthood, which in turn increases the proportion of people living to age 65 and beyond. In the United States, average life expectancy from birth has increased from 47 years in 1900 to 77.9 in 2005, with women continuing to outlive men. The growth in the population over age 85 has been most dramatic, reflecting major achievements in disease prevention and health care since the turn of the twentieth century. More recently, there has been increased attention given to learning about the aging process by studying centenarians. Those who live to be 100 and older may have a biological advantage over their peers who die at a younger age. Studies have found greater tolerance to stress and fewer chronic illnesses in centenarians. Ethnic minorities are less likely to live beyond age 65 than their white counterparts, but population projections anticipate a much higher rate of population growth for elders of color in the next 20 years. Because of the lower life expectancy of historically disadvantaged populations, increasing attention is given to health and economic disparities from birth to old age (Zarit and Pearlin, 2005).

The growth in the numbers and proportions of older people, especially the oldest-old, requires that both public and private policies affecting employment and retirement, health and long-term care, and social services be modified to meet the needs and enhance the quality of life of those who are living longer. Fundamental issues need to be resolved about who will receive what societal resources and what roles private and public sectors will play in sharing responsibilities of elder care.

Gerontology is growing as a field of study since early philosophers and scientists first explored the reasons for changes experienced with advancing age. Roger Bacon in the thirteenth century, Adolph Quetelet in the early nineteenth century, Botkin in the late nineteenth century, and Ivan Pavlov and G. Stanley Hall in the early twentieth century made pioneering contributions to this field. During the early 1900s, in Europe and the United States, the impact of an increasing aging population on social and health resources began to be felt. Social gerontological research has expanded since the 1940s, paralleling the rapid growth of the older population and its needs along with its resilience.

The growing older population and associated social concerns have stimulated great interest in gerontological research. However, existing research methodologies are limited in their ability to distinguish the processes of aging

per se from cohort, time, and measurement effects. Cross-sectional research designs are most often used in this field, but these can provide information only on age differences, not on age changes. Longitudinal designs are necessary for understanding age changes, but they suffer from the possibility of subject attrition and the effects of measuring the same individual numerous times. Newer methods in social gerontology, known as cohort-sequential, time-sequential, and cross-sequential designs, test multiple cohorts or age groups over time. They also are limited by possible confounding effects, but represent considerable improvement over traditional research designs.

Because research methods in gerontology have improved, today there is a better understanding of many aspects of aging. Research findings to date provide the empirical background for the theories and topics to be covered in the remaining chapters. Despite the recent explosion of knowledge in gerontology, gaps remain in what is known about older people and the aging process. The problem is particularly acute in our understanding of aging among historically underserved groups. Throughout the text, we will call attention to areas in which additional research is needed and suggest implications for gerontological practice and policy.

GLOSSARY

active aging   a model of viewing aging as a positive experience of continued growth and participation in family, community, and societal activities, regardless of physical and cognitive decline

active versus dependent life expectancy   a way of describing expected length of life, the term *active* denoting a manner of living that is relatively healthy and independent in contrast to being *dependent* on help from others

ageism   negative attitudes, beliefs, and conceptions of the nature and characteristics of older persons that are based on age that distort their actual characteristics, and abilities.

aging   changes that occur to an organism during its life span, from development to maturation to senescence

Baltimore Longitudinal Studies of Aging   a federally funded longitudinal study that has examined physiological, cognitive, and personality changes in healthy, middle-aged and older men since 1958, and in women since 1978

cohort   a group of people of the same generation sharing a statistical trait such as age, ethnicity, or socioeconomic status (for example, all African American women between the ages of 60 and 65 in 1999)

competence model   a conception or description of the way persons perform, focusing on their abilities vis-á-vis the demands of the environment

compression of morbidity   given a certain length of life, a term referring to relatively long periods of healthy, active, high-quality existence and relatively short periods of illness and dependency in the last few years of life

cross-sectional research   research that examines or compares characteristics of people at a given point in time and attempts to identify factors associated with contrasting characteristics of different groupings of people

environmental press   features of the social, technological, natural environment that place demands on people

geriatrics   clinical study and treatment of older people and the diseases that affect them

gerontology   the field of study that focuses on understanding the biological, psychological, social, and political factors that influence older people's lives

life expectancy   the average length of time persons, defined by age, sex, ethnic group, and socioeconomic status in a given society, are expected to live

life course   a broader concept than individual life span development that takes account of cultural, historical, and societal contexts that affect people as they age

longitudinal research   research that follows the same individual, over time, to measure change in specific variables

maximum life span   biologically programmed maximum number of years that each species can expect to live

person–environment (P–E) perspective   a model for understanding the behavior of people based on the idea that persons are affected by personal characteristics, such as health, attitudes, and beliefs, as they interact with and are affected by the characteristics of the cultural, social, political, and economic environment

resilience   capacity to overcome adversity, in part due to protective personal, family, community and societal factors

selective dropout   elders who drop out of longitudinal studies tend to be sicker, less educated, and more isolated

senescence   gradual decline in all organ systems, especially after age 30

sequential research designs   research designs that combine features of cross-sectional and longitudinal research designs to overcome some of the problems encountered in using those designs

RESOURCES

Log on to MySocKit (www.mysockit.com) for information about the following:

- ACTION—Older Americans Volunteer Programs
- AoA—Administration on Aging
- Alliance for Aging Research
- American Federation for Aging Research
- Gerontological Society of America
- MedWeb: Geriatrics
- National Institute on Aging (NIA)`

REFERENCES

AARP. *Global Aging Report.* 2000, 5, 4–5.

Alwin, D., and Wray, L. A life-span developmental perspective on social status and health. *Journals of Gerontology,* 2005, 60B, 7–14.

Bernstein, A.M., Willcox, B.J., Tamaki, H., Kunishima, N., Suzuki, M., Willcox, D.C., Yoo, J.S., and Perls, T.T. First autopsy study of Okinawan centenarian: Absence of many age-related diseases. *Journal of Gerontology: Medical Sciences,* 2004, 59A, 1195–1199.

Birren, J.E., and Clayton, V. History of gerontology. In D.S. Woodruff and J.E. Birren (Eds.),

Aging: Scientific perspectives and social issues. New York: Van Nostrand, 1975.

Botwinick, J. *Cognitive processes in maturity and old age* (3rd ed.). New York: Springer, 1984.

Bureau of Labor Statistics, Labor force data: Percent distribution of employed population aged 55 and over, 2004. Cited in W. He, M. Sengupta, V. Velkoff, and K.A. DeBarros. *65+ in the United States: 2005.* U.S. Census Bureau, Current Population Reports. Washington, DC: U.S. Government and Printing Office, 2005.

Burnette, D. Conceptual and methodological considerations in research with non-white ethnic elders. *Journal of Social Service Research,* 1998, *23,* 71–91.

Butler, R. Ageism: Another form of bigotry. *The Gerontologist,* 1969, *9,* 243.

Centers for Disease Control and Prevention (CDC). *Trends in causes of death among older persons in the United States: 2005.* Accessed September 2006, from http://www.cdc.gov/nchs/data/ahcd/agingtrends/06olderpersons.

Cohen, G. D. *The mature mind: The positive power of the aging brain.* Cambridge, MA: Perseus Books, 2005.

Cooney, T.M., Schaie, K.W., and Willis, S.L. The relationship between prior functioning on cognitive and personality dimensions and subject attrition in longitudinal research. *Journals of Gerontology,* 1988, *43,* P12–P17.

Fredriksen-Goldsen, K. Caregiving and resiliency: Predictors of well-being. *Journal of Family Relations,* in press.

Freedman, V.A., Martin, L.G., and Schoeni, R.F. Recent trends in disability and functioning among older adults in the United States. *Journal of the American Medical Association,* 2002, *288,* 3137–3146.

Fries, J.F. Aging, natural death, and the compression of morbidity. *New England Journal of Medicine,* 1980, *303,* 130–135.

Fries, J.F. The compression of morbidity: Near or far? *Milbank Quarterly,* 1990, *67,* 208–232.

Hayflick, L. *How and why we age* (2nd ed.). New York: Ballantine Books, 1996.

Hazzard, W. R. Aging, health, longevity, and the promise of biomedical research. In E.J. Masoro and S.N. Austad (Eds.), *Handbook of the biology of aging* (5th ed.). San Diego: Academic Press, 2001.

He, W., Sengupta, M., Velkoff, V., and DeBarros, K.A. *65+ in the United States: 2005.* U.S. Census Bureau, Current Population Reports. Washington, DC: U.S. Government and Printing Office, 2005, 23–29.

Hoover, D., Crystal, S., Kumar, R., Sambamoorthi, U., and Cantor, J. Medical expenditures during the last year of life. *Health Services Research,* 2002, *37,* 1625–1642.

International Longevity Center–USA. *The aging factor in health and disease.* (Report of an interdisciplinary workshop). New York: The Center, 1999.

Kaiser, F. *I say senior, you say senior, suddenly senior.* Accessed October 15, 2006, from http://www.suddenlysenior.com/boomerhatessenior.html.

Katz, S., Branch, L.G., Branson, M.H., Papsidero, J.A., Beck, J.C., and Greer, D.S. Active life expectancy. *New England Journal of Medicine,* 1983, *309,* 1218–1224.

Kaye, J.A. Oldest-old healthy brain function. *Archives of Neurology,* 1997, *54,* 1217–1221.

Lawton, M.P. Behavior-relevant ecological factors. In K.W. Schaie and C. Scholar (Eds.), *Social structure and aging: Psychological processes.* Hillsdale, NJ: Erlbaum, 1989.

Lawton, M.P., and Nahemow, L. Ecology and the aging process. In C. Eisdorfer and M.P. Lawton (Eds.), *Pychology of adult development and aging.* Washington, DC: American Psychological Association, 1973.

Lesnoff-Caravaglia, G. Response to "Ageism in Gerontological Language" or growing old absurd. *The Gerontologist,* 2002, *42,* 431.

Levy, B.R. Eradication of ageism requires addressing the enemy within. *The Gerontologist,* 2001, *41,* 578–579.

Manton, K.G., and Gu, X.L. Changes in the prevalence of chronic disability in U.S. black and non-black population above age 65 from 1982 to 1999. *Proceedings of the National Academy of Sciences,* 2001, *98,* 6354–6359.

Manton, K.G., and Land, K.C. Active life expectancy estimates for the U.S. elderly population. *Demography,* 2000, *37,* 253–265.

Manton, K.G., and Vaupel, J.W. Survival after the age of 80 in the United States, Sweden, France, England and Japan. *New England Journal of Medicine,* 1995, *333,* 1232–1235.

National Center for Health Statistics. *National Vital Statistics Reports,* 2006, *54* (www.cdc.gov/nchs).

O'Rand, A.M. and Hamil-Luker, J. Processes of cumulative adversity: Childhood disadvantage and increased risk of heart attack across the life course. *Journals of Gerontology,* 2005, *60B,* Special Issue II, S117–S124.

Parmelee, P.A., and Lawton, M.P. The design of special environments for the aged. In J.E. Birren and K.W. Schaie (Eds.), *Handbook of the psychology of aging* (3rd ed.). San Diego: Academic Press, 1990.

Perls, T.T., Alpert, L., Wagner, G.G., Vijg, J., and Kruglyak, L. Siblings of centenarians live longer. *Lancet,* 1998, *351,* 1560–1565.

Perls, T.T., and Silver, M.H. *Living to 100: Lessons in living to your maximum potential at any age.* New York: Basic Books, 1999.

Perls, T.T., and Terry, D.F. Genetics of exceptional longevity. *Experimental Gerontology,* 2003, *38,* 725–730.

Perls, T.T., and Wood, E.R. Acute care costs of the oldest old: They cost less, their care intensity is less, and they go to nonteaching hospitals. *Archives of Internal Medicine,* 1996, *156,* 754–760.

Poon, L.W., Johnson, M.A., Davey, A., Dawson, D.V., Siegler, I.C., and Martin, P. Psychosocial predictors of survival among centenarians. In P. Martin, A. Rott, B. Hagberg, and K. Mongan (Eds), *Centenarians.* New York: Springer Publishing, 2000.

Reville, R.T., and Schoeni, R.F. The fraction of disability caused at work. *Social Security Bulletin,* 2003–2004, *65,* 31–38.

Reynolds, C. Boomers, act II. *American Demographics,* 2004, *26,* 10–11.

Riley, M.W., and Riley, J. Longevity and social structure: The potential of the added years. In A. Pifer and L. Bronte (Eds.), *Our aging society: Paradox and promise.* New York: W.W. Norton, 1986.

Samuelsson, S.M., Baur, B., Hagberg, B., Samuelsson, G., Norbeck, B., Brun, A., Gustafson, L., et al. The Swedish Centenarian Study: A multidisciplinary study of five consecutive cohorts at the age of 100. *International Journal of Aging and Human Development,* 1997, *45,* 223–253.

Schaie, K.W. Age changes and age differences. *The Gerontologist,* 1967, *7,* 128–132.

Schaie, K.W. *Intellectual development in adulthood.* Cambridge: Cambridge University Press, 1996.

Schaie, K.W. (Ed.), *Longitudinal studies of adult psychological development.* New York: Guilford Press, 1983.

Schaie, K.W. Methodological problems in descriptive developmental research on adulthood and aging. In J.R. Nesselroade and H.W. Reese (Eds.), *Lifespan developmental psychology: Methodological issues.* New York: Academic Press, 1973.

Schaie, K.W. Quasi-experimental research designs in the psychology of aging. In J.E. Birren and K.W. Schaie (Eds.), *Handbook of the psychology of aging.* New York: Van Nostrand Reinhold, 1977.

Silver, M.H., Newell, K., Hyman, B., Growdon, J., Hedley, E.T., and Perls, T. Unraveling the mystery of cognitive changes in old age. *International Psychogeriatrics,* 1998, *10,* 25–41.

Social Security Administration. Accessed October 1, 2006, from http://www.ssa.gov/OACT/TR06/V_demographic.html.

Suzuki, M., Willcox, B.J., and Willcox, D.C. Implications from and for food cultures for cardiovascular disesase. *Asia Pacific Journal of Clinical Nutrition,* 2001, *10,* 165–171.

Terry, D.F., Willcox, M.A., McCormick, M.A., and Perls, T.T. Cardiovascular disease delay in centenarian offspring. *Journals of Gerontology: Medical Sciences,* 2004, *59A,* 385–389.

U.S. Census Bureau. Life expectancy at birth: United States 1940, 1950, 1960, 1970, and 1998. *National Vital Statistics Reports,* 48, No. 11, 2000.

U.S. Census Bureau. *Median age of the total population: 2005.* Accessed October 2006a, from http://www.factfinder.census.gov.

U.S. Census Bureau. Accessed October 1, 2006b, from http://www.census.gov/cgi-bin/ ipc/idbagg.

U.S. Census Bureau. Population Division, Interim Statistics.*Population projections by age: 2005.* Accessed October 1, 2006c, from http://www.census.gov/population/projections/SummaryTabC1.pdf.

White, N., and Cunningham, W.R. Is terminal drop pervasive or specific? *Journals of Gerontology,* 1988, *44,* S141–S144.

Whitfield, K.E., and Hayward, M. The landscape of health disparities among older adults. *Public Policy and Aging Report,* 2003, *13,* 1–7.

Williams, D. The health of U.S. racial and ethnic populations. *Journals* of *Gerontology*, 2005, *60B*, 53–62.

Willcox, B.J., Willcox, D.C., He, Q., Curb, J.D., and Suzuki, M. Siblings of Okinawan centenarians share lifelong mortality advantages. *Journal of Gerontology: Biological Sciences*, 2006b, *61A*, 345–354.

Willcox, D.C., Willcox, B.J., Todoriki, H., Curb, J.D., and Suzuki, M. Caloric restriction and human longevity: What can we learn from the Okinawans? *Biogerontology*, 2006a, *7*, 173–177.

World Health Organization (WHO). *Active Ageing: A Policy Framework*. Geneva, Switzerland: WHO, 2002.

Zarit, S.H., and Pearlin, L.I. Special issue on health inequalities across the life course. *Journals of Gerontology*, 2005, *60B*, Special Issue II, S5–S7.

2

Aging in Other Countries and across Cultures in the United States

This chapter describes the growth of the older population worldwide, including

- The increasing population of older adults in industrialized and developing countries
- The impact of demographic shifts on employment and retirement patterns in other countries
- How modernization has affected elders' roles in traditional societies
- The role of filial piety
- Challenges faced by older immigrants in the United States

Worldwide Trends

The rapid pace of economic development in most countries has resulted in shifts from rural, agricultural societies to more urbanized industrial landscapes with accompanying changes in social and family structures. Improved life expectancy has resulted in more people living into advanced old age, as noted for the U.S. population in Chapter 1. However, in many regions of the world where young adults must migrate to cities for job opportunities, older adults are left behind without family members living nearby. These changes in intergenerational contact are compounded when adult children immigrate to other countries for better job and educational opportunities. In this chapter we will explore the impact of the increased population of older adults worldwide, combined with the cultural changes and economic patterns that disrupt traditional family and social structures.

Demographic Changes

All world regions are experiencing an increase in the absolute and relative size of their older populations. The number of persons age 65 or older in the world is expected to increase from an estimated 420 million in 2000 to 974 million in 2030. This will result in a world population in which 12 percent will be 65 years of age or older by the year 2030, compared with 7 percent today (He et al., 2005). As seen in the projections for population growth in the United States, described in Chapter 1, the global age distribution will change from a pyramid to a cylindrical form (Figure 2.1). This is due to a reduction in fertility rates worldwide, even in the less developed countries of Africa and South America. It is estimated that

120 countries will reach total fertility rates below replacement levels (i.e., 2.1 children per woman) by 2025, compared to 22 countries in 1975 and 70 in 2000 (WHO, 2002). The situation is particularly critical in Japan, where the fertility rate in 2006 was 1.25.

The current numbers and expected growth of the older population differ substantially between the industrialized and developing countries. Currently 60 percent of older adults live in developing countries, which may increase to 75 percent by 2020. For example, in 2000 the population age 65 and older for most Western European countries was estimated to be greater than 15 percent:

- Italy and Japan currently have the highest proportion of elders in the world (19.5 percent each).
- Germany has 18.6 percent.
- Greece has 17.8 percent.
- Sweden has 17.3 percent (Haub, 2006).

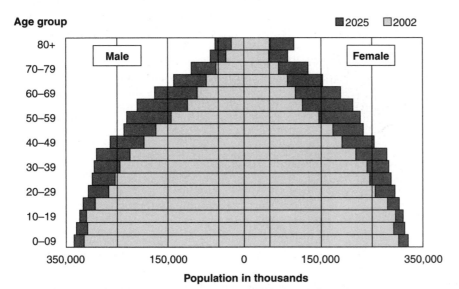

FIGURE 2.1   **Global Population Pyramid in 2002 and 2025**
SOURCE: World Health Organization, *Active ageing: A policy framework*. WHO, 2002. Reprinted by permission of the World Health Organization.

JAPAN'S AGING CRISIS

Japan is experiencing the most rapid rate of population aging in the world. In 1970, 7 percent of its population was 65 or older, but this has increased to 19.5 percent in 2006. This group will comprise 30 percent of Japan's population by 2050. Even more striking is the prediction that 7.2 percent will be age 80 and older in 2020, compared with 4.1 percent in the United States. By 2050, Japan is expected to have one million people aged 100 and older. Nevertheless, there is great resistance by politicians and society in general to immigration, which could increase the number of young workers contributing to the economic support of retirees in Japan. Reports by the United Nations and demographers project a need for 13 million to 17 million new immigrants by 2050 in order to prevent the collapse of Japan's pension system. Yet, in the past 25 years only 1 million foreigners have been accepted as immigrants in this insular country.

SOURCE: *New York Times*, July 24, 2003.

A major reason for such large proportions is increased life expectancy beyond age 65 in developed countries, as illustrated by trends in the United States and Japan (Figure 2.2). In less than

30 years, both countries have made great strides in keeping people alive into advanced old age. In particular, Japanese men and women have gained considerable advantage since 1970—almost 5 years for men and an additional 7 years for women (NCHS, 2005). In contrast, Sub-Saharan Africa and South Asia each counted only 3 percent of their population age 65 or over. The median age of these regions also varies:

- 23.5 worldwide
- 37 in Western Europe
- 36.5 in the United States
- 20 in Latin America

Even in Africa, with continued high fertility and high mortality rates, the median age will increase from 19 today to 27.4 in 2050. Figure 2.3 shows this projected increase in the median age of three developed countries and for Mexico. In less than 45 years, the median age in Italy, the "oldest" country, will be 52.5 followed closely by Japan at 52.3. The United States will show a much smaller increase, from a median age of 36.5 currently to 41.5 in 2050. This is due primarily to higher birthrates in the United States compared to these other countries. Mexico's median

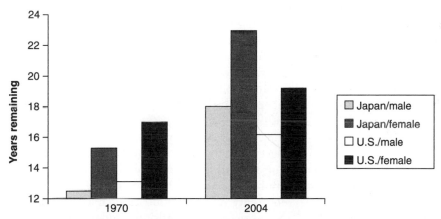

FIGURE 2.2   Life Expectancy at Age 65: United States and Japan
SOURCE: http://www.mhlw.go.jp/english/database/db-hw/lifetb04/1.html, accessed October, 2006, and http://www.ssa.gov/OACT/TR/TR06/V_demographic.html, accessed October, 2006.

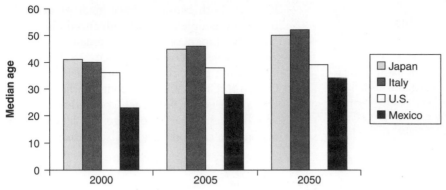

FIGURE 2.3 **Median Age: 2000 versus 2005 versus 2050**
SOURCE: United Nations, 2006a, 2006b.

age is also expected to increase significantly, from the current 25 to 38 by 2050, even though fertility rates in Mexico will remain high (United Nations, 2006b).

At the same time, the less-developed regions of the world expect to show a nearly fivefold increase in their oldest population, from 3.8 percent in 1975 to 17 percent in 2075. This five-fold growth rate is projected to occur in just 30 years (2000–2030) in Malaysia and Mexico, compared with slightly less than a doubling of the older population in the United States during this same period (Kinsella and Velkoff, 2001). An even greater rise in the proportion of the old-old (ages 75–84) and oldest-old is anticipated in these countries, from the current 0.5 percent to 3.5 percent in 2075. In absolute numbers, China currently has the largest number of people 65 and older (102 million), which is expected to reach 322 million by 2050. The Chinese population aged 80 and older is also the largest in the world (13 million vs. 9.2 million in the United States), and is projected to reach 100 million by 2050. This increase in the general population of elders and among the old-old is attributable mostly to China's continued low birth rate (Kaneda, 2006; Zeng, Liu, and George, 2003). This will result in a top-heavy rectangular population structure, as illustrated by Figure 2.4, which is much more dramatic than the increases

described globally in Figure 2.1. Reasons for the growth of the old-old in developing countries include:

- improved sanitation
- medical care
- immunizations
- better nutrition
- declining birth rates

Unfortunately, this rapid growth has not led to public policy and social planning in developing countries. While industrialized countries like France took more than 100 years to double their population of elders, it will take China only 26 years to do so. Such an increase requires government planning, but few developing countries have been able to focus on this coming crisis (Kalache and Keller, 2000; Kinsella and Phillips, 2005). It is also important to note that the less-developed regions of the world are currently coping with the tremendous impact of high fertility rates. Even with the continued high infant mortality rates in countries such as those in sub-Saharan Africa, children under 15 represent 37 percent of the population in less-developed regions, compared with 22 percent in more-developed regions (United Nations, 2006b).

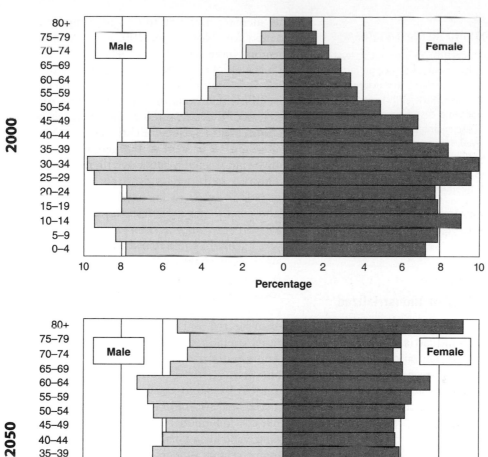

FIGURE 2.4 Population Pyramids, China: 2000 and 2050
SOURCE: *World Population Prospects: The 2004 Revision* (2005).

GOVERNMENT EFFORTS TO INCREASE BIRTHRATES

In response to dramatic declines in birth rates, leaders of several industrialized countries have proposed tax benefits and financial incentives to encourage women to bear more children. Russian President Vladimir Putin has proposed a cash bonus of $9000 per baby, as well as an increasing scale of cash and assistance with child care. However, economists are not optimistic that this will reverse the trend toward low fertility and a declining number of workers to support Russia's aging population. Meanwhile, French Prime Minister Dominique de Villepin has advocated national support for child care and foster grandparents to assist mothers working outside the home in France. (Chivers, 2006)

Economic Implications for Industrialized Countries

Life expectancy in industrial nations has improved by 6 years for men and 8.5 years for women since 1953. The rate has been greatest over the past 20 years, with a significant impact on the availability of workers to support retired persons. If current retirement patterns continue, the dependency ratio for older retired persons will drop from 3.5:1 (3.5 workers to support 1 retiree) in 1990 to about 2:1 in 2030 in the industrialized countries of Europe and in Japan. A report by the Economic Policy Committee of the European Union projects a decline in the working-age population by 7 percent between 2005 and 2030. In contrast, the population of elders is projected to rise by 52 percent (European Commission, 2005).

A parallel concern for European countries facing an aging population is the "graying" of their workforce. As middle-aged workers begin to retire, many companies are experiencing problems in replacing these skilled workers with new employees who have the necessary qualifications. European Union (EU) countries project a decline in their 20- to 29-year-old population by 20 percent in the next two decades, coupled with

an increase in the 50 to 64 age group by 25 percent (Von Nordheim, 2003). In response, EU leaders have set a goal of having 50 percent of their employees be age 55 to 64, partly by raising the age of full retirement by an additional 5 years by 2010 (Commission of European Communities, 2004). These are difficult objectives because across the 25-member EU the current average is less than 40 percent of workers in the 55 to 64 age range, with an average retirement age of 60. This ranges from an average retirement age of 57 in Poland to 63 in Portugal. Portugal's population age 65 and older is projected to grow from 17 percent today to 33 percent by 2050. This rapid growth, combined with concerns about the significant share of its gross domestic product (GDP) being spent for pension expenditures, has forced the national government to change its retirement policies. Portugal's Ministry of Labor and Social Security has recently placed restrictions on early retirement and calculation of pension benefits in an effort to encourage workers to postpone their retirement (SSA, 2005). As another example, the legal retirement age of 65 in Germany is older than in other EU countries, but the federal government has initiated legislation for raising this to 67. This represents a major reform of Germany's state pension system and will be done incrementally, beginning in 2012 and taking effect fully by 2029. At the same time, in response to growing numbers of retirees who depend on its pension fund, the German government will decrease full state pensions from the current 54 percent to 43 percent of the individual's salary by 2030 (Wagner, 2006).

The EU's stated objective of increasing the older workforce reverses the trend toward early retirement. Until recently, state pension plans and early retirement incentives to avoid layoffs made it attractive for workers to retire in their 50s and early 60s. This allowed companies and governments to hire less expensive younger workers. But with the decline in the younger population, many available positions are not being filled.

THE CRISIS IN EUROPE'S PENSION SYSTEMS

Pension programs in European nations have already started to feel the pinch of a growing population of retirees. The average portion of gross domestic product spent on pensions is 10 percent for the European Union; in Italy it is 14 percent. It will most likely rise in Italy if the current law that allows retirement at age 57 persists. Some regional government workers in Italy can retire even earlier; in Sicily, for example, male government workers can retire after 25 years on the job and women after 20 years. While other European countries like France and Germany are enacting legislation to require 40 years of employment or extending the retirement age to 67, efforts by the Italian government to protect its pension system by changing retirement laws have met with fierce resistance from labor unions.

The United Kingdom has taken a proactive position to prevent age discrimination in recruiting, selecting, and retaining workers. A program initiated in 2000 by the U.K. government, "New Deal 50," offers training grants of £1500 (almost $3000) to prepare older adults to return to the workforce and a working tax credit of £40–60 per week to supplement their earnings (Taylor, 2003). ASDA, a large U.K. retailer has been successful in recruiting and retaining mature workers. They proudly point to the fact that 19 percent of their workforce is age 50 and older. ASDA offers workshops to promote the company to potential employees over age 50; it also allows up to 3 months unpaid leave and a "grandparent leave" of one week after the birth of a grandchild. These actions have benefited the company directly; ASDA stores with the highest proportion of older workers report only one-third the absenteeism rates of the average in other stores (Personnelzone, 2004).

An innovative solution to preventing the "brain drain" of older workers was devised by Bosch, a German electronics company. Retiring employees complete a questionnaire about the knowledge they have gained during their careers. Project managers access this information from a database if they need workers with these specific abilities. These retirees are then employed for short periods on projects that require such skills (Bosch Management Support, 2004).

In response to these demographic changes and in recognition of the value of older workers, IBM Business Consulting Services (2005) offers several strategies for European companies to respond to this impending crisis:

1. Redirect recruiting and training to include older workers.
2. Retain valued employees by offering alternative, flexible working conditions (e.g. telecommuting).
3. Preserve the critical knowledge that mature workers possess.
4. Offer opportunities for worker retraining.
5. Facilitate intergenerational workforce communication.
6. Assist older workers in learning and using new technologies.

Although Australia is facing less of a workforce crisis than European countries, many Australian companies have recognized the importance of hiring and retaining experienced workers. One example is a financial services company, Wespac, which planned to expand its financial advising division. To do so, they recruited 900 experienced workers who were age 55 and older and interested in starting a second career. The company's leaders viewed older workers as an asset because they could communicate better with their older clients (Nixon, 2002).

In addition to raising the age for receiving full retirement benefits, industrialized countries may also need to permit more immigration of young workers from the developing world. Already, more than a quarter of all workers in Australia are immigrants. However, this is a controversial proposal for many countries where immigrants often are not easily assimilated because of languages, religions, and cultures divergent from those of the host country. Such tensions erupted into riots in late 2005 in the suburbs of Paris, where young Muslim immigrants from North Africa protested policies and practices by employers and the French government that discriminated against foreign workers. The challenges faced by older immigrants to the United States and other industrialized countries will be discussed later in this chapter.

The Impact of Modernization on Older Adults' Roles in Traditional Societies

Significant cultural variations affect the social position and experiences of older persons. Perhaps the greatest differences in the status of older adults are between traditional societies and those of the modernized world, with its rapidly changing values and norms. Examining the different ways that other societies have dealt with issues affecting their elders can shed light on the process of aging in our society. The field of "comparative sociocultural gerontology" or an "anthropology of aging" has helped researchers to differentiate what aspects of aging are universal or biological, and which factors are largely shaped by the sociocultural system (Sokolovsky, 1997; Infeld, 2002).

Understanding how aging in contemporary American society differs from that experienced elsewhere, and which factors are socioculturally determined, can also suggest strategies for improving environments in which to grow old. Within the constraints of this one chapter, we can only glance at a few other cultures. For a more complete view, we urge you to turn to the available literature on the anthropology of aging, including the *Journal of Cross-Cultural Gerontology*. While this chapter explores aging in other countries and among immigrants to the United States, Chapter 14 focuses on the cultural

Older people in Asian cultures enjoy teaching traditional arts to younger generations.

diversity represented by older ethnic minorities within contemporary American society.

Resources Held by Older Adults

Definitions of old age—as well as the authority exercised by older people—have traditionally rested on the material and political resources controlled by them. These resources include:

- traditional skills and knowledge
- security bestowed by property rights
- civil and political power
- information control
- general welfare from routine services performed by older people such as child care

Traditional systems of **social stratification** conferred respect and authority to some older adults if they controlled these resources or skills (Glascock, 1997). Within the constraints set by the social environment and its ideology, older people's social rank in traditional cultures was generally determined by the balance between the cost of maintaining them and the societal contributions they were perceived to make. As age became a less important criterion for determining access to and control of traditional and political resources, older members of society lost some of their status and authority.

Modernization Theory

A number of explanations have been advanced for the declining status of the old in modern society. Modernization theory is a major explanation. One of the first comparative analyses that raised this issue was reported by Leo Simmons in *The Role of the Aged in Primitive Society* (1945). He noted that the status of older persons, as reflected in their resources and the honor bestowed upon them, varied inversely with the degree of technology, social and economic diversity, and occupational specialization (or modernization) in a given society. **Modernization theory** was defined by Cowgill (1974a, 1974b, 1986) as:

> The transformation of a total society from a relatively rural way of life based on animate power, limited technology, relatively undifferentiated institutions, parochial and traditional outlook and values, toward a predominantly urban way of life, based on inanimate sources of power, highly differentiated institutions, matched by segmented individual roles, and a cosmopolitan outlook which emphasizes efficiency and progress (Cowgill, 1974a, p. 127).

As society becomes more modernized, older people lose political and social power, influence, and leadership. These social changes also may lead to disengagement of aging persons from community life. In addition, younger and older generations become increasingly separated socially, morally, and intellectually. Youth is glorified as the embodiment of progress and achievement, as well as the means by which society can attain such progress. Over time, the characteristics of modernization that contribute

to the lower status of older adults in traditional societies are:

- health technology
- scientific technology as applied in economic production and distribution
- urbanization
- literacy and mass education

Health technology has reduced infant mortality and maternal deaths, and prolonged adult life, thereby increasing the number of older persons. With more elders in the labor market, competition between generations for jobs intensified, and retirement developed as a means of forcing older people out of the labor market. However, as noted above, this has resulted in a shortage of workers in many industrialized countries.

Scientific technology creates new jobs primarily for the young, with older workers more likely to remain in traditional occupations that become obsolete. The rapid development of high-tech industries today and the gap between generations in the use of computers and the Internet illustrate this phenomenon. Unable to perform the socially valued role of contributors to a technologically skilled workforce, some older workers feel marginalized and alienated.

In the early stages of modernization, when the society is relatively rural, young people are attracted to *urban areas*, whereas older parents and grandparents remain on the family farm or in rural communities. The resulting residential segregation of the generations has a dramatic impact on family interactions. The geographical and occupational mobility of the young, in turn, leads to increased social distance between generations and to a reduced status of the old.

Finally, modernization is characterized by efforts to promote *literacy and education,* which tend to be targeted toward the young. As younger generations acquire more education than their parents, they begin to occupy higher-status positions. Intellectual and moral differences between the generations increase, with older members of society experiencing reduced leadership roles and influence (Cowgill, 1974a, 1974b).

Some social historians have criticized modernization theory, arguing that it idealizes the past and ignores the fact that older people in many preindustrial societies were treated harshly and at the whim of younger family members (Albert and Cattell, 1994; Kertzer and Laslett, 1994). However, there is considerable empirical support for this theory. For example, rapid urbanization in many developing countries has dislodged the tradition of family support for their elders. Modern migration programs in India, while providing resources for young and old, have resulted in younger people obtaining more education and creating a sense of superiority over their illiterate elders. Rapid urbanization has left almost 30 percent of old people in rural areas in India without family nearby to care for them (Dandekar, 1996; Vincentnathan and Vincentnathan, 1994). Meanwhile, families who eke out a meager living in urban areas have little with which to assist their elders who live with them. In the economically more successful countries of East Asia, such as Japan and South Korea, older people have benefited from improvements in health care, income, and longer life expectancy, but at the cost of power and prestige that was accorded previous generations of older adults (Silverman, Hecht, and McMillin, 2000).

Another example of how modernization has eroded traditional family supports is Taiwan, where young adults' support for multigenerational households declined from 76 percent in 1984 to 62.7 percent in 1995 (Hsu, Lew-Ting, and Wu, 2001). Adult children in China report feeling less obligated to help their parents if this conflicts with the demands of their job (Zhan, 2004). In such instances, it becomes vital for national and local governments to provide services such as public housing, health care, old-age pension plans, and policies that support family care of elders. These programs may serve to reduce tensions between generations. Some demographers have suggested that the improving

> **ROLE CHANGES AND SUICIDE AMONG OLDER ADULTS**
>
> Evidence of international differences in adaptation to role loss is reflected in suicide rates among older women. Although the rate among women in the United States *drops* from 11.6 per 100,000 among those aged 40 to 50 to 6.6 per 100,000 among women over 65, the suicide rate *increases* dramatically in Japan, tripling from 11.6 to 39.3 per 100,000. In Taiwan there is also a striking increase, from 10.4 to 34.6 per 100,000 in this same age range (Hu, 1995). In general, women aged 75 and older have higher suicide rates than their counterparts in English-speaking countries. Suicide rates for men aged 75 and older are higher than for any other age group in Asian countries, especially in rural China and Singapore, less so in Japan (Pritchard and Baldwin, 2002).

health and financial status of older populations has resulted in more older adults choosing to live apart from their adult children. In contrast to this concept of a normative trend toward individualism, other demographers have found that increases in older persons' income or that of their adult children do not result in significant changes in traditional family structures and the value of family interdependence (Cameron, 2000; Kinsella and Velkoff, 2001).

Occupation and education appear to have a reversed J-shaped relationship to modernization. In the early phases of rapid social change (illustrated by nations such as China and the Philippines), the occupational and educational status of older adults shows a decline, but then later improves (exemplified by New Zealand, Canada, and the United States). This suggests that, as societies move beyond an initial state of rapid modernization, status differences between generations decrease and the relative status of older people may rise, particularly when reinforced by social policies such as Social Security, which have improved older adults' financial status. Societies in advanced stages of modernization may become more aware of the older population's devalued status. Through public education, social policies, and the media, they then attempt to create more opportunities for, and positive images of, older people. This has already been occurring in the United States, in part because of the aging of the baby boomers, who have the political clout and resources to change popular stereotypes of aging. Advertising and television programs increasingly portray older persons as vital, active, involved, and physically attractive.

Impact of Modernization on Filial Piety

Most societies have some norms of favorable treatment toward their elders, but considerable variability exists in practice. For example, **filial piety**—a sense of reverence and deference toward elders—in China and Taiwan was not always manifested, but was affected by family resources, the number of living children, and geographic location (Ikels, 1997). The norms of filial piety were more often practiced by wealthy families in traditional rural China. Despite the Confucian reverence for age, known as "xiao," older people in lower-class families had fewer resources to give them status. But the tradition was maintained because of Confucian ideals that required children to always obey and serve their parents.

THE UNDERPINNINGS OF FILIAL PIETY IN ASIAN CULTURE

In his writings, Confucius emphasized that young people should respect, not just provide care for, their elders:

> Filial piety today is taken to mean providing nourishment for parents, but dogs and horses are provided with nourishment. If it is not done with reverence for parents, what is the difference between men and animals?

SOURCE: From *Analects*, Book 2, Chapter 7, quoted in Sung, 2000.

Life for older people in China has undergone a major transformation. The "political economy" has had an impact on elders' status as government policies have been altered. For example, women have benefited from changes such as not having to submit to arranged marriages or having their feet bound. Their work opportunities have expanded by opening up more jobs to women. National social insurance also benefits older Chinese citizens. However, the practice of educating sons and not daughters in traditional China has resulted in older cohorts in which women are illiterate and economically dependent on their children in old age. For this reason, researchers have found older women in China today to be more disadvantaged than men in their functional health as well as economic status (Zeng, Liu, and George, 2003). This problem is compounded by China's one-child-per-family policy that began in 1979. Although the policy is less rigid now, it has resulted in a disproportionate number of older adults to working-age younger adults. In addition, the break up of communes that provided support for childless elders in the past has also placed many elders at risk. These problems are expected to continue as future cohorts of older people contend with fewer children to care for them in times of need. These changes will also reduce multigenerational living arrangements in China (Cheng and Chan, 2006).

The rising standard of living in China has benefited many young adults, who often migrate to urban areas for job opportunities. This results in a concentration of older adults in rural areas, where 65 percent of China's general population and 76 percent of its older adults reside (United Nations, 2002). This pattern of migration by younger workers to urban areas also occurs in other Asian countries such as the Philippines, Indonesia, and Thailand, resulting in sharp declines in three-generational co-residence (Joseph and Phillips, 1999; Knodel and Ofstedal, 2002; Zhang, 2004). The loss of this long-held tradition of intergenerational living, an important pillar of filial piety, may significantly affect the older adult who is left behind. A recent survey in a rural region of China compared elders living in three-generational households or with grandchildren in **skipped generation households** (i.e., where grandparents were caring for grandchildren after the parents had relocated to urban areas for employment) with elders who lived alone or with a spouse. Those in traditional multigenerational households reported greater life satisfaction and less depression than their counterparts in single-generation households. Stronger emotional ties with and financial assistance from their adult children mitigated the negative effects of living alone on elders' well-being (Silverstein, Cong and Li, 2006).

In response to these population and economic demands, China has increased its publicly funded housing and government-funded welfare institutions for all older adults, not just for childless elders as in the past. A private residential-care-facility industry and community-based services are also emerging in response to the anticipated 24 percent older population by 2050 (Kaneda, 2006; Zhan et al., 2006). In Singapore a more radical approach to caring for a growing older population has emerged. In 1997, the government opened a special court where older persons can bring legal claims against their children for not providing assistance in their old age.

Overcoming the Impact of Modernization on Intergenerational Relations

Despite these changes in older adults' status and family relations in traditional societies, strong cultural values can mitigate many of the negative effects of modernization on older people. This is vividly illustrated in modern, industrialized, and urban Japanese society. Confucian values of filial piety and ancestor worship help to maintain older persons' relatively high status and integration in family life, as well as their leadership in national politics. Traditional values of reciprocity and lifelong indebtedness to one's parents are a major reason for continued three-generational house-

Even the oldest-old have important roles in most Asian families.

holds in Japan, even though the modernization of Japanese society has increased economic demands on the nuclear family. Almost half of working-age Japanese women today are employed outside the home. Unprecedented numbers of older people in Japan have increased the societal costs of maintaining older members and created dilemmas for younger family members who are responsible for their support. Therefore, it is not surprising that the majority of respondents to a survey by the Japanese Ministry of Health and Welfare (57.3 percent) viewed the aging population as a serious problem, and 68 percent thought that the birth rate in Japan should be encouraged to grow (National Institute of Population and Social Security Research, 2004).

Nevertheless, the majority of middle-aged persons in Japan still believe that care of older parents is the children's responsibility. Indeed, negligence toward one's parents is a source of great public shame. Society also assumes responsibility for the care of Japan's elders; all those age 70 and older receive free basic medical services, which is often viewed as a model by other Asian countries.

The Japanese government provides incentives for home care by families; they can receive subsidies to remodel their homes in order to accommodate joint households as well as a tax credit for providing elder parent care (Kim and Maeda, 2001). For these reasons, the proportion of older parents living in multigenerational households, although declining, is still higher than in any other industrialized nation. In 1995, 56 percent of people over age 65 lived with their children and grandchildren, but this is a decline from 1980, when 70 percent of older households were multigenerational. By 2010, this is projected to drop even further, to 42 percent (National Institute of Population and Social Security Research, 2006). Meanwhile, the number of households consisting of only the older couple has increased. In 1995 they comprised 26 percent of older households, compared with 19 percent in 1985 (Jenike, 1997; Kinsella and Velkoff, 2001; Maeda, 1998; Morioka, 1996). The number of nursing homes and long-stay hospitals in Japan has also grown, but more community-based options are needed. All these trends suggest that traditional customs of caring for aging parents in adult children's homes are changing. The percentage of parents living with children has declined, due to urbanization, industrialization, the growing number of employed women, and the declining number of children since 1950. Urban–rural differences in family expectations are demonstrated by the fact that 25 percent of people age 75 and older in Tokyo live alone, compared with 15 percent in rural regions. Despite the growth of long-term care facilities, institutionalization in any form is still viewed as abandonment by many older people. As a result, most elder care still takes place in private homes.

Even though the proportion of elders living with adult children has declined, middle-aged women remain the primary caregivers to Japanese elders, as in most other countries. As older adults continue to live longer, they may increasingly require goods and services at the perceived expense

> ### "RETIRED HUSBAND SYNDROME"
>
> A new medical diagnosis has been coined in Japan. Labelled "Retired Husband Syndrome" (or RHS), the condition has been observed among women whose husbands have retired by age 60 to 65 and remain at home full-time, demanding the attention and care of their wives. These wives, from a generation where wives remained at home and were subservient to their husbands, develop many psychosomatic symptoms related to the stress of having to serve their husbands full-time after retirement. With the projected increase in Japanese men retiring— almost 7 million between 2007 and 2009—RHS is expected to increase dramatically among women 60 and older in Japan.
>
> SOURCE: Faiola, A., *Washington Post*, October 17, 2005.

of younger members (e.g., children), and may place even greater demands on middle-aged women in Japanese society. With the increased proportion of educated, professional women and newer cohorts influenced more by Western values than by Confucianism, many women do not want to leave their jobs to become caregivers to their parents or parents-in-law. Because of public concerns about long-term care needs for its growing population of oldest-old, the Japanese Diet passed the Public Long Term Care Insurance Act in 1997 (Maeda, 1998). This national policy guarantees comprehensive long-term care for all Japanese persons age 65 or older, and for those age 40 to 64 who may require long-term care. Funding is provided by a combination of mandatory insurance premiums paid by older persons (estimated to be approximately equivalent to $19 per month in 2000 and $27 in 2010) and taxes that will be paid to federal, prefecture, and municipal governments. Users of this service also must co-pay 10 percent of all incurred expenses.

The current shortage of long-term care options needs to be addressed to fully implement this program. Nevertheless, if it succeeds, this universal long-term care program is expected to relieve somewhat the burden on Japanese families and hospitals, where most long-term care occurs. The program is being watched closely by policy makers in other developed countries to see if it can serve as a model for day-to-day care for their increasing populations of oldest-old while still maintaining filial piety.

A strong belief in filial piety also plays a dominant role in family attitudes and government policies regarding care for aging parents in South Korea, where the number of people 65 and older has increased threefold in 25 years. Surveys of young Koreans reveal that more than 90 percent believe that adult children must care for their older parents, and in fact 90 percent of older adults cite family as their primary source of support. These values are supported by the high proportion of people age 65 and older— 65 percent—who live with their adult children, even in urbanized areas like Seoul. In particular, daughters-in-law are expected to provide most of the day-to-day care for their aging parents-in-law. The government of South Korea promotes family-based caregiving by sponsoring a "Respect for Elders Day" and a "Respect for Elders Week," as well as prizes to honor outstanding examples of filial piety. These initiatives help reduce Koreans' expectations from the government, although changing demographics today have placed a greater burden on families, with average family size down to 3.0 and with 46 percent of all married women in Korea working outside the home (Kim, 1998; Levande, Herrick, and Sung, 2000; Sung, 1998, 2000, 2001).

Other Asian countries where filial piety has been maintained, despite changing work and family patterns, are Singapore, Thailand, and the Philippines, where 91 percent, 69 percent, and 67 percent of women 60 and older, respectively, live with their children (Kinsella and Velkoff, 2001). The importance of filial piety generally supersedes modern social and economic demands in these Asian countries.

A Cross-Cultural View of Elders' Roles in Contemporary Societies

As we have discussed, every society defines people as old on some basis, whether chronological, functional, or generational, and assigns that group a particular set of rights, privileges, and duties that differ from those of its younger members. For example, older persons in our society today qualify for Social Security and Medicare on the basis of their age, although the age of eligibility is increasing as life expectancy increases. In some religious groups, only the oldest members are permitted to perform the most sacred rituals. Societies generally distinguish two, sometimes three, classes of elders:

- those who are no longer fully productive economically, but are physically and mentally able to attend to their daily needs
- those who are totally dependent, who require long-term care, and who are regarded as social burdens and thus may be negatively treated
- those who continue to participate actively in the economy and the social system, through farming or self-employment, care of grandchildren, or household maintenance, while younger adults work outside the home

Consistent with social exchange theory discussed in Chapter 8, older people who can no longer work but who control resources essential to fulfill the needs of younger group members generally offset the societal costs incurred in maintaining them. In some social systems, political, judicial, or ritual power and privileges are vested in older people as a group, and this serves to mediate social costs. For instance, in societies such as those of East Africa, politically powerful positions are automatically assigned to men who reach a certain age (Keith, 1990). In other societies, the old do not inherently have privileges, but gain power as individuals, often through diplomatic skills and contacts with powerful others. The following examples from other cultures illustrate the balance between the costs and contributions made by older adults and the extent of power and respect that they command:

- Older Sherpas in Nepal today must cope with the indirect effects of modernization. Job opportunities for young adults in Darjeeling and other parts of India have increased in recent years, as young men have found jobs as porters for climbers in the Himalayas. As a result, adult children are not available or interested in living with their aging parents in many families, resulting in older adults who live alone and express a sense of abandonment (Goldstein and Beall, 2002). As younger sons have moved away from the community and are not available to share households and care for the old, Sherpa elders have resisted the traditional division of property and tend to keep the younger sons' shares for themselves. Sherpa elders are also becoming proponents of birth control; since they cannot count on sons to take care of them as they wish, they prefer to share their property among fewer children, keeping more for themselves (Keith, 1990).
- In Australia, the traditional respect accorded to elders in the Aborigine culture has resulted in a valuable role for older women. In one Aborigine community in central Australia, a group of women, all over age 70, have formed a night patrol that intervenes to stop rowdy parties and disco activity that result in excessive drinking and violence. These peacekeepers receive more cooperation from the young perpetrators than do police, and community leaders report a decline in assaults and arrests for drunken behavior over the past ten years since this group began its work (AARP, 2000).
- Older women play a valuable role in Zulu culture. Their pensions are a steady source of family income, and grandmothers provide an important caregiving function. Despite their contributions, these older women reported feeling

that younger Zulus did not respect them. Grandchildren indicated a schism between their new values of individualism and traditional tribal values of kinship held by their grandmothers (AARP, 1999).

- In some countries, rapid societal changes have placed unexpected burdens on elders. Older people in many African countries face multiple challenges created by sociodemographic shifts, poverty, and the HIV/AIDS epidemic. Although much smaller in proportion than in other regions of the world, people age 60 and older comprise a growing share of the population in most African countries, ranging from 6.8 percent in South Africa to 4.3 percent in Zimbabwe. With increasing migration of younger family members to urban centers, older adults in rural parts of Africa cannot rely on their adult children to care for them. In fact, many provide a critical role as caregivers themselves to grandchildren left behind by parents who seek employment in distant cities. In recent years, this responsibility has been compounded by the growing number of AIDS orphans, especially in sub-Saharan Africa. Of the 2.5 million deaths due to AIDS worldwide in 1998, 2 million occurred in sub-Saharan Africa. Given that the population age 15 to 49 has been hardest hit by AIDS, older adults are often left to care for their grandchildren as well as extended family members. In most cases, they receive very little government support for their surrogate parenting. To make matters worse, most African countries provide little if any social security or pension benefits for their older citizens (Darkwa and Mazibuko, 2002; UNAIDS, 2000).

In other cultures, respect toward functioning elders may be promoted, but a subtle acceptance of benign neglect may result in the demise of older persons who are physically and/or cognitively impaired. An ethnographic analysis of Niue, an independent Polynesian island, revealed significant discrepancies between the status of older people who were in good health and had important social and political functions, and those who were too frail to care for themselves. Although medical services are free on Niue, families and neighbors did not summon visiting doctors and public health nurses, even for infected sores, painful joints, and other treatable conditions in these frail elders. The basic needs of cognitively impaired elders were even more frequently ignored. This may stem from values of reciprocity. Like other societies where reciprocity is crucial for intergenerational exchanges, the frail elders of Niue can no longer contribute to the group's well-being. Therefore, such neglect may be seen as a way of merely hastening the inevitable death of these weaker members of that society (Barker, 1997; Glascock, 1997).

Control over knowledge, especially ritual and religious traditions, has traditionally provided elders with a critical source of power. The aged Shaman is an example, revered in many societies for knowledge or wisdom. The importance of older members of society in maintaining cultural values is illustrated in India, where traditional Hindu law prescribes a four-stage life cycle for high-caste men: student, householder, ascetic, and mendicant. In the last two stages, older religious men are expected to renounce worldly attachments to seek enlightenment in isolated retreats. This practice ensures that the pursuit of the highest form of knowledge is limited to older men of higher castes (Sokolovsky, 1997).

Knowledge as the basis of older people's power has been challenged as traditional societies become more urbanized or assimilated into the majority culture. Over the course of the twentieth century, American Indian elders lost their roles as mentors and counselors to younger tribal members. Their knowledge of tribal customs and stories, language, agricultural skills, and folk medicine were no longer valued as family structures changed and people migrated away from the reservation (Baldridge, 2001).

Among some cultural groups, however, including many American Indian tribes, a revival of interest and pride in native identity and spirituality has occurred, thus raising the esteem of elders who possess ritual knowledge. For example, they are the only ones who know the words and steps for many traditional songs and dances. Knowledge of the group's culture, particularly its arts and handicrafts, native songs and epics, has enhanced the social status of older persons in these societies; furthermore, the traditions of reverence for old age and wisdom remain strong, overriding the impact of modernization on elders' roles. The timing of such a revival is critical, however. A similar revival among Plains Indians did not have comparable positive consequences for the tribe's older members who were no longer expert in traditional ways. The growing desire for ethnic or tribal identity among many Indians, which has led to a conscious restoration of old forms, illustrates that modernization does not automatically erode the status of elders. Similarly, the search for one's heritage or roots has led to increased contacts between younger generations seeking this information from older persons who often are a great repository of family histories.

Immigrants from Traditional Cultures to the United States

The number of older immigrants to the United States has grown dramatically since 1965 when the Immigration and Naturalization Act was amended to allow entry from more diverse countries than in the past. Subsequent legislation expanded this process by eliminating the national origins quota system. As a result, there has been a shift from mostly European to primarily Asian and Latin American countries as the source of immigrants to the United States. Between 1991 and 2000, 9.1 million people arrived from other countries. The greatest proportion (49 percent) were from South and Central America; 31 percent came from Asia;

15 percent from Europe, and 4 percent from Africa. The proportion of the immigrant population ages 60 and older is still relatively small, despite rising from 3.2 percent of all immigrants in the 1990s to 7.6 percent in 2002. The majority of these older immigrants arrive as "immediate relatives of U.S. citizens," often following their adult children who preceded them to this country (Moon and Rhee, 2006; U.S. Census Bureau, 2002). This older immigrant population is:

- less likely to be educated (almost half have not completed high school)
- less likely to be proficient in English (including 58 percent of elders from Asian countries)
- more likely to live in poverty
- less likely to have health care coverage (45 percent of all elders who have no health insurance are foreign-born)
- less likely to use health and social services
- more likely than their U.S.-born peers to receive government benefits such as Medicaid (Asian American Justice Center, 2006; He, 2001; Moon and Rhee, 2006; U.S. Census Bureau, 2002).

Social activities with others from their native country can help older immigrants adapt to life in the United States.

Adult children who precede their parents to the new country often encourage them to immigrate because they are concerned about providing care for their aging parents from a distance, especially when other siblings are unavailable in the home country. In many cases, the assistance is mutually beneficial because the parents help their adult children in family-owned businesses and as caregivers for grandchildren. They often live with or near their adult children in order to provide full-time child care. However, elders' immigration for the sake of their children and grandchildren can disrupt their lives and psychological well-being at a time when their own health may be declining. Social isolation and depression often result. Depression rates as high as 26 percent have been found among immigrant elders, and may be linked to financial problems, lack of health coverage, multiple chronic diseases, and grief over leaving their home and friends in their home country (Gelfand, 2003; Min, Moon and Lubben, 2005; Mui and Kang, 2006; van der Geest, Mul and Vermeulen, 2004; Wilmoth, 2001). Many of these older immigrants lack economic and educational resources and are not proficient in English, thereby making acculturation more difficult. Language and cultural barriers compound the elder's difficulties in accessing Western health care. For example, older immigrants must rely on their adult children to seek health services and manage the accompanying paperwork, shifting the balance of power and respect, and making the older adult dependent on the child. In a study of older Chinese immigrants in Boston, the most depressed were elders with the most chronic diseases and worst self-ratings of health (Wu, Tran, and Amjad, 2004).

Older refugees to Western countries face even more problems adjusting to their new country. In the past 35 years, waves of Indochinese refugees have come to the United States from countries experiencing political strife, war and unrest. Property and other resources in

POINTS TO PONDER

Think about immigrant and refugee groups in the United States. In what ways are elders in such families involved or not involved in the lives of their children and grandchildren? What impact do a common language and shared cultural values have on their interactions? To what extent have cultural differences created family conflicts and reduced the status of elders?

Many immigrant elders prefer living in ethnic enclaves where others speak their native language.

their native lands that afforded them importance and power were generally stripped from them in their home country. Being in the United States has brought them a different life than the one they might have imagined for their later years. These older refugees do not have the ability to provide material goods, land, or other financial support, which has traditionally given them status. Accordingly, traditional power has been eroded as families have started new lives in this culture and the balance of power has shifted in these families. Indeed, financial self-sufficiency is a major determinant of adjustment to life in the United States among older Indochinese refugees, regardless of education, gender, and English proficiency. In a study of refugee elders from Cambodia, Vietnam, the Ukraines, and Jewish elders from the former Soviet Union, reports of loneliness and isolation were widespread. However, the majority of these refugees were unaware of any social or health services that could help them overcome these problems and adjust to their new situation (Strumpf et al., 2001). Refugees from countries in the midst of civil war often experience even greater mental health problems. Traumas such as torture, massacre of family and friends, and separation from family members can have long-lasting negative effects, even after escaping to the political safety of the United States (Morioka-Douglas, Sacks, and Yeo, 2004).

Living Arrangements of Older Immigrants

Co-residence with adult children varies across nationality among immigrants. In an analysis of U.S. census data on almost 64,000 older immigrants, Wilmoth (2001) compared the living arrangements of Latino (mostly Cuban and Mexican), Asian (mostly from China or Southeast Asia), and non-Hispanic white (mostly from Europe) immigrants. Significant differences emerged across immigrant groups, with the highest rates of independent living among white, Japanese, and Cuban immigrants. Living in another family member's home was more common among other Asian groups and elders from Mexico, especially among those who were unmarried, with lower incomes and less than a college education, and those with a physical disability. Co-residence may not always benefit the older immigrant. This is particularly true if their adult children live in a suburban community far from an ethnic enclave, such as Chinese and Southeast Asian neighborhoods in urban settings. Elders who choose to live in these ethnic enclaves lose their immediate access to family, but gain the benefit of socializing with their peers and finding health and social service providers who speak their native language. In some cases, immigrant elders who choose to live in ethnic enclaves in the city sacrifice the material comfort of life in the suburbs in order to be close to these reminders of "home." For these older adults, their residence takes on a meaning beyond physical safety and comfort, but can serve to ameliorate their sense of displacement from their home country (Becker, 2003).

When immigrant elders need long-term care, traditional norms of filial piety play a dominant role in the decision by elders and their adult children about what services to use. Research with immigrant Latino families has found that the family mobilizes a wide network of extended family and friends to provide care in the community (Gelfand, 2003). Among families from Southeast Asia, regardless of religion (Sikh, Hindu, Muslim, or Christian), those who continue to hold filial piety beliefs are less likely to feel burdened by caring for an older parent (Gupta and Pillai, 2002). Indeed, among some immigrant groups, placing an older family member in a nursing home is viewed as a denial of one's filial obligations. These values of

IMMIGRANTS WORKING IN LONG-TERM CARE FACILITIES

More and more workers in the direct services labor force are young immigrants. Their clients are often white, middle class, and old. Nowhere is this more evident than in long-term care facilities such as assisted living and nursing homes. In some communities, immigrants make up as many as half of the nurses, aides, and housekeeping staff of long-term care facilities. Communication with older clients may suffer because of poor English proficiency among staff, hearing impairments among elders, and stereotypes held by each group regarding the other. These facilities are a microcosm of the increasingly diverse American society. They can also create opportunities for cross-cultural dialog and celebration of diversity.

providing long-term care to frail elders at home can strengthen bonds in immigrant families. However, if adult children are already burdened by financial problems, demands at work, and interpersonal conflicts with their children or spouse, their parents' expectations of caregiving in the home can create psychological distress for those who provide such care (Moon and Rhee, 2006).

Financial Dilemmas Facing Immigrant Elders

Financial self-sufficiency is an important determinant of an elder's social position in the family, whether they are immigrants or native-born Americans. For many older immigrants, government benefits such as Medicaid and Supplemental Security Income (SSI) allow them greater options for long-term care and health care. However, major policy changes took place in 1996 that severely limited non-citizen immigrants' access to these benefits. Euphemistically labeled "welfare reform," this change enacted by the U.S. Congress placed significant limits on immigrants' eligibility for and access to public assistance benefits, especially SSI and Temporary Assistance to Needy Families (TANF). These changes, aimed at downsizing the federal government's costs at the time, transferred decisions and responsibility for welfare programs to state and local governments. The immediate and long-term effects of this policy change have been to reduce income security for poor families and older immigrants, especially those who were not U.S. citizens when welfare reform was enacted. This problem differentially affects non-immigrant elders, depending on the state where they reside. In states where budgetary and philosophical attitudes toward welfare programs are negative, immigrants have faced lower benefits, restrictions on eligibility and time limits. In states such as California, which has the largest number of non-citizen immigrants, the percentage of immigrant households receiving public assistance has sharply declined. Many who are eligible have not applied for the assistance they need because they think that they are ineligible or that it will affect their status in the United States (Angel, 2003; Caro and Morris, 2004; Carroll, 2002; Estes et al., 2006; Zimmerman and Fix, 1998).

Summary and Implications for the Future

The growth of the older population is a worldwide phenomenon. The largest proportions of elders are in industrialized countries, especially in Europe and Japan, where the median age has increased dramatically in the past 20 years. However, the majority of older people live in developing countries, increasing from 60 percent of the world's population today to 75 percent by 2020. China is already facing a crisis of its one-child-per-family policy resulting in fewer and fewer workers to support its burgeoning population of elders. Many developing countries have not yet established adequate public policies to address the growth of their older population. In contrast, many industrialized countries, especially in the European Union, are implementing new retirement and pension policies that will increase the number of older workers while reducing the burden on their state pension programs. Not surprisingly, these attempts to raise the retirement age and place restrictions on pensions are being met with resistance by many workers who expected to retire with full benefits between age 55 to 64, as in the past. Other industrialized countries are actively recruiting middle-aged adults as employees and offering incentives for their existing older workers to continue on the job.

A basic principle governing the status of older adults is the need to achieve a balance between older people's contributions to society and the costs of supporting them. Often, the process of modernization and technological development conflicts with traditions of filial piety. But the family continues to play an important role in supporting its oldest members in most societies. The extent to which older citizens are engaged in society appears to vary with the nature of their power resources, such as their material possessions, knowledge, and social authority. In most of their exchanges, older people seek to maintain reciprocity and to be active, independent agents in the management of their own lives. That is, they prefer to give money, time, or other resources in exchange for services or materials. This theoretical perspective, described as social exchange theory in Chapter 8, suggests that modern society should seek ways to increase older people's exchange resources so that they are valued by society.

Control of resources as a basis for social interactions between members of a society is important throughout the life course. However, it becomes even more crucial in old age, because retirement generally results in a decline in one's level of control over material and social resources. As their physical strength diminishes and their social world correspondingly shrinks, many older people face the challenge of altering their environments and using their capacities in ways that will help them to maintain reciprocal exchanges and to protect their competence and independence. This may be an even greater problem for older refugees who may still have full physical and cognitive functions, but have lost material resources in their homeland that would have given them power and prestige. Older people who immigrate to the United States often do so to be with their adult children and generally help with child care or the family business. Although this may represent a reciprocal exchange, immigration in the later years can also deprive elders of their autonomy and opportunities for active aging. Some experience psychological and physical health problems. Other older immigrants face financial burdens, especially since welfare reform in the mid-1990s placed restrictions on immigrants' access to Medicaid. These attempts to maintain control over one's environment in the face of changing personal capacities and resources are consistent with the person–environment model presented in Chapter 1. This issue will be discussed in detail in subsequent chapters on biological, psychological, and social changes with aging. The dearth of information on cross-cultural issues in gerontology suggests a need for more anthropologists to direct their research toward comparing how the aging process and elders are viewed in different cultures and countries.

GLOSSARY

filial piety   a sense of reverence and deference to elders that encourages care for one's aging family members.

modernization theory   advances in technology, applied sciences, urbanization, and literacy which, in this context, are related to a decline in the status of older people

skipped generation households   often because of economic necessity, the middle generation moves out of the home and grandparents assume responsibility for the day-to-day care of grandchildren

social stratification   divisions among people (e.g., by age, ethnic group) for purposes of maintaining distinctions between different strata by significant characteristics of those strata

REFERENCES

AARP. Adapting to a new social order. *Global aging report,* 1999, *4,* 6.

AARP. *Global aging report,* 2000, *5,* 4–5.

Administration on Aging (AOA). *Profile of Older Americans: 2005.* Washington, DC: 2005.

Albert, S.M., and Cattell, M.G. *Old age in global perspective.* New York: G.K. Hall and Co., 1994.

Angel, J.L. Devolution and the social welfare of elderly immigrants: Who will bear the burden? *Public Administration Review,* 2003, *63,* 79–89.

Angel, J.L., Angel, R.J., Lee, G.Y., and Markides, K.S. Age at migration and family dependency among older Mexican immigrants: Recent evidence from the Mexican American EPESE. *The Gerontologist,* 1999, *39,* 59–65.

Asian American Justice Center and Asian Pacific American Legal Center. *A community of contrasts: Asian and Pacific Islanders in the United States.* Washington, DC: Author, 2006.

Baldridge, D. Indian elders: Family traditions in crisis. *American Behavioral Scientist,* 2001, *44,* 1515–1527.

Barker, J.C. Between humans and ghosts: The decrepit elderly in a Polynesian society. In J. Sokolovsky (Ed.), *The cultural context of aging.* Westport, CT: Bergin and Garvey, 1997.

Becker, G. Meanings of place and displacement in three groups of older immigrants. *Journal of Aging Studies,* 2003, *17,* 129–149.

Bosch Management Support. *Handfeste unterstutzung statt allgemainer Ratschlage-eine feste verbindung auf Zeit.* 2004, 2.

Cameron, L. The residency decision of elderly Indonesians: A nested logit analysis. *Demography,* 2000, *37,* 17–27.

Caro, F.G., and Morris, R. Devolution and aging policy. *Journal of Aging and Social Policy,* 2004, *14,* 1.

Carroll, D. *TANF reauthorization: A California perspective.* Sacramento, CA: California Budget Project, 2002.

Cheng, S.T., and Chan, A.C.M. Filial piety and psychological well-being in well older Chinese. *Journal of Gerontology: Psychological Sciences,* 2006, *61B,* P262–P269.

Chivers, C.J. Russians, busy making shrouds, are asked to make babies. *New York Times,* May 14, 2006, p. 4.

Cowgill, D. Aging and modernization: A revision of the theory. In J.F. Gubrium (Ed.), *Late life communities and environmental policy.* Springfield, IL: Charles C. Thomas, 1974a.

Cowgill, D. *Aging around the world.* Belmont, CA: Wadsworth, 1986.

Cowgill, D. The aging of populations and societies. In F. Eisele (Ed.), *Political consequences of aging. The annals of the American Academy of Political and Social Science,* 1974b, *415,* 1–18.

Dandekar, K. *The elderly in India*. Thousand Oaks, CA: Sage, 1996.

Darkwa, O.K., and Mazibuko, F.N.M. Population aging and its impact on elderly welfare in Africa. *International Journal of Aging and Human Development*, 2002, *54*, 107–123.

Estes, C.L., Goldberg, S., Wellin, C., Linkins, K.W., Shostak, S., and Beard, R.L. Implications of welfare reform on the elderly: A case study of provider, advocate and consumer perspectives. *Journal of Aging and Social Policy*, 2006, *18*, 41–63.

European Commission. *Green paper on demographic change*. Brussels, EU: 2005.

Gelfand, D.E. *Aging and ethnicity: Knowledge and services* (2nd ed.) New York: Springer, 2003.

Glascock, A.P. When is killing acceptable: The moral dilemma surrounding assisted suicide in America and other societies. In J. Sokolovsky (Ed.), *The cultural context of aging* (3rd ed.). Westport, CT: Bergin and Garvey, 1997.

Goldstein, M.C., and Beall, C.M. Modernization and aging in the third and fourth world: Views from the rural hinterland in Nepal. In D.L. Infeld (Ed.), *Disciplinary approaches to aging: Anthropology of aging* (Vol. 4). New York: Routledge, 2002.

Gupta, R., and Pillai, V.K. Elder caregiving in South Asian families: Implications for social services. *Journal of Comparative Family Studies,* 2002, *33*, 565–576.

Haub, C. *2006 World population data sheet*. Cited in http://www.prb.org. Accessed October 15, 2006.

He, W. U.S. Census Bureau, Current Population Reports. *The older foreign-born population in the United States: 2000*. Washington, DC: Printing Office, 2001, 23–211.

He, W., Sengupta, M., Velkoff, V., and DeBarros, K.A. *65+ in the United States: 2005*. U.S. Census Bureau, Current Population Reports. Washington, DC: U.S. Government and Printing Office 2005, 23–29.

Hsu, H.C., Lew-Ting, C.Y., and Wu, S.C. Age, period, and cohort effects on the attitude toward supporting parents in Taiwan. *The Gerontologist,* 2001, *41*, 742–750.

Hu, Y.H. Elderly suicide risk in family context: A critique of the Asian family care model. *Journal of Cross-Cultural Gerontology,* 1995, *10*, 199–217.

IBM Business Consulting Services. *Addressing the challenge of an aging workforce*. Somers, NY: IBM Global Services, 2005.

Ikels, C. Aging. In C. Loue (Ed.), *Handbook of immigrant health*. New York: Plenum Press, 1998.

Ikels, C. Long-term care and the disabled elderly in urban China. In J. Sokolovsky (Ed.), *The cultural context of aging* (3rd ed.). Westport, CT: Bergin and Garvey, 1997.

Ikels, C., and Beall, C.M. Age, aging and anthropology. In R.H. Binstock, and L.K. George (Eds.), *Handbook of aging and the social sciences* (5th ed.). San Diego: Academic Press, 2001.

Infeld, D.L. (Ed.). *Disciplinary approaches to aging: Anthropology of aging* (Vol. 4). New York: Routledge, 2002.

Jenike, B.R. Gender and duty in Japan's aged society: The experience of family caregivers. In J. Sokolovsky (Ed.), *The cultural context of aging* (3rd ed.). Westport, CT: Bergin and Garvey, 1997.

Joseph, A.E., and Phillips, D.R. Aging in rural China: Impacts of increasing diversity in family and community resources. *Journal of Cross-Cultural Gerontology,* 1999, *14*, 153–158.

Kalache, A., and Keller, I. The graying world: A challenge for the 21st century. *Science Progress,* 2000, *83*, 33–54.

Kaneda, T. *China's concern over population aging and health*. Accessed October 28, 2006, from http://www.prb.org.

Keith, J. Age in social and cultural context: Anthropological perspectives. In R. Binstock, and L. George (Eds.), *Handbook of aging and the social sciences* (3rd ed.). New York: Academic Press, 1990.

Kertzer, D., and Laslett, P. (Eds.). *Demography, society and old age*. Berkeley: University of California Press, 1994.

Kim, I.K., and Maeda, D. Comparative study on sociodemographic changes and long-term care needs of the elderly in Japan and South Korea. *Journal of Cross-Cultural Gerontology,* 2001, *16*, 237–255.

Kim, K.H. A study of determinants of elderly people's coresidence living patterns. *Journal of the Korea Gerontological Society,* 1998, *18*, 107–122.

Kinsella, K., and Phillips, D. The challenge of global aging. *Population Bulletin*, 2005, *60*.

Kinsella, K., and Velkoff, V.A. *An aging world: 2001*. U.S. Census Bureau Series. Washington, DC: U.S. Government Printing Office, 2001, 95/01–1.

Knodel, J., and Ofstedal, M.B. Patterns and determinants of living arrangements. In A.I. Hermalin (Ed.), *Well-being of the elderly in Asia: A four-country comparative study*. Ann Arbor: University of Michigan Press, 2002.

Levande, D.I., Herrick, J.M., and Sung, K.T. Eldercare in the United States and South Korea. *Journal of Family Issues,* 2000, *21,* 632–651.

Maeda, D. *Recent policy of long term care in Japan.* Paper presented at meetings of the American Public Health Association, Washington, DC, November, 1998.

Min, J., Moon, A. and Lubben, J. Determinants of psychological distress over time among older Korean Americans and non-Hispanic white elders. *Journal of Mental Health and Aging,* 2005, 9, 210–222.

Moon, A., and Rhee, S. Immigrant and refugee elders. In B. Berkman, and S. D'Ambruoso (Eds.), *Handbook of social work in health and aging.* New York: Oxford Press, 2006.

Morioka, K. Generational relations and their changes as they affect the status of older people in Japan. In T. Harevan (Ed.), *Aging and generational relations.* New York: Aldine de Gruyter, 1996.

Morioka-Douglas, N., Sacks, T., and Yeo, G. Issues in caring for Afghan American elders: Insights from literature and a focus group. *Journal of Cross-Cultural Gerontology,* 2004, *19,* 27–40.

Mui, A.C., and Kang, S.Y. Acculturation stress and depression among Asian immigrant elders. *Social Work,* 2006, 51, 243–250.

National Center for Health Statistics (NCHS). *Health United States, 2005, with chartbook on trends in the health of Americans.* Hyattsville, MD: NCHS, 2005.

National Institute of Population and Social Security Research. *Housing with seniors: 1975–2010.* Accessed October 15, 2006, from http://www.jinjapan.org/insight/html/focus10/page08.html.

National Institute of Population and Social Security Research. *Key learning from the 2nd public opinion survey on population issues in Japan.* Accessed 2004, from http://www.ipss.go.jp/English/pospi_2nd/chosa.html.

New York Times. Insular Japan needs, but resists immigration. July 24, 2003, A1–A3.

Nixon, S. Looming labour crisis puts the focus on grey force. *Sydney Morning Herald,* October 2, 2002.

Pang, K.Y.C. Symptoms of depression in elderly Korean immigrants: Narration and the healing process. *Culture, Medicine and Psychiatry,* 1998, 22, 93–122.

Personnelzone Direct. *SAGA predicts thousands will delay retirement.* Accessed February 2004, from http://www.personnelzone.com.

Pritchard, C., and Baldwin, D.S. Elderly suicide rates in Asian and English-speaking countries. *Acta Psychiatrica Scandinavica,* 2002, *105,* 271–275.

Silverman, P., Hecht, L., and McMillin, J.D. Modeling life satisfaction among the aged: A comparison of Chinese and Americans. *Journal of Cross-Cultural Gerontology,* 2000, *15,* 289–305.

Silverstein, M., Cong, Z., and Li, S. Intergenerational transfers and living arrangements of older people in rural China. *Journal of Gerontology: Social Sciences,* 2006, *61B,* S256–S266.

Simmons, L.W. *The role of the aged in primitive society.* New Haven, CT: Yale University Press, 1945.

Social Security Administration (SSA). *International update.* SSA Publication No. 13–11712, 2005.

Sokolovsky, J. (Ed.) *The cultural context of aging* (3rd ed.). Westport, CT: Bergin and Garvey, 1997.

Strumpf, N.E., Glicksman, A., Goldberg-Glen, R.S., Fox, R.C., and Logue, E.H. Caregiver and elder experiences of Cambodian, Vietnamese, Soviet Jewish, and Ukrainian refugees. *International Journal of Aging and Human Development,* 2001, *53,* 233–252.

Sung, K.T. An exploration of actions of filial piety. *Journal of Aging Studies,* 1998, *12,* 369–386.

Sung, K.T. Family support for the elderly in Korea: Continuity, change, future directions and cross-cultural concerns. *Journal of Aging and Social Policy,* 2001, *12,* 65–77.

Sung, K.T. Respect for elders: Myths and realities in East Asia. *Journal of Aging and Identity,* 2000, *5,* 197–205.

Taylor, P. Policy-making towards older workers in the U.K. In H. Buck, and B. Dworschak (Eds.), *Ageing and work in Europe.* Stuttgart, 2003.

United Nations. *World Population Aging 1950–2050.* Department of Economic and Social Affairs: Population Division, 2006a.

United Nations. *World Population Prospects.* Volume III. Department of Economic and Social Affairs: Population Division, 2006b.

United Nations AIDS Programme (UNAIDS). *HIV/AIDS in Africa: Fact sheet.* Accessed 2000, from http://www.unaids.org.

U.S. Census Bureau. *Global Aging into the 21st Century.* Washington, DC: U.S. Department of Commerce, 1996.

U.S. Census Bureau. *The older foreign-born population in the United States: 2000.* Current Population Reports, Series 23–211, Washington, DC: U.S. Government Printing Office, 2002.

van der Geest, S., Mul, A., and Vermeulen, H. Linkages between migration and the care of frail older people: Observations from Greece, Ghana, and The Netherlands. *Ageing and Society,* 2004, *24,* 431–450.

Vincentnathan, S.G., and Vincentnathan, L. Equality and hierarchy in untouchable intergenerational relations and conflict resolutions. *Journal of Cross-Cultural Gerontology,* 1994, *9,* 1–19.

Von Nordheim, F. EU policies in support of member states' efforts to retain, reinforce and re-integrate older workers in employment. In H. Buck and B. Dworschak (Eds.), *Ageing and work in Europe.* Stuttgart, 2003.

Wagner, J. German government agrees to first-pillar reform. *Global Action on Aging.* Accessed October 16, 2006, from http://www.globalagin.org/pension/world/2006/firstpillar.htm.

Wilmoth, J.M. Living arrangements among older immigrants in the United States. *The Gerontologist,* 2001, *41,* 228–238.

Wilmoth, J.M. *Social integration of older immigrants in 21st century America.* Syracuse University Policy Brief No. 29. Syracuse, NY: Syracuse University, 2004.

World Health Organization (WHO). *Active Ageing: A policy framework.* Geneva, Switzerland: WHO, 2002.

Wu, B., Tran, T.V., and Amjad, Q.A., Chronic illnesses and depression among Chinese immigrant elders. *Journal of Gerontological Social Work,* 2004, *43,* 79–95.

Yee, B.W.K., The social and cultural context of adaptive aging by Southeast Asian elders. In J. Sokolovsky (Ed.), *The cultural context of aging* (3rd ed.). Westport, CT: Bergin and Garvey, 1997.

Zeng, Y., Liu, Y., and George, L.K. Gender differentials of the oldest old in China. *Research on Aging,* 2003, *25,* 65–80.

Zhan, H.J. Willingness and expectations: Intergenerational differences in attitudes toward filial responsibility in China. *Marriage and Family Review,* 2004, *36,* 175–200.

Zhan, H.J., Liu, G., Guan, X, and Bai, H.G. Recent developments in institutional elder care in China: Changing concepts and attitudes. *Journal of Aging Social Policy,* 2006, *18,* 85–108.

Zhang, H. Living alone and the rural elderly: Strategy and agency in post-Mao rural China. In C. Ikels (Ed.), *Filial piety: Practice and discourse in contemporary East Asia.* Palo Alto, CA: Stanford University Press, 2004.

Zimmerman, W., and Fix, M. *Declining immigrant applications for Medi-Cal and welfare benefits in Los Angeles County.* Washington, DC: The Urban Institute Press, 1998.

part two

The Biological and Physiological Context of Social Aging

If we are to understand how older people differ from younger age groups, and why the field of gerontology has evolved as a separate discipline, we must first review the *normal* changes in biological and physiological structures as well as diseases that impair these systems and affect the day-to-day functioning of older persons. Part Two provides this necessary background.

- Chapter 3 describes normal changes in major organ systems and how they may influence older persons' abilities to perform activities of daily living and to interact with their social and physical environments. This area of research has received considerable attention as scientists have explored the basic processes of aging. Numerous theories have emerged to explain observable changes such as wrinkles, gray hair, stooped shoulders, and slower response time, as well as changes in other biological functions that can only be inferred from tests of physiologic function. These include changes in the heart, lungs, kidneys, and bones. There are many normal changes in these organ systems within the same person that do not imply disease, but may slow down the older adult. Furthermore, significant differences in the degree of change experienced have been observed among people and among organ systems within the same person. The effects of health enhancement behaviors—such as vigorous exercise, nutrition, and an active lifestyle—on the extent of physical aging are discussed.
- Chapter 3 highlights some of the exciting new discoveries in biological research that show the potential of modifying cellular processes and using human growth hormones to slow down aging and even increase the maximum life span of humans. Some of the current debates surrounding potential ways to extend cell life and cell regeneration are also presented in Chapter 3.
- Age-related changes in the five major senses are also discussed in Chapter 3. Because sensory functions are so critical for our daily interactions with our social and physical environments, and because many of the normal declines observed in sensory systems are a model of changes throughout the body, it is useful to focus on each sensory system and its role in linking individuals with their environments. Recommendations are made for modifying the environment and for communicating effectively with older people who are experiencing significant declines in vision, hearing, taste, smell, touch, and kinesthetic functioning.

• Chapter 4 focuses on secondary aging—diseases of the organ systems described in Chapter 3, and how these diseases can affect active aging. Acute and chronic diseases are differentiated, and the impact of these diseases on the demand for health, long-term care, and social services among different segments of the older population is presented. The growing problem of HIV-AIDS among older persons and implications for long-term care are discussed. For nearly every chronic disease, inequities by gender, ethnic minority status and social class exist and affect life expectancy, morbidity, and mortality rates.

• Because automobile accidents among older people often result from psychomotor and vision changes associated with aging, methods to reduce auto fatalities through new programs in driver training and through better environmental design are considered. Differences across states in licensing older drivers are examined in Chapter 4.

• Chapter 4 also provides some striking statistics on older people's use of health services, barriers to their use, and recommendations for enhancing culturally competent services. Most existing medical, dental, and mental health services do not adequately address distinctive needs of the older population, especially those with low income and less education or who have been historically underserved. As a result, older people who could benefit most from the services often fail to use them.

• Health enhancement and wellness programs have proved successful in maintaining and even improving older people's health in many areas, including exercise, prevention of falls and osteoporosis, and nutrition. Chapter 4 describes some of these programs and the research evidence for the benefits of health promoting programs.

Throughout Part Two, the tremendous variations in how people age physically are emphasized. Because of lifestyle, environmental, and genetic factors, some people will show dramatic declines in all their organ systems at a relatively early age. Most older people, however, will experience slower rates of decline and at different levels across the organ systems. For example, some people may suffer from chronic heart disease, yet at the same time maintain strong bones and muscle strength. In contrast, others may require medications for painful osteoarthritis, even as their heart and lungs remain in excellent condition. The following vignettes illustrate these variations.

A HEALTHY OLDER PERSON: MRS. HILL

I am an 80-year-old widow and a retired librarian. I have been slightly deaf all my life because of a childhood illness. And now I am experiencing some loss of vision but it doesn't keep me from doing the things I like to do. I have to watch my high blood pressure, but I can keep it under control by taking the medications my doctor prescribes. I never go to my doctor except for a semiannual checkup and for him to review my medications. I sometimes get frustrated at not having as much energy as I did when I was raising my children, but for the most part, I just accept this as part of aging and I adjust my activities accordingly. Even though I'm slowing down a bit, I'm still able to volunteer at the local library two afternoons each week when I read new books to a group of children age 4 to 6. I can still drive, but I like to walk most places, and get good exercise that way. I try to keep active, and I was one of the first seniors to participate in a new wellness program at our local senior center. The staff even convinced me to help teach an exercise class at the center three times a week. My daughter is always worried about my falling or hurting myself in my kitchen. So my son-in-law made some minor modifications, like changing the height and location of my kitchen shelves, so I can reach things better. I guess I should be pleased that friends and relatives frequently tell me that I do not look my age. I think my optimistic attitude has helped "keep me young," although I'm proud of reaching age 80 as a healthy and active person. I think each one of us is responsible for how we age, and I get really irritated with some of my friends who stay home all the time, watch TV, and complain.

AN OLDER PERSON WITH CHRONIC ILLNESS: MR. JONES

When I was only 60, I had a stroke that paralyzed me on my left side and made me unable to walk. Ever since the stroke 10 years ago, I have trouble talking and often slur what I am trying to say. My wife says that my personality has changed, that I am not the kind, gentle man she married. I know I get irritable at having to be lifted from bed to chair and I just started being incontinent, which really upset both me and my wife. My wife first tried to care for me at home, but my incontinence was the "last straw." After that, she felt she could no longer take care of me, although it was a really tough decision for her to move me to a nearby nursing home. Both of us are having a really hard time adjusting to the nursing home. My mind still works fine but in some ways that is worse 'cause I am aware of all the changes I've been experiencing. I get so frustrated over what I can no longer physically do and with having to retire earlier than planned. And money is really tight these days since neither of us is working and we have to pay for the nursing home. Our kids live in another state so they've not been able to help their mother take care of me and they have their own families to worry about so they can't help us out financially. We are worrying that we will have spent all our life savings and will have to apply for Medicaid to

cover my being here. If I think about things too much, I start to cry easily. I was always in charge of things, but now I can't control anything in my life anymore, not even going to the bathroom. I never thought my life would end up like this. And my wife gets angry at me a lot 'cause I can sure be ornery and difficult and I am not very good at thanking her for all that she does for me.

These two vignettes point to the complexity of physiological aging. Chronological age is often a poor predictor of health and functional status, as illustrated by Mrs. Hill's excellent functional and emotional health and Mr. Jones's situation of physical dependency, even though he is 10 years younger than Mrs. Hill. As noted above, Part Two describes these variations in normal physiological aging. It contrasts these with changes due to disease, and presents factors that influence functional status in the later years.

3

The Social Consequences of Physical Aging

For most people, aging is defined primarily by its visible signs—graying hair, balding among some men, sagging and wrinkled skin, stooped shoulders, and a slower walk or shuffling gait. Although these are the most visible signs of old age among humans, numerous other changes occur in our internal organs—the heart, lungs, kidneys, stomach, bladder, and central nervous system. These changes are not as easy to detect because they are not visible. In fact, x-rays and computer-assisted images of organ systems are not very useful for showing most changes that take place. It is primarily by measuring the **functional capacity** of these systems (i.e., the performance capacity of the heart, lungs, kidneys, and other organs) that their relative efficiency across the life span can be determined. This chapter describes normal changes that all of us experience in our biological systems as we age. In the next chapter, the diseases of aging that may impair organ functions more than would be expected from normal aging processes are discussed.

As noted in Chapter 1, biological aging, or **senescence,** is defined as the normal process of changes over time in the body and its components. It is a gradual process common to all living organisms that eventually affects an individual's functioning vis-à-vis the environment but does not necessarily result in disease or death. It is not, in itself, a disease. But aging and disease are often linked in most people's minds, since declines in organ capacity and our immune system make us more vulnerable to sickness. Because certain diseases such as Alzheimer's, arthritis, and heart conditions have a higher incidence with age, we may erroneously equate age with disease. However, a more accurate conception of the aging process is a gradual accumulation of irreversible functional losses to which the average person tries to accommodate. As discussed in Chapter 1, people can maintain an active lifestyle as they experience age-related changes in their biological and physiological systems. In order to achieve active aging, individuals may alter their physical and social environments by reducing the demands placed on their remaining functional capacity (e.g., relocating to a one-story home or apartment to avoid stairs, driving only during the day, avoiding crowds). This is consistent with the person–environment model of aging; as their physical competence declines, older people may simplify their physical environment to reestablish homeostasis or their comfort zone. It also suggests their resilience as they cope effectively with changes.

Individual differences are evident in the rate and severity of physical changes, as illustrated by the vignettes of Mrs. Hill and Mr. Jones. As noted earlier, not all people show the same degree of change in any given organ system, nor do all the systems decline at the same rate and at the same time. Individual aging depends largely on genetic inheritance, nutrition and diet, physical activity, and environment. Thus, while one 78-year-old feels "old" because of aches and pains due to arthritis but uses her excellent cognitive skills at work every day, another 78-year-old may retain her physical ability but may live in a nursing home due to advanced dementia. One way of understanding these variations in biological aging is to examine the major theories that have been advanced to explain the changes in all living organisms over time.

Biological Theories of Aging

Popular culture, as reflected in books and magazines, is full of stories about "anti-aging therapies," "fighting aging," and "preventing death." The problem with these optimistic projections is that no single scientific theory has yet been able to explain what causes aging and death. Without a clear understanding of this process, it is impossible to prevent, fight, or certainly to stop this normal mechanism of all living organisms.

The process of aging is complex and multidimensional, involving significant loss and decline in some physiological functions, and minimal change in others. Scientists have long attempted to find the causes for this process. A theme of some theories is that aging is a process that is programmed into the genetic structure of each species. Yet, genetic heritability within a species accounts for only 35 percent of the variance in lifespan. More likely it is the rate of damage to DNA and its repair that predicts longevity (Rattan and Clark, 2005). Other theories state that aging represents an accumulation of stimuli from the environment that produce stress on the organism. Any theory of aging must be based on the scientific method, using systematic tests of hypotheses and empirical observations. It is generally agreed that in order to be viable, biological theories must meet four criteria:

1. The process must be universal; that is, all members of a species must experience the phenomenon.
2. The process must be deleterious, or result in physiological decline.

3. The process must be progressive, that is, losses must be gradual over time.
4. Finally, the losses must be intrinsic, that is, they cannot be corrected by the organism.

These guidelines are useful for excluding biological phenomena that are different from aging per se. For example, they help to distinguish disease from normal aging. While diseases are often deleterious, progressive, and intrinsic, they are not universal (e.g., not all older adults will develop arthritis or Alzheimer's disease). Each of the following biological theories meets these criteria, although the evidence to support them is not always clear. Even though these theories advance our understanding of aging, none of them is totally adequate for explaining what *causes* aging. The theories that will be discussed in this section are based on extensive research with animals and humans:

- Wear and tear
- Autoimmune
- Cross-linkage
- Free radical
- Cellular aging
- Endocrine and immunological

One of the earliest theories of biological aging, the **wear and tear theory,** suggests that, like a machine, the organism simply wears out over time (Wilson, 1974). In this model, aging is a preprogrammed process; that is, each species has a biological clock that determines its maximum life span and the rate at which each organ system will deteriorate. For example, fruit flies (drosophilae) have a natural life span of a few hours, butterflies a few weeks, dogs up to 20 years, and humans about 120 years. This process is compounded by the effects of environmental stress on the organism (e.g., nutritional deficiencies). Cells continually wear out, and existing cells cannot repair damaged components within themselves. This is particularly true in tissues that are located in the striated skeletal

and heart muscles and throughout the nervous system; these tissues are composed of cells that cannot undergo cell division. As we will see later, these systems are most likely to experience significant decline in their ability to function effectively with age.

Another early theory, the **autoimmune theory,** proposes that aging is a function of the body's immune system becoming defective over time and attacking not just foreign proteins, bacteria, and viruses, but also producing antibodies against itself. Older people become more susceptible to infections. This explanation of the immune system is consistent with the process of many diseases that increase with age, such as cancer, diabetes, and rheumatoid arthritis (Finch, 1990). Nevertheless, this theory does not explain *why* the immune system becomes defective with age; only the effects of this change are described. For example, the thymus gland, which controls production of disease-fighting white blood cells, shrinks with aging, but the *reasons* for both this reduction in size and the fact that more older people do not suffer from autoimmune diseases are unclear.

The **cross-linkage theory** (Bjorksten, 1974; Gafni, 2001) focuses on the changes in the protein called *collagen* with age. Collagen is an important connective tissue found in most organ systems; indeed, about one-third of all the protein in our body is collagen. As a person ages, changes in collagen, such as wrinkling of the skin, are clearly observable. These changes lead to a loss of elasticity in blood vessels, muscle tissue, skin, the lens of the eye and other organs, and to slower wound healing. Another visible effect of changes in collagen is that the nose and ears tend to increase in size. From this theoretical perspective, collagen changes are due to the binding of essential molecules in the cells through the accumulation of cross-linking compounds, which in turn slows the process of normal cell functions and shows signs of aging. These cross-links are necessary to join together the parallel molecules of collagen. However, in older animals and humans these links increase, making the tissue less pliable and rigid, as seen in wrinkled skin.

An extension of cross-linkage theory is the **free radical theory** of aging (Finch 1990; Harman, 1956, 1993). Free radicals are highly reactive molecules that break off in cells and possess an unpaired electron. They are produced normally by the use of oxygen within the cell but are multiplied by smoking, exposure to ultraviolet radiation, and psychological stress. They interact with other cell molecules and may cause DNA mutations, cross-linking of connective tissue, changes in protein behavior, and other damage. Such reactions continue until one free radical pairs with another or meets an *antioxidant*. These are chemical inhibitors that can safely absorb the extra electron and prevent oxygen from combining with susceptible molecules to form free radicals. They are produced by cells in the body but aging results in slower production of antioxidants. Some researchers have proposed that ingesting antioxidants such as vitamins E and C, beta carotene, and selenium can inhibit free radical damage; this can then slow the aging process by delaying the loss of immune function and reducing the incidence of many diseases associated with aging (Aldwin and Gilmer, 2004; Beckman and Ames, 1998; Grune and Davies, 2001).

Nevertheless, it appears that free radicals are not totally destroyed. Those that survive in the organism damage the proteins needed to make cells in the body by interacting with the oxygen used to produce protein. As a result, free radicals may destroy the fragile process of building cells and the DNA strands that transmit messages of genes. Some have argued that this continuous pounding by dangerous oxidants wears away the organism over time, not just by interfering with cell-building, but also by requiring antioxidants to be ever-vigilant. This damage to cell tissue by free radicals has been implicated in normal aging, as well as in the development of some cancers, heart disease, Alzheimer's disease, and Parkinson's disease.

Molecular biologists have explored this theory further by splicing genes to measure the cumulative effects of free radicals in cells, with the goal of developing ways to counter these effects. It may be that synthetic antioxidants can be developed and administered to older people as the body's natural supply is depleted. Animal studies have shown dramatic enhancements of memory and physical activity with high doses of antioxidants. For example, two drugs containing the enzymes superoxide dismutase and catabase (known to have antioxidant properties) have been found to extend the lifespan of worms by more than 50 percent. These drugs may also be effective in reducing the damage caused by strokes or Parkinson's disease (Melov et al., 2000). Until research with mice supports the promising results emerging from worm studies, it is difficult to predict whether humans will experience similar benefits. It may be that the free radical theory holds the greatest promise for slowing the aging process in the future. However, while increasing the intake of antioxidants may eventually result in more people achieving their *life expectancy*, there is no evidence that the *maximum human life span* of approximately 120 years will increase significantly (Hayflick, 1996). Indeed, there is little support for the positive impact of increasing antioxidant defenses (Grune and Davies, 2001).

The **cellular aging theory** suggests that aging occurs as cells slow their number of replications. Hayflick and Moorehead (1961) first reported that cells grown in culture (i.e., in controlled laboratory environments) undergo a finite number of replications, approaching 50 doublings. Cells from older subjects replicate even fewer times, as do cells derived from individuals with progeria and Werner syndrome—both rare genetic anomalies in which aging is accelerated and death may occur by age 15 to 20 in the former and by 40 to 50 in the latter condition. It appears that cells are programmed to follow a biological clock and stop replicating after a given number of times. The number of divisions a normal cell undergoes depends on the specific cell type. As the number of replications decreases, telomeres show a consistent shortening effect (Hornsby, 2001). In addition, proponents of this theory point out that each cell has a given level of DNA that is eventually depleted. This in turn reduces the production of RNA, which is essential for producing enzymes necessary for cellular functioning. Hence, the loss of DNA and subsequent reduction of RNA eventually result in cell death (Hayflick, 2000).

Another biological theory that suggests that aging is programmed into biological organisms is **endocrine and immunological theory.** Proponents of this theory point to the decline in testosterone in men and estrogen in women as a partial cause of some chronic diseases such as osteoporosis, as well as loss of muscle mass and strength (Harman et al., 2000). Similarly, loss of T-cells from the thymus gland begins by age 20 and accelerates before old age is reached. This reduces the organism's ability to fight infections in the later years (Effros, 2001).

Of all the theories of physiological aging, cellular aging appears to explain best what is going on. The role of cell replication, RNA production, and telomere shortening in aging is widely accepted in the scientific community. It should not be presumed, however, that the step from understanding to reversing the process of aging will be achieved soon. It is often erroneously assumed that scientific discoveries of the *cause* of a particular physiological process or disease can immediately lead to *changing* or reversing that condition. Unfortunately, that step is a difficult one to make, as evidenced by the challenges in advancing cancer research. Scientists have long observed the structural changes in cancer cells, but the reasons for these changes are far from being understood. Without a clear understanding of *why* a particular biological process takes place, it is impossible to move toward reversing that process. However, some hope is offered by recent scientific research that successfully forced cells to produce **telomerase,** the enzyme responsible for rebuilding telomeres and in this manner continued cell replication. The reverse process may be effective in preventing the rapid proliferation of cancer cells, which do not show any limits on replication. Researchers have identified methods of inhibiting or blocking the production of this enzyme replicating naturally occurring chemicals that block the production of telomerase, or **telomerase inhibitors** (Bodner et al., 1998). There is growing evidence that significant shortening of telomeres may play a role in some diseases, such as ulcerative colitis, cirrhosis of the liver, and colon cancer (Eastwood, 1995; Kinouchi et al., 1998; Rudolph et al., 2000). By controlling the biological mechanisms that cause telomeres to shorten, researchers may eventually reduce the prevalence of these diseases.

Can Aging Be Reversed or Delayed?

Growth Hormones

Genetic researchers have made great strides in the past 30 years in their understanding of the aging process. Indeed, contrary to our long-held assumptions about aging, many scientists have become convinced that aging is *reversible.* New research on telomeres is one example of this development. Another approach is the possibility of introducing new hormones into the body to replace the depleted hormones in genes that serve as chemical messengers. Researchers at the National Institute on Aging, Veterans Administration centers, and universities around the country are testing the effects of injecting growth

POINTS TO PONDER

How would you feel if the aging process could be reversed? What might happen to society if more people could achieve the maximum life span of 120 years? What are some of the ethical and resource allocation issues raised by scientific efforts to reverse or slow the aging process?

hormones into aging animals and humans. So far, many startling discoveries have been made, such as increased lean muscle mass and vertebral bone density, and reduced fat levels. These changes in turn have led to increased activity and vigor. While these effects are short-lived, it may not be long before a human growth hormone is marketed that can safely be administered on a regular basis, like daily doses of vitamins.

Some researchers have tested the effects of the hormone dehydroepiandrosterone, or DHEA on muscle strength, cardiovascular formation, and bone density. This hormone is secreted by the adrenal glands, and the body converts it into testosterone and estrogen. Production of DHEA increases from age 7 to 30, when it stabilizes, then begins to decline. By age 80, the body has less than 5 percent of the level of DHEA it produced in its peak. Animal studies have shown that administering DHEA to adult mice results in increased activity levels and learning speed. However, research evidence with humans is not sufficient to recommend the regular, long-term use of DHEA. One of the few long-term clinical trials with DHEA gave older men and women supplements for two years. Bone mineral density improved in only one area of several that were measured, while insulin sensitivity, muscle strength, and quality of life showed no improvement. The authors recommend physical exercise instead of DHEA to improve these parameters in older adults' well-being (Dhatariya and Nair, 2003; Nair et al., 2006).

Caloric Restriction

Several studies using animal models (mice, fruit flies, fish) have demonstrated that reducing caloric intake by 50 to 70 percent increased the life span of experimental animals by as much as 30 to 50 percent, because it delays the appearance of pathology. Dietary restriction did not, however, include limiting nutrients in these studies. Caloric restriction that is accomplished mostly through reducing fat intake has been found to be most successful in extending the life of experimental

---

STEM CELL RESEARCH

Advances in stem cell research were recognized as the "scientific breakthrough of the year" in 1999 by the journal *Science*. This is because of significant advances in guiding such cells into becoming organ-specific tissues. They are potentially valuable for replacing cells in dieseased or dead tissues as in Parkinson's disease, Alzheimer's disease, or strokes. Nevertheless, this new technology, even more than other emerging areas of genetic research, is fraught with ethical dilemmas. In order to obtain stem cells by current methods, human embryos are preferred. Such embryos are often derived from aborted fetuses, so this has stirred debate among people opposed to abortion. Indeed, in 1995, Congress banned the National Institutes of Health (NIH) from funding research using human stem cells. Researchers in private biotech firms that do not receive government funding continued their work in this area. In 2000, the NIH issued new rules that federally funded researchers could use stem cells derived from frozen embryos that are due to be discarded by fertility clinics. These rules were accompanied by strict guidelines on how embryonic cells are to be harvested. Ethical concerns regarding the harvesting of stem cells from embryonic tissue may be alleviated in the future as research with adult stem cells finds ways of differentiating them into organ-specific tissues as successfully as embryonic cells (Bloom, 1999).

---

animals without causing malnutrition. Yet, it is evident from these studies that restriction of fat, protein, or carbohydrate intake alone is not sufficient; total caloric intake must also be reduced. Nor have the same benefits been found from merely increasing the intake of antioxidants or specific vitamins. The benefits of caloric restriction are greatest when it is initiated soon after birth; however, even when mice were placed on such diets in early middle age, their maximum life span increased by 10 to 20 percent (Masoro, 2003). In fact, caloric restriction has even been found to extend the reproductive capacity of female mice (McShane, Wilson, and Wise, 1999).

Until the results of longitudinal studies with primates are available, these conclusions are not generalizable to humans. The first such major study with primates is an ongoing one by researchers at the Baltimore Longitudinal Studies of the Gerontology Research Center (Lane et al., 1997, 2002; Roth, Ingram, and Lane, 2001; Weed et al., 1997). This study has examined the effects of feeding rhesus monkeys 30 percent less than their normal caloric intake. After 6 years on this diet, these monkeys showed higher activity levels, lower body temperature, less body fat, lower fasting glucose and insulin levels, and a slower decline in DHEA levels produced by the adrenal glands than an age-matched control group of monkeys that were fed freely, with no caloric restrictions.

These results provide the first evidence in primates that caloric restriction may delay the aging process by slowing down metabolism, thereby reducing the number of free radicals created in the organism. Lower caloric intake may also maintain the production of adrenal steroids such as DHEA without artificially replacing them. Caloric restriction also reduces the growth of tumors, delays declines in kidney function, decreases the loss of muscle mass, and slows other age-related changes ordinarily found in these animals. It delays the onset of autoimmune disease, hypertension, Type II diabetes, cataracts, glaucoma, and cancers in these animals, and appears to improve immune response and wound healing. In one of the few human studies, 18 adults who reduced their calorie intake for six years showed improved cardiovascular function and lower blood pressure, triglycerides, low-density lipids, glucose, and insulin (Fontana et al., 2004). These studies offer further support that caloric restriction may help humans improve their active life expectancy (Li and Wolf, 1997; Masoro, 2001, 2003; Mattison et al., 2003).

Anti-Aging Compounds

Recent studies have found that living organisms produce specific enzymes that can be boosted to survive the damage caused by stressors such as ionizing radiation, and can delay cell death. Although this research has focused on simple organisms such as yeast, fruit flies, and worms (specifically the nematode *Caenorhabditis elegans*, or *C. elegans*), the findings provide evidence that cellular enzymes can be boosted by compounds such as *resveratrol* (Howitz et al., 2003). Resveratrol is a type of polyphenol, a chemical that is found in red wine and seems to be responsible for the preventive benefits observed in red wine against heart disease. In laboratory studies, Howitz and colleagues found that adding these enzyme boosters to yeast cells increased their life span by 70 percent. These findings may eventually lead to important discoveries that can slow the aging process in humans, but it will require many more years of research to move beyond single cell and simple organisms to complex mammals.

Researchers with the Baltimore Longitudinal Studies (described in Chapter 1) have also been searching for a medication that can alter cellular metabolism to mimic the effects of caloric restriction. One such compound is 2-deoxy-D-glucose (2DG), which has been found to reduce insulin levels in the blood and slow tumor growth in rodents. This compound causes cells to produce smaller amounts of glucose's byproducts in the same way as caloric restriction, and in turn slow the formation of free radicals. Research with mice has demonstrated significant benefits in reducing blood glucose, body temperature, and damage to nerve cells. However, the NIA researchers have also found that 2DG can have toxic effects in higher doses or when used for prolonged periods. This may limit its application to primates, but these findings may open the door to testing other compounds that can mimic caloric restriction (Lane et al., 2002). Instead of "anti-aging," biogerontologists today are focused on **prolongevity,** or the idea that length of life can be extended and some diseases associated with aging eliminated. The concept of prolongevity does not change the fundamental processes of aging, described in the remainder of this chapter (Hayflick, 2004a, 2004b; Olshansky, Hayflick, and Carnes, 2002).

PROMISING RESEARCH FOR PROMOTING HEALTHY AGING

Resveratrol is found in the skin of grapes and in red wine and has been offered as a partial explanation for the "French paradox," the puzzling fact that people in France enjoy a high-fat diet yet suffer less heart disease than Americans. Recent research on mice receiving a high-calorie diet concluded that resveratrol activated genes that protected against the effects of aging and extended the life span, even neutralizing the risks of diabetes from an unhealthy diet. While viewed as a major landmark on the molecular genetics of aging, the findings should not encourage people to think that red wine could reverse the effects of eating badly. In fact, a person would have to drink at least 100 bottles of red wine a day or take megadoses of resveratrol supplements to reach the levels of the substance given to mice. Scientists at this point caution against taking large doses of reservatrol nutritional supplements until more is known about its effects in humans. Their goal is to develop a safe and effective form of this product (Bauer et al., 2006).

Research on Physiological Changes with Age

It is difficult to distinguish normal, age-related changes in many human functions from changes that are secondary to disease or other factors. Until the late 1950s, much of our knowledge about aging came from cross-sectional comparisons of healthy young persons with institutionalized or community-dwelling older populations who had multiple chronic diseases. These comparisons led to the not-surprising conclusion that the organ systems of older persons function less efficiently than those of younger persons.

Since the 1950s, a series of longitudinal studies have been undertaken with healthy younger and middle-aged persons to determine changes in various physiological parameters. The first of these studies began in 1958 at the Gerontology Research Center in Baltimore, as described in Chapter 1 (Shock, 1962). Today, many of the people in the original sample are still participating in the study. Many other researchers around the country are examining physiological functions longitudinally. The information in this chapter is derived from their work.

Aging in Body Composition

In this section, *normal* changes in the human body—both visible and invisible—are reviewed. These include changes in:

- muscle mass, fat tissue, and water (body composition)
- skin
- hair

CHANGES IN BODY COMPOSTION   Although individuals vary greatly in body weight and composition, the proportion of body weight contributed by water generally declines for both men and women: on the average, from 60 percent to 54 percent in men, and from 52 percent to

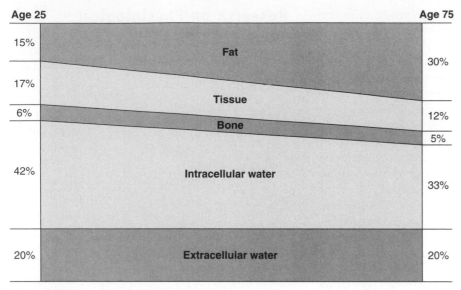

FIGURE 3.1 Distribution of Major Body Components
SOURCE: Reprinted with permission from the American Geriatrics Society. Speculations on vascular changes with age, by R.J. Goldman (*Journal of the American Geriatrics Society,* Vol. 18, p. 766, 1970).

46 percent in women (Blumberg, 1996). Lean body mass in muscle tissue is lost, whereas the proportion of fat increases (see Figure 3.1). This decline in muscle mass and increase in fat is known as *sarcopenia*. Because of an increase in fibrous material, muscle tissue loses its elasticity and flexibility. After age 50, the number of muscle fibers steadily decreases; muscle mass typically declines by 40 percent between ages 30 and 80 (Rincon, Muzumdar, and Barzilai, 2006). However, as illustrated by **master athletes,** older people who maintain a vigorous exercise program can prevent a significant loss of muscle tone, as described in Chapter 4. The loss of muscle mass and water, and increase in fat tissue, all have a significant effect on older adults' ability to metabolize many medications, which can lead to adverse reactions such as disorientation, falls, and overmedication. Some drugs are processed by muscle tissue, some in fat, and some in water throughout the human body. With the changes in body composition described here, these medications may remain in fat tissue longer than needed,

or may be too concentrated relative to the available water and muscle volume.

These changes in muscle mass, water, and fat are also associated with weight alterations, from increased weight for some people in the middle

LEARNING FROM MASTER ATHLETES

The National Senior Games Association, committed to promoting healthy lifestyles through sports and fitness, involves thousands of participants in competitive sports events known as Senior Olympics at the state and national levels. Older athletes defy expectations about inevitable physiological decline. For example, an 88-year-old shot-put thrower in the 1999 Senior Olympics claimed that his return to competitive track and field eliminated his migraine headaches. An 86-year-old who played guard for an NFL team in the 1930s broke records for his age group. Whether they have maintained their physical activity levels since youth or begun in middle or old age, older master athletes can teach gerontologists about the effects of healthy lifestyles on biological aging.

years, until after age 75 when there is a tendency toward lower weight and lower calorie intake. This is why we rarely see people in their 80s and 90s who are obese, but at the same time it is rare to see older adults with excellent muscle tone. The balance of sodium and potassium also changes, with the ratio of sodium increasing by 20 percent between ages 30 to 70, which has implications for restricting salt intake.

The changes in body composition that we have described have numerous implications for the diets of older people; although older adults generally need fewer total calories per day than active younger people, they need to consume a higher proportion of protein, calcium, and vitamin D to offset the depletion of these nutrients and to ensure that they obtain nutrient-rich calories (Blumberg, 1996). However, many older individuals do not change their diet during the later years unless advised specifically by a physician. Others, especially those living alone, eat poorly balanced meals. This combination of poor nutrition and age-associated changes in the body composition are found to be linked to diabetes and cardiovascular disease, because of alterations in carbohydrate metabolism and insulin resistance (Rincon et al., 2006).

CHANGES IN THE SKIN   As stated at the beginning of this chapter, changes in the appearance and texture of skin and hair are often the most visible signs of aging. These also tend to have deleterious consequences on how older people view themselves and are perceived by others. The human skin is unique among that of all other mammals in that it is exposed directly to the elements, with no protective fur or feathers to shield it from the direct effects of sunlight. In fact, ultraviolet light from the sun, which damages the elastic fibers beneath the skin's surface, is primarily responsible for the wrinkled, dried, and tougher texture of older people's skin, known as photoaging or extrinsic aging. Indeed, UV radiation may be the main culprit in skin aging, suggesting the value of protecting

the skin throughout the life span. Human skin cells collected from exposed parts of the body grow much more slowly than skin from areas protected by the sun (e.g., underarms). This is evident when one compares the appearance of the skin of two 75-year-olds: one a retired farmer who has worked under the sun most of his life, the other a retired office worker who has spent most of his years indoors. The farmer generally will have more wrinkles; darker pigmentation known as **melanin,** which has been produced by the body to protect it from ultraviolet rays; and drier skin with a leathery texture. He is also more likely to have so-called *age spots* or *liver spots*—harmless from a health standpoint but of concern sometimes for their appearance. As one might expect, people who spend most of their lives in sunny climates are more prone to these changes. Concern about the negative consequences of extensive exposure to the sun is more prevalent today, and younger people are taking more precautions, such as wearing sun screen regularly (Ramirez and Schneider, 2003).

Besides these environmental factors, the human body itself is responsible for some of the changes in the skin with age. The outermost layer of skin, the epidermis, constantly replenishes itself by shedding dead cells and replacing them with new cells. As the person gets older, the process of cell replacement is slowed, up to 50 percent between ages 30 and 70. More importantly, the connective tissue that makes up the second layer of skin, the *dermis,* thins because the number of dermal cells diminishes and makes it less elastic with age. These changes result in reduced elasticity and thickness of the outer skin layer, longer time required for the skin to spring back into shape, and increased sagging and wrinkling. Sometimes women in their 20s and 30s may experience these problems earlier than men. This is because women tend to have less oil in the sebaceous glands. However, the process of skin aging varies widely, depending on the relative amount of oil in the glands, exposure to the sun, and heredity. Despite its changing appearance, the skin can still perform its protective function throughout old age.

Wound healing is also slower in older persons. Thus, people over age 65 require more time than those under age 35 to form blisters as a means of closing a wound, and more time to form new epithelial tissue to replace blistered skin. This is one of the reasons why bed sores of nursing home residents can take so long to heal and may prove deadly.

The sebaceous and sweat glands, located in the dermis, generally deteriorate with age. Changes also occur in the deepest, or *subcutaneous,* skin layers, which tend to lose fat and water. The alterations in subcutaneous skin are compounded by a reduction in the skin's blood circulation, which can damage the effectiveness of the skin's temperature regulatory mechanism and make older people more sensitive to hot and cold temperatures. As a result, older persons' comfort zone for ambient temperature is generally three to five degrees warmer than that for younger persons. It also takes longer for an older person to adjust after being exposed to either hot or cold extreme temperatures. This leaves the older individual much more vulnerable to **hypothermia** (low body temperature, sometimes resulting in brain damage and death) and **hyperthermia** (heat stroke), as evidenced by reports of increased accidental deaths among older adults during periods of extremely cold winter weather and of prolonged heat spells. For example, the long heat wave in Europe during August, 2003, claimed over 15,000 lives in France alone, most of whom were older people who lacked adequate ventilation in their homes and apartments (*New York Times,* August 24, 2003). A similar heat wave in Europe in July, 2006 resulted in a far lower death rate, when only 112 French elders died. The lower death rate compared to 2003 was attributed to better preparation by the medical community and public service announcements reminding people to stay indoors and drink plenty of water.

To prevent hypothermia, it is recommended that indoor temperatures be set above 68°F during winter months in older people's homes, and that humidity be minimized. Some older people who are concerned about conserving energy and money may set their thermostats below 68°F. As a preventive measure, the Department of Health and Human Services, as well as many local governments, offer funds to help low-income individuals pay for heating costs (NIH, 2006).

CHANGES IN THE HAIR   As we age, the appearance and texture of our hair changes. Hair is thickest in early adulthood and decreases by as much as 20 percent in diameter by age 70. This is why so many older people have fine, limp-looking hair. This change is compounded by the increased loss of hair with age. Although up to 60 strands of hair are lost daily during youth and early adulthood, the hair is replaced regularly through the action of estrogen and testosterone. As we age, however, more hairs are lost than replaced, especially in men. Some men experience rapid hair loss, leading to a receding hairline or even complete baldness by their mid-40s. Some older women also find their hair thins so much that they cannot hide bald spots. Reasons for the observed variation in hair loss are not clear, but genetic factors appear to play a role.

Gray hair results from pigment loss in the hair follicles. As we age, less pigment is produced at the roots. Eventually all the hair becomes colorless, or white in appearance. The gray color of some people's hair is an intermediate stage of pigment loss. In fact, some people may never experience a total loss of pigment production, but will live into an advanced old age with relatively dark hair. Others may experience graying in their 20s. In our society, graying of hair tends to have more stigma associated with it for women than for men, and women are more likely to tint or color their hair.

Changes in Organ Systems

Although some change occurs with age in all organ systems, this chapter focuses on changes in the:

- musculoskeletal and kinesthetic system
- respiratory system
- cardiovascular system
- urinary system
- gastrointestinal system
- endocrine system
- nervous system

CHANGES IN THE MUSCULOSKELETAL AND KINESTHETIC SYSTEM   Stature or height declines an average of 3 inches with age, although the total loss varies across individuals and between men and women. Indeed, the Baltimore Longitudinal Studies found that a gradual reduction in height begins around age 30, averaging 1/16 inch per year. We reach our maximum size and strength at about age 25, after which our cells decrease steadily in number and size. This decline occurs in both the trunk and the extremities, and may be attributable to the loss of bone mineral. This loss of bone mineral density is, in turn, attributed to a decline in

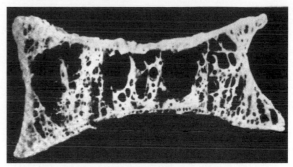

With osteoporosis, both trabecular and cortical bones become more brittle and lace-like.

estrogen levels with menopause in women. A decline in testosterone may explain the similar, but less dramatic, loss of bone mineral in older men (Rudman et al., 1991). The spine becomes more curved, and discs in the vertebrae become compacted. This is why older people are sometimes described as literally shrinking. Such loss of height is intensified for individuals with **osteoporosis,** a disease that makes the bones less dense, more porous, and hence more prone to fractures following even minor stress. For older people who have no natural teeth remaining, it is not unusual to lose a considerable volume of bone in the jaw or alveolar bone. This results in a poor fit of dentures and a painful feeling when chewing or biting with dentures. The loss of bone mass characteristic of osteoporosis is *not* a normal process of aging, but a disease that occurs more frequently among older women, as discussed in Chapters 4 and 15.

Another normal change with aging is that shoulder width decreases as a result of bone loss, weakened muscles, and loss of elasticity in the ligaments. This results in loss of range of motion, making it difficult for some older people to reach high cupboards or turn their head to see cars behind them. Regular exercise to strengthen shoulder muscles can slow such loss of upper body mobility. Crush fractures of the spine cause the vertebrae to collapse, such that over time, some older people (especially women) appear to

---

INCONGRUENCE BETWEEN THE ENVIRONMENT AND OLDER ADULT'S MOTOR FUNCTIONING AND BALANCE

Mrs. Guitierrez, age 83, lives alone and is determined to be as independent as possible. Her neighbors watch carefully, however, when she goes out to walk her small dog. She shuffles, moves very slowly, and often has to stop and grab hold of something to avoid falling. When her son and daughter-in-law visit, they shudder when she climbs on a stool to reach a can or bottle on the upper cabinet shelves. Her son has tried to make her home safer, by moving the food to lower shelves, putting grab bars in the bathroom, and removing throw rugs. These changes are necessary to accommodate normal age-related changes in her kinesthetic and motor functioning.

be stoop-shouldered or hunched—a condition known as **kyphosis.** Stiffness in the joints is also characteristic of old age; this occurs because cartilage between the joints wears thin and fluid that lubricates them decreases. Strength and stamina also decline with aging. Maximum strength at age 70 has been found to be 65 to 85 percent of the maximum capacity of a 25-year-old. This drops to 50 percent by age 80, although older persons who maintain an active physical fitness program show much less decline in strength. Grip strength declines by 50 percent in men between age 30 and 75, and to a lesser degree in women.

The **kinesthetic system** lets an individual know his or her position in space; adjustments in body position become known through kinesthetic cues. Because of age-related changes in the central nervous system, which controls the kinesthetic mechanism, as well as muscle weakness, diminished vision, and spinal injury, older people demonstrate a decreased ability to orient their bodies in space and to detect externally induced changes in body position. Other physiological and disease-related changes, such as damage to the inner ear, may exacerbate this problem. Older persons need more external cues to orient themselves in space, and can be incorrect by 5 to 20 degrees in estimating their position compared to younger people. If both visual and surface cues of position are lost, older people experience postural sway or inability to maintain a vertical stance. This is why healthy older adults may complain that "things are spinning."

Not surprisingly, these alterations in motor functioning and in the kinesthetic system result in greater caution among older persons, who then tend to take slower, shuffling, and more deliberate steps. Older people are more likely to seek external spatial cues and supports while walking. As a result, they are less likely to go outside in inclement weather for fear of slipping or falling. Some may complain of dizziness and vertigo. These normal, age-related changes combine with the problems of slower reaction time,

> ### POINTS AND PONDER
>
> Look around your own home, or your parents' home. What physical factors can you identify that would be a problem if you were an 80-year-old woman living there? Think about lighting, stairs, floor, cabinets, and so on. What changes could make the home congruent with an older person's needs?

muscle weakness, and reduced visual acuity make it far more likely that older people will fall and injure themselves. However, attempts to improve balance through general and aerobic exercise, alternative approaches such as Tai Chi, and systematic programs to increase visual cues are effective in enhancing the postural stability of healthy older persons (Nikolaus and Bach, 2003; Wolfe et al., 2003). Other advantages of exercise programs for older adults are discussed in Chapter 4.

CHANGES IN THE SENSE OF TOUCH   *Somesthetic,* or touch, sensitivity also deteriorates with age. This is partially due to changes in the skin and to age-related loss in the number of nerve endings. Reduced touch sensitivity is especially prevalent in the fingertips, palms, and lower extremities. Age differences in touch sensitivity of the fingertips are much more dramatic than in the forearm. Using two-point discrimination tests (i.e., the minimum distance at which the subject detects the two points of a caliper), researchers have found that older persons need two to four times the separation of two points that younger persons do. This has significant implications for daily tasks that require sensitivity of the fingertips, such as selecting medications from a pillbox.

Pain perception is an important aspect of touch sensitivity. Older adults are less able to discriminate among levels of painful stimuli than younger persons. One reason for this may be that nerve cells in the skin become less efficient with age. As a result, burns are often more serious in older people because they do not respond to the heated object or flame until it is too late.

The distinction between pain perception and pain behavior is a critical one. Tolerance for pain is a subjective experience, which may be related to cultural, gender, and personality factors. In older people, increased complaints of pain may be a function of depression and psychosomatic needs. On the other hand, some people may attempt to minimize their pain by not reporting above-threshold levels of unpleasant stimuli. This is consistent with a frequently observed attitude among many older adults that pain, illness, and discomfort are inevitable corollaries of aging and "just something to live with." In fact, most elders probably underreport actual pain experienced. For example, an older person may not report symptoms of a heart attack unless or until it is severe. This has significant implications for health-seeking behaviors, as described in Chapter 4.

CHANGES IN THE RESPIRATORY SYSTEM   Almost every organ system shows some decline in **functional (or reserve) capacity** with age, as illustrated by several physiological indices in Figure 3.2. It is important to keep in mind that this graph is based on *cross-sectional* data collected from healthy men in these age groups; results from the Baltimore Longitudinal Studies of Aging show more variability when longitudinal data for each cohort are examined. On average, many organ systems show a functional decline of about 1 percent per year after age 30. Complex functions that require the integration

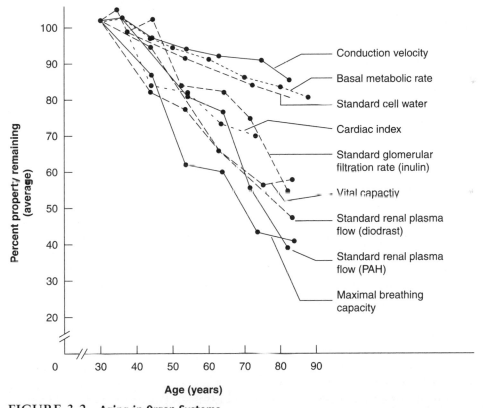

FIGURE 3.2   Aging in Organ Systems

SOURCE: N.W. Shock, The physiology of aging. *Scientific American,* 1962, *206,* 110. Copyright © 1962 by Scientific American, Inc. All rights reserved.

of multiple systems experience the most rapid decline. For example, maximum breathing capacity—which requires coordination of the respiratory, nervous, and muscular systems—is greatly reduced. Accordingly, normal changes in the respiratory and cardiovascular system become most evident with age. These changes are responsible for an individual's declining ability to maintain physical activity for long periods and the increasing tendency to fatigue easily. With aging, the muscles that operate the lungs lose elasticity so that respiratory efficiency is reduced. Gradual declines in organ function are caused by increasing rates of cell loss and inability of tissues to repair themselves with aging, resulting in impaired replication and reserve capacity of the organ. Indeed, this loss of reserve capacity with aging may be responsible for some diseases associated with aging (Hornsby, 2001).

Vital capacity, or the maximum amount of oxygen that can be brought into the lungs with a deep breath, declines. The average decline for men is estimated to be 50 percent between ages 25 and 70, or a decline from 6 quarts of air to 3 quarts. Breathing may become more difficult after exercise, such as climbing up several flights of stairs, but it does not necessarily impair the older person's daily functions. It may simply mean that the person has to move more slowly or rest on the stairway landing. However, the rate of decline in vital capacity is slower in physically active men, such as athletes, than in sedentary healthy men. A longitudinal study that followed well-trained endurance athletes (average age 62 at baseline) and a control group of sedentary men (average age 61 at baseline) over 8 years suggests that aging per se plays only a small role in the decline of the respiratory system:

- Maximum volume of oxygen declined in master athletes by 5.5 percent.
- Maximum volume of oxygen declined in sedentary men by 12 percent (Rogers et al., 1990).

Of all the organ systems, the respiratory system suffers the most punishment from environmental pollutants and infections. This makes it difficult to distinguish normal, age-related changes from pathological or environmentally induced diseases. Cilia, which are hairlike structures in the airways, are reduced in number and less effective in removing foreign matter, which diminishes the amount of oxygen available. This decline, combined with reduced muscle strength in the chest that impairs cough efficiency, makes older adults more susceptible to chronic bronchitis, emphysema, and pneumonia. Older people can avoid serious loss of lung function by remaining active, pacing their tasks, taking part in activities that do not demand too much exertion, and avoiding strenuous activity on days when the air quality is poor.

CARDIOVASCULAR CHANGES AND THE EFFECTS OF EXERCISE Structural changes in the heart and blood vessels include a reduction in bulk, a replacement of heart muscle with fat, a loss of elastic tissue, and an increase in collagen. Within the muscle fibers, an age pigment composed of fat and protein, known as *lipofuscin,* may take up 5 to 10 percent of the fiber structure. These changes produce a loss of elasticity in the arteries, weakened vessel walls, and **varicosities,** or an abnormal swelling in veins that are under high pressure (e.g., in the legs). In addition to loss of elasticity, the arterial and vessel walls become increasingly lined with lipids (fats), creating the condition of **atherosclerosis,** which makes it more difficult for blood to be pumped through the vessels and arteries. This buildup of fats and lipids occurs to some extent with normal aging, but it is exacerbated in some individuals whose diet includes large quantities of saturated fats. Such lifestyle risk factors for heart disease are reviewed in Chapter 4.

Blood pressure is expressed as the ratio of **systolic** to **diastolic pressure.** The former refers to the level of blood pressure (in millimeters)

Biking can help maintain respiratory and cardiovascular function.

during the contraction phase (systole), whereas the latter refers to the stage when the chambers of the heart are filling with blood. For example, a blood pressure of 120/80 indicates that the pressure created by the heart to expel blood can raise a column of mercury 120 millimeters. During diastole, in this example, the pressure produced by blood rushing into the heart chambers can raise a column of mercury 80 millimeters. In normal aging (i.e., no signs of cardiovascular disease), systolic blood pressure increases somewhat, but the diastolic blood pressure does not (see Figure 3.3). As with changes in the heart, extreme elevation of

blood pressure is not normal and is associated with unhealthy diet, obesity, and an inactive lifestyle, all of which have cumulative effects over the years. The harmful effects of abnormally high or low blood pressure are examined in Chapter 4.

Heart rate varies across individuals, remaining relatively high in physically active older persons. Resting heart rates also decrease with aging, although physically well-conditioned older people tend to have heart rates more similar to the average younger person.

These changes in the heart and lungs cause them to be less efficient in utilizing oxygen. This, in turn, reduces an individual's capacity to maintain physical activity for long periods. Nevertheless, physical training for older persons can significantly reduce blood pressure and increase their aerobic capacity (Vincent et al., 2002). Studies of master athletes show that physical training results in a greater volume of oxygen, more lean body weight, reduced levels of low density lipoprotein (LDL) cholesterol, also known as "bad cholesterol," and higher levels of high density lipoprotein (HDL), or good cholesterol, than is found in sedentary older persons (Yataco et al., 1997). However, these levels in master athletes are worse than in younger athletes, underscoring the reality that normal changes in the body's physiology and its operation cannot be eliminated completely. For example, world-class sprinters are generally in their late teens or early 20s, but marathon winners are normally in their late 20s or early 30s, since strength and neuromuscular coordination peak earlier than stamina. After age 30, running speed declines by a few percent each year (Hayflick, 1996).

Nevertheless, moderate exercise, such as a brisk walk 3 to 4 times per week, yard work, or even house work, appears to slow down these age-related changes. Researchers have found a significant increase in aerobic capacity, as measured by maximum volume of oxygen intake, among older persons after 24 weeks of low-intensity or

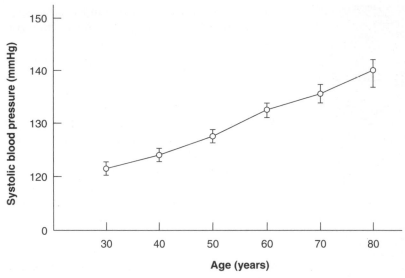

FIGURE 3.3   Effect of Age on Systolic Blood Pressure
SOURCE: J.D. Tobin, Physiological indices of aging. In D. Danon, N.W. Shock, and M. Marois (Eds.), *Aging: A challenge in science and society*, VoL 1 (New York: Oxford University Press, 1981).

high-intensity training (e.g., walking vs. jogging for 30 minutes). Both low and high intensity resulted in improved aerobic capacity (Vincent et al., 2002). However, high-intensity training can also lead to more **orthopedic injuries** than low-intensity training. For this reason, given that both high- and low-intensity training are effective for improving aerobic capacity, walking may be the best exercise for many older adults. It should be noted that exercise by itself may not be sufficient

for reducing LDL cholesterol levels in the blood, which has been associated with heart disease. Instead, reduced intake of animal fats, tropical oils, transfats, and refined carbohydrates appears to be essential for lowering these elements in the blood. Although there are limitations, such findings justify optimism that physical health can be considerably improved through lifestyle changes,

---

HOW TO CALCULATE MAXIMUM ACHIEVABLE HEART RATE

The maximum heart rate achievable by sustained exercise is directly associated with age. An easy way to calculate this is: 220 minus age in years.
For example:

- For a 25-year-old, 220 − 25 = 195 beats per minute
- For a 70-year-old, 220 − 70 = 150 beats per minute

AN OLDER ADULT CAN IMPROVE CARDIOVASCULAR FUNCTION

Mrs. Carson had gained weight after retiring at age 66. She was never very interested in exercise. However, a medical checkup at age 68 revealed high LDL and total cholesterol, as well as marginally high blood pressure. She began an exercise program of walking 30 minutes, five times weekly, and cut down her intake of red meat. After 6 months she had lost 10 pounds, her blood lipids were in the normal range, and her blood pressure was 120/70, ideal for a woman her age.

even after age 65. Aerobic exercise and a healthy lifestyle can significantly increase active life expectancy by postponing and shortening the period of morbidity (e.g., days of sickness) that one can expect in the later years. The significance of certain lifestyle habits for maintaining good health in old age is discussed further in Chapter 4.

CHANGES IN THE URINARY SYSTEM   Both kidney and bladder functions change with age. The kidneys play an important role in regulating the body's internal chemistry by filtering blood and urine through an extraordinary system of tubes and capillaries, known as glomeruli. As blood passes through these filters, it is cleaned, and the necessary balance of ions and minerals is restored. In the process, urea (e.g., water and waste materials) is collected and passed through the ureter and the bladder, where it is excreted in the form of urine. With age, the kidneys decrease in volume and weight, and the total number of glomeruli correspondingly decreases by 30 percent from age 30 to age 65. As a result, **renal function,** defined by the rate at which blood is filtered through the kidneys, declines by up to 50 percent with age. These changes have significant implications for an older person's tolerance for certain medications such as penicillin, tetracycline, digoxin, and others that are cleared by glomerular filtration. These drugs remain active longer in an older person's system and

may be more potent than in a younger person, indicating a need to reduce drug dosage and frequency of administration.

The kidneys also lose their capacity to absorb glucose, as well as their concentrating and diluting ability. This contributes to increased problems with dehydration and hyponatremia (i.e., a loss of salt in the blood). Of all organ systems, renal function deteriorates most dramatically with age, irrespective of disease.

Compounding this problem, bladder function also deteriorates with age. The capacity of the bladder may be reduced by as much as 50 percent in some older persons. At the same time, however, the sensation of needing to empty the bladder is delayed. The latter condition may be more a function of central nervous system dysfunction than changes in the bladder. As a result, **urinary incontinence** is common in older adults. As many as 30 percent of older people living in the community and at least 50 percent of those in nursing homes suffer from difficulties with bladder control. The problem may be made worse by a stroke, dementia, or other diseases associated with the nervous system, such as Parkinson's (Thom and Brown, 1998). Unfortunately, because of the social stigma associated with incontinence, older adults may be reticent to mention such problems to their physician or family members.

Because of these changes in the kidney and the bladder, older people may be more sensitive to the effects of alcohol and caffeine. Both of these substances inhibit the production of a hormone that regulates urine production. Ordinarily, this hormone, known as antidiuretic hormone (ADH), signals to the kidneys when to produce urine in order to keep the body's chemistry balanced. When it is temporarily inhibited by the consumption of alcohol, coffee, or tea, the kidneys no longer receive messages and, as a result, produce urine constantly. This, in turn, dehydrates the body. It appears that ADH production is slowed with aging, so substances that inhibit its production increase the load on the kidneys and the bladder. These changes can force older people to avoid

AN OLDER WOMAN WITH BLADDER CONTROL PROBLEMS

Mrs. RedHorse, age 75, has experienced increasing problems with urinary incontinence, especially since she began using diuretics for her high blood pressure. This has forced her to curtail many of her favorite activities, such as her daily walks with her dog, overnight visits to her daughter's home, and her afternoon tea breaks. She feels frustrated and embarrassed to talk with her physician or daughter about this problem.

social outings, even a trip to the grocery store, out of fear that they may not have access to a bathroom. Family members may be puzzled as to why their previously active relative is now isolating herself. Possible treatments for urinary incontinence, as well as ways that older people can alter their daily habits to accommodate bladder problems, are discussed more fully in Chapter 4.

CHANGES IN THE GASTROINTESTINAL SYSTEM   The gastrointestinal system includes the esophagus, stomach, intestines, colon, liver, and biliary tract. Although the esophagus does not show age-related changes in appearance, some functions show alterations. These may include a decrease in contraction of the muscles and more time for the cardiac sphincter (a valvelike structure that allows food to pass into the stomach) to open, thus taking more time for food to be transmitted to the stomach. The result of these changes may be a sensation of being full before having consumed a complete meal. This in turn may reduce the pleasure a person derives from eating, and result in inadequate nutrient intake. This sensation also explains why older people may appear to eat such small quantities at mealtimes.

Secretion of digestive juices in the stomach apparently diminishes after age 50, especially among men. As a result, older people are more likely to experience the condition of **atrophic gastritis,** or a chronic inflammation of the stomach lining. Gastric ulcers are more likely to occur in middle age than in old age, but older people are at greater risk for colon and stomach cancer. Because of this risk, older people who complain of gastrointestinal discomfort should be urged to seek medical attention for the problem, instead of relying on home remedies or over-the-counter medications for heartburn or digestive problems.

As with many other organs in the human body, the small and large intestines decrease in weight after age 40. There are also functional changes in the small intestine, where the number of enzymes is reduced, and simple sugars are absorbed more slowly, resulting in diminished efficiency with age. The smooth muscle content and muscle tone in the wall of the colon also decrease. Anatomical changes in the large intestine are associated with the increased incidence of chronic constipation in older persons.

Behavioral factors are probably more critical than organic causes of constipation, however, as discussed in Chapter 4. Spasms of the lower intestinal tract are an example of the interaction of physiological with behavioral factors. Although they may occur at any age, such spasms are more common among older persons. These spasms are a form of functional disorder—that is, a condition without any organic basis, often due to psychological factors. Many gastrointestinal conditions that afflict older people are unrelated to the anatomical changes described previously. Nevertheless, they are very real problems to an older person who experiences them. For these reasons, many physicians routinely do a complete checkup, including a colonoscopy, of the gastrointestinal system in their patients age 50 and older, every 2 to 3 years.

The liver also grows smaller with age, by about 20 percent, although this does not appear to have much influence on its functions. However, the ability to process medications that are dependent on liver function does deteriorate. Jaundice occurs more frequently in older people, and may be due to changes in the liver or the obstruction of bile in the gall bladder. In addition, high alcohol consumption may put excessive strain on the older person's liver, resulting in the disease condition of cirrhosis of the liver.

CHANGES IN THE ENDOCRINE SYSTEM   The endocrine system is made up of cells and tissues that produce a variety of hormones. One of the most obvious age-related changes in the endocrine system is **menopause,** resulting in a reduced production of two important hormones in women—**estrogen** and progesterone. Many other hormones besides estrogen and progesterone also decline with aging. These include testosterone, thyroid, growth hormones, and insulin. Changes in insulin levels with aging may affect the older person's ability to metabolize **glucose** in the diet efficiently, resulting in high blood sugar levels. It is unclear if the changes in hormone production are a cause or an effect of aging. Nevertheless, much of the research aimed at reversing or delaying aging has focused on replacing other hormones whose levels decline with aging. As noted earlier, some support for hormone replacement is found in animal studies; for example, by stimulating the hypothalamus in the brain (which produces growth hormones) of old female rats, researchers have stimulated the development of eggs and increased protein synthesis in these animals. Thyroid hormones administered to old rats have been found to increase the size of the thyroid and the efficiency of their immune systems (Hayflick, 1996).

CHANGES IN THE IMMUNE SYSTEM   There are many complex changes in the immune system with aging. The concept of *immunosenescence* implies that aging results in a significant decline in the immune system, increasing the older person's susceptibility to infectious disease and risk of death. However, recent research findings contradict the prevailing wisdom that the aging process always results in deterioration or immunodeficiency (i.e., an inadequate response to infectious organisms). Studies of centenarians show highly effective immune responses when compared to some young-old persons (Cossarizza et al., 1997; Effros, 2001; Franceschi et al., 1995; Solana, 2003). Nevertheless, the fact that most deaths in people age 80 and older are caused by infections implicates failure of the immune system in these cases. This may be because of lower production of T-cells, B-cells, and lymphocytes with aging. Declines in these critical cells for creating antibodies to infectious organisms are aggravated by a reduction in CD3, CD4, CD8, and CD28 molecules that are critical as a secondary activator signal for T-cells.

The variation across organ systems in cellular composition is noteworthy. Although healthy adults show declines in the production of these cells in blood, T-cells in the tonsil and spleen actually *increase* with age. Based on studies of old and young mice, aging appears to cause a qualitative change in immune responses. The quantity of antibody production may be high but it is activated more slowly and less efficiently in older animals. Age-related changes in some physiological processes, such as a decline in lipid metabolism and pulmonary function, reduced acid secretion in the gut, and reductions in sex hormones may all influence immune function. Altered immune function has been linked to some diseases of aging, including prostate and skin cancers as well as cardiovascular disease.

CHANGES IN THE NERVOUS SYSTEM   The brain is composed of billions of **neurons,** or nerve cells, and billions of glial cells that support these. We lose some of both types of cells as we grow older. Neuronal loss begins at age 30, well before the period termed *old.* It is compounded by alcohol consumption, cigarette smoking, and breathing polluted air. The frontal cortex experiences a greater loss of cells than other parts of the brain. A moderate degree of neuronal loss does not create a major decline in brain function, however. In fact, contrary to popular belief and common jokes about neuronal loss, we can function with fewer neurons than we have, so their loss is not the reason for mild forgetfulness in old age. Even in the case of Alzheimer's disease and other **dementias,** severe loss of neurons may be less significant than changes in brain tissue, blood flow, and receptor organs (Thomas et al., 1996).

Other aging-related changes in the brain include a reduction in its weight by 10 percent, an accumulation of lipofuscin (i.e., an age pigment composed of fat and protein), and slower transmission of information from one neuron to another. The reduction in brain mass occurs in all species, and is probably due to loss of fluids. The gradual buildup of lipofuscin, which has a yellowish color, causes the outer cortex of the brain to take on a yellow-beige color with age. As with the moderate loss of neurons, these changes do not appear to alter brain function in old age. That is, difficulties in solving problems or remembering dates and names cannot be attributed to these slight alterations in the size and appearance of the brain. Indeed, research comparing age-related changes in brain structures of healthy men and women shows that men experience greater loss of cerebrospinal fluid volume, but this does not translate to any greater or less change in memory or learning among men with normal aging (Coffey et al., 1998).

Age-related changes in neurotransmitters and in the structure of the synapse (the junction between any two neurons) are shown to impair cognitive and motor function. Electroencephalograms, or readings of the electrical activity of the brain, show a slower response in older brains than in the young. These changes may be at least partially responsible for the increase in reaction time with age. The Baltimore Longitudinal Studies of Aging found that reaction time slows by as much as 20 percent between age 20 and age 60 (Hayflick, 1996). Other hypotheses include neuronal loss and reduced blood flow; however, available data are inconclusive. Reaction time is a complex product of multiple factors, primarily the speed of conduction and motor function, both of which are slowed by the increased time needed to transmit messages at the synapses.

The reduced speed with which the nervous system can process information or send signals for action is a fairly widespread problem, even in middle age when people begin to notice lagging reflexes and reaction time. As a result, such tasks as responding to a telephone or doorbell, crossing the street, completing a paper and pencil test, or deciding among several alternatives generally take longer for older people than for the young. Most people adjust to these changes by creatively modifying their physical environment or personal habits, such as taking more time to do a task and avoiding rush situations; for example:

- leaving the house one hour before an appointment instead of the usual 15 minutes
- shopping for groceries when stores are not crowded
- shopping in smaller stores
- avoiding freeway driving

Such person–environment adaptations are perhaps most pronounced in the tasks associated with driving. The older driver tends to be more cautious, to slow down well in advance of a traffic signal, to stay in the slower lane, and to avoid freeways during rush hour. Many choose to drive larger cars that can survive collisions better than compact cars. Despite this increased caution, accident rates are high among older drivers, as discussed in the next chapter.

Changes in the central nervous system that accompany aging also affect the senses of hearing, taste, smell, and touch. Despite these alterations, intellectual and motor function do not appear to deteriorate significantly with age. The brain has tremendous reserve capacity that takes over as losses begin. It is only when neuronal loss, inadequate function of neurotransmitters, and other structural changes are severe that the older person experiences significant loss of function. The changes in the brain that appear to be associated with Alzheimer's disease are discussed in Chapter 6.

Changes in Sleep Patterns with Aging

One of the most common complaints of older people is that they can no longer sleep well, with up to 40 percent of older persons in community surveys complaining of sleep problems. These complaints have a basis in biological changes that occur with aging. Results of laboratory studies of sleep–wake patterns of adults have consistently revealed normal, age-related changes in electroencephalogram (EEG) patterns, sleep stages,

TIPS FOR IMPROVING SLEEP

Sleep disturbances can be alleviated by improving one's **sleep hygiene**. These include:

- increasing physical exercise
- increasing exposure to natural light during the day
- reducing the intake of caffeine and other medications
- avoiding napping during the day
- improving the sleeping environment (e.g., a quieter bedroom with heavy curtains to block out the light, because exposure to light can change circadian rhythms) (Vitiello, 1996)

total sleep time, longer time to fall asleep (latency), and sleep efficiency (Ohayon et al., 2004; Vitiello, Larsen, and Moe 2004). Sleep progresses over five stages:

- non-REM sleep; i.e., no rapid eye movements during sleep (stages 1–4)
- REM (rapid eye movement) sleep (stage 5)

Sleep stages occur in a linear pattern from stage 1 through stage 4, then REM sleep in stage 5. Stage 4 is when deep sleep takes place. Each cycle is repeated four or five times through the night. Brain wave activity differs in a characteristic pattern for each stage.

Many of these brain waves slow down with aging, and the length of time in each stage changes. In particular, comparisons of studies across the lifespan reveal increased time in stages 1 and 2, when sleep is lighter. Time spent in REM sleep declines and occurs earlier in the cycle. During these stages, older people, more so than the young, are easily awakened, apparently by environmental stimuli that would not disturb a younger person (Ohayon et al., 2004).

Changes in circadian rhythms, or the individual's cycle of sleeping and waking within a 24 hour period, are characterized by a movement from a two-phase pattern of sleep (awake during the day, asleep during the night) to a multiphasic rhythm that is more common in infants—daytime napping and shorter sleep cycles at night. These changes may be associated with changes in core body temperatures in older people, as discussed earlier in this chapter.

When older persons compensate by taking more daytime naps, night sleep can be further disrupted. Most often, older people who report sleep disturbances to their primary physician are prescribed sleeping pills (sedative-hypnotic medications); this age group represents the highest users of such medications, receiving almost one-half of all sedative-hypnotic drugs prescribed. Yet medications do not necessarily improve their sleep patterns, especially if used long-term (Vitiello, 2000). Many hypnotics used to treat sleep disorders can instead produce a paradoxical effect by resulting in insomnia if used for a long time.

It is important to emphasize that a true sleep disturbance is one that interferes with daytime activities. Researchers who have examined older people with sleep complaints have found that chronic diseases, psychiatric disorders, and alcohol and prescription drug use are more likely to cause disturbed sleep in this population than aging per se. Research by Vitiello, Moe and Prinz (2002) found that only 3.2 percent of one community-dwelling sample of older people and 1.4 percent of another could be classified as experiencing a significant sleep disorder, after excluding all persons who had medical or psychiatric conditions that could affect sleep. An even larger study of almost 12,000 people (ages 15+) in Canada found that increased age was not significantly related to insomnia, but life stress, smoking, low education and income, multiple health problems, and activity limitations were all associated with insomnia at any age (Sutton, Moldofsky, and Badley, 2001). There are a few true *disorders of sleep* that can occur with aging; these include respiratory problems, **sleep apnea,** which is defined as a 5- to 10-second cessation of breathing, and **nocturnal myoclonus** or **periodic limb movement disorder (PLMD),** which is a neuromuscular disturbance affecting the legs during sleep. Generally these conditions are treated with medications, although behavior training to modify sleeping position, weight loss, and devices to improve breathing are found to be useful for sleep apnea.

Sleep disturbance in older persons with dementia is not uncommon, and can disrupt both the patient's and caregiver's quality of life. This often leads to premature nursing home placement of elders with dementia. For these reasons, many families seek medical help for the patient's insomnia, resulting in the use of sedative-hypnotic medications that may further aggravate the elder's sleep disturbance. It is important to try non-pharmacological therapies along with behavioral and environmental interventions (e.g., preventing daytime napping, keeping the elder patient physically active during the day) to treat sleep problems in dementia patients. Medications should not be the treatment of first choice for this population (McCurry et al., 2000; Vitiello and Borson, 2001).

In general, sleep disorders in older persons should be treated because in some cases they can increase the risk of mortality. A large study of community-dwelling older adults found that daytime sleepiness was associated with increased death rates in men and women (1.40 times the rate for men with normal sleep, 2.12 times the rate for women with normal sleep). Frequent awakenings or early morning awakenings had no discernible effect on mortality (Newman et al., 2000). Poor sleep quality increases the risk of falls among older adults in residential care facilities. In one study, elders who reported sleep disturbance were 3.2 times more likely to have fallen in the past year, while those who awoke 2 times or more per night were 50 percent more likely to have fallen (Hill et al., 2007).

Changes in Sensory Functions

Our ability to see, hear, touch, taste, and smell has a profound influence on our interactions with our social and physical environments. Given the importance of our sensory functions for social interactions, and the gradual decline in our sensory abilities with aging, it is critical that we understand these changes and how they can influence our competence level as we age. A popular belief is that, as we get older, we cannot see, hear, touch, taste, or smell as well as we did when we were younger. This appears to be true. The decline in all our sensory receptors with aging is normal; in fact, it begins relatively early. We reach our optimum capacities in our 20s, maintain this peak for a few years, and gradually experience a decline, with a more rapid rate of deterioration after the ages of 45 to 55. Having said this, we should note that there is tremendous diversity among individuals in the rate and severity of sensory decline, as illustrated earlier by Mrs. Hill and Mr. Jones. Some older persons may have better visual acuity than most 25-year-olds; many 75-year-olds can hear better than most younger persons. And many elders have a more intense sense of smell than their younger counterparts. Although age per se does not determine deterioration in sensory functioning, it is clear that many internal changes do occur. The older person who has better visual or hearing acuity than a 25-year-old probably had even better sensory capacities in the earlier years. It is important to focus on *intraindividual* changes with age, not *interindividual* differences, when studying sensory and perceptual functions. Unfortunately, most of the research on sensory changes with age is cross-sectional—that is, based on comparing different persons who are older and younger.

POINTS TO PONDER

Think about the wine taster who, in old age, may still be considered the master of his trade, performing a job that requires excellent taste discrimination. Perfume developers also attain their expertise over many years. What other jobs require intrinsic sensory abilities as well as skills that take years to master?

DISTINCTIONS IN TERMINOLOGY RELATED TO SENSORY FUNCTIONS

- *Sensation* is the process of taking in information through the sense organs.
- *Perception* is a higher function in which the information received through the senses is processed in the brain.
- *Sensory threshold* is the minimum intensity of a stimulus that a person requires in order to detect the stimulus. This differs for each sensory system.
- *Recognition threshold* is the intensity of a stimulus needed in order for an individual to identify or recognize it. As might be expected, a greater intensity of a stimulus is necessary to recognize than to detect it.
- *Sensory discrimination* is defined as the minimum difference necessary between two or more stimuli in order for a person to distinguish between them.

For this reason, the reader needs to be aware that there are tremendous individual differences in how much and how severely sensory functions deteriorate with age.

Changes in different senses also vary within the same individual. Thus, the person who experiences an early and severe decline in hearing acuity may not have any deterioration in visual functioning. Some sensory functions, such as hearing, may show an early decline, yet others, such as taste and touch, change little until well into advanced old age. Over time, however, sensory decrements affect an older person's social functions.

Because these alterations are usually gradual, people adapt and compensate by using other, still-intact sensory systems. For example, they may use the following person–environment compensation strategies to maintain their level of competence by:

- standing closer to objects and persons in order to hear or see
- using nonverbal cues such as touch and different body orientations

- utilizing external devices such as bifocals or hearing aids
- reducing the level of excessive stimulation in their environment, such as moving to a quieter table in a restaurant

To the extent that people can alter their environment to conform to their changing needs, sensory decline need not be incapacitating. It becomes much more difficult for individuals to use compensatory mechanisms if the environment does not allow for modification to suit individual needs, if the decline in any one system is severe, or if several sensory systems deteriorate at the same time. Such problems are more likely to occur in advanced old age. This is because, with normal aging, sensory and recognition thresholds increase, and the individual needs a higher level of the stimulus and greater distinctions between multiple stimuli in order to distinguish between them.

Changes in Vision

Vision problems increase with age; when 55- to 64-year-olds are compared with those over age 85, the prevalence of visual impairments increases fourfold from 55 per 1000 people to 225 per 1000. As a result, older adults are more likely to experience problems with daily tasks that require good visual skills, such as reading small print or signs on moving vehicles, threading a needle, or adapting to sudden changes in light level when entering a dark room after being out in the sun. In addition, visual impairments can cause significant problems with activities of daily living, increase the risk of falls and fractures, and result in depression. In addition to eye charts, a widely used assessment tool is the Functional Vision Screening Questionnaire (Aldwin and Gilmer, 2004; Desai et al., 2001; Stuen, 2006).

EFFECTS OF STRUCTURAL CHANGES IN THE EYE   Most age-related problems in vision are attributable to changes in parts of the eye

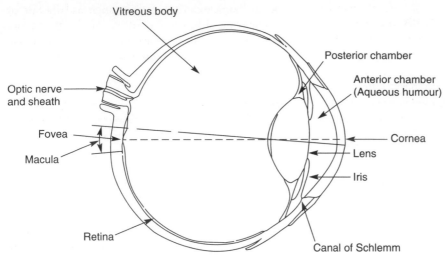

FIGURE 3.4   The Eye

(see Figure 3.4). However, these problems are aggravated by alterations in the central nervous system that block the transmission of stimuli from the sensory organs. Changes in the visual pathways of the brain and in the visual cortex may be a possible source of some of the alterations that take place in visual sensation and perception with age. The parts of the eye that show the greatest age-related modifications are:

- the cornea
- the pupil
- rods and cones in the retina
- the lens

The cornea is usually the first part of the eye to be affected by age-related changes. The surface of the cornea thickens with aging, and the blood vessels become more prominent. The smooth, rounded surface of the cornea becomes flatter and less smooth, and may take on an irregular shape. The older person's eye appears to lose its luster and is less translucent than it was in youth. In some cases, a fatty yellow ring, known as the *arcus senilis,* may form around the cornea. This is not a sign of

impending vision loss, however; in fact, it has no impact on vision.

At its optimal functioning, the pupil is sensitive to light levels in the environment, widening

> **PROBLEMS WITH RESTAURANT ENVIRONMENTS**
>
> Many older people may feel frustrated when they go to a special restaurant for an evening dinner, only to find that the tables are lit by candles. This makes it difficult to read the menu, to see the way to the table, and even to have eye contact with companions. Family and friends may be frustrated in such situations if they do not understand that the older person's complaints about the restaurant stem from these changes in vision, not from a lack of appreciation for their efforts. Some older people cope with these problems by avoiding such restaurants altogether or going there only during daylight hours.
>
> It is important for restaurant owners to provide good lighting at each table and write their menus in large, legible print against a white background. In response to the growing number of baby boomers who are experiencing problems of visual accommodation, some restaurants have begun to stock reading glasses with different levels of magnification to lend to their customers!

in response to low light levels and contracting when light levels are high. With aging, the pupil appears to become smaller and more fixed in size. The maximum opening of the pupil is reduced in old age, commonly to about two-thirds its original maximum. That is, the older person's pupil is less able to respond to low light levels by dilating or opening to the extent needed. The eye also responds more slowly to changes in light conditions. This problem is compounded by a slower shift from cones to rods under low-light conditions. As a result, the older person may have considerable difficulty functioning in low-light situations, or in adjusting to significant changes in ambient light. In fact, older people may need three times more light than younger persons to function effectively; for example, highway signs must be 65 to 75 percent closer than for younger drivers to be readable at night. Illumination levels also affect older people's ability to read text written in small font (such as a menu with less than 12 point font, in a dimly lit restaurant), and with low contrast between text and background. When 80-year-olds were compared with 30-year-olds, low levels of illumination (10-lux*) caused the former to make twice as many errors as the latter, even with high contrast between figure and ground. However, at the highest illumination levels (1000-lux), older adults benefited from high contrast and performed as well as young adults. Unfortunately, most homes and offices do not provide such high lighting levels (Fozard and Gordon-Salant, 2001).

These changes may also reduce the older person's ability to discern images in conditions of poor light contrast (e.g., driving at twilight or under foggy or rainy conditions), and to detect details in moving objects. Even among healthy older persons who are still driving, age-related visual changes may significantly alter their abilities

*Lux is a unit of measurement for illumination, referring to the amount of light received by a surface at a distance of one meter from a light source.

under marginal conditions. For example, a survey of participants aged 22 to 92 in the Baltimore Longitudinal Studies revealed that age was highly correlated with reports of problems with:

- sudden merging of other vehicles
- judging their own and other vehicles' speed
- driving under glare and hazy conditions
- reading street signs while driving (Kline et al., 1992)

For these reasons, older people may choose to avoid such activities, especially driving among fast-moving traffic on freeways at night when bright headlights create glare against asphalt surfaces, and in rain. Although this is a safe method of coping with age-related difficulties in low-light situations, it can restrict the older person's social activities. In such instances, families and professionals may have to encourage older people to use other forms of transportation, such as buses and taxis, thereby avoiding the problem of too little environmental stimulation relative to the person's competence. More often, however, older people want to keep driving as long as possible, even when they experience such difficulties, because driving is linked with autonomy and control in their daily lives (Horowitz and Higgins, 2000).

PROBLEMS RELATED TO OXYGEN AND FLUID LEVELS Problems in rod and cone function may be related to a reduced supply of oxygen to the retina. This may be due to a deficiency of vitamin A. However, there is little research evidence to suggest that increased intake of vitamin A in old age can improve visual functioning under low-light conditions.

As stated earlier, two fluid-filled chambers are in the eye: *aqueous humour* fills the anterior or front portion of the eye, and *vitreous humour* is found in the posterior chamber, behind the lens. The *aqueous humour* drains through the canal of Schlemm. In the disease state known as **glaucoma,** drainage is less efficient, or excess production of the aqueous humour occurs and causes pressure on the optic nerve. Glaucoma, which is not a normal part of aging, increases in frequency with age, and can be managed with regular medications if it is caught early. Unfortunately, it is an insidious disease that progresses slowly and may not be detected until it is more advanced. More severe cases may require surgery or, more recently, laser treatment. In its later stages, glaucoma may result in tunnel vision, which is a gradual narrowing of an individual's field of vision, such that peripheral vision is lost and the individual can focus only in the center, affecting elders' safe mobility. Untreated glaucoma is the second leading cause of blindness in the United States (Braille Institute, 2004), and the primary cause of blindness among African Americans. It is more prevalent and more difficult to treat in African Americans, with rates of 15 percent versus 7 percent in whites age 70 and older (Desai et al., 2001; Stuen, 2006).

EFFECTS OF AGING ON THE LENS   Perhaps the greatest age-related changes in the eye occur in the lens. In fact, the lens is a model system for studying aging because it contains some of the oldest cells in the body, formed during the earliest stages of the embryo's development. Furthermore, the lens is a relatively simple structure biochemically; all of its cells are of the same type and are composed of protein.

Collagen is the primary protein in the lens, and makes up 70 to 80 percent of the total tissue composition of the entire body. As it ages, collagen thickens and hardens. This change in collagen makes the lens less elastic, thereby reducing its ability to alter its shape (i.e., from rounded to elongated and flat) as it focuses from near to far. Muscles that help stretch the lens also deteriorate with age, thereby compounding the problem of changing the shape of the lens. This process, known as **accommodation,** begins to deteriorate in middle age and is manifested in increasing problems with close vision. By the

> **SUGGESTIONS FOR IMPROVING PERSON-ENVIRONMENT FIT FOR PEOPLE EXPERIENCING CHANGES IN THEIR VISION**
>
> - Use widely contrasting colors on opposite ends of the color spectrum, such as red and yellow, green and orange.
> - Define edges and corners such as stairs, walls, and doors clearly with color or texture.
> - Avoid using blue and green together to define adjoining spaces, such as stairs and stair landings, floors and ramps, and curbs and curbcuts, especially where the junction represents different levels.
> - Avoid shiny floor and wall surfaces that can cause glare.
> - Avoid placing a single, large window at the end of a long, dark corridor.

time many people reach their 40s and 50s, they need to hold their reading material at arm's length. As a result, many turn to reading glasses or bifocals.

By age 60, accommodative ability is significantly deteriorated. Decrements in accommodation may cause difficulties for the older person when shifting from near to far vision; for example, when looking across a room, walking up or down stairs, reading and glancing up, and writing notes while looking up at a blackboard or a lecturer. The hardening of the lens due to changes in collagen tissue does not occur uniformly. Rather, there is differential hardening, with some surfaces allowing more light to enter than others. This results in uneven refraction of light through the lens and onto the retina. When combined with the poor refraction of light through the uneven, flattened surface of the cornea, extreme sensitivity to glare often results. This problem becomes particularly acute in environments with a single source of light aimed at a shiny surface, such as a large window at the end of a long, dark corridor with highly polished floors, occasional streetlights on a rain-slicked highway, or a bright, single, overhead incandescent light shining on a linoleum floor. These conditions may contribute to older people's greater caution and anxiety while driving or walking.

From childhood through early adulthood, the lens is a transparent system through which light can easily enter. With normal aging, the lens becomes more opaque, and less light passes through it (especially shorter wavelengths of light); these changes compound the problems of poor vision in low light that were described earlier. Some older persons experience a more severe opacification (clouding of the lens) to the point that the lens prevents light from entering. This disease condition, known as a **cataract,** is the fourth leading cause of blindness in the United States and the primary cause of blindness worldwide (Braille Institute, 2004). Symptoms of cataracts include:

- cloudy or fuzzy vision
- double vision
- problems with glare from bright light
- problems with color discrimination

Researchers in the Framingham eye study examined the incidence of cataracts, that is, the development of the condition in the same individual over a number of years. In a reexamination of survivors almost 14 years later, the incidence rate was 50 percent for people who were age 55 to 59 at the beginning of the study. It jumped to 80 percent for older adults who had been age 70 to 74 at the start (Milton and Sperduto, 1991). In other words, the prevalence of cataracts increases tenfold between ages 52 and 85. There is strong evidence for a relationship between the development of cataracts with age and the lack of antioxidants such as vitamins A, C, and E (Jacques, Chylack, and Taylor, 1994; Seddon et al., 1994b; Stuen, 2006).

A cataract may occur in any part of the lens—in the center, the peripheral regions, or scattered throughout. If the lens becomes totally opaque, cataract surgery may be required to extract the lens. It carries relatively little risk, even for very old persons, and can significantly enhance quality of life. Indeed, this is the most common surgical procedure performed on people over age 65, with about 1.5 million extractions performed per year, usually as an outpatient procedure. A lens implant in place of the extracted lens capsule is the most common treatment. Almost half of these 85 years and older in a U.S. survey reported that they had undergone cataract surgery, compared with about 20 percent at age 70 to 74. Older women were more likely to report having had cataract surgery than their male counterparts (Desai et al., 2001). When the older person first obtains a replacement lens, it takes some time to adjust to performing daily activities. Patients who receive a lens implant show improvement not just in visual function, but also in objective assessments of activities of daily living and manual function within a few months.

In addition to getting harder and more opaque, the lens becomes more yellow with age, especially after age 60. The increasingly more opaque and yellowing lens acts as a filter to screen out wavelengths of light, thus reducing the individual's color sensitivity and ability to discriminate among colors that are close together in the blue-green range. Older people may have problems selecting clothing in this color range, sometimes resulting in poorly coordinated outfits. Deterioration in color discrimination may also be due to age-related changes in the visual and neural pathways.

OTHER CHANGES IN VISION *Depth and distance perception* also deteriorate with aging, because of a loss of convergence of images formed in the two eyes. This is caused by differential rates of hardening and opacification in the two lenses, uneven refraction of light onto the retina, and reduced visual acuity in aging eyes. As a result, there is a rapid decline after age 75 in the ability to judge distances and depths, particularly in low-light situations and in the absence of orienting cues, such as stairs with no color distinctions

DIAGNOSING MACULAR DEGENERATION

Mr. Lopez noticed over the past 5 years that objects appear blurry when he looks directly at them, but sharper as he glances more peripherally. He finally went for an eye exam after experiencing more problems with driving. The ophthalmologist diagnosed macular degeneration and was able to treat it with Visudyne. Mr. Lopez can now drive safely again and continue to play bridge and participate in other activities.

at the edges and pedestrian ramps or curb cuts with varying slopes. Another age-related change is narrower peripheral vision (the ability to see on either side without moving the eyes or the head). Since our peripheral vision makes us aware of approaching objects, older adults can be startled when a car or other fast-moving object seems to appear suddenly out of nowhere. This problem becomes particularly acute when driving; for example, an older person may not see cars approaching from the left or right at an intersection or passing.

Some older persons experiencing **age-related macular degeneration (AMD)** lose acuity in the center of their visual field. The macula is that point in the retina with the best visual acuity, especially for seeing fine detail. Macular degeneration is the leading cause of blindness in adults. (Braille Institute, 2004). It occurs if the macula receives less oxygen than it needs, resulting in destruction of the existing nerve endings. The incidence of macular degeneration increases with age, even more dramatically than cataracts. About 6 million Americans, mostly over age 65, have this condition. Rates of AMD increase significantly with age, from 18 percent among those age 70 to 74 to 47 percent among people 85 and older (Desai et al., 2001). The condition is more common in older women and in white elders than in men and African Americans. There is evidence for both a genetic basis and environmental risk factors, such as a lack of antioxidants for age-related macular degeneration. Researchers are searching for the specific genes responsible for AMD, with the goal of developing early detection and prevention programs. By studying a large family with a history of AMD, geneticists have identified *HEMICENTIN-1* as the gene where a mutation occurs in people with AMD. Future research will lead to animal models where the mutation can be created and treated, with the eventual goal of modifying the gene in humans before it manifests as AMD (Schultz et al., 2003). Studies that have supplemented older people's diets with carotenoid-rich foods or used zinc supplements have found positive effects on visual activity of AMD patients, but there is no cure for AMD at this time (Allikmets et al., 1997; Blumberg, 1996; Stuen, 2006).

The early stages of macular degeneration may begin with a loss of detail vision; then central vision gradually becomes worse. Total blindness rarely occurs, but reading and driving may become impossible. Older persons with this condition may compensate by using their remaining peripheral vision. They may then appear to be looking at the shoulder of someone they are addressing, but actually be relying on peripheral vision to see the person's face. Laser treatment in the early stages of this disease is effective, but it carries a risk of burning away the center of the retina entirely. A new form of therapy combines a light-activated drug treatment (Visudyne) with a low-power laser light to activate the drug. This procedure is effective in destroying the abnormal blood vessels and scar tissue in the eye without damaging the retina. Although macular degeneration cannot be cured, this new treatment can slow retinal damage and improve central vision.

Some older people, most often postmenopausal women, experience reduced secretion of tears. They may complain of "dry eyes" that cause irritation and discomfort. Unfortunately, this condition has no known cure, but it does not cause blindness and can be managed with artificial tears to prevent redness and irritation. Artificial tears can be purchased at most drugstores.

The muscles that support the eyes, similar to those in other parts of the body, deteriorate with age. In particular, two key muscles atrophy. These are the elevator muscles, which move the eyeball up and down within its socket, and the ciliary muscle, which aids the lens in changing its shape. Deterioration of the elevator muscles results in a reduced range of upward gaze. This may cause problems with reading overhead signs and seeing objects that are placed above eye level, such as on high kitchen shelves.

Assisting Adaptation and Active Aging through Environmental Modifications

As suggested above, many older adults report modest impairments in their activities of daily living, including reading small print, adjusting to dimly lit environments, tracking moving targets, and locating a sign in a cluttered background. Family and friends can help by improving the physical environment, such as replacing existing light bulbs with higher wattage, fluorescent lighting with color correction and three-way bulbs, moving low tables and footstools outside the traffic flow, and putting large-print labels on prescription bottles, spices, and cooking supplies. Older people can also take advantage of:

- large-print newspapers and books
- audiotapes of books that are available in community libraries and bookstores
- playing cards with large letters
- larger fonts on flat-screen computer monitors that are designed to reduce glare

Local agencies serving the visually impaired often provide low-vision aids at minimal cost. These include:

- needle threaders for sewing
- templates for rotary telephones, irons, and other appliances
- large-print phone books, clocks, and calendars

- magnifying glasses for situations where large-print substitutes are unavailable

Other environmental modifications may be more costly or require the use of a professional architect. Families and designers can help make the home and work environment safer for elders with visual impairments by:

- placing contrasting color strips on stairs, especially on carpeted or slippery linoleum stairs, to aid the older person's depth perception
- coloring and light coding ramps and other changes in elevation
- clearly marking changes in floor surfaces such as door sills
- increasing the number of light sources
- installing non-slip and non-glossy floor coverings
- using a flat paint instead of glossy finishes to reduce the problem of glare on walls
- installing venetian and vertical blinds to control glare throughout the day
- using indirect or task lighting (e.g., reading lamps, countertop lamps) rather than ceiling fixtures
- adding dimmer switches so that lighting levels can be adjusted

Age-related vision changes need not disadvantage people if they can be encouraged to adapt their activities and environment to fit their level of visual functioning with their needs. An older adult who is having difficulty adjusting to vision-related losses may initially resist such modifications. One way to address this resistance is to involve the older person in decisions about such changes to provide a sense of control and choice, despite vision loss.

Changes in Hearing

In terms of survival, vision and hearing are perhaps our most critical links to the world. Although vision is important for negotiating the

POINTS TO PONDER

Consider some ways in which we rely on our hearing ability in everyday life: in conversations with family, friends and coworkers; in localizing the sound of approaching vehicles as we cross the street or drive; and in interpreting other people's emotions through their tone of voice and use of language. How does a person function if these abilities gradually deteriorate?

physical environment, hearing is vital for communication. Because hearing is closely associated with speech, its loss disrupts a person's understanding of others and even the recognition of one's own speech. An older person who is experiencing hearing loss learns to make changes in behavior and social interactions, so as to reduce the detrimental social impact of hearing loss. Many younger hearing-impaired persons learn sign language or lip reading. But these are complex skills requiring extensive training and practice, and are less likely to be mastered by older adults.

THE ANATOMY AND PHYSIOLOGY OF THE EAR   It is useful to review the anatomy of the ear in order to understand where and how auditory function

deteriorates with age. The auditory system has three components, as illustrated in Figure 3.5. The outer ear begins at the pinna, the visible portion that is identified as the ear. The auditory canal is also part of the outer ear. Note the shape of the pinna and auditory canal; it is a most efficient design for localizing sounds.

The eardrum, or tympanic membrane, is a thin membrane that separates the outer ear from the middle ear. This membrane is sensitive to air pressure of varying degrees and vibrates in response to a range of loud and soft sounds. Three bones, or *ossicles,* that transfer sound waves to the inner ear are located in the middle ear (the *malleus, incus,* and *stapes*).

These very finely positioned and interrelated bones carry sound vibrations from the middle ear to the inner ear—that snail-shaped circular structure called the cochlea. Amplified sounds are converted in the cochlea to nerve impulses. These are then sent through the internal auditory canal and the cochlear nerve to the brain, where they are translated into meaningful sounds. The cochlea is a fluid-filled chamber with thousands of hair cells that vibrate two parallel membranes to move sound waves. The vibration of these hair cells is one of several factors involved in perceiving the pitch (or frequency) and loudness (intensity) of a sound.

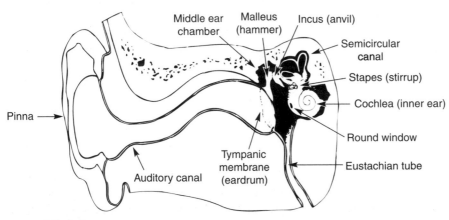

FIGURE 3.5   **The Ear**

AGE-RELATED CHANGES   The pinna appears somewhat elongated and rigid in some older adults. These changes in the outer ear, however, have no impact on hearing acuity. The supporting walls of the external auditory canals also deteriorate with age, as is true for many muscular structures. Arthritic conditions may affect the joints between the malleus and stapes, making it more difficult for these bones to perform their vibratory function. This is compounded by stiffening of the tympanic membrane, which also becomes thinner and less vascular with age. **Otosclerosis** is a condition in which the stapes becomes fixed and cannot vibrate. It is most likely to affect older persons.

The greatest decline with age occurs in the cochlea, where structural changes result in **presbycusis,** or sensorineural loss that accompanies aging. Changes in auditory thresholds can be detected by age 30 or even younger, but the degeneration of hair cells and membranes in the cochlea is not observed until much later. Age-related declines in the middle ear include:

- atrophy of hair cells
- vascular changes
- changes in the cochlear duct
- loss of auditory neurons
- deterioration of neural pathways between the ear and brain (Rees, 2000)

These alterations affect the older person's ability to detect and localize sounds, especially at lower volume and very high pitch or frequency. Tests of pure-tone thresholds (i.e., the level at which a tone of a single frequency can be detected) reveal a steady decline after age 60, over 15 years. Changes in the high-frequency range are about 1 dB per year. In the range of speech, changes are slow until age 60, then accelerate to a rate of 1.3 dB per year after age 80 (Brant and Fozard, 1990). About 26 percent of the population age 65 to 74 is estimated to have some loss of hearing, increasing to 35 percent of those over 75, and 50 percent among those age 85

and older. Rates are higher among white men (61 percent) than any other group at age 85 and older. Thirteen percent suffer from advanced presbycusis. Again, age differences are dramatic; 17 percent of people 85 and older were deaf in one epidemiological study compared with 5 percent of those age 70 to 74 (Desai et al., 2001; Stuen, 2006; Weinstein, 2000). The Screening Version of the Hearing Handicap Inventory for the Elderly (HHIE-S) is a widely used tool to assess the extent of hearing loss.

As with studies regarding visual changes, researchers suggest that age-related alterations in the brain are primarily responsible for the deterioration in auditory functioning. These may include cellular deterioration and vascular changes in the major auditory pathways to the brain. However, aging and disease-related pathological changes can damage the auditory system itself. Together with exposure to environmental noise over a lifetime, these factors can cause presbycusis.

Tinnitus, a high-pitched "ringing," is another problem that affects hearing in old age, although it can also occur earlier in life. It may occur bilaterally or in one ear only. The incidence increases threefold between youth and middle age, and fourfold between youth and old age, and may be aggravated by other types of hearing loss. Tinnitus may be related to occupational noise exposure; for example, men with tinnitus have been found to have 20 to 30 years of exposure to noisy work environments. It cannot be cured, but people suffering from tinnitus can generally learn to manage it or try alternative approaches such as acupuncture (Micozzi, 1997).

In contrast to visual changes, hearing loss appears to be significantly affected by environmental causes. People who have been exposed to high-volume and high-frequency noise throughout their lives (e.g., urban dwellers, construction workers who use jack hammers and factory workers) experience more hearing decrements in middle and old age than do those from rural, low-noise environments. Over the last three decades, hearing loss among people age 18 to 44 has increased significantly. This means that future cohorts will include more elders with hearing loss that was environ- mentally induced earlier in their lives, perhaps from listening to loud iPod music in adolescence and young adulthood! As shown in Figure 3.6, women generally show less decline than men; about 61 percent of people with

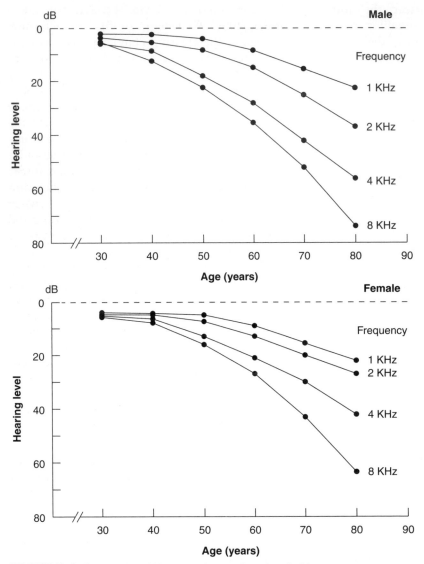

FIGURE 3.6   **Gender Differences in Hearing Thresholds**

SOURCE: Ordy, J.M., Brizzee, K.R., Beavers, T., and Medart, P. Age differences in the functional and structural organization of the auditory system in man. In J.M. Ordy and K.R. Brizzee (Eds.), *Sensory systems and communication in the elderly* (New York: Raven Press, 1979), p. 156. Reprinted with permission of the author and publisher.

hearing loss are men. Gender differences in hearing loss occur across the life course:

- 3 percent of men versus 2 percent of women at ages 18 to 44
- 8 percent versus 3 percent at ages 45 to 64
- 19 percent versus 10 percent among those 65 and older (National Academy, 1999)

It is interesting to speculate why these gender differences appear. Are they due to variations in noise exposure or to hormonal differences? The fact that severe hearing loss is found only in some women suggests that the former hypothesis may be more likely. If so, such gender differences may be less pronounced in future cohorts, where women have had access to occupations traditionally held by men and both men and women have been exposed to occupational and recreational noise.

COMPENSATION AND ADAPTATION Hearing loss can be of several types, involving limited volume and range or distortion of sounds perceived. Regardless of type, hearing loss results in some incongruence between the person and his or her environment. Older persons who have lost hearing acuity in the range of speech (250–3000 Hz) have particular difficulties distinguishing the sibilants or high-frequency consonants such as *z, s,*

sh, f, p, k, t, and g. Their speech comprehension deteriorates as a result, which may be the first sign of hearing loss. In contrast, low-frequency hearing loss has minimal impact on speech comprehension. As Figure 3.6 illustrates, higher-frequency sounds can be heard better by raising the intensity. The recognition of consonants (*p, t, k, b, d, g*) can be increased by 50 to 90 percent among older persons simply by raising their volume.

Thus, an individual may compensate by raising the volume of the TV and radio, moving closer to the TV, or listening to other types of music made by lower-pitched instruments such as an organ. When this occurs, it is imperative to determine whether a hearing loss exists, to identify the cause, and to fit the individual with an appropriate hearing aid, if possible. The older design of hearing aids, using analog technology, merely increases the volume of sound. A major difficulty with some of the less expensive types of hearing aids is that the volume of background noise is raised, in addition to the sound that the user of the device is trying to hear. This may compensate for loss of higher-frequency sounds, but cannot completely obliterate the problem of presbycusis. In fact, hearing aids may result in such major adaptation problems that older persons stop wearing them after several months.

Fortunately, developments in hearing aid technology are resulting in digital hearing aids with tiny computer chips that filter sounds to match each user's hearing loss profile, without amplifying background noises. These newer designs also are less obtrusive and fit well inside the ear. However, they can cost about twice as much as conventional hearing aids and are not covered by Medicare or by most private health insurance plans. The cost, stigma, and adjustment problems with hearing aids may explain why only 11.6 percent of older adults with reported hearing loss use a hearing aid (Crews and Campbell, 2004).

Other means of compensating for hearing loss are to design environments that dampen background noises or to select such settings for communicating with older persons. Sound levels

---

RELUCTANCE TO USE HEARING AIDS

The social stigma associated with wearing a hearing aid is greater than with wearing glasses. These are undoubtedly some of the reasons why only about one-third of older people with hearing loss use them. Nevertheless, after President Clinton was fitted with a new digital hearing aid in 1997, while he was still in office, there was a dramatic increase in the number of hearing aids sold. Sales jumped by 25 percent between 1996 and 1997; many of these were baby boomers like President Clinton who purchased a hearing aid for the first time (National Academy, 1999).

should not exceed 80 decibels. Soundproof rooms, while costly, are beneficial, particularly if housing for older people is built on busy streets or near freeways. Offices of health professionals should have at least one quiet area without the distraction of background noises. Older people can also benefit from new designs in telephones with volume adjusters and lights that blink when the phone rings.

When conversing with people who are experiencing age-related hearing loss, the following hints can help both younger and older persons enjoy their communication:

- Face an older person directly and maintain eye contact.
- Sit somewhat close (3 feet away) and at eye level with the older person.
- Do not cover your face with hands or objects when speaking.
- Speak slowly and clearly, but without exaggerating speech.
- Do not shout.
- Avoid distracting background noises by selecting a quiet, relaxing place away from other people, machines, and traffic sounds.
- Speak in a lower, but not monotonic, tone of voice.
- Repeat key points in different ways and with different words.
- If specific information is to be transmitted (e.g., how to take medications), structure the message in a clear, systematic manner (Kiyak, 1996; NIA, 2005).

Helping older people with hearing impairment compensate for this loss is essential to avoid harmful effects on interpersonal relationships, social engagement, and self-esteem. For some older adults, increasing levels of hearing impairment can disrupt functional abilities, resulting in social withdrawal and even clinical depression (Dalton et al., 2003; Strawbridge et al., 2000). One of the most frustrating experiences is the simultaneous deterioration of both hearing and vision. Although it is relatively rare for both functions to decline significantly with age, family, friends, and professionals must be particularly versatile in using the appropriate communication techniques suggested earlier. For example, when talking with an older person who is impaired in both hearing and vision, touching a hand, arm, or shoulder may aid communication.

Changes in Taste and Smell

Although older people may complain that food does not taste as good as it once did, these complaints are probably not due to an age-associated

Cooking with spices can enhance olfactory and taste sensitivity.

generalized loss of taste sensitivity. It was once thought that age brought dramatic decreases in the number of taste buds on the tongue, that this loss of receptor elements led to functional loss that was experienced as a dulling of taste sensation, and that these changes accounted for older people's reduced enjoyment of food. Subsequent studies, however, have challenged each link in this chain of reasoning. Aging does appear to cause some loss of taste buds, but this does not affect taste thresholds. Furthermore, threshold loss almost never involves more than one of the four basic taste qualities (Cowart, 1989).

The notion that various functions decline differentially has replaced the belief that older people experience a generalized taste loss. The research task now is to specify *which* aspects of taste function remain intact and which decline with normal aging or disease. Although the taste function of older people does not undergo a general decline in strength, it demonstrates specific changes. For example, while the relationship between taste intensity and stimulus strength is age-stable, judgments of taste intensity become less reliable with age. Older adults have more difficulty than younger people in discriminating between varying intensities of a flavor (e.g., tested by increasing the level of bitterness in coffee, saltiness of food), but such discrimination occurs less often with a stimulus that differs in its sweetness. These differences have been observed across age groups, from teens to people in their 80s. It is also important to note that in studies where the average taste performance of the older individuals is poorer, some perform as well as, or better than, many younger persons.

Appreciation of food does not depend on taste alone. The sense of smell clearly is involved. We have all experienced changes in the way food "tastes" while ill with a head cold and a stuffy nose, or if we suffer from allergies. These changes suggest that sensitivity to airborne stimuli plays a key role in the smell and taste of foods. Older people perceive airborne

stimuli as less intense than younger persons, and do less well on odor identification. External factors such as smoking and medications contribute to these differences, but even after accounting for these factors, age differences are dominant (Stuen, 2006; Tuorila, Niskanen, and Maunuksela, 2001). When parallel assessments are made in the same subject, age-related declines for smell are greater than for taste. This suggests that one way to increase older people's enjoyment of eating is to provide them with enhanced food odors. Classes in cooking with herbs and spices can be valuable for older people who are experiencing changes in their taste and olfactory abilities. These activities can also help older people in sharpening their sensitivity to tastes and odors, improve the palatability and intake of food, increase salivary flow and immunity, and ultimately enhance their quality of life (Schiffman and Graham, 2000).

Losing the ability to smell and taste is not just a matter of reduced enjoyment, but can foster risks such as unhealthy eating habits, social isolation, and being unable to smell dangers like smoke from fire or leaking gas. We have all known elders who keep adding salt and sugar to their food to enhance the taste, often doing the exact opposite of what their doctor recommends. Finding healthier ways to enhance the aroma and flavor of foods is important for both elders' nutrition and social engagement. Adding even a tablespoon of gravy or olive oil to food can dramatically improve its enjoyment by making the aroma and flavor chemicals more available to the taste buds without increasing fat content significantly. This is because fat in food is essential to flavor. Color in food also affects the perceived intensity of flavor, which suggests the importance of not overcooking food and attending to the visual presentation of a meal. As with all the age-associated sensory changes, families and health care providers need to be creative in modifying the environment.

Implications for the Future

As we proceed into the twenty-first century, new discoveries in genetics, pharmacology, biomedical technology, and surgical techniques hold great possibilities for enhancing the quality of life and extending the human life span. Today scientists can already place embryonic stem cells in culture at an early stage, and watch them maintain telomerase activity and indefinite replication. In the future they will be able to transplant stem cells to human organs in a successful attempt to reverse the decline or disease processes in these organs (Carpenter et al., 1999; Hornsby, 1999).

Someday people will know their predisposition to a wider array of genetically linked conditions beyond a few that are currently predictable with genetic testing, such as Huntington's disease. The long-term impact of caloric restriction and the use of enzyme boosters and antioxidants throughout adulthood on pathogenic conditions in old age as well as folic acid on atherosclerosis and heart disease will become clearer. We will also learn the long-term effects of pharmacological and exercise interventions to prevent insulin resistance and coronary artery disease, osteopenia, and functional decline. Drug dosing will become more individualized, so physicians can assess each elder's ability to metabolize and excrete drugs before prescribing a particular medication at specific doses. In many ways, biological aging in the twenty-first century will move away from the treatment of disease and genetic disorders to their prevention. Trends in microbiological research suggest that an important focus will be on ways to extend the average length of life while at the same time maintaining active lifestyles. Developments in robotics will assist older people to live independently with robots that serve as "personal aids" if their mobility, vision and hearing decline significantly.

Both scientific and technological advances in this field will result in the need for more skilled professionals to assist the aging population. These include scientists such as microbiologists and geneticists who focus on the basic mechanisms and genetics of aging, and researchers in computer sciences and engineering who can design external aids to reduce environmental press. There is also a growing need for therapists such as vision rehabilitation therapists who can orient and help keep visually impaired elders active. It will also be important to encourage professionals such as occupational and physical therapists, as well as audiologists, to specialize in aging. These clinicians can test the aging individual and prescribe activities to maintain function. It is important for health care providers to understand what is normal, age-associated decline, and what is disease, in order to help older adults who are experiencing significant loss of physiological functions. These experts also need skills to modify the environment and enhance elders' competence to accommodate such physiological changes. A significant barrier to the expansion of this necessary pool of professionals is that Medicare and many other health insurance policies do not reimburse for such specialized services to older adults.

Summary

As shown by this review of physiological systems, the aging process is gradual, beginning in some organ systems as early as the 20s and 30s, and progressing more rapidly after age 70, or even 80, in others. Even with 50 percent deterioration in many organ systems, an individual can still function adequately. The ability of human beings to compensate for age-related changes attests to their significant amount of excess reserve capacity. In most instances, the normal physical changes of aging need not diminish a person's quality of life if person–environment congruence can be maintained. Since many of the decrements are gradual and slight, older people can learn to modify their activities to adapt to their environments—for example, by pacing the amount of physical exertion throughout the day. Family members and professionals can be supportive by encouraging modifications in the home, such as minimizing the use of stairs, moving the focus of the older person's daily activities to the main floor of the home, and reinforcing their efforts to cope creatively with common vision or hearing impairments.

The rate and severity of decline in various organ systems vary substantially, with the greatest deterioration in functions that require coordination among multiple systems, muscles, and nerves. Similarly, wide variations across individuals in the aging process spring from differences in heredity, diet, exercise, culture, and living conditions. Many of the physiological functions that were once assumed to deteriorate and to be irreversible with normal aging are being reevaluated by researchers in basic and clinical physiology as well as by health educators. Examples of master athletes who continue their swimming, running, and other competitive physical activities throughout life show that age-related declines are not always dramatic. Even people who begin a regular exercise program late in life have experienced significant improvements in their heart and lung capacity. The role of preventive maintenance and health-enhancement programs in the aging process is discussed in Chapter 4.

Sleep patterns change with normal aging. Lab studies reveal changes in EEG patterns, sleep stages, and circadian rhythms with advancing years. However, recent studies demonstrate that true sleep disturbances are associated with physical and psychiatric disorders and the medications used to treat these conditions, and are not due to aging per se. Sedative-hypnotic drugs are widely used by older people who complain of sleep disturbance. However, improving sleep hygiene by increasing physical exercise, reducing the intake of alcohol, caffeine, and some medications, and modifying the sleep environment are generally more effective methods than sleeping pills for long-term use. This is particularly true for older persons with dementia. Medications are useful only in the case of true sleep disorders, such as sleep apnea and twitching legs during sleep.

Changes in sensory function with age do not occur at a consistent rate in all senses and for all people. Some people show rapid declines in vision while maintaining their hearing and other sensory abilities. Others experience an early deterioration in olfactory sensation, but not in other areas. All of us experience some loss in these functions with age, but interindividual differences are quite pronounced. Normal age-related declines in vision reduce the ability to respond to differing light levels; to function in low-light situations; to see in places with high levels of glare; to discern color tones, especially in the green-blue-violet range; and to judge distances and depth. Peripheral vision becomes somewhat narrowed with age, as does upward and downward gaze. Older people have more diseases of the eye, including glaucoma, cataracts, and macular degeneration; if these diseases are not treated, blindness can result. Older persons who experience significant declines in visual function with age should be encouraged to maintain former levels of activity, either by adapting the environment to fit changing needs or by substituting new activities for those that have become more difficult. Unfortunately, some older people prefer to withdraw from previous activities, thereby becoming more isolated and at risk of depression and deteriorating quality of life.

Decline in auditory function generally starts earlier than visual problems, and affects more people. Significant impairments in speech comprehension often result. Although hearing aids can frequently improve hearing by raising the intensity of speech that is in the high-frequency range, many older people feel uncomfortable and even stigmatized when using them. Hence, the solutions to communicating with hearing-impaired elders may lie mostly in the environment, not within older persons themselves. These include changes in communication styles, such as speaking directly at an older person in a clear voice, but not shouting; speaking in a lower tone; repeating key points; and sitting closer to a hearing-impaired person.

Environmental aids such as soundproof or quiet rooms and modified telephones can also be invaluable for older people with significant hearing declines.

Although many older people complain that food does not taste as good as it once did, changes with age in taste acuity are minimal. The decline in olfactory receptors with age is more significant than in taste receptors, and may be responsible for the perception of reduced taste acuity. These changes are more pronounced in people who smoke or drink heavily, but the use of medications has only modest effects. There is less change in people who have sharpened their taste and olfactory sensitivity, such as professional winemakers and perfumers. This pattern suggests that older people should be encouraged to participate in activities that enhance their taste and olfactory functions.

As we learn more from studies of normal physiological changes with aging, reports that once appeared definitive are found to be less so, and a complete understanding of some areas is shown to be lacking. This is particularly true in the areas of taste, smell, and pain perception. Research is needed to distinguish normal changes in these areas from those that are related to disease, and those that can be prevented. Longitudinal research would help to answer many of these questions. Finally, research that examines the impact of sensory deterioration on the older person's interactions with the environment is also needed.

GLOSSARY

accommodation   ability of the lens of the eye to change shape from rounded to flat in order to see objects that are closer or farther from the lens

age-related macular degeneration (AMD)   loss of vision in the center of the visual field caused by insufficient oxygen reaching the macula

atherosclerosis   accumulation of fats in the arteries and veins, blocking circulation of the blood

atrophic gastritis   chronic inflammation of the stomach lining

autoimmune theory   the hypothesis that aging is a function of the body's immune system becoming defective, producing antibodies against itself

cataract   clouding of the lens of the eye, reducing sight and sometimes leading to blindness; requires surgical extraction of the lens

cellular aging theory   the hypothesis that aging occurs as cells slow their number of replications, based on the observation that cells grown in controlled laboratory environments are able to replicate only a finite number of times

cross-linkage theory   the hypothesis that aging is a function of the reduction of collagen with age, causing loss of elasticity in most organ systems

dementia   diminished ability to remember, make accurate judgments, etc.

diastolic blood pressure   the level of blood pressure during the time that chambers of the heart are filling with blood

endocrine and immunological theory   focuses on loss of sex hormones and T-cells as the cause of many normal age-related declines and chronic diseases associated with aging

estrogen   a female sex hormone that declines significantly with aging; can be replaced alone (estrogen replacement therapy) or in combination with progesterone, another female sex hormone (hormone replacement therapy)

free radical theory   a special case of the cross-linkage theory of aging that posits that free radicals, highly reactive molecules, may produce DNA mutations

functional (or reserve) capacity   the ability of a given organ to perform its normal function, compared with its function under conditions of illness, disability, and aging

glaucoma   a disease in which there is insufficient drainage or excessive production of aqueous humor, the fluid in the front portion of the eye

glucose   a type of sugar found in plants and animals, serves as a major energy source and circulates in blood

hyperthermia   body temperatures several degrees above normal for prolonged periods

hypothermia   body temperatures several degrees below normal for prolonged periods

kinesthetic system   the body system that signals one's position in space

kyphosis   stoop-shouldered or hunched condition caused by collapsed vertebrae as bone mass is lost

master athletes   individuals who have continued to participate in competitive, aerobic exercise into the later years

melanin   skin pigmentation

menopause   one event during the climacteric in a woman's life when there is a gradual cessation of the menstrual cycle, which is related to the loss of ovarian function; considered to have occurred after 12 consecutive months without a menstrual period

neurons   nerve cells in the brain

orthopedic injuries   injuries to the bones, muscles, and joints

osteoporosis   a dramatic loss in calcium and bone mass resulting in increased brittleness of the bones and increased risk of fracture, more frequently found in white, small-stature women

otosclerosis   loss of hearing caused by hardening of stapes and inability to vibrate, not normal aging

periodic limb movement disorder (PLMD)   neuromuscular disturbance resulting in uncontrolled movement of legs during sleep (also known as *nocturnal myoclonus*)

presbycusis   age-related hearing loss

prolongevity   research aimed at increasing average life expectancy by reducing burden of disease but not disrupting fundamental aging processes

renal function   kidney function, defined by the rate at which blood is filtered through the kidneys

senescence   biological aging, i.e., the gradual accumulation of irreversible functional losses to which the average person tries to accommodate in some socially acceptable way

sleep apnea   five- to 10-second cessation of breathing, which disturbs sleep in some older persons

sleep hygiene   behaviors associated with sleep, e.g., location, lighting, regular vs. irregular bedtime, use of drugs that promote or hinder sleep

systolic blood pressure   the level of blood pressure during the contraction phase of the heart

telomerase   the enzyme responsible for rebuilding telomeres

telomerase inhibitors   chemicals produced by the organism that block the production of telomerase

telomeres   excess DNA at ends of each chromosome, lost as cells replicate

tinnitus   high-pitched ringing in the ear

urinary incontinence   diminished ability to retain urine; loss of bladder control

varicosities   abnormal swelling in the veins, especially the legs

vital capacity   the maximum volume of oxygen intake through the lungs with a single breath

wear and tear theory   one of the biological theories of aging; states that aging occurs because of the system simply wearing out over time

RESOURCES

Log on to MySocKit (www.mysockit.com) for information about the following:

- AARP Andrus Foundation publication, "Lighting the Way" (2002)
- American Foundation for the Blind, Unit on Aging
- American Printing House for the Blind
- American Speech-Language Hearing Association
- Better Hearing Institute
- International Hearing Aid Helpline of the International Hearing Society
- International Longevity Center
- Library of Congress, Blind and Physically Handicapped Division
- National Association for Continence
- National Sleep Foundation
- Self-Help for Hard of Hearing People (SHHH)

REFERENCES

Aldwin, C.M., and Gilmer, D.F. *Health, illness and optimal aging.* Thousand Oaks, CA: Sage, 2004.

Allikmets, R., Shroyer, N.F., Singh, N., Seddon, J.M., and Lewis, R.A. Mutation of the Stargardt disease gene (ABCR) in age-related macular degeneration. *Science,* 1997, *277,* 1805–1807.

Bauer, J., Pearson, K., Price, N., Jamieson, H., Lerin, C., et al. Resveratrol improves health and survival of mice on a high-calorie diet, *Nature,* 2006, *10,* 1038–1040.

Beckman, K.B., and Ames, B.N. The free radical theory of aging matures. *Physiological Reviews,* 1998, *78,* 547–581.

Bjorksten, J. Crosslinkage and the aging process. In M. Rockstein, M.L. Sussman, and J. Chesky (Eds.), *Theoretical aspects of aging.* New York: Academic Press, 1974.

Blumberg, J.B. Status and functional impact of nutrition in older adults. In E.L. Schneider, and J.W. Rowe (Eds.), *Handbook of the biology of aging* (4th ed.). New York: Van Nostrand, 1996.

Bodner, A.G., Ouelette, M., Frolkis, M., Holt, S.E., Chiu, C.P., Morin, G.B., Harley, et al. Extension of life-span by introduction of telomerase into normal human cells. *Science,* 1998, *279,* 349–352.

Braille Institute. *Statistics on sight loss.* Accessed 2004, from http://www.brailleinstitute.org/Education-Statistics.html.

Brant, L.J., and Fozard, J. Age changes in pure-tone hearing thresholds in a longitudinal study of normal human aging. *Journal of the Acoustical Society of America,* 1990, *88,* 813–820.

Carpenter, M.K., Cui, X., Hu, Z.Y., Jackson, J., Sherman, S., Seiger, A., and Wahlberg, L.U. In vitro expansion of a multipotent population of human neural progenitor cells. *Experimental Neurology,* 1999, *158,* 265–278.

Coffey, C.E., Lucke, J.F., Saxton, J.A., Ratcliff, G., Unitas, L.J., Billig, B., and Bryan, R.N. Sex differences in brain aging. *Archives of Neurology,* 1998, *55,* 169–179.

Cossarizza, A., Ortolani, C., Monti, D., and Franceschi, C. Cytometric analysis of immuno-senescence. *Cytometry,* 1997, *27,* 297–313.

Cowart, B.J. Relationships between taste and smell across the life span. In C. Murphy, W.S. Cain, and D.M. Hegsted (Eds.), Nutrition and the chemical senses in aging: Recent advances and current research needs. *Annals of the New York Academy of Sciences.* New York: New York Academy of Sciences, 1989.

Crews, J.E., and Campbell, V.A. Vision impairment and hearing loss among community-dwelling older Americans: Implications for health and functioning. *American Journal of Public Health,* 2004, *94,* 823–829.

Dalton, D.S., Cruickshanks, K.J., Klein, B.E.K., Wiley, T.L., and Nondahl, D.M. The impact of hearing loss on quality of life in older adults. *The Gerontologist,* 2003, *43,* 661–668.

Desai, M., Pratt, L.A., Lentzner, H., and Robinson, K.N. Trends in vision and hearing among older Americans. *Aging Trends,* 2001, *2,* Hyattsville, MD: National Center for Health Statistics.

Dhatariya, K.K., and Nair, K.S. Dehydroepiandrosterone: Is there a role for replacement? *Mayo Clinic Proceedings,* 2003, *78,* 1257–1273.

Eastwood, G.L. A review of gastrointestinal epithelial renewal and its relevance to the development of adenocarcinomas of the gastrointestinal tract. *Journal of Clinical Gastroenterology,* 1995, *21,* 1–11.

Effros, R.B. Immune system activity. In E.J. Masoro and S.N. Austad (Eds.), *Handbook of the biology of aging* (5th ed.). San Diego: Academic Press, 2001.

Finch, C.E. *Longevity, senescence and the genome.* Chicago: University of Chicago Press, 1990.

Fontana, L., Meyer, T.E., Klein, S., and Holloszy, J.O. Long-term calorie restriction is highly effective in reducing the risk for atherosclerosis in humans. *Proceedings of the National Academy of Sciences of the U.S.A.,* 2004, *101,* 6659–6663.

Fozard, J.L., and Gordon-Salant, S. Changes in vision and hearing with aging. In J.E. Birren, and K.W. Schaie (Eds.), *Handbook of the psychology of aging* (5th ed.). San Diego: Academic Press, 2001.

Franceschi, C., Monti, D., Sansoni, P., and Cossarizza, A. The immunology of exceptional individuals: The lesson of centenarians. *Immunology Today,* 1995, *16,* 12–16.

Gafni, A. Protein structure and turnover. In E.J. Masaro, and S.N. Austad (Eds.), *Handbook of the biology of aging,* (5th ed.) San Diego: Academic Press, 2001.

Grune, T., and Davies, K.J.A. Oxidative processes in aging. In E.J. Masoro, and S.N. Austad (Eds.), *Handbook of the biology of aging* (5th ed.). San Diego: Academic Press, 2001.

Harman, D. Aging: A theory based on free radical and radiation chemistry. *Journal of Gerontology,* 1956, 2, 298–300.

Harman, D. Free radical involvement in aging: Pathophysiology and therapeutic implications. *Drugs and Aging,* 1993, 3, 60–80.

Harman, S.M., Metter, E.J., Metter, J., Tobin, J.D., Pearson, J., and Blackman, M.R. Longitudinal effects of aging on serum total and free testosterone levels in healthy men. *Journal of Clinical Endocrinology and Metabolism,* 2000, 86, 724–731.

Hayflick, L. Anti-aging is an oxymoron. *Journal of Gerontology,* 2004a, B573–578.

Hayflick, L. From here to immortality. *Public Policy and Aging Report,* 2004b, 14, 1–7.

Hayflick, L. *How and why we age.* New York: Ballantine Books, 1996.

Hayflick, L. The illusion of cell immortality. *British Journal of Cancer,* 2000, 83, 841–846.

Hayflick, L., and Moorehead, P.S. The serial cultivation of human diploid cell strains. *Experimental Cell Research,* 1961, 25, 285–621.

Hill, E.L., Cumming, R.G., Lewis, R., Carrington, S., and LeCouteur, D.G. Sleep disturbances and falls in older people. *Journal of Gerontology: Medical Sciences,* 2007, 62A, 62–66.

Hornsby, P.J. Cell proliferation in mammalian aging. In E.J. Masoro, and S.N. Austad (Eds.), *Handbook of the biology of aging* (5th ed.). San Diego: Academic Press, 2001.

Hornsby, P.J. The new science and medicine of cell transplantation. *American Society for Experimental Microbiology News,* 1999, 65, 208–214.

Howitz, K.T., Bitterman, K.J., Cohen, H.Y., Lamming, D.W., Lavu, S., Wood-Zipkin, R.E., Chung, P., et al. Small molecule activators of sirtuins extend *Saccharomyces cerevisiae* lifespan. *Nature,* 2003, 425, 191–196.

Horowitz, A., and Higgins, K.E. Older drivers and failing vision: Time to surrender the keys! *Consultant,* 2000, 40, 1310–1316.

Jacques, P.F., Chylack, L.T., and Taylor, A. Relationships between natural antioxidants and cataract formation. In B. Frei (Ed.), *Natural antioxidants in human health and disease.* San Diego: Academic Press, 1994.

Kinouchi, Y., Hiwatashi, N., Chida, M., Nagashima, F., Takagi, S., Maekawa, H., and Toyota, T. Telomere shortening in the colonic mucosa of patients with ulcerative colitis. *Journal of Gastroenterology,* 1998, 33, 343–348.

Kiyak, H.A. Communication in the practitioner-aged patient relationship. In P. Holm-Pedersen, and H. Loe (Eds.), *Textbook of geriatric dentistry* (2nd ed.). Copenhagen: Munksgaard, 1996.

Kline, D.W., Kline, T.J.B., Fozard, J.L., Kosnik, W., Schieber, F., and Sekuler, R. Vision, aging, and driving: The problems of older drivers. *Journals of Gerontology,* 1992, 47, M27–34.

Lane, M.A., Ingram, D.K., Ball, S.S., and Roth, G.S. Dehydroepiandrosterone sulfate: A biomarker of primate aging slowed by calorie restriction. *Journal of Clinical Endocrinology and Metabolism,* 1997, 82, 2093–2096.

Lane, M.A., Ingram, D.K., and Roth, G.S. The serious search for an anti-aging pill. *Scientific American,* 2002, 287, 36–41.

Li, Y., and Wolf, N.S. Effects of age and long-term caloric restriction on the aqueous collecting channel in the mouse eye. *Journal of Glaucoma,* 1997, 6, 18–22.

Masoro, E.J. Caloric restriction, slowing aging, and extending life. *Science of aging knowledge environment,* 2003, 8, RE2.

Masoro, E.J. Dietary restriction: An experimental approach to the study of the biology of aging. In E.J. Masoro, and S.N. Austad (Eds.), *Handbook of the biology of aging* (5th ed.). San Diego: Academic Press, 2001.

Mattison, J.A., Lane, M.A., Roth, G.S., and Ingram, D.K. Calorie restriction in rhesus monkeys. *Experimental Gerontology,* 2003, 38, 35–46.

McCurry, S.M., Reynolds, F., Ancoli-Israel, S., Teri, L., and Vitiello, M.V. Treatment of sleep disturbance in Alzheimer's disease. *Sleep Medicine Reviews,* 2000, 4, 603–628.

McShane, T.M., Wilson, M.E., and Wise, P.M. Effects of lifelong moderate caloric restriction. *Journals of Gerontology: Biological Sciences,* 1999, 54A, B14–B21.

Melov, S., Ravenscroft, J., Malik, S., Gill, M.S., Walker, D.W., Clayton, P.E., Wallace, D.C., et al. Extension of life-span with superoxide dismutase/catalase mimetics. *Science,* 2000, 287, 1567–1569.

Micozzi, M. Exploring alternative health approaches for elders. *Aging Today,* 1997, 18, 9–12.

Milton, R.C., and Sperduto, R.D. Incidence of age-related cataract: 13.6 year follow-up in the Framingham eye study. *Investigations in Ophthalmic Vision Science,* 1991, *32,* 1243–1250.

Nair, K.S., Rizza, R.A., O'Brien, P., Dhatariay, K.K., Short, K.R., Nehra, A., Vittone, J.L, et al. DHEA in elderly women and DHEA or testosterone in elderly men. *New England Journal of Medicine,* 2006, *355,* 1647–1659.

National Academy on an Aging Society. *Hearing loss,* 1999, 2.

New York Times. In France, nothing gets in the way of vacation. August 24, 2003, p. 5.

National Institute on Aging (NIA). *Hearing loss age page.* Accessed 2005, from http://niapublications.org/engagepages/ hearing.asp.

National Institutes of Health (NIH). Hypothermia: A cold weather hazard for seniors. *NIH News,* February 15, 2006.

Newman, A.B., Spiekerman, C.F., Enright, P., Lefkowitz, D., Manolio, T., Reynolds, C.F., and Robbins, J. Daytime sleepiness predicts mortality and CVD in older adults. *Journal of the American Geriatrics Society,* 2000, *48,* 115–123.

Nikolaus, T., and Bach, M. Preventing falls in community-dwelling frail older people using a home intervention team (HIT): Results from the randomized Falls-HIT trial. *Journal of the American Geriatrics Society,* 2003, *51,* 300–305.

Nordin, S., Razani, L.J., Markison, S., and Murphy, C. Age-associated increases in intensity discrimination for taste. *Experimental Aging Research,* 2003, *29,* 371–386.

Olshansky, S.J., Hayflick, L., and Carnes, B.A. No truth to the fountain of youth. *Scientific American,* 2002, *286,* 92–95.

Ohayon, M.M., Carskadon, M.A., Guilleminault, C., and Vitiello, M.V. Meta-analysis of quantitative sleep parameters from childhood to old age in healthy individuals: Developing normative sleep values across the human lifespan. *Sleep,* 2004, *27,* 1255–1273.

Ramirez, R., and Schneider, J. Practical guide to sun protection. *Surgical Clinics of North America,* 2003, *83,* 97–107.

Rattan, S.I.S., and Clark, B.F.C. Understanding and modulating ageing. *UBMB Life,* 2005, *57,* 297–304.

Rees, T. Health promotion for older adults: Age-related hearing loss. *Northwest Geriatric Education Center Curriculum Modules,* Seattle: University of Washington NWGEC, 2000.

Rincon, M., Muzumdar, R., and Barzilai, N. Aging, body fat, and carbohydrate metabolism. In E.J. Masoro, and S.N. Austad (Eds), *Handbook of the biology of aging* (6th ed.), Amsterdam: Elsevier Academic Press, 2006.

Rogers, M.A., Hagberg, J.M., Martin, W.H., Ehsani, A.A., and Holloszy, J.O. Decline in VO2 max with aging in master athletes and sedentary men. *Journal of Applied Physiology,* 1990, *68,* 2195–2199.

Roth, G.S., Ingram, D.K., and Lane, M.A. Caloric restriction in primates and relevance to humans. *Annuals of the New York Academy of Sciences,* 2001, *928,* 305–315.

Rudman, D., Drinka, P.J., Wilson, C.R., Mattson, D.E., Scherman, F., Cuisinier, M.C., and Schultz, S. Relations of endogenous anabolic hormones and physical activity to bone mineral density in elderly men. *Clinical Endocrinology,* 1991, *40,* 653–661.

Rudolph, K.L., Chang, S., Millard, M., Schreiber-Agus, N., and DePinho, R.A. Inhibition of experimental liver cirrhosis in mice by telomerase gene delivery. *Science,* 2000, *287,* 1253–1258.

Schiffman, S.S., and Graham, B.G. Taste and smell perception affect appetite and immunity in the elderly. *European Journal of Clinical Nutrition,* 2000, *54,* S54–S63.

Schultz, D.W., Klein, M.L., Humbert, A.J., Luzier, C.W., Persun, V., et al. Analysis of the ARMD1 locus: Evidence that a mutation in *HEMICENTIN-1* is associated with age-related macular degeneration in a large family. *Human Molecular Genetics,* Accessed 2003, from http://hmg.oupjournals.org/content/abstract/ddg348v1.

Seddon, J.M., Ajani, U.A., Sperduto, R.D., Hiller, R., Blair, H.N., and Burton, T.C. Dietary carotenoids, vitamins A, C, and E, and advanced age-related macular degeneration. *Journal of the American Medical Association,* 1994a, *272,* 1413–1420.

Seddon, J.M., Christen, W.G., Manson, J.E., Lamotte, F.S., Glynn, R.J., Buring, J.E., and Hennekens, C.H. The use of vitamin supplements and the risk of cataract among U.S. male physicians. *American Journal of Public Health,* 1994b, *84,* 788–792.

Shock, N.W. The physiology of aging. *Scientific American,* 1962, *206,* 100–110.

Solana, R. *Immunosenescence in centenarians and the old-old.* Symposium presented at the International Association of Gerontology, Barcelona, July 2003.

Strawbridge, W.J., Wallhagen, M.I., Shema, S.J., and Kaplan, G.A. Negative consequences of hearing impairment in old age: A longitudinal analysis. *The Gerontologist,* 2000, *40,* 320–326.

Stuen, C. Older adults with age-related sensory loss. In B. Berkman (Ed.), *Handbook of Social Work in Health and Aging.* New York: Oxford, 2006.

Sutton, D.A., Moldofsky, H., and Badley, E.M. Insomnia and health problems in Canadians. *Sleep, 2001, 24,* 665–670.

Thom, D.H., and Brown, J.S. Reproductive and hormonal risk factors for urinary incontinence in later life: A review of the clinical and epidemiological literature. *Journal of the American Geriatrics Society,* 1998, *46,* 1411–1417.

Thomas, T., Thomas, G., McLendon, C., Sutton, T., and Mullan, M. Beta-amyloid-mediated vasoactivity and vascular endothelial damage. *Nature,* 1996, *380,* 168–171.

Tuorila, H., Niskanen, N., and Maunuksela, E. Perception and pleasantness of a food with varying odor among the elderly and young. *Journal of Nutrition, Health and Aging,* 2001, *5,* 266–268.

Vincent, K.R., Braith, R.W., Feldman, R.A., Kallas, H.E., Lowenthal, D.T. Improved cardiorespiratory endurance following 6 months of resistance exercise in elderly men and women. *Archives of Internal Medicine,* 2002, *162,* 673–678.

Vitiello, M.V. Effective treatment of sleep disturbances in older adults. *Clinical Cornerstone,* 2000, *2,* 16–27.

Vitiello, M.V., Larsen, L.H., and Moe, K.E. Age-related sleep change: Gender and estrogen effects on the subjective-objective sleep quality of healthy, non-complaining men and women. *Journal of Psychosomatic Research,* 2004, *56,* 503–510.

Vitiello, M.V., and Borson, S. Sleep disturbances in patients with Alzheimer's disease. *CNS Drugs,* 2001, *15,* 777–796.

Vitiello, M.V., Moe, K.E., and Prinz, P.N. Sleep complaints cosegregate with illness in older adults. *Journal of Psychosomatic Research,* 2002, *53,* 555–559.

Weed, J.L., Lane, M.A., Roth, G.S., Speer, D.L., and Ingram, D.K. Activity measures in rhesus monkeys on long-term calorie restriction. *Physiology and Behavior,* 1997, *62,* 97–103.

Weinstein, B.E. *Geriatric Audiology.* New York: Thieme Medical Publishers, 2000.

Wilson, D.L. The programmed theory of aging. In M. Rockstein, M.L. Sussman, and J. Chesky (Eds.), *Theoretical aspects of aging.* New York: Academic Press, 1974.

Wolf, S.L., Barnhart, H.X., Kutner, N.G., McNeely, E., Coogler, C., Xu, T., et al. Reducing frailty and falls in older persons: An investigation of Tai Chi and computerized balance training. *Journal of the American Geriatrics Society,* 2003, *51,* 1794–1803.

Yamauchi, Y., Endo, S., and Yoshimura, I. A new whole mouth gustatory test procedure: Effects of aging, gender, and smoking. *Acta Otolaryngologica Supplement,* 2002, *546,* 49–59.

Yataco, A.R., Busby-Whitehead, J., Drinkwater, D.T., and Katzel, L.I. Relationship of body composition and cardiovascular fitness to lipoprotein lipid profiles in master athletes and sedentary men. *Aging,* 1997, *9,* 88–94.

4

Managing Chronic Diseases and Promoting Well-Being in Old Age

No aspect of old age is more alarming to many of us than the thought of losing our health. Our fears center not only on the pain and inconvenience of illness, but also on its social-psychological consequences, such as loss of personal autonomy and economic security. Poor health, more than other changes commonly associated with aging, can reduce a person's competence in mastering his or her environment.

Defining Health

Most people would agree that good health is something more than merely the absence of disease or disability. As defined by the World Health Organization, **good health** is a state of complete physical, mental, and social well-being. Thus, health implies an interaction and integration of body, mind, and spirit, a perspective that is reflected in the growth of health promotion programs and alternative medicine, and is congruent with the concept of active aging used throughout this text.

As used by health care providers and researchers, the term **health status** refers to: (1) the presence or absence of disease, and (2) the degree of disability in an individual's level of functioning. Thus, activities that older people can do, or think they can do, are useful indicators of both how healthy they are and the services and environmental changes needed to cope with their impairments. Older people's ability to function independently at home is of primary concern. The concepts that capture this functional ability—**activities of daily living (ADLs)** and **instrumental activities of daily living (IADLs)**—are described in the box on page 116.

The World Health Organization (2002) defines **disability** as impairments in the ability to complete multiple daily tasks. About 20 percent of older people are estimated to have a mild degree of disability in their ADLs, but less than 4 percent are severely disabled (Federal Interagency Forum, 2006). The more disabled older population is limited in their extent and types of major activities and mobility, such as eating, dressing, bathing, or toiletry, and requires the assistance of family or paid caregivers. The extent of disabilities and need for help in personal care activities increase with age and differ by gender and poverty status, as shown in Figure 4.1.

Women age 90 and older are twice as likely to be disabled and to require assistance than those age 70 to 74. Men in both age groups are less likely to have IADL and ADL limits and show a smaller increase in disability with age. For example, only about half as many community-dwelling men over age 65 report ADL limitations as their female counterparts. This may be because men who survive to this age have a genetic advantage and are hardier than men who die at a younger age. African Americans and Latinos are twice as likely as whites to report problems with ADLs and IADLs, and have higher rates of disability, especially among low-income and less-educated elders (CDC, 2004a; Federal Interagency Forum, 2006; Ferraro and Kelley-Moore, 2005; Kelley-Moore and Ferraro, 2004).

In 2000, approximately 10 million persons 65 years or older needed some assistance to remain in the community (including 10.5 percent of those age 65–79 and 51 percent of those over age 85).

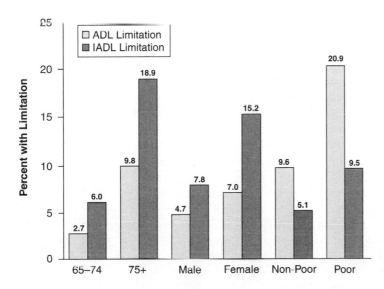

FIGURE 4.1 **Comparing ADL and IADL Limitations, 2002: Age, Gender, Poverty Status**
SOURCE: *Health, United States*, 2004a.

ASSESSING FUNCTIONAL HEALTH

The most commonly used measure of *functional health,* termed the *activities of daily living (ADL),* summarizes an individual's ability to perform basic personal care tasks such as:

- eating
- bathing
- dressing
- using the toilet
- getting in or out of a bed or chair
- caring for a bowel-control device
- walking (the most common ADL limitation for older adults)

Instrumental activities of daily living (IADL) summarize an individual's ability to perform more complex, multidimensional activities and interact effectively with the environment:

- home management
- managing money
- meal preparation
- making a phone call
- grocery shopping (the most common IADL problem)

This figure is expected to reach 15 million by the year 2020 and 21 million by 2030. Another way to describe these projections is to state that 30 percent of persons over age 65 will have activity limitations that require some assistance by 2030. About 20 percent of this group will have severe limitations in ADL (AoA, 2005). The implications of this growth for long-term care are described in Chapter 11.

Frailty is one way of describing such severe limitations in ADL. More specifically, frailty includes problems with walking speed, declining activity levels, weak grip strength, and chronic exhaustion. In many instances, frailty is complicated by **comorbidity,** defined as the coexistence of two or more chronic systemic or psychiatric conditions. For example, an older person's physical strength may be impaired by heart disease and the effects compounded by diabetes and arthritis. All these characteristics increase the risk of hospitalization, nursing home placement, and falls (Fried et al., 2001).

Quality of Life in Health and Illness

As noted in Chapter 1, the concept of active aging implies that aging need not be a time of decline or dependency. For most older adults, being able to do the things that they want at home and in the community is a primary component of active aging (Menec, 2003; Phelan et al., 2004). Even those who experience chronic diseases can usually maintain some degree of autonomy and choice and avoid disability that impedes their daily functioning. As we will illustrate in this chapter, social and health behaviors throughout life, such as diet, smoking, alcohol consumption, and physical activity, as well as the physical environment where we live and work, all play a role in the development and progress of chronic diseases. Health and wellness include a range of factors, such as health behaviors, social contributions, and access to health care (Putnam et al., 2003). To the extent that people practice health-enhancing habits and an active lifestyle in their younger years, many chronic conditions can be prevented, while others can be managed so they do not result in a severe disability that prevents active aging (Kalache and Kickbusch, 1997).

Not only are people living longer today, but they are more likely to manage their chronic conditions without resulting in frailty or physical disability. National surveys have found a decline in the proportion of older adults who reported problems with daily activities, from 26.5 percent in 1982 to slightly less than 20 percent in 2004–2005. Disability rates have declined in all age groups 65 and older, especially among the oldest-old (AARP, 2003; Federal Interagency Forum, 2006, Manton, Gu, and Lamb, 2006).

Regular swimming can relieve the pain of arthritis.

Nevertheless, chronic illnesses often accompany old age, and societal values affect our attitudes toward loss of health. The importance placed by our culture on being independent and highly active may underlie our relative inability to accept illness graciously. It may also underlie the relatively high rates of depression experienced by elders with chronic illnesses, especially cardiovascular disease and diabetes. These values of independence may partially explain why healthy older people often do not want to share housing or recreational activities with those who have mental or physical disabilities.

A reliable evaluation of health takes into account not only a physician's assessment of an older person's physical condition, but also their self-perceptions, observable behaviors, and life circumstances. **Quality of life** may be defined as this combination of an individual's functional health, feelings of competence, independence in ADL, and satisfaction with one's social circumstances. Most older people appear to adjust their perceptions of their health in response to the aging process. In the 2002 National Health Interview Survey (NHIS), 76 percent of non-Hispanic whites, 60 percent of African Americans, and 62 percent of Latinos 65 and older rated their health as excellent or very good. Self-ratings were slightly lower among those 85 and older: 67 percent of whites, 54 percent of African Americans, and 51 percent of Latinos gave high self-ratings (Figure 4.2) (Federal Interagency Forum, 2006). Not surprisingly, household income is also associated with self-assessed good health; higher income elders rate their health more positively (He et al., 2005). More objective assessments of the elder's health by family and health care providers may differ from the elder's self-assessment. Even older persons in nursing homes tend to rate their health positively. Older people who must take multiple medications, experience chronic pain, struggle with depression or have financial and ADL limitations are most likely to report lower quality of life (Merck Institute, 2004).

On the other hand, those who have recently had a successful medical or surgical intervention to alleviate the symptoms of their chronic conditions are more likely to report improved quality of life. It is noteworthy that physicians rate the quality of life of older persons with diabetes, arthritis, or even ischemic heart disease lower than do these elders themselves. This may indicate greater adaptation to disabling conditions among patients than physicians expect, or that medical professionals' definitions of quality of life are more constrained by health factors than are patients' own perceptions. The concept of resilience, described in Chapters 1 and 6, may also help explain the generally positive evaluations of their health by many older adults with chronic illness and disabilities. In general, older

POINTS TO PONDER

Think about your own health perceptions. To what extent do you compare your health to others of your age or gender? How does your ability to perform various ADLs affect your health perceptions? How does your day-to-day health affect your overall quality of life?

WHY OLDER ADULTS RATE THEIR HEALTH POSITIVELY

- compare themselves with peers
- sense of accomplishment from having survived to old age
- perception of competence to meet environmental demands
- a broad definition of quality of life to include meaning and life satisfaction

women rate their health more positively than men, even though they have more chronic diseases and are more likely to live in long-term care facilities (NCHS, 1999). The reasons for gender differences are unclear.

Perceptions of good health are generally associated with other measures of well-being, particularly life satisfaction. Older persons who view themselves as reasonably healthy tend to be happier, more satisfied, more involved in social activities, and less lonely. In turn, lower life satisfaction is associated with lower levels of self-perceived health. It has also been found that

self-ratings of health are correlated with mortality. That is, older people who report poorer health, especially poorer functional abilities, are more likely to die in the next 3 years than those who perceive their functional health to be good (Bernard et al., 1997).

Chronic and Acute Diseases

As noted in Chapter 3, the risk of disease and impairment increases with age. However, the extreme variability in older people's health status, as illustrated by Mrs. Hill and Mr. Jones in the vignettes in the introduction to Part Two, shows that poor health is not necessarily a concomitant of aging. The incidence of **acute** (or temporary) **conditions,** such as infections or the common cold, actually decreases with age. Those acute conditions that do occur, however, are more debilitating and require more care, especially for older women:

- The average number of days of restricted activity due to acute conditions is nearly three times greater for people age 65 and older than it is for those 17–44 years old.
- Older people report, on average, 33 days per year of restricted activity days, of which 14 are spent in bed (NCHS, 2003a).

An older person who gets a cold, for example, faces a greater risk of pneumonia or bronchitis

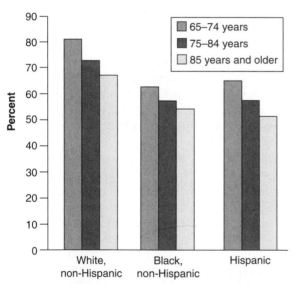

FIGURE 4.2   **Good to Excellent Health among Noninstitutionalized Persons 65 and Older, by Age, Race, and Hispanic Origin: United States, 2002–2004**
SOURCE: Federal Interagency Forum, 2006.

because of changes in organ systems (described in Chapter 3) that reduce his or her resistance and recuperative capacities. Thus, older people are more likely than their younger counterparts to suffer restrictions on their social activities as a result of temporary health problems.

In some cases, an acute condition that merely inconveniences a younger person may result in death for an older person. For example, respiratory infection rates are similar in young and old, but people age 65 and older account for 90 percent of all deaths due to pneumonia and influenza. Hospitalization for influenza-associated respiratory problems occurs much more frequently for older adults, increasing from less than 100 per 100,000 at age 50–64, to more than 400 at age 75–79, and 1200 per 100,000 among those 85 and older (Thompson et al., 2004). This is why it is important for older people to be vaccinated against pneumonia and influenza. These vaccines can reduce the risk of pneumonia by 67 percent and of flu by 50 percent among older people, saving medical costs and increasing days of healthy living. Even if older adults develop pneumonia after receiving a vaccine, the consequences are less severe. Their hospital stays are shorter; they are one-third less likely to have respiratory failure, and half as likely to die during hospitalization than elders who do not obtain the pneumococcal vaccine (Fisman et al., 2006). The proportion of older adults who obtained a pneumonia vaccine (58 percent) and flu vaccine (65 percent) in 2004 increased from less than 50 percent and 63 percent respectively in 1999. Rates are lower for African Americans and Latinos than for whites: 46 percent, 55 percent, and 67 percent, respectively, received flu vaccines in 2004; comparable figures for pneumonia vaccines were 39 percent, 34 percent, and 61 percent, respectively (CDC, 2003c; Federal Interagency Forum, 2006). Even though Medicare Part B reimburses for these vaccines, older adults who rely only on Medicare for their health insurance are less

likely to obtain flu shots than those with private insurance: 58 percent and 70 percent, respectively, in 2004 (Schoenborn, Vickerie, and Powell-Griner, 2006).

What is of greatest concern in terms of quality of life is that older people are much more likely than the young to suffer from **chronic conditions.** Chronic health conditions are:

- long-term (more than three months)
- often permanent, leaving a residual disability that may require long-term management or care rather than a cure

More than 80 percent of persons age 70 and over have at least one chronic condition, with multiple health problems occurring in 50 percent of the older population (CDC, 2003b). Chronic problems are often accompanied by continuous pain and/or distress. At the very least, the individual is inconvenienced by the need to monitor health and daily activities, although ADLs may not always be limited. Almost 40 percent of older persons with chronic diseases report limitations in their

---

ETHNIC MINORITY DIFFERENCES IN CHRONIC DISEASES

Among those 70 and older:

- African American and Latino elders are more likely to suffer from diabetes than non-Hispanic whites.
- Diabetes is twice as common among women of color as in white women.
- Hypertension is 1.5 times more likely in African Americans than in whites.
- Rates of stroke are also higher among the former groups, but only when comparing black vs. white women.
- In contrast, white men age 70 and older are more likely to report heart disease than their Latino or African American counterparts (Federal Interagency Forum, 2006).

ability to perform basic ADLs (NCHS, 1999). Only about 2 percent of those age 65 and over are confined to bed by their chronic illness or disability, and most older people with chronic conditions are not dependent on others for managing their daily routines. On the other hand, the small percentage who do need assistance with care have placed enormous pressures on health and long-term care services as well as on informal caregivers, as discussed in Chapters 10 and 17.

Although one can live a satisfying life with multiple chronic conditions, these diseases may influence the decision to continue working or to retire. In a 2005 national survey, 25 percent of retirees ages 50 to 58, and 35 percent of those ages 59 to 61 cited chronic health problems as their reason for retiring. This varied by type of disease, and heart conditions were mentioned most frequently (He et al., 2005).

Many of these late-middle-aged adults have converted to part-time work; as a result, their median income is lower during retirement than for their healthier peers, which can profoundly affect their economic well-being as they age, as discussed more fully in Chapter 12.

The most frequently reported chronic conditions causing limitation of activity in persons age 65 and over are shown in Figure 4.3. Hypertension, arthritis, and heart disease are the leading chronic diseases, but older women are less likely to suffer from heart disease than older men, although their rates of heart disease are increasing dramatically and approximating rates for men. The most common heart condition for both men and women is ischemic heart disease. Older women are more likely to report arthritis and hypertension. Not surprisingly, most chronic conditions increase in prevalence with age. For example, people age 65 and over are twice as likely to suffer from arthritis as those aged 45 to 64. Other conditions, such as heart disease and diabetes, show lower rates in the oldest-old, probably because of the higher mortality associated with these diseases at a younger age (Federal Interagency Forum, 2006).

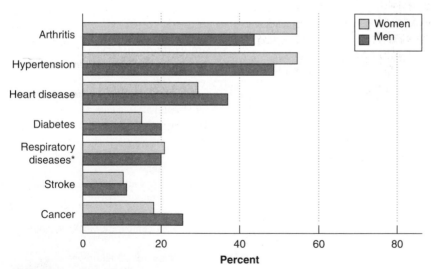

FIGURE 4.3   Percent of Persons 65 Years and Older Who Reported Selected Chronic Conditions by Gender: United States, 2003–2004
*(Includes emphysema, asthma, chronic bronchitis)
SOURCE: Federal Interagency Forum, 2006.

Disabling chronic diseases tend to occur earlier among African Americans, Latinos, and American Indians than among whites. In the 2001–2002 National Health Interview Survey, 66 percent of African Americans age 65 and older had hypertension, compared with 48.5 percent of whites, and 48 percent of Latinos. Diabetes rates also varied by race and ethnicity: 23 percent of blacks, 14 percent of whites, and 24 percent of Latinos (Federal Interagency Forum, 2006). These conditions result in higher rates of hospitalization, longer hospital stays, and shorter life expectancy. Therefore, it is not surprising that older persons of color with chronic conditions are less likely to describe their health as good or excellent than whites in every age group after 65, as shown in Figure 4.2 (Federal Interagency Forum, 2006). Health disparities, such as poorer self-assessments of health and lower life expectancies, are explained as products of discriminatory policies across the life course, whereby nonwhites have lower incomes and inadequate nutrition throughout their lives. An additional factor is that elders of color, because of their cultural values or negative experiences with formal services, may be less likely to utilize the health care system. The effects of ethnic minority status on the incidence and treatment of chronic conditions are further discussed in Chapter 14.

As noted above, comorbidity, or the problem of coping with two or more chronic conditions, is another concept central to understanding health status and its secondary consequences, such as depression, anxiety, and social isolation. Comorbidity is more common in older women than in men. Among women age 65 and older, 50 percent have at least two chronic diseases, and 25 percent have three or more such conditions. Older women of color, especially in the lower socioeconomic range, have a higher prevalence of chronic illness, functional limits on their ADLs, and disability, which reflects a lifetime of health and economic disparities. Because of their greater likelihood of coping with multiple chronic conditions, the old-old report more problems in performing ADLs. At age 65 to 74, 34 percent report significant ADL limitations, compared with 45 percent of people 75 and older (Clancey and Bierman, 2000).

Interactive Effects

Even though the majority of chronic conditions are not severely limiting, they can nevertheless make life difficult and lower older people's resistance to other illnesses. As noted earlier, the functional limits imposed by a chronic illness interact with the social limits set by others' perceptions of illness to influence an older person's daily functioning and quality of life. Therefore, it is important to look beyond the statistics on the frequency of chronic conditions to the nature of chronic illness, the interaction of physical changes with emotional and sociocultural factors, and the physiological differences between young and old that may make the older person more susceptible to health problems.

Certain types of chronic diseases (e.g., cancer, anemia, and toxic conditions) may be related to older people's declining **immunity,** that is, reduced resistance to environmental carcinogens, viruses, and bacteria. The accumulation of long-term, degenerative diseases may mean that a chronic condition, such as bronchitis, can have different and more negative complications than the same disease would have in a younger person. With reduced resistance to physical stress, an older individual may be less able to respond to treatment for any acute disease, such as a cold or flu, than a younger person would. The cumulative effect of chronic illness with an acute condition may become the crisis point at which the older person becomes dependent on others for care. The impact of any chronic condition appears to be mediated by the physiological changes that occur with age, the sociocultural context, and the person's mental and emotional outlook. This represents varying levels of P–E fit.

In sum, disabling health changes occur at different rates in different individuals and are not inevitable with age. We turn now to an examination of the chronic conditions that are the most common causes of death in older people.

Causes of Death in Later Years

Heart disease, cancer, and strokes accounted for 62 percent of all deaths among people age 65 and older in 2003 (Federal Interagency Forum, 2006). Even though it has declined rapidly over the past 30 years, heart disease remains the major cause of death among both men and women. It is the number-one risk factor among adults 65 and over, killing 40 percent more people than all forms of cancer combined, and accounting for 20 percent of adult disabilities. Heart disease accounts for 18 percent of hospital admissions, and 33 percent of deaths that occur among older people, with the highest rates among the oldest-old and among African Americans (American Heart Association, 2005; OMHRC, 2006). Since 1995, death rates from cancer among older adults have declined. But even if cancer were eliminated altogether as a cause of death, this would only extend the average life span by less than 2 years at age 65. Eliminating deaths due to major cardiovascular diseases, however, would add an average of 14 years to life expectancy at age 65. The benefits of eliminating cardiovascular diseases would be especially significant for older African American women (22 years) and white women (17.4 years). This would also increase the proportion of older persons in the total population. Declines in elders' deaths due to diseases of the heart since 1981, from 2600 per 100,000 to about 1500 per 100,000 in the year 2003, demonstrate progress in this area (Hayflick, 1996; NCHS, 2003b).

Stroke has also been decreasing as a leading cause of death among the oldest-old; it is the third leading cause for women over age 65 but fourth for men, slightly less than chronic obstructive pulmonary diseases (COPD) such as asthma and emphysema. Dramatic differences in rates of death due to heart disease and stroke are found across ethnic minority groups and gender (Sahyoun et al., 2001). As Figure 4.4 demonstrates for 55- to 64-year-olds (the "young-old"), African American men are at highest risk for death due to heart disease and cerebrovascular accidents (CVAs). Among women, African Americans are most likely to die of heart disease and CVAs, but have about the same death rates as Latina women for cancer. Lower death rates among whites are attributable to greater health care access across the life course, which allows early detection and management of these conditions so they become chronic diseases among whites rather than causing death. Likewise, Asian American adults are more likely to survive strokes and cancer, because these conditions are detected earlier than among African Americans, Latinos, and American Indians. Asian Americans also have the lowest incidence of heart diseases (NCHS, 2003a). For older African American and Latina women, diabetes is the fourth major cause of death. It accounts for more than twice the rate of deaths as COPD, which is sixth in this population group (NCHS, 2003b). Overall death rates are significantly higher among African Americans than whites until age 64 (by 80 percent), but lower among Latinos (by 20 percent) and Asian-Pacific Islanders (by 50 percent). These differences are less dramatic after age 75 (Williams, 2005).

Educational achievement moderates the effect of ethnic minority status on chronic disease and disability, especially among older women. While African American women who have completed 0 to 8 years of school can expect 18.4 years of unhealthy life, their counterparts with 13 or more years of school can anticipate 12.9 years. Among white women, the difference is 17.5 versus 11.8 years of unhealthy life, respectively. Differences between more- and less-educated men are less dramatic; African American men with 0 to 8 years

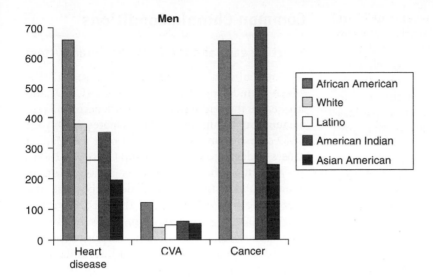

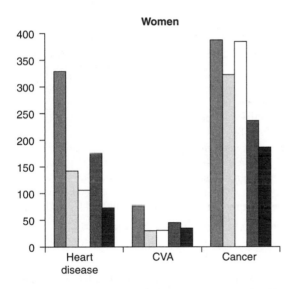

FIGURE 4.4   **Death Rates for Selected Diseases at Age 55 to 64 (per 100,000)**
SOURCE: NCHS, 2003b.

of education can expect 13.4 years of unhealthy life versus 9.0 for those with 13 or more years of education. Comparable patterns for white men have been reported: 14.1 versus 10.0 years. Thus, education benefits people into old age, especially women, by enhancing their awareness of and access to preventive health services (Crimmins and Saito, 2001).

Men have higher rates of heart disease and cancer than women. In fact, gender differences in mortality are due mainly to the greater incidence of the principal fatal chronic diseases among men. However, women experience more nonfatal chronic conditions, including arthritis, incontinence, osteoarthritis, osteoporosis, and cataracts, than do men. These diseases are less likely to result in death than cancer and heart disease, but they may lead to nearly as many days spent in bed. In other words, older women are more likely to be bothered by chronic conditions, many of which can cause functional disability and impair their quality of life and daily interactions. However, they are less likely to die of such chronic conditions than are older men.

When examining rates of chronic diseases among low-income and ethnic minority elders, a life course perspective highlights the interplay among generational influences and economic and health inequalities. For example, in both developing and developed countries, chronic diseases are linked to poor health and lower levels of quality of life. Poor people of all ages face an increased risk of health problems and disabilities. Although the likelihood of chronic illness increases with age, research increasingly shows that the origins of risk for chronic health conditions begin in early childhood or earlier (World Health Organization, 2002). Available research demonstrates the intergenerational transmission of specific health-risk behaviors and lifestyles, including eating behaviors, depression, and family functioning (Baker, Whisman, and Brownell, 2000; Jacob and Johnson, 2001; Lawson and Brossart, 2001). Furthermore, risk continues to be influenced by factors such as socioeconomic status and experiences across the life course. For example, childhood conditions explain a substantial portion of the difference in men's mortality by race, operating indirectly through adult socioeconomic achievement (Warner and Hayward, 2002). Alternatively, increases in socioeconomic status are related to people living longer and healthier lives (Lynch et al., 2000; Whitfield and Hayward, 2003). Thus, any analysis of chronic conditions in old age needs to consider the role of racial, gender, and socioeconomic inequities across the life course. We turn next to describing more fully the most common chronic illnesses in old age.

Common Chronic Conditions

Heart Disease and the Cardiovascular System

As noted above, cardiovascular diseases (CVD), which include coronary heart disease (CHD) and stroke, are the leading cause of death across all ethnic minority groups in the United States. Each year, CVD claims as many lives as the next five leading causes of death combined (Ai and Carrigan, 2006).

Coronary heart disease is a condition in which blood to the heart is deficient because of a narrowing or constricting of the cardiac vessels that supply it. This narrowing may be due to atherosclerosis,* in which fatty deposits (plaque formation) begin early in life and accumulate to reduce the size of the passageway of the large arteries. People in industrialized nations have

---

HEART DISEASE AS A CHRONIC CONDITION

The dramatic decline in deaths due to heart attacks and strokes in the United States became front-page news in the *New York Times* in 2003: "The stereotypical heart attack patient is no longer a man in his 50s who suddenly falls dead. Instead, the typical patient is a man or woman of 70 or older who survives." The article addressed the growing challenge of maintaining heart attack survivors who must cope with chronic heart disease, including congestive heart failure that can impair functional health.

SOURCE: *New York Times,* January 19, 2003, pp. 1, 16.

---

*The terms **atherosclerosis** and **arteriosclerosis** are often used interchangeably, causing confusion regarding their distinction. Arteriosclerosis, a generic term, sometimes called hardening of the arteries, refers to the loss of elasticity of the arterial walls. This condition occurs in all populations, and can contribute to reduced blood flow to an area. In atherosclerosis, the passageway of the large arteries narrows as a result of the development of plaques on their interior walls; atherosclerosis has been found to be age-related and of higher incidence in industrialized populations. Arteriosclerosis and atherosclerosis can be superimposed, but there is not a causative relationship between the degree of atherosclerosis and the loss of elasticity (arteriosclerosis).

HEALTH AND BEHAVIORAL FACTORS THAT INCREASE THE RISK OF ATHEROSCLEROSIS

- hypertension or high blood pressure
- elevated blood lipids (resulting from a dietary intake of animal products high in cholesterol)
- cigarette smoking
- diabetes mellitus
- obesity
- inactivity
- stress
- family history of heart attack

---

higher levels of atherosclerosis than those in developing countries, which may be due to differences in diet and lifestyle. However, this pattern is shifting with globalization, with the incidence of cardiovascular disease higher in India and China than in all developed countries combined (American Heart Association, 2003).

As the reduced blood flow caused by atherosclerosis becomes significant, angina pectoris may result. The symptoms of angina are shortness of breath and pain from beneath the breastbone, in the neck, and down the left arm. For older individuals, these symptoms may be absent or may be confused with signs of other disorders, such as indigestion or gallbladder diseases. In such instances, elders may delay seeking timely medical care. Treatment includes rest and nitroglycerine, which serves to dilate the blood vessels.

If deficient blood supply to the heart persists, heart tissue will die, producing a dead area known as an *infarct*. In other words, coronary artery disease can lead to a myocardial infarction (MI), or heart attack. The average age of a person experiencing a heart attack is 65.8 for men, 70.4 for women. After suffering an MI, 25 percent of men and 38 percent of women will die within a year. Black elders are more likely to die of heart disease than their white counterparts, a difference that is increasing. Among survivors, nearly 22 percent of men and 46 percent of women will be disabled within six years (American Heart Association,

2005). Accordingly, about 50 percent of older adults with heart disease report limitations in their ADLs, compared with 26 percent of their age peers who do not have this condition.

Acute myocardial infarction results from blockage of an artery supplying blood to a portion of the heart muscle. The extent of heart tissue involved determines the severity of the episode. Heart attacks may be more difficult to diagnose in older people, since their symptoms are often different from those in younger victims. These include:

- a generalized state of weakness
- dizziness
- confusion
- shortness of breath

These are different from the chest and back pain or numbness in the arms that characterizes heart attacks in younger people. Symptoms in older people may also merge with other problems, so that a heart attack may not be reported or treated until it is too late for effective help. Although women are far less likely to have heart attacks than men prior to menopause, their rates increase after age 65, and the gap between men and women narrows with advancing age.

The term *congestive heart failure*, or heart failure, indicates a set of symptoms related to the impaired pumping performance of the heart, so that one or more chambers of the heart do not empty adequately during the heart's contractions. Heart failure does not mean that the heart has stopped beating. But decreased pumping efficiency results in shortness of breath, reduced blood flow to vital body parts (including the kidneys), and a greater volume of blood accumulating in the body tissues, causing edema (swelling). Treatment involves drugs, dietary modifications (e.g., salt reduction), and rest. Depression is a common complication of coronary heart disease, and can affect the outcomes of cardiac surgery; this points to the importance of health care providers also treating depression (Ai and Carrigan, 2006).

PREVENTIVE MEASURES TO REDUCE CARDIOVASCULAR RISK

- weight control
- daily physical activity
- treatment of diabetes
- reduce intake of salt, saturated fat, processed carbohydrates
- increase intake of fruits and vegetables (rich in magnesium),
- fruits rich in potassium (e.g., bananas, oranges),
- foods high in calcium
- replacement of animal fat with olive oil
- avoidance of partially hydrogenated oils
- avoidance of cigarette smoking
- avoidance of excessive alcohol intake

Most cardiovascular problems are treatable and preventable through diet, exercise, and medications. As will be noted in our discussion of many chronic diseases, preventive steps are most important. For example, *hypertension,* or high blood pressure (defined as levels higher than 140 mm Hg for systolic or 90 mm Hg for diastolic pressure) is the major risk factor in the development of cardiovascular complications and can be prevented, as illustrated in the box above. As shown in Figure 4.3, the risk of hypertension is greater for women than men after age 65 (Federal Interagency Forum, 2006). This may partially explain why the incidence of coronary heart disease and strokes increases with age among women, although women with these conditions, on average, live longer than men. Older adults with hypertension, high cholesterol, and who are obese (body mass index greater than 30) are at greatest risk of coronary heart disease and stroke (NCHS, 2005). These modifiable lifestyle risk factors are more common among low-income individuals.

The prevalence of hypertension is significantly higher among older African Americans than whites (66 percent vs. 48.5 percent, respectively), but whether this difference is due to lifestyle or genetic factors is unclear. Significant increases in blood pressure should never be considered normal. For example, in some isolated primitive populations, a rise in blood pressure with age does not occur. Although genetic factors may come into play, this difference suggests that lifestyle can affect vulnerability to high blood pressure. Poverty is one risk factor associated with this condition; 50 percent of older adults with private insurance are hypertensive, compared with 63 percent who are on Medicaid (Merck Institute, 2004; Schoenborn et al., 2006).

Most people can control their hypertension by improving health habits, although some must also use antihypertensive medications. Older adults who have been prescribed an antihypertensive must continue using it consistently and correctly. Because hypertension is not easily recognized by laypersons, they may stop taking their medications if symptoms such as dizziness and headaches disappear. Some older adults discontinue their antihypertensive medications because they cannot afford the cost. This can lead to significant elevations in blood pressure, as well as a stroke or aneurysm.

Another cardiovascular problem, which is less frequently addressed than hypertension, is *hypotension,* or low blood pressure. Yet hypotension, characterized by dizziness and faintness from exertion after a period of inactivity and frequently related to anemia, is actually very common among older adults. Problems with

COMMONLY PRESCRIBED CLASSES OF MEDICATIONS TO CONTROL HYPERTENSION

- *diuretics* (also known as "water pills"),which reduce excess water
- *beta blockers,* which reduce heart rate
- *ACE inhibitors,* which block an enzyme that constricts blood vessels
- *calcium channel blockers,* which work by preventing calcium from causing muscle contractions in the heart and inside blood vessels

hypotension may be more pronounced after sitting or lying down (postural hypotension) or suddenly standing, after which a person may appear to lose balance and sway. Hypotension is not in itself dangerous, but can increase the risk of falls. Older people who have a history of low blood pressure or who are taking some types of antihypertensive medications need to change positions carefully.

Strokes and Other Cerebrovascular Problems

We have seen how heart tissue can be denied adequate nourishment because of changes in the blood vessels that supply it. Similarly, arteriosclerotic and atherosclerotic changes in blood vessels that serve the brain can reduce its nourishment and result in the disruption of blood flow to brain tissue and malfunction or death of brain cells. This impaired brain tissue circulation is called *cerebrovascular disease*. When a portion of the brain is completely denied blood, a cerebrovascular accident (CVA), or stroke, occurs. The severity of the stroke depends on the particular areas as well as the total amount of brain tissue involved. Many older adults who have heart problems also are at risk for cerebrovascular disease.

CVAs represent the fourth leading cause of death following accidents. Of the 200,000 deaths from strokes each year, 80 percent occur among persons age 65 and over. African American elders and men in general are at greater risk of experiencing a stroke than whites or other ethnic minority groups. The incidence of a stroke in 2000 was 11.8 percent for African Americans versus 7.9 percent for non-Hispanic whites and 7.5 percent for Latinos (NCHS, 2005). The rate of CVA incidents increases with age. The young-old stroke victim is twice as likely as the oldest-old to be discharged to home after recovery (63 percent and 32 percent, respectively). Conversely, the oldest-old stroke victim is twice as likely to die as the young-old (12.5 percent and 6.4 percent, respectively) (CDC, 2003a).

Atherosclerotic changes, in which fatty deposits gradually obstruct an artery in the brain or neck, are a common underlying condition. The most frequent cause of strokes in older persons is a *cerebral thrombosis,* a blood clot that either diminishes or closes off the blood flow in an artery of the brain or neck. Another cause of stroke is cerebral hemorrhage, in which a weak spot in a blood vessel of the brain bursts. This is less common in older adults, although more likely to cause death when it does occur. The risk of stroke appears to be related to social and personal factors, most prominently hypertension, but also:

- age
- previous lifestyle
- diet
- exercise patterns
- socioeconomic status
- access to and utilization of health care

Regular sustained exercise and low-fat diets are associated with the reduction of fatty particles that clog the bloodstream. The use of such over-the-counter drugs as aspirin and warfarin in preventing blood clots also reduces the risk of strokes. Indeed, the death rate from strokes has dropped by 40 percent in the last 20 years, especially among the older population, because of these preventive measures and improved and immediate treatment. The area of the brain that is damaged by a stroke dictates which body functions may be affected. These include:

- *aphasia,* or inability of the stroke victim to speak or understand speech if the speech center of the brain dies
- *hemiplegia,* or paralysis of one side of the body
- *heminanopsia,* or blindness in half of the victim's visual field

The treatment for stroke is similar to that for heart attack and hypertension: modulated activity and supervised schedules of exercise and drugs, along with interventions to address depression. The FDA has approved new drugs to dissolve blood clots within three hours of the stroke. However, many victims do not receive this treatment because it generally takes longer than three hours to reach a diagnosis of the stroke and the location of the clot. An alternative method is to deliver the clot-dissolving drug directly with a long, fine tube through the artery; this can be effective within 6 hours after symptoms begin. These newer techniques offer great hope for patients and their families, but do not entirely prevent the neurological losses caused by a stroke.

Stroke survivors often require physical, occupational, and speech therapy, and their recovery process can be slow, frustrating, and emotionally draining for the patient and family. It is important to assess carefully the effects of a stroke and determine what functions can be retrained. Newer, more aggressive and immediate rehabilitation methods are effective in reducing the rates of residual impairments following a stroke. Within a year, about 50 percent have regained most of their motor function, but many people report residual nonmotor impairments such as problems with vision, speech, cognitive abilities, memory and balance that can result in placement in a long-term care facility (Gubrium et al., 2003; Kugler et al., 2003; Mauk, 2006).

Rehabilitation must address not only physical conditions, but also mental health issues such as depression, anxiety, and the psychosocial needs for support and respite of stroke patients and their family caregivers. The recognition of this wider range of rehabilitation has led to the creation of stroke support groups and Internet sites for both the survivor and family members.

Cancer

Because older people are more likely to have cancer than other age groups, cancer is often classified as a disease of older adults (Marimaldi and Lee, 2006). Among those 65 and over, about 25 percent of deaths are due to cancer, especially cancers of the lungs, breast, colon, and pancreas. In fact, these malignancies in old age are the leading cause of death among women age 65 to 74, and roughly equal to heart disease among men. Fifty percent of all cancer occurs and is diagnosed after age 65. On the other hand, the incidence of cancer decreases among those who reach age 90 (Masoro, 2006). In 2001, 3.5 percent of the adult population were survivors of cancer; among these, 14 percent had survived for 20 years or longer. For those who survive into old age, cancer takes on the dimensions of a chronic disease rather than a life-threatening one (National Cancer Institute, 2005).

Breast cancer is the most common malignancy in women age 65 and over, as is prostate cancer among older men. Lung cancer has its highest incidence in men age 65 and over, but appears to be associated more with smoking than with age. Cancer of the colon is more common in women, whereas colorectal cancer is more frequent in men. Breast cancer is the second leading cause of cancer death in women age 65 and older, who account for as much as 67 percent of breast cancer mortality (Ershler, 2003). Both the incidence and mortality rates due to cervical and breast cancer are greater in older African American women than in older white women, primarily because of lower use of cancer screening services (SEER, 2004). However, when screenings are done regularly and the time between screening and diagnosis is minimized, both groups experience a similarly favorable prognosis (American Cancer Society, 2001; Dignam, 2000; Woolam, 2000). The greater risk of cancer with age may be due to a number of factors:

- the effects of a slow-acting carcinogen
- prolonged development time necessary for growth to be observable
- extended pre-exposure time
- failing immune capacity that is characteristic of increased age
- an accumulation of senescent cells with aging (Campisi, 2005)

Some cancers that have a high prevalence in the middle years and again in old age may have a different etiology. For example, breast cancer in premenopausal women appears to have a genetic basis and is related to family history, while that in postmenopausal women may have external or environmental causes. Certain dietary and lifestyle factors along with socioeconomic status and where one lives may also be related to cancer in older people. Diagnosing cancer in old age is often more difficult than at earlier life stages, because of the existence of other chronic diseases and because symptoms of cancer, such as weight loss, weakness, or fatigue, may be inaccurately attributed to aging, depression, or dementia. In addition, the current older generation's fear of cancer may be so great that they do not seek medical help to address their suspicions and fears. Nevertheless, many older adults today are cancer survivors and report cancer as a chronic rather than a life-threatening condition. Because of ethnic differences in screening and early diagnosis, described previously, cancer is more likely to be a chronic disease in whites age 70 and older (21 percent) than among Latinos (10.5 percent) and African Americans (9.1 percent) (Merck Institute, 2004). Although future cohorts are more likely to participate in cancer screening as well as preventive measures, the numbers of people with cancer will continue to increase simply because of the higher incidence of cancer among the rapidly growing population of older adults (Marimaldi and Lee, 2006).

Arthritis

Although not a leading cause of death, arthritis is the second most common chronic condition affecting older people after hypertension, and is a major cause of limited activity. In fact, 50 percent of those over age 65 and 58 percent over 70 report this problem (Federal Interagency Forum, 2006). Because arthritis is so common and the symptoms are so closely identified with the normal aging process, older people may accept arthritis as inevitable. If so, they may fail to seek treatment or to learn strategies to reduce pain and support their autonomous functioning. Although many treatments are used to control arthritic symptoms, little is known about ways to postpone or eliminate these disorders.

Arthritis is not a single entity, but includes over 100 different conditions of inflammations and degenerative changes of bones and joints. **Rheumatoid arthritis,** a chronic inflammation of the membranes lining joints and tendons, is characterized by pain, swelling, bone dislocation, and limited range of motion. It afflicts two to three times more women than men and can cause severe crippling. Rheumatoid arthritis is not associated with aging per se; many young people also have this condition, with initial symptoms most commonly appearing between 20 and 50 years of age.

Rheumatoid arthritis is characterized by acute episodes followed by periods of relative inactivity. Its cause is unknown; treatment includes a combination of rest, exercise, and use of aspirin, which provides relief from pain, fever, and inflammation. Use of other antiinflammatory agents, antimalarials, and corticosteroids, as well as surgical procedures to repair joints and correct various deformities, are effective for some people. There are extensive new developments in drug therapy for rheumatoid arthritis.

Osteoarthritis, which is presumed to be a universal corollary of aging, is a gradual degeneration of the joints that are most subject to stress—those of the hands, knees, hips, and shoulders. Pain

---

SYMPTOMS OF RHEUMATOID ARTHRITIS

- malaise
- fatigue
- loss of weight
- fever
- joint pain
- redness
- swelling
- stiffness affecting many joints

THERAPIES FOR OSTEOARTHRITIS

- antiinflammatory drugs
- steroids
- regular exercise
- heat and cold
- reduction of strain on weight-bearing joints through weight loss and the use of weight-bearing appliances
- surgical procedures that restore function to the hips and knees

and disfigurement in the fingers are manifestations of osteoarthritis, but are generally not disabling. Osteoarthritis of the lower limbs, however, can limit mobility, reduce social activities, and increase the need for long-term care. Heredity as well as environmental or lifestyle factors are identified as causes of osteoarthritis, particularly:

- obesity
- occupational stresses
- wear and tear on the joints

Some progress has been made in minimizing inflammation and pain through the use of several types of therapy. A natural supplement (chondroitin sulfate, or CS) is effective in managing the pain associated with osteoarthritis without significant side effects (Leeb et al., 2000). Unfortunately, however, none of these techniques can reverse or cure the disease.

An estimated 50 percent of adults age 70 and older who have arthritis need help with ADLs, compared with 23 percent of their peers without arthritis. Not surprisingly, the former group uses health services (physicians, hospitals, medications, physical therapy, and nursing homes) and social services at a higher rate than the latter. Even though African Americans experience more limitations in activity, they are less likely to use medical services and physical or occupational therapy (Mikuls et al., 2003). Because of the constant pain and discomfort experienced by elders with arthritis, it is highly associated with

self-reports of poor health. To illustrate, correlates of poor subjective health among people in their 60s include:

- arthritis
- poor vision
- few social resources

Among people in their 80s, subjective reports of poor health are associated with:

- arthritis
- heart disease
- low education
- poor mental health (Quinn et al., 1999)

It is noteworthy that arthritis is the only variable that appears as an important component of subjective health for both age groups.

The prime danger for people with arthritis is reducing their physical activity in response to pain. The adage "use it or lose it" has special meaning to a person with arthritis. Movement stimulates the secretion of synovial fluid, the substance that lubricates the surfaces between joints and increases blood flow to joint areas. Movement also tones the muscles that hold joints in place and that shield joints from excessive stress. When someone tries to avoid pain by sitting still as much as possible, the losses in lubricating fluid and muscular protection make movement even more painful. Eventually, the muscles surrounding immobilized areas lose their flexibility, and affected joints freeze into rigid positions called *contractures*. For these reasons, older people need to be encouraged to maintain physical activity in spite of pain. Researchers who tested a 6-month physical activity program for older adults with osteoarthritis in the knee and hip joints demonstrated significant improvements in lower extremity stiffness, pain, and walking speed (Hughes et al., 2004). Tai Chi, aerobics, and resistance training and fitness walking all show promise in decreasing the pain and stiffness associated with arthritis (Gallagher, 2003; Hughes et al., 2004).

The pervasive and unpredictable nature of the pain of arthritis can also result in social isolation and depression. A program to teach African American elders about managing their arthritis pain resulted in fewer symptoms of depression up to two years later than in elders who received no training (Phillips, 2000). Conversely, treating depression can reduce symptoms associated with arthritis. In a study testing antidepressant medications and psychotherapy with depressed older adults, 56 percent reported arthritis as a coexisting medical condition. Elders in the treatment group experienced a significant reduction in pain intensity and interference with ADLs due to arthritis, compared with those not receiving any treatment. They also gave higher subjective ratings of health and quality of life. These indirect benefits of treating depression illustrate the importance of psychological factors in a systemic condition like arthritis (Lin et al., 2003).

Congruent with the person–environment perspective and the concept of active aging, the environment may need to be restructured, so that a person with arthritis is able to walk around and keep up with daily activities, but is not burdened by extreme press or demands. For example, a smaller home on one level can reduce environmental press. Despite the relatively low cost of physically modifying private homes, this is not widely done. A national survey revealed that only 17 percent of women and 12 percent of men age 70 and older have installed railings; 13 percent and 11 percent, respectively, have installed ramps in their homes. Even the most frequently reported home modification—bathroom bars and shower seats—were made by only 43 percent of women and 36 percent of men (National Academy, 2000a). Families and health care providers can be instrumental in recommending such modifications and helping elders locate programs, such as minor home repair, to reduce their cost.

Osteoporosis

The human body is constantly forming and losing bone through the metabolism of calcium. As noted in Chapter 3, osteoporosis involves a more dramatic loss in bone mass. The increased brittleness of the bones associated with this condition can result in diminished height, slumped posture, backache, and a reduction in the structural strength of bones, making them susceptible to fracture. Compressed or collapsed vertebrae are the major cause of *kyphosis,* or "dowager's hump," the stooped look that many of us associate with aging.

Osteoporosis, together with its less serious counterpart, **osteopenia** (a significant loss of calcium and reduced bone density but without the risk of fractures), affect about 25 million Americans, 80 percent of whom are women. Caucasian and Asian American women are more

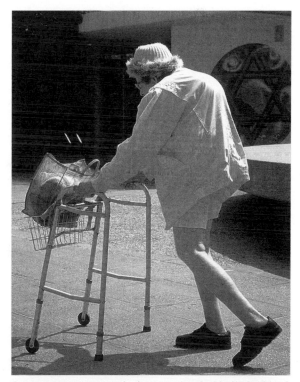

Even severe osteoporosis does not inevitably limit elders' independence.

likely to develop it than African American women; estimates are that 20 percent of white and Asian women age 50 and older have this condition, compared with 5 percent of African American and 10 percent of Latina women (NIA, 2001). The causes of osteoporosis are unclear, although risk factors include:

- small stature and low body weight
- loss of calcium and estrogen in menopausal women
- a sedentary lifestyle
- cigarette smoking
- excessive alcohol and caffeine consumption
- long-term dieting or fasting
- inadequate fluoride intake
- genetic factors that determine bone density
- family history of a hip fracture in a close relative (e.g., mother or sister)

The primary risk posed by osteoporosis is a fracture of the neck of the femur, or thigh. Many of the falls and associated hip fractures of old age actually represent an osteoporotic femoral neck that broke from bearing weight, causing the individual to fall. Osteoporosis results in 1.5 million fractures per year; one in two women will have an osteoporosis-related fracture in their lifetime. Some 20 percent of white women experience fractures by age 65, increasing to more than 30 percent by age 90. Although both men and women lose bone mass with aging, men rarely develop symptomatic osteoporosis before age 70. White men are far less likely than white women to experience hip fractures; African American men and women have even lower rates of fractures than white men. Increases in life expectancy are expected to double the number of hip fractures within the next 50 years.

The most common sites of fractures are:

- 47 percent vertebrae
- 20 percent hip
- 17 percent wrist
- 16 percent other sites (NIH, 2003).

Many older people have undiagnosed osteoporosis, often showing no symptoms until a fall or fracture occurs. Typically, no immediate precipitating event can be identified as the cause of the fracture.

Hip fractures are of great concern because of their impact on morbidity and mortality; about 24 percent of elders die within a year after a hip fracture (NIH, 2003). Even when death does not occur after a hip fracture, falls that result in hip fractures can cause long-term disability and are responsible for more days of restricted activity than any other health problem. Six months after a hip fracture, only about 15 percent of older people can walk across a room on their own (NIH, 2003). The costs to society are also high because of hospitalizations and long-term care.

Not all falls and fractures among older people result from osteoporosis, however. Cardiovascular disease underlies approximately 50 percent of them. Others are due to a decline in postural control, produced by impairments of the senses and the central nervous system, changes previously discussed in Chapter 3. Table 4.1 lists some of these risk factors.

PREVENTING OSTEOPOROSIS: THE CASE FOR AND AGAINST ESTROGEN Osteoporosis starts well before old age, perhaps as young as age 35. In the years immediately following menopause, the rate of bone loss can be as high as 5 percent, compared to a normal rate of 1 or 2 percent. Reduced estrogen—not calcium—is the primary cause of bone loss in the first 5 years after menopause. The goal in treating osteoporosis is to prevent further bone loss. Hormone replacement therapy (HRT), combining estrogen with progestin, or using estrogen alone (ERT), had been used for many years to prevent osteoporosis and bone fractures. This was because both HRT and ERT can decrease the risk of hip fractures and of spinal crush fractures. Since estrogen blocks the process of bone reabsorption, it can help the bones absorb dietary calcium and

TABLE 4.1   Risk Factors for Falls

RISK FACTOR	RELATIVE RISK**	
	FOR WOMEN	FOR MEN
Body mass index* less than 23.1 (i.e., a thin frame)	2.0	1.5
Daily alcohol consumption per day greater than 27 grams	2.9	1.9
No load-bearing exercise	2.0	3.4
No vigorous exercise in young adulthood	7.2	2.4
Two or more falls in past 12 months	3.0	3.4
History of stroke	3.8	3.6
Cigarette smoker (current or past)	1.5	not tested
Regularly uses sedatives	2.5	3.0
Regularly uses thyroid drugs	7.1	11.8

*Body mass index (BMI) is calculated by dividing weight (in kilograms) by height (in meters) squared: kg/m^2. To calculate your own BMI, check the Website: www.nhlbi.nih.gov/guidelines/obesity/bmi_tbl.htm.

**Increased risk relative to elders without these conditions

SOURCE: Lau et al., 2001.

thereby increase bone mineral density (BMD) 3 to 5 percent. However, the effects may not be permanent, and benefits may be lost after discontinuing HRT.

Findings from the Women's Health Initiative (WHI) raised serious questions about the benefits versus risks of HRT, and resulted in fewer women using HRT. As part of this large (more than 100,000 women age 65 and older) national randomized controlled trial of exercise, diet, and HRT for preventing osteoporosis, heart disease, and cancer, one arm of the study tested the effects of a combined estrogen with progesterone intervention (HRT) against a

A SUMMARY OF PREVENTIVE STRATEGIES AGAINST OSTEOPOROSIS

- increased intake of calcium daily
- increased intake of vitamin D
- moderate weight-bearing exercise such as vigorous walking and strength training
- possibly fluoride
- possibly natural estrogens (phytoestrogens)

placebo pill. Women enrolled in this arm did not know which drug they were using. Although the study was designed to measure health outcomes after 8.5 years of HRT or placebo use, it was stopped in 2002 after 5.6 years. This was because the research team found no benefits of HRT on their primary outcomes, and in fact showed that HRT had several adverse effects. The relative risk of coronary heart disease, breast cancer, and stroke was *higher* among women in the HRT group compared to those in the placebo condition, although this translated to a slightly higher absolute risk (i.e., number of women who actually developed these conditions). It should be noted that women using HRT were at much *lower* relative risk of developing colorectal cancer and hip fractures. In fact, their total bone and mineral density in the hip increased by 3.7 percent. These relative and absolute risks are shown in Table 4.2 (Cauley et al., 2003; WHI, 2002).

On the basis of these unexpected findings, the WHI researchers do not recommend using HRT to prevent chronic diseases, especially coronary heart disease. In early 2004, the WHI

TABLE 4.2   Risks and Benefits of Combined Estrogen Plus Progestin for Some Diseases

COMPARED TO PLACEBO	RELATIVE RISK	ABSOLUTE RISK
Blood clot	111% increase	18 more cases per 10,000 women
Stroke	41% increase	8 more cases
Heart attack	29% increase	7 more cases
Breast cancer	26% increase	8 more cases
Colorectal cancer	37% *decrease*	6 fewer cases
Hip fractures	33% *decrease*	5 fewer cases

SOURCE: WHI, 2002.

director instructed all participants in the estrogen-only arm of this clinical trial (ERT) to stop using their pills as well. After 6.8 years, women using estrogen had a higher incidence of strokes than women on a placebo (12 more per 10,000). No differences were found in heart disease incidence, or in breast or colorectal cancers. However, ERT did reduce the risk of hip fractures by 6 cases per 10,000 (WHI, 2003). Women coping with menopausal symptoms and attempting to prevent osteoporosis need to weigh the risks and benefits of HRT and ERT for their own health profile. Table 4.3 summarizes these findings.

As a result of these warnings, more women and health care providers are turning to non-hormonal or natural remedies during menopause, such as soy or red clover iofavone extracts, antidepressants, and other prescription drugs. However, a recent analysis of several clinical trials found that none of the non-hormonal therapies used to relieve vasomotor symptoms of menopause (e.g. hot flashes) were as effective as estrogen or progesterone. The researchers concluded that the lowest effective dose of hormones should be used by women with these menopausal symptoms (Nelson et al., 2006).

For women who cannot or choose not to use ERT or HRT, and because of their potential risks, new drugs, such as Fosamax, are approved by the Food and Drug Administration (FDA). Some of these can slow the rate of bone loss and

TABLE 4.3   Risks and Benefits of HRT

ADVANTAGES	DISADVANTAGES
Combined HRT	**Combined HRT**
• can reduce risk of osteoporosis and hip fractures	• can increase risk of blood clots
• can increase bone mineral density	• can increase heart attack and stroke risk
• can relieve hot flashes and night sweats	• can increase risk of breast cancer
• can relieve vaginal dryness	• may contribute to gallbladder disease (pill form only)
• can improve cholesterol levels	
• can reduce risk of colon cancer	
Estrogen Only	**Estrogen Only**
• can reduce risk of hip fractures	• can increase risk of strokes

SOURCES: NIA, 2001; WHI, 2002.

prevent vertebral fractures. However, none of these medications eliminates the need for increased intake of calcium and vitamin D among older women. Combinations of fluoride and calcium treatments are sometimes given, but may have negative side effects of gastrointestinal and rheumatic complaints. Researchers are also testing the effectiveness of phytoestrogenic or "natural" estrogens that are found in some foods such as wild yams.

Scientists are working on new forms of estrogen that will have the benefits of current forms without the risks. These "designer estrogens," or selective estrogen receptor modulators, appear to improve bone density and reduce levels of low density lipoprotein (LDL) (bad) cholesterol while increasing the levels of high density lipoprotein (HDL) (good) cholesterol, but do not have the adverse effects associated with HRT. Other researchers are exploring the effects of parathyroid hormone on advanced osteoporosis.

CALCIUM AND EXERCISE TO PREVENT OSTEOPOROSIS

Certain dietary and exercise habits may help prevent osteoporosis, especially increasing the amount of one's calcium intake after age 50. The National Institute on Aging (2001) recommends that women over age 50 consume between 1200 and 1500 mg of calcium daily. This is higher than what was previously recommended; 1500 mg of calcium is equivalent to five 8-ounce glasses of milk daily, far more than most women are accustomed to consuming. In fact, some studies have recommended doses as high as 2000 mg/day in older postmenopausal women. Given the difficulty of obtaining this much calcium from dietary sources, supplements may be the most effective way to increase calcium levels. Despite concerns about side effects related to high intake, such as kidney stones, there is little evidence that such supplementation harms older women (Chiu, 1999).

Calcium is absorbed better when combined with vitamin D. For this reason, milk in the United States is fortified with vitamin D. Unfortunately, many older women do not consume enough milk or milk products to obtain vitamin D in that manner. It is also produced by the human body after 15 to 20 minutes of exposure to sunlight each day, but many older women avoid the sun or are unable to get outside every day, especially in the winter. Older women who do not obtain an adequate intake of fortified milk or exposure to sunshine should take daily multivitamins with at least 400 international units (IUs) of vitamin D (600 IUs for those over age 70) (NIA, 2001). The WHI, described above, demonstrated that regular intake of a calcium and vitamin D supplement (at least four days per week) can reduce hip fractures by 29 percent (WHI, 2003).

Although increased calcium appears to be an important preventive measure, low dietary calcium may be only partly responsible for osteoporosis. Therefore, increasing calcium intake may not prevent fracturing after bone loss has occurred. One reason is that an estimated 40 percent of osteoporotic women have a deficiency of the enzyme that is needed to metabolize calcium (lactose), thus making it difficult for them to absorb calcium. An additional problem is that once one fracture is present, an individual has a 70 to 80 percent chance of developing another.

A combination of calcium and exercise (both aerobic and weight-bearing) appears to prevent bone loss. Researchers found that simple, vigorous walking on a daily basis for one year prevents bone loss in older women with osteopenia and osteoporosis. However, they concluded that this daily exercise program must continue longer to improve bone mineral density (BMD) levels (Yamazaki et al., 2004). On the other hand, new forms of exercise are found to increase BMD in the hip after just eight months (Gusi, Raimundo, and Leal, 2006). Other researchers have compared the BMD of postmenopausal women who have been running regularly (at least 5 years, more than 10 miles per week) in conjunction with hormone replacement therapy or without. Bone mass does not seem to be protected with exercise alone, but in this study the combination of HRT and running increased total BMD and BMD in the spine. However, this combination did not significantly improve hip BMD, which is the critical issue for preventing hip fractures (Hawkins et al., 1999).

Because of the increased attention to osteoporosis today, many entrepreneurial clinics are offering bone-density testing to postmenopausal women. These small, portable machines generally test bone density only at the wrist or ankle. This makes them less reliable and accurate than the large whole-body machines known as DEXA. Tests with portable machines show the obvious results; that most women over 50 have less bone mass than younger women. A major limitation is that such tests do not provide a comparison with any baseline data for a specific individual. Women should have a comprehensive baseline bone density test before they undergo menopause, and then be retested when they are in their 60s, 70s, and 80s. In fact, a committee of osteoporosis experts, convened by the U.S. Preventive Services Task Force in 2002, concluded that bone density testing should be targeted. DEXA testing should be done at the hip where many fractures occur, and primarily for women 65 and older, as well as women over 60 who weigh less than 127 pounds. These recommendations and other preventive suggestions can be found at http://www.ahrq.gov/clinic/uspstfix.htm.

Chronic Obstructive Pulmonary Disease or Respiratory Problems

Chronic bronchitis, fibrosis, asthma, and emphysema are manifestations of chronic obstructive pulmonary diseases (COPD) that damage lung tissue. They increase with age, develop slowly and insidiously, and are progressive and debilitating, often resulting in frequent hospitalizations, major

lifestyle changes, and death. In fact, by age 90, most people are likely to have some signs of emphysema, with shortness of breath and prolonged and difficult exhalation. Getting through daily activities can be extremely exhausting under such conditions. Causes of COPD are both genetic and environmental, especially prolonged exposure to various dusts, fumes, or cigarette smoke. Three to four times as many men as women have these diseases, probably due to a combination of normal age changes in the lung and a greater likelihood of smoking and exposure to airborne pollutants. This is especially true in older cohorts; men in the oldest-old group are three times more likely to die of COPD than their female counterparts. This pattern may shift over time with more women exposed to pollutants. Treatment is usually continuous, and includes:

- drugs
- respiratory therapy
- breathing exercises to compensate for damage
- avoidance of respiratory infections, smoking, pollution, and other irritants

Allergic reactions to bacterial products, drugs, pollutants and even foods increase with age. The greater incidence of drug allergies may be a function of decreases in physiological capacities and the increased use of many drugs, such as sedatives, tranquilizers, antidepressants, and antibiotics.

Diabetes

Compared with other systems of the body, the endocrine glands do not show consistent and predictable age-related changes, other than the gradual slowing of functioning. However, insufficient insulin, produced and secreted by the pancreas, can lead to **diabetes mellitus.** Diabetes mellitus is characterized by hyperglycemia or above-normal amounts of glucose (sugar) in the blood and urine, resulting from an inability to use carbohydrates. Diabetics may go into a coma

SYMPTOMS OF DIABETES

- excessive thirst
- increased appetite
- increased urination
- fatigue
- weakness
- loss of weight
- slower wound healing
- blurred vision
- irritability

when their blood glucose levels get very high. Low blood glucose (hypoglycemia) can also lead to unconsciousness. Older diabetics include people who:

- have had the disease since youth or juvenile onset diabetes (Type I);
- develop it in middle age (adult onset diabetes), most often between 40 and 50, and incur related cardiovascular problems (Type II)
- develop it late in life and generally show mild pathologic conditions (Type II)

Type II diabetes is most common in older adults, accounting for 90 to 95 percent of all diagnosed cases, and can generally be managed without insulin through careful diet and strict exercise regimen (American Diabetes Association, 2003). Although diabetes can occur at any age, diabetic problems related to the body's lessened capability to metabolize carbohydrates can be particularly severe in older adults. Older age, obesity, and ethnic minority status are among the most significant risk factors for Type II diabetes (ADA, 2004). Obesity is a primary risk due to changes in fat/muscle ratio and slower metabolism with aging. This is especially the case among older African American, American Indian, and Latina women, who have a higher rate of obesity and diabetes than do older white women. On average, African Americans, Latinos and American Indians are 1.6, 1.5, and 2.2 times more likely, respectively,

to have diabetes than non-Hispanic whites, 14 percent of whom have this condition (CDC, 2003d; OMHRC, 2006; Schoenborn et al., 2006). Glucose tolerance and the action of insulin are often compromised by poor diet, physical inactivity, and coexistent diseases, placing the individual at greater risk of diabetes. Poorly controlled diabetes can result in kidney failure and diabetic retinopathy, a disease of the eye described in Chapter 3. These conditions are more common among African Americans with diabetes than among their white counterparts.

The prevalence of diabetes has doubled among all age groups, from just under 6 million in 1980 to 12 million in 2000. The rate of Type II diabetes increased between 1990 and 1998 from 4.9 percent to 6.5 percent (a change of 33 percent) of the U.S. adult population (Mokdad et al., 2000). The fact that the greatest increase is among 30- to 39-year-olds has disturbing implications for future cohorts of older adults. By 2050, the largest increase in diabetes prevalence (336 percent) will be among today's mid-life individuals who will then be 75 years or older. It is estimated that 4 million in this age group will have diabetes in 2050, compared with 1 million today (CDC, 2003d; Francoeur and Elkins, 2006). When rates were compared across ethnic minority groups in this middle-aged population, Latinos showed the greatest increase in diabetes prevalence, followed by whites and African Americans. The researchers attributed these increases in rates of diabetes over a 20-year period to a rise in obesity during this same interval, from 12 percent to 20 percent. This growing rate of obesity, which is associated with low income, raises concerns about health risks for future cohorts of elders.

The symptoms of diabetes shown in the box above may not be present in older people, however. Instead, diabetes among the older population is generally detected incidentally through eye examinations, hospitalization, and testing for other disorders. Older people may experience fatigue, a sign of this disease, but attribute it to a slowing down often assumed to be normal with aging. Since blood glucose may be temporarily elevated under the stress of illnesses such as stroke, myocardial infarction, or infection, people should not be labeled as diabetic unless the high glucose level persists under conditions of reduced stress.

The cumulative effect of high blood glucose levels can lead to complications in advanced stages of diabetes. These include:

- hypertension
- infections
- painful nerves in the feet, legs, and hands
- blindness
- kidney disease or failure
- stroke
- cognitive impairment
- harm to the coronary arteries
- skin problems
- poor circulation in the extremities, leading to gangrene and amputations

Comorbidity of diabetes with other age-related physical problems such as hypertension can result in serious health difficulties, limitations in functional ability, and if left undetected or untreated, can have life-threatening consequences (DeCoster, 2001). Approximately 2 out of every 3 people with diabetes die from heart disease or stroke associated with their diabetic condition (CDC, 2003d). On average, life expectancy among diabetics is 15 years less than in the population without diabetes. The shorter life expectancy for diabetics may explain the decline in prevalence for this condition across older cohorts, from 17 percent among the young-old to 11 percent of the oldest-old (ADA, 2004, Schoenborn et al., 2006). Diabetes cannot be cured, but it can generally be managed at home primarily through changes in lifestyle and health behaviors. These include:

- a diet of reduced carbohydrates and calories
- regular exercise

- proper care of feet, skin, teeth, and gums
- monitored insulin intake for those who require it

To minimize forgetfulness and treatment errors, older people, especially those who acquire diabetes late in life, may need reminders from health care providers and family members regarding:

- the importance of diet
- daily examination of their skin
- urine testing
- the correct dosage of insulin or other drugs

Problems with the Kidneys and Urinary Tract

The various diseases and disorders of the urinary system characteristic of old age tend to be either acute infections or chronic problems resulting from the gradual deterioration of the structure and function of the excretory system with age. As seen in Chapter 3, the kidneys shrink in size, and their capacity to perform basic filtration tasks declines, leading to a higher probability of disease or infection. One of the most common age-related problems for women is the inability of the bladder to empty completely. This often results in cystitis, an acute inflammatory state accompanied by pain and irritation that can generally be treated with antibiotics.

Older men face an increased risk of diseases of the prostate gland, with cancer of the prostate being the most frequent malignancy and African American men having the highest rate (SEER, 2004). After age 40 the risk doubles every decade, and the mortality rate among men age 65 and older is 100 times greater than for those under age 65 (Coleman, Hutchins and Goodwin, 2004). For these reasons, the American Cancer Society and the American Urological Association recommend annual prostate evaluations for men age 50 and older by both a digital rectal exam and a test to determine levels of prostate-specific antigen

(PSA) in the blood. Cancer of the prostate frequently spreads to the bones, but surgery is rarely recommended for men over age 70 because the disease usually progresses slowly in this age group. Instead, more conservative treatment, such as hormonal therapy, and more frequent monitoring are usually recommended. Treatment of prostate cancer and its effects on men's sexual functioning are described more fully in Chapter 7. A more common problem for older men is **benign prostatic hypertrophy,** a condition in which the prostate gland becomes enlarged and causes discomfort, but is not associated with prostate cancer.

INCONTINENCE **Incontinence,** or the inability to control urine or feces, is a chronic urinary problem that can profoundly alter an older person's social and living situations. It has been estimated to occur in at least 17 percent of men and more than 35 percent of women over age 65 and living in the community (Thom, Nygaard, and Calhoun, 2005; Stothers, Thom, and Calhoun, 2005). Because older people and their families often consider incontinence a taboo topic, they tend to be unaware of methods to treat it. Most older adults do not discuss the problem with their doctors, and only a small percentage use any protective devices, such as absorbent pads that can be purchased in drug stores. Many health care providers, in turn, do not ask their older patients about incontinence. This widespread reluctance to acknowledge incontinence as a problem can have serious psychological and social implications, constraining an elder's social life and precipitating the decision for nursing home placement. For many families, frequent incontinence is often the "breaking point" in their ability to provide in-home care. As a result, up to 10 percent of nursing home admissions are attributed to incontinence. This has significant cost and quality of life implications (Morrison and Levy, 2006). There are two primary types of incontinence:

- *urge incontinence,* where the person has a strong urge to urinate, due to irregular bladder contractions, and is unable to hold urine long enough to reach a toilet
- *stress incontinence,* where leakage occurs during physical exertion or when sneezing or coughing because of weakened pelvic floor muscles. This phenomenon can also occur among younger women.

Many cases of incontinence represent a combination of these two types, referred to as *mixed incontinence.* Incontinence sometimes results from a specific precipitating factor, such as acute illness, infection, or even a change in residence. It can be treated if the cause is known. For example, temporary incontinence can be caused by bladder or urinary tract infections, which may be treated with antibiotics. Prescribed medications can also cause urgent and frequent urination. If informed of the detrimental effects of medication, a physician may reduce the drug dosage. With age, the bladder and urethra in women commonly descend, resulting in stress incontinence; leaking then occurs with the increased abdominal pressure brought on by coughing, sneezing, laughing, lifting, or physical exercise. Another type of incontinence, known as *functional incontinence,* often results from neurological changes and accompanies other problems, such as Parkinson's disease and dementia. Other physical causes that should be investigated

---

MANAGEMENT OF INCONTINENCE

- medications to increase bladder capacity
- surgery
- dietary changes
- Kegel exercises (at least 100 times per day)
- behavioral management techniques, such as reducing fluid intake when bathroom access is limited
- reduction in the intake of caffeine (e.g., coffee, tea, cola, even chocolate) can prevent the stimulation of the kidneys to excrete fluids
- weight loss can also help, as obesity is found to cause urine leakage

medically are prostate problems, pernicious anemia, diabetic neuropathy, and various cancers. Because the types and causes of incontinence vary widely, thorough diagnosis and individualized treatment programs are critical. Even habitual incontinence should not be assumed to be irreversible.

Although some physicians prescribe medications to increase bladder capacity or reduce urine production, these often have unpleasant side effects such as blurred vision and dry mouth. Noninvasive behavioral management techniques, such as frequent access to toilet facilities, restriction of fluid intake before bedtime, and systematic exercise of the pelvic muscle, are often just as effective. Even incurable problems can be managed through protective products (e.g., absorbent pads) and catheters (tubes draining the bladder) to reduce complications, anxiety, and embarrassment. Only a small proportion of older persons with incontinence, however, are so severely disabled that they are unlikely to regain continence and require a catheter or other external appliances to cope with the conditions. Physical exercise, known as Kegels, designed to promote and maintain sphincter muscle tone, can also prevent or reduce age-related incontinence, particularly among older women. All possible treatments, especially behavioral techniques, exercise, and biofeedback, should be explored, since older people's embarrassment and humiliation may result in their avoiding social gatherings out of fear of having their incontinence detected. Support groups, such as those sponsored by the National Association for Incontinence, exist nationwide.

Problems with the Intestinal System

Many older people experience problems in digestion and continuing gastrointestinal distress, due particularly to age-related slowing down of the digestive process. Most intestinal problems are, in fact, related to unbalanced diets or diets with limited fiber content. **Diverticulitis** is one of the most common difficulties, affecting as many as two-thirds of the oldest-old, especially women (Korzenik, 2006). It is a condition in which pouches or sacs (diverticula) in the intestines (especially in the colon) result from weakness of the intestinal wall; these sacs become inflamed and infected, leading to symptoms of nausea, abdominal discomfort, bleeding, and changes in bowel function. Diverticulitis, which is increasing in industrialized nations, may be associated with a highly refined diet lacking in fiber. Management includes a high-fiber diet and antibiotic therapy.

Many older people worry about constipation, but this is not an inevitable outcome of aging, as noted in Chapter 3. It is more prevalent among elders in long-term care facilities but is also reported by up to 26 percent of elders in the community, and accounts for about 2.5 million physician visits annually (Hsieh, 2005). Constipation may be a symptom of an underlying disease or obstruction. If this is not the case, treatment commonly includes:

- physical activity
- increased fiber intake
- increased fluid intake
- bowel training
- biofeedback
- laxatives and stool softeners

Because many older people are overly concerned about having regular bowel movements, they may become dependent on laxatives. Data from more than 5000 white and African American elders found that 10.2 percent of both groups used laxatives, with higher use among women,

---

CAUSES OF CONSTIPATION
- overuse of cathartics
- lack of exercise
- psychological stress
- gastrointestinal disease
- an unbalanced diet with respect to bulk

those using four or more prescriptions, those with four or more physician visits per year, and those with problems with ADLs (Ruby et al., 2003). Over time, laxatives can cause problems, such as irritating the colon and decreasing the absorption of certain vitamins.

Hiatus hernia appears to be increasing in incidence, especially among obese women; this occurs when a small portion of the stomach slides up through the diaphragm. Symptoms include indigestion, difficulty in swallowing, and chest pain that may be confused with a heart attack. Medical management includes weight reduction, elevation of the upper body when sleeping, changes in the size and frequency of meals, and medication. Although hiatus hernia in itself is not especially severe, it may mask the symptoms of more serious intestinal disorders, such as cancer of the stomach.

The incidence of gallbladder disease, especially gallstones, also increases with age and is indicated by pain, nausea, and vomiting, with attacks increasing in number and severity. Most cases in older adults are asymptomatic, and physicians debate whether to perform surgery or follow a more conservative course of medical management. Medical treatment usually involves a combination of weight loss, avoiding high-fat foods, and using antacids as needed.

Oral Diseases

Because of developments in preventive dentistry, newer cohorts of older people have better oral health than any preceding cohort. According to the 2002–2003 National Health Interview Survey (NHIS), only 27 percent over age 65 today are completely **edentulous** (i.e., no natural teeth remaining). As one might expect, edentulism increases with age.

- 24 percent of the young-old are edentulous
- 39 percent of the oldest-old are edentulous (Schoenborn et al., 2006)

This change is due entirely to historical differences in dental care delivery, not because of the aging process.

The common problems of tooth decay and periodontal diseases also appear to increase with age, although the evidence is limited and less clear. In national epidemiological surveys such as the National Health and Nutrition Examination Survey (NHANES III), the rate of root caries (cavities that develop on exposed root surfaces) was found to be more than three times greater among people over age 65 than in those under age 45. Rates of decay on the enamel surfaces of teeth, however, are not much higher among 65- to 74-year-olds compared with 35- to 44-year-olds. Differences are much greater when the older group is compared with people age 18 to 24, who have only about 10 percent of their tooth surfaces decayed or filled, compared with 31 percent of people age 65 to 74 (NCHS, 1999). These differences reflect changes over time in preventive dental care, such as the widespread use of water fluoridation. NHANES III also found an age-related increase in the incidence of periodontitis or gum disease, especially after age 45. As a result, 25 percent of older adults have poor bone support of existing teeth (USDHHS, 2000).

Cancers of the lip, tongue, mouth, gum, pharynx, and salivary glands increase with advanced age. In North America and Western Europe, cancer of the lip is the most frequent type of oral cancer and has the highest survival rates among those listed previously (between 65 and 90 percent over a five-year period). Smoking and heavy alcohol use are strongly linked to oral cancer (USDHHS, 2000).

HIV/AIDS in the Older Population

While it cannot be classified as a chronic disease in the same way as diabetes or chronic obstructive pulmonary disease, the growing number of older adults with HIV (human immunodeficiency virus) or AIDS (acquired immune deficiency syndrome), and the increasing time between infection, diagnosis, and death make this an important public health issue in gerontology. In years to come, HIV/AIDS will place greater demands on long-term care, especially home-based services and on informal caregiving networks. Since it is mandatory to report AIDS cases, the Centers for Disease Control and Prevention (CDC) receive reports from all state and territorial health departments on all diagnosed cases of AIDS. Because of stereotypes that AIDS only affects younger populations and that older people are not sexually active, many physicians and HIV-testing programs do not routinely test older adults for HIV/AIDS. Often, cases go undiagnosed because older people do not report symptoms, and in some cases symptoms such as nerve pain and vision problems are simply attributed to aging.

Almost one million Americans are living with HIV/AIDS. Although it is difficult to guess the actual prevalence of cases without a diagnosis, it is estimated that 27 percent of people with HIV/AIDS are age 50 and older (considered "older adults" by CDC). Men are at far higher risk than women, ranging from 86 percent of diagnosed AIDS cases among 50 to 54-year-olds, to 79 percent among those 65 and older. More than half of all cases among the population 50 and older are African Americans and Latinos (52 percent). Women of color are at greater risk than their white counterparts in this age group, representing 70 percent of women living with HIV/AIDS. The number of new HIV/AIDS cases in older women has risen sharply in the past ten years. This increase of 40 percent is due primarily to women becoming infected through unprotected sex with infected male partners. A notable minority obtained the virus by sharing needles for drug use. In 2003, 71 percent of all women diagnosed with AIDS had been exposed to the virus through heterosexual contact, and only 27 percent through intravenous drug use. The problem of exposure through unprotected sex is greatest for older women of color (CDC, 2001, 2006b; HRSA, 2001; Stark, 2006; Vosvick et al.,

2003; Zablotsky and Kennedy, 2003). Many older people do not seek medical attention during the early stages of this disease because they assume many of the symptoms are merely signs of normal aging or chronic diseases that they are already managing. These include:

- general aches and pains
- headache
- chronic cough
- lack of energy
- loss of appetite and weight
- problems with short-term memory

Because of such misunderstandings, older people who become infected with the HIV/AIDS virus often are unaware that they are at risk and may not suspect their sexual partners. One reason for the significant rise of this disease among older women is that, after the menopause, they may assume that they do not need to have their male partner use a condom and practice safe sex because they need not fear pregnancy. Menopause can also cause vaginal dryness and thinning of the vaginal lining. This may result in small abrasions and tears in the vaginal walls where the virus can penetrate. Older men may be at risk because of unprotected sex with male partners and paid sex workers. The latter may be male or female, and some may use injected heroin or crack cocaine with shared needles (HRSA, 2001; NIA, 1999b; Radda et al., 2003).

Older adults may also be at greater risk because already low levels of T-cells, part of the immune system, are lost more rapidly in older people with this infection. In elders with compromised immune systems, the HIV virus is more likely to attack than in younger people or in other older people who have a fully functioning immune system. This may also explain why the incubation period for HIV is shorter in older adults, an average of 5.7 years versus 7.3 years in people under age 50. Poorer immune reactions may also explain the shorter time between diagnosis and death for people over age 50 (Emlet and Farkas, 2002).

HIV/AIDS is not a major cause of death for older people, compared to heart disease, cancer, stroke, and diabetes. Nevertheless, it accounted for 2.2 per 100,000 deaths among people age 65 to 74 and 0.7 per 100,000 for those age 75 to 84. As with younger populations, the availability of antiretroviral drugs has reduced death rates due to HIV/AIDS among older populations, from a high of 3.6 per 100,000 in 1995 to 2.2 in 2000, which results in all age groups living longer with HIV/AIDS as a chronic rather than terminal illness (NCHS, 2003a).

Researchers question whether older adults with HIV/AIDS are more or less likely than younger people to use health services. An analysis of 571 cases in California compared 63 AIDS patients who were age 60 and older, with 190 age 50 to 59 and 318 age 30 to 49. In addition to age, functional status and diagnosis were hypothesized to be predictors of inpatient and outpatient medical care, in-home services, and mental health services. Age was not associated with functional health or service utilization. Both younger and older patients were more likely to use all types of services as their ADL limitations increased. Among all types of health care, mental health services were least likely to be used by all age groups (Emlet and Farkas, 2002). These findings demonstrate that older adults with HIV/AIDS do not seek health services at a higher rate than younger patients unless their functional health has deteriorated significantly. However, another study found age differences in perceptions of the importance of community-based services. In this case, adults age 50 and over who were living with HIV/AIDS were compared with their 20- to 39-year-old counterparts regarding the perceived importance of services. Older patients rated home-delivered meals, adult day care, home chore services, and physical therapy as more important than did their younger counterparts. Both groups rated drug programs to treat HIV/AIDS plus dental and primary medical care as most important. These results suggest that older HIV/AIDS patients highly value long-term care services to improve

their quality of life (Emlet and Berghuis, 2002). Recent budget cuts, however, are limiting the availability of community-based and home-care services. In addition, older HIV-positive persons may not seek services because of real or perceived homophobia and discrimination.

Unfortunately, many older persons with HIV/AIDS do not have an adequate social safety net to replace these needed community services. One survey of adults age 50 to 68 living with HIV/AIDS in New York City found that 42 percent perceived a lack of emotional support and 27 percent reported inadequate practical assistance. Those with a more advanced stage of the disease, who should have had *more* support, actually reported *less* emotional and practical help in coping with their activities of daily living (Schrimshaw and Siegel, 2003). In another survey of older adults with HIV/AIDS in New York, 71 percent lived alone and only about 33 percent had a partner. Most had lost contact with their families (Shippy and Karpiak, 2005). In general, older HIV-positive persons are more likely to live alone than their younger counterparts, which has implications for their caregiving and service needs to manage their condition (Poindexter and Emlet, 2006).

For all the reasons just described, it is essential to educate older adults about *their* risk for HIV/AIDS. Even those who know something about this disease may feel that it cannot affect them if they are not engaging in homosexual activity or intravenous drug use. Many older people have relied on the media for their knowledge in this area. Unfortunately, the media rarely reports on *older* adults contracting AIDS through heterosexual intercourse or blood transfusions. It is therefore not surprising that many older people are unaware that they may be infected. They are also less willing to be tested for the virus, and once diagnosed, are less likely to seek out AIDS support groups or other forms of emotional support. At the same time, ageist attitudes may prevent health providers from encouraging sexually active elders to be tested for this virus or even asking questions about their sexual history as part of a routine health screening.

Accidents among Older People

Although mortality statistics suggest that older people are less likely than the young to die of accidents (only 7 per 10,000 deaths compared with 10 per 10,000 among people 21 and younger), these numbers mask the true incidence of deaths due to accident-related injuries. For example, if an older person breaks a hip after falling down a flight of stairs or breaks a leg in an auto accident, she enters a hospital, often is discharged to a nursing home, and soon after may die from pneumonia. Pneumonia is then listed as the cause of death, when in fact this acute condition was brought on by the patient's problems in recovering from the accident.

Despite this underestimate, the risk of death from physical injuries is about four times greater for 80-year-olds than for 20-year-olds. Those age 60 and older are twice as likely as younger adults to be killed in a car crash. For drivers age 65 to 74, motor vehicle accidents are the leading cause of injury-related deaths. For those age 74 to 84, this is the second leading cause of injury-related deaths after falls. Older drivers and passengers are three times more likely to die than younger people following an auto crash. This is most likely due to older adults' greater physical vulnerability. Given these statistics, it is not surprising that many elders take refresher courses offered by AARP ("55 Alive Driver Safety Program") and the Automobile Association of America ("Safe Driving for Mature Operators") (Arfin, 2006).

Older Drivers

Currently 27.5 million drivers in the United States are age 65 and older. These numbers will grow as baby boomers age and more people live into their 80s and 90s and want to continue driving. Older people, both drivers and passengers, made up 10 percent of all auto fatalities in 1975, 17 percent

---

RETRAINING OLDER DRIVERS

It may be useful for state licensing departments to test all adults annually on some of the relevant physiological and cognitive abilities, and to retrain older drivers who are experiencing significant declines in these areas. The AARP, National Safety Council, and the Automobile Association of America (AAA) have developed such courses. For example, AARP estimates that some 500,000 older drivers enroll in their "Mature Driver Safety" program each year. This 8-hour course is offered through retirement homes, senior centers, shopping malls, libraries, and religious institutions. Older persons can obtain discounts of 5 to 10 percent on their auto insurance in many states after completing such courses.

---

in 1998, and are projected to represent 27 percent of auto fatalities in 2015, as more baby boomers reach old age. Between 2000 and 2020, the proportion of people age 65 and over who continue to drive will double (NHTSA, 2001).

Many older people view driving as an important part of maintaining their autonomy and active aging. However, a tragic accident in July 2003 attracted national attention to the issues raised by older drivers. In that accident, an 86-year-old driver in California mistakenly stepped on the accelerator instead of the brake, causing the deaths of 10 people and many injuries in a crowded market area. This unfortunate event raised many questions about the need for mandatory tests and restrictions on driving after a certain age. Only 21 states currently have special license requirements for older drivers. Some include:

1. Cannot renew licenses by mail after age 70: Alaska, California, and Louisiana
2. More frequent renewals (hence, more regular testing) required for older people than for younger drivers: Arizona, Colorado, Hawaii, Idaho, Illinois, Indiana, Iowa, Kansas, Maine, Missouri, Montana, New Mexico, and Rhode Island

3. More frequent vision tests for older drivers: Arizona, Florida, Maine, Oregon, and Utah
4. More frequent road tests for older drivers: Illinois and New Hampshire
5. Medical report required for drivers 70 and older: Nevada

Older drivers are less likely to drive in bad weather, at night, in freeway traffic, or in rush hour. They are also less likely to speed or to drive while drunk. As ways of managing, they generally select familiar routes of travel, and drive fewer miles per year than younger drivers. Nevertheless, they have more accidents per mile driven. A U-shaped pattern of fatal crashes has been observed, from a high rate among 17-year-olds, to a low at ages 30 to 64, to an increased rate among 75-year-olds (Bédard et al., 2001; Insurance Institute for Highway Safety, 2001). This higher rate of accidents in older drivers may be attributed to:

- changes in eye-hand coordination
- slower reaction time
- impaired vision (especially diminished night vision, sensitivity to glare, and poor peripheral vision)
- hearing impairments
- slower information processing and declining attention skills, especially divided attention
- problems with visual-spatial skills
- declines in physical strength

Even though most accidents by older drivers occur at low speeds, age-related declines in organ systems and brittle bones make the older person more vulnerable to injuries and death. Older drivers are more likely to sustain rib and pelvic fractures and thoracic injuries, but fewer head and brain injuries in an auto accident. Regardless of their injuries, older adults, especially those age 75 and older, have longer hospital stays, more pulmonary, cardiovascular, and renal complications, and greater need for rehabilitation services following trauma (Li, Braver

> **DESIGN CHANGES THAT COULD HELP OLDER DRIVERS**
> - wider rearview mirrors
> - pedal extensions
> - less complicated and legible instrument panels
> - electronic detectors in front and back of car that signal when too close to other cars
> - better protection on doors
> - booster cushions for shorter-stature drivers

and Chen, 2003; Salen et al., 2003). Some medications, especially those given for insomnia or anxiety, that have a long half-life in the bloodstream, increase the risk of motor vehicle crashes in older adults by as much as 45 percent (Hemmelgarn et al., 1997).

Although older adults diagnosed with Alzheimer's disease or other dementias generally stop driving, almost 4 percent of American men age 75 and older who drive have dementia (Foley et al., 2000). Many older adults with cognitive impairments restrict their driving to the community where they reside and avoid long highway trips. However, city driving may actually pose more hazards than highways, because of multiple intersections, traffic congestion, and other driving demands that require rapid information processing and reaction time. A national survey of more than 5000 older men and women revealed that the majority of women with cognitive impairment do not drive (75.6 percent) compared to 43 percent of their male counterparts, which may reflect traditional gender roles characteristic of the cohort age 75 and older where driving has been associated with masculinity. Men with mild and severe cognitive impairments apparently cope by avoiding long-distance driving. As one might expect, both men and women with dementia who have another driver in their household are more likely to stop driving themselves. In this same survey, elders with impaired vision and limitations in their ADLs were less likely to drive, but having heart disease, diabetes, or arthritis did not cause them to restrict their driving (Freund and Szinovacz, 2002).

Improved environmental design can help some older drivers. For example, older people have more accidents while making left turns; these could be avoided by designing better left-turn intersections with special lanes and left arrow lights. Road signs that are clearer and well lighted could reduce the high number of violations received by older drivers for improperly changing lanes or entering and exiting highways. For drivers who are prone to falling asleep at the wheel, a device inserted behind their ears will sound an alarm if they start to drift off.

Another approach to reducing person–environment discrepancies for older drivers is to install air bags that have lower power in cars; of 68 adults killed by air bags between 1991 and 2000, 40 percent were age 70 or older. The Ford Motor Company has installed "force limiters" in some models. These are part of a personal safety system to use sensors to adjust air bags and seat-belts according to the weight of the driver and passenger, and how close the driver is to the steering wheel. Other design options to modify the environment are summarized in the box on page 145.

Falls and Their Prevention

As noted earlier, older people are at a greater risk of falls than the young. Falls are the leading cause of injuries for people over age 65 in the United States, and account for 95 percent of all hip fractures. Up to 30 percent of older adults in the community, and even more in long-term care settings, experience a fall in a given year. Many older people who fall become more fearful of falling and therefore restrict their activity levels (Fletcher and Hirdes, 2004). They may also become more rigid or overly cautious in walking. This may, in turn, increase the likelihood of subsequent falls. In fact, 65 percent of those who fall

RISK FACTORS FOR FALLS

- inactivity that weakens muscles
- visual impairment
- multiple diseases
- medications (e.g., cardiac conditions and medications that cause postural hypotension; some antidepressants)
- gait disorders
- poor balance when standing
- low lighting levels
- hazards in the environment such as slippery floors, loose area rugs, poorly demarcated stairs, and slippery surfaces in showers and tubs
- unfamiliar environments

do so again within 6 months (CDC 2006c). The majority of elders who experience fall-related fractures do not recover their pre-fall functional level one year later. Therefore it is important to identify risk factors for falls and try to prevent them. The most common risk factors are lack of balance control, impaired gait, arthritis, cognitive impairment, increased age, use of four or more medications or any psychoactive drugs, visual impairment, and **sarcopenia** (Huang et al., 2003; Lord, Sherrington, and Menz, 2001; Moreland et al., 2004). Sarcopenia refers to the atrophy of muscles and can affect all muscle groups, weakening the upper body and arms. It can impair balance and cause difficulties in rising from a chair, bathtub or toilet, and in maintaining elders' functional independence. Both men and women are at increased risk for sarcopenia after age 75, especially if they do not exercise (Foldvari et al., 2000).

Despite many national and local public health efforts to prevent falls among older people, fall-related deaths and hip fractures due to falls have not declined dramatically, and falls continue to be the leading cause of accident mortality (Miltiades and Kaye, 2006). Between 1993 and 2003, there was an *increase* in the rate of deaths caused by falls, from 24 to 37 per

---

INTERVENTIONS TO PREVENT FALLS

- Environmental modifications of the homes of older people who have experienced multiple falls in the past can significantly decrease falls.
- An investment in home modifications and assistive devices saves health care costs for an older person.
- Training older women how to control their balance can prevent falls (Ray et al., 1997)
- In a large study of 14 nursing homes, 50 percent of the homes (the experimental group) made major modifications to their physical environment, in wheelchair safety, and in the use of psychotropic medications. No changes were made in the other 7 homes (control group). A significant decline in recurrent falls occurred among older residents of the experimental homes with environmental modifications when compared with the control group (19 percent vs. 54 percent, respectively) in the subsequent 2 years (Ray et al., 1997)

100,000 (CDC, 2006d; Merck Institute, 2004). In 1998, 163 deaths per 100,000 people age 85 and older were attributable to falls, much higher than the target of 105 per 100,000 in *Healthy People 2000*. Similarly, the target of 607 hip fractures per 100,000 older adults was exceeded in 1998, with 863 fractures per 100,000 among the age 65 and older population. In fact, both hip fractures and fall-related deaths have actually increased since 1990, in contrast to other health problems that have shown a gradual decline (Merck Institute, 2004).

Most falls are preventable. Education and exercise training of older adults and their caregivers along with preventive medications and environmental interventions are needed to reduce the risk of falls (see examples of intervention recommendations in the box above). New drugs can prevent fractures by strengthening bone. Researchers in the United States and Japan found alendronate (brand name, Fosamax) to be effective in reducing fractures of the spine and femoral

neck by 50 percent in one study and 44 percent in another. Other effective medications are risedronate (brand name, Actonel) and raloxifene (brand name, Evista); the latter drug has been particularly useful in preventing spinal fractures (Cranney et al., 2002). Findings from a study in the Netherlands suggest that thiazide diuretics used to treat hypertension may indirectly prevent bone loss. These drugs draw water from the blood but reduce calcium loss in the urine. Older adults using any one of many brands of thiazide diuretics for their hypertension for more than 1 year also lowered their risk for hip fractures by 50 percent, but the benefits diminished within 4 months of discontinuing the drug (Schoofs et al., 2003).

Informal social support, especially family networks and friendly visting by volunteers, are also associated with reducing the risks of falling (Fletcher and Hirdes, 2004). In addition to the guidelines for fall prevention established by the American Geriatrics Society (2001), comprehensive checklists and measures of physical ability are available to assess the risk of falls. The Get-up and Go Test is recommended as an initial assessment tool; older adults are asked to get up from a chair, walk 10 meters, return and sit down in the chair. Creating a slip-free, clutter-free home environment can also reduce falls. The Home Fall Hazard Assessment Tool evaluates environmental conditions in the home that could contribute to falls. By emphasizing balance stability and postural control, Tai Chi is found to reduce the risk of falling and fear of falling (Wolf et al., 2003).

Use of Physician Services by Older People

The increased incidence of many chronic and acute diseases among the older population would seem to predict a striking growth with age in the use of health care services. There is some support for a differential pattern of utilization among different age groups. The probability of seeing a doctor at least once in the previous year increases slightly with age. For example, 91 percent of 55- to 64-year-old women reported visiting a physician in the past 12 months in the 2002 NHIS, compared with 94 percent of those age 65 to 74, 95 percent at age 75 to 84, and 95.5 percent of those 85 and older (Schoenborn et al., 2006). However, the major difference across age groups is in *frequency* of use annually:

- 1.3 physician visits per person among those 25 to 44
- 7.3 visits for people 45 to 64
- 11.4 visits for people 65 to 84
- 15.0 visits for those 85 and older (Merck Institute, 2004).

When they visit physicians, both younger and older people do so primarily for acute symptoms and to receive diagnostic and therapeutic services. However, the larger number of yearly visits by older persons may indicate that they are seeking care for chronic conditions as well. It is noteworthy that only a small proportion of older adults are high users of all health services. Low use, however, does not necessarily mean that all health needs are being met. For example, low-income older adults, across all ethnic minority groups, report more unmet health needs than middle- or high-income elders (NCHS, 2000a).

- Among low-income elders, 22 percent report unmet health needs.
- Among middle- and upper-income elders, 2.5 percent have unmet health needs.

There is less difference between socioeconomic groups within the Latino population:

- Among low-income Latino elders, 18 percent have unmet health needs.
- Among middle- and upper-income Latino elders, 8 percent have such needs.

These differences in meeting health needs suggest that other factors, such as cost and cultural barriers, result in higher rates of unmet needs among certain groups. For example, African American elders report more outpatient visits than whites, but are also less likely to follow treatment recommendations, including medication use (Pathman, Fowler-Brown, and Corbie-Smith, 2006).

Use of Other Health Services

HOSPITALS Hospital utilization may reflect older people's need for health care more accurately than do elective visits to physicians' offices. Older people are more frequently hospitalized and for longer periods of time than younger populations, accounting for about 35 percent of all short-stay hospital days of care (Healthcare Cost and Utilization Project [HCUP], 2002). However, the average length of stay was dramatically reduced after the introduction of **diagnosis related groupings (DRGs)** for Medicare patients in 1983 (see Chapter 17). While DRGs prompted a transfer of care from inpatient hospitals to outpatient settings, home-based care after hospitalization by older people has decreased overall. This reflects more stringent eligibility and reimbursement criteria rather than a diminishing need for care. In addition, hospital utilization may be declining because of the growing number of procedures that are performed in community-based settings. Hospital emergency rooms (ER) are used for medical care more often among low-income populations. In the 2002 NHIS, 29 percent of elders classified as poor reported ER use in the past 12 months, compared with 22 percent of the non-poor (Schoenborn et al., 2006). Research with low-income African Americans shows that ER users are mostly people without a regular physician, without private health insurance, and who have an external locus of control regarding their health (i.e., the belief that others have more control than they do over their well-being) (Bazargan, Bazargan, and Baker, 1998).

MEDICATION USE   The use of prescription and nonprescription medications, including vitamins and mineral supplements, may indicate the older person's need for health care. Although they represent just over 12 percent of the population, older adults use 34 percent of all prescriptions and 30 percent of all nonprescription medications (Merck Institute, 2004). In a national survey of 2590 adults conducted in 2001, 94 percent of older women and 90 percent of older men reported taking at least one medication; 57 percent of the former took five or more. Prescription drugs represented 25 percent of these. Older women, especially white women, were most likely to report using both prescription and nonprescription drugs, Asians and Pacific Islanders least likely. The most common prescription medications used by older and middle-aged respondents were antihypertensives, heart medications, and diuretics (reflecting the high prevalence of hypertension and heart disease that these drugs are intended to treat). Aspirin was the most commonly used over-the-counter (OTC) drug, reported by 58 percent of older men and 51 percent of older women who took it to prevent heart attacks. Older adults were second only to middle-aged adults in their use of multivitamins and specific nutritional supplements (Kaufman et al., 2002).

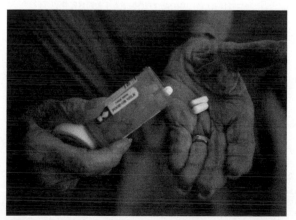

Older adults use more medications than other age groups.

An average older person living in the community takes 5.3 prescription medicines per day (Gurnack, Atkinson, and Osgood, 2002). Some older people take as many as 12 to 15 different medications (prescription and nonprescription) simultaneously, at an average annual cost of around $480. The burden falls especially hard on older women, who are most likely to experience chronic diseases and have the lowest incomes. With the growth of medications to manage a variety of chronic conditions, it is not surprising that the average older American increased their number of filled prescriptions from 18 in 1992 to 32 in 2002 (Federal Interagency Forum, 2006; Sambamoorthi, Shea, and Crystal, 2003). Not surprisingly, nursing home residents take more prescription drugs than do community-dwelling elders. It is estimated that the average nursing home resident uses 8.8 medications per day, and 32 percent use 9 or more (Doshi, Shaffer and Briesacher, 2005). It is therefore not surprising that adverse drug reactions are common among nursing home residents (Handler et al., 2006). Coverage for high prescription drug costs is affected by the 2006 prescription drug changes in Medicare. These changes are described more fully in Chapter 17.

Many older people take either too many medications or inappropriate drugs, making over-medication a concern. This is because the less-efficient excretion of drugs by the kidney and liver and the changing proportions of fat and muscle tissue (as discussed in Chapter 3) may prolong the effects of some drugs. Furthermore, combinations of medications can cause adverse drug reactions. Many hospital admissions of older people result from such adverse reactions, and many falls and sudden impairments in cognitive function may be due to inappropriate medication use or overmedication. Older people who are discharged from hospitals with a large number of medications are more likely to be rehospitalized because of drug complications. This is especially true if they are using 7 or more medications. This pattern occurs independent of the elder's diagnosis and type of medication. Researchers in one study of almost 400 elders, average age 79, found that as many as 32 percent of this group discharged from a hospital stay experienced adverse drug reactions. Elders on multiple medications prior to their hospitalization were at greater risk for such complications (Page and Ruscin, 2006). The higher rate of medication use among older adults also may result in reporting errors and incorrect use. Older people admitted to a hospital often give inconsistent medication reports. For these reasons, health and social service providers must exercise caution in relying on elders' self-reports of medication use (Flaherty et al., 2000).

DENTAL SERVICES   An area of elective health care, ignored even more than routine medical care, is the use of professional dental services. Although the rate of preventive dental service utilization has risen significantly over the past 20 years among younger cohorts, the use of dental services by older adults has increased only slightly. In the latest National Health Interview Survey, older persons continued to be the lowest users of professional dental care; 44 percent had not seen a dentist in the past year, and 33 percent had not obtained care in the past 5 years. Ethnic minorities are far less likely to visit a dentist; 65 percent of African Americans and 57 percent of Latino elders reported that they had not seen a dentist in 2004, compared with 40 percent of white elders (NHIS, 2006; Schoenborn et al., 2006). This rate is incongruent with the level of oral diseases that require professional attention. Yet, once older adults enter the dental care system, their average number of visits is similar to that of younger people. The current state of Medicare reimbursement, whereby physician visits are covered but dental care is not, plays an important role in this differential pattern of utilization. Therefore, it is not surprising that older adults who are not poor are twice as likely to make preventive dental visits as those who are poor (67 percent vs. 32 percent, respectively). Elders with private health insurance that covers dental care are also more likely to make

annual dental visits than those on Medicare only: 63 percent versus 31.5 percent (Kiyak and Reichmuth, 2005; Schoenborn et al., 2006).

Health Promotion with Older People

Health promotion is defined as a combination of health education and related organizational, political, and economic changes aimed at enhancing an individual's capacities for moving toward greater health, not just less disease. Some programs emphasize the "health enhancement" or "wellness" aspects of their health promotion efforts. This contrasts with disease prevention, which is focused on avoiding diseases that can result in impairment and disability. Health promotion encompasses a variety of interventions in recognition of the complex social, biological, cultural, and economic factors that influence health and health behavior. Accordingly, this definition includes altering individual health practices, such as diet and exercise, as well as creating healthier environments and changing cultural attitudes and expectations toward health. Health promotion represents a shift from a biomedical model, where the physician is responsible to treat disease, to a model that emphasizes control over

---

HEALTH PROMOTION CAN REDUCE HEALTH CARE COSTS

Several health promotion programs find that healthy lifestyles can reduce health care costs:

- A community-based, peer-led program for elders with chronic disease found that exercise and dietary interventions resulted in fewer hospitalizations, and health care savings up to $520 over 2 years.
- An individualized intervention program to reduce risks for falls resulted in a $2000 reduction in health care costs among participants compared to elders in the control group (Stepnick and Whitelaw, 2006).

one's health in an effort to improve physical well-being and quality of life.

Disease prevention is also important at all stages of a disease. It includes "primary prevention" (e.g., water fluoridation to prevent the onset of tooth decay), "secondary prevention" (e.g., screening for early detection of cancer), and "tertiary prevention" to manage a disease (e.g., using antihypertensive medications appropriately in order to maintain a healthy blood pressure while preventing side effects associated with the drugs). Preventive health behaviors can save the individual and society significant amounts of money for treating more advanced disease. For example, influenza vaccines can save $118 in treatment costs per $1.50 spent on the vaccine itself (Rothberg, Ballantonio, and Rose, 2003). Health promotion thus makes explicit the importance of people's *environments* and *lifestyles* as determinants of good health (Breslow, 1999).

The primary rationale for health promotion programs for older adults is to reduce the incidence of *disabling chronic diseases*. This can enhance the older person's functional ability and overall quality of life, not merely prolong life. Health promotion also recognizes that chronic conditions cannot be cured but can be prevented from causing functional disability. As suggested in our earlier discussion of disease, as many as 80 percent of the chronic illnesses that afflict older individuals may be related to social, environmental, and behavioral factors, particularly poor health habits. In addition, 90 percent of fatal and near-fatal episodes of strokes and heart attacks are believed to be preventable.

Longitudinal studies identify several unhealthy behaviors that increase chances of dying at a younger age than statistically expected. A study of older adults age 70 to 90 found that those who consumed a healthy diet, exercised 30 minutes daily, avoided smoking, and consumed alcohol in moderation were 50 percent less likely to die within the next 10 years than elders who did not practice these health promoting lifestyles (Knoops et al., 2004).

A viable health care goal, as noted in Chapter 1, is compression of morbidity—delaying the age at which chronic illness and possible disabilites begin (Fries, 1980, 2003). This goal of improvement in chronic disease rates seems feasible. Evidence is provided by studies of male master athletes in their 60s. These athletes experience very little decline in their cardiovascular functions, including maximum heart rate and maximum volume of oxygen used during exercise, especially when compared with age-matched sedentary men. Furthermore, HDL cholesterol levels are higher and their triglycerides are lower than in age-matched sedentary men, and are comparable to those of healthy young men (Yataco et al., 1997). Even moderate exercise performed regularly, together with healthy eating and not smoking, can delay the onset of disability by as much as 10 years (Stepnick and Whitelaw, 2006).

Only a small percentage of national health care dollar is spent on prevention, early detection, and wellness services. Medicare and many private

---

HEALTHY PEOPLE 2010

Two major goals of *Healthy People 2010*, released by the Secretary of Health and Human Services, are:

- to increase quality and years of healthy life for all Americans
- to eliminate health disparities among segments of the U.S. population

Although the 26 focus areas of *Healthy People 2010* do not specifically address elders or any particular age group, the health topics are relevant for current cohorts of older adults, as well as younger and middle-aged people today, who could improve their quality of life as they live longer. For example, by promoting healthy behaviors such as increasing levels of physical activity and fitness, improving nutrition and reducing tobacco use (focus areas #1–3), future cohorts will not only increase their life expectancy, but will improve the quality of those years.

SOURCE: *Healthy People 2010* (http://www.health.gov, 2000).

health insurance plans do not typically pay for prevention services. An encouraging sign, however, is the increasing number of health maintenance organizations, health care clinics, universities, and work sites that offer health promotion programs. Some of these programs have been carried into senior centers, adult day health care sites, and assisted living, retirement, and nursing homes. A growing number of older adults now obtain preventive services, in some cases higher than targets set by *Healthy People 2010*.

The Relationship of Health Practices to Health Outcomes

Considerable research demonstrates the relationship of personal health habits to active aging or aging well. Factors that are related to good health outcomes include:

- consuming more vegetables and fruits, less saturated fats and refined carbohydrates
- maintaining a regular exercise schedule
- not smoking
- limiting alcohol consumption
- maintaining one's weight in the ideal range
- sleeping seven to eight hours per night

The relationship between these behaviors and healthy aging appear to be cumulative and independent of age, sex, ethnic minority, and socioeconomic status. Additional epidemiological evidence demonstrates links between specific health habits and decreased longevity and increased health risks. These specific lifestyle

POINTS TO PONDER

Identify healthy and unhealthy behaviors in your lifestyle. Have you ever tried to modify these behaviors? If so, what techniques worked for you? What were some obstacles? To what extent can lifestyle changes after age 65 overcome the effects of poor health habits acquired earlier in life?

factors, discussed briefly below, include alcohol consumption, cigarette smoking, diet, and exercise.

ALCOHOL   The relationship between drinking alcohol and physical health in old age is U-shaped; the least healthy are those who drink heavily and those who abstain, although abstainers may include former heavy drinkers who have damaged their systems. Light drinking may have some cardiovascular benefits. Excessive drinking (5 or more drinks at a single sitting) contributes to poor physical health, more frequent hospitalizations, decreased cognitive function, poorer metabolism of prescription medications, and premature death.

While excessive alcohol use can cause significant health problems, moderate use is shown to have beneficial effects. As discussed in Chapter 3, consuming 1 to 2 servings of red wine with dinner, 2 to 4 times per week, appears to increase levels of HDL, the "good" cholesterol, in the blood while preventing oxidation of LDL. Polyphenols found in abundance in red wine (and less so in white wine) also reduce blood clotting and may lower the incidence of heart attacks, as demonstrated by the "French paradox," that is, the lower rates of heart attacks among the French, who consume more red wine than Americans. It is important to note that all these benefits derive from *moderate*, not excessive consumption of wine (Frankl, 2003).

SMOKING   The effects of cigarette smoking, especially in interaction with other risk factors, on heart disease, emphysema, and lung cancer are extensively documented. Smokers who use oral contraceptives, are exposed to asbestos, have excessive alcohol consumption, or are at risk for hypertension have a greater chance of experiencing a nonfatal myocardial infarction and are at significant risk for cancers of the oral cavity and lung. Smoking can reduce bone density and musculoskeletal strength and interfere with the absorption of some medications. The longer one is exposed to tobacco, the greater these risks. However, quitting smoking can gradually reduce some of these health risks. For example, people who quit smoking 5 or more years ago can reduce their risk of stroke to the same level as those who never smoked, and 15 years after quitting, they have the same life expectancy as their age peers who never smoked (Doll, 1999; Ostbyte and Taylor, 2004).

DIET   Poor diet is related to obesity, cancer, and heart disease. Obesity carries an increased risk of cardiovascular and pulmonary difficulties, aggravates other conditions such as hypertension, arthritis, and diabetes, and adds risk to surgery. Interpretation of the relationship between obesity and morbidity and mortality is difficult, however. This is because obesity is correlated with other risk factors, such as high blood pressure.

Clinical studies have identified the effects of specific dietary behaviors on health outcomes. A moderate reduction in dietary fat consumption, to 26 percent of total calories, may be more beneficial than a severe reduction (18 percent fat) in reducing cholesterol levels. Indeed, among men with high levels of LDL (bad cholesterol) and triglycerides (a type of fat found in blood), those who reduced their fat intake to 26 percent

showed the greatest reduction in LDL and triglycerides, while maintaining their HDL (good cholesterol) levels. When fat intake decreased to 18 percent, HDL levels also declined (Knopp et al., 1997). Subsequent research with 50- to 89-year-old adults who modified their fat intake to include two-thirds from vegetable sources and only one-third from animal fats demonstrated a decrease in cholesterol levels for adults whose baseline level was 233 mg/dL or higher, and a reduction in risk of death from coronary heart disease (Chernoff, 2001).

Another nutritional problem of older adults is insufficient intake of certain nutrients. As many as 40 percent of older people have diets that are deficient in three or more nutrients. Up to 15 percent may have vitamin B_{12} deficiency, which is necessary for the production of blood cells and healthy functioning of the nervous system. These deficiencies are in part due to inadequate intake of milk, eggs, vegetables, fruit, and other sources of these nutrients. They may also result from poorer absorption of nutrients by the gastrointestinal (GI) system in older adults, especially those on multiple medications that affect GI absorption. Antioxidants were described in Chapter 3 and include vitamins A, C, E, zinc, and selenium. Some middle-aged and older adults read claims in the media of a relationship between antioxidant intake and slowing of the aging process, prevention of cancer, and cognitive decline. Although many of these claims are not verified by research, they lead many people to use supplements of these nutrients in large doses. There is some evidence that use of supplemental antioxidants can indeed reduce the risk of developing some cancers, but it is better to obtain the necessary nutrients through a well-balanced diet of foods rich in these antioxidants. By following the National Cancer Institute's "Five-a-Day" campaign to consume at least five servings of fruits and vegetables per day, older adults can reduce their chances of developing colon and other types of cancer (Chernoff, 2001; Gray et al., 2003).

BENEFITS OF ANTIOXIDANTS IN THE DIET

Antioxidants bind with free radicals and prevent them from damaging cells. They are abundant in fruits and vegetables that are colorful, such as blueberries, cherries, grapes, cranberries, broccoli, kale, and spinach. Dark chocolate and red wine also are high in antioxidants. Antioxidants are shown to improve brain function because free radicals cause so much damage in this organ. Rats fed a diet rich in antioxidants show significant improvement in their learning ability and observable changes in neuronal function (Wang et al., 2005).

Exercise as Part of Health Promotion

Up to 50 percent of physical changes in older people that are mistakenly attributed to aging may be due to being physically unfit. Physically inactive people age faster and look older than physically fit persons of the same age, in part because of what has been termed **hypokinesia,** a disease of "disuse," or the degeneration and functional loss of muscle and bone tissue. Exercise can slow this loss of muscle mass or lean body mass. Older people who participate in higher-intensity resistance training 30 minutes per day can improve muscle mass and strength. Strength-training programs have been successful after just 8 to 12 weeks even with elders in nursing homes, improving their muscle strength, gait velocity (walking speed), and stair-climbing ability (DiPietro, 2001, Evans, 1999; Haber, 2003; Hewitt, 2003).

There is also considerable evidence of the relationship between regular, vigorous exercise and reduction in a person's chances of dying from heart disease and cancer, as well as hospital admissions for serious illness (DiPietro, 2001; Fried, Kronmal, and Newman, 1998). Moderate exercise is also found to increase life expectancy by 1.3 to 3.7 years longer than for those who do not exercise. Rigorous exercise, equivalent to running 30 minutes per day 5 days a week, extended life by 3.5 to 3.7 years, based on adults examined in the Framingham Heart Study over 40 years (Franco et al., 2005). Researchers found that exercise efficiency and capacity can be

Older people with all levels of ability can benefit from outdoor activities.

improved in older adults through physical training. Older adults (ages 65 to 79) had lower exercise capacity and cardiovascular efficiency than 20- to 30-year-olds before training, but 3 to 6 months of aerobic training resulted in greater improvements on indicators of exercise efficiency among older adults than among the young (Woo et al., 2006). Physical activity is also important for older adults who have chronic heart disease. People diagnosed with heart disease who participate in a regular, moderate exercise program can reduce their risk of cardiac death by 20 to 25 percent, as well as the possibility of disability. Both low- and high-intensity exercise programs can improve aerobic capacity and physical strength among the old-old. They can alleviate the problem of "stiff joints" and lower back pain by improving their flexibility and range of motion. Aerobic exercise and strength training are also shown to improve the functional health of older adults with Type II diabetes. Physical activity can even reduce the risk of falls among older people, thereby preventing disability and the high costs of

---

EXERCISE AND HEALTHY AGING

Researchers have found that strength-training exercises, 20 minutes a day for just 2 to 3 times per week, can help older adults gain 3 pounds of muscle and replace fat in just 10 to 12 weeks. Increased muscle tissue level improves metabolism and efficient use of glucose, reduces blood pressure, increases bone mass, and helps the gastrointestinal system function more efficiently (Crandell, 2006).

treatment and long-term care associated with falls (Evans, 1999; Vincent et al., 2002; Wolf et al., 2003).

Regular exercise is found to reduce the risk of breast cancer. A large study of almost 75,000 women age 50 to 79 who were enrolled in the Women's Health Initiative (described earlier) compared women who walked at least 10 hours per week with their counterparts who were sedentary. The former lowered their risk of developing breast cancer by 30 percent over the sedentary group. The greatest benefit was obtained by lighter-weight women, followed by women of normal weight and those who were slightly overweight. No racial or age differences emerged in the benefits of exercise. No additional benefits were accrued from more vigorous exercise such as jogging or tennis, suggesting that a simple but regular routine of walking daily can play an important role in preventing breast cancer (McTiernan et al., 2003). The box below summarizes some of the health benefits of a regular walking regimen, but it should be noted that the benefits are greatest if people begin this exercise habit during young adulthood or middle age and not wait until their 60s or 70s. Nevertheless, initiating regular exercise at any age, even after age 80, has beneficial effects.

BABY BOOMERS: THE MARATHON GENERATION

Future cohorts of older adults will include a growing number who participate in strenuous exercise. For example, in the United States, 43 percent of all marathoners in 2004 were age 40 and older, compared with 26 percent in 1980. In 2005, the average age of marathon runners was 36 for women and 40.5 for men. In the 2005 New York City Marathon, which requires minimum times to qualify, several participants were in their 70s. Among finishers, 16 percent were age 50 and older, compared with 4 percent in 1976. In the Boston Marathon that same year, 20 percent were over age 50.

SOURCE: Kadloe D., *Time,* June 26, 2006.

Despite the known benefits of exercise, only 22 percent of older Americans participate in *regular* physical activity (defined as 30 minutes or more at least 5 times per week). In the 2003–2004 National Health Interview Survey, 27.5 percent of those age 65 to 74 reported participating in regular physical activities, compared with 19.4 percent of the old-old, and 8.4 percent of oldest-old adults. Even fewer—12 percent—engaged in strength training exercises. Older non-Hispanic whites are more likely to report regular physical activity (23 percent) than are African American (13 percent) and Latino (14 percent) elders. In contrast, 47 percent of white women and 61 percent of African American women report that they do not engage in *any* physical activity (CDC, 2004b; Federal Interagency Forum, 2006). National recommendations to increase physical activity have made only a modest impact on older people. A significant barrier to exercise participation may be attitudinal. Elders who have low expectations about health-related quality of life in old age are less likely to value exercise and do not believe it can help them. Elders with high expectations were more likely to engage in moderate to vigorous exercise than those with low expectations (Sarkinsian et al., 2005).

BENEFITS OF A DAILY, BRISK 30-MINUTE WALK FOR OLDER ADULTS

- avoids obesity
- controls blood pressure
- boosts HDL cholesterol in blood
- boosts metabolic rate
- reduces body fat, improves lean muscle mass
- reduces risk of blood clots, heart attacks, strokes
- helps manage Type II diabetes
- reduces risk of osteoporosis
- improves long-term recovery from depression
- improves balance and prevents falls
- increases joint mobility for people with osteoarthritis

POINTS TO PONDER

Think about people you know who are between ages 75 to 85. What makes some of them look older, while others look younger than their chronological age? Compare their diets, smoking history, and exercise habits. Are there differences in their diets? Are any of them currently smokers or have they smoked in the past? What physical activities are they participating in, and what did they do in the past?

Exercise needs to occur regularly, not just once a week or less. For example, in the Physicians' Health Study with 21,481 men, those who exercised less than once a week were 74 times more likely to die during exertion than men who exercised 5 or more times per week. This study concluded that exercise should be vigorous and last at least 30 to 60 minutes each time (Albert et al., 2000). New national objectives for regular exercise state that adults and children over age 6 should engage in moderate physical activity at least 30 minutes each day (*Healthy People 2010*). But current activity levels among most older adults are so low that meeting objectives for *Healthy People 2010* will require significant behavioral changes among at least one-half of people 65 and older. Successful strategies to increase physical activity include goal-setting, self-monitoring, group support, regular telephone counseling with individualized motivational messages, and support of home-based activity programs. Older adults tend to adhere better to individualized home-based exercise programs than to classes with other elders (Castro and King, 2002; DiPietro, 2001; King, 2001; Stepnick and Whitelaw, 2006).

Increasing physical activity levels from sedentary to participation in 30 minutes of exercise even for 2 days per week can significantly reduce health care costs. In a study of more than 2000 adults whose average age was 63, comparisons in activity levels over 1 year revealed significant savings in both inpatient and outpatient health care costs. The greatest decline ($2200) was found for elders who increased their physical activity levels to 3 or more days per week from none or once a week, a relatively minor change. These savings compensated in part for the health care costs of people with multiple chronic conditions who increased their exercise levels (Martinson et al., 2003). In recognition of potential cost savings, some corporations and even local governments are providing insurance incentives for people who engage in healthy behaviors, while those who choose not to participate pay high premiums. The dramatic impact of self-care behaviors on health care costs and hospital and physician use is an important indicator of the benefits for both individuals and society of a healthy lifestyle in the later years.

SUSTAINING THE MOTIVATION TO CHANGE HEALTH BEHAVIORS

Motivating adults of any age to make and sustain changes in their health behaviors is a challenge. One program for older adults, Enhance Wellness, focuses on motivation first. A team of two professionals, typically a nurse and social worker, assess an individual's strengths and risks, then develops a plan in which the participant, not the professional, chooses the health behaviors they want to work on. As participants implement their individualized plan, a volunteer health mentor offers ongoing encouragement, feedback, and monitoring. Allowing elders to set their own goals and providing peer support are vital components of this program. It has reduced length of hospital stays, lowered medication use, alleviated symptoms of mood disorders, and enhanced elders' sense of self-efficacy. The Enhanced Fitness programs provides low-cost, evidence-based exercise programs that focus on stretching flexibility, balance, low-impact aerobics and strength-training exercises. Implemented in nearly 100 sites nationwide, Enhanced Fitness does not require expensive equipment or a large space (Accessed March 9, 2007, from, http://www.projectenhance.org/pro/fitness.hml).

Improving the Effectiveness of Health Promotion Programs

Modest gains have been made in reducing unhealthy behaviors among middle aged and older adults. For example, smoking rates among older white and African American women have declined to less than 8 percent, and for white men to 9.4 percent. However, older African American men still exceed the target set by *Healthy People 2010,* with 19.4 percent who report smoking (CDC, 2004a; NCHS, 2003b).

In contrast to gains in smoking reduction, nutritional and exercise habits have not improved to levels envisioned by *Healthy People 2000.* Although obesity is less common among older Americans than in other age groups, many chronic diseases such as heart disease and diabetes are associated with it. Yet obesity rates have increased among older adults, from 12 percent in 1990 to 19 percent in 2002 (Cole and Fox, 2004). Elders of color and low-income older persons are at greatest risk for obesity. Nevertheless, healthier nutritional patterns are reflected in the decreased consumption of saturated fats and increased intake of vegetables, fruits, and complex carbohydrates during the past decade. Surveys reveal that 32 percent of older adults have improved their nutritional intake, but this is considerably lower than the target of 50 percent set by *Healthy People 2000* (Butler, 2000).

Some of the most successful health promotion interventions have included older adults who have some chronic health conditions. For example, a dietary self-management program using interactive computer technology and individualized health messages for people with Type II diabetes resulted in significant improvements in nutritional habits and health care costs (Glasgow et al., 1997). Another study focused on an exercise and education program for older adults with osteoarthritis. Both aerobic and strength training exercise were prescribed over 8 weeks. This intervention was more effective than a control condition in reducing arthritis pain and stiffness over 6 months. Elders in the exercise group significantly increased their exercise self-efficacy and adherence to the program. (Ettinger et al., 1997). Long-term success in these programs appears to be related to improvements in the status of specific chronic diseases. Other factors that can enhance the effectiveness of health promotion programs include:

- utilizing social support, such as exercise groups or pairs
- opportunities for intergenerational activities (e.g., healthy eating programs for grandparents and grandchildren)
- utilizing available resources such as outdoor paths or malls for walking programs
- culturally competent nutritional and exercise interventions with written and oral materials in the elders' native language

In summary, health promotion programs must be designed to fit the lifestyle, preferences, social

---

HEALTH PROMOTION ON A LARGER SCALE

Health promotion efforts at a community and even a national level demonstrate dramatic effects. In the early 1970s, the government of Finland responded to high rates of cardiovascular disease in its southeastern region with the North Karelia Project. Local communities passed bans on smoking in public zones. Dairy farms were converted to growing berries that reduced residents' intake of fatty milk while simultaneously increasing their intake of berries high in vitamin C. By 1997, death rates from both lung cancer and heart disease had declined by 70 percent. On the other hand, just a few miles away, in northwestern Russia, the health of the local population had declined; death rates from heart disease, cancer, and emphysema increased because of worsening environmental and economic conditions with the collapse of the Soviet Union (*New York Times,* 2000).

class, and cultural values of older adults who are the targets of such efforts. Older adults can benefit from health promotion activities that take such structural factors into account.

Limitations of Health Promotion

Health promotion programs are sometimes criticized for their emphasis on individual responsibility for change, which minimizes the societal health and economic disparities, such as poverty, that underlie individual health practices. Likewise, some educational efforts ignore the roles of policy makers, health care providers, food manufacturers, and the mass media in creating social and economic environments that may counter health promotion interventions. In addition to educating individuals to adopt healthy habits, the broader social environment must be changed.

In general, organized health promotion programs have difficulty recruiting more than 50 percent of the target population. This is true even for programs focused on people diagnosed with a potentially deadly condition such as

---

POINTS TO PONDER

Think about a health habit that you have tried to change, such as increasing your daily exercise and intake of fruits and vegetables, What difficulties did you face in making the desired changes? What are some strategies that worked for you? Could these same methods be used to help older adults change lifelong habits?

---

post–myocardial infarct patients and those with high blood pressure. Attrition is also high, with rates of 30 to 60 percent. Older people most likely to participate in organized health promotion are those with a preventive attitude (e.g., regular users of physicians and dentists for checkups, nonsmokers, exercisers, and users of seat belts and smoke alarms), and those with higher participation rates in community services generally.

Another limitation is that, although the value of health promotion is widely publicized, individuals often do not act on this information. Think about the number of people who continue to smoke despite the empirical evidence linking smoking to lung cancer, or the fact that one third of white women and one-half of ethnic minority women do not get regular mammograms (Federal Interagency Forum, 2006). The gap between health knowledge and health practices can be very wide. Even when individual behavior change is a legitimate goal, sustaining health practices over time is difficult in the face of years of habit. More longitudinal research is needed to assess the long-range (10 years or more) consequences of health promotion interventions for individuals and for health care costs, especially since programs may initially be very costly before significant savings emerge.

Health promotion is clearly a growing area, especially in light of pressure from Medicare, health maintenance organizations (HMOs), and private insurers to reduce rising health care costs for older adults. However, it requires collaboration

---

LIFESTYLE AND LONGEVITY

Arthur is a 97-year-old who may be described as a "paragon of good living." He has never smoked, has maintained his ideal body weight throughout adulthood, mostly by eating a diet rich in vegetables, fruit and nuts, and by walking two miles daily in his hilly neighborhood. Arthur has no chronic diseases. Although he still grieves over the death of his wife of 60 years 5 years ago, Arthur's spiritual beliefs and strong family network of children, grandchildren, and great grandchildren who live nearby have all helped him cope with his loss. His lifestyle exemplifies the link between longevity and healthy habits (maintaining an ideal weight, eating a healthy diet, not smoking, regular exercise, strong support network, and spiritual values). Many of these individual behaviors were also found to predict survival of men in a 40-year study of Japanese men (Willcox et al., 2006).

among individuals, local, state, and federal organizations and governments. In 2001, several national organizations such as AARP, the American Geriatrics Society, and the National Council on the Aging joined forces with government agencies including the CDC and NIA, and with foundations concerned about health care and aging. They developed "The National Blueprint: Increasing Physical Activity among Adults Age 50 and Older." This partnership of more than 55 organizations developed 18 priority areas that recommended strategies at the individual, community, and policy levels. Community efforts included developing exercise programs in neighborhoods with large ethnic minority populations and building safe walking trails. This partnership also promoted efforts to provide low-income elders with low cost, healthy meals and fresh produce (Active Aging Partnership, 2006). Research and demonstration programs provide ample evidence for the effectiveness of a multi-pronged approach to health promotion in delaying the onset of chronic diseases, reducing disability and health care costs, and even extending life expectancy.

Implications for the Future

As baby boomers age, several trends may emerge First, this cohort includes more informed, health-conscious consumers than their predecessors. As a result, they will make more demands on the health care system, not just for themselves but for those for whom they are caregivers. A greater proportion than among previous cohorts will continue their self-care and wellness focus. Many will attain *Healthy People 2010* objectives that their parents have not been able to achieve. At the same time, however, a significant minority of baby boomers, particularly smokers and those who have lived a lifetime in poverty with little access to preventive services, will cope with multiple chronic diseases as their life expectancy increases.

HEALTHY AGING AMONG BABY BOOMERS

"Healthy aging" has become a goal of many middle-aged adults today. As noted in this and previous chapters, newer cohorts of adults are avoiding smoking, watching their weight, eating a healthy diet, and increasing their exercise frequency and level. It is no longer surprising to see midlife and young-old men and women competing in marathons and race walks. A popular phrase is, "Age 60 today is the old 50," with many 60 and older taking on new challenges. Some examples of baby boomers who have made the most of turning 60:

- A businessman who recently became a part-time certified meditation teacher.
- A pilot and motorcycle rider who celebrated his 60th birthday by riding 4000 miles from Seattle, Washington to North Carolina.
- An educator who assumed the position of vice president for a Fortune 500 company at age 60.

SOURCE: *Seattle Times*, 2005.

Changes in the health care system will also influence future cohorts' access to and use of health services. For example, because of increased cost containment efforts (described in Chapter 17), more adults are enrolled—often not by choice—in health maintenance organizations (HMOs) or other types of managed care for their health care. In 1998, 78 million Americans were enrolled in HMOs; the numbers are expected to rise to 125 million by 2010. About 25 percent are expected to be elders and people with disabilities who are enrolled in Medicare (RWJF, 2003). To the extent that these health care systems are focused on maintaining and enhancing health behaviors, elders will have opportunities to participate in health promotion activities. However, if services are limited and preventive programs such as exercise, smoking cessation, and nutritional counseling are not offered, future cohorts of elders will not have ready access to health enhancement programs. The growth of health technology, including telemedicine and home-based medication dispensers that prevent under- or overmedication, can help future elders manage their own health. The impact of these technologies on older adults' ability to age in place in their own homes is discussed in Chapter 11.

Because of improved health status and survival with multiple chronic diseases among the older population, there is a growing need for health care providers trained in gerontology and clinical geriatrics. Geriatricians (physicians who specialize in geriatric medicine), as well as dentists, pharmacists, nurses and nurse practitioners, social workers, health educators, physical therapists, and occupational therapists who have been trained in geriatrics and gerontology, are critical to helping future cohorts of elders manage their chronic conditions and maximize their functional abilities. The shortage of physicians and pharmacists trained in geriatrics is one reason why many older Americans experience adverse reactions to medications and high rates of emergency room and inpatient hospital visits. Health care providers who are trained in geriatrics are more likely to encourage exercise programs, smoking cessation, and dietary interventions for older people and less likely to endorse stereotypes of aging as a time of decline. Indeed, there is evidence for better health outcomes for older adults who receive specialized geriatric nursing and physician care (Kovner, Mezey, and Harrington, 2002).

The increasing need for geriatric nurse specialists comes at a time when the nursing profession is experiencing a shortage in all specialties and the median age of nurses today, 45, is higher than all other health professions. Over 1 million new and replacement nurses will be needed by 2012 (Rieder, 2006). These trends do not bode well for the field of geriatric nursing care. Today only about 10,000 of the 2.56 million registered nurses are certified in gerontological nursing, while only 3 percent of the 111,000 advanced practice nurses are certified in geriatrics (American Association of Colleges of Nursing, 2004). Likewise, the number of physicians specializing in geriatrics is far from adequate. In

2005, there was one geriatrician for every 5,000 adults age 65 and older. This is less than half the projected need for the current patient pool, and only one-fourth of the number needed by 2030. A primary reason for this gap in workforce needs is that only 9 of the 145 medical schools in the United States have departments of geriatrics; few schools require geriatric courses; and teaching hospitals graduate internists with as little as 6 hours of geriatric training (Gross, 2006). The situation in pharmacy is especially dire, with only 720 of 200,000 pharmacists who have received certification in geriatrics (Alliance for Aging Research, 2002; Scharlach, Simon, and Dal Santo, 2002).

Social workers, who are key members of interdisciplinary health care teams, are not yet prepared to meet the growing demand for geriatric social work. The National Institute on Aging has projected a need for 60,000 to 70,000 geriatric social workers by 2020; yet less than 10 percent of that projected need is currently available. In fact, only about 4 percent of social workers with Masters degrees work in services targeted at older adults. A 2005 survey of a national sample of licensed social workers found that 75 percent worked in some way with older adults but had generally not been prepared to do so (Bureau of Labor Statistics, 2004; NASW, 2005; Rosen, Zlotnik and Singer, 2002). Unless health professional schools become more proactive in recruiting faculty to develop geriatric curricula and students to consider a career in geriatrics or gerontology, the current situation will grow into a crisis. The federal government took an important first step by passing the Geriatric Care Act in 2001, aimed at improving Medicare reimbursement for geriatric care and offering incentives for health professionals to obtain training in this field. In addition, the John A. Hartford Foundation in New York City remains the primary source of funding for professional development and mentoring in geriatrics in many health care disciplines, especially in medicine, nursing, and social work.

Summary

Although older adults are at risk of more diseases than younger people, most rate their own health as satisfactory. Health status refers not only to an individual's physical condition, but also to her or his functional ability in various social and psychological domains. It is affected by a person's social surroundings, especially the degree of environmental stress and social support available. Although stress increases the risk of certain illnesses, such as cardiovascular disease, older people are generally less negatively affected by it; this may reflect maturity, resiliency, self-control, or a lifetime of developing coping skills.

Older people are more likely to suffer from chronic or long-term diseases than from temporary or acute illnesses. The majority of older persons, however, are not limited in their daily activities by chronic conditions. The impact of such conditions apparently varies with the physiological changes that occur with age, the individual's adaptive resources, and his or her mental and emotional perspective. The type and incidence of chronic illnesses also vary by gender, ethnic minority status, and socioeconomic status.

The leading causes of death among persons over age 65 are heart disease, cancer, stroke, and accidents. Diseases of the heart and blood vessels are the most prevalent. Because hypertension or high blood pressure is a major risk in the development of cardiovascular problems, preventive actions are critical, especially weight control, dietary changes, appropriate exercise, and avoidance of cigarette smoking. Cancers, especially lung, bowel, breast and colon cancers, are the second most frequent cause of death among older people; the risk of cancer increases with age. Cerebrovascular accident, or stroke, is the third leading cause of death among older persons. It may be caused by cerebral thrombosis, or blood clots, and by cerebral hemorrhage. Healthy lifestyle practices are important in preventing these deaths. Indeed, death rates due to heart disease and stroke have declined for older adults, while deaths attributable to cancer have declined among middle-aged adults. This is because of more preventive health care and early detection of cancer in the middle years. Similarly, accidents, particularly those associated with driving and falls, are often preventable through changes in environmental design as well as exercise.

Arthritis, although not fatal, is a major cause of limited daily activity and, to some extent, affects most older persons. Osteoporosis, or loss of bone mass and the resultant increased brittleness of the bones, is most common among older women, and may result in fractures of the hip, spine, and wrist. New research supports the benefits of physical exercise for preventing fractures and falls and managing arthritis. Chronic respiratory problems, particularly emphysema, increase with age, especially among men. Diabetes mellitus is a frequent problem in old age, and is particularly troubling because of comorbidity or the many related illnesses that may result. Problems with the intestinal tract include diverticulitis, constipation, and hiatus hernia. Cystitis and incontinence are frequently occurring problems of the kidneys and urinary system, especially among older women. Although the majority of older persons have some type of incontinence, most kinds can be treated and controlled.

The growth of the older population, combined with the increase in major chronic illnesses, has placed greater demands on the health care system. Nevertheless, older people seek outpatient medical, dental, and mental health services at a slightly lower rate than their incidence of chronic illnesses would predict. Like younger people, the older population is most likely to seek health services for acute problems, not for checkups on chronic conditions or for preventive care. Perceptions that physicians, dentists, and mental health professionals cannot cure their chronic problems may deter many older people from seeking needed care. The problem may be compounded by ageist beliefs of some health care providers and by cultural and linguistic barriers that result in health care disparities among historically underserved groups. More training in geriatrics and gerontology is needed for health care providers in order to improve their attitudes toward and competencies for working with older people and their families.

Health promotion is effective in improving the well-being and enhancing the quality of life of older people. The elimination or postponement of the chronic diseases that are associated with old age is a major goal for specialists in wellness and health enhancement, as well as biomedical researchers interested in delaying the aging process. Treatment methods for all these diseases are changing rapidly with the growth in medical technology and the increasing recognition given to such environmental factors as stress, nutrition, and exercise in disease prevention. If health promotion efforts to modify lifestyles are successful, and if aging research progresses substantially, the chronic illnesses that we have discussed will undoubtedly be postponed, and disability or loss of functional status may never happen to future cohorts.

GLOSSARY

acute condition   short-term disease or infection, often debilitating to older persons

acute myocardial infarction   loss of blood flow to a specific region of the heart, resulting in damage of the myocardium

Activities of Daily Living (ADLs)   summarize an individual's performance in personal care tasks such as bathing or dressing, as well as such home-management activities as shopping, meal preparation, and taking medications

arteriosclerosis   loss of elasticity of the arterial walls because of fatty deposits

atherosclerosis   narrowing of large arteries because of plague deposits

benign prostatic hypertrophy (BPH)   enlargement of the prostate gland in older men, without signs of cancer or other serious disease; may cause discomfort

chronic condition   long-term (more than three months), often permanent, and leaving a residual disability that may require long-term management or care rather than cure

comorbidity   simultaneously experiencing multiple health problems, both acute and chronic

diabetes mellitus   a disease that impairs the ability of the pancreas to produce insulin, a hormone that enables glucose from the blood to cells, and accumulates in the blood

diagnosis related groups (DRGs)   a system of classifying medical cases for payment on the basis of diagnoses; used under Medicare's prospective payment system (PPS) for inpatient hospital services

disability   an impairment in the ability to complete multiple daily tasks

diverticulitis   a condition in which pouches or sacs (diverticula) in the intestinal wall become inflamed and infected

edentulous   the absence of natural teeth

frailty   severe limitations in ADL

good health   more than the mere absence of infirmity, a state of complete physical, mental, and social well-being

health promotion   a model in which individuals are responsible for and in control of their own health, combined with health education and related organizational, political, and economic changes conducive to health

health status   the presence or absence of disease as well as the degree of disability in an individual's level of functioning

hiatus hernia   a condition in which a small portion of the stomach slides up through the diaphragm

hypokinesia   the degeneration and functional loss of muscle and bone due to physical inactivity

Instrumental Activities of Daily Living (IADLs)   daily activities involving use of the environment

immunity   ability of the organism to resist pathogens (viruses and bacteria)

incontinence   the inability to control urine and feces—of two types: urge incontinence, where a person is not able to hold urine long enough to reach a toilet, and stress incontinence, where leakage occurs during physical exertion, laughing, sneezing, or coughing

osteoarthritis   gradual degeneration of joints that are subject to physical stress

osteopenia a significant loss of calcium and reduced bone density not associated with increased risk of fractures

quality of life going beyond health status alone, this concept considers the individual's sense of competence, ability to perform activities of daily living, and satisfaction with social interactions, in addition to functional health

rheumatoid arthritis a chronic inflammation of the membranes lining joints and tendons, characterized by pain, swelling, bone dislocation, and limited range of motion; can occur at any age

sarcopenia atrophy of skeletal muscle mass, generally resulting from a sedentary lifestyle and some chronic diseases

REFERENCES

AARP. Beyond 50. *A report to the nation on independent living and disability.* Washington, DC: AARP Public Policy Institute, 2003.

Active Aging Partnership. National Blueprint: Increasing physical activity among adults aged 50 and older. Accessed February 13, 2006, from http://www.agingblueprint.org.

Ai, A., and Carrigan, L. Older adults with age-related cardiovascular disease. In B. Berkman (Ed.), *Handbook of Social Work in Health and Aging,* New York: Oxford. 2006.

Albert, C.M., Mittleman, M.A., Chae, C.U., Lee, I.M., Hennekens, C.H., and Manson, J.E. Triggering of sudden death from cardiac causes by vigorous exertion. *New England Journal of Medicine,* 2000, *343,* 1355–1361.

Alliance for Aging Research. *Medical never-never land: Ten reasons why America is not ready for the coming age boom.* Washington, DC: Alliance for Aging Research, 2002.

American Association of Colleges of Nursing. *Nursing Practitioner and Clinical Nurse Specialists Competencies for Older Adult Care.* Washington, DC, 2004.

American Cancer Society (ACS). *Breast cancer questions and answers; Cancer facts for men.* ACS, 2001.

American Diabetes Association (ADA). *National diabetes fact sheet: General information and national estimates on diabetes in the United States.* Accessed 2003, from http://www.diabetes.org/diabetes-statistics/nationaldiabetes-fact-sheet.jsp.

American Diabetes Association (ADA). Screening for Type 2 diabetes. *Diabetes Care,* 2004, *27,* S11–S13.

American Geriatrics Society. Guideline for the prevention of falls in older persons. *Journal of the American Geriatrics Society,* 2001, *49,* 664–672.

American Heart Association. *Heart disease and stroke statistics 2003 update.* Dallas, TX: American Heart Association, 2003.

American Heart Association. *Heart disease and stroke statistics 2005 Update.* Dallas, TX: American Heart Association, 2005.

Arfin, F. Older drivers turning to AAA, AARP for advice on road safety. *About: Senior Travel.* Accessed December 1, 2006, from http://seniortravel.about.com.

Baker, C.W., Whisman, M.A., and Brownell, K.D. Studying intergenerational transmission of eating attitudes and behaviors. Methodological and conceptual questions. *Health Psychology,* 2000, *19,* 376–381.

Bazargan, M., Bazargan, S., and Baker, R.S. Emergency department utilization, hospital admissions, and physician visits among elderly African American persons. *The Gerontologist,* 1998, *38,* 25–36.

Bédard, M., Stones, M.J., Guyatt, G.H., and Hirdes, J.P. Traffic-related fatalities among older drivers and passengers: Past and future trends. *The Gerontologist,* 2001, *41,* 751–756.

Bernard, S.L., Kincade, J.E., Konrad, T.R., Arcury, T.A., and Rabiner, D. Predicting mortality from community surveys of older adults: The importance of self-rated functional ability. *Journals of Gerontology: Social Sciences,* 1997, *52,* S155–S163.

Breslow, L. From disease prevention to health promotion. *Journal of the American Medical Association,* 1999, *281,* 1030–1033.

Bureau of Labor Statistics. *Social workers.* Accessed September 15, 2005, from http://stats.bls.gov/oco/ocos060.htm.

Butler, R.N., *Maintaining healthy lifestyles.* Workshop Report of the International Longevity Center, 2000.

Campisi, J. Aging, tumor suppression and cancer: Highwire act. *Mechanics of Aging and Development,* 2005, *126,* 51–58.

Castro, C.M., and King, A.C. Telephone-assisted counseling for physical activity. *Exercise and Sport Sciences,* 2002, *30,* 64–68.

Cauley, J.A., Robbins, J., Chen, Z., Cummings, S.R., Jackson, R.D., LaCroix, A.Z., LeBoff, M., Lewis, C.E., et al. Effects of estrogen plus progestic on risk of fracture and bone mineral density. *Journal of the American Medical Association,* 2003, *290,* 1729–1738.

Centers for Disease Control and Prevention (CDC). *Behavioral risk factor surveillance system online trends databases.* Accessed October 15, 2006a, from http://www.cdc.gov/brfss/.

Centers for Disease Control and Prevention (CDC). *Health, United States, 2004. Special excerpt: Trend tables on 65 and older population.* Atlanta, GA:CDC, 2004a.

Centers for Disease Control and Prevention (CDC). *HIV/AIDS Surveillance Report—Mid-Year Edition,* 2001, *13,* 14.

Centers for Disease Control and Prevention (CDC). *HIV/AIDS Surveillance in women, updated through 2003.* Accessed October 15, 2006b, from http://www.cdc.gov/hiv/graphics/htm.

Centers for Disease Control and Prevention (CDC). Hospitalizations for stroke among adults aged ≥65 years: U.S., 2000. *MMWR Public Health Report,* 2003a, *52,* 586–589.

Centers for Disease Control and Prevention (CDC). *National Center for Chronic Disease Prevention and Health Promotion.* Accessed 2003b, from http://www.cdc.gov/brfss.

Centers for Disease Control and Prevention (CDC). *National Center for Injury Control. U.S. Prevention programs for seniors.* Accessed February 13, 2006c, from http://www.cdc.gov/ncipc/falls/fallprev.pdf.

Centers for Disease Control and Prevention (CDC). National diabetes fact sheet: General information and national estimates of diabetes in the United States, 2003d.

Centers for Disease Control and Prevention (CDC). Percentage of persons aged >65 who reported receiving influenza or pneumococcal vaccine. Accessed 2003c, from http://www.cdc.gov/mmwr/preview/mmwrhtml/figures/m025a2tl.gif.

Centers for Disease Control and Prevention (CDC). Strength training among adults aged 65 and older—U.S. 2001. *Morbidity and Mortality Weekly Report,* 2004b, *53,* 25–26.

Centers for Disease Control and Prevention (CDC). Tips for preventing falls. Accessed December,
2006d, from http://www.cdc.gov/ncipc/duip/fallsmaterial.htm.

Chernoff, R. Nutrition and health promotion in older adults. *Journals of Gerontology,* 2001, *56A* (Special Issue II), 47–53.

Chiu, K.M. Efficacy of calcium supplements on bone mass in postmenopausal women. *Journals of Gerontology: Medical Sciences,* 1999, *54A,* M275–M280.

Clancey, C.M., and Bierman, A.S. Quality and outcomes of care for older women with chronic disease. *Women's Health Issues,* 2000, *10,* 178–192.

Cole, N., and Fox, M.K. *Nutrition and health characteristics of low-income populations: Older Adults* (Volume IV). U.S. Dept of Agriculture Economic Research Service, Food Assistance and Nutrition Research Program, 2004.

Coleman, E.A., Hutchins, L., and Goodwin, J. An overview of cancer in older adults. *MEDSURG Nursing,* 2004, *13,* 75–109.

Cramer, N. Promoting continence: Strategies for success. *Perspectives in Health Promotion and Aging,* 1993, *1,* 1–3.

Crandell, S. Living longer: Exercise. *AARP Magazine,* 2006, *49,* 90–93.

Cranney, A., Tugwell, P., Wells, G., and Guyatt, G. Osteoporosis Methodology Group and the Osteoporosis Research Advisory Group. Meta-analyses of therapies for postmenopausal osteoporosis. I. Systematic reviews of randomized trials in osteoporosis: Introduction and methodology. *Endocrine Reviews,* 2002, *23,* 496–507.

Crimmins, E.M. Trends in the health of the elderly. *Annual Review of Public Health,* 2004, *2,* 79–98.

Crimmins, E.M., and Saito, Y. Trends in healthy life expectancy in the United States: Gender, racial and educational differences. *Social Science and Medicine,* 2001, *52,* 1629–1641.

DeCoster, V.A. Challenges of type 2 diabetes and role of health care social work: A neglected area of practice. *Health and Social Work,* 2001, *26,* 26–37.

DiPietro, L. Physical activity in aging: Changes in patterns and their relationship to health and function. *Journals of Gerontology,* 2001, *56A* (Special Issue II), 13–22.

Dignam, J.J. Differences in breast cancer prognosis among African American and Caucasian women. *CA—A Cancer Journal for Clinicians,* 2000, *50,* 50–64.

Doshi, J.A., Shaffer, T., and Briesacher, B.A. National estimates of medication use in nursing homes. *Journal of the American Geriatrics Society.* 2005, *53,* 438–443.

Emlet, C.A., and Berghuis, J.P. Service priorities, use and needs: Views of older and younger consumers living with HIV/AIDS. *Journal of Mental Health and Aging,* 2002, *8,* 307–318.

Emlet, C.A., and Farkas, K.J. Correlates of service utilization among midlife and older adults with HIV/AIDS. *Journal of Aging and Health,* 2002, *14,* 315–335.

Ershler, W.B. Cancer: A disease of the elderly. *Journal of Supportive Oncology,* 2003, *1,* 5–10.

Ettinger, W.H., Burns, R., Messier, S.P., Applegate, W., Rejeski, W.J., et al. The fitness arthritis and seniors trial, *Journal of the American Medical Association,* 1997, *277,* 25–31.

Evans, W.J. Exercise training guidelines for the elderly. *Medical Science and Sports Exercise,* 1999, *31,* 12–17.

Federal Interagency Forum on Aging-Related Statistics. *Older Americans update 2006: Key Indicators of Well-Being.* Hyattsville, MD: Author, 2006.

Ferraro, K., and Kelley-Moore, M. Are racial disparities in health conditional on socioeconomic status? *Social Science and Medicine,* 2005, *60,* 191–204.

Ferrucci, L., Kittner, S.J., Corti, M.C., and Guralnik, J.M. Neurological conditions. In J.M. Guralnick, L.P. Fried, E.M. Simonsick, J.D., Kaspar, and M.E. Lafferty (Eds.), *The women's health and aging study.* Bethesda, MD: NIH/NIA, 1995.

Fisman, D.N., Abrutyn, E., Spaude, K.A., Kim, A., Kirchner, C., and Daley, J. Prior pneumococcal vaccination is associated with reduced death, complications, and length of stay among hospitalized adults with community-acquired pneumonia. *Clinical Infectious Diseases,* 2006, *42,* 1093–1101.

Flaherty, J.H., Perry, H.M., Lynchard, G.S., and Morley, J.E. Polypharmacy and hospitalization among older home care patients. *Journals of Gerontology: Medical Sciences,* 2000, *55A,* M554–M559.

Fletcher, P.C. and Hirdes, J.P. Restriction in activity associated with fear of falling among community-based seniors using home care services. *Age and Ageing,* 2004, *33,* 273–279.

Foldvari, M., Clark, M., Laviolette, L., Bernstein, M., Kaliton, D., Castaneda, C., et al. Association of muscle power with functional status in community-dwelling elderly women. *Journals of Gerontology Series A: Biological Sciences and Medical Sciences,* 2000, *55,* M192–M199.

Foley, D.J., Masak, K.H., Ross, G.W., and White, L.R. Driving cessation in older men with incident dementia. *Journal of the American Geriatric Society,* 2000, *48,* 928-930.

Franco, O.H., deLaet, C., Peeters, A., Jonker, J., Mackenbach, J., and Nusselder, W. Effects of physical activity on life expectancy with cardio-vascular disease. *Archives of Internal Medicine,* 2005, *165,* 2355–2360.

Francoeur, R., and Elkins, J. Older adults with diabetes and complications. In B. Berkman (Ed.) *Handbook of Social Work in Health and Aging.* New York: Oxford, 2006.

Frankl, W.S. Is alcohol good or bad for the heart? *Gerontology News,* 2003, *31,* 2.

Freund, B., and Szinovacz, M. Effects of cognition on driving involvement among the oldest old. *The Gerentologist,* 2002, *42,* 621–633.

Fried, L.P., Kronman, R.A., and Newman, A.B. Risk factors for 5-year mortality in older adults: The Cardiovascular Health Study. *Journal of the American Medical Association,* 1998, *279,* 585–592.

Fried, L.P., Tangen, C.M., Walston, J., Newman, A.B., Hirsch, C., Seeman, T., Tracy, R., et al. Frailty in older adults: Evidence for a phenotype. *Journals of Gerontology Series A: Biological Sciences and Medical Sciences,* 2001, *56,* M146–M156.

Fries, J.F. Aging, natural death, and the compression of morbidity. *New England Journal of Medicine,* 1980, *303,* 130–135.

Fries, J.F. Measuring and monitoring success in compressing morbidity. *Annals of Internal Medicine,* 2003, *139,* 455–459.

Gallagher, B. Tai Chi Chuan and Qigong: Physical and mental practice for functional mobility. *Topics in Geriatric Rehabilitation,* 2003, *19,* 172–182.

Glasgow, R.E., LaChance, P.A., Toobert, D.J., Brown, J., Hampson, S.E., and Riddle, M.C. Long-term effects and costs of a brief behavioral dietary intervention for patients with diabetes delivered from the medical office. *Patient Education and Counseling,* 1997, *32,* 175–184.

Gorelick, P.B., Shanmugam, V., and Pajeau, A.K. Stroke. In J.E. Birren (Ed.), *Encyclopedia of gerontology,* Vol. 2. San Diego: Academy Press, 1996.

Gray, S.L., Hanlon, J.T., Landerman, L.R., Artz, M., Schmeder, K.E., and Fillenbaum, G.G. Is antioxidant use protective of cognitive function in community-dwelling elderly? *American Journal of Geriatric Pharmacotherapy*, 2003, *1*, 3–10.

Gross, J. Geriatrics lags in age of high-tech medicine. *The New York Times*, October 18, 2006, http://www.nytimes.com/2006/10/18/health/18aged.

Gubrium, J., Rittman, M., Williams, C., and Boylstein, C. Benchmarking as everyday functional assessment in stroke recovery. *The Journals or Gerontology*, 2003, *588*, 5203–5211.

Gurnack, A.M., Atkinson, R., and Osgood, N. (Eds.). *Treating alcohol and drug abuse in the elderly*. New York: Springer, 2002.

Gusi, N., Raimundo, A., and Leal, A. Low-frequency vibratory exercise reduces the risk of bone fracture more than walking. *BMC Musculoskeletal Disorders*, 2006, *7*, 92–98.

Haber, D. *Health promotion and aging: Practical applications for health professionals* (3rd ed.), New York: Springer, 2003.

Handler, S.M., Wright, R.M., Rudy, C.M., and Hanlon, J.T. Epidemiology of medication-related adverse events in nursing homes. *American Journal of Geriatric Pharmacotherapy*, 2006, *4*, 264–272.

Hawkins, S.A., Wiswell, R.A., Jaque, S.V., Constantino, N., Marcell, T.J., Tarpenning, K.M., Schroeder, E.T., et al. The inability of hormone replacement therapy or chronic running to maintain bone mass in master athletes. *Journals of Gerontology: Medical Sciences*, 1999, *54A*, M451–M455.

Hayflick, L. *How and why we age*. New York: Ballantine Books, 1996.

He, W., Sengupta, M., Velkoff, V., and DeBerros, K. *65+ in the United States*. Washington, DC: U.S. Department of Health and Human Services, 2005.

Health Care Cost and Utilization Project (HCUP). 2002 National Statistics, Accessed 2002, from http://hcup.ahrq.gov/HCUPnet.asp.

Health Resources and Services Administration (HRSA). HIV disease in individuals ages 50 and above. *HRSA Care Action*, February 2001, 1–3.

Healthy People 2010. Understanding and Improving Health. U.S. Government Printing Office. No. 017-001-00547-9, 2000.

Hemmelgarn, B., Suissa, S., Huang, A., Boirin, J.F., and Pinard, G. Benzodiazepine use and the risk of motor vehicle crash in the elderly. *Journal of the American Medical Association*, 1997, *278*, 27–31.

Hewitt, M.J. *Growing older, staying strong: Preventing sarcopenia through strength training*. New York: International Longevity Center, 2003.

Hsieh, C. Treatment of constipation in older adults. *American Family Physician*, 2005, *74*, 715–718.

Huang, G., Gau, M., Lin, W., and Kernoham, G. Assessing risk of falling in older adults. *Public Health Nursing*, 2003, *20*, 399–411.

Hughes, S.L., Prohaska, T.R., Wong, M.D., Hirsch, S., and Mangione, C.M. Promoting physical activity among older people. *Generations*, 2005, *29*, 54–59.

Hughes, S.L., Seymour, R.B., Campbell, R., Pollak, N., Huber, G., and Sharma, L. Impact of the fit and strong intervention on older adults with osteoarthritis. *The Gerontologist*, 2004, *44*, 217–228.

Insurance Institute for Highway Safety (IIHS). *Fatality facts, elderly*. Arlington, VA: IIHS. http://www.hwysafety.org/safety%5Ffacts/fatality%5facts/elderly.htm.

Jacob, T., and Johnson, S.L. Sequential interactions in the parent-child communications of depressed fathers and depressed mothers. *Journal of Family Psychology*, 2001, *15*, 38–52.

Juvenile Diabetes Foundation. *Diabetes Facts*. Accessed 1998, from http://www.jdfcure.org.

Kalache, A., and Kickbusch, I. A global strategy for healthy aging. *World Health*, 1997, *4*, 4–5.

Kaufman, D.W., Kelly, J.P., Rosenberg, L., Anderson, T.E., and Mitchell, A.A. Recent patterns of medication use in the ambulatory adult population of the United States. *Journal of the American Medical Association*, 2002, *287*, 337–344.

Kelley-Moore, M. and Ferraro, K. The black-white disability gap: Persistent inequality in later life? *Journals of Gerontology*, 2004, *59*, S34–S43.

King, A.C. Interventions to promote physical activity by older adults. *Journals of Gerontology*, 2001, *56A* (Special Issue II), 36–46.

Kiyak, H.A. and Reichmuth, M. Barriers to and enablers of older adults' use of dental services. *Journal of Dental Education*, 2005, *69*, 975–986.

Knoops, K.T.B. Mediterranean diet, lifestyle factors and 10-year mortality in elderly European men and women. *Journal of the American Medical Association*, 2004, *292*, 1433–1439.

Knopp, R.H., Walden, C.E., Retzlaff, B.M., McCann, B.S., Dowdy, A.A., Albers, J.J., Gey, G.O., et al. Long-term cholesterol-lowering effects of 4 fat-restricted diets in hypercholesterolemic and combined hyperlipidemic men. The dietary alternatives study. *Journal of the American Medical Association,* 1997, *278,* 1509–1515.

Korzenik, J.R. Case closed? Diverticulitis: Epidemiology and fiber. *Journal of Clinical Gastroenterology,* 2006, *40,* Supplement 3, S112–S116.

Kovner, C.T., Mezey, M., and Harrington, C. Who cares for older adults? *Health Affairs,* 2002, *21,* 78–89.

Kugler, C., Altenhoner, T., Lochner, P., and Ferbert, A., Does age influence early recovery from ischemic stroke? A study from the Hession Stroke Data Bank, *Journal of Neurology,* 2003, *250,* 676–681.

Lau, E.M.C., Suriwongpaisal, P., Lee, J.K., Das De, S., Festin, M.R., Saw, S.M., et al. Risk factors for hip fracture in Asian men and women: The Asian Osteoporosis Study. *Journal of Bone and Mineral Research,* 2001, *16,* 572–580.

Lawson, D.M., and Brossart, D.F. Intergenerational transmission: Individuation and intimacy across three generations. *Family Process, 2001, 40,* 429–442.

Leeb, B.F., Schweitzer, H., Montag, K., and Smolen, J.S. A meta-analysis of chondroitin sulfate in the treatment of osteoarthritis. *Journal of Rheumatology,* 2000, *27,* 205–211.

Li, G., Braver, E.R., and Chen, L.H. Fragility versus excessive crash involvement as determinants of high death rates per vehicle-mile of travel among older drivers. *Accident Analysis and Prevention,* 2003, *35,* 227–235.

Lin, E.H.B., Katon, W., VonKorff, M., et al. Effect of improving depression on pain and functional outcomes among older adults with arthritis. *Journal of the American Medical Association,* 2003, *290,* 2428–2434.

Lord, S.R., Sherrington, C., and Menz, H.B. *Falls in older people: Risk factors and strategies for prevention.* New York: Cambridge University Press, 2001.

Lynch, J.W., Smith, G.D., Kaplan, G.A., and House, J.S. Income inequality and mortality: Importance to health of individual income, psychosocial environment and material conditions. *British Medical Journal,* 2000, *320,* 1200–1204.

Mann, W.C., Ottenbacher, K.J., Fraas, L., Tomita, M., and Granger, C.V. Effectiveness of assistive technology and environmental interventions in maintaining independence and reducing home care costs for the frail elderly. *Archives of Family Medicine,* 1999, *8,* 210–217.

Manton, K.G., Gu, X., and Lamb, V.L. Change in chronic disability from 1982 to 2004/2005 as measured by long-term changes in function and health in the U.S. elderly population, *Proceedings of the National Academy of Sciences,* 2006, *103,* 18374–18379.

Marimaldi, P., and Lee, J. Older adults with cancer. In B. Berkman, *Handbook of Social Work in Health and Aging.* New York: Oxford, 2006.

Martinson, B.C., Crain, A.L., Pronk, N.P., O'Conner, P.J., and Maciosek, M.V. Changes in physical activity and short-term changes in health care. *Preventive Medicine,* 2003, *37,* 319–326.

Masoro, E.J. Are age-associated diseases an integral part of aging? In E.J. Masoro and S.N. Austad (Eds), *Handbook of the Biology of Aging* (6th ed.), Amsterdam: Elsevier Academic Press, 2006.

Mauk, K. Nursing interventions within the Mauk model of poststroke recovery. *Rehabilitation Nursing,* 2006, *31,* 257–263.

McTiernan, A., Kooperberg, C., White, E., Wilcox, S., Coates, R., Adams-Campbell, L., Woods, N., et al. Recreational physical activity and the risk of breast cancer in postmenopausal women: The Women's Health Initiative Cohort Study. *Journal of the American Medical Association,* 2003, *290,* 1331–1336.

Menec, V., The relation between everyday activities and successful aging: A 6-year longitudinal study. *Journals of Gerontology,* 2003, *58B,* S74–82.

Merck Institute of Aging and Health. *The state of aging and health in America.* Washington, DC: Merck Institute, 2004.

Mikuls, T.R., Mudano, A.S., Pulley L.V., and Saag, K.G. Association of race/ethnicity with the receipt of traditional and alternative arthritis-specific health care. *Medical Care,* 2003, *41,* 1233–1239.

Miltiades, H., and Kaye, L., Older adults with orthopedic and mobility limitations. In B. Berkman (Ed.), *Handbook of Social Work in Health and Aging,* New York: Oxford, 2006.

Mokdad, A.H., Ford, E.S., Bowman, B.A., Nelson, D.E., Engelgau, M.M., Vinicor, F., and Marks, J.S. Diabetes trends in the U.S.: 1990–1998. *Diabetes Care,* 2000, *23,* 1278–1283.

Moreland, J.D., Richardson, J.A., Goldsmith, C.H., and Clase, C.M. Muscle weakness and falls in older adults: A systematic review of the literature. *Journal of the American Geriatrics Society,* 2004, *52,* 1121–1129.

Morrison, A., and Levy, R. Fraction of nursing home admissions attributable to urinary incontinence. *Value Health*, 2006, *9*, 272–274.

National Association of Social Workers. *Assuring the sufficiency of a frontline workforce: A national study of licensed social workers.* Preliminary report. Center for Workforce Studies, NASW, 2005.

National Cancer Institute. *Facts about Office of Cancer Survivorship.* Accessed February 10, 2005, from http://dccps.nci.nih.gov/ocs/ocs_factsheet.pdf.

National Center for Health Statistics (NCHS). *Adults' health status and health care.* Accessed 2000, from http://www.cdc.gov/nchs.

National Center for Health Statistics (NCHS). *Health, United States.* Hyattsville, MD: NCHS, 1999.

National Center for Health Statistics (NCHS). *Health, United States, 2003.* Accessed 2003a, from http://www.cdc.gov/nchs/ data/hus/hus03.pdf.

National Center for Health Statistics (NCHS). *Trends in health and aging.* Accessed 2003b, from http://www.cdc.gov/nchs/about/otheract/aging/trendsoverview.htm.

National Center for Health Statistics (NCHS). *Health, United States, 2005.* Accessed 2005, from http://www.cdc.gov/nchs/ data/hus/hus05pdf.

National Health Interview Survey (NHIS). Accessed November 27, 2006, from http://www.nchs.gov.

National Heart, Lung, and Blood Institute. *Sixth report of the Joint National Committee on Prevention, Detection, Evaluation and Treatment of High Blood Pressure.* NIH/NHLBI Publications, November, 1997.

National Highway Traffic Safety Administration (NHTSA). *Traffic safety facts 2000: Older population.* Washington, DC: U.S. Department of Transportation, 2001.

National Institute on Aging (NIA). *Exercise: A guide from the National Institute on Aging.* Bethesda, MD: NIH/NIA Publication No. 99–4258, 1999a.

National Institute on Aging (NIA). *Is HIV/AIDS different in older people?* Bethesda, MD: NIH/NIA, 1999b.

National Institute on Aging (NIA). *Menopause: A resource for making healthy choices.* Bethesda, MD: NIH/NIA, 2001.

National Institutes of Health (NIH). Osteoporosis and Related Bone Diseases—National Resource Center. Fast facts on osteoporosis. Accessed 2003, from http://www.osteo.org/fast+facts+on+osteoporosis&docty.

Nelson, H.D., Vesco, K.K., Haney, E., Fu, R., Nedrow, A., Miller, J., et al. Nonhormonal therapies for menopausal hot flashes: Systematic review and meta-analysis. *Journal of the American Medical Association*, 2006, *295*, 2057–2071.

New York Times. An ailing Russian lives a tough life that's getting shorter. December 3, 2000, 1–19.

Office of Minority Health Research (OMHRC). *HHS fact sheet: Minority health disparities at a glance.* Accessed December 1, 2006, from http://www.omhrc.gov/templates/content.aspx?ID=2139.

Ostbyte, T., and Taylor, D.H. Effect of smoking on years of healthy life lost among middlle-aged and older Americans. *Health Services Research*, 2004, *39*, 531–551.

Page, R.L., and Ruscin, J.M. Risk of adverse drug events and hospital-related morbidity and mortality among older adults. *American Journal of Geriatric Pharmacotherapy*, 2006, *4*, 297–305.

Pathman, D.E., Fowler-Brown, A., and Corbie-Smith, G. Differences in access to outpatient medical care for black and white adults in the rural South. *Medical Care*, 2006, *44*, 429–438.

Phelan, E., Anderson, L., LaCroix, A., and Larson, A. Older adults' views of "successful aging": How do they compare with researchers' definitions? *Journal of the American Geriatrics Society*, 2004, *53*, 211–216.

Phillips, R.S. Preventing depression: A program for African American elders with chronic pain. *Family and Community Health*, 2000, *22*, 57–65.

Poindexter, C., and Emlet, C. HIV-infected and HIV-affected older adults. In B. Berkman (Ed.), *Handbook of Social Work in Health and Aging* New York: Oxford, 2006.

Putnam, M., Greenen, S., Powers, L., Saxton, M., Finney, S., and Dautel, P. Health and wellness: People with disabilities discuss barriers and facilitators to well being. *Journal of Rehabilitation*, 2003, *69*, 37–45.

Quinn, M.E., Johnson, M.A., Poon, L.W., and Martin, P. Psychosocial correlates of subjective mental health in sexagenarians, octogenarians, and centenarians. *Issues in Mental Health Nursing*, 1999, *20*, 151–171.

Radda, K.E., Schensul, J.J., Disch, W.B., Levy, J.A., and Reyes, C.Y. Assessing human immunodeficiency virus (HIV) risk among older urban adults. *Family and Community Health*, 2003, *26*, 203–213.

Ray, W.A., Taylor, J.A., Meador, K.G., Thapa, P.B., and Brown, A.K. A randomized trial of a consultation service to reduce falls in nursing homes. *Journal of the American Medical Association*, 1997, *278*, 595–596.

Rieder, C. Building academic geriatric nursing capacity: The JAHN/AAN Partnership. *Nursing Outlook*, 2006, *54*, 169–171.

Robert Wood Johnson Foundation (RWJF). *Health and Health Care 2003* (2nd ed.). Washington, DC: RWJF, 2003.

Rosen, A.L., Zlotnik, J.L., and Singer, T. Basic gerontological competence for all social workers: The need to "gerontologize" social work education. *Journal of Gerontological Social Work*, 2002, *39*, 25–36.

Rothberg, M.B., Bellantonio, S., and Rose, D.N. Management of influenza in adults older than 65 years of age: Cost-effectiveness of rapid testing and antiviral therapy. *Annals of Internal Medicine*, 2003, *139*, 321–329.

Ruby, C.M., Fillenbaum, G.G., Kuchibhatla, M.N., and Hanlon, J.T. Laxative use in the community-dwelling elderly. *American Journal of Geriatric Pharmacotherapy*, 2003, *1*, 11–17.

Sahyoun, N.R., Lentzner, H., Hoyert, D., and Robinson, K.N. Trends in causes of death among the elderly. *Aging Trends*. National Center for Health Statistics (NCHS), 2001.

Salen, P.N., Kellwell, K., Baumgratz, W., Eberhardt, M., and Reed, J. How does octogenarian status affect mobility, mortality, and functional outcomes of elderly drivers in motor vehicle crashes in Pennsylvania? *Academy of Emergency Medicine*, 2003, *10*, 477–478.

Sambamoorthi, U., Shea, D., and Crystal, S. Total and out-of-pocket expenditures for prescription drugs among older persons. *The Gerontologist*, 2003, *43*, 345–359.

Sarkisian, C.A., Prohaska, T.R., Wong, M.D., Hirsch, S., and Mangione, C.M. Relationship between expectations for aging and physical activity among older adults. *Journal of General Internal Medicine*, 2005, *20*, 911–915.

Scharlach, A., Simon, J., and Dal Santo, T. Who is providing social services to today's older adults? *Journal of Gerontological Social Work*, 2002, *38*, 5–17.

Schoenborn, C.A., Vickerie, J.L., and Powell-Griner, E. Health characteristics of adults 55 years and over: U.S. 2000–2003. *Advance Data from Vital and Health Statistics*. No. 370. Hyattsville, MD: NCHS, 2006.

Schoofs, M., van der Klift, M., Hofman, A., de Laet, C., Herings, R., Stijnen, T., Pols, H., et al. Thiazide diuretics and the risk for hip fracture. *Annals of Internal Medicine*, 2003, *139*, 476–482.

Schrimshaw, E.W., and Siegel, K. Perceived barriers to social support from family and friends among older adults with HIV/AIDS. *Journal of Health Psychology*, 2003, *8*, 738–752.

Shippy, R.A. and Korpiak, S.E. The aging HIV/AIDS population: Fragile social networks. *Aging and Mental Health*, 2005, *9*, 246–254.

Stepnick, L., and Whitelaw, N. *A new vision of aging: Helping older adults make healthier choices*. Washington, DC: Center for the Advancement of Health, 2006.

Stark, S.W. HIV after age 55. *Nursing Clinics of North America*, 2006, *41*, 469–479.

Stothers, L., Thom, D.H., and Calhoun, E. Urologic diseases in America project: Urinary incontinence in males. *Journal of Urology*, 2005, *173*, 1302–1308.

Surveillance, Epidemiology, and End Result (SEER). *Cancer incidence in the United States: Changing patterns for major cancers by sex among whites and blacks*. Washington, DC, 2004.

Talbot, L.A., Fleg, J.L., and Metter, E.J. Secular trends in leisure-time physical activity in men and women across four decades. *Preventive Medicine*, 2003, *37*, 52–60.

Thom, D.H., Nygaard, I.E., and Calhoun, E. Urologic diseases in America project: Urinary incontinence in women. *Journal of Urology*, 2005, *173*, 1295–1301.

Thompson, W.W., Shay, D.K., Weintraub, E., Brammer, L., Bridges, C.B., and Cox, N.J. Influenza-associated hospitalizations in the U.S. *Journal of the American Medical Association*, 2004, *292*, 1333–1340.

U.S. Administration on Aging. http://www.aoa.dhhs.gov//aoa/stats, 2000.

U.S. Department of Health and Human Services (USDHHS). *Oral Health in America: A Report of the Surgeon General*. Bethesda, MD: NIDCR/NIH, 2000.

Vincent, K.R., Braith, R.W., Feldman, R.A., and Lowenthal, D.T. Improved cardiorespiratory endurance following 6 months of resistance exercise in elderly men and women. *Archives of Internal Medicine*, 2002, *162*, 673–678.

Vosvick, M., Koopman, C., Gore-Felton, C., Thoresen, C., Krumboltz, J., and Spiegel, D. Relationship of functional quality of life to strategies for coping with the stress of living with HIV/AIDS. *Psychosomatics: Journal of Consultation Liaison Psychiatry*, 2003, *44*, 51–58.

Wang, Y., Chang, C.F., Chou, J., Chen, H.L., Harvey, B.K., et al. Dietary supplementation with blueberries, spinach or spirulina reduces ischemic brain damage. *Experimental Neurology*, 2005, *193*, 75–84.

Warner, D.F., and Hayward, M.D. *Race disparities in men's mortality: The role of childhood social conditions in a process of cumulative disadvantage*. University of Pennsylvania, Unpublished manuscript, 2002.

Whitfield, K.E., and Hayward, M. The landscape of health disparities among older adults. *Public Policy and Aging Report*, 2003, *13*, 1–7.

Willcox, B.J., He, Q., Chen, R., Yano, K., Masaki, K.H., Grove, J.S., et al. Midlife risk factors and healthy survival in men. *Journal of the American Medical Association*, 2006, *296*, 2343–2350.

Williams, D.R. The health of U.S. racial and ethnic populations. *Journals of Gerontology*, 2005, *60B*, Special Issue II, 53–62.

Wolf, S.L., Barnhart, H.X., Kutner, N.G., McNely, E., Coogler, C., Xu, T., et al. Reducing frailty and falls in older persons: An investigation of Tai Chi and computerized balance training. *Journal of the American Geriatrics Society*, 2003, *51*, 1794–1803.

Women's Health Initiative Investigators (WHI). Risks and benefits of estrogen plus progestin in healthy postmenopausal women. *Journal of the American Medical Association*, 2002, *288*, 321–333.

Women's Health Initiative Investigators (WHI). Effects of estrogen plus progestin on gynecologic cancers and associated diagnostic procedures: The Women's Health Initiative randomized trials. *Journal of the American Medical Association*, 2003, *290*, 1739–1748.

Woo, J.S., Derleth, C., Stratton, J.R., and Levy, W.C. The influence of age, gender, and training on exercise efficiency. *Journal of the Amercian College of Cardiology*, 2006, *47*, 1049–1057.

Woolam, G.L. Cancer statistics 2000: A benchmark for a new century. *CA—A Cancer Journal for Clinicians*, 2000, *50*, 6–7.

World Health Organization (WHO). *Active aging: A policy framework*. Paper presented at the Second United Nations World Assembly on Aging, Madrid, Spain, 2002.

World Health Organization (WHO). *Growing older, staying well, aging and physical activity in everyday life*. Geneva, Switzerland: WHO, 1998.

Yamazaki, S., Ichimura, S., Iwamoto, J., Takeda, T., and Toyama, Y. Effect of walking exercise on bone metabolism in postmenopausal women with osteopenia/osteoporosis. *Journal of Bone and Mineral Metabolism*, 2004, *22*, 500–508.

Yataco, A.R., Busby-Whitehead, J., Drinkwater, D.T., and Katzel, L.I. Relationship of body composition and cardiovascular fitness to lipoprotein lipid profiles in master athletes and sedentary men. *Aging*, 1997, *9*, 88–94.

Zablotsky, D., and Kennedy, M. Risk factors and HIV transmission to midlife and older women: Knowledge, options and the initiation of safer sexual practices. *Journal of Acquired Immune Deficiency Syndrome*, 2003, *33*, Supplement #2, S122–S130.

part three

The Psychological Context of Social Aging

The dynamic interactions between people and their environments as they age, the population trends that make gerontology such an important field for practice, research, and policy, and the historical background of social gerontology were discussed in Part One. Part Two focused on the normal biological and physiological changes that take place with aging, and our growing understanding of how biological aging may be altered. The most common chronic health problems that afflict older people and may influence their social functioning were presented. The older population's use of the health care system was reviewed. Part Two concluded with a discussion of the growing field of health promotion, and how enhanced health behaviors can help people experience active aging.

In this section, the focus is on psychological changes with aging—both normal and abnormal—that influence older people's social behavior and dynamic relationships with their physical and social environments. As we have already seen, many changes take place in the aging organism that may make it more difficult to perform activities of daily living and to respond as quickly and easily to external demands as in youth. Many older people have chronic health problems, such as arthritis, diabetes, or heart disease, that compound the normal changes that cause some people to slow down. In a similar manner, some changes in cognitive functioning, personality, and sexuality are a function of normal aging. Other psychological changes may be due to the secondary effects of diseases.

Researchers have examined changes in intelligence, learning, and memory with aging. The literature in this area, reviewed in Chapter 5, suggests that normal aging does not result in significant declines. Although older subjects in the studies described do not perform as well as younger ones, their scores are not so low as to indicate significant impairments in social functioning. Laboratory tests also may be less than ideal as indicators of cognitive function in older people. Research on ways to improve memory in the later years is discussed. The chapter concludes with a discussion of wisdom and creativity in old age, and whether these abilities improve or decline with aging.

Chapter 6 describes personality development in the later years, the expression and regulation of basic and complex emotions, the importance of maintaining self-esteem, and threats to self-esteem that result from age-associated changes.

This chapter also focuses on coping and successful adaptation to such changes. Given the normal age-related alterations in physiological, sensory, and cognitive functions, personality styles, and older individuals' social networks, some gerontologists argue that older people experience more stress in a given time period than young adults. Furthermore, there has been considerable debate about whether aging results in the use of different types of coping strategies. However, longitudinal research in this area is insufficient to conclude with any certainty that aging is associated with more stressful life events than young adulthood. The concept of successful aging and its similarity to active aging is discussed. It is a concept that has drawn considerable research attention and debate, particularly because it may not be salient for low-income elders from historically underserved groups. Successful aging requires both high levels of physical and functional health and remaining active in cognitive and social functions, a lifestyle that may not be an option for those with limited financial and health care resources.

Certain forms of psychopathology, such as schizophrenia, are more common in young adults than in old age. However, as described in Chapter 6, some older people are at high risk for major depression, paranoia, and dementia. In the case of dementia, memory and problem-solving abilities decline quite dramatically, sometimes within a few years, other times over many years. Older individuals with a diagnosis of dementia experience significant impairments in their ability to interact with other people and to control their physical and social environments. To the extent that older people do not seek mental health services for treatable disorders such as depression or paranoia, their social interactions will deteriorate as well. Some may become reclusive and, in the case of severely depressed older white men, at greater risk of suicide. Despite the growing number of studies that document the benefits of therapeutic interventions for older

adults, the older population underutilizes mental health services. This is particularly true among elders of color. Most of the mental health care provided to older adults takes place in hospitals, not in community mental health centers or in private practice. Furthermore, most therapy is provided by family doctors who generally do not have special expertise in geriatric medicine or psychiatry.

An important aspect of personality is sexuality, the individual's ability to express intimate feelings through a wide range of loving and pleasurable experiences. Chapter 7 addresses the influence of social attitudes and beliefs, normal physiological changes, and diseases on older adults' sexuality. Contrary to popular belief, aging need not reduce sexual pleasure and capacity. More often, older people withdraw from sexual activity because of societal expectations and stereotypes or lack of available partners. As people become better informed about aging and sexuality, and as sexual taboos are reduced, the aging Baby Boomers, who experienced the sexual revolution of the 1960s, will more easily express their sexuality. New research on maintaining sexual activities in old age is discussed.

As with physical aging, the material in Part Three suggests that aging does not affect all people's psychological functions in the same way. Normal cognitive changes, such as mild forgetfulness, generally are not so dramatic as to impair older people's social functions. A relatively small segment of the older population experiences Alzheimer's disease or other types of dementia, but the incidence increases with age. Personality and patterns of coping also do not change so dramatically as to impair social functioning, although some gender-based behaviors become less pronounced with age. Coping and adaptation skills do not become impaired with normal aging; styles of coping vary widely among older people. Indeed, aging results in increasing differences in psychological functioning among people, not greater similarity. Some people experience active aging despite chronic diseases and deterioration in cognitive function, while others poorly adapt to these normal and secondary changes of aging. The following vignettes illustrate many contrasts in psychological aging.

AN OLDER PERSON WITH INTACT COGNITIVE ABILITIES: MR. WALLACE

I am a retired professor in a midwestern community. Now 85, I retired 20 years ago, after teaching history in a large state university for 40 years. I try to remain active by doing volunteer work in the local historical society, teaching part-time at the university, and traveling to Europe with my wife for three months every summer, occasionally leading groups of other retirees in tours of medieval European towns. My life goal that I'm determined to complete before I die is an historical novel about Charlemagne. This is a topic I've lectured and read extensively on. It also is a good topic to study on my trips to Europe. My wife tells me I'm busier these days than before my retirement. During the first few months after retirement, I had a mild bout of depression, but I found some relief through group therapy with other retirees. I enjoy intellectual challenges today as much as I did when I was employed, in fact, more so, because I'm pursuing these activities without the pressures of a day-to-day job. I'm determined to keep up this level of activity until I "run out of energy!"

AN OLDER PERSON WITH GOOD COPING SKILLS: MRS. JOHNSON

At age 83, I've probably suffered more tragedies than most. I was born to a poor farming family in Mississippi. My mother, my eight older sisters and brothers, and I moved north after my father died and the family farm was lost. We supported each other through hard work in the factories. I married young; my husband and I struggled through the years to buy our own home and raise our three children. My husband died 20 years ago, leaving me with a small pension. I worked at a manual labor job until age 70, when arthritis made it painful for me to do the heavy work needed on the job. During the past three

years, I've experienced too many losses: My son and daughter-in-law died in an auto accident; my last surviving sister died; and my oldest granddaughter, the one I could most depend on, moved west to attend medical school. My losses are painful, but I guess it's "God's will" that I experience them. I think God has a "master plan" for all of us, so I've learned to accept these losses. When I become too depressed, I turn to the Bible, and look forward to visits from my grandchildren and great-grandchildren to keep me busy.

AN OLDER PERSON WITH DEMENTIA: MR. ADAMS

I'm now 64, but I started showing signs of confusion and disorientation about 10 years ago. I was diagnosed as having Alzheimer's disease at age 58, five years before I planned to retire. My wife and I had made plans to travel around the world during retirement; now all our plans have completely changed. Most days I'm really agitated and disoriented; I wander during the night, and my wife complains that I'm occasionally abusive to her. The slightest change in routine will upset me. Sometimes I just cry and wonder what has happened to me. My wife is determined to keep me at home, even though she gets upset when I yell at her and don't recognize or appreciate all that she does for me. I go every day to an adult day-care center, where the staff try to keep me active and stimulated. My wife also attends meetings of a support group for family caregivers of Alzheimer's disease patients. She enjoys these meetings because she can express her feelings about how hard things are and gets lots of support. I'm grateful to her for trying to keep me at home and not talking about putting me in a nursing home, but I know she worries about how long she can manage me at home.

The next three chapters describe how the aging process influences cognitive abilities, personality styles, mental health, and intimacy and sexuality, as well as responses to major life events. They emphasize the wide variations in these processes with aging. The vastly different psychological status of Mr. Wallace, Mrs. Johnson, and Mr. Adams result in significant variations in the social aspects of their lives.

5

Cognitive Changes with Aging

One of the most important and most studied aspects of aging is cognitive functioning; that is, intelligence, learning, and memory. These are critical to an individual's performance in every aspect of life, including work and leisure activities, social relationships, and productive roles. Older people who have problems in cognitive functioning will eventually experience stress in these other areas as well, along with an increasing incongruence between their competence levels and the demands of their environments. Researchers have attempted to determine whether normal aging is associated with a decline in the three areas of cognitive functioning and, if so, to what extent such a decline is due to age-related physiological changes. Much of the research on these issues has evolved from studies of cognitive development across the life course. Other studies have been undertaken in response to concerns expressed by older persons or their families that they cannot learn as easily as they used to, or that they have more trouble remembering names, dates, and places than previously.

Intelligence and Aging

Intelligence is difficult both to define and to measure. Of all the elements of cognition, it is the least verifiable. We can only infer its existence and can only indirectly measure individual levels. **Intelligence** is generally defined as the "theoretical limit of an individual's performance" (Jones, 1959, p. 700). While the limit is determined by biological and genetic factors, the ability to achieve this limit is influenced by environmental opportunities, such as challenging learning experiences, as well as by environmental constraints, such as the absence of books or other intellectual stimulation. Intelligence encompasses a range of capabilities, including the ability to deal with symbols and abstractions, acquire and comprehend new information, adapt to new situations, and understand and create new ideas. Alfred Binet, who developed the first test of intelligence, emphasized the operational aspects of intelligence: "to judge well, to comprehend well, to reason well, these are the essentials of intelligence" (Binet and Simon, 1905, p. 106). In general, both experts and laypersons agree that intelligence consists of three major sets of abilities: problem-solving, verbal, and social competence (Cavanaugh and Blanchard-Fields, 2006). **Intelligence quotient (IQ)** refers to an individual's relative abilities in some of these areas compared to others of the same chronological age.

A multidimensional structure of intelligence is assumed by most contemporary tests of this concept. Most tests today measure a subset of intellectual skills known as **primary mental abilities (PMAs),** which include:

- number or mathematical reasoning
- word fluency or the ability to use appropriate words to describe the world
- verbal meaning or vocabulary level
- inductive reasoning or the ability to generalize from specific facts to concepts
- spatial relations or the ability to orient oneself in a three-dimensional space
- verbal memory, or the ability to retain and recall words, sentences, and passages from readings
- perceptual speed

A useful distinction is made between **fluid intelligence** and **crystallized intelligence** (Cattell, 1963; Horn, 1970, 1982; Horn and Donaldson, 1980). These two types of intelligence include some of the primary mental abilities described above. Fluid intelligence consists of skills that are biologically determined, independent of experience or learning, and may be similar to what is popularly called "native intelligence." It involves processing information that is not embedded in a context of existing information for the individual. It requires flexibility in thinking. Crystallized intelligence refers to the knowledge and abilities that the individual acquires through education and lifelong experiences. It includes social judgment and the ability to understand subtle meanings in verbal communication. These two types of intelligence show different patterns with aging, as discussed in the next section.

MEASURES OF FLUID INTELLIGENCE

- spatial orientation
- abstract reasoning
- word fluency
- inductive reasoning

MEASURES OF CRYSTALLIZED INTELLIGENCE

- verbal meaning
- word association
- social judgment
- number skills

There has been considerable controversy regarding intelligence in the later years. Many researchers have found significant differences between young and old persons on intelligence tests in cross-sectional studies, with older persons performing at a much lower level. Even when the same cohort is followed longitudinally, there is a decline in some intelligence tests that is independent of generational differences (Schaie, 1996a, 1996b). Others conclude that aging is not really associated with decrements in intelligence. However, standardized IQ tests and the time pressures on test-takers may be more detrimental to older persons than to the young. Still others point to methodological problems in conducting research in this area. Unfortunately, these mixed research findings serve to perpetuate the stereotype that older people are less intelligent than the young.

Many older persons are concerned that their intelligence has declined. This concern may loom so large for them that merely taking part in a study intended to "test their intelligence" may provoke sufficient anxiety to affect their test performance. Such anxieties may also influence daily functioning. Older people who are told by friends, family, test-givers or society in general that they should not expect to perform as well on intellectual tasks because aging causes a decline in intelligence may, in fact, perform more poorly.

The most widely used measure of adult intelligence is the Wechsler Adult Intelligence Scale (WAIS). It consists of 11 subtests, 6 of which are Verbal Scales (which measure, to some extent, crystallized intelligence), and 5 are Performance Scales (providing some measure of fluid intelligence). The performance tests on the WAIS are generally timed; the verbal tests are not.

Verbal scores are obtained by measuring an individual's ability to:

- define the meaning of words
- interpret proverbs
- explain similarities between words and concepts

In this way, accumulated knowledge and abstract reasoning can be tested.

Performance tests focus on an individual's ability to manipulate unfamiliar objects and words, often in unusual ways:

- tests of spatial relations
- abstract reasoning
- putting puzzles together to match a picture
- matching pictures with symbols or numbers
- arranging pictures in a particular pattern

Both psychomotor and perceptual skills are needed in performing these tasks. A consistent pattern of scores on these two components of the WAIS has been labeled the **Classic Aging Pattern.** People age 65 and older in some studies, and even earlier in others, perform significantly worse on Performance Scales (i.e., fluid intelligence), but their scores on Verbal Scales (i.e., crystallized intelligence) remain stable. This tendency to do worse on performance tasks may reflect age-related changes in noncognitive functions, such as sensory and perceptual abilities, and in psychomotor skills. These changes in turn may make the older person more susceptible to interference during the learning or performance process (Hasher et al., 2002). As seen in Chapters 3 and 4, aging results in a slowing of the neural pathways and of the visual and auditory functions. This slower reaction time, and the delay in receiving and transmitting messages through the sense organs, explains poorer performance on subtests requiring such capabilities. Some researchers therefore argue for the elimination of time constraints in performance tasks. Studies that have not measured speed of performance have still found significant age differences in these subtests, however (Salthouse, 1996a). Performance-related aspects of intellectual function appear to decline independent of psychomotor or sensory factors. Speed of cognitive processing, such as the time to perform simple math problems, also declines with age and, in turn, slows an individual's responses on tests of performance.

Turning to verbal skills, the Classic Aging Pattern suggests that the ability to recall stored verbal information and to use abstract reasoning tends to remain constant throughout life. Declines, where they exist, typically do not show up until advanced old age, or, in the case of cognitive impairment such as the dementias, they tend to begin early in the course of the disease.

When given logically inconsistent statements in cognitive studies, older subjects analyze these inconsistencies on the basis of their own knowledge, whereas younger adults tend to ignore the logic and attempt to reach conclusions quickly. Older subjects also reject simplified solutions and prefer a complex analysis of the problem. This finding from laboratory-based research is supported by surveys of attitudes and beliefs among respondents of varying ages. Younger respondents are more willing to provide a direct response, whereas many older persons attempt to analyze the questions and give more contingency responses; that is, analyzing the question and stating that the answer could be x in one situation and y in another, rather than an all-encompassing response. For example, on a measure of environmental preference, the respondent may be asked, "How much privacy do you generally prefer?" A younger respondent is more likely to focus on the "general" situation, whereas the older respondent is more likely to consider situations both in which privacy is preferred and where it is not. It thus is important to review older persons' responses to tests of problem solving and abstract reasoning from other perspectives beyond the traditional approaches that are grounded in cognitive theories developed with younger populations. Most tests of intelligence do not reward the more analytical or complex responses typical of some older adults.

Problems in the Measurement of Cognitive Function

A major shortcoming of many studies of intelligence in aging is their use of cross-sectional research designs rather than longitudinal approaches. Age differences that are obtained in cross-sectional studies may reflect cohort or generational differences rather than actual age changes. In particular, changes in educational systems, increasing levels of education, and the widespread access to computers, the Internet, and high-speed travel have profoundly influenced the experiences of today's youth when compared with those of people who grew up in the early to mid-twentieth century. These historical factors may then have a greater effect on intelligence scores than age per se (Schaie, 2005).

Subject attrition, or dropout from longitudinal studies of intelligence, is another problem. There is a pattern of *selective attrition,* whereby the people who drop out tend to be those who have performed less well, who perceive their performance to be poor, or whose health status and functional abilities are worse than average. The people who remain in the study (i.e., "the survivors") performed better in the initial tests than did dropouts. This is consistent with our earlier observation that older persons often become unduly anxious about poor performance on tests of intellectual function. Hence, the results become biased in favor of the superior performers, indicating stability or improvement

---

SUMMARY OF AGE-RELATED CHANGES IN INTELLIGENCE

- Peak performance varies by test, usually between the late 30s and early 40s.
- Performance on timed tests declines more than on non-timed tests.
- Performance on non-timed tests remains stable until the 80s.
- People rarely decline in all five PMAs.
- High scorers continue to do well even among oldest-old.
- Declines in tests of fluid intelligence begin earlier than in crystallized intelligence ("classic aging pattern").

over time. They do not represent the wider population of older adults, whose performance might have shown a decline in intelligence (Schaie, 1996a, 2005).

Longitudinal Studies of Intelligence

Several major classic longitudinal studies have examined changes in intellectual function from youth to old age (Schaie, 1996b). The Iowa State Study tested a sample of college freshmen in 1919 and retested them in 1950 and 1961 (Cunningham and Owens, 1983; Owens, 1953, 1966). The researchers found general stability in intellectual functioning through middle age, with a peak in their late 40s and 50s. Declines were observed after age 60 in many men, but the degree of change varied widely among the men and across variables. The New York State Study of Aging Twins began in 1946 and followed this group through 1973 (Kallmann and Sander, 1949). Average performance declined significantly on timed tests, but, as with the Iowa State Study, individual differences were pronounced. Among the individuals who were healthy enough to complete the final follow-up, performance on non-speed intelligence tests remained stable until they reached their ninth decade. The greatest declines were

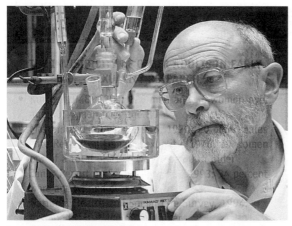

Intellectual stimulation can help sustain higher-level cognitive skills.

observed in the test of hand-eye coordination and in fluid intelligence. Both studies had less than 25 percent of the original sample available at the final follow-up, which raises questions whether survivors are representative of their cohort in cognitive functioning.

The Seattle Longitudinal Study (SLS) began in 1956 and has collected data on Thurstone's primary mental abilities every 7 years for the last 50 years (Schaie, 1996a, 1996b, 2005). At each follow-up assessment, individuals who are still available from the original sample are retested, along with a new, randomly selected sample from the same population. This study has provided the basis for the development of sequential research models, described in Chapter 1. Peak performance varies across tests and between men and women, ranging from age 32 on the test of numbers for men, and age 39 on the test of reasoning for women. Age decrements have been observed after age 60 on tests of word fluency, numbers, and spatial orientation that become progressively worse in later years. Tests of spatial orientation and inductive reasoning, both indicators of fluid intelligence, show greater decline with age. Men experience earlier declines in spatial abilities than in other tests, whereas women decline earlier on tests of word fluency than in other areas. However, other primary mental abilities, such as verbal meaning and numerical skills, show only minimal declines until the mid-70s. These results are consistent with cross-sectional results using the WAIS, as we have seen earlier. They are supported by other, shorter longitudinal studies that have found little change over three years (Christensen et al., 1999; Zelinski, Gilewski, and Schaie, 1993). The findings suggest that the Classic Aging Pattern holds up in both cross-sectional and longitudinal studies, and that some performance aspects of intelligence may begin to deteriorate after age 60, although substantial changes are generally rare until the 80s (Schaie, 2005, 2006).

In all these studies, most of the significant declines occur in intellectual abilities that are less practiced and require speed. Schaie (1996a,

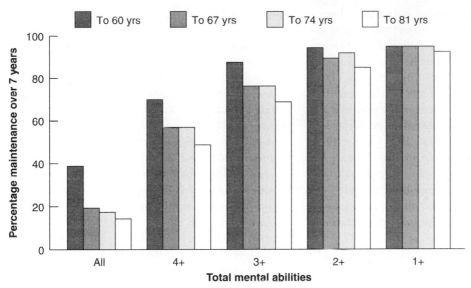

FIGURE 5.1 **Proportion of Individuals Who Maintain Scores on Multiple Abilities**
SOURCE: Schaie, K.W., The hazards of cognitive aging. *The Gerontologist*, 1989, *29*, 484–493. Reprinted with permission.

1996b, 2005) concludes that the changes observed in the SLS indicate a normative developmental transition from stability in general intelligence in the middle years, to a gradual decline that begins around age 60. Most people in the SLS maintained their abilities in one or more areas well into their advanced years, as shown in Figure 5.1. When comparing performance on the WAIS at age 60 versus age 67, the researchers found that only about 33 percent of participants showed decrements. About 40 percent declined between ages 67 and 74, and even between ages 74 and 81 only 50 percent experienced notable declines. Schaie and his colleagues found no linear decline in all five primary mental abilities for any participants as old as age 88. In fact, recent findings from the SLS suggest that declines during the middle years (ages 46–60) on delayed recall and word fluency tests and on tests of psychomotor speed may predict cognitive impairment in old age (Schaie, 1996a, 1996b, 2005, 2006).

The Duke Longitudinal Studies, described in Chapter 1, assessed intelligence and memory, in addition to many health variables. This series of three longitudinal samples, each measured several times, provides useful information about the relationship between intellectual function and health status, especially cardiovascular disease (Palmore, 1985; Siegler, 1983). The findings regarding age changes generally are consistent with the other longitudinal studies described in this section. That is, declines in cognitive function were not observed until individuals reached their 70s. Scores on performance tests were found to decline earlier than scores on verbal measures.

Factors That May Influence Intelligence in Adulthood

Researchers who have compared intelligence test scores of older and younger persons have found wide variations in scores of both groups. Older test-takers generally have obtained poorer scores, but age per se is only one factor in explaining differences.

As mentioned earlier, there is also a biological factor in intelligence, such that some people are innately more intelligent than others. However, it is difficult to determine the relative influence of biological factors, because it is impossible to measure the specific mechanisms of the brain that account for intelligence. Structural changes in the brain and in neural pathways occur with aging, as seen in Chapter 3. These changes, however, are generally diffuse and not focused in a particular region of the brain. It is therefore impossible to determine what specific changes in the brain and its pathways may account for the age-related deterioration that is observed.

Other variables that have been examined are educational attainment, involvement in complex versus mechanistic work, cardiovascular disease, hypertension, and sensory deficits. Some studies have found cohort differences on tests of intelligence, with newer cohorts of older people performing better than previous cohorts who took the same test at about the same age. These differences emerge primarily on tests of crystallized and less on fluid intelligence and psychomotor speed, even when comparing adult children and their parents (Schaie et al., 1992; Schaie and

---

INTELLECTUALLY ACTIVE ELDERS

Increasingly, more older adults continue to participate in intellectually challenging jobs well beyond their 60s and 70s. For example, college campuses are full of retired faculty who retain emeritus status and who continue to teach or conduct research well into their 80s. One of the Poet Laureates of the United States was Stanley Kunitz, appointed at age 95. Another active octogenarian is Dr. Hilary Koprowski, whose research in 1948 led to the widespread adoption of a live vaccine to immunize children against polio. Koprowski, now age 91, continues to conduct medical research at Thomas Jefferson University in Philadelphia. Meanwhile, James Wiggins continued to edit a weekly newspaper in Ellsworth, Maine well into his 90s.

Willis, 1995; Willis and Schaie, 2006). Newer cohorts' advantage has been attributed to higher educational attainment. Therefore, it is important to control statistically for educational differences when analyzing the relationship between age and intelligence. Significant positive effects of education were found on all tests of cognitive function when comparing healthy independent adults age 70 to 79 with different educational levels. In particular, participants with the highest level of education (12+ years) did three times better on a test of abstract thinking than did people with 7 or fewer years of education (Inouye et al., 1993).

Occupational level, which is generally associated with educational level, also influences intelligence test scores. Older people who still use their cognitive abilities in jobs or activities that require thinking and problem-solving (such as Mr. Wallace in the introductory vignette) show less decline on cognitive tests than those who do not use these skills. This is because most of the observed declines in intellectual abilities occur in highly challenging, complex tasks. In addition, people whose occupations demand more verbal skills (e.g., lawyers and teachers) may continue to perform very well on these aspects of intelligence tests. Those who use more abstract and fluid skills in their occupations (e.g., architects and engineers) are more likely to do well on the performance tests of the WAIS, well into their 70s and 80s. In general, older people who do not participate in any intellectual pursuits perform worse on intelligence tests than do their peers who are "cognitively engaged." The nature of intellectual activities is also important; those who participate in complex work and leisure activities with more opportunities for self-direction show consistently higher scores, even among the oldest-old (Mackinnon, 2003; Schooler and Mulatu, 2001; Schooler, Mulatu, and Oates, 1999, 2004).

The effects of declining physical health and sensory losses on intelligence become more severe in the later years, and may displace any positive influence due to education and occupation for people who are 75 years and older. Several studies have identified poorer performance on intelligence tests by older people with conditions such as diabetes, hypertension, and cardiovascular disease, particularly in tests that demand psychomotor speed (Elias et al., 2004; Hassing et al., 2004; Knopman et al., 2000; Rosnick et al., 2004). In the Seattle Longitudinal Study, participants with cardiovascular disease declined at younger ages on all tests of mental abilities than did those with no disease; people who had hypertension in middle age performed worse on most tests after age 70 (Launer et al., 1995; Schaie, 1996a, 2006).

Nutritional deficits may also impair an older person's cognitive functioning. One study of community dwelling, healthy older persons (ages 66–90) examined their performance on multiple tests of cognitive functioning and nutritional status longitudinally. Older people with low intake of vitamins E, A, B_6, and B_{12} at baseline performed worse on visiospatial and abstraction tasks 6 years later; those who used vitamin supplements did better (Larue et al., 1997). These findings reinforce the results of research on the impact of nutritional deficiencies on physical performance, described in Chapter 4.

Depression, or even mild dysphoria (i.e., feeling "blue" or "down in the dumps," but not clinically depressed) can influence cognitive function. Indeed, in a large study of people age 50 to 93 that controlled for the effects of age, education, and occupation, older adults with worse scores on a measure of depression had significantly lower scores on tests of both crystallized and fluid intelligence (Rabbitt et al., 1995). In another study that measured changes in memory, spatial functioning, and perceptual speed, older adults with symptoms of depression showed the most decline over 4 years (Christensen et al., 1999). Given the prevalence of depression in the older population, this may be a cause of poorer cognitive performance rather than aging per se.

As noted in Chapter 3, hearing loss is common in older persons, especially moderate levels of loss that affect their ability to comprehend speech. Visual deficits become more severe in advanced old age. Poorer performance by some test-takers who are very old may be due primarily to these sensory losses, not to a central cognitive decline. Older persons with hearing or vision loss do especially poorly on tests of verbal meaning and spatial relations (Lindenberger and Baltes, 1994).

An apparent and rapid decline in cognitive function within 5 years of death is another physical health factor that appears to be related to intelligence test scores. This phenomenon is known as the *terminal drop* or **terminal decline hypothesis,** first tested by Kleemeier (1962). In longitudinal studies of intelligence, older subjects who decline more sharply are found to die sooner than good performers. This has been observed on many different tests, especially in verbal meaning, spatial and reasoning ability, and psychomotor speed (Bosworth et al., 1999). This suggests that time since birth (i.e., age) is not as significant in intellectual decline as is proximity to death.

Finally, anxiety may negatively affect older people's intelligence test scores. As noted earlier, older people in laboratory tests of learning and memory are more likely than the young to express high test anxiety and cautiousness in responding. These same reactions may occur in older people taking intelligence tests, especially if they think that the test really measures how "intelligent" they are. Anxieties about cognitive decline and concerns about becoming cognitively

HEALTH IMPAIRMENTS THAT AFFECT PERFORMANCE

- cardiovascular disease
- hypertension
- nutritional deficits
- depression
- hearing loss
- terminal drop

impaired may make older people even more cautious, and hence result in poorer performance on intelligence tests.

The Process of Learning and Memory

Learning and *memory* are two cognitive processes that must be considered together. That is, learning is assumed to occur when an individual is able to *retrieve* information accurately from his or her memory store. Conversely, if an individual cannot retrieve information from memory, it is presumed that learning has not adequately taken place. Thus, *learning* is the process by which new information (verbal or nonverbal) or skills are *encoded,* or put into one's memory. The specific parts of the brain involved in this process are the hippocampus, which first receives and processes new stimuli, and the cerebral cortex, where memories are stored. Some of the most exciting research in this field is focused on the process of neuronal development as learning occurs. *Memory* is the process of retrieving or recalling the information that was once *stored.* Memory also refers to a part of the brain that retains what has been learned throughout a person's lifetime. Researchers have attempted to distinguish three separate types of memory: sensory, primary or short-term, and secondary or long-term.

Sensory memory, as its name implies, is the first step in receiving information through the sense organs and passing it on to primary or secondary memory. It is stored for only a few tenths of a second, although there is some evidence that it lasts longer in older persons because of slower reaction times of the senses. Sensory memory has been further subdivided into **iconic** (or visual) and **echoic** (or auditory) **memory.** Examples of iconic memory are:

- words or letters that we see
- faces of people with whom we have contact
- landscapes that we experience through our eyes

Of course, words can be received through echoic memory as well, such as when we hear others say a specific word, or when we repeat words aloud to ourselves. A landscape can also enter our sensory memory through our ears (e.g., the sound of the ocean), our skin (e.g., the feel of a cold spray from the ocean), and our nose (e.g., the smell of salt water). To the extent that we focus on or rehearse information that we receive from our sense organs, it is more likely to be passed into our primary and secondary memories.

Despite significant changes in the visual system with aging (as described in Chapter 3), studies of iconic memory find only small age differences in the ability to identify stimuli presented briefly. Such modest declines in iconic memory would not be expected to influence observed decrements in secondary or long-term memory. However, some researchers suggest that even small declines in sensory memory may result in a large decline in long-term memory (Craik and Jennings, 1994). Although research on iconic memory is limited, there has been even less with echoic memory and less still that has compared older persons with younger. We have all experienced the long-term storage of memories gained through touch, taste, or smell. For example, the aroma of freshly baked bread often evokes memories of early childhood. However, these sensory memories are more difficult to test. As a result, very little is known about changes with these other modes of sensory memory.

Working or **primary memory** is a temporary stage of holding, processing, and organizing information, and does not necessarily refer to a storage area in the brain. Despite its temporary nature, working memory is critical for our ability to process new information. We all experience situations where we hear or read a bit of information such as a phone number or someone's name, use that name or number immediately, then forget it. In fact, most adults can recall seven, plus or minus two pieces of information (e.g., digits, letters, or words) for 60 seconds or

RETRIEVING OLD MEMORIES

A person may have learned many years ago how to ride a bicycle. If this skill has been encoded well through practice, the person can retrieve it many years later from his or her memory store, even if he or she has not ridden a bicycle in years. This applies to many other skills learned early in life, from remembering childhood prayers to diapering a baby.

less. It is not surprising, therefore, that local phone numbers in most countries are seven digits or fewer, although the addition of area codes for local dialing makes it more difficult to retain this information in our permanent memory store (**secondary** or **long-term memory**). In order to retrieve information later, it first must be rehearsed or "processed" actively. This is why primary memory is described as a form of "working memory" that decides what information should be attended to or ignored, which is most important, and how best to store it. If we are distracted while trying to retain the information for the 60 seconds that it is stored in short-term memory, we immediately forget it, even if it consists of only two or three bits of information. This happens because the rehearsal of such material is interrupted by the reception of newer information in our sensory memory. Most studies of primary memory have found minimal age differences in its storage capacity, but the encoding process which occurs in primary memory declines. This requires some organization or elaboration of the information received. Older persons are less likely than young people to process new information in this manner. Indeed, some argue that aging leads to a decline in "attentional resources," or mental energy, to organize and elaborate newly acquired information in order to retain it in secondary memory (Bopp and Verhagen, 2005; Craik, 1994; Smith, 1996; Zacks, Hasher, and Li, 2000). In fact, many of the age-related changes observed in different components of attention may explain these problems with working memory.

Another explanation for this slowing process is that **perceptual speed**—the time required to recognize a stimulus and respond to it—deteriorates with aging. According to this theory, older people have more problems holding information in their working memory while receiving new stimuli through sensory memory ("simultaneity"). This is compounded by the possibility that it takes longer for older people to ignore irrelevant stimuli and complete working memory tasks (Salthouse, 1996b). For example, if an older driver is trying to locate a street address that was just given, but is also listening to news on the radio, the driver is less likely to remember the street address than would a younger driver in the same situation.

True learning implies that the material we acquire through our sensory and primary memories has been stored in "secondary memory." For example, looking up a telephone number and immediately dialing it does not guarantee that the number will be learned. In fact, only with considerable rehearsal can information from primary memory be passed into secondary memory. This is the part of the memory store in which everything we have learned throughout our lives is kept; unlike primary memory, it has an unlimited capacity. The different components of secondary memory are described in Table 5.1. Researchers have demonstrated significant declines in some components, but very little or no change in others.

Older adults consistently recall less information than younger people in paired associates tests with retention intervals as brief as one hour or as long as eight months. Age differences in secondary memory appear to be more pronounced than in sensory or primary memory and are often frustrating to older people and their families. Indeed, middle-aged and older people are frequently concerned that they cannot remember and retrieve information from secondary memory. The perception that one has poor memory can seriously harm older adults' self-concept, as well as their performance on many tasks, and may even result in depression. Such concern, growing out of a fear of dementia, is generally out of proportion to the actual level of decline (Pearman and Storandt, 2004; Verhaeghen, Geraerts, and Marcoen, 2000). Older individuals can benefit significantly from methods to help organize their learning, such as imagery and the use of mnemonics. Examples of such techniques to improve learning and memory are discussed later in this chapter.

The Information Processing Model

The **information processing model** of memory is presented in Figure 5.2. This is a conceptual model; that is, it provides a framework for understanding how the processes of learning and memory take place. It is not necessarily what goes on in the neural pathways between the sense organs and the secondary memory store. Having described each of the components in this model, here we review the steps involved in processing some information that we want to retain. One example is the experience of learning new names at a social gathering. Sensory memory aids in hearing the name spoken, preferably several times by other people, and seeing the face that is associated with that name. Primary memory is used to store that information temporarily, so that a person can speak to others and address them by name (an excellent method of rehearsing this information), or manipulate the information in order to pass it on to secondary memory. This may include repeating the name several times, trying to isolate some aspect of the person's physical features and relating it to the name, and associating the name with other people one has known in the past who have similar names. In the last type of mental manipulation, information from secondary memory (i.e., names of other people) is linked with the new information. This is a useful method because the material in secondary memory is permanent, and associating the new information with well-learned information aids in its storage and subsequent recall.

During any stage of this cognitive processing, the newly obtained information can be lost. This may occur if the sensory memory is flooded with similar information; in this case, if a person is being introduced to multiple new names and faces at a party, it is almost impossible to distinguish the names or to associate each name with a face. Information may also be lost during the primary memory stage. In our example, if a person is trying to use the newly heard name and is distracted by other names and faces, or receives unrelated but relevant information (e.g., a telephone call) while rehearsing the new

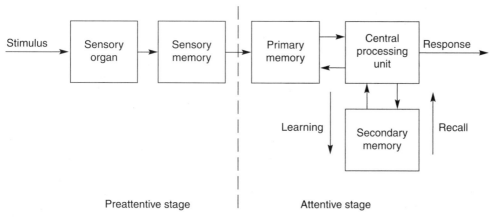

FIGURE 5.2   **Schematic Representation of the Information Processing Model**

name, the name has not been sufficiently processed in working memory to pass into secondary memory.

The learning process may also be disrupted because of inability to retrieve information efficiently from secondary memory. For example, a person may associate the newly heard name with someone known in the past; if he or she has difficulty retrieving the stored name from secondary memory, however, this may be so frustrating as to redirect the individual's attention from the new name to the old name. How often have you ignored everything around you to concentrate on remembering a name that is "on the tip of the tongue" (i.e., in secondary memory) but not easily retrievable? As noted above, aging appears to reduce the efficiency of *processing* information in sensory and primary memory (i.e. encoding), and has less effect on retrieval from secondary memory. It does *not* influence the storage capacity of primary or secondary memories. That is,

contrary to popular opinion, these memory stores are not physical spaces that become overloaded with information as we age. Table 5.1 lists some key types of secondary memories. Although researchers have linked some types of memory to specific regions of the brain (e.g. episodic memory occurs in the medial temporal lobe while procedural memory takes place in the striatum), this does not mean that they take up physical space in these areas. Episodic memory has been shown to decline the most with aging, especially after age 60. Nevertheless, more educated older adults and those given more practice opportunities during the learning process show less decline. These advantages have been demonstrated for both episodic and semantic memory (Hoyer and Verhaeghen, 2006; Rönnlund et al., 2005). Not surprisingly, semantic memory shows the least decline with aging because it is stimulated by words and concepts learned throughout one's lifetime. Procedural memory is also retained into

TABLE 5.1   Types of Secondary Memory

It is important to recognize that secondary memory is not unilateral but has several components. The types of memory listed here (and many others) appear to be influenced differently by the aging process.

MEMORY TYPE	DESCRIPTION
Episodic memory	Consciously recalling specific events or episodes.
Explicit memory	Consciously attempting to keep a stimulus in one's mind, in a specific order (e.g , a poem, a mental "to do" list).
Flashbulb memory	Remembering specific events that have personal relevance, and the emotions triggered by the events (e.g., remembering where one was and how one reacted to the September 11, 2001, terrorist attacks on the World Trade Center).
Implicit memory	Unintentionally remembering stimuli that were acquired without paying attention (e.g., words or music to an old song that one did not even realize one knew).
Procedural memory	Often nonverbal, this type of memory relies on motor functions, such as riding a bike or playing a piece on the piano without reading the music.
Semantic memory	The storehouse of words and facts that have accumulated over one's lifetime.
Source memory	Remembering where one saw or heard a new piece of information (e.g., source of an article read on healthy aging).
Prospective memory	The task of remembering to do something in the future (e.g., remembering to keep a medical appointment)

AIDS TO WORKING MEMORY

The popularity of phones with digital memory for storing multiple phone numbers attests to the problem that people of all ages have with primary memory. Rather than looking up important phone numbers or attempting to memorize them, we can store these in the phone and retrieve them with the push of one or two buttons. Another technological development that can help reduce the information we must store in our minds is the personal digital assistant. These hand-held devices are useful for storing phone numbers, addresses, memos and even helping with orientation to physical space via a global positioning system (GPS). As older adults become more comfortable with these new technologies, they may experience less stress about retaining newly acquired information.

advanced old age; even people who have not ridden a bike in 50 years can get on and start pedaling, albeit perhaps somewhat wobbly at first. There is some age-related decline in procedural memory, where the elder is asked to remember a future event or time. But the effect is less dramatic than for episodic memory. Some researchers have demonstrated that source memory is not independent, but a component of episodic memory (Hoyer and Verhaeghen, 2006; Johnson, 2005; Siedlecki, Salthouse, and Berish, 2005).

The Importance of Learning and Memory in Everyday Life

As noted above, one of the most common complaints of older people is the difficulty they experience when attempting to learn and remember new names. Researchers find that older learners have more problems than young adults in experiments of face and name learning tests. Even among younger people, recalling a person's name is more difficult than remembering their occupation. This is because information about an occupation is

meaningful (e.g. we can visualize a person "doing" or "performing" their job or relate it to our own work), but names often do not have a semantic association to help process the new information (Fraas et al., 2002; Reese and Cherry, 2004; Rendell, Castel, and Craik, 2005). The best learning of new names occurs when older adults are told they will be asked to recall the names later. Information about the name to be recalled (e.g. facial features, link between face and name) can help older learners, whether they are given this information or they generate the descriptors themselves (Troyer et al., 2006).

Executive Function in Older Adults

An important component of learning is **executive function,** which is the ability to organize one's learning. It includes planning, decision making, avoiding interference or distraction from other stimuli while trying to learn new content, and the ability to shift attention from one task to another and to modify cognitive and spatial sets as new information is received. Normal aging is associated with mild declines in executive function, but older adults with dementia, as well as younger and older adults with depression or obsessive compulsive disorders experience significant impairment in this ability to organize their learning (Brooks, Weaver, and Scialfa, 2006; Gunstad et al., 2006; Watkins et al., 2005). Elders who exhibit declines in executive function over time also show signs of decline in instrumental activities of daily living (IADL), described in Chapter 4 as the ability to perform daily self-care activities (Royall et al., 2004). Problems with executive function and working memory may predict problems with medication adherence (i.e. the number of days that medications were taken as prescribed) among older adults using prescription drugs. Scores on executive function and working memory explained more variance in elders' ability to take their drugs as prescribed than did their age, level of education, or illness severity. Executive function was even better than total memory scores in predicting medication adherence (Insel et al., 2006).

Factors That Affect Learning in Old Age

The Importance of Attention

A critical component of cognition, especially in the learning process, is attention. Researchers have addressed three components of attention as central to people's ability to perform many different functions, including learning new skills and facts. These include selection, vigilance (or sustained attention), and attentional control under conditions of divided attention (Parasuraman, 1998).

Selective attention requires both conscious and unconscious skills; the learner must be able to select information relevant to a task while ignoring irrelevant information. Researchers who have tested age differences in selective attention have used visual search tasks, in which subjects must search for a target item in an array of items shown under different conditions. Older people do somewhat worse than young research subjects in such studies, but only under more complex conditions. **Vigilance, or sustained attention,** requires the individual to look out for a specific stimulus over time. This is the type of attention that air traffic controllers must use when watching for blips (each one representing an airplane) on a radar screen. In complex tasks in which each signal requires some decision (e.g., directing a plane to change its flight course upon seeing the blip), older people do worse than young adults. However, few differences between young and old are found when the task is simple or does not place significant demands on memory, or when participants have had practice with that type of vigilance, or are told to ignore irrelevant information. Age effects emerge when an event to be attended to shows up in an unpredictable pattern

(Einstein, Earles, and Collins, 2002; Rogers and Fisk, 2001). **Attentional control** is the individual's ability to determine how much attention should be directed at specific stimuli, and when to shift focus to other stimuli. This is particularly important under conditions of **divided attention.** In such cases the individual attempts to perform multiple tasks at the same time, such as listening to the radio or conversing on a cell phone while driving, or speaking on the phone in the kitchen while cooking a multicourse dinner. Experiments with divided attention tasks have used stimuli in the same sensory mode (e.g., listening to two channels of music or words simultaneously) or different sensory systems (e.g., listening to spoken words while reading a different set of words). As with the other two components of attention, age differences are not as dramatic as once thought. If the older person has had practice with managing multiple tasks (e.g., an experienced cook who can prepare multiple dishes simultaneously), it is just as easy for old and young subjects to shift their attention. To the extent that a task becomes practiced or "automatic," even if these skills were developed many years ago, an older person can perform them without any more attentional control than a young person. However, the more complex the activities demanded by each task, the more it affects an older person's ability to perform these tasks simultaneously. Furthermore, if the individual is anxious while performing tests that require divided attention, older adults do worse than do younger test-takers (Hogan, 2003; Whiting, 2003).

Practical Implications of Attention Changes with Aging

A better understanding of what causes age-related changes in attention and the nature of such changes can improve the person–environment (P–E) interface for older people, and their responses for maintaining active aging and P–E competence. For example, by examining each step of the task of driving under different conditions, researchers can focus on specific elements of selective attention, vigilance, and attentional control. Drivers must attend to important cues such as changes in traffic signals, traffic flow, and the speed of other cars. Vigilance plays an important role in long-distance driving, especially on monotonous stretches of interstate highways. By breaking down each component of driving and determining which conditions help or hinder older drivers, designers of traffic systems can place warning signs or traffic lights in the most complex locations in order to prevent accidents. Concurrently, classes aimed at older drivers can take advantage of this knowledge to improve their selective attention and vigilance skills under diverse driving conditions. As described in Chapter 4, older adults are disproportionately involved in motor vehicle accidents. A better understanding of age-related attention changes can reduce their high accident rates.

IMPROVING WEB PAGES FOR OLDER USERS

- Avoid using a patterned background behind text material.
- Use dark type or graphics against a light background.
- Avoid excess graphics and animation.
- Avoid pop-up menus that can confuse the main text.
- Use a consistent layout in different sections of the Web site.
- Limit how much information is presented on each page.
- Distinctly identify all links with a specific convention, such as underlining or a unique graphic.
- Identify clearly the content that is included under each heading.
- If animation or video is used, select short segments to reduce download time.
- Provide a telephone number and e-mail for users who want direct contact.

SOURCES: Adapted from Mead, Lamson, and Rogers, 2002, and National Library of Medicine, 2002.

The design of computers and Web pages is another area in which knowledge of age-related changes in attention can improve older persons' ability to maintain active aging in terms of cognitive functioning and social interaction. Given the significant growth in the number of baby boomers learning to use the computer, primarily for accessing the Internet, it behooves Web designers to consider older users' special needs (Mead, Lamson, and Rogers, 2002; Morrell, Mayhorn, and Bennett, 2000). In addition to the changes in attention processes just described, Web and software designers must recognize that many older people experience problems with language comprehension, fine motor movement, and reading small print. Some suggestions for Web designers are presented in the box on this page.

Environmental and Personal Factors

One problem with assessing learning ability is that it is not possible to measure the process that occurs in the brain while an individual is acquiring new information. Instead, we must rely on an individual's performance on tests that presumably measure what was learned. This may be particularly disadvantageous to older persons, whose performance on a test of learning may be poor because of inadequate or inappropriate conditions for expressing what was learned (Hess, Rosenberg, and Waters, 2001). For example, an older person may in fact have learned many new concepts in reading a passage from a novel, but not necessarily the specific concepts that are called for on a test of learning. Certain physical conditions may affect performance and thus lead to underestimates of what the older person has actually learned. These include:

- an unfamiliar learning environment
- poor lighting levels and small font size
- tone and loudness of the test-giver's voice in an oral exam
- time constraints placed on the test-taker

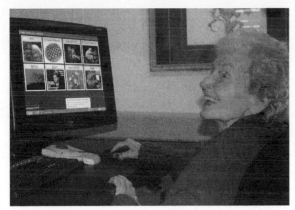

Computers provide elders with intellectual and social opportunities.

The learning environment can be improved, however. Some ways to do this include:

- glare-free and direct lighting
- lettering of good quality
- larger fonts
- color contrast
- a comfortable test-taking situation with minimal background noise
- a relaxed and articulate test-giver

As noted above, time constraints are particularly detrimental to older people. Although the ability to encode new information quickly is a sign of learning ability, it is difficult to measure. Instead, response time is generally measured. As we have already seen, psychomotor and sensory slowing with age has a significant impact on elders' response speed. Declines in perceptual speed, which can be measured separately from memory skills per se, may be a major reason why older people do worse on memory tests. Researchers have shown that perceptual speed accounts for a significant part of the observed age-related variance in memory performance. Even when older research subjects are given more time to complete tests of memory, their perceptual speed still plays a significant role in their performance (Ratcliff,

Spieler, and McKoon, 2000; Salthouse 1993, 1994a, 1996b).

The **general slowing hypothesis** proposed by Salthouse (1996a) suggests that processing of information slows down in the nervous system with aging. This results in more problems with responding to complex tasks, with older subjects doing worse on tests with more decisions than do younger people. This hypothesis also implies that older people perform worse under multi-tasking conditions (e.g., working on a computer while speaking on the phone and listening to the radio) than do younger people. Research on paired associates tasks has demonstrated that older persons make more *errors of omission* than *errors of commission*. That is, older persons are more likely not to give an answer than to guess and risk being wrong. This phenomenon was first recognized in middle-aged and older adults in tests of psychomotor functioning. The older the respondent, the more likely he or she was to work for accuracy at the expense of speed. This occurs even when the older learner is encouraged to guess and is told that it is acceptable to give wrong answers (i.e., commission errors). Conditions of uncertainty and high risk are particularly difficult for older persons, where they are far more cautious than the young. Low-risk situations elicit less caution from older adults and greater willingness to give responses in a learning task. The aging process may create an increased need to review multiple aspects of a problem, probably because of past experiences with similar dilemmas. Errors of omission may be reduced somewhat by giving rewards for both right and wrong answers, thereby forcing an answer.

Verbal ability and educational level are important factors in learning verbal information. Studies that entail learning prose passages show age deficits among those with average vocabulary abilities and minimal or no college education. In contrast, older persons with high verbal ability and a college education perform as well as younger subjects in such experiments. This may be due to greater practice and facility with such tasks on the part of more educated persons and those with good vocabulary skills. It may also reflect differences in the ability to organize new information, a skill that is honed through years of education and one that assists in the learning of large quantities of new material.

Stability in performing familiar perceptual-motor tasks may also occur because the accomplished performer of a specific task makes more efficient moves than does a less-skilled person. Such differences are evident in many areas demanding skill, from typing and driving to playing a musical instrument or operating a lathe. Therefore, older workers can overcome the effects of slower psychomotor speed and declines in learning skills by their greater experience in most occupations. As described above with respect to divided attention, older people who are experienced in performing specific tasks show no age decrements in these activities.

The conditions under which learning takes place affect the old more than the young, just as test conditions are more critical. Older persons respond differently to varied testing situations; people tested under challenging conditions ("this is a test of your intelligence") are likely to do worse than those in supportive conditions ("the researcher needs your help"). Positive feedback appears to be a valuable tool for eliciting responses from older adults in both learning and test situations. Fatigue may also play a role. Older adults performed better on tests of working memory in the morning when they were more alert. They performed worse than young adults on these same tasks when tested in the evening (West et al., 2003).

Pacing the rate of information flow makes it suitable to learners of any age and gives them opportunities to practice the new information (e.g., writing down or spelling aloud newly learned words). Self-pacing is most beneficial for older learners, followed by a moderate pace

> **EXAMPLES OF RETRIEVAL**
>
> **Recall**
>
> > **Free recall** "List the capitals of each state." "Describe how to repair a bicycle tire."
> >
> > **Cued recall** "The capital of New York begins with the letter 'A'; what is it?"
>
> **Recognition**
>
> > "Which of these three cities is the capital of New York?"
> >
> > "All but one of the following is a type of memory. Select the one that is not."

set by the test-giver. Older adults do much worse than younger adults when information is presented in a fast-paced manner. Another condition that supports learning is the presentation of familiar and relevant material compared to material perceived by the older learner to be unimportant. Older people do worse in recalling recently acquired information than do younger people when the new information is unfamiliar or confusing. Age differences also emerge when the material to be learned has low meaning and personal significance to the learner. Laboratory studies of cognitive functioning often seem artificial and meaningless to older adults who are unaccustomed to such research methods, and even more so to those with little academic experience. Many people will complain that such tests are trivial, nonsense, or that these tasks have no connection to the "real world." Indeed, it may appear odd to anyone to be learning meaningless words and symbols in a lab study. But for older people who are unfamiliar with test-taking situations, it may appear particularly foolish and not worth the effort required. This may also serve a useful ego-defensive function for individuals who feel uncomfortable or threatened by a test-taking situation. It is generally easier for people to blame the environment or the test itself for their poor performance than to accept it as a sign of a decline in their intelligence or their capacity to learn.

Spatial memory, that is, the ability to recall where objects are in relationship to each other in space (e.g., using a map or finding one's way back to where the car is parked), also appears to decline with aging. It is unclear, however, if older people do worse than the young because they have difficulty encoding and processing the information, or if the problem is in retrieval. It appears that there is an age-related decline in encoding ability for spatial information. Older people have more difficulty than younger persons in reading maps that are misaligned relative to the user. For example, when older people stand in front of a "You are here" map that is aligned 180° away from themselves, they take up to 50 percent more time and make 30 percent more errors than younger persons in the same condition. However, when the map is aligned directly with the user, no age differences are observed. This may be attributable to increased problems with mental rotation of external images and with perspective-taking as we age. Older adults also perform less well than younger people when they are shown a set of items in a certain arrangement, then the items are removed, and they are asked to reconstruct the objects in the same arrangements (Aubrey, Li, and Dobbs, 1994; Das and Agarwai, 2000).

Age-Related Changes in Memory

As we have seen, learning involves encoding information and storing it into secondary or long-term memory, so that it can be retrieved and used later. Studies of this process have focused on two types of retrieval: recall and recognition. **Recall** is the process of searching through the vast store of information in secondary memory, perhaps with a cue or a specific, orienting question. **Recognition** requires less

search. The information in secondary memory must be matched with the stimulus information in the environment. Recall is demanded in essay exams, recognition in multiple-choice tests.

Not surprisingly, most researchers identify age-related deficiencies in recall, but few differences in recognition. This may be due to the context in which multiple stimuli are presented, triggering cues for the test-taker (Sharps and Martin, 1998; Smith, 1996). Recall tasks have been further divided into *free recall* and *cued recall* situations. In the former, no aids or hints are provided for retrieving information from secondary memory. In the latter case, the individual is given some information to aid in the search (e.g., category labels and first letter of a word). Older people tend to do less well than the young in tests of free recall, but are aided significantly by cueing. In particular, use of category labels (semantic cues) at the learning stage is found to be more helpful to older persons than the use of structural cues—for example, giving the respondent the first letter of a word to be recalled (Smith, 1996). However, cued recall tests are not as helpful as recognition tests for older learners.

The question of whether older people have better recall of events that occurred in the distant past than recent situations is unclear. Many events are firmly embedded in secondary memory because they are unique or so important that subsequent experiences do not interfere with the ability to recall them. The birth of a child, one's wedding ceremony, or the death of a parent, partner, or sibling are events that most people can recall in detail 40 or more years later. This may be because the situation had great personal significance or—in the case of world events, such as the bombing of Hiroshima or President Kennedy's assassination—had a profound impact on world history. Some distant events may be better recalled because they have greater personal relevance for the individual's social development than recent experiences, or because they have been rehearsed or thought about more. Another possibility is that cues that helped the older person recall events in the past are less effective with recalling recent occasions because of "cue-overload." That is, the same cues that were once helpful in remembering certain information are also used to recall many recent events. But the cues are so strongly associated with one's earlier life experiences that the newer information becomes more difficult to retrieve. For example, older people may have difficulty memorizing new phone numbers because the cues that helped them recall phone numbers in the past may be so closely associated with previous ones that they confuse recent phone numbers with old ones.

One problem in determining whether recall of distant situations is really better than recall of recent events is the difficulty in validating an older person's memories. In many cases, there are no sources that can be checked to determine the accuracy of such recollections. We can all identify with this process of asking an old friend or family member, "Do you remember the time when . . . ?" If others have no recollection of the event, it may make us wonder if the situation really took place, or it may mean that the event was so obscure that it made no impact on other people. Hence, such memories are difficult to measure accurately.

Several theories are offered to explain *why* older people may have problems with retrieving information from secondary memory. One explanation is that not using the information results in its loss (the **disuse theory**). This theory suggests that information can fade away or decay unless it is exercised, as in the adage, "Use it or lose it." However, this explanation fails to account for the many facts that are deeply embedded in a person's memory store and that can be retrieved even after years of disuse.

A more widely accepted explanation is that new information interferes with the material that has been stored over many years. As we

have noted earlier, interference is a problem in the learning or encoding stage. When the older person is distracted while trying to learn new information, this information does not become stored in memory. Poor retrieval may be due to a combination of such distraction during the learning stage and interference by similar or new information with the material being searched in the retrieval stage. Although researchers in this area have not conclusively agreed on any of these explanations, the **interference theory** appears to hold more promise than others for explaining observed problems with retrieval.

Tip-of-the-Tongue States

Tip-of-the-tongue states (TOTs) represent a specific type of difficulty in retrieval. We all experience situations when we know the name of a place or person but cannot immediately recall it. This might be the name of a favorite restaurant or park, or a famous actor or character in a story, or an acquaintance we have not seen in many years. Features of TOTs are that the target word is familiar and will be recalled by searching through one's memory, drawing associations from similar names, or mentally focusing on an image of the place or person. TOTs are also distinguished by a feeling of *imminence,* the sense that one can "almost" remember it, or that it is on the "tip of one's tongue" (Schwartz, 2002).

Although all people experience TOTs, both anecdotal evidence and cross-sectional studies show that TOTs increase with age. Two different theories have been offered to explain this. The *decrement model* suggests that memory networks deteriorate with aging, and TOTs are a manifestation of these impaired networks (Brown and Nix, 1996). The second model focuses on *incremental knowledge gain* with aging, whereby the cumulative knowledge and vocabulary of older adults can cause more names in secondary memory to interfere with the name to be recalled (Dahlgren, 1998). When we experience a TOT, most of us can rely on:

1. spontaneous retrieval of the name (i.e., letting it pop into our primary memory later, when we are removed from the immediate pressure to remember the words),
2. using specific search strategies such as cues (e.g., listing similar names or going through the alphabet), or
3. using other sources to aid recall, such as asking another person or looking in a dictionary or thesaurus.

Older people seem to use spontaneous recall more often, and search strategies of any type less often than young adults. These differences may be explained by the decrement model and incremental knowledge model. The former would posit that aging causes deterioration in one's efficient use of cues; the latter attributes it to a larger bank of names in one's memory that makes it difficult to search for a specific word (Schwartz, 2002).

Improving Cognitive Abilities in Old Age

Cognitive Retraining

In the Seattle Longitudinal Study (SLS) described earlier in this chapter, the researchers tested the effects of **cognitive retraining**—teaching research participants how to use various techniques to keep their minds active and maintain good memory skills. This approach to retraining is based on the premise of maximizing one's remaining potential, a widely accepted concept in physical aging but only recently applied to cognitive aging. Intellectual activities that involve problem-solving and creativity, such as Scrabble and crossword puzzles, are described by Willis and colleagues as effective ways for older people to maximize their intellectual abilities. In the SLS, cognitive retraining resulted in a reversal of declines that had been

LIFELONG LEARNING

Continuing education is an excellent way to maintain intellectual skills in old age. Elderhostel is a popular international program that offers older adults learning options based on college campuses and through tours to educational and historic sites. "Summer College for Seniors" is a program offered by Shoreline Community College in Seattle. Each summer, more than 100 elders participate in week-long college classes on topics as wide-ranging as constitutional law and classical music. College faculty who teach these older students enjoy the perspectives they bring, and praise their maturity both intellectually and emotionally. As one 65-year-old Summer College student noted, "The people here may be gray on top but they're not dull between the ears." Another participant, age 75, added, "I think, as a senior, mental stimulation is as important as physical exercise."

Seattle Times, July 25, 2000, p. B1 (F. Vinluan, staff reporter).

observed over the preceding 14 years in 40 percent of research participants. Many elders maintained these gains over the next testing period (Willis, 2001; Willis and Nesselroade, 1990; Willis and Schaie, 1988, 1986). However, cognitive training in some areas may be more effective than others. Elders in the SLS trained in reasoning ability demonstrated more long-term gains than those trained in spatial orientation, especially 14 years later (Boron, Willis, and Schaie, 2007). Teaching older adults strategies for remembering lists of words, themes, and details in stories by using practice and performance feedback can significantly improve their memory. In one large-scale study, a 10-session memory-training intervention resulted in 26 percent of elders improving their memory immediately after the intervention, and continued for two years (Ball et al., 2002). This same study assessed the impact of memory retraining on IADLs up to five years later. Elders who received inductive reasoning training showed the greatest improvement in IADLs such as reading road signs, following directions on a medication bottle, and looking up telephone numbers. Booster sessions at 11 and 35 months improved skills even more. Training in memorization and speed of processing was less beneficial (Willis et al., 2007). However, the effectiveness of cognitive retraining programs depends on the mental status and physical health of participating elders (Nyberg, 2005).

There has been considerable experimentation with chemical interventions to improve memory. Researchers have tested products that enhance the chemical messengers in neurons or improve the function of neural receptors. Ginkgo biloba, a natural extract derived from leaves of the maidenhair tree, has received attention because it seems to improve memory by improving circulation in the brain. Systematic research on the effects of ginkgo biloba for mild memory loss, as well as for people with Alzheimer's disease, has not shown significant benefits (van Dongen et al., 2003). Vitamin E is an antioxidant (described in Chapter 3) that may help enhance memory by reducing oxidative damage resulting from normal aging. No long-term human studies are yet available to support these claims for the benefits of vitamin E or other possible supplements such as lecithin, vitamin B_{12}, and folic acid. It is also important to recognize that therapeutic doses of these and other supplements (i.e., levels that are high enough to show improved memory function) can cause harmful side effects such as internal bleeding, and megadoses may even increase mortality (Bjelakovic, et al., 2007). Nevertheless, there may be some FDA-approved memory-enhancing drugs within the next few years.

Other researchers have examined the benefits of practical memory-enhancing methods, such as cognitive aids. Although useful at any age, cognitive aids may be particularly helpful for an older person who is experiencing increased problems with real-world cognitive abilities, such as recalling names, words, phone numbers, and daily chores. However, elders are more likely to use external aids such as notes and lists than cognitive aids. That is,

---

DIET AND COGNITIVE CHANGE

The results of a large cohort study of almost 4000 community-dwelling elders found that vegetable consumption may reduce the rate of cognitive decline with aging. Older adults who averaged 2.8 servings per day of vegetables (especially leafy greens, broccoli, squash, and collards) had 40 percent slower decline over six years on tests of immediate and delayed recall, perceptual speed, attention, and short-term memory than did elders who consumed an average of 0.9 servings per day. High levels of fruit intake or use of vitamin supplements did not affect cognitive scores over time. The benefits of higher vegetable intake were greater for the old-old in this study. These results support the findings of a national study of women (the Nurses Study), which showed that high intake of vegetables, but no fruit, slowed cognitive decline (Kang, Ascherio, and Grodstein, 2005; Morris et al., 2006).

---

they are more likely to reduce environmental press to enhance their competence in learning as a means of improving P–E congruence. One way of improving personal competence may be to enhance cardiovascular fitness. Research has demonstrated significant benefits of exercise and physical activity for cognitive functioning, especially for the oldest-old. One explanation for the positive effects of cardiovascular fitness on learning and memory may be that exercise improves blood flow to the brain. Another factor may be that synaptic connections in the frontal lobes increase with cardiovascular activity (Colcombe and Kramer, 2003; Kramer, Erickson, and Colcombe, 2006).

Older adults who are most concerned about declining memory use external and cognitive aids as a way of coping with the problem. This is particularly true for elders with a strong internal locus of control—that is, a belief that they have control over their well-being rather than attributing their problems to external forces (Verhaeghen et al., 2000). Similarly, the belief that one has a good memory helps older adults do well on tests of memory (Zelinski and Gilewski, 2004). Recognizing that low self-efficacy can affect older people's learning ability, researchers have used cognitive restructuring techniques to convince older learners to change their views of aging and memory. By focusing on their strengths and believing that they could control how much they retain of newly acquired information, elders in one study improved their scores on memory tests more than their counterparts who did not receive self-efficacy training (Caprio-Prevette and Fry, 1996).

Memory Mediators

Most memory improvement techniques are based on the concept of **mediators,** that is, the use of visual and verbal links between information to be encoded and information that is already in secondary memory. Mediators may be visual (e.g., the method of locations) or verbal (i.e., the use of mnemonics). **Visual mediators**—the method of locations (or loci)—are useful for learning a list of new words, names, or concepts. Each word is associated with a specific location in a familiar environment. For example, the individual is instructed to "walk through" his or her own home mentally. As the person walks through the rooms in succession, each item on the list is associated with a particular space along the way. Older persons using this technique are found to recall more words on a list than when they use no mediators. One advantage of the method of loci is that learners can visualize the new information within a familiar setting, and can decide for themselves what new concept should be linked with what specific part of the environment. Imaging is a useful technique in everyday recall situations as well. For example, an older person can remember what he or she needs to buy at the grocery story by visualizing using these items in preparing dinner. This type of exercise to strengthen memory in one task can help improve performance on other memory tasks (Colcombe and Kramer, 2003).

Another way of organizing material to be learned and to ensure its storage in secondary memory is to use **mnemonics,** or verbal riddles, rhymes, and codes associated with the new information. Many teachers use such rhymes to teach their students multiplication, spelling (e.g., "*i* before *e* except after *c*"), and the calendar ("30 days hath September, April, June, and November/all the rest have 31, except February alone, and that has 28 days clear/except every leap year"). Many other mnemonics are acquired through experience as well as our own efforts to devise ways to learn a new concept (e.g., making up a word to remember the three components of cognition: intelligence, learning, memory might

LOOK, SNAP, AND CONNECT

A practical method for retaining information efficiently in order to recall it later is the "Look, Snap and Connect" technique, recommended by Small (2002), who suggests that we can improve our memory at every age by using an encoding and retrieval system that is personally meaningful. The components of this method are:

Look: Actively focus on what you want to learn in order to take in the information, and record the information received through multiple senses.

Snap: Create a mental snapshot or image of the object or person or word(s) to be remembered; the more bizarre or unusual the image, the better it will be recalled (e.g., remembering Mr. Brown's name by visualizing him covered with brown paint).

Connect: Visualize a link to associate the images created through mental snapshots, thereby retaining the information through its link with existing memories (e.g., remembering a grocery list by connecting items together, such as *flour* poured over *apples* that are swimming in a bowl of *milk*).

SOURCE: From G. Small, *The memory bible.* New York: Hyperion, 2002.

become "IntLeMe"). These can assist older people, particularly the young-old, to learn more efficiently, especially if the mnemonics are specific to the memory task at hand. Older people with mild or moderate dementia can also benefit from visual methods of recall (e.g., method of loci), but less from list-making. Whatever method is used, however, it is important to train the older adult in the use of a specific mnemonic and to provide easy strategies to help the person apply these techniques to everyday learning events. In one study, researchers provided half the sample with a "memory handbook" and 30 minutes of practical instruction; the other half were given just a pamphlet that gave examples of useful mnemonics (but no face-to-face instruction in their use). The former group demonstrated significant improvements in two subsequent memory tests; the pamphlet group did not (Andrewes, Kinsella, and Murphy, 1996). Other mediators to aid memory include:

1. using the new word or concept in a sentence,
2. associating the digits in a phone number with symbols or putting them into a mathematical formula (e.g., "the first digit is 4, the second and third are multiplied to produce the first"),
3. placing the information into categories,
4. using multiple sensory memories, and
5. combining sensory with motor function.

In this last technique, one can write the word (iconic memory), repeat it aloud to oneself (echoic memory), or "feel" the letters or digits by outlining them with one's hand. Unfortunately, many older persons do not practice the use of newly learned memory mediators. They may not be motivated to use the techniques, which often seem awkward, or they may forget and need to be reminded. Perhaps the major problem is that these are unfamiliar approaches to the current cohort of older adults. As future cohorts become more practiced in these memory techniques through their educational experiences, the use of such strategies in old age may increase.

The most important aspect of memory enhancement may be the ability to relax and to avoid feeling anxious or stressed during the learning stage. As noted earlier, many older people become overly concerned about occasional memory lapses, viewing them as a sign of deterioration and possible onset of dementia. Thus, a young person may be annoyed when a familiar name is forgotten, but will probably not interpret the memory lapse as loss of cognitive function, as an older person is likely to do. Unfortunately, society reinforces this belief. How often are we told that we are "getting old" when we forget a trivial matter? How often do adult children become concerned that their parent sometimes forgets to turn off the stove, when in fact they may frequently do so themselves? Chronic stress can also impair older people's memory performance. Research with animals and humans has shown that some hormones released under high-stress conditions (e.g., cortisol and corticosterone) cause the subject to make more errors in memory tests (McGaugh, 2000).

In addition to mediators, **external aids** or devices are often used by older people to keep track of the time or dates, or to remember to turn the stove on or off. Simple methods such as list-making can significantly improve an older person's recall and recognition memory, even if the list is not used subsequently. A list that is organized by topic or type of item (e.g., a chronological "to-do" list or a grocery list that groups produce, meats, dry goods together) also is found to aid older people's memory significantly. Older adults with higher educational attainment and

---

A MEMORY EXERCISE

Use the method of loci to help you remember *seven* items that you need to buy at the grocery store. Go to the store without a list, but imagine yourself walking through the kitchen at home after your trip to the grocery store, placing each of the seven items in a specific location.

better vocabulary skills, which will be true of baby boomers, benefit even more from list-making methods (Burack and Lackman, 1996). Older people can develop the habit of associating medication regimens with specific activities of daily living, such as using marked pill boxes and taking the first pill in the morning before their daily shower, or just before or after breakfast, taking the second pill with lunch or before their noontime walk, and so on. These behaviors need to be associated with activities that occur every day at a particular time, so that the pill-taking becomes linked with that routine. Charts listing an individual's daily or weekly routine can be posted throughout the house. Alarm clocks and kitchen timers also can be placed near an older person while the oven or stove is in operation. This will help in remembering that the appliance is on without the person's needing to stay in the kitchen. With the increased availability of home computers, daily activities and prescription reminders can be programmed into an older person's computer. Finally, for older people who have serious memory problems and a tendency to get lost while walking outdoors, a bracelet or necklace imprinted with the person's name, address, phone number, and relevant medical information can be a lifesaver.

Wisdom and Creativity

Wisdom and creativity are difficult to define and measure. Most people have an image of what it means to be wise or creative, but it is impossible to quantify an individual's level of wisdom or creativity. It is suggested that *wisdom* requires the cognitive development and self-knowledge that come with age (Cohen, 2005; Levitt, 1999). Wisdom is a combination of experience, introspection, reflection, intuition, and empathy; these are qualities that are honed over many years and that can be integrated through people's interactions with their environments. Thus, younger people may have any one of these skills individually, but their integration requires more maturity. Based on research

Younger generations can benefit from the wisdom of elder scholars.

with older adults who had been nominated as "wise" by other people, the following five criteria can be used to assess if the individual demonstrates wise behavior (Baltes and Kunzmann, 2003; Baltes and Staudinger, 2000; Staudinger, 1999):

- *Factual knowledge*—possessing both general and specific information about life conditions and relevant issues.
- *Procedural knowledge*—using decision-making strategies, planning, and interpretation of life experiences to a given situation.
- *Lifespan contextualism*—considering the context in which events are occurring and the relationship among them.
- *Value relativism*—considering and respecting values and priorities brought to the situation by other participants.
- *Managing uncertainty*—developing back-up plans or alternative strategies if one's performance is hampered by external factors.

Wisdom is achieved by transcending the limitations of basic needs such as health, income, and housing. The individual must have continued opportunities for growth and creativity in order to develop wisdom (Ardelt, 1997). Wisdom implies that the individual does not act on impulse, has good insights, and can reflect on all aspects of a given situation objectively. This makes the wise older person better at conflict resolution. In many cultures, as noted in Chapter 2, older persons are respected for their years of experience and ability to mediate conflicts, and the role of "wise elder" is a desired status. One perspective on wisdom is that it requires such lifelong experiences, insights, and emotional maturity in order to impart to younger generations the skills, family and cultural values, and community traditions (Cohen, 2000, 2005). This approach combines the focus on emotional maturity and regulation of feelings that is typical of Eastern concepts of wisdom with the emphasis on cognitive maturity that is characteristic of Western perspectives, as shown by the five criteria above (Takahashi and Overton, 2002). The balance theory of wisdom suggests that a wise individual is one who can balance different components of intelligence—practical, analytical, and creative—and use them to solve problems that will benefit society, rather than focusing on using one's intelligence for personal gain (Sternberg, 1998; Sternberg and Lubart, 2001).

Not all older people achieve wisdom, however. Wisdom suggests the ability to interpret knowledge, or to understand the world in a deeper and more profound manner. Such reflectiveness and the reduced self-centeredness that this requires allow older people to take charge of their lives and become more accepting of their own and others' weaknesses. Indeed, among older men and women in the Berkeley Guidance Study, those who scored high on the three components of wisdom (cognitive, reflective, affective thinking) also scored high on a measure of life satisfaction. This suggests that active aging (described in Chapters 1 and 6) is enhanced when wisdom has been attained (Ardelt, 1997). Older people who have achieved this level of wisdom can play productive roles in many businesses, government and voluntary agencies, where their years of experience and ability to move beyond the constraints presumed by others could help such organizations. (Such functions are discussed in more detail in Chapter 12.)

Creativity refers to the ability to apply unique and feasible solutions to new situations and to come up with original ideas or material products. We generally think of creativity in terms of extraordinary products that have been created (e.g., composers or artists). However, people who come up with unique but smaller scale products (e.g., an attractive garden or beautiful quilts) also are displaying their creativity (Cohen, 2000, 2005). A person may be creative in science, the arts, or technology. Although we can point to well-known creative people in each of these areas (e.g., Albert Einstein in science, Wolfgang Amadeus Mozart and Georgia O'Keeffe in the arts, and Thomas Edison in technology), it is difficult to determine the specific characteristics that make such persons creative. As with intelligence in general, creativity is inferred from the individual's output, but cannot really be quantified or predicted. One measure of creativity is a test of *divergent thinking,* which is part of Guilford's (1967) structural model of intelligence. This is measured by asking a person to devise multiple solutions to an unfamiliar mental task (e.g., name some different uses for a flower). Later still, Torrance (1988) developed a test of creativity that also measures divergent thinking. Children who scored high on this test were found to be creative achievers as young adults (i.e., the test has good predictive and construct validity), but the test has not been used to predict changes in creativity across the life course.

Divergent thinking may be only one component of creativity, however. A creative person must also know a great deal about a particular body of knowledge such as music or art before he or she can make creative contributions to it. However, this neglects the contributions to scientific problem-solving or the arts by people who may have expertise in one area and bring a fresh perspective to a different field. To date, there have been no systematic studies of divergent thinking among people who are generally considered to be

CREATIVITY IN LATE LIFE

In his insightful book, *The Creative Age*, Dr. Gene Cohen examines how creativity and creative expression can expand with aging. He provides numerous examples of scientists, artists, writers, and composers who produced their most innovative works in their later years. These include:

- Sir Isaac Newton (1642–1727), the father of calculus, revised his influential book describing the three laws of motion at age 71 and again at age 84.
- The German mathematician Carl Friedrich Gauss (1777–1855) made many discoveries well into old age. He updated his fundamental theory of algebra at age 71.
- The Renaissance painter Titian painted several masterpieces between age 78 and 83, and began experimenting with an impressionistic style in his later years.
- Hanya Holm (1893–1992) choreographed popular Broadway plays in her young-old stage, including *My Fair Lady* when she was 63 and *Camelot* at age 67.
- Three early leaders of the women's rights movement started the six-volume *History of Women's Suffrage*, in 1875. Elizabeth Cady Stanton was 72; Susan B. Anthony was 67, and Matilda Gage was 61 when the book was published.

creative. Much of the research on creativity has been performed as analyses of the *products* of artists and writers, not on their creative *process* directly. Indeed, no studies have been conducted to compare the cognitive functioning of artists, scientists, technologists, and others who are widely regarded as creative with that of persons not similarly endowed. Researchers who have examined the *quantity* of creative output by artists, poets, and scientists have found that the average rate of output at age 70 to 80 drops to approximately half that of age 30 to 40. However, a secondary peak of productivity often occurs in the 60s, although not as high as the first peak (Simonton, 1989, 1991, 1999). The second peak of creativity may produce even better works. Indeed, Simonton's analysis of the last works of 172 classical composers in their final years revealed compositions that were judged highly by musicologists in terms of aesthetics, melody, and comprehensibility.

Some have suggested that creativity actually increases with age because the individual becomes more self-confident, experienced, and free from social constraints. This results in the ability to make novel decisions to solve problems. Indeed, these researchers have found that older adults with high physical and cognitive functioning use both hemispheres of the brain more equally than do younger adults, and have a greater density of synapses accruing from a lifetime of learning and experiences. As a result of this increased capacity of the brain, combined with a feeling of being liberated from the commitments and priorities of younger years, older adults can explore and express their creativity in multiple ways (Cabeza et al., 2002; Cohen, 2000, 2005).

Opportunities for creative expression can have other significant benefits, as illustrated by a study of the impact of a structured and sustained arts program on elders' physical and emotional well-being. Older adults were randomly assigned to a 35-week arts education and activity program, or to a control condition. When these elders were assessed again one year later, those in the arts and activity program had made fewer physician visits, had used fewer medications, had lower scores on a measure of depression, and higher morale than did elders in the control group (Cohen, 2005). This suggests the value of encouraging elders' creativity in a wide range of forms.

Implications for the Future

Advances in neuroscience will eventually uncover the specific changes in the brain that account for age-related changes in memory, attention, and learning ability. New techniques of brain research are evolving with the use of magnetic resonance imaging (MRI) and positron emission tomography (PET) that can determine which areas of the brain are responsible for different types of attention, learning, and memory. These noninvasive techniques adopted from the medical diagnostic field are already being used to study differences in attention tasks between young and old subjects, and between older persons with different types of dementia. PET scans can reveal differences in brain activity among people with varying educational levels, and in the early stages of Alzheimer's disease (Greenwood and Parasuraman, 1999; Parasuraman and Greenwood, 1998; Silverman, Small, and Chang, 2001; Small, 1999).

Unfortunately, however, these high-tech methods of early detection may not be accessible to all people as they age because of their high cost. Unless Medicare and private insurers recognize the benefits of screening for dementia, as they do with cancer, these techniques will be limited to older adults who can afford to pay for them. This is true for other computer-assisted devices and systems that can be used in older adults' homes to help them maintain person–environment competence, as will be described in Chapter 11.

Many career opportunities are emerging for students interested in the interface of cognitive psychology, education, technology, and gerontology. Especially among future cohorts, older adults will increasingly search for opportunities to learn and become retrained. With the extension of life expectancy and changes in retirement patterns (as discussed in Chapter 12), many people will seek second and third careers that will require new cognitive and motor skills. Educators and software designers can apply the concepts presented in this chapter to respond to the needs of older learners.

Summary

This chapter presented an overview of major longitudinal studies of cognitive functioning. Researchers have examined age-related changes in intelligence, learning, and memory, and what factors in the individual and the environment affect the degree of change in these three areas of cognitive functioning.

Of all the cognitive functions, intelligence in older adults has received the greatest attention and is most controversial. It is also the area of most concern for many older persons. One problem with this area of research is the difficulty of defining and measuring what is generally agreed to be intelligence. In examining the components of intelligence measured by the Wechsler Adult Intelligence Scale (WAIS), fluid intelligence (as measured by performance scales) has been shown to decline more with aging than verbal, or crystallized, intelligence. This may be due partly to the fact that the former tests are generally timed, while the latter are not. However, age differences emerge even when tests are not timed, and when variations in motor and sensory function are taken into account. This decline in fluid intelligence and maintenance of verbal intelligence is known as the Classic Aging Pattern. To the extent that older persons practice their fluid intelligence by using their problem-solving skills, they will experience fewer decrements in this area. In contrast, aging does not appear to impair the ability for remembering word and symbol meanings. This does not imply that the ability to recall words is unimpaired, but when asked for definitions of words, older people can remember their meanings quite readily.

One problem with studying intelligence in aging is that of distinguishing age *changes* from age *differences*. To determine changes with age, people must be examined longitudinally. The problems of selective attrition and terminal drop make it difficult to interpret the findings of longitudinal studies of intelligence. These factors may result in an underestimate of the decline in intelligence with aging. The problem of cross-sectional studies of intelligence is primarily that of cohort differences. Even if subjects are matched on educational level, older persons have not had the exposure to computers and early childhood learning opportunities that are available to recent cohorts. The Seattle Longitudinal Study, which initiated the approach of testing multiple cohorts longitudinally, provides valuable insights into the impact of cohort differences in education and health on intelligence. This study also determined that changes on some tests of cognitive function in the middle years can predict cognitive impairment in the later years. Occupation, sensory decline, poor physical health, and severe hypertension also have been found to have a significant impact on intelligence test scores.

Learning and memory are cognitive functions that are usually examined because tests of memory are actually tests of what a person has learned. According to the information processing model, learning begins when information reaches sensory memory, and then is directed via one or more sensory stores to primary memory. It is in primary memory that information must be organized and processed if it is to be retained and passed into secondary memory. Information is permanently stored in this latter region. Studies of recall and recognition provide evidence that aging does not affect the capacity of either primary or secondary memory. Instead, it appears that the aging process makes us less efficient in "reaching into" our secondary memory and retrieving material that was stored years ago. Tip-of-the-tongue states are an example of problems in remembering familiar names and words, and the role of stress in the retrieval process. Recognition tasks, in which a person is provided with a cue to associate with an item in secondary memory, are easier than pure recall for most people, especially those who are older. Some types of memory, such as semantic and procedural memory, are retained into advanced old age. Others, like episodic memory, show significant age-related decrements.

The learning process can be enhanced for older people by reducing time constraints, making the learning task more relevant for them, improving the physical conditions by using bright but glare-free lights and large letters, and providing visual and verbal mediators for learning new information. Helping the older learner to relax and not feel threatened by the learning task also ensures better learning. Such modifications are consistent with the goal of achieving greater congruence between older people and their environment.

Significant age-related declines in intelligence, learning, and memory are not inevitable. Older people who continue to perform well on tests of intelligence, learning, and memory are characterized by higher levels of education, good sensory functioning, maintenance of physical activities and good nutrition, and employment and leisure activities that require complex problem-solving skills. People who do not have serious cardiovascular disease or severe hypertension also perform well, although there is some slowing of cognitive processing and response speed. Even such slowing is not a problem for older people whose crystallized knowledge in the targeted area is high. Natural products and vitamins that may improve memory in older people but whose benefits are not proven should be researched.

Although there is some agreement that wisdom is enhanced by age and that creativity reaches a second peak for some people in old age, there has been less research emphasis in these areas. Indeed, these concepts are more difficult to measure in young and old persons. These and other issues in cognition must be studied more fully with measures that have good construct validity before gerontologists can describe with certainty cognitive changes that are attributable to normal aging rather than disease.

GLOSSARY

attentional control   ability to allocate one's attention among multiple stimuli simultaneously

Classic Aging Pattern   the decline observed with aging on some performance scales of intelligence tests versus consistency on verbal scales of the same tests

cognitive retraining   teaching research participants how to use various techniques to keep their minds active and maintain good memory skills

crystallized intelligence   knowledge and abilities one gains through education and experience

disuse theory   the view that memory fades or is lost because one fails to use the information

divided attention   ability to focus on multiple stimuli simultaneously

echoic memory   auditory memory, a brief period when new information received through the ears is stored

executive function   cognitive skills required to organize one's learning function

external aids   simple devices used by older people to keep track of the time or dates, etc., such as list-making

fluid intelligence   skills that are biologically determined, independent of experience or learning, similar to "native intelligence," requiring flexibility in thinking

general slowing hypothesis   physiological changes that cause slower transmission of information through the nervous system with aging

iconic memory   visual memory, a brief period when new information received through the eyes is stored

information processing model   a conceptual model of how learning and memory take place

intelligence   the theoretical limit of an individual's performance

intelligence quotient (IQ)   an individual's abilities relative to population standards in making judgments, in comprehension, and in reasoning

interference theory   the view that memory fades or is lost because of distractions experienced during learning or interference from similar or new information to the item to be recalled.

mediators   visual and verbal links between information to be memorized and information that is already in secondary memory

mnemonics   the method of using verbal cues such as riddles or rhymes as aids to memory

perceptual speed   time, in milliseconds, required to perceive and react to a stimulus

primary mental abilities (PMAs)   the basic set of intellectual skills, including mathematical reasoning, word fluency, verbal meaning, inductive reasoning, and spatial orientation

recall   the process of searching through secondary memory in response to a specific external cue

recognition   matching information in secondary memory with the stimulus information

secondary (long-term) memory   permanent memory store; requires processing of new information to be stored and cues to retrieve stored information

selective attention   being able to focus on information relevant to a task while ignoring irrelevant information

sensory memory   the first step in receiving information through the sense organs and passing it on to primary or secondary memory

spatial memory   the ability to recall where objects are in relationship to each other in space

terminal decline hypothesis   the hypothesis that persons close to death decline in cognitive abilities

tip-of-the-tongue states (TOTs)   difficulty retrieving names from secondary memory but often spontaneously recalled later

vigilance (sustained attention)   keeping alert to focus on a specific stimulus over time

visual mediators   the method of locations; memorizing by linking each item with a specific location in space

working (primary) memory   holding newly acquired information in storage; a maximum of 7 ± 2 stimuli before processing into secondary memory or discarding

REFERENCES

Andrewes, D.G., Kinsella, G., and Murphy, M. Using a memory handbook to improve everyday memory in community-dwelling older adults with memory complaints. *Experimental Aging Research*, 1996, 22, 305–322.

Ardelt, M. Wisdom and life satisfaction in old age. *Journals of Gerontology*, 1997, *52B*, P15–P27.

Aubrey, J.B., Li, K.Z.H., and Dobbs, A.R. Age and sex differences in the interpretation of misaligned "You-are-Here" maps. *Journals of Gerontology*, 1994, *49*, P29–P31.

Ball, K., Berch, D.B., Hemers, K.F., Jobe, J.B., Leveck, M.D., Mariske, M., et al. Effects of cognitive training interventions with older adults. *Journal of* the American Medical Association, 2002, 288, 2271–2281.

Baltes, P.B. The aging mind: Potential and limits. The Gerontologist, 1993, 33, 580–594.

Baltes, P.B., and Kunzmann, U. Wisdom. Psychologist, 2003, 16, 131–133.

Baltes, P.B., and Staudinger, U.M. Wisdom: A meta-heuristic to orchestrate mind and virtue toward excellence. American Psychologist, 2000, 55, 122–126.

Berg, S. Aging, behavior, and terminal decline. In J.E. Birren and K.W. Schaie (Eds.), Handbook of the psychology of aging (4th ed.). San Diego: Academic Press, 1996.

Binet, A., and Simon, T. Méthodes nouvelles pour le diagnostique du niveau intellectuel des anormaux. Année Psychologique, 1905, 11, 102–191.

Bjelakovic, G., Nikolova, D., Gluud, L.L., Simonetti, R.G., and Gluud, C. Mortality in randomized trials of antioxidant supplements for primary and secondary prevention. Journal of the American Medical Association, 2007, 297, 842–857.

Bopp, K.L., and Verhaeghen, P. Aging and verbal memory span: A meta-analysis. Journals of Gerontology: Psychological Sciences, 2005, 60B, P223–P233.

Boron, J.B., Willis, S.L., and Schaie, K.W. Cognitive training gain as a predictor of mental status. Journals of Gerontology: Psychological Sciences, 2007, 62B, P45–P52.

Bosworth, H.B., Schaie, K.W., and Willis, S.L. Cognitive and sociodemographic risk factors for mortality in the Seattle Longitudinal Study. Journals of Gerontology: Psychological and Social Sciences, 1999, 54B, 273–282.

Brooks, B.L., Weaver, L.E., and Scialfa, C.T. Does impaired executive functioning differentially impact verbal memory measure in older adults with suspected dementia? The Clinical Neuropsychologist, 2006, 20, 230–242.

Brown, A.S., and Nix, L.A. Age-related changes in the tip-of-the-tongue experience. American Journal of Psychology, 1996, 109, 79–91.

Bruce, P.R., and Herman, J.F. Adult age differences in spatial memory. Journal of Gerontology, 1986, 41, 774–777.

Burack, O.R., and Lackman, M.E. The effects of list-making on recall in young and elderly adults. Journals of Gerontology, 1996, 51B, P226–P233.

Cabeza, R., Anderson, N.D., Locantore, J.K., and McIntosh, A.R. Aging gracefully: Compensatory brain activity in high-performing older adults. Neuroimage, 2002, 17, 1394–1402.

Caprio-Prevette, M.D., and Fry, P.S. Memory enhancement program for community-based older adults: Development and evaluation. Experimental Aging Research, 1996, 22, 281–303.

Cattell, R.B. Theory of fluid and crystallized intelligence: A critical experiment. Journal of Educational Psychology, 1963, 54, 1–22.

Cavanaugh, J.C., and Blanchard-Fields, F. Adult development and aging (5th ed.). Belmont, CA: Thomson Wadsworth, 2006.

Christensen, H., Mackinnon, A.J., Korten, A.E., Jorm, A.F., Henderson, A.S., Jacomb, P., and Rodgers, B. An analysis of cognitive performance of elderly community dwellers: Individual differences in change scores as a function of age. Psychology and Aging, 1999, 14, 365–379.

Cohen, G.D. The creative age. New York: Aron Books, 2000.

Cohen, G.D. The mature mind: The positive power of the aging brain. Cambridge, MA: Perseus Books, 2005.

Colcombe, S.J., and Kramer, A.F. Fitness effects on the cognitive function of older adults: A meta-analytic study. Psychological Science, 2003, 14, 125–130.

Craik, F.I.M. Memory changes in normal aging. Current directions in psychological science, 1994, 5, 155–158.

Craik, F.I.M., and Jennings, J.M. Human memory. In F.I.M. Craik and T.A. Salthouse (Eds.), The handbook of aging and cognition. Hillsdale, NJ: Erlbaum, 1994.

Cunningham, W.R., and Owens, W.A. The Iowa State study of the adult development of intellectual abilities. In K.W. Schaie (Ed.), Longitudinal studies of adult psychological development. New York: Guilford Press, 1983.

Dahlgren, D.J. Impact of knowledge and age on tip-of-the-tongue rates. Experimental Aging Research, 1998, 24, 139–153.

Das, I., and Agarwai, S. Effect of aging on memory for spatial locations of objects. Psycho-Lingua, 2000, 30, 17–20.

Einstein, G.O., Earles, J.L., and Collins, H.M. Gaze aversion: Spared inhibition for visual distraction in older adults. *Journals of Gerontology: Psychological Sciences*, 2002, *57B*, P65–P73.

Elias, P.K., Elias, M.F., Robbins, M.A., and Budge, M.M. Blood pressure-related cognitive decline: Does age make a difference? *Hypertension*, 2004, *44*, 1–6.

Fraas, M., Lockwood, J., Neils, S., Trunjas, J., Shidler, M., Krikorian, R., and Weiler, E. "What's his name?" A comparison of elderly participants' and undergraduate students' misnamings. *Archives of Gerontology and Geriatrics*, 2002, *34*, 155–165.

Gold, D.P., Andres, D., Etezadi, J., Arbuckle, T., Schwartzman, A., and Chaikelson, J. Structural equation model of intellectual change and continuity and predictors of intelligence in older men. *Psychology and Aging*, 1995, *10*, 294–303.

Greenwood, P.M., and Parasuraman, R. Scale of attention focus in visual search. *Perception and Psychophysics*, 1999, *1*, 837–859.

Gruber-Baldini, A.L. *The impact of health and disease on cognitive ability in adulthood and old age in the Seattle Longitudinal Study.* Unpublished doctoral dissertation. Pennsylvania State University, 1991.

Guilford, J.P. *The nature of human intelligence.* New York: McGraw-Hill, 1967.

Gunstad, J., Paul, R.H., Brickman, A.M., Cohen, R.A., Arns, M., Roe, D., et al. Patterns of cognitive peformance in middle-aged and older adults. *Journal of Geriatric Psychiatry and Neurology*, 2006, *19*, 59–64.

Hasher, L., Chung, C., May, C.P., and Foong, N. Age, time of testing, and proactive interference. *Canadian Journal of Experimental Psychology*, 2002, *56*, 200–207.

Hassing, L.B., Grant, M.D., Hofer, S.M., Pedersen, N.L., Nilsson, S.E., Berg, S., et al. Type 2 diabetes mellitus contributes to cognitive change in the oldest old. *Journal of the International Neuropsychological Society*, 2004, *4*, 599–607.

Hess, T.M., Rosenberg, D.C., and Waters, S.J. Motivation and representational processes in adulthood: The effects of social accountability and information relevance. *Psychology and Aging*, 2001, *16*, 629–642.

Hogan, M.J. Divided attention in older but not younger adults is impaired by anxiety. *Experimental Aging Research*, 2003, *29*, 111–136.

Horn, J.L. The aging of human abilities. In B.B. Wolman (Ed.), *Handbook of developmental psychology.* Englewood Cliffs, NJ: Prentice-Hall, 1982.

Horn, J.L. Organization of data on life-span development of human abilities. In L.R. Goulet and P.B. Baltes (Eds.), *Life-span developmental psychology: Research and theory.* New York: Academic Press, 1970.

Horn, J.L., and Donaldson, G. Cognitive development in adulthood. In O.G. Brim and J. Kagan (Eds.), *Constancy and change in human development.* Cambridge, MA: Harvard University Press, 1980.

Hoyer, W.J., and Verhaeghen, P. Memory Aging. In J.E. Birren and K.W. Schaie (Eds.), *Handbook of the Psychology of Aging* (6th ed.). Burlington, MA: Elsevier Academic Press, 2006.

Hultsch, D.F., Hammer, M., and Small, B.J. Age differences in cognitive performance in later life: Relationships to self-reported health and activity lifestyle. *Journals of Gerontology*, 1993, *48*, P1–P11.

Inouye, S.K., Albert, M.S., Mohs, R., and Sun-Kolie, R. Cognitive performance in a high-functioning, community-dwelling elderly population. *Journals of Gerontology*, 1993, *48*, M146–M151.

Insel, K., Morrow, D., Brewer, B., and Figueredo, A. Executive function, working memory, and medication adherence among older adults. *Journals of Gerontology: Psychological Sciences*, 2006, *61B*, P102–P107.

Johnson, M.K. The relation between source memory and episodic memory: Comment on Siedleckie et al. (2005). *Psychology and Aging*, 2005, *20*, 529–531.

Jones, H.E. Intelligence and problem-solving. In J.E. Birren (Ed.), *Handbook of aging and the individual: Psychological and biological aspects.* Chicago: University of Chicago Press, 1959.

Kallmann, F.J., and Sander, G. Twin studies on senescence. *American Journal of Psychiatry*, 1949, *106*, 29–36.

Kang, J.H., Ascherio, A., and Grodstein, F. Fruit and vegetable consumption and cognitive decline in aging women. *Annals of Neurology*, 2005, *57*, 713–720.

Kleemeier, R.W. Intellectual change in the senium. *Proceedings of the Social Science Statistics Section of the American Statistical Association*, 1962, *1*, 290–295.

Knopman, D.S., Boland, L.L., Folsom, A.R., Mosley, T.H., McGovern, P.G., Howard, G., et al. Cardiovascular risk factors and longitudinal cognitive changes in middle age adults. *Neurology,* 2000, *54* (supplement).

Kramer, A.F., Erickson, K.I., and Colcombe, S.J. Exercise, cognition, and the aging brain. *Journal of Applied Physiology,* 2006, *101,* 1237–1242.

Larue, A., Koehler, K.M., Wayne, S.J., Chiulli, S.J., Haaland, K.Y., and Garry, P.J. Nutritional status and cognitive functioning in a normally aging sample: A 6-year reassessment. *American Journal of Clinical Nutrition,* 1997, *65,* 20–29.

Launer, L.J., Masaki, K., Petrovitch, H., Foley, D., and Havlik, R.J. The association between midlife blood pressure levels and late-life cognitive function. *Journal of the American Medical Association,* 1995, *274,* 1846–1851.

Levitt, H.M. The development of wisdom: An analysis of Tibetan Buddhist experience. *Journal of Humanistic Psychology,* 1999, *39,* 86–105.

Lindenberger, U., and Baltes, P.B. Sensory functioning and intelligence in old age. *Psychology and Aging.* 1994, *9,* 339–355.

Mackinnon, A., Christensen, H., Hofer, S.M., Korten, A.E., and Jorm, A.F. Use it and still lose it? The association between activity and cognitive performance established using latent growth curve techniques in a community sample. *Aging, Neuropsychology and Cognition,* 2003, *10,* 215–229.

McGaugh, J.L. Memory: A century of consolidation. *Science,* 2000, *287,* 248–251.

Mead, S.E., Lamson, N., and Rogers, W.A. Human factors guidelines for web site usability: Health-oriented web sites for older adults. In R.W. Morrell (Ed.), *Older adults, health information, and the World Wide Web.* Mahwah, NJ: Erlbaum, 2002.

Morrell, R.W., Mayhorn, C.B., and Bennett, J. A survey of World Wide Web use in middle-aged and older adults. *Human Factors,* 2000, *42,* 175–182.

Morris, M.C., Evans, A., Tangney, C.C., Bienias, J.L., and Wilson, R.S. Associations of vegetable and fruit consumption with age-related cognitive change. *Neurology,* 2006, *67,* 1370–1376.

Mouloua, M., and Parasuraman, R. Aging and cognitive vigilance: Effects of spatial uncertainty and event rate. *Experimental Aging Research,* 1995, *21,* 17–32.

National Library of Medicine. *Making your web site senior friendly: A checklist.* Bethesda, MD: NIH/NLM, 2002.

Nyberg, L. Cognitive training in healthy aging: A cognitive neuroscience perspective. In R. Cabeza, L. Nyberg, and D. Park (Eds.), *Cognitive neuroscience of aging: Linking cognitive and cerebral aging.* New York: Oxford University Press, 2005.

Owens, W.A. Age and mental abilities: A longitudinal study. *Genetic Psychology Monographs,* 1953, *48,* 3–54.

Owens, W.A. Age and mental ability: A second adult follow-up. *Journal of Educational Psychology,* 1966, *57,* 311–325.

Palmore, E. (Ed.). *Normal aging II: Reports from the Duke Longitudinal Study.* Durham, NC: Duke University Press, 1974.

Palmore, E. (Ed.). *Normal aging III: Reports from the Duke Longitudinal Study.* Durham, NC: Duke University Press, 1985.

Parasuraman, R. The attentive brain: Issues and prospects. In R. Parasuraman (Ed.), *The attentive brain.* Cambridge, MA: MIT Press, 1998.

Parasuraman, R., and Greenwood, P.M. Selective attention in aging and dementia. In R. Parasuraman (Ed.), *The attentive brain.* Cambridge, MA: MIT Press, 1998.

Pearman, A., and Storandt, M. Predictors of subjective memory in older adults. *Journals of Gerontology Series B: Psychological and Social Sciences,* 2004, *59,* P4–P6.

Poon, L.W. Differences in human memory with aging: Nature, causes, and clinical implications. In J.E. Birren and K.W. Schaie (Eds.), *Handbook of the psychology of aging* (2nd ed.). New York: Van Nostrand Reinhold, 1985.

Rabbitt, P., Donlan, C., Watson, P., McInnes, L., and Bent, N. Unique and interactive effects of depression, age, socioeconomic advantage, and gender on cognitive performance of normal healthy older people. *Psychology and Aging,* 1995, *10,* 307–313.

Ratcliff, R., Spieler, D., and McKoon, G. Explicitly modeling the effects of aging on response time. *Psychonomic Bulletin and Review,* 2000, *7,* 1–25.

Reese, C.M., and Cherry, K.E. Practical memory concerns across the lifespan. *International Journal of Aging and Human Development,* 2004, *59,* 237–255.

Rendell, P.G., Castel, A.D., and Craik, F.I.M. Memory for proper names in old age: A disproportional impairment? *Quarterly Journal of Experimental Psychology,* 2005, *58,* 54–71.

Rogers, W.A., and Fisk, A.D. Attention in cognitive aging research. In J.E. Birren and K.W. Schaie (Eds.), *Handbook of the psychology of aging* (5th ed.). San Diego: Academic Press, 2001.

Rönnlund, M., Nyberg, L., Bäckman, L., and Nillson, L.G. Stability, growth, and decline in adult life span development of declarative memory. *Psychology and Aging,* 2005, *20,* 3–18.

Rosnick, C.B., Small, B.J., Graves, A.B., and Mortimer, J.A. The association between health and cognitive performance in a population-based study of older adults. *Aging Neuropsychology and Cognition,* 2004, *11,* 89–99.

Royall, D.R., Palmer, R., Chiodo, L.K., and Polk, M.J. Declining executive control in normal aging predicts change in functional status. *Journal of the American Geriatrics Society,* 2004, *52,* 346–352.

Salthouse, T.A. Age-related differences in basic cognitive processes: Implications for work. *Experimental Aging Research,* 1994a, *20,* 249–255.

Salthouse, T.A. General and specific speed mediation of adult age differences in memory. *Journals of Gerontology,* 1996a, *51B,* P30–P42.

Salthouse, T.A. The processing speed theory of adult age differences in cognition. *Psychological Review,* 1996b, *103,* 403–428.

Salthouse, T.A. Speed and knowledge as determinants of adult age differences in verbal tasks. *Journals of Gerontology,* 1993, *48,* P29–P36.

Schaie, K.W. *Developmental influences on adult intelligence: The Seattle Longitudinal Study.* New York: Oxford University Press, 2005.

Schaie, K.W. Intellectual development in adulthood. In J.E. Birren and K.W. Schaie (Eds.), *Handbook of the psychology of aging* (4th ed.). San Diego: Academic Press, 1996a.

Schaie, K.W. Intelligence. In R. Schulz (Ed.), *Encyclopedia of aging* (4th ed.). New York: Springer, 2006.

Schaie, K.W. *Intellectual development in adulthood: The Seattle Longitudinal Study.* Cambridge: Cambridge University Press, 1996b.

Schaie, K.W. The primary mental abilities in adulthood: An exploration in the development of psychometric intelligence. In P.B. Baltes and O.G. Brim, Jr. (Eds.),

Life-span development and behavior (Vol. 2). New York: Academic Press, 1979.

Schaie, K.W., Plomin, R., Willis, S.L., Gruber-Baldini, A., and Dutta, R. Natural cohorts: Family similarity in adult cognition. In T. Sonderegger (Ed.), *Psychology and aging: Nebraska symposium on motivation.* Lincoln: University of Nebraska Press, 1992.

Schaie, K.W., and Willis, S.L. Perceived family environments across generations. In V.L. Bengston, K.W. Schaie, and L. Burton (Eds.), *Societal impact on aging: Intergenerational perspectives.* New York: Springer, 1995.

Schooler, C., and Mulatu, M.S. The reciprocal effects of leisure time activities and intellectual functioning in older people: A longitudinal analysis. *Psychology and Aging,* 2001, *16,* 466–482.

Schooler, C., Mulatu, M.S., and Oates, G. The continuing effects of substantially complex workers. *Psychology and Aging,* 1999, *14,* 483–506.

Schooler, C., Mulatu, M.S., and Oates, G. Occupational self-direction in older workers: Findings and implications for individuals and societies. *American Journal of Sociology,* 2004, *110,* 161–197.

Schwartz, B.L. *Tip-of-the-tongue states.* Mahwah, NJ: Lawrence Erlbaum Associates, 2002.

Sharps, M.J., and Martin, S.S. Spatial memory in young and older adults: Environmental support and contextual influences at encoding and retrieval. *Journal of Genetic Psychology,* 1998, *159,* 5–12.

Siedlecki, K.L., Salthouse, T.A., and Berish, D.E. Is there anything special about the aging of source memory? *Psychology and Aging,* 2005, *20,* 19–32.

Siegler, I.C. Psychological aspects of the Duke Longitudinal Studies. In K.W. Schaie (Ed.), *Longitudinal studies of adult psychological development.* New York: Guilford Press, 1983.

Silverman, D.H.S., Small, G.W., and Chang, C.Y. Evaluation of dementia with positron emission tomography: Regional brain metabolism and long-term outcome. *Journal of the American Medical Association,* 2001, *286,* 2120–2127.

Simonton, D.K. Career landmarks in science: Individual differences and interdisciplinary contrasts. *Developmental Psychology,* 1991, *27,* 119–127.

Simonton, D.K. Creativity from a historiometric perspective. In R.J. Sternberg (Ed.), *Handbook of creativity.* New York: Cambridge University Press, 1999.

Simonton, D.K. The swan-song phenomenon: Last works effects for 172 classical composers. *Psychology and Aging*, 1989, *4*, 42–47.

Small, G.W. *The memory bible.* New York: Hyperion, 2002.

Small, G.W. Positron emission tomography scanning for the early diagnosis of dementia. *Western Journal of Medicine*, 1999, *171*, 293–294.

Smith, A.D. Memory. In J.E. Birren and K.W. Schaie (Eds.), *Handbook of the psychology of aging* (4th ed.). San Diego: Academic Press, 1996.

Staudinger, U.M. Older and wiser? Integrating results on the relationship between age and wisdom-related performance. *International Journal of Behavioral Development*, 1999, *23*, 641–664.

Sternberg, R.J. A balance theory of wisdom. *Review of General Psychology*, 1998, *3*, 347–365.

Sternberg, R.J., and Lubert, T.I. Wisdom and creativity. In J.E. Birren and K.W. Schaie (Eds.), *Handbook of the psychology of aging* (5th ed.). San Diego: Academic Press, 2001.

Takahashi, M., and Overton, W.F. Wisdom: A culturally inclusive developmental perspective. *International Journal of Behavioral Development*, 2002, *26*, 269–277.

Torrance, E.P. The nature of creativity as manifest in its testing. In R.J. Sternberg (Ed.), *The nature of creativity: Contemporary psychological perspectives.* Cambridge: Cambridge University Press, 1988.

Troyer, A.K., Hafliger, A., Cadieux, M.J., and Craik, F.I.M. Name and face learning in older adults: Effects of level processing, self-generation, and intention to learn. *Journals of Gerontology: Psychological Sciences*, 2006, *61B*, P67–P74.

van Dongen, M., van Rossum, E., Kessels, A., Sielhorst, H., and Knipscheld, P.G. Ginkgo for elderly people with dementia and age-associated memory impairment: A randomized clinical trial. *Journal of Clinical Epidemiology*, 2003, *56*, 367–376.

Verhaeghen, P., Geraerts, N., and Marcoen, A. Memory complaints, coping and well-being in old age: A systematic approach. *The Gerontologist*, 2000, *40*, 540–548.

Watkins, L.H., Sahakian, B.J., Robertson, M.M., Veale, D.M., Rogers, R.D., Pickard, K.M., et al. Executive function in Tourette's syndrome and obsessive-compulsive disorder. *Psychological Medicine*, 2005, *35*, 571–582.

West, R., Murphy, K.J., Armilio, M.L., Craik, F.I.M., and Stuss, D.T. Effects of time of day on age differences in working memory. *Journals of Gerontology: Psychological Sciences*, 2002, *57*, P3–P10.

Whiting, W.L. Adult age differences in divided attention: Effects of elaboration. *Aging, Neuropsychology, and Cognition.* 2003, *10*, 141–157.

Willis, S.L. Methodological issues in behavioral intervention research with the elderly. In J.E. Birren and K.W. Schaie (Eds.), *Handbook of the psychology of aging* (5th ed.). San Diego: Academic Press, 2001.

Willis, S.L., and Nesselroade, C.S. Long-term effects of fluid ability training in old-old age. *Developmental Psychology*, 1990, *26*, 905–910.

Willis, S.L., and Schaie, K.W. A co-constructionist view of the third age: The case of cognition. *Annual Review of Gerontology and Geriatrics*, 2006, *26*, 131–151.

Willis, S.L., and Schaie, K.W. Cognitive trajectories in midlife and cognitive functioning in old age. In S.L. Wilkie and M. Martin (Eds.), *Middle adulthood: A lifespan perspective.* Thousand Oaks, CA: Sage, 2005.

Willis, S.L., Tennstedt, S.L., Marsiske, M., Ball, K., Elias, J., Koepke, K.M., Morris, J.N., et al. Long-term effects of cognitive training on everyday functional outcomes in older adults. *Journal of the American Medical Association*, 2006, *296*, 2805–2814.

Zacks, R.T., Hasher, L., and Li, K.Z.H. Human memory. In F.I.M. Craik and T.A. Salthouse (Eds.), *The handbook of aging and cognition* (2nd ed.). Mahway, NJ: Erlbaum, 2000.

Zelinski, E.M., Gilewski, M.J. 10-item Rasch modeled memory self-efficacy scale. *Aging and Mental Health*, 2004, *8*, 293–306.

Zelinski, E.M., Gilewski, M.J., and Schaie, K.W. Individual differences in cross-sectional and 3-year longitudinal memory performance across the adult life span. *Psychology and Aging*, 1993, *8*, 176–186.

6

Personality and Mental Health in Old Age

We have all had the experience of watching different people respond to the same event in different ways. For example, you probably know some students who are extremely anxious about test-taking while others are calm, and some students who express their opinions strongly and confidently while others rarely speak in class at all. All these characteristics are part of an individual's personality.

Defining Personality

Personality can be defined as a unique pattern of innate and learned behaviors, thoughts, and emotions that influence how each person responds and interacts with the environment. An individual may be described in terms of several personality traits, such as passive or aggressive, introverted or extroverted, independent or dependent. Personality can be evaluated with regard to particular standards of behavior; for example, an individual may be described as being adapted or maladapted, resilient or feeling hopeless. Personality styles influence how we cope with and adapt to the changes that occur as we age. The process of aging generally involves some stressful life experiences. How an older person attempts to alleviate such stress has an influence on that individual's long-term well-being. The person–environment congruence model presented in Chapter 1 suggests that our behavior is influenced and modified by the environment in interaction with our competence in multiple areas, and that we shape the environment around us. An individual's behavior is often quite different from one situation to another, and depends both on each situation's social norms and expectations, and on that person's needs and motives.

Although personality remains relatively stable with normal aging, some older people who showed no signs of psychopathology earlier in their lives may experience some types of mental disorders in late life. For other older people, psychiatric disorders experienced in their younger years may continue or may reemerge. In some individuals the stresses of old age may compound any existing predisposition to psychopathology. These stresses may be internal, resulting from the physiological and cognitive changes, or external, a function of role losses and the deaths of partners, friends, or children. Such conditions may significantly impair older people's competence, so that they become more vulnerable to environmental press and less able to function at an optimal level.

Stage Theories of Personality

Most theories of personality emphasize the developmental **stages** or phases of personality and posit that the social environment influences development. As we focus on stages of adult development, however, it is important to avoid the image of rigid, immutable stages and

inevitable transitions, with no room for individual differences. In fact, people *do* make choices regarding their specific responses to common life changes. This results in diverse expressions of behavior under similar life experiences such as adolescence, parenting, midlife caregiving, retirement, and even the management of chronic diseases. There has been disagreement about whether this pattern of development continues through adulthood. Sigmund Freud's focus on psychosexual stages of development through adolescence has had a major influence on developmental psychology. In most of his writings, Freud suggests that personality achieves stability by adolescence. Accordingly, Freud views adult behavior as a reflection of unconscious motives and unsuccessful resolution of early childhood stages. Freud's work subsequently shaped the stage theories of personality developed by Jung and Erikson in the mid-twentieth century.

Jung's Psychoanalytic Perspective

Carl Jung's model of personality assumes changes throughout life, as expressed in the following statement from one of his early writings:

> We cannot live the afternoon of life according to the program of life's morning, for what was great in the morning will be little at evening, and what in the morning was true will at evening have become a lie. (1933, p. 108).

The development of consciousness and the ego proceeds from the narrow focus of the child to

---

JUNG'S PERSPECTIVE ON INTROVERSION WITH AGING

In contrast to the young, older persons have:

a duty and a necessity to devote serious attention to (themselves). After having lavished its light upon the world, the sun withdraws its rays in order to illuminate itself (Jung, 1933, p. 109).

POINTS TO PONDER

Think about an older person you know who appears to have achieved the stage of ego integrity. What adjectives would you use to describe this individual? How would you describe your interactions with this person?

the otherworldliness of the older person. Jung suggests that the ego moves from *extraversion,* or a focus on the external world in youth and middle age when the individual progresses through school, work, and marriage, to *introversion,* or to a focus on one's inner world in old age. Like Erikson, Jung examined the individual's confrontation with death in the last stage of life. He suggested that life for the aging person must naturally contract, and that the individual in this stage must find meaning in inner exploration and an afterlife.

Jung (1959) also focused on changes in archetypes with age. That is, according to Jung, all humans have both a feminine and a masculine side. An **archetype** is the feminine side of a man's personality (the anima) and the masculine side of a woman's personality (the animus). As they age, people begin to adopt psychological traits more commonly associated with the opposite sex. For example, older men may show more signs of passivity and nurturance while women may become more assertive as they age. This allows the individual to express oneself more fully and to satisfy their personal needs rather than being constrained by society's stereotypes of masculine versus feminine qualities. The concepts of personality stages and shifts from gender-typed to archetypal characteristics with aging have influenced subsequent theories of personality development.

Erikson's Psychosocial Model

Although trained in psychoanalytic theory, Erikson moved away from this approach and focused on psychosocial development through-

out the life cycle. According to his model (Erikson, 1963, 1968, 1982; Erikson, Erikson, and Kivnick, 1986), the individual undergoes eight stages of development, with the unconscious goal of achieving *ego identity.* Three of these stages are beyond adolescence, with the final one occurring in mature adulthood. At each stage the individual experiences a major task to be accomplished and a conflict to be resolved; the conflicts of each stage of development are the foundations of successive stages. Depending on the outcome of the crisis associated with a particular stage, the individual proceeds to the next stage of development in alternative ways. Erikson also emphasized the interactions between genetics and the environment in determining personality development. His concept of the *epigenetic principle* assumed an innate plan of development in which people proceed through stages as they become cognitively and emotionally more capable of interacting within a wider social radius. Hence, each subsequent stage requires additional cognitive and emotional development before it can be experienced.

The individual in the last stage of life is confronted with the task of **ego integrity versus despair.** According to Erikson, the individual accepts the inevitability of mortality, achieves wisdom and perspective, or despairs because he or she has not come to grips with death and lacks ego integrity. A major task associated with this last stage is to look inward in order to integrate the experiences of earlier stages and to realize that one's life has had meaning, whether or not it was "successful" in the traditional sense. Older people who achieve ego integrity feel a sense of connectedness with younger generations, and share their experiences and wisdom with them. This may take the form of:

- informal visiting
- counseling
- mentoring
- sponsoring an individual or group of younger people

ERIKSON'S PSYCHOSOCIAL STAGES

Stage	Goal
I: Basic trust vs. mistrust	To establish basic trust in the world through trust in the parent.
II: Autonomy vs. shame and doubt	To establish a sense of autonomy and self as distinct from the parent; to establish self-control vs. doubt in one's abilities.
III: Initiative vs. guilt	To establish a sense of initiative within parental limits without feeling guilty about emotional needs.
IV: Industry vs. inferiority	To establish a sense of industry within the school setting; to learn necessary skills without feelings of inferiority or fear of failure.
V: Ego identity vs. role diffusion	To establish identity, self-concept, and role within the larger community, without confusion about the self and about social roles.
VI: Intimacy vs. isolation	To establish intimacy and affiliation with one or more others, without fearing loss of identity in the process that may result in isolation.
VII: Generativity vs. stagnation	To establish a sense of care and concern for the well-being of future generations; to look toward the future and not stagnate in the past.
VIII: Ego integrity vs. despair	To establish a sense of meaning in one's life, rather than feeling despair or bitterness that life was wasted; to accept oneself and one's life without despair.

- writing memoirs or letters or sharing oral traditions
- assuming a leadership role in one's community
- life review

The process of sharing one's memories and experiences with others (orally or written) is described as **life review,** and is a useful mode of therapy with older adults, as described later in this chapter. Life satisfaction, or the feeling that life is worth living, may be achieved through these tasks of adopting a wider historical perspective on one's life, accepting one's mortality, sharing experiences with the young, and leaving a legacy to future generations. Erikson's theory is a widely accepted framework for studying personality in late life because it suggests that personality is dynamic throughout the life cycle. Indeed, this theory fits the person–environment model; we interact with a variety of other people in different settings, and our personality is affected accordingly. Both longi-

tudinal and sequential research methods support the developmental stages postulated by Erikson. Standardized measures of personality demonstrate developmental changes in self-confidence, dependability, identity, and **generativity,** or the desire to help and mentor younger persons (Ryff, Kwan, and Singer, 2001).

Jane Loevinger extended Erikson's theory by expanding the stages of ego development in adulthood (Loevinger, 1976, 1997, 1998). According to her theory, one's interactions with the environment shape one's thoughts and values. Instead of two stages occurring in adulthood as Erikson's model proposes, Loevinger describes six. The individual must successfully progress through the preceding one to reach the next one, although most people remain at the second one forever. These stages are:

- conformist
- conscientious conformist

- conscientious
- individualistic
- autonomous
- integrated

Each stage requires a transition in several domains, including the individual's personal standards and life goals, interpersonal style, primary preoccupations in life, and cognitive style. Loevinger's last stage, labeled *integrated,* resembles that of Erikson, because in both cases, individuals integrate their identity, personal conflicts, and values. People who reach this level of ego development have come to peace with themselves and their achievements. By testing this theory of ego development with the Sentence Completion test, researchers have shown how ego development predicts cognitive development and social judgments (Blanchard-Fields and Norris, 1994; Loevinger, 1998).

A recent perspective on stages of personality development in adulthood has been provided by Gene Cohen, a psychiatrist, whose qualitative research with older adults reveals that progress from one stage to another is not always linear. In his interviews with older people, he found many who experienced setbacks in some aspects of their lives while moving forward in others. For example, some elders may have achieved integrity of their intellectual and spiritual selves, but may not have been successful with the generativity stage. Cohen suggests that these older adults can resolve the conflicts of an earlier stage even as they proceed through the subsequent stage of development (Cohen, 2005).

Empirical Testing of These Perspectives

In testing the validity of stage theories, subsequent research has contributed to our understanding of personality development in late adulthood. Many of these studies are cross-sectional; that is, they derive information on age *differences,* not age changes. There are notable exceptions to this approach, including the Baltimore Longitudinal Studies (described in Chapter 1) and the Kansas City Studies, which examined changes in physiological, cognitive, and personality functions in the same individuals over a period of several years. Research by Costa and McCrae (1994, 1995) in the Baltimore Longitudinal Studies is related to Erikson's work, since it identifies changes in *adjustment* with age, but stability in specific *traits* (described later in this chapter). Cross-sectional studies by De St. Aubin and McAdams (1995), and by Peterson and Klohnen (1995) examined age differences in generativity, Erikson's seventh stage. These researchers consistently found that middle-aged and older adults express more generative concerns (i.e., attribute more importance to the care of younger generations than to self-development) than young adults. "Generative adults" exhibit concerns not just toward their own children, but toward the younger population in general.

AGE CHANGES IN MASTERY

Young men tend to:

- be more achievement-oriented
- take more risks
- be more competitive
- be more concerned with controlling their environments

Compared to young men, older men:

- are more expressive
- are more nurturant
- have greater need for affiliation and accommodation

Young women tend to:

- be more affiliative
- be more expressive

Compared to young women, older women:

- are more instrumental
- express more achievement-oriented responses

SOURCE: Gutmann, 1992.

Other researchers have found empirical support for Jung's observations regarding decreased sex-typed behavior in old age. David Gutmann (1977, 1980, 1992), who examined personality across the life span in diverse cultures from a psychoanalytic perspective, identified a shift from **active mastery** to **passive mastery** as men age. In contrast, women appear to move from passive to active mastery. The increased passivity of older men may allow them to explore their inner worlds and move beyond the external orientation of their younger years.

The Grant Study of Harvard University Graduates is a longitudinal investigation that followed 268 men, beginning in 1938 when they were students, through age 65 when 173 of the men were still available to take part in these life reviews and qualitative interviews. This unique research has identified support for stage theories of personality (Vaillant, 1977, 1994, 2002; Vaillant and Vaillant, 1990). The men who remained for long-term follow-ups were observed to follow a common pattern of stages:

- establishment of a professional identity in their 20s and 30s
- career consolidation in their 40s
- exploration of their inner worlds in midlife (a major transition similar to the stage of ego integrity versus despair that Erikson described as occurring in late life)

Men who were most emotionally stable and well adjusted in their 50s and 60s were characterized by:

- greater generativity (i.e., responsibility for and care of coworkers, children, charity)
- less gender stereotyped in their social interactions
- more nurturant and expressive

These changes observed in men as they moved from youth to middle to old age have implications for contemporary family care and responsibilities, as discussed in Chapters 9 and 10.

Dialectical Models of Adult Personality

Another model of adult personality development has been proposed by Levinson (1977, 1986) and his colleagues (Levinson et al., 1978). This model is based on secondary analyses of American men described in published biographies and in interviews with working-class men. In a subsequent study, this model was also found to apply to women (Levinson, 1996). In contrast to Erikson who focused on stages of ego development, Levinson and colleagues have examined developmental stages in terms of **life structures,** or the underlying characteristics of a person's life at a particular period of time. Of all stage theories of adult development, this model is the most explicit in linking each stage with a specific range of chronological age. Each period in the life structure (defined as four "eras" by Levinson) represents developmental stages, each one lasting about 20 years. These are separated by *transitions* of about 5 years, each of which generally occurs as the individual perceives changes in the self, or as external events such as childbirth and retirement create new demands on one's social relationships with others (see the box on the next page).

Levinson's model represents an example of a *dialectical approach* to personality development that is consistent with the person–environment model; it proposes that growth occurs because of interactions between a person who is changing biologically *and* psychologically, and a dynamic environment. To the extent that an individual is sensitive to the changing self, he or she can respond to shifting external conditions by altering something within the self or by modifying environmental expectations. This process thereby reestablishes equilibrium with the environment. For example, older people who deny normal biological and physiological changes

---

LEVINSON'S "SEASONS" OF LIFE

Era I   Preadulthood (Age 0–22)

(An era when the family provides protection, socialization, and support of personal growth)

Early Adult Transition (Age 17–22)*

Era II   Early Adulthood (Age 17–45)

(An era of peak biological functioning, development of adult identity)

Entering the adult world, entry life structure for early adulthood

Age 30 transition*

Settling down, culminating life structure for early adulthood

Mid-Life Transition (Age 40–45)*

Era III   Middle Adulthood (Age 40–65)

(Goals become more other-oriented, compassionate roles, mentor roles assumed; peak effectiveness as a leader)

Entering life structure for middle adulthood

Age 50 transition*

Culmination of middle adulthood

Late Adulthood Transition (Age 60–65)*

Era IV   Late Adulthood (Age 60+)

(An era when declining capacities are recognized; anxieties about aging, loss of power and status begin)

Acceptance of death's inevitability

*Indicates major transitions to a new developmental era.

SOURCE: D. Levinson, C.M. Darrow, E.B. Klein, M.H. Levinson, and B. McKee, *The seasons of a man's life* (New York: Alfred A. Knopf, 1978). Reprinted with permission of the author and publisher.

---

they are experiencing may have difficulty in modifying their lifestyles and environment.

Trait Theories of Personality

Another theoretical perspective on personality is to examine characteristic behaviors specific within individuals that reflect **trait theories.** Traits are relatively stable personality dispositions; together they make up a constellation that distinguishes each individual. For example, we can describe people along a continuum of personality attributes such as extroverted to introverted, passive to aggressive, and optimistic to pessimistic, as well as high or low on need for achievement and affiliation. Most personality theorists agree that traits do not change unless the individual makes a conscious effort to do so—for example, undergoing psychological counseling to become more nurturant or more assertive.

This assumption of stability has led trait researchers to examine personality traits longitu-

dinally in the middle and later years. Proponents of this approach are McCrae and Costa (1997, 2003; McCrae, 2002), who measured specific traits of participants in the Baltimore Longitudinal Studies (described in Chapter 1). They propose a *five-factor model of personality traits,* consisting of five primary, independent dimensions:

- neuroticism
- extraversion
- openness to experience
- agreeableness
- conscientiousness

Within each component are six *facets* or subcategories of traits listed above; people who score high on the primary trait would demonstrate higher tendencies toward these behaviors and emotions.

Standardized tests such as the Guilford-Zimmerman Temperament Survey (GZTS) are used to compare individuals with population norms on these traits. By administering the GZTS to the same research subjects three times over

Maintaining an active lifestyle can enhance an older person's self-confidence.

12 years in the Baltimore Longitudinal Studies, researchers found stability in the five traits described above, independent of environmental influences. Using a cross-sectional approach, they also identified consistency in these traits in middle-aged and older adults. Both groups differed from young adults on some personality factors, especially in neuroticism, extraversion, and openness to experience (Costa and McCrae, 1994, 1995). Their research supports the idea of lifelong stability, and even heritability of some personality traits. Subsequent studies by McCrae and Costa, with collaborators from diverse countries, demonstrate universal patterns of linear declines with age in neuroticism, extraversion, and openness, and an increase in agreeableness and conscientiousness. Although not all age differences were significant, the greatest difference was consistently between the youngest and oldest cohorts (McCrae et al., 1999, 2000; McCrae and Terracciano, 2005; McCrae et al., 2004).

Life events play an important role in the pattern of these changes in personality traits. Negative life events occurring in the late 70s are associated with significant declines in extraversion and an increase in neuroticism. On the other hand, positive life events such as remarriage after age 70

are followed by increased extraversion (Maiden et al., 2003; Mroczek and Spiro, 2003; Mroczek, Spiro, and Griffin, 2006). The Baltimore Longitudinal Studies tracked personality scores for as long as 42 years. The pattern of decline in neuroticism, extraversion, and openness, and the increase in agreeableness and conscientiousness observed in cross-sectional and shorter longitudinal observations was supported by these longer assessments. However, the researchers also identified significant individual variability in these changes as well as in specific facets of the extraversion factor (Terracciano, McCrae, and Costa, 2006).

Cohort and cultural influences on some personality traits have also been identified. Using a cross-sequential research design, Schaie and Willis (1991) found few changes in specific traits of the same individuals over 7 years in the Seattle Longitudinal Study (described in Chapters 1 and 5), but they did find cohort differences. That is, the oldest participants in the first wave were less flexible and adaptable than were the same age persons in the second wave of testing 7 years later. Cultural factors may also play a role in the development of certain traits. For example, traditional societies, including the United States before the feminist movement of the 1960s, reinforced "agreeableness" as a trait in women; several facets of this trait such as altruism, compliance, modesty, and tender-mindedness are viewed in traditional societies as important "feminine" traits. However, as women move into more diverse roles and enter occupations that were once considered "masculine," there is less gender stereotyping of traits.

Emotional Expression and Regulation

Basic emotions such as fear, anger, happiness, and shame are hardwired, or part of the core personality of every human being. However, as the individual develops and ages, feelings may become more cognitively complex and expressed differently. For example, a young child often expresses every emotion under any circumstance, but with socialization and a lifetime of interpersonal experiences, older adults know how to modulate their expressive behavior, including not expressing certain emotions like anger or fear. Experiences throughout life also help adults anticipate others' emotional responses. Part of the development process is to achieve control over one's environment by expressing emotions (primary control), as well as controlling one's expressiveness through secondary control (Schulz and Heckhausen, 1998). Other personality theorists have suggested that emotion regulation serves the goal of achieving or fulfilling interpersonal relations and minimizing interpersonal conflict (while at the same time maintaining a positive emotional state) in the later years (Carstensen et al., 1996; Carstensen, Pasupathi, and Mayr, 2000).

The role of family and culture on emotional expression and regulation has also been examined. People in the same age cohort may differ in their ability to express or deny emotions, based on the social conditioning they received from their parents and the cultural milieu regarding how, when, and where emotions can be expressed. Parents who discourage their children from crying in public or verbally expressing anger often set the stage for a lifetime of controlling one's emotions. Thus, emotional development depends not just on physiological and cognitive maturation, but also on familial and cultural influences (Magai, 2001; Magai et al., 2001). These early familial and cultural expectations that can influence emotional expression across the life course remain powerful messages in old age and need to be considered by social and health care providers working with older adults.

Self-Concept and Self-Esteem

A major adjustment required in old age is the ability to redefine one's **self-concept,** or one's cognitive image of the self, as some previous social roles shift and as new roles are assumed. Our self-concept emerges from our interactions with the social environment, our social roles, and accom-

---

PERSONALITY FACTORS IMPORTANT FOR MAINTAINING SELF-ESTEEM

- Reinterpretation of the meaning of self, such that an individual's self-concept and self-worth are independent of any roles he or she has played ("I am a unique individual" rather than "I am a doctor/teacher/wife").
- Acceptance of the aging process, its limitations, and possibilities. That is, individuals who realize that they have less energy and respond more slowly than in the past, but that they can still participate in life, will adapt more readily to the social and health losses of old age.
- Reevaluation of one's goals and expectations throughout life. Too often people establish life goals at an early age and are constantly disappointed as circumstances change. The ability to respond to internal and external pressures by modifying life goals appropriately reflects flexibility and harmony with one's environment.
- The ability to look back objectively on one's past and to review one's failures and successes. *Life review* entails an objective review and evaluation of one's life. An older person who has this ability to reminisce about past experiences and how these have influenced subsequent personality development, behavior, and interpersonal relationships can call upon coping strategies that have been most effective in the past and adapt them to changed circumstances. Life review can also help the older person come to terms with unresolved conflicts from one's past, resulting in greater ego integrity.

---

plishments. Through continuous interactions with the environment, people can confirm or revise these self-images. They do so either by:

- *assimilating* new experiences into their self-concept, or
- *accommodating* or adjusting their self-concept to fit the new reality.

Accommodation is more difficult and requires greater adaptive skills (Whitbourne and Primus,

1996). For example, how does a retired teacher identify himself or herself after giving up the work that has been that individual's central focus for the past 40 or 50 years? How does a woman whose self-concept is closely associated with her role as a wife express her identity after her husband dies?

Many older persons continue to identify with the role that they have lost (think of those who continue to introduce themselves as a "teacher" or "doctor" long after retiring from those careers). This would represent a type of *identity assimilation*. Others experience *role confusion*, particularly in the early stages of retirement, when cues from other people are inconsistent with an individual's self-concept. This may require *identity accommodation*. Still others may undergo a period of depression and major readjustment to the changes associated with role loss. To the extent that a person's self-concept is defined independently of particular social roles, one adapts more readily to the role losses that may accompany old age. Both assimilation of new social roles to a stable self-concept, and some accommodation to changing realities, are indicators of successful adaptation of one's self-concept. Older adults who have not been able to develop a sense of themselves as differentiated from their past roles are more likely to experience negative outcomes. However, research with the oldest-old demonstrates that self-concept remains essentially unchanged among most elders. Even with declining health and loss of significant others, those who survive to advanced old age maintain their identity (Diehl, Hastings and Stanton, 2001; Troll and Skaff, 1997).

For an older person whose self-concept is based on social roles and others' expectations, role losses have a particularly significant impact on that individual's **self-esteem**—defined as an evaluation or feeling about his or her identity relative to some ideal or standard.

- *Self-concept* is the cognitive definition or self-perception of one's identity.
- *Self-esteem* is based on an emotional assessment of the self.

The affective quality of self-esteem makes it more dynamic and more easily influenced by such external forces as retirement, widowhood, health status, and both positive and negative reinforcements from others (e.g., respect, deference, or ostracism). Social roles integrate the individual to society and add meaning to one's life. As a result, alterations in social roles and the loss of status that accompanies some of these changes often have a negative impact on an older person's self-esteem. Think, for example, of an older woman whose social roles have emphasized that of caregiver to her family. If she herself becomes dependent on others for care because of a major debilitating illness such as a stroke or dementia, she is unwittingly robbed of this "ideal self," and her self-esteem may suffer.

An individual who experiences multiple role losses must not only adapt to the lifestyle changes associated with aging (e.g., financial insecurity or shrinking social networks), but must also integrate the new roles with his or her "ideal self" or learn to modify this definition of "ideal." Older persons who are experiencing major physical and cognitive disabilities simultaneously with role losses, or worse yet, whose role losses are precipitated by an illness (e.g., early retirement due to stroke or nursing home placement because of Alzheimer's), must cope with multiple challenges at a time in their lives when they have the fewest resources to resolve them successfully. Grief and depression are common reactions in these cases.

Some studies have shown a generalized decrease in self-esteem from age 50 to 80, although many others have found improvement from adolescence through the young-old period. These varied findings may be attributed to the cross-sectional nature of research on self-esteem and age. An analysis of 50 published studies of self-esteem among people ranging in age from 6 to 83 found a common pattern of stability in self-esteem between midlife and old age. This pattern resembles the stability of personality traits described earlier in this chapter

(Trzesniewski, Donallen, and Robins, 2003). Stressful life events and disabilities such as severe hearing loss can impair older adults' self-esteem. For example, older people who are socially isolated and have significant physical disabilities often have the poorest self-esteem. In contrast, those who practice active aging by maintaining a strong social network and participating in voluntary or civic activities do better psychologically (Ryff, Kwan, and Singer, 2001). Volunteering can enhance the older person's self-esteem because it contributes to the elder's sense of personal competence. However, the long-term impact of volunteering on self-esteem is greater for people from upper socioeconomic classes than for low-income elders (Herzog et al., 1998; Krause and Shaw, 2000).

Stress, Coping, and Adaptation

Life changes, both positive and negative, place demands on the aging person's abilities to cope with new life situations. Together with health and cognitive functioning, personality characteristics influence coping responses. Self-concept and self-esteem are two important elements that play a role in coping styles, and may help explain why some older people adjust readily to major life changes, while others have difficulty. Indeed, self-esteem, health, and cognitive skills all contribute to an individual's sense of competence. Major life events and situations represent environmental stressors that place demands on an individual's competence.

Some Useful Definitions

The concept of life events and life challenges forms the basis for this section. These terms refer to *internal or external stimuli* that cause some change in our daily lives. They may be positive or negative, gains or losses, discrete or continuous.

Life events are identifiable, discrete life changes or transitions that demand a response

> **EXAMPLES OF INTERNALLY AND EXTERNALLY CREATED EVENTS**
>
> **Internal**
> - changes in eating or sleeping habits
> - effects of a chronic disease such as arthritis or diabetes
>
> **External**
> - starting a new job
> - losing one's job, or retirement
> - widowhood

from the individual because they disrupt one's person–environment balance or homeostasis. Improvement in one's own health or in a family member's health are examples of *positive life*

Intergenerational celebrations are examples of positive life events.

events, whereas deteriorating health and death of a loved one are *negative events*. Some life experiences may have both positive *and* negative aspects. For example, older workers may view their pending retirement with great joy and make numerous plans for the post-retirement years. However, they may also experience some negative consequences, such as reduced income and feelings of not being productive or contributing to society. *Life challenges* refer to the combination of discrete critical life events and chronic stressors that may be present but are not appraised as consistently difficult. Caregiving of an adult child with disabilities is a life challenge that is ongoing and not a specific life event, but it includes both gains and losses (Nelson-Becker, 2004; Snyder, 2001).

Another distinction is made between *on-time* and *off-time* events. This concept distinguishes life experiences that a person can anticipate because of one's stage in the life cycle (on-time) from those that are unexpected at a given stage (off-time). Other researchers have used the terms *normative* and *non-normative* events, suggesting that an individual anticipates some life experiences because they are the norm for most people of a given age. For example, a man married to a 75-year-old woman is more likely to expect the death of his wife than is the husband of a 35-year-old woman. As shown later in this chapter, researchers have found differences in how people respond to on-time and off-time events.

The concept of *stress*, as defined in Chapter 4, is also important for this chapter. Since Selye's (1946) introduction of this term, many researchers have explored the antecedents, components, and consequences of stress. In fact, Selye (1970) defined aging as the sum of stresses experienced across one's lifetime. Not everyone perceives the same events to be stressful, however. Lazarus and DeLongis (1983) have introduced the concept of **cognitive appraisal**—the way in which a person perceives the significance of an encounter for his or her well-being. Cognitive appraisal serves to

> ### THE IMPORTANCE OF COGNITIVE APPRAISAL
>
> Life events can represent a positive or negative stressor for the individual. Cognitive appraisal means that different people can view the same situation differently. One may see it as a challenge (i.e., a positive stressor), while another views it as a threat (i.e., a negative stressor). This evokes different coping responses in the two people. For example, an older woman who moves voluntarily to a retirement apartment may view it as an exciting and desirable change in her lifestyle, or she may resent the change as too demanding and disruptive. In the former case, she will adapt more readily and will experience less negative stress than in the latter. On the other hand, if this person views the move as totally benign and does not expect it to place any demands on her, she will probably be unpleasantly surprised by the level of stress that she eventually encounters, no matter how minimal.

minimize or magnify the importance or stressfulness of an event by attaching some meaning to it. If a situation is construed as benign or irrelevant by an individual, it does not elicit coping responses. On the other hand, if a person appraises a situation as challenging, harmful, or threatening, it becomes a stressor, and calls on the individual's adaptation responses. This concept of cognitive appraisal can help to explain why older individuals may react quite differently to the same stressor.

Aging and Life Events

Some researchers distinguish between life events and chronic stressors, such as poor health and financial difficulties, but both require adaptive or coping skills (McLeod, 1996). There has been considerable discussion among researchers about the nature of life events in the later years, the older person's ability to cope with them, and whether old age is associated with more or fewer life events than youth. Significant life events that are more likely to occur in old age include widowhood, retirement, and relocation to a long-term care facility. The nature of such roles and the challenge associated with assuming a social role for the first time result in major changes in an individual's daily functioning and demand adaptation to the new situation. Few studies have compared the relative stressfulness of role losses, role gains or replacements, and role extensions in old age, although research on life stress among younger populations is extensive. Chapter 12 examines in greater detail the losses and gains in both paid and nonpaid roles in the later years.

The first systematic studies of the physiological and psychological impact of increased sources and amounts of stress on humans were undertaken by Holmes and colleagues (Holmes and Masuda, 1974; Holmes and Rahe, 1967; Rahe, 1972). They introduced the concept of *life change units,* a numerical score indicating the typical level of change or stress that a particular event produces in an individual's day-to-day life. It appears that the life change units assigned to some events by young respondents may not reflect the degree of stress actually produced by events that they have not yet experienced (e.g., a partner's death). Research comparing older and younger people's ratings of life events reveals:

- Some items such as "death of spouse" are perceived to be equally stressful by all ages.
- Younger people view "death of a close friend" and "marital reconciliation" as more stressful than do older people.
- Older individuals who have experienced a life event such as "retirement" and "death of spouse" assign lower readjustment scores than those who have not experienced them.

These findings suggest that the anticipation of an event is more stressful than the actual experience, and that previous experience with a life event can help the person cope better when a similar event occurs. In addition, many older people have developed resilience and maturity through their previous coping experiences; they may be the most adaptive members of their cohort if they have survived beyond the life expectancy predicted for them. A more recent conceptualization suggests that it is not the major, catastrophic life events that demand effective coping responses. Instead, it is "daily hassles" such as problems related to work, family, or financial stability that create stress. Conversely, the "daily uplifts" of life, such as a friendly phone call from a grandchild who lives across the country, can help elders tolerate these hassles (Lazarus, 2000).

What Determines Stress Responses in Old Age?

Both social and personal factors act as mediators and affect the process of coping with stressful events. The former encompasses friendships and family support, while the latter includes the individual's functional ability, cognitive status, and self-esteem, as well as aspirations, values, vulnerabilities, and needs that mediate between a particular stressful situation and its outcomes. As noted above, it is important to know if the individual appraises a situation as stressful. The relative desirability or undesirability of an event, whether or not it is anticipated, and previous experiences with similar events also determine how an individual responds to the situation. The availability of social supports is significant too. A person who must face a crisis alone may use different coping strategies than one who has family and friends.

POINTS TO PONDER

Think about some life experiences that you personally have undergone. These should include both positive and negative life events. What made each event stressful to you? Did your cognitive appraisal of the situations make them easier or more difficult for you to cope with them? What specific coping techniques did you use with each event?

Personality styles also may affect responses to stress. For example, a person with a passive style may not feel powerful enough to directly influence his or her fate, whereas one with an active style may rely more on personal abilities and less on other people. Differences in responses to stress by older people with these different styles would be expected; however, research has not provided sufficient evidence for such hypothesized variations.

Locus of control is another closely related personality characteristic that may influence responses to stress. This is an individual's belief that events in his or her life result from personal actions (internal locus), or are determined by fate or powerful others (external locus). Internal locus of control and a sense of mastery appear to be related to successful coping in both young and old. For example, they can help the individual maintain functional ability in old age and improve adaptation to widowhood (Kemper, van Sonderen, and Ormel, 1999).

Adaptation in the Later Years

As noted earlier in this chapter, a critical personality feature in the later years is an individual's ability to adapt to major changes in life circumstances, health and social status, and social and physical environments. **Adaptation** includes a range of behaviors such as coping, goal-setting, problem-solving, and other attempts to maintain psychological homeostasis (Ruth and Coleman, 1996). Given older people's numerous experiences with life events, role loss, and environmental changes, it would appear that adaptation in old age should occur with relative ease. Indeed, in one sense, an individual who has reached age 75 or 80 has proved to be the most adaptable of his or her generation, since the ultimate proof of adaptation is survival. As we have seen, older persons face challenges to their well-being in the form of personal and family illness, age-related declines in sensory and physiological functions, and changes in their social and physical environments. To the

extent that older people are capable of using coping skills that were effective in youth and middle age, they will continue to adapt to change successfully.

Does coping change with age? Before answering, we must first define and consider the functions of coping. **Coping** is the manner in which a person responds to stress. It includes cognitive, emotional, and behavioral responses made in the face of internally and externally created events. It differs from **defense mechanisms** in that people are generally conscious of how they have coped in a particular situation and, if asked, can describe specific coping responses to a given stressor. Coping strategies may be described as "planful behavior" in response to a stressful situation. Some forms of coping are aimed not at resolving the problem, but at providing psychological escape, as illustrated by the categories of coping defined by some researchers (see the box on page 222). Coping reactions generally serve two functions:

- *problem-focused* coping to solve a problem that has produced stress for the individual
- *emotion-focused* coping to reduce the emotional and physiological discomfort that accompanies the stressful situation (Lazarus, 1999; Lazarus and Folkman, 1984)

In some cases, an individual may focus only on solving the problem or on dealing with the emotional distress that it creates. Such reactions tend to be incomplete and do not resolve both the emotional and functional impact of the situation. Coping must fulfill both emotion-regulating and problem-solving functions in order to alleviate stress.

The question of whether coping styles change with age has been explored by researchers focused on specific challenges such as caregiving for a frail partner, or on different types of problems (e.g., relocation vs. death of a loved one), or on general styles of appraising coping with diverse challenges (Ryff et al., 2001). One study found that older adults used more impulse

CLASSIFICATION OF COPING RESPONSES

General Strategies of Coping	Coping Responses to Terminal Illness	Dimensions of Coping
(Lazarus, 1975a, 1975b; Lazarus and Launier, 1978; Lazarus and Folkman, 1984)	(Moos, 1977)	(Kahana and Kahana, 1982)
• Information search in an attempt to understand the situation • Direct action to change the situation • Inhibition of action • Psychological responses to the emotional arousal created by the situation	• Searching for information • Setting goals • Denying or minimizing the problem • Seeking emotional support • Rehearsing alternative outcomes	• Instrumental (taking action, alone or with the assistance of others) • Intrapsychic (cognitive approaches, acceptance of the situation) • Affective (releasing tensions, expressing emotions) • Escape (avoiding or denying the problem, displacement activities such as increased exercise, eating, and smoking) • Resigned helplessness (feeling impotent, unable to cope)

control and positive appraisal, while adolescents and young adults tended to rely on more aggressive strategies. Gender differences emerged in the use of internalizing versus outwardly expressing emotions in stressful conditions (Diehl, Coyle, and Labouvie-Vief, 1996). The extent to which life events are generated by the individual (e.g., deciding to retire) or are externally created with no choice by the person who experiences the event (e.g., being forced to take early retirement) can disrupt the individual's coping style, regardless of age. Nevertheless, uncontrollable events can often propel the older person toward further growth and development (Diehl, 1999).

Religious coping is an important strategy, especially among African American elders (Mattis and Jagers, 2001; Musick, 2000). Indeed, in the Duke Longitudinal Study, 45 percent of the respondents age 55 to 80 mentioned trust and faith in God, prayer, and seeking help from God as a coping strategy for at least one of three major life events. Over 70 percent of adults had used religion in coping with major life events. Religious coping among churchgoing adults is identified to be associated with positive mental health (e.g., lower rates of depression) and better perceived general health (e.g., lower blood pressure and coronary artery disease risk, and improved survival rates after heart surgery) (Ai and Carrigan, 2006; George, 2002; Idler, 2002; Koenig and Brooks, 2002; Miller and Thoresen, 2003; Wong and Ujimoto, 1998). Social supports and a sense of belonging to a larger group are components of religious coping that influence well-being in older adults (Reiss, 2000).

Studies of coping among the old-old indicate that acceptance of change in one's life (e.g., nursing home placement, divorce of children or grandchildren) may be the most adaptive coping response. Control over external events may be less important than the need to make uncontrollable events more acceptable to one's values and beliefs. In most cases, the coping styles chosen by an older person are appropriate for the problem at hand and result in successful adaptation. When cognitive deterioration is significant, however, there is a restriction in the range of coping responses and a tendency to resort to more primitive reactions, such as denying or ignoring the problem. The majority of older people appear capable of using a wide repertoire of coping responses and call on the most effective ones for a given situation. In sum, most people maintain their coping styles into old age, and use appropriate responses.

Successful Aging

Early gerontological studies focused on quality of life and subjective well being, concepts that no longer dominate gerontological research. Instead, researchers and clinicians are increasingly interested in the concepts of successful, robust, vital, or positive aging and resilience, with the most attention given to defining and measuring **successful aging** (Danner, Snowden and Friesen, 2001; George, 2006; Hendricks and Hatch, 2006; Rowe and Kahn, 1987, 1997, 1998; Seeman et al., 1994). This interest has been sparked by the growing number of older people who have avoided the disabling chronic health problems and declining cognitive skills and have managed to cope effectively in their daily lives. What are the characteristics of such elders who age successfully that distinguish them from their less hardy peers? Successful aging is defined as a combination of:

- physical and functional health
- high cognitive functioning
- active involvement with society

This definition implies that the successful older person has low risk of disease and disability (i.e., healthy lifestyle factors such as diet, not smoking, physical activity), is actively using problem-solving, conceptualization, and language skills to ensure mental stimulation, is maintaining social contacts, exhibits emotional optimism, and is participating in productive activities (e.g., volunteering, paid or unpaid work). The concept of personal agency — individual choices and behaviors—is also central. The model of successful aging proposed by Rowe and Kahn (1997, 1998), shown in Figure 6.1, integrates these components.

The MacArthur Studies of Successful Aging, on which this model was based, examined longitudinally a cohort of men and women (aged 70–79 at baseline) in three East Coast communities. They were selected because they represented the top third of their age group in

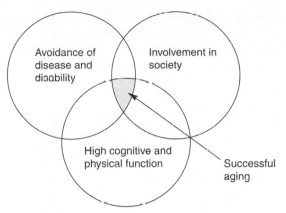

FIGURE 6.1   A Model of Successful Aging
This model assumes that all three components must exist for successful aging to occur.
SOURCE: Reprinted with permission, Rowe and Kahn, 1997.

cognitive and physical function. Within this selective group of "robust" older persons, more specific tests of cognitive and physical abilities, as well as physiological parameters, were conducted in 1988 and 1991. Those with the highest performance scores in this group at follow-up and those who survived three years later had fewer chronic conditions (especially cardiovascular diseases), better self-rated health, and higher educational and income levels. The majority of these robust older adults reported no problems with daily physical activities such as walking, crouching, and stooping without help, and 55 percent maintained their baseline performance levels after three years. Although 23 percent showed a decline on the performance tests, 22 percent actually *improved*. Those who declined or died in the interim had greater weekly variability in their physical performance, blood pressure, balance, and gait, and had entered the study with some chronic diseases (Nesselroade et al., 1996; Seeman et al., 1994). Participants in the MacArthur Studies were also assessed on their physical functioning over 7 years. Those with a strong support system showed less deterioration in their functional health than elders without strong networks. Such social supports were particularly valuable for men and those who had poorer physical health at baseline. Based on these findings, the MacArthur Studies researchers recommend that people remain actively engaged with life and connected to others as they age (Rowe and Kahn, 1997, 1998; Unger et al., 1999).

As noted above, successful aging also implies maintenance of cognitive functioning. In the MacArthur Studies, *educational level* was the best predictor of continued high levels of cognitive ability. Rather than innate intelligence, higher educational achievement in those who aged successfully was most likely due to lifelong interest in intellectual activities as well as a beneficial effect of education on the development of complex networks in the brain. Other predictors of maintaining cognitive abilities were *involvement in strenuous physical activity*. A higher level of **self-efficacy,** that is, a feeling of competence in one's ability to deal with new situations, was also a significant predictor of high physical and cognitive function at follow-up (Seeman et al., 1999). A recent review of 28 studies that examined correlates of successful aging confirmed that cognitive activity, absence of disability, more physical activity, non-smoking, and absence of depression, diabetes, and debilitating arthritis were significantly correlated with objective measures of this concept (Depp and Jeste, 2006).

The concept of "robust aging" represents a broader perspective on successful aging, one that considers exceptional functioning on measures of physical health, cognitive abilities, and emotional well-being even among the oldest-old (Garfein and Herzog, 1995; Suzman et al., 1992). Others have labeled this "optimal aging," an ideal state that is theoretically but not practically possible for most people (Schulz and Heckhausen, 1996). Four important characteristics appear to distinguish robust older adults from their less-robust peers:

- productive involvement (defined as 1500 hours or more of paid or unpaid work, home maintenance, or volunteer activity in the past year)

- absence of depressive symptoms (i.e., high affective well-being)
- high physical functioning
- no cognitive impairment (Garfein and Herzog, 1995)

Robust elders reported more social contacts, better physical health and vision, and fewer significant life events (e.g., death of partner, child, close friend) in the past 3 years than did poorly functioning elders. For the oldest-old, robust aging also implies the ability to perform independently basic activities of daily living, higher-level work, and leisure and social activities (Horgas, Wilms, and Baltes, 1998).

A related concept is **resilience,** or the ability to thrive under adversity or multiple life challenges, turning adversity into a catalyst for growth and development. The concept of resilience takes account of background characteristics (e.g. gender, ethnic minority status, and age) and personal, family, cultural, and community capacities that can protect against or moderate adversity and influence meaning and well-being in later life. For example, people who have positive interpersonal relationships, strong cultural values, and a supportive community can enhance their resilience even in the face of chronic health problems and economic adversity (Fredriksen-Goldsen, in press; Kahn, 2003; Neimeyer, 2001; Ryff et al., 2001).

A comparison of three large longitudinal studies provides insights into personality and coping styles that result in what some researchers call "positive aging" (i.e., actively responding to changes in one's health and interpersonal relations). The Grant Study of Harvard Graduates studied a cohort of men born in the 1920s from their student days through old age. The Glueck Study of Inner City Adolescent Boys followed a cohort born in the 1930s, while the Terman Study of Gifted Children examined both males and females starting in 1922. Vaillant continued to interview survivors of these three groups during their middle and older years, starting with the Grant sample in 1967, the Glueck men in 1970, and the surviving 90 women in the Terman study after 1987 (Vaillant, 1977, 1994, 2002). Vaillant found important commonalities across these diverse samples of men and women, despite their different childhood and family experiences and socioeconomic status during their youth and middle years. He concluded from these studies that:

- personality and coping strategies in youth and during college years predict adaptive ability in old age if the person does not have a psychological disorder
- childhood social class and parental problems had little impact on outcomes during these participants' old age
- self-confidence and preferences evolve with age

Vaillant observed that those who had aged "positively" shared the quality of resilience, which he defined as adaptability and taking life in stride. This trait was expressed by one of the Grant study subjects whose closest friends and relatives had died: "Life is like a book filled with many chapters. When one chapter is finished, you must go on to the next chapter" (Vaillant, 2002, p. 9). Based on his analysis of the early childhood and young adulthood experiences of surviving elders, Vaillant summarized qualities that predicted positive aging:

1. long-term "healing relationships" in which elders help others and accept help from these close friends and family members
2. a supportive marriage or long-term partnership
3. continued involvement with life, making new friends to replace those lost through death or relocation, as well as the ability to accept the inevitability of death
4. mature defense mechanisms and active coping responses rather than passive acceptance when faced with crises in health and interpersonal relations (Vaillant, 2002)

Other researchers emphasize that a sense of purpose, meaning, or contribution to society is a critical element of successful aging. This sense of purpose is more than reflection, acceptance, and ego integrity as Erikson describes in his eighth stage of adult development. It requires that older persons continue giving back to society, the hallmark of the seventh stage—generativity. For example, research with participants in the Foster Grandparents Program reveals that those who have aged successfully believe they have achieved higher-order needs, such as helping children, are making a difference in others' lives, and feeling that their lives have a purpose (Fisher, 1995). These are elements of both generativity and ego integrity, and support the importance of both types of developmental tasks for successful aging. As noted in Chapter 12, older adults who volunteer generally experience greater life satisfaction than their peers who do not, a pattern that underlies the current emphasis on civic engagement of elders (Hudson, 2006). Even those who do not volunteer but maintain social ties can increase their chances of life satisfaction in old age. In a study of community-dwelling older adults, greater activity levels, resilience, and number of close friends were all correlated with subjective reports of successful aging, but having multiple chronic illnesses or a disability was not (Montross et al., 2006). A 12-year follow-up of almost 3000 community-dwelling elders showed that people who were socially disengaged (i.e., no social contacts) were 2.4 times more likely to experience cognitive impairment than elders of the same age, gender, ethnic minority status, and health status who had 5 or 6 close social ties (Bassuk, Glass, and Berkman, 1999).

A Critique of the Successful Aging Paradigm

The concept of successful aging has been widely critiqued for conveying a middle-age, middle-class norm of remaining active as a way to show that one is an exception to their age peers, that is, "not really old, not aging."

The unspecified but clearly preferred method of successful aging is, by most accounts, not to age at all, or at least to minimize the extent to which it is apparent that one is ageing, both internally and externally (Andrews, 1999, p. 305)

Since normal physical changes do occur with age, an implicit message of successful aging is to develop strategies (or "lifestyle industries") to preserve "youthfulness" in order not to be seen as old. The focus on physical and mental activity is reinforced by mass marketing and advertising of exceptionally fit and physically attractive older adults who have the resources to slow decline (Calasanti and Slevin, 2001; Hendricks and Hatch, 2006; Katz, 2000; McHugh, 2000). In such instances, successful aging assumes that everyone has autonomy and lifestyle options. But such options across the life course may not be available to low-income and historically disadvantaged elders who lack the resources or supports to engage in the lifestyle habits identified for successful aging. Instead, assumptions about appropriate lifestyles for happiness and successful aging are often class-based and may unintentionally overlook or blame older adults who have not had such lifestyle and genetic advantages (Wray, 2003). The concept of successful aging also minimizes the extent to which physical and social environments are structured to limit choices to engage in an active lifestyle (Hendricks and Hatch, 2006; Holstein and Minkler, 2003). Admonitions to choose healthy lifestyles do not generally resonate with low income elders who are preoccupied with having enough to eat (Grzywacz and Marks, 2001). Based on these concerns, the MacArthur Studies researchers later emphasized the importance of altering policies (e.g., funding prevention under Medicare) and environments (e.g., free public exercise areas) to increase opportunities to age successfully (Hendricks and Hatch, 2006; Kahn, 2003; Riley, 1998).

Another limitation of the successful aging model is its emphasis on activity and productivity characteristic of mainstream Western culture. This overlooks elders—often from other cultures—who are contemplative and engage in spiritual activities and may experience a high degree of subjective well-being. A narrow definition of successful aging can also be stigmatizing to older adults with chronic illnesses who develop strategies to compensate for their functional disabilities and are able to experience a high level of a subjective well-being or quality of life, even though they do not fit "successful aging" in terms of Rowe and Kahn's criteria (Minkler and Fadem, 2002; Moody, 2005). In effect, the concept of successful aging is an ambiguous and controversial one. As such, it raises questions about whose standards define "success," and overlooks the fact that older adults may perceive their quality of life to be high, even though they would not be classified as such by the theoretical models of successful aging (George, 2006). Indeed, in a study of 867 community-dwelling elders, 50.3 percent rated themselves as aging successfully, but when objectively assessed with Rowe and Kahn's three criteria, only 18.8 percent were classified in this manner (Strawbridge, Wallhagen, and Cohen, 2002). Similarly, a study of low-income older women found that they developed strategies to remain involved in personally meaningful activities and to experience quality of life, even though their lives did not fit the prevailing models of successful aging (Wray, 2003). It is important to note that "success" in the Rowe and Kahn model should not be viewed as a dichotomous state, but a continuous variable where elders may be more successful in one of the three criteria than in others, and still be viewed as having aged well (Kahn, 2003). Nevertheless, because of some of the class, race, and gender biases implicit in successful aging, the concept of active aging or resilience may be more applicable to historically underserved populations that display remarkable strengths despite adversities in their lives. Their strengths may derive from internal resources (e.g., spirituality, religiosity, self-concept, and sense of mastery) and from social and cultural resources (e.g., social supports, community resources, and cultural values). Resilience was described earlier as adaptability in the review of longitudinal studies of personality and adaptation across the life span (Vaillant, 2002), and is discussed in Chapters 14 and 15 in the context of aging among ethnic minorities and women.

Psychological Disorders among Older Persons

As shown in Chapter 5 and in the earlier sections of this chapter, normal psychological development with aging includes some changes in cognitive processes such as attention, memory, and learning, as well as maturation of coping responses, stability in personality traits, and a natural progression through different stages of personality development. The majority of older adults experience these changes without major disruptions in their behavior or mental health. However, some older people experience more severe problems in cognitive function, coping ability, emotional stability, or interpersonal behavior. **Psychopathology** consist of conditions that impair the individual's interpersonal and self-care behaviors, and often result in feelings of distress and loss of autonomy. These conditions are not unique to older adults and are found across the life course. However, they may be more difficult to diagnose among older people due to co-morbidities, such as chronic systemic diseases and impaired sensory function. The major forms of psychological disorders in older adults include mood disorders, anxiety disorders (including phobias and panic disorders), schizophrenia, and substance-related disorders.

Depression is the primary mood disorder of old age, and accounts for a significant number of suicides, especially among older men. Alzheimer's disease and other dementias are cognitive disorders that are more likely to affect the oldest-old. Alcoholism and drug abuse are less common in older individuals, although their effect on older people's physical health and cognitive functioning is more detrimental than on younger persons. Paranoid disorders and schizophrenia are conditions that are first diagnosed in youth or middle age. Each of these conditions is reviewed in the following sections.

The prevalence of psychological disorders among older persons who are living in the community ranges from 15 to 25 percent, depending on the population studied and the categories of disorders examined. Even higher rates can occur in the institutionalized older population, with estimates of 10 to 40 percent of older patients with mild to moderate impairments, and an additional 5 to 10 percent with significant impairments. Twenty percent of all first admissions to psychiatric hospitals are persons over age 65. Older psychiatric patients are more likely to have chronic conditions and to require longer periods of inpatient treatment than are younger patients, as evidenced by the fact that 25 percent of all beds in these hospitals are occupied by older persons, even though older adults comprise just over 12 percent of the U.S. population. Most older patients with chronic psychiatric conditions live in the community; fewer live in nursing homes or psychiatric institutions. Overall, fewer than 25 percent of older adults who need mental health services ever receive treatment, a pattern that is true across all service areas. Older patients comprise only 4 percent of psychiatric outpatient clients and less than 2 percent of those served by private practitioners. A major barrier to treatment is a shortage of geriatric mental health professionals (Gatz and Smyer, 2001; Jeste et al., 1999; Kaskie and Estes, 2001; Rosen, 2005).

One problem with describing the prevalence of mental disorders of older people is the lack of criteria distinguishing conditions that emerge in old age from those that continue throughout adulthood. In fact, the major classification system for psychiatric disorders, the *Diagnostic and Statistical Manual of Mental Disorders*, fourth edition with text revisions (DSM-IV-TR), (2000), makes such a distinction only for dementias that begin in late life. No other mental disorders are differentiated for old age, although other diagnostic categories are described specifically for adulthood as separate from childhood or adolescence. The problem of inadequate criteria for late-life psychopathology (or psychological disorders) is compounded by the lack of age-appropriate psychological tests for diagnosing these conditions. An increasing number of tests are being developed, especially for diagnosing depression and dementia in older people.

Depression

Depression, dementia, and paranoia are the three most prevalent forms of late-life psychopathology. Of these, **depression** is the most common. It is important to distinguish *unipolar* depression from *bipolar* disorders (that is, ranging from a depressed to a manic state), as well as severe conditions such as sadness, grief reactions, and other affective disorders. Most of the depressions of old age are unipolar; bipolar disorders are rare. Still other cases in late life are *minor* or *reactive* depressions, which arise in response to a significant life event with which the individual cannot cope. For example, physical illness and the loss of loved ones through death and relocation may trigger depressive reactions in older people. The vegetative signs, suicidal thoughts, weight loss, and mood variations from morning to night that are observed in major depression are not found in minor depression. Studies of older individuals in community settings and in nursing homes suggest that the prevalence of major depression is generally lower than the rates of minor or reactive depression. Depression in nursing home residents is often misdiagnosed. Rates as high as 20 to 30 percent have been found among such residents (Blazer, 1999; Gallo and Lebowitz, 1999; Harralson et al., 2002; Jones, Marcantonio, Rabinowitz, 2003). **Dysthymic disorder** is a less

Untreated depression in older men is a risk factor for suicide.

acute type of depression but with symptoms that last longer than major depression.

Estimates of depression for community-dwelling elders are:

- 8–20 percent for minor depression
- 1 percent for major depression
- 2 percent for dysthymic disorder
- 0.1 percent for bipolar disorder

Clinically relevant depressive symptoms are more common among older women and among both men and women 75 and older (12.5 percent and 18.7 percent, respectively), compared with men and women ages 65 to 74 (9.8 percent and 17.1 percent, respectively) (Health and Retirement Survey, 2002). These rates are about the same for whites and African Americans. However, depression is more likely to be undetected or misdiagnosed in ethnic minority elders, in part because of cultural barriers to diagnosis and treatment (Lincoln, 2003). Asian American elders, for example, attach a strong stigma to mental illness, which can result in an under-diagnosis (Surgeon General, 2001). Rates of depression among Latinos tend to be higher than among whites, especially among Mexican Americans (25.6 percent). This is explained partially by the following sociodemographic and health-related correlates of depression: lack of insurance, financial strain, low locus of control regarding health, chronic health conditions, and functional disability. In addition, cultural factors, such as immigrant status, recency of immigration, and low levels of acculturation are all associated with increased risk of depressive symptomatology (Aranda, Lee, and Wilson, 2001; Mui and Kang, 2006). Health care providers need to recognize such risk factors and be sensitive to cultural differences in order to diagnose accurately and treat depression effectively.

As noted earlier in this chapter, most role *gains* (e.g., paid worker, driver, voter, partner, or parent) occur in the earlier years, whereas role *losses* may multiply in the later years. As we have seen, loss of roles may be compounded by decrements in sensory abilities, physical strength, and health. These role losses often result in grief, which may be misdiagnosed as depression or may be discounted by health care providers as a normal part of old age. Although depression usually does not result from any one of these losses alone, the combination of several losses in close sequence may trigger a reactive depressive episode. This may be due to changes in the brain caused by multiple stressors that affect the production of mood-regulating chemicals in the brain. It appears that acute life events can lead to a recurrence of major depression, but do not necessarily trigger its first onset (Kessler, 1997). Older people with major physical conditions such as stroke, cancer, diabetes, or chronic pain and those who do not have a supportive social network are at greatest risk. In addition, older persons who have experienced depression in the past are at greater risk for a recurrence than

those whose first episode occurs in old age, especially if the depression is triggered by a major life event (Mitchell and Subramaniam, 2005). Risk factors for depression in older adults include:

- female gender
- unmarried
- co-morbidity (i.e., multiple chronic diseases)
- chronic financial strain
- family history of depressive illness
- lack of social support (Aranda et al., 2001; Garrard et al., 1998)

Psychiatric symptoms that persist beyond 6 months in older persons may indicate the development of a major depressive episode. Consistent with the approach of person–environment fit, environmental and social interventions, as well as psychotherapy, are more effective than antidepressant medications for minor depression. However, medications and sometimes electroconvulsive therapy are necessary to treat major depression and prevent suicide, as described later in this chapter.

Death rates are higher among older persons with a diagnosis of depression, almost twice that for nondepressed people within 1 year. Depressed older adults, especially if they have cognitive impairment, have a significantly higher mortality risk. The more severe a patient's depressive symptoms, the more likely he or she is to die sooner (Blazer, Hybels, and Pieper, 2001; Schulz et al., 2000). Medical hospital stays are often twice as long and health care costs in general are higher for those with depression. In addition, depressed older adults take longer to recover from a hip fracture or stroke, or from a cardiovascular disease episode (Ai and Carrigan, 2006; Chiles, Lambert and Hatch, 1999). This may be because older persons with depression are more apathetic, less motivated to improve their health, and more likely to entertain thoughts of suicide than younger depressives. The Diagnostic and Statistical Manual (DSM-IV-R) of the American

Psychiatric Association (2000) lists the following criteria for major depression:

1. depressed mood most of day, nearly every day
2. markedly diminished interest or pleasure in activities, apathy
3. significant weight loss or weight gain, or appetite change
4. sleep disturbance (insomnia or hypersomnia) nearly every day
5. agitation or lack of activity nearly every day
6. low energy level or fatigue nearly every day
7. self-blame, guilt, worthlessness
8. poor concentration, indecisiveness
9. recurrent thoughts of death, suicide

At least five of these symptoms are present during the same 2-week period and represent a change from previous function. Among these, number 1 or 2 on the list should be at least one of the symptoms.*

Below are some symptoms of depression that may be confused with normal aging and therefore overlooked by health care providers:

- reports or evidence of sadness
- feelings of emptiness or detachment with no precipitating major life event such as bereavement
- expressions of anxiety or panic for no apparent cause
- loss of interest in the environment
- neglect of self-care
- changes in eating and sleeping patterns

The depressed person may complain of vague aches and pains, either generally or in a specific part of the body. Occasional symptoms or symptoms associated with a specific medication, physical illness, or alcoholism need to be distinguished from the somatic complaints associated with depression. When multiple

*Adapted with permission from the *Diagnostic and statistical manual of mental disorders,* 4th ed. Copyright 1994 American Psychiatric Association, Washington, DC, p. 327.

MEDICATIONS THAT MAY PRODUCE SYMPTOMS OF DEPRESSION

- antihypertensives
- digoxin (used for some heart conditions)
- corticosteroids (used for preventing joint inflammation)
- estrogen
- some antipsychotic drugs
- anti-Parkinsonism drugs such as L-dopa

---

symptoms appear together and persist *for at least 2 weeks,* an elder and his or her family should suspect major depression, especially if an older person speaks frequently of death or suicide.

One problem with detecting depression in older people is that they may be more successful than their younger counterparts at masking or hiding symptoms. In fact, many cases of depression in older persons are not diagnosed because the individual either does not express changes in mood or denies them in the clinical interview. A *masked depression* is one in which few mood changes are reported. Instead, the patient complains of a vague pain, bodily discomfort, and sleep disturbance; reports problems with memory; is apathetic; and withdraws from others (Blazer, 2003; Gallo and Lebowitz, 1999). This is a common condition in current cohorts of elders, especially Asian immigrants, because many of them were raised in environments that discouraged open expression of feelings.

Health care professionals and family members need to distinguish depression from medical conditions and changes due to normal aging or from grief. For example, an older woman with arthritis who complains of increasing pain may actually be seeking a reason for vague physical discomfort that is related to a depressive episode. People with masked depression are more likely to complain of problems with memory or problem-solving. Their denial or masking of symptoms may lead the physician to assume that the individual is experiencing dementia, a condition that is generally irreversible. It is for this reason that depression in older persons is often labeled *pseudodementia*.

Because of such likelihood of denial, a physician's first goal with an older patient who has vague somatic and memory complaints should be to conduct a thorough physical exam and lab tests. This is important in order to determine if an individual is depressed or has a physical disorder or symptoms of dementia. If the cognitive dysfunction is due to depression, it will improve when the depression is treated. On the other hand, some medical conditions may produce depressive symptoms. These include:

- Parkinson's disease
- rheumatoid arthritis
- thyroid dysfunction
- diseases of the adrenal glands

As noted earlier, depression can coexist with medical conditions such as heart disease, stroke, arthritis, cancer, diabetes, chronic lung disease, and Alzheimer's disease, compounding the dysfunction associated with these medical problems and delaying the recovery process. Certain medications may also produce feelings of depression. In fact, any medication that has a depressant effect on the central nervous system can produce depressive symptoms, specifically lethargy and loss of interest in the environment. For these reasons, older adults with depressive symptoms should be examined thoroughly for underlying physical illness, hypothyroidism, vitamin deficiencies, chronic infections, and reactions to medications. Physicians must frequently conduct medication reviews to determine if their older patients begin to show side effects to a drug, even after using it for several months or years. Late-life depression is costly not just for the individual's physical and psychological well-being, but it exacts a large economic toll. The interaction of symptoms of depression with many somatic conditions results in more visits to primary care physicians and emergency rooms as well as longer hospital stays for older adults. Because elders with depression are most likely to be seen in these settings than in community mental health clinics, primary care physicians and emergency room personnel should be trained to detect signs of depression (Surgeon General, 1999a; Unutzer et al., 2003).

THERAPEUTIC INTERVENTIONS   It is important to treat both major and secondary depressions upon diagnosis, because the older depressed patient is at higher risk of self-destructive behavior and suicide. Older adults are more likely to seek help for depressive symptoms from their family doctor than from mental health professionals. Primary care physicians who diagnose depression in an older person must provide psychological support for acute symptoms, including empathy, attentive listening, and encouragement of active coping skills and problem solving. For patients with minor depression, this may be all they need to show a decrease in symptoms. For more severely depressed elders, alternative therapies may be required. There is some disagreement, however, about the efficacy of such therapies. Although short-term improvements may be achieved through treatment, the long-range prognosis is not always successful, and some older people will experience a relapse (Mitchell and Subramaniam, 2005).

The most common therapeutic intervention with depressed older individuals is pharmacological, which is particularly useful for those experiencing a major depression or bipolar depression (Frazer, Christensen, and Griffiths, 2005; Wilson et al., 2004). Therapy with antidepressants is generally long-term because the higher doses used during the acute episode must be followed by a maintenance dose in order to reduce the risk of relapse. Although antidepressants work well for some older persons, many cannot use these drugs because of other medications they are taking, such as antihypertensives, or because the side effects are more detrimental

---

COMBINED THERAPIES MAY BE MOST EFFECTIVE WITH OLDER ADULTS

In the six months since the death of his wife of 52 years, Mr. Simon has lost interest in all the activities that he and his wife enjoyed together. He has lost weight and sleeps irregularly. His complaints of poor memory and loss of energy have alarmed his adult children, who insisted he see his family physician. The doctor prescribed an antidepressant upon recognizing the symptoms of depression. However, Mr. Simon stopped taking these medications after two weeks because they made him feel dizzy and caused dry mouth. The physician spent time discussing the immediate benefits from medications, but also arranged for Mr. Simon to participate in one-on-one psychotherapy sessions with an expert in geriatric psychotherapy. After 2 months, Mr. Simon has already seen the benefits of combining these two therapies for his condition. He now attends a local senior center daily, and has begun a regular exercise program of walking for one hour every day.

---

than the depression itself. These effects include postural hypotension (i.e., a sudden drop in blood pressure when rising from a prone position), increased vulnerability to falls and fractures, cardiac arrhythmias, urinary retention, constipation, disorientation, skin rash, and dry mouth (Ensrud et al., 2003; Richards et al., 2007). Because of these potentially dangerous reactions, it is important to start antidepressant therapy at a much lower dose (perhaps 50 percent lower) in older than in younger patients and to monitor its effects regularly.

Many older persons who turn to a general practitioner for treatment of depression often receive antidepressants as a first line of attack rather than psychotherapy, or in combination. There is increased evidence that a combination of well-monitored pharmacotherapy and counseling can reduce symptoms in up to 80 percent of chronically depressed older adults, even in the oldest-old (Blazer, 2003; Reynolds and

Kupfer, 1999). This combination was found to reduce symptoms of bereavement-related depression in 69 percent of elders in a 16-week treatment program, compared with 45 percent for drugs alone, and 29 percent for psychotherapy alone (Reynolds et al., 1999). In another study, older adults with clinically diagnosed major depression showed the least recurrence of symptoms if they were treated with an antidepressant and psychotherapy (35 percent recurrence) than medication alone (37 percent recurrence) or psychotherapy alone (68 percent recurrence). Recurrence was 2.4 times more likely among those given a placebo rather than the antidepressant (Reynolds et al., 2006). Therapy lasting at least one year has also been shown to stabilize bouts of mania and depression in adults with bipolar disorder. This suggests that patients with clinical depression can benefit from combined therapeutic interventions (Frank et al., 1999; Keller et al., 2000).

Older people are just as likely as younger persons to benefit from the insight and empathy provided by a therapist trained in geriatric psychotherapy. In particular, secondary depression responds well to supportive therapy that allows the patient to review, and come to terms with, the stresses of late life. Supportive psychotherapy is useful because it allows older patients to reestablish control and emotional stability. Older depressed persons appear to benefit from short-term, client-centered, directive therapy more than from therapy that is nondirective or uses free association to uncover long-standing personality conflicts. **Reminiscence therapy** allows older people with depression to work through difficult memories and process their grief and loss, but requires more sessions than other forms of psychotherapy (Bohlmeijer, Smit, and Cuijpers, 2003; Cully, LaVoie, and Gfeller, 2001). *Cognitive-behavioral interventions* use active, time-limited approaches to change the thinking and behavior that affect depression, such as self-monitoring of negative thoughts about oneself, daily monitoring of

A SUCCESSFUL THERAPY FOR MINOR DEPRESSION

The Program to Encourage Active, Rewarding Lives for Seniors (PEARLS) is an innovative and effective therapy for minor depression. It was developed by researchers at the University of Washington Health Promotion Center with funds from the CDC. It consists of 8 in-home visits by a counselor over 8 months. Older adults diagnosed with *minor depression* (characterized by loss of interest, feelings of sadness or hopelessness) are helped by this structured behavior therapy and positive event scheduling. Together with their counselors, PEARLS clients develop and evaluate solutions to their depression. This technique has been found to be effective in eliminating depression completely for about a third of elders and reduced depressive symptoms by half in another 43 percent. PEARLS also lowers hospitalization rates compared to a control group (http://apps.nccd.cdc.gov).

SUMMARY OF THERAPEUTIC INTERVENTIONS FOR DEPRESSED OLDER ADULTS

Pharmacotherapy (antidepressants)

Electroconvulsive therapy

Psychotherapy
- supportive
- directive
- cognitive-behavioral

Combination of therapies

moods, and increased participation in pleasant events for depressed elders who are caring for a frail spouse or partner. It is the most effective form of psychotherapy when combined with antidepressant medication (Frazer, Christensen, and Griffiths, 2005; Goisman, 1999; Teri et al., 1997). *Problem-solving therapy* teaches patients effective techniques for coping with their concerns related to their depression. In a systematic testing of this approach in elders with minor depression or dysthymia, researchers combined problem-solving therapy with social and physical activities, and antidepressants as needed. Elders in the intervention, Program to Encourage Active, Rewarding Lives for Senior (PEARLS) and described in the box above, experienced a 50 percent reduction in depressive symptoms and better quality of life than those treated by more conventional methods (Ciechanowski et al., 2004). Despite these benefits of some forms of psychotherapy for depressed older adults, primary care physicians are more likely to prescribe antidepressants and less likely to refer

elders for counseling. In many cases they receive only limited sessions of psychotherapy, because of the cost of counseling; this is especially the case among older men, Latinos, and African Americans (Unutzer et al., 2003).

Because older adults with depression are more likely to be seen in hospital settings than community mental health centers, hospital-based interventions need to be developed. One such intervention, Improving Mood—Promoting Access to Collaborative Treatment for Late-Life Depression (IMPACT) in Washington State, developed a model of care coordination for patients with concurrent depression and mental illness. A depression care manager, who is a psychologist, psychiatric nurse, or social worker, provides patient education in the hospital with follow-up, treatment support, and brief psychotherapy after discharge. In a randomized control of 400 providers and 1802 patients, those receiving the IMPACT intervention showed a greater reduction in depression and more depression-free days than those receiving usual care. Re-engineering Systems for Primary Care Treatment (RESPECT), in Colorado, uses a similar coordinated care intervention involving patient and provider education, and close coordination with the primary care physician. Patients with the care coordination intervention showed significant improvements in depression symptoms. Both care coordination models have been implemented in hospitals across the country (Capers, 2004).

As noted above, psychotherapy must be accompanied by **pharmacotherapy** or electroconvulsive therapy in severely depressed elders. Despite past controversy about its use, **electroconvulsive** or **electroshock therapy (ECT)** is sometimes used in cases of severe depression. This involves delivering a brief electric current to the brain; it is a quick and effective method, even in patients older than 80, for treating major depression in patients who:

- have not responded to medications
- have a higher risk of suicide
- refuse to eat
- are severely agitated
- show vegetative symptoms
- express feelings of hopelessness, helplessness, or worthlessness
- have experienced delusions
- cannot tolerate or are unresponsive to medication

Unilateral nondominant hemisphere ECT is often preferred because it is capable of alleviating depression without impairing cognitive functioning. In fact, for some older adults, ECT can improve cognitive dysfunction associated with the depression. However, older adults with a recent history of a myocardial infarct, irregular heartbeat, or other heart conditions must be treated with caution because ECT can place a significant load on the cardiovascular system. Maintenance treatment with ECT may be necessary for older depressed persons (as often as once a month). In some cases, antidepressants are used after a course of ECT to prevent relapse. ECT remains a major form of treatment for severe depression, but not as commonly used as pharmacotherapy (Bosboom and Deijen, 2006; Rapaport, Mamdani and Herrman, 2006; Rudorfer, Henry, and Sackheim, 1997; van der Wurff, 2004).

Suicide among Older People

Older people are at greater risk of suicide than any other age group. It has been estimated that 17 to 25 percent of all *completed* suicides occur in persons aged 65 and older. In 2003, the national rate was 11.0 suicides per 100,000 population. The rate increased from 13.5 per 100,000 for persons 65 and older to 18 per 100,000 among those over age 85 (CDC, 2006a, 2006b). The highest suicide rates are among white males age 85 and older. The prevalence of suicide in this group, 51.6 per 100,000, is more than:

- twice the rate for white men age 65 to 74 (23.1 per 100,000)
- 14.5 times the rate for white women age 85 and older
- 4.5 times the rate for African American men age 85 and older

Note that these statistics reflect direct or clearly identifiable suicides. There are probably a significant number of indirect suicides that appear to be accidents or natural deaths (e.g., starvation or gas poisoning), and cases where family members and physicians do not list suicide as the cause of death; therefore these rates may underrepresent the actual incidence of suicides.

One explanation for the higher rates of suicide among older white males is that they generally experience the greatest incongruence between their ideal self-image (that of worker, decision maker, or holder of relatively high status in society) and the realities of advancing age. With age, the role of paid worker is generally lost; chronic illness may diminish one's

RISK FACTORS FOR SUICIDE IN OLDER ADULTS

- a serious physical illness with severe pain
- the sudden death of a loved one
- a major loss of independence or financial inadequacy
- statements that indicate frustration with life and a desire to end it
- a sudden decision to give away one's most important possessions
- a general loss of interest in one's social and physical environment
- isolation and a feeling of being cut off from others

sense of control, and an individual may feel a loss of status. Social isolation also appears to be a salient factor; suicide rates among older widowed men are more than five times greater than for married men, but no differences are found between married and widowed women. This is because older widowed Caucasian men are most likely to lack strong social support networks. In contrast, African American, Latino and Chinese men are less likely to commit suicide because of more extensive family support systems, spiritual beliefs, and the importance of religious institutions in their lives (Oquendo, 2001). In fact, suicide rates peak for African Americans in young adulthood, with a slight rise at ages 50 to 55, then decline significantly. Suicide risk is greatest among white males who are widowed, age 85 and older, with recurrent major depression, and with chronic pain, cardiopulmonary diseases, or cancer. However, contrary to popular belief, older suicide victims are no more likely than other older people to have been diagnosed with a terminal illness prior to the suicide (Blazer and Koenig, 1996; Joe, et al., 2006; Li, 1995; Yin, 2006). There are fewer nonfatal suicide attempts in older men compared to their younger counterparts. That is, the rate of completed suicides is far greater among older men— one for every eight attempts, compared with one completed suicide for every 100 to 200 attempts by the young. This difference may be due to the use of more lethal methods of suicide, such as shotguns. Firearms were used in 73 percent of suicides committed by older adults, compared with 54 percent of suicides committed by 15- to 24-year-olds (Anderson and Smith, 2003; CDC, 2006a).

Because attempts at suicide are more likely to end in death for older white men, family members and health care providers need to be sensitive to clues of an impending suicide. The National Institute of Mental Health (2006) estimates that 70 percent of older persons who commit suicide had seen a primary care physician in the preceding month, but their psychological disturbances had not been detected or were inadequately treated. In most cases, these older persons had not sought psychiatric care. For this reason, the Surgeon General in 1999 issued a "Call to Action to Prevent Suicide." This effort, aimed at mental health providers and the older population directly, focused on increasing awareness of depression, its symptoms, and potential outcomes. However, it is crucial for primary care physicians to recognize symptoms of depression in their older patients and know how to refer them to mental health professionals *before* the older person demonstrates suicidal intentions (Surgeon General, 1999b). Unfortunately, this rarely happens because the average visit to a primary care physician is only 17 minutes, providing little time for elders to express their concerns about depression (Heisel and Duberstein, 2005).

Watching for subtle cues is also important, since older people are less likely to make threats or to announce their intentions to commit suicide than are young people. Clearly, not all older people displaying such symptoms will attempt suicide, but recognizing changes in an older family member's or client's behavior and moods can alleviate a potential disaster.

Dementia

Normal aging does not result in significant declines in intelligence, memory, and learning ability, as described in Chapter 5. Mild impairments do not necessarily signal a major loss, but often represent a mild form of memory dysfunction known as **benign senescent forgetfulness.** Only in the case of the diseases known collectively as the dementias does cognitive function show marked deterioration. **Dementia** includes a variety of conditions that are caused by or associated with damage of brain tissue, resulting in impaired cognitive function and, in more advanced stages, impaired behavior and personality. Such changes in the brain result in progressive deterioration of an individual's ability to learn and recall items from the past. Previously, it was assumed that all

---

**CARE FOR DEMENTIA PATIENTS
WITH ACUTE ILLNESS**

In the late stages of many irreversible dementias such as Alzheimer's disease, the patient is often physically frail and unable to survive an acute condition such as pneumonia or a hip fracture. A recent study followed people age 70 or older who were hospitalized for one of these conditions, and *also* had a late-stage dementing illness. Six months later, mortality rates were much higher for elders with pneumonia and dementia than for those with no dementia (53 percent vs. 13 percent). Those with hip fractures and dementia also died at higher rates than elders without dementia (55 percent vs. 12 percent). Both patients with and without dementia received as many life-saving procedures. Only 7 percent of the former had written documents to forgo such treatment and only 24 percent had requested analgesics. These findings point to the need to establish guidelines for palliative treatment for an older person with dementia who is dying of an acute illness (Morrison and Siu, 2000).

---

these syndromes were associated with cerebral arteriosclerosis ("hardening of the arteries"). In fact, we now know that a number of these conditions occur independently of arteriosclerosis. Some features are unique to each type of dementia, but all dementias have the following characteristics:

- a change in an individual's ability to recall events in recent memory
- problems with comprehension, attention span, judgment
- disorientation to time, place, and person

The individual with dementia may have problems in understanding abstract thought or symbolic language (e.g., be unable to interpret a proverb), particularly in the later stages of the disease. Although not part of normal aging, the likelihood of experiencing dementia does increase with advancing age. Depending on the criteria used, estimates range from 2 to 7 million people over age 65 having

some type of dementia; almost 2 million have severe dementia, and up to 5 million are mildly to moderately impaired (Hendrie, 1997; Teri, McCurry, and Logsdon, 1997). Because of problems in differentially diagnosing dementia, and variations in the criteria used by available tests and classification systems, prevalence rates vary greatly. Nevertheless, there is general agreement among epidemiological studies that the incidence of dementias increases with age, especially between ages 75 and 90. For example, it is estimated that:

- 12 percent of the 75 to 79 age group have some dementia
- 54 percent of 85- to 89-year-olds have signs of dementia
- 84 percent of people over age 90 have some symptoms (Kukull et al., 2002)

However, as noted in Chapter 1, rates of dementia among "hardy" centenarians may actually be lower than among 85- to 90-year-olds because of genetic advantages experienced by those who live to age 100 and beyond.

The major types of dementias are shown below. Note the distinction between *reversible* and *irreversible* dementias.

REVERSIBLE	IRREVERSIBLE
Drugs	Alzheimer's
Alcohol	Vascular
Nutritional deficiencies	Lewy Body
Normal pressure hydrocephalus	Huntington's
	Pick's disease
Brain tumors	Creutzfeldt-Jacob
Hypothyroidism/ Hyperthyroidism	Kuru
	Korsakoff
Neurosyphilis	
Depression (pseudodementia)	

The first refers to cognitive decline that may be caused by drug toxicity, hormonal, or nutritional disorders, and other diseases that may be reversible. Sources of potentially reversible dementias include tumors in and trauma to the brain, toxins, metabolic disorders such as hypo- or hyperthyroidism, diabetes, hypo- or hypercalcemia, infections, vascular lesions, and hydrocephalus. Severe depression may produce confusion and memory problems in some older people. Some medications may also cause dementia-like symptoms. This problem is aggravated if the individual is taking multiple medications or is on a dosage that is higher than can be metabolized by the older kidney or liver. An individual who appears to be suffering from such reactions should be referred promptly for medical screening.

Irreversible dementias are those that have no discernible environmental cause and cannot yet be cured. Although there is considerable research on the causes and treatments for these conditions, they must be labeled irreversible at the present time. Some of these are more common than others; some have identifiable causes, while others do not. Pick's disease is one of the rarest; in this type, the frontal and temporal lobes of the brain atrophy. Of all the dementias, it is most likely to occur in younger persons (age of onset is usually 40–50), and to result in significant personality changes. Creutzfeldt-Jacob and Kuru diseases have been traced to a slow-acting virus that can strike at any age. In the former type of dementia, decline in cognitive abilities occurs quite rapidly, as seen in the epidemics of "mad cow disease" in the past 10 years that have been attributed to consuming tainted beef in Great Britain, Europe, and the United States. Kuru disease is quite rare. Huntington's disease is a genetically transmitted condition that usually appears in people in their 30s and 40s. It results in more neuromuscular changes than do the other dementias. Attention and judgment declines in the earlier stages, but memory remains intact until the later stages when dementia symptoms become more severe. Korsakoff syndrome is associated with long-term alcoholism and a deficiency of vitamin B1. This form of dementia results in severe loss of memory.

Vascular dementia is estimated to represent 20 to 50 percent of all irreversible dementias. This form of dementia was labeled "multi-infarct" in the past. In this type, blood vessels leading to the brain become occluded, with the result that several areas of the brain show infarcts, or small strokes. The primary risk factor for vascular dementia is the same as for strokes, that is, hypertension. Because of this, vascular dementia may be prevented by controlling hypertension. Nevertheless, once it occurs, this type of dementia is irreversible (Lis and Gaviria, 1997). Recent research suggests that the onset of vascular dementia may be predicted by abnormal walking patterns or gaits. In fact, elders with one of three types of abnormal gaits were 3.5 times more likely to develop vascular dementia (but no other type of dementia) in one study. Older people who walked with their legs swinging outward in a semicircle, took short steps with minimal lifting of their feet, or had an unsteady, swaying gait and no physical condition that would have caused this problem were eventually found to have vascular dementia. These movement patterns may reflect changes in the brain that trigger this condition (Verghese et al., 2002).

Delirium

Delirium is a reversible dementia that has a more rapid onset than other types of dementia. Signs of delirium are:

- abrupt changes in behavior
- fluctuations in behavior throughout the day
- worse at night and when first awake
- inability to focus attention on a task
- problems with short-term memory
- hallucinations
- speech that makes no sense or is irrational
- disturbance in sleep patterns

Delirium is usually caused by some external variables such as a reaction to an injury (especially head injury) or infection, malnutrition, reaction to alcohol or prescription medications, high fever, or even a fecal impaction or urinary problems. Up to 50 percent of older adults show symptoms of delirium after major surgery, possibly due to general anesthesia. A thorough medical assessment can help diagnose and reverse delirium and its symptoms by determining its causes (Logsdon and Teri, 2000; Qualls, 1999).

Alzheimer's Disease

Senile dementia of the Alzheimer's type (Alzheimer's disease or AD) is the most common irreversible dementia in late life, accounting for 45 to 55 percent of all dementias. Prevalence rates are difficult to obtain, but it is estimated that about 4.5 million Americans or 10 percent of all persons age 65 and over, and 29 percent of those age 85 and older have clinical symptoms of AD (Hebert et al., 2003).

With the increased survival of older adults beyond age 85, it is estimated that as many as 13 million Americans will be diagnosed with AD by 2050. This increased prevalence is projected for most regions of the world; for example, in China and India the number of elders with dementia is expected to double between 2005 and 2025, and to triple by 2050 (Alzheimer's Disease International, 2006). The dramatic rise in projected rates of AD underlies much of the research focus on the causes of and therapies for AD.

Although a distinction was made in the past between pre-senile (i.e., before age 65) and senile dementia, there is now agreement that these are the same disease. Researchers do, however, make

---

ALZHEIMER'S DISEASE VERSUS NORMAL CHANGES IN MEMORY

Many people in middle and old age become alarmed that they may have Alzheimer's disease at the first signs of forgetting. Here are some distinctions between *normal*, age-related changes in memory (as described in Chapter 5) and AD:

Normal Aging
- Forgetting to set the alarm clock
- Forgetting someone's name and remembering it later
- Forgetting where you left your keys and finding them after searching
- Having to retrace steps to remember a task
- Forgetting where you parked your car

Possible AD
- Forgetting *how* to set the alarm clock
- Forgetting a name and never remembering it, even when told
- Forgetting places where you might find your keys
- Forgetting how you came to be at a particular location

THE EXPERIENCE OF DEMENTIA

Thomas DeBaggio, a writer, describes what it feels like to experience Alzheimer's disease firsthand:

> I thought I was breaking into pieces. Shards of memory kept disappearing. When, after the tests, the doctor told me I had Alzheimer's disease, the statement exploded in my head. There was no cure, only the hope that my brain's eager course of self-destruction could be slowed for awhile. . . . Now writing is like walking through a dark room. Sometimes I have to get down on my knees and crawl. Words slice through my mind so fast that I cannot catch them. I will soon be stripped of language and memory. I am on the cusp of a new world, a place I will be unable to describe. It is the last hidden place, and marked with a headstone. (DeBaggio, 2002)

A daughter writes about her father's experiences with dementia:

> His memory is blank; words float by him in a soup. He can't button a shirt or negotiate a toilet. Yet when I look at him—at his body, his face—I see . . . him. Warm, enraged, rejecting, beseeching, profane, silly; much of his mind is gone, but his self is still there. . . . There may be no drug (yet) to cure Alzheimer's but relationships are always possible, as long as the person of sounder mind holds up his or her end. (Levine, 2004)

a distinction between the more common, late-onset form of AD and a rarer, early-onset form that appears in multiple generations of the same family, usually when the individual is in middle age (40s, even 30s). This is known as "familial AD." The rate of decline for those who are diagnosed with early-onset AD is faster and their lives often more severely affected than for the late-onset form, but it represents a very small proportion of all AD cases.

POTENTIAL CAUSES OF AND RISK FACTORS FOR ALZHEIMER'S DISEASE AND OTHER DEMENTIAS   Several hypotheses are proposed to explain the causes of Alzheimer's disease. Case control studies that focused on the incidence or development of AD have not found support for environmental hypotheses, such as a previous head injury, thyroid disease, exposure to therapeutic radiation, anesthesia, or the accumulation of metals such as aluminum in the brain (Kokmen et al.,

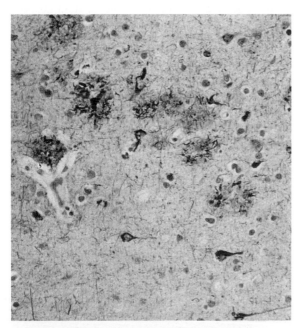

The dark patches in this brain section are neuritic plaques with a core of amyloid protein, characteristic of Alzheimer's disease.

1996). Even though the abnormal tangles (a web of dead brain cells) found in the neurons of the brains of Alzheimer's victims contain more aluminum than is found in brains of normal controls, there is no evidence that such an accumulation *causes* AD.

Although it is difficult to assess with great accuracy an older person's childhood development, two verifiable early-life characteristics may increase one's risk of AD. In a community-based case-control study comparing 393 people diagnosed with AD and 377 controls, researchers examined the effects of mother's age at patient's birth, birth order, number of siblings, and area of residence before age 18. They found only the last two variables associated with AD risk. The more children in one's family, the greater one's AD risk. Similarly, patients were half as likely as controls without dementia to have grown up in the suburbs (Moceri et al., 2000). These results suggest that receiving more attention as a child and living in a more secluded environment may serve as a protective factor against AD in old age.

In another case-control study, information was obtained about activity patterns during ages 20 to 60 among 193 older persons with AD and 358 healthy controls who were currently in their 60s and 70s. These activities included nonoccupational pastimes that could be classified as intellectual, physical or passive. Elders with no signs of dementia had participated in more intellectual and physical recreational activities during their middle years than did those in the control group. The greatest effect was for intellectual pastimes such as learning a new language, taking challenging courses, or learning a new activity; the more such activities an individual participated in, the lower the probability of AD. This was true regardless of educational level, gender, and current age. Although the findings must be interpreted with some caution, the dramatic differences observed suggest that participation in intellectual activities may have a protective effect against AD (Friedland et al., 2000).

Another research group tracked the physical activity levels of 1740 older adults for 6 years who had no signs of dementia at the start of the study. During this period, almost 10 percent began to show symptoms of dementia. The incidence rate of dementia for people who exercised three or more times per week (including walking, swimming, weight training, and stretching) was 13.0 per 1000 person-years, compared with 19.7 per 1000 person-years among elders who developed dementia. The researchers suggest that regular exercise may delay or prevent dementia by stimulating blood flow to the brain (Larson et al., 2006). The findings are consistent with earlier studies that found regular exercise can decrease the risk for AD (50 percent) and any dementia (36 percent), and more varied physical activities further reduces the risk (Laurin et al., 2001; Podewils et al., 2005). This same longitudinal study also found that participants with poor physical functioning (poor standing balance, slower walking speed, weak handgrip) were three times more likely to develop dementia, including Alzheimer's disease, than elders with good physical functioning. Regular physical activity can improve these functions (Larson et al., 2006).

The Nun Study offers insights into the association between education, lifestyle, and cognitive and physical aging without the bias of socioeconomic status, diet, and health care that is a problem with many other studies of aging among the general population. The 678 members of the School Sisters of Notre Dame who participated in this longitudinal study, including the analysis of their brains at autopsy, shared an adulthood of identical lifestyles. Therefore the differences seen among the nuns are attributable primarily to their educational levels and intellectual and physical activities throughout their lives. By analyzing the autobiographies these nuns had written at age 22, researchers found an association between linguistic skills in youth and the risk of dementia 50 to 70 years later. Greater atrophy and more plaques and tangles were found in the brains of women whose writings during their youth had fewer complex ideas, a simpler vocabulary, and lower "idea density" (Riley et al., 2005; Snowdon, Greiner, and Markesbery, 2000). The emotional content of these early autobiographies was also examined for their positive, negative, or neutral tone. By adjusting statistically for age and education, the researchers found a significant link between positive emotions and mortality; those in the highest quartile of positive emotional content in their early writings decreased their risk of death in old age by a factor of 2.5 compared with nuns whose writings lacked much positive expression. This may be because positive emotions triggered a lifetime of positive behaviors in the survivors. In addition, early samples of written language appear to be better than oral samples at distinguishing between high and low functioning (Danner, Snowdon, and Friesen, 2001; Mitzner and Kemper, 2003). The Nun Study also demonstrated that clinical manifestations of dementia may not always parallel the neuropathological changes experienced in these conditions. That is, many of the nuns at autopsy had the hallmarks of advanced dementia in their brain samples (e.g., neurofibrillary tangles in the neocortex), but they did not demonstrate any clinical symptoms of dementia before their death (e.g., disorientation to time, place, person) (Snowdon, 2001, 2003).

Physical health may also be related to AD. A recent study points to obesity as a risk factor for AD in women but not in men. Women who were overweight at age 70, 75, and 79 were more likely to develop dementia by age 88. The researchers suggest that being overweight may raise blood pressure and restrict blood flow to the brain, thereby indirectly increasing women's risk for AD, although a parallel effect was not observed in men (Gustafson et al., 2004). Experiencing a stroke may also increase an elder's risk for AD and having a stroke during the course of AD can accelerate the decline of cognitive function in AD patients (DeCarli, 2006). There is some evidence that a severe head injury during one's younger years (resulting in unconsciousness lasting more than 24 hours) can increase the risk of AD in old age. A study of more than 2000 veterans of World War II with documented head injuries revealed four times greater likelihood of AD in severe head injury victims, and twice the risk in victims of a moderate head injury (Plassman et al., 2000).

Lack of estrogen is another potential risk factor that has drawn research interest. As estrogen secretion declines with aging, proteins associated with neuronal growth decrease, resulting in the synaptic impairments typical of AD. However, estrogen replacement therapy (ERT) does not appear to be an effective treatment or preventive mechanism against AD. The Women's Health Initiative Memory Study (ancillary to the WHI Study described in Chapter 4) found that, among more than 4500 women who were placed on a combination of estrogen and progestin, or placebo for 5 years, there was no difference in the rates of developing mild cognitive impairment. In fact, twice as many women using the combination hormone developed dementia—40 versus 21—in this large sample (Shumaker et al., 2003).

The brains of AD patients experience a reduction in the number of cholinergic nerve cells (up to 80 percent loss in some key areas). These brain cells are important for learning and memory because they release an important chemical "messenger," *acetylcholine,* that transfers information from one cell to another (i.e., neurotransmitters). Their loss reduces the acetylcholine available for this important function. The noradrenergic system is another chemical messenger system that becomes impaired with AD, further complicating our understanding of why and how these neurochemical systems appear to break down in this disease.

Still another neurochemical change observed in Alzheimer brains is the accumulation of *amyloid,* a protein. It appears that there may be a genetic defect in one of the normal proteins located in brain regions responsible for memory, emotions, and thinking. Amyloid is actually a group of proteins found in the neurofibrillary tangles that characterize an Alzheimer's brain.

The precursor protein to amyloid, *beta-amyloid,* is coded by a gene located in chromosome 21, which is also the chromosome responsible for Down syndrome. This may explain why AD appears with greater frequency in families with a member who has Down syndrome. Deposits of amyloid or its precursor beta-amyloid have been found in the brains of Down patients as young as age 8, and in those who die later with AD. Beta-amyloid may be responsible for the death of brain cells in these patients. In fact, many Down patients have the characteristic brain changes of AD, but not the clinical symptoms. As with other changes observed in the brains of AD patients, it is not yet clear whether these beta-amyloid deposits are the *cause* of AD or secondary to other structural or biochemical changes (Mrak and Griffin, 2004).

Genes on at least four different chromosomes may be involved in the development of AD. In addition to mutations of the gene encoding amyloid precursor protein on chromosome 21, presenilin 1 on chromosome 14, presenilin 2 on chromosome 1, and the apolipoprotein E gene on chromosome 19 have been implicated in this disease. While the mutations on chromosomes 1, 14, and 21 are associated with familial or early-onset AD, the more common late-onset form of AD appears to be linked to a genetic mutation on chromosome 19. Subsequent researchers have focused on a protein called *apolipoprotein* or *APOE* on this chromosome. APOE is responsible for transporting cholesterol in the blood, and beta-amyloid in the brain. There are three genes associated with APOE: E2, E3, E4. The risk for Alzheimer's disease is associated with the E4 gene; people who inherit this gene from one parent have three times the risk of developing AD, and those who inherit one from each parent have eight times the risk (Olichney, 1997).

Characteristics of Alzheimer's Disease

As illustrated by Mr. Adams in the introduction to Part Three AD is characterized by deficits in attention, learning, memory, language skills and, in some instances, problems in judgment, abstraction, and orientation. These changes in cognitive function appear to be related to structural changes in the brain. They include:

- a premature loss of nerve cells in some areas of the brain
- a loss of synapses
- deterioration of the free radical metabolism process described in Chapter 3
- impaired neurotransmitter function such as the cholinergic system, resulting in plaques and tangles throughout these areas

The *hippocampus* is a region in the limbic system deep inside the brain that is involved in learning new information and retrieving old information (see Chapter 5). It is one of the first regions where plaques and tangles occur, so it is not surprising that patients in the earlier stages of the disease often have difficulties with verbal memory, attention span, and orientation to the environment, as well as increased anxiety, restlessness, and unpredictable changes in mood. Researchers examined the volume of the hippocampus and severity of neurofibrillary tangles at autopsy of 56 women in the Nun Study. Those with the greatest hippocampal atrophy and the most tangles had performed worse on a test of delayed verbal recall one year before death (Mortimer et al., 2004). Family members may complain about personality changes such as the older person becoming more aggressive or, in some cases, more passive than in the past. Depression may set in as the individual realizes that he or she is experiencing these problems. In the more advanced stages of the disease, as it spreads to the *neocortex*, which controls higher-level brain functions, and links new stimuli with information stored in the brain, the elder may experience problems recalling appropriate words and labels, perseveration (i.e., continually repeating the same phrase and thoughts), apathy, and problems with comprehension. Alzheimer's victims at this stage may not recognize their partners, children, and long-time friends. However,

some patients in the intermediate stages of AD may describe quite articulately and vividly events that took place many years ago. In the advanced phases, as the neurons in the motor cortex die, the patient may need assistance with bodily functions such as eating and toileting. At autopsy, there is a generalized deterioration of cortical tissue, which appears to be tangled and covered with plaque. These plaques and tangles appear first in a region near the base of the skull (entorhinal cortex), and move higher and deeper to the hippocampus and eventually to the neocortex as the disease advances (Snowdon, 2001).

ARE THERE STAGES OF ALZHEIMER'S DISEASE? There have been some attempts to determine if AD proceeds through a series of stages, such that symptoms become more prevalent and severe over

---

GLOBAL DETERIORATION SCALE

Stage 1: No cognitive or functional decrements

Stage 2: Complaints of very mild forgetfulness and some work difficulties

Stage 3: Mild cognitive impairment on cognitive battery; concentration problems; some difficulty at work and in traveling alone

Stage 4: Late confusional stage; increased problems in planning, handling finances; increased denial of symptoms; withdrawal

Stage 5: Poor recall of recent events; may need to be reminded about proper clothing and bathing

Stage 6: More advanced memory orientation problems; needs assistance with activities of daily living; more personality changes

Stage 7: Late dementia with loss of verbal abilities; incontinent; loss of ability to walk; may become comatose

SOURCE: Reisberg, B., Ferris, S.H., De-Leon, M.J., and Crook, T., The Global Deterioration Scale for assessment of primary degenerative dementia. *American Jorunal of Psychiatry, 139,* pp. 1136–1139, 1982. Copyright 1982, the American Psychiatric Association. Reprinted by permission.

time. This is a difficult task because the course of AD varies so widely. Some patients may experience a rapid decline in memory, while their orientation to time, place, and people may remain relatively intact. Other patients may experience mood and personality changes early, whereas still others maintain their pre-morbid personality for many years after the symptoms first appear.

A broad distinction is often made among early, middle, and advanced stages of AD. These categories are based on the patient's levels of decline in memory, orientation, and activities of daily living. Assessment tools such as the Mini-Mental Status Exam (MMSE) and the Dementia Rating Scale (DRS) can help in categorizing levels of decline (Folstein, Folstein, and McHugh, 1975; Mattis, 1976). These give clues to the patients' levels of deterioration on the basis of their test scores. Perhaps the most extensive research to determine the stages of AD has been conducted by Reisberg et al. (1982), who developed a Global Deterioration Scale that delineates 7 stages of the disease, as shown in the box on page 242.

Because of attention on Alzheimer's disease by the media and by researchers, there is some tendency to overestimate its occurrence and to assume that it is the cause of all dementias. In many ways, it has replaced vascular dementia as a label given without a thorough diagnosis. The most confirmatory diagnosis of Alzheimer's disease today can still be made only at autopsy, when the areas and nature of damaged brain tissue can be identified. However, psychological measures of cognitive functioning such as the MMSE and DRS, and a thorough physical exam can provide clues to its existence in the earlier stages. Or they may indicate that the observed changes in behavior and/or personality are due to a reversible condition. Early diagnosis can be made with some certainty after an extensive patient workup. In fact, it is primarily through a process of elimination of other conditions that some dementias such as AD may be diagnosed. In such diagnoses, it is particularly important to rule out depression, prolonged grief, drug toxicity, and nutritional

DIAGNOSING ALZHEIMER'S DISEASE

- a medical and nutritional history
- laboratory tests of blood, urine, and stool
- tests for thyroid function
- a thorough physical and psychological examination
- in some cases, a CT (computerized tomography) scan, a PET (positron emission tomography) scan, or MRI (magnetic resonance imaging) in order to detect any tumors, strokes, blood clots, or hydrocephalus, and to test the response of specific areas of the brain

deficiencies because, as stated earlier, these conditions may be reversed. Recent findings using protein biomarkers in cerebrospinal fluid show that these new techniques may be useful in diagnosing and distinguishing between Alzheimer's, Parkinson's, and Lewy body dementia (Zhang, Goodlett, and Montine, 2005).

THERAPY FOR PATIENTS WITH ALZHEIMER'S DISEASE Unfortunately, no completely successful treatment for AD is yet available. If the evidence for high levels of certain abnormal proteins in Alzheimer brains proves correct, future treatment might involve the use of drugs that interrupt the production of those proteins and their precursors so they cannot accumulate in brain tissue. Some researchers have focused on nerve growth factor, a naturally occurring protein that replenishes and maintains the health of nerve cells. Animal studies show remarkable success in repairing damaged brain cells.

Currently, only a few drugs are approved for treating AD. Other medications in the testing phase include some drugs that restore the activity of neurotransmitters in the brain and some that even replace lost neurochemicals. In the last several years, one drug has been found to slow the decline of memory loss by about 5 percent in the early to moderate stages of AD. This medication, donepezil (marketed as Aricept), is a cholinesterase inhibitor and slows the loss of acetylcholine in the brains of AD patients. More recently, two other cholinesterase inhibitors, rivastigmine (marketed as Exelon) and galantamine (Razadyne), were approved for use in AD. These drugs also prevent the breakdown of acetylcholine and slow the decline in cognitive ability, ADLs, and normal behavior while other studies have found modest improvements for up to 36 months (Feldman, 2002; Raskind et al., 2004; Seltzer, 2006). Another drug used to manage symptoms of AD is memantine (Namenda). This drug is designed to treat patients in the moderate to severe stages of AD. It works by lowering levels of the neurotransmitter glutamate, which can damage neurons at high levels (Reisberg et al., 2003; Tariot et al., 2004). However, none of these drugs reverses the destruction of brain tissue by plaques and tangles. They must be used with caution, or avoided altogether, in patients with liver disease, peptic ulcers, severe COPD, and bradycardia.

Some researchers have begun to explore the possibility that AD may be related to inflammation of brain tissue. This has led to the hypothesis that nonsteroidal antiinflammatory drugs (NSAIDs), such as ibuprofen, can prevent or delay the onset of AD. Although many older people currently use low doses of NSAIDs to prevent heart attacks, few controlled clinical trials have tested whether NSAIDs have similar benefits for AD. A review of studies that followed NSAID users found that regular use for two or more years reduces the risk of AD by 40 to 50 percent (Szekely et al., 2004). Animal studies demonstrate that a daily dose of ibuprofen reduced inflammation in the brain, and resulted in about half the number of plaques and half the amyloid deposits as in the mice that were not given NSAIDs (Lim et al., 2000). The drug may act as a preventive by improving the production of chemicals that control amyloid build-up or by clearing amyloid more efficiently. Another promising pharmacotherapy for AD may be a combination of vitamin E (described in Chapter 3 as an antioxidant that appears to prevent or reduce the symptoms of other chronic diseases)

HEALTH CARE COSTS OF DEMENTIA

Health care costs for patients with AD and other dementias are much higher than for adults in the same age range without dementia. Average annual costs for AD patients were almost $8000 in 2004, and for those with vascular dementia almost $14,000 (Hill et al., 2005). This is partly due to "co-morbidity," or the presence of other medical problems along with dementia. One study found that 35 percent of AD patients also had cardiovascular disease, compared with 10 percent of a control group of elders without AD; 25 percent had congestive heart failure, compared with 15 percent of controls. This results in greater expenditures for visits to physicians' offices, for hospital, and home health care, but the greatest difference between AD patients and controls is for skilled nursing care at three times the rate for controls (Fillit et al., 2002). By preventing AD and other dementias, researchers can help to improve the quality of life for older adults and their families, while reducing these skyrocketing health and long-term care costs.

and selegiline hydrochloride (marketed as Eldepryl and generally prescribed for Parkinson's disease). In one clinical trial, patients in the moderate stage of AD who were given this combination did not decline as rapidly as those given a placebo (Sano et al., 1997). Vitamin E may also be effective in reducing the risk of AD. In one study that examined almost 5000 older adults for five years, the incidence of AD was lower among elders who used vitamin E supplements in combination with vitamin C than among those who did not use any vitamin supplements or only one of these vitamins alone (Zandi et al., 2004). However, it is important to review AD patients' medications with their physicians to confirm that vitamin E will not interact with their other medications, in particular with blood thinners.

Ginkgo biloba is an extract from the dried leaves of the maidenhair tree. Some families report that regular use of this product improves the memory of an AD patient in the early to intermediate stages. However, a study in the Netherlands casts some doubt on the benefits of this treatment. Researchers studied 214 nursing home residents with mild to moderate AD or vascular dementia. Each person was given a usual dose of ginkgo biloba (84 elders) or an elevated dose (82 elders), and compared with a group (48 elders) that used a placebo over 24 weeks. No effects were observed on tests of memory or depression, but those using ginkgo performed slightly better on self-reported ADLs (van Dongen et al., 2000).

Researchers have made dramatic strides toward understanding the neurochemical basis of this disease and are rapidly moving toward its treatment. There is even some promise of a vaccine that can help the immune system produce antibodies against amyloid proteins and clear amyloid deposits from the brain. Successful research with mice gives scientists hope that such a vaccine may be effective with humans (Schenk et al., 1999).

Medications are often prescribed to manage behavioral problems in some AD patients, including agitation, hallucinations, physical aggressiveness, and wandering. In particular, risperidone, a drug used to treat psychotic symptoms in schizophrenic patients, appears to calm aggressive, delusional behaviors in a significant segment of this population (Goldberg and Goldberg, 1997). Because of their potential side effects, however, it is important to weigh the harm caused by these patient behaviors against the possible side effects of medications. Furthermore, the prescribing physician must regularly reevaluate the need to continue or reduce the dosage of any drugs used for behavior management, perhaps as frequently as every 3 to 4 months.

Behavioral Treatment and Environmental Interventions

As noted earlier, new medications that are being approved by the FDA show some promise of slowing the rate of decline with AD. To date, however, neither these medications nor psy-

---

CARING FOR AD PATIENTS AT EACH STAGE OF THE DISEASE

Depending on the stage of the disease, caregivers of elders with AD can help them in different ways. Using the Global Deterioration Scale described in the box on page 242, families can try the following ways of helping the patient:

Stages 1–3 (Mild dementia)
- Set up an orientation area in the home where the patient's critical items (e.g., wallet, keys, glasses) can always be found.
- Watch for signs of driving problems.
- Encourage physical and social activities.

Stages 4–5 (Moderate dementia)
- Make changes in home environment to assure safety and autonomy, but maintain familiarity (e.g., improved, constant light levels).
- Put labels on important doors (e.g., patient's bedroom, bathroom) and drawers.
- Keep in visible areas photos of family and close friends taken with patient, names clearly written on photos.

Stages 6–7 (Advanced dementia)
- Visit alternative long-term care facilities that fit P–E needs of the particular patient.
- Simplify daily routines but still encourage some physical activity (e.g., walks in fenced-in yard).
- Try alternative means of communication (e.g., touch, sharing old family photos).

---

chotherapy can restore the cognitive functions lost with most irreversible forms of dementia. Nevertheless, many older persons can benefit from behavioral and exercise therapies, and from some environmental modifications. For example, exercise training combined with behavioral management training for family caregivers can help both the AD patient and their caregivers. One study tested the effects of a 3-month exercise program for AD patients, together with teaching behavioral management to their caregivers. Compared with AD patients who received only routine medical care, those in the exercise program had significantly fewer days of restricted activity, lower scores on a measure of depression, and less likelihood of nursing home placement up to two years later (Teri et al., 2003).

Individual competence can be enhanced somewhat and the social and home environments simplified considerably in an effort to maintain P–E congruence and maintain some independent functioning. Simple changes, such as removing sources of glare and making lighting levels consistent throughout the house, can prevent confusion and "sundowning," a condition that affects some AD patients as natural light levels change and they become more fatigued later in the day. It is important to maintain a regular schedule, to keep the patient moderately active, and to prevent withdrawal from daily interactions. Written schedules of activities, simplified routes from room to room, and written directions for cooking, bathing, and taking medications can aid a person in finding his or her way around and prevent the frustration of getting lost or not recognizing once-familiar people and places. AD patients can be encouraged to perform more ADLs if their grooming supplies (e.g., toothbrush, toothpaste, comb) are kept visible and in a familiar sequence of use. These items can also help AD patients recognize their own bathroom or bedroom as the disease progresses. A useful device for some patients in the intermediate stages of Alzheimer's is a "memory box" that contains photos from the individual's past on the outside and mementoes on the inside, placed on his or her door to identify the bedroom. Physical activity during the day can also help the patient sleep better through the night. Productive activities such as setting the table, folding laundry, and raking leaves in a secure backyard can also help patients maintain a sense of continuity with their past lives and use their excess energy. However, the frequency and intensity of such activities should not overwhelm or confuse the patient.

Wandering is another problem that can be prevented with some environmental changes.

These can be restrictive, such as locking all exterior doors, or more protective, such as providing a safe backyard or garden area for the AD patient to explore, within easy sight of the home's windows and doors to orient the patient. ID bracelets with silent or audible alarms that can help locate the AD patient are becoming more common for use in the home, given their demonstrated benefits in nursing homes. One company has even developed a model where family or close friends can record a message on a tape attached to the bracelet to guide the wandering person back home. Some local chapters of the Alzheimer's Association offer the "safe return" program, which provides ID bracelets for AD patients, maintains records, and assists emergency teams in locating, identifying, and returning home the AD patient who becomes lost in the community. Agitation may also accompany AD; elders may display irritable behavior, pacing, restlessness, and general expressions of distress. These behaviors are not a normal outcome of AD but are triggered by environmental changes, fear, fatigue, loss of control, or medical conditions such as infections or adverse reactions to medications. The patient displaying signs of agitation should first be evaluated and treated for possible underlying medical conditions. If no systemic conditions are found, behavioral and environmental interventions can be used, such as

NEW WAYS OF HELPING AD PATIENTS

Until a few years ago, reality orientation was a popular therapeutic method that was used in nursing homes and by many families caring for AD patients. The emphasis was on reorienting confused older adults to the present and correcting them when they referred to a dead spouse as being alive now, or talking about getting to work despite being retired for over 20 years. However, these techniques can frustrate and agitate the patient. Most experts today agree that it is better to acknowledge the patient's memories of the past and not argue with them about the accuracy of these memories.

adapting the home environment to the older person's needs and providing stability in ADLs.

Ultimately, the goal of managing these dementias is to slow the rate of deterioration and to prevent nursing home placement for as long as possible. For the AD patient who does enter a nursing home, it is important to find a facility that can maximize the individual's remaining abilities as the disease progresses (i.e., environments that can maintain the patient's P–E congruence). During the 1990s, the number of special care units (SCUs) in nursing homes grew. These units are generally designed for residents with advanced dementia, especially AD, and staffed by nurses and therapists with special training in this field. Many provide a higher staff-to-resident ratio, a safe environment where patients can move about without getting lost, and special services aimed at maintaining the patients' remaining cognitive capacities. They are less likely to use chemical and physical restraints with disruptive residents. However, because there are no national licensing regulations for SCUs, the nature of services and quality of care provided vary widely. That is, the designation of a nursing home unit as a SCU does not necessarily imply richer or more tailored services than non-SCU units that also house AD and other dementia patients (Day, Carreon, and Stump, 2000).

Newer options include assisted living facilities, adult family homes, and adult day care (described in Chapter 11). However, like SCUs, families must determine if these alternative housing options can provide a safe and supportive environment for AD patients, especially as the disease progresses.

CAREGIVER NEEDS   One of the most important considerations with Alzheimer's disease and other dementias is to provide social and emotional support to the family as well as the patient. It is estimated that 60 to 80 percent of all people with AD remain in the community, cared for by family. In fact, about 19 million family caregivers

provide basic instrumental ADLs for their relatives with AD. It has been estimated that these informal caregivers provide as much as $100 billion in care. (Bloom, de Pouvourville, and Straus, 2003; Czaja, 2000). The typical caregiver of an AD patient is a 46-year-old woman, employed full-time, and caring for a 77-year-old mother. On average they provide care for 4.5 years. Chapter 10 describes the challenges faced by these caregivers as they balance the role of caregiver to their loved ones with the need to maintain their jobs, family, and personal life.

Parkinson's Disease

Parkinson's is a neurodegenerative disorder that begins as a loss of muscle control, with tremors in the feet and hands, gradually progressing to slow and limited movements. Speech can become impaired, muscles become rigid, and the person moves more slowly and with a shuffling gait. In its later stages, Parkinson's can manifest dementia-like symptoms. Today about one million Americans have this condition. It usually strikes people over age 60, although some people—such as the actor Michael J. Fox—are first diagnosed in their 30s.

Parkinson's differs from AD in many ways. First, the degeneration and loss of cells in the brain occurs mostly in the *substantia nigra,* located in the center of the brain. This is the region where dopamine is produced, the brain chemical responsible for initiating voluntary movement. This is why Levodopa (L-dopa) is the drug of choice for most people with Parkinson's, as a way of replacing dopamine. However, in some people L-dopa can cause such side effects as hallucinations, agitation, and uncontrollable movement. Newer drugs known as dopamine agonists have been developed as an alternative for such patients. One of the most exciting research developments in this area is the possibility of implanting stem cells (described in Chapter 3) into the brain of Parkinson's patients. These cells appear to revitalize damaged regions and resume production of dopamine in the substantia nigra. Another promising development is new surgical methods in the brain to stop tremors and involuntary movement. Behavioral techniques such as meditation, biofeedback, and dietary modification are also recommended. The Internet is increasing the accessibility of information about Parkinson's disease for both family caregivers and professionals. For example, the Parkinson's Association provides e-tutorials on characteristics and stages, treatment basics, mobility and safety, digestion and bladder problems, communication and sleep, and mood and thinking problems. Parkinson's is often cited as a disease that could benefit from stem cell research, and the Parkinson's Association has actively lobbied for the harvesting of stem cells.

Alcoholism

For most older people, alcohol use is associated with socializing and occurs in moderation (i.e., less than once a week, and no more than 2 drinks each time). However, those who consume 4 or more drinks per occasion and do so frequently and routinely are more likely to use alcohol as a way to cope with stressful life events and to relax. Obtaining accurate statistics on the prevalence of alcoholism in older adults is difficult, because of the stigma associated with this condition among older cohorts. Estimates vary from 1 to 5 percent of all older people living in the community. In general, alcohol consumption declines sharply after age 65, from a peak of 2.9 drinks per day among men aged 26 to 29 to 1.02 among those 65 and older. Similarly, older women report consuming 0.5 drinks per day, compared with 1.5 among women 26 to 29 (Chan et al., 2006). Older adults also have lower rates of alcohol abuse than any other age group, even when compared with middle-aged adults; however, in one study, 3.2 percent of older adults reported heavy alcohol use (DHHS, 2005; Hasin and Grant, 2005). A national survey revealed that 80 percent of people over age 65 reported at least

one alcoholic drink once a month or more frequently. Of this group, 10 percent reported consuming 5 drinks in one sitting, at least once a month. Another 5 percent had that many every time they drank (Reid et al., 1999). Alcoholism in older adults is accompanied by depression in 30 percent of cases, and by dementia in 20 percent, although the direction of causality is not always clear (Conway et al., 2006). Those at greatest risk are widowers and well-educated white men who have never married. Older men are four times more likely to have alcohol problems than are older women. Women at greatest risk of alcohol abuse are those who are smokers, not married, not religious, and with little social support. Prevalence rates are higher for African American elders than for Caucasians. The lowest rates for alcohol abuse are found in older Latina women (Hasin and Grant, 2004; Holroyd et al., 1997). Researchers from the Substance Abuse and Mental Health Services Administration (SAMHSA, 2001) estimate a 50 percent increase in the number of older adults with substance abuse problems (both alcohol and drugs) and a 70 percent increase in the rate of treatment need among older adults between 2001 and 2020.

It is important to distinguish lifelong abusers of alcohol from those who began drinking later in life. Alcoholics are less likely to be found among the ranks of persons over age 60 because of higher alcohol-related death rates at a young age. Those who continue to drink in old age tend to decrease their consumption. Surveys of alcoholism rates among older persons have revealed that approximately two-thirds began to drink heavily before age 40 (Shibusawa, 2006). Some older persons who are diagnosed as alcoholics have had this problem since middle age, but increasing age may exacerbate the condition for two reasons:

- The central nervous system (CNS), liver, and kidneys become less tolerant of alcohol with age because of the physiological changes described in Chapter 3 (e.g., loss of muscle tissue, reduction in body mass, and reduced efficiency of liver and kidney functions). For this reason, a smaller dose of alcohol can be more deleterious in the later years. In fact, current thinking is that people age 60 and older who drink should consume about half the amount acceptable for younger persons; that is, about one 4-oz glass of alcoholic beverage per day for men and somewhat less for women.

- An individual who has been drinking heavily for many years has already produced irreversible damage to the CNS, liver, and kidneys, creating more problems than those due to normal aging alone.

Perhaps because of the damage to their CNS, men who began drinking heavily before age 40 are more likely to experience depression, restlessness, sleeplessness, and tension than those who started later. It is difficult to determine the incidence of alcoholism among older persons who have no previous history of this disease. Physiological evidence is lacking, and drinking is often hidden from friends, relatives, and physicians. The older person may justify overconsumption of alcohol on the grounds that it relieves sadness and isolation. Even when family members are aware of the situation, they may rationalize that alcohol is one of the older person's few remaining pleasures. Denial is a common problem among many alcoholics, young or old; some older people may feel that they should be able to cope with their alcoholism on their own and not have to rely on health professionals or even on support groups such as Alcoholics Anonymous.

Physicians may overlook the possibility that alcohol is creating a health problem because the adverse effects of alcohol resemble some physical diseases or psychiatric and cognitive disorders that are associated with old age. For example, older alcoholics may complain of confusion, disorientation, irritability, insomnia or restless sleep patterns, heart palpitations, weight loss, depression, or a dry cough. Beliefs held by health

care providers that alcoholism does not occur in older people may also prevent its detection. Because of the problems caused by heavy alcohol use in old age, primary care physicians must screen their older patients by asking questions about the quantity, frequency, and context of drinking. This can help in the diagnosis and referral of older alcoholics to treatment programs, which currently are underutilized by older adults. This can also reduce the emotional, physical, and cognitive deterioration caused by alcoholism in older people and the subsequent hospitalizations and use of emergency medical services for conditions that are secondary to heavy alcohol consumption (Shibusawa, 2006).

Treatment for older alcoholics has not been differentiated from that for younger alcoholics. However, it is probably more important to focus on older alcoholics' medical conditions because of physical declines that make them more vulnerable to the secondary effects of alcohol. As with younger alcoholics, counseling and occupational and recreational therapy are important for treating older people experiencing alcoholism. Recovery rates for older alcoholics are as high as for younger alcoholics, especially if the problem began in late life.

Drug Abuse

As noted in Chapter 4, older persons use a disproportionately large number of prescription and over-the-counter (OTC) drugs, representing approximately 36 percent of outpatient prescription drug expenditures (Sambamoorthi, Shea, and Crystal, 2003). In particular, older people are more likely than the young to use tranquilizers, sedatives, and hypnotics, all of which have potentially dangerous side effects. They also are at risk of abusing aspirin compounds, laxatives, and sleeping pills, often because of misinformation about the adverse effects of too high a dosage or too many pills. It is not unusual to hear older patients state that they took twice or three times as much aspirin as they were

MEDICATION MANAGEMENT CAN THREATEN ELDERS' INDEPENDENCE

Their inability to manage their medications can be a threat to older people's independence. Families often cannot be present at every medication administration, and neighbors may help only intermittently. Even assisted living facilities cannot provide the daily help with medications that is needed, unless the older adult pays an additional fee. Some elders use plastic pillboxes with the days of the week printed on each section, or egg cartons or other small cups that the family has labeled with instructions. However, these devices cannot help an older person remember the time of day he or she must take the medication, and are not effective at all for someone with dementia.

prescribed because they did not feel that their pain was being alleviated with the lower dose. Yet, changes in body composition and renal and liver functions that occur with age, combined with the use of multiple medications, make older persons more likely to experience adverse drug reactions. Noncompliance with therapeutic drug regimens is often unintentional; older patients may take too much or too little of a drug because of nonspecific or complicated instructions by the physician, and they may use OTC drugs without reading warning labels about side effects and interactions with other drugs they are using. Intentional noncompliance generally takes the form of older patients' deciding that they no longer need the medication or that it is not working for them. Such noncompliance is found to be a factor in hospital admissions among the older population.

Both health care providers and older people themselves are more aware of the effects of "polypharmacy" today. Older persons do not abuse drugs to the extent that younger populations do, nor are they as likely to use illicit drugs such as heroin, cocaine, and marijuana. They also do not use hallucinogens, amphetamines, or mood-enhancing inhalants in noticeable numbers.

However, it is expected that the rate of substance abuse will increase by 50 percent between 2001 and 2020, with the aging of the baby boom generation (SAMHSA, 2001).

Paranoid Disorders and Schizophrenia

Paranoia, defined as an irrational suspiciousness of other people, takes several forms. It may result from:

- social isolation
- a sense of powerlessness
- progressive sensory decline
- problems with the normal "checks and balances" of daily life

Still other changes in the aging individual, such as memory loss, may result in paranoid reactions. Some suspicious attitudes of older persons, however, represent accurate readings of their experiences. For example, an older person's children may in fact be trying to institutionalize him or her in order to take over an estate; a nurse's aide may really be stealing from an older patient; and neighborhood children may be making fun of the older adult. It is therefore important to distinguish actual threats to the individual from unfounded suspicions. To the extent that the individual has some control over his or her environment, the older person's perception of a threatening situation is reduced. The diagnosis of paranoid disorders in older people is similar to that in younger patients; the symptoms should have a duration of at least one week, with no signs of schizophrenia, no prominent hallucinations, and no association with signs of dementia (APA, 2000).

As with depression, counseling can be useful for paranoid older persons. In particular, cognitive behavioral approaches, in which an individual focuses on changing negative, self-defeating beliefs or misconceptions, may be useful in treating paranoid older adults who often attribute causality to external factors (e.g., the belief that someone took their pocketbook, that they themselves did not misplace it). Therapy with paranoid older persons may be effective in redirecting beliefs about causality to the individuals themselves.

Schizophrenia is considerably less prevalent than depression or dementia in old age. Its peak prevalence is about 1.3 percent at age 18 to 54, declining to 0.6 percent in people age 65 and older (Howard et al., 2000; Meeks, 2000). Most older persons with this condition were first diagnosed in adolescence or middle age and continue to display behavior symptomatic of schizophrenia. However, the severity of symptoms appears to decrease and to change with age; older schizophrenics are less likely to manifest thought disorders, loss of emotional expression and problems with learning and abstraction, and more likely than younger schizophrenics to experience depression and social isolation. They also require lower doses of antipsychotic medications to manage their symptoms (Gellis, 2006).

Schizophrenics of any age, but especially older patients, need monitoring of their medication regimens and structured living arrangements. This is because pharmacotherapy with antipsychotic medications is the most effective treatment for older schizophrenic patients. However, many of the current cohort of older chronic schizophrenics residing in the community were deinstitutionalized in the 1960s as part of the national Community Mental Health Services Act of 1963. After spending much of their youth and middle age in state hospitals, these patients were released with the anticipation that they could function independently in the community, with medications to control their hallucinations and psychotic behavior. Although this approach has proved effective for many former schizophrenic inpatients, some have not adjusted well to deinstitutionalization, as witnessed by the number of homeless older schizophrenics on the streets in most major cities.

Anxiety

Anxiety disorders are another type of functional disorder or emotional problem with no obvious physiologic cause. The most common forms of anxiety disorders and their estimated prevalence in the older community-dwelling population are:

- generalized anxiety disorders in 1.1 percent to 7.1 percent
- phobias in 0.7 percent to 12.0 percent
- obsessive-compulsive disorder in 0.1 percent to 1.5 percent
- panic disorders in up to 0.3 percent of elders (Krasucki, Howard, and Mann, 1998)

Although more common than schizophrenia and paranoid disorders, anxiety disorders are not diagnosed as frequently in older populations as they are in the young. This may be because the older person develops more tolerance and better ability to manage stressful events. More likely, however, it may be that clinicians cannot diagnose anxiety disorders as accurately in older adults because they are often masked by physical health complaints or symptoms of depression (Gellis, 2006; Scogin, Floyd, and Forde, 2000). A study of 182 people age 60 and older who had been diagnosed with depression found that 35 percent had also been diagnosed with an anxiety disorder at some point in their lives. A significant proportion (23 percent) had a current diagnosis of panic disorder or specific phobias (Lenze et al., 2000). As with other psychiatric disorders that can be masked by physical symptoms, primary care physicians must probe further when older patients complain of diffuse pain, fast or irregular heart rate, fatigue, sleep disturbance, and restlessness. Although 2 to 5 percent of older adults are estimated to have some form of anxiety disorder, as many as 20 percent have symptoms of generalized anxiety disorder. Once the condition is diagnosed, older people can benefit from cognitive-behavioral therapy, psychosocial support, and in some cases, pharmacotherapy. Cognitive-behavioral therapy that challenges the elder's dysfunctional beliefs and maladaptive behaviors is found to be more effective in reducing anxiety symptoms than supportive counseling (Barrowclough et al., 2001; Gellis, 2006).

Older Adults Who Are Chronically Mentally Ill

The plight of older persons who are chronically mentally ill has not been addressed widely by mental health providers and advocates. This population is defined as people who suffer mental or emotional disorders that erode or prevent the development of their functional capacities in ADLs, self-direction, interpersonal relations, social interactions, learning, or recreation. Many chronically mentally ill older persons were institutionalized in their young adult years and released into the community after the deinstitutionalization movement began in 1963. Since then, they have been in and out of hospitals as their conditions have become exacerbated. These people have survived major upheavals and social neglect in their lives under marginally functional conditions. The social disruption and years of treatment with psychotropic drugs have taken their toll on many of them who are physiologically old in their 50s and 60s. Obtaining medical care for purely physical symptoms may be difficult because health care providers may dismiss a complaint as hypochondriasis or attribute it to the patient's psychiatric disorder. Health professionals in this situation need to perform a thorough exam to exclude conditions caused by the mental disorder or by aging per se, and to treat any systemic diseases that are diagnosed.

Psychotherapy with Older Persons

Despite early doubts by Freud (1924) and others about the value of psychotherapy for older patients, many researchers and therapists have developed and tested psychotherapeutic interventions specifically for this population, or have modified existing approaches. One challenge in working with older individuals is to overcome misconceptions about psychotherapy. For this reason, short-term, goal-oriented therapies may be more effective with older patients because they can begin to experience benefits immediately. On the other hand, older patients who are reluctant and unwilling to open up to a therapist may benefit more from long-term treatment in which rapport and trust between the therapist and the client can be established gradually. Several different types of therapy have been explored with this population.

As noted earlier, *life review* is one therapeutic approach that has been successfully used with older adults. Such therapy encourages introspection through active reminiscence of past achievements and failures, and may reestablish ego integrity in depressed older persons. This method may also be used effectively by social service providers who are not extensively trained in psychotherapy but have the opportunity to work one-on-one with older clients. It has been found to reduce symptoms of depression, and to increase life satisfaction and self-esteem in nursing home residents up to 3 years after completion of life review therapy (Haight, Michel, and Hendrix, 2000). An alternative form of life review, known as *reminiscence therapy,* has been compared with a more focused, problem-solving therapy. Although it has short-term benefits for depressed older people, it is less effective in long-term (i.e., greater than 3 months) reduction of depressive symptoms (Arean et al., 1993; Cully et al., 2001).

Group therapy is often advocated for older persons experiencing mental disorders, especially depression. Groups offer the opportunity for peer support, social interaction, and role modeling. Life review may be used effectively as part of group therapy. The opportunity to share life experiences and to learn that others have had similar challenges in their lives seems to enhance insight, self-esteem, and a feeling of catharsis. Group reminiscence therapy appears to reduce symptoms of depression immediately after the sessions have been completed, but its long-term benefits are unclear. Groups are also used for improving memory and enhancing cognitive skills. They are an ideal setting for teaching memory skills with the use of games and puzzles as well as reminiscence exercises (Gatz et al., 1998).

Empirical studies have been conducted to compare the efficacy of alternative therapeutic interventions. For example, *cognitive-behavioral* (i.e., active, structured, and time-limited therapy) and *brief psychodynamic therapy* (i.e., helping the patient to develop ego strength and feelings of control) both appear to be equally effective in alleviating minor depression, even up to 12 months following treatment. Psychodynamic therapy uses psychoanalytic concepts such as insight, transference, and the unconscious to relieve symptoms of depression and to prevent its recurrence by attempting to understand why the individual behaves in self-defeating ways. Each type of therapy may be appropriate for different types of older patients.

The therapeutic interventions just described are more frequently used in community settings than in nursing homes. The latter setting lends itself to more intense, long-term therapies: behavior-change programs, milieu therapy, and *remotivation therapy.* Behavior-change techniques using operant reinforcement and token economies have been successfully implemented in long-term care settings with psychiatrically impaired young and old patients. These methods are found to increase self-feeding and self-care and to reduce dependency. *Milieu therapy* is consistent with Lawton and Nahemow's competence model described in Chapter 1. This approach focuses on improving the therapeutic environment of the nursing home or enhancing an individual's sense of control over some important aspects of life. All staff members are encouraged to work as a team to improve the therapeutic environment of the facility.

Remotivation therapy has been used successfully with older persons with some cognitive impairment and who are withdrawn from social activities. They meet under the guidance of a trained group leader. The purpose is to discuss events and experiences by bringing all group members into the discussion, emphasizing the event's relevance for each member, and encouraging them to share what they have gained from the session. This approach is found to be effective in psychiatric hospitals and nursing homes as well as in adult day health centers.

Despite these positive reports about the benefits of psychotherapy with older adults, mental health professionals must take account of some differences in effectiveness between older and younger adults. Patients older than age 70 are more likely to experience relapse if treatment is discontinued or no booster sessions are offered. Relapse, or at least fading of treatment effects, is observed 6 to 12 months after these therapeutic interventions are discontinued (Reynolds et al., 2006; Reynolds and Kupfer, 1999).

Use of Mental Health Services

As noted in Chapter 4, older persons use physician services somewhat more than the young do, and are hospitalized at a much higher rate. In contrast, mental health services are significantly underutilized by older people, especially ethnic minority and low-income elders. Community-based care is used by older people at a far lower rate than inpatient hospital treatment, far below their representation in the U.S. population and less than the estimated prevalence of mental disorders in this group. In fact, fewer than 25 percent of older adults who need mental health care ever receive treatment; in addition, this lack of treatment provision to older adults is found across all service settings—community based, inpatient hospitals, residential care and nursing facilities (Kaskie and Estes, 2001). One major barrier to treatment is a serious shortage of mental health professionals with adequate training to meet the mental health, substance abuse, and psychosocial needs of older adults and their family caregivers (Rosen, 2005).

Older persons may be more likely to seek help from their primary physicians and to be hospitalized for mental disorders than to seek community mental health services. This may be because medical care does not carry the stigma of mental health services, especially for older ethnic minorities. For example, Asians and Pacific Islanders tend to view psychiatric disorders with shame. A disproportionate number of older persons represent the population of patients in state mental hospitals that house the chronically mentally ill. Despite the deinstitutionalization movement of the 1960s, the great majority of all psychiatric services to older people are in hospital settings.

BARRIERS TO OLDER PERSONS' USE OF MENTAL HEALTH SERVICES   Older adults are generally unwilling to interpret their problems as psychological, preferring instead to attribute them to physical or social conditions or to normal aging. In addition, the current cohort of adults over age 70 may be less oriented to the use of mental health services because of societal stigma, limited knowledge about mental disorders, and a lack of confidence in mental health workers. This requires a good "psychological ear" on the part of the older person's primary care physician. Therefore the physician must be attuned to the underlying emotional distress of the physical symptoms presented by the older patient.

Accessibility is perhaps the greatest barrier to older individuals' obtaining mental health services. In addition to the physical access issues of transportation and architectural barriers, there are significant problems of fragmented services, and older people's lack of knowledge about seeking mental health services on their own or obtaining appropriate referrals from physicians and social service providers. Cultural barriers, including communication problems, underlie the low utilization rates of mental health services by ethnic minority elders. These barriers are discussed in greater detail in Chapter 14. Fortunately, many innovative programs have arisen to overcome these barriers and respond to

---

OVERCOMING BARRIERS TO USING MENTAL HEALTH SERVICES

- Home visits by a psychiatrist, social worker, and a nurse are made to low-income, isolated older people in Baltimore through the "Psychogeriatric Assessment and Treatment in City Housing" (or PATCH) program.
- Rural elders in Iowa are served by mental health professionals through the Elderly Outreach Program (or EOP) of the community mental health system.
- The Family Services Program of greater Boston offers a community mental health program aimed especially at ethnic minority elders, entitled Services for Older People (or SOP).
- In Seattle, a mental health team from the community mental health network provides on-site evaluation and therapy to area nursing homes on a regular basis.
- In many communities, "gatekeepers" (non-traditional referral sources such as meter readers, postal carriers, and apartment and mobile home managers who have contact with isolated older people in the community) are trained to identify older persons who may require psychiatric care. These isolated older adults are typically chronically mentally ill.

---

the mental health needs of older adults, as highlighted in the box above. For example, many senior centers employ social workers trained in geriatrics to conduct support groups, education programs, and individualized counseling sessions on coping with grief, loss, and loneliness, and on methods to improve memory. Such programs reduce the stigma of psychotherapy by their informal structure in a familiar environment.

Reimbursement for psychological services is a major barrier. For example, Medicare Part A pays for no outpatient mental health expenditures, and only for a limited number of days for inpatient treatment. Furthermore, copayment by the subscriber for mental health services is greater than for physical health services. It should be noted that this lack of parity for mental health services occurs in many health insurance programs used by younger persons as well. Because of attitudes held by older patients toward mental disorders and by therapists toward older clients, however, these reimbursement issues are greater barriers to older persons' use of mental health services than they are for the young. In contrast, baby boomers may be more likely to seek such services in community mental health centers because of increased awareness of mental disorders and treatment modalities.

Implications for the Future

During the past 20 years, there has been more research emphasis on normal, age-related changes in personality, as well as psychological disorders such as depression and dementia. Larger, cross-national, and longitudinal studies are providing insights into the universality of stability in some personality traits and change in others. The inclusion of larger samples of women and ethnic minorities in more recent studies offers valuable information on gender and ethnic minority differences in psychological processes with aging. Researchers have identified differences in rates and symptoms of some psychological disorders by race and gender. This information can help health and social service providers who work with older adults recognize signs of depression, dementia, anxiety disorders, and other conditions as discussed in Chapters 14 and 15, and help them obtain the treatment they need.

With the growth of the older population and increased numbers of elders who live into their 80s and 90s, the sheer numbers of people with psychological disorders will expand over the next 30 years. More emphasis will be placed on alternatives to medications to treat these conditions, as well as culturally competent methods of psychotherapy such as problem-solving and cognitive-behavioral interventions, and communication with older adults and their families. Support groups for elders and their families who are coping with psychological disorders will continue

to grow. New research on the biochemistry of Alzheimer's disease and Parkinson's may offer hope for victims of these diseases, including early diagnosis and, potentially, stem cell transplants to repair affected areas of the brain. The Internet has already proven to be a valuable resource for older adults and their families as a means of learning more about their medical diagnoses, and even offers possibilities for group support and counseling by mental health professionals.

The discussion of normal personality development with aging and psychological disorders in this chapter should encourage students interested in research and clinical careers. There is a great need for evidence-based psychosocial care by psychologists, social workers, psychiatrists, and nurses to work in direct mental health services with older adults and, in the case of elders with dementia, to provide therapeutic services to their caregivers. Geriatricians are needed who can understand the difference between normal and abnormal psychological functioning in older adults, and who can distinguish dementia and depression from adverse reactions to medications and from grief responses to losses associated with aging. Even nurses and physicians who elect to go into primary care should develop these skills; as seen from the research described in this chapter, many older people with mood disorders and dementia seek a diagnosis and treatment from their primary care provider, not from a mental health specialist.

There is also a need for more researchers in gerontology who can advance the field of basic personality development and psychological disorders with aging. Whether you are interested in social or behavioral sciences, biological sciences, pharmacology or technology, there are many opportunities to test interventions to improve older persons' quality of life, both those who are healthy and those experiencing psychological disorders. In an era of limited resources for mental health services, it is essential to know what interventions are most effective with different groups of older adults.

Summary

Personality development in adulthood and old age has received increasing attention over the past 30 years. Earlier theories of personality suggested that development takes place only during childhood and adolescence, and stabilizes by early adulthood. Beginning with Erik Erikson, however, several theorists have suggested that personality continues to change and evolve into old age. According to Erikson's theory of psychosocial development, the individual experiences stages of development, with crises or conflicts at each stage, and the outcome of each has an impact on ego development in the next stage. The seventh stage, generativity versus stagnation, takes place mostly during the middle years, but increasingly researchers find that continued generativity in old age is important for active aging. Programs such as Foster Grandparents encourage older people to experience ongoing generativity or giving back to society by working with young children. The eighth and last stage of personality development occurs in old age and poses the conflict of ego integrity versus despair in dealing with one's impending death. Both cross-sectional and longitudinal studies have found evidence for these last two stages of development, particularly using Loevinger's model of ego development, which expands Erikson's stage theory.

The work of Carl Jung also emphasizes the growth of personality across the life span, but does not specify stages of development. Jung's model, like Erikson's, focuses on the individual's confrontation with death in this last stage. In addition, Jung described a decrease in sex-typed behavior with aging. Researchers have found that men become more accepting of their nurturant and affiliative characteristics as they age, whereas women learn to accept their ego-centric and aggressive impulses. Levinson's life structures model also examines personality from a developmental stage perspective. This model is consistent with the person–environment approach in emphasizing the interaction between the individual and his or her environment as the impetus for change.

Trait theories of personality have been tested systematically in the Baltimore Longitudinal Studies of Aging, using the five-factor model of personality that consists of five primary traits (neuroticism, extroversion, openness to experience, agreeableness, and conscientiousness), and several subcategories of traits. Costa, McCrae, and their colleagues have found considerable stability in these traits from middle age to old age when tested longitudinally and internationally, and age differences between young and old when tested cross-sectionally. It is recognized that older persons' self-concepts must be redefined as they move from traditional roles of worker, partner, and parent to less well-differentiated roles such as retiree or widow. But the process by which such changes take place and, more important, how they influence life satisfaction and self-esteem in old age is unclear.

Somewhat more research has been devoted to age-related changes in the nature of life events and the stress associated with them. Cognitive appraisal is an important consideration in understanding people's reactions to life events. To the extent that people perceive a situation as a threat, or as a negative stressor, the response may be avoidance or ineffective coping. If a particular life event is viewed as benign or unimportant, coping responses will not be activated. If an event proves to be more stressful than anticipated, an older person will be unprepared to cope with these demands. On the other hand, many elders display resilience in coping with life challenges.

Adaptation is influenced by an individual's access to a support network, cognitive skills, and personality traits such as active versus passive "mastery style" and "locus of control." Although ego defense mechanisms are observed to become more mature in middle and old age, it is difficult to describe coping styles in a similar manner. Age differences in the use of coping styles have been identified in cross-sectional studies, but longitudinal comparisons reveal considerable stability in coping.

Successful or active aging may be defined as the ability to avoid disease and disability, to function at a high level cognitively, to remain involved in society, and to cope effectively with life events and chronic hassles. An individual who has survived to the age of 75 or older has proved to be adaptable to new situations. Hence, older people who remain physically, cognitively, and socially active are the most resilient of their cohort. The concept of successful aging is often criticized for overlooking socioeconomic, racial, and gender barriers to adopting healthy lifestyles.

The prevalence of mental disorders in old age is difficult to determine, although estimates range from 5 to 45 percent of the older population. Research in acute and long-term care institutional settings provides higher estimates than epidemiological studies conducted in the community. This is because older persons with mental disorders are more likely to be treated in institutional settings and by primary care physicians than through community mental health services.

Depression is the most common mental disorder in late life, although estimates of its prevalence also vary widely depending on the criteria used to diagnose it. Bipolar disorders are rare in old age; major depression is more common. Reactive or minor depression that is secondary to major life changes is found frequently in older persons. This condition responds well to environmental and psychosocial interventions, whereas antidepressant medications combined with psychotherapy such as problem-solving and cognitive-behavioral therapies are more effective for major depression. It is important that older adults continue treatment for several months in order to improve their condition. Electroconvulsive therapy has been found to be effective for severe depression in older people who do not respond to other forms of therapy. Diagnosing depression in older people is often difficult. Both older adults and some health care providers deny it and accept "feeling blue" as a normal part of growing old, while others attribute it to medical conditions. On the other hand, it is important to screen for medical conditions and medications that may produce depressive symptoms as a side effect.

Depression is a risk factor for suicide in older people, particularly for white men over age 85. Life changes that result in a loss of social status and increased isolation may explain why this group is more likely to commit suicide than other segments of the population. The increased risk of suicide in older adults highlights the need for family members and service providers to be sensitized to clues of an impending suicide.

Dementia includes numerous reversible and irreversible conditions that result in impaired cognitive function, especially recall of recent events, comprehension, learning, attention, and orientation to time, place, and person. It is essential to perform a complete diagnostic workup of older people who have symptoms of dementia. A medical history, physical examination, assessment of medications, lab tests, psychological and cognitive testing, as well as neurological testing will aid in distinguishing reversible dementias that can be treated from the irreversible dementias, such as Alzheimer's disease, that currently can be managed but not cured. The biological basis of Alzheimer's disease is receiving much more research attention today. Future treatments may involve medications that replace or prevent the loss of brain chemicals, as well as vaccines and even gene therapy. Family members and service providers should be aware of changes in the older person's cognitive functioning and behavior that may signal dementia, and must avoid labeling such changes as normal aging or as the catchall phrase—"senility." The Nun Study has provided useful insights into early life experiences and activities that may prevent or delay the onset of dementia.

Although cognitive functioning cannot be restored in irreversible dementias, older persons in the early stages of these conditions often benefit from some medications, memory retraining, education, and counseling or psychotherapy to cope with the changes they are experiencing. Environmental modifications that simplify tasks and aid in orienting the patient may slow the rate of deterioration and postpone placement in a long-term care facility. It is also important to provide emotional and social support to family caregivers of elders with AD and other dementias. Support groups, education, adult day care, and other such respite programs are valuable for partners and other caregivers who assume full-time care for these patients at home, although they are limited by funding constraints.

Alcoholism and drug abuse are less common in older persons than in the young, although accurate estimates of prevalence are difficult to obtain. Physical health and cognitive function are significantly impaired in older alcoholics. Older men with a history of alcohol abuse also have a greater risk of suicide than do younger men or young and old women who are alcoholics. Drug abuse in older persons is rarely associated with illicit drugs, but often takes the form of inappropriate use or overuse of some prescription and over-the-counter drugs. Adverse reactions are more likely to occur in older persons because of age-related physiological changes that impair the ability to metabolize many medications and because of the greater likelihood of polypharmacy.

Paranoia and schizophrenia are far less common than depression and dementia in older persons. Most elders with these conditions first developed them in middle age; life changes such as relocation and confusion that result from dementia may trigger paranoid reactions in old age, and may aggravate preexisting schizophrenic symptoms. Psychotherapy, especially using cognitive-behavioral strategies, may be effective in treating paranoia, although it is important first to determine and to verify the underlying causes of the condition.

Many researchers have explored the feasibility of psychotherapy with older patients. Both short-term, goal-oriented therapy and long-term approaches have been advocated. Specific modes of therapy with older patients include life review, reminiscence, brief psychodynamic, and cognitive-behavioral techniques. These interventions are particularly effective with depressed older people in community settings. Nursing homes are ideal settings for long-term, intense therapies using groups, but staff may not have the time or training to implement them. Behavior change and milieu therapy have resulted in significant improvements in the mental well-being of elders who participate in short-term experimental interventions.

Despite the demonstrated efficacy of many forms of therapy with older persons, they significantly underutilize mental health services. Most treatments for psychological problems in this population take place in hospitals. Many older people prefer to seek treatment for depression and other mental disorders from their primary physician. This may result in an overuse of pharmacological treatment and an underutilization of counseling in cases where the latter may be more effective. Such behavior may be attributed to reluctance among the current cohort of elders to admit they have a psychological disorder, a lack of knowledge about such conditions and their treatment, and access problems. Barriers include attitudes of mental health and social service providers about the value of counseling for older persons, as well as the shortage of geriatric mental health services. As discussed in Chapter 14, cultural competence among mental health providers is needed to improve access for historically underserved groups. As more programs evolve that integrate services, and as future cohorts become aware of mental disorders and their treatment, acceptance and use of mental health services by older people will increase.

GLOSSARY

active and passive mastery interactions with one's social environment that are more controlling and competitive versus more affiliative and docile

adaptation ability to change personal needs, motivations, behaviors, and expectations to fit changing environmental demands or conditions

anxiety disorder functional psychological disorder often triggered by external stress; accompanied by physiological reactivity such as increased heart rate and sleep disorders

archetypes masculine and feminine aspects of personality, present in both men and women

benign senescent forgetfulness mild age-related decline in memory and learning ability; not progressive as in dementia

cognitive appraisal the individual's interpretation of an event as stressful, benign, or pleasant; determines individual's response to situation

coping (problem-focused versus emotion-focused) conscious responses to stress, determined by nature of stressor, personality, social support, and health

defense mechanisms unconscious responses to stress, affected by the individual's basic personality and early experiences

delirium a reversible dementia characterized by sudden onset, generally caused by environmental factors.

dementia progressive, marked decline in cognitive functions associated with damage to brain tissue; may affect personality and behavior; may be reversible or irreversible type

depression (major versus minor or reactive) the most common psychiatric disorder in old age, diagnosed if several behavioral and affective symptoms (e.g., sleep and eating disturbances) are present for at least two weeks; bipolar disorders are less common in older people than reactive (or minor) and major depression

dysthymic disorder a less acute type of depression, but often lasts longer than major depression

ego integrity versus despair the eighth and last stage of psychosocial development in Erikson's model; aging individual achieves wisdom and perspective, or despairs because he or she views one's life as lacking meaning

electroconvulsive or electroshock therapy (ECT) a form of therapy for severely depressed patients in which a mild electrical current is applied to one or both sides of brain

generativity the seventh stage of psychosocial development in Erikson's model; goal of middle-aged and older persons is to care for and mentor younger generations, look toward future, and not stagnate in past

life events identifiable, discrete life changes or transitions that require some adaptation to reestablish homeostasis

life review a form of psychotherapy that encourages discussion of past successes and failures

life structures in Levinson's model, specific developmental stages consisting of eras and transitions

paranoia a psychiatric disorder characterized by irrational suspiciousness of other people

pharmacotherapy use of medications to treat symptoms of physical or psychiatric disorders

psychopathology abnormal changes in personality and behavior that may be caused or triggered by a genetic predisposition, environmental stress, and/or systemic diseases

reminiscence therapy a type of psychotherapy used with depressed, anxious, sometimes confused older adults, stimulating the older person's memory of successful coping experiences and positive events in the past

resilience the ability to cope with life challenges and maintain one's optimism and psychological well-being

schizophrenia a psychiatric disorder characterized by thought disorders and hallucinations, psychotic behavior, loss of emotional expression.

self-concept cognitive representation of the self; emerges from interactions with social environment, social roles, accomplishments

self-efficacy perceived confidence in one's own ability to know how to cope with a stressor and to resolve it

self-esteem evaluation or feeling about one's identity relative to an "ideal self"; differs from self-concept in being more of an emotional, not cognitive, assessment of self

stage theories of personality development of individual through various levels, each one necessary for adaptation and for psychological adjustment

successful aging achievement of good physical and functional health, cognitive and emotional well-being in old age, often accompanied by strong social support and productive activity

trait theories personality theories that describe individuals in terms of characteristics or "typical" attributes that remain relatively stable with age

RESOURCES

Log on to MySocKit (www.mysockit.com) for information about the following:

- Alzheimer's Disease Education and Referral Center (ADEAR)
- Alzheimer's Disease and Related Disorders Association Inc. (ADRDA)
- Alzheimer's Research Forum
- American Association for Geriatric Psychiatry
- American Parkinson's Disease Association, Inc.
- Eldercare Web
- Elder Care Locator
- National Family Caregivers Association
- National Institute of Neurological Disorders and Stroke

REFERENCES

Ai, A.L., and Carrrigan, L. Older adults with age-related cardiovascular disease. In B. Berkman and S. D'Ambruoso (Eds.), *Handbook of social work in health and aging.* New York: Oxford University Press, 2006.

Alzheimer's Disease International. *Dementia in the Asia Pacific region: The epidemic is here.* Report submitted September 21, 2006. Accessed December 15, 2006, from http://www.alz.co.uk/research/files/apreport.

American Psychiatric Association (APA). Task Force on DSM-IV-TR. *Diagnostic and statistical manual of mental disorders* (4th ed., Text Revision). Washington, DC: APA, 2000.

Anderson, R.N., and Smith, B.L. Deaths: Leading causes for 2001. *National Vital Statistics Report,* 2003, *52,* 1–86.

Andrews, M. The seductiveness of agelessness. *Ageing and society,* 1999, *19,* 301–318.

Aranda, M.P., Lee, P.J., and Wilson, S. Correlates of depression in older Latinos. *Home Health Care Services Quarterly,* 2001, *20,* 1–20.

Arean, P.A., Perri, M.G., Nezu, A.M., Schein, R.L., Christopher, F., and Joseph, T.X. Comparative effectiveness of social problem-solving therapy and reminiscence therapy as treatments for depression in older adults. *Journal of Consulting and Clinical Psychology,* 1993, *61,* 1003–1010.

Barrowclough, C., King, P., Colville, J., Russell, E., Burns, A., and Tarrier, N. A randomized trial of the effectiveness of cognitive-behavioral therapy and supportive counseling for anxiety symptoms in older adults. *Journal of Consulting and Clinical Psychology,* 2001, *69,* 756–762.

Bassuk, S.S., Glass, T.A., and Berkman, L.F. Social disengagement and incident cognitive decline in community-dwelling elderly persons. *Annals of Internal Medicine,* 1999, *131,* 165–173.

Blanchard-Fields, F., and Norris, L. Causal attributions from adolescence through adulthood: Age differences, ego level, and generalized response style. *Aging and Cognition,* 1994, *1,* 67–86.

Blazer, D.G. Depression. In W.R. Hazzard, J.P. Blass, J.W.H. Ettinger, D.B. Halter, and J.G. Ouslander (Eds.), *Principles of geriatric medicine and gerontology* (4th ed.). New York: McGraw-Hill, 1999.

Blazer, D.G. Depression in late life: Review and commentary. *Journals of Gerontology, Series A: Biological and Medical Sciences,* 2003, *58A,* M249–M265.

Blazer, D.G., Hybels, C.F., and Pieper, C.F. The association of depression and mortality in elderly persons: A case for multiple independent pathways. *Journals of Gerontology: Medical Sciences,* 2001, *56A,* M505–M509.

Bloom, B.S., de Pouvourville, N., and Straus, W.L. Cost of illness of Alzheimer's disease: How useful are current estimates? *The Gerontologist,* 2003, *43,* 158–164.

Bohlmeijer, E., Smit, F., Cuijpers, P. Effects of reminiscence and life review on late-life depression: A meta-analysis. *International Journal of Geriatric Psychiatry,* 2003, *18,* 1088–1094.

Bosboom, P.R., and Deijen, J.B. Age-related cognitive effects of ECT and ECT-induced mood improvement in depressive patients. *Depression and Anxiety,* 2006, *23,* 93–101.

Calasanti, T.M., and Slevin, K.F. *Gender, social inequalities and aging.* Walnut Creek, CA: Altimira Press, 2001.

Capers, M. Conference Panel: Depression and illness: Coordinating care, *SMHSA News,* 2004 12. Accessed February 28, 2007, from http://www. SAMHSA_News/index.html.

Carstensen, L.I., Graff, J., Levenson, R.W., and Gottman, J.M. Affect in intimate relationships. In C. Magai and S.H. McFadden (Eds.), *Handbook of emotion, adult development and aging.* San Diego: Academic Press, 1996.

Carstensen, L.I., Pasupathi, M., and Mayr, U. Emotional experience in everyday life across the adult life span. *Journal of Personality and Social Psychology,* 2000, *79,* 644–655.

Centers for Disease Control and Prevention (CDC), National Center for Injury Prevention and Control (producer). Web-based Injury Statistics Query and Reporting System (WISQARS). Accessed September 28, 2006a, from http:// www.cdc.gov/ncipc/wisqars/default.htm.

Centers for Disease and Prevention (CDC), National Center for Injury Prevention and Control. Suicide fact sheet. Accessed September 27, 2006b, from http://www.cdc.gov/ncipc/factsheets/suifacts.htm.

Chan, K.K., Neighbors, C., Gilson, M., Larimer, M.E., and Marlatt, A. Epidemiological trends in drinking by age and gender: Providing normative feedback to adults. *Addictive Behaviors,* 2007, *32,* 967–976.

Chiles, J.A., Lambert, M.J., and Hatch, A.L. The impact of psychological interventions on medical cost offset: A meta-analytic review. *Clinical Psychology: Science and Practice,* 1999, *6,* 204–220.

Ciechanowski, P., Wagner, E., Schmaling, K., Schwartz, S., Williams, B., Diehr, P., et al. Community-integrated home-based depression treatment in older adults. *Journal of the American Medical Association,* 2004, *291,* 1569–1577.

Cohen, G.D. *The mature mind: The positive power of the aging brain.* Cambridge, MA: Perseus Books, 2005.

Col, N., Fanale, J.E., and Kronholm, P. The role of medication noncompliance and adverse drug reactions in hospitalizations of the elderly. *Archives of Internal Medicine,* 1990, *150,* 841–845.

Conway, K.P., Compton, W., Stinson, F.S., and Grant, B.F. Lifetime comorbidity of DSM-IV mood and anxiety disorders and specific drug use disorders. *Journal of Clinical Psychiatry,* 2006, *67,* 247–257.

Cook, A.E. Strategies for containing drug costs: Implications for a Medicare benefit. *Health Care Financing Review,* 1999, *20,* 29–38.

Costa, P.T., and McCrae, R.R. Solid ground in the wetlands of personality: A reply to Block. *Psychological Bulletin,* 1995, *117,* 216–220.

Costa, P.T., and McCrae, R.R. Stability and change in personality from adolescence through adulthood. In C.F. Halverson, G.A. Kohnstamm, and R.P. Martin (Eds.), *The developing structure of temperament and personality from infancy to adulthood.* Hillsdale, NJ: Erlbaum, 1994.

Cully, J.A., LaVoie, D., and Gfeller, J.D. Reminiscence, personality, and psychological functioning in older adults. *The Gerontologist, 2001, 41,* 89–95.

Czaja, S.J., Eisdorfer, C., and Schulz, R. Future directions in caregiving: Implications for intervention research. In R. Schulz (Ed.), *Handbook of dementia caregiving intervention research.* New York: Springer, 2000.

Danner, D.D., Snowdon, D.A., and Friesen, W.V. Positive emotions in early life and longevity: Findings from the Nun Study. *Journal of Personality and Social Psychology,* 2001, *80,* 804–813.

Day, K., Carreon, D., and Stump, C. The therapeutic design of environments for people with dementia: A review of the empirical research. *The Gerontologist,* 2000, *40,* 397–406.

De Baggio, T. *Losing my mind.* New York: The Free Press, 2002.

De Carli, C.S. When two are worse than one: Stroke and Alzheimer disease. *Neurology,* 2006, *67,* 1326–1328.

De St. Aubin, E., and McAdams, D.P. The relations of generative concern and generative action to personality traits, satisfaction/happiness with life, and ego development. *Journal of Adult Development,* 1995, *2,* 99–112.

Department of Health and Human Services (DHHS), Office of Applied Studies (2005). *Substance use among older adults: 2002 and 2003 update. The National Survey on Drug Use and Health Report.* Rockville, MD: Substance Abuse and Mental Health Services Administration. Accessed April 28, 2006, from http://oas.samhsa.gov/2k5/olderadults/olderadults.htm.

Depp, C.A., and Jeste, D.V. Definitions and predictors of successful aging: A comprehensive review of larger quantitative studies. *American Journal of Geriatric Psychiatry,* 2006, *13,* 6–20.

Diehl, M. Self-development in adulthood and aging: The role of critical life events. In C.D. Ryff and V.W. Marshall (Eds.), *The self and society in aging processes.* New York: Springer, 1999.

Diehl, M., Coyle, N., and Labouvie-Vief, G. Age and sex differences in strategies of coping and defense across the life span. *Psychology and Aging,* 1996, *11,* 127–139.

Diehl, M., Hastings, C.T., and Stanton, J.M. Self-concept differentiation across the adult life span. *Psychology and Aging,* 2001, *10,* 478–191.

Ensrud, K.E., Blackwell, T., Mangione, C.M., Bowman, P.J., Bauer, D.C., Schwartz, A., et al., Central nervous system active medications and risk for fractures in older women. *Archives of Internal Medicine,* 2003, *163,* 949–957.

Erikson, E.H. *Childhood and society* (2nd ed.). New York: Norton, 1963.

Erikson, E.H. *Identity, youth and crisis.* New York: Norton, 1968.

Erikson, E.H. *The life cycle completed: A review.* New York: Norton, 1982.

Erikson, E.H., Erikson, J.M., and Kivnick, H.Q. *Vital involvement in old age.* New York: Norton, 1986.

Feldman, H.H. Treating Alzheimer's disease with cholinesterase inhibitors: What have we learned so far? *International Psychogeriatrics,* 2002, *14* (Supplement), 3–5.

Fillit, H., Hill, J.W., Futterman, R., Loyd, J.R., Mastey, V. *Costs of comorbid medical conditions are increased in Alzheimer's disease.* Paper presented at annual meeting of the American Association for Geriatric Psychiatry, February, 2002.

Fisher, B.J. Successful aging, life satisfaction, and generativity in later life. *International Journal of Aging and Human Development,* 1995, *41,* 239–250.

Folstein, M., Folstein, S., and McHugh, P.R. Mini-mental state: A practical method for grading the cognitive state of patients for the clinician. *Journal of Psychiatric Research,* 1975, *12,* 189–198.

Frank, E., Swartz, H.A., Mallinger, A.G., Thase, M.E., Weaver, E.V., and Kupfer, D.J. Adjunctive psychotherapy for bipolar disorder: Effects of changing treatment modality. *Journal of Abnormal Psychology,* 1999, *108,* 579–587.

Frazer, C.J., Christensen, H., and Griffiths, K.M. Effectiveness of treatments for depression in older people. *Medical Journal of Australia,* 2005, *182,* 627–632.

Fredriksen-Goldsen, K. Caregiving and resiliency: Predictors of well-being. *Journal of Family Relations,* in press.

Freud, S. *Collected papers, Volume I.* London: Hogarth Press, 1924.

Friedland, R.P., Fritsch, T., Smyth, K., Koss, E., Lerner, A.J., Chen, C.H., Petot, G., et al. Participation in nonoccupational activities in midlife is protective against the development of Alzheimer's disease: Results from a case-control study. *Neurology,* 2000, *54,* Abstract #P05.076.

Gallagher-Thompson, D., and Steffan, A. Comparative effectiveness of cognitive-behavioral and brief psychodynamic psychotherapy for treatment of depression in family caregivers. *Journal of Consulting and Clinical Psychology,* 1994, *62,* 543–549.

Gallo, J.J., and Lebowitz, B.D. The epidemiology of common late-life mental disorders in the community: Themes for the new century. *Psychiatric Services,* 1999, *50,* 1158–1166.

Garfein, A.J., and Herzog, A.R. Robust aging among the young-old, old-old, and oldest-old. *Journals of Gerontology,* 1995, *50B,* S77–S87.

Garrard, J., Rolnick, S.J., Nitz, N.M., Luepke, L., Jackson, J., Fischer, L.R., Leibson, C., et al. Clinical detection of depression among community-based elderly people with self-reported symptoms of depression. *Journals of Gerontology Series A: Biological Sciences and Medical Sciences,* 1998, *53,* M92–M101.

Gatz, M., Fiske, A., Fox, L.S., Kaskie, B., Kasl-Godley, J.E., McCallum, T.J., and Wetherell, J.L. Empirically validated treatments for older adults. *Journal of Mental Health and Aging,* 1998, *4,* 9–26.

Gatz, M., and Smyer, M.A. Mental health and aging at the outset of the 21st century. In J.E. Birren and K.W. Schaie (Eds.), *Handbook of the psychology of aging* (5th ed.). San Diego: Academic Press, 2001.

George, L.K. The links between religion and health: Are they real? *Public Policy and Aging Report,* 2002, *12,* 4, 3–6.

George, L.K. Perceived quality of life. In R. Binstock and L.K. George (Eds.), *Handbook of aging and the social sciences* (6th ed.), New York: Academic Press, 2006.

Gellis, Z.D. Older adults with mental and emotional problems. In B. Berkman and S. D'Ambruoso (Eds.), *Handbook of social work in health and aging.* New York: Oxford University Press, 2006.

Gfroerer, J., Penne, M., Pemberton, M., and Folsom, R. Substance abuse treatment need among older adults in 2020: The impact of the aging baby-boom cohort. *Drug and Alcohol Dependence,* 2003, *69,* 127–135.

Goisman, R.M. Cognitive-behavioral therapy, personality disorders, and the elderly. In E. Rosowsky, R.C. Abrams, and R.A. Zweig (Eds.), *Personality disorders in older adults.* Mahwah, NJ: Lawrence Erlbaum Associates, 1999.

Goldberg, R.J., and Goldberg, J. Risperidone for dementia-related disturbed behavior in nursing home residents. *International Psychogeriatrics,* 1997, *9,* 65–68.

Grzywacz, J.G. and Marks, N.E. Social inequalities and exercise during adulthood: Toward an ecological perspective. *Journal of Health and Social Behavior,* 2001, *42,* 202–220.

Gustafson, D., Rothenberg, E., Blennow, K. Steen, B., and Skoog, I. An 18-year follow-up of overweight and risk of Alzheimer disease. *Archives of Internal Medicine,* 2004, *163,* 1524–1528.

Gutmann, D.L. The cross-cultural perspective: Notes toward a comparative psychology of aging. In J.E. Birren and K.W. Schaie (Eds.), *Handbook of the psychology of aging.* New York: Van Nostrand Reinhold, 1977.

Gutmann, D.L. Culture and mental health in later life. In J.E. Birren, R.B. Sloane, and G.D. Cohen (Eds.), *Handbook of mental health and aging* (2nd ed.). New York: Academic Press, 1992.

Gutmann, D.L. Psychoanalysis and aging: A developmental view. In S.I. Greenspan and G.H. Pollock (Eds.), *The course of life: Psychoanalytic contributions toward understanding personality development. Vol. 3: Adulthood and the aging process.* Washington, DC: U.S. Government Printing Office, 1980.

Haight, B.K., Michel, Y., and Hendrix, S. The extended effects of the life review in nursing home residents. *International Journal of Aging and Human Development,* 2000, *50,* 151–168.

Harralson, T.L., White, T.M. Regenberg, A.C., Kallan, M.J., and Have, T.T. Similarities and differences in depression among black and white nursing home residents. *American Journal of Geriatric Psychiatry,* 2002, *10,* 175–184.

Hasin, D.S., and Grant, B.F. Co-occurrence of DSM-IV alcohol abuse in DSM-IV alcohol dependence. *Archives of General Psychiatry,* 2004, *61,* 891–896.

Health and Retirement Survey (HRS). *A longitudinal study of health, retirement, and aging.* Accessed 2002. http://hrsonline.s.umich.edu.

Hebert, L.E., Scherr, P.A., Bienias, J.L., Bennett, D.A., and Evans, D.A. Alzheimer disease in the U.S. population: Prevalence estimates using the 2000 census. *Archives of Neurology,* 2003, *60,* 1119–1122.

Heisel, M.J., and Duberstein, P.R. Suicide prevention in older adults, *Clinical Psychology,* 2005, *12,* 243.

Hendrie, H.C. Epidemiology of Alzheimer's disease. *Geriatrics,* 1997, *52,* S4–S8.

Hendricks, J., and Hatch, L.R. Lifestyle and aging. In R. Binstock, and L. George (Eds.), *Handbook of aging and the social sciences,* New York: Academic Press, 2006, 301–319.

Herzog, A.R., Franks, M.M., Markus, H.R., and Holmberg, D. Activities and well-being in old age: Effects of self-concept and educational attainment. *Psychology and Aging,* 1998, *13,* 179–185.

Hill, J.W., Fillit, H., Shah, S.N., del Valle, M.C., and Futterman, R. Patterns of healthcare utilization and costs for vascular dementia in a community-dwelling population. *Journal of Alzheimer's Disease,* 2005, *8,* 43–50.

Holmes, T.H., and Masuda, M. Life change and illness susceptibility. In B.S. Dohrenwend and B.P. Dohrenwend (Eds.), *Stressful life events: Their nature and effects.* New York: Wiley, 1974.

Holmes, T.H., and Rahe, R. The social readjustment rating scale. *Journal of Psychosomatic Research,* 1967, *11,* 213–218.

Holroyd, S., Currie, L., Thompson-Heisterman, A., and Abraham, I. A descriptive study of elderly community-dwelling alcoholic patients in the rural south. *American Journal of Geriatric Psychiatry,* 1997, *5,* 221–228.

Holstein, M. and Minkler, M. Self, society and the "new gerontology." *The Gerontologist,* 2003, *43,* 787–796.

Horgas, A.L., Wilms, H.U., and Baltes, M.M. Daily life in very old age: Everyday activities as an expression of successful living. *The Gerontologist*, 1998, *38, 556–568.*

Howard, R., Rabins, P., Seeman, M., and Jeste, D. Late onset schizophrenia and very late onset schizophrenia-like psychosis: An international consensus. *American Journal of Psychiatry*, 2000, *157, 172–178.*

Hudson, R. Terms of engagement: The right and left look at elder civic activism. *Public Policy and Aging Report*, 2006, *16,* 13–18.

Idler, E.L. The many causal pathways linking religion to health. *Public Policy and Aging Report*, 2002, *12,* 7–12.

Jeste, D.V., Alexopoulos, G.S., Bartels, S.J., Cummings, J.L., Gallo, J.J., Gottlieb, G.L., et al. Consensus statement on the upcoming crisis in geriatric mental health: Research agenda for the next two decades. *Archives of General Psychiatry*, 1999, *56,* 848–853.

Joe, S., Baser, R.E., Breeden, G., Neighbors, H.W., and Jackson, J.S. Prevalence of and risk factors for lifetime suicide attempts among Blacks in the United States. *Journal of the American Medical Association*, 2006, *296,* 2112–2123.

Jones, R.N., Marcantonio, E.R., and Rabinowitz, T. Prevalence and correlates of recognized depression in U.S. nursing homes. *Journal of the American Geriatrics Society*, 2003, *51,* 1404–1409.

Jung, C.G. Concerning the archetypes, with special reference to the anima concept. In *C.G. Jung, Collected works,* Vol. 9, Part I. Princeton, NJ: Princeton University Press, 1959.

Jung, C.G. *Modern man in search of a soul.* San Diego: Harcourt Brace and World, 1933.

Kahana, E.F., and Kahana, B. Environmental continuity, discontinuity, futurity and adaptation of the aged. In G. Rowles and R. Ohta (Eds.), *Aging and the milieu: Environmental perspectives on growing old.* New York: Academic Press, 1982.

Kahn, R.L. Successful aging: Intended and unintended consequences of a concept. In L.W. Poon, S.H. Gueldner, and B.M. Sprouse (Eds.), *Successful aging and adaptation with chronic diseases.* New York: Springer, 2003.

Kaskie, B., and Estes, C.L. Mental health services policy and the aging. *Journal of Gerontological Social Work*, 2001, *36,* 99–114.

Katz, S. Busy bodies: Activity, aging and the management of everyday life. *Journal of Aging Studies*, 2000, *14,* 135–152.

Keller, M.B., McCullough, J.P., Klein, D.N., Arnow, B., Dunner, D.L, Gelenberg, A.J., et al. A comparison of nefazodone, the cognitive-behavioral analysis system of psychotherapy, and their combination for the treatment of chronic depression. *New England Journal of Medicine*, 2000, *342,* 1462–1470.

Kempen, G.I., van Sonderen, E., and Ormel, J. The impact of psychological attributes on changes in disability among low-functioning older persons. *Journals of Gerontology: Psychological Sciences*, 1999, *54B,* P23–P29.

Kessler, R.C. The effects of stressful life events on depression. *Annual Review of Psychology*, 1997, *48,* 191–214.

Koenig, H.G., and Brooks, R.G. Religion, health, and aging: Implications for practice and public policy. *Public Policy and Aging Report*, 2002, *12,* 13–19.

Kokmen, E., Beard, C.M., O'Brien, P.C., and Kurland, L.T. Epidemiology of dementia in Rochester, Minnesota. *Mayo Clinic Proceedings*, 1996, *71,* 275–282.

Krasucki, C., Howard, R., and Mann, A. The relationship between anxiety disorders and age. *International Journal of Geriatric Psychiatry*, 1998, *13,* 79–99.

Krause, N., and Shaw, B.A. Giving social support to others, socioeconomic status, and changes in self-esteem in later life. *Journals of Gerontology: Social Sciences*, 2000, *55B,* S323–S333.

Kukull, W.A., Higdon, R., Bowen, J.D., McCormick, W.C., Teri, L., Schellenberg, G., van Belle, G., et al. Dementia and Alzheimer disease incidence: A prospective cohort study. *Archives of Neurology*, 2002, *59,* 1737–1746.

Larson, E.B., Wang, L., Bowen, J.D., McCormick, W.C., Teri, L., Crane, P., and Kukull, W. Exercise is associated with reduced risk for incident dementia among persons 65 years of age and older. *Annals of Internal Medicine*, 2006, *144,* 73–81.

Laurin, D., Verreault, R., Lindsay, J., Mactherson, K., and Rockwood, K. Physical activity and risk of cognitive impairment and dementia in elderly persons. *Archives of Neurology*, 2001, *58,* 498–504.

Lazarus, R.S. Psychological stress and coping in adaptation and illness. In S.M. Weiss (Ed.), *Proceedings* of the National Heart and Lung Institute working conference on health behavior. DHEW Publication #NIH 76–868, 1975a.

Lazarus, R.S. The self-regulation of emotions. In L. Levi (Ed.), *Emotions: Their parameters and measurement.* New York: Raven Press, 1975b.

Lazarus, R.S. *Stress and emotion: A new synthesis.* New York: Springer, 1999.

Lazarus, R.S. Toward better research on stress and coping. *American Psychologist,* 2000, *55,* 665–673.

Lazarus, R.S., and DeLongis, A. Psychological stress and coping in aging. *American Psychologist,* 1983, *38,* 245–254.

Lazarus, R.S., and Folkman, S. *Stress, appraisal and coping.* New York: Springer, 1984.

Lazarus, R.S., and Launier, S. Stress-related transactions between person and environment. In L.A. Pervin and W. Lewis (Eds.), *Perspectives on interactional psychology.* New York: Plenum, 1978.

Lenze, E.J., Mulsant, B.H., Shear, M.K., Schulberg, H.C., Dew, M.A., Begley, A.E., Pollock, B.G. and Reynolds, C.F. Comormid anxiety disorders in depressed elderly patients. *American Journal of Psychiatry,* 2000, *157,* 722–728.

Levine, J. *Do you remember me? A father, a daughter, and a search for self.* New York: Free Press, 2004.

Levinson, D.J. A conception of adult development. *American Psychologist,* 1986, *41,* 3–13.

Levinson, D.J. Middle adulthood in modern society: A sociopsychological view. In G. DiRenzo (Ed.), *We the people: Social change and social character.* Westport, CT: Greenwood Press, 1977.

Levinson, D.J. *Seasons of a woman's life.* New York: Knopf, 1996.

Levinson, D.J., Darrow, C.M., Klein, E.B., Levinson, M.H., and McKee, B. *The seasons of a man's life.* New York: Knopf, 1978.

Li, G. The interaction effect of bereavement and sex on the risk of suicide in the elderly. *Social Science and Medicine,* 1995, *40,* 825–828.

Lim, G.P., Yang, F., Chu, T., Chen, P., Beech, W., et al. Ibuprofen suppresses plaque pathology and inflammation in a mouse model for Alzheimer's disease. *Journal of Neuroscience,* 2000, *20,* 5709–5714.

Lincoln, K. *Race differences in social relations and depression among older adults.* Paper presented at the Hartford Foundation Scholars Orientation, Washington, DC, 2003.

Lis, C.G., and Gaviria, M. Vascular dementia, hypertension, and the brain. *Neurological Research,* 1997, *19,* 471–480.

Loevinger, J. *Ego development.* San Francisco: Jossey-Bass, 1976.

Loevinger, J. Sentence completion test. In J. Loevinger (Ed.), *Technical foundations for measuring ego development.* Mahwah, NJ: Erlbaum, 1998.

Loevinger, J. Stages of personality development. In R. Hogan and J.A. Johnson (Eds.), *Handbook of personality psychology.* St. Louis: Washington University, 1997.

Logsdon, R.G., and Teri, L. *Evaluating and treating behavioral disturbances in dementia.* University of Washington: NW Geriatric Education Center Curriculum Modules, 2000.

Magai, C. Emotions over the life span. In J.E. Birren and K.W. Schaie (Eds.), *Handbook of the psychology of aging* (5th ed.). San Diego: Academic Press, 2001.

Magai, C., Cohen, C., Milburn, N., Thorpe, B., McPherson, R., and Peralta, D. Attachment styles in older European American and African American adults. *Journals of Gerontology: Psychological Sciences,* 2001, *56B,* S28–S35.

Maiden, R.J., Peterson, S.A., Caya, M., and Hayslip, B. Personality changes in the old-old. *Journal of Adult Development,* 2003, *10,* 31–39.

Masoro, E.J. "Successful aging"—Useful or misleading concept? *The Gerontologist,* 2001, *41,* 415–418.

Mattis, J.S., and Jagers, R.J. A relational framework for the study of religiosity and spirituality in the lives of African Americans. *Journal of Community Psychology,* 2001, *29,* 519–539.

Mattis, S. Mental status examination for organic mental syndrome in the elderly patient. In R. Bellack and B. Karasu (Eds.), *Geriatric psychiatry.* New York: Grune and Stratton, 1976.

McCrae, R.R. The maturation of personality psychology: Adult personality development and psychological well-being. *Journal of Research in Personality,* 2002, *36,* 307–317.

McCrae, R.R., Costa, P.T., *Personality in adulthood: A five-factor theory perspective* (2nd ed.). New York: Guilford Press, 2003.

McCrae, R.R., and Costa, P.T. Personality trait structure as a human universal. *American Psychologist,* 1997, *52,* 509–516.

McCrae, R.R., Costa, P.T., deLima, M.P., Simoes, A., Ostendorf, F., Angleitner, A., et al. Age differences in personality across the adult life span: Parallels in five cultures. *Developmental Psychology,* 1999, *35,* 466–477.

McCrae, R.R., Costa, P.T., Hrebickova, M, Urbánek, T., Martin, T.A., Oryol, V.E., et al. Age differences in personality traits across cultures: Self-report and observer perspectives. *European Journal of Personality,* 2004, *18,* 143–157.

McCrae, R.R., Costa, P.T., Ostendorf, F., Angleitner, A., Hrebickova, M., Avia, M.D., et al. Nature over nurture: Temperament, personality and life span development. *Journal of Personality and Social Psychology,* 2000, *78,* 173–186.

McCrae, R.R., and Terracciano, A. Universal features of personality traits from the observer's perspective: Data from 50 cultures. *Journal of Personality and Social Psychology,* 2005, *88,* 547–561.

McHugh, K. The "ageless self": Emplacement of identities in Sun Belt retirement communities. *Journal of Aging Studies,* 2000, *14,* 103–115.

McLeod, J.D. Life events. In J.E. Birren (Ed.), *Encyclopedia of gerontology,* San Diego: Academic Press, 1996.

Meeks, S. Schizophrenia and related disorders. In S.K. Whitbourne (Ed.), *Psychopathology in later life.* New York: Wiley, 2000.

Miller, W.R., and Thoresen, C.E. Spirituality, religion and health: An emerging research field. *American Psychologist,* 2003, *58,* 3–16.

Minkler, M., and Fadem, P. Successful aging: A disability perspective. *Journal of Disability Policy Studies,* 2002, *12,* 229.

Mitchell, A.J., and Subramaniam, H. Prognosis of depression in old age compared to middle age: A systematic review of comparative studies. *American Journal of Psychiatry,* 2005, *162,* 1588–1601.

Mitzner, T.L., and Kemper, S. Oral and written language in late adulthood, Findings from the Nun Study. *Experimental Aging Research,* 2003, *29,* 457–474.

Moceri, V.M., Kukull, W.A., Emanuel, I., van Belle, G., and Larson, E.B. Early-life risk factors and the development of Alzheimer's disease. *Neurology,* 2000, *54,* 415–420.

Montross, L.P., Depp, C., Daly, J., Reichstadt, J., Golshan, S., Moore, D., et al. Correlates of self-rated successful aging among community-dwelling older adults. *American Journal of Geriatric Psychiatry,* 2006, *14,* 43–51.

Moody, H. From successful aging to conscious aging. In M. Wykle, P. Whitehouse, and D. Morris (Eds.), *Successful aging through the lifespan.* New York: Springer, *55–69.*

Moos, R. *Coping with physical illness.* New York: Plenum Press, 1977.

Morrison, R.S., and Siu, A.L. Survival in end-stage dementia following acute illness. *Journal of the American Medical Association,* 2000, *284,* 47–52.

Mortimer, J.A., Gosche, K.M., Riley, K.P., Markesbery, W.R., and Snowdon, D.A. Delayed recall, hippocampal volume and Alzheimer neuropathology: Findings from the Nun Study. *Neurology,* 2004, *62,* 428–432.

Mrack, R.E., and Griffin, W.S. Trisomy 21 and the brain. *Journal of Neuropathology and Explorational Neurology,* 2004, *63,* 679–685.

Mroczek, D.K., and Spiro, A. Modeling intraindividual change in personality traits: Findings from the Normative Aging Study. *Journals of Gerontology: Psychological Sciences,* 2003, *58B,* P153–P165.

Mroczek, D.K., Spiro, A., and Griffin, P.W. Personality and aging. In J.E. Birren, and K.W. Schaie (Eds.), *Handbook of the psychology of aging* (6th ed). Burlington, MA: Elsevier Academic Press, 2006.

Mui, A.C., and Kang, S.Y. Acculturation stress and depression among Asian immigrant elders. *Social Work,* 2006, *51,* 243–250.

Musick, M.A. Theodicy and life satisfaction among black and white Americans. *Sociology of Religion,* 2000, *61,* 267–287.

National Institute of Mental Health. *Research on mental illnesses in older adults.* http://grants.nih.gov/grants/guide/pa-files/PA-03-014.html. Accessed February 18, 2006.

Neimeyer, R.A. (Ed.) *Meaning reconstruction and the experience of loss.* Washington, DC: American Psychological Association, 2001.

Nelson-Becker, H. Meeting life challenges: A hierarchy of coping styles in African American and Jewish American older adults. *Journal of Human Behavior in the Social Environment,* 2004, *10,* 155–174.

Nesselroade, J.R., Featherman, D.L., Agen, S.H., and Rowe, J.W. *Short-term variability in physical performance and physiological attributes in older adults: MacArthur successful aging studies.* Unpublished manuscript, University of Virginia, 1996.

Olichney, J.M., Sabbagh, M.N., Hofstetter, C.R., Galasko, D., Grundman, M., Katzman, R., and Thal, L.J. The impact of apoliprotein E4 on cause of death in Alzheimer's disease. *Neurology*, 1997, *49*, 76–81.

Oquendo, M.A. Ethnic and sex differences in suicide rates relative to major depression in the United States. *American Journal of Psychiatry*, 2001, *158*, 1656.

Peterson, B.E., and Klohnen E.C. Realization of generativity in two samples of women at midlife. *Psychology and Aging*, 1995, *10*, 20–29.

Plassman, B.I.., Havlik, R.J., Steffens, DC., Helms, M.J., Newman, T.N., Drosdick, D., et al. Documented head injury in early adulthood and risk of Alzheimer's disease and other dementias. *Neurology*, 2000, *55*, 1158–1166.

Podewils, L.J., Guallar, E., Kuller, L.H., Fried, L.P., Lopez, O.L., and Carlson, M. Physical activity, APOE genotype, and dementia risk. *American Journal of Epidemiology*, 2005, *161*, 639–651.

Qualls, S.H. Mental health and mental disorders in older adults. In J.C. Cavanaugh and S.K. Whitbourne (Eds), *Gerontology: An interdisciplinary perpective*. New York: Oxford University Press, 1999.

Rahe, R.H. Subjects' recent life changes and their near future illness reports: A review. *Annals of Clinical Research*, 1972, *4*, 393.

Rapaport, M.J., Mamdani, M., and Herrman, N. Electroconvulsive therapy in older adults: 13-year trends. *Canadian Journal of Psychiatry*, 2006, *51*, 616–619.

Raskind, M.A., Peskind, E.R., Truyen, I., Kershaw, P., and Damaraju, C.V. The cognitive benefits of galantamine are sustained for at least 36 months. *Archives of Neurology*, 2004, *61*, 252–256.

Reid, M.C., Concato, J., Towle, V.R., Williams, C.S., and Tennetti, M.E. Alcohol use and functional disability among cognitively impaired adults. *Journal of the American Geriatrics Society*, 1999, *47*, 854–859.

Reisberg, B., Doody, R., Stoffler, A., Schmitt, F., Ferris, S., Mobius, H.J. Memantine in moderate-to-severe Alzheimer's disease. *New England Journal of Medicine*, 2003, *348*, 1333–1341.

Reisberg, B., Ferris, S.H., De Leon, M.J., and Crook, T. The Global Deterioration Scale for assessment of primary degenerative dementia. *American Journal of Psychiatry*, 1982, *139*, 1136–1139.

Reiss, S. Why people turn to religion: A motivational analysis. *The Journal for the Scientific Study of Religion*, 2000, *39*, 47–52.

Reynolds, C.F., Dew, M.A., Pollock, B.G., Mulsant, B.H., Franks, E., Miller, M.D., et al. Maintenance treatment of major depression in old age. *New England Journal of Medicine*, 2006, *354*, 1130–1138.

Reynolds, C.F., and Kupfer, D.J. Depression and aging: A look to the future. *Psychiatry Services*, 1999, *50*, 1167–1172.

Reynolds, C.F., Miller, M.D., Pasternak, R.E., Frank, E., Perel, J.M., et al. Treatment of bereavement-related major depressive episodes in later life. *American Journal of Psychiatry*, 1999, *156*, 202–208.

Richards, J.B., Papaioannou, A., Adachi, J.D., Joseph, L., Whitson, H.E., Prior, J.C., et al., Effect of selective serotonin reuptake inhibitors on the risk of fracture. *Archives of Internal Medicine*, 2007, *167*, 188–194.

Riley, K.P., Snowdon, D.A., Desrosiers, M.F., and Markesbery, W.R. Early life linguistic ability, late in life cognitive function and neuropathology: Findings from the Nun Study. *Neurobiology of Aging*, 2005, *26*, 341–347.

Riley, M.W. Letters to the editor. *The Gerontologist*, 1998, *38*, 151.

Rosen, A. *The Shortage of an Adequately Trained Geriatric Mental Health Workforce*. Testimony to the Policy Committee of the White House Conference on Aging. Accessed February 18, 2006, from http://www.whcoa.gov/about/policy/meetings/Jan_24/Rosen%20WHCOA%20testimony.pdf.

Rowe, J.W., and Kahn, R.L. Human aging: Usual and successful. *Science*, 1987, *237*, 143–149.

Rowe, J.W., and Kahn, R.L. Successful aging. *The Gerontologist*, 1997, *37*, 433–440.

Rowe, J.W., and Kahn, R.L. *Successful aging*, New York: Pantheon Books, 1998.

Rudorfer, M.V., Henry, M.E., and Sackheim, H.A. Electroconvulsive therapy. In A. Tasman, J. Kay, and J.A. Lieberman (Eds.), *Psychiatry*. Philadelphia: Saunders, 1997.

Ruth, J.E., and Coleman, P. Personality and aging: Coping and management of the self in later life. In J.E. Birren and K.W. Schaie (Eds.), *Handbook of the psychology of aging* (4th ed.). San Diego: Academic Press, 1996.

Ryff, C.D., Kwan, C.M.L., and Singer, B.H. Personality and aging: Flourishing agendas and future challenges. In J.E. Birren and K.W. Schaie (Eds.), *Handbook of the psychology of aging* (5th ed.). San Diego: Academic Press, 2001.

Sambamoorthi, U., Shea, D., and Crystal, S. Total and out-of-pocket expenditures for prescription drugs among older persons. *The Gerontologist,* 2003, *43,* 345–359.

Sano, M., Ernesto, C., Thomas, R.G., Klauber, M.R., Schafer, K., and Grundman, M. A controlled clinical trial of selegiline, alpha-tocopherol or both as treatment for Alzheimer's disease. *New England Journal of Medicine,* 1997, *336,* 1216–1222.

Schaie, K.W., and Willis, S.L. Adult personality and psychomotor performance. *Journals of Gerontology,* 1991, *46B,* P275–P284.

Schenk, D., Barbour, R., Dunn, W., Gordon, G., Grajeda, H., Guido, T., Hu, K., et al. Immunization with amyloid-B attenuates Alzheimer-disease-like pathology in the PDAPP mouse. *Nature,* 1999, *400,* 173–177.

Schulz, R., Beach, S.R., Ives, D.G., Martire, L.M., Ariyo, A.A., and Kop, W.J. Association between depression and mortality in older adults. *Archives of International Medicine,* 2000, *160,* 1761–1768.

Schulz, R., and Heckhausen, J. Emotion and control: A life-span perspective. In K.W. Schaie and M.P. Lawton (Eds.), *Annual Review of Gerontology and Geriatrics* (Vol. 17). New York: Springer, 1998.

Schulz, R., and Heckhausen, J. A life span model of successful aging. *American Psychologist,* 1996, *51,* 702–714.

Scogin, F., Floyd, M., and Forde, J. Anxiety in older adults. In S.K. Whitbourne (Ed.), *Psychopathology in later life.* New York: Wiley, 2000.

Seeman, T.A., Charpentier, P.A., Berkman, L.F., Tinetti, M.E., Guralnick, J.M., Albert, M., Blazer, D., et al. Predicting changes in physical performance in a high functioning elderly cohort: MacArthur Studies of Successful Aging. *Journals of Gerontology,* 1994, *49A,* M97–M108.

Seeman, T.E., Unger, J.B., McAvay, G., and Mendes de-Leon, D. Self-efficacy beliefs and perceived declines in functional ability. *Journals of Gerontology,* 1999, *54B,* 214–222.

Seltzer, B. Cholinesterase inhibitors in the clinical management of Alzheimer's disease: Importance of early and persistent treatment. *Journal of International Medical Research,* 2006, *34,* 339–347.

Selye, H. The general adaptation syndrome and the diseases of adaptation. *Journal of Clinical Endocrinology,* 1946, *6,* 117–230.

Selye, H. Stress and aging. *Journal of the American Geriatrics Society,* 1970, *18,* 660–681.

Shibusawa, T. Older adults with substance/alcohol abuse problems. In B. Berkman and S. D'Ambruoso (Eds.), *Handbook of social work in health and aging.* New York: Oxford University Press, 2006.

Shumaker, S.A., Legault, C., Rapp, S.R., et al. Estrogen plus progestin and the incidence of dementia and mild cognitive impairment in postmenopausal women. *Journal of the American Medical Association,* 2003, *289,* 2651–2662.

Snowdon, D. *Aging with grace: What the Nun Study teaches us about leading longer, healthier, and more meaningful lives.* New York: Bantam, 2001.

Snowdon, D. Healthy aging and dementia: Findings from the Nun Study. *Annals of Internal Medicine,* 2003, *139,* 450–454.

Snowdon, D., Greiner, L.H., and Markesbery, W.R. Linquistic ability in early life and the neuropathology of Alzheimer's disease: Findings from the Nun Study. In R.N. Kalaria and P. Ince (Eds.), *Annals of New York Academy of Sciences,* New York: New York Academy of Sciences, 2000.

Snyder, C.R. *Coping with stress: Effective people and processes.* New York: Oxford University Press, 2001.

Sramek, J.J., and Cutler, N.R. Recent developments in the drug treatment of Alzheimer's disease. *Drugs and Aging,* 1999, *14,* 359–373.

Stewart, W.F., Kawas, C., Corrada, M., Metter, E.J., Risk of Alzheimer's disease and duration of NSAID use. *Neurology,* 1997, *48,* 626–632.

Strawbridge, W., Wallhagen, M., and Cohen, R.D. Successful aging and well-being: Self-rated compared with Rowe and Kahn. *The Gerontologist,* 2002, *42,* 727–733.

Substance Abuse and Mental Health Services Administration (SAMHSA). *Summary of the findings from the National Household Survey on Drug Abuse.* NHSDA Series H-13, DHHS Publication SMA 01-3549. Rockville, MD: NHSDA, 2001.

Surgeon General. *Mental health: A report of the surgeon general.* Accessed 1999a, from http://www.surgeongeneral.gov/library/mentalhealth/home.htm.

Surgeon General. *Mental health: Culture, race, ethnicity supplement to "Mental health: Report of the surgeon general."* Accessed 2001, from http://www.mentalhealth.org/cre.

Surgeon General. *The Surgeon General's Call to Action to Prevent Suicide.* Accessed 1999b, from http://www.surgeongeneral.gov/library/calltoaction/fact2.htm.

Suzman, R.M., Harris, T., Hadley, E.C., Kovar, M.G., and Weindruch, R. The robust oldest old: Optimistic perspectives for increasing healthy life expectancy. In R.M. Suzman, D.P. Willis, and K.G. Manton (Eds.), *The oldest old.* New York: Oxford Press, 1992.

Szekely, C.A., Thorne, J.E., Zandi, P., Ek, M., Messias, E., Breitner, J.C.S., and Goodman, S.N. Non-steroidal anti-inflammatory drugs for the prevention of Alzheimer's disease: A systematic review. *Neuroepidemiology,* 2004, *23,* 153–169.

Tariot, P.N., Farlow, M.R., Grossberg, G.T., Graham, S.M., McDonald, S., and Gergel, I. Memantine treatment in patients with moderate to severe Alzheimer's disease already receiving donepezil. *Journal of the American Medical Association,* 2004, *291,* 317–324.

Teri, L., Gibbons, L.E., McCurry, S.M., Logsdon, R.G., Buchner, D.M., Barlow, W.E., Kukull, W.A., LaCroix, A.Z. McCormick, W., Larson, Exercise plus behavioral management in patients with Alzheimer disease, *Journal of the American Medical Association,* 2003, *290,* 2015–2022.

Teri, L., Logsdon, R.G., Uomoto, J., and McCurry, S.M. Behavioral treatment of depression in dementia patients: A controlled clinical trial. *Journals of Gerontology,* 1997, *52B,* P159–P166.

Teri, L., McCurry, S.M., and Logsdon, R.G. Memory, thinking, and aging: What we know about what we know. *Western Journal of Medicine,* 1997, *167,* 269–275.

Terracciano, A., McCrae, R.R., and Costa, P.T. Longitudinal trajectories in Guilford-Zimmerman Temperament survey data: Results from the Baltimore Longitudinal Study of Aging. *Journals of Gerontology: Psychological Sciences,* 2006, *61B,* P108-P116.

Troll, L.E., and Skaff, M.M. Perceived continuity of self in very old age. *Psychology and Aging,* 1997, *12,* 162–169.

Trzesniewski, K.H., Donellan, M.B., and Robins, R.W. Stability of self-esteem across the life span. *Journal of Personality and Social Psychology,* 2003, *84,* 205–206.

Tufts University Health and Nutrition Letter. Anti-aging or successful aging? 2001, *19,* 1–2.

Unger, J.B., McAvay, G., Bruce, M.L., Berkman, L., and Seman, T. Variation in the impact of social network characteristics on physical functioning in elderly persons. *Journals of Gerontology,* 1999, *54B,* S245–S251.

Unutzer, J., Katon, W., Callahan, C.M., Williams, J.W., Hunkeler, E., Harpole, L., et al. Depression treatment in a sample of 1801 depressed older adults in primary care. *Journal of the American Geriatrics Society,* 2003, *51,* 505–514.

Vaillant, G.E. *Adaptation to life.* Boston: Little, Brown, 1977.

Vaillant, G.E. *Aging well.* Boston: Little, Brown, 2002.

Vaillant, G.E. Ego mechanisms of defense and personality psychopathology. *Journal of Abnormal Psychology,* 1994, *103,* 44–50.

Vaillant, G.E., and Vaillant, C.O. Natural history of male psychological health: A 45-year study of predictors of successful aging. *American Journal of Psychiatry,* 1990, *147,* 31–37.

Van der Wurff, F.B., Stek, M.L., Hoogendijk, W.L., and Beekman, A.T. Electroconvulsive therapy for depressed elderly (Cochrane review). *The Cochrane Library,* 2004, *1.*

Van Dongen, M.C., van Rossum, E., Kessels, A.G.H., Sielhorst, H.J.G., and Knipschild, P.G. The efficacy of ginkgo for elderly people with dementia and age-associated memory impairment: New results of a randomized clinical trial. *Journal of the American Geriatrics Society,* 2000, *48,* 1183–1194.

Verghese, J., Lipton, R.B., Hall, C.B., Kuslansky, G., Katz, M.J., and Buschke, H. Abnormality of gait as a predictor of non-Alzheimer's dementia. *New England Journal of Medicine,* 2002, *347,* 1761–1768.

Whitbourne, S.K., and Primus, L.A. Physical identity. In J.E. Birren (Ed.), *Encyclopedia of gerontology,* San Diego: Academic Press, 1996.

Wilson, K., Mottram, P., Sivanranthan, A. Antidepressants vs. placebo for the depressed elderly (Cochrane Review). *The Cochrane Library,* 2004, *1.*

Wong, P., and Ujimoto, V. The elderly: Their stress, coping and mental health. In C.L. Lee and W. Zane (Eds.), *Handbook of Asian American psychology.* Thousand Oaks, CA: Sage, 1998.

Wray, S. Women growing older: Agency, ethnicity and culture. *Sociology,* 2003, *37,* 511–527.

Yin, S. *Elderly white men afflicted by high suicide rates.* Washington, DC: Population Reference Bureau, 2006.

Zandi, P.P., Anthony, J.C., Khachaturian, A.S., Stone, S.V., Gustafson, D., Tschantz, J.T., Norton, N.C., et al. Reduced risk of Alzheimer's disease in users of antioxidant vitamin supplements. *Archives of Neurology,* 2004, *61,* 82–88.

Zhang, J., Goodlett, D.R., and Montine, T.J. Proteomic biomarker discovery in cerebrospinal fluid for neurodegenerative diseases. *Journal of Alzheimer's Disease,* 2005, *8,* 377–386.

7

Love, Intimacy, and Sexuality in Old Age

This chapter reviews

- The prevalent attitudes and beliefs about sex and love in old age that frequently affect an older person's sexuality
- Age-related physiological changes that may alter the nature of older men's and women's sexual response and performance, but do not interfere with their overall experience of sexuality
- Chronic illness, medication use, and sexuality
- Gay, bisexual, transgender, and lesbian (GLBT) relationships
- Importance of late-life affection, love, and intimacy
- Implications for families and professionals who work with older people

The previous chapter focused on personality: who one is and how one feels about oneself. An important aspect of one's personality is sexuality. In fact, **sexuality** encompasses many aspects of one's being as a man or a woman, including one's self-concept, identity, and relationships. **Sex** is not just a biological function involving genital intercourse or the sexual excitement of **orgasm;** it also includes the expression of feelings—loyalty, passion, affection, esteem, and affirmation of one's body and its functioning, which are part of one's intimate self and part of healthy and active aging. A person's speech and movement, vitality, and ability to enjoy life are all parts of sexuality. As with other aspects of aging discussed throughout this text, sexuality encompasses physiological, emotional, intellectual, spiritual, behavioral, and sociocultural components.

Older people, family members, and professionals need to understand the normal physiological changes that may affect sexual functioning and intimacy across the life course. To assess and treat potential negative effects of aging on sexuality, components of sexual desire need to be addressed: drive, beliefs/values, and motivation, as well as the sexual equilibrium within the primary relationship (Kingsberg, 2000). Since our sexual nature goes far beyond whether we are sexually active at any particular point in life, elders need to be comfortable with their decisions regarding expression of their sexuality. Accordingly, professionals need to respect older adults' choices and values. Although most older individuals can and do engage in intercourse, some genuinely do not desire to engage in the physical aspects of sexual behavior—patterns of sexual expression vary at all ages.

Congruent with the P–E model throughout this text, sexual activity is also affected by nonphysiological factors—self-esteem, chronic illness, psychosocial conditions, living arrangements and professionals' attitudes. In many instances, these dynamic contextual factors may exert greater influence than physiological changes. To summarize, sexual behavior in old age is especially likely to be affected by

- physiological changes
- the physical and social environment, especially the availability of sexual partners
- the individual's personal sexual history, self-concept, and self-esteem
- the psychological meaning attached to one's experiences
- the degree of physical fitness and functional ability
- the attitudes of others (e.g., family, health care providers, nursing home staff)

Attitudes and Beliefs about Sexuality in Later Life

It is striking that at a time when safe sex for nearly every segment of our population is publicly discussed, outdated ideas related to sex

> **POINTS TO PONDER**
>
> Reflect on jokes or stories you have heard about older adults and sexuality. What have they conveyed? How did they affect your understanding of sexuality and aging?

and aging persist, and research on sexuality and aging is relatively limited (Calasanti and Slevin, 2001). Despite its powerful role in many elders' lives, sexuality remains one of the least understood and visible aspects of active aging (Henry and McNab, 2003; Pangman and Seguire, 2000). Widespread stereotypes, misconceptions, and jokes about old age and sexuality can powerfully and negatively affect older people's sexual experience. Jokes often center on performance "He can't get it up any more," in part because of our society's emphasis on productivity and physical appearance. Many of these attitudes and beliefs stem from ageism generally, such as the perceptions of older people, especially women, as physically unattractive and therefore asexual. Another example of ageism is the stereotype that elders lack energy and are devoid of sexual feeling, and therefore are not interested in sex. Since sexuality in our society tends to be equated with youthful standards of attractiveness, older women and individuals with chronic illness and disability may experience the most negative consequences from ageist and sexist definitions. In some instances, sexual interaction between older persons may be viewed as socially unacceptable and even physically harmful for elders (e.g., a health care provider who advises a person with a terminal illness against engaging in sexual activity) (DeLamater and Friedrich, 2002; Pangman and Seguire, 2000; Zeiss and Kasl-Godley, 2001).

Such attitudes and beliefs may stem from misinformation, such as the perception that sexual activity and drive do and should decline with old age. Accordingly, older people who speak of enjoying sexuality may be viewed by some as exaggerating or deviant. Alternatively, older people who express caring and physical affection for one another may be infantilized, defined as "cute" and teased by professionals, their age peers, and family members. Such public scrutiny and ridicule frequently occur among residents and staff of long-term care facilities. Another barrier is that the oldest-old grew up in periods of restrictive guidelines regarding appropriate sexual behavior and taboos against other forms of sexual activity, such as masturbation. Many of these attitudes and beliefs of both elders and their families reflect a more conservative morality that views sex only as intercourse and intercourse as appropriate only for conception.

Surrounded by society stereotypes and fearing ridicule or censure, older people may unnecessarily withdraw from all forms of sexual expression, thereby depriving themselves and their partners of the energy and vitality inherent in sexuality. Yet for many older adults, sexual activity, in the broadest sense of encompassing both physical and emotional interaction, is necessary for them to feel alive, to affirm their identity, and to communicate with their partners. As a source of reinforcement and pleasure, sexual relations broadly defined can enhance well being and compensate for some losses in old age (Henry and McNab, 2003; Trudel, Turgeon, and Piche, 2000). Fortunately, the media, gerontologists, and other professionals are beginning to convey the message that sex is acceptable in old age. This is especially true among aging baby boomers, who experienced the sexual revolution of the 60s. One sign of change is that current cohorts of older people, especially the young-old, appear more accepting of and permissive in their attitudes toward sexuality and intimacy than in the past (AARP, 2004). Understanding the natural physiological alterations in sexual response associated with the aging process is an essential first step toward dispelling myths.

Myths and Reality about Physiological Changes and Frequency of Sexual Activity

One of the most prevalent societal myths is that age-related physiological changes detrimentally affect sexual functioning. Such misconceptions were shaped by the early research on sexuality. In part because of assumptions that older people do not engage in sex or are embarrassed to talk about it, most early surveys of sexual attitudes did not even question older adults about their sexuality. Such avoidance of the topic fostered further misinformation and misperceptions.

Other early studies included questions about sexuality, but focused on the frequency of sexual intercourse. These researchers overlooked the subjective experience or qualitative aspects of sexuality in old age. For example, from 1938 to 1948, Kinsey and his colleagues studied primarily

Sexuality and intimacy are important throughout the later years.

16- to 55-year-olds, and their discussion of respondents over age 60 emphasized the frequency of sexual intercourse. In fact, their 735-page report devoted only three pages to the topic of sex and aging (Schiavi, 1996). Using the number of orgasms or ejaculations as the measure of good sex, Kinsey and his colleagues found that by age 70, 25 percent of men experienced sexual dysfunction. Women were portrayed as reaching the peak of their sexual activity in their late 20s or 30s, then remaining on that plateau through their 60s, after which they showed a slight decline in sexual response capability (Kinsey, Pomeroy, and Martin, 1948, 1953). Because Kinsey and colleagues minimized the broader psychological aspects of sexuality, they failed to address the subjective meaning and importance of sex at different ages. Older individuals may have sexual intercourse less often, but it is not necessarily less meaningful than at a younger age. In fact, few age-related physiological changes prevent continued sexual enjoyment and activity in old age.

One reason that sexual activity and enjoyment may appear to decline with age is because of cross-sectional research designs used. Many of the methodological issues described in Chapter 1 are reflected in studies of sexuality in old age when younger and older cohorts are compared at one point in time. For example, the 1954 Duke Longitudinal Study, which examined the incidence of sexual intercourse and interest in sex,

---

POINTS TO PONDER

Is older adults' sexuality largely invisible to you? Or have you heard about it mostly through jokes, the media, the Internet, or on birthday greeting greeting cards? If so, what did these images convey to you? How did they affect your understanding of sexuality and aging?

---

found gradual age-related declines in frequencies of sexual activity for older adults compared to their young and middle-aged counterparts, especially for women and unmarried individuals. The median age for stopping intercourse was 68 in men and 60 in women (Pfeiffer and Davis, 1972). This study had several additional limitations as well. The definition of sexual activity was confined to heterosexual intercourse, and the respondents constituted a cohort of individuals raised during a period of strict sexual conservatism. As discussed in Chapter 1, we now know that such cross-sectional data fail to give a lifetime picture of an individual's sexual behavior. Because the cohort effect was not identified, the low levels of sexual activity reported may be related to the attitudes, values, and reluctance to report on sexual behavior among a cohort of elders who grew up in an era still influenced by Victorian values rather than any age-related physiological changes in sexual functioning (Schiavi and Rehman, 1995).

A subsequent reanalysis of the 1954 Duke Longitudinal Study data to control for a possible cohort effect and the second Duke Longitudinal Study over a six-year period revealed stability of sexual activity patterns from mid- to late life. In other words, those who were sexually conservative and inactive in young adulthood and mid-life, perhaps because of their social upbringing, carried that pattern through their later years. Similarly, those who were more sexually involved in young adulthood and middle age remained active in old age. A later analysis of the Duke data also found older women to be more

---

THE INVISIBILITY OF OLDER ADULTS IN EARLY SEXUALITY RESEARCH

- Kinsey, 1948, 1953: 126 men and 56 women over age 60; 4 men over age 80
- Masters and Johnson, 1966, 1970: 20 older males
- Hite Report on Female Sexuality, 1976: 19 women out of a total of 1844 were age 60 or older
- Janus Report on Sexual Behavior, 1993: 34 percent were age 51 and over
- National Health and Social Life Survey, 1994: excluded those age 60 and over

interested in sex than older men. However, the rate of sexual activity among older women declined, partly because of the absence of partners or because husbands tended to curtail or discontinue sexual activities. In fact, marital status and relationship issues appear to be more important in influencing women's sexual behavior than it is for men's (AARP, 1999; Matthias et al., 1997). In the Baltimore Longitudinal Studies of Aging, sexual dysfunction or impotence was identified to be the main barrier to men's sexual activity. Yet the men did not report feeling sexually deprived or lacking in self-esteem (Schiavi, 1999). Since most of the early studies focused on sexual performance, sexual satisfaction was neglected as an independent measure that is theoretically and clinically relevant (Schiavi, 1999). When sexual activity is defined more broadly than intercourse to encompass touching and caressing, rates of activity increase to over 80 percent for men and over 60 percent for women (Schiavi, Mandeli, and Schreiner-Engel, 1999; Wiley and Bortz, 1999). Recent studies that include open-ended questions identify the excitement, enjoyment, and pleasure—the passion and romance—of late-life sexuality and the value older adults place on the quality and meaning of intimate relationships. Accordingly, sexual activity and satisfaction are found to be related to 53 percent of older men's and 37 percent of older women's sense of self-worth, quality of life, and competence (AARP, 2004).

One of the first large-scale studies that provided evidence for continued sexual satisfaction in old age was the work of Masters and Johnson (1981). In their classic study of sexual responsiveness across the life span, Masters and Johnson determined that the capacity for both functioning and fulfillment does not disappear, even though physiological changes occur with age. They concluded that age-based limits to sexual behavior do not exist. Later studies, with predominantly white samples, identified that most older adults, especially men, and even among those over age 80, remain sexually active. As with most behaviors, there is a wide range. Some individuals even experience an increase in sexual activity with age, perhaps because of the absence of children in the home (Matthias et al., 1997; Schiavi and Rehman, 1995; Weg, 1996). For others, their sexual activity in old age may represent a continuation of activity earlier in life (Willert and Semans, 2000). Overall, sexual inactivity appears to depend on life circumstances, not lack of interest or desire.

The methodological limitations of most studies of older adults and sexuality are summarized in the box below.

The most recent large-scale research on aging and sexuality was an AARP telephone survey of 2930 men and women over age 45, which sought to understand the factors affecting sexuality and quality of life of midlife and older adults, and to compare the results to those of a 1999 survey. A major difference in the survey was the addition of Latino (3 percent), Native American (1 percent), African American (8 percent), and Asian (1 percent) respondents.

METHODOLOGICAL LIMITS OF RESEARCH ON SEXUALITY AND OLDER ADULTS

- Emphasis on frequency of intercourse, not its meaning or quality
- Small sample size in most studies
- Non-random and non-representative nature of sample, including lack of elders of color
- Because of taboo nature of sexuality, respondents may not be honest, may over- or underestimate sexual activity, or provide socially acceptable responses
- Cohort influence: The current cohort is likely to be less forthcoming than baby boomers because of their socialization not to discuss private issues such as sex
- Researchers' discomfort or biases about sex and aging influence the nature of their questions and interactions with respondents
- Reliance primarily on self-reports

The following patterns were identified among the sub-group age 70 and older:

- 87 percent of men and 63 percent of women had engaged in various forms of sexual expression (kissing, hugging, sexual touching or caressing, intercourse, self-stimulation or oral sex) in the past 6 months
- 85 percent of men and 55 percent of women indicated that they always or usually have an orgasm when engaging in sexual intercourse
- Of those with a partner, 85 percent of men and 81 percent of women reported getting moderate to extreme physical pleasure from their relationship
- Of those with a partner, 88 percent of men and 83 percent of women noted getting moderate to extreme emotional satisfaction from their relationship with their partner
- Patterns of sexual activity and satisfaction were similar across ethnic minority groups (AARP, 2004).

Based on a relatively small number of studies, the following is a summary of recent findings about older people and sexuality:

- Older people who remain sexually active do not differ significantly in the frequency of sexual relations compared with their younger selves (longitudinal data). Rather, sexual activity appears to decrease significantly when older people are compared with younger persons at the same point in time (cross-sectional data). Table 7.1 illustrates this decline with a cross-sectional survey.

POINTS TO PONDER

When you were growing up, how did you perceive you parents' and grandparents' sexuality? What were your sources of information about older adults and sexuality? How did these affect your thinking? Then and now?

TABLE 7.1 Percent of Older Adults Who Report Having Sexual Intercourse Once a Week or More

AGE	MALE	FEMALE
45–59	62%	61%
60–74	30%	24%
75+	26%	24%

SOURCE: American Association of Retired Persons, 1999.

- When a partner is available, the rate of sexual behavior is fairly stable throughout life. Sexually active older people perceive their sex lives as remaining much the same as they grow older.
- Although good physical and mental health are predictors of sexual activity and satisfaction, even older people with chronic health problems, depression, and cognitive dysfunction can achieve sexual satisfaction.
- Relationships are more important than sexual activity per se. Regardless of the length or nature of a late-life relationship, its quality is enhanced by emotional intimacy, an ability to manage stress and external distractions, and achieving a mutually respectful sexual balance (AARP, 2004; Kingsberg, 2000; Willert and Semans, 2000).

To review, as our biological clocks change with age, it is not necessarily for the better or worse in terms of the frequency or the nature of sexual experience. Individuals who have been sexually responsive all their lives will still enjoy sexual satisfaction in their later years, although their experience may differ subjectively from earlier in life (DeLamater and Friedrich, 2002; Zeiss and Kasl-Godley, 2001). Yet, this difference can be positive. For example, 75 percent of the respondents in the classic Starr and Weiner study (1981), which explored the meaning and significance of sexuality in old age, stated that sex is the same or better than when they were younger.

Although the majority of female respondents considered orgasm as essential to a good sexual experience, they also emphasized mutuality, love, and caring as central to their enjoyment and willingly varied their sexual practices to achieve satisfaction. Male respondents stated that not only is the physical stimulation of sex important, but also that sex is necessary for them to feel alive, reaffirm their identity, and communicate with a person they care about. Although the actual level of activity may be less important than one's satisfaction with it, a number of age-related physiological changes can nevertheless affect the nature of the sexual response.

Women and Age-Related Physiological Changes

With the growing numbers of women in the 45- to 54-year-old age group, increasing attention is being given to menopause. As noted in Chapter 4, the major changes for women as they grow older are associated with the reduction in estrogen and progesterone, the predominant hormones produced by the ovaries, during menopause. The **climacteric**—loss of reproductive ability—takes place in three phases: perimenopause, menopause, and postmenopause, and may extend over many years.

Perimenopause is marked by a decline in ovarian function in which a woman's ovaries stop producing eggs and significantly decrease their monthly production of estrogen, resulting in widely fluctuating estrogen levels and unpredictable menstrual cycles. It can occur as long as 10 years before menopause, starting as young as age 35. Only recently have researchers and health care providers recognized that perimenopause brings hot flashes around the head and upper body, concentration gaps and memory lapses, mood swings, sleep troubles, irritability, and migraines typically associated with menopause. Unfortunately, perimenopause often is not included in medical school curricula, and some health care providers may still dismiss a woman's early symptoms as "all in her head." **Menopause,** in the strictest sense as one event during the climacteric, is a period in a woman's life when there is a gradual cessation of the menstrual cycle, including irregular cycles and menses, which are related to the loss of ovarian function. Menopause is considered to have occurred when 12 consecutive months have passed without a menstrual period (**postmenopause**). The average age of menopause is 52 years, although it can begin as early as age 40 and as late as age 58. Surgical removal of the uterus—hysterectomy—also brings an end to menstruation (NIA, 2003a).

Physiological changes related to the decrease in estrogen in menopause and postmenopause include:

- hot flashes
- urogenital atrophy
- urinary tract changes
- bone changes (osteoporosis)

Hot flashes are caused by vasomotor instability, when the nerves over-respond to decreases in hormone levels. This affects the hypothalamus

HOME REMEDIES FOR MENOPAUSAL SYMPTOMS

Sharon "Missy" Peat described herself as a 51-year-old woman on the verge of a nervous breakdown. After her sleep was continuously interrupted by hot flashes, one night she opened her freezer, grabbed a box of frozen peas, and applied it to the back of her neck. After a few minutes, she felt better. The sweating subsided, the panic was gone and she went back to bed within 5 minutes. During the night, she experienced no more perspiration or clamminess. Since then, she has manufactured a cold, flexible gel pack sold for the relief of hot flashes. The success of her cold pack suggests the growing market for menopause products (Jacobson, 2000).

(the part of the brain that regulates body temperature), causing the blood vessels to dilate or constrict. When they dilate, blood rushes to the skin surface, causing perspiration, flushing, and increased pulse rate and temperature. Hot flashes are characterized by a sudden sensation of heat in the upper body, often accompanied by a drenching sweat and sometimes followed by chills. Gradually diminishing in frequency, hot flashes generally disappear within a few years.

Hormonal changes and vasomotor instability such as hot flashes and sweats can disrupt and reduce sleep, with sleep deprivation leading to irritability and moodiness that are often associated with menopause. Contrary to stereotypes and taboos regarding menopause, most women do not experience hot flashes or night sweats sufficiently severe to warrant treatment. They generally do not interfere with a woman's daily activities or sexual functioning or cause psychological difficulties. More Caucasian women report symptoms such as hot flashes and insomnia than Asian American and Latina women, but the reasons for this are probably cultural or social rather than physiological differences. For example, African American women are generally more positive than other groups about this period in their lives. This wide variability in

symptoms and responses suggests that there is not an inevitable "menopausal syndrome." Nor is there any scientific explanation for why symptoms such as hot flashes occur in some women and not in others (Gonyea, 1998; NIA, 2003b).

Estrogen loss combined with the normal biological changes of aging leads to **urogenital atrophy**—a reduction in the elasticity and lubricating abilities of the vagina approximately 5 years after menopause. As the vagina becomes drier and the layer of cell walls thinner, the amount of lubricants secreted during sexual arousal is reduced. Although vaginal lubrication takes longer, these changes have little impact on the quality of orgasms and do not result in an appreciable loss in sensation or feeling (Zeiss and Kasl-Godley, 2001). Nevertheless, discomfort associated with urogenital atrophy is an important contributor to decline in sexual activity with menopause. Artificial lubricants such as KY jellies and vaginal creams can help minimize discomfort. In addition, regular and consistent sexual activity, including masturbation, maintains vaginal lubricating ability and muscle tone, thereby reducing discomfort during intercourse (Gelfand, 2000).

Because of the thinning of vaginal walls, which results from estrogen degeneration and which offers less protection to the bladder and the urethra, lower urinary tract infections such as cystitis and burning urination may occur more frequently. These problems can be treated, however. Incontinence is found to inhibit sexual desire and response; unfortunately, many older women are reluctant to discuss incontinence with others, which precludes their finding ways to prevent its negative impact on sexual activity. Loss of estrogen during menopause also affects the absorption of calcium in the bones, resulting in osteoporosis (see Chapters 4 and 15).

The primary medical response to the symptoms of hot flashes and vaginal atrophy has been hormone replacement therapy (HRT), using estrogen alone (ERT) or in combination with progestin (EPT), which restores women's hormones to levels similar to those before menopause. As noted in Chapter 3, estrogen can alleviate hot flashes and vaginal changes, including atrophy, dryness, itching, pain during intercourse, urinary tract problems, and frequent urination (NIA, 2003b). However, recent studies suggest that the risk of breast cancer, blood clots, heart attacks, and strokes with long-term use may be substantially greater than previous research indicated, as described in Chapter 4. For these reasons, women who choose to use HRT for menopausal systems should receive the lowest effective dose (Nelson et al., 2006; NIH, 2004).

Because of the risks of HRT, many women have turned to alternative therapies. Some therapies appear to help moderate the symptoms of menopause and perimenopause; these include eating foods that are high in calcium, vitamin E, and fiber and lower in fat; weight-bearing and aerobic exercise; acupuncture; biofeedback; and herbal or naturopathic treatments, as shown in the box above (NIA, 2003a; Phillip, 2003). In a survey of 886 women age 45 to 65, the majority of women who used such alternative therapies found them to be beneficial, although there was no comparison group (Newton et al., 2002) At the same time, women need to be cautious about the use of alternative therapies not yet proven empirically to be effective.

In many non-Western cultures, menopause is viewed as a time of respect and status for women. Our cultural view is that women are expected to have difficulty at this period of life,

---

ALTERNATIVES TO ESTROGEN REPLACEMENT THERAPY

- herbal remedies, including soy, wild yams, beans, and black cohosh—a folk medicine made from a shrub root, but their effectiveness is unproven
- drugs already proven for other conditions that may reduce hot flashes (e.g., some antihypertensives; certain antidepressants; Neurontin, an antiseizure drug)
- combination of fluoride and calcium, but these may have gastrointestinal side effects

---

although this too has shifted as the baby boomers redefined menopause. The incidence of insomnia, depression, and anxiety may be traced to the meaning or psychosocial significance that women attach to menopause, as well as the cultural value placed on body image and on women's roles as mothers. Other symptoms reported by menopausal women, such as headaches, dizziness, palpitations, and weight increase, are not necessarily caused by menopause itself, but may be due to underlying psychosocial reasons. A growing number of women view menopause as a potentially positive transition characterized by relief rather than as a loss of fertility or a cause of depression. It can be a new and fulfilling time of opportunities, self-accomplishment, meaning, and greater autonomy (Brice, 2003; Defey et al., 1996; Gonyea, 1998; Jones, 1997). In sum, like other transitions experienced by women, menopause is affected by physiological and health factors, personality, self-esteem, and culture.

Despite some uncomfortable symptoms, menopause does not impede full sexual activity from a physiological point of view. In fact, many women, freed of worries about pregnancy and birth control, report greater sexual satisfaction after the menopause, including after a hysterectomy (NIA, 2003b). Generally, an older woman's sexual response cycle has all the dimensions of her younger response, but the time it takes for

---

RELIEF OF HOT FLASHES DURING MENOPAUSE

- avoid spicy foods, caffeine, and alcohol
- drink cold water or juice as a hot flash comes on
- wear breathable clothing (e.g., cotton), not synthetics
- dress in layers of clothing that can be gradually removed
- sleep in a cool room

her to respond to sexual stimulation gradually increases. The subjective levels of sexual tension initiated or elaborated by clitoral stimulation do not differ for older and younger women. The **preorgasmic plateau phase,** during which sexual tension is at its height, is extended in duration. Older women's capacity for orgasms may be slowed, but not impaired. The orgasm is experienced more rapidly, somewhat less intensely, and more spasmodically. The resolution phase, during which the body returns to its baseline prearousal state, occurs more rapidly than in younger women (Blonna and Levitan, 2000; Zeiss and Kasl-Godley, 2001). With more men turning to **sexupharmaceuticals,** such as Viagra, to treat erectile difficulties, little is known about the experiences of their female sexual partners and possible detrimental effects for them. Although the publicity surrounding Viagra—and its wide availability—may facilitate more positive attitudes to sexuality in old age, it may also create a societal expectation that a healthy and "normal" life for older adults requires the continuation of "youthful" (energetic) sex lives focused on penetrative intercourse. When prescribing these drugs, health care providers need to be sensitive to partners' perspectives and desires and to relationship dynamics (Potts et al., 2003).

In summary, no physiological impediment exists to full sexual activity for postmenopausal women. Changes such as the thinning of vaginal walls and loss of vaginal elasticity may render intercourse somewhat more painful but these effects can be minimized by sexual regularity. Instead, older women's sexuality tends to be influenced more by sociocultural expectations than by physiological changes—by the limited number of available male partners for heterosexual women, persistent stigma about lesbian relations in old age, and common cultural definitions of older women as asexual and unattractive, which can negatively affect women's self-image. These psychosocial barriers are discussed more fully later in this chapter.

Men and Age-Related Physiological Changes

Relatively little attention has been given to men's hormonal rhythms compared to women's. One reason for this is that men generally maintain their fertility and their capacity to father children, making hormonal and sexual changes less abrupt and visible. There is, however, increasing evidence that **male menopause** or **"viropause"** occurs and can affect the psychological, interpersonal, social, and spiritual dimensions of a man's life. Nevertheless, the male climacteric differs from women's in two significant ways: it occurs 8 to 10 years later than for women, and progresses at a more gradual rate. This is because the loss of testosterone (approximately 1 percent a year on average), while varying widely among men, is not as dramatic nor as abrupt as the estrogen depletion for menopausal women.

VIAGRA

Viagra has been touted as a wonder drug for men, with flashy ads typically featuring a romantic man and woman. The benefits described by the ads have been empirically supported. For example, a 1998 study of over 500 men, reported in the *New England Journal of Medicine,* confirmed Viagra's effectiveness. The most common side effects were headache, flushing, and disturbed digestion. For men and their partners who have been frustrated by impotence, the side effects are undoubtedly viewed as minor irritants. About 20 percent of men, however, do not experience any benefits from taking Viagra. New drugs such as Levitra and Cialis are advertised to be more vigorous and longer-lasting than Viagra. Viagra is sometimes prescribed for women, and has resulted in marked improvement in arousal, orgasm, and sexual enjoyment. However, Viagra does not alter women's sexual desire, which is a key factor in older women's sexuality and sexual satisfaction. (American Federation for Aging Research, 2000).

Some of the effects of this loss of testosterone are summarized as follows:

- reduced muscle size and strength
- increased calcium loss in the bones
- declines in response by the immune system
- lessened sexual response
- reduced interest in sex, anxiety and fear about sexual changes
- fatigue, irritability, indecisiveness, depression, loss of self-confidence, listlessness, poor appetite, and problems of concentration
- increased relationship problems and arguments with partners over sex, love, and intimacy
- loss of erection during sexual activity
- changes in secondary sexual characteristics such as a man's voice becoming higher pitched, his facial hair growing more slowly, and muscularity giving way to flabbiness (Diamond, 1997; Weg, 1996).

These changes, which occur in varying degrees, require some adaptation. But they do not necessarily interfere with sexual performance nor reduce sexual enjoyment and desire.

The normal physiological changes that characterize men's aging can alter the nature of the sexual response, however. The preorgasmic plateau phase, or excitement stage, increases in length, so

> ### POINTS TO PONDER
>
> Imagine the appeal of a recent Internet ad to some older men:
>
> Internet Advertising of Herbal Viagra—No prescription, no doctor, less than $1 a pill
>
> Welcome to the new sexual revolution. It's the all-natural male potency and pleasure pill that men everywhere are buzzing about. Herbal V is safe, natural and specifically formulated to help support male sexual function and pleasure. You just take two easy-to-swallow tablets one hour before sexual activity. . . . Herbal V—Bringing back the magic.

> ### AGE-RELATED PHYSIOLOGICAL CHANGES IN SEXUAL FUNCTION
>
> **Normal Changes in Aging Women**
> - Reduction in vaginal elasticity and lubrication
> - Thinning of vaginal walls
> - Slower response to sexual stimulation
> - Longer preorgasmic plateau phase
> - Fewer and less intense orgasmic contractions
> - Rapid return to prearousal state after orgasm
>
> **Normal Changes in Aging Men**
> - Erection may require more direct stimulation.
> - Erection is slower, less full, and disappears quickly after orgasm.
> - Orgasm is experienced more rapidly, less intensely, and more spasmodically.
> - Decreased volume and force of ejaculation.
> - Increased length of time between orgasm and subsequent erections (longer refractory period).
> - Occasional lack of orgasm during intercourse.
> - More seepage or retrograde ejaculation.

that response to sexual stimulation is slower. An **erection** may take longer to achieve and may require more direct stimulation. For example, in 18-year-old males, full erection is achieved on stimulation in an average of 3 seconds. At age 45, the average time is 18 to 20 seconds, while a 75-year old man requires 5 minutes or more. Erections tend to be less full with age and the erect penis may be less firm. The frequency and degree of erections can be studied while a man is sleeping. The recording of nocturnal penile tumescence—(sleep-related erections)—offers an opportunity to evaluate sexual functioning objectively under relatively controlled conditions. Such studies have found that the volume and force of the ejaculation are decreased in older men as they sleep. The two-stage orgasm—the sense of ejaculation inevitably followed by actual semen expulsion that is experienced by younger males—often blurs into a one-stage ejaculation for older men. Yet these erectile changes do not necessarily alter a man's sexual satisfaction (Blonna and Levitan, 2000; DeLamater and Friedrich, 2002; Masters and Johnson, 1981).

Another physiological change is that orgasm is experienced less intensely, and more spasmodically and rapidly, occurring every second or third act of intercourse rather than every time. The length of time between orgasm and subsequent erections increases (i.e., the **refractory period** after ejaculation, before a second ejaculation is possible, is longer). However, although these changes may alter the nature of the sexual experience, none of them causes sexual inactivity or impotence. As a result, the subjectively appreciated levels of sensual pleasure may not diminish (Bortz and Wallace, 1999a, 1990b; Masters and Johnson, 1981). In recent years, as noted in Chapter 3, there has been increasing attention to hormones such as DHEA, which are produced by the adrenal glands, the brain, and the skin, to revive men's sexual interest.

Although not an inevitable consequence of aging, **erectile dysfunction** or **impotence** (i.e., an inability to get and sustain an erection) is the chief cause of older men's withdrawing from sexual activity. (Note that erectile dysfunction is a more accurate medical term than impotence, although the two terms are used interchangeably here.) In one survey, 15 to 25 percent of men by age 64 experience impotence at least one out of every four times that they have sex (NIA, 2002). In the 2004 AARP survey, 24 percent of older male respondents had been diagnosed with erectile dysfunction. Most dysfunction is caused by disease or by age-induced deterioration of the blood vessels. Other problems are low testosterone levels and excessive use of tobacco or alcohol. Older men and their partners need to be informed that erectile dysfunctions are both common and treatable. Although impotence and lowered testosterone levels are not significantly correlated, declines in DHEA levels with aging appear to be associated with erectile dysfunction (American Prostate Society, 2003).

Despite the underlying pathologies frequently associated with impotence, it tends to be under-diagnosed because of the embarrassment and reluctance of older men and their health care providers to discuss sexual matters candidly. Since medical treatments can be effective in altering erectile dysfunction, health care providers must be sure to rule out the physiological basis of impotence, which tends to be more important than psychosocial factors (NIA, 2002). Physical risk factors include cardiovascular disease, the effects of drugs (especially antihypertensives, antidepressants, and tranquilizers), diabetes, hypertension, endocrine or metabolic disorders, neurological disorders, depression, alcohol, or prostate disorders. Most types of prostate surgery do not cause impotence, as discussed in the next section. In recent years, new ways to treat impotence have drawn increased attention. The marketing of a wide range of products reflects, in part, drug companies' awareness of baby boomers' buying power and their greater openness to talking about and wanting to experience sexual pleasure than prior cohorts of older men.

Clinical trials of sexupharmaceuticals, such as Sildenafil or Viagra, found that 60 to 80 percent of the men who participated and who had varying degrees of impotence benefited in terms of increased sexual satisfaction and improved relationships with their partners. However, only 8 percent of men and 2 percent of women age 65 and older report that they have taken any medicine, hormone, or other treatment to enhance sexual performance (AARP, 2004). This suggests that more attention should be given to the psychological factors related to intimacy and sexual enjoyment in old age, not just to chemical solutions. As noted earlier, one potential negative impact of Viagra and other erectile dysfunction drugs is reinforcing the cultural expectations that aging men are required to retain their youthful virility (Gross and Blundo, 2005). A theme of this chapter is that sexuality in old age needs to be expanded to include more than erection and ejaculation during intercourse, and both partners' needs must be considered. For example, health care providers and counselors must encourage couples to communicate their fears about impotence and suggest ways that they can openly enjoy fulfilling sexual experiences and intimacy without an erection. Medical treatments for erectile dysfunction should also be carefully explored, including:

- oral medications that cause erections
- pellets inserted into the urethra with an applicator that dilate the arteries and relax the erectile tissues, thereby triggering involuntary erections
- injection therapy
- vacuum pumps
- penile implants
- vascular surgery

However, less than 50 percent of men with erectile dysfunction/impotence receive treatment for this condition (AARP, 2004).

As is true for older women, the physiological changes that affect sexual activities in older men do not necessarily alter sexual satisfaction.

Chronic Diseases and Sexuality

Although normal physiological changes do not inevitably reduce sexual satisfaction, sexuality is associated with good physical and mental health, including being physically active and fit. Since sexual response requires the coordination of multiple systems of the body—hormonal, circulatory, and nervous systems if any of these are disrupted, sexual functioning can be affected. As a result, chronic diseases can play a major role in the decline of sexual function, and is often cited as a reason for refraining from sexual activity (Nusbaum, Hamilton, and Lenahan, 2003). Even when an illness does not directly affect the sexual organs themselves, systemic diseases can affect sexual functioning because of the following factors:

- their effects on mediating physiological mechanisms such as hypertension and arrhythmia
- chronic pain

> **PSYCHOLOGICAL TREATMENT OF SEXUAL PROBLEMS ASSOCIATED WITH CHRONIC ILLNESS: SUGGESTIONS FOR HEALTH CARE PROVIDERS**
>
> - provision of information about normal sexual responses and impact of the illness on sexual function
> - creation of a welcoming open atmosphere that encourages elders to talk about sexual concerns
> - change of attitudes, from exclusive emphasis on intercourse to acceptance of a wide range of sexual behaviors that enhance mutual pleasure, arousal and intimacy
> - review of medications that may interfere with sexual fulfillment
> - increased mutual communication about sexual preferences and needs
> - reduction of psychological factors that inhibit sexual response
> - facilitation of acceptance and adjustment to the limitations imposed by the chronic illness
> - creation of living arrangements that provide opportunities for sexual intimacy between partners
>
> SOURCE: Schiavi, 1999.

- complications of medication, especially from antihypertensive drugs
- negative effects on well-being and self-perceptions
- the all-consuming distraction of the illness may deplete the emotional energy needed for sexual interest and responsiveness (NIA, 2002)

Given these factors, it is not surprising that 30 percent of men and 16 percent of women cite better health as something that would improve their satisfaction with their sex lives (AARP, 2004). As is true across the life course, an older adult's personal characteristics combined with the specific challenges imposed by an illness influence how they adjust to disease and respond to treatment. Accordingly, how individuals appraise threats to sexual identity, sexual intimacy, body image, and control over bodily functions determines the nature of their adaptive responses (Shiavi, 1999). The way in which older people approach sexual losses entailed by chronic illness probably reflects how they have coped with other losses throughout their lives. Fortunately, health care providers now know more about how adults can compensate for disease to have satisfying sex lives, as shown in the box on page 283 regarding psychological treatment of sexual problems. There is also growing recognition that sexual activity can be a major component of treatment following a major illness or surgery and is a minimal risk to a person's health (Nusbaum et al., 2003). In this section, the chronic illnesses that commonly affect sexual functioning—diseases of the prostate, diabetes, heart disease and strokes, degenerative and rheumatoid arthritis, depression and dementia—are briefly discussed.

More than 50 percent of men age 65 and older have some degree of **prostate enlargement,** known as benign prostatic hypertrophy or BPH, and will experience prostate difficulties, usually inflammation or enlargement of the prostate gland, pain in the uro-genital area, and urinary flow dysfunction (Bostwick, MacLennan, and Larson, 1996; Diamond, 1997). Infections can be successfully treated with antibiotics, and new drugs are available to shrink the prostate. Some prostate problems can be reduced through simple treatments such as warm baths and gentle massage or antibiotics. However, when urination is severely restricted or painful, surgery is necessary. After surgery, semen is no longer ejaculated through the penis, but is pushed back into the bladder and later discharged in the urine. After healing occurs, the capacity to ejaculate and fertility may return in some men. The feeling of orgasm or climax can still be present, and sexual pleasure is not inevitably lessened.

Prostate cancer, the most common male cancer, affects one in eight American men. The rate at which this cancer kills men is similar to that of breast cancer in women. About 80 percent of all prostate cancers are found in men age 65 and older. Men who have a family history of prostate cancer and African American men are at increased risk of developing it, and should have more frequent screening exams. A major problem in diagnosis is that prostate cancer may have no symptoms in its early and middle stages while it is confined to the prostate gland and more likely to be amenable to treatment. After it spreads, symptoms include pain or stiffness in the lower back, hips, or upper thighs. Because the early symptoms are often masked, the American Cancer Society recommends that all men 40 years of age and older have an annual rectal exam, and that men age 50 and older receive an annual prostate specific antigen (PSA) test (American Federation for Aging Research, 2000; Gallagher and Gapstur, 2006).

The most extreme but effective treatment for prostate cancer is radical perineal prostatectomy, which includes cutting nerves. Although most prostate cancer treatments do not cause impotence, irreversible erectile dysfunction and incontinence can result from radical prostatectomy. Recent findings, however, suggest that potency and continence outcomes may be similar to other forms of treatment for prostate cancer (Han et al., 2004; Peschel and Colberg, 2003). Nerve-sparing surgery also has been developed, and may reduce the incidence of impotence among some men who undergo radical prostatectomy. Of course, the urologist's priority is to rid the patient of cancer tissue, and nerves very close to the prostate gland must often be severed. Nevertheless, even in these cases, men who have lost their normal physiologic response can still achieve orgasm (Donatucci and Greenfield, 2006; Harris, Weiss, and Blaivas, 2004; Rogers et al., 2006; Saranchuk et al., 2005). Fortunately, there are an increasing number of alternatives for early prostate cancer, such as radioactive pellet implantation, other forms of radiation therapy, or microwave energy to produce heat that can destroy cancer cells. Other promising developments are the clinical testing of a variety of vaccinations; brachytherapy, which precisely places radioactive seeds into the prostate gland to kill cancer cells and reduces the rates of impotence and incontinence; and new chemotherapy regimens that have produced a survival advantage (Doust et al., 2004; Gallagher and Gapstur, 2006; Han et al., 2004; Peschel and Colberg, 2003; Swanson, 2006). New options to restore sexual functioning after treatment of the cancer are **penile implants** and smooth muscle relaxants that are injected into the penis to reverse impotence; more research on their effectiveness is needed. Health care providers must provide older men with as much information as possible about the implications of prostate surgery, radiation, and hormonal treatments for sexual functioning. In some instances, men with prostate cancer place more weight on quality of life considerations than on improving survival through aggressive treatment, even though survival rates are greater for men who choose a definitive therapy (Afrin and Ergul, 2000; McNeel and Disis, 2000; Tward et al., 2006; Van Tol-Geerdink et al., 2004).

Although prostate surgery does not cause impotence in the majority of cases, between 5 and 40 percent of men who have undergone such surgery can no longer achieve an erection (Gotay, Holup, and Muraoka, 2002). In addition, since treatment of prostate cancer often involves methods that lower testosterone levels or block the effects of testosterone, a large percent of men undergoing such treatment lose their sexual desire, and up to 40 percent actually experience hot flashes (Diamond, 1997). In some instances, a man's postoperative "impotence" may be a convenient excuse for not engaging in sexual activity, or may represent fears of additional illness. When this occurs, psychological factors need to be addressed through counseling, and couples should be encouraged to try alternate methods of sexual satisfaction. When impotence is irreversible, partners need to be encouraged to pursue other means of sexual pleasure or consider a penile implant or vacuum pump.

Masturbation, more leisurely precoital stimulation, and use of artificial lubricants can all provide satisfying sexual experiences for partners dealing with erectile dysfunction.

While most older men fear that prostate surgery will interfere with their sexual functioning and satisfaction, women may fear that a hysterectomy (surgical removal of the uterus), an ovariectomy (surgical removal of both ovaries), or a mastectomy (surgical removal of one or both breasts) will negatively affect their sexuality. In most instances, however, women's sexual satisfaction and long-term functioning are not affected by these surgeries, particularly if their partners are sensitive and supportive. On the other hand, some hormonal changes associated with a complete hysterectomy may affect sex drive. When women experience menopause as a result of a hysterectomy, perhaps earlier than the average age of onset for menopause, short-term, low dose hormone replacement therapy is advisable except when the hysterectomy was due to cancer.

More common medical causes of male impotence than prostate surgery are arteriosclerosis—the vascular hardening that leads to heart attacks and strokes—and diabetes, particularly for lifelong diabetics. Anything that damages the circulatory system—smoking, inactivity, poor diet—can cause erectile dysfunction. Older people who have experienced a heart attack or heart surgery may assume that sexual activity will endanger their lives and give it up. Unfortunately, many health care providers are not sensitive to such fears and fail to reassure individuals that sexual activity can be resumed after they undergo a stress test without pain or arrhythmia (Nusbaum et al., 2003). Another precaution for post–heart attack patients who have been prescribed nitroglycerin is to take their usual dose 15 to 30 minutes before engaging in sexual activity (Schiavi, 1999). Stroke patients may also feel compelled to abstain from sexual activity because of an unfounded fear that sex could cause another occurrence. Generally, strokes do not harm the physiology of sexual functioning or the ability to experience arousal.

However, some antihypertensive drugs can cause impotence or inhibit ejaculation. Fortunately, ACE inhibitors are a class of antihypertensive drugs that are reported to cause fewer side effects on sexual function.

Impotence in life-long diabetics occurs because diabetes interferes with the circulatory and neurologic mechanisms responsible for the supply of blood flowing to the penis for erection. In such instances, a penile implant may be an option. With late-onset diabetes, impotence may be the first observable symptom of the disease. When the diabetes is under control, however, potency generally returns. The sexual functioning of women diabetics appears to be relatively unimpaired. When diabetes is controlled through balanced blood chemistry, sexual problems other than impotence that are attributable to the disease should disappear or become less severe. Other less common diseases that may cause erectile dysfunction are illnesses that affect the vascular and endocrine systems, kidney diseases, and neurological lesions in the brain or spinal cord (Schiavi, 1999).

Arthritis does not directly interfere with sexual functioning, but can make sexual activity painful. Some medications used to control arthritic pain may also affect sexual desire and performance. Yet sexual behavior can serve to maintain some range of motion of the limbs and joints and thereby help sore joints; it can also stimulate the body's production of cortisone, which is one of the substances used to treat the symptoms of rheumatoid arthritis. Experimenting with alternative positions can minimize pain during sexual intercourse. A warm bath, massage of painful joints, and timing the use of pain-killing medications approximately 30 minutes prior to intercourse may also help to control arthritic pain. As with most chronic diseases, communication with the partner about what is comfortable and pleasurable is essential. Unfortunately, the majority of older adults with arthritis do not receive treatment that could minimize its effects on sexual activity (AARP, 2004; Nusbaum et al., 2003).

It is estimated that up to 70 percent of patients with depression, especially men, experience sexual dysfunction. Depression also has differential effects on sexual interest, activity, and satisfaction. On the other hand, it is not clear that depression *causes* erectile dysfunction; it may be that the depression is a *reaction* to difficulties in sexual functioning. An alternative explanation is that sexual dysfunction is a side-effect of antidepressants and therefore may be prevented or treated (Balon, 2006; Werneke, Northey, and Bhugra, 2006). Although the reason for this association of depression with sexual dysfunction is unclear, health care providers should ask about sexual function to identify problems early among patients who exhibit depressive symptoms as well as those who are taking antidepressants. Tailoring the treatment of depression to minimize adverse effects on sexual function can increase treatment compliance and improve quality of life (Phillips and Slaughter, 2000).

Despite the high prevalence of Alzheimer's disease and other dementias, along with concerns expressed by partners and caregivers, there is limited empirical data about the impact of these disorders on sexual function. Partners faced with early stage dementia may find that sexual intimacy remains a vital means of communication and support. However, as the dementia progresses, changes in functional capacity and sexual expression can be extremely distressing to partners. Erectile problems commonly occur among male patients with Alzheimer's disease. Other sources of distress are awkward sequencing of sexual activity, requests for activities outside of the couple's sexual repertoire, and lack of regard for the healthy partner's sexual satisfaction. Healthy partners are often troubled by changes in the perceived nature of the relationship and their own loss of sexual desire as the disease progresses, often furthered by their exhaustion of being full-time caregivers. Although concerns have been raised whether sexual activity with a partner who has dementia and cannot consent is unethical and in some instances abusive, it can be argued that from a relationship-centered perspective, sexual activity between loving spouses is morally permissible, even if the partner lacks the cognitive ability to consent (Lingler, 2003). Health care providers need to help couples deal with losses in the relationship bond and sexuality, and changes in communication and intimacy (LoboPraabhu et al., 2005). Issues of competency arise when a patient with dementia attempts to initiate a relationship with a new sexual partner, which may occur in long-term care facilities. Although such behavior may be disturbing to health care providers and families, they raise concerns about individuals' rights as well as the difficult task of determining a person's capacity to make informed judgments regarding new relationships. Staff in such facilities often express fears about inappropriate sexual behavior by patients with dementia. However, the incidence of sexually aggressive behaviors toward staff or other patients is actually quite low. This suggests that the same degree of skill needed by health care staff to manage other symptoms of dementia is required to address inappropriate or ambiguous sexual behaviors when they occur. Training in sexual matters may assist health care providers to assist family members as well as patients themselves in dealing with this often ignored aspect of Alzheimer's disease and other dementias (LoboPraabhu et al., 2005; Loue, 2005).

Closely related to the effects of chronic illness on sexuality are those of drugs, including alcohol. Diagnosing drug effects on sexuality may be particularly difficult, since drugs affect individuals differently, and drug interactions frequently occur. Drugs that inhibit the performance of any organ system can alter sexual response. For men, some medications that are prescribed for chronic conditions may cause impotence, decrease sexual drive, delay ejaculation, or result in an inability to ejaculate. Medications such as SSRIs that are used to treat depression and psychosis are particularly likely to impair erectile functioning (Balon, 2006). Of patients taking antipsychotics such as thioridazine, 49 percent will experience impaired ejaculation, and 44 percent impotence. Yet this is one of the first drugs that a physician prescribes for an older person who is agitated, depressed, schizophrenic, or anxious. Similarly, erectile dysfunction occurs in 40 percent of cases involving the drug amoxapine for treatment of depression. As noted above, other types of drugs likely to affect sexual functioning are antihypertensive medications used to treat high blood pressure, drugs to control diabetes, and steroids. As a whole, medication use and the rate of adverse effects of drug therapy are consistently higher in female than in male older patients (Gelfand, 2000). For women, drugs can be associated with decreased vaginal lubrication, reduced sexual drive, and a delay or inability to achieve orgasm. Fortunately, both physicians and older people are now more aware of potential negative effects of drug regimes on sexual functioning. Likewise, more drugs are available that do not have negative side effects on sexual desire and ability. These include ACE inhibitors among the antihypertensives; fluoxetine, trazodone, and maprotiline among the antidepressants; desipramine among the tricyclic antidepressants; and lorazepam, alprazolam, and buspirone among antianxiety agents (Balon, 2006).

Alcohol, when used excessively, acts as a depressant on sexual ability and desire (Johnson, Phelps, and Cottler, 2004). Alcohol consumption affects male sexual performance by making both erection and ejaculation difficult to attain; consequently, a man's anxiety about performance may increase and result in temporary impotence. Prolonged alcoholism may lead to erectile dysfunction as a result of irreversible damage to the nervous system. Although there is little research on the effects of alcohol on women's sexual performance, some women who misuse alcohol are found to experience less sexual desire and no orgasms. More research is needed to differentiate the extent to which alcohol may be a means to cope with sexual problems or whether concerns about sexual performance are a consequence of alcohol misuse and contribute to sustaining the addiction (Schiavi, 1999).

Gay, Lesbian, Bisexual, and Transgender (GLBT) Partners in Old Age

Although most examples of sexual activity in this chapter are presented in terms of heterosexual marital relationships, this should not be assumed to always be the case. Although there are no reliable data, gay men and lesbians are estimated to comprise between 6 and 10 percent of the total population, which would suggest a similar pattern among older adults. In the most recent AARP national survey, 5 percent of men and 1 percent of women age 70 and older reported having current same-sex partners (AARP, 2004). These rates may be even higher because of beliefs among the current cohort of elders that homosexuality is taboo and therefore under-reported (Bennett and Gates, 2004). Older people, their families, and health and social service professionals need to be sensitive to heterosexual relationships outside of marriage and to same-gender, or homosexual, relationships. Such sensitivity includes discarding

Many lesbian and gay couples maintain long-term commitments to each other.

stereotypical views of the nature of GLBT relationships. Contrary to commonly held images, the varieties of gay and lesbian bonding are similar to those within heterosexual communities—ranging from monogamous life partners and non-monogamous primary relationships to serial monogamy and episodic liaisons. Gay and lesbian life partners face many of the issues that confront long-term heterosexual spouses, such as fears about the loss of sexual attractiveness, the death or illness of a sexual partner, or diminished interest or capacity for sex because of chronic disease. On the other hand, after a lifetime of discrimination or ostracism from family members, coworkers, or society generally, GLBT couples face additional issues related to intimacy and sexuality, which are discussed in this chapter and in Chapter 9 (Butler, 2006).

Although sexual activity for GLBT elders differs as much as it does for heterosexuals, there is also a consistent pattern of relatively high life satisfaction with being gay, positive adjustment to aging, and ongoing sexual interest and activity. Both lesbians and gay men are more likely to

---

REDEFINING SEXUAL ORIENTATION IN LATER LIFE

After her husband left her for a younger woman, a bout with breast cancer, and the death of her 26-year-old daughter, Isabel found herself increasingly drawn to spending time only with women: in a mothers' support group, in a group of midlife women coping with divorce, and through her work. She started attending workshops and lectures through the local college's Women's Information Center. At one of those courses, she met Carla, also recovering from a bitter divorce. They began to spend nearly all their free time together, enjoying the equality and closeness in their relationship. Within a year, Carla moved in with Isabel. Although their adult children were initially shocked by their mothers' behavior, they soon saw the value of the loving support and intimacy that their mothers experienced for the next 26 years.

report a high level of life satisfaction if they are happily partnered and communicating effectively with one another. Satisfaction is also high if they have a strong informal social support system, often defined as family and friends of choice, and have reconstituted what it means to be GLBT into something positive (Barranti and Cohen, 2000; Grossman, D'Augelli, and Hershberger 2000; Grossman, D'Augelli, and O'Connell, 2001; Healy, 2002; Orel, 2004).

Older lesbians, often closeted about their sexual orientation, have been labeled the *invisible minority*. They have generally practiced serial monogamy throughout their lives. The hiding of one's sexual orientation has been a survival strategy for some lesbians because maintaining employment was paramount to being self-sufficient. Nevertheless, most usually report a positive self-image and feelings about being identified as a lesbian (Clunis et al., 2005; Martin and Lyon, 2001; Morrow, 2001). Older lesbians generally do not fear changes in physical appearance, loneliness, or isolation in old age as much as some heterosexual women do. This may be because of the strong friendship networks that characterize many lesbian relationships or flexibility in gender roles that allows them to adjust more effectively to the socially constructed beliefs of aging and being old. Most lesbians remain sexually active, although sexual frequency generally declines. The extent to which sexual activity is considered to be an integral part of a lesbian relationship varies, although sexuality in a broader sense of intimacy continues to be important. For some, lesbianism is a wider female interdependence and sense of positive self-identity rather than a sexual relationship as such (Jones and Nystrom, 2002).

The number of gay men with partners increases with age and peaks among those age 46 to 55. After age 60, the percent of gay couples and the frequency of sexual activity decreases because of death, illness, cautiousness, or rejection of the notion of having a single, lifelong partner. But most gay men report that they are

---

STAFF SENSITIVITY TO GLBT RESIDENTS

In a nursing home in San Francisco, a chronically ill, wheelchair-bound African American man, who had become depressed and withdrawn, confided to a psychiatrist that "he liked men." That clue was the catalyst for a collaborative project between concerned staff and local gay and lesbian leaders to develop a social support system to draw out presumed closeted and lonely GLBT residents. Staff participated in sensitivity training, and a GLBT Rainbow group was formed. Social workers and nursing staff sensitively and discretely directed invitations to individuals who might be interested in coming to a Halloween party. Fifteen GLBT residents came, danced in wheelchairs, laughed, and sang. A year later, the Rainbow group had become the largest social support group at the facility (Martin and Lyon, 2001).

---

sexually active and are satisfied with their partners and their sex lives. They are more likely to be in long-term relationships (with an average length of 10 years) or none at all, rather than in short-term relationships of a year or less. Similar to their heterosexual peers, gay men are devalued in their own community for the natural features of aging: graying hair, wrinkles, added weight. Looking fit and youthful—that is, "not your age"—tends to increase a gay man's acceptability as a partner (Adam, 2000). Nevertheless, they generally maintain positive feelings about themselves and their appearance in old age. Similarly, gay men report a positive sense of self-esteem, well-being, and contentment, and adapt fairly well to the aging process (Berger and Kelley, 2001; Morrow, 2001). Despite fears of loneliness and social isolation, most gay men have closer friendships in old age than do heterosexual men, and these friends and confidants may serve to resolve some existing fears of aging. For many gay men, friendships may replace family ties disrupted by declaration of their homosexuality. Older gay men are just as likely to be involved in the homosexual network, satisfied with their social lives and sexual orientation, and confident in their popularity with other gays as their younger counterparts (MetLife, 2006; Murray and Adam, 2001; Yoakam, 1999). On the other hand, compared with their younger counterparts, gay men in today's older cohort tend to:

- fear exposure of their homosexuality
- hide their sexual orientation
- view their relatives, friends, and employers as less accepting of their homosexuality
- see their sexual orientation as outside of their personal control

However, these differences largely reflect cohort effects, rather than the aging process per se. The social support function of gay and lesbian relationships as "families of choice" is discussed further in Chapter 9. Health care providers, especially staff in long-term care facilities, need to recognize GLBT relationships and modify the environment to support GLBT elders' desire for intimacy.

As noted in Chapter 4, the increase in HIV/AIDS among the older population is of growing concern. Despite the risks, most older gay men remain sexually active, although they engage less frequently in one-night encounters and are more knowledgeable about safe sex than comparably aged heterosexual males. With the increasing public awareness about the importance of safe sex, future cohorts of gay men may be less likely to engage in high-risk sexual behavior. Of concern, however, is the increase in high-risk sexual behavior among younger gay men. Ongoing, accessible, and culturally relevant public education about safe sex is essential. Older persons with HIV/AIDS are found to be less likely to use emotional support and mental health services than the younger population. Such services may need to be reconfigured and presented differently in order to meet the emotional needs of elders diagnosed with HIV/AIDS. Preventive and support interventions need also to be culturally relevant (Emlet, 1996).

Psychosocial Factors and Late-Life Affection, Love, and Intimacy

In addition to the effects of normal physiological changes and chronic disease on sexual activity and enjoyment, a number of psychosocial factors affect the ways in which older people express their sexuality. These include:

- Past history of sexual activity and availability of a partner. Those who were most sexually active in middle age generally remain so in old age.
- Negative attitudes toward sexual activities and intimate behavior other than intercourse such as kissing, petting, holding and being held, dancing, massage, and masturbation interfere with the openness to try new ways of expressing intimacy.
- Emotional reactions to physiological changes and to illness-induced or doctor-induced changes.
- Responses to others' attitudes, including the societal norm that one is "too old" for sex.
- Societal misconceptions regarding sexuality in later life can powerfully affect one's self-concept as remaining sexually attractive and interesting.
- Living arrangements. For example, older adults in assisted living or nursing homes may face barriers to sexual expression, including lack of privacy, partners and, negative attitudes among staff and family.

A primary psychosocial factor, especially for women, is the availability of a partner. Although the nature of sexual relationships is becoming increasingly varied, most sexual activity for the current cohort of older people occurs within the context of a marital relationship. For women in heterosexual relationships, a central problem is differential life expectancy and the fact that most women have married men older than themselves. Because of older women's lower marriage and

Older adults find many ways to express intimacy.

remarriage rates, their opportunities for sexual activity within heterosexual relationships is dramatically reduced with age, but their capacity for sexual enjoyment is not altered.

The current cohort of older women, for whom sexual activity was generally tied to marriage, have relatively few options for sexual relationships. Unfortunately, these options are even more limited by the lack of socially approved models of sexuality for older women. For many women, their only models for sexuality may be the young. In addition, the pairing of older women with younger men is still rare, largely because of the double standard of aging in which older men are often viewed as "distinguished" while older women are perceived as unattractive and asexual. Women are also more likely than men to face socioeconomic barriers to meeting new partners, given the higher incidence of poverty among women compared to men. When a woman is preoccupied with financial or health worries, sexual activity may be a low priority.

Gender differences in sexual interest and participation may also be a barrier to finding satisfying intimate heterosexual relationships. Women generally report that the relational aspects of sexual activities—sitting and talking, making oneself more attractive, and saying loving words—are more important to them than to men. Men, however, often view sexual activities such as erotic readings and movies, sexual daydreams, and physically intimate activities, such as body caressing, intercourse, and masturbation, as more important than do women. Men tend to perceive women more sexually than women perceive men, although women who rate their partners as physically attractive also attribute positive qualities to their partner and to the interaction (Johnson, 1997; Levesque, Nave, and Lowe, 2006).

As noted earlier, the presence of a partner is a primary factor affecting sexuality in both men and women. Accordingly, a man who has not had sexual intercourse for a long time following the loss or illness of a partner may experience what has been called **widower's syndrome.** He may have both the desire and new opportunities for sexual activity, but his physiological system may not respond and he may be unable to maintain an erection. If he subscribes to the myth that in sex, performance counts (how many orgasms, how long an erection), rather than focusing on pleasuring and closeness, he is likely to experience performance anxiety and fear. Since anxiety tends to block sexual interest and response, he may be caught in a bind—the more he is concerned about performing well, the harder he tries and the more difficult it becomes. In such instances, older men need to be reminded that there is no right way to enjoy sex. Rather, sex can be whatever they and their partners find satisfying at the moment. Unhurried, nondemanding sexual interaction with an understanding partner can help resolve anxieties associated with widower's syndrome.

Similarly, women may face **widow's syndrome.** After a year or more of sexual inactivity, women are likely to experience a reduction in the elasticity of the vaginal walls. With less response to sexual stimulation, vaginal lubrication is slowed and reduced. Although these are all symptoms that arise from estrogen deficiency, they become more severe after a long period of no sexual contact. For men and women, frequent contact is important to ensure sexual responsiveness and comfort. Both men and women who are grieving the loss of a partner are initially unlikely to have the energy or interest in someone beyond themselves—both essential features of successful sexual activity.

Another critical factor in the physical and social environment is whether living arrangements provide opportunities for privacy. Such opportunities are most likely to be limited for those in adult family homes or nursing homes. Lack of privacy, negative staff attitudes, administrative rules, and the unromantic atmosphere of institutional environments all reduce the opportunities for residents to be sexually interested or involved. On the other hand, when conjugal rooms are set aside, some residents may be uncomfortable using them (Hu and Za, 2006; Loue, 2005).

Staff attitudes, which tend to reflect those of the larger society, may be the greatest barrier in long-term care facilities. Staff may assume that frail residents no longer need sexual intimacy. If older residents express a desire for sexual activity, staff may ignore, infantilize, tease, or ridicule them, or report it to administrators, thereby adding to a sense of embarrassment. Other staff may believe that chronic illness makes sexual activities impossible or harmful. Despite such obstacles, some residents in such settings are sexually active, and others would be if opportunities were available. The placement of older persons in long-term care facilities does not mean the end of their sexual interest. As noted earlier, even older people with dementia in nursing homes may maintain the competency to initiate sexual relationships (Hu and Za, 2006). Although there are significant legal and ethical issues in forming institutional policy and procedures to address residents' intimacy needs, nursing homes are developing such policies. These policies encom-

Staff in long-term care facilities can provide emotional support through touch.

pass residents' sexual rights to ensure privacy, establish conjugal rooms or home visits, evaluate residents' concerns about sexual functioning, encourage varied forms of sexual expression, and educate both staff and residents about sexuality and aging (Loue, 2005). It is important for staff to respect their residents' sexuality.

To summarize, the psychological and social factors that may affect sexual activity among older people include:

- past history of sexual activity
- attitudes toward sexual activities other than intercourse
- reactions to physiological or illness-induced changes
- reactions to others' attitudes
- availability of a partner, especially for women
- performance anxiety, which is often exacerbated for widowers and widows
- opportunities for privacy
- staff attitudes, including homophobia and ageism, and institutional policies

As noted throughout this chapter, it is also important to recognize and to convey to older individuals that sexuality and affection may be expressed in a wide variety of ways other than through sex. In fact, older people are more experienced at loving than any other age group, but this experience is often discounted. As stated above, **intimacy**—defined as the freedom to respond to and express human closeness—love, attachment, and friendship are cherished aspects of life, vital to an older person's well-being, quality of life, and active aging. When elders are experiencing assaults on their self-esteem, the need for affection may become even more intense. Without such affection, older individuals may feel lonely, even though they may be surrounded by other people and not physically alone.

Avenues for expressing intimacy are sensory, sensual, and sexual. Intimacy can involve flirting, laughing, smiling, communicating love through words, singing, touching, holding, as well as genital expression (Genevay, 1999). With age, long-term relationships frequently move toward deeper levels of intimacy expressed as loyalty, commitment, sharing, and mutual emotional response. This is not the case, however, in relationships characterized by conflict, emotional distance, and emotional or physical abuse throughout the years. In addition, many older people dealing with the feelings of loss and loneliness occasioned by the death of a partner or divorce may find it difficult to reinvest the energy needed to develop intimate relationships.

Touch is an important aspect of most intimate relationships. The need to be touched is life-long; physical contact through touching and caressing is as powerful in old age as in infancy, childhood, and early adulthood. Since the sense of touch is the most basic sense, older individuals may rely on it to a greater extent in their social interactions than other age groups (Weil, 2005). Just beneath an older person's expression of loneliness or of missing a former partner may lie the desire for someone to touch him or her. A hand clasp or hand laid gently on the shoulder or arm, a child's hug, or a massage can all be vital to addressing older persons' needs for

---

THE IMPORTANCE OF TOUCH

Val, a widow for 12 years, lives in a central Boston neighborhood. Her son and daughters live on the West Coast, and rarely see her. Fortunately, her neighborhood is a close-knit one and younger neighbors keep watch for her. They are accustomed to seeing her out, walking her three small dogs, talking to the dogs and giving them lots of affection. Last week, she was out walking her dogs for the first time in 3 weeks after a severe bout of flu. One of her 35-year-old male neighbors came up to her, said how glad he was to see her, and hugged her. She began to cry in response to the human warmth of the hug. It had been nearly 2 years since someone had hugged her like that.

---

affection and can increase their responsiveness. Staff in long-term care facilities especially need to be sensitive to the life-affirming role of touch for most older people, including those with dementia and those who are withdrawn or disoriented. On the other hand, health and human service professionals must recognize cultural differences regarding the meaning and appropriateness of touch. They need to be aware that, in some cultures, differential social status, gender, age, and the setting may influence the older person's acceptance of a friendly touch.

Friends are often important sources of intimacy, especially after a major role transition such as death of a partner, divorce, or retirement. The presence of a close confidant appears to be related to life satisfaction and a sense of belonging, worth, and identity. In any senior center or congregate meal site, gatherings of same-sex companions are frequent. Among women especially, same-sex friends frequently greet each other warmly with a hug and kiss, may join arms while walking, and spend considerable time together. These contacts are nonsexual in the narrow definitions of the term, but can be important to sexual health and to a person's psychological adaptation to aging. The importance of friendship for well-being in old age is discussed further in Chapter 9.

Facilitating Older Adults' Sexual Functioning

Given the importance of sexuality and sexual satisfaction, any clinical assessment or evaluation should address the elder's sexuality and intimacy. Concerns about sexuality may surface when health care professionals initiate discussion of multiple losses and loneliness, what older people miss in terms of intimacy, their history of loving relationships, and their interest in repairing old relationships and establishing new ones. Treatment should address issues relative to sources of intimacy, the meaning of past intimacies, grief over losses, and permission to explore new intimate relationships. Unfortunately, many health care providers have been taught little about sexuality and intimacy in late adulthood. Professionals may be uncomfortable or intimidated when addressing the lifelong intimacy needs of people as old as their own parents or grandparents. Physicians and nurses are often in a central position to respond to concerns about sexuality and intimacy, yet they may be more likely to prescribe treatment for physical symptoms, such as vaginal dryness, than to respond to the older person's emotional concerns or need for information. It is important for health care providers to recognize that the loss of intimacy may underlie other disorders that are being treated, such as depression. This can help ensure treatment of the underlying cause of the problem, not just its symptoms (Genevay, 1999).

As noted above, when an older person raises concerns about sexual functioning, such as impotence, the physician must first differentiate potential physical causes, including medications, from psychological ones. This can be done through a careful medical and social history, a thorough physical assessment, and basic hormone tests (Kingsberg, 1998). Such an approach can help to distinguish short-term problems that many individuals experience, such as transitory erectile dysfunction, from problems that persist under all circumstances with different sexual partners over a prolonged time period.

Increased knowledge of sexuality and aging tends to be associated with more accepting attitudes and enhanced sexual activity (Willert and Semans, 2000; Zeiss and Kasl-Godley, 2001). Health care providers can encourage and assure continuity of sexual expression for those for whom this has been an important part of their lives. One of the first health professionals to address this issue, Alex Comfort (1980), noted that sexual responsiveness should be fostered but not preached. In an AARP survey of older adults and sexual functioning, older respondents suggested guidelines for health care providers (Johnson, 1999). These included using clear and easy-to-understand terms; being open-minded, respectful, and nonjudgmental; and encouraging discussion. An older person who raises sexual concerns may most want support, acceptance, and listening. Elders who are concerned about their sexual functioning should be encouraged to focus on giving and receiving pleasure rather than on genital sex. As noted earlier, professionals should convey that intercourse is only one way of relating sexually and that there is no prescribed way for sex to proceed, but instead many options. When a partner is not available, masturbation may be an acceptable release of sexual tension. Explicit discussion of masturbation

---

SEX THERAPY WITH OLDER PERSONS

- Eliminate or control medical problems, including drug interference, that may directly impair genital functions or indirectly affect sexual functioning.
- Include practical behavioral techniques in the form of specifically structured sexual interactions that the couple can conduct in the privacy of their home
- Emphasize activities that encompass intimacy, giving pleasure, communicating with the partner, and letting the partner know when pleasure is experienced.
- Provide opportunities to discuss problems encountered as well as concerns about performance.
- Employ a holistic approach that includes exercise, nutrition, and interventions to build self-esteem (Kingsberg, 2000).

with older people may relieve anxiety caused by earlier prohibitions during their adolescence and young adulthood. Alternatively, professionals need to be sensitive to the fact that some elders do not want to engage in any sexual activity and must not put undue pressure on them to engage in or even discuss sexuality. Practitioners also need to take account of an older person's values, culture, religious beliefs, life experiences, and right to autonomy, and support them in making their own choices about sexual behavior and sexuality.

Many older people need to be encouraged to develop alternative definitions of sexual activity in order to gain intimacy, joy, and fulfillment through a broad spectrum of sensual interactions. Sex education and opportunities for group discussion and support can increase their awareness, knowledge, interest, and enjoyment of a range of sexual activities. As noted above, sex education is also essential for staff who work with elders, who must be careful not to impose their values or assumptions on older people. For example, nursing home employees need to recognize that the desire for intimacy and closeness continues throughout life among heterosexual and GLBT adults. With older people who are experiencing memory loss or disorientation, staff need to evaluate the elder's competencies in developing a care plan that allows the expression of appropriate sexual behavior. These include assessing the older person's awareness of the relationship, ability to avoid exploitation, and awareness of potential risks, including family members' disapproving attitudes (Hu and Za, 2006; Kuhn, 1999).

Implications for the Future

Compared to other areas, research on sexuality and aging remains relatively limited, suggesting that myths of older adult asexuality may still persist. However, baby boomers are likely to influence these attitudes as they age, just as they are affecting nearly every aspect of aging. One primary factor is that more boomers are single than any previous cohort of adults age 40 to 60,

largely because of divorce or never marrying. And many of them date regularly, although men are more likely to be looking for someone to live with than women, who tend to place a higher value on independence and personal freedom. The senior boomers are also more likely to be more comfortable expressing their sexuality than prior cohorts who were influenced by Victorian era values and norms (Henry and McNab, 2003; Kingsberg, 2000). The boomers' attitudes toward sexuality were strongly colored by the open, permissive atmosphere of the 1960s. The "sexual revolution," along with increased options for birth control, especially influenced women, giving them permission to express their sexual needs and desires and to be more assertive in relationships. Baby boomers' focus on physical fitness, antiaging treatments, and cosmetic surgery to enhance their physical appearance will also affect how sexuality in old age is viewed. Aging boomers may also press for more research on sexual dysfunction and ways to manage the negative effects of chronic illness and medications on sexuality. They will view sexuality as a quality of life issue that is central to wellness and active aging (Henry and McNab, 2003). Recognizing the wide range of ways in which sexuality and intimacy can be expressed, they will probably expect health care providers to consider their sexual needs when prescribing medications or other treatments. They are also likely to ask for drugs such as Viagra that can improve their sexual function and to buy products to enhance their sexual pleasure.

The boomers are likely to search online as a way to meet others, with some Websites catering specifically to those over age 50. A long-range health concern, however, is that the majority of boomers who have sex regularly do not use any protection. This is of particular concern for women who are at risk of developing HIV from heterosexual sex because their thinner vaginal walls are more susceptible to cuts and tears. The sexual needs of baby boomer GLBT partners are likely to be discussed more openly, although they also tend to engage increasingly in unprotected sex. Educating health care providers in the community and in long-term care facilities about the importance of sexuality across the life course is also helping to improve societal attitudes toward sexual expression in old age. Overall, senior boomers are likely to dramatically alter our images of sexuality in old age, push for more opportunities to form intimate relationships, and accept sexuality as a continuation of normal lifelong pleasures.

These trends suggest the need for mental health counselors, medical personnel, and social workers to acquire basic knowledge and skills regarding older adults' sexuality. Such training needs to encompass attitudes and values as well, so that professionals are more comfortable and sensitive in discussing sexual issues with elders, including GLBT partners. Increased professional knowledge and understanding are essential because older adults, like younger adults, may be less likely to be seen by a specialist such as a sex therapist and more likely to be treated by health care providers in a wide range of clinical settings.

Summary

As highlighted throughout this chapter, sexuality is affected by physical, psychological, and disease-related changes. The normal physiological changes that men and women experience in their sexual organs as they age do not necessarily affect their sexual pleasure or lead to sexual incapacity. Even chronic disease does not necessarily eliminate sexual capacity. For example, many older persons, after adequate medical consultation, can resume sexual activity following a heart attack or stroke. Contrary to the myths about sexuality in old age, many people in their 70s and 80s enjoy sexual activities.

Older couples can adapt to age-related changes in sexual functioning in a variety of ways. Simply knowing that such changes are normal may help older people maintain their sexual self-esteem. For both older men and women, long, leisurely foreplay can enhance sexual response. Avoiding alcohol prior to sexual activity can be helpful, since alcohol increases desire, but decreases sexual ability. Health professionals need to be alert to medications that adversely affect sexual functioning, such as antihypertensives, tranquilizers, and antidepressants.

This chapter emphasizes how psychosocial factors also can influence an older person's sexual behavior. Myths, stereotypes, and jokes pervade views of sexuality in old age. Unfortunately, societal expectations about reduced sexual interest may mean that older people stop sexual activity long before they need to. In future years, these myths may change as the media, gerontologists, and other professionals convey the message that sex is not only permissible but desirable in old age.

In professional work with older partners, definitions of sexuality need to be broadened beyond sexual intercourse. A variety of behaviors, such as touching, kissing, hugging, massage, and lying side by side, can contribute to sexual intimacy and satisfaction, even for older persons in long-term care facilities and those with dementia. Touching older people—a hand clasp or back rub, for example—is especially important in home-bound and institutional settings, but needs to be tempered with awareness of cultural differences.

Practitioners need to be sensitive to their clients' values and life experiences and to support them in making their own choices about sexual behavior and sexuality. Many of the current cohort of oldest-old grew up with taboos relating not only to intercourse but also to other forms of sexual activity, such as masturbation. Hence, such older individuals are likely to need encouragement from professional counselors or others if they are to be free to affirm their sexuality and to experience intimacy with others.

GLOSSARY

climacteric in women, the decline in estrogen production and the loss of reproductive ability; in men, the decline in testosterone

erection the swelling of the penis or clitoris in sexual excitement

erectile dysfunction   inability to get and sustain an erection

hot flashes   a sudden sensation of heat in the upper body caused by vasomotor instability as nerves overrespond to decreases in hormone level during menopause

impotence   the inability to have or maintain an erection

intimacy   feelings of deep mutual regard, affection, and trust, usually developed through long association

male menopause   a term that suggests a significant change experienced by men as their production of testosterone decreases in later life; although male fertility is maintained, some men experience both psychological and physiological changes

menopause   cessation of the menstrual cycle

orgasm   climax of sexual excitement

penile implant   a device surgically implanted in the penis to reverse impotence and allow an erection

perimenopause   unpredictable menstrual cycles—up to 10 years before menopause

postmenopause   when 12 months have passed without a menstrual cycle

preorgasmic plateau phase   in men and women, the phase of lovemaking prior to orgasm and in which sexual tension is at its height

prostate enlargement   growth of the prostate, due to changes in prostatic cells with age, which can result in pain and difficult urination

prostate cancer   the most common cancer among men age 65 and older

refractory period   in men, the time between ejaculation and another erection

sex   in the most narrow sense, a biological function involving genital intercourse or orgasm; in a broader sense, expressing oneself in an intimate way through a wide-ranging language of love and pleasure in relationships

sexuality   feelings of sexual desire, expression, and intimacy, not only sexual activity

sexupharmaceuticals   prescribed medications, such as Viagra, to treat men's erectile difficulties

urogenital atrophy   reductions in the elasticity and lubricating abilities of the vagina approximately 5 years after menopause

viropause   male menopause

widow(er)'s syndrome   a term coined by Masters and Johnson describing sexual dysfunction following a long period of abstinence due to a partner's illness and/or death

REFERENCES

Adam, B. Age preferences among gay and bisexual men. *GLQ: A Journal of Lesbian and Gay Studies*, 2000, *6*, 413–433.

Afrin, L.B., and Ergul, S.M. Medical therapy of prostrate cancer. *Journal of South Carolina Medical Association*, 2000, *26*, 77–84.

American Association of Retired Persons (AARP). *Modern Maturity sexuality survey.* Washington, DC: American Association of Retired Persons, 1999.

American Association of Retired Persons (AARP). *2004 Update of attitudes and behavior: Sexuality at midlife and beyond.* Washington, DC: American Association of Retired Persons, 2004.

American Federation for Aging Research. Research news on older men's health. *Lifelong Briefs*, 2000.

American Prostate Society. *Impotence.* Washington, DC: American Prostate Society, 2003.

Balon, R. SSRI—associated sexual dysfunction. *The American Journal of Psychiatry*, 2006, *163*, 1504–1509.

Barranti, C. and Cohen, H. Lesbian and gay elders: An invisible minority. In R. Schneider, N. Kropf, and A. Kisor (Eds.), *Gerontological social work: Knowledge, service settings and special populations.* Belmont, CA: Brooks/Cole, 2001.

Bennett, L., and Gates, G. *The cost of marriage inequality to gay, lesbian and bisexual seniors.* Washington, DC: Human Rights Campaign, 2004.

Berger, R., and Kelly, J.J. The older gay man. In B. Berzon (Ed.), *Positively gay: New approaches to gay and lesbian life.* Berkeley, CA: Celestial Arts, 2001.

Blonna, R., and Levitan, J. *Healthy sexuality.* Colorado: Morton, 2000.

Bortz, W.M., and Wallace, D.H. Physical fitness, aging and sexuality. *Western Journal of Medicine*, 1999a, *170*, 167–169.

Bortz, W.M., and Wallace, D.H. Sexual function in 1202 aging males: Differentiating aspects. *Journals of Gerontology*, 1999, *54B*, M237–M241.

Bostwick, D.G., MacLennan, G.T., and Larson, T. *Prostate cancer: What every man—and his family—needs to know.* New York: Villard, 1996.

Brice, C. *Age ain't nothing but a number: Black women explore midlife.* Boston: Beacon Press, 2003.

Butler, S. Older gays, lesbians, bisexuals and transgender persons. In B. Berkman (Ed.), *Handbook of social work in health and aging.* New York: Oxford, 2006.

Calasanti, T.M., and Slevin, K.F. *Gender, social inequalities and aging.* Walnut Creek, CA: Altamira Press, 2001.

Cauley, J.A., Robbins, J., Chen, Z., Cummings, S.R., Jackson, R.D., LaCroix, A.Z., et al. Effects of estrogen plus progestic on risk of fracture and bone mineral density. *Journal of the American Medical Association,* 2003, *290,* 1729–1738.

Clunis, M., Fredriksen-Goldsen, K., Freeman, P., and Nystrom, N. (Eds.), *Lives of lesbian elders. Looking back, looking forward.* Binghamton, NY: Haworth Press, 2005.

Comfort, A. Sexuality in later life. In J.E. Birren and R.B. Sloane (Eds.), *Handbook of mental health and aging.* New York: Van Nostrand Reinhold, 1980.

Defey, D., Storch, E., Cardozo, S., and Diaz, O. The menopause: Women's psychology and health care. *Social Science and Medicine,* 1996, *42,* 1447–1456.

DeLamater, J., and Friedrich, W.N. Human sexual development. *Journal of Sex Research,* 2002, *39,* 10–14.

Diamond, J. *Male menopause.* Naperville, IL: Sourcebooks, 1997.

Donatucci, C.F., and Greenfield, J.M. Recovery of sexual function after prostate cancer treatment. *Current Opinion in Urology,* 2006, *16,* 444–448.

Dorfman, R., Walters, K., Burke, P., Hardin, L., Karanik, T., Raphael, J., and Silverstein, E. Old, sad and alone: The myth of the aging homosexual. *Journal of Gerontological Social Work,* 1995, *24,* 29–44.

Doust, J., Miller, E., Duchesne, G., Kitchener, M., and Weller, D. A systematic review of brachytherapy: Is it an effective and safe treatment for localized prostate cancer? *Australian Family Physician,* 2004, *33,* 525–52.

Emlet, C.A. Case managing older people with AIDS: Bridging systems—recognizing diversity. *Journal of Gerontological Social Work,* 1996, *27,* 55–71.

Gallagher, E., and Gapstur, R. Hormone-refractory prostate cancer: A shifting paradigm in treatment. *Clinical Journal of Oncology Nursing,* 2006, *10,* 233–240.

Gelfand, M.M. Sexuality among older women. *Journal of Women's Health and Gender-based Medicine,* 2000, *9,* S15–20.

Genevay, B. Intimacy and older people: Much more than sex. *Dimensions.* San Francisco: American Society on Aging, 1999, pp. 1, 7.

Gonyea, J. Midlife and menopause: Uncharted territories for baby boomer women. *Generations,* Spring 1998, 87–89.

Gotay, C.C., Holup, J.L., and Muraoka, M.Y. The challenges of prostate cancer: A major men's health issue. *International Journal of Men's Health,* 2002, *1,* 59–72.

Gross, G., and Blundo, R. Viagra: Medical technology construction aging masculinity. *Journal of Sociology and Social Welfare,* 2005, *32,* 85–97.

Grossman, A.H., D'Augelli, A.R, and O'Connell, T.S. Being lesbian, gay, bisexual and 60 or older in North America. *Journal of Gay and Lesbian Social Services,* 2001, *13,* 23–40.

Grossman, A.H., D'Augelli, A.R., and Hershberger, S.L. Social support networks of lesbian, gay and bisexual adults 60 years of age and older. *Journals of Gerontology: Series B,* 2000, *55,* P171–O179.

Han, M., Nadler, R.B., Catalona, W.J., Thrasher, J.B., Tewari, A., and Menon, M. Point and counterpoint. Radical prostatectomy: Should the retropubic approach remain the standard of care? *Contemporary Urology,* 2004, *16,* 38–50.

Harris, M.J., Weiss, J.P., and Blaivas, J.G. The renaissance of nerve-sparing radical perineal prostatectomy. *Contemporary Urology,* 2004, *16,* 16–22.

Healy, T. Culturally competent practice with elderly lesbians. *Geriatric Care Management Journal,* 2002, *12,* 9–13.

Henry, J., and McNab, W. Forever young: A health promotion focus on sexuality and aging. *Gerontology and Geriatrics Education,* 2003, *23,* 57–74.

Hite, S. *The Hite report: A nationwide study on female sexuality.* New York: Macmillan, 1976.

Hu, L., and Za, A. Sexual expression among the institutionalized elderly with dementia and strategies for sexual care. *Archives of Internal Medicine,* 2006, *53,* 73–8.

Jacobson, S. Menopause. *The Seattle Times,* November 2000.

Janus, S.S., and Janus, C.L. *The Janus Report on sexual behavior.* New York: John Wiley and Sons, 1993.

Johnson, B. Older adults' suggestions for health care providers regarding discussions of sex. *Geriatric Nursing,* 1997, *18,* 65–66.

Johnson, B. Sexuality and aging. In M. Stanley and P.G. Beare (Eds.), *Gerontological nursing: A health promotion/prevention approach.* Philadelphia: FA Davis, 1999.

Johnson, S.D., Phelps, D.L., and Cottler, L.B. The association of sexual dysfunction and substance use among a community epidemiological sample. *Archives of Sexual Behavior,* 2004, *33,* 55–63.

Jones, J.B. Representations of menopause and their health care implications: A qualitative study. *American Journal of Preventive Medicine,* 1997, *13,* 58–65.

Jones, T., and Nystrom, N. Looking back . . . looking forward: Addressing the lives of lesbians 55 and older. *Journal of Women and Aging,* 2002, *14,* 59–73.

Kingsberg, S.A. Postmenopausal sexual functioning: A case study. *International Journal of Fertility and Women's Medicine,* 1998, *43,* 122–128.

Kingsberg, S.A. The psychological impact of aging on sexuality and relationships. *Journal of Women's Health and Gender-Based Medicine,* 2000, *9,* S33–38.

Kinsey, A., Pomeroy, B., and Martin E. *Sexual behavior in the human female.* Philadelphia: W.B. Saunders, 1953.

Kinsey, A., Pomeroy, B., and Martin, E. *Sexual behavior in the human male.* Philadelphia: W.B. Saunders, 1948.

Kuhn, D. Nursing home residents with Alzheimer's: Addressing the need for intimacy. *Dimensions,* San Francisco: American Society on Aging, 4–5.

Levesque, M., Nave, C., and Lowe, C. Toward an understanding of gender differences in inferring sexual interest. *Psychology of Women Quarterly,* 2006, *30,* 150–158.

Lingler, J.H. Ethical issues in distinguishing sexual activity from sexual maltreatment among women with dementia. *Journal of Elder Abuse and Neglect,* 2003, *15,* 85–102.

LoboPraabhu, S., Mollinari, V., Arlinghaus, K., Barr, E., and Lomax, J. Spouses of patients with dementia: How do they stay together 'till death do us part'? *Journal of Gerontological Social Work,* 2005, *44,* 161–174.

Loue, S. Intimacy and institutionalized cognitive impaired elderly. *Care Management Journals,* 2005, *6,* 185–190.

Mahoney, S. Seeking love. *AARP Magazine,* Nov./Dec., 2003, 59–67, 85.

Martin, D., and Lyon, P. Positively gay: New approaches to gay and lesbian life. In B. Berzon (Ed.), *Positively gay: New approaches to gay and lesbian life.* Berkeley, CA: Celestial Arts, 2001.

Masters, W., and Johnson, V. *Human sexual response.* Boston: Little Brown, 1966.

Masters, W., and Johnson, V. *Human sexual inadequacy.* Boston: Little Brown, 1970.

Masters, W.H., and Johnson, V.E. Sex and the aging process. *Journal of the American Geriatrics Society,* 1981, *29,* 385–390.

Matthias, R.E., Lubben, J.E., Atcheson, K.B., and Schweitzer, S.O. Sexual activity and satisfaction among very old adults: Results from a community-dwelling Medicare population survey. *The Gerontologist,* 1997, *37,* 6–14.

MetLife Mature Market Institute. *Out and aging: The MetLife study of lesbian and gay baby boomers.* Westport, CT: MetLife. 2006.

McNeel, D.G., and Disis, M.L. Tumor vaccines for the management of prostate cancer. *Archives,* 2000, *48,* 85–93.

Morrow, D.F. Older gays and lesbians: Surviving a generation of hate and violence. *Journal of Gay and Lesbian Social Services,* 2001, *13,* 151–169.

Murray, J., and Adam, B.D. Aging, sexuality and HIV issues among older gay men. *The Canadian Journal of Human Sexuality,* 2001, *10,* 75–90.

National Health and Social Life Survey. *The social organization of sexuality.* Chicago: The National Organization for Research, 1994.

National Institute on Aging (NIA), *Hormones and menopause.* Washington, DC: NIA, 2004. Accessed February 28, 2007, from http://www.niapublications.org/tipsheets/hormones. asp.

National Institute on Aging (NIA). *Age page: Menopause.* Washington, DC: NIA, 2003a.

National Institute on Aging. *Menopause: One woman's story, every woman's story: A companion guide 2003.* NIH Publication No. 03–5383. Washington, DC: NIA, 2003b.

National Institute on Aging. *Sexuality in later life.* Washington, DC: National Institute on Aging, 2002.

Nelson, H.D., Vesco, K.K., Haney, E., Fu, R., Nedrow, A., Miller, J., Nicolaidis, C., et al. Nonhormonal therapies for menopausal hot flashes: Systematic review and meta-analysis. *Journal of the American Medical Association,* 2006, *295,* 2057–2071.

Newton, K.M., Buist, D.S.M., Keenan, N.L., Anderson, L.A., and LaCroix, A.Z. Use of alternative therapies for menopause symptoms: Results of a population-based survey. *Obstetrics and Gynecology,* 2002, *100,* 18–25

Nusbaum, M.R.H., Hamilton, C., and Lenahan, P. Chronic illness and sexual functioning. *American Family Physician,* 2003, *67,* 347–54.

Orel, N.A. Gay, lesbian and bisexual elders: Expressed needs and concerns across focus groups. *Journal of Gerontological Social Work,* 2004, *43,* 57–77.

Pangman, V., and Seguire, M. Sexuality and the chronically ill older adult: A social justice issue. *Sexuality and Disability,* 2000, *18,* 49–59.

Peschel, R.E. and Colberg, J.W. Surgery, brachytherapy and external-beam radiotherapy for early prostrate cancer. *Lancet Oncology,* 2003, *4,* 233–241.

Pfeiffer, E., and Davis, G.C. Determinants of sexual behavior in middle and old age. *Journal of the American Geriatrics Society,* 1972, *20,* 151–158.

Phillip, H.A. Hot flashes—a review of the literature on alternative and complementary treatment approaches. *Alternative Medicine Review,* 2003, *8,* 284–302.

Phillips, R.L., and Slaughter, J.R. Depression and sexual desire. *American Family Physician,* 2000, *64,* 782–786.

Potts, A., Gavey, N., Grace, V. M., and Vares, T. The downside of Viagra: Women's experiences and concerns. *Sociology of Health and Illness,* 2003, *25,* 697–719.

Rogers, J. Su, L.M., Link, R.E., Sullivan, W., Wagner, A., and Pavlovich, C.P. Age stratified functional outcomes after laparoscopic radical prostatectomy. *Journal of Urology,* 2006, *176,* 2448–2452.

Saranchuk, J.W., Kattan, M.W., Elkin, E., Touijer, A.K., Scardino, P.T., and Eastham, J.A. Achieving optimal outcomes after radical prostatectomy. *Journal of Clinical Oncology,* 2005, *23,* 4146–4151.

Schiavi, R.C. *Aging and male sexuality.* Cambridge, UK: Cambridge University Press, 1999.

Schiavi, R.C. Sexuality and male aging: From performance to satisfaction. *Journal of Sex and Marital Therapy,* 1996, *11,* 9–13.

Schiavi, R.C., Mandeli, J., and Schreiner-Engel, P. Sexual satisfaction in healthy aging men. *Journal of Sex and Marital Therapy,* 1994, *20,* 3–13.

Schiavi, R.C., and Rehman, J. Sexuality and aging. *Urologic Clinics of North America,* 1995, *22,* 711–726.

Starr, B.D., and Weiner, M.B. *The Star-Weiner report on sex and sexuality in the mature years.* New York: Stein and Day, 1981.

Swanson, G.P. Management of locally advanced prostate cancer: Past, present, future. *Journal of Urology,* 2006, *176,* S34–41.

Trudel, G., Turgeon, L., and Piche, L. Marital and sexual aspects of old age. *Sexual and Relationship Therapy,* 2000, *15,* 381–406.

Tward, J.D., Lee, C.M., Pappas, L.M., Szabo, A., Gaffney, D.K., and Shrieve, D.C. Survival of men with clinically located prostate cancer treated with prostatectomy, brachytherapy, or no definitive treatment: Impact of age at diagnosis. *Cancer,* 2006, *107,* 2392–2400.

Van Tol-Geerdink, J.J., Stalmeier, P.F., van Lin, E.N., Schimmel, E.C., Huizenga, H., van Daal, W.A., et al. Do patients with localized prostate cancer treatment really want more aggressive treatment? *Journal of Clinical Oncology,* 2006, *24,* 4581–4586.

Weg, R.B. Sexuality, sensuality, and intimacy. *Encyclopedia of gerontology: Age, aging, and the aged,* 1996, *2,* 479–488.

Weil, A. *Healthy Aging,* New York: Knopf, 2005.

Werneke, U., Northey, S., and Bhugra, D. Antidepressants and sexual dysfunction. *Acta Psychiatrica Scandinavica,* 2006, *114,* 384–397.

Wiley, D., and Bortz, W.M. Sexuality and aging—Usual and successful. *Journals of Gerontology,* 1996, *51A,* M142–M146.

Willert, A., and Semans, M. Knowledge and attitudes about later life sexuality: What clinicians need to know about helping the elderly. *Contemporary Family Therapy,* 2000, *22,* 415–435.

Yoakam, J.R. Beyond the wrinkle room: Challenging ageism in gay male culture. *Dimensions,* San Francisco: American Society on Aging, 1999, pp. 3, 7.

Zeiss, A.M., and Kasl-Godley, J. Sexuality in older adult's relationships. *Generations,* 2001, *25,* 18–25.

part four

The Social Context of Aging

Throughout the previous three sections, we have identified how changes in the physical and psychological aspects of aging have numerous consequences for older people's cognitive and personality functioning, sexuality, and mental health. We have also seen how social factors (e.g., the presence of strong family and friendship ties) can affect physical changes (e.g., being at risk for certain chronic illnesses) as well as psychological experiences (e.g., the likelihood of depression and suicide). Within this framework of the dynamic interactions among physical, psychological, and social factors, we turn now to a more detailed discussion of the social environment of aging and its congruence with older people's level of functioning.

We begin with a review in Chapter 8 of the major social theories of aging—explanations of changes in social relationships that occur in late adulthood. Congruent with the person–environment perspective, these theories address optimal ways for people to relate to their changing social and physical environments as they age. The early positivist social gerontological theories, such as role, activity, and disengagement, were concerned with adaptation to age-related changes. These differ substantially from later theories, including continuity, age stratification, and exchange theory, which recognize the diverse and dynamic nature of the aging experience. The most recent theories are described as taking a "qualitative leap" over prior theories; these include social phenomenology, social constructionism, critical and feminist theory, and postmodernism, all of which raise fundamental questions about positivist or empirical approaches to studying aging and emphasize the highly subjective nature of the aging experience. These social gerontological theories or perspectives provide the basis for examining the primary dimensions of older people's social environments: family, friends, and other social supports; housing and community; paid and nonpaid productive roles and activities; and changes in one's social network through death and loss. These later theoretical approaches, in particular, recognize how older people's experiences along with their social environments can vary by ethnic minority status, social class, gender, and sexual orientation.

Chapter 9 begins by examining the important contribution of informal social supports, particularly family and friends, to quality of life. Chapter 1 identified how longer life expectancies, combined with earlier marriages and childbearing, have reduced the average span in years

301

between generations. This has also increased the number of three-, four-, and sometimes five-generation families. The growth of the multigenerational family has numerous ramifications for relationships between partners, grandparents and grandchildren, adult children and older relatives, and siblings and other extended family members. Generally, these relationships are characterized by reciprocity, with older family members providing resources to younger generations and trying to remain as autonomous as possible. The normal physical and psychological changes of aging usually are not detrimental to family relationships, although caring for an older relative with a long-term illness can burden family members. Compared to the earlier years, late-life family relationships are more often characterized by losses that demand role shifts and adjustments. A widower may cope with the loss of his wife by remarrying, whereas a widow tends to turn to adult children and friends.

Although some older people live alone—including a growing number who are homeless—friends, neighbors, and even acquaintances often perform family-like functions for them. More conducive to reciprocal and spontaneous exchanges, non-kin may be an even more important source of support for an older person than one's family, especially if family relationships are conflictual. As gerontologists have recognized the importance of informal social networks for older people's well-being, programmatic interventions, including intergenerational programming, have been developed specifically to strengthen these ties, which are described briefly in Chapter 9.

While most families and friends provide social support to older adults, in the case of frail elders, informal caregiving provided by partners, children, and others can become burdensome. The positive and negative impact of informal caregiving on both the care recipient and the caregiver is examined in Chapter 10. Elder mistreatment, although rare, can occur when caregivers feel extremely stressed and lacking in social supports. Generally, however, mistreatment

occurs because of the abuser's own psychological difficulties, such as substance abuse or mental illness.

Where people live—the type of housing, urban–suburban location, and safety of the community—affects their social interactions. Chapter 11 illustrates the importance of achieving congruence between older people's social, psychological, and physical needs and their physical environments. Relocation is an example of a disruption of this congruence or fit between the environment and the older person. Another illustration of a physical environment that no longer fits a person's social needs occurs when older residents become so fearful of victimization that they dare not leave their homes. Characteristics of the neighborhood can enhance older persons' social interactions and, in some instances, their feelings of safety. Elder-friendly communities, planned housing, home-sharing, congregate housing, assisted living facilities with multiple levels of care, adult family homes, home health care, and nursing homes are alternative forms of housing to support older people's changing and diverse needs. Chapter 11 also includes a discussion of housing policies and community-based social and health services that affect older people, as well as an analysis of the problem of homelessness among older adults.

Throughout our discussion of the social context for aging, the effects of socioeconomic status on types of interactions and activities are readily apparent. This status is largely determined by past and current employment patterns and by the resulting retirement benefits. Chapter 12 shows changing rates of labor-force participation among both men and women age 65 and over. Most people choose to retire early, provided their public or private pensions will enable them to enjoy economic security. Although most older adults apparently do not want to work full-time, many enjoy the option of flexible part-time jobs, increasingly for economic reasons. For most people, retirement is not a crisis, although for those without good health, adequate finances, or prior planning, retirement can be a difficult transition. Accordingly, women, ethnic minorities, and unskilled workers are most vulnerable to experiencing poverty or near-poverty in old age.

Chapter 12 also examines how people's interactions change with age in terms of their nonpaid productive roles, including involvement in community, organizational, religious, and political activities. The extent and type of civic engagement are influenced not only by age, but also by gender, ethnic minority status, health, socioeconomic class, and educational level. Therefore, declines in participation may not necessarily be caused by age-related changes but instead represent the influence of other variables. Generally, involvement tends to be fairly stable across the life course; leisure, volunteer and community activities, and roles formed in early and middle adulthood are maintained into later life. This does not mean, however, that older people do not develop new interests and skills. Many people initiate new forms of productivity through senior centers, volunteering, civic organizations, political activism, and education programs. Or think about the reports of older athletes who complete their first marathon or mountain ascent in their 60s, or become Peace Corps volunteers in their 80s. Given older adults' extensive knowledge and skills, they contribute to families, communities, and society in numerous ways, even when they are not compensated. These are all ways in which people can maintain active aging.

Chapter 13 examines attitudes toward death and dying, the process of dying, and the importance of palliative or end-of-life care. The impacts of social and cultural values, as well as individual factors such as the relationship between the dying person and caregivers, are discussed in reviewing research on grief and mourning. An individual's right to die, the legal and ethical debates about active and passive euthanasia, and the role of advance directives also are reviewed in this chapter. It concludes by examining the process of widowhood and how adults cope with this major life event.

Because of the predominance of social problems faced by older women and ethnic minorities, their distinctive needs and relevant practice and policy interventions are discussed in Chapters 14 and 15. Economic and health disparities experienced in young and middle adulthood by these groups tend to be perpetuated across the life course and into old age. These are not isolated problems, but rather of increasing concern to gerontologists and policy makers. This is because women over age 65 form the majority of older people and the number of older persons of color, although a small percentage of the total older population today, is growing rapidly. These populations nevertheless display considerable strength and resilience in the face of disadvantages.

The following vignettes illustrate the diversity of social interactions experienced by older people and set the stage for our discussion of the social context of aging.

MR. VALDRES: LIMITED SOCIAL RESOURCES

At 73 I live alone in a small room in an inner-city hotel. My wife left me 20 years ago. I've worked all sorts of odd jobs all my life, often as a migrant farm laborer. But for all those years of hard work, I get only the minimum amount of Social Security. Some months it is very hard to get by and I'm lucky if I get one good meal a day. Although I never hear from my ex-wife or even my six kids, I've got a group of buddies in the area who watch out for one another. We often get together at night to have a beer and watch TV in the hotel lobby. I've been a smoker all my life and I am paying for it now; the doctor says it's emphysema. But I have no use for doctors and have not been to one or even to the medical clinic in my neighborhood for over five years. I've been told my life would be easier if I would apply for public assistance, like SSI or food stamps. But I don't understand what these programs are and I definitely don't want to take any "handouts" from the government. I'm lucky that our hotel manager keeps track of what I do and will occasionally even slip me some extra money or food.

MRS. HOWARD: EXTENSIVE SOCIAL RESOURCES

At 78, I live with my husband of 53 years in a small town. I am fortunate that most of my relatives, including 3 of my children and 8 grandchildren, live nearby. We always get together as a family after church on Sundays and holidays. I taught elementary school for 25 years until I retired at age 71, and my husband was a successful local realtor until he retired at age 75. We're fortunate to have considerable savings. Even though we have enough money, we are proud of living simply and frugally. We've always saved for our retirement and for the possibility that we may need someone to help care for us someday. We've lived in the same house for the past 42 years—and plan to stay here as long as we can. We both work hard to keep it up and added a new kitchen, bath, and a guest bedroom just last year. I'm never bored. I keep myself busy by gardening, doing housework, reading, and visiting friends and relatives. I've always been active in our church, serve on the Advisory Board to our county's Area Agency on Aging, and believe that it's important to be involved in our town's politics. Recently, I started tutoring children with learning disabilities at our local school. So my days are filled with housework, talking to friends, neighbors, or relatives, or helping someone out, whether a grandchild or a neighbor. Even so, there are times when I feel so lonely and useless.

MR. MANSFIELD: COPING WITH MULTIPLE LOSSES

My wife and I made a good life for ourselves in Chicago, where I was a successful businessman and we raised 6 kids. When I retired at age 66, we moved to a small town in the South 'cause my wife loved sunshine. We became active in our church, volunteered at our local hospital, and enjoyed going to plays and keeping up with our children, whose careers took them all over the United States. We were really enjoying retirement until my wife of 50 years suddenly died three years ago. I was heartbroken and didn't know what to do without her. It seemed that at age 80, my life was

over. But then I got involved in a support group for widowers offered through our church and I also started teaching adult education classes. One thing led to another and soon I was really involved in this small southern town, even helping to put on an annual peace conference. While I still get teary when I talk about my deceased wife, I have found new meaning and purpose in my church work. But now I am facing new challenges in my life. My youngest and my oldest children both died in the past year. My oldest died in her early 50s of a drug overdose of pills she was taking for chronic pain. Her husband is so distraught that he has turned to me to help their two middle school children with homework and to stay with them when he has to be out of town. My youngest, a son, died 6 months later after a long battle with HIV/AIDS. Although losing a child seems to be the worst thing that can happen to a parent, I am managing to get by because I have so many friends through my church and my volunteering. The pain is still there every day, but I can share it with others and I have started to attend a support group for bereaved parents. Because my own health is beginning to deteriorate, I worry about having the energy to help out with my grandkids. I notice my eyesight is deteriorating so I am concerned about being able to drive and pick them up after school. Somehow, the death of my adult children has made me think even more about my own death and what lies ahead. But I know that my faith and my beliefs will help me deal with my own health, my grandkids, and my own concerns about death and dying.

These vignettes show the importance of informal social support networks, whether for an apparently isolated person in a low-income hotel such as Mr. Valdres, or for an older person, such as Mr. Mansfield, coping with multiple social losses. We turn now to a review of some of the social theories relevant to satisfying and active aging.

8

Social Theories of Aging

The Importance of Social Theories of Aging

All of us develop interpretive frameworks or lenses, based on our experiences, by which we attempt to explain the aging process and answer questions we all wonder about:

- What makes for successful, active, or vital aging?
- Who defines what is active aging?
- What are government roles and responsibilities toward older people in our society?
- What enhances older people's life satisfaction and well-being?

We observe older people in our families and communities and make generalizations about them. For example, some of our stereotypes of older people may be the result of unconscious theorizing about the meaning of growing old. Or we may devise our own recommendations for policies or programs based on our informal and implicit theories. In effect, we all develop theories based on our own experiences.

In contrast to our personal observations about age changes, the scientific approach to theory development is a systematic attempt to explain *why* an age change or event occurs. *Theory building*—the cumulative development of explanation and understanding about observations and findings—represents the core of the foundation of scientific inquiry and knowledge (Bengtson, Burgess, and Parrott, 1997). By using scientific methods, researchers seek to understand phenomena in a manner that is reliable and valid across observations, and then to account for what they have observed in the context of previous knowledge in the field. Scientists never entirely prove or disprove a theory. Instead, through empirical research, they gather evidence that may strengthen their confidence in it or move them closer to rejecting the theory by demonstrating that parts of it are untrue. Scientific theories not only lead to the accumulation of knowledge, but point to unanswered questions for further research and suggest directions for practical interventions. In fact, a good theory is practical! For example, some of the biological theories of aging discussed in Chapter 3 are useful in guiding people's health behaviors and health care programs and policies. If the theory is inadequate, the research, intervention, or public policy may fail by not achieving its intended goals (Bengtson et al., 1997).

As noted in Chapter 1, the biomedical study of aging, with its emphasis on disease and decline, has dominated the disciplinary development of gerontology since the beginning of the twentieth century. This chapter focuses on social theories of aging—explanations of changes in social relationships that occur in late adulthood—which are less well developed than biological explanatory frameworks and thus limit understanding of the social aspects of aging (Powell, 2006; Powell and Longino, 2002). Most social gerontological theories have been developed only since the 1950s and 1960s, and some have not been adequately tested.

In fact, some social theorists assert that the theoretical interpretations of aging are in their infancy (Estes, Biggs, and Phillipson, 2003). One reason for what has been called the theoretically sterile nature of gerontology is that early research in the field of gerontology tended to be applied rather than theoretical; it attempted to solve problems facing older people. Researchers were concerned with individual life satisfaction and older people's adjustment to the presumably "natural" conditions of old age—retirement, ill health, or poverty, which resulted in definitions of aging itself as a problem (Biggs and Powell, 2001; George, 1995; Powell, 2006). Despite their relatively recent development, social theories of aging can be classified into first, second, and third generations, or first and second *transformations of theoretical development*, or evolution of new modes of consciousness. Others categorize early theories as modernist, later ones as postmodernist (Bengtson et al., 1997; Lynott and Lynott, 1996; Powell, 2006). The order in which theories are presented in this chapter basically reflects the temporal dimensions of this intellectual history. Although there is some overlap of the central theoretical concepts across time, the later social theories are distinguished by a shift from:

- a focus on the individual to structural factors and interactive processes that affect aging, and
- largely quantitative methods in the positivist scientific tradition to a range of more qualitative methodologies that seek to understand the meaning of age-related changes among those experiencing them.

Social Gerontological Theory before 1961: Role and Activity

Much of the early social gerontological research was organized around the concept of adjustment, with the term "theory" largely absent from the literature (Lynott and Lynott, 1996).

The perspectives on roles and activities, however, later came to be called *theories*. Identified as functionalist gerontology because of its emphasis on the consequences of role loss, theories of adjustment focused on personal characteristics (health, personality, needs), while others emphasized society's demands on and expectations of the aging individual. Growing old was conceptualized as the individual encountering problems of adjustment due to role changes in later life. Role and activity theories not only postulated how individual behavior changes with aging, but also implied how it should change (Powell, 2006).

Role Theory

One of the earliest attempts to explain how individuals adjust to aging involved an application of **role theory** (Cottrell, 1942). In fact, this theory has endured, partially because of its applicable and self-evident nature. Individuals play a variety of social roles across the life course, such as student, mother, wife, daughter, businesswoman, grandmother, and so on. Such roles identify and describe a person as a social being and are the basis of self-concept and identity. They are typically organized sequentially, so that each role is associated with a certain age or stage of life. In most societies, especially Western ones, chronological age is used to determine eligibility for various positions, to evaluate the suitability of different roles, and to shape expectations of people in social situations. Some roles have a reasonable biological basis related to age (e.g., the role of mother), but many can be filled by individuals of a wider age range (e.g., the role of volunteer). Age alters not only the roles expected of people, but also the manner in which they are expected to play them. For example, a family's expectations of a 32-year-old mother are quite different from those of her at age 72. How well individuals adjust to aging is assumed to depend on how well they accept the role changes typical of the later years.

Age norms serve to open up or close off the roles that people of a given chronological age can play. Age norms are assumptions of age-related capacities and limitations—beliefs that a person of a given age can and ought to do certain things. As an illustration, a 76-year-old widow who starts dating a younger man may be told by family members that she should "act her age." Her behavior is viewed as not *age appropriate*. Norms may be formally expressed through social policies and laws (e.g., mandatory retirement policies that existed prior to 1987). Typically, however, they operate informally. For example, even though employers cannot legally refuse to hire an older woman because of her age, they can assume that she is too old to train for a new position. Individuals also hold norms about the appropriateness of their own behavior at any particular age, so that social clocks become internalized and age norms operate to keep people on a time track (Hagestad and Neugarten, 1985). Most people

---

ROLE LOSS: GIVING UP THE CAR KEYS

A major role loss for many older people, especially older men, is that of driver. Families often worry about an older relative's driving, especially if he or she has had a minor accident or some near collisions. They fear that their older relative will cause a major accident as a result of slow driving or abrupt shifting of lanes without first checking and signaling. Yet, the older driver often refuses to stop driving, blaming close calls on other drivers, poor brakes, or road conditions. The driver may deny the problem and resist giving up the keys, because the loss of role of driver carries many consequences: loss of independence, identity, personal satisfaction, the ability to carry out daily tasks, and the sense of personal power and control. For most older people, losing one's ability to drive—to go where they want to and when they want to—is a major role transition, symbolizing loss of autonomy. Any efforts to convince an older driver to give up the car keys must take account of what this role loss means to the older person.

in American society, for example, have *age-normative expectations* about the appropriate age at which to graduate from school, start working, marry, have a family, reach the peak of their career, and retire. These expectations have been shifting among baby boomers and their children, however, with more persons marrying later, and in middle age entering second or third careers.

Every society conveys age norms through *socialization,* a lifelong process by which individuals learn to perform new roles, adjust to changing roles, relinquish old ones, learn a "social clock" of what is age appropriate, and thereby become integrated into society. Older adults become socialized to new roles, such as grandparenting, that accompany old age. In addition, they must learn to deal with *role losses,* such as the loss of the spouse role with widowhood or divorce or the worker role with retirement. These losses can lead to an erosion of identity and self-esteem (Rosow, 1985). Older people may also experience *role discontinuity,* whereby what is learned at one age may be useless or conflict with a subsequent period in one's life. For example, learning to be highly productive in the workplace may be antithetical to adjusting to more ambigu-

ous roles in retirement. Although institutions or social situations that help older people prepare for such role changes are limited, older adults often display considerable flexibility in creating or substituting roles in the face of major changes in life circumstances. In fact, a process of *role exit* has been identified, whereby individuals discard roles which have been central to their identity, such as the employee role. Interventions such as retirement planning can encourage a process of gradually ceasing to identify with the worker role, shifting to leisure roles or a different workplace (Ekerdt and DeViney, 1993).

Some older people lack desirable role options. Until recently, few positive role models existed; those in the media and the public realm have tended to be youthful in appearance and behavior, maintaining middle-age standards that can hinder socialization to old age. In addition, some groups, such as women and ethnic minorities, may lack the resources to move into new roles or to emulate younger, physically attractive models. Fortunately, with the growth and visibility of the older population, there are more models of role gains and active aging as well as alternative roles for older people to play than in the past. There is also wider recognition that the role of

---

AGE-NORMATIVE EXPECTATIONS

Within a 5-year age range, how would you respond to the following questions *for most people, for your parents, and for yourself?* If your responses differ across these three groups, reflect upon why there are disparities. What does this tell you about how you view aging?

	For Most People	For Your Parents	For Yourself
Best age for a man to marry	_____	_____	_____
Best age for a woman to marry	_____	_____	_____
When most people should become grandparents	_____	_____	_____
When most men should be settled on a career	_____	_____	_____
When most women should be settled on a career	_____	_____	_____
When most people should be ready to retire	_____	_____	_____
When a man accomplishes the most	_____	_____	_____
When a woman accomplishes the most	_____	_____	_____

"dependent person" is not inevitable with age. Rather, the life course is characterized by varying periods of greater or lesser dependency in social relationships, with most people interdependent on others regardless of age. Even a physically impaired elder may still continue to support others financially and emotionally and may be able to devise creative adaptations to ensure competence at home. For example, older people who volunteer as "phone pals" in a telephone reassurance program for latchkey children provide valuable emotional support.

Activity Theory

Activity theory is also an attempt to answer how individuals adjust to age-related changes and problems, such as retirement, poor health, and role loss. It views successful aging largely as an extension of middle age in which older people seek to maintain roles, relationships, and status in later life. Based on Robert Havighurst's (1963, 1968) analyses of the Kansas City Studies of Adult Life, it was believed that the well-adjusted older person takes on age-appropriate replacements for past roles, through **productive roles** in voluntary, faith-based and leisure associations. The more active the older

---

ROLE MODELS FOR OLDER PEOPLE

Flip through a popular magazine or newspaper, noting how older adults are portrayed in both the ads and in news articles. What roles do older people play in the print media? Are there differences between magazines aimed at younger versus older audiences (e.g. *Wired* vs. *Time*)? Are the roles mostly positive or negative images? Exceptional or realistic? To what extent is diversity portrayed in terms of race/ethnicity, gender, age, social class, sexual orientation, or disability? Or are the images mostly homogeneous? Reflect on how these images fit with or contradict your own perspectives on others' aging as well as your own. We encourage you to develop a critical eye with regard to the role models for older adults portrayed in the media.

KEEPING ACTIVE

The following two cases illustrate the possible link between activity theory and life satisfaction:

- Bob lives in the northwest region of the United States. He retired at age 62 after 30 years of work in a management position for an aerospace company. He and his wife of 40 years carefully saved money so that they could be very active in their retirement. They spent their winters as "snowbirds," traveling in their mobile home to the Sun Belt. Now at age 69, they have spent 7 years in the same community in Arizona where they have a network of good friends who are also retired and from many parts of the United States. In the summer, they usually take one extended trip to the mountains. They enjoy good health and believe that keeping active is the key to their zest for life.

- Rose was a nurse for 30 years. In her career in direct patient care and teaching, she held positions of authority. She has always liked learning new things. Now 74 and retired, she is very active in her church and directs the adult education program. She has participated in Elderhostel four times, and has had the opportunity to travel to Asia and Europe. She has taken two trips with her teenage grandchildren as well. Staying active means always learning and expanding her knowledge, so Rose consistently looks forward to new challenges. She has taken several photography classes at a community college, and loves showing her travel photos to others.

---

person, the greater his or her life satisfaction, positive self-concept, and adjustment. Accordingly, age-based policies and programs are conceptualized as ways to develop new roles and activities, often consistent with middle-aged behavior, and to encourage social integration. To a large extent, activity theory is consistent with the value placed by our society on paid work, wealth, and productivity and reflects an anti-aging perspective (Powell, 2000; 2001b). Losing any of these characteristics is viewed as evidence of decline. Many older people themselves have adopted this perspective and believe that being active helps them to maintain life satisfaction, as illustrated by the vignettes in the boxes on page 309.

Activity theory, however, fails to take account of how personality, socioeconomic status, and lifestyle variables may be more important than maturational ones in the associations found between activity and life satisfaction, health, and well-being (Covey, 1981). The value placed by older people on being active probably varies with their life experiences, personality, and economic and social resources. Activity theory defined aging as an individual social problem that can be addressed by trying to retain status, roles, and activities similar to those of earlier life stages. A challenge to this perspective was formulated in 1961 as disengagement theory, which shifted attention away from the individual to the social system as an explanation for successful adjustment to aging.

The First Transformation of Theory

Disengagement Theory

The development of **disengagement theory** represents a critical juncture—as the first public statement wherein social aging theory is treated as a form of objective scientific inquiry using surveys and questionnaire methods separate from policy and practice applications (Lynott and Lynott, 1996). In fact, disengagement theory was the first comprehensive, explicit, and multidisciplinary theory advanced in social gerontology (Achenbaum and Bengtson, 1994). Cumming and Henry, in their classic work, *Growing Old* (1961), argued that aging cannot be understood separate from the characteristics of the social system in which it is experienced. All societies need orderly ways to transfer power from older to younger generations and to prepare for the disruption entailed by the death of its oldest members. Therefore, the social system deals with the problem of aging or "slowing down" by institutionalizing

mechanisms of disengagement or separation from society. Disengaging was assumed to benefit older adults as well by their decreased activity levels, more passive roles, less frequent social interaction, and preoccupation with their inner lives. *Disengagement* is thus viewed as inevitable and adaptive, allowing older people to maintain a sense of self-worth while adjusting through withdrawal to the loss of prior roles, such as occupational or parenting roles, and ultimately preparing for death (Powell, 2000, 2001a). Since disengagement is presumed to have positive consequences for both society and the individual, this theory challenges assumptions that older people have to be "busy" and engaged in order to be well-adjusted. In contrast to activity theory, it views old age as a separate period of life, not as an extension of middle age.

Disengagement theory is now widely discounted by most gerontologists. While attempting to explain both system- and individual-level change with one grand theory, it has generally not been supported by later empirical research (Achenbaum and Bengtson, 1994). Elders, especially in other cultures, may move into new roles of prestige and power. Likewise, not everyone in our culture disengages, as evidenced by the growing numbers of older people who remain employed, healthy, and politically and socially active. As demonstrated by the MacArthur Studies, described in Chapter 6, successful aging is more likely to be achieved by people who remain involved in society. Disengagement theory also fails to account for variability in individual preferences, personality, culture and environmental opportunities within the aging population (Estes and Associates, 2000; Marshall, 1994). Likewise, it cannot be assumed that older people's withdrawal from useful roles is necessarily good for society. For example, policies to encourage retirement have resulted in the loss of older workers' skills and knowledge in the workplace and altered the dependency ratio described in Chapter 1. Although disengagement theory has largely disappeared from the empirical literature, and transcendent one, normally accompanied by an increase in life satisfaction (Tornstam, 2000). This connection with the cosmic world may be expressed as wisdom, spirituality, and one's "inner world," and a shift away from activity, materialism, rationality, superficial social contacts, and preoccupation with the physical body. Like disengagement theory, gerotranscendence places value on the need for contemplation in old age. The aging experience causes elders to feel increased affinity to prior generations, smaller time gaps between historical periods, and a smaller divide between life and death. Gerotranscendence is viewed as the highest level of human development, but Western culture, with its emphasis on consumerism, productivity and physical attractiveness, creates barriers to such an achievement characterized by wisdom, self-acceptance, and purpose (Moody, 2005; Tornstam, 1989; 1994, 1996a). The theory of gerotranscendence is criticized for not considering the historical and cultural context in which aging occurs and for postulating a universal aging process. Critics contend that a theoretical perspective is needed that encompasses elders who are active or passive, participating or withdrawn,

as the first attempt to define an explicit multidisciplinary theory of aging, it nevertheless had a profound impact on the field.

Gerotranscendence Theory

Gerotranscendence theory to some extent parallels disengagement theory by its aim of developing a metatheory of a universal phenomenon of normal aging. This theory places greater focus on the inner self as a positive characteristic of old age, however. Gerotranscendence represents a shift in the elder's perspective from a materialistic, rational view of the world to a more cosmic

cosmic or worldly, angry or cheerful (Thorsen, 1998). Nevertheless, gerotranscendence theory has practical applications for both elders and health care providers working with older adults and may be reflected in life review, reminiscence therapy, and increased attention to spirituality (Tornstam, 1996b; Wadensten, 2005; Wadensten and Carlsson, 2001).

Continuity Theory

While challenging both activity and disengagement theory, **continuity theory** maintained the focus on social-psychological theories of adaptation that were developed from the Kansas City Studies. According to continuity theory, individuals tend to maintain a *consistent* pattern of behavior as they age, substituting similar types of roles for lost ones and maintaining typical ways of adapting to the environment. In other words, individuals do not change dramatically as they age, and their personalities remain similar throughout their adult lives unless changed by illness. Life satisfaction is determined by the consistency between current activities or lifestyles with one's lifetime experiences (Neugarten, Havighurst, and Tobin, 1968). This perspective states that, with age, we become more of what we already were when younger. Central personality characteristics become more pronounced, and core values more salient with age. For example, people who have always been passive or withdrawn are unlikely to become active upon retirement. In contrast, people who were involved in many organizations, sports, or religious groups are likely to continue these activities or to substitute new ones for those that are lost with retirement or relocation. An individual ages successfully and "normally" if she or he maintains a mature, integrated personality while growing old.

Continuity theory has some face validity because it seems reasonable. However, it is difficult to test empirically, since an individual's reaction to aging is explained through the interrelationships among biological and psychological changes and the continuation of lifelong patterns. Another limitation is that, by focusing on the individual as a unit of analysis, it overlooks the role of external social factors in modifying the aging process. It thus could rationalize a laissez-faire or "live and let live" approach to addressing problems facing older people.

Alternative Theoretical Perspectives

Activity, disengagement, and continuity theories have often been framed as directly challenging one another, even though they differ in the extent to which they focus on individual behavior or

---

CONTINUITY AND ADAPTATION

The following two cases illustrate the benefits of continuity for some elders:

At age 80, Rabbi Green, who has taught rabbinical students for 40 years, still makes the trip from his suburban home into the city to work with students one day per week. He speaks with considerable excitement about his reciprocal relationships with his students, how much he learns from them and how he enjoys mentoring. When students talk about their relationship with him, it becomes clear how much they value him as a mentor. Being a teacher is who he is now and who he has always been.

Mary, 90, has always been the "cookie jar" mother to her children and their friends. She was there to offer goodies and a listening ear. Now her children and the generation of young persons who were their friends live far away. But a new generation of children has moved into the neighborhood in the small town where she lives. She has become acquainted with many of them and their parents as they stop to talk with her while she works in her beloved yard. Now many of the children stop by for a cookie and a glass of milk after school. She is fondly called the "cookie jar grandma." The children say that, along with giving them cookies, she always listens to them.

Many adults continue to play golf into old age.

social systems/social structure (Lynott and Lynott, 1996; Marshall, 1996). None fully explains successful or active aging nor adequately addresses the social structure or the cultural or historical contexts in which the aging process occurs. During this early period of theory development, the factors found to be associated with optimal aging were, for the most part, individualistic—keeping active, withdrawing, "settling" into old age. When macro-level phenomena were considered, they were not conceptualized as structurally linked between the individual and society. Nor were race, ethnicity, sexual orientation, and social class explicitly identified as social structural variables. A number of alternative theoretical viewpoints have emerged since the 1960s, each attempting to explain "the facts" of aging better than another (Estes and Associates, 2000; Powell, 2006). Many of these perspectives emphasized a macro-level of structural analysis, and include symbolic interactionism or subcultures of aging, age stratification, social exchange, and political economy.

Symbolic Interactionism and Subculture of Aging

Consistent with the person–environment perspective outlined in Chapter 1, these **interactionist theories** focus on the person–environment trans-

action process, emphasizing the dynamic interaction between older individuals and their social world. It is assumed that older people must adjust to ongoing societal requirements. When confronted with change, whether relocation to a nursing home or learning to use a computer, elders are expected to try to master the new situation while extracting from the larger environment what they need to retain a positive self-concept.

Attempting to bridge the gap between the activity and disengagement points of view, **symbolic interactionism** argues that the interactions between individuals, their environment, and their encounters in it can significantly affect their experience of the aging process (Gubrium, 1973). This perspective emphasizes the importance of considering the meaning of the activity for the individuals concerned, since any activity may be valued in some environments, while devalued in others. Whether a new activity increases or decreases life satisfaction depends on an elder's resources (health, socioeconomic status, and social support), along with the environmental norms for interpreting activities (Lynott and Lynott, 1996). Symbolic interactionists view both the self and society as able to create new alternatives. Therefore, low morale and withdrawal from social networks are not inevitable with aging, but are one possible outcome of an individual's interactions that can be altered. Policies and programs based on the symbolic interactionist framework optimistically assume that both environmental constraints and individual needs can be changed.

Labeling theory, derived from symbolic interaction theory, states that people derive their self-concepts from interacting with others. In other words, we tend to think of ourselves in terms of how others define us and react to others. Once others have defined us into distinct categories, they react to us on the basis of these categorizations. As a result, our self-concept and behavior may change. For example, an older person who forgets where she or he parked the car is likely to be defined by relatives as showing signs of dementia, while younger people who do so are viewed as busy and distracted.

Proponents of the **subculture of aging theory** believe that older people maintain their self-concepts and social identities through their membership in a subculture (Rose, 1965). Behavior, whether of older persons or others, cannot be evaluated in terms of some overall social standard or norm. Rather, it is appreciated or devalued against the background of its members' expectations. Older people are presumed to interact with each other more than they do with others because they have developed an affinity for each other through shared backgrounds, problems, and interests. At the same time, they may be excluded from fully interacting with other segments of the population either because of self-segregation in retirement communities or "involuntary" segregation, such as younger people leaving inner city or rural areas and thereby isolating older residents. The formation of an aging subculture is viewed as having two significant consequences for older people:

- an identification of themselves as old, and thus socially and culturally distinct from the rest of our youth-oriented society
- a growing group consciousness that may create the possibility of political influence and social action

Age stratification theory and the subculture of aging suggest that older people prefer socializing within their own cohorts.

> ### SUBCULTURE OF AGING
>
> Roy, 63, has resided in a subsidized senior housing project in the Pacific Northwest for the past 4 years. A logger for many years, he never married, living alone in the woods for most of his work life and coming into town only when he needed supplies. When logging was curtailed, he "retired" early. Now he lives with many other older people in the senior apartments, where they look out for each other and occasionally share lunch in a nearby coffee shop. He is able to make use of a low-income clinic for health care, and goes daily to the downtown senior center for his lunch and to play cards.

Although the interactionist and subculture perspectives have implications for how to restructure environments, the focus is primarily on how individuals react to aging rather than on the broader sociostructural factors that shape the experience and meaning of aging in our society. As with some of the other theories described above, the subculture theory of aging also fails to recognize that older adults have important intergenerational roles and relationships, as grandparent, parent, friend, mentor, or employer. Instead, most people move into and out of a succession of different roles and statuses as they age, which is congruent with age stratification theory.

Age Stratification Theory

Just as societies are stratified in terms of socioeconomic class, gender, and race, every society divides people into categories or strata according to age—"young," "middle-aged," and "old." Age stratification is defined in terms of differential age cohorts. This means that individual experiences with aging, and therefore their roles, vary with their age strata. An older person's evaluation of life cannot be understood simply as a matter of being active or disengaged. Instead, changes in the system of age stratification influence how a person's experiences affect life satisfaction (Lynott and Lynott, 1996).

The **age stratification theory,** first conceptualized and developed by Matilda White Riley (Riley, 1971; Riley, Johnson and Foner, 1972; Riley, Foner and Riley, 1999), challenges activity and disengagement theories. It directs attention away from individual adjustment to that of the age structure of society (Marshall, 1996). This theory adds a structured time component in which cohorts pass through an age structure viewed as an age-graded system of expectations and rewards (Riley, Johnson, and Foner, 1972). Such an approach recognizes that the members of one stratum differ from each other in both their stage of life (young, middle-aged, or old) and in the historical periods they have experienced. Both the life course and the historical dimensions explain differences in how people behave, think, and, in turn, contribute to society. Differences due to the historical dimension are referred to as cohort flow. As we saw in our discussion of research designs in gerontology (Chapter 1), people born at the same time period (cohort) share a common historical and environmental past, present, and future. They have been exposed to similar events, conditions, and changes, and therefore come to see the world in similar ways (Riley, 1971). For example, older people who were at the early stage of their occupational and childrearing careers during the Depression tend to value economic self-sufficiency and "saving for a rainy day," compared to younger cohorts who have experienced periods of economic prosperity during early adulthood. This may create difficulties across generations in understanding each other's behavior with regard to finances or lifestyle.

Because of their particular relationship to historical events, people in the old-age stratum today are very different from older persons in the past or in the future, and they experience the aging process differently. This also means that cohorts as they age collectively influence age stratification. When there is a lack of fit in terms of available roles, cohort members may challenge the existing patterns of age stratification. For example, as successive cohorts in this century have experienced increased longevity and formal educational levels, this has changed the nature of how they age, how they view aging, and the age stratification system itself. Similarly, aging baby boomers are likely to alter the age stratification system profoundly, given their sheer size, higher education and income levels, and the social structural changes that they have experienced in their lifetimes.

Consider how the first of the baby boomers to retire in the early twenty-first century may differ

INTERGENERATIONAL CONFLICT AND AGE STRATIFICATION

Edna is a 90-year-old retired teacher who grew up during the Depression and was a young bride during World War II. These two major historical events have shaped her life, because she learned to make do with whatever resources were available to her. As a result, she has always been frugal with her spending, to the point of saving a large nest egg to pass on to her grandchildren when she dies. However, she is often critical about the way her grandchildren seem to spend every penny they earn. Even worse, they use credit cards freely and don't worry about carrying debt. She has expressed her concerns to her daughter, telling her these young people have not learned to save for a rainy day. Her daughter listens patiently but does not agree with what she considers her mother's penny-pinching ways. And her grandchildren try to explain to her that being in debt is a good way to build up credit for when they need a loan. She responds that she and her husband never took out a loan for anything but always paid in cash.

Many social theories view caregiving as integral to healthy aging.

from the cohort that retired in the 1950s. Although heterogeneous, this later cohort will tend to:

- view retirement and leisure more positively
- be physically active and healthier
- be more likely to challenge restrictions on their roles as workers and community participants through age discrimination lawsuits, legislative action, and political organization
- live long enough to become great-grandparents
- be more planful and proactive about the aging and dying processes

These variations, in turn, will affect the experiences and expectations of future cohorts as they age. In other words, as successive cohorts move through the age strata, they alter conditions to such a degree that later groups never encounter the world in exactly the same way, and therefore age differently.

Age stratification theory, with its focus on structural, demographic, and historical characteristics, can help us understand the ways in

which society uses age to fit people into structural niches in the social world, and how this age structure changes with the passage of time. By viewing aging groups as members of status groups within a social system, as well as active participants in a changing society, stratification theory can provide useful sociological explanations of age differences related to time, period, and cohort.

The concept of **structural lag** emerged from the age and society perspective (Riley, Kahn, and Foner, 1994; Riley and Riley, 1994). Structural lag occurs when social structures cannot keep pace with the changes in population and individual lives (Riley and Loscocco, 1994). For example, with the increases in life expectancy, societal structures are inadequate to accommodate and utilize postretirement elders. In some cases, the workplace, religious institutions, and voluntary associations may fail to recognize the resources that older people could contribute. Proponents argue that an age-integrated society would compensate for structural lag by developing policies, such as extended time off for education or family caregiving across the life course, to bring social structures into balance with individuals' lives (Estes and Associates, 2001).

Social Exchange Theory

Social exchange theory also challenged activity and disengagement theory. Drawing on economic cost-benefit models of social participation, Dowd (1980) attempts to answer why social interaction and activity often decrease with age. He maintains that withdrawal and social isolation are not the result of system needs or individual choice, but rather of an unequal exchange process of "investments and returns" between older persons and other members of society. The balance of interactions existing between older people and others determines personal satisfaction. Accordingly, individual adjustment depends on the immediate costs and benefits/rewards between persons, although exchange may also be driven by emotional needs and resources, such as social support (Bengtson et al., 1997). Because of the shift in **opportunity structures,** roles, and skills that accompanies advancing aging, elders typically have fewer resources with which to exert power in their social relationships, and their status declines accordingly (Hendricks, 1995). Society is at an advantage in such power relationships, reflected in the economic and social dependency of older people who have outmoded skills. With fewer opportunity structures and resources to exchange in value, some older people are forced to accept the retirement role in order to balance the exchange equation (Lynott and Lynott, 1996).

Despite their limited resources, older adults seek to maintain some degree of reciprocity, and to be active, autonomous agents in the management of their lives. In this model, adaptability is a dual process of influencing one's environment as

Our personal experiences with older adults affect our perceptions and social exchanges with elders.

well as adjusting to it. Although older individuals may have fewer economic and material resources to bring to the interaction or exchange, they often have nonmaterial resources such as respect, approval, love, wisdom, and time for civic engagement and giving back to society. Similarly, policies and services might aim to increase opportunity structures for elders' nonmaterial resources that are to be valued by society. For example, many intergenerational programs recognize the value of social exchange between young and old. Exchange theory is relevant to contemporary debates about intergenerational transfers across generations through public policies such as Social Security and within families through caregiving relationships. Social exchange can also be viewed across the life course. For example, parents who provided affection and tangible resources to their children during their early years are more likely to receive social, emotional, and financial support from their adult children in old age. In this instance, social exchange is a long-term interaction between generations (Silverstein et al., 2002).

Political Economy of Aging

The focus of exchange theory on power and opportunity structures is related to the development of the **political economy of aging,** a macro-analysis of structural characteristics that

---

FOSTER GRANDPARENT PROGRAMS

Ten-year-old Ann lives with her mother and older brother in a public housing high-rise apartment. Her mother has to work two jobs in order to make ends meet. This means that Ann is often left at home alone after school. Through the Foster Grandparent Program administered by the local senior services and available in Ann's school, Ann has someone to call after school if she is lonely or needs help with homework. And twice a week her foster grandmother comes to visit her, taking her on neighborhood outings, making clothes for her favorite doll, buying a special treat, or tutoring her. Ann benefits from her foster grandmother's attention and love. And her foster grandmother, a widow in her mid-70s, feels a sense of satisfaction, accomplishment, and responsibility in her relationship with Ann. She looks forward to her time with Ann and speaks with pride to her friends about Ann's achievements as if she were her real granddaughter. Most of all, the young girl and the older woman love each other—an emotional component of exchange relationships that makes it less appropriate to analyze relationships in strictly economic terms.

determine how people adapt in old age and how social resources are allocated. Political economy theorists rejected biomedical, activity, and disengagement models of aging. Instead, social class is viewed as the primary determinant of older people's position in a capitalist society, with dominant groups trying to sustain their own interests by perpetuating class inequities (Estes, 2001; Estes and Associates 2001; Minkler and Estes, 1998). Socioeconomic and political constraints, not individual factors, thereby shape the experience of aging, and are patterned not only by age and class but also by gender, sexual orientation, and ethnic minority status. These structural factors, often institutionalized and reinforced by economic and public policy, limit opportunities, choices, and experiences of later life. This means that the process of aging and how individuals adapt are not the problem. Rather, the major problems faced by older people are socially constructed in a capitalist society. In fact, policy solutions, such as Social Security, Medicare, and Medicaid, are viewed as a means of social control that perpetuates the "private" troubles of older people while meeting the dominant needs of the economy (Estes and Associates, 2001). Estes and colleagues (1996, 2001) argue that the marginalization of the older population is furthered by the development of the "Aging Enterprise," a service industry of service providers and planners funded largely by the Administration on Aging that reaffirm older adults' marginality in order to maintain their own jobs. Accordingly, policies and programs have often focused on socializing elders to adapt to their status, rather than efforts to fundamentally alter social and economic structures and inequities that underlie the challenges facing older people. Political economy still influences gerontological theorizing, but has been reframed as "critical gerontology," which remains concerned with structural inequities but also aims to challenge the marginality of elders (Powell, 2006; Phillipson, 1998).

A POLITICAL ECONOMY PERSPECTIVE ON OLDER WOMEN OF COLOR: LIFE COURSE INEQUITIES

Discrimination during their younger years and lack of opportunity throughout life have placed today's cohort of older African American women at a disadvantage. Because of racial and gender discrimination in education and employment throughout the life course, many did not have access to good jobs with retirement and health benefits. As a result, today many subsist on minimum Social Security benefits as their only source of income and Medicaid as their primary form of health insurance. This means that their health care options are structurally limited to providers who will accept Medicaid. And because of encounters with institutionalized racism in their past, they may resist other age-based services. They may not even apply for Supplemental Security Income (SSI), because of past negative experiences with public welfare. Subsisting on limited income and often busy caring for grandchildren, admonishments from care providers to keep active and volunteer do not take account of demands faced daily just to get by.

In addition to critiquing the marginalization of older adults through aging network services, political economy theorists criticize the current emphasis on civic engagement for implicitly devaluing the worth of elders who cannot or choose not to participate in these programs in their communities (Biggs, 2001; Martinson and Minkler, 2006). As discussed in Chapter 12, civic engagement includes local and national participation through volunteering and activism in programs such as Foster Grandparents and the Older Women's League. The growing call for civic engagement is viewed by critical gerontologists as a way to meet service gaps created by reduced public funding for health and social services and the federal deficit. Despite the benefits of volunteerism and productivity for successful aging, described in Chapter 6, there is an implicit assumption that older people have a *responsibility* to give back to their communities.

From a political economy perspective, social and structural factors affect the older person's choices in volunteering or remaining productive. For example, caregivers for a spouse with dementia or custodial grandparents of young children often cannot take on the additional role of a volunteer. The growing emphasis on civic engagement and productive aging can also divert the aging person from gerotranscendence, described earlier, in which contemplation allows the older person to find coherence and meaning in life (Biggs, 2001; Holstein, 1999). Even though proponents of the volunteering and civic engagement movement for older adults recognize the dangers of this "one-size-fits-all" approach to healthy aging, they continue to promote the desirability of elders contributing to society (Harvard School of Public Health/Metlife Foundation, 2004). A paradigm of aging that only values productivity and civic-engagement can stigmatize and disempower elders who cannot contribute to their communities because of illness, disability, or limited time and resources (Holstein and Minkler, 2003; Moody, 2005).

Life Course Perspective

The **life course perspective** is not necessarily a theory, but a framework pointing to a set of problems requiring explanation (George, 1996; 2007). As noted in Chapter 1, it attempts to bridge sociological and psychological constructs about processes at both the macro (population) and micro (individual) levels of analysis. In contrast with the more individualistic approach of role theory, the life course perspective attempts to explain how aging and its meaning are shaped by time, period, cohort, history, culture, and location in the social structure. Individual development in cognitive function and personality interact with these larger social forces and cohort experiences. Age stratification theory, described earlier, laid a critical foundation for the life course perspective (Bengtson et al., 1997; George, 2007; Marshall, 1996). This approach

> ### BENEFITING FROM LIFE COURSE SOCIAL CAPITAL
>
> James is a 72-year-old civil engineer who retired from the Army Corps of Engineers at age 66. But his expertise in designing large bridges has resulted in a second career as a consultant to state and federal projects where he is asked to assess the safety of bridges and to evaluate them after natural disasters. He is doing so well in his consulting job that he withdraws only the minimum from his pension benefits. He enjoys the respect and friendship of his new colleagues, as well as the opportunities to use his professional skills in this second career. The chance to still feel useful is more important to him than what he gets paid to consult.

takes account of the diversity of roles and role changes across the life span, since it contends that development is not restricted to any one part of the life span, but rather is a lifelong and highly dynamic process. This is consistent with Erikson's theory of psychosocial development throughout life, described in Chapter 6. The life course perspective expands on this idea, however, by emphasizing that human development cannot be solely equated with steady incremental growth, but instead is an interactive, nonlinear process characterized by the simultaneous appearance of role gains and losses, continuity and discontinuity. Accordingly, development is multidirectional, with stability in some functions, decline in others, and improvement in others. For example, an older person may experience some decrement in short-term memory but still be very creative. In addition, patterns of development are not the same in all individuals, as reflected by the considerable heterogeneity of life trajectories and transitions among older individuals. The life course perspective can provide a critical analysis of how caregiving for older relatives is now a standardized part of the life course, "on-time" for growing numbers of middle-aged adult children, because of increased life expectancy among their parent's generation. As noted in Chapter 1, growing research on health disparities take account of how gender, race, and social class structure the life course and result in cumulative disadvantage in old age (Estes, 2001). For example, because of care responsibilities, women have limited opportunities to accumulate savings and private pensions across their lives, resulting in lower income and higher rates of poverty in old age as compared to men (O'Rand, 2006). The life course perspective also considers the role of "human agency," or individual decisions that affect one's future. For example, dropping out of high school can have lifelong consequences on economic and social well-being (George, 2007).

This text's multidisciplinary person-in-environment approach, encompassing biological, psychological, physiological, and social changes, draws on many of the concepts of intraindividual change, interindividual variability, and historical, social, and cultural contexts or environments that are central to a life course approach.

Life Course Social Capital

Life course capital is a more recent approach to life course research that recognizes both the exchange of resources across the life course (social exchange theory) and persistent inequalities in our society (health and economic disparities). Human capital encompasses the idea of "stock"—or the accumulation of resources, such as skills and productive knowledge—as capital that can be allocated to satisfy basic human needs and wants. Capital can be social (e.g., informal social relationships), psychological and physical-well-being, or biological (e.g., genetic or developmental). Environmental factors, including community capital, institutional capital, and collectively held moral capital, in turn, affect the extent to which individuals possess such human capital. Over the life course, the accumulation of human capital, by acquiring valued skills and knowledge and participating in the paid labor force, is a primary mechanism of social inequality within cohorts. This differential increase in income sources and health

benefits affects individual well-being. The interactions among these forms of life course capital thus have implications for outcomes in wealth, morbidity, and mortality. Whatever the formative causal sequence in early life among these different forms of capital, the subsequent developmental course is one of interdependent exchange of capital. Life course research aims to uncover the patterns of relationship among forms of capital (both individual and structural) and their effects on different groups within the aging population (O'Rand, 2006; Rosen, 1998).

Recent Developments in Social Gerontological Theory: The Second Transformation

Social Phenomenology and Social Constructionism

The "second transformation" in theoretical development, occurring since the early 1980s, is described as a qualitative leap in gerontological thought (Lynott and Lynott, 1996; Powell, 2006). Phenomenological theorists take issue with the presumed "facts of aging," questioning the nature of age and how it is described and whose interests are served by thinking of aging in particular ways. Proponents of **social phenomenology** and **social constructionism** claim that the approach, orientation, and other subjective features of researchers are significantly connected to the nature of

---

POINTS TO PONDER

A debate before Congress in 2003 was whether to differentially allocate Medicare drug benefits according to income. What assumptions did this debate make about the older population as a whole? About upper income elders? What is your position on differential allocation of such prescription drug benefits? What theoretical perspective guides your thinking?

objective data. This means that the data or facts of aging cannot be separated from the researcher's perceptions about time, space, and self—or those of the individuals being studied. People actively participate in their everyday lives, creating and maintaining social meanings for themselves and those around them. No one, including researchers, directly or objectively sees a fixed reality. Rather, each of us actively constructs meanings that influence what we each call reality. For phenomenologists and social constructionists, it is not the objects or facts but rather the assumptions and interpretations of them that are critical (Lynott and Lynott, 1996; Ray, 1996). For example, this theoretical perspective would attempt to understand how policy makers interpret the growth of the older population in deciding whether to increase or decrease Medicare or Social Security benefits (Estes and Associates, 2001). If they perceive the aging population to be economically homogeneous, then policy solutions will not take account of need or class differences.

The emphasis of phenomenologists is on understanding, not explaining, individual processes of aging that are influenced by social definitions and social structures (Bengtson et al., 1997). Instead of asking how factors such as age cohorts, life stages, or system needs organize and determine one's experience, they reverse the question and ask how individuals, whether professionals or laypersons, draw on age-related explanations and justifications in how they relate to and interact with one another. Individual behavior produces a "reality," which in turn structures individual lives. In other words, the realities of age and age-related concepts are socially constructed through interpersonal interactions. For example, labeling older people as dependent, asexual, frail, or marginal is defined through social interactions by health care providers, family members, and society in general. Accordingly, social reality and the meaning of being old shift over time, reflecting the differing life situations and social roles that occur with maturation (Kaufman, 1994).

Not only do theorists construct versions of reality, but people do so in their everyday lives; similarly, in the everyday world, people often use or critique the constructions of theories (Marshall, 1996). Gubrium (1993a) used life narratives to discern the subjective meanings of quality of care and quality of life for nursing home residents—meanings that cannot be uncovered by predefined measurement scales. Similarly, Diamond (1992) utilized participant observation techniques as a nursing assistant to learn about the social world of nursing homes. He described the social construction of his job, how the meanings of care are constantly negotiated as the invisible work of caring for older residents' emotional needs clashes with the daily physical tasks of a nursing assistant. Because of their focus on individual interactions, social constructionists and phenomenologists tend to use ethnographic or more qualitative methods to understand the multifaceted aging experience. This contrasts with the **positivism** (or *quantitative approach*) of earlier theories. In order to

---

SOCIAL CONSTRUCTION OF AGING

At age 85, Martha enjoys a brisk, daily 30-minute walk around the park near her home. She manages her household on her own, participates in exercise classes at the local senior center, and enrolls in one history class each semester at the local community college. She is proud to be independent, healthy, and involved in her community. Nevertheless, the young people she meets at the park and in her college classes are always amazed at her vigor and intellectual curiosity. They often express surprise that she can do all she does "at her age," and ask her about her "secret to aging well." Martha tells them they need to expand their view of aging and discard their ageist stereotypes of growing older as an illness, and to stop viewing active older people as "exceptional." But many of these young adults rely on the negative images of aging that they have seen on TV or in popular magazines.

gather extensive verbal or observational data, ethnographic samples tend to be small. To positivists, phenomenological and social constructionist theories may seem impossible to test, and closer to assumptions about meaning than propositions that can be proved or disproved (Bengtson et al., 1997).

From the social constructionist perspective, what is considered to be old age varies with the economic, cultural, historical, and societal context. As noted in Chapter 1, chronological age is a poor predictor of social, physical, and mental abilities. Yet most of us, even gerontological scholars, may make positive or negative assumptions about someone simply on the basis of chronological age (Schaie, 1993). Many depictions of old age in the United States present it as a negative experience, something to be avoided, a disease to be dealt with by medical interventions—or what Estes refers to as the biomedicalization of old age (Estes and Associates, 2001). In fact, a recent survey by AARP found that both young and old respondents defined "old" as negative (e.g., decline and loss of roles or abilities). Older adults may shun the label "old," reserving it for those with obvious physical or mental decline (e.g., "I don't want anything to do with those old people"). Even the current preoccupation with healthy, successful aging, and turning to exercise or beauty products still portrays aging as something to be forestalled for as long as possible. In addition, the visual images associated with many of these antiaging activities are unattainable by the majority of Americans.

The negative ways in which age is socially constructed has numerous consequences for social policy, employer practices, public perception, and self-concept. As noted by the political economy theorists, problems related to aging and long-term care are to some degree socially constructed (Olson, 2003). Consider how public resources are disproportionately allocated toward skilled nursing care rather than toward supplementing the personal assistance provided by families and low-wage workers. Accordingly,

the majority of public funds go toward medical or long-term care, not psychosocial services that might enhance elders' quality of life and active aging. Similarly, the general public tends to think of old age as homogenizing, overlooking the tremendous diversity (by genetic makeup, history, personal experiences) that exists across at least one third of our lifetimes. From a social constructionist perspective, we need to deconstruct the concept *old,* and recognize how one's position or location (gender, race/ethnicity, social class, sexual orientation, level of ability) shapes the experiences of old age. This also suggests that gerontologists focus not only on the problems facing the old, but also on their strengths, resilience, how they overcome barriers, and ways in which cumulative disadvantage can nevertheless serve as an advantage in certain contexts (Calasanti and Slevin, 2001; Estes, 2001; Olson, 2003).

Critical Theory and Feminist Perspectives

Social constructionist theories have influenced other contemporary social gerontology theories, especially **critical** and **feminist theories.** Critical theorists critique the transformation of the relationships between subjects and objects from being genuine to being alienated, not the research procedures or the objective state of objects per se. Critical theorists are concerned with how positivist conceptualizations of aging represent a language serving to reify experiences as something separate from adults experiencing aging (Lynott and Lynott, 1996). They contend that a more critical and humane approach would allow older people themselves to define the research questions. Arguing for humanistic discourse in gerontology, Moody (1988, 2002) identifies four goals of critical gerontology:

1. to theorize subjective and interpretive dimensions of aging
2. to focus not on technical advancement but on "praxis," defined as active involvement in practical change, such as public policy

3. to link academics and practitioners through praxis

4. to produce "emancipatory knowledge," which is a positive vision of how things might be different or what a rationally defensible vision of a "good old age" might be (Moody 2002, p. xvii)

To achieve such knowledge requires moving beyond the conventional confines of gerontology to explore contributions toward theory development from more reflective modes of thought that are derived from the humanities (Cole et al., 1993). What is yet unknown is what "a good old age" means, as well as how it can be attained and what type of "emancipatory knowledge" is possible. Dannefer (1994) suggests that critical gerontology should not merely critique existing theory, but create positive models of aging that emphasize strengths and diversity. For example, Atchley (1993) maintains that critical gerontology must question traditional positivistic assumptions and measures to try to understand the multiple dimensions of retirement, including retirement as a freeing stage in the life course. Critical thinking has the potential to expand the field of social gerontology. It can do so by providing insight into, and critical self-reflection on, the continuing effort to understand the aging experience (Lynott and Lynott, 1996).

Because most gerontologists have been trained in the positivist tradition, critical theory, with its abstractionist approach, is often not cited nor yet well understood. Nevertheless, it has become a topic of considerable theoretical discourse in contemporary social gerontology (Minkler, 1996; Moody, 2002; Phillipson, 1996; Powell, 2006). By questioning traditions in mainstream social gerontology, critical theory calls attention to other perspectives relevant to understanding aging, especially the humanistic dimension, and has influenced feminist theories of aging. In addition, the self-reflexive nature of critical theory constantly challenges

A FEMINIST PERSPECTIVE ON CAREGIVING

Maria grew up with the expectation that she would marry, have children, and take care of her family. She fulfilled this expectation, raising four children, caring for her husband when he suffered a heart attack in his early 60s, and then later caring for both her mother and her mother-in-law. She never held a full-time job outside the home, instead occasionally working part-time in order to supplement her husband's income. When he died at age 65, she was left with only his Social Security. All her years of caregiving work, which had contributed to her family's well-being and to the economy, were not compensated in any way. She feels that she is being penalized for following the "rules" expected of her throughout her life. If her caregiving work were valued by our society and viewed as legitimate, Social Security would be altered to provide benefits for such in-home care. This would mean that caregivers such as Maria would receive Social Security benefits in their own right in old age.

gerontologists to understand the impact of social research and policy on older individuals. With growing attention to ethnographic and other qualitative methodologies, the interpretive approach of critical theory will increasingly be brought to bear on empirical observations of aging. This will encourage researchers to integrate critical theory with the strengths of positivist approaches.

One way that current theories and models of aging are viewed as insufficient by critical theorists is by their failure to include gender relations and women's experiences in the context of aging (Calasanti and Slevin, 2001; Cruikshank, 2003; Estes, 2001; Olson, 2003). For example, women were traditionally ignored in retirement research, often because paid employment was assumed to be unimportant to them (Calasanti and Slevin, 2001). Or women were not included in early health studies because men were defined as the norm.

In addition to critical theorists, feminist theories draw on a number of perspectives discussed thus far:

- political economy by focusing on the economic and power relations between older men and women
- symbolic interactionism, phenomenology, and social constructionism in the belief that gender must be examined in the context of social structural arrangements

Feminist theories attempt to integrate micro- and macro-approaches to aging through the links between individuals and social structures, or between personal problems and public responses. In particular, they focus on gender-based power relations across the life course and the utilization of both quantitative and qualitative methodologies (Browne, 1998; Estes and Associates, 2001; Moody, 2000; Ray, 1996).

From a feminist perspective, gender should be a primary consideration in attempts to understand aging, since women form the majority of the older population. Because gender is an organizing principle for social interactions across the life course, men and women experience the aging process differently. The intersections of gender with race, social class, sexual orientation, and disability are also examined by feminist theorists (Ginn and Arber, 1995; Moen, 2001; Calasanti and Slevin, 2001). Although feminism encompasses a wide range of intellectual paradigms and political/ideological positions, most feminist theories in aging have drawn on *socialist feminism*. This model argues that women occupy an inferior status in old age as a result of living in a capitalist and patriarchal society (Arber and Ginn, 1991, 1995; Browne, 1998).

Socialist feminism points to inequities in the gender-based division of labor and argues for major changes in how society defines, distributes, and rewards "work." Socialist feminists theorists attempt to understand women's aging

experiences in light of macro-level social, economic, and political forces rather than as isolated results of individual choices. Caregiving, women's retirement, health, and poverty across the life course are examined in light of women's differential access to power in the paid labor force, childrearing, and unpaid housework throughout their lives. As noted under the life course approach, such unequal access leaves women without economic resources to manage challenges in later life (Browne, 1998; Calasanti, 1999; Garner, 1999; Hooyman and Gonyea 1995; Hooyman et al., 2003). Social policy is criticized for defining the problems facing women as private responsibilities, rather than taking account of how existing structural

Intergenerational activities promote social exchange.

arrangements create women's limited choices in old age. For example, the lack of public and private pensions for a lifelong career as homemaker and caregiver leaves older women economically vulnerable. Feminists also point to our society's failure to take domestic labor seriously in life course analyses of work (Marshall, 1996). From a feminist view, work in the home is integral to economic productivity, but is devalued. Similarly, feminists contend that the consequences of caregiving should not be evaluated on the basis of individual characteristics such as burden. Instead, the underlying problem for women of all ages is inadequate and gender-based public policies, not their own stress level; the long-range solution is reorganizing work, including the work of caregiving, as a societal rather than an individual responsibility. Feminists argue that unpaid caring by families and underpaid work by direct care workers are interconnected and must be fundamentally changed to be more equitable and humane both for the givers and the recipients of care (Gonyea and Hooyman, 2005; Hooyman et al., 2002; Meyer, 1997).

New to the field, and sometimes ideologically based, feminist gerontological theories are less frequently cited than established models of explanation, such as social constructionism, life course, and exchange theories. Nevertheless, they can make significant contributions to gerontology and to the development of feminist theory generally. Not only are they focusing on the needs of the majority of older adults, but they also take account of diversity by ethnic minority status, social class, education, sexual orientation, and functional ability. Addressing issues that are relevant to women's lives, they draw explicit linkages to practice. In addition, they provide models for integrating micro- (personal) and macro- (political) levels of analysis. They thus encompass both structural and individual levels of theory and change in order to improve the social and economic positions of all women as they age. Lastly, they challenge

"mainstream" feminist theories, which typically have focused on issues pertaining to younger women, to take account of age, since gender shapes everyday experiences throughout the life course. The merger of feminist and aging scholarship has the potential for formulating politically sustainable solutions that permit women and men, young and old, to balance the burdens and satisfactions of caregiving and paid (Bengtson et al., 1997; Meyer, 1997; Moen, 2001; Powell, 2006).

Postmodern Constructions of Aging

Postmodern theory (or **deconstructionism**), which in itself is atheoretical, represents a decisive break with modernity or a positivist scientific approach to an "objective" truth. Since knowledge is socially constructed and social life highly improvisational, all forms of meaning and "knowledge" are not to be taken for granted. Constructs such as "social class" and "gender" relegate individual elders to socially constructed categories and overlook human agency to organize to change political and economic systems and life conditions. Even the political economy perspective is critiqued by postmodernists for treating aging as an object to be predicted or problematized (Powell and Longino, 2002). When postmodern and feminist theories are integrated, for example, the primary deconstructionist task is to critique language, discourse, and research practices that constrict knowledge about older women. To illustrate, caregiving is viewed not as the result of women's natural tendencies toward nurturing, but as the outcome of socialization processes and polices that reify gendered patterns of care and depend on the unpaid labor of women as efficient and cost-effective (Calasanti and Slevin, 2001; Hooyman and Gonyea, 1995; Hooyman et al., 2002). A postmodern feminist approach in gerontology draws on a variety of methodologies to understand women's experiences. The extent to which researchers' assumptions, values, and beliefs influence the research process is made explicit. Accordingly, postmodernist research, oriented to changing conditions that face women, is conducted to benefit women, and includes women as active participants.

More recent postmodern constructions of aging emphasize the cultural interaction between the complexity of the aging body and the social context in shaping people's "lived experience" across the life course. The notion of the aging body not as a medical or biological phenomenon but as a social and cultural practice of everyday life is an important narrative in the social construction of the aging identity of individuals. And, while external physical appearance changes with age, a person's essential identity does not. Consider how we often hear older adults state that they don't feel old until they see themselves in a mirror. The body is not passive material that is only acted upon but is always in the process of becoming. People derive their sense of identity in later life from their past achievements and what they hope to achieve in the future, not stereotypical attributes of old age (Longino and Powell, 2004; Powell, 2006). At the same time, the aging body is exploited by popular culture, especially glamorized representations of old age in advertisements oriented to foster consumption and a continual flight from the "symptoms" of aging to "aging well" (Gilleard and Higgs, 2000; Powell and Longino, 2001).

Postmodernism also addresses biotechnology and the reconstruction of aging bodies to reinvent aging through biomedical and information technologies. In fact, biotechnology can sell a dream of "not growing old" to people who have the resources to afford such technology (Longino and Powell, 2004). While biomedical and computer advances can provide new options for persons with chronic illness or disability, they also mean that "bodies can be reshaped, remade, fused with machines, empowered through technological devices and extensions" (Featherstone and Wernick, 1995). Closely related to the active adoption of consumer practices such as biotechnology is a growing emphasis on personal responsibility for one's health whereby those who do not engage in adequate "self-care" may not be deserving of societal resources to address their illness (Powell and Biggs, 2004). This attitude of "blaming the victim" is increasingly reflected in public policies oriented toward privatization and individual responsibility, which are discussed fully in Chapters 16 and 17.

The "Foucault Effect" on Gerontological Theory

The concepts of Michel Foucault, a French social theorist, have profoundly impacted social science disciplines and are relevant to analysis of professional power and aging. Even though Foucault did not specifically address gerontological theory, several gerontologists have used his work to deconstruct commonly held assumptions about aging (Biggs and Powell, 2001; Estes, Biggs and Phillipson, 2003; Katz, 1996; Powell, 2001). Concepts central to Foucault's work are the "expert gaze" on the aging body by the health and medical professions, discourse, and professional power. A discourse is a set of ideas, practices, and beliefs that coalesce to produce an overarching picture of society. The medical gaze refers to discourses or ways of seeing that shape the understanding of aging into a scientific problem and thereby advance the power of health professionals, foster the "scientific" management of aging, and dominate the individual will or human agency (Powell, 2006). Foucault's critique centered on both the medical and social work professions for their "gaze" that distances themselves from elders and treats them as dependent "objects." Professional regulation and techniques of surveillance are means by which professionals exercise their power, most visibly expressed through public "welfare," psychoanalytic thought, and "case

POSTMODERNISM AND FOUCAULT'S "EXPERT GAZE"

Nursing homes have traditionally been based on a hierarchical medical model in which professional staff, who often have little direct interaction with the residents (e.g., the "distant expert gaze"), believe that they know what is "best" for them. The medicalization of nursing homes has meant that most institutions are viewed as places to die, not to live. Rules and regulations, including the use of restraints, tend to be oriented to efficiencies and staff needs, not those of residents. When to get up and go to bed, when to eat meals, and when to have a bath are all typically determined by administrative staff and licensing requirements. In addition, staff members are assigned particular tasks, such as the medication nurse or the bath aide, without taking account of the needs of the elder resident as a whole. In contrast to this "expert gaze" on nursing homes, recent efforts to transform their organizational culture encompass resident-directed care where the residents choose when to get up, eat breakfast, and the timing of all other daily activities. Past assumptions and even licensing requirements are questioned, and creative approaches to regulations implemented. Services are decentralized and task-focused roles eliminated so that staff can work with the same residents over time and build a relationship. Other adults are resisting the "expert gaze" by starting intentional communities and co-housing where they make all decisions about communities for living, not for dying. While the traditional nursing home has tended to be a microcosm of how our society has viewed elders from a distance, these new options typically put older adults in central decision-making roles.

management" (e.g., the older person as a case to be maintained). One example of these surveillance principles is vividly reflected in the relationship between the controller and those being controlled in nursing homes (Wahidin and Powell, 2001, 2003). Although professional opinion is more widely heard than elders' voices, older people must be encouraged to actively "resist" the practices of professional power and scientific knowledge to control them.

Summary and Implications for the Future

This review of theoretical perspectives has highlighted the multiplicity of lenses through which to view and explain the aging process. Although we have emphasized the importance of utilizing explicit theoretical perspectives to build, revise, and interpret how and why phenomena occur, it is apparent that no single theory can explain all aging phenomena. Instead, these theories or conceptual frameworks vary widely in their emphasis on individual adjustment to age-related changes, their attention to social structure, power, and economic conditions, the methodologies utilized, and their reflective nature on the meaning of the aging experience. As noted early in the chapter, they represent different times or historical periods in the development of social theories. Some, such as disengagement theory, have been largely rejected by empirical data, while others, such as critical theory and feminist theory, are only now evolving and capturing the attention of a new generation of gerontological researchers. Other earlier perspectives, such as social exchange and symbolic interactionism, still influence research questions and social policy. As a whole, these theoretical perspectives point to new ways of seeing aging phenomena and new modes of analysis, laying the framework for future research directions. As the social, economic, and political conditions affecting older people change, new theoretical perspectives must develop or former ones must be revised through the gathering of information from diverse cultures, contexts, and circumstances. The theme of the Gerontological Imagination for the 2006 Gerontological Society Annual meeting reflects the growing interest in alternative perspectives across a wide range of disciplines. Given the increasing heterogeneity of the aging process, interdisciplinary research and theory building are essential. Such research must take account of both individual and macro-level changes. It must encompass the role of gender, race, class, sexual orientation, and functional ability, and allow for the dynamic nature and meaning of the aging experience. We turn next to the social context and relationships addressed by many of the social theories of aging: the vital role of social supports in old age; how physical living arrangements can affect social interactions; the concept of productive aging, which encompasses both paid and nonpaid roles and activities; and coping with loss in dying, bereavement, and widowhood.

GLOSSARY

activity theory a theory of aging based on the hypothesis that (1) active older people are more satisfied and better adjusted than those who are not active, and (2) an older person's self-concept is validated through participation in roles characteristic of middle age, and older people should therefore replace lost roles with new ones to maintain their place in society

age stratification theory a theoretical perspective based on the belief that the societal age structure affects roles, self-concept, and life satisfaction

continuity theory a theory based on the hypothesis that central personality characteristics become more pronounced with age or are retained through life with little change; people age successfully if they maintain their preferred roles and adaptation techniques

critical theory the perspective that genuine knowledge is based on the involvement of the "objects" of study in its definition and results in a positive vision of how things might be better rather than an understanding of how things are

disengagement theory a theory of aging based on the hypothesis that older people, because of inevitable decline with age, become decreasingly active with the outer world and increasingly preoccupied with their inner lives; disengagement is useful for society because it fosters an orderly transfer of power from older to younger people

feminist theory the view that the experiences of women are often ignored in understanding the human condition together with efforts to attend critically to those experiences

gerotranscendence theory a theory which places greater emphasis on the inner self; as people age, they move away from a focus on materialism and productivity to contemplation, spirituality, and a value placed on close relationships

interactionist theory a perspective that emphasizes the reciprocal actions of persons and their social world in shaping perceptions, attitudes, and behavior, etc., including person–environment, symbolic interaction, and labeling perspectives

labeling theory a theoretical perspective derived from symbolic interactionism, premised on the belief that people derive their self-concepts from interacting with others in their social milieu, in how others define us and react to us

life course capital an expansion of the life course perspective that addresses the impact of differential acquisition of resources among different members of a cohort

life course perspective a view of human development that focuses on changes with age and life experiences in the larger social context

opportunity structures social arrangements, formal and informal, that limit or advance options available to people based on such features as social class, age, ethnicity, and gender

political economy of aging a theory based on the hypothesis that social class determines a person's access to resources and that dominant groups within society try to sustain their own interests by perpetuating class inequities

positivism the perspective that knowledge is based solely on observable facts and their relation to one another (cause and effect or correlation); the search for ultimate origins is rejected

postmodern theory (or **deconstructionism**) the critique of language, discourse, and research practices that constrict knowledge

productive roles a concept central to activity theory; activities in volunteer associations, employment, politics, and faith-based organizations

role theory a theory based on the belief that roles define us and our self-concept, and shape our behavior

social constructionism   what is considered to be old varies with the economic, cultural, historical, and societal context

social exchange theory   a theory based on the hypothesis that personal status is defined by the balance between people's contributions to society and the costs of supporting them

social phenomenology and constructionism   a point of view in studying social life that places an emphasis on the assumptions and meanings of experience rather than the "objective" facts, with a focus on understanding rather than explaining

socialist feminism   feminist theory that attributes women's lower status in old age to capitalist and patriarchal social structures

structural lag   the inability of social structures (patterns of behavior, attitude, ideas, and policies) to adapt to changes in population and individual lives

subculture of aging theory   a theoretical perspective based on the belief that people maintain their self-concepts and social identities through their membership in a defined group (subculture)

symbolic interactionism   a theoretical perspective based on the belief that the interactions of such factors as the environment, individuals, and people's encounters in it can significantly affect their behavior and thoughts, including the aging process

REFERENCES

Achenbaum, W.A., and Bengtson, V.C. Re-engaging the disengagement theory of aging: Or the history and assessment of theory development in gerontology. *The Gerontologist,* 1994, *34,* 756–763.

American Association of Retired Persons (AARP). *Attitudes toward aging.* Washington, DC: AARP, 2004.

Arber, S., and Ginn, J. (Ed.). *Connecting gender and aging: A sociological approach.* Philadelphia: Open University Press, 1995.

Arber, S., and Ginn, J. *Gender and later life: A sociological analysis of constraints.* Newbury Park, CA: Sage, 1991.

Atchley, R.C. Critical perspectives on retirement. In T.R. Cole, W.A. Achenbaum, P.L. Jakobi, and R. Kastenbaum (Eds.), *Voices and visions:*

Toward a critical gerontology. New York: Springer, 1993.

Bengtson, V.L., Burgess, E.O., and Parrott, T.M. Theory, explanation and a third generation of theoretical development in social gerontology. *Journals of Gerontology,* 1997, *52B,* S72–S88.

Biggs, S. Toward a critical narrativity: Stories of aging in contemporary social policy. *Journal of Aging Studies,* 2001, *15,* 303–316.

Biggs, S., and Powell, J.L. A Foucauldian analysis of old age and the power of social welfare. *Journal of Aging and Social Policy,* 2001, *12,* 93–111.

Browne, C. *Women, feminism, and aging.* New York: Springer, 1998.

Calasanti, T.M. Feminism and gerontology: Not just for women. *Hallym International Journal on Aging* 1999, *1,* 44–55.

Calasanti, T.M., and Slevin, K.F. *Gender, social inequalities and aging.* Walnut Creek, CA: Altamira Press, 2001.

Cole, T.R., Achenbaum, W.A., Jacobi, P.L., and Kastenbaum, R. *Voices and visions of aging: Toward a critical gerontology.* New York: Springer, 1993.

Cottrell, L. The adjustment of the individual to his age and sex roles. *American Sociological Review,* 1942, *7,* 617–620.

Covey, H. A reconceptualization of continuity theory: Some preliminary thoughts. *The Gerontologist,* 1981, *21,* 628–633.

Cruikshank, M. *Learning to be old.* Lanham, MD: Rowman & Littlefield, 2003.

Cumming, E., and Henry, W.E. *Growing old.* New York: Basic Books, 1961.

Dannefer, W.D. *Reciprocal co-optation: Some reflections on the relationship of critical theory and social gerontology.* Revised version of paper presented at the International Sociological Association, Bieleveld, Germany, July 1994.

Diamond, T. *Making grey gold: Narratives of nursing home care.* Chicago: University of Chicago Press, 1992.

Dowd, J.J. *Stratification among the aged.* Monterey, CA: Brooks Cole, 1980.

Ekerdt, D.J., and DeViney, S. Evidence for a preretirement process among older male workers. *Journals of Gerontology,* 1993, *48,* S35–S43.

Estes, C.L. From gender to the political economy of ageing. *European Journal of Social Quality,* 2001, *2,* 28–46.

Estes, C.L., and Associates. *Social policy and aging: A critical perspective.* Thousand Oaks: Sage, 2001.

Estes, C.L., Biggs, S., and Phillipson, C. *Social theory, social policy and ageing.* Milton Keynes, U.K.: Oxford University Press, 2003.

Estes, C.L., Linkins, K.W., and Binney, E.A. The political economy of aging. In R.H. Binstock and L.K. George (Eds.), *Handbook of aging and the social sciences* (4th ed.). San Diego: Academic Press, 1996.

Featherstone. M. and Wernick, A. *Images of aging: Cultural representations of later life.* London: Routledge, 1995.

Garner, J.D. Feminism and feminist gerontology. *Fundamentals of feminist gerontology,* 1999, 3–13.

George, L.K. Missing links: The case for a social psychology of the life course. *The Gerontologist,* 1996, *36,* 248–255.

George, L.K. Age structures, aging, and the life course. In J.M. Wilmoth and K.F. Ferraro (Eds.), *Gerontology: Perspectives and issues* (3rd ed.). New York: Springer, 2007.

George, L.K. The last half century of aging research—and thoughts for the future. *Journals of Gerontology,* 1995, *50B,* S1–3.

Gilleard, C., and Higgs, P. *Culture of ageing.* London: Prentice Hall, 2000.

Ginn, J., and Arber, S. Only connect: Gender relations and aging. In S. Arber and J. Ginn (Eds.), *Connecting gender and aging: A sociological approach.* Philadelphia: Open University Press, 1995.

Gonyea, J., and Hooyman, N. Reducing poverty among older women: The importance of Social Security. *Families in Society.* 2005, *86,* 338–346

Gubrium, J.F. *The myth of the golden years.* Springfield, IL: Charles C. Thomas, 1973.

Gubrium, J.F. *Speaking of life: Horizons of meaning for nursing home residents.* New York: Aldine de Gruyter, 1993a.

Gubrium, J.F. Voice and context in a new gerontology. In T.R. Cole, W.A. Achenbaum, P.C. Jakobi, and R. Kastenbaum (Eds.), *Voices and visions of aging: Toward a critical gerontology.* New York: Springer, 1993b.

Hagestad, G., and Neugarten, B. Age and the life course. In R.H. Binstock and E. Shanas (Eds.), *Handbook of aging and the social sciences* (2nd ed.). New York: Van Nostrand, 1985.

Harvard School of Public Health/MetLife Foundation. *Reinventing aging: Baby boomers and civic engagement.* Boston: Harvard School of Public Health, Center for Health Communication, 2004.

Havighurst, R.J. Personality and patterns of aging. *The Gerontologist,* 1968, *38,* 20–23.

Havighurst, R.J. Successful aging. In R. Williams, C. Tibbits, and W. Donahue (Eds.), *Processes of aging,* Vol. 1. New York: Atherton Press, 1963.

Holstein, M. Women and productive aging: Troubling implications. In M. Minkler and C. Estes (Eds.), *Critical gerontology.* Amityville, NY: Baywood, 1999.

Holstein, M., and Minkler, M. Self, society, and the "new gerontology." *The Gerontologist,* 2003, *43,* 787–796.

Hooyman, N.R., Brown, C., Raye, R., and Richardson, V. Feminist gerontology and the life course: Policy, research and teaching issues. *Gerontology and Geriatrics Education,* 2002, *22,* 3–26.

Hooyman, N.R., and Gonyea, J. A feminist model of family care: Practice and policy directions. In J.D. Garner (Ed.), *Fundamentals of feminist gerontology,* New York: Haworth Press, 1999.

Hooyman, N.R., and Gonyea, J. *Feminist perspectives on family care: Policies for gender justice.* Thousand Oaks, CA: Sage, 1995.

Kaufman, S.R. The social construction of frailty: An anthropological perspective. *Journal of Aging Studies,* 1994, *8,* 45–58.

Katz, S. *Disciplining old age: The formation of gerontological knowledge.* Charlottesville: University Press of Virginia, 1996.

Longino, C.F., and Powell, J.L. Embodiment and the study of aging. In V. Berdayes (Ed.), *The Body in Human Inquiry: Interdisciplinary Explorations of Embodiment.* New York: Hampton Press, 2004.

Lynott, R.J., and Lynott, P.P. Tracing the course of theoretical development in the sociology of aging. *The Gerontologist,* 1996, *36,* 749–760.

Marshall, V.W. The state of theory in aging and the social sciences. In R.H. Binstock and L.K. George, (Eds.), *Handbook of aging and the social sciences* (4th ed.). San Diego: Academic Press, 1996.

Martinson, M., and Minkler, M. Civic engagement and older adults: A critical perspective. *The Gerontologists,* 2006, *46,* 318–324.

Meyer, M.H. Toward a structural life course agenda for reducing insecurity among women as they age. Book review. *The Gerontologist*, 1997, *37*, 833–834.

Minkler, M. Critical perspectives on aging: New challenges for gerontology. *Aging and Society*, 1996, *16*, 467–487.

Minkler, M., and Estes, C. (Eds.) *Critical gerontology: Perspectives from political and moral economy*. New York: Baywood, 1998.

Moen, P. The gendered life course. In R. Binstock and L.K. George (Eds.), *Handbook of aging and the social sciences* (5th ed.). San Diego: Academic Press, 2001.

Moody, H.R. *Aging: Concepts and controversies* (4th ed.). Thousand Oaks, CA: Sage, 2002.

Moody, H.R. From successful aging to conscious aging. In M. Wykle, P. Whitehouse, and D. Morris (Eds.), *Successful aging through the life span*. New York: Springer, 2005.

Moody, H.R. Toward a critical gerontology: The contribution of the humanities to theories of aging. In J.E. Birren and V.L. Bengtson (Eds.), *Emergent theories of aging*. New York: Springer, 1988.

Neugarten, B., Havighurst, R.J., and Tobin, S.S. Personality and patterns of aging. In B.L. Neugarten (Ed.), *Middle age and aging*. Chicago: University of Chicago Press, 1968.

Olson, L.K. *The not so golden years: Caregiving, the frail elderly and the long-term care establishment*. Lanham, MD: Rowman and Littlefield, 2003.

O'Rand, A.M. The precious and the precocious: Understanding cumulative disadvantage and cumulative advantage over the life course. *The Gerontologist*, 1996, *36*, 230–238.

O'Rand, A.M. Stratification and the life course. Life course capital, life course risks and social inequality. In R. Binstock and L.K. George (Eds.), *Handbook of aging and the social sciences* (6th ed.). San Diego: Academic Press, 2006.

Phillipson, C. Interpretations of aging: Perspectives from humanistic gerontology. *Aging and Society*, 1996, *16*, 359–369.

Powell, J.L. *Social theory and aging*, Lanham, MD: Rowman and Littlefield, 2006.

Powell., J.L. Aging and social theory: A sociological review. *Social Science Paper Publisher*, 2001, *4*, 1–12.

Powell, J.L. The importance of a "critical" sociology of old age. *Social Science Paper Publisher*, 2000, *3*, 105.

Powell, J.L., and Biggs, S. Aging, technologies of self and bio-medicine. A Foucauldian excursion. *International Journal of Sociology and Social Policy*, 2004, *25*, 96–115.

Powell, J.L., and Longino, C.F. Modernism vs. postmodernism. Rethinking theoretical tensions in social gerontology. *Journal of Aging Studies*, 2002, *7*, 115–25.

Powell, J.L., and Longino, C.F. Toward the postmodernization of aging: The body and social theory. *Journal of Aging and Identity*, 2001, *6*, 20–34.

Ray, R.E. A postmodern perspective on feminist gerontology. *The Gerontologist*, 1996, *36*, 674–680.

Riley, M.W. Social gerontology and the age stratification of society. *The Gerontologist*, 1971, *11*, 79–87.

Riley, M.W., Foner, A. and Riley, J.W. The aging and society paradigm. In V.L. Bengtson and K.W. Schaie (Eds.). *Handbook of theories of aging*. New York: Springer, 1999.

Riley, M.W., Johnson, J., and Foner, A. *Aging and society: A sociology of age stratification*, vol. 3. New York: Russell Sage Foundation, 1972.

Riley, M.W., Kahn, R.L., and Foner, A. (Eds.). *Age and structural lag: Society's failure to provide meaningful opportunities in work, family and leisure*. New York: John Wiley, 1994.

Riley, M.W., and Loscocco, K.A. The changing structure of work opportunities: Toward an age-integrated society. In R.P. Abeles, H.C. Gift, and M.G. Ory (Eds.), *Aging and quality of life*. New York: Springer, 1994.

Riley, M.W., and Riley, J.W. Age integration and the lives of older people. *The Gerontologist*, 1994, *34*, 110–115.

Rose, A.M. A current theoretical issue in social gerontology. In A.M. Rose and W.A. Peterson (Eds.), *Older people and their social worlds*. Philadelphia: F.A. Davis, 1965.

Rosen, S. Human capital. In P. Newman (Ed.), *The new Palgrave dictionary of economics and the law* (vol. 2). London: Macmillan, 1998.

Rosow, J. Status and role change through the life cycle. In R.H. Binstock and E. Shanas (Eds.), *Handbook of aging and the social sciences* (2nd ed.). New York: Van Nostrand, 1985.

Schaie, K.W. Ageist language in psychological research. *American Psychologist,* 1993, *48,* 49–51.

Silverstein, M., Conroy, S.J., Wang, H., Giarusso, R., and Bengtson, V.L. Reciprocity in parent-child relations over the life course. *Journals of Gerontology,* 2002, *57B,* S3–S13.

Stoller, E.P., and Gibson, R.C. Advantages of using the life course framework in studying aging. In E.P. Stoller and R. Gibson (Eds.), *Worlds of difference: Inequality in the aging experience.* Thousand, Oaks, CA: Pine Forge Press, 2000.

Thorsen, K. The paradoxes of gerotranscendence: The theory of gerotranscendence in a cultural gerontological and post-Modernist perspective. *Norwegian Journal of Epidemiology,* 1998, *8,* 165–176.

Tornstam, L. Transcendence in later life. *Generations,* 2000, *23,* 1014.

Tornstam, L., Gero-transcendence: A meta-theoretical reformulation of the disengagement theory. *Aging: Clinical and Experimental Research,* 1989, *1,* 55–64.

Tornstam, L. Gero-transcendence—A theory about maturing into old age. *Journal of Aging and Identity,* 1996a, *1,* 37–50.

Tornstam, L. Caring for the elderly: Introducing the theory of gerotranscendnece as a supplementary frame of reference for the care of the elderly. *Scandinavian Journal of Careing Sciences,* 1996b, *10,* 144–150.

Tornstam, L. Gerotranscendence—A theoretical and empirical exploration. In L.E. Thomas and S.A. Eisenhandler (Eds.), *Aging and the religious dimension.* Westport: Greenwood, 1994.

Wadensten, B. Introducing older people to the theory of gerotranscendence. *Journal of Advanced Nursing,* 2005, *42,* 381–388.

Wadensten, B., and Carlsson, M. A qualitative study of nursing staff members' interpretations of signs of gerotranscendence. *Journal of Advanced Nursing,* 2003, *41,* 462–470.

Wahidin, A., and Powell, J.L. Reconfiguring old bodies: From the biomedical model to a critical epistemology. *Journal of Social Sciences and Humanities,* 2003, *26,* 1–10.

Wahidin, A., and Powell, J.L. The loss of aging identity, social theory, old age and the power of special hospitals. *Journal of Aging and Identity,* 2001, *6,* 31–49.

c h a p t e r

9

The Importance of Social Supports: Family, Friends, Neighbors, and Communities

This chapter focuses on informal social support systems, including

- Social networks, social engagement, and their importance for health and active aging
- Multigenerational families
- Different types of family relationships
  Gay and lesbian families
  Grandparents and grandchildren
  Grandparents as primary caregivers
- Friends, neighbors, and acquaintances as social supports
- Social support interventions
- Intergenerational programming
- Pets as social support

As people age, their social roles and relationships change. Earlier chapters have noted and Part Four's introductory vignettes have illustrated that physiological, social, and psychological changes, as well as opportunities for social engagement in the larger environment, affect how older people interact with others. For example, with children typically gone from the home and without daily contacts with co-workers, older people may lose a critical context for social integration. At the same time, their need for social support may increase because of changes in health, cognitive, and emotional status. Such incongruence between needs and environmental opportunities can negatively influence elders' well-being.

The Nature and Function of Informal Supports

A common myth is that many older adults are lonely and isolated from family and friends. Contrary to this misperception, even older people who appear isolated generally are able to turn to an informal network, for information, financial advice, emotional reassurance, or concrete services. **Social networks** encompass interrelationships among individuals that affect the flow of resources and opportunities. Families, friends, neighbors, and acquaintances, such as postal carriers and grocery clerks, can be powerful antidotes to some of the negative social consequences of the aging process, as in the description of Mr. Mansfield on page 304. Elders can draw on these informal networks as a source of **social support** that may be informational, emotional, or instrumental (e.g., assistance with tasks of daily living). Older adults first turn to informal networks for support and move to formal assistance only when necessary, typically when they live alone. As suggested by the person-environment model, elders draw on their informal networks as a way to enhance their competence (Moren-Cross and Lin, 2006). It is important to note that definitions and measures of social support vary widely. Most research on social supports differentiates social networks, social integration, social capital, and assistance-related and nonassistance-related (e.g., feelings of worth, emotional closeness and belonging), support along with the importance of perceived social support. In fact, perceptions of support may be more important than the actual support received (Lyyra and Heikkinen, 2006).

Social integration, which encompasses both social networks and support, refers to the degree to which an individual is involved with others in the larger social structure and community. This concept captures the degree of emotional closeness, the availability of support when needed, and the perception of oneself as an individual actively engaged in social exchanges, such as civic engagement. The social structure shapes the individual, but the individual may also affect the social structure (Antonucci, Sherman, and Akimaya, 1996; Berkman, 2000; Moren-Cross and Lin, 2006). Both of these concepts, social support and social integration, take account of (1) the specific types of assistance exchanged within social networks; (2) the frequency of contact with others; (3) how a person assesses the adequacy of supportive exchanges; and (4) anticipated support or the belief that help is available if needed. Social integration, however, tends to emphasize the giving as well as the receiving of support, and thus takes account of cross-generational interdependence in old age. Consistent with theories of social exchange and social capital described in Chapter 8, most older adults try to maintain **reciprocal exchanges**— being able to help others who help them—in their interactions with others. Even frail elders who require personal care from their families may still contribute through financial assistance or child care. The meaningful role of helping others also benefits the helper, and is associated with positive affect, self-esteem, a sense of purpose, life satisfaction, and physical and mental health. As is true across the life course, older adults support others because of a sense of purpose, altruism, social norms, maintenance of a lifelong pattern of helping, or investing in a social network as a way to build social capital (Boaz, Hu, and Ye, 1999; Keyes, 2002; Krause and Shaw, 2000; Morrow-Howell et al., 2001;

POTENTIAL OUTCOMES OF SOCIAL SUPPORTS

- Physical and mental well-being (increased morale, self-confidence, reduced depression)
- Feelings of personal control, autonomy, and competence
- Improved cognitive abilities
- Active aging and resilience
- Reduced negative effects of stressful life events (bereavement, widowhood)
- Reduced disability and mortality risk

SOCIAL SUPPORT AMONG FRIENDS

After 40 years of marriage, Nan was devastated by her husband's decision to divorce her. Her children lived across the country and she had no close relatives in the town where they had raised their children. Nan turned to two women whom she had confided in for more than 30 years as they shared child-rearing, and the ups and downs of their marriages. These other women, both divorced, provided emotional support as Nan grieved the loss of her marriage and a life of economic security. They helped her find a good divorce attorney and financial advisor, who in turn helped her obtain an adequate settlement from her husband. Most importantly, they were available 24/7 to help her cope with this unexpected phase in her life, giving her more strength than her children or other relatives could have done.

Kawachi and Berkman, 2001; Uchino, 2004). As noted in Chapter 6, supportive networks foster active aging and characterize resilient elders.

The Impact of Informal Networks and Social Supports on Well-Being

The importance of emotional and instrumental support within older adults' informal networks is extensively documented. Informal reciprocal relationships are a crucial concomitant of an older person's physical and mental well-being, cognitive functioning, feelings of personal control, sense of meaning, morale, and even later onset of disability and mortality risk (Berkman, 2002; Kraus, 2006; Lubben and Gironda, 2003a, 2003b; Lubben et al., 2006; Lyyra and Heikkinen, 2006; Uchino, 2004). In fact, one study found that older adults with limited social support were 3.6 times more likely to die within the next five years than those with extensive support (Blazer, 2006). Provision of support, like its receipt, contributes to elders' perceptions of support availability, which is in turn generally linked with good physical and mental health. Face-to-face

interactions and size of informal networks are also associated with improved cognitive functioning (Cohen, Gottlieb, and Underwood, 2001; Eng et al., 2002; Holtzman et al., 2004; Liang, Krause, and Bennett, 2001; Moren-Cross and Lin, 2006; Seeman et al., 2002). Social support can also mediate the effects of adversity and other negative life circumstances, such as retirement, widowhood, illness, or relocation (Cohen, 2004; DuPertuis, Aldwin, and Bosse, 2001; Everard et al., 2000). It is unclear, however, whether such supports act as buffers against the negative impact of life events on health, or whether they have a more direct effect, independent of the presence or absence of major life events (Moren-Cross and Lin, 2006).

Alternatively, loss of social support through divorce, widowhood, or death of loved ones may contribute to health problems. For example, older adults who live alone and are not tied into informal networks are more likely to use formal services and to be placed in a long-term care facility. Their self-reported well-being tends to be lower. In fact, several longitudinal studies found an association between social support structures and reduced mortality risk. Similarly, social isolation may be conducive to a higher risk of disability, poor recovery from illness, and earlier death, although it is not clear if social support reduces the risk of mortality (Findlay, 2003; Lyyra and Heikkinen, 2006; Moren-Cross and Lin, 2006). The Lubben Social Network Scale, a widely used measure to assess social integration and to screen for social isolation among community-dwelling elders, has been used with culturally diverse elders and in many countries. Low scores on this scale—indicating social isolation—are correlated with a wide range of health problems (Lubben et al., 2006).

The extent to which networks vary with age is not clear-cut. While some studies have identified a decline in friendship networks, others have found that changes occur primarily in network composition (e.g., less contact with couples, more with informal helpers), or in the role played by this network (e.g., increased need for instrumental support) (Cantor, 1994; Kalmijh, 2003; Van Tilburg, 1998). In fact, elders active in retirement communities and voluntary associations may actually expand and diversify their networks. A process of social selection may occur whereby healthy people are more likely to have supportive social relationships precisely because they are healthy. Conversely, poor health may hinder them from initiating or sustaining social relationships (Wethington et al., 2000). In some instances, negative interactions with one's informal networks can have adverse effects on physical and mental health. In addition to conflictual relationships within informal networks, other types of negative interactions may be due to inconsistency between an older person's needs and competence level, such as disappointment that one's children are not doing enough to help after their hospitalization or relatives' being overprotective (Krause, 2004, 2006).

The family—the basic unit of social relationships—is the first topic considered here. We examine the rapid growth of the multigenerational family and how relationships with spouses, partners, adult children, parents, grandparents, and siblings change with age.

Changing Family Structure

Contrary to commonly held perceptions of elders as separate from families or families who "happen" to have an older relative, the lives of young and old, even at a geographic distance, are intertwined through cross-generational support. The family is the primary source of such support for older adults; nearly 94 percent have living family members. These include partners, adult children, grandchildren or great-grandchildren, and siblings. Approximately 80 percent of adults over age 65 have children (Uhlenberg, 2004).

About 66 percent of older adults live in a family setting—with a partner, child, or sibling—although not necessarily in a multigenerational household (Figure 9.1). Given the higher rates of widowhood among women than men, older men are more likely to live in a family setting, typically with a spouse or partner, than are women (81 and 61 percent, respectively). Only about 6 percent of older men and 17 percent of older women live with children, siblings, or other relatives, not with a spouse or partner (Federal Interagency Forum, 2006). However, the majority have at least one child living close

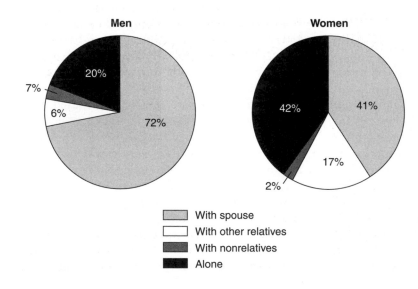

FIGURE 9.1   Living Arrangements of Persons 65+
SOURCE: Federal Interagency Forum on Aging, 2006.

by and see them regularly. Older adults typically do not want to live with their adult children. Nevertheless, declining health, loss of a former caregiver or partner, desire for companionship, and lower income often precipitate the move to a shared residence. Widowed mothers are more likely to live with a child than are divorced, single, or married mothers (Wilmouth, 2000). In a growing number of households, adult children are moving back into the family home, typically for financial reasons or following a divorce.

Factors associated with geographic proximity to the nearest child are:

- family size
- parent's health: as health declines, parents tend to move closer to an adult child
- parent's age: parents over age 80 live closer to adult children
- parents' socioeconomic status: higher social class tends to be associated with greater geographic distance
- marital status: widowed mothers live closest to daughters; remarried parents tend to live at a greater geographic distance than parents who remain married to each other

Geographic distance in itself does not impair the quality of parent–adult children relationships.

Family gatherings help maintain multigenerational ties.

In fact, as described in Chapter 10, adult children often provide care at a geographic distance.

The Growth of the Multigenerational Family

The term **multigenerational family** encompasses the growing reciprocity across three or more generations, both in the United States and globally. Among Americans over age 35, 80 percent report being members of a three-generation family and 16 percent are four-generation families (U.S. Census Bureau, 2001). For individuals born in 1900, the chances of both parents dying before the child reached age 18 were 18 percent; by age 30, only 21 percent had any grandparents alive. In contrast, 68 percent of individuals born in 2000 will have four grandparents alive when they reach age 18; by age 30, 76 percent will have a grandparent alive—almost four times that of the cohort born in 1900. In fact, 20-year-olds today are more likely to have a grandmother living (92 percent) than 20-year-olds in 1900 had their mother alive (83 percent) (Bengtson, 2001; Kleyman, 2006). Another indicator of changing multigenerational dynamics is that increasing numbers of people over age 65 have a child who is also over 65, who may then be both a child and a grandparent at the same time. In sum, persons at all stages of life are more likely to have kin relationships involving older people than in the past. This has resulted in parents and children now sharing 5 decades of life; siblings perhaps sharing 8 decades; and the grandparent-grandchild bond lasting 3 or more decades (Gonyea, in press).

Increased life expectancy may create multigenerational kinship networks to provide family continuity, along with instrumental or emotional support when needed. Yet increased longevity may also mean extended years of family differences and caring for relatives with chronic disabilities (Bengtson, 2001; Gonyea, in press). Although families are experiencing more cross-generational relationships, paradoxically, fewer people within each generation are available to provide care for older family members.

Demographic and societal trends that underlie this paradox include a decrease in overall fertility that has reduced family size, an increase in family dissolutions, and more women employed. As the birthrate has declined, delaying the age of childbearing has become common, and life expectancy has increased. This has resulted in a shift in the age structure for most families, from a "pyramid" to a "beanpole" (Bengtson, Rosenthal, and Burton, 1996). This means that American families are smaller today (averaging 2.6 people in the nuclear family) than ever before, with 20 percent of women not having their first child until after age 35 (Population Resources Center, 2006).

The number of women entering the paid workforce has increased dramatically in the past 50 years; over 60 percent compared to 33 percent of women in the 1950s (Bureau of Labor Statistics, 2006). The distribution of women in the paid workforce across the life course is also striking, with women in their childbearing years most likely to be employed. These women may also face multiple care responsibilities across the life course: for young children and young adult children with disabilities or chronic illnesses, for parents or grandparents during the woman's middle age, a partner in old age, or an adult child with developmental disabilities until the woman reaches advanced old age. Moving in and out of the labor force to be unpaid caregivers may mean socioeconomic and health inequities in old age. These caregiving patterns and life course inequities by gender, age, and race are discussed more fully in Chapters 10, 14, and 15.

Other societal trends are increasing the heterogeneity of the American family structure, including:

- a growth in divorce and **blended families** (e.g., families reconstituted by divorce and remarriage)
- more people living alone
- more single-parent households

- never-married individuals living together as **nontraditional families** (e.g., grandparents raising grandchildren, gay and lesbian families, and single parents choosing to raise children on their own)

For the first time, only 23.5 percent of U.S. households are composed of nuclear families. Similarly, the number of children living in single-parent households grew from about 12 percent in 1950 to about 32 percent today, with the highest rates among low-income families of color. As a result, the "first married nuclear family" is no longer the norm, but one of numerous family structures. In fact, the blended family may soon outnumber are other forms (Doodson and Morley, 2006; Population Resources Center, 2006; Scharlach and Fredriksen-Goldsen, 2001).

Defining Multigenerational Families

Consistent with social constructionist theory described in Chapter 8, definitions of families are socially constructed, and vary by culture and socioeconomic class. In this text, family is broadly defined by interactional quality, not necessarily by members' living together or blood ties. Kinship is a matter of social definition, particularly within ethnic minority families, as reflected in the role of fictive kin, grandparents as primary caregivers to grandchildren, "play relatives," godparents, and friends. Among gays and lesbians, chosen or "friendship" families are common. Gerontological practitioners and policy-makers need to be sensitive to the ways in which elders and their networks define family in order to work effectively with family members.

A life course and multigenerational perspective on families captures the interdependence of lives in three ways: the interdependence of cohorts in societies, of generations in families, and individual life paths in relation to these interdependencies. It also takes account of individual, family, and historical time (Hagestad, 2003).

More options are available today for GLBT couples and individuals who want to raise children.

Multigenerational families are characterized by cross-generational reciprocity and interdependence rather than dependence or independence. None of us, no matter what our age, is ever totally independent; we are embedded in networks of reciprocal interactions. Generations are interdependent across the life course—each contributes to the other, through families and nontraditional informal supports (e.g., friends, neighbors, "community gatekeepers," gay and lesbian partners). Contrary to stereotypes of egocentric older adults, most exchanges are from the older to younger generations, unless older adults require caregiving assistance (Silverstein et al., 2002). In fact, older adults' unacknowledged functions within families encompass role models for socialization, economic transfers, bearers of family history and continuity, and daily assistance, especially to young single mothers and divorced parents. As described more fully in Chapter 12, older adults typically remain productive in the broadest sense of the term, contributing to their communities through both paid and nonpaid work—as volunteers or leaders in community institutions or government, or supporting and encouraging younger family members. They often devote time, financial resources, and skills and experience to strengthening families and communities.

Regardless of the particular family structure, family relationships inevitably involve both solidarity and conflict. Cohesion appears to be based on sharing across generations along a variety of dimensions, including the extent of shared activities, the degree of positive sentiment, consensus on lifestyle choices and habits, and the exchange of assistance. Less is known about tensions, disagreements, or conflicts within the context of solidarity across generations over the life course (Clarke et al., 1999; Hagestad, 2003; Hummert and Morgan, 2001). Gerontological practitioners increasingly assess and work with families, not just with the older person, since family dynamics inevitably affect the well-being and quality of life of its oldest members. They also can encourage families to value their elder relatives' history and the sharing of stories across the generations. As discussed in Chapter 10, these assumptions of interdependence result in social policies that expect families to be the primary providers of care to older relatives.

THE STRENGTH OF MULTIGENERATIONAL TIES

During the summer of 2000, the governments of North and South Korea agreed to an unprecedented reunion of families that had been torn apart during the Korean War. Siblings who had not seen each other since their teens, and parents now in their 80s and 90s were reunited with their children who were themselves in their 60s. The fortunate 100 families were selected by lottery from the citizens of North Korea and flown to South Korea for a brief visit. This bittersweet reunion lasted only one week, when those from North Korea were required to return home. Nevertheless, the stories shared by these families provided a dramatic illustration of the endurance of family bonds across generations and over time.

Cultural Variations in Multigenerational Families

Due to the significant aging of the global population, as described in Chapter 2, other countries are also experiencing an increase in multigenerational families. In contrast to the United States, three- and four-generation families are more likely to live together in countries such as Japan, Korea, India, and Mexico (NIA, 2001). Within the United States, multigenerational families living together are more common among ethnic minorities than Caucasian populations and have been a source of strength historically. For example, older African American women, especially widows, are more likely to live in extended or multigenerational family households than are older white women. Grandparents or other "fictive kin" among African American households have traditionally played a central role in caring for children, and multigenerational exchanges are often necessary for economic survival. Even when controlling for need, ethnic minority families are more likely to live in multigenerational families or to depend on non-kin (e.g., friends and neighbors), who provide both social and instrumental support, especially for unmarried children and parents (Dilworth-Anderson, Williams, and Gibson, 2002).

This greater incidence of cross-generational households in communities of color may underlie the higher levels of assistance to elders and the generally positive parent-adult child relationships reported by African American, Latino, and Asian American families compared with their Caucasian counterparts (Dilworth-Anderson et al., 2002). On the other hand, the existence of extended family arrangements and fictive kin may carry financial and emotional costs and divert elders from accessing formal supports. These patterns may shift over time with increased economic and geographic mobility and levels of acculturation by younger generations.

By contrast, American culture and economic pressures often weaken multigenerational support networks within immigrant and

FAMILY HISTORIES: PRESERVING THE LEGACY OF AN OLDER RELATIVE

Along with the growth of multiple generations within families, younger family members are encouraging their older relatives to write or record on DVD or CD-ROM their family history. Life stories are typically not just about one older person, but that individual in the context of the whole family history. In fact, Websites to assist with writing personal histories advertise journalistic or service professionals to assist with this age-old task. While families have always passed stories across generations, the baby boomers are "professionalizing" storytelling, sometimes paying up to $30,000 for a written record of their ancestry. Multimedia legacies can include mementos, photos, and music and provide archived materials from the relevant historical period. Such storytelling not only leaves a legacy for younger generations, but the process of life review can have psychological and physical health benefits for older adults. Perhaps most important to families who are often separated by geographic and psychological distance, "capturing the richness of mature lives can at least ensure that yesterday will keep providing gifts to tomorrow."

SOURCE: S.S. Stitch, Stories to keep. *Newsweek*, November 11, 2002, A3.

refugee populations. Among Asian American immigrants, grandparents frequently provide child care to enable both parents to work outside the home, but younger generations' sense of filial responsibility toward older relatives may be eroded by their upward mobility, as described in Chapter 2. Latino immigrant families typically have strong cross-generational cohesion, but smaller family size, increased employment of women, and economic pressures may compromise such supportive interactions (Beyene, Becker, and Mayen, 2002). As an example, Cuban American elders place a high value on extended family relationships, but those now living in Florida tend to live alone, in part because of declining family size related to their immigration history. They often compensate for the lack of large geographically nearby family supports, however, by engaging in social networks and activities through religious organizations or senior centers (Martinez, 2003).

Despite pressures for assimilation and rapid economic and social changes, cultural variations remain salient in how multigenerational relations are defined and experienced. Even when behaviors such as dress, appearance, and material goods differ markedly across generations, some cultural values may nevertheless be shared. Cultural notions of "family" are strong, but are reinterpreted in rapidly changing economic and social conditions. As a result, living arrangements for elders often represent a balance of cultural convictions, functional ability, and actual choices. What is most important to elders, however, is not the structural makeup of family exchanges, but the subjective or emotional quality of the relationships (Martinez, 2003). Regardless of the particular family structure or nature of relationships, practitioners must be sensitive to cultural variants when working with multigenerational families.

Older Partners*

The marital or partnered relationship plays a crucial support function in most older people's lives, especially men's. Of all family members, partners are most likely to serve as confidants, provide support, facilitate social interaction, foster emotional well-being, and guard against loneliness. Nearly 55 percent of the population age 65 and older is married and lives with a spouse in an independent household. Less is known about the percentage living with a gay or lesbian partner. Significant differences exist, however, in living arrangements by gender and age. Because of women's longer life expectancy, higher rates of widowhood, and fewer options for remarriage, only 57 percent of women age 65 to 74 are married and living with a spouse, as compared to 79 percent of men. These percentages decline dramatically with age, with only 15 percent of women age 85 and older married compared to 58 percent of men, as shown in Figure 9.2 (DHHS, 2006; Federal Interagency Forum, 2006). Marital status affects living arrangements and the nature of caregiving that is readily available in case of illness. Accordingly,

Intergenerational work activities can benefit all participants.

*Less research has been conducted on gay, lesbian, *bisexual,* and *transgender* partners. Although we use the term *partner* throughout the text where relevant, in some instances data are only available on married heterosexual couples.

women represent 80 percent of older individuals who live alone. Among noninstitutionalized older men, only about 19 percent live without a partner, compared to 40 percent of their female counterparts (Federal Interagency Forum, 2006). Older men living alone typically have higher levels of depression, loneliness, and social isolation, and are more likely to use formal social services compared to those living with a partner. Married people, especially men, are found to be healthier and to live longer than their unmarried counterparts. They seem to benefit from social support, health monitoring, economic resources, and stress reduction. In fact, marital status appears to be related to physical and psychological health, life satisfaction, happiness, and well-being, especially for men, although we can all think of exceptions to these associations (Connidis, 2001; Lyyra and Heikkinen, 2006). While not having the legal option of marriage, GLBT elders who have partners tend to be less lonely and enjoy better physical and mental health than those living alone (Grossman, D'Augelli, and Hershberger, 2000; Grossman, D'Augelli, and O'Connell, 2001).

Couples are faced with learning to adapt to changing roles and expectations throughout their relationship. As partners change roles through retirement, post-parenthood, illness or disability, they face the strain of relinquishing previous roles, adapting to new ones, and experiencing cumulative losses. Failure to negotiate role expectations, such as the division of household tasks after retirement, can result in disagreements and divergent paths. Retirement can be an especially difficult transition, especially when partners do not retire at the same time, or where marital satisfaction was already low before retirement. Some retired couples experience changes in the emotional quality of their relationship, along with conflict over too much time together and the loss of personal space. On the other hand, increased time together in shared activities and with friends during retirement can have favorable effects on marital satisfaction (Hilbourne, 1999; Mohr, 2000; Smith and Moen, 1998).

Strains may be heightened by the fact that long-lived relationships are a contemporary phenomenon. At the end of the nineteenth century, the average length of marriage at the time of a spouse's death was about 28 years; now it is over 45 years. Never before in history have the lives of so many couples remained interwoven long enough to encounter the variety of life-changing events that later stages of marriage now bring. This pattern will change, however, for baby boomers who have

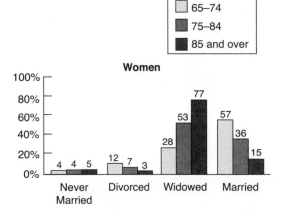

FIGURE 9.2   **Marital Status of Persons 65+**
SOURCE: Federal Interagency Forum on Aging, 2006.

experienced a decline in first marriage rates and an increase in never-marrying rates, divorce, and cohabitation. Many boomers will enter old age as single after experiencing multiple marital transitions (Bianchi and Casper, 2000; Pienta, Hayward, and Jenkins, 2000; Zhang, 2006).

Marital Satisfaction

Marital quality tends to vary by gender and life course. Men consistently experience increased levels of marital satisfaction over time than do women (Umberson and Williams, 2005; Umberson et al., 2006). Marital satisfaction is high among those recently married, lower among those in the childrearing period—especially in middle age—and higher in the later stages, when children typically leave home and household division of labor often equalizes with age (Frisco and Williams, 2004; Ward and Spitze, 2004). Contrary to stereotypes, most women are not depressed when their children leave home, but rather view the **empty nest** as an opportunity for new activities. However, children today are leaving the nest later and are more likely to return home, often for financial reasons (known as "boomerang children" who leave and come back multiple times), which can negatively affect the marriage (Ward and Spitze, 2004). Older partners' ability to negotiate these role transitions depends, in large part, on their prior adaptability and satisfaction in their marital relationship. Marital satisfaction may also increase in middle to early old age, because of developmental and structural changes, with couples becoming more similar in their attitudes, beliefs, roles, and behaviors (Davey and Szinovacz, 2004). As noted in Chapter 6, sex-role expectations and behaviors are often relaxed in old age. If relationships become more central to men's lives as they age, husbands and wives may experience less conflict in their relationship. Happy marriages in old age are characterized by more equality and joint decision-making through a gradual relaxation of boundaries and a decreas-

ing division of labor based on traditional male/female roles, although elder care roles typically remain gender-differentiated (Bogard and Spilka, 1996). Freed from the demands of work and parental responsibilities, and with more opportunities for companionship, partners may discover or develop common interests and a greater sense of interdependence. As a consequence, expressive aspects of the marriage—affection and companionship—may emerge more fully.

Studies of marital longevity found that couples celebrating golden anniversaries are characterized by intimacy, commitment, congruent values, religious faith, communication, and an ability to accommodate one another as needs change. For happily married older couples, their relationship is central to a "good life" and subjective well-being (George, 2006). As noted earlier, married persons are generally healthier, experience higher levels of self-esteem, make fewer demands on the health care system, and live longer than widowed or divorced persons of the same age, although this varies by gender (Diener et al., 2000; Pinquart and Sorenson, 2001). In fact, marital quality may be more important for men than age, health, life expectancy, education, or retirement in predicting life satisfaction and quality of life. These positive effects appear to emanate from three major functions of marriage for older couples: intimacy, interdependence, and a sense of belonging. However, a recent study of older Swedes found that the relationship between marital status and subjective well-being was explained more by living arrangement than by marital status per se (Jakobsson, Hallberg, and Westergren, 2004). Not surprisingly, unhappy marriages tend to affect older adults' health negatively, especially for women. One reason may be that physiological changes occur during marital conflict, which can impair immune response and increase cardiovascular reactivity (Robles and Kiecolt-Glaser, 2003; Umberson and Williams, 2005).

A small proportion of older adults remarry after widowhood or divorce later in life. Women have fewer options to remarry, because they generally outlive their male peers, and men tend to marry women younger than themselves. The likelihood that widowed men will remarry is seven times greater than for widowed women. Moreover, divorced people are more likely to remarry than are the widowed. Desire for companionship and having sufficient economic resources are central considerations in remarriage. Most older people who remarry choose someone they have previously known, with similar backgrounds and interests. Factors that appear to be related to successful late-life remarriages are long prior friendship, family and friends' approval, adequate pooled financial resources, and personal adaptability to life changes. Some older couples choose to live together but not to marry, generally for economic and inheritance reasons.

Divorce in Old Age

Even though the majority of older marriages are reasonably happy, an increasing proportion of older couples are choosing to divorce. The estimated 9 percent of adults age 65 and older who are divorced is almost double that of 1970, and demonstrates the growing acceptance of divorce as an option among all age groups. Rates are higher among ethnic minority elders. The percentage divorced is higher for all age groups under age 65 than for those over age 65, although more elders in future cohorts will be divorced and single. The growing divorce rate in the baby boom cohort has profound implications for the types of services provided by families and government. The increase in the divorce rate affects all ages, both directly and indirectly, in terms of repercussions across generations (Kreider, 2005).

For both men and women, increasing age decreases the likelihood of remarriage following divorce, making rates of remarriage in old age rel-

---

DATING IN OLD AGE

Divorce, widowhood, and increased life expectancy of adults who chose to remain single earlier in life have created growing numbers of single older adults engaged in a "dating game." As being single in later life is becoming the norm, the stigma of looking for a new partner is diminishing, although women still face more barriers than men. In fact, baby boomers, accustomed to dating services, personal ads, and Club Med singles vacations, are redefining dating and turning to creative ways to finding a partner. Already accustomed to the Internet for a range of services, they are generally comfortable with Internet dating services tailored to specific interests (adventure travel, hiking, science and nature, religious affiliation, environmental issues, vegetarianism, to name a few). Aware of the higher rate of divorce among remarried partners, older singles are often more interested in companionship—someone to do things with—than in marriage, especially when their children may be critical of potential partners or they fear needing to care for an older spouse.

SOURCE: AARP, 2003.

---

atively low, although more baby boomers will enter old age having been married more than once (Kreider, 2005). As noted earlier, rates of remarriage are higher for men of all ages than for women. Socioeconomic status affects the chances of remarriage among divorced women but not divorced men. Women who remain divorced as they age are more likely to experience financial difficulties. The smaller pool of potential partners partially explains gender differences in remarriage. On the other hand, the desire to remarry tends to be lower among divorced women than those who are widowed. Such reluctance is probably related to past negative experiences with marriage. Being divorced in old age typically means economic hardships and diminished interactions with adult children for women; men tend to lose the "kin keeping" and intimacy functions performed by their wives and have less contact than women with their children and grandchildren. In fact, most older divorced fathers do not consider their children as likely sources of support should they be in need. Generally, divorced mothers receive more advice, financial help, emotional support, and service assistance from their adult children than do divorced fathers. Among the estimated 75 percent of men and 60 percent of women across all ages who remarry, more than 40 percent are estimated to divorce again, creating complex stepfamily relationships among divorced adults in old age (Connidis, 2001).

Gay, Lesbian, Bisexual, and Transgender (GLBT) Partners

Although gerontological family research has traditionally focused on spouses in heterosexual couples, the concept of families in old age needs to be broadened to include gay, lesbian, bisexual and transsexual (GLBT) individuals. More than 25 percent of same sex partners include a partner age 55 or older, and more than 10 percent a partner over age 65, but the proportion may be higher because these relationships may have been hidden over the years (Bennett and Gates, 2004; Lambert, 2005). The general invisibility of being old is heightened for those who are old and gay or lesbian. Research on GLBT aging is relatively new, and studies of aging transsexual and bisexual persons are rare (Smith, 2002). In addition, little attention has been given to the intersections of race, ethnicity, culture, and social class with sexual orientation in old age. Older lesbians also have been ignored in research on women's health status and health care. Some studies suggest that the aging experience of gay men and lesbians is qualitatively different as a result of their sexual orientation and identity, in part because of a double stigma from the interaction of age and sexual orientation (Barranti and Cohen, 2001; Butler, 2006; Gabbay and Wahler, 2002). GLBT elders are referred to as the "twice hidden" and the "most invisible of an already invisible minority" (Blando, 2001, p. 87). The taboo of identifying as GLBT in an interview or survey means that

prevalence rates—probably underestimated—are ranging from 3 to 8 percent of the older adult population (Butler, 2006).

Although the majority of gays and lesbians are part of a live-in couple at any one time, as older adults they are more likely to live alone (66 percent) and less likely to be living with life partners and to have children than their heterosexual counterparts (Cahill et al., 2000; Hecht, 2004; Kurdek, 2005). However, their higher rates of living alone do not necessarily translate into being lonely and isolated. Instead, GLBT elders tend to have well-developed social networks of choice—partners and friends, members of their family of origin, and the larger community (Barranti and Cohen, 2001; Grossman et al., 2000, 2001; Healy, 2002; Orel, 2004). Whether GLBT elders are more concerned with age-associated changes in physical appearance is unclear (Adam, 2000; Calasanti and Slevin, 2001). Gay culture tends to be youth-focused and even ageist, viewing what is old as less attractive and worthy than what is young (Brotman, Ryan, and Cormier, 2003; Jones, 2001). Gay men, who generally value physical appearance, often express dissatisfaction with age-associated physical changes. Lesbians who conform to cultural stereotypes of beauty for women may be at risk for a more difficult transition to old age, since they already bear an internal cultural stigma. On the other hand, intimate relationships may not be as strongly predicated on youth or youthful physical appearance as for heterosexual women. In such instances, older lesbians appear to demonstrate greater flexibility with regard to the age of intimates, thereby increasing the pool of possible partners (Gabbay and Wahler, 2002; McDonald, 2001; Wahler and Gabbay, 1997).

Older GLBT individuals share concerns similar to other older adults—health, income, caregiving, living arrangements—but what is unique is that they have lived the majority of their lives through historical periods actively hostile and oppressive toward homosexuality.

Some older gay men and lesbians are concerned with "passing" or "being invisible" in a heterosexual society and only marginally accept their homosexuality. Coming out to family may be more difficult for members of ethnic minorities and for working-class men (Chapple, Kippas, and Smith, 1998; Connidis, 2001).

When the social and historical context is considered, the choice of some older lesbians and gay men to remain silent about their sexual orientation is understandable. Adults age 65 and over generally are the pre-Stonewall, or pre-liberation era, cohort; they did not benefit from the 1969 clash between the NYC police and gay and transgender persons, which was a watershed for gay pride. For many in the older cohort, coming out was instead viewed as being "incompetent" and a failure to successfully manage identity disclosure, and typically resulted in loss of social support (Rosenfeld, 1999). The current cohort of older lesbians and gay men lived through historical periods where homosexuality was a reason to be placed in an institution for the mentally ill. For example, until 1973, homosexuality was classified as a mental illness by the American Psychiatric Association and was not removed from the *Diagnostic and Statistical Manual of Mental Disorders* (DSM) until 1986. In addition, they also lived during the McCarthy era, when subversion and homosexuality were linked. Unlike their younger counterparts, older GLBT persons may not have benefited from antidiscrimination laws and supports for same-sex partners. In fact, they may even encounter ageism among younger GLBT persons and feel like outcasts, unwelcome to participate in the primarily youth-oriented gay community (Calasanti and Slevin, 2001; Wojciechowski, 1998). In addition, the experience of GLBT elders who have "come out" in middle age or late adulthood is likely to be different from those who identified as GLBT in their youth, during the more oppressive preliberation years (Butler, 2006).

If GLBT adults reveal their sexual orientation later in life, they must integrate their past lives of children, friends, and other partners into the coming-out process. Yet they may be ostracized by their children and family of origin at the stage when they most need support. They may also encounter insensitivity, discrimination, and, in some cases, hostility from health care providers. For example, the partners of those who are hospitalized or in a skilled nursing or assisted-living facility may be denied access to intensive care units and to medical records; staff may limit their visits and discourage expressions of affection. In a 2006 MetLife survey of 1100 self-identified GLBT adults age 40 to 61, 32 percent of gay men and 26 percent of lesbians cited their greatest concern about aging is discrimination due to their sexual orientation. And 19 percent of the respondents had little or no confidence that health care providers will treat them with dignity and respect (MetLife, 2006).

GLBT elders also face legal and policy barriers. To illustrate, domestic partners do not qualify for bereavement or sick leave in most companies, or for family leave under the 1993 Family and Medical Leave Act. When a partner is hospitalized or relocates to a nursing home, if a durable power of attorney for health care is not in place, blood relatives, who may be unaware of or opposed to the relationship, can control visitation, treatment options, and discharge planning. They can completely exclude

---

CARE NETWORKS OF OLDER LESBIANS

A group of seven lesbians with varying backgrounds took turns taking care of an 84-year-old, terminally ill, single lesbian, providing transport to medical appointments and leisure activities, coordinating the access to needed services, and talking with her about her life, politics, and dying. The primary physician, a woman with a specialty in geriatrics, became part of the network by responding to calls from the group, making home visits, and supporting their role as caregivers. As death neared, one year later than expected, the woman felt supported in making arrangements to die where and how she wanted.

partners from decision making, and any rights to an inheritance, (McFarland and Sanders, 2003; Orel, 2004). Because the federal government does not recognize gay marriage, Social Security's treatment of GLBT partners—they are ineligible for benefits—may be the most blatant and costly instance of discrimination based on sexual orientation. In addition, GLBT surviving partners are charged an estate tax on a jointly owned home and may accrue taxes after inheriting a retirement plan—negative financial consequences that do not apply to heterosexual married couples (Cahill et al., 2000; Hecht, 2004).

Fortunately, many families are more accepting of GLBT partners today than in the past, with groups such as Parents and Friends of Lesbians and Gays, supporting families in the process of coming to terms with a family member's sexual orientation. In addition, recent legislation in some states is gradually addressing some of the local legal and health care barriers faced by earlier cohorts of gay men and lesbians, but this does not address federal policies such as Social Security.

On the other hand, lifelong marginalization because of sexual orientation may stimulate adaptive strategies to meet the challenges of aging, even while older GLBT individuals typically are constrained by social constructions of gender, sexual orientation, and age. In the 2006 MetLife survey, about 40 percent of respondents believed that being GLBT has helped them prepare for aging through positive character traits, greater resilience, or better support networks. Latino and African American respondents were more likely than the sample as a whole to agree their GLBT identities have helped them approach midlife, and anticipate an easy transition to old age (MetLife, 2006). A successful transition to one stigmatized status—being a lesbian or gay man—may contribute to resilience and future successful transitions to another stigmatized status—being old (Berger and Kelly, 2001; Clunis et al., 2005; Gabbay and Wahler, 2002). This may occur because older gays and lesbians have learned

psychological skills throughout their lives in managing their sexual orientation and dealing on a daily basis with their nontraditional roles.

Through the painful process of "coming out," or confronting legal, religious, and familial barriers, GLBT elders enhance their strength and competence in adjusting to age-related changes, thereby buffering other normative age changes, such as friends and family moving away or dying. Across the life course, they are less likely to have adhered to a traditional male/female division of labor of tasks; this increases their role flexibility in retirement and lays the foundation for greater financial security since both partners are likely to have been employed. Experiencing greater blurring of gender-role definitions throughout their lives, gays and lesbians tend to be more independent, nontraditional, and self-affirming than their heterosexual peers, and to adapt more readily to the role changes associated with aging. Overall, older GLBT individuals, especially among the young-old, generally emphasize positive aspects about aging, experience self-acceptance and self-esteem, and have satisfying long-term relationships (Clunis et al., 2005; Jones and Nystrom, 2002; Morrow, 2001).

By having confronted real or imagined loss of family support earlier in life, gays and lesbians are also less likely to assume that biological families, including their adult children, will provide for them in old age and are more likely to plan for their own financial security and health care arrangements. Having learned self-reliance and other skills that serve them well in old age, they may more readily adjust to care tasks. Most gay men now approach old age having experienced multiple losses through deaths of friends and lovers to AIDS; their accumulated grief may paradoxically enhance their acceptance of other losses associated with age, including the loss of friends to help care for them.

Since approximately 90 percent of older gay men and lesbians are childless, they typically build a "surrogate family" through a strong mixed-age network of friends and significant others, which either complements or replaces family of origin supports. In effect, they create "friendship families" or a family of choice (Calasanti and Slevin, 2001; MetLife, 2006). In fact, lesbians with at least one significant friendship/relationship generally adapt well to aging (Gabbay and Wahler, 2002). Some gays and lesbians share innovative housing arrangements and are surrounded by empowering communities that include social support and advocacy organizations. These include Senior Action in a Gay Environment (SAGE), the Lavender Panthers, Older Lesbians Organizing for Change, and the National Association of Lesbian and Gay Gerontologists organized by the American Society on Aging. SAGE, for example, has chapters nationwide that sponsor intergenerational friendly visitors' services, housing and legal advocacy, professional counseling as well as SAGE Net, a consortium of groups offering similar services around the nation (Butler, 2006; Yoakam, 1997). Although the growing number of gay retirement communities cannot discriminate against heterosexual individuals, they do convey a welcoming message to GLBT elders (Hecht, 2004). Those who have such support through informal networks, social organizations, and housing alternatives tend to be characterized by high self-esteem and life satisfaction, less fear of aging, and greater effectiveness in managing the societal aspects of aging (Slusher, Mayer, and Dunkle, 1996).

Health care providers need to be sensitive and avoid **heterosexism,** whereby they assume that all clients are heterosexual and engaged in relationships with opposite sex partners (Zodikoff, 2006). Assessment, psychosocial histories, and care planning practices all need to recognize that older GLBT individuals may have distinctive needs related to their sexual orientation and a lifetime of dealing with stigma and discrimination that may deter them from seeking services (Fredriksen-Goldsen et al., in press). In addition, GLBT elders who are concerned with maintaining privacy may be

---

POINTS TO PONDER

Imagine being a gay or lesbian elder who attends daily an adult day health or senior center. Because of fear of ostracism, you need to respond to every question without mentioning a lifelong partner—either a partner at home or your grief over a partner's death. And imagine maintaining that silence day after day, perhaps year after year. This is what life is like for many older GLBT adults.

---

uncomfortable with allowing formal caregivers into their homes (Cook-Daniels, 1997). Staff committed to enhancing the quality of life in long-term care settings also need to advocate for non-homophobic policies and practices that allow older gay and lesbian partners to be together and to participate in critical end-of-life decisions. Fortunately, such needs are being recognized by some service providers, and agency culture is being changed to be more inclusive of GLBT elders, often through staff training. The inclusion of GLBT elders through an expanded definition of minority populations in the *Report of the 2005 White House Conference on Aging* is a tangible recognition of their needs (Hecht, 2004; Smith and Calvert, 2001).

Sibling Relationships

Sibling relationships represent the one family bond with the potential to last a lifetime. The likelihood of having a sibling in old age has increased most dramatically over the past 100 years. Given current life expectancy, most persons will not experience the death of a sibling until they are past 70 years of age. About 80 percent of older people have at least one sibling, and about 33 percent see a sibling monthly, although yearly visits are most typical. As with other kin-keeping responsibilities, sisters are more likely than brothers to maintain frequent contact with same-sex siblings, whether by phone, e-mail, or face-to-face interaction (Bank and Kahn, 1997; Connidis, 2001; Uhlenberg, 2004).

The sibling relationship in old age is characterized by a shared history, egalitarianism, and increasing feelings of closeness and affection, particularly among sisters. Siblings often renew past ties as they age, forgive past conflict and rivalry, and become closer than they were in young and middle adulthood, frequently through shared reminiscence (Bengtson et al., 1996). Siblings are particularly vital sources of psychological support in the lives of never-married older persons, widowed persons, and those without children, although their ability to provide support declines with age (Barrett and Lynch, 1999). Assistance generally increases after a spouse's death and enhances the widowed person's psychological well-being. Although siblings are less frequently caregivers to each other than are partners and adult children (with the exception of caring for the never-married), they do supplement the efforts of others during times of crisis or special need. The very existence of siblings as a possible source of help may be important, even if such assistance is rarely used (Cicirelli, 1995). Given these ties, it is not surprising that some studies have found that bereaved siblings were more impaired and rated their overall health as worse than bereaved spouses or friends (Hays, Gold, and Peiper, 1997).

The increasing rate of divorce and remarriage will undoubtedly affect sibling relationships. With the growth in blended families through remarriage, there will be more half-siblings and step-siblings. For divorced older people who do not remarry, interactions with siblings may become more important than when they were married. The sibling relationship is also important to gay men and lesbians in old age, presuming because their siblings have accepted their differences in sexual orientation (Connidis, 2001).

Never-Married Older People

Approximately 4 percent of the older population has never married (Federal Interagency Forum, 2006). Contrary to a commonly held image of loneliness and isolation, the majority of never-married older persons typically develop reciprocal relationships with other kin, especially siblings, and with friends and neighbors. While living alone in old age is often interpreted as a risk factor, it may not negatively affect health, emotional well-being, and social integration when an older person is accustomed to living independently. Elders who have lived alone all their lives may not feel lonely or isolated. Families and health care providers often assume that co-residence is desirable; but simply living with others tells little about the quality of relationships and life satisfaction. It may be that lack of social support most negatively affects mental and physical well-being when loss of a partner or other relatives occurs later in life, rather than a lifelong pattern. Service providers and families need to be cautious in making assumptions about preferred living arrangements in old age (Connidis, 2001; NIA, 2001).

As another example of resilience among those who have lived alone most of their adult lives, never-married adults, who typically have had lifelong employment, tend to enjoy greater financial security in old age. In addition, they may be more socially active and resourceful, with more diversity in their social networks—especially more

POINTS TO PONDER

If you have a brother or sister, try to imagine what your relationship will be like in old age. If you are an only child, have you created other networks that might support you as you grow older?

interactions with younger persons, friends, neighbors, and siblings—than their married counterparts. This pattern of greater social and economic resilience tends to differentiate never-married women from their married, divorced, or widowed counterparts. Compared with widowed peers, they tend to be more satisfied with their lives, self-reliant, and focused on the present. When they do need others' assistance, they are more likely to turn to siblings, friends, neighbors, and paid helpers than are their married peers (Barrett and Lynch, 1999; Tennstedt, 1999).

Organizations specifically for single people are growing, although many of these are for younger singles. Alternative living arrangements, such as cross-generational home-sharing programs, co-op arrangements and assisted living facilities, may appeal to single older adults who choose not to live alone. The proportion of single older adults is likely to increase in the future, because singlehood is increasingly common (approximately 28 percent currently) at earlier life stages (Population Resource Center, 2006).

Childless Older Adults

Although most elders have living children, approximately 20 percent of those age 85 and older, who married in the Depression and the immediate post-Depression years, are childless. This rate is likely to increase as baby boomers age. Childless older adults lack the natural support system of children and grandchildren. For childless elders, relatives are most important for performing instrumental tasks, while friends typically give emotional support. When faced with health problems, childless elders turn first to their partners/spouses (if available) for support, then to siblings, then to nieces and nephews. They also have a higher probability of illness, limited emotional support, and are more likely to live alone. Given these factors, it is not surprising that unmarried childless elders

utilize services and nursing homes more than do married childless persons (Connidis, 2001; Uhlenberg, 2004). On the other hand, simply having children does not guarantee adequate care in old age.

Some childless and unmarried older people, particularly women, develop kin-like or "sisterly" non-kin relations and may be quite satisfied with their lives. Yet they may not want these relationships to be a source of care, fearing the change from voluntary mutuality into dependency (Wu and Pollard, 1998). The growing number of childless and unmarried older individuals may affect the proportion of older people who will seek formal and informal supports and develop alternative living arrangements in the future. The numbers of elders who have no grandchildren will also increase proportionately. The percentage of women age 60 to 64 who never experience grandparenthood will increase from the current 13 percent to over 20 percent in 2020 (Uhlenberg, 2004).

Other Kin

Interaction with secondary kin—cousins, aunts, uncles, nieces, and nephews—appears to depend on geographic proximity, availability of closer relatives, and preference. Extended kin can replace or substitute for missing or lost relatives, especially during family rituals and holidays. For example, compared to their white counterparts, African American childless elders often turn to nieces and nephews when siblings are not available. Accordingly, family reunions are a vital source of connections among African American extended kin in both rural and urban areas (Chadiha et al., 2005). Personal or historical connections that allow for remembering pleasurable events may be more important than closeness of kinship in determining interactions.

THE REALITIES OF AGING FAMILIES

- The family is the primary source of support for older people.
- Most older people have family members.
- Most older people, especially elders of color, live in a community-based family setting.
- Multigenerational (4 and 5 generations) families are growing.
- The rate of divorce, single parenting, remarriage, and blended families is increasing.
- The range of alternative family structures is expanding, broadening our definition of family.
- Spouses/partners are the most important family relationship.
- Spouses/partners are the primary family caregivers, followed by adult children.
- Sibling relationships increase in importance with age.
- Never-married and childless older adults are not necessarily lonely, unhappy, or dissatisfied.
- Intergenerational relationships tend to be reciprocal.

Intergenerational Relationships: Adult Children

After spouses/partners, adult children are the most important source of informal support and social interaction in old age. Typically, the flow of support is not unidirectional from adult child to older parent, but rather is reciprocal (Silverstein et al., 2002). Over 80 percent of persons age 65 and over have surviving children, although the number of children in most families has decreased—a trend expected to continue. The majority of older adults live near at least one adult child, sharing a social life but not a home (Connidis, 2001). Most older people state that they prefer not to live with their children, generally for reasons of privacy and a sense of autonomy. As stated earlier in this chapter, the percent of older persons who live in their children's households increases with advancing age and

extent of functional disability, and for those who are widowed, separated, and divorced (Population Resource Center, 2006). Most older adults who need long-term care prefer to live with their children rather than be placed in a nursing home, although children are less willing than their parents to share a residence. When older parents do live with their children, they usually live with a daughter (Boaz et al., 1999). Less than 14 percent of the young-old and 4 percent of the oldest-old live in multigenerational households composed of parents, children, and grandchildren (Connidis, 2001). These proportions are higher, however, among some families of color, especially African Americans (Dilworth-Anderson et al., 2002).

Although most older parents and adult children do not live together, they nevertheless see each other frequently. Studies over the past two decades indicate the following patterns:

- Approximately 50 percent of older people have daily contact with their adult children
- Nearly 80 percent see an adult child at least once a week
- More than 75 percent talk on the phone at least weekly with an adult child (AOA, 2002; Population Resource Center, 2006)

Less is known about the quality than about the frequency of interactions between older parents and their adult children. Nevertheless, most intergenerational relationships involve some types of conflict, with parents concerned about their children's habits and lifestyle choices, and children noting differences in communication and interaction styles. Despite such widely occurring differences most intergenerational families report affection, mutual support, and a desire for more satisfying relationships with each other. This reflects the paradoxical nature of family relationships, in which solidarity and conflict fluctuate over the life course (Clarke et al., 1999).

Geographic separation of family members is generally due to adult children's mobility, not that of the older relatives. For many families, holidays may be the only times adult children return home; and these special occasions often have to be distributed among in-laws, step-in-laws, and other complex family arrangements. Older parents who live closer to their children have more contact with them, greater affection for them, and are more involved with grandchildren, although geographic separation does not necessarily weaken socioemotional bonds and **intimacy at a distance** can occur (Silverstein and Angelelli, 1998). Older parents expect to move closer to an adult child out of need (poor health, living alone, adult child who is financially better-off than they are) and tend to select the child with the greatest potential to provide support (most often the oldest daughter). Health care providers need to recognize how each generation faces its own developmental transitions as well as complex cross-generational issues.

Patterns of Intergenerational Assistance

Generally, families establish a pattern of reciprocal support between older and younger members that continues throughout an individual's lifetime. Consistent with social exchange theory discussed in Chapter 8, those with more valued resources (e.g., money or good health) assist those with less. Not only concrete assistance, but also emotional and social support are exchanged. At various points, older parents provide substantial support, especially financial assistance, to their children and grandchildren. Regardless of socioeconomic status, most **intergenerational transfers** of resources, especially of knowledge and financial support, go from parent to child. On the other hand, adult children who are not married are more likely to transfer resources to parents. Contrary to stereotypes, most adult children who assist their parents are not motivated by the expectation of an inheritance (Boaz et al., 1999; Silverstein et al., 2002).

In some instances, parents continue to provide care to adult children beyond normative

expectations of "launching" them to be more independent. For example, parental care remains a central role late in life for parents of adult children who are developmentally or physically disabled or chronically mentally ill. Yet many such parental caregivers are facing their own age-related limits in functional ability, energy, and financial resources, which can affect their caregiving ability. The history and cumulative nature of care demands can make their situation particularly stressful. A major worry is how their child will be cared for after their own deaths or if they themselves develop a debilitating illness. Despite such concerns, most caregiving parents do not make long-term plans about where their children will eventually live. Not surprisingly, when parental caregivers of adult children with psychiatric disorders die, their children often experience housing disruptions and potentially traumatic transitions (Lefley and Hatfield, 1999). As the population of adults with chronic illness and developmental disabilities grows, the aging, mental health, and disability service networks are initiating new support systems. These include respite care, more residential alternatives, and assistance with permanency planning (e.g., developing plans for permanent housing in the community) (McCallion, 2006). Fortunately, the Planned Lifetime Assistance Network (PLAN) is now available in some states through the National Alliance for the Mentally Ill. PLAN provides lifetime assistance to individuals with disabilities whose parents or other family members are deceased or can no longer provide care.

Grandparenthood and Great-Grandparenthood

At the turn of the twentieth century, three-generation families were less common, with only 6 percent of 10-year-olds having all four grandparents alive compared to 41 percent in 2000. More older people are experiencing the role of grandparenthood and, increasingly, of great-grandparenthood, although they have proportionately fewer grandchildren than preceding generations. Among parents age 90 and older, 90 percent are grandparents and nearly 50 percent are great-grandparents, with some women experiencing grandmotherhood for more than 40 years. This is because the transition to grandparenthood typically occurs in middle age, not old age, with about 50 percent of all grandparents under the age of 60. As a result, there is wide diversity among grandparents, who vary in age from their late 30s to over 100 years old, and grandchildren ranging from newborns to retirees (Reitzes and Mutran, 2004a). A 40-year-old woman and a 2-year-old boy may form a grandparent-grandchild dyad, as does a 90-year-old man and a 40-year-old woman. The issues faced by each vary by the life course position of each generation, as well as the historical and spatial context for cohorts.

The grandchild experience is another way of grasping the significance of increased years spent in grandparenting. For example, the proportion of 30-year-olds with a grandparent alive tripled between 1900 and 2000—from 21 to 75 percent (Silverstein and Marenco, 2001; Uhlenberg, 2004). Contrary to stereotypes, most emotional and social interactions between grandchildren and grandparents are typically with adolescents and young adults, not with young children, and often involve reciprocal exchanges.

The vast majority of grandparents do not live with grandchildren, but approximately 80 percent see a grandchild at least monthly and nearly 50 percent see a grandchild weekly. Geographic proximity and the nature of the grandparents' relationship with their adult child are major factors that determine frequency of visits. On the other hand, geographic distance does not markedly affect the quality of the grandchild–grandparents' emotional bonds. Parents primarily determine the degree of interaction when grandchildren are young. The

> ### PELOSI CHANGES THE IMAGE OF GRANDMOTHERS
>
> Immediately after the 2006 election, Nancy Pelosi, the first female Speaker of the House, was on the phone with her daughter about to give birth to Pelosi's sixth grandchild, while a White House aide tried to connect her with the President. Pelosi believes that "everything stops" when a grandchild is coming. The grandmother story reflects the profound changes in our society—with people living longer and healthier lives—and as grandparents, wanting influence in the political discourse. Pelosi has made it chic to be a grandma (Trafford, 2006).

parental or middle generation shapes their children's ties to grandparents by modeling behaviors, expressing their own attitudes toward the grandparent, and providing means for contact, although adult grandchildren's ties to grandparents depend less on the middle generation. Because women traditionally have stronger ties to their family of origin than do men, bonds between aging mothers and adult daughters tend to be closest. While both grandmothers and grandfathers perceive ties to daughters as stronger and closer than to sons, relationships tend to be closest between grandmothers and granddaughters. Family size also affects these relationships. Grandparents with many children and grandchildren tend to be less invested in any particular grandchild (Chan and Elder, 2000; Davis and Williams, 2002; Dubas, 2001; Fingerman, 2004).

Because of the wide diversity among people in a phase of the life course that can encompass more than 40 years, there are multiple grandparenting roles and meanings. Age of the grandparent/grandchild and life course position, frequency of contact, and parental influences all affect grandparents' satisfaction from the role. Early research found this role to be peripheral, and not a primary source of identity, meaning, or satisfaction for older adults (Neugarten, 1964; Wood and Robertson, 1976). The prime significance of grandparenthood was reported to be biological renewal and/or continuity (e.g., seeing oneself extended into the future) and emotional self-fulfillment, especially the opportunity to be a better grandparent than parent. In terms of style, older grandparents were more apt to be formal and distant, whereas younger ones emphasized mutuality, informality, and playfulness. Surprisingly, about 30 percent did not derive satisfaction from the role, describing it as difficult, disappointing, and unpleasant. Satisfaction tended to be higher among grandmothers than grandfathers (Neugarten and Weinstein, 1964).

More recent research concludes that grandparents generally derive great emotional satisfaction from interacting with their grandchildren and from opportunities to observe their grandchildren's development and share in their activities. They want to have an influence on their grandchildren, typically to encourage high moral standards, integrity, a commitment to succeed, and religious beliefs and values. Age influences the types of grandparent–grandchild interactions; younger grandparents, especially grandmothers, typically live closer and have more frequent contact through child care and shared recreational activities, while older grandparents with higher income provide financial and other types of instrumental assistance (Davies and Williams, 2002; Musil, 2006; Reitzes and Mutran, 2004a; Silverstein and Marenco, 2001; Uhlenberg, 2004). These age differences may shift, however, as baby boom grandparents remain employed longer or choose to travel more during retirement than past cohorts. In many cases, they turn to the Internet for communication with their computer-savvy grandchildren. Consistent with role theory, grandparenthood provides opportunities for older adults to experience a sense of meaning, morale and positive role identity, relive their lives through their grandchildren, and indulge them with unconditional love. Overall, the grandparent role and identity tends

to be associated with embeddedness in the family, along with life satisfaction and psychological well-being (Drew and Silverstein, 2004; Mueller and Elder, 2003; Reitzes and Mutran, 2004a, 2004b). The box below illustrates the diversity of grandparenting styles.

The **intergenerational stake hypothesis** refers to a pattern whereby the older generation tends to be more invested in imbuing future generations with their values and therefore are more committed to relationships with younger generations. In contrast, younger generations, as a whole, place a higher value on establishing autonomy from older generations and thus

---

STYLES OF GRANDPARENTING

Companionate, Friend, or Apportionate Style
Grandparent feels close and affectionate to grandchildren without taking on a particular role; gives advice informally, talks about family history, serves as confidant and occasionally indulges the grandchild.

Remote Style
Grandparent is less involved, often because of geographic distance.

Involved Style
Grandparent is geographically close; often assumes parent-like responsibilities in response to a family crisis (e.g., separation or divorce) or to enable the parents to work outside the home.

Individualized Style
This grandparent is emotionally closer than the remote grandparent, but does not contribute substantially to the lives of grandchildren.

Authoritative or Influential
Grandparents, typically grandmothers, provide extensive support, sometimes assuming parental responsibilities; this style is more characteristic of African American families.

SOURCE: Adapted from Davies and Williams, 2002; Roberto and Stroes, 1995.

report lower levels of intergenerational solidarity (Reitzes and Mutran, 2004a). Congruent with exchange and social capital theory described in Chapter 8, this differential stake may reflect the greater investment by elders in raising younger generations and the fact that grandparents often view their relationship with their grandchildren as closer and more positive than do the grandchildren. On the other hand, grandchildren may perceive the relationship as an active, supportive one and less authoritative than their relation with their parents. For the most part, young adult children, whose relationship with their grandparents is no longer mediated by their parents, perceive their grandparents as "helping them out" and a sign of their emotional support and investment in them (Harwood, 2001). When young adults develop open communication patterns with their grandparents—telling stories, mutual self-disclosure, chatting on the phone—both grandparents and grandchildren recognize the mutual benefits of their relationship. Such communicative and beneficial aspects of this relationship tend to foster shared family identity with and positive attitudes toward the grandparent. Grandparents as friends with their grandchildren is compatible with the concept of active aging (Soliz and Harwood, 2006; Uhlenberg, 2004).

Gender also influences grandparenting. Grandmothers and grandfathers both report aiding and being interested in grandchildren, but grandmothers generally emphasize closeness, open communication, warmth, and fun (i.e., an expressive approach) and attribute greater importance to family relationships. Grandfathers place greater emphasis on their role as advisors (i.e., an instrumental approach), and their sense of obligation and love to grandchildren (Roberto, Allen, and Bleiszner, 2001).

Some studies point to greater interactions through an extended kin network and more grandparent responsibility for childrearing among ethnic minorities. African American grandparenting tends to be characterized as

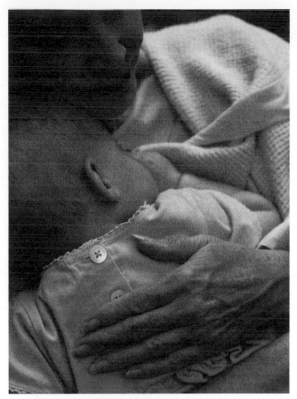

Grandparents as primary caregivers for grandchildren is a growing phenomenon.

authoritative or influential. In Asian immigrant families, grandparents who provide child care help support the family's economic success. Mexican American families tend to have strong grandparent-grandchild ties, with the flow of financial assistance generally from the older to young generations. Historically, grandparent–grandchildren relationships were characterized by norms of non-interference, with grandparents assuming only occasional or short term responsibility in responding to emergencies. The dramatic increase in the number of grandparents as primary caregivers to grandchildren reflects a profound shift in this pattern. The most common reasons are their adult children's substance abuse and incarceration (Davies and Williams, 2002; Hayslip and Kaminski, 2005).

Grandparents as Primary Caregivers of Grandchildren

Grandparents and other extended family members have traditionally provided care for grandchildren across families of color and in many other countries, as described in Chapter 2. (Cox, 2002). Such care provided by grandparents in three-generation households was often to supplement parental care or to support the young parents while they worked outside the home or faced short term disruptions. What has changed in the past two decades is the rapid growth of grandparents (or great-grandparents) who are the primary or sole caregivers for grandchildren because their adult sons or daughters are unable or unwilling to provide care. With over 2.4 million grandparents providing such primary care, such **skipped-generation households** are currently the fastest growing type in the United States (Simmons and Dye, 2003; Wallace, 2001).

CHALLENGES FACING GRANDPARENT CAREGIVERS

In Washington state, a 56-year-old woman who is blind, cares for her severely disabled 13-year-old grandson, who was violently shaken, struck, and thrown as a baby, suffering brain damage that left him with cerebral palsy and unable to walk, talk, drink, or eat solid food. Blind since age 16, she relies on Braille, a guide dog, and a few close friends to try to provide as full a life as possible for him. A case aide provides some daily assistance and can drive the teenager to school and other activities, but has an old, unreliable car. She survives on disability for both herself and her grandson, which does not cover additional costs entailed by the intensity of level of care that she must provide. Both grandmother and grandson dreamed of owning a van so that friends could drive him to sports events, church, and other activities that bring some joy into both of their lives. Fortunately, after her moving story ran in the *Seattle Times,* local contributors helped them realize their dream of an accessible van.

Skipped generation refers to the absence of the parental generation; this structure is also referred to as *downward extended households*. At the same time, the number of children living in a home with both a parent and grandparent present has declined (Casper and Bianchi, 2002; Fuller-Thompson and Minkler, 2001). These shifts represent a 30 percent increase in **custodial grandparenting** (i.e., those who have legal custody) since 1990 (U.S. Bureau of the Census, 2006).

Over 6 percent of all children live in grandparent-headed households. Of these, an estimated 30 percent are in such households without either of their parents for more than 6 months at a time, and where grandparents have assumed sole care responsibility. More than 10 percent of grandparents raise a grandchild for at least 6 months, but typically for far longer periods, in some cases for more than a decade. Although grandparent caregiving crosscuts social class, race, and ethnicity, African American children are more likely to live in a skipped-generation household than their white counterparts. Approximately 4 percent of Caucasian children, 6.5 percent of Latino, and 13.5 percent of African American children live with grandparents or other relatives. Although most grandparents are under age 65, 20 percent are age 65 and older and may be facing their own age-related changes and chronic diseases, as well as dealing with age-appropriate developmental tasks (Hayslip and Kaminski, 2005; Kropf and Yoon, 2006).

The majority of custodial grandparents are female, married, and live in the South. However, unmarried women and African Americans tend to predominate among grandparents who do not have legal custody (Hayslip and Kaminscki, 2005; U.S. Bureau of the Census, 2003). Even among older couples, women still predominate as the primary caregivers of their grandchildren. Although national studies indicate that the majority of sole grandparent caregivers are white (62 percent), Latinos (10 percent) and African Americans (over 30 percent) are disproportionately represented, given their percentage of the total population (Fuller-Thompson and Minkler, 2001; Hayslip and Kaminscki, 2005). Relatives such as aunts and siblings, who provide similar amounts of care as do grandparents, distinguish Latino households from other ethnic minority groups. Latino caregivers face the additional burden of anti-immigration sentiments and their legal manifestations, making them less likely to seek formal assistance with care tasks even if they hold legal status (Burnette, 1999; Cox, 2002; Cox, Brooks, and Valcarcei, 2000). Interventions to support grandparent caregivers need to take account of their wide diversity in terms of race, culture, socioeconomic status, age, and social class.

FACTORS ASSOCIATED WITH THE INCREASE IN GRAND-PARENT CAREGIVING   One factor underlying the dramatic increase in grandparent caregivers is a 2003 Supreme Court decision which upheld a lower court's decision that federal foster care benefits could not be denied to relatives who were otherwise eligible. This resulted in the practice of **formal kinship care**—the placement of children with relatives by the state—as opposed to the widespread **informal kinship** arrangements that do not involve state foster care or adoption systems. The majority of states now require that preference be given to relatives for placement of foster children. Federal and state laws and policies, however, that promote kinship care do not explain the concomitant growth in the number of informal arrangements of children living with grandparents (Cuddeback, 2004). In fact, a primary reason that grandparents assume the care role informally, typically well before any legal custody relationship is established, is their intent to keep a grandchild out of the state foster care system. Ironically, the only way that grandparents can be partially compensated is by meeting the state requirements for foster parents. Contrary to conservative arguments that grandparent caregivers take in grandchildren for financial gain, caring for grandchildren typically exacerbates already difficult economic circumstances. Even if grandparents do qualify for foster kinship care payments, they may experience delays and eligibility problems and their payment is lower than that for nonrelative foster parents (Goodman et al., 2004).

Rather than financial motivation, the predominant factors underlying increased grandparent caregiving are the parents' drug and alcohol abuse, especially the meth epidemic, HIV-AIDS, unemployment, divorce, incarceration, teen pregnancy, and death. Many of these factors will continue to increase the incidence of grandparent caregiving in the future (Hayslip

GRANDPARENTS AS CAREGIVERS

Mary long ago earned her stripes as a mom. She raised five children alone, in a tough Los Angeles neighborhood, and managed to put them through college or vocational training. She had looked forward to retirement and being a loving grandmother, to spoiling her grandchildren on visits and then sending them home. But her life has not turned out as expected. Instead, she's raising her 8-year-old grandson, James, alone, since the incarceration of her daughter and the boy's father for selling drugs.

When Mary's daughter was charged for possession of drugs, Mary could not bear the thought of her grandson being raised by strangers in the foster care system. She petitioned the courts to become his guardian. Her daughter has only contacted her son twice in the past four years. This has made the adjustment difficult for Mary and James, who often lashes out at his grandmother. Mary tries to provide as much love and stability for him as possible, helping him with his homework, assisting with his Cub Scout troop, and attending all his school events. She derives some emotional rewards from these activities with James, but misses activities with her peers. Many of her friends have dropped away, as they have more freedom to "take off and do things." She also struggles with guilt about her daughter and her situation. She has turned her anger and grief into organizing local support groups for others like herself and pressuring legislators to recognize caregiving grandparents' needs.

and Kaminski, 2005; Joslin, 2002). It is important to note that all of these factors are tied in fundamental ways to the growing problem of poverty, although many grandparent caregivers are not poor. Nevertheless, policy changes to address the factors contributing to the rise in skipped-generation households cannot be made without a commitment to confronting the underlying causes of poverty (Haglund, 2000).

THE GAINS AND COSTS OF CARE As with care responsibility across the life course, women predominate in the caregiving role, and experience both gains and costs. Although some grandparents enjoy emotional closeness and pleasure with grandchildren and a sense of being productive and needed (i.e., keeping the "family together and out of foster care"), they also experience significant costs (Giarrusso, Silverstein, and Feng, 2000; Kropf and Yoon, 2006; Haglund, 2000). Not surprisingly, stress is greatest with older grandchildren, because of difficult social, behavioral, and academic issues faced by some pre-teens and adolescents (Musil et al., 2002).

Economic costs of custodial grandparenting are significant. Compared to noncustodial grandmothers, they are more likely to live in poverty. As many as 50 percent of grandparent caregivers are living on a limited income and are not employed, even though the majority are age 45 to 64 and therefore not the typical retirement age (Hayslip and Kaminski, 2005; Smith et al., 2000). Those who are employed may need to reduce their hours or quit their jobs in order to care for their grandchild. Others may not suffer a decline in income caused by caregiving, but instead perceive a need to remain employed to cover basic costs entailed in raising a child, such as day care, clothing, food, sports, and special occasions. Such financial stress can exacerbate other types of distress, intensify feelings of being overwhelmed by multiple roles, and compromise their health. Grandparents who are sole caregivers are found to have higher levels of psychological distress compared

with those who provide only supplemental care to grandchildren. This distress, including depression, increases when they are caring for grandchildren with behavioral or emotional problems. They also tend to rate their health poorly, experience multiple chronic health problems, and avoid seeking care for themselves, especially for mental or emotional health problems (Burnette, 2000; Fuller-Thompson and Minkler, 2000; Simmons and Dye, 2003; Whitley, Kelley, and Sipe, 2001). These mental and physical problems tend to be magnified for grandparents who are raising a chronically ill or "special needs" child; 13 percent of children cared for by a custodial grandparent have emotional or behavioral problems, often due to past traumatic family circumstances, compared with 7 percent in two-parent families (Kolomer, McCallion and Janicki, 2002; Musil et al., 2006; Trute, 2003).

INFORMAL AND FORMAL SUPPORTS Grandparent caregiving also carries social costs. About 30 percent of grandmother caregivers are not married and therefore lack a partner's support. The non-normative nature of grandparent caregiving can intensify feelings of loneliness and loss from their own age peers who do not share similar responsibilities. Grandparents may grieve the loss of the adult children whom they knew as children and young adults (Waldrop and Weber, 2000). When adult children are incarcerated, drug addicted, or mentally ill, this is described as being "present but not present." Regardless of the reasons for this placement, most grandparents experience disappointment, embarrassment, shame, resentment, and guilt over their failure as parents who produced an adult child who relinquished their children. In this manner, grandparents may experience loss of identity and self-esteem as "good parents" along with alienation from their children. Society may reinforce this negative self-judgment because of common misconceptions of grandmothers as nondeserving poor (e.g., "they could not have been good parents or their children would not have turned out the way they did"). Other losses that intensify grandparent distress encompass the loss of retirement time or income anticipated in the child-free time of old age and dreams about their family and their life as an older adult, along with envying friends who pursue their leisure instead of being constrained by child care responsibilities (Giarrusso, Silverstein, and Feng, 2000; Goodman, 2003; Hayslip and Kaminski, 2005; Kelley et al., 2000).

Nevertheless, most grandparents assume the role willingly, often acting out of a deep sense of duty and obligation (Testa and Slack, 2002). Their grandchildren, however, may be embarrassed by having an older relative caring for them, and may repeatedly long for their parents, further intensifying the grandparent's sense of loss. Grandparents may pretend to be the parent and ask the child to call them "mother" in public settings, such as schools, as a way to increase the probability of support from others, and to minimize their grandchild's embarrassment. What can be especially painful is when other family members and friends pull away and fail to help out, intensifying feelings of alienation, isolation, and loneliness. Custodial grandparent caregivers also report more strain and conflict with other family members than their peers who are not providing daily care. Such strains and resultant feelings of being alone are often worse among those who assumed the care role because of their adult child's substance abuse, incarceration, or AIDS. Not surprisingly, custodial grandmothers perceive less support from others than other grandmothers. Losses are exacerbated by the lack of public recognition for the hard work of caregiving. Even their grandchildren and their adult children may not appreciate their hard work. In the largest study of children at risk born to unmarried mothers, grandparents were never mentioned as a critical support to grandchildren (McLanahan et al., 2003; Musil et al., 2006).

Despite the burdens of unanticipated caregiving, most custodial grandparents do not seek help for themselves, which increases their vulnerability, and most believe that they would still take responsibility for their grandchildren, despite the costs (Baird, 2003; Ehrle, 2001; Hayslip and Kaminski, 2005; Hayslip and Shore, 2000; Wohl, Lahner, and Jooste, 2003). Some grandparents may experience the cumulative effects of lifelong structural inequities due to race, gender, or disability, exacerbating the challenges they face as primary caregivers, as illustrated in the box on the next page. To outsiders, grandparent caregivers may be invisible, largely because of their age and gender (i.e., most are women), even though they may be the primary caregivers for the majority of their grandchild's life. Service systems, such as public child welfare, community mental health, and the public schools, are not prepared to work effectively with grandparents or to recognize the losses faced by the grandchild (Wallace, 2001).

The Temporary Assistance for Needy Families Program (TANF), under the 1996 Personal Responsibility Act that replaced Aid to Families with Dependent Children (AFDC), states that teen mothers can only receive benefits by living with their parents and being in school or having a job. An unintended consequence of this policy change is an increase in grandparents becoming primary caregivers for their grandchildren born to teenage parents. The employment requirements and 5-year lifetime benefit limits of TANF create obstacles for grandparents in accessing services and financial support through the welfare system (Minkler, Berrick, and Needell, 1999). Most grandparents receive the child-only benefit through TANF, with no financial support for themselves. Although foster care payments are higher than welfare benefits, grandparents can qualify for such payments only by transferring custody of the children to the state. In other words, they cede their own parental authority and become "foster parents" to their own grandchildren. However, foster care payments received

CHALLENGES AND OPTIONS FOR GRANDPARENTS IN RAISING THEIR GRANDCHILDREN

Legal Options
- Guardianship and custody, which provide parental authority to grandparents, but allow parental visitation rights
- Adoption, which gives grandparents all authority
- Foster parenthood (informal or formal; if the latter, grandparent qualifies for foster care payment, though at a lesser amount than non-relative foster parents)

Financial Options
- Temporary Assistance for Needy Families (TANF): Benefits only for children
- Food stamps
- Supplemental Security Income (SSI)
- Public housing/age-segregated retirement communities
- Foster care payment
- Adoption assistance

Child Care (day care, preschool, babysitters, respite)

Medical Insurance
- Medicaid but not Medicare
- Private insurance

Schooling
- Legal custody is necessary for grandchild to:
    Attend a public school
    Be tested for learning disabilities
    Qualify for remedial education

Psychological/Emotional Challenges for the Child
- Loss and grief, confusion, anger

Psychological/Emotional Challenges for the Grandparent
- Loss and grief over adult child, retirement plans, or employment
- Social isolation from age peers
- Concern about own health and mortality affecting child care responsibilities.

by kinship caregivers are less than what is received by licensed foster parents who are biologically unrelated. Some grandparent caregivers, especially among immigrants, may be unable to meet foster care regulations for home size, even though child welfare experts agree that relative placement is preferable. Some studies suggest that the state's reliance on kinship caregivers for low- or no-cost out-of-home foster placements results in an inequitable burden on informal support systems (Hayslip and Kawarski, 2005; Smith, 2000). And informal kinship caregivers—for example, those who have chosen not to transfer custody to the state—do not qualify for any state-funded services.

Fortunately, child welfare policy makers are now recognizing the need to develop services to support grandparent caregivers outside the traditional foster care or TANF programs. Education and support groups as well as Internet resources are available, including Kinship Care Navigators that can help grandparents. Support groups tend to be most effective when they provide information on how to access resources, enhance parenting skills, build on strengths, use a constructive problem-solving focus, and are combined with respite care. While social support is vital, the major need remains economic. Advocates for kinship care providers maintain that, at a minimum, grandparents should receive full foster care rates as well as other benefits accorded to unrelated foster parents, and should have the possibility of kinship adoption with federal subsidies for low-income families. In an effort to encourage permanent family placements, the Kinship Caregiver Support Act of 2005 gives states the option to use federal funds for subsidized guardianship payments to relative caregivers of children in foster care. This would make it easier for grandparents to become legal guardians and reduce barriers to services (Hayslip and Kawaski, 2005; Kelley, Whitley, and Sipe, 2000; Strom and Strom, 2000; Wohl et al., 2003). As noted by Weinberg (1998),

"It may be true that it takes a village to raise a child, but if children, the poor and the elderly are not to be confined to the ghettoes of that village, the community as a unit needs to recognize the value of caregiving" (p. 270).

An area for further multigenerational research and practice is to understand the needs of the "invisible" middle generation of parents who are unwilling or unable to raise their offspring and how this affects cross-generational exchanges across a family's life cycle. The lack of attention to this middle generation reflects in part our societal values on who is "deserving" of public benefits; but such neglect will have long-term consequences in terms of the middle generation's ability to be contributing members of society and to care for their parents in old age. Social workers in child welfare settings, schools, mental health clinics, hospitals, and senior centers can play pivotal roles in providing education and support to grandparental caregivers, advocating for economic resources and meeting the treatment needs of parents. Teachers, pediatricians, and other health care providers must be cognizant of the distinctive needs of grandparent caregivers as well as those of their grandchildren.

Great-Grandparents

The role of great grandparent has expanded as life expectancy has increased, although the attendant expectations and responsibilities are ambiguous (Drew and Silverstein 2004). Two predominant styles of performing the great-grandparenthood role have been noted. The most common, which tends to characterize generations separated by physical distance, is remote, involving only occasional and somewhat ritualistic contact on special occasions such as holidays and birthdays. Despite the irregular nature of contacts, however, great-grandparents derive considerable emotional satisfaction and a sense of personal and familial renewal from seeing a fourth generation as representing family continuity. Living long enough to be a great-grandparent is viewed positively. The other common style occurs when great-grandparents are geographically close (within 25 miles) to the fourth generation, and thus have frequent opportunities for physical and emotional closeness to great-grandchildren as well. Even great-grandparents who are in their 70s and 80s may serve as babysitters, go shopping, and take trips with their great-grandchildren. These activities provide diversions in their lives and can lead to renewed zeal and psychological well-being. Such positive interactions will undoubtedly be more common in the future, when great-grandparenthood is the norm and the oldest-old generations are healthier than current cohorts. Consistent with the reciprocal nature of most intergenerational relationships, growing numbers of adult grandchildren today help care for frail great-grandparents.

The Effects of Divorce and Changing Marital Patterns on Grandparenthood

A number of social trends affect the role of grandparent. Since 1950, marriage and remarriage rates have declined while rates of divorce, cohabitation, and births occurring to unmarried mothers have increased. A growing proportion of unmarried mothers are in a cohabiting relationship with the biological father. But 75 percent of the children born into such informal arrangements experience a single family household before reaching age 15 (Heuveline, Timberlake, and Furstenberg, 2003). The decline of the proportion of available fathers negatively affects paternal grandparents' roles while often increasing the involvement of maternal grandmothers to play an active role in their grandchildren's lives. Although grandparents of children in two-parent families tend not to influence significantly their grandchildren's overall well-being, maternal grandparents when the father is absent provide the safety net and protect their grandchildren from some of the risks of family disruptions (Elder and Conger, 2000; Uhlenberg, 2004).

The growing divorce rate profoundly affects the meaning of the grandparenthood experience.

As noted earlier, at least 50 percent of all persons marrying today will face divorce. The consequences of this for younger generations—over 30 percent of children living in one-parent families or with neither parent—is that it will affect the nature of the grandchild–grandparent relationship (Uhlenberg, 2004; U.S. Bureau of the Census, 2006). Since the tie between young grandchildren and their grandparents is mediated by the grandchildren's parents, divorce disrupts these links, changes the balance of resources within the extended family, and requires renegotiating existing bonds. Who is awarded custody affects the frequency of interaction with grandchildren; the grandparents whose adult child is awarded custody have more contact. Generally, grandmothers maintain more contact with their grandchildren than do grandfathers after an adult child's divorce, although emotional bonds and grandparents' feelings of responsibility toward grandchildren may endure even without frequent interaction (Copen and Silverstein, 2004; Ehrenberg and Smith, 2003; Uhlenberg, 2004).

Controversies regarding **grandparents' rights** for visiting and proposed state legislation to ensure such rights highlight the issues faced by grandparents when the other parent is awarded custody and reduces the amount of grandchild–grandparent interactions. Complex issues have also emerged concerning the liability of grandparents and step-grandparents for support of grandchildren in the absence of responsible parents. When parents divorce, the norm of noninterference by grandparents generally disappears. Instead, many grandparents, especially those related to the custodial parent, provide substantial assistance to their grandchildren, function as surrogate parents, and mediate tensions.

Since the mid-1960s, all states passed laws granting grandparents the right to petition a court to legally obtain visitation privileges with their grandchildren. This resulted from the passage of a 1983 uniform nationwide statute to ensure grandparents visitation rights even if parents object.

> ### GRANDPARENTING AND LEGAL ISSUES
>
> Laura and David's son was killed in an auto accident. He left behind two girls, ages 3 and 5 and their biological mother, who was his girlfriend. They had always been close to the grandchildren, and involved in their care. After his death, his girlfriend returned to assume responsibility for the girls. In her grief and anger, the girlfriend claimed the grandparents had no legal right to visit the girls and refused to allow contact. She later married, and her new husband felt even more strongly that Laura and David should not be allowed to visit the girls. The grandparents took their case to court, but the court ruled in favor of the biological mother.

However, in June 2000, the U.S. Supreme Court ruled by a 6–3 vote that the right of responsible parents to raise their children as they see fit takes precedence over prior state laws that give grandparents visitation rights. Any state law must respect the parents' wishes, although grandparents have the right to petition in cases of parental death or divorce. It is rare for grandparents to successfully petition for visitation rights when their grandchildren reside with both parents (Davitt, 2006). These rulings raise complex issues and may place children at the center of an intergenerational conflict played out in the courts. The long-term effects for grandchildren from visiting noncustodial grandparents over their parents' objections are unclear.

Despite the dramatic growth of blended families and thus of nonbiological grandparents, there is little research on step-grandparenting relationships. Based on marriage and divorce patterns during the 1990s, it is estimated that, by 2030, the population age 70 to 85 may have 1 step-grandchild for every 1.7 biological grandchildren. A grandchild may have step-grandparents, ex-step-grandparents, parents of a cohabiting partner of a parent, or GLBT grandparents (Uhlenberg, 2004). Not surprisingly, grandparents' sense of responsibility toward biological grandchildren is greater than toward step-grandchildren (Ganong and Coleman, 2006). From a grandparent's perspective, the growing phenomenon of divorce-remarriage means sharing grandchildren with their newly acquired relatives under conditions in which grandchildren will be scarcer because of declining birthrates. Grandchildren, in turn, may find themselves with 8 or more grandparents. Kinship systems are further complicated by the fact that, with the increased divorce rate after 20 or more years of marriage, grandparents may no longer be married to one another. With the aging of cohorts who have experienced high divorce rates, a growing proportion of grandparents will be divorced. It is estimated that the percent of new grandfathers who are no longer married to their grandchild's grandmother increased from 19 percent in the late 1970s to 37 percent now (Uhlenberg, 2004).

Divorce among grandparents is found to have negative repercussions on the grandparent–grandchild relationship; divorced elders, especially grandfathers, have less interaction with their grandchildren because of weaker ties with their adult children (King, 2003). Groups such as the Foundation for Grandparenting and The National Center for Grandparents'–Children's Rights, play important roles in disseminating up-to-date resources to grandparents regarding the complexities created by divorce of either generation and step-grandparenting.

Friends and Neighbors as Social Supports

Although the majority of older people live with others, approximately 16 percent of men, 30 percent of women age 65 to 74 live alone. After age 75, these rates increase to 23 percent of men and 50 percent of women. In fact, the rate of older persons living alone increased by 1.5 times the growth rate for older people in general since 1970. Those living alone are most likely to be women, elders of color, the oldest-old, adults of

low socioeconomic status, and those in rural areas (Federal Interagency Forum on Aging, 2006).

Among those living alone, the most vulnerable are the homeless. While the majority of homeless are age 25 to 45, 6 percent are estimated to be 55 to 64, and 2 percent 65 and older (National Law Center on Homelessness and Poverty, 2006). The absolute number of older adults who are homeless is increasing, especially among women. Characterized by higher rates of chronic stress, physical or mental disorders, economic deprivation, and alcohol misuse than the older population in general, homeless elders typically have fewer social supports. The needs of homeless elders are discussed more fully in Chapter 11.

After the homeless, men, the widowed, and the childless are the segments of the older population that are most vulnerable to lack of social supports, and increased risk of health problems and placement in a long-term care facility. Although time with friends may decline, the majority of older adults have at least one close friend with whom they are in frequent contact and to whom they can turn in emergencies. Non-kin care is provided to an estimated 5 to 10 percent of community-dwelling elders. Even older adults who have kin may nevertheless turn first to friends and neighbors for assistance, partially because friendship involves more voluntary and reciprocal exchanges between equals, consistent with social exchange theory (Barker, 2002; Wilmouth, 2000). The average friendship network is from 5 to 10 persons, which typically declines after age 85 when the need for assistance with personal care increases (Kalmijn, 2003; Litwin, 2003). Older adults who refuse to leave their own communities to live with or near adult children may recognize the importance of friends as companions essential to their well-being and know that replacing friends can be difficult in old age (Bleiszner and Adams, 1998). On the other hand, many older people steadily make new friends, and relationships generally get closer with age, particularly among women. Some friendship networks may even expand in old age if the elder moves to a retirement community or becomes more engaged in civic activities (Van Tilburg, 1998).

According to socioemotional selectivity theory, individuals over the life course are surrounded by an informal network of family, friends, and neighbors who exchange social support. With age and awareness that time is limited, they may choose deliberately to narrow their social networks to devote more time and energy to fewer relationships with people they most care about (Ajrouch, Blandon and Antonucci, 2005; Antonucci and Akiyama, 1987; Lansford, Sherman, and Antonucci, 1998). Such selective engagement, which is captured in the theory of gerotranscendence described in Chapter 8, is not the same as disengagement or withdrawal from social relationships. Instead, older adults may prefer to derive emotional comfort and meaning from familiar or intimate social interactions—or even from solitude—rather than expending the effort required to create and maintain a wide network of acquaintances that may provide less meaning to their lives. Careful selection of social network members is viewed as adaptive since it determines the degree to which elders have access to

---

FRIENDSHIPS AMONG OLDER WOMEN

Five women had gone to high school together, married their high school sweethearts, and remained in the same midwestern town, raising their children, volunteering, and working part-time. They met occasionally to play bridge, helped watch each other's children, and shared in the joys and sadness of family life. Within an eight-year time period, all became widows. They began to meet more often than when their husbands were alive—joining each other for meals, shopping trips, and bridge. When one of the women, Marge, suffered a stroke, the other four became her primary caregivers—bringing her food, accompanying her to the doctor, visiting with her daily, and helping to clean her home. This friendship network greatly relieved the caregiving burden for Marge's daughter.

---

social resources that can satisfy their socioemotional needs. Whether family, friends, or neighbors become involved appears to vary with the type of task to be performed, as well as the helper's characteristics, such as proximity, extent of long-term commitment, and degree of interaction. Friends and neighbors are well-suited to provide emotional support (e.g., stopping by to chat) and to assist spontaneously and occasionally, such as "checking in," providing transportation and running errands, while families are best equipped for long-term personal care. Even friends facing chronic health problems may still be able to assist others, such as by listening and offering advice and support. Among populations of color, friends often link older persons to needed community services. In fact, African American peers are more likely than whites to provide and receive both instrumental and emotional support, often through the church (Barker, 2002; Nocon and Pearson, 2000; Porter, Ganong, and Armer, 2000).

Friends are important for intimacy and exchange of confidences, especially when compared to relatives other than marital partners and after major role transitions such as widowhood or retirement. For example, an older widow generally prefers help from confidantes because relatives may reinforce her loss of identity as "wife," be overly protective or alternatively, minimize her loss. To the extent that friendships are reciprocal and satisfy social and instrumental needs, they can compensate for the absence of a partner and help mitigate loneliness (Stevens et al., 2006).

The role of friend can be maintained long after the role of worker, organization member, or partner is lost. The extent of reciprocity and quality of interaction, not the quantity, appear to be the critical factors in the maintenance of friendship networks. For instance, an intimate friendship with a confidant can be as effective as several less-intimate ones in coping with the grief of widowhood. Friendship quality, including reciprocity among friends, is frequently related to psychological well-being and happiness (Adams, Blieszner, and de Vries, 2000; Hogan, Linden, and Najarian, 2002). Given the general importance of friendships, professionals need to understand and encourage older adults to sustain these relationships or build new ones, despite the challenges faced by many elders in doing so.

Gender differences in informal supports are more pronounced than life course differences, with men showing greater declines than women in the number of new friends, their desire for close friendships, the intimate nature of friendships, and involvement in activities beyond the family (Field, 1999). Women in general, such as Mrs. Howard in the introductory vignette to Part Four, have more emotionally intimate, diverse, and intensive friendships than men. For many men, their wives are their only confidants, a circumstance that may make widowhood devastating for them. In contrast, women tend to satisfy their needs for intimacy throughout their lives by establishing close friendships with other women and therefore are less dependent emotionally on the marital relationship. When faced with widowhood, divorce, or separation, they often turn to these friends. Accordingly, widowed older women tend to receive more help and emotional support from friends than married older women. The resilience of some older women, in fact, may be rooted in their ability to form close reciprocal friendships (Moen, Erickson, and Dempster-McClain, 2000; Stevens et al., 2006).

Both men and women tend to select friends from among their social peers—those who are similar in age, sex, marital status, sexual orientation, and socioeconomic class. Most choose age peers as their friends, even though common sense would suggest that intergenerational friendship networks can reduce their vulnerability to losses as they age. Age homogeneity plays a strong role in facilitating friendships in later life, in part because of shared life transitions, reduced cross-generational ties with children and work associates, and possible parity of exchange. Adult children are not likely to be chosen as confidants, primarily because they are from different cohorts at different phases in the life cycle. Although friends are important resources, their helping efforts usually do not approach those of family members in duration or intensity, and do not fully compensate for the loss of a partner or children, especially for low-income elders with chronic illnesses. Friendships can also be characterized by negative interactions, such as unwanted advice or assistance, or by responses that minimize the challenges facing elders, and may become strained by excessive demands for assistance (Hogan et al., 2002; DeMallie et al., 1997; Litwin, 2003).

Interventions to Strengthen or Build Social Supports

Because of the importance of peer-group interactions for well-being, efforts are increasing to strengthen existing community ties or to create new ones if networks are nonexistent. Consistent with the person–environment model, such interventions can make the environment more supportive of the older person. They can be categorized as personal network building, volunteer linking, mutual help networks, and neighborhood and community development. Despite an extensive literature on the benefits of social supports, evidence is limited about how—and how well—social support interventions work (Hogan et al., 2002).

Personal network building aims to strengthen existing ties, often through **natural helpers**—nonfamily members to turn to because of their concern, interest, and innate understanding. Such natural helpers provide emotional support, assist with problem-solving, offer concrete services, and act as advocates. Neighbors often perform natural helping roles, and may strengthen these activities through organized block programs and block watches. Even people in service positions, often referred to as **gatekeepers,** can fulfill natural helping functions, because of the visibility of their positions and the regularity of their interactions with elders. For example, postal alert systems, whereby postal carriers observe whether an older person is taking in the mail each day, build on routine everyday interactions. Pharmacists, ministers, bus drivers, local merchants, beauticians, and managers of housing for older people, as in the case of Mr. Valdres in the introductory vignette, are frequently in situations to provide companionship, advice, and referrals. In high-crime areas, local businesses, bars, and restaurants may have a "safe house" decal in their windows, indicating where residents of all ages can go in times of danger or medical emergencies. These and other community-based supports are further described in Chapter 11.

Religious or faith-based institutions may also serve to strengthen and build personal networks, in some cases providing a surrogate family for older people. Through intergenerational programs, members of religious institutions can provide help with housework, home repair, transportation, and meal preparation, as well as psychological support. At the same time, older members may take on leadership and teaching roles within the church, synagogue, or mosque, thereby enhancing their sense of belonging and self-worth, as in the example of Mr. Mansfield on page 304. In many private and public programs, volunteers are commonly used to develop new networks or expand existing ones for older persons. For example, volunteers provide chore services in older people's homes, offer peer counseling and senior center outreach activities, and serve as friendly visitors. The role of voluntarism and social support is discussed more fully in Chapter 12.

By providing access to online support groups and chat rooms, referral links and informational support, and e-mail, the Internet and interactive television provide new opportunities for network building with peers and across generations for those with access to such information technology (Segrist, 2004; Willis, 2006). Websites, such as Third Age, have emerged as a means to build virtual community connections and reduce social isolation. Chat rooms, for example, are modeled upon community members' interests and needs; they can be altered by the changing will of the community of users. People may be drawn to such virtual communities as a way to readily connect with others in the anonymity of their home or office. Creating an electronic community, however, is obviously limited to older people who can access computers and the Internet. "Computer support" holds promise for elders with debilitating illnesses that present physical barriers to attending support groups, for rural and other isolated populations, and for those who desire anonymity. Some research suggests that computer interventions can improve cognitive functioning and promote active aging (Charness and Holley, 2004; Yange et al., 2006; Kramp and Battes, 2006). Findings on the effectiveness of telephone support are mixed (Davison, Pennebaker and Dickerson, 2000; Hogan et al., 2001).

Another approach aims to create or promote the supportive capacities of *mutual help networks,* especially through joint problem-solving and reciprocal exchange of resources. Mutual assistance may occur spontaneously, as neighbors watch out for each other, or may be facilitated by professionals. They may also be formed on the

---

INFORMATION TECHNOLOGY AND COMMUNITY BUILDING

When the public library in a small Massachusetts town began to offer computer training, they expected the classes to be filled with teenagers and young adults. Instead, the classes were filled with adults over age 55, eager to learn how to e-mail their friends and families around the country, and to use the Internet to search for health information and facts about their town's history.

basis of neighborhood ties or around shared problems, such as widow-to-widow programs and support groups for caregivers of family members with chronic impairments. Interacting with peers who share experiences may reduce feelings of being alone and expand problem-solving capacities, but may also inadvertently increase stress when groups lack a professional facilitator and participants share primarily negative or widely varying experiences. Support that does not meet the recipients' needs or is perceived as critical or dismissive of problems can increase negative effects. Self-help groups tend to be most effective for diseases considered stigmatizing (e.g., alcoholism, cancer, HIV/AIDS). Overall, the kind of support, who provides it and contextual issues all play a role in determining whether support interventions are perceived as beneficial (Davison et al., 2000; Hogan et al., 2001).

Increasingly, boomers are creating their own communities and support systems, sometimes called Circles of Caring, to meet their emotional, spiritual, and physical needs as they age. A group called Fiercely Independent Seniors in a rural area of Washington State meets weekly; members reciprocate by assisting each other with tasks like writing advance directives, and regularly checking up on each other. It is not surprising that the cohort who engaged in consciousness raising during the 1960s is fostering movements identified as "conscious aging," "pro-active aging," or "aging on your own terms." Such an approach is consistent with findings that it is not only the recipients of peer support who benefit, but also those who provide support (Hogan et al., 2001, King, 2006; Scharlach, 1988; Trenshaw, 2004).

Neighborhood and community building is another approach to strengthening a community's self-help and problem-solving capabilities and may involve social action through lobbying and legislative activities. They aim to build upon the strengths and resources of local communities, including communities of color, and many include an intergenerational component. The Tenderloin Project, which has existed for over

> **OLDER ADULTS AND THE INTERNET**
>
> A 78-year-old British man was the first older adult to upload a video on YouTube in August 2006. His first video begins with the streaming text, "geriatric gripes and grumbles," but he does not fit that stereotype. Not only is he enthusiastically embracing this medium typically used by 20-somethings, he is an avid blues and motorcycle enthusiast. His first five videos received more than 154,000 hits in less than two weeks, and he received about 4000 messages via YouTube in a single morning. He represents the future when it is anticipated that computer-savvy baby boomers will use the Internet for entertainment, shopping, and communication.

25 years in a low-income area of single-room occupancy units in San Francisco, is an example of neighborhood development. Nearby residents acted cross-generationally on the immediate problem of crime and victimization of older people and then dealt with community-wide issues such as nutrition, child care, and prostitution. In the process, social networks were strengthened and weekly support groups formed. Neighborhood-based intergenerational helping networks can connect the formal service system to provide personal care services to frail elders. Similarly, social supports can buffer the effects of neighborhood stressors on elders such as crime or traffic congestion (Schieman and Meersman, 2004).

Intergenerational Programming

Intergenerational programs, linking older people with schoolchildren, high-risk youth, children with special needs, and young families, are a rapidly growing type of mutual help. This can also be extended to address cross-generational neighborhood and community problems, such as safety and the environment. The most common type of intergenerational programming involves older adults serving children and youth.

For example, after-school telephone support, tutoring, and assistance at day-care programs are provided through Retired Senior Volunteer Programs (RSVP). Kinder Korps and the Foster Grandparents Program both provide tutoring and mentoring, generally to low-income youth. The Computer Pals Program fosters youth and elder e-mail partnerships, with adolescents often teaching computer skills to older adults. Some programs involve elders and youth in social action projects, such as Caring Communities, that seek to improve the environment through music, gardening, and art. Older adults can also assist young families with parenting skills, literacy training, social support, and job hunting, and in creating supportive communities for foster and adoptive families or other families with high-risk children. Residential facilities for high risk youth sometimes involve older adults as mentors and "surrogate" grandparents. Adolescents can in turn assist older neighbors with yard work, home maintenance, and friendly visiting (Eheart, Power, and Hoping, 2003; Hamilton et al., 1999; Kincade et al., 1996; Skilton-Sylvester and Garcia, 1998).

Sharing physical space can also encourage intergenerational contact, such as child care programs housed in nursing homes or assisted living facilities, or offering senior center activities within public schools. In such instances, however, it is important to respect the needs of both elders and children; for example, some older adults in nursing homes may not want to interact with children and may resent an environment that is too child-centered. Careful planning is necessary to ensure that interactions are age and developmentally appropriate, and ensure choice and autonomy for elders (Hayes, 2003; Salari, 2002). One program that took account of these factors implemented Montessori-based activities for both children and adults with dementia in an adult day care setting that had positive outcomes for both age groups (Camp et al., 2005). Both young and old generations may benefit from training on how to interact successfully; for example, young

AN INTERGENERATIONAL GRAN PAL PROJECT

A second-grade public school teacher involves his class in visiting regularly with their "Gran Pals" in a nearby skilled nursing care facility. In preparation for their visits, he first has them participate in a simulation of what it feels like to be "old and frail" by wearing glasses with Vaseline on the lens, being pushed in a wheelchair, wearing gloves while opening a bottle, learning to speak clearly and directly to someone while wearing earplugs, and so on. Such simulations are frequently created for undergraduate students, but this program involves 6- and 7-year-olds, who then write and talk about what they experience when their usual activities are restricted. Each visit to the skilled care facility begins with the teacher talking with the children about what they might experience, and is then followed by the children's writing and discussing what they learned. The teacher is motivated not only by the social benefits for the older residents, but also by the recognition that by the time his second graders enter the job market, 20 percent of the population will be older adults.

children are more spontaneous and comfortable with elders with disabilities, while teenagers may need some tips on ways to interact with a person in a wheelchair. Successful programs are characterized by reciprocal benefits for both young and old, and understanding of both human development and differences in communication styles. They typically enhance the self-esteem and social engagement of both young and old and may, in some instances, foster empathy and positive attitudes toward aging (Lewis, 2006). This was the case in an Intergenerational School in a center serving older adults, where elders serve as reading mentors and computer pals in the classroom, and students volunteer in affiliated nursing homes, each generation valuing their shared educational experiences (Whitehouse, Fallcreek, and Whitehouse, 2005).

Consistent with the broad concept of productivity discussed in Chapter 12, intergenerational programs are likely to grow in the future as a way to match elders' resources with the needs of younger generations. This is also congruent with the federal government's emphasis on cost-effective, private solutions to social problems. Practitioners in schools, senior centers, long-term care facilities, and other community-based settings can play pivotal roles in fostering cross-generational exchanges that benefit young and old. On the other hand, because public funding tends to be based on age, sustainable fiscal support for intergenerational programs is limited, and many depend on volunteers to keep the program going. Nearly everyone will agree that intergenerational programs are a good idea, but neither the government nor private funders readily provide the necessary support. The Association of Gerontology in Higher Education, Generations United, and Generations Together are national groups that promote intergenerational policy and practice.

Relationships with Pets

Many older adults talk to and confide in their pets and believe that animals are sensitive to their moods and feelings. Outcomes of owning a pet or participating in pet therapy are relatively unclear, and findings are mixed. Anecdotal accounts of the benefits of pets are more common than rigorous empirical studies (Banks and Banks, 2002; Saito et al., 2001). What is clear, however, is that having a pet to feed, groom, or walk can provide structure, a sense of purpose, and an anchor in days that might otherwise lack meaning, and may even serve to reduce depression (Johnson et al., 2003). Older adults who care for pets may experience meaning, purpose, and sense of control over their environment. Pets, with their unconditional love, may compensate for lack of family members in the home (Zasloff and Kidd, 1994). In some studies, pet owners score higher than their peers without pets on measures of happiness, self-confidence, morale, self-care, alertness,

responsiveness, and dependability. At the same time, these benefits may be partially because pet owners are more likely to be younger, physically active, and married or living with someone (Dembicki and Anderson, 1996; Raina et al., 1999). Less is known about its health benefits, although some studies have found that pet ownership is associated with greater survival among patients with coronary heart disease (Friedmann and Thomas, 1995). A study of 2,500 adults age 72 to 81 identified the mobility benefits from walking a dog (Thorpe et al., 2006). Interaction with animals can be an effective coping strategy for cancer patients to reduce anxiety and despair by providing distraction, focusing on the positive, and seeking and using social support. Pet visitation with nursing home residents has been found to improve health, self-concept, life satisfaction, and mental functioning. Given the apparent benefits of this relationship, the loss of a pet can result in intense grief; when this grief is minimized by others, elders' feelings of loss tend to be further intensified (Doka, 2001; Johnson et al., 2003).

The perceived benefits of pets has led to an increase in pet-facilitated programs for older adults in long-term care settings, as well as loan-a-pet or pet daycare programs for elders in their own homes. Some long-term care facilities, particularly those using the Eden Alternative, create a more homelike setting by having pets living in the facility (Coleman et al., 2002). However, a pet should not be viewed as a substitute for human relationships (some cases of self-neglect involve homes filled with pets, but lacking food, hygiene, and other social interaction for the elder). Nevertheless, pet ownership can enhance well-being and enrich elders' quality of life. In recognition of these benefits, the National Institute of Health's definition of complementary/alternative medicine (CAM) includes human-animal interaction as pet ownership, animal-assisted activity (e.g., pet visitation) or animal-assisted therapy (structured sessions with treatment goals) (Johnson et al., 2003). Differentiating pet ownership from occasional interaction with a pet in long-term care settings is important in future research and practice interventions with pets and elders. More research is also needed on ethnic minority differences in pet ownership patterns, pet attachment, health beliefs, and health practices to determine the relevance of animal-assisted techniques with culturally diverse elders (Johnson and Meadows, 2002).

Implications for the Future

Increases in life expectancy and declining family size will continue to produce more diverse and complex family structures. The vertical or "beanpole" family structure will grow—that is, an increasing number of living generations in a family, accompanied by decreasing numbers of family members within the same generation due to declining fertility rates. These trends, combined with growth in the number of unmarried persons and childless partners, will mean that future cohorts of adult children will have a greater number of aging parents and grandparents to care for, but fewer siblings to assist them. Top-heavy kin networks will raise caregiving challenges for both families and society, along with questions of intergenerational equity and reciprocity.

Delayed childbearing and smaller family size also will result in greater age differences between each generation and blurring of demarcations between generations, especially among Caucasian families. Active involvement in the daily demands of raising children will be fully completed by the time women are grandmothers, although some grandmothers will then become primary caregivers of grandchildren. Some women will simultaneously be both grandmothers and granddaughters. But baby boomers will have, on average, fewer grandchildren than the prior cohort who gave birth to the baby boomers. Growing proportions of parents, children, and grandchildren will share such

critical adulthood experiences as school, work, parenthood, retirement, and widowhood. On the other hand, generational differences of 30 years, along with geographic mobility, may contribute to difficulties in building affective bonds across multiple generations due to different values or lifestyles. The increasing divorce rate may mean that multiple generations will invest time in building reconstituted or blended families, which later may be dissolved. How these changes translate into new forms of family structure in the future remains unclear, since the extent to which acculturation and economic conditions will modify more traditional family arrangements is unknown. For both Caucasians and ethnic minority families, life course variations will grow as longer-lived men and women move in and out of various relationships, caregiving arrangements, living and employment situations, and communities.

All of these changes highlight the need for gerontological practitioners in a wide range of settings to gain skills in assessing and intervening with families, not only with the older person. Providers need to be sensitive to the wide variation of family forms, including grandparents as caregivers, GLBT partners, mothers who have delayed childbearing and are simultaneously caring for a toddler and a frail elder, single or never-married older adults with extensive friendship networks, and elders of color with fictive kin networks.

Health and human service providers in schools, community clinics, public child welfare, hospitals and mental health centers, regardless of their area of expertise, will increasingly encounter multigenerational families. This trend suggests the need for all such professionals to have basic knowledge and skills in working effectively with older adults and their increasingly complex families. In times of shrinking resources, professional creativity regarding intergenerational and multigenerational programs is needed to build on the resources and contributions of multiple generations to addressing social problems. Such collaborations are ways for both younger and older adults to engage in meaningful roles. In addition, service systems may shift from categorical, age-based services to ones that meet human needs across the life course. For example, the Lifespan Respite Bill passed by Congress in 2006, and programs such as the National Family Caregiver Support Program and the federal Family and Medical Leave Act address caregiving demands across the life course, not just for a particular age group. Given the dramatic growth in multigenerational families and the complexity of family forms, professionals will be challenged to think outside traditional age-based silos and models of service delivery, and develop new ways to utilize older adults as a civic resource.

Summary

The importance of informal social support networks for older people's physical and mental well-being is widely documented. Contrary to stereotypes, very few older people are socially isolated. The majority have family members with whom they are in regular contact, although they are unlikely to live with them. Their families serve as a critical source of support, especially when older members become impaired by chronic illness. The marital relationship is most important, with more than half of all persons age 65 and over married and living with a partner in independent households. Most older couples are satisfied with their marriages, which influences their life satisfaction generally. The older couple, freed from childrearing demands, has more opportunities to pursue new roles and types of relationships.

Less is known about sibling, grandparent, and other types of family interactions in old age, although the importance of their support is likely to increase in the future. Also, comparatively little research has been conducted on lesbian and gay relationships in old age and on never-married older persons who may rely primarily on friendship networks to cope. Siblings can be crucial

in providing emotional support, physical care, and a home. Interaction with secondary kin depends on geographic proximity and whether more immediate family members are available.

Contrary to the myth that adult children are alienated from their parents, the majority of older persons are in frequent contact with their children, either face-to-face or by phone. Filial relationships are characterized by patterns of reciprocal aid throughout the life course, until the older generation becomes physically or mentally disabled. At that point, adult children—generally women—are faced with providing financial, emotional, and physical assistance to older relatives, oftentimes with little support from others for their caregiving responsibilities. In ethnic minority and lower-income families, older relatives are most likely to receive daily care from younger relatives and to be involved in caring for grandchildren.

Most families, regardless of socioeconomic class or ethnic minority status, attempt to provide care for their older members for as long as possible, and use long-term care facilities only when they have exhausted other resources. Such caregiving responsibilities are affected by a number of social trends, most notable among them the increasing percentage of middle-aged women who are more likely to be employed, and the number of reconstituted families resulting from divorce and remarriage. The needs of caregivers are clearly a growing concern for social and health care providers and policy makers, and are discussed in Chapter 10.

With the growth of three- and four-generation families, more older persons are experiencing the status of grandparenthood and great-grandparenthood. Most grandparents are in relatively frequent contact with their grandchildren, and most derive considerable satisfaction from the grandparent role. The demands of grandparenthood are changing, however, as a result of divorce and remarriage. Perhaps the most dramatic change in the past decade has been the increase in the number of grandparents who are the primary or custodial caregivers to young grandchildren because their adult children are unable or unwilling to provide care.

For many older persons, friends and neighbors can be even more helpful than family members to maintaining morale and a quality of life. Generally, women interact more with friends than do men. In recognition of the importance of informal networks to physical and mental well-being, mutual support, neighborhood and community-based interventions have been developed to strengthen friendship and neighborhood ties. In recent years, many of these programs have attempted to foster intergenerational contacts. In sum, the majority of older persons continue to play a variety of social roles—partner, parent, grandparent, friend, and neighbor—and to derive feelings of satisfaction and self-worth from these interactions.

GLOSSARY

blended families families whose memberships comprise blood and nonblood relationships through divorce or remarriage

custodial grandparents grandparents who have legal custody of their grandchildren, when adult children are unable to provide adequate care

empty nest normative for middle-aged parents when adult children leave home for college or employment

formal kinship care placement of children with relatives by the state child welfare system

gatekeepers people in formal (e.g., physicians, nurses) or informal (e.g., friends and neighbors) service roles who regularly interact with older adults and can watch for signs indicating a need for assistance

grandparents' rights legal rights of grandparents to interact with grandchildren following divorce of the grandchildren's parents; liabilities of grandparent and step-grandparents as custodians of grandchildren in the absence of responsible parents

heterosexism assumptions of male–female relationships as the norm; bias against GLBT individuals

informal kinship care relatives, especially grandparents, provide care without any state involvement

intergenerational programs services that facilitate the interaction of people across generations; typically young and old

intergenerational stake hypothesis pattern whereby the older generation tends to be more invested in future generations around transmission of values and resources

intergenerational transfers exchange of knowledge, finances, and other resources among family members of different generations

intimacy at a distance strong emotional ties among family members even though they do not live near each other

kinship care the formal placement of children with extended family members, often grandparents

multigenerational family a family with three or more generations alive at the same time; considers the needs of middle generation, not just young and old

natural helpers people who assist others because of their concern, interest, and innate understanding

nontraditional families new family structures derived through gay and lesbian partnerships, cohabitation, informal adoption, etc.

reciprocal exchange sharing resources and assistance among individuals

skipped generation household where the parent generation is absent

social integration encompasses both social networks and support; degree to which a person is involved with others in the larger social structure and community

social networks the interrelationships and interactions among individuals that affect the flow of resources and support

social support informational, emotional, or instrumental (e.g., help with tasks of daily living) assistance from social networks

RESOURCES

Log on to MySocKit at (www.mysockit.com) for information about the following:

- AARP Grandparent Information Center
- Association for Gerontology in Higher Education (AGHE)

- Child Welfare League of America
- Foster Grandparents
- Foundation for Grandparenting
- Gatekeeper Program
- Generations Together, University of Pittsburgh
- Generations United
- National Center on Grandparents and other Relatives Raising Grandchildren
- National Center for Resource Family Support, the Casey Family Program
- National Coalition of Grandparents (NCOG)
- National Center for Grandparents Childrens Rights

REFERENCES

Adam, B.D. Age preferences among gay and bisexual men. *GLQ: A Journal of Lesbian and Gay Studies*, 2000, *6*, 413–433.

Adams, R.G., Blieszner, R., and de Vries, B. Definitions of friendship in the third age: Age, gender, and study location effects. *Journal of Aging Studies*, 2000, *14*, 117–133.

Administration on Aging (AOA). *Profile of Older Americans*. Washington, DC: 2002.

Administration on Aging (AOA). *Profile of Older Americans*. Washington, DC: 2004.

Ajrouch, K.J., Blandon, A.Y., and Antonucci, T.C. Social networks among men and women: The effects of age and socioeconomic status. *Journals of Gerontology*, 2005, *60B*, S311–S317.

Allen, S.M., Goldscheider, F., and Ciambrone, D.A. Gender roles, marital intimacy, and nomination of spouse as primary caregiver. *The Gerontologist*, 1999, *39*, 150–158.

American Association of Retired Persons (AARP). *AARP's Singles Survey*. Washington, DC: Author, 2003.

Antonucci, T.C., and Akimaya, H. Social networks in adult life and a preliminary examination of the convoy model. *Journal of Gerontology*, 1987, *42*, 519–527.

Antonucci, T.C., Sherman, A.M., and Akimaya, H. Social networks, support, and integration. In I.J. Birren (Ed.), *Encyclopedia of gerontology* (vol. 2). New York: Academic Press, 1996.

Baird, A. Through my eyes: Service needs of grandparents who raise their grandchildren from the perspective of a custodial grandmother. In B. Hayslip and J. Patrick (Eds.), *Working with custodial grandparents*. New York: Springer, 2003.

Bank, D.P., and Kahn, M.D. *The sibling bond*. New York: Basic Books, 1997.

Banks, M.R., and Banks, W.A. The effects of animal-assisted therapy on loneliness in an elderly population in long-term care facilities. *Journals of Gerontology*, 2002, *57A*, M428–M432.

Barker, J. Neighbors, friends and other non-kin caregivers of community-living dependent elders. *Journals of Gerontology*, 2002, *57B*, S158–167.

Barranti, C., and Cohen, H. Lesbian and gay elders: an invisible minority. In R. Schneider, N. Kropf, and A. Kisor (Eds.). *Gerontological Social Work: Knowledge, service settings and special populations*. Belmont, CA: Brooks/Cole, 2001.

Barrett, A.E., and Lynch, S.M. Caregiving networks of elderly persons: Variation by marital status. *The Gerontologist*, 1999, 695–704.

Baydar, N., and Brooks-Gunn, J. Profiles of grandmothers who help care for their grandchildren in the United States. *Family Relations*, 1998, *47*, 385–394.

Bengtson, V.C. Beyond the nuclear family: The increasing importance of multigenerational bonds. *Journal of Marriage and the Family*, 2001, *63*, 1–16.

Bengtson, V.C., Rosenthal, C.J., and Burton, L.M. Paradoxes of family and aging. In R.H. Binstock and L.K. George (Eds.), *Handbook of aging and the social sciences* (4th ed.). New York: Academic Press, 1996.

Bennett, L., and Gates, G. *The cost of marriage inequaltiy to gay, lesbian and bisexual seniors*. Washington, DC: Human Rights Campaign, 2004.

Berger, R.M., and Kelly, J.J. What are older gay men like? An impossible question? *Journal of Gay and Lesbian Social Services*, 2001, *13*, 55–65.

Berkman, B., and Harootyan, L. *Social work and health care in an aging society: Education, policy, practice and research*. New York: Springer, 2002.

Berkman, L.F. Social support, social networks, social cohesion, and health. *Social Work and Health Care*, 2000, *31*, 3–14.

Berrick, J., Needell, B., and Barth, R. Kin as a family and child welfare resource. In R. Hegar and Scannapieco (Eds.), *Kinship foster care: Policy, practice and research*. New York: Oxford Press, 1999.

Beyene, Y., Becker, G., and Mayen, N. Perception of aging and sense of well-being among Latino elderly. *Journal of Cross-Cultural Gerontology*, 2002, *17*, 155–172.

Blando, J.A. Twice hidden: Older gay and lesbian couples, friends and intimacy. *Generations*, 2001, *25*, 87–89.

Blazer, D. "How do you feel about . . . ? Self perceptions of health and health outcomes in late life. Kleemeier Award lecture delivered at Annual Meeting of the Gerontological Society of America, November 18, 2006, Dallas, Texas.

Blieszner, R., and Adams, R.G. Problems with friends in old age. *Journal of Aging Studies*, 1998, *12*, 223–238.

Boaz, R.F., Hu, J., and Ye, Y. The transfer of resources from middle-aged children to functionally limited elderly parents: Providing time, giving money, sharing space. *The Gerontologist*, 1999, *39*, 648–657.

Bogard, R., and Spilka, B. Self-disclosure and marital satisfaction in mid-life and late-life remarriages. *International Journal of Aging and Human Development*, 1996, *42*, 161–172.

Bradbury, T.N., Fincham, F.D., and Bench, S.R.H. Research on the nature and determinants of marital satisfaction: A decade in review. *Journal of Marriage and Family Relations*, 2000, *62*, 964–980.

Brotman, S., Ryan, B., and Cormier, R. The health and social service needs of gay and lesbian elders and their families in Canada. *The Gerontologist*, 2003, *43*, 192–202.

Brown, L.B., Alley, G.R., Sarosy, S., Quarto, G., and Cook, T. Gay men: Aging well. *Journal of Gay and Lesbian Social Services*, 2001, *13*, 41–54.

Bryson, K., and Casper, L.M. *Current populations reports*. Washington, DC: U.S. Bureau of the Census. Accessed April 27, 2007, from http://www.census.gov.

Bryson, K., and Casper, L.M. *Coresident grandparents and grandchildren: Current populations reports: Special studies*. Washington, DC: U.S. Bureau of the Census, 2000, P23–P198.

Bureau of Labor Statistics. *The employment situation: September 2006*. Washington, DC: U. S. Department of Labor, 2006.

Burnette, D. Latino grandparents rearing grandchildren with special needs: Effects on depressive symptomatology. *Journal of Gerontological Social Work*, 2000, *33*, 1–16.

Burnette, D. Physical and emotional well-being of custodial grandparents in Latino families. *American Journal of Orthopsychiatry*, 1999, *69*, 305–318.

Butler, S. Older gays, lesbians, bisexuals and transgender persons. In B. Berkman (Ed.), *Handbook of social work in health and aging*. New York: Oxford, 2006.

Cahill, S., South, K., and Spade, J. *Public policy issues affecting gay, lesbian, bisexual and transgender elders*. New York: The Policy Institute of the National Gay and Lesbian Task Force, 2000.

Camp, C., Orsulic-Jeras, S., Lee, M., and Judge, K. Effects of a Montessori-based intergenerational program on engagement and affect for adult day care clients with dementia. In M. Wykle, P. Whitehouse, and D. Morris (Eds.), *Successful aging through the life span: Intergenerational issues in health*. New York: Springer, 2005.

Cantor, M. Family caregiving: Social care. In *Family caregiving: Agenda for the future*. San Francisco: American Society on Aging, 1994.

Calasanti, T., and Slevin, K. *Gender, social inequalities and aging*. Walnut Creek, CA: Altima, 2001.

Casper, L.M., and Bianchi, S.M. *Continuity and change in the American family*. Thousand Oaks, CA: Sage, 2002.

Chadiha, L.A., Miller-Cribbs, J.E., Rafferty, J., Adams, P., Pierce, R., and Kommidi, S. Urban and rural African American female caregivers' family reunion participation. *Marriage and Family Review*, 2005, *37*, 129–146.

Chan, C.G., and Elder, G.H. Matrilineal advantage in grandchild-grandparent relations. *The Gerontologist*, 2000, *40*, 179–190.

Chapple, M.J., Kippas, S., and Smith, G. "Semi-straight sort of sex:" Class and gay community attachment explored within a framework of homosexually active men. *Journal of Homosexuality*, 1998, *35*, 65–83.

Choi, N.G. The never-married and divorced elderly: Comparison of economic and health status, social support, and living arrangement. *Journal of Gerontological Social Work*, 1996, *26*, 3–25.

Cicirelli, V.G. Strengthening sibling relationships in the later years. In G.C. Smith, S. Tobin, E.A. Robertson-Tchabo, and P. Power (Eds.), *Strengthening aging families: Diversity in practice and policy.* Thousand Oaks, CA: Sage, 1995.

Clarke, E.J., Preston, M., Raskin, J., and Bengtson, V.L. Types of conflicts and tensions between older parents and adult children. *The Gerontologist,* 1999, *39,* 261–270.

Clunis, M., Fredriksen-Goldsen, K., Freeman, P., and Nystrom, N. (Eds.), *Lives of lesbian elders. Looking back, looking forward.* Binghamton, NY: Haworth Press, 2005.

Cohen, G.D. Marriage and divorce in later life (Editorial). *American Journal of Geriatric Psychiatry,* 1999, *7,* 185–187.

Cohen, S., Social relationships and health. *American Psychologist,* 2004, *59,* 676–684.

Cohen, S., Gottlieb, B.H., and Underwood, L.G. Social relationships and health: Challenges for measurement and intervention. *Advanced Mind Body Medicine,* 2001, *17,* 129–41.

Coleman, M.T., Looney, S., O'Brien, J., Ziegler, C., Pastorino, C.A., and Tumer, C. The "Eden Alternative." Findings after one year of implementation. *Journals of Gerontology, 2002, 57A,* M419–M421.

Combs, A. Pet therapy and increased socialization among elderly clients. *Kentucky Nurse,* 2002, *50,* 15–16.

Connidis, I.A. *Family ties and aging.* Thousand Oaks, CA: Sage, 2001.

Connidis, I.A., and Campbell, L.D. Closeness, confiding and contact among siblings in middle and late adulthood. *Journal of Family Issues,* 1995, *16,* 722–745.

Cook-Daniels, L. Lesbian, gay male, bisexual and transgendered elders: Elder abuse and neglect issues. *Journal of Elder Abuse and Neglect,* 1997, *9,* 35–49.

Copen, C., and Silverstein, M. Predictors of grandparent-grandchild closeness after parental divorce. *The Gerontologist,* 2004, *44,* 91–92.

Cox, C. Empowering African American custodial grandparents. *Social Work,* 2002, *47,* 262–267.

Cox, C., Brooks, L.R., and Valcarcel, C. Culture and caregiving: A study of Latino grandparents. In C. Cox (Ed.), *To grandmother's house we go and stay: Perspectives on custodial grandparents.* New York: Springer, 2000.

Cuddeback, G.S. Kinship family foster care: A methodological and substantive synthesis of research. *Children and Youth Services Review,* 2004, *26,* 623–639.

Czaja, S., Charness, N., Fisk, A., Hertzog, C., Nair, S., et al., Factors predicting the use of technology. Findings from the Center for Research and Education on Aging and Technology Enhancement (CREATE) *Psychology and Aging,* 2006, *21,* 333–352.

D'Augelli, A.R. and Grossman, A.H. Disclosure of sexual orientation, victimization and mental health among lesbian, gay and bisexual older adults. *Journal of Interpersonal Violence,* 2001, *16,* 1008–1027.

D'Augelli, A.R., Grossman, A.H., Hershberger, S.L., and O'Connell, T.S. Aspects of mental health among older lesbian, gay and bisexual adults. *Aging and Mental Health,* 2001, *5,* 149–158.

Davey, A., and Szinovacz, M.E. Dimensions of marital quality and retirement. *Journal of Family Issues,* 2003, *25,* 431–464.

Davies, C., and Williams, D. *Grandparent study.* Washington, DC: American Association of Retired Persons, 2002.

Davison, K.P., Pennebaker, J.W., and Dickerson, S.W. Who talks: The social psychology of illness support groups. *American Psychologist,* 2000, *55,* 205–217.

Davitt, J. Policy to protect the rights of older adults. In B. Berkman (Ed.), *Handbook of social work in health and aging.* New York: Oxford Press, 2006, 923–934.

DeMallie, D.A., North, C.S., and Smith, E.M. Psychiatric disorders among the homeless: A comparison of older and younger groups. *The Gerontologist,* 1997, *37,* 61–66.

Dembicki, D., and Anderson, J. Pet ownership may be a factor in improved health of the elderly. *Journal of Nutrition and the Elderly,* 1996, *15,* 15–31.

Department of Health and Human Services. *Trends in Health and Aging.* Washington, DC: 2006.

Dilworth-Anderson, P., Williams, I.C., and Gibson, B.E. Issues of race, ethnicity, and culture in caregiving research: A 20-year review. *The Gerontologist,* 2002, *42,* 237–272.

Doka, K.J. *Caregiving and loss: Family needs, professional responses.* Washington, DC: Hospice Foundation of America, 2001.

Doodson, L., and Morley, D. Understanding the roles of non-residential stepmothers. *Journal of Divorce and Remarriage,* 2006, *45,* 109–130.

Drew, L., and Silverstein, M. Intergenerational role investments of great-grandparents: Consequences for psychological well-being. *Ageing and Society,* 2004, *24,* 95–111.

Dubas, J.S. How gender moderates the grandparent-grandchild relationship. *Journal of Family Issues,* 2001, *22,* 407.

DuPertuis, L.L., Aldwin, C.M., and Basse, R. Does the source of support matter for different health outcomes? *Journal of Aging and Health,* 2001, *13,* 494–510.

Eheart, B.K., Power, M.B., and Hopping, D.E. Intergenerational programming for foster-adoptive families: Creating community at Hope Meadows. *Intergenerational Relationships,* 2003, *1,* 17–28.

Ehrenberg, M., and Smith S. Grandmother-grandchild contacts before and after an adult daughter's divorce. *Journal of Divorce and Remarriage,* 2003, *39,* 27.

Ehrle, G.M. Grandchildren as moderator variables in the family: Social, physiological and intellectual development of grandparents who are raising them. *Family Development and Intellectual Functions,* 2001, *12,* 223–241.

Elder., G.H., and Conger, R.D. *Children of the land: Adversity and success in rural America.* Chicago: University of Chicago Press, 2000.

Eng, P.M., Rimm, E.B., Fitzmaurice, G., and Kawachi, I. Social ties and change in social ties in relation to subsequent total and cause-specific mortality and coronary heart disease incidence in men. *American Journal of Epidemiology,* 2002, *155,* 700–709.

Everard, K.M., Lach, H.W., Fisher, E.B., and Baum, M.C. Relationship of activity and social support to the functional health of older adults. *Journals of Gerontology,* 2000, *55B,* S208–S212.

Federal Interagency Forum on Aging-related Statistics. *Older Americans 2006: Key indicators of well-being.* Washington, DC: Federal Interagency Forum on Aging, 2006.

Field, D. Continuity and change in friendships in advanced old age: Findings from the Berkeley older generation study. *International Journal of Aging and Human Development,* 1999, *48,* 325–346.

Fields, J., and Casper, L.M. America's families and living arrangements. *Current Population Reports.* Washington, DC: U.S. Census Bureau, 2001.

Findlay, RA. Interventions to reduce social isolation among older people: Where is the evidence? *Ageing and Society,* 2003, *23,* 647–658.

Fingerman, K. The role of offspring and in-laws in grandparents' ties to their grandchildren. *Journal of Family Issues,* 2004, *25,* 1026–1049.

Fredriksen-Goldsen, K., Muraco, A., Barrett, R, and Williams, M. Aging and sexual orientation: A 25-year review of the literature (1980–2005). *The Gerontologist,* in press.

Friedmann, E., and Thomas, S.A. Pet ownership, social support and one-year survival after acute myocardial infarction in the Cardiac Arrhythmia Suppression Trial (CAST). *American Journal of Cardiology,* 1995, *76,* 1213–1217.

Frisco, M.L., and Williams, K. Perceived housework equity, marital happiness and divorce in dual-earner households. *Journal of Family Issues,* 2003, *24,* 51–73.

Fuller-Thompson, E., and Minkler, M. The mental and physical health of grandmothers who are raising their grandchildren. *Journal of Mental Health and Aging,* 2000, *6,* 311–323.

Fuller-Thompson, E., and Minkler, M. American grandparents providing extensive child care to their grandchildren: Prevalence and profile. *The Gerontologist,* 2001, *41,* 201–209.

Furlong, M. Creating online communities for older adults. *Generations,* 1997, *21,* 33–35.

Gabbay, S., and Wahler, J. Lesbian aging: Review of a growing literature. *Journal of Gay and Lesbian Social Services,* 2002, *14,* 1–21.

Ganong, L., and Coleman, M. Patterns of exchange and intergenerational responsibilities after divorce and remarriage. *Journal of Aging Studies,* 2006, *20,* 265.

George, L.K. Perceived quality of life. In R. Binstock and L.K. George (Eds.), *Handbook of aging and the social sciences,* New York: Academic Press, 2006.

Giarrusso, R., Silverstein, M., and Bengtson, V.L. Family complexity and the grandparent role. *Generations,* 1996, *20,* 17–23.

Giarrusso, R., Silverstein, M., and Feng, D. Psychological costs and benefits of raising grandchildren: Evidence from a National Survey of Grandparents.

In C.B. Cox (Ed.), *To grandmother's house we go and stay: Perspectives on custodial grandparenting.* New York: Springer, 2000.

Giarrusso, R., Stallings, M., and Bengtson, V.L. The "intergenerational stake" hypothesis revisited: Parent-child differences in perceptions of relationships 20 years later. In V.L. Bengtson, K.W. Schaie, and L.M. Burton (Eds.), *Intergenerational issues in-aging: Effects of societal change.* New York: Springer, 1995.

Goldman, N., Korenman, S., and Weinstein, R. Marital status and health among the elderly. *Social Science and Medicine,* 1995, *40,* 1717–1730.

Goldscheider, F.K. Divorce and remarriage: Effects on the elderly population. *Reviews in Clinical Gerontology,* 1994, *4,* 258–259.

Gonyea, J. Midlife, multigenerational bonds, and caregiving. In R. Talley (Ed.), *Caregiving: Science to practice.* New York: Oxford Press, in press.

Goodman, C. Multigenerational triads in grandparent-headed families. *Journals of Gerontology,* 2003, *58B,* S281–S289.

Goodman, C., Potts, M, Pasztor, E., and Scorzo, D. Grandmothers as kinship caregivers: Private arrangements as compared to public child welfare oversight. *Children and Youth Services Review,* 2004, *26,* 287–305.

Grann, J.D. Assessment of emotions in older adults: Mood disorders, anxiety, psychological well-being, and hope. In R.L. Kane and R.A. Kane (Eds.), *Assessing older persons: Measures, meaning, and practical applications.* New York: Oxford Press, 2000.

Grossman, A.H. The virtual and actual identities of older lesbians and gay men. In M. Duberman (Ed.), *A queer world: The Center for Lesbian and Gay Studies Reader.* New York: New York University Press, 1997.

Grossman, A.H., D'Augelli, A.R., and O'Connell, T.S. Being lesbian, gay, bisexual and 60 or older in North America. *Journal of Gay and Lesbian Social Services,* 2001, *13,* 23–40.

Grossman, A.H., D'Augelli, A.R., and Hershberger, S.L. Social support networks of lesbian, gay and bisexual adults 60 years of age and older. *Journals of Gerontology,* 2000, *55B,* P171–O179.

Hagestad, G.O. Interdependent lives and relationships in changing times: A life course view of families and aging. In R.A. Settersten, Jr. (Ed.), *Invitation to the life course: Toward new understandings of later life.* Amityville, NY: Baywood, 2003.

Haglund, K. Parenting a second time around: Ethnography of African American grandmothers parenting grandchildren due to parental cocaine abuse. *Journal of Family Nursing,* 2000, *6,* 120–135.

Hamilton, G., Brown, S., Alonzo, T., Glover, M., Mersereau, Y., and Wilson, P. Building community for the long term: An intergenerational commitment. *The Gerontologist,* 1999, *39,* 235–238.

Hanson, E.J., Tetley, J., and Clarke, A. A multimedia intervention to support family caregivers. *The Gerontologist,* 1999, *39,* 736–741.

Harwood, J. Comparing grandchildren's and grandparent's stake in their relationship. *International Journal of Aging and Human Development,* 2001, *53,* 195–210.

Hayes, C. An observational study in developing an intergenerational shared site program: Challenges and insights. *Journal of Intergenerational Relations,* 2003, *1,* 113–132.

Hays, J.C., Gold, D.T., and Peiper, C.F. Sibling bereavement in late life. *Journal of Death and Dying,* 1997, *35,* 25–42.

Hayslip, B., and Kaminski, P. Grandparents raising their grandchildren. In R. K. Caputo (Ed.), *Challenges of aging in U.S. families: Policy and practice implications.* Binghamton, NY: The Haworth Press, 2005.

Hayslip, B. and Patrick, J. Custodial grandparent viewed from within a lifespan perspective. In B. Hayslip and J. Patrick (Eds.), *Working with custodial grandparents.* New York: Springer, 2003.

Hayslip, B., and Shore, R. J. Custodial grandparenting and mental health services. *Journal of Mental Health and Aging,* 2000, *6,* 367–384.

Healy, T. Culturally competent practice with elderly lesbians. *Geriatric Care Management Journal,* 2002, *12,* 9–13.

Hecht, R. No straight answers. *AARP The Magazine,* May–June 2004. Accessed November 29, 2006, from www.aarpmagazine.org/people/Articles/.

Heuveline, P., Timberlake, J.M. and Furstenberg, F.F., Jr. Shifting childbearing to single mothers: Results from 17 Western countries. *Population and Development Review,* 2003, *29,* 47–71.

Hilbourne, M. Living together full time? Middle class couples approaching retirement. *Aging and Society,* 1999, *19,* 161–183.

Hilton, J.M., and Macari, D.P. Grandparent involvement following divorce: A comparison in single-mother and single-father families. *Journal of Divorce and Remarriage,* 1997, *28,* 203–224.

Hobbs, F.B., and Damon, B.C. *65+ in the United States.* Washington, DC: U.S. Bureau of the Census, Current Population Reports, 1996.

Hogan, B., Linden, W., and Najarian, B. Social support interventions: Do they work? *Clinical Psychology Review,* 2002, *22,* 381–440.

Holtzman, R.E., Rebok, G.W., Saczynski, J.S., Kouzis, A.C. Doyle, K.W., and Eaton, W.W. Social network characteristics and cognition in middle-aged older adults. *Journals of Gerontology,* 2004, *59B,* P278–P283.

Hummert, M.L, and Morgan, M. Negotiating decisions in the aging family. In M.L. Hummert and J.F. Nussbaum, *Aging, communication and health.* Mahwah, NJ: Lawrence Erlbaum Associates, 2001.

Jakobsson. U., Hallberg, I.R., and Westergren, A. Overall and health related quality of life among the oldest in pain. *Quality of Life Research,* 2004, *13,* 125–136.

Johnson, R.A., and Meadows, R.G. Older Latinos, pets and health. *Western Journal of Nursing Research,* 2002, *24,* 609–620.

Johnson, R., Meadows, R., Haubner, J., and Sevedge, K. Human–animal interaction: A complementary/alternative medical intervention for cancer patients. *American Behavioral Scientist,* 2003, *47,* 55–69.

Jones, B.E. Is having the luck of growing old in the gay, lesbian, bisexual, transgender community good or bad luck? *Journal of Gay and Lesbian Social Services,* 2001, *13,* 13–14.

Jones, T.C. and Nystrom, N. Looking back . . . looking forward: Addressing the lives of lesbians 55 and older. *Journal of Women and Aging,* 2002, *14,* 59–76.

Joslin, D. *Invisible caregivers: Older adults raising children in the wake of HIV/AIDS.* New York: Columbia University Press, 2002.

Kalmijn, M. Shared friendship networks and the life course: Analysis of survey data on married and cohabiting couples. *Social Networks,* 2003, *25,* 232–249.

Kawachi, I., and Berkman, L.F. Social ties and mental health. *Journal of Urban Health: Bulletin of the New York Academy of Medicine,* 2001, *78,* 458–467.

Kelley, S.J., Whitley, D.M., Sipe, T.A., and Yorker, B. Psychological distress in grandmother kinship care providers: The role of resources, social support and physical health. *Child Abuse and Neglect,* 2000, *24,* 311–321.

Kelley, S.J., Yorker, B., Whitley, D., and Sipe, T. A multimodal intervention for grandparents raising grandchildren: Results of an exploratory study. *Child Welfare,* 2001, *LXXX,* 27–50.

Keyes, C.L. The exchange of emotional support with age and its relationship with emotional well-being by age. *Journals of Gerontology: Psychological Sciences,* 2002, *57B,* 518–525.

Kincade, J.E., Rabiner, D.J., Bernard, S.L., Woomert, A., Konrad, T.R., DeFrisse, G.H., and Ory, M.G. Older adults as a community resource: Results from the National Survey of Self-Care and Aging. *The Gerontologist,* 1996, *36,*474–482.

King, M. Elderly seek to grow old together, form new support groups. *The Seattle Times,* May 1, 2006, A1, A11.

King, V. The legacy of a grandparent's divorce: Consequences for ties between grandparents and grandchildren. *Journal of Marriage and the Family,* 2003, *65,* 170–183.

Kleyman, P. Families for the 21st century: A multigenerational affair. *Aging Today,* San Francisco American Society on Aging, 2006.

Kolomer, S., McCallion, P., and Janicki, M. African American grandmother carers of children with disabilities: Predictors of depressive symptoms. *Journal of Gerontological Social Work,* 2002, *37,* 45–64.

Krause, N., Church-based social support and mortality. *Journals of Gerontology,* 2006, *61B,* S140–S146.

Krause, N. Social relationships in late life. In R. Binstock and L. George (Eds.), *Handbook of aging and the social sciences* (6th ed.). New York: Academic Press, 2006.

Krause, N. Stressors in highly valued roles, meaning in life and the physical health status of older adults. *Journals of Gerontology,* 2004, *59B,* S87–S117.

Krause, N., and Shaw, B. Giving social support to others, socioeconomic status and changes in self-esteem in late life. *Journals of Gerontology,* 2000, *55B,* S323–S333.

Kreider, R. *Number, timing and duration of marriages and divorces: 2001. Current Population Reports.* Washington, DC: U.S. Bureau of the Census, 2005.

Kropf, N., and Yoon, E. Grandparents raising grandchildren. Who are they? In B. Berkman (Ed.), *Handbook of social work in health and aging.* New York: Oxford Press, 2006.

Kruk, E. Grandparent-grandchild contact loss: Findings from a study of "Grandparent Rights" members. *Canadian Journal on Aging,* 1995, *14,* 737–754.

Kulik, L. Continuity and discontinuity in marital life after retirement: Life orientations, gender role ideology, intimacy, and satisfaction. *Families in Society,* May–June 1999, *80,* 286–294.

Kurdek, L.A. What do we know about gay and lesbian couples? *Current Directions in Psychological Science,* 2005, *14,* 251.

Lambert, S. Lesbian and gay families: What we know and where to go from here. *The Family Journal: Counseling and Therapy for Couples and Families,* 2005, *13,* 43–51.

Lang, F.R., and Cartensen, L.L. Close emotional relationships late in life: Further support for proactive aging in the social domain. *Psychology and Aging,* 1994, *9,* 315–324.

Lansford, J.E., Sherman, A.M., and Antonucci, T.C. Satisfaction with social networks: An examination of socioemotional selectivity theory across cohorts. *Psychology and Aging,* 1998, *13,* 544–552.

Lefley H.P., and Hatfield, A.B. Helping parental caregivers and mental health consumers cope with parental aging and loss. *Psychiatric Services,* March 1999, *50,* 369–375.

Lewis, L. Intergenerational programs that really work. *Caring for the Ages.* American Medical Directors Association, Columbia, MD, 2006, 1–7.

Liang, J., Krause, N., and Bennett, J. Is giving better than receiving? *Psychology and Aging,* 2001, *16,* 511–523.

Litwin, H. The association of disability, sociodemographic background, and social network type in later life. *Journal of Aging and Health,* 2003, *15,* 391–408.

Lowenthal, M.F., and Haven, C. Interaction and adaptation. *American Sociological Review,* 1968, *33,* 20–30.

Lubben, J., Blozik, E. Gillmann, G., Iliffe, S., Kruse, W., Beck, J., and Stuck, A. Performance of an abbreviated version of the Lubben Social Network Scale among three European community-dwelling older adult populations. *The Gerontologist,* 2006, *46,* 505–513.

Lubben, J.E., and Gironda, M.W. *Centrality of social ties to the health and well-being of older adults.* New York: Springer, 2003a.

Lubben, J.E. and Gironda, M.W. Measuring social networks and assessing their benefits. In C. Phillipson, G. Allan, and D. Morgan (Eds.), *Social networks and social exclusion.* Hants, England: Ashgate, 2003b.

Lyyra, T.M., and Heikkinen, RL. Perceived social support and mortality in older people. *Journals of Gerontology,* 2006, *61B,* S147–S153.

MacDonald, B., with C. Rich. *Look me in the eye: Old women, aging and ageism.* Denver: Spinsters Ink Books, 2001.

Martinez, I.L. The elder in the Cuban American family: Making sense of the real and ideal. *Journal of Comparative Family Studies,* 2003, *33,* 359–370.

Martin, D., and Lyon, P. Positively gay: New approaches to gay and lesbian life. In B. Berzon (Ed.), *Positively gay: New approaches to gay and lesbian life.* Berkeley, CA: Celestial Arts, 2001.

McCallion, P. Older adults as caregivers to persons with developmental disabilities. In B. Berkman (Ed.), *Handbook of social work in health and aging:* New York: Oxford Press, 2006.

McFarland, P.L., and Sanders, S. A pilot study about the needs of older gays and lesbians: What social workers need to know. *Journal of Gerontological Social Work,* 2003, *40,* 67–80.

McLanahan, S., Garfinkel, I., Reichman, N., Teitler, J., Carlson, M., and Audiger, C.N. *The fragile families and child well-being study: Baseline national report.* Princeton, NJ: Princeton University, 2003.

MetLife Mature Market Institute. *Out and aging: The MetLife study of lesbian and gay baby boomers.* Westport, CT: Metropolitan Life Insurance, 2006.

Metropolitan Life Insurance Company. *MetLife study of employer costs for working caregivers.* Westport, CT: Metropolitan Life Insurance, 1998.

Miller, B., and Cafasso, L. Gender differences in caregiving: Fact or artifact? *The Gerontologist,* 1992, *32,* 498–507.

Miller, B., Campbell, R., Farron, C., Kaufman, J., and Davis, L. Race, control, mastery, and caregiver distress. *Journals of Gerontology,* 1995, *50B,* S376–S382.

Miller, R.B., Hemesath, K., and Nelson, B. Marriage in middle and later life. In T.D. Hargrave and S.M. Hanna (Eds.), *The aging family: New visions in theory, practice, and reality.* New York: Brunner/Mazel, 1997.

Minkler, M. Intergenerational households headed by grandparents: Context, realities, and implications for policy. *Journal of Aging Studies,* 1999, *13,* 199–218.

Minkler, M., Berrick, J.D., and Needell, B. Impacts of welfare reform on California grandparents raising grandchildren: Reflections from the field. *Journal of Aging and Social Policy,* 1999, *10,* 45–63.

Minkler, M., and Fuller-Thomson, E. Depression in grandparents raising grandchildren. *Archives of Family Medicine,* 1997, *6,* 445–452.

Moen, P., Erickson, M.A., and Dempster-McClain, D. Social role identities among older adults in a continuing care retirement community. *Research on Aging,* 2000, *22,* 559–579.

Mohr, R. Reflections on golden pond. In P. Papp (Ed.), *Couples on the fault line: New directions for therapists.* New York: Guilford, 2000.

Moren-Cross, J., and Lin, N. Social networks and health. In R. Binstock and L. George (Eds.), *Handbook of aging and the social sciences* (6th ed.). New York: Academic Press, 2006.

Morrow, D.F. Older gays and lesbians: Surviving a generation of hate and violence. *Journal of Gay and Lesbian Social Services,* 2001, *13,* 151–169.

Morrow-Howell, N., Sherraden, M., Hinterlong, J., and Rozario, P.A. *The productive engagement of older adults: Impact on later-life well-being.* St. Louis: Longer Life Foundation, 2001.

Morrow-Kondos, D., Weber, J.A., Cooper, K., and Hesser, J.L. Becoming parents again: Grandparents raising grandchildren. *Journal of Gerontological Social Work,* 1997, *28,* 35–46.

Mui, A.C., and Burnette, J.D. A comparative profile of frail elderly persons living alone and those living with others. *Journal of Gerontological Social Work,* 1994, *21,* 5–26.

Musil, C.M. Health of grandmothers as caregivers: A ten month follow up. *Journal of Women and Aging,* 2000, *12,* 129–145.

Musil, C.M., Warner, C., Zauszniewski J., Jeanblanc, A., and Kercher, K. Grandmothers, caregiving and fam-

ily functioning. *Journals of Gerontology,* 2006, *69B,* 89–98.

Musil, C.M., Youngblut, J., Ahn, S., and Curry, V. Parenting stress: A comparison of grandmother caretakers and mothers. *Journal of Mental Health and Aging,* 2002, *8,* 197–210.

Mueller, M., and Elder, G. Family contingencies across the generations: Grandparent-grandchild relationships in holistic perspective. *Journal of Marriage and Family,* 2003, *65,* 404–417.

National Academy on an Aging Society. *Helping the elderly with activity limitations: Caregiving, 7.* Washington, DC: author, 2000.

National Institute on Aging. *An aging world.* Washington, DC: U.S. Census Bureau, 2001.

National Law Center on Homelessness and Poverty. Key factors concerning homeless person in America, 2006. Accessed from www.nlchp.org/FA_HAPIA/Home lessnessFactsJune2006.pdf.

National Research Council. *New horizons in health: An integrative approach.* Washington, DC: National Academy Press, 2001.

Neugarten, B. *Personality in middle and late life: Empirical studies by Bernice L. Neugarten in collaboration with Howard Berkowitz and others.* New York: Atherton Press, 1964.

Neugarten, B., and Weinstein, K. The changing American grandparent. *Journal of Marriage and the Family,* 1964, *26,* 199–204.

Nocon, A., and Pearson, M. The roles of friends and neighbors in providing support for older people. *Ageing and society,* 2000, *20,* 341–367.

Orel, N.A. Gay, lesbian and bisexual elders: Expressed needs and concerns across focus groups. *Journal of Gerontological Social Work,* 2004, *43,* 57–77.

Pienta, A., Hayward, M.D., and Jenkins, K.R. Health and marriage in later life. *Journal of Family Issues,* 2000, *21,* 559–586.

Pinquart, M., and Sorensen, S. Influences of socioeconomic status, social networks, and competence on subjective well-being in later life: A meta-analysis. *Psychology and Aging,* 2001, *14,* 187–224.

Population Resource Center. *Executive summary: The changing American family.* Washington, DC: 2006, www.prcdc.org/summaries/family/famly.html.

Porter, E.J., Ganong, L.H., and Armer, J.M. The church, family and kin: An older rural black woman's support network and preferences for care providers. *Qualitative Health Research,* 2000, *10,* 452–470.

Raina, P., Walther-Toews, D., Bennett, B., Woodworth, C., and Abernathy, T. Influence of companion animals on the physical and psychological health of older people: An analysis of a one-year longitudinal study. *Journal of the American Geriatrics Society,* 1999, *47,* 323–329.

Reid, J.D. Development in late life: Older lesbian and gay lives. In A.R. D' Augelli and C.J. Patterson (Eds.), *Lesbian, gay and bisexual identities across the lifespan: Psychological perspectives.* New York: Oxford Press, 1995.

Reitzes, D.C., and Mutran, E.J. Grandparent identity, intergenerational identity and well-being. *Journals of Gerontology,* 2004a, *59B,* S213–S220.

Reitzes, D.C., and Mutran, E.J. Grandparenthood: Factors influencing frequency of grandparent–grandchildren contact and grandparent role satisfaction. *Journals of Gerontology,* 2004b, *59B,* S9–S16.

Ren, X.S., Skinner, K., Lee, A., and Kazis, L. Social support, social selection and self-assessed health status: Results from the veteran's health study in the United States. *Social Science and Medicine,* 1999, *48,* 1721–1734.

Reynolds, W. Marital satisfaction in later life: An examination of equity, equality, and reward theories. *International Journal of Aging and Human Development,* 1995, *40,* 155–173.

Riley, M.W., and Riley, J. Structural lag: Past and future. In M.W. Riley, R.L. Kahn, and A. Foner (Eds.), *Age and structural lag: Society's failure to provide meaningful opportunities in work, family and leisure.* New York: John Wiley & Sons, 1994.

Roan, C.L., and Riley, R. Intergenerational co residence and contact: A longitudinal analysis of adult children's response to their mother's widowhood. *Journal of Marriage and the Family,* 1996, *58,* 708–717.

Roberto, K.A., Allen, K.R., and Blieszner, R. Grandfathers' perceptions and expectations of relationships with their adult grandchildren. *Journal of Family Issues,* 2001, *22,* 407–426.

Roberto, K.A., and Stroes, S.J. Grandchildren and grandparents: Roles, influences, and relationships. In J. Hendricks (Ed.), *The ties of later life.* Amityville, NY: Baywood, 1995.

Robles, T.F., and Kiecolt-Glaser, J.K. The physiology of marriage: Pathways to health. *Physiology and Behavior,* 2003, *79,* 409–416.

Rogers, S.J., and Amato, P.R. Have changes in gender relations affected marital quality? *Social Forces,* 2000, *79,* 731–753.

Rook, K.S. *Stressful aspects of older adults' social relationships: Current theory and research.* New York: Hemisphere, 1990.

Rosenfeld, D. Identity work among lesbian and gay elderly. *Journal of Aging Studies,* 1999, *13,* 121–144.

Saito, T., Okada, M., Ueji, M., Kikuchi, K., and Kano, K. Relationship between keeping a companion animal and instrumental activity of daily living: A study of Japanese elderly living at home in Satomi Village. *Nippon Koshu Eisei Zasshi,* 2001, *48,* 47–55.

Salari, S.M. Intergenerational partnerships in adult day centers: Importance of age-appropriate environments and behaviors. *The Gerontologist,* 2002, *42,* 321–333.

Scharlach, A., Peer counselor training for nursing home residents. *The Gerontologist,* 1988, *28,* 499–502.

Scharlach, A., and Fredriksen-Goldsen, K. *Families and work: New directions in the twenty first century.* New York: Oxford University Press, 2001.

Schieman, S., and Meersman, S. Neighborhood problems and health among older adults: Received and donated social support and the sense of mastery as effect modifiers. *Journals of Gerontology,* 2004, *59B,* S89–S97.

Seeman, T.E. Health promoting effects of friends and family on health outcomes in older adults. *American Journal of Health Promotion,* 2000, *14,* 362–370.

Seeman, T.E., Singer, B.H., Ryff, C.D., Love, G.D., and Levy-Storms, L. (2002). Social relationships, gender and allostatic load across two age cohorts. *Psychosomatic Medicine,* 2002, *64,* 395–406.

Segrist, K. A computer training program for older adults: Identifying and overcoming barriers to continued computer usage. *Activities, Adaptation and Aging,* 2004, *28,* 13–26.

Shye, D., Mullooly, J.P., Freeborn, D.K., and Pope, C.R. Gender differences in the relationship between social network support and mortality: A longitudinal study of an elderly cohort. *Social Science and Medicine,* 1995, *41,* 935–947.

Silverstein, M., and Angelelli, J. Older parents' expectations of moving closer to their children. *Journals of Gerontology*, 1998, *53B*, S153–S163.

Silverstein, M., Conroy, S.J., Wang, H., Giarrusso, R., and Bengtson, V. Reciprocity in parent-child relations over the adult life course. *Journals of Gerontology*, 2002, *57B*, S3–S13.

Silverstein, M., and Marenco, A. How Americans enact the grandparent role across the family life course. *Journal of Family Issues*, 2001, *22*, 493–522.

Simmons, T., and Dye, J. *Grandparents living with grandchildren: 2000.* Washington, DC: US Census Bureau, 2003.

Skilton-Sylvester, E., and Garcia, A. Intergenerational programs to address the challenge of immigration. *Generations*, 1998/99, *22*, 58–63.

Slusher, M.P., Mayer, C.J., and Dunke, R.E. Gays and Lesbians Older and Wiser (GLOW): A support group for older gay people. *The Gerontologist*, 1996, *36*, 118–123.

Smith, C.J. Grandparents raising grandchildren: Emerging program and policy issues for the 21st century. *Journal of Gerontological Social Work*, 2000, *34*, 81–94.

Smith, C.J., Beltran, A., Butts, D., and Kingson, E.R. Grandparents raising grandchildren: Emerging program and policy issues for the 21st century. *Journal of Gerontological Social Work*, 2000, *34*, 81–94.

Smith, D., and Moen, P. Spousal influence on retirement: His, her and their perceptions. *Journal of Marriage and the Family*, 1998, *60*, 734–744.

Smith, G.C., Tobin, S.S., and Fullmer, E.M. Assisting older families with lifelong disabilities. In G.C. Smith, S. Tobin, E.A. Robertson-Tchabo, and P. Power (Eds.), *Strengthening aging families: Diversity in practice and policy,* Thousand Oaks, CA: Sage, 1995.

Smith, H., and Calvert, J. *Opening doors: Working with older lesbians and gay men.* London: Aging Concern, 2001.

Smith, P.R., Bisexuality: Reviewing the basics, debunking the stereotypes of professionals in aging. *Outward:* Newsletter of LGAIN, 2002, 8, 2, 8.

Soliz, J., and Harwood, J. Shared family identity, age salience and intergroup contact: Investigation of the grandparent-grandchild relationships. *Communication Monographs*, 2006, *73*, 87–107.

Stephens, M.A., and Franks, M. Spillover between daughters' role as caregiver and wife: Interference or enhancement? *Journals of Gerontology*, 1995, *50B*, P9–P17.

Stevens, N.L., Camille, M.S., Martina, M.A., and Westerhof, G.J. Meeting the need to belong: Predicting effects of a friendship enrichment program for older women. *The Gerontologist*, 2006, *46*, 495–502.

Stitch, S.S. Stories to keep. *Newsweek,* November 11, 2002, p. A3.

Strom, R.D., Buki, L.P., and Strom, S.K. Intergenerational perceptions of English-speaking and Spanish-speaking Mexican-American grandparents. *International Journal of Aging and Human Development*, 1997, *45*, 1–21.

Strom, R.D. and Strom, S.K. Goals for grandparent caregivers and support groups. In B. Hayslip and R. Goldberg-Glen (Eds.), *Grandparents raising grandchildren: Theoretical, empirical and clinical perspectives.* New York: Springer, 2000.

Stroup, A.L., and Pollock, G.E. Economic well being among white elderly divorced. *Journal of Divorce and Remarriage*, 1999, *31*, 53–68.

Subramanian, S.V., Kubzansky, L., Berkman, L., Fay, M., and Kawachi, I. Neighborhood effects on the self-rated health of elders: Uncovering the relative importance of structural and service-related neighborhood environments. *Journals of Gerontology*, 2006, *61B*, S153–S160.

Szinovacz, M.E., DeViney, S., and Atkinson, M.P. Effects of surrogate parenting on grandparents' well-being. *Journals of Gerontology*, 1999, *54B*, S376–S388.

Taylor, R., and Chatters, L. Extended family networks of older black adults. *Journals of Gerontology*, 1991, *46B*, S210–S218.

Temkin-Greener, H., Bajorska, A., Peterson, D.R., Kunitz, S.J., Gross, D., Williams, T.F., et al., Social support and risk-adjusted mortality in a frail older population. *Medical Care*, 2006, *42*, 779–788.

Tennstedt, S. *Family caregiving in an aging society.* Washington, DC: Administration on Aging 1999, Symposium.

Testa, M.F., and Slack, K.S. The gift of kinship foster care. *Children and Youth Services Review,* 2002, *24*, 79–108.

Thorpe, R.J., Simonsick, M., Ayonayon, H., Satterfield, S., et al. Dog walking behavior and maintaining mobility in later life. *Journal of the American Geriatric Society,* 2006, *54,* 1419.

Trafford, A. Power to the grandparents. *Washington Post,* November 1, 2006, 1.

Trenshaw, C. *A harvest of years: A PeerSpirit guide for proactive aging circles.* Langley, WA: PeerSpirit, 2004.

Trute, B. Grandparents of children with developmental disabilities: Intergenerational support and family well-being. *Families in Society,* 2003, *84,* 119–126.

Tucker, J.S., Friedman, H.S., Tsai, C.M., and Martin, L.R. Playing with pets and longevity among older people. *Psychology and Aging,* 1995, *10,* 3–7.

Turvey, C.L., Carney, C., Arndt, S., Wallace, R.B., and Herzog, R. Conjugal loss and syndromal depression in a sample of elders aged 70 years and older. *American Journal of Psychiatry,* 1999, *156,* 1596–1601.

Uchino, B.N. *Social support and physical health: Understanding the health consequences of relationships:* New Haven, CT: Yale University Press, 2004.

Uhlenberg, P. The burden of aging: A theoretical framework for understanding the shifting balance of caregiving and care receiving vs. cohort ages. *The Gerontologist,* 1996, *36,* 761–767.

Uhlenberg, P. Historical forces shaping grandparent-grandchild relationships: Demography and beyond. *Health and Medical Complete,* 2004, *24,* 77.

Uhlenberg, P., and Kirby, J.B. Grandparenthood over time: Historical and demographic trends. In M.E. Szinovacz (Ed.), *Handbook on grandparenthood.* Westport, CT: Greenwood Press, 1998.

Umberson, D., and Williams, K. Marital quality, health and aging: Gender equity? *Journals of Gerontology,* 2005, *60B,* 109–113.

Umberson, D., Williams, K., Powers, D.A., Chen, M.D., and Campbell, A. As good as it gets? A life course perspective on marital quality. *Social Forces,* 2005, *84,* 493–511.

Umberson, D., Williams, K., Powers, D.A., Liu, H., and Needham, B. You make me sick: Marital quality and health over the life course. *Journal of Health and Social Behavior,* 2006, *47,* 1–16.

U.S. Bureau of the Census. *Grandparents living with grandchildren: Census 2000 Brief.* Washington, DC: U.S. Government Printing Office, 2003b, 1–10.

U.S. Bureau of the Census. Marital status and living arrangements. *Current Population Surveys.* Washington, DC, 2003a.

U.S. Bureau of the Census. *Multigenerational households for the United States and Puerto Rico: 2001.* Accessed from http://www.census.population/ cen2000/phc_t17.pdf.

U.S. Census Bureau. Median age of the total population: 2005. Accessed October 2006a, http://www. factfinder.census.gov.

U.S. Census Bureau. Accessed October 1, 2006b, http://www.census.gov/cgi-bin/ipc/idbagg.

U.S. Bureau of the Census. *Statistical Abstract of the United States.* Washington, DC: 2006.

Van Tilburg, T. Losing and gaining in old age: Changes in personal network size and social support in a four-year longitudinal study. *Journals of Gerontology,* 1998, *53B,* S313–S323.

Wahler, J.J., and Gabbay, S.G. Gay male aging: A review of the literature. *Journal of Gay and Lesbian Social Services,* 1997, *6,* 1–20.

Waldrop, D., and Weber, J. From grandparent to caregiver: The stress and satisfaction of raising grandchildren. *Families in Society: The Journal of Contemporary Human Services,* 2001, *82,* 461–472.

Wallace, G. Grandparent caregivers: Emerging issues in elder law and social work practice. *Journal of Gerontological Social Work,* 2001, *34,* 127–134.

Ward, R.A., and Spitze, G.D. Marital implications of parent-adult child coresidence: A longitudinal view. *Journals of Gerontology,* 2004, *59B,* S2–S8.

Weinberg, J. Caregiving, age and class in the skeleton of the welfare state: 'And Jill came tumbling after.' In M. Minkler and C.L. Estes (Eds.), *Critical gerontology: Perspectives from political and moral economy.* Amityville, NY: Baywood, 1998.

Wethington, E., Moen, P., Glasgow, N., and Pillemer, K. Multiple roles, social integration, and health. In P. Moon, K. Pillemer, E. Wethington, and N. Glasgow (Eds.), *Social integration in the second half of life.* Baltimore: Johns Hopkins University Press, 2000.

Whitehouse, C., Fallcreek, S., and Whitehouse, P. Using a learning environment to promote intergenerational relationships and successful aging. In M. Wykle, P. Whitehouse, and D. Morris (Eds.), *Successful aging through the life span:*

Intergenerational issues in health. New York: Springer, 2005.

Whitley, D.M., Kelley, S.J., and Sipe, T.A. Grandmothers raising grandchildren: Are they at increased risk for health problems? *Health and Social Work,* 2001, *26,* 105–114.

Willis, S. Technology and learning in current and future generations of elders. *Generations,* 2006, Summer, 44–48.

Wilmouth, J.M. Unbalanced social exchanges and living arrangement transitions among older adults. *The Gerontologist,* 2000, *40,* 64–74.

Wohl, E., Lahner, J., and Jooste, J. Group process among grandparents raising grandchildren. In B. Hayslip and J. Patrick (Eds.), *Working with custodial grandparents.* New York: Springer, 2002.

Wojciechowski, W.C. Issues in caring for older lesbians. *Journal of Gerontological Nursing,* 1998, *24,* 28–33.

Wood, V., and Robertson, J. The significance of grandparenthood. In J. Gubruim (Ed.), *Time, roles and self in old age.* New York: Human Sciences Press, 1976.

Wu, Z., and Pollard, M.S. Social support among unmarried childless elderly persons. *Journals of Gerontology,* 1998, *53B,* S324–S335.

Yange, L., Krampe, R.T., and Baltes, P.B. Basic forms of cognitive plasticity extended into the oldest-old: Retest learning, age and cognitive functioning. *Psychology and Aging,* 2006, *21,* 372–378.

Yoakam, J. Playing bingo with the best of them: Community initiated programs for older gay and lesbian adults. *Journal of Gay and Lesbian Social Services,* 1997, *6,* 27.

Yoakam, J.R. Beyond the wrinkle room: Challenging ageism in gay male culture. *Dimensions.* San Francisco: ASA Mental Health and Aging Network, 1999, *3,* 7.

Zasloff, R.C., and Kidd, A.H. Loneliness and pet ownership among single women. *Psychological Reports,* 1994, *75,* 747–752.

Zodikoff, B.D. Services for lesbian, gay, bisexual and transgender older adults. In B. Berkman (Ed.), *Handbook of social work in health and aging.* New York: Oxford Press, 2006.

10

Opportunities and Challenges of Informal Caregiving

This chapter addresses informal family caregiving, including

- Benefits and costs of caregiving
- Objective and subjective burden
- The gendered nature of family care
- Partners as caregivers
- Adult children as caregivers
- Caregivers in families of color
- Caregivers of elders with dementia, especially Alzheimer's disease
- Policies and programs to support family caregivers
- Caregivers' use of formal services and informal support networks
- Elder mistreatment
- Placement in a nursing home
- Direct care workers in long-term care

As noted in Chapter 9, the majority of long-term care to adults age 65 and over is provided not in nursing homes, but informally and privately, at little or no public cost, within elders' homes or other community-based settings. Over 80 percent of older adults with limitations in three or more activities of daily living (ADL) are able to live in the community primarily because of informal assistance. Among elders in the community, only 8 percent rely exclusively on formal care, 14 percent use a combination of informal and paid assistance, while nearly 80 percent receive care solely from family, friends, and neighbors. The availability of such supports can determine whether elders can remain at home; 50 percent of those with long-care needs but no informal caregiving supports are in nursing homes, compared to only 7 percent of those who have

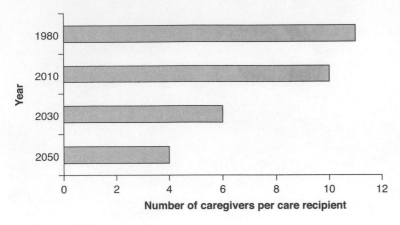

FIGURE 10.1 **The Shrinking Pool of Potential Caregivers**
SOURCE: U.S. Census Bureau, 2006.

informal care supports (Family Caregiving Alliance, 2006b; O'Brien and Elias, 2004; Schmieding, 2006; Thompson, 2004). The growing demand for such informal assistance is illustrated in Figure 10.1.

Who Are Informal Caregivers?

The terms *family* and **informal caregiving** are often used interchangeably, although informal caregivers also encompass friends, neighbors and even acquaintances. **Caregiving**, whether informal or formal, denotes supportive, non-medical, mostly low-tech services, such as help with bathing or eating, and some medical services, such as administering medications and attending to wounds (Schmieding, 2006). The primary forms of care provided by families are:

- emotional support
- instrumental activities inside and outside the home (e.g., transportation, meal preparation, shopping)
- personal care (e.g., bathing, feeding, dressing)
- contacting and monitoring agencies for services

The vast majority of family caregivers help older relatives daily; 50 percent assist with one or more ADLs, most often getting in and out of bed and chairs and getting dressed, and 80 percent with three or more IADLs, primarily with transportation, grocery shopping, and housework (National Alliance for Caregiving and AARP, 2004). The type and extent of family care is largely determined by the older adult's functional status, intensity of needed care, co-residence, and the caregiver's gender.

The number of family caregivers is estimated at 28.8 million. On average, family caregivers provide care for 21 hours per week and for more than four years, with 33 percent providing care for five years or longer (Arno, 2006; National Alliance for Caregiving and AARP, 2004; Wakabayashi and Donato, 2004). Not surprisingly, the number of hours of care each week and the length of care increase for those caring for persons with dementia. The average caregiver is age 46, female, married, and working outside the home earning an income of $35,000 (Family Caregiver Alliance, 2006b). However, caregiving for elders occurs across the life course; a growing number of young caregivers, ages 8 to 18, are helping parents or grandparents with activities of daily living as well as caregivers who are in their 60s or even 70s (National Alliance for Caregiving and United Hospital Funds, 2005).

Even though families have always been the primary caregivers of elders, family care was perceived by policy makers as nonexistent and by researchers as largely invisible until the mid-1980s. Although Shanas's groundbreaking research (1979) refuted the prevailing social myth of families' alienation from their elders, policy makers and frequently the general public still assumed that many families abandoned their elders to institutional care. After three decades of caregiver research and numerous testimonials regarding care demands, the central role played by families in the lives of elders with chronic illness is now widely recognized, and the term *family caregiver* is used by policy makers and the popular press (Gonyea, in press).

Families' patterns of support are characterized by complexity and diversity in terms of geographic proximity, gender, socioeconomic class, sexual orientation, ethnic minority status, family structure, and the history and nature of the relationship between caregiver and care recipient (Fredriksen-Goldsen, 1999, in press; Karlawash et al., 2001; Martin-Matthews, 2000). Distance—both geographic and emotional—often inhibits family members' provision of care. Among primary family caregivers, 97 percent live within an hour of the elder and nearly 65 percent of them visit care recipients at least an hour a week. But among the remainder, an estimated 5 million caregivers who live more than an hour away, only 16 percent visit an hour a week. Not surprisingly, caregivers at a geographic distance are more likely to spend their time arranging for services, checking that care is provided, and managing finances than providing personal care (MetLife, 2004; Parker, Church, and Toseland, 2006). Emotional distance in the caregiving dyad may have a greater impact on quality of care than physical. It may occur when caring for a partner or parent after years of conflictual relationships and family disruption, neglect, abuse, or separation. With growing rates of divorce, adult children may face the challenge of caring for parents who did not care for them as children. As noted in Chapter 9, changes in family relationships through divorce

and remarriage can negatively affect interaction with children—especially for men—and may limit adult children's availability as potential sources of support in old age. The effects of the nature of the care dyad, gender, ethnic minority status, and sexual orientation on caregiving are discussed more fully below.

Costs and Benefits of Informal Care

For Society

Because of the many hours of unpaid care provided by family, it is not surprising that informal caregiving saves the American health care system substantial dollars; the value of such care is estimated at $306 billion. If informal supports were unavailable, total long-term care costs would more than double (Arno, 2006).

While informal care is not a new phenomenon, demographic and social changes are intensifying demands on families to provide more complex care for longer periods of time and for multiple family members (Bengtson, 2001). These changes include the rapid growth of the oldest-old with chronic illness and disability, more women employed outside the home, more complex family structures (e.g., multigenerational, single-parent, GLBT "families of choice," blended families and skipped-generation households), and increasing racial and economic inequities. These are compounded by changes in managed care and other cost-cutting health care measures, particularly to Medicaid. In addition, families are increasingly expected to provide both "high-tech" and "high-touch" care, because of policies that provide incentives to discharge Medicare patients quickly from hospitals. As a result, families, who typically are unprepared for caregiving generally, often must also face the challenge of providing medically oriented acute care along with post-acute and

---

SUMMARY OF SOURCES OF CAREGIVER STRESS

Financial

- direct costs of care, such as home care equipment and medicine
- travel costs for long-distance caregivers
- reduced hours (and income) at work
- early retirement
- absenteeism and disruptions at work
- reduced productivity at work
- missed opportunities in career
- inadequate accommodations at the workplace

Physical

- health problems (headaches, stomach disturbances, and weight changes)
- use of prescription drugs and health services
- sleep disorders and exhaustion
- neglect of self and others
- increased morbidity and mortality

Emotional

- grief, loss, and hopelessness
- guilt, anger, resentment, and denial
- giving up time for oneself (and family)
- strained social and family relationships
- social isolation
- worry and anxiety
- feelings of being alone and isolated
- negative attitudes or behaviors toward care recipient (anger)
- depression

---

rehabilitative care, such as intravenous drug therapy, ventilator assistance, and wound care (Stone, 2000).

For Informal Caregivers

Of greater concern to gerontologists and geriatricians are the costs and negative consequences experienced by caregivers; these costs are conceptualized as primary and secondary stressors that typically result in objective and subjective burden. **Primary stressors** are events that derive directly from the elder's illness, such as cognitive deficits

and behavioral problems. **Secondary stressors** are not secondary in terms of their importance, but are so called because they do not arise directly from the older person's illness. Common secondary stressors are role strains and deterioration of the caregivers' sense of mastery, self-esteem, and competence (Family Caregiver Alliance, 2006b). These stressors create a sense of burden:

> **Objective burden** refers to the daily physical demands, tasks, and behavioral phenomena of caregiving: the older relative's symptomatic behaviors, disruptions of family life and roles, and legal, employment, health, and mental health problems.
>
> **Subjective burden** encompasses the feelings and emotions aroused in family caregivers, such as grief, anger, guilt, worry, tension, loneliness, and sadness.

The caregiver's individual appraisal of the situation or subjective burden appears to be more salient than objective burden or the actual tasks performed. This is consistent with findings in Chapter 9 on how perceptions of social support are more important to quality of life than the actual support given. Similarly, caregiving stress is multidimensional, and not assessed or modified by focusing on only one cause or manifestation of stress (Family Caregiver Alliance, 2006b; Zarit and Leitsch, 2001). On the other hand, living with the care recipient, being a woman, coping with the elder's behavioral problems, especially those associated with dementia, and long hours of intensive levels of care without any break are associated with increased caregiver stress (Chappel and Reid, 2002; Savundranagam, Hummert and Montgomery, 2005). Families experience costs or burdens in three primary areas:

1. *Physical and mental health outcomes:* A growing body of evidence documents that increases in caregiving stress are related to poor

health outcomes over time (Beach et al., 2005; Cannuscio et al., 2002; Kiecolt-Glaser and Glaser, 2003; Lee, Colditz, Berkman, and Kawachi, 2003; Schmieding, 2006; Vitaliano, Zhang, and Scanland, 2003). Physical health problems affect 25 to 30 percent of caregivers, most often among African American, female, unemployed, and middle-aged caregivers and those providing highest levels of care, such as for persons with dementia (Family Caregiver Alliance, 2006c; Navaie-Waliser et al., 2002). These problems include headaches, exhaustion, pain, arthritis, back troubles, sleep disorders, intestinal disturbances, weight changes, inappropriate use of prescription drugs, elevated blood pressure, and poorer functioning immune systems, which results in more colds and viral illnesses (Mittelman, 2002; Polen and Green, 2001). In one study, women who spent 9 or more hours a week caring for a spouse increased their coronary heart disease risk twofold (Lee, et al., 2003). Not surprisingly, caregivers whose health is compromised by caregiving stress may face an increased risk of mortality. In fact, an 8-year study of over 500,000 couples enrolled in Medicare found that hospitalization of a spouse for serious illness, especially one that interferes with the patient's physical or mental ability, also increases their partner's risk of death, with the biggest impact on wives (Christakis and Allison, 2006).

Poorer physical health and lower physical stamina are associated with emotional distress and mental health problems, especially depression and anxiety (Beach et al., 2005). Among caregivers, 40 to 60 percent are estimated to have clinical depression, with 25 to 50 percent of these suffering from major depression (Family Caregiver Alliance, 2006b). One 4-year study identified that middle-aged and older women who provided care for a spouse with chronic illness were almost six times as likely to suffer symptoms of depression or anxiety as those who

> **SELF-CARE NEEDS OF THE CAREGIVER**
> - Learn to accept help.
> - Take time for relaxing and pleasurable activities by asking others for help or utilizing respite/adult day care.
> - Find ways to incorporate exercise into your daily routine.
> - Take time to eat healthy food.
> - Set limits on your older relative's demands.
> - Attend to your spiritual needs.
> - Participate in caregiver support groups.

had no care responsibilities, and those caring for parents were twice as likely to manifest such symptoms (Cannuscio et al., 2002). Depression is found to increase with the length of caregiving and the amount of time (36 hours or more) devoted to weekly care. It appears that a threshold of time involvement may exist beyond which the likelihood of negative mental health consequences rapidly escalates. Levels of depression and loneliness remain high for caregivers even after the care ends (Family Caregiver Alliance, 2006b; Gallagher-Thompson, 2003; Marks, Lambert and Choi, 2002; Pinquart and Sorenson, 2006; Prigerson, 2003; Robinson-Whelen et al., 2001).

2. *Financial:* These encompass the direct costs of medical care, adaptive equipment, or hired help as well as indirect opportunity costs of lost income, missed promotions, or unemployment. Excluding those who care for a spouse/partner, 50 percent of informal caregivers contribute financially to the care of their relative, an average of $200 monthly. Not surprisingly, the greater the burden of care responsibilities, the higher the probability of negative work-related adjustments; caregivers of elders with dementia must make the most changes in employment. Among such caregivers, more than 80 percent go to work later or leave earlier than scheduled; nearly 40 percent move from

full-time to part time jobs, which may be a transitional step to leaving the labor force (National Alliance for Caregiving and AARP, 2004). Compared to their Caucasian counterparts, African American caregivers are more likely to continue in the labor force by relying on close friends (Bullock, Crawford, and Tennstedt, 2003). Averaging 12 years out of the paid work force to care for children or elders, women suffer long-term economic costs of caregiving, including higher rates of poverty in old age (Wakabayashi and Donato, 2004). These costs are discussed more fully in Chapter 15. Disruptions and

---

THE FINANCIAL BURDEN OF PARENTAL CAREGIVING

About half of all adult children contribute to their parents' support. For some baby boomers, the costs of accessible housing, medical supplies, and other expenses for caring for their parents that are not covered by Medicare or private insurance can deplete their savings. Unlike spousal caregivers, they cannot even claim the expenses on their income tax unless they pay more than half of the parent's support. This may force the middle-aged child to work beyond their preferred retirement age and leave them fearful of their own aging. In some cases, this financial devastation for adult child caregivers occurs because they are reluctant to use their parents' savings; in many cases the elder does not have sufficient savings yet does not qualify for Medicaid. As one example, a vice president at the Federal Reserve Bank in New York borrowed against her 401K retirement plan, sold her house, and depleted 20 years of savings in order to care for her 97-year-old father. She spent $50,000 for lawyers' fees to win a contested guardianship, $3000 for home care equipment, $400 a month for home delivered meals, $330 per trip for a wheelchair accessible van to get him to doctor's appointments, and an additional $1600 each month to rent an apartment large enough for herself, her dad, and a home aide. She does not keep track of what she spends, stating that you "just have to buy what you have to buy" (Gross, 2006).

---

absenteeism due to caregiver responsibilities not only affect the employee financially, but also cost employers up to $33.6 billion per year in lost productivity (MetLife Mature Market Institute and NAC, 2006a).

3. *Emotional:* Subjective burdens tend to be of greatest concern. They encompass worry, anxiety, feeling alone, isolated, and disconnected from others; "erosion of self" with one's identity completely submerged in the care role; and feeling overwhelmed, out of control, inadequate, and fearful over the unpredictability of the future. Loss of time for oneself, family and friends; giving up vacations, hobbies, and social activities; and getting less exercise than before are frequently cited by caregivers as the most negative impacts (Braithwaite, 2000; Moen, Erickson, and Dempster-McClain, 2000; National Alliance for Caregiving and AARP, 2004). Emotional costs tend to increase with difficult levels of care, and are experienced by women more than men. Caregivers who feel trapped in the role are at risk of neglect, burnout, or "compassion fatigue" (National Academy, 2000; Ory et al., 1999; Prescop et al., 1999).

Caregiver Gains

Given the problem-focused nature of gerontological research, most caregiving studies have examined stress, burden, and the losses entailed. As noted above, however, caregiving is multidimensional and includes both negative and positive experiences (Family Caregiver Alliance, 2006b; Nijboer et al., 2000). Caregiving of older adults can be lonely, stressful, moving, and satisfying all at the same time. In other words, psychological well-being can coexist with distress under adverse life circumstances for both caregivers and care recipients. This means that caregivers may experience losses of identity, privacy, and time for self, while simultaneously feeling a sense of purpose and personal enrichment. Similar to other types of

POWERFUL TOOLS FOR CAREGIVERS

Powerful Tools for Caregivers (PTC), available in nearly 20 states, is based on a self-efficacy model that teaches caregivers to manage their emotions, engage in self-care behaviors (e.g., take time to relax), and communicate assertively and effectively. For example, caregivers learn and rehearse changing "You" messages into "I" messages to communicate their thoughts and feelings. They enact plans to take time for themselves without feeling guilty. Emotion-focused coping skills are taught that help caregivers reframe difficult care situations and view self-care as essential to being a good caregiver. Caregivers create weekly action plans for self-care. After taking part in PTC, caregivers, spouses and adult children report significant improvements on all outcome measures, especially participation in relaxation activities and physical exercise. Most of these gains in physical and mental health are sustained six months later (Boise, Congelton, and Shannon, 2005; Kuhn, 2004; Schmall, Cleland, and Sturdevent, 2000).

difficulties and loss throughout the life course, caregivers often experience personal benefits, such as self-efficacy, confidence, self-affirmation, pride, marital satisfaction, and greater closeness with the care recipient and other family members. These gains can buffer some of the adverse effects of care-related stressors (Beach et al., 2000; Kramer, 1997; Narayn et al., 2001; Rapp and Chao, 2000). And for parents and children who have had a conflictual relationship, caregiving may offer an opportunity to work through these issues (Donorfio and Sheehan, 2001).

Some caregivers find personal meaning in their role, such as preservation of values and ideals and feelings of giving back to older generations. In fact, a greater sense of meaning in life can enhance caregiver well-being (Acton and Wright, 2000; Gonyea, in press; Sherrell, Buckwalter, and Morhardt, 2001). These findings regarding caregiver gains reflect its qualitative or subjective nature and the role of individual appraisal; for example, what one caregiver experiences as

stressful, another may find to be a source of satisfaction. In addition, benefits and costs vary over time in the caregiving process, especially at points of entry and exit from the role. These patterns also point to the need for practitioners to recognize both role gains and strains as intervening processes in understanding caregiver well-being outcomes (Gonyea, in press; Kramer, 1997; Narayn et al., 2001; Seltzer and Li, 2000).

Caregivers' well-being and costs of care (and the interaction between gains and costs) are thus affected by two clusters of factors: *contextual* (e.g., level of care, care recipient's behavior and symptoms, quality of relationship with care recipient, socioeconomic status) and *dynamic* (e.g., the caregiver's internal capacities and social, cultural, and spiritual resources). The following factors, which are often more important than the elder's disability status or the amount or type of care provided, influence whether caregivers experience primarily costs or gains:

1. The nature of the relationship between the caregiver and recipient dyad (e.g., past history of conflict/neglect between them; recipient unappreciative, making unreasonable demands, adopting manipulative behavior). A good relationship prior to caregiving minimizes stress, even in the face of heavy care demands.
2. Family support or disharmony, co-residence or geographic distance, financial resources.
3. The salience and timing in the caregiver's life course (e.g., when faced with multiple demands at midlife)
4. Gender (women typically experience caregiving as more stressful than men who provide similar levels of care).
5. Race and ethnicity, with ethnic minority caregivers generally using fewer services but experiencing less depression and stress.
6. Social networks and degree of reciprocity between caregiver and care recipient (Almberg, Grafstroem, and Winblad, 2000; Sebern, 2005).

Caregiving research has focused on caregiver outcomes. Yet both the stress of care and reciprocity in the caregiving dyad can affect the well-being of the caregiver and care recipient. The importance of such reciprocity across the life course suggests the importance of studying family care from the perspective of both members of the care dyad. Even caregivers of relatives with dementia may experience some reciprocity in the relationship, especially when there is a family history of solidarity, deeply established attachments, and rich memories. To illustrate, a care recipient who can no longer manage daily chores can nevertheless entertain the caregiver with stories of family history (Fredriksen-Goldsen and Hooyman, 2003). A future direction for caregiver research is further analysis of how resilience, as discussed in Chapters 1 and 6, may reduce potentially negative effects of caregiver burden on well-being (Fredriksen-Goldsen, in press). Similarly, interventions should address both the caregiver and the care recipient in the dyad, prevent negative interactions, and provide elders with no more assistance than what is required, in efforts to help them maintain competence and self-efficacy (Beach et al., 2005; Liang, Krause, and Bennett, 2001; Martire et al., 2004; Whitlatch et al., 2006). Types of interventions that can facilitate congruence between the degree of environmental press and level of competence are discussed more fully below.

The Gendered Nature of Family Care

Caregivers are generally adult children (41 percent), followed by partners or spouses (23 percent). This division of labor is due, in part, to high rates of widowhood among older adults. Along with the sharing of care responsibilities by multiple siblings, children outnumber spouses as active carers. However, among primary caregivers (e.g., one family member assumes most of the responsibility), 62 percent are spouses, often living with the care recipient. Regardless of the type of care

> ### LOSS OF SELF IN THE CAREGIVING ROLE
>
> "By definition, caregiving does not affect your life; it becomes your life. Outside activities disappear. In eight years, I have been to the movies three times" (McLeod, 1999, p. 81). As noted by a daughter, "It is culturally expected to care for a parent in the home, yet it is viewed as women's work, and we don't value that very much in our society. Society thinks 'it's just an old person,' and 'it's just a woman.' So there are no benefits—no unemployment insurance, no vacations. It's insulting, and yet this is important work" (McLeod, 1999, p. 36).

relationship, women form up to 75 percent of primary family caregivers. Although gender roles are changing in our society, women are still the primary nurturers and kin keepers. In fact, 50 percent of all women provide elder care at some point in the life course, whether as partners, daughters, or daughters-in-law (Family Caregiver Alliance, 2006c; NASUA, 2003). Among all types of caregivers (primary and secondary), 36 percent are wives, 29 percent are daughters, 20 percent are other females (nieces, daughters-in-law, granddaughters, etc.), and the remainder are male relatives. When men are primary caregivers, they

Growing numbers of younger women will assume both elder-care and employment responsibilities.

are usually husbands, secondarily sons, and least often sons-in-law. Although the number of male caregivers is increasing, family caregiver is a euphemism for one primary caregiver, typically female (Family Caregiver Alliance, 2006c; Gonyea, in press).

From the feminist theory perspective discussed in Chapter 8, women predominate not only because they are socialized to be carers, but also because society devalues women's unreimbursed responsibilities in the home as well as their paid work through employment. That is, because women typically earn less than men, an implicit assumption is that they can more willingly and readily give up paid employment to provide care (Calasanti and Slevin, 2001). Types of care also vary by gender and family relationship. While the participation of sons as caregivers is increasing, daughters are still twice as likely to become the primary caregiver as are sons. Of those who provide constant care—40 or more hours per week—80 percent are women (Calasanti and Slevin, 2001). Daughters predominate as the primary caregivers for older widowed women and older unmarried men, and they are the secondary caregivers in situations where the partner of an older person is still alive and able to provide care. Daughters are more likely than sons to be involved in *caring for* (e.g., help with daily tasks such as bathing, dressing, and eating), as well as *caring about* the care recipient (e.g., relational aspects of care that involve trust, rapport, compassion, comfort, communication, and sense

of psychological responsibility). Such personal care tasks are physically draining, involve daily interruptions, and entail intimate or bodily contact. On the other hand, men are most often the primary caregivers of people with HIV/AIDS, and may become more comfortable over time in providing personal care (Thompson, 2002).

As a whole, sons tend to focus on more circumscribed, instrumental, and sporadic tasks, such as house and yard maintenance, financial management, and occasional shopping. While committed to care, they are more likely to adopt an attitude of "you do what you have to do" and use a "work" paradigm in approaching caregiving (Greenberg, Seltzer, and Brewer, 2006; Sanders and McFarland, 2002). They provide less personal care, especially to mothers, although they are more likely to perform "nontraditional" tasks (e.g., bathing, meals, dressing) when caring for a parent in the home. In addition, sons place less importance on emotional well-being and more on completing care goals. In other words,

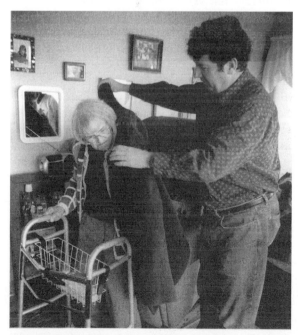

More sons today are caregivers to aging parents than in the past.

CHARACTERISTICS OF WOMEN AS CAREGIVERS

- form the majority of caregivers, even when male family members are available, except for spouses
- feel more psychological responsibility
- are more likely to give up or modify employment
- face multiple demands and roles from employment and/or dependent children
- caregiving is often a "career" over the life course and affects economic well-being in old age

women more often feel responsible for their relative's physical *and* psychological well-being, and perceive caregiving demands as disrupting their personal and social lives than do men. In contrast, male caregivers are more likely to separate boundaries of employment and caregiving, and to engage in self-care, such as preventive health behaviors, than female caregivers (Campbell and Martin-Matthews 2000; Kramer and Thompson, 2002; Seltzer and Li, 2000; Thompson, 2002; Yee and Schulz, 2000).

Given these gender-based differences and the distinction between caring for and caring about, most research has found that daughters tend to experience more stress and feelings of psychological burden than sons, even when both are performing similar tasks across similar time periods (Gerstel and Gallagher, 2001; Martin, 2000; Yee and Schulz, 2000). Accordingly, women caregivers report higher levels of depression, anxiety, psychiatric symptomatology, and lower life satisfaction than their male counterparts. A recent meta-analysis of 229 caregiver studies suggests that while female caregivers have higher rates of depression and health problems than their male counterparts, this difference may be associated with depression and poor health among women generally and not due to caregiver stress (Pinquart and Sorensen, 2006). Another limitation is that most studies of gender differences are cross-sectional and thus do not capture how caregiving stress may change over time for both men and women. Nevertheless, gender-based patterns are identifiable and generally consistent across cultures. For example, as noted in Chapter 2, although norms of filial support are weakening in Asian countries, daughters-in-law are still expected to provide care, without emotional or tangible support from other family members (Navaie-Waliser et al., 2001; Yee and Schulz, 2000).

Increasingly, researchers are exploring not only how men and women differ in performing the caregiving role, but also how gender influences the meaning, social context, and consequences of caring (Pinquart and Sorensen, 2006). Women, for example, generally have more extensive social networks than do men. Although these may be useful resources, the networks themselves may also be sources of stress if they are characterized by conflict or other negative interactions (Gonyea, in press). Women experience greater economic costs from the undervalued work of care across the life course than do men, which are exacerbated by policies such as Social Security. These economic inequities for older women are discussed more fully in Chapter 15.

Spouses/Partners as Caregivers

The most frequent caregiving pattern is between partners; 22 percent of those who care for older adults are themselves age 65 and older (Family Caregiver Alliance, 2006b). Since most caregiving studies have focused on heterosexual couples, the term *spouse* is used most frequently in this discussion; nevertheless, it is important to recognize the distinctive structural challenges faced by gay and lesbian partner caregivers, who are discussed in Chapter 9. The extent to which caring for a spouse is a normative experience—part of the marital contract and necessary for sustaining the quality of the marital relationship—affects the nature of the care experience. When the marital tie is not supportive, emotional intimacy may be more important than gender in the selection of a caregiver (Allen, Goldscheider, and Ciambrone, 1999). Spouses, who are the most likely to be primary caregivers, perform

---

POINTS TO PONDER

Spouses/partners account for:

- 28 percent of the caregivers of Caucasian elders
- 20 percent of caregivers of Latinos
- 15 percent of African American caregivers

What factors may account for these differences?

80 percent of all care tasks, spending 40 to 60 hours per week on household chores and personal care. Because of differences in life expectancy, more wives than husbands over age 65 care for a partner with chronic illness. Men receive more care on average, typically from only one person—their wife. In contrast, women receive help from a larger number of caregivers, including children and grandchildren (Family Caregiver Alliance, 2006c).

Within the gender-based differences described above, husbands are more likely to provide care than are sons or sons-in-law, and they predominate among the 25 to 28 percent of caregivers who are male. In fact, husbands of women with chronic disabilities are more likely to provide care than are other relatives. As a result, husbands comprise nearly 40 percent of spousal caregivers and are predicted to grow in the future because of increases in men's life expectancy. Husbands tend to be the first person called on to care for their wives, to be the oldest subgroup of caregivers, and to spend the greatest number of hours in care compared with other caregivers. Caregiving husbands are found to experience more strain in the marital relationship and higher rates of depression and unhappiness than caregiving wives. Not surprisingly, the caregiver's health and the quality of the marital relationship (e.g., high levels of partner interaction and communication) affect the continuation of the care relationship (Harris, 2002; Kramer and Lambert, 1999; Tennstedt, 1999).

Older spouses experience more negative consequences from caregiving than do younger adult children (Ory, Tennstedt, and Schulz, 2000). Both husband and wife caregivers report considerable stress and feelings of grief and loss. These problems may be exacerbated because the caregivers are also facing their own aging-related changes, physical illnesses, or reduced finances. Emotional stress, particularly depression, tends to be highest among spouses caring for partners with cognitive impairment. The nature of the relationship also affects the consequences of care. For example, caregiving is found to be more stressful for wives than daughters, since wives more frequently experience losses in marital and family relationships and social involvement. Wives' sense of well-being, however, may increase when a husband dies (Seltzer and Li, 2000). As a whole, spousal caregivers experience more negative consequences than do adult children.

Gay and lesbian partners' caregiving experiences are made more difficult by legal and structural barriers in most societies. For example, they may be denied visitation rights in the hospital or nursing home, overlooked by health care providers as the primary support, and excluded from decision-making about end of life care (Zodikoff, 2006). In a national survey of 1000 self-identified GLBT baby boomers age 40 to 61, 25 percent of respondents indicated that they had provided care for a friend or family member within the past six months. Of these, 36 percent were caregivers for parents, 18 percent for partners, and 26 percent for friends and other non-relatives. In contrast with surveys of heterosexual individuals, about the same proportion of GLBT men and women serve as caregivers. In addition, both perform care management and care provider tasks, which suggests greater role flexibility than in the heterosexual population. GLBT caregivers' time commitment was also found to

---

CULTURAL EXPECTATIONS OF WOMEN AS CAREGIVERS

A researcher in Seoul, Korea, who studies women's labor market issues, has cared for her mother-in-law for 22 years. Although her husband and in-laws help pay for a personal assistant to care for her mother-in-law during the day, the middle-aged professional assumes all the care after her 8- to 10-hour workday and on weekends, without any assistance from her husband. She has had only one vacation during that time period, has little social life, but rarely questions her obligation to her mother-in-law.

be greater than the population as a whole. In fact, 17 percent of caregivers who are full-time employees reported providing 40 or more hours of care per week (MetLife, 2006b). The extent to which these greater time demands are due to caring for persons with HIV/AIDs is not clear.

Adult Children/Grandchildren as Caregivers

The importance of the parent-child bond across the life course is underscored by the fact that adult children represent the largest group of active carers for aging parents with chronic illness or disability. Parent care has become a predictable and nearly universal experience across the life course, yet many adults are not adequately prepared for it, because they are typically thrust into the role with little advance warning. Although often referred to as a "role reversal," an adult child never becomes a parent's parent. Instead, caring for parents is about letting go of outmoded patterns to meet current family needs, a process that can lead to feelings of grief and loss among adult children caregivers and that persist even after a parent's death (McLeod, 1999).

The average woman today can expect to spend more years caring for an older family member (18 years) compared to 17 years for her children. The concept of "sandwiched generation" refers to middle-aged women faced with competing responsibilities of parental and child care. Such **women in the middle** may be juggling extensive family responsibilities along with employment and their own age-related transitions. This latter issue is particularly important because the age group 35 to 64 is most likely to be providing parent care (Brody, 2004; Guberman and Maheu, 1999; Ingersoll-Dayton, Neal, and Hammer, 2001). Women in the middle generation are also centrally involved in maintaining family communication and cohesion across generations. Compared to their male

SANDWICH GENERATION

A woman in her mid-50s with teenage children and a full-time job, Annette had cared for both her parents. Her mother, disabled with rheumatoid arthritis, lived with Annette's family for 5 years before she died. Within a year, Annette's father suffered a stroke and lived with the family for 3 years before his death. Annette's teenagers had resented the amount of time she gave to her parents, and her husband became impatient with how little time they had alone together. They had not had a vacation in 5 years. Since family and friends were not interested in helping her with the care of her parents, Annette and her husband rarely even had a night out alone together. As an employed caregiver, Annette frequently missed work and was distracted on the job whenever she had to consult doctors or take her parents for therapy during normal business hours. She felt alone, isolated, and overwhelmed by the stress. She was physically and mentally exhausted from trying to meet too many demands, unaware that some support services were available in her community, and feeling that she had to handle these responsibilities on her own. When her mother-in-law became too frail to live alone, Annette knew her family and job would suffer once again if she tried to balance household duties, a full-time job, and the care of both older and younger relatives. She began to explore assisted living options for her mother-in-law.

counterparts, they are more likely to give up employment, which can result in a loss of income (both current and retirement) and a source of identity and self-esteem. More recent data, however, indicate that women caring for older relatives typically do not have dependent children (under age 18) for whom they are responsible. This means that they are more likely to face the competing demands of caring for older relatives and paid employment than the dual responsibilities of child and elder care. Nevertheless, middle-aged women may still feel psychologically and financially responsible for their young adult children, who frequently return home to

> ### WOMEN IN THE MIDDLE
>
> A woman in her early 40s had given up a rewarding career to care for her mother-in-law with Alzheimer's disease, her 11-year-old daughter, and 8-year-old son. Her husband's siblings, who had no children, provided only occasional financial assistance, refusing to help by giving her respite or time off. Her husband worked two jobs, and although he was supportive, he was rarely present to help. Caring for her mother-in-law dominated her life, and she had little time to attend her children's special events or sports. Her son had had to give up his room for his grandmother, and her daughter complained about how her mother never spent time with her. In the 2 years of caring for her mother-in-law, she had not had a day just for herself. When she learned about the availability of respite services, she started to sob, recognizing how much she had been grieving the loss of time for herself and her children.

the "empty nest" out of economic necessity or because of divorce (Arnett, 2000; Brody, 2004; Goldscheider, Thornton, and Yang, 2001; Spillman and Pezzin, 2000).

Juggling multiple roles, however, may not always be a primary source of stress. In fact, women who lack any meaningful social roles may experience greater stress compared with women with multiple roles. Others' support for the caregiving role may be more important than the multiplicity of roles per se (Dautzenberg et al., 1999; Reid and Hardy, 1999).

Family Caregivers of Color

Caregiving research has focused on U.S.-born whites; less is known about care in ethnic minority communities or other cultures. African Americans and Latinos are the most likely to be providing informal care compared to other ethnic minority groups. For both African Americans and Latinos, caregivers are less likely to be spouses and more likely to be another family member or a friend. Both groups are likely to experience more physical health problems compared to their white counterparts (Haley et al., 2004; National Alliance for Caregiving and AARP, 2004; Pinquart and Sorenson, 2005; Weiss et al., 2005). African American caregivers tend to provide higher levels of care, to be more likely to assist extended family members, and to be more economically disadvantaged than their white counterparts. They also are less likely to have alternative caregivers to assist them on an ongoing basis, even though they often face more severe care situations and are less likely to use formal supports. Despite these objective burdens, African American caregivers report less stress, anxiety, feelings of "bother" and depression; higher levels of self-efficacy; and greater rewards compared to other groups. Their greater satisfaction and perceived gains (e.g., pride, belief that they will be rewarded by God) may be partially due to the mediating effects of religion, spirituality, prayer, and faith; to strong beliefs about filial support; and to more positive, respectful views of elders (Chadidha et al., 2002; Cuellar, 2002; Dilworth-Anderson, Williams, and Gibson, 2002; Foley, Tung, and Mutran, 2002; Haley et al., 2004; Roff et al., 2004). On the other hand, younger African American caregivers who are facing financial and other pressures may experience a contradiction between what they believe they should do for relatives and what they can actually do. Accordingly, rates of nursing home placement among African American elders have increased in recent years, from 4.2 percent in 1985 to 5.6 percent in 1999 (Groger and Mayberry, 2001; NCHS, 2006).

Latinos are identified as experiencing greater burden and rates of depression and less positive appraisals and feelings of competence than whites or African Americans, despite strong norms of filial responsibility. This pattern may occur because of Latinos' high rates of poverty, poor health, and limited access to insurance and other services (Adams et al., 2002; Magana, 2006; Navaie-Waliser et al., 2001). Cultural values of familism and collectivism mean that Latinos typically feel obligated to provide care and are at high risk for putting the needs of family and community above their own well-being.

Among Chinese and Korean immigrant families, older members often experience shifts in their expectations of filial piety. While parents often sacrificed for their children's education and economic advancement, their adult children in the United States, who may not live in close physical proximity, may not perceive a filial obligation to care for their parents as strongly as adult children in Korea and China. As daughters-in-law enter the paid workforce and sons develop financial independence in the United States, they may feel less obligated to provide care. Yet, seeking help within the family remains a strong Asian American value, reducing the likelihood that elders will turn to services for support to reduce their social isolation (McCormick et al., 2002; Wong, Yoo, and Stewart, 2006). Caregiving expectations and experiences among ethnic minorities are explored more fully in Chapter 15.

Inconsistent findings related to caregiving consequences among ethnic minorities are partially due to methodological limitations, such as using a "grouping variable" by race/ethnicity, culture, or national origin to attribute differences between groups of caregivers (Gonyea, in press). Whether identified differences are largely due to cultural factors (e.g., language, values, beliefs, or norms) or to ethnic minority status, with the latter implying the effects of inequality and discrimination, requires further research. What is clear is that sociodemographic variables (i.e., gender, race, marital status, sexual orientation) per se are not the primary causes of caregiver outcomes. It is also known that ethnic minorities are at higher risk of morbidity and mortality across the life course. The greater incidence of health

Caregiving is an intergenerational responsibility in many cultures.

problems does not, however, translate into higher rates of institutional care; a smaller percentage of elders of color (3 percent) than Caucasian elders (4.2 percent) live in nursing homes. Yet, even among ethnic minorities with strong norms of filial piety and familism, economic and social forces are increasingly influencing their abilities and willingness to care for aging family members and rates of institutional care are likely to increase. Evidence for this shift comes from the increasing proportions of older African Americans using nursing homes, as noted above (Groger and Mayberry, 2001; NCHS, 2006; Ness, Ahmed, and Aronow, 2004; Olson, 2001).

Caregiving for Relatives with Dementia

The demands and losses associated with caregiving tend to be intensified when caring for a relative with dementia (Prigerson, 2003). Almost 70 percent of adults with Alzheimer's disease (AD) are cared for at home by family for the entire duration of the disease (Alzheimer's Association, 2001; Kramer, 2000). This translates into families providing up to 80 percent of the care for relatives with AD. In a national survey that compared caregivers of relatives with dementia to other caregivers, the former were found to provide the most difficult kinds of personal care (bathing, feeding, dealing with incontinence), to spend more hours per week providing care ("constant care") and to do so for longer periods of time. Not surprisingly, they are at higher risk of strain, mental and physical health problems, and family conflicts. Over 40 percent report high levels of emotional stress compared to 30 percent of all caregivers; 20 percent rate their health as fair or

WHEN CAREGIVING IS CREATED BY A NATURAL DISASTER

When Hurricane Katrina devastated the Gulf Coast, it hit especially hard on elders with dementia, whose confusion was intensified by the chaotic situation. And many families suddenly found themselves providing more care or needing to replace whatever care arrangements had been in place for their older relatives. The Alzheimer's Association sent staff to the devastated area to help locate elders with dementia, ensure that they were wearing the Safeguard identification bracelets, and link them with their family caregivers from outside the region. As a result of how public systems failed elders after Katrina, more agencies serving older adults, including the Alzheimer's Assocation and long-term care facilities, are developing disaster preparedness guidelines to assist elders and their paid and unpaid caregivers.

INTENSIFICATION OF PAST BEHAVIORS WITH ALZHEIMER'S DISEASE

In *Elder Rage: or Take my Father . . . Please!,* Marcell (2000) tells of caring for her father, who had always had a bad temper and was a controlling, dominating, explosive, and verbally abusive husband and father. Afflicted with Alzheimer's disease at age 83, he constantly raged and cursed at his daughter and his wife, threatened physical violence, and refused to take his medications.

poor, and 18 percent state that caregiving has made their health worse (Mittelman et al., 2004b). In one study that found greater risk of death among spousal caregivers, the spouse's diagnosis with dementia or cognitive impairment increased the caregiver husband's death risk by 22 percent and wives' risk by 28 percent, which is higher than for those caring for elders with less-debilitating illnesses (Christakis and Allison, 2006). Caregivers of relatives with dementia must live with behavior problems, such as marked confusion, anxiety and agitation, suspicion, and sleep disturbances (Alzheimer's Association and National Alliance for Caregiving, 2004; National Alliance for Caregiving and AARP, 2004). Rates of depression in caregivers range from 25 to 87 percent, along with a high incidence of anger, grief, and anxiety (Connell, Janevic, and Gallant, 2001; Mittelman, 2002; Mittelman et al., 2004b; Ory et al., 2000; Schulz et al., 2003a, Vitaliano et al., 2002). Physical health indicators, such as blood lipids and glucose levels, are also higher among caregivers of elders with dementia than among noncaregiving older partners.

The concept of "learning to bend without breaking" refers to the high level of unpredictability and continual changes to which families of AD patients must accommodate (Gwyther, 1998). For long-term partners, their roles and relationships are profoundly redefined by the pervasiveness of care responsibilities and the perception of no end in sight. When care recipients with Alzheimer's disease are no longer psychologically present or when their personalities are markedly changed, new disruptive behaviors may emerge (e.g., emotional and verbal abuse, increased aggressive or violent behavior) that increase their caregivers' sense of loss. Adult children typically grieve the loss of their relationship with their parent and of opportunities missed because of care responsibilities. Older partners, on the other hand, may experience a loss of couple identity and intimacy, uncertainty, and aloneness (Meuser and Marwit 2001).

Caregivers of relatives with dementia, who tolerate an ambiguous situation for long periods of time, often experience anticipatory grief or "quasi-widowhood." They refer to their loved one as having died twice: first the psychological death of the person they knew and loved, and then the physical death. This can result in multiple waves of grief—denial, anger, guilt, resentment, and depression. Similarly, older adult caregivers for partners with brain injury, a stroke that has affected the loved one's personality, or who are comatose experience their partner's psychological death years before the physical death. These emotional responses are similar to the feelings of loss and grief that occur when a loved one dies (Adams and Sanders, 2004; Boss, 1999; Dupuis, 2002). Health care providers must be aware that caregivers of relatives with dementia often are grieving as they provide end-of-life care (Sanders and Corley, 2003; Schulz et al., 2003).

THE "ABSENCE" OF ALZHEIMER'S PATIENTS

As described by a 36-year-old daughter, "She is not the way she used to be as my mother. Just looking in her bedroom at home, it is feeling like she is gone. Yet she's still alive. Her things are still where they have been for years, even when she was well. She sits and looks at the things that once made up her life and to her that life never existed. I ask myself daily, 'Is my mother alive or dead?'" (Sanders and Corley, 2003).

DAILY GRIEVING BY THE AD CAREGIVER

According to a 71-year-old husband, "being married to someone for over 50 years and seeing her with this disease, I am daily grieving over her loss. Upon death, you will grieve for a while, but your life goes on. Seeing your loved one daily die for over 6 years just makes your feelings stronger. I just wish I could have killed her and myself and just got this whole thing over really quickly" (Sanders and Corley, 2003).

Such instances of prolonged stress from caring for a loved one with dementia, as illustrated by the daughter and husband caregivers in the boxes on this page, can create a sense of desperation over lacking control of a difficult situation. This chronic sorrow or "long good-bye" can negatively affect caregivers' physical and mental health and increase their risk of mortality, with grief often misdiagnosed as clinical depression. Compared with caregivers of older adults in nursing homes who experience sadness and guilt, those providing care at home for relatives with dementia tend to experience more anger (Mittelman, 2002; Sanders and Corley, 2003). Fortunately, more supports and skills training are now available to caregivers of relatives with dementia including interventions that teach effective strategies to change behaviors of both caregiver and the care recipient, using in-person, telephone, and Internet support groups (Bourgeois et al., 2002; Burgio et al., 2001; Logsdon et al., 2005). The Alzheimer's Association provides specific suggestions for managing behavioral issues, as well as extensive educational materials for caregivers.

The Internet has emerged in the last few years as a way for caregivers to share their experiences with others facing similar burdens and frustrations. Some of these Websites include advice and updated information from experts, such as the Alzheimer's Association, while others encourage caregivers to offer support and suggestions to their peers who have recently become caregivers. The opportunity to log on to a chat room on the Internet also avoids the need to find alternative care or respite for the AD patient at home while attending support groups in person. The growth of adult day centers is another response to the need to maintain persons with dementia in the community, to help them remain active and retain learned skills, and to provide respite for caregivers. Caregivers who regularly take their AD patients to such centers have shown lower levels of anger, depression, and stress than those who do not (Zarit et al., 1998). The need for publicly funded adult day-centers, respite, and support groups is greater than the availability of services. However, caregivers of AD elders are less likely to use such services to treat their depression and their sense of burden than other type of caregivers (Brodaty et al., 2005).

Legislation to Support Family Caregivers

A barrier to the development of services for family caregivers has been policy makers' fears that service accessibility will reduce, curtail, or substitute for informal care. This is often referred to as families "coming out of the woodwork" to utilize services. This concern persists, despite almost two decades of empirical documentation that formal in-home services do not substitute for informal care (Family Caregiver Alliance, 2006c; Penning, 2002).

Despite policy makers' concerns that formal care would substitute for informal support at public expense, two federal policy initiatives aim to support families: the **Family and Medical Leave Act** of 1993 (FMLA) and the **National Family Caregiver Support Program** of 2000 (NFCSP). Under the FMLA, businesses with 50 or more employees are required to grant up to 12 weeks of unpaid leave annually when a child is born or adopted, when an immediate family member with a serious health condition needs

care, or when the employee is unable to work because of a serious health condition. Health coverage and reinstatement of employment after the leave are guaranteed.

Because the FMLA does not apply to small employers, less than 10 percent of private sector worksites are covered. Even though this relatively small percentage of businesses employs almost 60 percent of American workers, not all workers of covered employers are eligible for FMLA benefits, because of requirements related to duration and amount of work. When these eligibility criteria are applied, only about 40 percent of private sector employees are eligible for leave. Additional barriers to using FMLA are lack of knowledge of the act and the unpaid nature of the leave. From a political economy perspective (described in Chapter 8), FMLA benefits only those who can afford to forgo income while on leave. Workers who cannot manage the loss of wages entailed by family care leave are more likely to be African American, hourly wage earners who are predominantly women, and have lower levels of household income (Wisensale, 2001). The FMLA also does not recognize extended family members, characteristic of many ethnic minority families or GLBT caregivers. Proposals to reform FMLA continue to be debated along partisan lines in the U.S. Congress (Hudson and Gonyea, 2000). The Family and Medical Leave Extension Act was introduced in 2003 for a pilot program to help states develop partially paid leave, but is unlikely to be continued in the near future. California was the first state to offer paid leave in 2004, and 26 other states have some form of paid leave in their legislative sessions. Most recently, Massachusetts has considered legislation for the nation's most generous paid leave policy. Workers would be paid their full salary (up to $750 a week) for up to 12 weeks to care for newborns or ill family members. Paid leave would be funded by a small employee contribution ($1.50 to $2.50 a week) and provide job protection for those who take leave. Proponents of paid leave contend that employers would actually save money when factoring in less turnover and fewer paid sick days. In contrast, most western European countries provide paid leave and special pensions for family caregivers of dependents across the life course, along with attendant care allowances to allow older adults with disabilities to purchase and manage at least some in-home services. Under the Medicaid waiver system, described more fully in Chapter 17, some states now allow relatives (with the exception of spouses) to be paid as personal care providers.

The National Family Caregiver Support Program (NFCSP) was funded by the Administration on Aging in 2000. For the first time in the history of the Older Americans Act, state units on aging and area agencies on aging are required to serve not only older adults but also family caregivers. This includes family caregivers of elders and grandparents or other older kin caregivers of children/grandchildren. States are expected to partner with the local Area Agencies on Aging (AAAs) and other service providers to establish a network of services, although states have flexibility on what specific services to provide. The NFCSP gives a higher priority to services for low-income, older caregivers and for those caring for persons with developmental disabilities.

In recognition of the growing phenomenon of grandparents as sole caregivers for grandchildren, each state may use up to 10 percent of the total funds to help grandparents and other family caregivers over age 60. Funds are also designated for American Indian caregivers. The primary service funded to date is information and referral (AOA, 2004). Although NFCSP is important public policy recognition of the central role of informal care in our society, the program is modest in its impact. This is because of limited funding, the shift in thinking required by service workers to conceptualize the caregivers as clients, the resulting limited attention to assessment of the family caregiver, and the challenges of reaching caregivers when they are most likely to accept help but before they are

> **SERVICES UNDER THE NATIONAL FAMILY CAREGIVER SUPPORT PROGRAM**
> - information and assistance
> - individual counseling
> - support groups and caregiver training
> - respite care
> - supplemental services to complement family care

in crisis. Overall, most federal and state policies continue to focus on the care recipient rather than supporting the caregiver (Feder and Levine, 2004; Feinberg et al., 2004; NASUA, 2003).

Use of Services

Consistent with the person–environment (P–E) model, interventions to support caregivers seek to increase the family's capacities for care and reduce the environmental press created by the elder's need for care. Such supports to caregivers can help sustain care of their older relative at home and thereby reduce costly nursing home care. Ideally, services are provided to both members of the care dyad. For example, adult day health care provides socialization and health services for older adults, but also gives their caregivers a break from care. Services targeted to older adults in general are discussed in Chapters 11 and 16. This section focuses on services for informal caregivers.

> **FORMAL SUPPORTS FOR CAREGIVERS**
> - adult day care
> - respite care
> - home health care
> - counseling in person or by phone
> - psychoeducational groups
> - training programs/skill development
> - self-care techniques
> - support groups
> - Internet resources, chat rooms

Supportive Services for Family Caregivers

Caregiver Assessment

In the past, health care providers focused primarily on the care recipient, overlooking the needs of family caregivers who were the "hidden patients" needing care themselves (Family Caregiver Alliance, 2006a; Levine et al., 2004; Guberman and Maheu, 2002). Fortunately, the importance of assessing the caregiver as well as the older person is increasingly recognized. Assessment of caregivers helps identify issues that might otherwise be overlooked, gives the family a defined role in the treatment process, validates family's experiences, and reduces risks to caregivers' well being (Family Caregiver Alliance, 2006a; Feinberg, 2004; Guberman et al., 2003; Pickard, 2004). Because of the costs of care and their impact on the well-being of both members of the caregiving dyad, it is essential for health professionals to assess **caregiver burden** and well-being, especially for those caring for relatives with dementia. Assessments take account of the caregiving context, caregiver's health, knowledge and skills, the care recipient's functional level, and the nature of care tasks. The Caregiver Burden Interview (CBI) and the Revised Memory and Behavior Problems Checklist (RMBPC) are two of the most frequently used assessment instruments. The RMPBC also assesses subjective burden. However, both scales should be used cautiously with families of color (Gottlieb, Thompson, and Bourgeois, 2003; Richardson and Barusch, 2006). Most caregiver assessments are not culturally sensitive because they were developed for research purposes, with small, primarily white, middle-class samples (Feinberg, 2003–2004; Gaugler et al., 2000a, 2000b). Home assessments are shown to be better than clinic-based ones at identifying potentially serious caregiving issues (Ramsdell et al., 2004). In general, caregivers are preoccupied with having their loved one's needs evaluated, which suggests that caregiver assessment is most likely to be effective if it takes place after this process is complete (Family Caregiver Alliance, 2006a). Outcomes of caregiver assessment include maintaining health and well being, preventing social isolation, and locating appropriate supportive services (Nicholas, 2003). Unfortunately, fewer than 50 percent of programs funded by the National Family Caregiver Support Program of the Older Americans Act and Medicaid waiver programs uniformly assess caregiver needs (Feinberg et al., 2004; Feinberg and Newman, 2004).

Service Utilization

Although the Aging Network, especially through the National Family Caregiver Support Program, now provides more services for caregivers, increased service availability does not in itself enhance the caregiver or care recipient's well-being. As noted earlier, most family caregivers do not use services; or they do so selectively to supplement informal care for limited time periods or wait until services are absolutely necessary. Whether reliance on informal networks is a result or cause of underutilization of formal services is unclear. To some extent, patterns of lower service use may persist because families are unaware of services, unwilling to accept them, or lack the time and resources to access them. For example, taking the time to partner with service providers may be perceived as stressful (NASUA, 2003). Yet services tend to be underutilized even by caregivers who perceive a need for greater formal support (Dilworth-Anderson et al., 2002; Family Caregiver Alliance, 2006b; Montgomery and Kosloski, 2000). Another reason for underutilization of services is that family caregivers typically self-select into their role, and often do not identify themselves as caregivers needing support. For example, a daughter who begins by assisting her mother with shopping may not think of herself as a caregiver when she starts to provide more intensive levels of care. Yet this discrepancy between her care behavior and her identity as daughter can itself increase the stress of caring. When her identity changes to that of caregiver, she may be more open to accepting services (Brodie and Gadling-Cole, 2003; Dobrof and Ebenstein, 2003–2004; Franks, Pierce, and Dwyer, 2003; Montgomery and Kosloski, 2000).

Gender and race affect service utilization, with women and ethnic minority caregivers the least likely to turn to formal services. Some caregivers of color may not utilize services because of inaccessibility due to economic, religious, insurance, and other barriers, or because of discriminatory experiences that cause them to feel like unwelcome outsiders to agencies (Dilworth-Anderson et al., 1999, 2002; Magana, 2006).

Even when formal services are used, the overall effects are relatively modest in terms of caregiver well-being, hours of care provided, or number of tasks performed for the care recipient. This pattern may occur because services may prolong the duration of caregiving, but not necessarily reduce subjective burden. Interventions may occur too late in the caregiving cycle after stress has already spilled over into other aspects of caregivers' lives (e.g., secondary stressors) or problems have become too complex to solve through short-term strategies. More likely, services may not meet what caregivers perceive to be their needs (i.e., their subjective appraisal of their situation). For example, many services are oriented toward crisis intervention, short-term support, and residential care rather than in-home, long-term personal care to assist with daily tasks. In other instances, families may be too poor to purchase private pay services, but not poor enough to be eligible for Medicaid-reimbursed services.

Compared to narrowly focused interventions, the most effective interventions are multi-component ones that incorporate multiple strategies and services (respite, adult day health, and support groups), that target services early in the caregiving process, are 8 to 12 weeks in duration, and are tailored to fit the care context. Interventions to promote caregiver mastery,

realistic appraisals of their situations, and skills to manage the situation have been found to reduce depression (Hepburn et al., 2003; Hooyman, 2003; Mittelman et al., 2004a, 2004b; Schulz et al., 2002). The largest six-site multicomponent intervention program, REACH, aimed to reduce depression and burden among caregivers of relatives with Alzheimer's. The face-to face intervention attempted to change the nature of specific stressors along with caregivers' appraisal of and response to stressors (Wisniewski et al., 2003). On the other hand, multicomponent interventions may not uncover the relative impact of specific problems, making it difficult to target particular services (Kennet, Burgio, and Schulz, 2000). For instance, counseling may reduce emotional stress, but typically requires that the caregiver travel for this service; in such instances, telephone-based assistance is sometimes utilized to address time and geographic barriers (Coon, Ory, and Schulz, 2003; NASUA, 2003; Pinquart and Sorensen, 2003; Sorensen, Pinquart, and Duberstein, 2002). Health and social service providers need to be attuned to the fact that caregiving is a dynamic process, changing over time as the care recipient's needs shift, and thus the types of supports needed also vary over time. We turn now to describing some specific services to support caregivers.

Support Groups

Although findings are somewhat contradictory, support groups for caregivers are generally effective, especially if organized around particular illnesses or caregiver needs. For example, posttest measures of a support group for early-stage caregivers indicated a significant increase in preparedness for the caregiving role, competence, and use of positive coping strategies, and a decrease in their levels of perceived strain (subjective burden). This suggests that during the early phase of caregiving, families can promote their wellness and enhance their ability to face challenges through increased emotional strength and coping skills. Support group participation is also associated with decreased depression and increased morale; lower rates of institutionalization; greater knowledge of illness and resources; and increased informal support. In contrast to these benefits, some studies report that support groups are less effective than individual counseling for reducing strain and improving psychological well-being. Although support groups can provide emotional assistance, they may not necessarily lower the level of caregiver stress. In fact, they may actually be perceived as an additional burden by caregivers who have to travel and arrange respite care for their elder in order to attend, or if the support groups tend to focus primarily on the negative aspects of caregiving. Support group facilitators should consider that men typically prefer to talk to other men, and that the needs of spouses and adult children caregivers tend to differ (Gartska, McCallion, and Toseland, 2001; Harris, 2002; Mittelman, 2002; Toseland and Smith, 2003).

Psychoeducational Groups and Skills Training

Psychoeducational groups, which usually combine education and social support, are found to enhance caregiver well-being, delay nursing home placement, and increase the utilization of supportive services (Bourgeois et al., 2002; Burgio et al., 2003b; Kuhn and Fulton, 2004; Mittelman et al., 2004a, 2004b). Caregivers point to the value of understanding the nature of the illness and having knowledge of relevant resources. Some groups educate and empower caregivers to advocate for policy and programmatic changes (Morano, 2002; Schulz et al., 2002).

Training programs can enhance caregivers' problem-solving skills. For example, the Environmental Skill-Building Program teaches caregivers how to use environmental and personal resources to modify the troublesome behaviors of their relative. Caregivers are also taught distraction tech-

niques and how to enhance communication with their care recipient. Such skill-building benefits male caregivers in particular, who may be less likely to attend support groups that focus on expressing their feelings (Richardson and Barusch, 2006; Femiano and Coonerty-Femiano, 2002; Gitlin and Gwyther, 2003).

Individual and Family Counseling

Individual interventions, such as cognitive behavioral therapy, tend to be more effective than groups in addressing issues such as family conflict, emotional reactions such as grief to a care recipient's chronic illness, and problems resulting from a care recipient's cognitive or emotional disorders (Barusch and Richardson, 2006; Mittelman et al., 2003; Sorensen et al., 2002; Toseland and Smith, 2003). Family-level interventions need to address not only how much other members do, but the manner by which assistance is provided. In some instances, other family members may increase the caregiver's subjective burden by giving too much advice or criticism. When this occurs, interventions need to promote the useful help that families give the primary caregiver and reduce family conflict (Eisdorfer et al., 2003; Mittelman et al., 2004a, 2004b). The effectiveness of individual and family counseling will vary with the caregivers' gender, ethnic minority status, education, and social class (Gallagher-Thompson et al., 2003).

Respite Care

Respite care is planned for emergency, short-term relief to caregivers from the demands of ongoing care. Accessible and affordable respite and adult day care can provide caregivers with a break from their daily demands. Both can be part of a multimodal approach to reducing both caregiver distress and institutionalization (Silberg, 2001). Respite encompasses a range of services and may be in- or out-of-home care, for example, through adult day health, or overnight care in a long-term care facility. As noted by one caregiver interviewed for an Administration on Aging study, "Respite is my number one need. I've been caring for Mom for seven years . . . in that time, I have had one vacation for three days" (AOA, 2003). Respite is one of the services offered under the National Family Caregiver Support Program. Most caregivers state that they would like respite services, but often face barriers to their use, including their own willingness to entrust their relative's care to someone else or guilt over taking a much needed break. When adult day health is used as respite, caregiver depression, role overload, and worry are reduced, and nursing home admission may be delayed (Leitsch et al., 2001; Gaugler et al., 2003; Kagan, 2006).

After a 4-year debate, Congress passed the Lifespan Respite Act in 2006. Based on state models of life span respite, it will fund competitive grants to states and local bodies to develop coordinated systems of accessible, community-based respite care services for caregivers and care recipients regardless of age or disability. Giving one agency authority to integrate funds, ensure care coordination, control costs, and identify gaps is intended to make respite more accessible. This integrated approach recognizes the fragmentation and insufficient funding for adequate respite services based on categorical age groups (Kagan, 2003, 2006). Such an approach is also congruent with a multigenerational framework, as discussed in Chapter 9, which recognizes shared needs of caregivers across the life course. Despite these efforts, federal funding for life course respite falls far short of the need.

Electronic Supports

Many Websites provide caregivers with information on community resources, including living facilities, and an opportunity to connect with other caregivers on a 24-hour basis. Teleconferencing is being used to create virtual support groups among caregivers and can be accessed through caregiver Websites. A growing number of Websites through AARP, AOA, and the Assisted Living Federation of America (ALFA) allow caregivers to complete an interactive assessment online to determine the services they most need. These strategies are generally not systematic or targeted early on in caregiving, but instead are randomly used across the caregiving career. Use of the Internet for service accessibility and support is likely to increase with computer-savvy baby boomers and their adult children. Some corporations provide elder-care information, referral, education, and adult daycare through employee assistance programs. Toll-free information and referral lines are vital, with a national elder-care locator service sponsored by the Administration on Aging. However, research on the effectiveness of computer, phone, and workplace interventions is relatively limited. (Fredriksen-Goldsen and Scharlach, 2001).

Future Service Directions

Regardless of the specific service configuration, support services should be culturally competent and in accessible locations, such as faith-based institutions, schools, primary care clinics, the workplace, and senior and community centers. Ideally, support services are provided early in the caregiving cycle or even before it begins. This enables caregivers to plan before they are abruptly thrust into a burdensome role. Unfortunately, it is human nature that most people do not seek out information and assistance until they need it. General information sessions about services and supports for older adults and their caregivers are typically not well attended, often because few people like to think about these late life challenges. An effective early preventive strategy would engage the caregiver in planning shortly after experiencing the first acute incident or receiving the diagnosis of a chronic disease.

Self-care for caregivers is an essential component in reducing stress and preventing out-of-home placement. A goal of self-care is to prevent the onset of stress and, if such signs do occur, to reduce the care demands. Learning how to accept limits and ask others to help, attending to one's physical and spiritual needs such as through exercise, meditation or time for reflection, and creating moments of joy with friends or family are critical to both self-care and to providing effective care over the long haul. Professionals can encourage caregivers to take care of their own health in order to sustain quality care for their loved ones. Yet the demands of caregiving that underlie stress often interfere with finding the time and resources for self-care. Self-care activities are most realistic when they can be integrated with other daily routines.

Yoga is an excellent way to reduce caregiver stress, and can be practiced at home.

Elder Mistreatment

In some cases, caregivers may mistreat older relatives, although this is not typically due to caregiver stress, but rather to caregivers' emotional or behavioral problems. Elder mistreatment, often invisible, has become a public issue only within the past 20 years, after the 1987 Amendments to the Older Americans Act provided guidelines for identifying mistreatment, and as a result of the visible advocacy of the National Center for the Prevention of Elder Abuse.

Elder mistreatment encompasses any knowing, intentional, or negligent act by a caregiver or other person that harms or causes risk of harm to a vulnerable adult (National Center on Elder Abuse, 2006). Our focus is on domestic abuse in the home, but elder abuse also occurs in institutional settings (e.g., nursing homes, adult family homes, group homes). Types of mistreatment

---

TYPES AND SIGNS OF ELDER MISTREATMENT

- *Physical:* willful infliction of pain and injury, such as restraining, slapping, hitting, malnutrition
- *Emotional:* verbal assault, threats, fear, insults, humiliation, infantilization, isolation, exclusion from activities
- *Sexual:* nonconsensual sexual contact
- *Material or financial:* theft; misuse or concealment of the elder's funds, property, or estate; telemarketing fraud; investment schemes; usurious home loans; home repair scams
- *Medical:* withholding or improper administration of needed medications, aids such as dentures, glasses, or hearing aids, and visits to physicians
- *Neglect:* refusal or failure to fulfill any part of a person's obligations to an elder, withholding of food, medications, funds, or medical care
- *Violation of rights:* removal from home or into long-term care setting without elder's consent
- *Abandonment:* desertion of elder by someone responsible for the elder's care

---

PROSECUTING ELDER NEGLECT

Neglect cases are often the most difficult to prosecute, because of the challenge of proving "failure to act." Investigating cases of elder neglect can also be complicated by the victim's underlying disease: Was the disease or neglect responsible for the person's death? When King County prosecutors in Washington State charged a daughter with killing her mother through reckless neglect, the case broke new ground. It was the first time the county medical examiner had declared a death to be homicide by elder neglect, and it sent an aggressive new message that crimes of neglect would no longer be ignored. A fire department aid crew found the mother in her garbage-littered, foul-smelling suburban home. The mother was lying in the fetal position, her head and body covered with feces. She was taken to the hospital, where she died a week later of dehydration and hypothermia. Her daughter, who had called 911 and reported that her mother had fallen, was charged with first-degree manslaughter. The daughter said she had brought her mother shampoo, assumed she was bathing, and had not noticed an unusual smell about her mother.

---

range from physical, sexual, or emotional to financial exploitation and neglect (either self-imposed or by another person) that result in unnecessary suffering. In a large longitudinal study, elders who were mistreated were 3.1 times more likely to die within a 3-year period than those who had not experienced abuse (Lachs and Pillemer, 2004). Up to 90 percent of mistreatment cases are committed by family members. Abusers are primarily men, and approximately 60 percent are adult children or spouses/partners. Although findings on the incidence of abuse vary because of methodological problems, an estimated 2 to 10 percent of older adults are abused by someone who lives with them, and the rate increases among those over age 85 (Lachs and Pillemer, 2004; National Center on Elder Abuse, 2006; Taylor et al., 2006; Tomita, 2006). For every case of mistreatment that is reported to

authorities, there may be as many as five unreported cases (APA, 2006).

Although financial and emotional abuse and self-neglect are most common, neglect and physical abuse (e.g., slapping, hitting, bruising) are reported most frequently. Emotional mistreatment, neglect, sexual assault, and abandonment are harder to document and often unreported (Schofield and Mishra, 2003; Teaster and Roberto, 2004; Wilber and McNeilly, 2001). Underreporting also occurs because some abusive behavior is enmeshed within complicated familial relationships (e.g., a family that has always yelled at one another), and because elders who are dependent on their abusers fear retaliation if they report mistreatment.

A CASE OF FINANCIAL ABUSE

At age 85, Jean moved in with her son, her daughter-in-law and two teenage granddaughters. She brought with her assets from the sale of her home and her husband's Social Security and railroad pension. Anxious not to burden her son, who was a consultant and often unemployed, she helped him buy two cars, paid part of the family's monthly rent, and assisted with her granddaughters' private school tuition. What began as Jean's being helpful soon became financial abuse, with her son driving her to the bank to withdraw cash for him from her account and writing checks to himself. At first, Jean did not experience this as abusive since her son always had a "good reason" for "borrowing" the money. In addition, her son would often tell her that "it was going to be his money some day anyway, so what was the difference if he spent it now or later?" The lines between financial and emotional abuse began to blur; Jean was left alone all day and her son threatened that he would put her in a nursing home if she complained. When Jean had only $8000 left in her bank account, she finally stood up to her son, insisting that the remaining funds needed to be saved for a burial plot and funeral expenses. Shortly after that, her son left his wife and daughters, who became supportive and loving of Jean and invited her to continue to live with them.

Psychological and financial abuse is even further complicated by the victims' dependency on the abusers or the abusers' economic dependency on the victims (Muehlbauer and Crane, 2006).

Undue influence is an abusive behavior that is especially difficult to detect. It occurs when a person uses his or her role and power to exploit the trust, dependency, and fear of another, often isolating and creating a world controlled by the abuser. If the abuser is a family member, older victims have trouble separating their feelings of care and love from the loss and trauma experienced at the hands of the abuser. The abusive situation becomes more complicated when the abuser is dependent on the older victim financially, emotionally, and for housing. A web of mutual dependency is created when both the abuser and the victim rely on each other for a portion of their livelihood. Abuser dependency occurs more often than the reverse; for example the dependent caregiver relies on the elder's financial resources, but the older person accepts such exploitation over being placed in a nursing home (Blum, 2000; Quinn, 2000; Wilber and Nielsen, 2002).

Elder neglect or deprivation, whether deliberate or unintentional, accounts for 60 to 70 percent of all reported elder mistreatment cases (Fulmer et al., 2005). It occurs when the caregiver does not provide assistance, goods or services necessary to avoid physical harm or mental anguish of the care recipient, such as denying food or health-related services to the elder. It can range from withholding appropriate attention to intentionally failing to meet the elders' needs, including failure to manage older adults' money responsibly (Muehlbauer and Crane, 2006). The elder's personality, childhood trauma experiences, and cognitive status are identified as risk factors for neglect. Some research on the relationship between self-reported childhood trauma and later-life neglect has found that elders who suffered from neglect or abuse in childhood are more likely to tolerate poor care in later life, because they view it as normative (Fulmer et al., 2005).

Self-neglect occurs when the older adult engages in behavior that threatens his or her safety, even though he or she is mentally competent and understands the consequences of decisions. In some instances, the inability to perform essential self-care activities (e.g., providing for food, shelter, medical care, and general safety) may reflect a lifelong lifestyle choice and a way of preserving identity and remaining in preferred environments. Elders who save everything may be trying to maintain control of their space. Yet such self-preservation behaviors are typically socially unacceptable (Bozinovski, 2000; Tomita, 2006). Self-neglect is also associated with mental impairment such as dementia, isolation, depression, and alcohol abuse, although all of these conditions negatively affect the elder's cognitive abilities. The incidence of self-neglect is highest among women living alone (Heath et al., 2005). Professional interventions, typically by social workers or nurses, generally focus on building trust with the elder to allow some services to reduce dangerously unhealthy living situations, while still protecting the elder's autonomy regarding his or her living situation. In some instances, professionals need to accept that there is nothing they can do to change the situation (Anetzberger et al., 2000; Otto, 2002; Wilber and Nielsen, 2002).

SIGNS AND SYMPTOMS OF SELF-NEGLECT

- dehydration, malnutrition, untreated or improperly managed medical conditions, poor personal hygiene
- hazardous or unsafe living conditions (e.g., improper electrical wiring, no indoor plumbing, no heat, no running water)
- unsanitary or unclean living quarters (e.g., animal/insect infestation, no functioning toilet, fecal/urine smells)
- inappropriate and/or inadequate clothing, lack of necessary medical aids (e.g., eyeglasses, hearing aids, dentures)
- grossly inadequate housing or homelessness

Whether behavior is labeled as abusive or neglectful depends on its frequency, duration, intensity, and severity, and varies across states. Lacking a national policy on elder mistreatment, each state determines standards for what constitutes abuse, who should be protected, and how. Regardless of state statutory definitions, however, the older person's perception of the action and the sociocultural context of the mistreatment also affect its identification and consequences (Hudson and Carlson, 1999; Wold, 2000).

Although ethnic minority groups vary in their opinions about what constitutes abuse, cultural differences should never be used as a justification for abuse. Nevertheless, culture, degree of acculturation, and filial values and beliefs can influence the definition of abuse and the elder's response to it (Lachs and Pillemer, 2004). In Korean families, for example, an elder may tolerate financial abuse because of the traditional patriarchal property transfer system, where sons enjoy exclusive family inheritance rights. Korean elders are also less likely to report mistreatment out of shame or fear of creating conflict (Moon, Tomita, and Jung-Kamei, 2001; Tomita, 2006). Underreporting of abuse among ethnic minority communities, especially among Asian Americans, may also reflect language barriers or mistrust of the legal and health care systems. The extent of elder mistreatment among GLBT relationships is unknown. Many in the current cohort who are uneasy being candid about their sexual orientation might have a difficult time admitting that they are abuse victims. However, this may shift in the future with greater societal acceptance of same sex partnerships (MetLife and the Lesbian and Gay Aging Issues Network of the American Society on Aging, 2006b). With the increasing numbers of grandparents as primary caregivers for grandchildren, the hidden problem of mistreatment of grandparents by older grandchildren may also become more visible (Brownell and Berman, 2000).

MR. JONES'S EMERGENCY ROOM VISIT

As an intern in a regional hospital, you have been called in to the emergency room by a nurse supervisor to talk with Mr. Jones, an 80-year-old widower. The nurse, while leaving to respond to another emergency, asks you to "deal with this senile patient." Mr. Jones is sitting in a chair beside a 65-year-old man, Mr. Sloan, who brought Mr. Jones to the emergency room.

The two men have been living together for the past 16 years, after Mr. Jones became widowed. Mr. Sloan has a history of mental illness and heavy drinking, and has been unable to hold a steady job for the past 10 years. Nevertheless, the two men appear to care for one another and Mr. Sloan says that he cooks, cleans, and cares for Mr. Jones's needs. Mr. Sloan keeps repeating that he "doesn't know how much longer he can do this," and just does not understand what is wrong with Mr. Jones.

Mr. Jones is disheveled and has visible bruises on his face and arms. You learn from the nurse that he is waiting to have his broken right wrist set. You greet Mr. Jones and ask him what happened, and Mr. Sloan answers for him. He says he found Mr. Jones after he had fallen off a chair when trying to change a light bulb. As he describes this, Mr. Jones is silent and unresponsive. Mr. Sloan tells you that both the hospital-intake worker and emergency room nurse admonished Mr. Jones for climbing on a chair, saying he should know better. Mr. Sloan says that he just can't control Mr. Jones every minute to prevent accidents from happening. Mr. Jones looks away. He is confused and tells you that he couldn't find his Medicare card when the intake worker asked for it. He says he can't remember whether he took his wallet with him when he left home.

When Mr. Jones is taken into an examining room, Mr. Sloan insists on accompanying him. Mr. Jones begins an agitated monologue that does not seem to make sense. Mr. Sloan explains to you that his behavior is typical and there is no point in talking with him. Mr. Sloan says that he will answer any questions. Mr. Jones becomes increasingly agitated and starts to cry.

If you were seeing these men in the emergency room, what information would you want to gather?

> ### WARNING SIGNS OF ABUSE AND NEGLECT
> * depression, fear, or anxiety on the part of the elder
> * discrepancy in psychosocial and medical history between elder and possible abuser
> * vague, implausible explanations of illness or injuries
> * illness that does not appear to be responding to treatment; lab findings inconsistent with history provided
> * frequent visits to the emergency room; unexplained injuries or illnesses

As noted earlier, while caregiver burden and the elder's limited functional ability may be contributing factors, caregiving stress does not in itself lead to abuse or explain its occurrence. In fact, assumptions of such stress as the cause of mistreatment can lead to inappropriate interventions for the caregiver rather than a criminal investigation (Anetzberger, 2000; Quinn and Heisler, 2002). Consistent with the P–E model, causes are embedded in the interplay of individual characteristics of the abuser and the victim within familial, cultural, and social contexts that result in adaptive or maladaptive behaviors (Carp, 2000). Congruent with feminist and social exchange theories discussed in Chapter 8, power inequities are more plausible explanations than family stress. There is growing recognition that elder mistreatment should be viewed largely from the perspective of power and control and thus treated as a criminal matter, whereas neglect may be a crisis in caregiving and therefore a health and social issue (Fulmer, Paveza, and Quadagno, 2002). In fact, case descriptions of abusers and victims reflect such power dynamics and marginalization of elders (especially women and the oldest-old), with the abuser exerting control over the vulnerable elder. Given gender inequities, it is not surprising that older women are mistreated at higher rates than men, comprising approximately 70 percent of reported victims. Nor should we be surprised that those over age 85 are abused at two to three times their proportion of the older population. Power differentials may also underlie the fact that sexual abuse is the least acknowledged, detected and reported type of elder mistreatment (National Center on Elder Abuse, 2006; Teaster and Roberto, 2004).

Spousal abuse may reflect lifelong patterns of "domestic violence grown old." In such instances, older women may stay in an abusive relationship for years, hoping the situation will get better or unaware of any other options. Silently enduring violence into their 70s or 80s, they tend to become increasingly isolated and "fall between the cracks"—too old to go to domestic violence shelters designed for younger women, and invisible to providers of age-based services. Spousal abuse may also occur in new, first-time relationships or may be "late-onset" domestic violence, perhaps triggered by retirement, illness, reduced income, cognitive decline, and dementia. Few shelters promote themselves to older women or are equipped to handle their distinctive needs; but even when such shelters exist, they are underutilized by older women. As noted by one advocate, "when we advertised an elder-domestic violence support group, no one came. But when we relaunched it as a quilt-making group, women felt comfortable to come forward" (France, 2006, p. 82).

As noted earlier, abuser impairment is one of the strongest explanations for elder mistreatment. Abusers typically have more mental or physical health problems, alcohol or drug dependence, financial problems, and resentment toward and social isolation of the older person

> ### CHARACTERISTICS OF THE ABUSER THAT REFLECT POWER INEQUITIES
> * being male
> * dependent on the elder for housing, finances, or other services (e.g., meals, laundry)
> * mental illness, substance abuse, a history of problem behaviors, and lack of empathy for those with disabilities

compared to non-abusers (Lachs and Pillemer, 2004; Schofield and Mishra, 2003; Tomita, 2006). The history of the relationship is also salient; for example, a history of alcoholism, financial problems, child abuse and neglect, conflict and violence in the relationship are other risk factors (Barusch and Richardson 2006). The following behavioral characteristics of the care recipient are associated with greater probability of abuse: being aggressive, critical, complaining, combative, and excessively dependent or unrealistic in expectations. Given these factors, it is not surprising that older adults who are socially isolated, and those with dementia, who may display aggressive, unpredictable behavior and who are typically less able to report abuse and access services, are the most vulnerable to mistreatment (Anetzberger et al., 2000; McConnell and McConnell, 2000; National Center on Elder Abuse, 2006; Wilber and Nielsen, 2002).

Assessment, Interventions, and Reporting

Families and health care providers need to be alert to signs of potential mistreatment, although it may still be difficult for the abused to talk openly about their experience. And abusers are typically effective at presenting themselves as overly concerned about their older victim and thus at masking signs. A range of screening and assessment tools for professionals to evaluate both caregivers and care recipients for risk of elder mistreatment are available. Two with excellent psychometric properties are the Elder Assessment Instrument (EAI), used by clinicians (Fulmer, 2003), and an index of risk factors as part of a comprehensive geriatric assessment (Shugarman, et al., 2003). The use of elder abuse screening tools with family caregivers is problematic; not surprisingly, families are reluctant to report risk factors. For this reason, some researchers recommend the use of self-report measures with elders, such as the Vulnerability to Abuse Screening Tool (VAT) (Schofield and Mishra, 2003). Others argue for a comprehensive

assessment that takes account of the caregiver, care recipient, environmental, housing, and community factors (Anetzberger, 2005; Anetzberger et al., 2000; Carp, 2000).

Multilevel interventions aim to take account of such person–environment characteristics. One intervention program successfully coordinated the work of adult protective services and the Alzheimer's Association in educating caregivers to prevent mistreatment (Anetzberger et al., 2000). Another intervention model focused on empowerment and strengthening the elder's resources and educating the caregiver, including home care interventions, empowerment support groups for elders, and family support groups for caregivers (Nahmiash and Reis, 2000). Because of the high incidence of behavioral and emotional problems of abusers, targeted individual interventions with caregivers are also important (Reay and Brown, 2002).

All 50 states have developed procedures for reporting domestic abuse (including 24-hour toll-free numbers for receiving confidential reports of abuse), and all but 6 have made such reporting mandatory for health care providers. This means that providers' failure to report elder abuse to public agencies is a criminal offense. In fact, 8 states require "any person," not just professionals, to report suspicion of mistreatment. Every state also has a long-term care ombudsman to investigate and resolve complaints about nursing homes but only 37 states require Adult Protective Services (APS) investigation in institutional settings (Teaster and Roberto, 2004). All states have established APS programs, which generally have the authority to investigate reported cases or to refer them to appropriate legal authorities such as district attorneys.

Adult Protective Services is the state or county system that investigates reports of mistreatment. They evaluate risk, assess the elder's capacity to agree to services, develop and implement care plans, and monitor ongoing service delivery (Otto, 2002). Since mandatory reporting laws require that APS accept all

THE COMPLEXITIES OF DOMESTIC VIOLENCE GROWN OLD

Married for 41 years, Audrey was first abused two months after their wedding. Her husband's attacks increased in frequency and cruelty. Once he caught her fingers in his car window and let her loose only when her screams drew a crowd. She camouflaged her bruises. But her psychological wounds were painfully visible. He made her believe she was dumb and fat, though she slimmed down to a fashion model's stature, and made her totally dependent on him. He refused to let her see family and friends alone and had the telephone removed from the house. She prayed that time would temper his moods, though it never did. Retirement seemed to make him angrier. Even when he sank into a feeble old age, he would strike at her with his cane. Only a few years ago, a doctor, alerted by her sad demeanor, asked if she was experiencing trouble at home. Unloading her secret brought Audrey a sense of liberation she hadn't felt in years. Although the doctor introduced her to a domestic abuse intervention program, and she attended weekly meetings, she remained with her husband. Even when her husband was totally reliant on her because of his heart disease, high blood pressure, and diabetes, the physical abuse never ebbed. Right before he died, he put his arm around her and told Audrey he loved her. When he died, she was finally free of his abuse (France, 2006).

substantiated after investigation, but relatively few are prosecuted, often because witnesses or victims are unable or unwilling to testify (Choi and Mayer, 2000; Fulmer et al., 2002; Wilber and Nielsen, 2002; Wold, 2000). Other reasons for underreporting include the isolation of older adults and our society's value on family privacy (which make concealment possible), lack of uniform reporting laws, and professionals' reluctance to report suspected cases. Screening measures for abuse typically assume that the alleged victim has the cognitive ability to respond to questions. In addition, the unknown consequences from reporting abuse (e.g., removal from the home, nursing home placement, abuser's anger) may be more traumatic to the abused than remaining in the negative situation. Reporting abuse may make visible to others the emotionally painful reality that a child can abuse a parent. If the abuser is arrested, restrained from the home, or abandons the elder, the older adult suffers the loss of a caregiver and companion, no matter how harmful the relationship may be. The elder may grieve the loss of the family member who was abusive as well as the other multifaceted losses entailed by abuse (Bergeron, 2000; Sprecher and Fehr, 1998).

Since reports of abuse to APS appear to be only the "tip of the iceberg," large, rigorous probability samples of community-dwelling older adults' self-reports are needed. In addition,

reports, heavy caseloads typically are filled with complex and difficult cases that other agencies are unwilling or unable to accept (Wilber and Nielsen, 2002). Another barrier is that few community-based living options and in-home supports exist for elders removed from high-risk situations. In addition, professionals are often biased toward home care and resist placing the elder in a long-term care facility, even when the latter would be safer for the abused elder than remaining at home with a suspected abuser.

Only about 16 percent of cases of mistreatment are reported; of these, over 60 percent are

PRINCIPLES THAT SHAPE ADULT PROTECTIVE SERVICES PRACTICE

- the client's right to self-determination and autonomy
- the use of the least restrictive alternative
- the maintenance of the family unit whenever possible
- the use of community-based services rather than institutions
- the avoidance of ascribing blame
- the presumption that inadequate or inappropriate services are worse than none (Otto, 2000)

it is important to conduct longitudinal follow-ups of APS use. Such information can better clarify the magnitude of the problem (Branch, 2002; Otto, 2002; Thomas, 2000).

Ethical issues typically emerge in instances of elder mistreatment. Elders' rights to self-determination and to refuse treatment, which are difficult to assess in ambiguous situations, are central to any systems to prevent mistreatment. In addition, professional ethics places a high value on confidentiality and protection of client's rights and autonomy. As a result, less than 10 percent of APS clients receive services without the client's consent (Otto, 2002). In contrast to instances of child abuse, an older person has the right to refuse assistance even if he or she is found to be incompetent. In such instances, however, APS would move to have a guardian appointed who would assume authority over the elder's personal financial and estate affairs and could authorize nursing home placement against the elder's wishes (Lachs et al., 2002). However, a court-appointed guardian may also mistreat the elder, typically through financial exploitation. Issues of confiden-

tiality are salient in caregiver support groups where caregivers self-disclose abuse, but the health care provider is mandated to report this information (Bergeron and Gray, 2003).

In the past decade, cases of mistreatment have become criminalized under state statutes. This means that law enforcement may conduct a criminal investigation while APS supports the victim with counseling and services designed to provide safe medical and physical care. Some intervention models include teaming law enforcement professionals (e.g., police, district attorneys) with social workers and other health and human service professionals from a wide range of agencies to address the needs of both the victim and the abuser (Brownell, 2002). Elder Justice Act legislation was introduced to Congress in 2006 to provide more funds to detect, prevent, and prosecute elder abuse, but was not passed.

Placement in Long-Term Care Facilities

Although living alone is a major predictor of placement in long-term care facilities, some 50 percent of those in nursing homes have children (Tennstedt, 1999). In most cases, families turn to nursing homes only after exhausting their own resources, although adult daughters and husbands resort to out-of-home placement earlier than do other family members. The decision to seek nursing home placement is frequently precipitated by the family caregiver's illness or death, or by severe family strain. Placement is thus often the result of a breakdown in the balance between the older person's care needs and self-care abilities; the primary caregiver's internal and external resources; and the larger support network. For example, the characteristics of the caregiving context, especially perceived burden, negative family relationships, and low confidence in care, are better predictors of whether an Alzheimer's patient will enter a nursing home than are the illness characteristics or symptoms of the care

A MODEL FOR MULTIDISCIPLINARY COLLABORATION TO PREVENT AND PROSECUTE ABUSE

In King County in Seattle, Washington, a county-wide Elder Abuse Project sponsors an elder abuse council that includes police, prosecutors, nurses, medical examiners, and social service workers. It meets monthly to figure out how "the system" can better prevent, treat, and respond to the abuse of older and disabled adults. A criminal mistreatment review panel helps policymakers decide whether elder neglect cases can be prosecuted. The project also trains police, emergency room staff and medical technicians, and long-term care workers to detect signs of elder abuse and familiarize themselves with state laws. Recognizing that neglect is one of the most underreported and least understood crimes by police and prosecutors, the project is currently focusing on adult neglect cases.

> **PRECIPITANTS TO NURSING HOME PLACEMENT**
>
> Caregiving stress becomes intensified when older adults experience:
>
> - Falls
> - Incontinence that cannot be managed
> - Aggressiveness
> - Sleep problems
>
> Nursing home placement may result.

recipient (Gaugler et al., 2000b; Gaugler et al., 2005; Seltzer and Li, 2000).

Most people hold negative attitudes toward nursing homes, even though the quality of care in many residential care settings is excellent. Given such attitudes, moving an older relative to a nursing home is typically a stressful family event, especially for wives who vowed to care for their husbands "in sickness and in health" (Seltzer and Li, 2000). Accordingly, the placement decision often arouses feelings of grief, loss, guilt, and fear, and may renew past family conflicts. However, some families experience improved relationships with their relatives and continue to visit and assist with hands-on care in long-term care facilities. In other words, the role of "caregiver" does not cease after out of home placement, but the nature of tasks and stressors change (Gaugler, Kane and Kane, 2002; Polivka, 2005). Families typically still feel psychologically responsible, even though they must relinquish control over daily care decisions to staff and learn how to be "visitors" rather than primary caregivers (Schulz et al., 2003b). These role changes can initially trigger the family's dissatisfaction with their elder's care. However, when staff–family partnerships develop, families generally experience less stress and are more satisfied with the care received by their elder (Maas, 2000).

With the growth of the oldest-old, placement in a long-term care setting may come to be viewed as a natural transition in the life cycle. Geriatric care managers can assist with the timing of this transition and with negotiating a positive role for

the caregiver's continued involvement in the facility. To ease the transition to the post-placement phase, many nursing homes have developed support and educational groups for families and special training for staff. Internet-based services can also assist families with locating an appropriate long-term care facility (Tanase, 2003).

Underpaid Caregivers: Direct Care Workers

Underpaid **direct care workers** (e.g., nurses aides, personal assistants, home care workers, etc.) are second only to families as the primary providers of long-term care. Of the total number of direct care jobs in long-term care, 56 percent are in nursing and personal care facilities, 17 percent in assisted living and other residential care settings, and the remaining 27 percent in home health care, either through an agency or as independent providers (Howes, 2004). As the "eyes and the ears" of the long-term care system, direct or chronic care workers provide "high-touch" intimate, personal, and physically/emotionally challenging care. These hands-on providers are expected to be compassionate in their care, yet usually do not feel prepared, respected, or valued—similar to the experiences of many family caregivers. The typical paraprofessional or aide is an immigrant single mother of children under age 18, with minimal education and living in poverty. Racial and gender inequities in education and employment opportunities across the life course partially explain the predominance of African American, Asian, and Latina women, many of whom are immigrants, among direct care workers. Language and cultural differences in communication may interfere with meeting older persons' needs. Our society's lack of public recognition of the socially and economically important work of caregiving is, in turn, reflected in relatively negative working conditions. These include poverty-level wages, limited training, inadequate supervision, and low status (DHHS, 2003; Howes, 2004).

The heavy workload is often a repetition of single tasks, and the risk of personal injury from physical work is high. Workers of color may be treated disrespectfully, even verbally and physically abused, by some older care recipients. In addition, there are few incentives for obtaining more training or education to enhance quality of care. Not surprisingly, the turnover rate among direct care workers is high, with 45 to 100 percent replaced annually in nursing homes and 30 percent in home care. Turnover not only disrupts continuity of care, but is expensive, costing providers from $1400 to $3900 per direct care worker for recruitment, training, and lost productivity. The total costs of turnover among direct care workers is estimated to exceed $4 billion annually (Harris-Kojetin et al., 2006). Today, over 40 states face a shortage of direct care workers, and many large nursing homes and home care agencies recruit workers from developing countries. The problem will be exacerbated as the population of older adults increases, with projections of nearly 70 percent growth in long-term care workers between 2000 and 2010 (DHHS, 2003; Howes, 2004; Institute for the Future of Aging Services [IFAS], 2004; Montgomery et al., 2005). The public policy and structural factors that exacerbate this shortage, along with Medicaid waiver programs that allow adults with disabilities and elders to hire family members, are discussed further in Chapter 17.

Fortunately, employers and policy makers are beginning to recognize the centrality of direct care workers to quality long-term care. In 2001, a report by the Institute of Medicine emphasized that the quality of long-term care depends on the performance of the caregiving workforce and recommended more attention to education, training, and supports for direct care workers. In California, Oregon, and Washington, home care workers have unionized; coalitions of organized labor, disabilities activists, senior citizens' lobbies, and community groups share the goal of changing the structure of employment in home health care (Schneider, 2003). Because of unionization in California, roughly 25 percent of home care workers earn more than the minimum wage and have access to health, dental, and vision care insurance. As a result, being a home care worker is now considered a good job in California (Howes, 2004). In addition to improved wages and benefits, it is important to provide direct care workers with more opportunities to be involved in decision making. This is because these staff often know the older resident best and can enhance decision-making autonomy, job satisfaction, and retention (IFAS, 2004). Culture change efforts in nursing homes have also reduced turnover significantly as described in Chapter 11.

Implications for the Future

With the aging of the baby boomers and increased longevity, family care of older adults will undoubtedly encompass a longer phase of the life span, with adults devoting 40 to 50 years to caring for older relatives. Care networks will be larger and more complex because of the diversity of family structures and the effects of divorce, remarriage, blended families, more single parents, unmarried heterosexual couples, and GLBT families raising children. Women are likely to remain the primary caregivers for elders. Even though 75 percent of married mothers work outside the home, women still assume primary responsibility for children. In fact, women still devote nearly as much time to household tasks as they did 50 years ago, even though the expectation and necessity for women to enter the paid workforce has grown. The persistence of this gender-based pattern in child care and household tasks thus tempers expectations that men will soon become the majority of primary care providers of frail elders, although the percent of male caregivers is already increasing (Family Caregiver Alliance, 2006b).

The workforce need for direct care workers in home health and residential care will outpace the supply among women ages 25 to 54. In fact, the job growth rate for direct care workers is projected to be twice as high as health care employment in general (45 percent vs. 25 percent) and 3 times as high as all other industries (45 percent vs. 16 percent) (Montgomery et al., 2005). Possible solutions to this looming shortage are to recruit more workers from other countries (although this is more difficult with new immigration restrictions), expand the number of training programs, offer retraining for older and displaced workers, improve worker safety, wages and benefits, and explore the possibility of technology to assist with direct care monitoring, as described in Chapter 11 (DHHS, 2003).

The role of government in supporting family caregivers in the near future is unclear, and will undoubtedly be affected by the escalating federal deficit. Current federal cutbacks, increased military spending, and the devolution of responsibility for services to the states suggest that public funding to support informal caregivers will probably be limited. More corporations may offer elder-care services as an employee benefit, because of the effects of family caregiving on worker productivity. Other private sector initiatives, such as faith-based programs, may provide incremental supports for families, but these are unlikely to reduce substantially the burdens faced by families who may be caring for relatives with cognitive impairments for many years. For-profit geriatric care management businesses are likely to grow, especially to address issues of caregiving at a geographic distance. However, these services to locate and coordinate resources will be primarily accessible to upper-middle-class adult children. Unless patterns of public funding change dramatically, low-income families who are not poor enough to qualify for Medicaid-funded services will typically lack such supports.

Health care providers' assessments of older adults will increasingly include family caregivers' capacities. Nurses and social workers will play a key role in identifying supportive resources for families to enhance their caregiving capability and reduce stress. The issues of grief and loss inherent in family care, especially for an older adult with dementia, will need to be addressed by hospice workers, bereavement counselors, and other providers. The professional preparation of health care providers must include more information about how family history and relationships affect care, how to work effectively with family systems, and how to identify supportive resources for caregivers. Providers will also need training on detecting and reporting elder mistreatment.

FOR BETTER OR WORSE © 2006 Lynn Johnston Productions. By Universal Press Syndicate. Reprinted with permission. All rights reserved.

The use of information technology to provide family caregivers with informal and mutual support will grow. Living in a networked society, senior boomers, facile with computers and the Internet throughout their adult lives, will be more comfortable than current cohorts in accessing information and support from others, including resources for family caregivers, through computer-based technology. The Internet can already provide a wealth of information for family caregivers. These include free e-mail question-and-answer sites, bulletin board structures for sharing concerns and joint problem-solving, digital photos of long term care facilities, and links to national resources. Services such as these will continue to grow. Family caregivers will increasingly turn to other caregivers for 24-hour mutual support as well as accessing medical information via the Internet. The growth of assistive technology and computerized "smart homes," as described in Chapter 11, will enable more frail elders to remain safely in their own homes. However, such innovative supports will be more readily available to those who can privately purchase them than to low-income elders and their families. Whether computer technology can, over time, reduce inequities and barriers to services among low-income elders of color remains unknown, and will probably mirror racial and class gaps among younger generations.

Summary

Most families, regardless of socioeconomic class or ethnic minority status, attempt to provide care for their older members for as long as possible, and seek nursing home placement only when they have exhausted other resources. Without informal caregiving, the costs of long-term care to society would be staggering. Adult children—generally women—are faced with providing financial, emotional, and physical assistance to older relatives, oftentimes with little support from others. In ethnic minority and lower-income families, older relatives are likely to receive daily care from younger relatives and to be involved themselves in caring for grandchildren. But there are often numerous financial, physical, and emotional costs to caregiving. Elder mistreatment is one tragic outcome of a stressful caregiving situation, although most likely a result of caregivers' own behavioral problems. Responsibilities for caregiving are affected by a number of social trends, most notable among them the increasing percentage of middle-aged women—traditionally the caregivers—who are more likely to be employed, and the number of reconstituted families resulting from divorce and remarriage. The needs of caregivers are clearly a growing concern for social and health care providers and policy makers.

GLOSSARY

caregiving   the act of assisting people with personal care, household chores, transportation, and other tasks associated with daily living; provided primarily by families without compensation or by direct care workers.

caregiver burden   physical, emotional, and financial costs associated with assisting persons with long-term care needs

direct care workers   nurse aides, personal assistants, and home care staff who provide hands-on care in both home and long-term care settings; also referred to as chronic care workers

elder mistreatment   maltreatment of older adults, including physical, sexual, and psychological abuse, and financial exploitation, and neglect

elder neglect   deprivation of care necessary to maintain elders' health by those trusted to provide the care (e.g., neglect by others) or by older persons themselves (self-neglect)

Family and Medical Leave Act   federal legislation passed in 1993 that provides job protection to workers requiring short-term leaves from their jobs for the care of a dependent parent, seriously ill newborn or adopted child

informal caregiving   unpaid assistance provided by family, friends, and neighbors for persons requiring help with ADL and IADL's.

National Family Caregiver Support Program of 2000   requires state and area agencies on aging to provide services to support family caregivers

objective burden   reality demands that caregivers face (income loss, job disruption, etc.)

primary stressors   events that derive directly from the elder's illness, such as memory loss or wandering

respite care   short-term relief (rest) for caregivers; may be provided in the home or out of home (e.g., adult day health centers)

secondary stressors   do not arise directly from the older person's illness, such as role strains and loss of time for self; however these are not secondary in terms of their importance

self-neglect   the older adult engages in behavior that threatens own safety, even though mentally competent

subjective burden   the caregiver's experience of caregiver burden; differential appraisal of stress

women in the middle   women who have competing demands from older parents, spouses, children, or employment

RESOURCES

Log on to MySocKit (www.mysockit.com) for information about the following:

- Administration on Aging, National Family Caregiver Support Program
- Alzheimer's Association
- Elders in Action
- Eldercare Locator
- Eldercare Web
- Family Caregiver Alliance
- The Home Care Page
- National Alliance for Caregiving
- National Association of Geriatric Care Managers
- National Center on Elder Abuse

- National Family Caregivers Association
- National Institute on Aging, Family and Professional Caregiver Programs
- National Respite Coalition Task Force: Lifespan Respite

REFERENCES

Acton, G.J., and Wright, K. Self-transcendence and family caregivers of adults with dementia. *Journal of Holistic Nursing*, 2000, *18*, 143–58.

Adams, B., Aranda, M., Kemp, B., and Takagi, K. Ethnic and gender differences in distress among Anglo-American, African American, Japanese American and Mexican American spousal caregivers of persons with dementia. *Journal of Clinical Geropsychology*, 2002, *8*, 279–301.

Adams, K.B., and Sanders, S. Alzheimer's caregiver differences in experience of loss, grief reactions and depressive symptoms across stage of disease. *Dementia*, 2004, *3*, 195–210.

Administration on Aging (AOA). *The Older Americans Act: National Family Caregiver Support Program (Title III-E and Title VI-C): Compassion in Action.* Washington, DC: U.S. Department of Health and Human Services, 2004.

Allen, S., Goldscheider, F., and Ciambrone, D.A. Gender roles, marital intimacy, and nomination of spouse as primary caregiver. *The Gerontologist*, 1999, *39*, 150–158.

Almberg, B., Grafstroem, M., and Winblad, B. Caregivers of relatives with dementia: Experiences encompassing social support and bereavement. *Aging and Mental Health*, 2000, *4*, 82–89.

Alzheimer's Association of America. *Statistics and chapter information.* Chicago, 2001.

Alzheimer's Association of America and National Alliance for Caregiving. *Family care: Alzheimer's caregiving in the United States, 2004.* Author, 2004.

American Psychological Association (APA). *Elder abuse and neglect. In search of solutions.* Accessed December 21, 2006, from http://www.apa.org.

Anetzberger, G.J. (2005). Clinical management of elder abuse: General considerations. *Clinical Gerontologist, 28*, 27–41.

Anetzberger, G.J. Caregiving: Primary cause of elder abuse? *Generations,* Summer 2000, *24,* 46–51.

Anetzberger, G.J., Palmisano, B.R., Sanders, M., Bass, D., Dayton, C., Eckert, S., and Schimer, M.R. A model intervention for elder abuse and dementia. In E.S. McConnell (Ed.), Practice Concepts. *The Gerontologist,* 2000, *40.*

Arnett, J.J. Emerging adulthood: A theory of development from the late teens through the twenties. *American Psychologist,* 2000, *55,* 469–480.

Arno, P.S. *Prevalence, hours and economic value of family caregiving.* Kensington, MD: National Family Caregivers Association and San Francisco, CA: Family Caregiver Alliance, 2006.

Beach, S., Schulz, R., Williamson, G., Miller, L., Weiner, M., et al., Risk factors for potentially harmful informal caregiver behavior. *Journal of the American Geriatrics Society,* 2005, *53,* 255–261.

Beach, S., Schulz, R., Yee, J., and Jackson, S. Negative and positive health effects of caring for a disabled spouse: Longitudinal findings from the Caregiver Health Effects Study. *Psychology and Aging,* 2000, *15,* 259–271.

Bengtson, V.L. Beyond the nuclear family: The increasing importance of multigenerational bonds. *Journal of Marriage and the Family,* 2001, *63,* 1–16.

Bergeron, R. Serving the needs of elder abuse victims. *Policy and Practice of Public Human Services,* 2000, *58,* 40–45.

Bergeron, R., and Gray, B. Ethical dilemmas of reporting suspected elder abuse. *Social Work,* 2003, *48,* 96–105.

Blum, B. *Elder abuse.* Paper presented at the Elder Abuse Conference, Tucson, Arizona, 2000.

Boise, L., Congelton, L., and Shannon, K. Empowering family caregivers: The powerful tools for caregiving program. *Educational Gerontology,* 2005, *31,* 1–14.

Boss, P. Ambiguous loss: Living with frozen grief. *Harvard Mental Health Letter,* 1999, *16,* 4–7.

Bourgeois, M.S., Schulz, R., Burgio, L., and Beach, S. Skills training for spouses of patients with Alzheimer's disease: Outcomes of an intervention study. *Journal of Clinical Geropsychology,* 2002, *8,* 53–73.

Bozinovski, S. Older self-neglectors: Interpersonal problems and the maintenance of self-continuity. *Journal of Elder Abuse and Neglect,* 2000, *12,* 37–56.

Braithwaite, V. Making choices through caregiving appraisals. *The Gerontologist,* 2000, *40,* 706–717.

Branch, L. The epidemiology of elder abuse and neglect. *Public Policy and Aging Report,* 2002, *12,* 19–23.

Brodaty, H., Thompson, C., Thompson, C., and Five, M. Why caregivers of people with dementia and memory loss don't use services. *International Journal of Geriatric Psychiatry,* 2005, *20,* 537–546.

Brodie, K., and Gadling-Cole, C. The use of family decision meetings when addressing caregiver stress. *Journal of Gerontological Social Work,* 2003, *41,* 89–100.

Brody, E. *Women in the middle.* New York: Springer, 2004.

Brownell, P. The application of the culturagram in cross-cultural practice with elder abuse victims. *Journal of Elder Abuse and Neglect,* 1997, *9,* 19–33.

Brownell, P. *Project 2015: The future of aging in New York state.* New York: Department for the Aging, 2002.

Brownell, P., and Berman, J. Elder abuse and the kinship foster care system: Two generations at risk. In C. Cox (Ed.), *To grandmother's house we go and stay.* New York: Springer, 2000.

Bullock, K., Crawford, S., and Tennstedt, S. Employment and caregiving: Exploration of African American caregivers. *Social Work,* 2003, *48,* 150–162.

Burgio, L., Corcoran, M., Lichstein, K.L., Nichols, L., Czaja, S.J., Gallagher-Thompson, D., et al. Judging outcomes in psychosocial interventions for dementia caregivers: The problems of treatment implementation. *The Gerontologist,* 2001, *41,* 481–489.

Burgio, L., Solano, N., Fisher, S., Stevens, A., and Gallagher-Thompson, D. Skill-building: Psychoeducational strategies. In D.W. Coon. D. Gallagher-Thompson, and L. Thompson (Eds.), *Innovative interventions to reduce dementia caregiver distress: A clinical guide.* New York: Springer, 2003b.

Burgio, L., Stevens, A., Guy, D., Roth, D.L., and Haley, W.E. Impact of two psychosocial interventions on white and African American family caregivers of individuals with dementia. *The Gerontologist,* 2003a, *43,* 568–581.

Calasanti, T.M., and Slevin, K.F. *Gender, social inequalities and aging.* Walnut Creek, CA: Altima Press, 2001.

Campbell, L.D., and Martin-Matthews, A. Primary and proximate. *Journal of Family Issues,* 2000, *21,* 1006–1031.

Cannuscio, C. Jones, C., Kawachi, I., Colditz, G., Berkman, L., and Rimm, E. Reverberations of family illness: A longitudinal assessment of informal caregiving and mental health status in the nurses' health study. *American Journal of Public Health,* 2002, *92,* 1305–1311.

Carp, F. *Elder abuse in the family: An interdisciplinary model for research.* New York: Springer, 2000.

Chadidha, L., Adams, P., Phorano, O., Ong, S., and Byers, L. Stories told and lessons learned from African American female caregivers' vignettes for empowerment practice. *Journal of Gerontological Social Work,* 2002, *40,* 135–144.

Chappell, N.L., and Reid, R.C. Burden and well being among caregivers: Examining the distinction. *The Gerontologist,* 2002, *42,* 772–80.

Choi, N.G., and Mayer, J. Elder abuse, neglect and exploitation: Risk factors and prevention strategies. *Journal of Gerontological Social Work,* 2000, *33,* 5–25.

Christakis, N., and Allison, P. Spouse's hospitalization increases partner's risk of death. *New England Journal of Medicine,* 2006, *54,* 719–730.

Connell, C.M., Janevic, M.R., and Gallant, M.P. The costs of caring: Impact of dementia on family caregivers. *Journal of Geriatric Psychiatry and Neurology,* 2001, *14,* 179–187.

Coon, D., Ory, M., and Schulz, R. Family caregivers: Enduring and emerging themes. In D. Coon, D. Gallagher-Thompson, and L. Thompson (Eds.), *Innovative interventions to reduce caregiver distress.* New York: Springer, 2003, 327.

Cuellar, N. A comparison of African American and Caucasian American female caregivers of rural, post-stroke, bed bound older adults. *Journal of Gerontological Nursing,* 2002, *28,* 36–45.

Dautzenberg, M.G., Diedricks, J.P., Philipsen, H., and Tan, F.E. Multigenerational caregiving and well-being: Distress of middle aged daughters providing assistance to elderly parents. *Women's Health,* 1999, *29,* 57–74.

Department of Health and Human Services (DHHS). *The future supply of long-term care workers in relation to the aging of the baby boom generation. Report to Congress.* Washington, DC: 2003.

Dilworth-Anderson, P., Williams, S.W., and Cooper, T. Family caregiving to elderly African Americans: Caregiver types and structures. *Journals of Gerontology: Social Sciences,* 1999, *54B,* S237–S241.

Dilworth-Anderson, P., Williams, S.W., and Gibson, R.E. Issues of race, ethnicity, and culture in caregiving research: A 20-year review. *The Gerontologist,* 2002, *42,* 237–272.

Dobrof, J., and Ebenstein, H. Family caregiver self-identification: Implications for healthcare and social service professionals. *Generations,* 2003/2004, *27,* 33–38.

Donorfio, L.M., and Sheehan, N.W. Relationship dynamics between aging mothers and caregiving daughters: Filial expectations and responsibilities. *Journal of Adult Development,* 2001, *8,* 39–49.

Dupuis, S. Understanding ambiguous loss in the context of dementia care: Adult children's perspective. *Journal of Gerontological Social Work,* 2002, *37,* 93–114.

Eisdorfer, C., Cazja, S.J., Loewenstein, D., Rubert, M., Arguelles, S., et al. The effect of a family therapy and technology-based intervention on caregiver depression. *The Gerontologist,* 2003, *43,* 521–531.

Family Caregiver Alliance. Caregiver assessment: *Principles, guidelines, and strategies for change. Report from a National Consensus Development Conference.* San Francisco: National Center on Caregiving, 2006a.

Family Caregiver Alliance, *Selected caregiver statistics.* San Francisco: Family Caregiver Alliance, 2006b.

Family Caregiver Alliance. *Women and caregiving: Facts and figures.* San Francisco: Family Caregiver Alliance, 2006c.

Feder, J., and Levine, C. Explaining the paradox of long-term care policy. In C. Levine and T. Murray (Eds.), *The cultures of caregiving: Conflict and common ground among families, health care professionals and policy makers.* Baltimore: Johns Hopkins University Press, 2004, 103–112.

Feinberg, L.F. The state of the art of caregiver assessment. *Generations.* 2003–2004.

Feinberg, L.F., and Newman, S.A study of 10 states since passage of the National Family Caregiver Support Program: Policies, perceptions and program development. *The Gerontologist,* 2004, *44,* 760–769.

Feinberg, L.F., Newman, S., Gray, L., Kolb, K., and Fox-Grage, W. *The state of the states: A 50-state study.* San Francisco: Family Caregiver Alliance, 2004.

Femiano, S., and Coonerty-Femiano, A. Principles and interventions for working therapeutically with caregiving men: Responding to challenges. In E. Kramer and L. Thompson (Eds.), *Men as Caregivers,* New York: Springer, 2002.

Foley, K.L., Tung, H.J., and Mutran, E.J. Self gain and-self loss among African American and white caregivers. *Journals of Gerontology,* 2002, *57,* S14–S22.

France, D. And then he hit me. *AARP Magazine,* Jan/Feb., 2006, 73–77.

Franks, M., Pierce, L., and Dwyer, J. Expected parent-care involvement of adult children. *Journal of Applied Gerontology,* 2003, 22, 104–117.

Fredriksen, K.I. Family caregiving among lesbians and gay men. *Social Work,* 1999, *44, 142–155.*

Fredriksen-Goldsen, K.I. Caregiving and resiliency: Predictors of well being. *Journal of Family Relations,* in press.

Fredriksen-Goldsen, K.I., and Hooyman, N. *Multigenerational health, development and equality.* Seattle: University of Washington School of Social Work, Concept paper, 2003.

Fredriksen-Goldsen, K.I., and Scharlach, A.E. *Families and work: New directions in the twenty first century.* New York: Oxford University Press, 2001.

Fulmer, T. Try this: Elder abuse and neglect assessment. *Journal of Gerontological Nursing,* 2003, *29,* 8–10.

Fulmer, T., Paveza, G., and Quadagno, L. Elder abuse and neglect: Policy issues for two very different problems. *Public Policy and Aging Report,* 2002, *12,* 15–18.

Fulmer, T., Paveza, G., VandeWeerd, C., Fairchild, S., Guadagno, L., Bolton-Blatt, M., et al. Dyadic vulnerability and risk profiling for elder neglect. *The Gerontologist,* 2005, *45,* 525–535.

Gallagher-Thompson, D., Hargrave, R., Hinton, L., Arean, P., Iwamasa, G., and Zeiss, L. Interventions for a multicultural society. In D. Coon, D. Gallagher-Thompson and L. Thompson (Eds.), *Innovative interventions to reduce dementia caregiver distress.* New York: Springer, 2003.

Gartska, T., McCallion, P., and Toseland, R. Using support groups to improve caregiver health. In

M.L. Hummert and J.F. Nussbaum (Eds.), *Aging, communication, and health.* Mahwah, NJ: Lawrence Erlbaum Associates, 2001.

Gaugler, J.E., Edwards, A., Femia, E., Zarit, S., Stephens, M., et al. Predictors of institutionalization of cognitively impaired elders: Family help and the timing of placements. *Journals of Gerontology,* 2000b, *55B,* P247–255.

Gaugler, J.E., Jarrot, S., Zarit, S., Stephens, M., Townsend, A., and Greene, R. Adult day service use and reductions in caregiving hours: Effects on stress and psychological well-being for dementia caregivers. *International Journal of Geriatric Psychiatry,* 2003, *18,* 55–62.

Gaugler, J.E., Kane, R.L., and Kane, R.A. Family care for older adults with disabilities: Toward more targeted and interpretable research. *International Journal of Aging and Human Development,* 2002, *54,* 205–231.

Gaugler, J.E., Kane, R.L., Kane, R.A., Clay, T., and Newcomer, R. The effects of duration of caregiving on institutionalization. *The Gerontologist,* 2005, *45,* 78–89

Gaugler, J.E., Leitsch, S.A., Zarit, S.H., and Pearlin, L.I. Caregiver involvement following institutionalization: Effects of preplacement stress. *Research on Aging,* 2000a, *22,* 337–360.

Gerstel, N., and Gallagher, S. Men's caregiving: Gender and the contingent character of care, *Gender and Society,* 2001, *15,* 197–217.

Gitlin, L., and Gwyther, L. In-home interventions. Helping caregivers where they live. In Coon, D. Gallagher-Thompson, and L. Thompson. *Innovative interventions to reduce dementia caregiver distress.* New York: Springer, 2003.

Goldschieder, F.K., Thornton, A., and Yang, LS. Helping out the kids: Expectations about parental support in young adulthood. *Journal of Marriage and the Family,* 2001, *63,* 727–740.

Gonyea, J. Midlife, multigenerational bonds, and caregiving. In R. Talley (Ed.), *Caregiving: Science to practice.* New York: Oxford Press, in press.

Gottlieb, B.H., Thompson, L., and Bourgeois, M. Monitoring and evaluating interventions. In D. Coon, D. Gallagher-Thompson, and L. Thompson. *Innovative interventions to reduce dementia caregiver stress.* New York: Springer, 2003.

Greenberg, J., Selzter, M., and Brewer, V. Caregivers to older adults. In B. Berkman (Ed.), *Handbook of social work in health and aging,* New York: Oxford, 2006.

Groger, L., and Mayberry, P. S. Caring too much? Cultural lag in African Americans' perceptions of filial responsibilities. *Journal of Cross-Cultural Gerontology,* 2001, *16,* 21–39.

Gross, J. Elder care costs deplete savings of a generation. *New York Times,* Dec. 30, 2006, A1, A16.

Guberman, N., and Maheu, P. Combining employment and caregiving: An intricate juggling act. *Canadian Journal of Aging,* 1999, *18,* 84–106.

Guberman, N., and Maheu, P. Conceptions of family caregivers: Implications for professional practice. *Canadian Journal of Aging,* 2002, *21,* 25–35.

Guberman, N., Nicholas, E. Nolan, M., Rembicki, D., Lundh, U., and Keefe, J. Impacts on practitioners of using research-based carer assessment tools: Experiences from the UK, Canada and Sweden, with insights from Australia. *Health and Social Care in the Community,* 2003, *11,* 345–355.

Gwyther, L. Social issues of the Alzheimer's patient and family. *Neurological Clinics,* 1998, *18,* 993–1010.

Haley, W.E., Gitlin, L., Wisniewski, S., Mahoney, D., Coon, D., Winter, L., Corcoran, M., Schnifeld, S., and Ory, M. Well-being, appraisal and coping in African American and Caucasian dementia caregivers: Findings from the REACH study. *Aging and Mental Health,* 2004, *8,* 316–329.

Harris, P.B. The voices of husbands and sons caring for a family member with dementia. In E. Kramer and L. Thompson, *Men as caregivers.* New York: Springer, 2002.

Harris-Kojetin, L., Lipson, D., Fielding, J., Kiefer, K., and Stone, R. *Recent findings on frontline long-term care worker: A research synthesis 1999–2003.* Accessed December 2, 2006, from http://aspe.hhs.gov/daltcp/reports/insight.pdf.

Heath, J. Brown, M. Kobylarz, F., and Castano, S. The prevalence of undiagnosed geriatric health conditions among adult protective service clients. *The Gerontologist,* 2005, *45,* 820–823.

Hepburn, K., Lewis, M., Sherman, C., and Tornatore, J. The Savvy Caregiver Program: Developing and testing a transportable dementia family caregiver training program. *The Gerontologist,* 2003, *43,* 908–915.

Hooyman, N. The prevention of caregiver stress in older adulthood. In T.P. Gullotta and M. Bloom

(Eds.), *The encyclopedia of primary prevention and health promotion.* New York: Kluwar, 2003.

Howes, C. Upgrading California's home care workforce: The impact of political action and unionization. *The State of California's Labor,* 2004, 71–105.

Hudson, M.F., and Carlson, J.R. Elder abuse: Its meaning to Caucasians, African Americans, and Native Americans. In T. Tattara (Ed.), *Understanding elder abuse in minority populations.* Philadelphia: Taylor and Francis, 1999.

Hudson, R.B., and Gonyea, J.G. Time not yet money: The promise and politics of the Family and Medical Leave Act. *Journal of Social Policy and Aging,* 2000, *11,* 189–200.

Ingersoll-Dayton, B., Neal, M.B., and Hammer, L.B. Aging parents helping adult children: The experience of the sandwiched generation. *Family Relations,* 2001, 262–271.

Institute for the Future of Aging Services (IFAS). *Better Jobs, Better Care.* Washington, DC, 2004.

Janevic, M., and Connell, C.M. Racial, ethnic and cultural difference in the dementia caregiving experience: Recent findings. *The Gerontologist,* 2001, *41,* 334–337.

Kagan, J. *Lifespan Respite Act now goes to President's desk to be signed into law.* Annandale, VA: National Respite Coalition. Press Release from Hilary Rodham Clinton, December 8, 2006.

Kagan, J. *Lifespan respite. Fact sheet number 7.* Annandale, VA: National Respite Coalition, 2003.

Karlawash, J.H., Casaretti, D., Klocinski, J., and Clark, C.M. The relationships between caregivers' global ratings of Alzheimer's disease patients' quality of life, disease severity, and the caregiving experience. *Journal of the American Geriatrics Society,* 2001, *49,* 1066–1070.

Kennet, J., Burgio L., and Schulz, R. Interventions for in-home caregivers: A review of research 1990 to present. In R. Schulz (Ed.), *Handbook of dementia caregiving.* New York Springer, 2000.

Kiecolt-Glaser, J., and Glaser, R. Chronic stress and age-related increases in the proinflmmatory cytokine IL-6. *Proceedings of the National Academy of Sciences,* 2003, *100,* 9090–9095.

Kramer, B.J. Gain in the caregiver experience: Where are we? What next? *The Gerontologist,* 1997, *37,* 218–232.

Kramer, B.J. Husbands caring for wives with dementia: A longitudinal study of continuity and change. *Health and Social Work,* 2000, *25,* 97–107.

Kramer, B.J., and Lambert, J.D. Caregiving as a life course transition among older husbands: A prospective study. *The Gerontologist,* 1999, *39,* 658–667.

Kramer, B.J., and Thompson, E.H. *Men as caregivers: Theory, research and service implications.* New York: Springer, 2002.

Kuhn, D., Empowering family caregivers. *Social Work Today,* 2004, *4,* 38.

Kuhn, D., and Fulton, B. Efficacy of an educational program for relatives of persons in the early stages of Alzheimer's disease. *Journal of Gerontological Social Work,* 2004, *42,* 109–130.

Lachs, M., and Pillemer, K., Elder abuse. *The Lancet,* 2004, *364,* 1263–1272.

Lachs, M., Williams, C., O'Brien, S., and Pillemer, K. Adult protective service use and nursing home placement. *The Gerontologist,* 2002, *42,* 734–739.

Lee, S., Colditz, G., Berkman, L., and Kawachi, I. Caregiving and risk of coronary heart disease in U.S. women: A prospective study. *American Journal of Preventive Medicine,* 203, *24,* 113–119.

Leitsch, S., Zarit, S., Townsend, A., and Greene, R. Medical and social adult day service programs. *Research on Ageing,* 2001, *23,* 473–498.

Levine, C., Reinhard, S., Feinberg, L., Albert, S., and Hart, A. Family caregivers on the job: Moving beyond ADLS and IADLs. *Generations,* 2004, *27,* 17–23.

Liang, J., Krause, N., and Bennett, J., Social exchange and well-being: Is giving better than receiving? *Psychology and Aging,* 2001, *16,* 511–523.

Logsdon, R., McCurry, S.M., and Jeri, L. STAR caregivers: A community-based approach for teaching family caregivers to use behavioral strategies to reduce affective disturbances in persons with dementia. *Alzheimer's Care Quarterly,* 2005, *6,* 146–153.

Loucks, C. *But this is my mother!* Acton, MA: Vander Wyk and Burham, 2000.

Maas, M. When elders transition, so do their caregivers: Invited Commentary. *Transitions,* Wayne State University Institute of Gerontology, 2000, *7,* 8.

Magana, S. Older Latino family caregivers. In B. Berkman (Ed.), *Handbook of social work in health and aging.* New York: Oxford University Press, 2006.

Marcell, J. *Elder rage or take my father . . . please!* Irvine, CA: Impressive Press, 2000.

Marks, N., Lambert, J., and Choi, H. Transitions to caregiving, gender and psychological well being: A prospective U.S. national study. *Journal of Marriage and Family,* 2002, *64,* 857–879.

Martin, C.D. More than the work. *Journal of Family Issues,* 2000, *21,* 986–1006.

Martin-Matthews, A. Change and diversity in aging families and intergenerational relations. In N. Mandell and A. Duffy (Eds.), *Canadian families: Diversity, conflict and change.*Toronto: Harcourt Brace, 2000.

Martire, L., Lustig, A., Schulz, R., Miller, G., and Helgeson, V. Is it beneficial to involve a family member? A meta-analysis of psychosocial interventions for chronic illness. *Health Psychology,* 2004, *23,* 599–611.

McConnell, B.R., and McConnell, E.S. Treating excess disability among cognitively impaired nursing home residents. *Journal of the American Geriatrics Society,* 2000, *48,* 454–455.

McCormick, W.C., Ohata, C.Y., Uomoto, J., Young, H., and Graves, A.B. Similarities and differences in attitudes toward long-term care between Japanese Americans and Caucasian Americans. *Journal of the American Geriatrics Society,* 2002, *50,* 1149–1155.

McLeod, B.W. *Caregiving: The spiritual journey of love, loss and renewal.* New York: John Wiley and Sons, 1999.

MetLife Mature Market Institute and the Lesbian and Gay Aging Issues Network of the American Society on Aging. *Out and aging: The MetLife study of lesbian and gay baby boomers.* Westport, CT: MetLife Market Institute, 2006b.

MetLife Mature Market Institute and National Alliance for Caregiving. *The MetLife caregiving cost study: Productivity losses to U.S. business.* Westport, CT: MetLife Mature Market Institute, 2006a.

MetLife Insurance Company. *Miles away: The MetLife study of long-distance caregiving.* Westport, CT: MetLife Mature Market Institute, 2004.

Meuser, T.M., and Marwit, S.J. A comprehensive stage sensitive model of grief in dementia caregiving. *The Gerontologist,* 2001, *41,* 658–670.

Meuser, T.M., and Marwit, S.J. Development and initial validation of an inventory to assess grief in caregivers of persons with Alzheimer's disease. *The Gerontologist*, 2002, *42*, 751–767.

Mittelman, M. Family caregiving for people with Alzheimer's disease: Results of the NYU Spouse Caregiver Intervention Study. *Generations*, 2002, *3*, 104–106.

Mittelman, M., Roth, D., Coon, D., and Haley, W. Sustained benefit of supportive intervention for depressive symptoms in caregivers of patients with Alzheimer's disease. *American Journal of Psychiatry*, 2004a, *161*, 850–856.

Mittelman, M., Roth, D., Haley, W., and Zarit, S. Effects of a caregiver intervention on negative caregiver appraisals of behavior problems in patients with Alzheimer's disease. Results of a randomized trial. *Journals of Gerontology*, 2004b, *59B*, P27–P34.

Mittelman, M., Zeiss, A., Davies, H., and Guy, D. Specific stressors of spousal caregivers: Difficult behaviors, loss of sexual intimacy and incontinence. In Coon, D., Gallagher-Thompson, D., and Thompson, L. *Innovative interventions to reduce dementia caregiver distress*. New York: Springer, 2003.

Moen, P., Erickson, M.A., and Dempster-McClain, D. Social role identities among older adults in a continuing care retirement community. *Research on Aging*, 2000, *22*, 559–579.

Montgomery, R.J.V., Holley, L., Deichert, J. and Kosloski, K. A profile of home care workers from the 2000 census. *The Gerontologist*, 2005, *45*, 593–600.

Montgomery, R.J.V., and Kosloski, K. Family caregiving: Change, continuity and diversity. In M.P. Lawston and R.L. Rubenstein (Ed.), *Alzheimer's disease and related dementias: Strategies in care and research*. New York: Springer, 2000.

Montgomery, R.J.V., and Kosloski, K. Pathways to a caregiver identity for older adults. In R.C. Talley and R. Montgomery (Eds.), *Caregiving across the life span*. New York: Oxford, in press.

Moon, A., Tomita, S.K., and Jung-Kamei, S. Elder mistreatment among four Asian-American groups: An exploratory study on tolerance, victim blaming and attitudes toward third party intervention. *Journal of Gerontological Social Work*, 2001, *36*, 153–169.

Morano, C. A psycho-educational model for Hispanic Alzheimer's disease caregivers. *The Gerontologist*, 2002, *42*, 122–126.

Muehlbauer, M., and Crane, P. Elder abuse and neglect. *Journal of Psychosocial Nursing*, 2006, *44*, 43–48.

Nahmiash, D., and Reis, M. Most successful intervention strategies for abused older adults. *Journal of Elder Abuse and Neglect*, 2000, *12*, 53–70.

Narayn, S., Lewis, M., Tornatore, J., Hepburn, K., and Corcoran-Perry, S. Subjective responses to caregiving for spouses with dementia. *Journal of Gerontological Nursing*, 2001, *27*, 19–28.

National Academy on an Aging Society. *Helping the elderly with activity limitations: Caregiving*, #7 Washington, DC: May 2000.

National Alliance for Caregiving and AARP. *Caregiving in the U.S.* Bethesda: National Alliance for Caregiving, and Washington, DC: AARP, 2004.

National Alliance for Caregiving and the United Hospital Fund. *Young caregivers in the U.S.: Findings from a national survey*. Author, 2005.

National Association of State Units on Aging (NASUA). *The aging network implements the National Family Caregiver Support Program*. Washington, DC: Administration on Aging, 2003.

National Center on Elder Abuse. *National elder abuse incidence study*. Washington, DC: American Public Health Services Association, 2003.

National Center on Elder Abuse. *The 2004 Survey of State Adult Protective Services: Abuse of adults 60 years of age and older*. Washington, DC: National Center on Elder Abuse, 2006.

National Center for Health Statistics (NCHS). *Health, United States*. Accessed December 20, 2006, from http://www.cdc.gov/nchs/hus.htm.

Navaie-Waliser, M., Feldman, P.H., Gould, D.A., Levine, C., Kuerbis, A.N., and Donelan, K. The experiences and challenges of informal caregivers: Common themes and differences among whites, blacks and Hispanics. *The Gerontologist*, 2001, *41*, 733–741.

Navaie-Waliser, M., Feldman, P.H., Gould, D.A., Levine, C., Kuerbis, A.N., and Donelan, K. When the caregiver needs care: The plight of vulnerable caregivers. *American Journal of Public Health*, 2002, *92*, 409–413.

Ness, J., Ahmed, A., and Aronow, W.S. Demographics and payment characteristics of nursing home residents in the U.S.: A 23-year trend. *Journals of Gerontology* 2004, *59*, BS1213–BS1217.

Nicholas, E. An outcomes focus in carer assessment and review: Value and challenge. *British Journal of Social Work,* 2003, *33,* 31–47.

Nijboer, C., Triemstra, M., Tempelaar, R., Mulder, M., Sanderman, R., and van den Bos, G.A. Patterns of caregiver experiences among partners of cancer patients. *The Gerontologist,* 2000, *40,* 738–746.

O'Brien, E., and Elias, R. *Medicaid and long-term care.* Washington: DC: Kaiser Commission on Medicaid and the Uninsured, 2004.

Olson, L.K. *Age through ethnic lenses: Caring for elderly in a multicultural society.* Baltimore: Rowman and Littlefield, 2001.

Ory, M., Hoffman, R.R. III, Yee, J.L., Tennstedt, S.L., and Schulz, R. Prevalence and impact of caregiving: A detailed comparison between dementia and nondementia caregivers. *The Gerontologist,* 1999, *39,* 177–185.

Ory, M., Tennstedt, S.L., and Schulz, R. The extent and impact of dementia care: Unique challenges experienced by family caregivers. In R. Schulz (Ed.), *Handbook of dementia caregiving: Evidence-based interventions for family caregivers.* New York: Springer, 2000.

Otto, J.M. Program and administrative issues affecting adult protective services. *Public Policy and Aging Report,* 2002, *12,* 3–7.

Parker, M., Church, W., and Toseland, R. Caregiving at a distance. In B. Berkman (Ed.), *Handbook of social work in health and aging,* New York: Oxford Press, 2006.

Penning, M.J. Hydra revisited: Substituting formal for self- and informal in-home care among older adults with disabilities. *The Gerontologist,* 2002, *42,* 4–16.

Pickard, L. *The effectiveness and cost-effectiveness of support and services for informal carers of older people.* London: Audit Commission, 2004.

Pinquart, M., and Sorensen, S. Ethnic differences in stressors, resources and psychological outcomes of family caregiving. A meta-analysis. *The Gerontologist,* 2005, *45,* 90–106

Pinquart, M., and Sorensen, S. Gender differences in caregiver stressors, social resources and health: An updated meta-analysis. *Journals of Gerontology,* 2006, *61B,* P33–P45

Pinquart, M., Sorensen, S., and Peak, T. Helping older adults and their families develop and implement care plans. *Journal of Gerontological Social Work,* 2003, *43,* 3–23.

Polen, M.R., and Green, C.A. Caregiving, alcohol use and mental health symptoms among HMO members. *Journal of Community Health,* 2001, *26,* 285–301.

Polivka, L. Always on call: When illness turns families into caregivers/Caring for our elders. *The Gerontologist,* 2005, *45,* 557–561.

Prescop, K.L., Dodge, H.H., Morycz, R.K., Schulz, R., and Ganguli, M. Elders with dementia living in the community with and without caregivers: An epidemiological study. *International Psychogeriatrics,* 1999, *11,* 235–250.

Prigerson, H.G. Costs to society of family caregiving for patients with end-stage Alzheimer's disease. *New England Journal of Medicine,* 2003, *20,* 1891–1892.

Quinn, M.J. Undoing undue influence. *Journal of Elder Abuse and Neglect,* 2000, *12,* 9–17.

Quinn, M.J., and Heisler, C.J. The legal system: Civil and criminal responses to elder abuse and neglect. *Public Policy and Aging Report,* 2002, *12,* 8–16.

Ramsdell, J., Jackson, J., Guy, H., and Renvall, M. Comparison of clinic-based home assessment to a home visit in demented elderly patients. *Alzheimer Disassociation Disorder,* 2004, *18,* 145–153.

Rapp, S., and Chao, D. Appraisals of strain and of gain: Effects on psychological wellbeing of caregivers of dementia patients. *Aging and Mental Health,* 2000, *4,* 142–147.

Reay, A., and Brown, K.D. The effectiveness of psychological interventions with individuals who physically abuse or neglect their elderly dependents. *Journal of Interpersonal Violence,* 2002, *17,* 416–431.

Reid, J., and Hardy, M. Multiple roles and well-being among midlife women: Testing role strain and role enhancement theories. *Journals of Gerontology,* 1999, *54B,* S329–S338.

Richardson, V., and Barusch, A. *Gerontological practice for the twenty-first century.* New York: Columbia University Press, 2006.

Robinson-Whelen, S., Tada, Y., McCallum, R.C., McGuire, L., and Kiecolt-Glaser, J.K. Long term caregiving: What happens when it ends?

Journal of Abnormal Psychology, 2001, *110*, 573–584.

Roff, L.L., Burgio, L., Gitlin, L., Nichols, L., Chaplin, W. et al. Positive aspects of Alzheimer's caregiving: The role of race. *Journals of Gerontology*, 2004, *59B*, P185–P190.

Sanders, S., and Corley, C. Are they grieving: A qualitative analysis examining grief in caregivers of individuals with Alzheimer's disease. *Health and Social Work*, 2003, *37*, 35–53.

Sanders, S., and McFarland, P. Perceptions of caregiving role by son's caring for a parent with Alzheimer's disease. *Journal of Gerontological Social Work*, 2002, *37*, 61–75.

Savundranayagam, M.Y., Hummert, M.L., and Montgomery, R.J.V. Investigating the effects of communication problems on caregiver burden. *The Journals of Gerontology*, 2005, *60B*, S48–S55.

Schmall, V., Cleland, M., and Sturdevent, M. *The caregiver help book*. Oregon Gerontological Association: Legacy Health System, 2000.

Schmieding, L. *Caregiving in America: At home there's always hope*. New York: International Longevity Center and Arkansas: Schmieding Center for Senior Health and Education of Northwest Arkansas, 2006.

Schneider, S. Victories for home health care workers. *Dollars and Sense*, September/October 2003, 25–27.

Schofield, M., and Mishra, G. Validity of self-report screening for elder abuse: Women's Health Australia Study. *The Gerontologist*, 2003, *43*, 110–120.

Schulz, R., Burgio, L., Burns, R., Eisdorfer, C., Gallagher-Thompson, D., Gitlin, L., and Mahoney, D. Resources for enhancing Alzheimer's caregiver health (REACH): Overview, site-specific outcomes and future directions. *The Gerontologist*, 2003a, *43*, 514–520.

Schulz, R., Mendelsohn, A.B., Haley, W.E., Mahoney, D., Allen, R.S., Zhang, S., Thompson, L., and Belle, S.H. End of life care and the effects of bereavement on family caregivers of persons with dementia. *The New England Journal of Medicine*, 2003b, *20*, 1936–1942.

Schulz, R., O'Brien, A., Czaja, S., Ory, M., Norris, R., Martire, L.M., Belle, S.H., et al. Dementia

caregiver intervention research: In search of clinical significance. *The Gerontologist*, 2002, *42*, 589–682.

Sebern, M. Psychometric evaluation of the shared care instrument in a sample of home health care family dyads. *Journal of Nursing Measurement*, 2005, *13*, 175–191.

Seltzer, M., and Li, L.W. The dynamics of caregiving: Transitions during a three-year prospective study. *The Gerontologist*, 2000, *40*, 165–178.

Shanas, E. The family as a social support in old age. *The Gerontologist*, 1979, *19*, 169–174.

Sherrell, K., Buckwalter, K., and Morhardt, D. Negotiating family relationships: Dementia care as a midlife developmental task. *Families in Society*, 2001, *82*, 383–392.

Shugerman, L., Fries, R., Be, E., Wolfe, R.S., and Morris, J.N. Identifying older adults at risk for abuse during routine screening practices. *Journal of the American Geriatrics Society*, 2003, *51*, 24–31.

Silberg, M. *Respite care: State policy trends and model programs*. San Francisco: Family Caregiver Alliance, 2001.

Sorensen, S., Pinquart, M., and Duberstein, P. How effective are interventions with caregivers? An updated meta-analysis. *The Gerontologist*, 2002, *42*, 356–372.

Spillman, B.C., and Pezzin, L.E. Potential and active family caregivers: Changing networks and the "sandwich generation." *Milbank Quarterly*, 2000, *78*, 347–374.

Sprecher, S., and Fehr, B. The dissolution of close relationships. *Perspectives on loss: A sourcebook*. Philadelphia: Bruner Mazel, 1998.

Stone, R. *Long term care for the elderly with disabilities: Current policy, emerging trends and implications for the 21st century*. New York: The Milbank Memorial Fund, 2000.

Tanase, T. *Alzheimer's educator*. Seattle, WA: Total Living Choices, 2003.

Taylor, D., Ghassan, B., Evans, J., and Jackson-Johnson, V. Assessing barriers to the identification of elder abuse and neglect: A community survey of primary care physicians. *Journal of the National Medical Association*, 2006, *98*, 403–404.

Teaster, P., and Roberto, K. Sexual abuse of older adults: APS cases and outcomes. *The Gerontologist*, 2004, *44*, 788–796.

Tennstedt, S.L. *Family caregiving in an aging society.* U.S. Administration on Aging, 1999, Symposium.

Thomas, C. The first national study of elder abuse and neglect: Contrast with results from other studies. *Journal of Elder Abuse and Neglect,* 2000, *12,* 1–14.

Thompson, E.H. What's unique about men's caregiving? In B.J. Kramer, and E.H. Thompson, Jr. (Eds.), *Men as caregivers; Theory, research and service implications.* New York: Springer, 2002.

Thompson, L., *Long-term care: Support for family caregivers.* Washington, DC: Georgetown University, Long-term care Financing Project, 2004.

Tomita, S. Mistreated and neglected elders. In B. Berkman (Ed.), *Handbook of social work in health and aging.* Oxford Press, 2006.

Toseland, R., and Smith, G. *Supporting caregivers through education and training.* Washington, DC: National Family Caregiver Support Program, Administration on Aging, 2003.

Vitaliano, P.P., Scanlan, J.M., Zhang, J., Savage, M.V., Hirsch, I.B., and Siegler, I.C. A path model of chronic stress; the metabolic syndrome, and coronary heart disease. *Psychomatic Medicine,* 2002, *64,* 418–435.

Vitaliano, P., Zhang, J., and Scanlan, J. Is caregiving hazardous to one's physical health? A meta analysis. *Psychological Bulletin,* 2003, *129,* 946–972.

Wakabayashi, C., and Donato, K. *The consequences of caregiving for economic well-being in women's later life.* Presented at the annual meeting of the American Sociological Association, San Francisco, 2004.

Weiss, C., Gonzalez, H., Kabeto, M., and Langa, K. Differences in the amount of informal care received by non-Hispanic whites and Latinos in a nationally representative sample of older Americans. *Journal of the American Geriatrics Society,* 2005, *53,* 146–151.

Whitlatch, C., Judge, K., Zarit, S., and Femia, E. Dyadic counseling for family caregivers and care receivers in early stage dementia. *The Gerontologist,* 2006, *46,* 688–694.

Wilber, K.H., and McNeilly, D.P. Elder abuse and victimization. In J.E. Birren and K.W. Schaie (Eds.), *Handbook of the psychology of aging* (5th ed.). San Diego: Academic Press, 2001.

Wilber, K.H., and Nielsen, E.K. Elder abuse: New approaches to an age-old problem. *Public Policy and Aging Report,* 2002, *12,* 24–26.

Wisendale, S. Federal initiatives in family leave policy: Formulation of the FMLA. In S. Wisendale (Ed.), *Family leave policy: The political economy of work and family in America.* New York: M.E. Sharpe, 2001.

Wisniewski, S., Belle, S., Coon, D., Maracus, S., Ory, M., Burgio, L. et al. The Resources for Enhancing Alzheimer's Caregiver Health (REACH): Project design and baseline characteristics. *Psychology and Aging,* 2003, *7,* 622–631.

Wold, R. Introduction: The nature and scope of elder abuse. *Generations,* 2000, *24,* 6–12.

Wong, S., Yoo, G., and Stewart, A. The changing meaning of family support among older Chinese and Korean immigrants. *Journals of Gerontology,* 2006, *61B,* S4–S9.

Yee, J.L., and Schulz, R. Gender differences in psychiatric morbidity among family caregivers: A review and analysis. *The Gerontologist,* 2000, *40,* 147–164.

Zarit, S., and Leitsch, S. Developing and evaluating community-based intervention programs for Alzheimer's patients and their caregivers. *Aging and Mental Health,* 2001, S84–S98.

Zarit, S.H., Stephens, M.A.P., Townsend, A., and Greene, R. Stress reduction for family caregivers: Effect of adult day care use. *Journals of Gerontology,* 1998, *53B,* S267–S277.

Zodikoff, B.D. Services for lesbian, gay, bisexual and transgender older adults. In B. Berkman (Ed.)., *Handbook of social work in health and aging,* Oxford Press, 2006.

11

Living Arrangements and Social Interactions

This chapter will examine elders' interactions with their physical environment, from the community to the private home and long-term care setting. Chapter 17 addresses the cost of long-term care and sources of payment for this type of housing and services. As we have discussed, active aging depends on physical and functional health, cognitive and emotional well-being, and a level of engagement that is congruent with an individual's abilities and needs. Another important element that affects the aging process is the environment, both social and physical, that serves as the context for activities as well as the stimulus that places demands on the individual. According to person–environment (P–E) theories of aging, an individual is more likely to experience life satisfaction and quality of life in an environment that is congruent with his or her physical, cognitive, and emotional needs and competence.

Age-related changes and disease conditions tend to make older people more sensitive to characteristics of the physical environment that may have little effect on the typical younger person. They may impair the older person's ability to adapt to and interact with complex and changing environments. On the other hand, many older people function as well as younger persons in a wide range of physical surroundings. Observation of these differences in individual responses has led to the concept of *congruence* or *fit* between the environment and the individual. This concept is explored in other P–E theories below.

Person–Environment Theories of Aging

The impact of the environment on human behavior and well-being is widely recognized in diverse disciplines. Environment as a complex variable entered the realm of psychology in the early work of psychologist Kurt Lewin and his associates (Lewin, 1935, 1951; Lewin, Lippitt, and White, 1939). Lewin's field theory (1935, 1951) emphasizes that any event is the result of multiple factors, individual and environmental; or more simply stated, B = f(P,E) (i.e., behavior is a function of personal and environmental characteristics). Accordingly, any change in characteristics of either the person or the environment is likely to produce a change in that individual's behavior.

Murray's theory of personality (1938), known as *personology*, provides the earliest

framework for a P–E congruence model. This theory depicts the individual in dynamic interaction with his or her setting, which is the type of interaction portrayed throughout this book. The individual attempts to maintain equilibrium as the environment changes. Murray's concepts of *need* and *press* are relevant for theories of P–E congruence. Need is viewed as a force in the individual that works to maintain equilibrium by attending and responding to, or avoiding, certain environmental demands (i.e., the concept of press in the P–E model).

According to Murray's and others' theories of P–E congruence, optimal well-being is experienced when a person's needs are in equilibrium with environmental characteristics. For example, an older woman who has lived on a farm will adjust more readily to a small nursing home in a rural area than to a large urban facility. In contrast, an older couple who are city-dwellers may be dissatisfied if they decide to retire to a small home on a lake far from town; adaptation may be more difficult and perhaps never fully achieved. To the extent that individual needs are not satisfied because of existing environmental characteristics and level of "press," it is hypothesized that the person is likely to experience frustration and strain.

P–E Congruence Models in Gerontology

The environment plays a more dominant role for older people with ADL limitations because their capacity to control their surroundings, such as leaving an undesirable setting, is considerably reduced. Changes in physical, social, and psychological competence constrain the individual's range of adaptive behaviors to stressful environments. Therefore, this perspective may be even more useful for understanding frail elders' behavior than for understanding the behavior of healthier older adults and younger populations.

The *competence model*, described in Chapter 1, provides an important perspective on person–environment transactions in old age.

AN EXAMPLE OF P–E INCONGRUENCE HARMING AN OLDER PERSON

An older man who lives with his daughter and teenage grandchildren in a small home may feel overwhelmed and unable to control the high level of activity (and choice of music!) by the younger family and their friends. In contrast, an older man who lives alone in a quiet neighborhood has greater control over the level of activity in his home, even though the house may seem too quiet and boring to his grandchildren when they visit.

This model assumes that the impact of the environment is mediated by the individual's level of abilities and needs. Competence is defined as "the theoretical upper limit of the individual to function in areas of biological health, sensation-perception, motives, behavior, and cognition" (Lawton, 1975, p. 7). *Environmental press* refers to the potential of a given environmental feature to influence behavior (for example, the level of stimulation, physical barriers, and lack of privacy). For older adults who experience functional decline, as measured by increasing dependence in ADLs and IADLs, the environment must be simplified and more supportive, but when the environment does not change appropriately the individual experiences P–E incongruence (Golant, 2003; Iwarsson, 2005).

The practical implications of the P–E model are illustrated by examples of older persons with Alzheimer's disease or other forms of dementia who cannot readily re-establish P–E congruence or adapt to incongruence. Their cognitive deterioration may make them unable to recognize the incongruence between their needs and the environment, and certainly reduces their ability to re-establish congruence. The patient with dementia may become behaviorally disturbed unless others intervene to reestablish congruence. Caregivers can simplify the environment to

---

AN ENVIRONMENT THAT PLACES EXTREME DEMANDS ON ELDERS' COMPETENCE

In February 2006, 82-year-old Mayvis Coyle received a traffic ticket for the first time in her life. Her crime was jaywalking at a crosswalk on a busy 5-lane boulevard in Los Angeles, where the pedestrian light is green for only 20 seconds. Mayvis was fined $114 for continuing to cross the street after the light had turned red. Others, including a 78-year-old woman using an electric cart, have complained that the light changes when they are only halfway across the boulevard. The policeman who issued the ticket defended his action by responding that his job was to assure pedestrian safety. Clearly the timing of this light places unrealistic *environmental press* on people whose physical *competence* declines because of age or disability (Associated Press, 2006).

---

make it fit the individual's cognitive competence; for example, by providing cues and orienting devices in the home to help the person find his or her way without becoming lost or disoriented. The ultimate goal of any modification should be to maximize the older person's ability to negotiate and control the situation, and to minimize the likelihood that the environment will overwhelm the person's competence.

Geographic Distribution of the Older Population

The Aging Experience in Rural, Urban, and Suburban Areas

As the United States and other industrialized countries have become more urbanized, a smaller proportion of all population subgroups, including those age 65 and over, currently reside in rural communities. The great majority of older Americans (77.4 percent) live in metropolitan areas (i.e., urban and suburban communities), compared with only 5 percent in communities with fewer than 2500 residents. Older ethnic

---

COPING WITH DECLINING COMPETENCE

As competence in cognition, physical strength and stamina, health, and sensory functioning decline with advanced age, the individual may experience increased problems with high environmental press. For example, grocery shopping in a large supermarket on a busy Saturday morning may become an overwhelming task for an older person who has difficulties with hearing and walking. The older adult might decide to shop in a smaller store at nonpeak hours, or to avoid supermarkets altogether and use a neighborhood grocery store or order groceries by phone or online.

minorities are more likely to live in central cities, placing them at greater risk for victimization and poor-quality housing.

There is also a "graying of the suburbs"; that is, a greater proportion of people who moved into suburban developments in the 1960s have raised their children and remained in these communities after retirement. Since 1977, increasing numbers of older people are living in the suburbs rather than in central cities, as shown in Figure 11.1. Compared to their urban counterparts, elders in suburban communities tend to have higher incomes, are less likely to live alone, and report themselves to be in better functional health.

However, the lower density of housing, greater distance to social and health services, and lack of mass transit make it difficult for older suburban dwellers to continue living independently in these suburbs if they become frail or unable to drive. Many suburban communities are responding to their changing resident needs by developing community transit (e.g., vans or special buses) programs to take older adults and persons with disabilities to social and health services, senior centers, shopping, restaurants, and places of worship. Future cohorts of older adults will expect more of these services and businesses to be located in the suburbs, in the

same way that shopping centers and retirement housing options are now constructed in these population centers.

Older persons who live in nonmetropolitan areas generally have lower incomes (near the poverty level) and poorer health than those in urban areas. A greater proportion relies on Social Security benefits for their primary source of income. This is particularly true for African Americans who reside in small towns and rural areas. Limitations in mobility and activity are greater among elders in rural communities and least among those in suburbs. This may be a function of income and cohort differences. The greater availability of services such as hospitals, clinics, senior centers, private physicians, transportation in urban and suburban communities compared to rural settings may also explain these differences. Despite attempts to offset urban–rural differences in health and social services, significant gaps remain in terms of access and availability. Transportation is a critical problem for older rural residents, both to transport them to medical and social services and to bring service providers to their homes. For example, only 14 percent of rural elders live within a half mile of a bus stop or mass transit station, compared with 43 percent of urban and suburban elders (AARP, 2002).

Despite their lower income and poorer health, older persons in small communities are found to interact more with neighbors and friends of the same and younger ages than do those in urban settings. Mr. and Mrs. Howard in the introductory vignette to Part Five illustrate the positive aspects of smaller communities for older people. These include greater proximity to neighbors, stability of residents, and shared values and lifestyles. Proportionately few rural elders live near their children and most do not receive financial and social support from them. However, friendship ties appear to be stronger and more numerous among rural elders than among those in urban settings. In sum, older persons who remain in rural areas and small

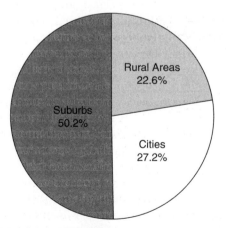

FIGURE 11.1   **Population of Older Americans Living in Urban, Suburban, and Rural Areas**
SOURCE: AOA, 2006.

towns are more disadvantaged in terms of income, health, and service availability than are those in metropolitan areas. On the other hand, P–E fit suggests that those who have a high need for social interaction and have lived most of their lives in rural areas would be most satisfied in such settings, and would experience severe adaptation problems in more anonymous urban environments.

Elder-Friendly/Livable Communities

An emerging concept in the physical environment for older adults—one that is consistent with the need for P–E congruence—is that of **elder-friendly** or **livable communities**. While P–E congruence focuses on the individual's level of competence, needs, and preferences, this concept examines elders at the community level. Researchers who have studied older adults' perspectives define elder-friendly communities as:

- Addressing basic needs of safe neighborhoods, affordable housing, and adequate nutrition
- Optimizing physical and mental health by providing access to social and health services, preventive and health promotion activities, chronic disease management, and end-of-life care
- Promoting social and civic engagement, including opportunities for employment, volunteering, and cross-generational interaction
- Maximizing autonomy for frail and disabled elders by providing accessible public transportation and resources to help them remain at home (Advantage Age Initiative, 2007; Austin, et al., 2001; Hanson and Emlet, 2006).

To determine if communities fulfill these criteria for elder-friendliness, researchers have conducted surveys of older residents in diverse areas. A 2005 national survey of 1000 adults 50 and older by AARP found that the availability of community services such as dependable transportation, nearby grocery and drugstores, hospitals, and affordable housing affected residents' satisfaction with their community. Urban dwellers were more satisfied than those in suburbs where these services were less available. Dissatisfied residents also felt isolated and disengaged from their neighbors and the larger community. Findings from such surveys are useful for guiding city officials and leaders in the aging network to improve housing, services, and employment and volunteering opportunities for older citizens (AARP, 2005; Austin et al., 2001; Feldman and Oberlink, 2003; Hanson and Emlet, 2006; Kochera and Bright, 2005–2006).

Relocation

Relocation, or moving from one setting to another, also represents P–E incongruence or discontinuity between the individual's competence and environmental demands. Anyone who has moved from one city or one house to another has experienced the problems of adjusting to new surroundings and to different orientations, floor plans, and design features in the home. A healthy person can usually adjust quite easily. An older person who has lived in the same home for many years will require more time to adapt, even if the move is perceived as an improvement to a better, safer, or more comfortable home. This is because the older person has adjusted to a particular level of P–E fit over a long time. A relocation that entails extensive lifestyle changes, such as a move to a retirement community or a nursing home with its rules and policies governing the residents, requires greater adjustments and a longer time to adapt. Whatever psychological and physiological distress elders experience generally disappears within three months after the move, however (Lutgendorf et al., 2001). Older adults who move voluntarily often feel more stress before the move than after.

Regardless of the nature of the move, many elders experience feelings of loss associated with giving up possessions and a familiar setting.

Older homeowners are far more likely than younger families to have lived in their current homes for at least 30 years (50 percent vs. 4 percent). This difference also occurs among renters (16 percent vs. 1 percent, respectively), and may explain why older people are less likely to relocate. Indeed, less than 5 percent of people age 65 to 85 move in a given year, compared with 34 percent of adults age 20 to 29 (Longino and Bradley, 2003). A national survey by AARP revealed an overwhelming desire by people age 50 and older to remain in their own homes and communities:

- 69 percent were very satisfied with their residence
- 73 percent preferred to remain in the same community (AARP, 2006c)

Among those who had moved in 2004, 76 percent had done so within the same state (AOA, 2006). In general, older people are less likely to move to a new community than are younger families, but are more likely to move to a different type of housing within the same community. In their life course model of retirement migration, Litwak and Longino (1994) proposed that the large migrant stream of retirees to the Sunbelt from northern states is accompanied by a smaller counterstream in the opposite direction. In their subsequent work, these researchers suggest that older people generally relocate in response to changes in life conditions, such as retirement, or disabilities that make their existing home environments incongruent with their needs (Litwak and Longino, 1994; Longino and Bradley, 2006). As a result, the type of housing chosen varies according to the reasons for the move. Their three-stage model of migration is described as:

- Stage 1 occurs most often among the young-old and recent retirees, generally to retirement communities in the Sunbelt—Florida, California, Arizona, or Texas. This may include "snow-birds" who spend their winters in the warmer climate and the remaining months in their home states. Both patterns have resulted in a significant increase in the population age 65 and older in Sunbelt states in the past 30 years.
- Stage 2 is often precipitated by chronic illness that limits elders' abilities to perform ADLs. They may move to retirement communities or assisted living facilities nearby that offer some amenities (e.g., meals, housekeeping), but remain relatively independent.
- Stage 3 is not experienced by most elders, but occurs when severe or sudden disability (e.g., stroke) makes it impossible to live even semi-independently. In some cases the frail older person relocates from a Sunbelt community to a nursing home near family members. One indicator of this shift is that Florida has the highest population of people age 65 and older but ranks twenty-fourth in its proportion of oldest-old (Longino, 2004).

ADAPTING TO P–E INCONGRUENCE IN ONE'S HOME

It may seem odd to family, friends, and service providers that an older person does not wish to leave a home that is too large and too difficult to negotiate physically, especially if he or she is frail and mobility-impaired. The problem is compounded if the home needs extensive repairs that an older person cannot afford. Despite such seemingly obvious needs for relocating, it is essential to consider older people's preferences before encouraging them to sell a home that appears to be incongruent with their needs. Families should not ignore the meaning of home to the older person as a symbol of self-identity, control, autonomy, and emotional and cognitive bonding with their social and physical environment (Oswald and Wahl, 2004).

Relocation implies a loss of familiar surroundings and possessions.

For many other elders, an intermediate stop may be the home of an adult child before relocating to a long-term care facility. In other cases, older persons remain in their home, but receive some home care and other support services. To the extent that older retirees who relocate to the Sunbelt have children and siblings living in their state of origin, and the more visits they make back home, the more likely they are to make a "counterstream migration" by moving back to their home state. However, having children who live nearby in the Sunbelt state where they have relocated and being satisfied with their new residence make it less likely that retirees will return to their home state (Stoller and Longino, 2001).

The oldest-old are most likely to relocate, often into or near their children's homes. Such moves are precipitated by widowhood, significant deterioration in health, or disability (Castle, 2001). Not surprisingly, relocation is more difficult for elders with multiple or severe physical or cognitive disabilities. As we have seen in Chapter 6, these individuals have more difficulty coping with stressful life events than healthy older people. Unfortunately, they are often the very people who must relocate to skilled nursing facilities, environments that may be most incongruent with their needs. Relocation stress can be reduced if the older person has some control over the decision to move and is involved in the decision process, such as selecting the facility and deciding what possessions to keep.

The stress of adapting to a new setting is one reason why many frail older people who can no longer maintain their own homes are reluctant to move, even though they may recognize that they "should" be in a safer environment. Indeed, the 2005 housing survey by AARP found overwhelming support for the statement, "I'd like to stay in my home and never move." Among all respondents 50 and older, 89 percent agreed with the statement, and this preference increased with age:

- 84 percent among those 50–64
- 95 percent among those 75+ (AARP, 2006c)

WHAT TO DO WITH A LIFETIME OF POSSESSIONS?

Older adults who move to a smaller home—whether a condo, apartment, assisted living, or nursing home—are typically faced with the task of disposing of a lifetime of possessions. The memories associated with a favorite possession can result in wrenching decisions for elders and their families, intensifying the feelings of loss associated with a move. This task can be even more daunting for elders from the Depression era cohort who have saved material items throughout their lives. For other elders, who are classified as hoarders, their living spaces are so cluttered that they are not usable and can pose a fire risk. Another complicating factor in disposing of lifelong possessions is when family members live far from the elder or disagree over who should inherit which cherished possessions. To assist with this process, new services have recently emerged, including Senior Move Managers, Professional Organizers, and even support groups for hoarders.

A major reason for this large proportion of elders who prefer to remain in their own home, regardless of its condition, is the almost universal desire for **aging in place.** This is the preference to stay in their homes where the environment is familiar, neighbors can be relied on for assistance and socializing, and the aging person has control. As aging occurs, however, an increasing number of services may be required to allow aging in place. To the extent that these resources are accessible in the neighborhood or local community, people are more likely to remain in such settings and to avoid or delay relocation to a long-term care facility. Some of these support services are described later in this chapter.

Some older people may live in communities that were not planned for this population (unlike a Sun City or Leisure World, for example), but have become **naturally occurring retirement communities (NORCs).** Such places have, over the years, attracted adults who have eventually "aged in place" there. As the population of older adults with health and social service needs increases in NORCs, some state and local governments are offering needed services. For example, city funds and philanthropic grants pay for an on-site team of social workers and nurses to care for elders in a Queens, New York, apartment complex where more than 60 percent of residents are over 60. This program has been a model for communities in 20 other states (Larson, 2006).

Another type of community where people are aging in place is a collaborative neighborhood known as **co-housing** (Co-housing Association of the U.S., 2006; deLaGrange, 2006; Greene, 2006; Vierck, 2005). Adapted from Denmark in the late 1980s, co-housing communities are clusters of 10 to 70 residences (attached or single-family homes) where families of all ages live independently, but share a "common house" where social and recreational activities, community meetings, and occasional group meals are shared. Most of the co-housing communities today are intergenerational, and have only recently begun to deal with issues of

RETIREES CAN REVITALIZE AMERICA'S SMALL TOWNS

New cohorts of retirees who practice active aging have revitalized once-dying communities by relocating there, spending money for goods and services, sometimes continuing to work part-time, and creating jobs for other residents. One estimate is that a retiree who relocates to a community can have as great an economic impact as three to four factory workers because, in general, they are wealthier and have more disposable income. In 2000, new residents age 50 and older brought twice as much revenue to Florida as they cost the state in services (*Seattle Times,* 2003).

some residents who are growing older with chronic diseases and dementia. Physical barriers such as inaccessible entries and multistory dwellings become increasingly difficult for those with disabilities. The principles of participatory decision making and resident management that characterize co-housing may elude those experiencing cognitive decline. In recognition of the potential incongruence of age-integrated co-housing for frail older adults, a new trend has emerged in co-housing, targeting those 55 and older (deLaGrange, 2006; ElderCohousing.org, 2006). Many of these neighborhoods are being built near intergenerational co-housing communities, but often with fewer homes (15 to 20 households), physical features and social services that respond to declines in physical and cognitive function. Another more recent model of housing that encourages aging in place is **intentional communities.** These are more communal housing projects, both intergenerational or targeted only at older adults, where people with a common interest (e.g., religious, political, professional or sexual orientation) collaborate in the construction of a community of apartments, townhouses, or detached single-family homes. Residents of intentional communities generally share more activities than those in co-housing (Christian, 2003; Yeoman, 2006).

The Impact of the Neighborhood

All of us live in a neighborhood, whether this is a college campus, a mobile home park, an apartment complex, or the several blocks surrounding our homes. Because of its smaller scale, the neighborhood represents a closer level of interaction and identification than does the community. Results of the American Housing Survey by the U.S. Census Bureau reveal:

- Seventy-six percent of older people in general are satisfied with their neighborhoods.
- Seventy-one percent in poorer neighborhoods are satisfied (HUD, 1999).

Among those who reported problems, noise and traffic concerns topped the list, followed by complaints about people and crime in the neighborhood.

Satisfaction with one's neighborhood increases if amenities such as a grocery store, bank, laundromat, or senior center are located nearby. These services also can provide a social network. For many older people, however, special vans or other types of transportation are necessary to access such services. Older adults are willing to travel farther for physician services, entertainment, family visits (although friends need to be nearby for regular visiting to occur), and club meetings, probably because these activities occur less frequently than

---

PRACTICAL HELP FROM NEIGHBORS

Neighbors can provide a security net, as partners in a Neighborhood Watch crime-prevention program, or in informally arranged systems of signaling to each other. The older neighbor who lives alone might open her living room drapes every day by 9:00 A.M. to signal to her neighbors that all is well. Other neighbors might check in on the older person on a daily or weekly basis to make sure that home-delivered meals are being eaten regularly.

---

grocery shopping and laundry. Because of the importance of family ties, visits to family members may occur more often, regardless of proximity. Distance is less important if family members drive older relatives to various places, including their homes.

Proximity and frequent contact with families may not be as critical if neighbors and nearby friends can provide necessary social support. As discussed in Chapter 9, neighbors play an important role in older people's social networks. When adult children are at a geographic distance, neighbors are needed to help in emergencies and on a short-term basis, such as minor home repairs, yard maintenance, or transportation. It is often more convenient for neighbors than family to drive an older individual to stores and doctors' offices. This does not mean that neighbors can or should replace family support systems because of the family's central caregiving role. Nevertheless, neighbors are an important additional resource.

Victimization and Fear of Crime

A common stereotype is that crime affects the older population more than other age groups. However, national surveys by the U.S. Department of Justice's Bureau of Justice Statistics consistently show that people over age 65 have the lowest rates of all types of victimization among all age groups over 12. As Table 11.1 illustrates, when compared to people age 16 to 19, those age 65 and older are:

- 17 times less likely to be victims of an assault
- 12 times less likely to experience a robbery
- 4 times less likely to be attacked by a purse snatcher or pickpocket

In fact, these rates have steadily declined for all age groups since 1996. For example, in 2005, 5 percent of all homicide victims were age 65 or older, indicating a victimization rate of less than 2 per 100,000 population, compared with

TABLE 11.1   Victimization Rates per 1000 Persons or Households, 2005

AGE	VIOLENT CRIME	ROBBERY	ASSAULT	PURSE SNATCHING/ PICKPOCKETING
16–19	45.8	7.0	33.9	1.6
25–34	23.6	3.1	19.9	1.0
50–64	11.4	1.4	9.3	0.6
65+	2.4	0.6	1.9	0.4

SOURCE: Bureau of Justice Statistics, 2006.

3.5 per 100,000 in 1996 (Bureau of Justice Statistics, 2006b). Nevertheless, some segments of the older population are at greater risk:

- The young-old are more likely than those age 75 and older to face all types of crime.
- African American elders are 25 percent more likely than whites to be assault victims, and 4 times more likely to be victims of purse snatching and pickpocketing.
- Older Americans with incomes less than $7500 are most likely to become victims of

all crimes, including violent crime and assault (more than 1.7 times and 1.5 times the rate for those with incomes over $50,000, respectively).
- Not surprisingly, older people in urban centers are 1.6 times more likely than suburban or rural elders to experience violent crimes, 1.3 times more likely to be assaulted, and 1.5 times more likely to be victims of property crimes. African American elders in urban settings are even more likely than their rural counterparts to experience these crimes (Bureau of Justice Statistics, 2006a).

Contrary to common beliefs, older white and African American women are at lowest risk for violent crimes:

- For all types of assault, 1.4 per 1000 versus 2.2 for older white men and 5.6 for older African American men.
- For all crimes of violence, 1.8 per 1000 among white women, less than 0.3 for older African American women, compared to 3.2 for older white men and 5.6 for black men. This compares with the highest-risk group, males age 20 to 24, who experience 58.8 violent crimes per 1000 population (Bureau of Justice Statistics, 2006a).

The conditions under which crimes are committed against older people differ from those of other age groups. For example, they tend to be

NEIGHBORHOOD CRIME PREVENTION PROGRAMS

In response to concerns about crime, Neighborhood Watch and other programs encourage neighbors to become acquainted and to look out for signs of crimes. Such crime-prevention programs increase older people's access to their neighbors. They break down the perception of neighbors as strangers and the fear of being isolated in a community, both of which foster fear of crime. Some large communities have established special police units to investigate and prevent crimes against older people. These units often train police to understand processes of aging, and to communicate better with older people to help them overcome the trauma of a theft or physical assault. Improvements in community design can also create a sense of security. For example, brighter and more uniform street lighting, especially above sidewalks and in alleys, can deter many would-be criminals.

victimized during the day, by strangers who more often attack alone, in or near their homes, and with less use of weapons. This suggests that perpetrators of crimes feel they can easily overtake the older victim without a struggle. The sense of helplessness against an attacker may make older persons more conscious of their need to protect themselves, and produce levels of fear that are incongruent with the statistics about their relative vulnerability to violent crimes. Such fear of crime results in dissatisfaction with their neighborhood among vulnerable elders. In the 2005 AARP housing survey, 87 percent of those 65 to 74 and 84 percent 75 and older were satisfied with the security of their neighborhood. However, those in urban areas were twice as dissatisfied with the safety of their neighborhood as their counterparts in suburbs and 50 percent more than elders in rural areas. Similarly, elders with household incomes less than $25,000 were much less satisfied with neighborhood safety than those with incomes over $50,000, mostly because they lived in areas with higher crime rates (AARP, 2006c).

It is not unrealistic for older adults in high crime areas to be concerned, given the potential negative consequences of a physical attack or theft for an older person. Even a purse snatching can be traumatic, because of the possibility of an injury or hip fracture during a struggle with the thief and the resulting economic loss. Experiencing a violent crime can even result in nursing home placement. In a study of over 2300 older adults in New Haven, Connecticut, 5 percent had experienced a violent crime and 21 percent any type of victimization prior to their move to the nursing home. Over the next 10 years, 32 percent entered a nursing home other than for post-hospitalization rehabilitation. Those who had been victims of violent crimes were 2.1 times more likely to enter a nursing home than their nonvictimized counterparts, compared with 1.6 times likelihood for elders with cognitive impairment. These findings illustrate the potential long-term consequences of victimization against older persons (Lachs et al., 2006). Being a crime victim can also disrupt the victim's sense of competence and subjective well-being. Older women are particularly fearful of crime, although, as described above, they are even less likely to be victims. Although seemingly irrational, such fear of crime is an important determinant of older women's behavior that requires more community efforts to empower and strengthen their environmental competence. For example, older women can benefit from education in self-defense and from neighborhood support networks. In sum, the significance of the fear of crime is not whether it is warranted, but the effect it has on elders' psychological well-being.

Although less likely to be victims of violent crime, older people are more susceptible to economically devastating crimes such as fraud and confidence games. Police departments in major cities report higher rates of victimization against older adults by con artists and high-pressure salesmen. Medical quackery and insurance fraud are also more common, perhaps because many older people feel desperate for quick cures or overwhelmed by medical care costs. They therefore become easy prey for unscrupulous people who exploit them by offering the "ultimate medical cure" or "low-cost, comprehensive long-term care insurance" coverage. Older adults are also more vulnerable to commercial fraud by funeral homes, real estate brokers, and investment salespeople. Perhaps more devastating than the financial consequences of fraud is the negative impact on elders' trust and self-confidence. Such feelings can prevent the older person from seeking appropriate professional services for medical conditions, insurance, and other transactions. And families may perceive their older relatives as no longer competent to live autonomously. AARP's classes on how to prevent victimization by fraud are currently their most popular educational offering.

Housing Patterns of Older People

In this section, the residential arrangements of older persons are reviewed, including independent housing, planned housing, retirement communities, and residential long-term care. We also discuss newer models of long-term care, both community-based and residential. Policies that govern such long-term care options are described in Chapter 17.

By far the most common type of housing for older adults is traditional independent housing (93 percent of those 65 and older live in such housing), followed by long-term care (LTC) facilities (4 percent), and community housing with services, such as continuous care retirement communities (3 percent). However, for the oldest-old, these latter options are more common; 75 percent live in independent housing, 17 percent in LTC, and 8 percent in community housing with services (Federal Interagency Forum on Aging, 2006).

Independent Housing

In 2003, of the 21.6 million elder households, 80 percent were homeowners, and 20 percent were renters. The former spent 35 percent of their income for housing, less than half that spent by renters (76 percent). Rather than indicating low mortgages, this difference may be explained by the fact that homeowners, on average, have higher median income levels than renters ($26,889 versus $13,377 in 2003). Older people are more likely than any other age group to occupy housing that they own free and clear of a mortgage (65 percent in 2005) (U.S. Census Bureau, 2006). These include condominiums, mobile homes, and even congregate facilities that offer "life care" for retired persons; but by far the greatest proportion of owned units are single-family homes. As shown in Figure 11.2, home ownership varies considerably among the older population. Married couples, non-Hispanic whites, especially those with an annual income of $40,000 or more, and those residing in rural communities are most likely to own their homes. However, the cost of utilities, taxes, insurance, and repair and maintenance can be prohibitive because their homes tend to be older and poorly constructed. In addition, the older person's current competence level may be incongruent with their physical environment, so that they require more appropriate housing.

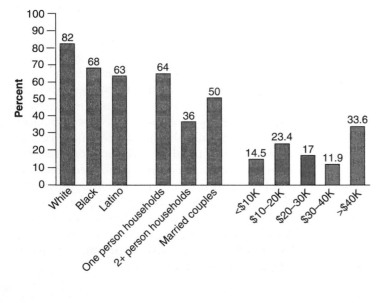

FIGURE 11.2 **Characteristics of Older Homeowners**
SOURCE: U.S. Census Bureau, 2006.

Many of the houses owned by the older population are old; 32 percent were built before 1949, compared with 27 percent of homes in general (NCOA, 2002). As a result, many have inadequate weatherproofing and other energy-saving features, with large indoor and outdoor spaces that are difficult to maintain. Exposed wiring, lack of sufficient outlets, and worn-out oil furnaces can be hazards. A 2003 survey revealed that 5.2 percent of homes occupied by older homeowners had physical problems (AOA, 2006). Severe problems with the quality of housing units are seen in renter-occupied dwellings at about twice the rate as than in owner-occupied units (Commission on Affordable Housing, 2002).

It is not unusual to hear news stories during winter months of fires in older homes that result from faulty wiring, overloaded circuits, and the use of space heaters because of an inadequate furnace. The latter situation is particularly troublesome for older persons who have difficulties in maintaining body heat and prefer warmer ambient temperatures (see Chapter 3). Many communities attempt to prevent these problems by providing free or low-cost home repairs for low-income elders and special assistance to all older persons to make their homes more energy efficient (e.g., no interest loans for weatherproofing and installing storm windows). Some cities that have experienced sudden increases in their electricity and natural gas rates have also developed programs to aid low-income people of all ages, but this is becoming more difficult with current high energy costs and cuts in public services.

Since 1989, the U.S. Department of Housing and Urban Development (HUD) has had the authority to offer insurance for home equity conversion mortgages (HECM, or "reverse mortgages"). With insurance from HUD, numerous lenders across the country provide reverse mortgages to homeowners age 62 and older with little or no mortgage debt remaining, and who qualify as low or moderate-income. Lenders estimate that 83 percent of older adults have paid off their mortgages, and their average equity exceeds $55,000. A reverse mortgage is a useful option for people age 62 and older who are "house-rich but cash-poor." It can help people age in place and pay for needed repairs and maintenance. In effect, reverse mortgages lend the older person money via a credit line on his or her mortgage. The title is retained by the lender, or the lender puts a lien on the home. The older person receives a lump sum or monthly payment (or annuity) from the lender and still lives in the house. This can mean an additional $1000 or more each month for many older homeowners. When the older person dies or sells the house, the lender generally deducts the portion of the mortgage that has been paid, including interest, as well as a portion (usually about 10 percent) of the home's appreciated value or equity since the date of the reverse mortgage.

Reverse mortgages may carry long-term risks for the lender; currently, there are no guidelines for the duration of such mortgage plans. For example, what if the older homeowner outlives the home's equity? Lenders do not want to evict such a person, but at the same time they do not want to lose their investment. In addition, homeowners must consider the initial costs of such a mortgage. These include a 2 percent mandatory mortgage insurance fee, a loan origination fee, and standard closing costs. Together with interest, a borrower could pay an annualized credit-line rate of 13 to 17 percent for this loan. The Federal Housing Administration (FHA) has developed a program to reduce these costs, especially for elders with small or no mortgages. Depending on the homeowner's age, they may be able to borrow up to 56 percent of their home's value at a reasonable interest rate (AARP, 2006b). For older people with other assets to use as collateral, other types of loans may be more cost-effective than a reverse mortgage. HUD offers information about reverse mortgages on its Website and its toll-free phone number.

On the other hand, many people in their 50s and 60s have considerable equity in their homes because of housing prices rising steeply since the early 1990s. As their children leave, some prefer to sell these homes and move to smaller dwellings. A growing trend, however, is represented by aging baby boomers, who prefer a large home with many amenities that will help them remain independent and age in place. These include features such as master bedrooms and full bathrooms on the main floor, universal design in the kitchen and bathroom that allows autonomy for people in wheelchairs and walkers, wireless computer systems and "smart homes" (discussed later in this chapter). Builders and architects need to recognize that boomers will expect more options in the size and amenities of homes, and in the ability to adapt their homes to allow aging in place than any previous generation.

Planned Housing

During the past 40 years, federal and local government agencies and some private organizations, such as faith-based groups, have developed planned housing projects specifically for older persons. These include subsidized housing for low-income elders and age-segregated housing for middle- and upper-income older persons.

"SUMMER CAMP FOR ADULTS"

Many housing developers are expanding their markets by building active retirement communities for newer cohorts of older adults. Unlike the huge developments of the past, such as Sun Cities in California and Arizona with over 9000 homes, recent projects have less than 1000 units. They offer golf courses, tennis courts, and swimming pools for active adults age 60 and older. Indeed, these developments have so many recreational amenities that some are marketed as "full-time summer camps for adults."

Gerontologists have attempted to understand the effects of the quality and type of housing on older persons' satisfaction level and behavior following relocation to such environments. It appears that planned housing can indeed improve low-income elders' quality of life, but it is difficult to generalize to other older populations, particularly those with higher income.

Where to locate planned housing projects raises a number of complex issues. Developers must consider such factors as whether the area is zoned for residential, commercial, or industrial use, as well as access to social and health services. As stated earlier in the discussion of neighborhood characteristics, older adults are most likely to use services if they are on site and if public transportation is easily accessible. If a particular site is not already near a bus stop, residents and developers may be able to convince the local public transportation authority. Some larger developments provide van services for their older residents to obtain medical and social services, as well as planned excursions to theaters, museums, parks, senior centers, and shopping malls.

The topography of the site, crime rates, and security of the community are other important considerations, along with the need to integrate the housing project into the neighborhood. This last item is especially crucial; in a housing project that is architecturally distinct and separated by walls and vegetation from the rest of the neighborhood, residents are likely to experience a lack of fit with their environment and to feel physically and psychologically isolated from the larger neighborhood. Examples of this are a tall, multilevel structure in the midst of single-family homes, or a sprawling "retirement community" on the edge of an industrial area. The lack of fit may also be felt by the residents of the larger neighborhood, who may reject the presence of an entire community of older people in their midst, even if the project is architecturally consistent with other buildings. On the other hand, the growing number of elders with higher incomes has led to the expansion of somewhat exclusive retirement communities with units costing $500,000 and more, offering computer access, marinas, restaurants, golf courses, hiking trails, and some communal services. These are known as "active adult communities."

Continuous Care Retirement Communities

Another option for elders with financial resources is the growing number of **continuous care retirement communities (CCRCs).** These multilevel facilities offer a range of housing, from independent to congregate living arrangements and intermediate to skilled care, with units for 400 to 600 elders. These options are more widely available in housing that is purchased, less so for rental housing. Such alternatives are particularly important for couples, who face the likelihood that one partner will require skilled nursing care eventually. A report by the American Association of Homes and Services for the Aging (AAHSA, 2006) estimates that 98 percent of CCRCs provide apartment style living; 81 percent assisted living or other types of intermediate care, and 95 percent have a nursing home on-site or nearby. When several levels of care are available

Retirement communities offer opportunities for social interaction and physical activity.

at one site, older couples can feel assured that they can remain near each other, even if one becomes placed in intermediate or skilled care. Reasons for choosing a CCRC include:

* a desire to plan ahead if care is needed in the future
* not wanting to be a burden on family members
* guaranteed health care
* freedom from home maintenance
* availability of supportive services, social and educational programs (Krout et al., 2002; Moen and Erickson, 2001).

Many housing plans for older people that offer options in living arrangements have either *lifecare contracts* or *life lease contracts*. Under these plans, the older person must pay an initial entry fee, often quite substantial, based on projections of life expectancy and on the size of the living quarters. In the case of a *lifecare contract*, the individual who eventually needs increased care is provided nursing home care without paying more for these services. This is a form of long-term care insurance that provides care as needed. With a *life lease contract*, the individual is guaranteed lifetime occupancy in the apartment. However, in the

ADVANTAGES AND DISADVANTAGES OF CCRCs

Considering the high cost of CCRCs with lifecare contracts or founders' fees, potential buyers should consider the pros and cons of these commitments. Their greatest advantages are access to services that permit independent living and, for married respondents, the opportunity to continue to live together if one spouse needs nursing home care. A potential risk for older people who enter into a lifecare contract is that the facility will declare bankruptcy. In an attempt to avoid this, many states that license lifecare housing projects require providers to establish a trust fund for long-term care expenses.

latter case, if more expensive care is required, such services are generally not provided by the facility, and the older person must give up the apartment and find a nursing home. These contracts also charge monthly fees, but these are generally not as high as those in facilities that rely only on month-to-month payments. The advantage of lifecare contracts is that the individual is guaranteed lifetime care; this is important, given the actuarial tables of life expectancy for those who reach age 65. However, elders who pay month-to-month may use up all of their life savings long before dying, if skilled care is needed, unless they have long-term care insurance. In contrast, a lifecare contract may provide a sense of security for the older person who can pay a large lump sum. The individual is taking the chance that higher levels of care will eventually be needed, so the costs are averaged out over a long period. The variation in services guaranteed by CCRCs results in a wide range of entry fees, from $20,000 to $400,000, with monthly payments ranging from $200 to $2500 (Netting and Wilson, 2006). For those who die soon after moving in, some facilities refund part of the entry fee to the family. In many cases, however, there is a policy of no refunds. Obviously, the ability to purchase these contracts is limited to the small percentage of older people who have considerable cash assets. Indeed, older persons in these facilities are better educated and have greater financial resources than the general older population.

Long-Term Care

Even though most older adults prefer to live in their own homes, in some cases the loss of physical and cognitive abilities may impair the elder's competence so much that P–E congruence cannot be achieved and long-term care services are required. Traditionally this has meant relocation to a nursing home, but as described in this section, community-based long-term care options have expanded in the past 20 years. Following a description of nursing homes and the cultural changes taking place in this industry, we discuss newer options in both residential and community-based long-term care.

Nursing Homes

People who are unfamiliar with the residential patterns of older people mistakenly assume that the majority live in nursing homes; however, the actual proportion is only 4.5 percent of the population 65 and older, or 1.6 million. This is a decline from 1985, when 5.4 percent resided in nursing homes (U.S. Census Bureau, 2000). The lifetime risk of admission to a nursing home increases with age, from 39 percent at age 65 to 49 percent at age 85. Approximately 47 percent of women and 33 percent of men older than 65 use nursing homes at some point in their lives, often for a short stay after hospitalization (Seperson, 2002; Spillman and Lubitz, 2002).

As shown in Figure 11.3, the oldest-old disproportionately use nursing homes; when all ethnic groups are combined, rates increase from 1.1 percent of the young-old, to 17 percent of the oldest-old, to almost 50 percent of those who are age 95 and older (Federal Interagency Forum on Aging, 2006; NCHS, 2005; Seperson, 2002). Each year more than 1 million older persons leave long-term care facilities, almost evenly divided among discharges to the community, transfers to other health facilities, and death. Therefore, the statistic of 4.5 percent is a cross-sectional snapshot of the population in long-term care facilities that does not take account of movement into and out of such settings.

With the increase in alternative long-term care options, such as assisted living and adult family homes (described later in this chapter), rates of nursing home admissions are changing substantially. More elders, even those with multiple physical and cognitive impairments, are selecting or are placed in long-term care facilities other than nursing homes, while many others receive health care in their own homes. This

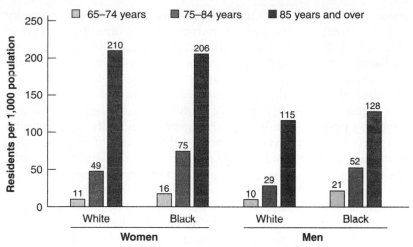

FIGURE 11.3 **Nursing Home Residents among Persons 65 Years of Age and Over, by Age, Gender, and Race: United States, 1999**
SOURCE: National Center for Health Statistics, 2005.

has resulted in a decline in nursing homes, from 19,100 in 1985 to about 16,000 today. These newer options in LTC have also reduced the proportion of elders in nursing homes, from 1.3 percent in 1985 to 1.1 percent among the young-old and from 22 to 17 percent among the oldest-old (Federal Interagency Forum on Aging, 2006; NCHS, 2005). The total number of beds and average number of beds per home have both increased, however. This reflects a decline in the number of smaller nursing homes. The lower rates of nursing home admissions will probably continue, despite the significant growth of the oldest-old. This is because of increasing LTC options and a preference for remaining in one's own home. Nevertheless, nursing homes are often the best choice for the oldest, most frail and vulnerable segment of the population. As a result of more community-based options, nursing home residents today are much sicker and require more intensive services than their counterparts 20 to 30 years ago. This greater intensity of services has raised the cost of living in a nursing home, not including specialized care such as for dementia (MetLife, 2003). The average age of nursing home residents is 81,

and women are disproportionately represented. The typical nursing home includes:

- 72 percent women
- 66 percent widowed or divorced elders
- 40 percent of residents with a diagnosis of dementia
- 82 percent requiring assistance with two or more ADLs (NCHS, 2000)

The gender differential in nursing homes, shown in Figure 11.3, is due to women's longer life expectancy, their greater risk of multiple chronic illnesses, and their greater likelihood of being unmarried. The last factor is a critical one, since the absence of a partner or other caregiver is a major predictor of nursing home placement.

In a 6-year follow-up of 634 community-dwelling persons aged 70 and over who had some disabilities at baseline, 41 percent had died and 23 percent had entered a nursing home for some time in those 6 years. Those whose primary caregiver was a male were more than twice as likely to enter a nursing home as elders with a female caregiver. Living with the primary caregiver reduced nursing home placement by one-half. The use of formal services such as adult day care diminished the risk for cognitively impaired older persons, but increased the risk for physically frail persons by a factor of 2.5 when both formal and informal care were required. This apparent dichotomy may mean that formal services can relieve the burden of caregiving in cases of dementia, thereby postponing or preventing nursing home placement. In contrast, older people with disabilities who need both formal and informal care may be too impaired to live in the community, even when multiple services are brought into their homes. These elders represent the segment of the population that will continue to require nursing homes in the future, even with the growth of other, less restrictive and less costly LTC alternatives (Jette, Tennstedt, and Crawford, 1995). Inequities in social exchange in the caregiver–care recipient dyad, as discussed in Chapter 10, can also result in placement. That is, if the adult child must help an increasingly frail parent, and the older adult cannot reciprocate, the likelihood of nursing home placement increases. Elders with incontinence, hallucinations, impaired communication, and severe ADL and IADL limitations are more likely to move to a nursing home, whether or not they have a family caregiver (Friedman et al., 2006; Wilmoth, 2000). About 87 percent of nursing home residents are white, compared to 10.4 percent who are African American, and 3 percent who are Latino, American Indian, or Asian-Pacific Islander (NCHS, 2000). African Americans have historically been less likely to live in nursing homes, but since 1985 there has been an increase in the proportion who turn to nursing home care:

- In 1985, 5.6 percent of whites and 4.2 percent of African Americans lived in nursing homes.
- In 2000, the proportions were reversed, such that 4.2 percent of whites and 5.6 percent of African Americans were nursing home residents (NCHS, 2006).

The under-representation of ethnic minority groups in nursing homes appears to reflect cultural differences in the willingness to place older persons in such facilities, greater availability of family supports, or institutionalized discrimination. For low-income elders of color, options may be limited by the lack of Medicaid beds in nursing homes. This under-representation may also reflect the dearth of facilities that address ethnic minorities' distinctive needs, thereby forcing them to enter nursing homes that are incongruent with their cultural needs. In some communities with large ethnic minority populations, nursing homes have been built under the auspices of nonprofit organizations or faith-based groups. For example, in San Francisco and Seattle, Japanese and Chinese American elders can enter nursing homes operated and staffed by people who speak their language and serve culturally specific foods. In most of the Chinese facilities, for example, employees can communicate with residents in many dialects of Chinese (*New York Times,* 2003).

Most nursing homes (about 65 percent) are *proprietary* or *for-profit,* and thus operate as a business that aims to make a profit for the owners or investors. There has been an increase in nursing homes owned by large multifacility chains. Another 6 percent are owned by federal, state, or local governments. *Nonprofit* homes (29 percent of the total) are generally sponsored by faith-based or fraternal groups (Cowles, 2006). Although profit is not their goal, they must be self-supporting. These are governed by a board or advisory group, rather than owners or investors, as in the case of proprietary homes. Although instances of reimbursement fraud by proprietary homes are highly publicized, the terms *proprietary* and *nonprofit* do not designate type or quality of care, but rather how the home is governed and how its earnings are distributed. The extent to which nursing home care is shaped by federal funding mechanisms (e.g., Medicare, Medicaid) and regulations is discussed in Chapter 17.

Because of stereotypes and media stories about poor-quality facilities, few older people choose to live in a nursing home. Most enter after receiving informal care from family members, formal home care services, and, in some cases, following a stay in facilities such as assisted living or adult family homes. African Americans are more likely than other groups to enter directly from a hospital and therefore have less control over the placement decision. Nevertheless, nursing home life offers some advantages over other types of long-term care. These include:

- increased social interaction
- accessible social activities
- intensive rehabilitation services not provided by other long-term care alternatives
- relief from the stress of caregiving on family

Although the media report instances of abuse and violation of regulations, many excellent nursing homes exist. Increased efforts to improve nursing homes and the development of innovative options signal an important change in skilled nursing facilities. Such options include subacute care for post-hospital discharge residents, palliative and hospice care for terminally ill persons, and special care units (SCUs) for residents with cognitive or severe physical impairments. These services are becoming more important as newer residents enter with worse functional status than previous cohorts, including many with dementia and needing assistance with multiple ADLs (Gwyther and Kane, 2006; Teresi, Holmes, and Ory, 2000; Vourlekis and Simons, 2006).

Increasingly, residents of nursing homes and their families have more influence over their lives, through resident councils, patients' bills of rights, nursing home ombudsmen, and the advocacy of groups such as the National Citizens Coalition for Nursing Home Reform (NCCNHR). In its resident surveys, this organization found that a major concern of cognitively intact older people is to be involved in decisions about their daily lives in the facility. Through such efforts,

along with increased gerontological training, nursing home staff are also implementing ways to involve family, friends, and the larger community in their policies, procedures, and activities.

Congress enacted provisions in nursing home regulations in the Omnibus Budget Reconciliation Act (OBRA) that were intended to recognize and respect residents' rights. This law requires every nursing home that participates in Medicare or Medicaid to respect residents' dignity, choice, and right of self-determination. Most states have a nursing home ombudsman or a complaint-resolution unit where residents and their families can report their concerns and grievances. An important component of OBRA was to discourage pharmacological and physical restraints for managing behavior problems among residents with dementia. Staff training in behavior management techniques was recommended by the Health Care Financing Administration in 1990 (now the Centers for Medicare and Medicaid Services, or CMS). These actions have resulted in research and demonstration initiatives to test alternative approaches to behavior management. One successful strategy is to train nurse aides in effective nonverbal and communication skills, as well as specific staff behaviors that can prevent the onset of problematic resident behaviors. Such training reduced agitation in residents and resulted in improved communication skills up to 6 months after the intervention (Burgio et al., 2002).

Culture Change in Nursing Homes

In response to growing concerns about the "warehousing" of frail elders in nursing homes, new paradigms are emerging. Since the 1990s, there has been a major **culture change** and a focus on **resident-centered care** in nursing homes. Culture change focuses not just on the physical environment, but also decision making that encourages more input by residents, family members and staff, and a less hierarchical organizational structure than the traditional nursing home model. Nursing homes that have adopted this paradigm shift focus on individualizing services to each resident's needs and preferences (i.e., resident-centered care), offering them choices in waking and eating time, and in some cases even selecting which staff members serve them. One of the first national efforts aimed at changing the nursing home culture was labeled the **Eden Alternative** by its founder, Dr. Bill Thomas. This approach to nursing home policy and operations emphasizes the "home" aspect of nursing homes, as a place where residents can continue to grow, rather than institutions where they come to die. According to this paradigm, elders should continue to make decisions for themselves and engage in meaningful activities, including caring for plants and pets in the home, or volunteering in a child care center if there is one on site. Facilities that have adopted the Eden Alternative deemphasize strictly scheduled activities and focus on humanizing staff–elder interactions (Thomas, 1999; Thomas and Stermer, 1999). To date, few systematic evaluations of these facilities have assessed whether the Eden Alternative philosophy has any impact on residents. In one study, overall quality of care had improved in a Canadian home that implemented the Eden Alternative (Schmidt and Beattie, 2005). In another study, elders in a home that adopted the Eden Alternative were assessed at baseline and one year after the program began and compared with elders in a typical nursing home. Lower levels of boredom and helplessness were found among residents in the Eden Alternative facility, but the groups did not differ in loneliness scores (Bergman-Evans, 2004).

Other paradigms of culture change have been promoted by the **Pioneer Network,** a growing coalition of long-term care administrators and advocates for improving the quality of care in nursing homes. The Pioneer Network also emphasizes the importance of supporting individual residents' rights rather than rigid adherence to institutional regulations. Unlike the policy and operations focus of the Eden Alternative, this model modifies the physical environment to make nursing homes more home-like, create "neighborhoods," and offer residents more privacy. Organizational changes such as expanding staff roles, leadership and decision making are also intended to provide a resident-centered facility (Angelelli and Higbie, 2005; Grant, 2006; Yeatts, et al., 2004). One of the first nursing homes in the country to implement these physical and organizational changes was Mt. St. Vincent Home in Seattle. In this dramatic example, each floor was divided into "neighborhoods" of 20 residents per group, with their own small dining rooms, with resident-directed care, integration of cognitively alert elders and those with dementia, and assignment of staff to each "neighborhood" (Boyd, 2003).

The **Green House** concept also focuses on deinstitutionalizing long-term care by converting large nursing facilities into multiple intentional communities of 8- to 10 residents. Its goal is to empower residents with as much autonomy and choice as possible. These smaller houses are linked together organizationally but residents remain part of the 8- to 10-person home. The community of residents interacts in a shared living room and dining area, but residents have private rooms and bathrooms. The homes do not have nursing stations, unlike the typical nursing home design. Each unit has a lower resident to staff ratio, and all staff are taught to provide direct or hands-on care. These **universal workers** perform multiple services, including meal preparation, personal care, and housekeeping, rather than specializing in one task. This allows greater opportunities for staff and residents to know each other. One licensed nurse is available for 2 to 3 houses, depending on the level of skilled care needed. Preliminary evaluations suggest less depression and agitation, and less antipsychotic medication use among elders with dementia in Green House homes. Job satisfaction among staff appears to be higher and turnover lower

> **IMPLEMENTING RESIDENT-CENTERED CARE IN ASSISTED LIVING**
>
> One facility that has combined technology with a resident-centered model of long-term care is Oatfield Estates or Elite Care, located just outside Portland, Oregon. The campus is comprised of multiple houses with 12 private suites for up to 15 elders who eat and socialize with their house-mates and staff who are assigned to that house. Family members are encouraged to visit and volunteer, and can monitor their elder's daily activities 24 hours a day, with the resident's permission. This is because residents wear an unobtrusive electronic monitoring device that can track their activities, where they are spending their time, and how well they are sleeping. Such monitoring also allows elders to wander throughout Oatfield Estates' gardens and houses, without concerns about being lost. This combination of technology and resident-centered care has allowed the facility to care for many elders with dementia who would ordinarily be placed in a nursing home. Elite Care has garnered international attention for this ability to combine technology and humanistic care for even the most frail elders.

than in traditional nursing homes (Lustbader and Williams, 2006; Rabig et al., 2006). This philosophy has been enhanced by the implementation of technology to assist universal workers and further improve the quality of life of frail residents at Oatfield Estates, near Portland, Oregon, as described by the box on this page. These significant paradigm shifts in their organizational philosophy and structure, physical design and staff caregiving practices are improving the quality of care for frail elders in nursing homes (Angelelli, 2006; Day, Carreon, and Stump, 2000; Fagan, 2004).

Newer Options for Long-Term Care

In response to perceived needs for elders with some limitations in their ADLs, **community residential care** options (CRCs) have also grown dramatically in the past 15 years. This LTC model is defined as group housing with additional services such as meals, basic health care, and some personal assistance. Examples include assisted living and adult family homes (or adult foster care), described more fully below. At a minimum, CRCs provide room and board, at least one meal per day, and 24-hour security, although not as extensively as nursing homes (Hawes, 2001; Hawes, Rose, and Phillips, 1999; Quinn et al., 1999). Community residential care can help older people maintain their independence, even if they have multiple ADL limitations. Because they cost less to operate, more individuals and organizations are investing in this type of housing. Large health care systems, insurance companies, and nonprofit and for-profit corporations have built CRCs or added new apartment or cottage units to their existing nursing home campuses. The great majority of CRC residents are age 75 and older. Many would have been placed in nursing homes in the past, but are now entering CRCs. The lower cost of CRCs has made them a more desirable option for states with growing numbers of frail elders who need public assistance. One reason for this is the trend toward state licensure and Medicaid reimbursement, albeit at lower levels, for these alternatives. This increasing use of Medicaid waivers is discussed in Chapter 17.

Assisted Living

Assisted living (AL) is seen by its advocates as a more humane model of housing for elders who need assistance with personal care and with some ADLs, but who are not so severely impaired physically or cognitively that they need 24-hour skilled medical care (Regnier, 2002; Wilson, 1993, 1995). The Assisted Living Federation of America (ALFA) defines assisted living as "a special combination of housing, personalized supportive services, and healthcare" (www.alfa.org). It is based on a social model of long-term care, rather than a medical model such as nursing homes. As such, it is not necessarily a specific building type but a philosophy of care. Nevertheless, AL facilities usually provide private apartments, which typically include:

- a small kitchen
- a full bathroom
- in some, a bedroom, sitting room, and an additional partial bath

These features provide a more homelike, less-institutional setting that encourages frail elders to maintain active aging and continuity with their previous lifestyles (Frank, 2002; Marsden, 2005). Some assisted living facilities offer shared units as a lower-cost alternative. Most provide congregate meals in a common dining room, as well as housekeeping, laundry, and help with some ADLs, such as medication use. Staff generally include at least one nurse, a social worker, and one or more people to provide case management services. Access to health care is provided for specific residents as needed (often contracting the services of physicians, physical therapists, mental health specialists). As a result, staffing costs are lower than in nursing homes, thereby keeping the average cost of AL lower. An extensive analysis of such facilities throughout the United States and northern Europe led Regnier (2002) to develop nine criteria for a successful assisted living project. According to these guidelines, AL facilities that want to achieve excellent resident outcomes should:

1. appear residential in character
2. be perceived as small in scale
3. provide residents with privacy
4. recognize each resident's uniqueness
5. encourage independence and interdependence
6. emphasize health maintenance, mental stimulation, and physical activity
7. support involvement by residents' families
8. maintain contact with the immediate community
9. serve frail elders

Assisted living facilities often develop individual service plans, based on each resident's functional abilities. Families considering these options must ask what the facility will provide as their older relatives decline physically or cognitively. Like nursing homes, AL providers that offer a variety of services generally charge "tiered" rates, that is, increasingly costly fees for elders who need more services. Therefore, even though AL on average costs half that of a nursing home, some facilities with extensive amenities and health services can cost as much as a nursing home (MetLife, 2003).

Assisted living generally offers residents more autonomy, privacy, and participation in care decisions than do nursing homes. The trade-off, of course, is that the individual may decide to participate in activities that are risky or that do not comply with health care regimens recommended by a professional. These may include choices such as refusing to use a walker or not following a specific diet. As a result of this conflict between assuring resident autonomy versus safety, many facilities have moved toward a policy of managed or **negotiated risk.** Under such policies, residents (and often their family or guardian) must sign a written agreement that allows the resident to accept greater risk of personal injury in exchange for autonomy in decisions about lifestyle. Many elders and their families are willing to accept greater risk in exchange for autonomy and privacy in assisted living, despite the fact that elders in AL today are more frail than was intended by this type of housing:

- Their average age is 84
- 23 percent have a diagnosis of Alzheimer's disease
- About 33 percent have a significant hearing impairment and/or visual impairments
- 72 percent need some help with bathing and 57 percent with dressing
- More than 75 percent need help with managing medications and money
- Only 20 percent can perform all ADLs independently (Marsden, 2005)

When the assisted living model was first proposed (Wilson, 1993, 1995), the focus was on creating a home-like setting, smaller in scale than nursing homes, that allowed resident control and privacy. These facilities were intended to provide apartments with private baths, food preparation and storage areas, and doors that residents could lock. The goal was to allow elders to age in place by providing services as needs changed, but with shared responsibility and negotiated risk, recognizing that AL could not offer all the medical services available in nursing homes. Over time, however, the concept has changed, so that many facilities do not offer private apartments. In addition, the lack of state and federal legislation defining assisted living has resulted in diverse models of this concept, depending on ownership and location. Because of wide variations in definitions, estimates range from 10,000 to 40,000 facilities, serving between 350,000 to 1 million elders (Hawes, 2001; Kane and Wilson, 2001; Pynoos and Matsuoka, 2001). Some AL facilities can accommodate older people with multiple disabilities, many of whom traditionally would be placed in nursing homes. However, some have argued that many AL facilities are not good settings for aging in place because they do not provide adequate services as residents become more frail. Some states have policies against admitting elders with cognitive impairment or behavioral problems unless staff receive special training, but exceptions are common (Hernandez, 2005–2006; Zimmerman, Munn, and Koenig, 2006).

Assisted living is most prominent in Oregon, where the concept was first introduced. Because of flexible regulations about residents' ADL limitations, only 20 percent leave AL for nursing homes, compared with 60 percent in other states (Phillips et al., 2003; Golant, 2004). Oregon currently has an equal mix of nursing home and AL beds (30 percent each) for elders who need long-term care. Another 40 states and the District of Columbia have adopted the concept of assisted living. They provide **Medicaid waivers**

THE DOWNSIDE OF CRCs

Despite its many advantages, housing for older adults that is based on a social model of long-term care can have its downside. These problems are aggravated in states that have few or no licensure requirements for assisted living or other CRCs. For example, state officials and industry representatives in Alabama agreed to enforcing stricter rules after reviewing complaints against 200 unlicensed facilities. Two particularly egregious examples are a 92-year-old man who climbed out of a window in the assisted living facility where he lived, walked away, and died of exposure; and a frail resident, in another facility, who became bedridden, lost 40 pounds and died when no medical attention was provided.

for elders to use AL as an alternative to nursing homes for elders who have fewer ADL limitations. Some, such as Oregon and Washington, have implemented programs that encourage the use of AL and other community-based long-term care options. Interest in assisted living is growing, but costs are prohibitive for many low and middle income elders, and many facilities do not accept elders who are covered by Medicaid because of reimbursement rates lower than fees charged to private pay residents. In some cases, elders must move out because they have run out of funds and must turn to nursing homes that accept Medicaid, even though they might benefit from the greater autonomy and self-care at AL facilities. As more states provide Medicaid waivers for assisted living as an alternative to nursing homes, greater P–E congruence can be achieved between needs of elders with fewer ADL limitations and available housing options (Hernandez, 2005–2006). Medicaid waivers are described in detail in Chapter 17.

Since most elders and their families prefer AL over nursing homes, there is growing interest in whether these LTC options differ in resident outcomes. In a comparison of 76 elders living in a nursing home with 82 in an assisted living facility within the same CCRC campus, medical records were examined and residents were interviewed 4 times over a 12-month period. At the baseline assessment, cognitive status did not differ between groups, but nursing home residents had more symptoms of depression and poorer functional health than AL residents. During the 12-month follow-up, mortality rates and relocation to units or facilities with more assistance did not differ between the two sites. Residents' age was the best predictor of mortality, whereas their functional and cognitive ability, educational level, and payment status (i.e., private vs. Medicaid) predicted whether or not they would relocate to higher levels of care. No differences emerged on these variables between the two types of facilities. These findings suggest that older adults who need residential long-term care may do just as well in terms of health outcomes in the less restrictive and less costly assisted living setting as they would in a nursing home (Pruchno and Rose, 2000). These positive findings have led many housing policy advocates to promote the expansion of AL for lower-income elders. One result has been an allocation of funds from HUD to states to convert existing multifamily units into assisted living. To date, five states (California, Connecticut, New Jersey, New York, and Pennsylvania) have received these funds to accommodate their low-income, frail elders who could not otherwise afford it (HUD, 2006a).

Private Homes That Provide Long-Term Care

Adult foster care (AFC) or **adult family homes (AFH)** are other options for older persons who do not need the 24-hour medical care of skilled nursing homes. Like assisted living residents, older residents in AFCs can generally decide for themselves whether to take their medications or to exercise, unlike the more structured nursing home schedule. AFC is generally provided in a private home by the owners who may have some health care training but are not required to be professionals in the field. The owner and, in some

cases, auxiliary staff provide housekeeping, help with some ADLs, personal care, and some delegated nursing functions, such as giving injections, distributing medications, and changing dressings on wounds if they have been trained and certified by a registered nurse. These homes are licensed to house up to 5 or 6 residents. Some specialize in caring for adults with physical disabilities or psychiatric disorders; others refuse to care for people with advanced dementia; while still others offer services to dementia patients only.

In 2000, 39 states covered services in AFH or AL through Medicaid waivers (Mollica, 2001). Medicaid reimbursement rates for AFC are one-third to one-half the rates paid to nursing homes. This works well for residents who do not require heavy care (e.g., those who are not bedridden or with severe behavioral problems due to dementia). However, for more frail older clients, or for those who have aged in place (i.e., have become more impaired while living in that AFC), the reimbursement rates do not reflect the time and effort required of the facilities' caregivers. For this reason, a survey of 290 AFH providers in Washington State revealed high levels of dissatisfaction with reimbursement rates and complaints that case managers were not disclosing the severity of clients' needs when referring them to AFH (Curtis, Kiyak, and Hedrick, 2000).

This trend toward placing more impaired older persons in AFC or AFH is driven by states' efforts to control long-term care costs and most elders' and families' preferences for a social, rather than a medical, model of care. Similar to the study described above that compared residents' health outcomes in nursing homes versus assisted living facilities (Pruchno and Rose, 2000), Hedrick and colleagues (2003) compared health, relocation, and mortality over a 12-month period among residents of assisted living, adult family homes (AFH), and adult residential care (ARC) facilities. They followed 349 adults in 219 facilities (including AL, AFH, and ARC), from 3 months after the individual entered the facility to 12 months later.

At baseline, AFH residents were more likely than the other two groups to require help with multiple ADLs (especially bathing and dressing), even though the oldest group resided in AL settings. General health status was similar across the three types of settings, and cognitive impairment was more common in AFH and AL residents than among those in ARC (58, 43, and 23 percent, respectively). However, there were no significant differences across the three types of long-term care in mortality rates, declines in health, or relocation to different settings over the 12 months of follow-up.

These results support the findings of the study comparing nursing homes and AL—that a less restrictive and less costly LTC setting can accommodate frail elders as well as the more costly option. Furthermore, residents' health outcomes as measured by mortality, morbidity, and relocation are similar across these settings. Aging in place appears to be possible without relocating to the more expensive setting, whether that is AFH versus AL, or AL versus nursing homes. To the extent that these CRCs provide some help with ADLs, they can reduce the costs for elders and their families who pay out-of-pocket, as well as states that must allocate their Medicaid dollars for eligible elders (Chapin and Dobbs-Kepper, 2001).

Because outcomes such as mortality, morbidity, and relocation are often similar, despite wide variations in the cost and range of services offered by residential LTC options, it is also important to consider other outcomes. Improving the older person's quality of life, not just extending life, should become a primary goal for long-term care providers. Critical elements of quality of life to be considered by such facilities should be

- a sense of safety, security, and order
- physical comfort and freedom from pain
- enjoyment of daily life
- meaningful activities
- meaningful interpersonal relationships

- maintaining functional competence (or "active aging" within the limits of the elder's capacities)
- maintaining dignity
- a sense of privacy
- a sense of individuality, autonomy, and choice
- spiritual well-being (Kane, 2001)

Services to Assist Aging in Place

As noted earlier, long-term care has evolved in the past 15 years from an emphasis on purely institutional care to a broad range of services to help older adults age in place in the least restrictive environment possible. Under this broader definition, homemaker services, nutrition programs, adult day care, and home health care are all long-term care services which can assist the older person in maintaining P–E congruence. As shown in Figure 11.4, some of these services (e.g., home care) are brought to the older person, whereas others (e.g., adult day health) require the individual to leave home to receive the services.

Home Care

Despite the increasing array of residential options for older adults, most prefer to age in place. Surveys of older adults, even those in substandard housing, reveal that more than 90 percent want to stay in their own homes for as long as possible (AARP, 2003, 2006a, 2006c). While some home care alternatives are motivated by elders' desire to age in place, other changes are being driven by cost concerns. As third-party payers (e.g., Medicare) have searched for alternatives to escalating hospital and nursing home costs, home care services have grown dramatically. Medicare reimburses home health care services, defined as skilled nursing or rehabilitation benefits that are provided in the patient's own home and prescribed by a physician. Not surprisingly, the average home health client is a woman age 70 and has 1.7 ADL impairments. The oldest-old generally receive more home

In Home
- Home care
- Home health services
- Home-delivered meals
- Home improvement

Older Adult at Home

In Community
- Senior center
- Adult day care
- Transportation
- Shopping

FIGURE 11.4   Services Needed by Elders at Home with Long-Term Care Needs

health visits on average than any other age group, about 4 times as many as for those age 65 to 66 (Hughes and Pittard, 2001; Peng, Navaie-Waliser, and Feldman, 2003).

As demand has increased, home care agencies have expanded their services beyond health care to include a broad array of home- and community-based services (HCBS) to support aging in place:

- assistance such as chore services to maintain the home
- personal care to help the person perform ADLs

- home-delivered meals
- automatic safety response systems

Other HCBS options, such as adult day care and care management, are offered in community settings. These services provide respite to family caregivers and opportunities for social interaction for isolated elders. The checklist in the box below summarizes factors that families should consider when selecting home health care services.

Chore workers and other home- and community-based services can help older people remain in their homes.

A CHECKLIST FOR CHOOSING HOME HEALTH CARE SERVICES

- Is the agency licensed, accredited, and certified to give home health care?
- Is the agency Medicare-certified/approved?
- Does it have a written statement about its services, eligibility, costs, and payment procedures?
- Does it do background checks on potential employees?
- Are homemakers and home health aides trained? For how long? By whom?
- How are employees supervised?
- Will the same person provide care on a regular basis?
- What are the hourly fees? Minimum hours required?
- How does the agency handle theft and other unacceptable behaviors?
- Will you be given a copy of the treatment/ service plan?
- Does the agency have a Bill of Rights for clients?

Adult Day Care and Adult Day Health Care

Adult day care (ADC) is another long-term care option that allows the older person to remain at home and receive some health and social services. In this case, users attend a local ADC center one or more times per week, for several hours each day. ADC goes beyond senior centers in providing structured health and social services for older people with cognitive and functional impairments. These facilities are smaller than most senior centers, with an average daily attendance of less than 25 elders; about 75 percent are non-profit. Some ADCs are based on a health rehabilitative model of long-term care with individualized care ("Adult Day Health Care" or ADHC), while others fit into a social psychological model ("social day care"). Although both may provide recreation, meals, transportation to and from the facility, and memory-retraining programs, ADHCs are more likely to offer nursing care, physical and speech therapy, health monitoring, and scheduled medication distribution. The greatest advantage of ADHCs over home health care is to bring together older people for social interaction. Equally important, they provide respite and support for family caregivers, as noted in Chapter 10. This is an important function, especially since it can reduce caregivers' feelings of stress, worry, and overload (Gaugler et al., 2003). Clearly, such services are not suitable for the most impaired or bedbound older person; but they are an invaluable resource for elders with moderate levels of dementia or with serious physical impairments and chronic illnesses who still benefit from living in the community.

Technology to Help Aging in Place

An important consideration in helping older adults to age in place is to design housing that is adaptable to their changing competence levels. These include private homes where all amenities are on one level, with easy access to a bathroom

---

PLANNING FOR AGING IN PLACE

When Mr. and Mrs. Pond bought their last home, they were in their late 60s. They chose a house on one level, installed grab bars in the bathroom, nonslip surfaces, and other safety features. When Mr. Pond was 78, he had a stroke that restricted his mobility. Mrs. Pond's vision became more impaired. However, with help from a weekly chore worker, daily meals delivered to their home, and twice-weekly visits to an adult day care facility, they were able to remain in their home until they died, he at age 82, she at 85.

---

and kitchen. If the home was not initially built with these design principles, modifications should be made to improve visual and physical accessibility, and to ensure autonomy by the aging homeowner.

Even among middle-aged adults, new home buyers are demanding "flexible housing." In response to this growing demand, the Master Builders Association has developed a training program to help contractors build and remodel homes that can be used throughout a lifetime. This interest on the part of home builders is clearly more than academic. It reflects the trend of first-time buyers to select neighborhoods where they will want to live for many years. As a result, architects and builders are already designing homes with movable walls that can expand or shrink a room as needs change, or plumbing that can convert a small room on the main floor of the house into a bathroom. This gives families the flexibility to adapt their homes as they assume caregiving roles, or if one of the current residents needs community-based in-home care in the future. Other options are modifiability in the number and size of bedrooms, and using a cluster design so that multiple generations and even unrelated renters can live under the same roof while retaining their privacy.

Knowledgeable about the Americans with Disabilities Act (ADA), builders and architects are aware of the need to make main-floor hallways and doorways in private homes wide enough for wheelchair access. Even though the ADA does not require accessibility in private homes, these trends are occurring because builders recognize the growing market for such housing features. Computerized controls for heat, artificial lighting, and window coverings are too costly for most of today's home buyers, but will become more prevalent in homes of the future. With portable keypads, these features can help frail older persons maintain ambient temperatures, lighting, and sound at levels that are congruent with their competence level.

Newer cohorts of elders are also benefiting from the **Universal Design** movement, first proposed by an activist for the rights of persons with disabilities (Mace, 1998). This concept of designing the environment to allow the widest range of users possible (i.e. inclusive design) and facilitate active aging attracts the attention of architects, landscape architects, and interior and furniture designers. What began as an attempt to make street curbs and hallways and bathrooms in homes accessible to people in wheelchairs has grown to a movement that makes all environments—parks, wilderness areas, automobiles, and computer workstations— accommodate people who are able-bodied, as well as those with limited mobility, vision, and hearing. The principles behind universal design are to:

- maximize autonomy
- enhance personal dignity
- enable full participation in society
- provide opportunities for self-fulfillment (Preiser and Ostroff, 2001)

Some architects are working on cost-effective means of applying new technology to home and long-term care design. For example, systems that make a room light up through sensors in the floor can help prevent accidents when an older person gets up at night. Bed sensors that detect weight change can be used to monitor how often the older person gets out of bed during the night. Remote controls for operating thermostats, windows, and their coverings can help an older adult change the room temperature as needed, as well as open and close windows and shades to control the ambient temperature and to prevent glare. Other design features that can be built into housing to assist aging in place include:

- bathrooms with roll-in showers
- hands-free sensors on faucets
- nonskid flooring
- low-pile carpeting
- uniform lighting throughout the house
- elevator shafts that are built into the home and used as closets until they are needed as elevators

For example, today nearly 35 percent of individuals age 75 and older use at least one assistive device or have had their home modified for accessibility. This proportion will increase dramatically in the future, especially among baby boomers. The most popular modification is to install grab bars in bathrooms (in about 30 percent of homes owned by 65 and older adults). Other changes are far less frequent, perhaps because of cost concerns:

- Twenty-three percent added brighter lighting in their homes.
- Sixteen percent added more handrails.
- Four percent replaced doorknobs and water faucets with lever handles.
- Four percent installed ramps in place of steps or stairs (AARP, 2000).

The field of **gerontechnology** (or *gerotechnology*), where gerontologists and industrial and human factors engineers work together to create **assistive technology** has expanded in the past 10 years. Technology is being built into housing and products to improve P–E congruence for older adults. Many of these products are designed to help people remember tasks such as medication schedules; one product already on the market uses verbal and tone reminders, as well as flashing lights and a single red button to dispense medications on a predetermined schedule. Family members or health providers can set up a prescription routine on a specific schedule for up to 11 different drugs for 30 days. Other devices can be attached to each prescription container; a prerecorded voice announces the schedule and dose needed for that particular medication. This technique is especially useful for older people with dementia who would benefit from hearing a family member's voice reminding them what medications to take (Logue, 2002). These new devices are not necessarily better than hands-on care by caregivers, but they may allow the elder to remain self-sufficient longer, reduce caregiver burden, and are often more cost-effective than paid caregivers (Agree and Freedman, 2003; Pinto et al., 2001; Rialle et al., 2002).

Computer programs have been developed to describe potential side effects of various medications and interactions among them. Currently, these software programs are aimed at physicians, pharmacists, and other health professionals. However, programs will soon be available, written in layman's language, where elders can type in the names and doses of

medications they are taking, and then obtain a printout of potential side effects and special precautions. This would be particularly useful to the many older adults who are using multiple prescriptions and over-the-counter medications. It is also technically possible to conduct remote monitoring between a patient's home and a local health care facility for such information as blood pressure and heart-rate measures. Indeed, as Figure 11.5 illustrates, such monitoring consists of wearing a bracelet or armcuff attached to a computer or a cell phone that transmits health data to a centralized database in a hospital or health provider's office. After paying for the necessary hardware and software, however, the costs of regular monitoring by a health care provider may be prohibitive for many older adults. In the future, health insurance plans may provide this benefit.

Assistive technology can include home monitoring for people with diabetes and hypertension. In this case, the patient's relevant health variables (e.g., weight, blood pressure, blood glucose, and cholesterol) are transmitted to a centralized health care database, as shown in Figure 11.5. Indeed, the field of **telehealth,** where health information is transmitted electronically from the patient's home to their physician's office, or from an ambulatory care setting such as a health clinic to a specialist's office, has grown 40 percent annually since 1997. These systems can increase patients' compliance with medication regimens and reduce their hospitalization rates (Lehmann, 2002, 2003). Information about the elder's health status can also be transmitted online to family members who live or work at a distance from the elder. This allows long-distance surveillance by caregivers.

Other developments include monitoring systems installed in the homes of elders with early-stage dementia so they can remain at home while their family caregivers are employed. Also known as *aware home technology,* these systems support aging in place by monitoring daily

---

LESSONS FROM OTHER COUNTRIES

The United States can learn from developments in other countries with larger proportions of older adults in their population. For example, new homes in Sweden are required by housing codes to include a full bathroom on the main floor. Such foresight is important when one considers the high likelihood that a very old homeowner may no longer be able to go up and down stairs to use a bathroom in the traditional upstairs sleeping quarters (Riley, 1999).

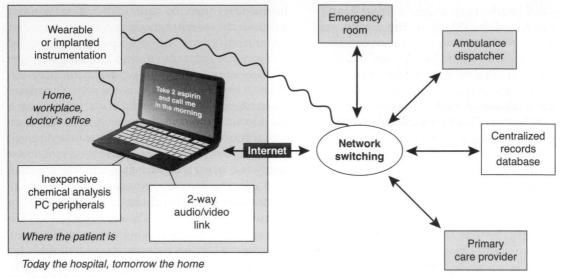

FIGURE 11.5 **Schematic Diagram of a Proposed Interface between the Patient and the Health Care System**
SOURCE: Reprinted with permission of Professor Paul Yager.

activities such as medication use, mapping trends in ADLs, and assisting elders' communication. Caregivers can obtain real time data on their work computers or only emergency information. Alarms can alert family members if the frail elder has fallen, left the stove on beyond a predesignated time, or walked beyond the home's boundaries (e.g., "safe" doors may lead to a protected garden while "alarm" doors lead to the street). Sensors can be placed under mattresses to determine if the elder is sleeping, restless, or out of bed during the night. Because they work by detecting weight on the bed, these sensors can also track the elder's weight and notify caregivers if significant weight loss occurs (Rogers and Fisk, 2005).

Researchers and engineers at the Massachusetts Institute of Technology, Sony, Honda, and other Japanese companies are testing robots that can be used by frail elders to perform routine housework and personal services, and even socialize with their owners. The Intel Corporation is developing a digital photo frame that is activated when someone calls the elder. If the

caller's information is stored on the digital frame, it can identify the caller with a photo and a description of when they last called and what they discussed.

As the fields of gerontechnology and telehealth grow, elders and their families must be alert to the ethical issues of privacy and confidentiality, and must recognize that technology cannot substitute for personal attention and caring by a loved one. They may also be too expensive for many elders. However, these new developments can lengthen the time a frail elder can live independently and reduce caregiver burden (Agree & Freedman, 2003; Pew and Van Hemel, 2004; Rogers and Fisk, 2005).

Technology also can be used to enhance options for older adults' recreation and enrichment. For example, computers are commonly used for obtaining information via the Web and for leisure (e.g., games linked by telecommunication channels, books read on a computer monitor with adjustable font size, programs that convert written to spoken text for visually impaired users). Interactive television, CD-ROM and DVD, closed-caption TV programming, and online education can greatly expand the social worlds of homebound elders and stimulate intellectual functioning through active participation in learning. For example, Senior Net is a nationwide computer network that encourages discussion on diverse topics and offers hands-on classes in computer use. For a small membership fee, users can attend local classes on computer literacy, word processing, database management, and how to access useful sites on the Internet. Computer game companies such as Nintendo are marketing games specifically to older adults.

Given trends toward Internet banking and shopping, future cohorts with computer skills may not need to leave their homes to obtain many services. More older adults are using computers for accessing the Web at home or in nearby libraries and senior centers. But cohort differences are evident in this area; 40 percent of households headed by those age 70 to 79 had a computer in 2003, compared with 58 percent of households headed by adults 60 to 69. Only 25 percent of the former and 44 percent of the latter group reported using the Internet (U.S. Census Bureau, 2005). These rates of computer and Internet use among older Americans are higher than among older adults in the United Kingdom (20 percent of people 65 and older, compared with 63 percent of all ages) and in the European Union (8 percent among 65- to 74-year-olds) (Whitney and Keith, 2006). The majority of elders who use computers do so for e-mail communication, for online social support, banking, shopping, and for the latest health information. This increasing recognition of the scope of the Internet has resulted in a 47 percent growth in elders' use of the Internet between 2000 and 2004, with an almost equal interest by men and women. As baby boomers reach old age and as computers become as ubiquitous as telephones, far greater usage of the Internet is expected (AOA, 2006; Fox, 2004; Morgan, 2004).

Housing Policy and Government Programs

Housing policy for older people is less well developed than in the areas of income security and health care. This is due, in part, to the influence of well-organized interest groups, such as builders and real estate developers.

The major housing programs that benefit older adults involve subsidies to suppliers of housing to enable them to sell or rent housing for less than the prevailing market price. Since 1959, two special housing programs for very low-income older people and those with disabilities have given loans for the construction of housing for these groups. The program for elders is known as *Section 202* grants; that for low-income people with disabilities is the *Section 8* grants. Both are administered by HUD. Section 202 provides housing for people age 62 and older whose incomes are less than 50 percent of the median income in their areas; in most communities this translates to less than $20,850 per year for a one-person household (HUD, 2006b). This program subsidizes rent for qualified elders, so they pay only 30 percent of their adjusted gross income as rent and the federal government covers the remainder. Section 202 grants also provide loans with no or low interest to private nonprofit organizations or consumer cooperatives for the financing, construction, or rehabilitation of housing for older people. These loans do not need to be repaid as long as the housing is available to very low-income elders for at least 40 years. These subsidized housing projects must provide some support services such as meals and transportation.

Section 8 housing programs represent an additional form of housing subsidy for very low-income persons, regardless of age. Qualifying elders or families of persons with disabilities receive rent vouchers to subsidize their rent in the private housing market. Landlords receive from federal and state governments the difference

Federal funds for Section 8 vouchers have been reduced, and many owners have lost interest in the low-income housing market, especially in urban centers undergoing renewal or "gentrification." Some landlords have converted their buildings into higher-rent apartments or condominiums, hotels, or office spaces, or have sold the property outright to local developers. These changes in federal funding and local priorities have reduced the supply of Section 8 housing, which will continue to decline in this century. Some relief has come in the form of vouchers given directly to low-income renters to find market-rate housing, although they may pay more than 30 percent of their income in rent, higher than the traditional form of Section 8 units. Older people make up 15 percent of low-income households with these vouchers (AARP, 2001; Commission on Affordable Housing, 2002). Other policies that indirectly affect older homeowners are:

- property tax relief
- energy assistance
- home equity conversion or reverse mortgages described earlier in this chapter
- energy assistance for low-income homeowners to offset air conditioning and heating costs is provided under the federal government's allocation of block grant money to cities and states

Less than 5 percent, or 1.5 million older people, benefit from federally funded housing assistance programs. The numbers are declining as HUD reduces its subsidies directly to older adults in the form of rent vouchers (Section 8 and 202) or indirectly through low-cost loans to builders of housing for older people (Section 202). Reasons for the decline in housing subsidies are federal cutbacks and public perceptions that most older people can afford to pay their housing costs directly. Most recent federal activity in the housing arena has maintained the programs and housing stock that currently exist, modifying

between the rental cost of a housing unit and 30 percent of the tenants' income available for rent. Older people make up about 40 percent of users of this rent supplement program (AARP, 2001). Although two million households currently benefit from Section 8 vouchers, private landlords are less likely to accept them in cities with low vacancy rates in the rental market (National Coalition for the Homeless, 2006).

programs only incrementally to serve larger numbers of older adults. The goal is to make better use of existing housing resources through accessory apartments and home equity conversions, rather than to increase the overall housing supply for older adults. Another major need is for more congregate housing services. As described earlier, congregate housing is an important link in the long-term care network, enabling frail and low-income older people to maintain P–E congruence. Innovations are needed that modify existing communities and neighborhoods to meet elders' changing housing needs. This may include creating "granny flats" or accessory housing as part of existing homes to accommodate older people in smaller units near family or close friends.

SRO Housing

Single-room-occupancy (SRO) hotels in urban centers have traditionally served as minimal housing for the urban poor, particularly single men, who make up the largest group of SRO residents. Indeed, the typical SRO resident is a white, middle aged or older man with less than 10 years of education and an income level 20 percent lower than that of his non-SRO peers, who reports multiple chronic conditions, and who has lived in his room for at least 5 years. Most are unemployed or unemployable. Increasingly, however, these facilities are becoming home to younger people who are drug abusers, with psychiatric disorders, and often HIV-positive. Older SRO residents may feel threatened in such environments (Foley, 1998).

The Section 8 program described above also provides funding, under the McKinney-Vento Homeless Assistance Act (McKinney, 1987) to rehabilitate existing structures such as unused schools and hotels, converting them into SRO housing for homeless individuals. In most cases, the only private space is a bedroom and a toilet; shared space includes bathrooms, kitchens, and living rooms. Although HUD does not require landlords to do so, 47 percent provide some support services such as job and substance abuse counseling, basic health services, and literacy training. HUD covers the difference between the unit's rental price and the portion paid by the low-income renter. However, SRO housing is rapidly disappearing. As urban cores become more "gentrified," and as more upper-income people discover the advantages of living downtown, the trend of demolishing SRO hotels and using this valuable land for upscale condominiums and office and retail space will continue, as discussed above for Section 8 and Section 202 housing. One result of this has been a dramatic increase in the number of homeless older people in urban centers over the past 20 years (National Coalition for the Homeless, 2006).

The Problems of Homelessness

Although this chapter focuses on elders' housing and community service options, a growing segment of the older population is homeless, often unable to afford basic housing and unaware of services to which they are entitled. Homeless people generally include those who, "for whatever reason, do not have a fixed, regular, and adequate night-time residence" (McKinney, 1987). Today's homeless elders (defined as age 50 and older because physiologically they are often 10 to 20 years older than their chronological age) are largely the chronic homeless who have lived on the streets for many years and have lost contact with their families. People over age 50 comprise about 10 percent of the homeless population. This includes an increasing number of women, although there are approximately 4 times more men in this population (U.S. Conference of Mayors, 2005). Older homeless men are more likely to have lived this way longer than their female counterparts. Many suffer from psychiatric disorders, alcoholism, or

Older people often offer assistance to their homeless peers.

dementia, and lack strong social support. As a result, older adults are the most vulnerable segment of the homeless population. Unfortunately, the trend is toward increased homelessness among older adults. This is due primarily to the loss of affordable housing, and reductions in HUD's housing assistance programs (Section 8 and Section 202) directed at persons 62 and older. Although most homeless adults receive Supplemental Security Income (SSI) (described in Chapter 17), the current monthly maximum SSI benefit of $579 for an individual is inadequate to cover their food, medicine, and health care costs. Most cannot find rental housing with this extremely low income level, even with Section 8 vouchers. Affordable housing for homeless elders is difficult to find even in communities with low housing costs (NLIHC, 2006).

Homeless people who become redomiciled (i.e., find permanent housing) tend to be mostly older women with some social support, who attend community facilities (and become more familiar to service providers), and who do not display psychotic symptoms (Cohen, Sokolovsky, and Crane, 2001; Stergiopoulos and Herrmann, 2003). One epidemiological study interviewed 900 homeless persons using standard diagnostic criteria for psychiatric disorders. Although the rates for other psychiatric diagnoses did not differ by age or gender, alcohol abuse was significantly more prevalent among men age 50 and older than among younger men (81 percent vs. 60 percent); the reverse was true for drug abuse (16 percent vs. 43.5 percent). No differences emerged in rates of substance abuse or other psychiatric diagnoses between younger and older homelesss women (DeMallie, North, and Smith, 1997).

Homeless people also lack food, clothing, medical care, and social supports. Such a disorganized lifestyle can magnify the usual age-related declines in biological and psychological processes described in earlier chapters. A life at the edge, in which the individual is constantly trying to fulfill basic human needs (food, shelter, safety from predators) does not leave much energy for these elders to maintain even a modicum of health and well-being; their problems are compounded by chronic psychiatric disorders, alcoholism, drug abuse, and cognitive impairment (often a result of long-term alcohol abuse). Due to their unstable lifestyles and frequent disruptions in mental well-being, homeless elders with chronic health problems often do not have the physical, social, or psychological resources to seek regular medical care for these conditions, or even to follow the necessary medication schedules and dietary restrictions. The prevalence of chronic diseases in this group is higher than for other segments of the older population, yet their access to health services is inadequate and sporadic at best (Folsom et al., 2002). They generally obtain health care through public hospital emergency rooms; clinical appointments and follow-up visits are rarely kept. Thus, they often die because of diseases that are neglected, accidents, and victimization on the streets. The number of homeless elders is estimated to double in the future, due to an increase in the number of younger persons with risk factors of lifelong poverty, substance abuse, incarceration, marital disruption, and loss of family contacts (Cohen, 1999; Crane et al., 2004).

The McKinney-Vento Homeless Assistance Act provides limited funds to respond to some of these needs. These funds, administered by HUD, are given as grants to communities to develop services that address the multiple problems of shelter, food, health care, and victimization faced by homeless adults and families. The grants are intended for programs that provide supportive and SRO housing with services, and emergency shelters. Unfortunately, the available funds are inadequate for most communities to respond to the growing homeless population.

Aging in Place among Older Prisoners

The U.S. Department of Justice and state departments of corrections or criminal justice categorize prisoners 50 and older as "older." This is because of the small number of inmates over age 65, and because inmates generally age faster as a result of more chronic diseases and a history of drug and alcohol abuse. The cohort age 50 and older represents 8.6 percent of the total U.S. prison population, while those 55 and older make up about 5 percent. The average age among older prisoners is 57. This population is increasing, attributable to the large numbers who have aged in prison with life terms, mandatory minimum sentences with no parole, and older adults committing more serious crimes. In some cases, prison is a "haven" for those who consciously commit new crimes to avoid life on the streets. As with younger populations of prisoners, African Americans are disproportionately

represented among older inmates: about 700 per 100,000 African American adults 55 and older are in prison, compared with 420 per 100,000 Latinos and 130 per 100,000 whites (Aday, 2006; Gallagher, 2001; Harrison and Beck, 2006; Loeb and AbuDagga, 2006).

The rapidly increasing costs of health care for older inmates have gained the attention of correctional officials. Lifestyles and incarceration have accelerated the aging process for many inmates whose health and diet are compounded in prison. The most common chronic diseases among older prisoners are hypertension, arthritis, and chronic obstructive pulmonary disease. These are typical in the older population generally, but rates are 25 percent higher among prisoners, and occur at younger ages. Psychiatric conditions, especially depression, are often lifelong problems in prisoners and go untreated in as many as half of prisoners (Loeb and AbuDagga, 2006; Mitka, 2004; Regan, Alderson, and Regan, 2002; Williams et al., 2006).

Several recommendations have been offered to improve the health status of older prisoners and reduce state and federal corrections systems' health care costs. These include reallocating budgets to provide more health services to older inmates (currently prison budgets are determined on a per-inmate basis, although older prisoners' costs are 3 times higher than the general inmate population); providing separate geriatric health facilities and hospice services; making physical accommodations in older inmates' cells and in bathrooms (e.g. installing handrails, removing top bunks), and training younger inmates as caregivers to older inmates with functional impairments (this would also provide job training for future parolees). A more controversial proposal is early release, known as **compassionate release,** for nonviolent older inmates. Efforts by the Project for Older Prisoners Program have led to the early release of over 100 older prisoners without any subsequent recidivism (Aday, 2006; Mitka, 2004; Turley, 2006; Williams et al., 2006).

Implications for the Future

As baby boomers age, larger numbers of older adults will reside in suburbs and fewer in central cities. Future cohorts will create a demand for services in the suburbs rather than traveling to city centers for their health care, social, recreational, and shopping needs. These trends are already evident as more businesses, medical and dental providers, senior centers, and shopping malls relocate to suburbs. This will reduce the demand for public transportation between suburbs and city centers, which has become too costly for most municipalities to provide. Boomers will be more likely than their parents' generation to continue driving or to use specialized transportation such as vans provided by community agencies.

Because of earlier experiences with relocation and more travel opportunities during their youth, baby boomers will feel more confident about relocating to other parts of the United States, including less costly rural communities and small towns. Some will even choose to move to other countries, such as Mexico, where their retirement income can buy more, or as a form of reverse migration to their homeland. Instead of large, isolated retirement communities, future cohorts of elders are more likely to select independent housing in the communities where they relocate, integrating by volunteering, obtaining paid employment, and becoming active participants in these settings. More cohousing and intentional communities will emerge as groups of older adults choose to live near people who share their interests and lifestyle, but where they can age in place in their own homes. Others will opt to live in continuous care retirement communities (CCRCs) that provide choices in housing and services if the elder becomes frail with age.

As the number of people living to age 85 and older increases, demand for more choices in long-term care will also increase. Aging in place will become a more viable option than it is today, thanks to technological advances that can create more P–E congruence. Technology allows older people to communicate with family members and health and social service providers via the Internet and telehealth. New developments in this area can provide electronic reminders to take medications, exercise, eat healthy meals and record their vital signs. Families may find that caregiving burdens are reduced if they can leave the elder at home and monitor them from a distance. The use of technology will be aided by the growth in "flexible housing" that is being demanded by baby boomers today. Middle-aged adults, who are building new homes or remodeling existing homes to accommodate their aging parents, often find that the home can benefit them as they age in place. They are discovering that elder-friendly home design, including bedroom, bath, and kitchen facilities on the entry floor, easy-to-operate mechanical and electronic devices, and temperature controls for each area of the home, is practical and can be built with minimal construction costs. Such homes can create a more supportive environment for aging baby boomers, but will be limited to those who can afford it.

Although future cohorts of elders will have more options, these choices will depend on their financial resources. As a result, economic disparities will become greater than during their youth. Those who have adequate resources will be able to travel and relocate to more desirable communities. They can purchase services and technology that can help them age in place. If they eventually need long-term care services, they can select from among multiple options in types and quality. Middle-aged people today with adequate financial resources are more likely to purchase long-term care insurance, creating a wider range of options for those who may need such services in their later years. Some of these LTC insurance policies include home health care, adult day health care, and other non-residential services, as described in Chapter 17. Older adults who do not have adequate income or who could not afford to purchase such insurance in their younger years will have to retire on the limited options available to them through Medicaid and Social Security. These elders often have little choice in the type or quality of services they obtain. Homelessness may also rise among older people, especially for those who have severed ties from their families due to divorce, alcohol and drug abuse. These trends suggest an increasing schism between older adults who have aged with sufficient social and financial resources, and those who have faced adversity throughout their lives, including homeless adults and those growing old in prison.

Health and social service providers who serve future cohorts of elders should be aware of the growing options in housing and long-term care. These professionals must be sensitive to the impact of the home and neighborhood on elders' security, comfort, social connectedness, and ultimately their quality of life. If these features are incongruent with elders' needs, knowledgeable experts can play a significant role in helping them make necessary environmental changes, including relocating to a setting that fits their needs (Gonyea, 2006). Long-term care providers, especially in nursing homes, must also change existing paradigms of caring for frail elders, from institutional models that focus on maintaining policies and regulations, to more resident-centered care. Nursing homes, in particular, are experiencing culture change where many employees of the future will be trained as "universal workers." These expanded roles for LTC workers can reduce staff turnover and improve quality of care for frail elders (Noelker and Ejaz, 2005; Perez-Pena, 2003; Wiener, 2003).

Summary

This chapter presented ways in which environmental factors affect the physical and psychological well-being of older people, and the importance of achieving P–E congruence in housing. Perhaps the most important lesson to be gained from this discussion is that a given environment is not inherently good or bad. Some environments are more conducive for achieving active aging among *some* people, while other older adults need an entirely different set of features. For example, an older person who has a high need for activity and stimulation and has always lived in an urban setting will be more satisfied with an assisted living facility in a metropolitan center than will the individual who has always lived in a single-family dwelling in a rural community. Most P–E models point to the necessity of examining each older person's specific needs, preferences, and abilities, and designing environments that can flexibly respond to these differences. To the degree that environmental press can be reduced to accommodate personal abilities and needs, the aging person can function more effectively and enhance well-being. The growing options in LTC provide one way of achieving P–E fit for elders with diverse preferences and needs. Relocation represents a special case of P–E incongruence that can disturb the well-being of an impaired older person by raising the level of environmental press.

Differences in housing quality and services for rural older residents are of concern. Current cohorts are more likely than previous ones to live in suburbs, although disproportionately more elders of color than whites live in urban centers. The neighborhood and neighbors play a significant role in older adults' well-being. With retirement and declining health, the older person's physical lifespace becomes more constricted. The neighborhood takes on greater significance as a source of social interactions, health and social services, grocery shopping, banking, and postal services. Neighbors represent an important component of older people's social and emotional network, especially when family is unavailable.

Fear of crime among older persons is widespread but is incongruent with actual victimization rates. Older people experience far lower rates than younger people for violent crimes, and somewhat lower for other types of crime. Victimization rates have declined for all age groups, particularly for older women. African American men, however, are at greater risk for crimes than any other group of elders. The potential danger of injury and long-term disability, as well as the fear of economic loss, may contribute to this incongruence between actual victimization rates and fear of crime.

The high rate of home ownership and long-term residence in their homes make it difficult for older people to relocate to new housing, even when the new situation represents a significant improvement over the old. The poor condition of many older people's homes and the high costs of renovating and maintaining them sometimes make relocation necessary, even when an older homeowner is reluctant. Better living conditions and a safer neighborhood in which several other elders reside are found to improve older people's morale and sense of well-being, especially following a move to a planned housing project from substandard housing. The growth of planned and congregate housing for older adults raises the issue of site selection for such housing. It is especially important when designing housing that public transportation be located nearby and that facilities such as medical and social services, pharmacies, and groceries be within easy access. Services need to be integrated from the beginning, because many who move in as young adults continue to live there for many years and age in place.

As people live longer and healthier lives beyond retirement, the need for housing that provides a range of care options will continue to grow. The growth in housing and long-term care alternatives benefits elders who can afford to pay for them, but they face limited choices if they cannot pay out-of-pocket or have not purchased long-term care insurance. Assisted living and adult foster care or adult family homes are rapidly becoming a cost-effective option to nursing homes for older people who need help with ADLs but not necessarily 24-hour care. Many of these community residential care facilities provide greater autonomy, more options for privacy, and less direct supervision than nursing homes. Home care is now the fastest-growing component of personal health care expenditures. It allows older people to age in place while bringing services such as skilled nursing care, rehabilitation, and personal and household care to the person's home. Adult day care or adult day health care, both as a rehabilitative and social model, provides opportunities for social integration of frail older people who are living at home alone or with a family caregiver. The older person can attend adult day health care for several hours each day and receive nursing and rehabilitation services, while the caregiver obtains respite from care tasks. Many adult day care programs also offer counseling and support groups for caregivers.

Single-room-occupancy hotels have traditionally been a low-cost housing option for older people, especially for older men living alone. However, as these buildings have been demolished or remodeled, and rents have exceeded what elders can afford, SRO residents have become displaced; some have become homeless. Many older homeless people have chronic medical, psychiatric, and cognitive disorders that often go unattended because of inadequate access to health services. As a result, these homeless elders grow physiologically old more rapidly than do their more stable peers. A growing concern is the number of older people in prisons, mostly because many have aged in place, but also because of mandatory minimum sentences with no parole, and older adults committing more serious crimes. By age 55, many of these prisoners have chronic diseases and disabilities found in much older adults in the community. The escalating costs of care for this population, as well as the incongruence between prison environments and frail older persons, have stimulated discussions about the need for geriatric facilities in prisons, physical accommodations, and even early release.

GLOSSARY

adult day care (ADC)   a community facility that frail older people living at home can attend several hours each day; when based on a health rehabilitation model, it provides individualized therapeutic plans; those based on a social model focus on structured social and psychotherapeutic activities

adult foster care (AFC)/adult family home (AFH)   a private home facility, licensed by the state, in which the owner of the home provides housekeeping, personal care, and some delegated nursing functions for the residents

aging in place   continuing to live in a private home or apartment, even when declining competence reduces P–E congruence and more assistance with ADL is needed

assisted living (AL)   a housing model aimed at elders who need assistance with personal care, e.g., bathing and taking medication, but who are not so physically or cognitively impaired as to need 24-hour attention

assistive technology   a range of electronic and computer technologies that assist people with disabilities to perform as many ADLs as possible without assistance from others

co-housing   a community of families or elders who share some activities in a common house but live independently

community residential care (CRC)   a general label for residential long-term care options other than nursing homes; includes adult foster care, adult family homes, and assisted living

continuous care retirement community (CCRC)   a multilevel facility offering a range from independent to congregate living arrangements, including nursing home units; generally requires an initial entry fee to assure a place if long-term care is needed in the future

culture change   new models of nursing home care that attempt to humanize these facilities and make them more home-like and less insitutional

Eden Alternative   a paradigm for nursing home care that encourages active participation by residents and greater staff decision-making

elder-friendly (livable) communities   cities, suburbs, and towns that offer transportation, social and health services, and safe and adaptable housing to help older residents age in place

gerontechnology   a recent field of research and practice, aimed at using technology to improve older adults' autonomy

Green House   an expansion of the Eden Alternative that focuses on smaller groups of residents served by a core group of workers who perform multiple tasks.

home health care   a variety of nursing, rehabilitation, and other therapy services, as well as assistance with personal care and household maintenance, that are provided to people who are homebound and have difficulty performing multiple ADLs

intentional communities   a group of families or elders with common values (e.g. political, religious, lifestyle) who live independently but share meals, activities, and some expenses

long-term care (LTC)   a broad range of services geared to helping frail older adults be autonomous as long as possible; offered in nursing homes and other types of facilities, or in their own home through nutritional programs, adult day care, and home health services

Medicaid waivers   exceptions to state Medicaid rules that allow use of Medicaid funds for services that are traditionally not covered by Medicaid, such as chore services and home care

naturally occurring retirement community (NORC)   a neighborhood or larger area occupied mostly by older people, but without having been planned specifically for this population

negotiated risk   agreement between a resident, family, or guardian, and facility administration that the resident in a CRC setting will assume risks if problems such as falls and accidents result from maintaining autonomy

nursing homes   facilities with three or more beds staffed 24 hours per day by health professionals who provide nursing and personal-care services to residents who cannot remain in their own homes due to chronic disease, functional disabilities, or significant cognitive impairments

Pioneer Network   a coalition of nursing home administrators and LTC advocates focused on improving quality of care and residents' quality of life by making organizational changes

resident-centered care a model of long-term care in which frail elders have the right and ability to determine their own needs and how these should be met

single-room-occupancy (SRO) hotels older buildings in urban centers that have been converted to low-cost apartments; often these are single rooms with no kitchen and bathrooms shared with other units

telehealth transmitting a patient's health status and vital signs via computer or telephone lines directly to a health provider

universal design designing a product, building or landscape to make it accessible to and usable by the broadest range of users

universal worker nursing home staff who perform multiple services, including meal preparation, personal care, and housekeeping, rather than specializing in one task

RESOURCES

Log on to MySockit (www.mysockit.com) for information about the following:

- Advantage Age Initiative
- AgeNet, LLC
- American Association of Homes and Services for the Aging (AAHSA)
- American Association of Retired Persons (AARP)
- American College of Health Care Administrators (ACHCA)
- American Seniors Housing Association
- Assisted Living Federation of America (ALFA)
- Caring Concepts
- Citizens for the Improvement of Nursing Homes (CINH)
- Gatekeeper Program
- Department of Housing and Urban Development (HUD)
- National Adult Day Services Association (NADSA)
- National Association for Home Care (NAHC)
- National Association of Directors of Nursing in Long Term Care (NADONAILTC)

- National Association of Senior Move Managers (NASMM)
- National Citizens Coalition for Nursing Home Reform (NCCNHR)
- National Institute on Adult Day Care

REFERENCES

AARP. *Across the states: Profiles of long-term care and independent living.* Washington, DC: AARP Public Policy Institute, 2006a.

AARP. *Beyond 50.03: A report to the nation on independent living and disability.* Washington DC: AARP Public Policy Institute, 2005.

AARP. *Federally insured loans.* Accessed December 7, 2006b, from http://www.aarp.org/money/revmort/revmort_federal.

AARP. *Fixing to stay: A survey on housing and home modification issues.* Washington, DC: AARP Public Policy Institute, 2000.

AARP. *The state of 50+ America 2006.* Washington, DC: AARP Public Policy Institute, 2006c.

AARP. *A summary of federal rental housing programs.* Washington, DC: AARP Public Policy Institute, 2001.

AARP. *These four walls: Americans 45-plus talk about home and community.* Washington, DC: AARP Public Policy Institute, 2003.

AARP. *Transportation: The older person's interest.* Washington, DC: AARP Public Policy Institute, 2002.

Aday, R.H. Aging prisoners. In B. Berkman and S. D'Ambruoso (Eds.), *Handbook of social work in health and aging.* New York: Oxford Press, 2006.

Administration on Aging (AOA). *A profile of older Americans: 2005.* Accessed November 3, 2006, from http://www.aoa.gov/stats/profile.

AdvantageAge Initiative. *AdvantageAge Communities.* New York, NY: Visiting Nurse Service of New York, 2007. Accessed March 18, 2007, from: http://www.vnsay.org/advantage.html.

Agree, E.M., and Freedman, V.A. A comparison of assistive technology and personal care in alleviating disability and unmet need. *The Gerontologist,* 2003, *43,* 335–344.

American Association of Homes and Services for the Aging (AAHSA). *Continuing care retirement communities.* Accessed November 15, 2006, from http://www.aahsa.org/consumer_info/homes_svcs_directory.

Angelelli, J. Promising models for transforming long term care. *The Gerontologist*, 2006, *46*, 428–430.

Angelelli, J., and Higbie, I. Unfolding the culture change map and locating ourselves together. *Journal of Social Work in Long-Term Care*. 2005, *3*, 121–135.

Associated Press, *Woman, 82, gets ticket for slow crossing.* April 11, 2006.

Austin, C., Flux, D., and Ghali, L. *A place to call home: Final report of the elder friendly communities project.* Calgary, Alberta, 2001. Accessed 2001 from http://www.elderfriendlycommunities.org/pdf/A-place-to-call-home.pdf.

Bergman-Evans, B. Beyond the basics: Effects of the Eden Alternative model on quality of life issues. *Journal of Gerontological Nursing*, 2004, *30*, 27–34.

Boyd, C. The Providence Mt. St. Vincent Experience. *Journal of Social Work in Long Term Care*, 2003, *2*, 245–268.

Bureau of Justice Statistics. *Criminal victimization in the United States 2005: Statistical tables.* Washington DC: U.S. Department of Justice, 2006a.

Bureau of Justice Statistics. *Homicide trends in the United States: Eldercide.* Accessed December 10, 2006b, from http://www.ojp.usdoj.gov/bjs/homicide/elders.htm.

Burgio, L.D., Stevens, A., Burgio, K.L., Roth, D.L., Paul, P., and Gerstle, J. Teaching and maintaining behavior management skills in the nursing home. *The Gerontologist*, 2002, *42*, 487–496.

Castle, N.G. Relocation of the elderly. *Medical Care Research and Review*, 2001, *58*, 291–333.

Chapin, R., and Dobbs-Kepper, D. Aging in place in assisted living: Philosophy versus policy. *The Gerontologist*, 2001, *41*, 43–50.

Christian, D.L. *Creating a life together.* New York: New Society, 2003.

Cohen, C.I. Aging and homelessness. *The Gerontologist*, 1999, *39*, 5–14.

Cohen, C.I., Sokolovsky, J., and Crane, M. *International Journal of Law and Psychiatry*, 2001, *24*, 167–181.

Co-housing Association of the U.S. *What is co-housing?* Accessed December 8, 2006, from http://www.cohousing.org/overview.aspx.

Commission on Affordable Housing and Health Facilities Needs. *A quiet crisis in America: A report to Congress.* Washington, DC: U.S. Government Printing Office, 2002.

Coronel, S. *Research Findings: Long term care insurance in 2002.* America's Health Insurance Plans [formerly Health Insurance Association of America], Washington, D.C. 2004.

Cowles, C.M. Nursing homes: A growth industry? Accessed December 20, 2006, from http://www.longtermcareinfo.com/crg/index.html.

Crane, M., Byrne, K., Fu, R., Lipmann, B., Mirabelli, F., Bartelink, A., et al. *Causes of homelessness in later life: Findings from a 3-nation study.* Washington, DC: Committee to End Elder Homelessness, 2004.

Curtis, M.P., Kiyak, H.A., Hedrick, S. Resident and facility characteristics of adult-family home, adult residential care, and assisted living facilities in Washington state. *Journal of Gerontological Social Work*, 2000, *34*, 25–41.

Day, K., Carreon, D., and Stump, C. The therapeutic design of environments for people with dementia: A review of the empirical research. *The Gerontologist*, 2000, *40*, 397–406.

Deatrick, D. Senior-Med: Creating a network to help manage medications. *Generations*, 1997, *21*, 59–60.

deLaGrange, K. Elder cohousing: How viable is cohousing for an aging population? Accessed December 1, 2006, from http://www.cohousing.org/livingincoho_seniors.aspx.

DeMallie, D.A., North, C.S., and Smith, E.M. Psychiatric disorders among the homeless: A comparison of older and younger groups. *The Gerontologist*, 1997, *37*, 61–66.

ElderCohousing.org. Getting started workshops for elder cohousing, 2006.

Fagan, R.M. Culture change in long term care: Creating true independence for elders. *Maximizing Human Potential*, 2004, *11*, 1–6.

Federal Interagency Forum on Aging-Related Statistics. *Older Americans: 2006.* Washington DC: Government Printing Office, 2006.

Feldman, P.H., and Oberlink, M.R. The AdvantAge Initiative: Developing community indicators to promote the health and well-being of older people. *Family and Community Health*, 2003, *26*, 268–274.

Foley, D. Hellish conditions at single-room occupancy hotels. *Body Posit,* 1998, *11,* 18–23.

Folsom, D.P., McCahill, M., Bartels, S.J., Lindamer, L.A., Ganiats, T.G., and Jeste, D.V. Medical comorbidity and receipt of medical care by older homeless people with schizophrenia or depression. *Psychiatric Services,* 2002, *53,* 1456–1460.

Fox, S. *Older Americans and the Internet.* Accessed November 2006, from http://www.pewinternet. org/pdfs/PIP_Seniors_Online_2004.pdf.

Frank, J.B. *The paradox of aging in place in assisted living.* Westport, CT: Bergin and Garvey, 2002.

Friedman, S.M., Steinwachs, D.M., Temkin-Greener, H., and Mukamel, D.B. Informal caregivers and the risk of nursing home admission among individuals enrolled in PACE. *The Gerontologist,* 2006, *46,* 456–463.

Gallagher, E.M. Elders in prison: Health and well-being of older inmates. *International Journal of Law and Psychiatry,* 2001, *24,* 325–333.

Gaugler, J.E., Jarrott, S.E., Zarit, S.H., Stephens, M.A., Townsend, A., and Greene, R. Adult day service use and reductions in caregiving hours: Effects of stress and psychological well-being for dementia caregivers. *International Journal of Geriatric Psychiatry,* 2003, *18,* 55–62.

Golant, S.M. Conceptualizing time and behavior in environmental gerontology. *The Gerontologist,* 2003, *43,* 638–648.

Golant, S.M. Do impaired older persons with health care needs occupy U.S. assisted living facilities? *Journals of Gerontology,* 2004, *59B,* S68–S79.

Gonyea, J.G. Housing, health, and quality of life. In B. Berkman and S. D'Ambruoso (Eds.), *Handbook of social work in health and aging.* New York: Oxford Press, 2006.

Grant, L. *Culture change in for-profit nursing homes.* The Commonwealth Fund. Accessed November 12, 2006, from http://www.cmwf. org/spotlights/spotlights_show.htm?doc.

Greene, K. When it comes to finding a new place to live, today's retirees are looking for something completely different. *Wall Street Journal,* October 2, 2006.

Gwyther, L.P., and Kane, R.A. Dementia special care units in residential care. In B. Berkman and S. D'Ambruoso (Eds.), *Handbook of social work in health and aging.* New York: Oxford Press, 2006.

Hanson, D., and Emlet, C.A. Assessing a community's elder friendliness. *Family and Community Health,* 2006, *29,* 266–278.

Harrison, P.M., and Beck, A.J. Prisoners in 2005. *Bureau of Justice Statistics Bulletin,* 2006, NCJ 215092, 7–8.

Hawes, C. Introduction. In S. Zimmerman, P.D. Sloan, and J.K. Eckert (Eds.), *Assisted living: Needs, practices and policies in residential care for the elderly.* Baltimore: Johns Hopkins University Press, 2001.

Hawes, C., Rose, M., and Phillips, C.D. *A national study of assisted living for the frail elderly executive summary: Results of a national survey of faciliies.* Washington, DC: Public Policy Institute, AARP, 1999.

Hedrick, S.C., Sales, A.E.B., Sullivan, J.H., Gray, S.L., Tornatore, J., Curtis, M., and Zhou, X.A. Resident outcomes of Medicaid-funded community residential care. *The Gerontologist,* 2003, *43,* 473–482.

Hernandez, M. Assisted living in all its guises. *Generations,* Winter 2005–2006, *29,* 16–23.

Housing and Urban Development (HUD). *Housing our elders.* Washington, DC: Office of Policy Development and Research. 1999.

Housing and Urban Development (HUD). *News Release: Bush administration awards $7.9 million to convert multifamily projects into assisted living facilities.* Accessed December 15, 2006a, from http://www.hud.gov/news/release.cfm?CONTEN T=pr06-144.cfm.

Housing and Urban Development (HUD). *Section 202 supportive housing for the elderly.* Accessed December 5, 2006b, from http://www.hud.gov/ offices/hsg/mfh/progdesc/eld202.cfm.

Hughes, S.L., and Pittard, M.A. Home health. In C.J. Evashwick (Ed.), *The continuum of long-term care* (2nd ed.). Albany, NY: Delmar, 2001.

Iwarsson, S. A long-term perspective on person-environment fit and ADL dependence among older Swedish adults. *The Gerontologist,* 2005, *45,* 327–336.

Jette, A.M., Tennstedt, S., and Crawford, S. How does formal and informal community care affect nursing home use? *Journals of Gerontology,* 1995, *50B,* S4–S12.

Kane, R.A. Long-term care and a good quality of life: Bringing them closer together. *The Gerontologist,* 2001, *41,* 293–304.

Kane, R.A., and Wilson, K.B. *Assisted living at the crossroads: Principles for its future.* Portland, OR: The Jessie F. Richardson Foundation, 2001.

Kochera, A., and Bright, K. Livable communities for older people. *Generations,* Winter 2005–2006, *29,* 32–36.

Krout, J.A., Moen, P., Holmes, H.H., Oggins, J., and Bowen, N. Reasons for relocation to a continuing care retirement community. *Journal of Applied Gerontology,* 2002, *21,* 236–256.

Lachs, M., Bachman, R., Williams, C.S., Kossack, A., Bove, C., and O'Leary, J.R. Violent crime victimization increases risk of nursing home placement in older adults. *The Gerontologist,* 2006, *46,* 583–589.

Larson, C. Finding a good home: Taking care of your parents. *U.S. News and World Report,* November 27, 2006.

Lawton, M.P. Competence, environmental press, and the adaptation of older people. In P.G. Windley and G. Ernst (Eds.), *Theory development in environment and aging.* Washington, DC: Gerontological Society, 1975.

Lehmann, C.A. *Economic benefits of telehealth in managing diabetes patients in ambulatory settings.* Paper presented at SPRY Foundation Conference on Technology and Aging, Bethesda, MD, October 2003.

Lehmann, C.A. The future of home testing— Implications for traditional laboratories. *Clinica Chimica Acta,* 2002, *323,* 31–36.

Lewin, K *Dynamic theory of personality.* New York: McGraw-Hill, 1935.

Lewin, K. *Field theory in social science.* New York: Harper and Row, 1951.

Lewin, K., Lippitt, R., and White, R. Patterns of aggressive behavior in experimentally created social climates. *Journal of Social Psychology,* 1939, *10,* 271–299.

Litwak, E., and Longino, C.F. Migration patterns among the elderly: A developmental perspective. In R. B. Enright (Ed.), *Perspectives in social gerontology.* Boston: Allyn and Bacon, 1994.

Loeb, S.J., and AbuDagga, A. Health-related research on older inmates. *Research in Nursing and Health,* 2006, *29,* 556–565.

Logue, R.M. Self-medication and the elderly: How technology can help. *American Journal of Nursing,* 2002, *102,* 51–57.

Longino, C.F. Socio-physical environments at the macro level: The impact of population migration. In H.W. Wahl, R.J. Scheidt and P.G. Windley (Eds.), *Annual Review of Gerontology and Geriatrics,* 2004, *23,* 110–129.

Longino, C.F., and Bradley, D.E. A first look at retirement migration trends in 2000. *The Gerontologist,* 2003, *43,* 904–907.

Longino, C.F., and Bradley, D.E. Internal and international migration. In R.H. Binstock and L.K. George (Eds.), *Handbook of aging and the social sciences* (6th ed). San Diego: Academic Press, 2006.

Lustbader, W., and Williams, C.C. Culture change in long-term care. In B. Berkman and S. D'Ambruoso (Eds.), *Handbook of social work in health and aging.* New York: Oxford Press, 2006.

Lutgendorf, S.K., Reimer, T.T., Harvey, J.H., Marks, G., Hong, S., Hillis, S.L., and Lubaroff, D.M. Effects of housing relocation on immunocompetence and psychosocial functioning in older adults. *Journals of Gerontology: Medical Sciences,* 2001, *56A,* M97–M105.

Mace, R.L. Universal Design in housing. *Assistive Technology,* 1998, *10,* 21–28.

Manton, K.G., Stallard, E., and Corder, L.S., The dynamics of dimensions of age-related disability 1982–1994 in the U.S. elderly population. *Journals of Gerontology,* 1998, *53A,* B59–B70.

Marsden, J.P. *Humanistic design of assisted living.* Baltimore: Johns Hopkins University Press, 2005.

McKinney, S.B. *Homeless Assistance Act,* P.L. 100-77 (1987)

MetLife. *Market survey of nursing home and home care costs.* Westport, CT: Metropolitan Life Insurance, Mature Market Institue, 2003.

Mitka, M. Aging prisoners stressing health care system. *Journal of the American Medical Association,* 2004, *292,* 423–424.

Moen, P., and Erickson, M.A. Decision-making and satisfaction with a continuing care retirement community. *Journal of Housing for the Elderly,* 2001, *14,* 53–69.

Mollica, R.L. State policy and regulations. In S. Zimmerman, P.D. Sloan, and J.K. Eckert (Eds.), *Assisted living: Needs, practices and policies in residential care for the elderly.* Baltimore: Johns Hopkins University Press, 2001.

Morgan, R. Computer-based technology and caregiving for older adults. *Public Policy and Aging Report,* 2004, *14,* 1–5.

Murray, H.A. *Explorations in personality.* New York: Oxford University Press, 1938.

National Center for Health Statistics (NCHS). Data from the 1997 National Nursing Home Survey. *Vital and Health Statistics,* No. 311, 2000.

National Center for Health Statistics (NCHS). *Health, United States.* Accessed December 20, 2006, from http://www.cdc.gov/nchs/hus.htm.

National Center for Health Statistics (NCHS). *Data warehouse on trends in health and aging: Nursing home residents by age, sex, and race: 1977–1999.* Hyattsville, MD: NCHS, 2005.

National Coalition for the Homeless (NCH). Federal housing assistance programs. Accessed December 5, 2006, from http://www.nationalhomeless.org.

National Council on the Aging (NCOA). Facts about older Americans. Accessed December, 2002, from http://www.ncoa.org/content.cfm?sectionID.

National Low Income Housing Coalition (NLIHC). Out of reach. Accessed December 6, 2006, from http://www.nlihc.org.

Netting, F.E., and Wilson, C.C. Continuing care retirement communities. In B. Berkman and S. D'Ambruoso (Eds.), *Handbook of social work in health and aging.* New York: Oxford Press, 2006.

New York Times. Immigrants now embrace homes for elderly. October 20, 2003, pp. A1, A10.

Noelker, L.S., and Ejaz, F.K. Training direct-care workers for person-centered care. *Public Policy and Aging Report,* 2005, *15,* 17–19.

Oswald, F., and Wahl, H.W. Dimensions of the meaning of home in later life. In G.D. Rowles and H. Chaudhury (Eds.), *Home and identity in late life.* New York: Springer, 2005.

Peng, T.R., Navaie-Waliser, M., and Feldman, P.H. Social support, home health service use, and outcomes among four racial-ethnic groups. *The Gerontologist,* 2003, *43,* 503–513.

Perez-Pena, R. Overwhelmed and understaffed, nursing home workers vent anger. *New York Times,* June 8, 2003, p. 1.

Pew, R.W., and Van Hemel, S.B. (Eds.), *Technology for adaptive aging.* Washington DC: National Academies Press, 2005.

Phillips, C.D., Munoz, Y., Sherman, M., Rose, M., Spector, W., and Hawes, C. Effects of facility characteristics on departures from assisted living. *The Gerontologist,* 2003, *43,* 690–696.

Pinto, M.R., DeMedici, S., VanSant, C., Bianchi, A., Zlotnicki, A., and Napoli, C. Ergonomics, gerontechnology, and design for the home environment. *Applied Ergonomics,* 2001, *31,* 317–322.

Preiser, W., and Ostroff, E. (Eds.), *Universal design handbook.* New York: McGraw Hill, 2001.

Pruchno, R.A., and Rose, M.S. Effect of long-term care environments on health outcomes. *The Gerontologist,* 2000, *40,* 429–436.

Pynoos, J., and Matsuoka, C.A.E. Housing. In C.J. Evashwick (Ed.), *The continuum of long-term care* (2nd ed.). Albany, NY: Delmar, 2001.

Quinn, M.E., Johnson, M.A., Andress, E.L., McGinnis, P., and Ramesh, M. Health characteristics of elderly personal care home residents. *Journal of Advance Nursing,* 1999, *30,* 410–417.

Rabig, J., Thomas, W., Kane, R.A., Cutler, L.J., and McAlilly, S. Radical redesign of nursing homes: Applying the Green House concept in Tupelo, Mississippi. *The Gerontologist,* 2006, *46,* 533–539.

Regan, J.J., Alderson, A., and Regan, W.M. Psychiatric disorders in aging prisoners. *Clinical Gerontologist,* 2002, *26,* 8–13.

Regnier, V. *Design for assisted living.* Hoboken, NJ: John Wiley & Sons, 2002.

Rialle, V., Duchene, F., Noury, N., Bajolle, L., and Demongeot, J. Health "smart" homes: Information technology for patients at home. *Telemedicine Journal and e-Health,* 2002, *8,* 395–409.

Riley, C.A. *High access home.* New York: Rizzoli International Publications, 1999.

Rogers, W.A., and Fisk, A.D. Aware home technology: Potential benefits for older adults. *Public Policy and Aging Report,* 2005, *15,* 28–30.

Schmidt, K., and Beatty, S. Quality improvement: The pursuit of excellence. *Quality Management in Health Care,* 2005, *14,* 196–198.

Seattle Times. Retirees gaining popularity in towns yearning for growth. May 27, 2003, p. A5.

Seperson, S.B. Demographics about aging. In S.B. Seperson and C. Hegeman (Eds.), *Elder care and service learning: A handbook.* Westport, CT: Auburn House, 2002.

Spillman, B.C., and Lubitz, J. New estimates of lifetime nursing home use. *Medical Care,* 2002, *40,* 965–975.

Stergiopoulos, V., and Herrmann, N. Old and homeless: A review and survey of older adults who use shelters in an urban setting. *Canadian Journal of Psychiatry,* 2003, *48,* 374–380.

Stoller, E.P., and Longino, C.F. "Going home" or "leaving home"? The impact of person and place ties on anticipated counterstream migration. *The Gerontologist,* 2001, *41,* 96–102.

Teresi, J.A., Holmes, D., and Ory, M.G. The therapeutic design of environments for people with dementia. *The Gerontologist,* 2000, *40, 64–74.*

Thomas, W.H. *The Eden alternative handbook.* Sherburne, NY: Eden Alternative Foundation, 1999.

Thomas, W.H., and Stermer, M. Eden Alternative principles hold promise for the future of long-term care. *Balance,* 1999, *3,* 14–17.

Turley, J. Release elderly inmates. Accessed December 13, 2006, from http://www.LATimes.com/news/opinion/commentary.

U.S. Census Bureau. American housing survey for the U.S.: 2005. *Current Housing Reports.* Series H150-05. Washington DC: U.S. Government Printing Office, 2006.

U.S. Census Bureau. Computer and internet use in the U.S.: 2003. *Current Population Reports.* Series P23-208. Washington DC: U.S. Government Printing Office, 2005.

U.S. Census Bureau. Household and family characteristics. *Current Population Reports.* Series P20-515. Washington, DC: U.S. Government Printing Office, 1998.

U.S. Census Bureau. *Moving rates among Americans declines.* Accessed March 20, 2000, from http://www.census.gov.

U.S. Conference of Mayors. *Hunger and homelessness survey: A status report on hunger and homelessness in America's cities.* Accessed December 2005, from http://www.usmayors.org/uscm/hungersurvey/2005/HH2005final.pdf.

Vierck, B. Cohousing comes of age. *Aging Today,* Sept–Oct 2005, *27,* 1–5.

Vourlekis, B., and Simons, K. Nursing homes. In B. Berkman and S. D'Ambruoso (Eds.), *Handbook of social work in health and aging.* New York: Oxford Press, 2006.

Whitney, G., and Keith, S. Active ageing through universal design. *Gerontechnology,* 2006, *5,* 125–128.

Wiener, J.M. An assessment of strategies for improving quality of care in nursing homes. *The Gerontologist,* 2003, *43* (Special Issue), 19–27.

Williams, B.A., Lindquist, K., Sudore, R.L., Strupp, H.M., Wilmott, D.J., and Walter, L.C. Being old and doing time: Functional impairment and adverse experiences of geriatric female prisoners. *Journal of the American Geriatrics Society,* 2006, *54,* 702–707.

Wilmoth, J.M. Unbalanced social exchanges and living arrangement transitions among older adults. *The Gerontologist,* 2000, *40, 64–74.*

Wilson, K.B. Developing a viable model of assisted living. In P. Katz, R.L. Kane and M. Mazey (Eds.), *Advances in long-term care.* New York: Springer, 1993.

Wilson, K.B. Redefining quality in assisted living. *Provider,* 1995, 73–74.

Yeatts, D.E., Cready, C., Ray, B., DeWitt, A., and Queen, C. Self-managed work teams in nursing homes: Implementing and empowering nurse aide teams. *The Gerontologist,* 2004, *44,* 256–261.

Yeoman, B. Rethinking the commune. *AARP Magazine,* Accessed December 8, 2006, from http://www.aarpmagazine.org/lifestyle/rethinking_the_commune.html.

Zimmerman, S., Munn, S. and Koenig, T. *Assisted living settings.* In B. Berkman and S. D'Ambruoso (Eds.), *Handbook of social work in health and aging.* New York: Oxford Press, 2006.

12

Productive Aging: Paid and Nonpaid Roles and Activities

What Do We Mean by Productive Aging? Definitions and Critique

Productivity is typically thought of as paid work. In fact, disengagement and role theories focus on the losses associated with withdrawal from the employment role. Many older adults, however, are productive without being employed or engaged in obligatory activities. As described in Chapters 1 and 6, the model of successful, robust, or active aging implies that productivity is broader than paid work; it includes any paid or unpaid activity that produces goods and services for the benefit of society, such as household tasks, child care, volunteerism, and helping family and friends. We use the concept of productivity throughout this chapter because of the myriad ways in which older adults contribute to their families, neighborhoods, communities, and society, as well as the reciprocal benefits that elders may experience through such contributions.

Older adults are viewed individually and collectively as a resource to meet their own and society's needs. Engagement in such productive activity, particularly the concept of civic engagement, is assumed to have a positive influence on older adults' mental and physical well-being (American Society on Aging, 2005; Gerontological Society of America, 2005; Hinterlong, Morrow-Howell, and Sherraden, 2001; Sherraden, et al., 2001).

The concept of productivity is subject to criticisms similar to those leveled at successful aging (see Chapter 6 for a critique of successful aging). From the perspectives of feminist, political economy and social constructionist theories, an emphasis on productivity may lead to further marginalization and blaming of low-income women and elders of color who cannot attain middle-class standards of productive activity. If such groups are not productive enough, are they then defined as failures? Accordingly, are those who are disabled or who prefer to be contemplative a problem for society (Estes and Mahakian, 2001; Martinson and Minkler, 2006; Moody, 2005)? Similarly, if an individual is sitting and thinking, it is difficult to quantify the value of an idea that can lead to tremendous productivity gains in society, but may not appear to be "productive behavior." Likewise, cognitive and emotional exchanges, such as Erikson's concept of generativity or giving back to younger generations, as described in Chapter 6, cannot be quantified (Birren, 2001). Critical gerontologists maintain that the concept of productive activity has class, race, and gender biases because of implicit middle-class norms of what is considered a "productive" way to spend time. They caution against "prescribing" active engagement for elders, and emphasize fostering opportunity and choice. Accordingly, class, race, ethnicity, and gender inequities across the life course all affect an older adult's ability to engage in meaningful and productive experiences. The meaning of productive aging is shaped by the increasing inequality in society and the aging population, which creates different life chances and opportunities for elders. Overall, critics of the concept

Gardening provides older adults with physical exercise and creative expression.

of productive aging urge caution regarding who defines productive aging, which segments of the older population this concept applies to, and who benefits (Calasanti and Slevin, 2001; Estes and Mahakian, 2001; Holstein, 2007; Moody, 2001).

Given this context, we use the concept of productivity in this text in the broadest sense of engagement with and contributions to others—

DEFINING PRODUCTIVE AGING

A retired mathematics teacher, Yakov, a 67-year-old immigrant from Eastern Europe, volunteers in the Senior Companion program. He spends a day each week with Harry, a postman who is legally blind, assisting with daily tasks that enable Harry to remain in his own home. Theirs is a reciprocal relationship: Each is convinced that he is the helper and the other is the recipient of the help. Harry helps Yakov with his English, correcting grammatical errors, while Yakov receives a stipend to help with household tasks. They often go out to lunch at the local Burger King, their favorite restaurant. The waiter who takes their order looks to be about their age, but he is wearing an orange and blue polyester outfit and a Burger King beanie, and working alongside giggling 15-year-olds acquiring their first job experience. Which of these three older adults is "productive"?

SOURCE: Adapted from Freedman, 2001, p. 246.

family, neighbors, friends, and community. But the contributions need not be "goods and services" in a traditional sense. The active aging model, described in Chapter 1, suggests that productivity can benefit society, the community, the family, or even just oneself. It can include social, psychological, and spiritual dimensions, such as self-improvement through learning, personal fulfillment, and searching for life's meaning. Productivity is not the same as "staying busy," since a contemplative elder may nevertheless be contributing to his or her own or others' well-being. This broad definition recognizes that even a homebound, chronically disabled elder may be productive by teaching family and friends about how to age with dignity, placing phone calls to check up on other neighbors, reading to a young child, listening to a grieving friend, or providing encouragement and life lessons to a confused adolescent. The older woman who prefers to spend hours working alone in her garden may be contributing to the "common good" by creating beauty for neighbors to enjoy, even though she may not view herself as contributing directly to the community. Regardless of our life circumstances, there is a universal human need to be of use, and reaching out and giving to others in a wide variety of ways can be a powerful antidote to loneliness, isolation, and depression.

An assumption throughout this text is that older adults represent our society's greatest underutilized asset. They bring the resilience and hardiness of survivors, and the wisdom of life experiences and lessons learned. As such, elders are a civic treasure that can provide leadership in community and religious organizations, volunteer formally or informally, and influence decision-making and legislative processes. What is critical is for older adults to be able to exercise choice over how they spend their time. Public resources are then needed to support such choices. Although the concept of productive aging may imply that older adults *should* be outwardly productive and exert pressures on them to

engage in activities that they would prefer not to undertake, the greater danger appears to be that our society has provided limited opportunities for older adults to be engaged and make contributions. Consistent with the person–environment (P–E) framework of this book, older adults need opportunities to choose and adjust their behavior and aspirations to maintain a sense of competence in a changing environment. Accordingly, modifications are needed in public policy and societal institutions to allow older adults to contribute to others and to play meaningful roles in old age (Freedman, 2001, 2002).

Race, ethnicity, gender, social class, sexual orientation, cohort experiences, living arrangements, and neighborhoods are structural or societal factors that influence the choices available to older adults. Personal capacities, such as the normal physical and psychological changes of aging, health status, personality, cognitive capacity, and values also influence how individuals choose to spend their time in old age. Self-esteem and self-concept are powerful factors. Some older adults may believe that they are "too old" or lack the capacity to perform certain activities, even though they have the objective resources of finances and a supportive family or lifestyle. Others with limited objective resources (e.g., in poor health or poverty) may nevertheless possess the inner resources to seek out new opportunities in old age, because of their zest for living and learning new things. In other words, people's use of time and arenas of involvement all vary with the opportunities provided by the larger environment, as well as with their personal capacities at each phase in the life course. Nevertheless, the meanings, options, and outcomes for productive aging and engagement vary among different populations; social class appears to be the most salient structural factor in shaping whatever may be possible in aging, since class is found to be related to every measure of health, illness, and disability (Estes and Mahakian, 2001). As noted throughout this text, poor health, reduced income, transportation difficulties, or social isolation across the life course often disrupt and reduce choices in old age and lead to further inequities. Nevertheless, as noted by Cohen (2005) and discussed in Chapter 6, many individuals pursue new activities, including art, music, running, hiking, meditating, or teaching for the first time in old age. Even with decreased competence in health and physical functioning, older people can enjoy active aging by modifying their activities to establish congruence between their needs and abilities and environmental demands. Consistent with the concept of selective optimization discussed in Chapter 9, older adults generally become more selective about how they invest their time and energy, and with whom, than in the past. Having the option to decide how one spends time is a salient factor differentiating retirement from earlier life phases of obligatory school, employment, or dependent care.

This chapter reviews the choices and opportunities as well as the constraints that older adults face related to productivity: retirement, employment, pursuit of leisure, religious participation and spirituality, membership in community associations and volunteerism, education, and political involvement. It concludes by recognizing how societal institutions need to change to provide options for older adults to choose how they wish to remain engaged and contributing to others, whether through lifelong learning, volunteerism, contemplative activities, or religious involvement. Community and societal responsibility, including policy changes and resource commitments, are essential elements of any program to promote productive aging, and to reduce inequities in opportunities for active engagement. We turn now to retirement, which removes older adults from paid forms of productivity and shapes opportunities for their engagement in nonpaid activities.

Retirement

With increased longevity and changing work patterns, **retirement** may define a third or more of the life course and be as much an expected phase as raising children, completing school, or working outside the home. Men in particular, but increasingly women among younger cohorts, develop age-related expectations about the rhythm of their careers—when to start working, when to be at the peak of their careers, and when to retire. They typically assess whether they are "on time" according to these socially defined schedules.

The value placed on work and paid productivity in our society shapes how individuals approach employment and retirement. Those over age 65 were socialized to a traditional view of hard work, job loyalty, and occupational stability. Current demographic trends and social policies mean that values and expectations about work and retirement are changing, as many of the young-old exit and re-enter the workforce through partial employment or new careers. As individuals live longer, a smaller proportion of their lifetime is devoted to paid employment, even though the number of years worked is longer. For example, a man born in 1900 could expect to live about 47 years. He would work for 32 years (70 percent of his lifetime) and be retired for about one year (2 percent of his lifetime). In contrast, a man born today can anticipate living about 75 years, working for about 55 percent of his life, and being retired for 18 percent. Women, too, are living longer beyond retirement and are devoting a smaller portion of their lives to raising children. A woman born in 1900 could expect that 6 years of her 48-year life span (or 12 percent) would be spent in the labor force. The comparable figure for a woman today is nearly 21 percent of her 78-year life span (Urban Institute, 2007).

POINTS TO PONDER

How does your view of work and retirement differ from that of your parents and/or grandparents? What does retirement mean to you? At what age do you see yourself retired, and what type of planning should you do to achieve that goal? How many careers do you anticipate having?

Conceptions of work and leisure took on new meanings in the industrialized world, with the institutionalization of retirement a relatively recent phenomenon in Western society (Hardy, 2002; Moen, 2003). Retirement developed as a twentieth century social institution, along with industrialization, surplus labor, and a rising standard of living. **Social Security** legislation, passed in 1935, established the right to financial protection in old age and thus served to institutionalize retirement. Based on income deferred during years of employment, Social Security was viewed as a reward for past economic contributions to society and a way to support people unable to work because of illness or disability. At the same time, Social Security served to create jobs for younger people by removing adults age 65 and over from the labor force. From the perspective of critical gerontology, discussed in Chapter 8, retirement serves a variety of institutional functions in our society. It can stimulate and reward worker loyalty; it is a way to remove older, presumably more expensive, workers and replace them with younger employees, who are assumed to be more productive.

Nevertheless, some societal and individual consequences from retirement are negative. Earlier retirement, combined with longer life expectancies, has created prolonged dependence on Social Security and other retirement benefits, as well as a loss of older workers' skills. This shift from nearly all adults working to near-universal retirement raises concerns about Social Security's viability for future generations. Since retirement is associated in the public mind with the chronological age of 65 (the age of eligibility for full Social Security and Medicare benefits), it also carries the connotation of being old, and no longer physically or mentally capable of full-time employment. In fact, society has come to associate aging with decreased employment capacity, with little regard for the older population's heterogeneity. This limits implementation of more flexible work arrangements and retraining opportunities for older adults who want or need to continue in the paid workforce.

The Timing of Retirement

Retirement policies, labor market conditions, and individual characteristics all converge on the decision to retire and affect the timing of retirement. Prior to 1986 when mandatory retirement for most jobs was eliminated, federal laws influenced the retirement age. Even so, this factor was not as salient as financial incentives, since less than 10 percent of employees were forced to retire because of legal requirements (Quinn and Burkhauser, 1993). The limited effect of mandatory retirement is also shown by the fact that federal workers retire at the average age of 61, even though they have never had a mandatory retirement age. The arbitrary nature of a specific age for retirement is illustrated by the pattern that, since World War II and until the twenty-first century, most people retired between the ages of 60 and 64, and very few continued to work past age 70. In fact, during this time period, age 65 has not been the "normal" retirement age, largely because chronological age alone does not explain the diversity of health status, disability, and economic factors. Instead, in 2000, 14 years after mandatory retirement laws disappeared, 61.5 years was the average age for retirement compared to 74 years in 1910, largely due to continued incentives to move older workers out of the labor force. Each

POINTS TO PONDER

You may have some questions about retirement, such as what do retired adults do all day? How can one be sure to have enough money to retire, especially if a person lives a long time? How can I ensure a successful retirement for myself? Will Social Security still be around when I want to retire? Will I even want to retire? It's never too early to be thinking about these issues.

year, 75 percent of all new Social Security beneficiaries retired before their 65th birthday, and most began collecting reduced benefits at age 62.5. The average retirement age in heavy industries, such as steel and auto manufacturing, has been even lower because of private pension inducements. Those who retired from the military in their early 40s after the minimum required 20 years often moved on to other careers that enabled them to draw two pensions after age 65. This five-decade trend toward early retirement was not markedly slowed by the 1983 amendments to the Social Security Act, which delayed the age of eligibility for full benefits and increased the financial penalty for retiring at age 62 (Rix, 2006).

A noticeable shift in this trend is now occurring, however. The average age of retirement is rising and participation in the labor force is increasing, suggesting an emphasis on retaining older workers and a desire among some to remain on the job or to change careers (Korczyk, 2004; Quinn, 2003; Hardy, 2006; Rix, 2006). A number of factors underlie this shift:

- the strong economy of the late 1990's;
- the decline in defined benefits and early retirement benefits of private pension plans;
- changes to Social Security that eliminated disincentives to remain in the labor force;
- the scheduled increase in age for receipt of full Social Security benefits (age 67 by 2022);
- technological advances;
- improvements in health and longevity; and
- projected slow growth in the labor force, resulting in worker and skill shortages.

For example, the health care sector, faced with an inadequate supply of skilled workers, has sought ways to retain older workers or to encourage them to return from retirement (Harvard/MetLife, 2004; Rix, 2006; U.S. Congressional Budget Office, 2004a). In addition, changing the terms of pension eligibility, increasing the taxation of

Social Security benefits, and reducing employer-sponsored health insurance have probably increased the proportion of older workers who need to work primarily for financial reasons, especially among ethnic minorities and women. As a result, labor force growth over the next decade will be primarily in the age 55 and older population among two broad categories: women and workers of color who have to keep working for financial reasons, as well as professionals and those in upper management whose skills are valued in the labor market (O'Rand, 2005). In some surveys, 70 percent or more of the respondents age 55 and older indicate that they plan to work during retirement, and a portion say they will work beyond age 70 or will never retire (AARP, 2004, 2006).

Over time, this shift in retirement age will have societal benefits, because older adults will be contributing longer as taxpayers. In fact, if every worker contributed to the Social Security system for an additional five years, more than 50 percent of the projected Social Security shortfall would be offset (Urban Institute, 2006). According to the Congressional Budget Office, continuing to earn and postponing receipt of Social Security benefits until age 70 could nearly double payments to what they would be if collected at age 62 (Hardy, 2006; U.S. Congressional Budget Office, 2004b). But later retirees also will receive larger monthly retirement benefits that could counter these gains to the Social Security Trust Fund. Longer work lives also mean more years to save and keep investments growing and fewer years to spend such savings. This trend toward later retirement is likely to continue since baby boomers report that they expect to retire, on average, at age 65; and 80 percent state that they plan to work in retirement, cycling between periods of work and leisure (Merrill Lynch, 2005). Having redefined earlier stages of life, boomers may reject a pattern of fixed, early, or permanent retirement and reinvent the concept of retirement in doing so. Nevertheless, a higher retirement age to qualify for benefits is not favored by most workers age 50 and over;

workers may expect and even want to work in retirement, but they want to choose for themselves (Rix, 2006).

FACTORS THAT AFFECT THE TIMING OF RETIREMENT
This section discusses five P–E characteristics that affect retirement decisions:

1. an adequate retirement income and/or economic incentives to retire
2. health status, functional limitations, and access to health insurance other than Medicare
3. the nature of the job, employee morale, and organizational commitment
4. gender and ethnic minority status
5. family and gender roles (whether a partner is working, degree of marital satisfaction)

An *adequate income,* through Social Security, a private pension with a defined benefit schedule, or interest income, is a major factor affecting retirement timing. Similarly, financial adequacy, followed by access to health care, is the single most important factor in decisions to keep working rather than retire (AARP, 2003b; Rix, 2006). Despite our society's work-oriented values and the importance of income, employment and retirement/pension policies since the 1900s encouraged early retirement. Until 10 to 15 years ago, 9 out of 10 U.S. pension plans, particularly for white-collar workers, provided financial incentives for early retirement along with employer-sponsored health insurance for former employees, creating the "pension elites" of the 1980s (O'Rand, 2005). Even employees who were not planning to retire were offered benefits too attractive to turn down. In a national AARP survey of more than 1000 elders in 2000, over 70 percent reported that their savings and Social Security benefits were sufficient for them to retire (Cutler, Whitelaw, and Beattie, 2002). Economic factors thus directly affect decisions about the feasibility of retirement and indirectly contribute to worker health and job

satisfaction. When given a choice, and with financial security and adequate health insurance, most people have elected to retire as soon as they could. Workers accumulated a significant proportion of the financial resources to finance their retirement in the decade preceding retirement. As noted above, changes in Social Security and a shift from defined benefits pension plans toward defined contributions plans (such as 401Ks) have now increased incentives to work beyond the minimum age of eligibility for benefits (Harvard/MetLife, 2004).

Functional limitations and access to health insurance are also important factors in the retirement decision. Two categories of early retirees are identified:

1. those with good health and adequate financial resources, especially private pension incentives
2. those with health problems that make their work burdensome and often result in underemployment or job dislocation

Poor health, when combined with an adequate retirement income and health insurance, usually results in early retirement. In contrast, poor health, an inadequate income, and lack of health insurance generally delay retirement out of necessity, as is often the case with low-income, ethnic minority workers. Disability and functional limitations are greater motivations for retirement from physically demanding and stressful jobs for workers of color, for men with employed wives, and for men with limited, nonwork financial resources (Cutler et al., 2002). What remains unclear, however, is whether those in poorer health and with disabilities are more likely to lose their jobs because of underemployment, job displacement, or plant closures, or conversely, whether job loss itself leads to poorer health, or both (Kasl and Jones, 2000). But once a person is not working, poor health often acts as a barrier to reentering the labor force (O'Rand, 2005).

A third factor affecting timing is the *nature of one's job,* including job satisfaction, employee morale, and organizational commitment. Some workers retire to escape boring, repetitive jobs such as assembly line and service positions. Workers who have a positive attitude toward retirement and leisure but a negative view of their jobs, often because of undesirable and stressful working conditions, are likely to retire early. Employees with a high school education or less tend to retire earlier than well-educated employees, as illustrated by Mr. and Mrs. Howard in the Part Four introductory vignette. In contrast, older women who are well educated and in professional jobs are the most likely to continue working (Moen, 2001).

While *gender and ethnic minority status* can exacerbate economic inequities in old age, their effects on the timing of retirement are not clear-cut. Although both men and women overall choose early retirement, women of retirement age are less likely to be fully retired than their male counterparts. Their retirement decisions may also be determined by variables such as marital status and years devoted to childrearing; women at any age are more likely to exit the labor market to assume family care obligations (Cutler et al., 2002; Moen, 2001). Nevertheless, current income and receipt of a pension other than Social Security are primary factors in women's retirement decisions, as is the case for men. Women who entered the labor force in middle age or later, after performing family caregiving roles or because of divorce or widowhood, often need to continue in low-wage jobs without pensions in order to get by financially (McLaughlin and Jensen, 2000; O'Rand, 2005). African American women are more likely to have been employed steadily most of their adult lives, but to retire later than their white counterparts, largely for economic reasons (Flippen, 2005). To a large extent, the retirement system exacerbates inequalities of the labor market earlier in life. Employment histories that fit the expectation of lifelong work with few disruptions tend to be associated with a smoother transition to retirement. In contrast, the timing of retirement for persons of color, particularly African Americans and Latinos, differs from the traditional pattern for white males. White males with a desire for leisure, low-income African Americans, and Latinos experiencing involuntary market exits are most likely to retire. Ethnic minorities' lifetime employment patterns often result in an unclear line between work and nonwork, however; lengthy periods of unemployment or underemployment at an earlier age limit their access to retirement benefits. Yet, diminished opportunities may have "pushed" them into retirement (Flippen 2005). Black men up to age 61 have higher rates of retirement than Caucasian men. After age 61, African American males have lower rates. One factor affecting African American men's earlier retirement may be that those who are moderately disabled are more likely to identify themselves as partly or fully retired. This is because self-identification with the retiree role has more psychological benefits and social legitimacy than identifying with a sick role. Furthermore, their greater likelihood of multiple chronic illnesses (discussed in Chapters 4 and 14) makes declining health a more salient reason for retirement among African Americans than among whites (Angel and Angel, 2006).

In some cases, retirement due to poor health and adverse work conditions results in older adults perceiving their early retirement as forced. In an analysis of the Health and Retirement Survey, those who retired early were more likely than older retirees to perceive their retirement as forced, that is, needing to leave the workforce earlier than they had planned or wanted to. Nearly 33 percent of retirees felt their choices had been restricted by health limitations; job displacement created by plant closings, layoffs or downsizing, and caregiving obligations (Prisuta, 2004). In other studies, race and ethnicity did not affect perceptions of involuntary retirement among men, but did so among women (Szinovacz and Davey, 2005).

Satisfaction with Retirement

Early gerontological studies emphasized the negative impacts of retirement as a life crisis due to loss (Atchley, 1976; Streib and Schneider, 1971). Later research has identified the positive effects of retirement on life satisfaction and health, especially during the first few years after retiring. For most employees, retirement is desired, and their decision is not whether to retire but when. Not surprisingly, similar factors (e.g., financial security and health status) also influence the degree of satisfaction with retirement. In general, control over the timing of retirement, financial security, and health appear to be the major determinants of retirees' life satisfaction, rather than retirement status per se. Not surprisingly, retirees with higher incomes or at least adequate finances report being more satisfied and having a more positive retirement identity than those with lower incomes. Regardless of socioeconomic status, however, most retirees remain engaged in some type of productive activity, whether paid or non-paid. Activities other than paid work that provide autonomy, a sense of control, and a chance to learn new things are all related to retirement satisfaction (Drentea, 1999, 2002; Fast, Dosman, and Moran, 2006; Moen, 2001). It is useful to examine retirement as a *process* or *transition* that affects people's life satisfaction and self-identity in multiple ways. This concept encompasses not only the timing and type of retirement situation as a life stage, but also the phases and the development of a retiree identity. Similarly, an individual's degree of satisfaction with the outcome depends to some extent on how the retirement process is experienced, especially the extent of choice or autonomy, preparation and planning, and congruence with prior employment roles. Overall, whether individuals adopt a retiree identity (i.e., what they make of the retiree role) depends on their prior employment status, amount of retirement income, and extent of disability (Szinovacz and Davey, 2004b; Szinovacz and DeViney, 1999). While a major transition, retirement is often blurred, with the majority of retirees experiencing minimal stress and being relatively satisfied with their lives.

Retirement does not *cause* poor physical or mental health (e.g., depression), as is commonly assumed (Drentea, 2002; Moen, 2001; Moen, Kim, and Hofmeister, 2001). Although functional health does deteriorate for some after retirement, for others both physical and mental health improves, perhaps because they are no longer subject to stressful, unhealthy, or high-risk work conditions. Contrary to stereotypes about retirement's negative health effects, people who die shortly after retiring were probably in poor health before they retired. In fact, deteriorating

Many older adults discover their artistic side with retirement.

health is more likely to cause retirement than vice versa. The misconception that people become ill, depressed, or die as a consequence of retirement undoubtedly persists on the basis of findings from cross-sectional data, as well as anecdotal reports of isolated instances of such deaths. In addition, the traditional American ideology that life's meaning is derived from paid work may reinforce the stereotype that retirement has primarily negative consequences. Retirees may also be motivated to exaggerate their health limitations to justify their retirement. In fact, health status is interconnected with other factors, such as the normative acceptability of not working and the desire for a retirement lifestyle.

Personal and social characteristics that contribute to satisfaction in retirement include:

- perceptions of daily activities as useful
- internal locus of control
- a sense of having chosen the timing of retirement
- access to an adequate social support system of friends and neighbors
- marital or partner relationships that are supportive of the retiree role

Consistent with continuity theory, *preretirement self-esteem and identity* influence postretirement self-esteem. Individuals whose primary source of meaning was not employment and with weaker work values adjust to a satisfying routine more readily than do those with strong work ethics who did not develop leisure activities when employed. Conversely, retirees who do not adjust well typically have poor health, inadequate family finances, marital problems, and difficulties making transitions across the life course. Those who retire early because of poor health or lack of job opportunities or who feel pushed out of their jobs are less satisfied with retirement. But they are also dissatisfied with other aspects of their lives, such as their housing, standard of living, and leisure (Butrica and Shaner, 2005; Drentea, 2002; Smith and Moen, 2004).

Occupational status, which is frequently associated with educational level, is also an important predictor of retirement satisfaction. Not surprisingly, lower-status workers have more health and financial problems and are therefore less satisfied than higher-level white-collar workers. The more meaningful work characteristics of higher-status occupations may "spill over" to a variety of satisfying nonwork pursuits throughout life. These are conducive to more social contacts and structured opportunities during retirement. For example, a college professor may have a work and social routine that is more readily transferable to retirement than that of a construction worker. Differences between retirees in upper- and lower-status occupations do not develop with retirement, but rather reflect variations in social and personal resources throughout life. This view of retirement as a long-term process that presents continual challenges as retirees adapt is consistent with continuity theory, discussed in Chapter 8.

The nature of the *spouse/partner relationship* and the partner's role in the decision-making process affect retirement satisfaction in a range of ways. In one study, retirees' and spouses' individual and joint reports of retirement satisfaction were related to perceptions of spousal influence on the retirement decision, with the effects varying by gender. Couples who reported both individual and joint satisfaction were ones where the wives reported that their husbands did not influence their retirement decision (Smith and Moen, 2004). Control over the timing of retirement and the marital context such as a partner's disability, influence postretirement well-being, although these effects differ by gender. Women caring for a partner with a disability, combined with perceptions of being forced into an abrupt or too-early retirement, reported more depressive symptoms than others (Szinovacz and Davey, 2004b). Another study found that women reported more depressive symptoms than men when their spouses were already retired while the woman continued to work. For recently retired men, however, the positive effect of a wife's retirement was contingent on the couple's enjoyment of joint activities (Szinovacz and Davey, 2004a). A wife's continued employment tended to cause greater conflict in the marital relationship than men's employment, because of the effect on joint time together (Davey and Szinovacz, 2004). These examples of the nature of the partner relationship and how it affects retirement illustrate the common saying, "I married you for life, but not for lunch." Quite simply, conflicts are more likely when partners do not enjoy spending leisure time together and when wives feel they did not control the timing of retirement.

Gender and ethnic minority status markedly influence retirement satisfaction. Women's retirement plans and well-being, like men's, are influenced by their health and their own pension and Social Security eligibility, not by their husbands'. Their slightly lower levels of retirement satisfaction seem to be due to their lower retirement incomes, typically because of the lack of a private pension and because they have spent more years out of the paid labor force to assume dependent care responsibilities. For women who enjoy the routine, rewards, and sociability of paid employment, adjusting to a full-time stay-at-home role can be difficult. Those who entered the workforce in midlife, after raising their children, may not be ready to retire when their husbands are (Moen et al., 2001).

Reentry to the labor force (or "unretirement") is distinct from "partial" retirement (reducing hours worked per week or weeks worked per year). As noted above, retirement for African Americans and Latinos is not a single, irreversible event that represents the culmination of career employment. Instead, those who faced discontinuous work patterns and ongoing financial needs, because of lack of pensions and other nonwage resources, generally do not define themselves as retired. As "unretired-retired," they spend a greater percentage of their lives working intermittently and in temporary jobs beyond

---

SUMMARY OF FACTORS AFFECTING RETIREMENT SATISFACTION

- a retirement process that involves choice, autonomy, adequate preparation and planning, and congruence with prior job roles
- retirement activities that provide autonomy, sense of control, chance to learn and to feel useful
- financial security
- good health
- a suitable living environment
- a strong social support system of reciprocal relationships
- a higher-status occupation prior to retirement
- personal capacities, such as a positive outlook and sense of mastery

---

retirement because of their low wage base. Elders of color are more vulnerable to job displacement and more adversely affected by it. Their reemployment rates, personal and household income, and rates of health insurance coverage following displacement are lower than that of white workers. Displaced older workers must often move into lower-paying jobs to bridge the years to retirement. In addition, African American men tend to have higher rates of disability and mortality across the life course and especially in the years preceding retirement, which result in retirement inequities (Flippen, 2005; Hardy, 2006).

For all retirees, however, retirement is now less a single phase in a person's life course and more a dynamic process with several stages where the retired/nonretired roles overlap, and individuals move in and out of the workforce. Instead of a "crisp" or unidirectional one-step shift, blurred transitions often involve complex patterns such as returning to employment, flexible hours and part time options, "unretirements," and later, second or third partial or full retirements. About 50 percent of older workers currently pass through a period of partial retirement on the way to complete retirement, or reverse the process by reentering the labor force (Hardy, 2006). This means that the end of a career often differs from the end of a working life. The propensity to work on a part-time or part-year basis—exiting and reentering the workforce—is primarily for economic reasons and is not specific to a particular job. Those who change jobs shortly before retirement are the most likely to work afterward, suggesting that "unretirement" is part of a repertoire of adaptive behaviors in the later years. Money is not the only reason why older adults move from retirement to employment, however; many say they enjoy work, see it as a way to remain active and productive, and to socialize (AARP, 2003b, 2004). In sum, consistent with the life-course perspective discussed in Chapter 8, there is growing diversity regarding the timing and flexibility of retirement, with changing norms about the sequencing of paid and nonpaid roles, or repeated work exits and reentry as personal and societal economic circumstances change.

The Importance of Planning

Because retirement is a process, preparation and planning for productive roles in old age are important for transitioning to retirement. Comprehensive preparation, an orientation toward the future, and a belief in one's ability to adapt to change are associated with a generally positive retirement experience (Ekerdt, Kosloski, and DeViney, 2000; Moen, 2001). In addition, occupations that demand more complex thinking, decision making, and intellectual challenge (e.g., professional and highly paid positions) may better prepare people for retirement decision making and planning. Additionally, if nonwork interests and skills are not developed prior to retirement, cultivating them afterward may be more difficult (Drentea, 1999; McLaughlin and Jensen, 2000).

Comprehensive *retirement planning programs* that address social activities, financial resources, health promoting behaviors, and family relationships are one way of encouraging a positive transition. Unfortunately, such programs are not widespread. Even when they exist, programs may

be underutilized, in part because of the human tendency to deny that one is getting old. When boomers were asked about retirement, only 13 percent of respondents in a national survey felt economically secure and looking forward to retirement and the leisure that they believe they have earned. In contrast, 32 percent were "strugglers" and "anxious," primarily women who feared retirement as a time of financial hardship and worried about health care costs (Prisuta, 2004). Ironically, this latter group, typically lower-income workers, is also the least likely to have access to resources to plan for retirement. Government employees and older men with more years of education, higher occupational status, and private pensions have greater access to retirement planning opportunities, thereby perpetuating inequities in old age.

Another approach to retirement preparation is for employers to *restructure work patterns* during the preretirement years, gradually allowing longer vacations, shorter work days, flex-time, job-sharing, and opportunities for community engagement, thereby easing the transition to many leisure time. This is probably unrealistic for many employers because of the potential added cost of such options. Most workers would like to retire gradually, phasing down from full-time to part-time work. In one study, 33 to 50 percent of people who left their full time career moved into *bridge jobs*—full or part-time jobs other than those in which they spent the better part of their working years and that "bridge" the transition from work to retirement (Harvard/MetLife, 2004; Quinn, 2003). This preference for bridge jobs emerges because of financial, health insurance, and social needs, as well as a desire for creative and challenging opportunities after many years in a traditional worker role. Such options are contingent on whether employers will retrain them for a new job, make pension contributions after age 65, or transfer them to jobs with less responsibility, fewer hours, and less pay as a transition to full retirement. Until recently, only about 33 percent of firms offered such opportunities.

Employers are more likely to permit flexible schedules, part-time work, job sharing, and a reduced work week than a formal phased retirement program. When available, phased retirement that permits a gradual shift tends to be an individualized ad hoc decision, not employer policy, and more readily available to higher level employees than to those in low-paying positions (Hutchens, 2003).

Employment Status

As noted above, some older adults never fully retire, and employment remains their primary means of productivity. In 2004, 14.4 percent of adults age 65 and over were in the labor force (working or actively seeking work), including 19 percent of older men, and 11 percent of older women. These numbers decline for those over age 70, to 13 percent for men, and 7 percent for women (AOA, 2005; Federal Interagency Forum, 2006). Nearly 46 percent of men and

11 percent of women age 65 and over were employed in 1950 (U.S. Census Bureau, 2002). Between 1963 and 1993, there was a decline among working men ages 62 and older, but since 1993 their participation in the labor force has increased to 52.5 percent in 2005 among men age 62 to 64, and 13.5 percent among those 70 and older. In contrast, the proportion of women 62 and older in the labor force has steadily increased since 1983, with 40 percent of women age 62 to 64 and 7 percent of those over 70 employed in 2005. These changes are illustrated in Figure 12.1 (Federal Interagency Forum, 2006). Reasons for this gradual increase in the proportion of older adults employed include the elimination of the Social Security "earnings test" in 2000, changes in the design of employer-sponsored pensions, and the decline in the proportion of older adults in positions that initially require a longer education and training (e.g., managerial and professional positions or self-employment), or those with flexible retirement policies (AOA, 2005). Compared with

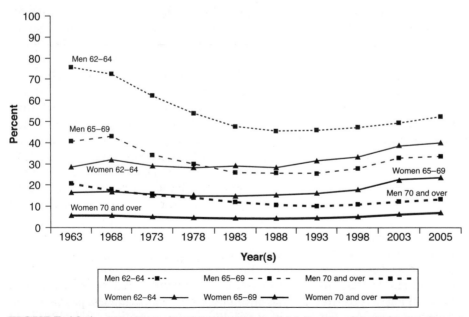

FIGURE 12.1 **Labor Force Participation Rates of Adults 62 and Over, by Age Group, Annual Averages, 1963–2005**
SOURCE: Federal Interagency Forum on Aging-Related Statistics, 2006.

their younger counterparts, older workers are less likely to be in physically demanding or high-tech jobs (Federal Interagency Forum, 2006; Hardy, 2006; Wan et al., 2005).

Individuals who continue to work past age 55 remain almost as likely to work full-time as their younger counterparts until about age 62, the prior age of eligibility for partial Social Security benefits. Part-time work has increased more than full-time employment and is generally preferred by older adults. Among women age 65 to 69 who are employed, nearly 50 percent are part-time workers compared to 35 percent among their male counterparts. These proportions among employed people age 70 and older are 61 and 47 percent, respectively. Figure 12.2. (Purcell and Whitman, 2006; Wan et al., 2005). As noted above, part-time work that allows gradual retirement is perceived by the working public of all ages as a desirable alternative, especially when a flexible work schedule is combined with the ability to draw partial pensions. Older workers are more likely to be self-employed than younger workers (approximately 20 percent versus 7 percent, respectively) (Hipple, 2004; Wan et al., 2005). Depending on one's definition of career, 25 to 50 percent of all older people, especially those who are self-employed, remain in the labor force in some capacity after they leave their primary career jobs. It is unclear, however, to what extent part-time work represents underemployment of adults whose hours of work have been reduced because of slack work or company downsizing, feeling pressured to leave full-time work, or inability to find full-time employment. Furthermore, several obstacles exist to obtaining part-time work:

- Older persons may not be able to find part-time work at a wage level similar to full-time employment.
- Employer policies may prevent part-time workers from drawing partial pensions.
- Employers resist the additional administrative work and higher health insurance costs

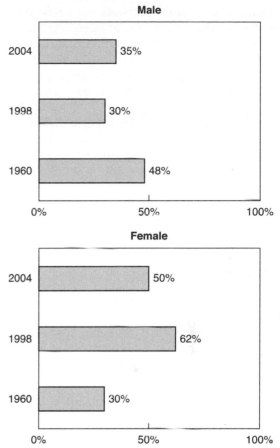

FIGURE 12.2 **Persons 65 to 69 Who Work Part-Time**
SOURCE: Purcell and Whitman, 2006.

entailed in hiring part-time or temporary older workers. Those costs, however, may be tempered by the advantage of fewer employer-paid benefits for dependents among older workers.

More Older People Seek Employment

The rate of employment seeking is high among older adults, especially among older persons of color (U.S. Census Bureau, 2002). A decreasing pool of younger workers, a healthier and better educated cohort of older persons who are oriented toward lifelong careers, economic expectations to continue a similar lifestyle, and increasing health and long-term care expenses contribute to the desire of more people to continue working beyond age 65. Other reasons why older people, especially among the young-old, seek employment, are:

• *Financial need:* A primary factor is that many people choose to retire and then find it harder to live on a lower than anticipated retirement income. In fact, over 50 percent of retired workers return to work within 3 to 4 years, largely for economic reasons. As noted above, they move back and forth from full or partial retirement into nonretirement, or accept jobs in the service sector

Part-time work can provide both income and satisfaction.

and in smaller firms of lower pay in order to get by financially. Such movement in and out of the labor force is a common pattern with negative economic and health consequences in old age for African Americans and Latinos. The problem has been exacerbated in the past few years as major companies have gone into bankruptcy and their pension plans have collapsed or shrunk. The stock market plunge after 2000 also reduced the value of employer-provided (defined benefit) pensions, leaving retirees with a much smaller income than they had anticipated.

• *Desire to feel productive:* Others work after retirement in order to feel productive, share expertise, and reduce boredom. Continued employment into old age is associated with

---

STRATEGIES TO RECRUIT AND RETAIN OLDER WORKERS

As many as 40 percent of the workforce in some companies will be eligible to retire within the next five years. To address this, more companies are adapting the workplace to hire or retain older workers. John Deere & Company, an industrial equipment manufacturer, has employees in their 70s who benefit from flexible working hours and telecommuting. The company also deals with the ergonomics of the workplace to make jobs less tiring for older workers. IBM uses its networks to recruit retired alumni for special projects, creating "boomerangs"—former employees who return after an absence. Automobile manufacturers, such as BMW and Toyota, have adapted their workstations to older workers. At the same time, some of these companies have trimmed retirement benefits, making retirement a less-attractive option. Companies such as Lockheed Martin and PepsiCo have initiated phased-retirement packages that offer workers in their 50s a chance to work shorter hours and receive some pension income. This approach allows employers to retain skilled employees at a lower cost than full-time workers, while older workers benefit from the flexibility of part-time employment with an adequate income.

SOURCE: Turning boomers into boomerangs, *The Economist*, February 18, 2006.

RETIREES WHO DON'T

The number of employees age 75 and older has increased more than 80 percent in the past 25 years. Marge, who is 79, is one such employee. She still works 2 days a week as a waitress in a family restaurant. She states that she would rather work than go to a social club or senior center. Marge brings a strong work ethic and commitment to the job. A younger co-worker maintains that "sometimes she runs us under the table" (Hollingsworth, 2002). Another is Waldo, who began working when he was 13, guiding a lead team of horses pulling a wheat thrasher. After a series of various jobs, he started a business cleaning seeds for planting in the 1950s and ran it until he was 91 years old. He then took a decades-long hobby of bee keeping and went into the honey business, which he is still running at age 104 (Manning, 2006). And Arthur, who worked 72 years repairing Los Angeles buses, eventually retired at age 100.

higher morale, happiness, adjustment, and longevity, in part because of the social support networks with coworkers. For some older people, a job represents a new career, a continuation of earlier work, or a way to learn new skills and form new friendships (Chen and Scott, 2006).

• *Job restructuring and contingent, temporary service jobs.* When older workers feel pushed out of their jobs by company closures, technological change, downsizing, mergers, or reorganization, retirement is not "voluntary." Instead, it may border on age discrimination and be associated with poorer physical and mental health (Gallo et al., 2000). In the past two decades, more employers have tried to reduce costs and increase productivity by creating labor force structures that can be readily altered at management discretion. With each successive recession since the early 1990s, the risk of under or unemployment for older workers has increased. This has resulted in the growth of a contingent or temporary workforce,

even for highly skilled professional positions, that does not provide financial security and benefits based on workers' seniority or skills. Contingent employees work less than 34 hours a week and may be on-call workers or independent contractors. Workers displaced by these market changes may be too old to have good job prospects, but may nevertheless need to work and accept temporary employment just to make ends meet. Those who do find jobs, often in the service industry, typically experience downward mobility to low wages and to temporary or part-time work in smaller firms with fewer benefits. This trend disproportionately affects women and older adults of color (Flippen, 2005; Hardy, 2006; Siegel, Muller, and Honig, 2000). Although the unemployment rate remains lower among older workers, they stay out of work longer, suffer a greater loss of earnings in subsequent jobs, experience longer periods of unemployment, and are more likely to become discouraged and stop looking for work. For older adults needing to work for economic reasons or wanting to stay active, unemployment can result in dissatisfaction with life and higher rates of illness (Chen and Scott, 2006; Gallo et al., 2000).

Barriers to Employment

Why do unemployed older workers have a difficult time with their job search? Several reasons have been discussed:

• They may have been in one occupation for many years and therefore lack job-hunting skills.

• They are more vulnerable to skill obsolescence created by changes in the economy, including the shift away from product manufacturing and medium-wage manufacturing jobs toward low-wage positions in the service industries and high-wage positions in high-tech fields. For example, older workers are generally not hired for jobs that require extensive use of computers (Hirsch, Macpherson, and Hardy, 2000).

IS THIS AGE DISCRIMINATION?

A bank announces that it is opening a new branch and advertises for tellers. Jane Feld, age 53 with 22 years of banking experience, applies. The employment application includes an optional category for age. Rather than pausing to think about whether to indicate her age, she answers the question voluntarily and truthfully. The next week, Ms. Feld receives a polite letter from the bank, complimenting her on her qualities, but turning her down because she is overqualified. She later finds out that a 32-year-old woman with only 4 years' experience is hired.

Sarah Nelson, age 55, is a manager with a large advertising company. For the past 5 years, she has received outstanding performance reviews. Two months after a strong review and pay increase, she was abruptly fired for "poor performance." Her replacement, age 35, started a week after she was fired.

- Until recently, many businesses did not alter the work environment, such as allowing part time work, to prepare older workers for rapid changes.
- Only a few programs, such as the federal **Senior Community Service Employment Program (SCSEP),** specifically target low-income older adults through retraining and subsidized employment.
- Age-based employment discrimination persists, even though mandatory retirement policies are illegal for most jobs. Age discrimination alleged as the basis for loss of employment is the fastest-growing form of unfair dismissal complaints submitted to the Equal Employment Opportunity Commission. In a 2002 AARP survey, 67 percent of older workers perceived age discrimination in the workplace, although only 9 percent reported having been passed up for a promotion because of their age, and 5 percent said they had not received a raise because of their age (AARP, 2003b). The **Age Discrimination in Employment Act (ADEA)** has reduced blatant

forms of age discrimination (e.g., advertisements that restrict jobs to younger people), but has been less effective at promoting the hiring of older workers.

- More subtle forms of discrimination endure, such as expectations of attractiveness in dress, makeup, and hairstyle, or making jobs undesirable to older workers by downgrading title or salary.
- Negative stereotypes about aging and productivity persist. Some employers assume that older workers will not perform as well as younger ones because of poor health, declining energy, diminished intellectual ability, or different work styles, even though this is not empirically supported, as discussed below.
- Others perceive older workers as less cost effective, given their proximity to retirement, less flexible in a changing workplace with new technology, expensive to train, and incurring higher health care costs (Hardy, 2006).
- Human resource managers typically offer older workers little support for career development or career counseling (DeLong, 2004).

Despite such concerns, however, most employers rate older workers high on loyalty, dependability, emotional stability, and ability to get along with co-workers.

Creating New Employment Opportunities

Advocacy organizations for older people maintain that judging a person's job qualifications solely on the basis of age, without regard to job suitability, is inequitable, and that chronological age alone is a poor predictor of job performance. Instead, experience is viewed as a better predictor of job performance than age. Not hiring older workers deprives society of their skills and capacities. To address future labor shortages, government and corporate policies and pensions should be modified to extend employment opportunities and offer financial incentives to older workers. For example, tax

LAWS TO PREVENT OR ADDRESS DISCRIMINATION BASED ON AGE

- The Age Discrimination in Employment Act (ADEA), passed in 1967, protects workers age 45 and over from denial of employment strictly because of age.
- This act was amended in 1978 to prohibit the use of pension plans as justification for not hiring older workers and to raise the mandatory retirement age to 70. In 1986, mandatory retirement was eliminated.
- In 1990, the Older Workers Benefit Protection Act prohibited employers from treating older workers differently from younger workers during a reduction in workforce.
- The Americans with Disabilities Act (ADA) of 1990 also offers protection to older adults. Employers are expected to make work-related adjustments and redesign jobs for workers with disabilities, including impairments in sensory, manual, or speaking skills.

incentives could be given to employers who hire older workers. With willing and supportive employers, work environments can be modified and job-referral, training, and counseling programs provided to link older adults and potential employers. As industries become more knowledge-based, employers need to reassess the value of older workers, the organizational roles they play, the institutional memory they represent, and the array of experiences they have accrued (DeLong, 2004; Hardy 2006).

POINTS TO PONDER

Next time you are talking to an employer, ask whether the firm has older workers. How are their skills utilized? Are there opportunities for training and development? What have the firm's experiences been with older workers in terms of absenteeism, productivity, and morale?

Economic Status: Sources of Income in Retirement

In terms of the P–E model, economic status in old age is largely influenced by environmental conditions, especially past and current employment patterns and resultant retirement income and benefits. Although economic resources in themselves do not guarantee satisfaction, they affect older people's daily opportunities and competence that can enable them to experience active aging. Economic status is consistent for most people across the life course.

The median household income of people age 65 and older was $25,210, compared to a median income of approximately $50,500 for all households in 2004 (DeNavas-Walt, Proctor, and Lee, 2005; Purcell and Whitman, 2006). However, this difference needs to be viewed in the context that households of elders are smaller and generally do not have work-related and child-rearing expenses facing younger households. Median net worth increases with extent of education, and the lowest median incomes are found in households headed by elders of color (AOA, 2005). Older adults are estimated to need 65 to 80 percent of their pre-retirement income to maintain their living standard in retirement. Since retirement can reduce individual incomes by one-third to one-half, retirees who do not fall into upper-income brackets must markedly adjust their standard of living downward—while their out-of-pocket spending for items such as health care typically increases.

Sources of income for the older population include Social Security earnings, savings, assets, and private pensions, which comprise nearly 97 percent of all income received (Purcell and Whitman, 2006). The sources of aggregate income for persons over age 65 are illustrated in Figure 12.3. The distribution of income sources varies widely, however, with women, elders of color, and the oldest-old most likely to rely on Social Security and to lack private pensions and other assets. Those at the

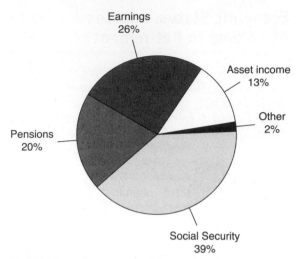

FIGURE 12.3 **Sources of Older Adults' Aggregate Income**

SOURCE: Federal Interagency Forum, 2006.

bottom of the income range rely largely on Social Security and/or Supplemental Security Income (SSI), as described below.

Social Security

Older people depend largely on Social Security for their retirement income.

- Nearly 40 percent of all income received by older units (i.e., a married couple with one or both members age 65 and older and living together, or a person age 65 or older not living with a spouse) is from Social Security.
- The average Social Security benefit is approximately $955 per month for retired workers, or $11,460 per year. Monthly benefits for men averaged $1076, compared to $826 for women.
- Approximately 95 percent of all older people receive Social Security, with women more likely to have this as their only source of income compared to their male counterparts.

- Without Social Security, 48 to 55 percent of older adults would be poor.
- Of those age 65 and over, 66 percent receive at least 50 percent of their income and 18 percent receive all their income from Social Security (see Figure 12.4).
- Marital status often determines the extent of reliance on Social Security; for approximately 75 percent of single older women, Social Security represents more than 50 percent of their income compared to an estimated 50 percent of married couples.
- Among low-income households and the oldest-old, 83 percent of their income is from Social Security (Federal Interagency Forum, 2006; Gist, 2007; Purcell and Whitman, 2006; SSA, 2006).

Social Security was never intended to provide an adequate retirement income, but only a floor of protection or the first tier of support. It was assumed that additional pensions and individual savings would help support people in their later years. This assumption has not been borne out, as reflected in the proportionately lower income received by retirees from savings and private pensions. Not surprisingly,

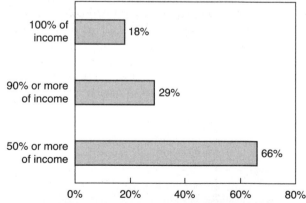

FIGURE 12.4 **Percent of Beneficiary Units with Social Security Benefits as a Major Source of Income, 2003**

SOURCE: National Center for Policy Analysis, 2003.

older individuals with the lowest total income have Social Security as their *sole* income source (Yee, 2005).

As described further in Chapter 16, the Social Security system is a public trust into which all workers pay and from which all are guaranteed an income floor in old age or disability. To be insured, a worker retiring now must be age 62.5 or older and must have been employed at least 10 years in covered employment. The level of benefits received is based on a percentage of the retired worker's average monthly earnings that were subject to Social Security tax. Insured persons are eligible for full benefits at age 65 (note that the age is rising from 65 to 67 by 2022 at a rate of two months each year, beginning with workers and spouses born in 1938—who must be 65 years and two months for full benefits). If workers choose to

retire at age 62.5, their monthly benefits are permanently reduced and are not increased when they reach age 65. Since 1975, Social Security benefits are automatically increased annually whenever the Consumer Price Index increases by 3 percent or more. This is known as the cost-of-living adjustment, or COLA, which protects benefits from inflation. Since benefits are related to a worker's wage and employment history, women and people of color, with patterns of intermittent or part-time work, tend to receive less than the average monthly benefit. Another inequity inherent within Social Security is that GLBT partners cannot qualify for benefits based on their partner's earnings. In addition, some of the oldest-old have never qualified for Social Security, because they were employed in occupations such as domestic work not covered by the system. Future retirees who are immigrants or GLBT partners will not be covered, unless federal legislation broadens the definition of who is eligible.

The Social Security payroll tax is regressive (i.e., paying the same rate of 12.4 percent for both the rich and the poor). This means that low-income workers, often women and people of color, pay a larger proportion of their monthly salary for the Social Security tax compared to higher-income workers. On the other hand, lower-income workers benefit proportionately more from Social Security when they retire, receiving benefits equal to 56 percent of their working wages, while high-income workers' benefits on average are only 28 percent of their prior salary. In addition, higher income workers must now pay income tax on 50 percent of their Social Security benefits. Unfortunately, most low- and middle-income adults do not plan sufficiently for their retirement income, because they assume that Social Security will be adequate and they fail to assess the impact of inflation and reduced income levels. Some are able to supplement their Social Security income with assets, pensions, job earnings, and Supplemental Security Income (SSI).

GENDER INEQUITIES AND SOCIAL SECURITY

- A widow may start to collect surviving dependents' benefits when she reaches age 60. However, she will lose about 28 percent of what she would have received if she had waited until age 65.

- Widows and divorcees under age 60 who are not disabled and who do not have children under age 18 entitled to Social Security, or who are not responsible for disabled persons, cannot receive Social Security benefits. This group of women, who generally do not have a paid work history and do not qualify for any public benefits, are sometimes referred to as **displaced homemakers.** Since the average age at widowhood is 66 years, many women face this "widow's gap."

- A woman who is divorced after at least 10 years of marriage and who reaches retirement age may collect up to 50 percent of her ex-husband's retirement benefits, but only when he turns 62 and if she remains single. Because many widows or divorced women do not meet these criteria, a large percentage of single older women live in poverty or near-poverty conditions (Older Women's League, 2002).

Asset Income

Income from **assets** (e.g., savings, investments home equity, and personal property), the next most important source of income, is received by about 56 percent of older adults. This represents a decline since 1986, coinciding with a long period of falling interest rates and dividend yields. But assets comprise only 12 percent of the total income of all older people. Not surprisingly, the median income of those with assets is more than twice the median income of those without. Over 33 percent of older households—typically the oldest-old, women, and persons of color—report no asset income (Federal Interagency Forum, 2006; Purcell and Whitman, 2006).

Home equity represents the major component of older people's assets, and is about 50 percent of their net worth. Approximately 80 percent of older people own their homes, although this percentage declines among elders of color. Yet 50 percent of older homeowners spend almost half of their incomes on property taxes, utilities, and maintenance (SSA, 2002). Home equity therefore does not represent liquid wealth or cash and cannot be relied on to cover daily expenses. Reverse mortgages, described in Chapter 11, are one way to convert the accumulated value of a home into regular monthly income, but relatively few older people participate. Other assets are primarily interest-bearing savings and checking accounts, although today most of these accounts generate low earnings from interest.

Even though older adults with fixed incomes cannot depend on assets to meet current expenses, their net worth tends to be greater than for those under age 35. As an indicator of vast income differences among older people, overall net worth is approximately $27,000 for African American households, but above $215,000 for white households. Education is a primary factor affecting total assets; across all groups, the net worth of those with no high school diploma is approximately $59,000 compared to $376,000 for those with some college or more (Federal Interagency Forum, 2006).

Pensions

Although nearly all jobholders are covered by Social Security as a general public pension, not all have *job-specific pensions*. Most such pensions are intended to supplement Social Security, not to be the sole source of income. They are available only through a specific employment position and are administered by a place of employment, union, or private insurance company. Job-specific pensions include public employee pensions (for those who work for federal, state, or local governments) and private pensions. In 2004, an estimated 36 percent of private sector workers and 90 percent of civilian government workers age 65 and older received pension income. Women are less likely than men to receive a

---

PENSIONS AND GENDER INEQUITIES

- Women are half as likely as men to receive a pension, and when they do, the benefit is only about 50 percent of what men receive.
- Women are more likely than men to be "in and out" of the labor force, and therefore less likely to achieve the required length of service and level of seniority for vesting pension benefits.
- Women's earnings in their longest career job, used as the base for calculating a pension, are relatively low.
- Nonemployed women face an additional problem: Most pension plans reduce benefits for those who elect to protect their spouses through survivors benefits. In the past, many men chose higher monthly benefits rather than survivors benefits; when they died, their wives were left without adequate financial protection. As married women's employment experiences increasingly resemble those of men, the gender gap in pensions may narrow. But this is also due to a decline in the number of men with pensions (Burnes and Schulz, 2000).

private pension, either as a retired worker or as a surviving spouse (28 percent compared to 44 percent, respectively). Since 1995, the gap between the proportion of men and women receiving pensions has declined, primarily because of reductions in the percentage of men receiving pension income rather than an increase among women (Purcell and Whitman, 2006). Relatively few workers are enrolled in private pension programs that provide the replacement rate of income necessary for retirement. Instead, job-specific pensions comprise approximately 20 percent of the older population's aggregate income, and even less among the lowest income elders: 2 percent. Only about 3 percent of pension plans provide cost-of-living increases, so most plans are adversely affected by inflation. Economic recessions and escalating health care costs have also reduced pension assets. In recent years, employee pension coverage, especially among persons of color, has declined. This is a problematic trend for older adults' future well-being (Federal Interagency Forum, 2006; O'Rand, 2005).

Pension benefits are generally based on earnings or a combination of earnings and years of service. Eligibility is usually between ages 60 and 65, with a range from 50 to 70. Federal policies have supported private pension programs by postponing taxation of pension benefits, as well as allowing benefits to be invested to generate earnings that are not taxed. Tax has been paid only when the pension is drawn, after the money has produced many years of earnings.

Until the late 1990s, defined benefit pension plans provided incentives for building seniority (typically 30 years), as well as disincentives for quitting mid-career and delaying retirement. Defined benefit pension plans were also used to encourage early retirement, especially connected with plant closures and a priority on retaining younger workers (Hardy, 2006). Health insurance benefits have also been jeopardized by company bankruptcies. Think about airline pilots and flight attendants who have lost pensions and other benefits when their company

declared bankruptcy. In such instances, a company can "shed" its union contracts by arguing that the financial burden of pension obligations makes it unattractive to prospective buyers. Once sold, companies can be re-opened as nonunion operations (Hardy, 2006).

As a whole, private pensions go to workers with long, continuous service in jobs that have such coverage. In general, these are higher-income, relatively skilled positions of 30 or more years concentrated among large, unionized firms and financial service sectors. As a result, retirees who benefit from private pensions tend to be white, well-educated males in middle- and upper-income brackets, with lowest-income older persons receiving, on average, only 4 percent of their income from pensions (Wu, 2003). Pension coverage thus varies dramatically by class, race, gender, and age. It is relatively low for women, workers of color, and lower-income workers in small nonunion plants and low-wage industries such as retail sales and services, and for retirees currently over age 65 (Purcell and Whitman, 2006).

The Employment Retirement Income Security Act (ERISA), enacted in 1974 to strengthen private pension systems, was the first comprehensive effort to regulate them. As a result, defined benefit pension plans required vested benefits (**vesting** refers to the amount of time a person must work on a job in order to acquire rights to a pension). When vested, all covered workers are guaranteed a full or defined benefit for life upon retirement after 10 or 15 years with the company, regardless of whether or not they remain with that organization until retirement. A person could work for one firm for 12 years, move to a second company until retirement at age 65, and then receive pensions from both based on years of service. In addition, the person could anticipate the size of the pension benefit. ERISA also strengthened standards for financing, administering, and protecting pension plans. Tax-exempt individual retirement accounts (IRAs) were made available to all workers in

TYPES OF PENSION PLANS

- **Defined benefit:** Guarantees a specific or defined amount of pension income for the remainder of a worker's life (e.g., a lifetime annuity). The company must set aside funds to cover the benefits promised.
- **Defined contribution:** Employers, employees, or both contribute to the fund, such as 401K plans, over the years; the success of the fund's benefits depends on the nature of investments. Growing in use, they create greater risks for the economic security of future retirees.
- **Cash balance plans:** Combine elements of both defined benefit and defined contribution plans. These are likely to erode the value of what defined benefit plans have promised.

1981, in an effort to increase personal savings for retirement. Workers could save by deferring income taxes on some contributions and on investment earnings. Over time, this has resulted in the growth of defined contribution plans, IRAs or 401Ks, that require workers to manage their own retirement portfolios. This shift has also been fostered by increased federal regulation of pensions, ballooning pension liabilities, and employers' desire for flexibility in making labor force adjustments. The growth of defined contribution plans influences retirement indirectly by removing penalties for delayed retirement and allowing more individualized timing of retirement, with some workers remaining employed longer in order to retire with a larger account balance (Hardy, 2006; Purcell and Whitman, 2006). Yet only about 10 percent of all workers have IRAs, primarily those earning $50,000 or more who have disposable income (Verma, 2006). Lower-income workers generally cannot spare the money, and the tax benefit is considerably less for them. Ironically, then, the people who need retirement income the most generally cannot take advantage of IRAs.

As with employer pension plans, the tax deferral of IRAs provides the equivalent of a long-term interest-free loan (e.g., tax shelter) to the predominantly high-income taxpayers who use them. Sweeping changes in laws affecting pension plans in the 2006 Pension Protection Act gave companies the latitude to change pension plans, such as converting a defined benefit pension to a less favorable cash-balance plan. New regulations will make it more expensive for companies to offer pension plans, further reducing the number of private plans available. On the other hand, this legislation will encourage more defined contribution plans or 401Ks (Caudill, 2006).

Earnings

Overall, current job *earnings* form 18 to 26 percent of the aggregate income of older units, and are reported by about 18 percent of men and 13 percent of women, although they may increase if boomers remain in the workforce longer than prior cohorts. In fact, the proportion of income from earnings has already grown, partially because of increased employment among older people and a drop in interest and dividend income (Purcell and Whitman, 2006). Not surprisingly, percent of income from earnings differs markedly by age and class; elders in the lowest fifth of aggregate incomes garner only 1 percent of income through earnings, while earnings comprise 40 percent of aggregate income among the highest fifth. Although earnings are an important income source to the young-old and to those with the highest income from assets and pensions, they decline in importance with age (Federal Interagency Forum, 2006).

In sum, the equity goals of Social Security are outweighed by private pensions, asset income, IRAs, and other preferential tax treatment for a small percentage of wealthy older adults. This creates greater economic inequality among the older population over time. In general, older households' wealth is characterized by modest holdings, limited prior savings, and large inequities.

Poverty among Old and Young

The economic status of older adults has improved dramatically since the 1960s. In 1969, 35 percent of those age 65 and over fell below the official poverty line. Today, 9.8 percent of older people are poor, compared with 11.3 percent of those under age 65, and 17.8 percent of children under age 18. The percent of people in poverty does not give a complete picture of the economic status of older adults, however, since 27.5 percent of elders are considered high income, and 34.6 percent middle income. On the other hand, while the *proportion* of poor people age 65 and older has fallen, the *number* of elders living in poverty has remained constant since the 1970s due to the growth in the total number of older adults (Federal Interagency Forum, 2006; Purcell and Whitman, 2006). A primary factor in reducing poverty among elders has been Social Security, including the 1972 increases in Social Security benefits and COLAs that began in 1975 and were described earlier. Other factors include:

- the strong performance of the economy and labor productivity in the 1950s and 1960s
- the growth of real wages that older adults experienced during their working lives
- accumulation of home equity
- existence of Medicare
- pension protection (although this is now declining)
- implementation of the Supplemental Security Income (SSI) program
- changes in the definition of the poverty threshold for older adults

As a result of such gains, the public perception is that *all* older persons are financially better off than other age groups. This perception is also fueled by the increase in poverty among children under age 6, who are the poorest age group. However, this decline in the income status of children is largely structural, caused by economic, political, and demographic forces, especially cuts in child welfare and income maintenance programs, not by the growth of the older population.

Poverty Differentials over Time

When viewed over time, many older people are not financially comfortable, despite their overall improved income status. Forty percent of Americans between the ages of 60 and 90 experience at least one year below the poverty line, and 48 percent at least a year in which their income falls below 125 percent of the poverty line (Rank and Hirschl, 1999). A larger proportion (6.7 percent) of older people than younger (4.5 percent) fall just above the poverty line and thus are "near poor" and at risk for poverty, making 16.5 percent poor or near poor (AOA, 2005). These "tweeners" are caught between upper-income and poor older people—not well enough off to be financially secure but not poor enough to qualify for the means-tested safety net of Medicaid and SSI. Paradoxically, the only way they can improve their economic well-being is to qualify for Medicaid and SSI by spending down (using up their assets). The percentage of subgroups that are poor, even with Social Security, and the percentage kept out of poverty by Social Security, are illustrated in Figure 12.5.

These figures also do not reflect the fact that the federal poverty standard for a single adult age 65 and over is 8 to 10 percent lower than for younger adults. In setting this lower threshold to quality for benefits as "poor," the Census Bureau assumes that the costs of food and other necessities are lower for older people, even though many have special nutritional needs and spend proportionately more on housing, transportation, and health care than do younger groups. If the same standard were

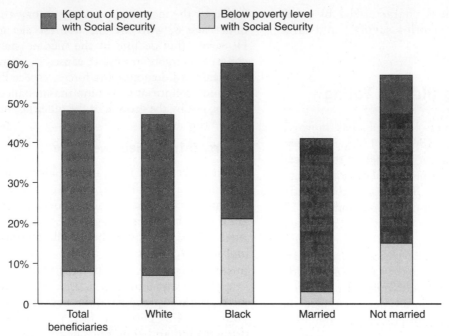

FIGURE 12.5   **Aged Units and Poverty Status**
SOURCE: Social Security Administration, Social Security Bulletin Annual Statistical Supplement, 2000.

applied to the older population as to the other age groups, the poverty rate for older people would increase to over 15 percent. Another factor that increases the economic vulnerability of older adults is that they are less likely to have reserve funds to cover emergencies such as catastrophic medical expenses. As a result, low-income elders often face impossible trade-offs, such as giving up medications or food in order to pay for housing or medical care. If older people are facing health care needs or living alone in inadequate, poorly heated housing, they may have greater difficulty coping with economic hardship than younger adults (Richardson and Barusch, 2006).

Contrary to the static nature of poverty that is suggested by cross-sectional data at a single point in time, many older people move in and out of poverty over time, often because of health and long-term care costs. The uncertainty of economic hardship in itself can negatively affect

elders' well being. When such individual movements are identified, the risk of falling below the poverty line at some time during a specified period more than doubles the highest average risk for older couples, and by almost 30 percent for widows. For example, many women become poor for the first time in their lives after depleting their assets while caring for a dying partner. Once an older person moves into poverty, she or he is less likely to exit than are younger age groups. Many "hidden poor" among the older population are either living with relatives or in long-term care facilities and thus not counted in official census statistics. In sum, more older people are at marginal levels of income and at greater risk of poverty than the population 18 to 64 years; they are also more likely to be trapped in long-term poverty. As noted throughout this text in discussions of disparities, wide socio-economic diversity exists within the older population, with economic marginality most

WHO ARE THE OLDER POOR?

- 7.5 percent of older whites
- 14 percent of older Asians and Pacific Islanders
- 19 percent of older Latinos
- 25 percent of older African Americans
- 29 percent of older American Indians
- 18 percent of older people living alone
- 17 percent of nonmarried elders
- 14 percent of those over age 85
- 13 percent of those in central cities
- 11 percent of those in rural areas (AOA, 2005).

pronounced among older women, those who live alone or in rural areas, ethnic minorities, and the oldest-old.

Poverty Differentials by Gender

Older women comprise one of the poorest groups in our society. In fact, the risk of poverty among couples and single men has fallen sharply leaving poverty in old age a characteristic primarily of single frail women over age 85, especially women of color, in rural areas, and who have outlived their husbands (McLaughlin and Jensen, 2000; Wu, 2003). Nearly 13 percent of older women are poor, compared to approximately 7 percent of older men (U.S. Census Bureau, 2006). Widows account for over 50 percent of all older poor, reflecting the loss of pension income and earned income often associated with the death of a wage-earner spouse. In contrast, the wife's death *reduces* the risk of poverty for widowers (Purcell and Whitman, 2006; SSA, 2004). As implied above, the primary reasons for women's lower retirement income are:

- their interrupted employment histories because of family responsibilities
- their greater likelihood of being divorced, widowed, and unmarried

- their lower wages across the life course and resultant lower Social Security benefits
- their greater likelihood of having worked part time, often in temporary positions
- their lower likelihood of having private pensions to supplement Social Security
- their lower probability of having worked in higher-level or professional occupations (Heinz, Lewis, and Hounsell, 2006; Herd, 2006; Lee, 2005; McLaughlin and Jensen, 2000).

These factors that lead to higher proportions of poor older women are referred to as the **feminization of poverty** and are discussed more fully in Chapter 15.

Poverty Differentials by Ethnic Minority Status

African American and Latino elders of both genders have substantially lower incomes than their white counterparts, as described earlier. Almost 25 percent of older African Americans and 19 percent of older Latinos are poor, compared with 7.5 percent of older whites (AOA, 2005). The median income of older African American and Latino men living alone is about 33 percent lower than older white men living alone. Although the differences are less pronounced among women, the median incomes of older African American and Latina women are generally 25 to 33 percent lower than those of white women. Minority women's slight economic advantage relative to that of their male peers stems from minority men's higher rates of unemployment and unsteady work histories. Not only are median incomes lower, but the average black or Latino household has no financial or liquid assets. Within each population of color, poverty is more common for women, especially divorced women, than for men (Federal Interagency Forum, 2006). These higher rates of poverty among elders of color are discussed more fully in Chapter 14.

Poverty Differentials by Age and Living Status

Poverty rates among the young-old are lower, in part due to continued employment or the greater likelihood of retirement with good pension plans. In contrast, older cohorts continue to experience income loss as they age, and therefore economic deprivation relative to younger cohorts. The poverty rate for those 65 to 74 years is nearly 10 percent; for those over age 85, nearly 15 percent. The fact that median income declines with age is due in part to the disproportionate number of unmarried women among the oldest-old. The economic hardships of older cohorts are often compounded by a lifetime of discrimination, by historical factors such as working at jobs with no pension or inadequate health insurance, and by recent events such as loss of a partner or declining health. Accordingly, older cohorts are more likely to live alone, which is associated with poverty. Of all older people living alone, 18 percent are poor, compared with 6 percent of those living with others. When the poor and the near-poor are grouped together, 45 percent of older adults living alone fall into this category. In every successively older age group, unmarried women have a lower median income than unmarried men or married couples. Because the poverty rate increases with age, nearly 50 percent of those age 85 and over are either poor or near-poor (AOA, 2005; U.S. Census Bureau, 2006).

In sum, despite the overall improved financial situation of the older population, large pockets of poverty and near-poverty exist among women, elders of color, those over age 75, those who live alone, and elders in rural areas. As a result, economic inequities are actually greater among older people than among other age groups. Aging advocates maintain that strategies to alleviate poverty among today's older Americans cannot rely on the labor market. Instead, they must be immediate, such as increasing levels of Social Security for those with low lifetime earnings and ensuring that women and men have full access to benefits accrued by their spouses.

Public Assistance

Only about 5 percent of the older population receives some type of public assistance, primarily in the form of **Supplemental Security Income** (SSI). This percentage is greater among persons of color and women (U.S. Census Bureau, 2005). SSI was established in 1974 to provide a minimum income for elders living on the margin of poverty. The basic federal payment in 2005 was $579 a month for a single person and $869 for a couple. Although these payments change each year to reflect cost-of-living increases, the increase between 2003 and 2005 averaged just $40 (SSA, 2006).

SSI is intended to provide a minimum guaranteed income to older adults and persons of all ages who are visually impaired or disabled. In contrast to Social Security, SSI does not require a history of covered employment contributions. Instead, eligibility is determined at the state level by a categorical requirement that the recipient be 65 years of age, blind, or disabled, with a strict means-test based on monthly income and assets. Nevertheless, many eligible older poor do not participate in SSI, and others are denied benefits because they are immigrants. For those who do so, the federal SSI benefits fall substantially below the poverty line, especially for women who live alone, because benefit levels are higher for couples than for individuals. Only a few states have supplemented federal benefits; even in those instances, levels remain low, so that SSI supplies only about 14 percent of the income of poor older people. Those who receive SSI may also qualify for Medicaid and food stamps, but only a fraction of eligible elders receive food stamps. The amount of SSI benefits depends on income, assets, and gifts or contributions from family members for food, clothing, or housing. These gifts may be counted as income and may result in a reduction in benefits. Becoming eligible for SSI is a time-consuming and often demeaning process, requiring extensive documentation and the ability to deal with conflicting criteria for benefits from SSI, Medicaid, and food stamps. Additionally, even legal immigrants are denied access to these programs. Despite these barriers, increasing numbers of "poor" or "near-poor" older adults rely on public assistance, through SSI, Medicaid, or food stamps.

As noted earlier, along with health, living arrangements, and marital status, economic status influences the nonpaid roles and activities in old age. This is particularly important for organizational membership, volunteerism, religious participation and spirituality, and political involvement. We turn now to discuss these other forms of productive aging.

Patterns and Functions of Nonpaid Roles and Activities

Leisure

The term **leisure** evokes different reactions in people. For some, it signifies wasting time. For others, it is only the frenzied pursuit of "leisure activities" on the weekends that sustains them through the work week. Leisure can be defined as any activity characterized by the absence of obligation, which in itself is inherently satisfying. Free time alone is not necessarily leisure. Instead, the critical variable is how a person defines tasks and situations to bring intrinsic meaning. Individuals who do not experience feelings of freedom and satisfaction may still be at "work" rather than at "leisure." People's

reactions to the concept of leisure are clearly influenced by cultural values attached to paid work and a mistrust of nonwork time. Because of American values of productivity and hard work—especially among the current generation of older persons—many older adults have not experienced satisfying nonwork activities at earlier phases in their lives. Societal values are changing, however, with more legitimacy given to nonwork activities across the life course, as evidenced by the growing number of classes and businesses that specialize in leisure for middle-aged adults. For low-income or ethnic minority elders, however, leisure may be a meaningless concept if they have to continue working to survive, lack resources for satisfying recreational time, or cope with functional disabilities.

Disagreement regarding the value of leisure pursuits for older people is reflected historically in the gerontological literature. An early perspective was that leisure roles cannot substitute for employment because they are not legitimated by societal norms. Since work is a dominant value in U.S. society, it was argued that individuals cannot derive self-respect from leisure. A closely related view is that retirement is legitimated in our society by an ethic that esteems leisure that is earnest, occupied, and filled with activity—a "busy" ethic, which is consistent with the activity theory of aging (Ekerdt, 1986). For those with strong work values, work-like activities were defined as important for achieving satisfaction in retirement. The prevalence of the "busy" ethic is reflected in a question commonly asked

---

POINTS TO PONDER

What does leisure mean to you? How have your values, socioeconomic status and culture influenced your definition of leisure? How is this different from your parents' or grandparents' definition? How do you see yourself spending leisure time when you are old?

of retirees: What do you do all day? "Keeping busy" and engaging in productive activities analogous to work were presumed to ease the adjustment to retirement by adapting retired life to prevailing societal norms, even though the "busy" ethic is contrary to the definition of leisure as intrinsically satisfying. A counterargument is that leisure can replace the employment role and provide personal satisfaction in later life, especially when the retired person has good health and an adequate income, and their activities build upon preretirement skills and interests. In fact, leisure activities that challenge a person's cognitive and physical abilities, such as dancing, playing a musical instrument, using the computer, and playing board games, can enhance their sense of competence, control, and mastery (Cohen, 2005).

Although wide variations exist, *patterns of meaningful nonpaid activity* among older individuals are identified.

- Most activity changes are gradual, reflecting a consistency and a narrowing of the repertoire of activities as individuals age.
- Compared to younger people, older adults are more likely to engage in solitary and sedentary pursuits, such as watching television, visiting with family and friends, and reading.
- The time spent on personal care, sleep and rest, "doing nothing in particular," hobbies, and shopping composes a larger fraction of older adults' days than among younger and middle-aged individuals (Johnson and Schaner, 2005; Prisuta, 2004).

When judged by younger persons or by middle-class standards, these essential and universal activities may be viewed as "boring and nonproductive." Yet, the ability to perform these more mundane non-work activities—personal care, cooking, doing errands, puttering around the house or garden, or sitting in quiet reflection—can be critical to maintaining older

people's competence, self-esteem, and life satisfaction, especially among the oldest-old. Furthermore, these routines may represent realistic adjustments to declining energy levels and incomes. Such routine pursuits, consistent with the broader concept of productive aging, may thus reflect rational choices about ways to cope that are congruent with environmental changes and may also enhance quality of life, but do not always fit the narrow definition of leisure.

Non-work activities also vary by gender and socioeconomic status. Older men tend to do more household and yard maintenance, while older women perform more housework, child care and other types of caregiving, as well as volunteering and participating in more voluntary associations. Not surprisingly, higher-income older people, especially those living in planned retirement communities, tend to be more active in leisure pursuits with others than low-income elders. Such differences in activities are attributable primarily to the costs of pursuing them, not necessarily to inherent differences by social class. Not surprisingly, a wide range of leisure-oriented businesses, including group travel and adventure programs, are marketing services to higher-income older adults, especially baby boomers. Nevertheless, several benefit programs are designed to reduce financial barriers to leisure. For instance, Golden Passports issued by federal agencies give older people reduced admission fees to national parks. Similar programs at the local or state level as well as AARP membership provide reduced admission to parks, museums, and cultural activities, and discounted prices from businesses and transportation services.

The *psychological benefits of leisure* perceived by older participants include:

- companionship (e.g., playing cards or going dancing)
- compensation for past activities (e.g., walking instead of hiking in the mountains)
- temporary disengagement (e.g., watching TV)
- comfortable solitude (e.g., reading)

- expressive solitude (e.g., knitting, wood-working)
- civic engagement (e.g., volunteering, attending meetings of social groups or political events)

The major benefits of nonpaid activities appear to be building networks with others and providing new sources of personal meaning and competence. Not surprisingly, leisure activities enhance elders' positive identity and self-concept. Accordingly, activities that result in a sense of being valued and contributing to society are found to be positively related to life satisfaction and mental well-being in retirement (Menec, 2003). This relationship does not mean, however, that leisure activity itself creates well-being, since active older people also tend to be healthier and of higher socioeconomic status. The quality of interactions with others in nonwork activities may be more salient for well-being than the number or frequency of interactions.

Religious Participation, Religiosity, and Spirituality

Of the various options for organizational participation, religious affiliation is the most common choice for older persons. After family and government, religious groups or denomination are an important source of instrumental and emotional support for elders (Cutler and Hendricks, 2000). The role of religion and spirituality varies across the life course; attendance at religious institutions is lowest among those in their 30s, peaks in the late 50s to early 60s (with approximately 60 percent of this age group attending), and begins to decline in the late 60s or early 70s. Despite this slight decline, the level of organizational religious involvement for older adults exceeds that of other age groups, with 50 percent of persons over age 65 attending a religious institution in an average week, and many more attending less frequently. Aside from participation in organized

---

DO WE BECOME MORE RELIGIOUS WITH AGE?

It remains unclear whether people become more religious with age, or whether the increased religiosity among older adults is a cohort or period effect. Although no definitive data support either of these perspectives, consistent of findings from Gallup Poll data tend to support the view that religiosity increases with age:

- In 1975, 45 percent of persons age 18 to 29 indicated their religious beliefs were "very important" to them, compared with 63 percent of those ages 50 and older.
- In 2001, 58 to 60 percent of that same cohort (age 44 to 55) indicated their religious beliefs were "very important" to them, compared with 65 to 75 percent of those age 65 and older.
- In 1966, 38 percent of persons age 18 to 29 attended religious services in a typical week, compared to 51 percent of those age 50 and older.
- In 2001, 44 percent of persons in that cohort (now age 54 to 65) attended religious services in a typical week, compared with 32 percent of 18- to 29-year-olds and 60 percent of those older than age 75.
- In 2006, more than 50 percent of adults age 65 and older indicated that religion was very important to them, compared to less than 50 percent of young adults age 18 to 29.

These data suggest that the young in the previous generation also tend to be less religious than the old; however, as they have become older, they too have become more religious. On the other hand, if religiousness is related to better health, those who are less religious may be more likely to die at a younger age, leaving those who are more religious alive at a later age (i.e., a selection effect).

SOURCE: Gallup Poll, 2002, 2006; Idler, 2006; Koenig, 2002; Koenig and Brooks, 2002; Wink and Dillon, 2001.

---

religion, the meaning and importance of religion are stronger in old age than in earlier phases of life (Wink and Dillon, 2001). In a 2006 Gallup Poll, more than 60 percent of adults age 65 and older indicated that religion was "very important" to them, compared to less than 50 percent of people 18 to 29 (Gallup, 2006; Hodge, 2003). Furthermore, adults 65 and over are the most likely of any age group to belong to religiously affiliated groups that can provide a loving, supportive community and a way to contribute. In contrast to other types of voluntary organizations, leadership positions in churches, temples, and synagogues tend to be concentrated among older people. Religiosity can be examined in terms of three factors:

1. Participation in religious organizations
2. The personal meaning of religion and private devotional activities within the home
3. Its benefits for mental and physical well-being, mortality, and quality of end of life

Religion typically is a narrower concept than religiosity, referring to an organized system of spiritual beliefs, values, and behaviors shared by a community (a denomination) and transmitted over time. Religion encompasses communal ties and practices within formal religious institutions, rather than individual behavior (Nelson-Becker, 2004; Nelson-Becker, Nakashama, and Canda, 2006). Declines in rates of such formal participation after age 70 may reflect health and transportation difficulties and functional limitations more than lack of religiousness and spirituality per se. In fact, while attendance at formal services declines slightly with age, older individuals apparently compensate by an increase in internal religious practices—reading the Bible or other religious books, listening to or watching religious broadcasts, prayer and meditation, or studying religion, often in their homes. They also report higher levels of subjective religious experiences than other age groups, such as having had life-changing religious experiences, having daily spiritual experiences, using religiosity to cope with adversity, and thinking of themselves as religious or spiritual persons (Canda, Nakashama, and Furman, 2004; Idler, 2006; Idler et al., 2003; Nelson-Becker, 2004; Nelson-Becker et al., 2006). For many elders, religiosity, as encompassing trust

and faith in a power greater than oneself, prayer, and strength from a greater being, is an effective way to cope. Older adults pray, asking help from a divine being, more often than other age groups. The emotions of hope, gratitude, and forgiveness may represent significant components by which prayer exerts a salutary influence on elders' mental health. Religious beliefs, as contrasted with attendance at religious events, appear to be relatively stable from the late teens until age 60 and to increase thereafter. Thus, some older people who appear to be disengaged from religious organizations may be fully engaged nonorganizationally, experiencing a sense of spirituality, and strong and meaningful subjective ties to religion (Idler, 2006; Nelson-Becker et al., 2006).

Most surveys on religiosity are limited by cross-sectional research, as discussed in Chapter 1. That is, they do not attempt to measure adults' past religious values and behaviors and changes with age. The few available longitudinal studies suggest that cohort differences (e.g., a strong period effect of a rise in church attendance in the 1950s and early 1960s) may be more important than the effects of age and have produced mixed findings of increased, decreased, or stable religiousness over the life course (Hays et al., 2001; Ingersoll-Dayton, Krause, and Morgan, 2002). Thus, although religious convictions appear to become more salient over the years, this may be a generational phenomenon captured by the cross-sectional nature of most of the research. The current cohort of older persons, raised during a time of more widespread religious involvement, had their peak rates of attendance in the 1950s, when this country experienced a church revival. All cohorts, not only older people, have shown a decline in church or synagogue attendance since 1965. This is now changing, however, with younger families increasingly turning to organized religion. Despite the cross-sectional limitations of most studies in this field, religious involvement appears to increase with age, and then declines among the oldest-old, but subjective religiousness does not decline and may actually increase prior to death (Benjamin et al., 2003; Idler, 2006).

Studies of religious activity identify both gender and racial differences. Consistent with participation patterns in other organizations, women have higher rates of religious involvement than men (Miller and Stark, 2002; Taylor, Chatters, and Levin, 2004). Religion appears to be central to the lives of most older African Americans and Latinos of both genders, and related to their sense of meaning, life satisfaction, feelings of self-worth, personal well-being, and sense of resilience and integration in the larger community (Idler, 2006; Krause, 2003; Taylor et al., 2004). The high esteem afforded African American elders in the church may partially underlie these positive associations. Historically, African Americans have had more autonomy in their religious lives than in their economic and political lives. The negative effects of life stress for older African Americans are found to be offset by increased religious involvement through prayer and other private religious activities, and a cognitive reframing of the situation in positive terms (e.g., "I have been through a lot before and I'll get through this too") (Kessler, Mickelson, and Williams, 1999; Mattis and Jagers, 2001; Taylor et al., 2004). For some African American caregivers, the church and God are considered part of their informal system of support and respite (Dilworth-Andersen, Williams, and Cooper, 1999; Idler, 2006). The church also provides social services such as in-home visitation, counseling, meals, household help, and transportation for African American elders, and links them with formal agencies. Such instrumental support reflects the African American church's historical responsibility for improving its parishioners' socioeconomic and political conditions.

Benefits of Religious Participation and Religiosity

The association between religion or spirituality and health is receiving growing attention by gerontological researchers, educators, and practitioners—along with increased visibility in the popular press. A primary reason for this greater attention is that the benefits of religion for physical and mental well-being appear to be significant and consistent. Perhaps the most compelling finding is that religious participation may reduce the risk of mortality and is associated with a lower prevalence of physical illness. For example, religious participation has been shown to reduce the risk of death and decrease time until recovery among patients undergoing cardiac surgery. Religious activity in later life is also associated with better immune functioning, lower blood pressure, greater longevity overall, as well as enhanced quality of life at the end of life (Idler, 2006; Koenig, 2002; Nelson-Becker, 2004; Powell, Shahabi, and Thoresen, 2003; Seeman, Dubin, and Seeman, 2003; Schaie, Krause, and Booth, 2004).

What is unclear is the extent to which religion has protective effects on health, and therapeutic effects on the course and outcomes of illness. It does appear that religious participation (e.g., attending religious services) is associated with later onset of disability, and for those who experience functional limitations, increased likelihood of improving their physical functions. Although service attendance decreases with the onset of disability, it is typically temporary, with attendance levels later returning to almost the level observed before the disability occurred. Accordingly, individuals who report that they turn to religion to cope with their problems exhibit better health outcomes. Because religion provides a world view that infuses the present with meaning and the future with hope, it may help people cope with health problems (Hudson, 2002; Koenig, 2002; Miller and Thoresen, 2003; Oman and Thoresen, 2002; Smith, McCullough, and Poll, 2003).

Religion also has benefits for mental well-being, self-esteem, life satisfaction, a sense of usefulness, and morale. Religious participation is associated with decreased prevalence of mental illnesses, such as major depression, anxiety disorders, substance abuse, and suicide.

In instances of depression, religious involvement is linked with both greater likelihood of recovery from depression and shorter time until recovery. In fact, level of religious service attendance is a significant predictor of better and quicker recovery. As is the case with recovery from physical illness, religious coping is the facet of religious experience most strongly related to recovery from depression (Idler, 2002, 2006; Koenig, McCullough, and Larson, 2001; Van Ness and Larson, 2002). Across all religions, the more devout members are usually less afraid of dying and less prone to depression and loneliness than the less devout. Accordingly, individuals for whom faith provides meaning in their lives experience greater feelings of internal control and a more positive self-concept. Among African American women in particular, spirituality is found to engender self-esteem and positive interpretations of life circumstances (Black, 1999).

The strong association between religion and physical and mental well-being does not imply that religious factors are the only or the primary factors causing good health. Religion has beneficial effects on health because there are so many different pathways to it, through the modification of known risk factors, the provision of social support, a sense of control over unhealthy behaviors such as substance use, and the availability of belief systems for coping with adverse circumstances (e.g., the stress-buffering effect described in Chapter 6). Regardless of the particular pathway, a growing body of evidence shows that religious participation has protective effects on health and helps older adults cope more effectively with their health problems. In fact, the strength of these relationships between religious involvement and well-being increases over time (Bosworth et al., 2003; Idler, 2006; Musick, 2000).

Although religiousness itself is beneficial, the sense of belonging and social support derived from the organizational aspects also enhance well-being (Idler, 2006). Across the life course, religious groups provide social support and reduce stress in people's lives. Older people list among its benefits both the meaning religion gives to life and the social interaction, support, and security that it affords. Congruent with the broad concept of productivity, religious institutions also provide innumerable opportunities to care for and serve others in need. The connection between religious activity and health appears to be especially strong among those who volunteer within religious settings. Volunteers, who typically are externally oriented, are happier, healthier, live longer, and use fewer health services (Krause et al., 1999; Oman, Thoresen, and McMahon, 1999).

A growing number of religious institutions reach out to their aging members by providing transportation to services, making large print publications and hearing assistance devices available, and visiting those who are homebound or in hospitals (Cnaan, 2002; Idler, 2006). Religious institutions are also distinctive for having memberships that cut across the entire life course, providing opportunities for intergenerational interaction and reciprocity. Given the importance of the social networks within religious settings, practitioners need to consider how social support through churches and synagogues complements and interacts with religious beliefs and activities. Yet religious institutions often face the paradox that as their congregation ages and faces increased need, fiscal resources diminish (Cnaan, 2002). In addition, as public social services continue to be reduced, religious institutions are expected to play a greater role in providing counseling, referral to services, and illness prevention/health promotion. The role of faith-based services that receive federal support is, however, raising complex issues regarding the role of church and state that require ongoing dialogue among religious leaders, ethicists, constitutional scholars, and gerontological practitioners (Brooks and Koenig, 2002; Cnaan and Boddie, 2002).

The Value of Spiritual Well-Being

Spirituality is a broader concept than religion, defined in a wide variety of ways:

- a human quest for meaning, sense of purpose, and moral principles in relation to one's deepest convictions and experiences about the nature of reality
- a relationship with that which is sacred in life and transcending the ordinary limits of the body, ego, linear space, and time
- self-determined wisdom in which the individual tries to achieve balance in life
- self-transcendence or crossing a boundary beyond the self, being supported by some power greater than oneself
- achievement of meaning and purpose for one's continued existence
- sense of the wholeness of life and connectedness to the universe, and nature, and a higher power
- awe or unconditional joy
- giving and receiving support through affiliation with others
- intuitive nonverbal understanding of how to cope with life's circumstances (Canda and Smith, 2001; Hodge, 2003; Nelson-Becker et al., 2006)

Spirituality—or belief in a relationship with a higher power—can be differentiated from organized religion but not necessarily religiousness. And some elders may find the term spirituality confusing, even though they are able to define their practical philosophy toward life (Nelson-Becker, 2003). With illness and end of life, older adults are likely to express a sense of spirituality by seeking the meaning and purpose of life, looking at the significance of past events, and wondering what will happen after death. They may also turn to spirituality as they contemplate the legacy they hope to leave behind. Although small proportions of the population in national studies describe themselves as "spiritual but not religious," the majority of adults describe themselves as both religious and spiritual, which makes it difficult to determine their unique effects on physical and mental well-being. Those who view themselves as spiritual but not religious appear to be rejecting participation in organized religion, but emphasizing personal spiritual practices—praying or meditating, appreciating nature, applying spiritual principles to everyday life, and practicing positive emotions such as gratitude and forgiveness. For example, 85 percent of Americans pray frequently, but only 40 percent attend religious services regularly (George, 2002). Baby boomers are less likely than the pre-World War II cohort to say they are "religious and spiritual" or "religious only," but they are more likely to say "spiritual only." Less than half of boomers in an AARP survey were satisfied with their religious and spiritual life, but indicated that this was an area where they wanted to make positive change in the next five years (Keegan et al., 2002). With increased spiritual diversity in our society, boomers are likely to relate to a wider set of both religious and spiritual possibilities (Marler and Hadaway, 2002; Nelson-Becker, 2004).

High levels of spirituality, as measured by closeness to a supreme power, are found to be associated with mental health indicators such as purpose and meaning in life, self-esteem, and perceived quality of life (Idler, 2006). Similarly, spiritual beliefs influence definitions of health, the prevention of illness, the interaction with health care providers, and coping with illness. Spirituality can be an effective coping strategy that provides mental and social support and the ability to derive meaning from everyday lives. Such findings are consistent with the relationships between religiousness and health, since many of the private forms of religious participation (e.g., prayer, meditation, personal rituals) are similar, whether people define themselves as religious or spiritual (George, 2002, Van Hook, Hugen, and Aguilar, 2001).

Spiritual well-being is related not only to the quality of life but also to the will to live. Some gerontologists and theologians maintain that the person who seeks meaning in life will have a reason to live, despite losses and challenges associated with aging. When death is near, spirituality is important for coping with disease, disability, and pain. Mr. Mansfield, in the introduction to Part Four, illustrates the role of spirituality in helping older persons cope with tragic losses in their lives.

Aging can be characterized as a spiritual journey in which the person aims to achieve integration across a number of areas—biological, psychological, social, and spiritual. An ageless self, that is, a person who is not preoccupied or discouraged by his or her aging, has an identity that maintains continuity and is on a spiritual journey in time, despite age-related physical and social changes. For such an individual, being old per se is neither a central feature of the self nor the source of its meaning. Confronting negative images of aging, loss, and death is believed to be essential for psychological-spiritual growth and healthy aging. In fact, dealing with loss can be one of aging's greatest spiritual challenges. Autobiographical storytelling, journal keeping, and empathic interactions with others are useful in supporting older persons' spiritual integration.

The central role of spirituality in many older adults' lives, especially among ethnic minorities and immigrants, has numerous implications for professionals working with them. Spirituality is a quality that can be acknowledged in any situation. Many faith traditions emphasize the importance of silence in creating space to experience spirituality, with the silence of meditation or prayer as a way

to nourish our spirituality. In hospice programs, for instance, patients, workers, and families can experience profound togetherness out of shared silence. In nursing homes, residents, staff, and families may also find that silence has value. Spiritual deepening can also come from confronting and working through doubt and uncertainty. For others, spirituality is a state of being rather than of doing, of approaching each other with kindness and openness to their unique way of manifesting their spirituality. It is a way to experience others authentically without judging or evaluating them. Spiritual reflections and experiences can also be a source of insight for both practitioners and older clients. Contemplative understanding includes feelings and thoughts, and can counterbalance overly rational decision-making processes. In some instances, spirituality can provide a more balanced understanding of what is available compared to what is needed. When practitioners learn to focus on experiences of spirituality with older adults, they can create common experiential ground that can transcend the confines of specific faith traditions, open opportunities for incorporating spirituality into all aspects of everyday life, and develop interventions that take account of spiritual differences (Nelson-Becker, 2006).

Historically, the medical profession has taken a predominantly biological perspective toward aging, overlooking psychological, emotional, and spiritual factors. Whether and in what context physicians should introduce questions of religion or spirituality into patient care continue to be debated and may be a divisive issue in our increasingly religiously diverse society (Idler, 2006; Miller and Thoresen, 2003). Health care practitioners who view spiritual well-being as important to older people's physical and-mental health have developed instruments to measure an individual's spiritual interests and resources, such as personal values, philosophy, and sense of purpose. Some have developed spiritually sensitive practices. Ideally, comprehensive assessments include spiritual assessment (Larrimoe, Parker and Crowther, 2002; Nash and Stewart, 2002; Nelson-Becker, 2005b). One recent assessment

---

MEDITATION AS A FORM OF SPIRITUALITY

Carl, age 68, is an active volunteer and employed part-time. No matter how busy he is, however, he always manages to set aside a half hour in the morning to meditate. Since he started meditating at age 62, his blood pressure has decreased; he has fewer health problems, and he has a calm, positive outlook on life. He describes his meditation to his friends as the center of his spiritual journey.

POINTS TO PONDER

Ask an older person—a relative, neighbor, close friend—whether he or she perceives himself or herself as spiritual. What does spirituality mean to the individual? How has that meaning developed over time?

tool includes 11 spiritual domains, definitions for each, and relevant questions (Nelson-Becker, Nakashima, and Canda, 2007). Increasingly, health providers are encouraged to be sensitive to, and to ask questions about, religion and spiritual well-being that may guide health care choices. A spiritual assessment conducted in an open, inquiring manner, would include questions such as:

- What helps you to experience a deep sense of meaning, purpose, and moral perspective in your life?
- Do you consider yourself religious or a person of faith? Do you consider yourself to be spiritual?
- If so, what terms for referring to spirituality, religion, or faith do you prefer?
- Would you like to incorporate spirituality or religion in our work together?

Some health-promotion screening tools include questions on the individual's spiritual or philosophic values, life goal-setting, and approach to answering questions, such as: What is the meaning of my life? How can I increase the quality of my life? Depending on elders' responses to such questions, health care providers may encourage them to seek religious support or reconnect with a spiritual community (Hodge, 2003, 2004; Nelson-Becker et al., 2006).

Civic Engagement

Closely related to the concept of productive aging is the role of **civic engagement** for elders. Both perspectives emphasize individual responsibility,

self-reliance, and contribution. Fueled by the concern that civil society is weakened by Americans' growing focus on private activities, increasing attention is given to tapping the vast civic potential—a non-monetized form of activity—of older adults. According to Mark Freedman, whose national organization, **Civic Ventures**, provides guidance to older adults seeking civic engagement opportunities, "older adults might produce a windfall for American communities in the twenty-first century . . . and along the way bring opportunities for greater fulfillment and purpose in later years" (Freedman, 2002, p. 86; Freedman and Adler, 2005). Additionally, the Gerontological Society of America, American Society on Aging, and National Council on the Aging have major civic engagement initiatives. For the first time, the 2006 reauthorization of the Older Americans Act called for strategies to utilize older adults to address critical local needs of national concern. Civic engagement is generally defined as the process in which individuals actively participate in the life of their communities, through individual and collective activities such as voting, joining community groups, and volunteering, (Harvard/MetLife, 2004). However, some studies equate civic engagement with volunteerism only and overlook other activities associated with civic life such as voting, community activism, staying informed about current events, caregiving, and building informal connections (Martinson and Minkler, 2006).

Both conservatives and progressives advocate civic engagement, but for different reasons. Conservatives distinguish between the civil and the political, and favor voluntary involvement as a way to address social problems rather than governmental solutions. Older adults as volunteers, often through faith-based organizations, are viewed as a way to fill gaps created by budgetary shortfalls. Core concepts of governmental programs to protect elders, such as Social Security, are viewed as inconsistent with civic engagement. In contrast, progressives advocate for elders to be more politically active to ensure that public policies safeguard the rights of vulnerable elders (Eberly and Streeter, 2002; Holstein and Minkler, 2003; Hudson, 2007). The conservative definition of civic engagement overlooks organizations of elders that try to foster social change and promote social justice, such as the Gray Panthers and the Older Women's League. This social justice perspective was often articulated by Maggie Kuhn, the founder of the Gray Panthers: the "old, having the benefit of life experience, the time to get things done and the least to lose by sticking their necks out, are in a perfect position to serve as advocates for the larger public good" (1991, 38). Progressives also contend that a narrow focus on volunteering and individual betterment devalues and detracts from other types of civic engagement, promotes engagement as "social therapy," and minimizes the need for broader institutional and policy-level changes (Holstein, 2007; Martinson and Minkler, 2006). "Volunteering in a soup kitchen will help hungry individuals in a town, but will do nothing to address broader problems of homelessness and poverty" (Theiss-Morse and Hibbing, 2004, 237–238). This tension between individual and government responsibility for basic human needs, intertwined with civic engagement, was at the heart of the 2005 White House conference on Aging, which emphasized individual, family, and community responsibilities over those of government (Hudson, 2006; Moody, in press).

From a social constructionist perspective, as discussed in Chapter 8, the current focus on civic engagement—similar to productive and successful aging—may inadvertently devalue those for whom engagement is neither possible nor chosen, such as elders caring for partners with dementia, caring for grandchildren, or having to work minimum wage jobs to make ends meet. Civic engagement is also criticized for excluding low- and middle-income elders who cannot afford to volunteer and may have the highest rates of disability and poor health. Some programs—such as Senior Community Service

and Employment, funded by AOA, and Foster Grandparents—provide small stipends and must be brought in the national discourse about civic engagement. While some might argue that such paid public service is not volunteerism in the pure sense (i.e., non-paid work), policy makers need to recognize that the only way that some older adults, especially elders of color, can participate in civic engagement initiatives is to offset their costs by a modest stipend, child care, reimbursement for gas and transportation, and, if necessary, support for time away from employment or caregiving responsibilities. From a social justice perspective, such programmatic supports are essential to ensure that low-income elders' voices are heard by policy makers (Holstein, 2007).

Civic engagement may also overlook other ways of attaining meaning and fulfillment in later life, as reflected in the concept of gerotranscendence. Social constructionists argue for defining civic engagement as ways to flourish, grow, and live a good old age in whatever ways are possible and desired. They also contend that all elders should be honored and their dignity respected, regardless of whether they are engaged in this manner (Holstein, 2007; Minkler, 2000). From their viewpoint, civic engagement should be broadened to encompass a wide range of activities that foster social connectedness—or the "social capital of the community" (Putnam, 2002). Generalized reciprocities that foster connectedness across the community—keeping an eye on each other's house or the children in the neighborhood—may be more salient for both individual and community well-being than formal volunteering. In fact, what people do may matter less than the fact that they are involved in their community and that they experience a feeling of belonging (Putnam, 2002). Since most elders seek meaning and purpose—personal, spiritual, religious, artistic, political—in their lives, the challenge for modern society is to create purposeful roles for all older adults (Emerman, 2006).

Membership in Voluntary Associations

Given our societal emphasis on being active and productive, voluntary association membership is often presumed to be a "good" leisure activity, with positive effects on physical and mental health. These benefits appear to be associated with having a sense of control and social engagement (Newson and Kemps, 2005; Verghese et al., 2003). For example, one study found that participating in a formal, community-based cultural program had positive effects on overall health, doctor visits, prescription use, loneliness and morale among older adults, whose mean age was 80 (Cohen, 2005; Cohen et al., 2006). Overall, older people tend to be more involved in voluntary organizations than are younger people, although membership in faith-based organizations is the only type that actually increases with age (Prisuta, 2004). Membership is most closely tied to social class and varies among cultures. When socioeconomic status is taken into account, older adults show considerable stability in their general level of voluntary association participation from middle age until their 60s (Cutler and Hendricks, 2000). Similar to most retirement activities, characteristics that influence voluntary association membership include age, gender, ethnic minority status, prior activities and memberships, health, and socioeconomic status. Older women are more active in voluntary associations than older men, perhaps because of their multiple roles in earlier years, that involved volunteer work. Older African Americans have higher rates of organizational membership than do older whites or other elders of color. Nevertheless, for both blacks and whites, membership is highest among those with better health and higher income and education levels. Some ethnic minority differences exist in the types of associations joined. Older African Americans are especially likely to belong to church-related groups and social and recreational clubs; older whites frequently are members of nationality organizations and senior citizen groups. Latinos participate in fraternal and service-oriented organizations, mutual aid societies, and "hometown" clubs.

Senior centers encourage voluntary association activities. With over 16,000 such centers nationally, they vary greatly in the type of services offered, ranging from purely recreational events to social action, or the delivery of social and health services, including nutrition programs, health screening, health promotion, and support groups for caregivers and grandparents. In fact, the Older Americans Act identifies senior centers as preferred focal points for comprehensive, coordinated case management service delivery, especially social and nutritional supports, to promote elders' autonomy and remaining in the community. In

Older adults' leisure time often involves teaching younger generations.

> **REASONS FOR LOW LEVELS OF PARTICIPATION IN SENIOR CENTERS BY OLDER ADULTS**
>
> - lack of interest in the center's activities (i.e., lack of fit between elder's needs and services of the center)
> - programming that does not address the needs of young-old and oldest-old
> - poor health
> - inadequate transportation to the center
> - desire not to be with only old people; don't identify as "senior"
> - the low proportion of men in many centers
> - the lower percentage of elders of color in many centers
> - inability to speak English

recent years, programs focused on "aging in place," such as health promotion, adult day health, mental health services, caregiver support, and community ombudsman, have increased. A study of 734 centers in 8 states found that participants experienced improved physical and mental health, enhanced friendships, and health promoting behaviors (Aday, 2003). Despite the range of activities and services, available, only about 15 percent of older persons participate in senior centers (Pardasani, 2004a). Furthermore, centers typically draw from a relatively narrow population, reaching primarily healthy, lower- to middle-class individuals under age 85 with a "lifetime of joining groups." Nationwide, individuals who are generally less advantaged, but not the least advantaged, are most likely to join in senior center activities. Those who participate are already socially active and view centers as arenas for enhanced social interaction (Pardasani, 2004a).

Senior centers face programmatic challenges. Their membership has become older as their users have aged in place, and the young-old are less inclined to attend at the same time that the oldest-old are too frail to participate. Senior center staff are concerned that rapidly aging participants are not being replaced by the young-old, and some centers are eliminating "senior" from their names, marketing and developing more inclusive language such as community centers. They are faced with offering programs, often for a fee, that attract the young-old while trying to retain their current participants who are growing older and increasingly frail. To do so will not only require innovative programming, but also low-cost, efficient, and reliable forms of transportation (Pardasani, 2004a). The Older Americans Act requires that agencies receiving public funding concentrate on providing services to those most in need, who tend to be low-income, rural, ethnic minority, or frail elders (Wacker, Roberto, and Piper, 2003). But elders of color are consistently underrepresented in senior center participation, even in diverse communities (Pardasani, 2003). When senior center programs do take account of culture, socioeconomic status, specific needs, and kinship ties, African American elders are slightly more likely than whites to attend centers. Similarly, Latino participation increases if centers serve congregate meals on site and offer socialization opportunities with members of their own communities (Pardasani, 2004b). Asian American elders are more likely to participate if they are in relatively good health, and if the senior centers are located in their own neighborhood and offer recreational and acculturation programs in their native language (Lai, 2001).

Lack of transportation, inadequate facilities, limited culturally competent staff, and relevant programming are the primary barriers to senior center participation by elders of color (Miko and Sanchez, 2001). Increasing the representation of ethnic minority and bilingual staff and culturally specific and linguistically diverse programming can foster the participation of elders of color in centers. However, some observers contend that such targeting of services runs counter to the universal nature of the Older Americans Act and may reduce the participation of those relatively more-advantaged older people who currently attend centers. The challenge for senior centers is to reach out to the broadest cross-section of the older population, while increasing the participation of young-old and elders of color in their service areas (Pardasani, 2004b).

Older persons who are active in community organizations such as senior centers derive a variety of benefits. In general, activity level is positively associated with well-being, improved functional and cognitive status and physical health, although the benefits and protective effects may differ by gender (Greenfield and Marks, 2004, 2007; Menec, 2003; Van Willigen, 2000). Socializing is a primary reward for participation in voluntary associations, and aids in achieving active aging, as described in Chapters 1 and 6. Because these organizations are typically age-graded, people interact with others who are similar in age and interests. These interactions often result in friendships, support, a sense of belonging, mutual exchanges of resources, and collective activity. Consistent with the broader concept of productivity, voluntary associations can also serve to maintain the social integration of older people, countering losses in roles and in interactions with others. Older people in voluntary organizations are found to have higher morale and perceived well-being, although this may be attributed to their higher levels of health, income, and education. When these other characteristics are taken into account, organizational membership is not necessarily related to overall life satisfaction (Cutler and Hendricks, 2000). The most satisfied members of organizations are those who become involved in order to have new experiences, achieve something, be creative, and help others. Such members, in turn, participate actively through planning and leadership. Opportunities for more active participation are found in senior advocacy groups such as the Older Women's League and AARP, or in organizations such as advisory boards to Area Agencies on Aging where older people must, by charter, be in leadership roles. Overall, voluntary association membership appears to be most satisfying when it provides opportunities for active, intense involvement and significant leadership roles.

Volunteer Work and Organizations

Similar to participation in voluntary associations, volunteering is more characteristic of our society than others (Independent Sector, 2006a, 2006b). Volunteer work is distinguished by choosing to serve or help others, rather than by its unpaid nature or by formal activity, and can be formal within an organization, or informal, such as time spent helping others not in the household. Volunteering thus has value both to the individual because of its association with autonomy and choice and to society because of its service component. With cutbacks in public funding, nonprofit, service, educational, and religious organizations increasingly rely on volunteers to accomplish their missions and provide services. The Depression era cohort of older adults, who had the children who became the baby boomers, were generally actively engaged in community service and civic engagement in middle age, and have continued this pattern in old age. The boomers are different in terms of how they spend their time. They vote

---

VOLUNTEERING AS A SUBSTITUTE FOR PAST ROLES

Ted was a teacher of sixth-grade science in an inner-city public school for 35 years. When he retired at age 57, he began a successful second career selling real estate. Now, at age 72, he continues to work on average 2 days per week. He enjoys the contact with people and finds his work very different from teaching. Because he believes it is important to give back to his community, he also volunteers as a tutor in an after-school program run by his church for neighborhood "latchkey" children.

less, read newspapers less, and are less likely to join religious or civic organizations (Putnam, 2002, 2004). In addition, female baby boomers are more likely to be employed and therefore have less time to volunteer (Morrow-Howell, Hinterlong, and Sherraden, 2001).

Rates of volunteerism are highest among adults at midlife:

- 51 percent at age 34 to 44,
- 48 percent of those age 45 to 54,
- 41 percent among 65 to 74 years,
- 9 percent among those ages 75 and older.

The higher rates earlier in life are often associated with work or family roles, and thus with having more rather than fewer obligations and commitments (Prisuta, 2004). It may also reflect that younger adults are likely to volunteer in ways that will benefit their children, such as Parent-Teacher-Student Associations (PTSA). It is estimated that 22 to 23 percent of older adults volunteer, a rate that is lower than adults as a whole (27 percent) (Corporation for National and Community Service, 2006). When volunteering is redefined to include informal contributions (e.g., helping neighbors), however, 51 percent of middle-aged and older adults report some type of formal volunteerism and an additional 36 percent volunteer informally (AARP, 2003a). Older adults who volunteer invest more hours into their volunteer work (median of 96 hours) than do younger volunteers. This suggests that, once engaged, they are often reliable and committed (Independent Sector, 2002; Peter D. Hart Research Associates, 2002). Among the older population, *rates of community involvement and volunteerism* are highest among adults with the following characteristics:

- high income and education
- discretionary time
- good health
- a history of volunteering across the life course
- employed part time: although retirees, on average, devote more hours to volunteering, a higher percentage of employed elders volunteer
- a broad range of interests
- a belief that they can make valuable contributions
- greater religious commitment and affiliation (Kutner and Love, 2003; Zedlewski and Schaner, 2006)

The primary type of volunteer work is through religious organizations (45.2 percent), followed by social and community service (17.6 percent), and hospitals (10.5 percent), with the lowest rate in environmental or animal care organizations (U.S. Bureau of the Census, 2006).

GENDER DIFFERENCES IN VOLUNTEERISM As is the case generally in voluntary activities, women, especially widows, are more likely to volunteer than men. This may shift, however, as more women enter the paid workforce. Although women generally view volunteering as a way to help others, men more frequently define it as a substitute for the worker role (Moen, 2001).

ETHNIC MINORITY DIFFERENCES IN VOLUNTEERISM Ethnic minority elders are less likely to participate in formal volunteering. In fact, the term "volunteering" and "community service" can have negative connotations in some communities of color,

---

AN ACTIVE VOLUNTEER AT AGE 80

Edna was an elementary school librarian, forced to retire in 1986, when mandatory retirement still existed. After a few months at home, she was back in the local school, working 4 or 5 days a week as a substitute librarian. She is widely loved by the kids, and the parents and teachers respect her ability to relate to a wide range of children, managing to hook them into "listening to reading."

VOLUNTEERING AS A SOURCE OF SUPPORT

Mary, a homemaker and mother of four children, spent her early years involved with Scouts and PTA and teaching Sunday school. Her last child left home when Mary was 52, and she felt "lost" because there was no one to "need" her in the same ways her children had. At 53, she began volunteering, answering the phone for a community center that served children and elders, and found a new role. When she was widowed at age 70, she increased the hours of volunteering to fill the lonely hours when she especially missed her husband. Since she has never driven, she takes the bus one day a week to the community center. Now at age 80, she was recently honored by the city at a special reception for her 8000 hours of volunteer service.

similar to court-ordered community service. Immigrant groups often have values tied to helping others, but the concept of volunteer is uniquely American and does not translate into their familiar concept of informal service. Nevertheless, volunteering as a way to help others through informal networks is frequent in communities of color, such as through African American churches. It may represent a history of self-reliance and incorporation of a lifetime of hard work into leisure experiences and services to others (Calasanti and Slevin, 2001). Mutual aid (e.g., providing food and lodging to older persons) is common in American Indian communities. Volunteer activities among Asian and Pacific Islander elders reinforce the continuation of their value systems. Older Chinese, for example, often work through family associations or benevolent societies. Some Japanese elders participate in clubs that are an extension of the "family helping itself" concept rooted in traditional Japanese culture. The Latino community emphasizes informal volunteering, such as self-help, mutual aid, and neighborhood assistance, but has the lowest rate of formal volunteering (Zedlewski and Schaner, 2006). Given these diverse meanings, organizations are changing the way they define and pro-

mote volunteering by emphasizing terms of "neighboring" and "community involvement." More programs are recognizing that they need to help volunteers in underserved communities address their economic needs. For example, **Experience Corps** sponsors school-based programs, where older adults work one-on-one with young children, create before- and after-school programs, and receive a modest stipend for their service. The **Senior Companion Program** also offers low-income elders a stipend (Harvard/MetLife, 2004).

PROGRAMS TO EXPAND VOLUNTEERISM   Within the past 40 years, a number of public and private initiatives have been designed to expand community service and civic engagement by older persons, as summarized in the box on the next page. Other approaches seek to expand volunteer involvement; for example, workplace volunteering allows companies to improve their communities while building teamwork skills and morale and improving corporate public image. In some instances, employees use set hours of paid time each month to participate in community service, and involvement in children's education. As a sign of the times, Single Volunteers, an organization with 18 chapters nationally, brings single adults together for service events and indirectly as a way to make new friendships.

BENEFITS OF VOLUNTEERISM   Volunteer programs serve *two major social benefits:* (1) provide individuals with meaningful social roles that enhance their well-being; and (2) furnish organizations with experienced, reliable workers at minimal cost.

Volunteering is increasingly viewed as a central component of active aging and healthy communities (O'Neill and Lindberg, 2005). As described above for participants in community organizations, older volunteers generally experience psychological and health benefits, such as greater life satisfaction, self-rated health, sense of accomplishment, and feelings of

**VOLUNTEER OPPORTUNITIES
FOR OLDER ADULTS**

- Ask a Friend Campaign: aims to increase the number of volunteers benefiting local communities
- Civic Ventures Experience Corps: tutors and mentors in public schools
- Civic Ventures: offer the Purpose Prize to recognize older individuals for exemplary service and BreakThrough Award for innovative organizations
- Environmental Alliance for Senior Involvement: environmental protection activities
- Family Friends: advocates and mentors to young children
- Foster Grandparents: offer support to children with special needs
- National Council on the Aging: RespectAbility provides technical assistance to non-profits to more effectively utilize older volunteers
- Older Americans Act programs: assisting at meal sites, escort and transportation services, home repair, counseling, legal aid
- Senior Medicare patrol: retired professionals assist Medicare and Medicaid beneficiaries
- Peace Corps: places older volunteers to meet needs in other countries
- Retired and Senior Volunteer Program (RSVP): funds volunteers in schools, hospitals and other community settings
- Service Corps of Retired Executives (SCORE): retired executives and small business owners assist small businesses and first-time entrepreneurs
- Volunteers in Parks: volunteer programs with the National Parks Service
- Senior Community Service Employment Program (SCSEP): provides stipends to low-income elders who volunteer in non-profits
- Senior Companionship Program; give financial support to low income adults age 60 and older to provide in-home services to elders in need

Wilson, 2003). Continuous volunteering across the life course fosters higher levels of psychological well-being by buffering against losses in the face of declining functional health. This may result from expanded social networks, resources, power, and emotional gratification. In fact, both moderate levels of physical fitness and volunteering are found to lower the risk of mortality. This may occur when volunteering provides older adults who lack other major sources of role identity with an opportunity to develop more meaning and purpose in their lives and to enhance their roles (Fried et al., 2004; Greenfield and Marks, 2004, 2007; Harris and Thoresen, 2005; Lum and Lightfoot, 2005; Zedlewski and Schaner, 2006). On the other hand, the positive effects decline when the time spent volunteering is more than 100 hours a year (Morrow-Howell et al., 2003; Musick and Wilson, 2003). Other factors such as self-identity, role strain, and meaningfulness also may underlie the curvilinear relationship between volunteering and mortality (Shmotkin, Blumstein, and Modan, 2003).

Contrary to the assumptions of activity theory, the desire to replace lost roles (e.g., employee or spouse) is not a primary motivator for older volunteers. Instead, older people are more likely to volunteer if they are married, well educated, involved in other organizations, and employed part-time (Morrow-Howell et al., 2003). For most retirees, volunteering is apparently not a work substitute, although it may protect them from any negative effects of retirement. Most elders want roles that fully engage their capacities and interests and in ways that are meaningful to them or matter to their communities (Freedman, 2001, 2002). Given this motivator, national service programs, such as the **Foster Grandparents Program** and **Retired Senior Volunteer Program (RSVP),** are effective in recruiting volunteers. From the perspective of social exchange theory, volunteering may ensure valued social resources as a basis of exchange, primarily by assisting others and contributing to

usefulness; they also have lower rates of functional disability and depression (Greenfield and Marks, 2004; Hendricks and Cutler, 2004; Lum and Lightfoot, 2005; Menec, 2003; Morrow-Howell et al., 2003; Musick and society rather than being perceived as dependent. This in turn enhances older volunteers' life satisfaction, mental health, and self-rated health (Gartland, 2001). Consistent with the continuity theory of aging, most older volunteers have felt a sense of responsibility to others throughout their lives. Volunteerism is part of a productive lifestyle across the life course that unfolds in a person's employment, education, and organized activities, with volunteers' long-standing involvement either remaining constant or expanding as they age. This partially explains why recruiting volunteers in old age is more difficult than during midlife.

The experience of Edna and Ted (see boxes on page 513) illustrates how some older adults achieve life satisfaction when volunteering builds on previous professional skills as teachers and mentors. Mary's activities, described in the box on page 515, illustrate how volunteering can support older adults in generative roles. A number of trends will influence the meaning and functions of volunteerism for older persons. Those who are critical of the growing emphasis on civic engagement see volunteerism as a way to fill gaps in services created by growing federal and state budget cuts (Holstein, 2007). With increased national attention on self-help and mutual aid, some people may choose to become more active in cross-generational neighborhood and community activities. Regardless of the type of volunteer and informal helping networks, the challenge remains of whether and how to involve older people who are low-income, persons of color, living alone, frail and disabled, or from areas with inadequate public transportation. Volunteer programs in the future may need to expand outreach capacities to such elders, allow flexible schedules, provide accessible training, compensate them monetarily, or provide other benefits such as transportation and meals. Regardless of the type of volunteerism, the documented benefits suggest that efforts to encourage volunteering among older persons should continue (Freedman, 2001, 2002; Menec, 2003; Morrow-Howell et al., 2003; Zedlewski and Schaner, 2006).

Educational Programs

Many educational programs have been oriented toward enrichment or practical personal assistance in such areas as health and finances, rather than civic engagement or community improvement. This has occurred in part because most higher education institutions have not viewed older learners as a priority, nor have they fully recognized the market potential for education among senior boomers. Even though 80 percent of state universities offer tuition-free, space-available enrollment in college classes for older people, state legislatures typically have provided little funding for older adult programs.

Fortunately, some creative late-life learning initiatives have developed in higher education that are constructed around images of productive aging, not of decline or need. Lifelong learning institutes (LLI), which offer courses (usually non-credit) for 200 to 500 mid-life to older adults each year, are flourishing. Over 100 programs are funded by the Osher Foundation at 4-year colleges or universities, with the aim of funding 100 endowed Osher Lifelong Learning Institutes serving 500 to 1000 or more members annually. Types of course offerings vary, with some programs hiring expert faculty and others utilizing volunteers and hosting special events to bring together members of diverse communities (Corley and Monnier, 2007).

ELDERHOSTEL One of the best known is **Elderhostel,** where older learners attend "learning adventures" on campuses and affiliated locations throughout the country and the world. Each one has an educational component and is often associated with a college or university, whether the group is studying architecture in London, seals in Antarctica, monkeys in Belize, antiquities in Greece, or archaeology in the Southwest United States. Elderhostel involves over 150,000 participants age 55 and older a year in 8000 programs at over 1500 different academic institutions. Offered in all 50 states and 90 countries,

Elderhostel can include active learning experiences such as sailing.

the oldest participant to date is 103 (Elderhostel, 2007). To cater to the young-old and boomers, Elderhostel now offers private rooms and baths rather than dormitory accommodations.

Some gerontology certificate programs are committed to preparing significant numbers of older people for roles as advocates and service providers. Community colleges, because of their accessibility, are ideal settings in which to develop educational programs that offer older adults ways to be productive. A few states recognize the market for lifelong learning and are funding a range of programs, including liberal arts education, peer learning groups, health promotion, training of older volunteers, and intergenerational service learning programs, such as older adults offering younger undergraduates career guidance. With the growth of distance learning and Web-based instruction, baby boomers provide a growing market for educational programs. Even for the current cohort, programs such as **Senior Net** teach computer skills and how to communicate online.

As suggested in Chapter 5, educational programs need to take account of older learners'

particular needs, such as self-paced learning, and sensitivity to hearing and vision problems, and avoiding time pressures. Lifelong learning programs for all elders represent an area in need of further development and funding, especially as baby boomers age and seek new opportunities to "reinvent themselves" and contribute in new ways after retirement.

Political Participation

Another major arena of participation is political life. Political acts range from voting to participation in a political party or a political action group, to running for or holding elective office. In examining older people's political behavior, three factors make interpretation of the relationship between age and political behavior complex:

1. stages in the life course
2. cohort effects
3. historical or period effects, as discussed in Chapter 1

Historical factors influence interpretations of older people's political behavior, particularly analyses of the extent of conservatism. Some early studies found older people to be more conservative than younger people, as measured by preference for the Republican Party and voting behavior (Campbell, 1962). Older people's apparent conservatism partially reflects the fact that people born and raised in different historical periods tend to have perspectives reflecting those times—in this instance, the historical effect of party realignments in the late 1920s and 1930s. Before the New Deal of the 1930s and 1940s, people entering the electorate identified with the Republican Party to a disproportionate extent; they have voted Republican ever since, and form the majority of the oldest-old population. This apparent association of Republicanism with age thus reflects cohort differences, not the effects of aging per se. Conclusions about older people's political behavior and attitudes are thus limited by the cross-sectional nature of many studies that did not take account of historical and cohort effects. In short, how a person thinks and acts politically can be traced largely to environmental and historical factors, not to the individual's age.

Age differences in conservatism/liberalism are less a matter of people becoming more conservative or liberal than of their maintaining these values throughout life. Successive generations entering the electorate since World War II have become comparatively more liberal, with older people more likely to identify with the Democratic Party since the mid-1980s. This shift may be due in part to increases in low-income and retired blue-collar people who are opposed to the stance of the Republican Party on issues such as Social Security and Medicare. In fact, older adults are more likely to favor major health care reforms than are younger people, in part because of escalating costs not covered by Medicare. At the same time, increasing numbers of young people, including many among the baby boom generation, have identified with conservative Republicans and independent candidates since the 1980s (Alwin, 1998; Binstock, 2000).

Overall, various cohorts of older adults during the past 50 years have tended to distribute their votes among presidential candidates in roughly the same proportions as other age groups. In other words, voting differences are greater within than between age groups. Individuals of all ages are not ideologically consistent in their issue-specific preferences, such as Medicare, Social Security, or taxes. Furthermore, both older and younger people may hold beliefs on specific issues that contradict their views on more general principles. Given the older population's heterogeneity, differences of opinion on any political issue are likely to equal or exceed variations between age groups and are more likely to be due to economic status and partisanship than age (Binstock, 2000, 2006).

Voting Behavior

Older Americans are more likely than younger adults to vote in national elections, although rates of electoral participation are low for all age groups in our society. The voting rates of older adults have remained steady while those of other age groups have declined overall (Binstock, 2006). The participation rate of older people in the last four presidential elections has averaged 68 percent. This is higher than the rates for all other age groups and the overall rate of 58 percent, although in the 2004 election, all age groups turned out at a higher rate than in 2000. Older voters cast almost 22 percent of the votes in the 2004 Presidential election, even though they were slightly less than 17 percent of the voting-age population (Binstock, 2006; Hudson, 2007; U.S. Census Bureau, 2005). Votes for Bush and Kerry were distributed in nearly the same proportion as the rest of the electorate, although a higher proportion of voters age 60 to 64 voted for Bush. Reasons for the older population's higher rate of registration and voting include:

- Older adults are more likely to pay attention to the news and to be more knowledgeable about politics and public affairs generally, demonstrating higher levels of "civic competence."
- Strong partisans are more likely to vote, and the current cohort of older people identifies with the major political parties more strongly than younger persons, who are more likely to identify with independent parties (Binstock, 2000, 2006; Binstock and Quadagno, 2001).

In instances where voter turnout among older adults is low, factors other than aging are probably the reason, including gender, ethnic minority status, education, and generational variables as well as access to the polls. For example, the voter turnout among ethnic minorities is lower than that of whites. The lack of political acculturation of Latinos appears to influence their relatively low rates of participation; for example, Mexican American elders, fearful of deportation, are more cautious and conservative in their political involvement. On the other hand, older African Americans who are active in their communities, with a strong sense of responsibility, a Democratic identity, and higher levels of education, are more likely to vote. These and earlier findings suggest that differences in the rates of political participation among older people of color do not reflect age or ethnic minority identity per se, but rather lower educational levels, feelings of powerlessness, cohort and immigration experiences, and real or perceived barriers to voting and other political activities. To public officials and the media, the older electorate is viewed as exerting substantial political influence beyond what their numbers might suggest, as reflected in the following perspectives on senior power.

Senior Power

Research on "senior power" reflects an ongoing debate about whether age serves as a catalyst for a viable political movement.

PROPONENTS OF THE "SENIOR POWER" MODEL OF POLITICS   Older people are a powerful political constituency in the policy-making process because legislators and appointed officials are influenced by public opinion—especially by those who vote and are political party leaders, as is the case with older people. This perspective of senior power is consistent with the subculture theory of aging, discussed in Chapter 8. This theory suggests that older people, because of common values and experiences, develop a shared political consciousness that is translated into collective action on old-age-related issues (Rix, 1999). Because baby boomers are better educated, healthier, and have higher incomes, it is presumed that they will have more resources essential to political power. It also assumes that older people

Many older people advocate for their rights.

in the future will experience increasing pride, dignity, and shared consciousness about old age and thus define problems collectively. From this perspective, age will become a more salient aspect of politics, even if all older persons and their organizations do not speak (or vote) with a unified political voice. Heterogeneity among the older population does not preclude age—as with gender and ethnic minority status—from exerting political influence (Binstock and Day, 1996).

Although there is little evidence of old-age voting blocs, mass membership interest groups that cast themselves as "representatives" of older voters (e.g., AARP) generally have significant political influence. This occurs because policy makers find it useful and incumbent to invite them to participate in policy activities, and thus to reach older adults. The symbolic legitimacy that old-age organizations have for participation in interest group politics gives them power in the following ways:

- They have relatively easy informal access to public officials, members of Congress and their staffs, and administrative officials.
- Their legitimacy enables them to obtain public platforms in the national media, congressional

hearings, national conferences, and commissions dealing with issues affecting older adults.

- Mass membership groups can mobilize their members in large numbers to contact policy makers and register displeasure (Binstock and Quadagno, 2001).

"Senior citizens" have traditionally been a prime target of campaign efforts in critical states with large blocs of electoral votes, as vividly illustrated in the 2000 Presidential election in Florida. Both political parties strategize about how to target older adults, given their aggregate numerical importance as voters. In fact, an important form of power available to old-age interest groups is "the electoral bluff": the perception of being powerful is, in itself, a source of political influence, even though old-age organizations have been unable to swing a decisive bloc of older voters (Binstock and Quadagno, 2001).

COUNTERARGUMENT: OLDER PEOPLE DO NOT CONSTI-
TUTE A SIGNIFICANT AGE-BASED POLITICAL FORCE
Early critics of the subculture theory argue that the diversity of the older population precludes their having shared interests around which to coalesce. Most older people, especially the young-old, do not identify themselves as "aged," behave as an old-age-benefits voting bloc, or define problems as stemming from their age. Rather than a unified age group, they distribute their votes among candidates in roughly the same proportion as the electorate as a whole. In fact, it is difficult for those who identify on the basis of age to determine differences between candidates' positions on old-age-policy issues, since no candidate wants to alienate "the senior vote." In addition, older voters are not captives of any single political philosophy, party, or mass organization. In fact, some argue that "the elderly" is really a category created by policy analysts, pension officials, key political figures, and outdated models of interest-group politics and not a sound basis for political mobilization (Hudson, 2007). Since age is only one of many personal characteristics,

it cannot predict political behavior or age-group consciousness based on differential access to resources. Nor are these self-interests or old-age policy issues the most important factors in elders' electoral decisions (Binstock and Quadagno, 2001; Hudson, 2006).

Instead, differences by socioeconomic class, ethnic minority status, gender, and religion increasingly influence older people's political interests (Hudson, 2006). For example, upper- and lower-income older adults are not unified on Social Security or Medicare, since some older people have more at stake than others in proposals to reduce, maintain, or enhance benefits. Another example of voting on the basis of age identity is that older people are rarely unified about issues affecting the young, such as school levies, and do not vote as a bloc against increasing property taxes to support public schools. Instead, they generally recognize the importance of education for economic productivity in the future. This example suggests that old-age–related issues are not necessarily more important than other issues, partisan attachments, or the characteristics of specific candidates. In fact, it appears that older and younger people are more likely to form alliances along economic, racial, ethnic, and ideological lines than to unite horizontally on the basis of age. **Generations United** is an umbrella organization composed of over 130 national organizations of different age groups and represents one such vertical intergenerational coalition. Such organizations acknowledge the mutual interdependence of generations, suggesting common ground on which to build a more inclusive sense of community (Prisuta, 2004).

As examples of a cross-age, cross-class alliance, poor older people may work with younger welfare beneficiaries for health insurance for all ages. Middle-income people of all ages may come together around issues of climate change and preserving the environment for future generations. With threatened federal cuts to Medicare and Medicaid, subgroups of older people may become more politically organized in the future, with political agendas different from most of today's senior organizations, especially around issues of means-testing, higher eligibility ages for government benefits, and debates about privatizing of Medicare and Social Security.

HISTORICAL DEVELOPMENT OF AGE-BASED GROUPS   At first glance, the number, variety, and strength of age-based national organizations appear to support the perspective that older people are a powerful political force. Age-based organizations are able to build memberships, conduct policy analyses, marshal grassroots support, and utilize direct mail and political action. The first age-based politically oriented interest group grew out of the social and economic dislocations of the Depression. The Townsend Movement proposed a tax on all business transactions to finance a $200/month pension for every pensioner over age 60. However, passage of the Social Security Act in 1935, in which groups of older people played a supporting but not a leading role, took away the Townsend Movement's momentum, and the organization died out in the 1940s. Most political divisions during the turbulent period of the Depression were class- and labor-based rather than age-based. The Townsend Movement did demonstrate, however, that old age could be a short-term basis for organizing (Binstock and Day, 1996). New Deal legislation on behalf of older people (e.g., Old Age Insurance) owed its birth to the hardships of the Great Depression,

President Roosevelt's leadership, and reformers' invoking the plight of older people as a strategy for introducing social insurance, not to the influence of an organized bloc of older people (Hudson, 2007). The McClain Movement, another early age-based organization, aimed to establish financial benefits for older persons through a referendum in the 1938 California elections, but lost followers after economic conditions improved in the 1940s. These early groups nevertheless furnished older people with a collective voice and identity.

Organized interest groups representing older people did not re-emerge until the 1950s and 1960s. Even so, the passage of Medicare in 1965 was due more to key political leaders than to the political influence of older people. However, the presence of successful public policies galvanized elders into a self-identified political constituency and created the political base to advocate for aging network services. Over 1000 separately organized groups for older adults now exist at the local, state, and national levels, with approximately 100 major national organizations involved in political action on behalf of older persons (Hudson, 2007; Walker, 2006). In many ways, the diversity of the older population is reflected in the variety of organizations themselves, ranging from mass membership groups to nonmembership staff organizations and associations of professionals or service providers. Yet, the very diversity of these groups reduces their potential to act together as a unified bloc. For example, the National Caucus for the Black Aged, National Hispanic Council on Aging, and National Indian Council on Aging were created to address political inequities facing specific groups of elders of color. They may not act in concert with each other or with organizations such as the **American Association of Retired Persons** (AARP) that represent primarily a white, middle-class constituency.

Three of the largest *mass-membership organizations* are the **National Council of Senior Citizens (NCSC)**, the **National Association of**

A NEW IMAGE FOR AARP

AARP ads feature themes such as "Age is just a number, and life is what you make it" or "You're ready to make this the time of your life. We help make it happen." A cover of AARP's magazine promised "Great Sex," and carried a picture of actress Susan Sarandon wearing a deep V-necked sweater.

Retired Federal Employees (NARFE), and the AARP. NCSC was developed by organized labor in the early 1960s with the objective of passing Medicare. It now is composed of over 2000 senior clubs and sponsors housing for low-income elders and persons with disabilities. NARFE was also formed for a specific political purpose—the passage of the Federal Employees Pension Act in the 1920s. It has since concentrated on bread-and-butter issues for federal employees, such as labor/management relations, rather than broader political issues affecting older persons generally.

The best known and largest of these organizations is **AARP,** which began in 1958 with a small number of older adults working to provide a special group health insurance program. It now has grown to a membership of over 35 million encompassing nearly 50 percent of the nation's population over age 50, and over 13 percent of the population generally. Now using only its acronym rather than its full name, AARP seeks to recruit the young-old and baby boomers who may not consider themselves to be retirees or old. In fact, the minimum age of membership has been lowered from 55 to 50. It has merged its two magazines—*My Generation* for adults ages 50 to 59 and *Modern Maturity* for those older than 60 into *The Magazine,* which does not make age explicit on the cover. An assumption of this merger is that both the young-old and the old-old (who may be their parents) share interests related to health, financial security, and travel. Nevertheless, AARP continues to publish three slightly different versions of *The Magazine* to appeal to cohorts in their 50s, 60s, and beyond. It is also published in Spanish to reach out to the rapidly growing young-old Latino population. In addition, AARP spends millions to advertise in popular magazines such as *Time* and *Newsweek* with ads of healthy, robust, and often physically attractive older adults. In a similar spirit, they now sponsor 10 K runs, marathons, a wide range of fitness activities and adventure travel. Such ads and "repackaging" reflect AARP's recognition of the huge market for their products with the baby boomers. In fact, by 2010, over 50 percent of all AARP members will be boomers.

Members are attracted by the benefits of lower-cost health insurance, credit cards, travel, rental car discounts, discount prescriptions by mail, and a myriad of other services, available to members for the current membership fee of only $12.50 a year. AARP has had a substantial impact on policies and practices for older adults, most recently through its support of the 2003 Prescription Drug Coverage Bill, Medicare Part D. As noted in Chapter 17, AARP was seen as responding to drug company and insurance interests in their support of Part D. Critics contend that AARP has moved away from advocacy on behalf of the older population and has become a big business that markets products and services. In addition, AARP is now joining with nonaging organizations, such as the Child Welfare League and Generations United, to address issues related to grandparenting and kinship care. They are committed to intergenerational programming as well, most visibly evidenced by their national partnership with Big Brothers/Big Sisters.

A wide range of trade associations, professional societies, and coalitions concerned with

---

SERVICES OFFERED BY AARP

- free tax preparation services
- peer grief and loss counseling
- legal council for older adults
- driver safety course
- classes in personal safety
- money management program
- home, auto, and life insurance
- mobile home insurance
- Grandparent Information Center
- AARP Health Care Options (supplemental health insurance)
- legal services network
- fraud prevention courses

aging issues also exists. *Trade associations* include:

- American Association of Homes and Services for the Aged (AAHSA)
- American Nursing Home Association (ANHA)
- National Council of Health Care Services (NCHCS), consisting of commercial enterprises in the long-term care industry, such as the nursing home subsidiary of major hotel chains
- National Association of State Units in Aging (NASUA), which is composed of administrators of state area agencies on aging

Trade associations work to obtain federal funds and influence the development of regulations for long-term care facilities and service delivery. Two *professional associations* active in aging policy issues, the **Gerontological Society of America (GSA)** (which now also encompasses the **Association for Gerontology in Higher Education**) and **American Society on Aging (ASA)**, are composed primarily of gerontological researchers, educators, and practitioners from many disciplines. The major confederation of social welfare agencies concerned with aging is National Council on Aging (NCOA), which encompasses over 2000 organized affiliates, including public and private health, social work, and community action agencies.

Several organizations that began at the grassroots level now have nationwide membership and recognition. The **Older Women's League (OWL)**, founded in 1981, brings together people concerned about issues affecting older women, especially health care and insurance, Social Security, pensions, and caregiving. It advocates for older women both in the federal policy-making process and within the programs of national associations such as the GSA. Women activists within OWL represent a trend away from the comparatively lower rates of past political participation among older women. The **Gray Panthers,** founded by the late Maggie Kuhn, aims to form grassroots intergenerational alliances around issues affecting all ages. Since Maggie Kuhn's death, the Gray Panthers' visibility has declined, but they are still involved in social change related to cross-generational issues.

On certain issues such as health care reform, the influence of organizations of older people has been limited relative to powerful interest groups such as the insurance, medical, and pharmaceutical industries. For example, none of President Clinton's 1997 appointments to the National Bipartisan Commission on the Future of Medicare represented organized old-age interests (Binstock, 2000). Accordingly, pharmaceutical and insurance companies and private managed care organizations exerted more influence on the 2003 Medicare Prescription Drug Bill than did older adults. Nevertheless, until recently, most politicians did not want to offend age-based organizations and constituencies. After higher-income older people organized to influence Congress to repeal the 1988 Medicare Catastrophic Coverage Act that would have benefited low-income elders, no proposals concerning older adults emerged from committees in the next Congressional election year.

Whether older people act as a unified bloc or not, many policy makers act as if there were a "politics of age" founded on cohort-based interest groups, and politicians continue to count elders' votes. Presidential candidates in the 2000 election actively courted the senior vote, advocating widely different proposals for Social Security and prescription drug coverage. Even if older people cannot affect the passage of legislation, they are seen as blocking changes in existing policies, especially when programs such as Social Security and Medicare are threatened. Perceptions of such influence then affect the feasibility of major changes in policies on aging, even though the political legitimacy of old-age interest groups has eroded over the past decade (Binstock, 2000; Hudson, 2006).

POLITICAL ACTIVISM AND OLDER WOMEN

Tish Sommers is an example of the increasing political activism of older women. Sommers, a long-time homemaker, learned about the vulnerability of older women when she was divorced at age 57. She found that newly single homemakers her age had a hard time getting benefits that people who have been employed take for granted. She coined the term *displaced homemaker* and built a force of women. They successfully lobbied for centers where displaced homemakers had job training during the late 1970s. In 1980, she and Laurie Shields founded the Older Women's League (OWL), a national organization that has grown to over 14,000 members and over 100 chapters. Her maxim was "Don't agonize, organize." During the 6 years of organizing OWL, Sommers also fought a battle with cancer. Even at her death in 1986, she was still fighting, organizing groups nationally around the right to maintain control over end-of-life care.

Some national age-based organizations are viewed as being biased toward the interests of middle- and upper-working-class older people. AARP, for example, has been criticized for advancing only the interests of its primarily middle-class membership, for recruiting members largely on the basis of selective incentives and direct member services (e.g., insurance, drug discounts, and travel, and for imposing its policy agenda on its members). In recent years, however, age-based organizations have not only reached out to lower-income older persons, but also collaborated with other groups. This is reflected by the cross-age coalitions that have formed around health and long-term care. In addition to national associations, a wide range of organizations at the local and state levels have mobilized around intergenerational and cross-class issues such as affordable public transportation, environmental issues, safe streets, and low-cost health care.

In sum, despite the growth of age-based organizations, the senior-power model appears to have little validity with respect to older adults'

voting behavior and political attitudes. Old age per se is currently not a primary basis for political mobilization, despite images of homogenous senior groups put forth by politicians, the media, and age-based organizations. With regard to the future, we can predict that the senior boomers will cast a higher total vote in national elections than voting rates today; on the other hand, the heterogeneity of the baby boom cohort suggests that age will not form the primary basis for political behavior (Binstock, 2000; Hudson, 2006). Cross-generational alliances are likely to be most important in influencing policies and programs, as further discussed in Chapters 16 and 17.

Implications for the Future

As they have moved through life, boomers have continued to reshape many of the social conventions around marriage and family, parenting, and workplace behavior. Entering old age with greater economic resources than prior cohorts, they will shape new paradigms of work, productivity, and retirement. They also will seek opportunities that provide them with a sense of meaning and purpose. Baby boomers' ability to earn more during their lifetimes results from economic and demographic shifts, such as deferred marriage, reduced and later child-bearing, increased labor force participation of women, higher levels of educational attainment, and greater investments. For example, they have acquired real estate more than prior cohorts; 36 percent of homeowners age 50 to 60 report that the equity in their primary residences totals 51 to 100 percent of their total household worth (Harney, 2006). At the same time, because of low birth rates in the cohorts following baby boomers, businesses in the next two decades will face a shortage of skilled workers. More people over age 70 are likely to choose to continue to be employed, preferably on a part time basis, or may pursue second or third careers. This will reflect a relatively new concept of "bridge jobs" to retain older workers, offer them new experiences, and provide work/life flexibility between careers or before they leave the paid work-force permanently (Harvard/MetLife, 2004). Senior boomers will also benefit from the full lifting of the Social Security cap on outside earnings, which will allow them to continue working without financial penalty. Their continued employment may reflect their limited confidence about their financial futures and concerns about outliving their retirement savings, in part because they typically borrowed more and saved less than their parents. Despite their greater lifetime earnings and extensive equity in real estate than prior cohorts, 75 percent in a recent survey of baby boomers reported that they do not feel financially prepared to retire and that they expect to keep working, health permitting (Harney, 2006).

The numbers of economically vulnerable elders will not diminish dramatically. Instead, a permanent underclass of boomers is projected, with disproportionate representation of African Americans and Latinos, those with a sporadic employment history, single women, and the poorly educated. This pattern is unlikely to change without interventions earlier in the life course to prevent poverty and chronic illness, and ensure educational and employment opportunities in young adulthood and middle age.

Retirement will continue not to be a single irreversible event. Instead, more adults will change careers two or three times throughout their lives and move in and out of the workforce. They will cycle between periods of work and leisure well beyond age 65. The retirement transition will be eased by businesses that provide sabbaticals, extended vacations and leaves, retraining programs, and career-development alternatives. Educational opportunities will become more accessible through distance-learning formats that use information-based technology. Such educational options benefit employees by allowing them to explore new careers and volunteer and leisure interests. This in turn can prevent job burnout or boredom, so that early retirement is not perceived as the only viable option. Incentives to encourage

people to work longer are a pragmatic response to the projected labor shortage, especially in the service sector. Although more companies are beginning to modify the workplace in order to retain older workers longer, such workplace modifications do not adequately meet the growing interest in part-time employment. The economic downturn and high unemployment of the early part of this century has also adversely affected efforts to retrain and retain older workers, especially when it is more cost-efficient to encourage their early retirement and hire lower-paid younger workers. As illustrated in the box on page 488, more companies are developing innovative ways such as flexible hours and telecommuting, to recruit and retain boomers with many years of expertise.

From a societal perspective, a work-retirement continuum for a population with a longer life expectancy requires modifying our expectations regarding lifelong education and training. Changing societal values about the "appropriate age" for education, employment, retirement, and leisure demand a reexamination of employment policies and norms. The traditional linear life cycle of education for the young, employment for the middle aged, and retirement for the old is already undergoing major changes. This is occurring as more middle-aged and older persons enter college for the first time, move into new careers, or begin their studies for graduate or professional degrees. Other countries provide models for reconceptualizing work and retirement. A "gliding out" plan of phased retirement in Japan and some European countries permits a gradual shift into a part-time schedule. Some Scandinavian countries give workers year-long sabbaticals every 10 years as a time to reevaluate their careers or to take a break instead of working straight through to retirement. Jobs can also be restructured, gradually allowing longer vacations, shorter workdays, and more opportunities for community involvement during the preretirement working years. Barriers to such changes in our society, however, include the fact that

Americans have fewer vacation days than any other Western industrialized society and tend to work more days per week. On the other hand, movement in and out of the workforce and new retirement options may come to be viewed as legitimate alternatives for both men and women because of the following factors:

- increasing numbers of career-oriented women who are committed to an ideology of shared family responsibilities, with a modest increase in the number of fathers who share or assume primary responsibility for child care
- growing awareness of the possibility of two or three careers over the life course
- younger generations who are less likely to compartmentalize employment and leisure, and who are more open to modified work schedules, job sharing, and phased retirement
- increasing numbers of retirees who work part-time and also volunteer
- growing corporate awareness of employee needs, such as on-the-job exercise and fitness programs, child care, staff training, and counseling.

To some extent, these factors reflect a shift from the traditional 40-plus-hours a week work ethic to a more balanced view of employment and leisure. Future cohorts of older adults may view leisure in retirement merely as a continuation of prior non-work activities and not regard it as a new stage in life. Integration of leisure and other nonpaid activities across the life course will undoubtedly smooth the transition to retirement for those who had the economic resources to enjoy leisure throughout their lives.

Whether the economy will create such work and leisure alternatives is unclear. Many new jobs are in the service sector (e.g., health and social services, food, and recreation) rather than in manufacturing. Many of these jobs cannot provide older workers with financial security. Whether technological advances will produce new jobs or result in net job losses is also unknown. What is certain is greater labor market diversity among the older population and greater variations in the reasons for retirement, unemployment, and economic well-being. Definitions of the nature of work, family, careers, and retirement will gradually reshape cultural and organizational expectations.

The concept of the *Third Age* moves beyond focusing only on employment roles; instead, it denotes the stage in life that occurs after middle age but before the final stage, and is conceptualized as a time of continued involvement and development in areas of life beyond employment and family. This concept is congruent with the broad perspective of productivity, discussed throughout this chapter, which seeks new ways to develop and use our human potential in old age. The vitality of the older population must be recognized as a way to involve their skills and wisdom through both paid and unpaid positions for the benefit of society and of older adults themselves. Increasingly, questions will be raised about how work should be defined and contributions measured. Advocates of a productive aging society point to the need to place a real value on unpaid volunteer and caregiving activities. Volunteer effort may be perceived as contributing more to the common good than paid work and therefore as deserving greater rewards than currently exist. However, flexible options for productive activity by older adults are unevenly distributed across all sectors of society. Therefore, initiatives to encourage volunteerism and other types of unpaid productive contributions must occur within a broader framework that seeks to eliminate economic inequities across the life course and in old age. On the other hand, a national survey of boomers found that they did not envision civic engagement in their retirement years, and felt they deserved time to do whatever they wanted (Prisuta, 2004).

These changes in work, retirement, and productivity will require new skills and knowledge among social and health care providers and planners of services for older adults. Preretirement counseling, lifelong distance learning opportunities, career development and retraining programs, and expanded volunteer programs all pose new roles for gerontological practitioners and researchers. Professionals and laypersons alike will be challenged to reconceptualize the use of time and human resources, given reduced rates of disability and increased longevity.

Summary

Paid employment is typically associated with productivity in our society. While early retirement was the norm for the past five decades, more older adults are continuing to be employed, often in multiple careers. Health status, income, and attitudes toward the job influence decisions about when to retire. Most retirees adjust well to this important transition and are satisfied with the quality of their lives. Those with good health, higher-status jobs, adequate income, and existing social networks and leisure interests are most likely to be satisfied. Not all retirement is desired, however; many older people would prefer the opportunity for part-time work, but are unable to find suitable and flexible options. Preparation for the retirement transition is beneficial, but planning assistance is generally not available to those who need it most—workers who have less education, lower job status, and lower retirement incomes. Retirement by itself does not cause poor health or loss of identity and self-esteem. Dissatisfaction in this stage of life is more often due to poor health and low income.

Although a smaller percentage of older people have incomes below the poverty line than was true in the past, more older than younger people live at marginal economic levels. In addition to older adults who are officially counted as living below the poverty line, many others live near this level, and many are "hidden" poor who live in nursing homes or with their families. Frail, unmarried women—especially older African American women—are the most likely to live in or near poverty. Public assistance programs such as SSI have not removed the very serious financial problems of the older poor. Social Security is the major source of retirement income for a large proportion of the older population; those who depend on Social Security alone are the poorest group. Private pensions tend to be small in relation to previous earnings, are subject to attrition through inflation, and go primarily to workers in large, unionized, or industrialized settings. Income from assets is distributed unequally among the older population, with a small number of older persons receiving sizable amounts from savings and investments. The most common asset of older people is their home, which provides no immediate income.

As earlier chapters documented, changes in employment and parenting roles, income, and physical and cognitive capacities often have detrimental social consequences for older adults. Nevertheless, there are arenas in which older people may still experience meaningful involvement and develop new opportunities and skills, consistent with the broader definition of productive aging that includes nonpaid contributions to society. This chapter has considered six of these arenas: leisure pursuits, voluntary association membership, volunteering and civic engagement, education, religious involvement, and political activity. The meaning and functions of participation in these arenas are obviously highly individualized. Participation may be a means to strengthen and build informal social networks, influence wider social policies, serve other persons, and substitute new roles for old. The extent of involvement is influenced not by age alone, but also by a variety of other salient factors including gender, ethnic minority status, health, social class, and educational level.

Because of the number of interacting variables, age-related patterns in participation are not clearly defined. There are some general age-related differences in types of leisure pursuits; with increasing age, people tend to engage in more sedentary, inner-directed, and routine pursuits in their homes rather than social activities or obligations outside the home. Changes in organizational participation and volunteering are less clearly age-related. Participation in voluntary associations stabilizes or declines only slightly with old age; declines that do occur are associated with poor health, inadequate income, and transportation problems. Volunteering, which is higher among today's older population than other age groups, tends to represent a lifelong pattern of community service that peaks in middle age.

Past research on religious and political participation has pointed inaccurately to declines in old age. Although formal religious participation such as church or synagogue attendance appears to diminish slightly, other activities such as reading religious texts, listening to religious broadcasts, and praying increase. Religiosity appears to be an effective way of coping, particularly among ethnic minority elders. Spirituality is differentiated from religion as a positive and broader factor in older people's physical and mental well-being and their quality of life.

Voting by older people has increased since the 1980s. Declines in voting and political participation in the past may have been a function of low educational status or physical limitations, not age per se. In fact, older persons' skills and experiences may be more valued in the political arena than in other spheres. The extent to which older people form a unified political bloc that can influence politicians and public policy is debatable. Some argue that older adults form a subculture with a strong collective consciousness; others point to their increasing diversity and political inequity, as apparent in the number of elders critical of AARP's support of Medicare Part D.

Most forms of organizational involvement appear to represent stability across the life course; the knowledge and skills necessary for a varied set of activities in old age are generally developed in early or middle adulthood and maintained into later life. On the other hand, preretirement patterns of productivity are not fixed. Individuals can develop new interests and activities in later life, often with the assistance of senior centers, continuing education programs, and community or special interest organizations.

GLOSSARY

Age Discrimination in Employment Act (ADEA) federal law that protects workers age 45 and over from denial of employment strictly because of age

American Association of Retired Persons (AARP) national organization open to all adults age 50 and over, offering a wide range of informational materials, discounted services and products, and a powerful political lobby

American Society on Aging (ASA) association of practitioners and researchers interested in gerontology

assets an individual's savings, home equity, and personal property

Association for Gerontology in Higher Education (AGHE) the only national membership organization devoted primarily to gerontological education

civic engagement active participation in one's community by voting, volunteering, joining community groups

Civic Ventures an organization that provides resources for civic engagement and awards to innovators and agencies working for the common good

displaced homemakers widowed or divorced women under age 60 who do not yet qualify for Social Security benefits but may lack the skills for employment

Elderhostel program in which older adults can take inexpensive, short-term academic courses associated with colleges and universities around the world

Employment Retirement Income Security Act (ERISA) 1974 legislation to regulate pensions

Experience Corps trains adults age 55 and older to serve in inner-city schools

feminization of poverty a variety of factors that lead to higher proportions of poverty among women than men

Foster Grandparents Program volunteer program pairing seniors with children with special needs

Generations United a national intergenerational coalition, involving AARP, the Child Welfare League, and the Children's Defense Fund

Gerontological Society of America (GSA)   an association of researchers, educators, and practitioners interested in gerontology and geriatrics

Gray Panthers   a national organization, founded by Maggie Kuhn, which encourages intergenerational alliances around social issues

National Association of Retired Federal Employees (NARFE)   national organization of adults retired from the federal government, primarily involved in political and social issues

National Council of Senior Citizens (NCSC)   mass-membership organization involved in political action for older adults

National Council on the Aging (NCOA)   national organization of over 2000 social welfare agencies concerned with aging that provides technical consultation and is involved in federal legislative activities

Older Women's League (OWL)   a national advocacy organization, concerned about issues affecting older women

Retired Senior Volunteer Program (RSVP)   federally sponsored program that places older adult volunteers in a wide range of service settings

retirement   the period of life, usually starting between age 60 and 65, during which an individual stops working in the paid labor force

Senior Community Services Employment Program (SCSEP)   programs sponsored by the federal government that provide subsidies for non-profit groups and businesses to employ older workers

Senior Companion Program   a volunteer program in which seniors receive a stipend to assist homebound elders

senior learning programs   academic programs specially designed for older adults, or programs of tuition waivers that allow older adults to take college courses at no cost

Senior Net   national educational program that teaches older adults computer skills and provides opportunities for on-line communication

Social Security   federal program into which workers contribute a portion of their income during adulthood and then, beginning sometime between age 62 and 65, receive a monthly check based on the amount they have earned and contributed

spirituality   believing in one's relationship with a higher power without being religious in the sense of organized religion

Supplemental Security Income (SSI)   federal program to provide a minimal income for low-income older people (and other age groups with disabilities)

vesting of pension benefits   length of time a person must work on a job in order to acquire rights to a pension

RESOURCES

Log on to MySocKit (www.mysockit.com) for information about the following:

- Action
- American Association of Retired Persons (AARP)
- American Society on Aging (ASA)
- Association for Gerontology in Higher Education (AGHE)
- Elderhostel
- Federal Council on Aging
- Generations United
- Gerontological Society of America (GSA)
- Grey Panthers
- National Association of Retired Federal Employees (NARFE)
- National Council on Aging (NCOA)
- National Council of Senior Citizens (NCSC)
- National Senior Citizens Education and Research Center (NSCERC)
- The Leadership Council of Aging Organizations

REFERENCES

Achenbaum, A. Civic ventures: Looking backward, planning forward. *Public Policy and Aging Report*, 2007, 16, 9–12.

Aday, R.H. *Identifying important linkages between successful aging and senior center participation.* Presented at the joint conference of the National Council on Aging and American Society of Aging, Chicago, Illinois. March 12, 2003.

Administration on Aging (AOA). *Profile of Older Americans: 2005*. Washington, DC: Author, 2005.

American Association of Retired Persons (AARP). *Enhancing volunteerism among aging boomers*. Washington, DC: AARP, 2003a.

American Association of Retired Persons (AARP). *Staying ahead of the curve: The AARP work and career study*. Washington, DC: AARP, 2002.

American Association of Retired Persons (AARP). *Baby boomers envision retirement II: Survey of boomers' expectations for retirement*. Washington, DC: AARP, 2004.

American Association of Retired Persons (AARP). *Boomers turning 60*. Washington, DC: AARP, 2006.

American Society on Aging. *Atlantic philanthropies supports ASA's new project to promote civic engagement. ASA Connections* Newsletter. Accessed December 30, 2005, from http://www.asaaging.org/asaconnection/05mar/top.cfm.

Angel, R., and Angel, J. Diversity and aging in the United States. In R. Binstock and L.K. George (Eds.), *Handbook of aging and the social sciences*. (6th ed). New York: Academic Press, 2006.

Atchley, R.C. *The sociology of retirement*. New York: Wiley/Schenkman, 1976.

Barusch, A.S. Religion, adversity and age: Religious experiences of low income elderly women. *Journal of Sociology and Social Welfare*, 1999, *26*, 125–142.

Benjamin, M., Musick, M., Gold, D., and George, L.K. Age-related declines in activity level: The relationship between chronic illness and religious activities, *Journals of Gerontology*, 2003, *58B*, S377–S385.

Binstock, R.H. Some thoughts on a faith-based initiative in long-term care. *Public Policy and Aging Report*, 2002, *12*, 20–22.

Binstock, R.H. Older people and voting participation: Past and future. *The Gerontologist*, 2000, *40*, 18–31.

Binstock, R.H. Older voters and the 2004 election. *The Gerontologist*, 2006, *46*, 382–384.

Binstock, R.H., and Day, C.L. Aging and politics. In R.H. Binstock and L.K. George (Eds.), *Handbook of aging and the social sciences* (4th ed.). San Diego, CA: Academic Press, 1996.

Binstock, R.H., and Quadagno, J. Aging and politics. In R.H. Binstock and L.K. George (Eds.), *Aging and the social sciences* (5th ed.). San Diego: Academic Press, 2001.

Birren, J. Psychological implications of productive aging. In N. Morrow-Howell, J. Hinterlong, and M. Sherraden (Eds.), *Productive aging: Concepts and challenges* (5th ed.). Baltimore: Johns Hopkins University Press, 2001.

Black, H.K. Life as gift: Spiritual narratives of elderly African-American women living in poverty. *Journal of Aging Studies*, Winter 1999, *13*, 441–455.

Bosworth, H., Park, K., McQuoid, D., Hays, J., and Steffens, D. The impact of religious practice and religious coping on geriatric depression. *International Journal of Geriatric Psychiatry*, 2003, *18*, 905–914.

Brooks, R.G., and Koenig, H.G. Having faith in an aging health system:Policy perspectives. *Public Policy and Aging Report*, 2002, *12*, 23–26.

Bureau of Labor Statistics. *Volunteering in the United States*, U.S. Department of Labor, 2002.

Burnes, J., and Schulz, J.H. *Older women and private pensions in the United States*. Waltham, MA: National Center on Women and Aging, 2000.

Butrica, B., and Shaner, G. Satisfaction and engagement in retirement. *Perspectives on Productive Aging, 2, 2005*. Washington, DC: The Urban Institute, The Retirement Project, 2005.

Calasanti, T.M., and Slevin, K.F. A gender lens on old age. In *Gender, social inequalities and aging*. Walnut Creek, CA: Altamira Press, 2001.

Campbell, A. *How policies make citizens: Senior political activism and the American welfare state*. Princeton: Princeton University Press, 2002.

Campbell, A. Social and psychological determinants of voting behavior. In W. Donohue and C. Tibbits (Eds.), *Politics of age*. Ann Arbor: University of Michigan, 1962.

Canda, E. and Smith, E. (Eds.), *Transpersonal perspectives on spirituality in social work*. Binghamton, NY: Haworth Press, 2001.

Canda, E., Nakashama, M., and Furman, L. Ethical considerations about spirituality in social work: Insights from a national qualitative survey. *Families in Society*, 2004, *85*, 27–35.

Caudill, A. *Changing the retirement landscape—the Pension Protection Act of 2005*. Accessed February 1, 2007, from http://web.ebscohost.com/ehost/ pdf.

Chen, Y.P., and Scott, J. *Phased retirement. Who opts for it and toward what end?* AARP, 2006. Accessed February 7, 2007, http://assets.aarp.org/rgcenter/econ/2006.

Cnaan, R. *The invisible caring hand.* New York: New York University Press, 2002.

Cnaan, R., and Boddie, S. Charitable choice and faith-based welfare: A call for social work. *Social Work,* 2002, *47,* 224–235.

Cohen, G.D. *The mature mind: The positive power of the aging brain.* New York: Avon Books, 2005.

Cohen, G.C., Perlstein, S., Chapline, J. Kelly, J., Firth, K., et al., The impact of professionally conducted cultural programs on the physical health, mental health and social functioning of older adults. *The Gerontologist,* 2006, *46,* 726–734.

Corporation for National and Community Service. *2005 Key volunteer stats.* Washington, DC: CNCS, 2006. Accessed February 8, 2007, from http://www.nationalservice.org/pdf/VIA/VIA_key_stats.pdf.

Cutler, N.E., Whitelaw, N.A., and Beattie, B.L. *American perceptions of aging in the 21st century.* Washington DC: National Council on the Aging, Publication No. APA100, December 2002.

Cutler, S.J., and Hendricks, J. Age differences in voluntary association memberships: Fact or artifact. *Journals of Gerontology,* 2000, *55B,* S98–S107.

Davey, A., and Szinovacz, M.E. Dimensions of marital quality and retirement. *Journal of Family Issues,* 2004, *25,* 431–464.

DeLong, D. *Lost knowledge: Confronting the threat of an aging workforce.* New York: Oxford University Press, 2004.

DeNavas-Walt, C., Proctor, B., and Lee, C. Income, poverty and health insurance coverage in the United States: 2005. Washington, DC. U.S. Census Bureau, U.S. Government Printing Office, 2005.

Dentrea, P. The best or worst years of our lives? The effects of retirement and activity characteristics on well-being. *Dissertation Abstracts International, A: The Humanities and Social Sciences,* 1999, *60,* 1771A.

Dentrea, P. Retirement and mental health. *Journal of Aging and Health,* 2002, *14,* 167–194.

Dilworth-Anderson, P., Williams, S.W., and Cooper, T. Family caregiving to elderly African Americans: Caregiver types and structures. *Journals of Gerontology,* 1999, *54B,* S237–S241.

Eberly, D., and Streeter, R. *The soul of civil society: Voluntary associations and the public value of moral habits.* Lanham, MD: Lexington Books, 2002.

The Economist. Turning boomers into boomerangs. February 18, 2006, 65–67.

Ekerdt, D.J. The busy ethic: Moral continuity between work and retirement. *The Gerontologist,* 1986, *26,* 239–244.

Ekerdt, D.J., Kosloski, K., and DeViney, S. The normative anticipation of retirement by older workers. *Research on Aging,* 2000, *22,* 3–22.

Elderhostel. *Adventures in Lifelong Learning.* Accessed February 7, 2006, from http://www.elderhostel.org.

Emerman, J. On life's new stage—and its challenge to the field of aging. *Aging Today,* September–October, 2006, 3–4.

Estes, C., and Mahakian, J.L. The political economy of productive aging. In N. Morrow-Howell, J. Hinterlong, and M. Sherraden (Eds.), *Productive aging: Concepts and challenges.* Baltimore: Johns Hopkins University Press, 2001.

Fast, J., Dosman, D., and Moran, L. Productive activity up in later life. *Research on Aging,* 2006, *28,* 691–712.

Federal Interagency Forum on Aging-related Statistics. *Older Americans 2006: Key indicators of well-being.* Washington, DC: Federal Interagency Forum on Aging, 2006.

Flippen, C. Minority workers and pathways to retirement. In R. Hudson (Ed.), *The new politics of old age policy.* Baltimore: John Hopkins University Press, 2005, 129–156.

Freedman, M. Civic windfall? Realizing the promise in an aging America. *Generations,* 2002, *26,* 86–89.

Freedman, M. Structural lead: Building new institutions for an aging America. In N. Morrow-Howell, J. Hinterlong, and M. Sherraden (Eds.), *Productive aging: Concepts and challenges.* Baltimore: Johns Hopkins University Press, 2001.

Freedman, M., and Adler, R. Capturing the windfall: Older adults in the social sector workforce. *Elders as resources: Intergenerational strategies series.* Baltimore: Annie E. Casey Foundation, 2005.

Fried, L., Carlson, M., Freedman, M., Frick, K., and Glass, T., et al., A social model for health promotion for an aging population: Initial evidence on the Experience Corps model. *Journal of Urban Health,* 2004, *81,* 64–78.

Gallo, W.T., Bradley, E.H., Siegel, M., and Kasl, S.V. Health effects of involuntary job loss among older workers: Findings from the health and retirement survey. *Journals of Gerontology,* 2000, *55B,* S131–S140.

Gallup Poll. *Poll topics and trends: Religion.* March 18–20, 2002b. Accessed July 1, 2002, from http://www.gallup.com/poll/topics/religion2.asp.

Gallup Poll. *Religion most important to Blacks, women and older Americans* 2006. Accessed February 7, 2007, from http://www.gallup.com/poll/topics.

Gartland, J.P. (2001). *Senior volunteer participation: An effective means to improve life satisfaction.* Report prepared for the Corporation for Community National service. Accessed February 6, 2007, from http://www.nationalservice.org/jobs/fellowships/2000–01.html.

George, L.K. The links between religion and health: Are they real? *Public Policy and Aging Report,* 2002, *12,* 3–6.

Gerontological Society of America. Press release: *The Gerontological Society of America announces initiative on civic engagement in older Americans.* Accessed December 30, 2005, from http://www.geron.org/press/engagement.htm.

Gist, J. Population aging, entitlement growth and the economy. ARRP. Accessed February 1, 2007, from http://assets/aarp.org/rgcenter/econ/2007_01_security.pdf.

Greenfield, E., and Marks, N. Continuous participation in voluntary groups as a protective factor for the psychological well-being of adults who develop functional limitations: Evidence from the National Survey of Families and Households. *Journals of Gerontology,* 2007, *62B,* S60–S68.

Greenfield, E., and Marks, N. Formal volunteering as a protective factor for older adults' psychological well-being. *Journals of Gerontology,* 2004, *59B,* S258–S264.

Hardy, M. Older workers. In R. Binstock and L. George (Eds.), *Handbook of aging and the social sciences* (6th ed.). New York: Academic Press, 2006.

Hardy, M. The transformation of retirement in 20th century America. *Generations,* 2002, *26,* 9–16.

Harney, K. Study finds boomers bigger on real estate. *The Seattle Times,* October 22, 2006, E1, E6.

Harris, A., and Thoresen, C. Volunteering is associated with delayed mortality in older people: Analysis of the longitudinal study of aging. *Journal of Health Psychology,* 2005, *10,* 739–752.

Harvard School of Public Health/MetLife Foundation. *Reinventing aging: Baby boomers and civic engagement,* Harvard School of Public Health, Center for Health Communication, 2004.

Hays, J., Meador, K., Branch, P., and George, L. The Spiritual History Scale in four dimensions (SHS-4): Validity and reliability. *The Gerontologist,* 2001, *41,* 239–249.

Heinz, T., Lewis, J., and Hounsell, C. *Women and pensions: An overview.* Washington, DC: Women's Institute for a Secure Retirement (WISER), 2006.

Hendricks, J., and Cutler, S.J. Volunteerism and socioemotional selectivity in later life. *Journals of Gerontology,* 2004, *59B,* S251–S257.

Herd, P. Crediting care or marriage: Reforming Social Security family benefits. *Journals of Gerontology,* 2006, *61B,* S24–S34.

Hinterlong, J., Morrow-Howell, N., and Sherraden, M. Productive aging: Principles and perspectives. In N. Morrow-Howell, J. Hinterlong, and M. Sherraden (Eds.), *Productive aging: Concepts and challenges.* Baltimore: Johns Hopkins University Press, 2001.

Hipple, S. *Self-employment in the United States: An update.* Bureau of Labor Statistics Monthly Labor Review, 2004. Accessed February 6, 2007, from http://www.bls.gov/opub/mlr/2004/07/art2full.pdf.

Hirsch, B., Macpherson, D., and Hardy, M. Occupational age structure and access for older workers. *Industrial and Labor Relations Review,* 2000, *53,* 401–418.

Hodge, D. The intrinsic spirituality scale: A new six-item instrument for assessing the salience of spirituality as a motivational construct. *Journal of Social Service Research,* 2003, *31,* 41–61.

Hodge, D. Working with Hindu clients in a spiritually sensitive manner. *Social Work,* 2004, *49,* 27–38.

Hollingsworth, B. Retirees who don't. *The Seattle Times,* November 10, 2002, H1.

Holstein, M., and Minkler, M. Self, society and the "new gerontology." *The Gerontologist,* 2003, *43,* 787–796.

Holstein, M. A critical reflection on civic engagement. *Public Policy and Aging Report,* 2007, *16,* 21–26.

Hudson, R. Terms of engagement: The right and left look at elder civic activism. *Public Policy and Aging Report,* 2007, *16,* 17–18.

Hudson, R.B. Religion and health: Legal and policy implications. *Public Policy and Aging Report,* 2002, *12,* 2.

Hudson, R.B. The 2005 White House Conference on Aging: No Time for Seniors. *Public Policy and Aging Report,* 2006, *16,* 1–3.

Hutchens, R. *The Cornell Study of employer phased retirement policies: A report on key findings.* Ithaca, NY: Cornell University School of Industrial and Labor Relations, 2003.

Idler, E.L. The many causal pathways linking religion to health. *Public Policy and Aging Report,* 2002, *12,* 7–12.

Idler, E.L. Religion and aging. In R. Binstock and L.K. George, (Ed.), Religion and aging. *Handbook of aging and the social sciences* (6th ed.). New York: Academic Press, 2006.

Idler, E.L., Musick, M., Ellison, C., George, L., Krause, N. et al., Measuring multiple dimensions of religion and spirituality for health research. *Research on Aging,* 2003, *25,* 327–365.

Independent Sector. *Giving and volunteering in the United States, 2001.* Washington, DC: Independent Sector, 2002.

Independent Sector. *Giving answers,* 2006a. Accessed December 18, 2006, from http://www.giving answers.com/nmrd/nonprofitsectoroverview/ organizations/Independent.

Independent Sector. Research: *Value of volunteer time.* 2006b. Accessed December 18, 2006, from http://www.independentsector.org/[programs/ research/volunteer_time.html.

Ingersoll-Dayton, B., Krause, N., and Morgan, D. Religious trajectories and transitions over the life course. *International Journal of Aging and Human Development,* 2002, 51–70.

Johnson, R., and Schaner, S. Value of unpaid activities by older Americans tops $160 billion per year. Washington, DC: The Urban Institute, *Perspectives on Productive Aging,* Brief No. 4, 2005.

Kasl, S.V., and Jones, B.A. The impact of job loss and retirement on health. In L.F. Berkman and I. Kawachi (Eds.), *Social epidemiology.* New York: Oxford University Press, 2000.

Keegan, C., Gross, S., Fisher, L., and Remez, S. *Boomers at midlife: The AARP life stage study.* Washington, DC: AARP, 2002.

Kessler, R.C., Mickelson, K.D., and Williams, D.R. The prevalence, distribution, and mental health correlates of perceived discrimination in the United States. *Journal of Health and Social Behavior,* 1999, *40,* 208–230.

Koenig, H.G. An 83-year-old woman with chronic illness and strong religious beliefs. *Journal of the American Medical Association,* 2002, *288,* 487–493.

Koenig, H.G., and Brooks, R.G. Religion, health, and aging: Implications for practice and public policy. *Public Policy and Aging Report,* 2002, *12,* 13–19.

Koenig, H.G., McCullough, M.E., and Larson, D.B. *Handbook of religion and health.* New York: Oxford University Press, 2001.

Korczyk, S. Is early retirement ending? AARP, 2004. Accessed February 7, 2007, from http://assets/ aarp.org/ rgcentre/post-import/2004.

Krause, N. Religious meaning and subjective well-being in late life. *Journals of Gerontology,* 2003, *58B,* S160–S170.

Krause, N., Ingersoll-Dayton, B., Liang, J., and Sugisawa, H. Religion, social support and health among Japanese elderly. *Journal of Health and Human Behavior,* 1999, *40,* 405–421.

Kuhn, M. *No stone unturned.* New York: Ballatine Books, 1991.

Kutner, G., and Love, J. *Time and money: An in-depth look at 45 + volunteers and donors.* Washington, DC: AARP, 2003.

Lahey, J. *Do older workers face discrimination? An Issue in Brief No. 3.* Chestnut Hill, MA: Center for Retirement Research at Boston College, 2005.

Lai, D. Use of senior center services by the elderly Chinese immigrants. *Journal of Gerontological Social Work,* 2001, *35,* 59–79.

Larrimore, W., Parker, M., and Crowther, M. Should clinicians incorporate positive spirituality into their practices: What does the evidence say? *Annals of Behavioral Medicine,* 2002, *24,* 69–73.

Lee, S. *Women and Social Security: Benefit types and eligibility.* Washington, DC: Institute for Women's Policy Research, 2005.

Lum, T., and Lightfoot, E. The effects of volunteering on the physical and mental health of older people. *Research on Aging*, 2005, 27, 31–55.

Manning, C. 104-year-old is a lifelong laborer. *The Seattle Times*, December 3, 2005, A15.

Marler, P., and Hadaway, C. 'Being religious' or 'being spiritual' in America: A zero sum proposition? *Journal for the Scientific Study of Religion*, 2002, 41, 289–300.

Martinson, M., and Minkler, M. Civic engagement and older adults: A critical perspective. *The Gerontologist*, 2006, 46, 318–324.

Mattis, J., and Jagers M. A relational framework for the study of religiosity and spirituality in the lives of African Americans. *Journal of Community Psychology*, 2001, 29, 519–539.

McCrea, J.M., Nichols, A., and Newman, S. (Eds.), *Intergenerational service-learning in gerontology: A compendium*. The Corporation for National Service, Generations Together, University Center for Social and Urban Research, University of Pittsburgh, 1998.

McLaughlin, D.K., and Jensen, L. Work history and U.S. elders' transitions into poverty. *The Gerontologist*, 2000, 40, 469–479.

Menec, V. The relation between everyday activities and successful aging: A 6-year longitudinal study. *Journals of Gerontology*, 2003, 58B, S74–S82.

Merrill Lynch. "The new retirement survey" from Merrill Lynch reveals how baby boomers will transform retirement. *Merrill Lynch News*, press release, February 22, 2005.

Miko, P., and Sanchez, M. Activity patterns of elderly Hispanic men. *Activities Adaptation and Aging*, 2001, 26, 1–12.

Miller, A., and Stark, R. Gender and religiousness: Can socialization explanations be saved? *American Journal of Sociology*, 2002, 107, 1399–1423.

Miller, W.R., and Thoresen, C.E. Spirituality, religion, and health: An emerging research field. *American Psychologist*, 2003, 58, 3–66.

Minkler, M. New challenges for gerontology. In E.W. Markson and L.A. Hollis-Sawyer (Eds.), *Intersections of aging: Readings in social gerontology*. Los Angeles, CA: Roxbury, 2000.

Moen, P. The gendered life course. In R. Binstock and L.K. George (Eds.), *Aging and the social sciences* (5th ed.). San Diego: Academic Press, 2001.

Moen, P. Midcourse: Reconfiguring careers and community service for a new life stage. *Contemporary Gerontology*, 2003, 9, 87–94.

Moen, P., Kim, J., and Hofmeister, H. Couples' work status transitions and marriage quality in late midlife. *Social Psychology Quarterly*, 2001, 64, 55–71.

Moody, H.R. Productive aging and the ideology of old age. In N. Morrow-Howell, J. Hinterlong, and M. Sherraden (Eds.), *Productive aging: Concepts and challenges*. Baltimore: Johns Hopkins University Press, 2001.

Moody, H.R. Productive aging and the ideology of old age. In N. Morrow-Howell (Ed.), *Perspectives on productive aging*. Baltimore: John Hopkins University Press, in press.

Moody, R. From successful aging to conscious aging. In M. Wykle, P. Whitehouse, and D. Morris (Eds.), *Successful aging through the life span*. New York: Springer, 2005.

Morrow-Howell, N., Hinterlong, J., Rozario, P., and Tang, F. The effects of volunteering on the well-being of older adults. *Journals of Gerontology*, 2003, 58B, S137–S146.

Morrow-Howell, N., Hinterlong, J., and Sherraden, M.W. *Productive aging: Concepts and challenges*. Baltimore: Johns Hopkins University Press, 2001.

Musick, M.A. Theodicy and life satisfaction among black and white Americans. *Sociology of Religion*, 2000, 61, 267–287.

Musick, M.A., and Wilson, J. Volunteering and depression: The role of psychological and social resources in different age groups. *Social Science and Medicine*, 2003, 56, 259–269.

National Academy on an Aging Society. *Who are retirees and older workers?* Data Profile. Washington, DC: June 2000.

National Center for Policy Analysis. *Annual Report of the Board of Trustees of the Federal Old age and Survivors' Insurance Trust Funds*. Washington, DC: 2003.

Nash, M., and Stewart, B. *Spirituality and social care: Contributing to personal and community well-being*. London: Jessica Kingsley, 2002.

Nelson-Becker, H. Meeting life challenges: A hierarchy of coping styles in African-American and Jewish elders. *Journal of Human Behavior in the Social Environment*, 2004, 10, 155–174.

Nelson-Becker, H., Religion and coping in older adults: A social work perspective. *Journal of Gerontological Social Work,* 2005a, *45,* 51–68.

Nelson-Becker, H. Development of a spiritual support scale for use with older adults. *Journal of Human Behavior in the Social Environment,* 2005b, *11,* 195–212.

Nelson-Becker, H., Nakashima, M., and Canda, E. Spirituality in professional helping interventions with older adults. In B. Berkman (Ed.), *Handbook of social work in health and aging.* New York: Oxford Press, 2006.

Nelson-Becker, H., Nakashima, M., and Canda, E. Spiritual assessment in aging: A framework for clinicians. *Journal of Gerontological Social Work,* 2007, *48,* 331–347.

Newson, R., and Kemps, E. General lifestyle activities as a predictor of current cognition and cognitive change in older adults: A cross-sectional and longitudinal examination. *Journals of Gerontology,* 2005, *60B,* P113–P120.

Older Women's League (OWL). *Social Security privatization: A false promise for women.* Washington, DC: Older Women's League, 2002.

Oman, D., and Thoresen, C.E. Does religion cause health? Different interpretations and diverse meanings. *Journal of Health Psychology,* 2002, *4,* 301–326.

Oman, D., Thoresen, C.E., and McMahon, K. Volunteerism and mortality among the community-dwelling elderly. *Journal of Health Psychology,* 1999, *4,* 301–316.

O'Neill, G., and Lindberg, B. *Civic engagement in an older America.* Gerontological Society of America. Accessed February 7, 2007, from www.agingsociety.org/agingsociety/Pages%20from%20GeronNLSept05.pdf.

O'Rand, A.M. When old age begins: Implications for health, work and retirement. In R. Hudson (Ed.), *The new politics of old age policy.* Baltimore: Johns Hopkins, 2005.

Pardasani, M. Senior centers: Focal points of community-based services for the elderly. *Activities, Adaptation and Aging,* 2004a, *28,* 27–44.

Pardasani, M. Senior centers: Increasing minority participation through diversification. *Journal of Gerontological Social Work,* 2004b, *43,* 41–56.

Pardasani, M. Senior Centers: Patterns of programs and services. *Dissertation Abstracts.* New York: Yeshiva University, 2003.

Pargament, K.I., Smith, B.W., Koenig, H.G., and Perez, L. Patterns of positive and negative religious coping with major life stressors. *Journal for the Scientific Study of Religion,* 1998, *37,* 710–724.

Peter D. Hart Research Associates. *Older Americans and volunteerism.* New York: Peter D. Hart Research Associates, 2002.

Powell, L., Shahabi, L., and Thorsesen, C. Religion and spirituality: Linkages to physical health. *American Psychologist,* 2003, *58,* 36–52.

Prisuta, R. Enhancing volunteerism among aging boomers. Harvard School of Public Health and MetLife. *Reinventing aging: Baby boomers and civic engagement.* Boston: Harvard School of Public health, Center for Health Communication, 2004.

Purcell, P., and Whitman, D. Income of Americans age 65 and older, 1969 to 2004. *Journal of Deferred Compensation,* 2006, *12,* 1–41.

Putnam, R. Bowling together. *The American Prospect,* 2002, 13, 3.

Putnam, R. *Democracies in flux.* New York: Oxford University Press, 2004.

Quadagno, J., and Hardy, M. Work and retirement. In R.H. Binstock and L.K. George (Eds.), *Handbook of aging and the social sciences* (4th ed.). San Diego, CA: Academic Press, 1996.

Quinn, J.F. *Retirement trends and patterns among older Americans.* Presentation to the Harvard School of Public Health—MetLife Foundation Conference on Baby Boomers and Retirement; Impact on Civic Engagement, Cambridge, MA, October 9, 2003.

Quinn, J.F., and Burkhauser, R.V. Labor market obstacles to aging productively. In S.A. Bass, F.G. Caro, and Y.P. Chen (Eds.), *Achieving a productive aging society.* Westport, CT: Auburn House, 1993.

Rank, M.R., and Hirschl, T.A. Estimating the proportion of Americans ever experiencing poverty during their elderly years. *Journals of Gerontology,* 1999, *54B,* S184–S193.

Reilly, S. Transforming aging: The civic engagement of adults 55+. *Public Policy and Aging Report,* 2007, *16,* 1, 3–8.

Richardson, V.E., and Barusch, A.S. Poverty and aging. In V.E. Richardson, and A.S. Barusch, *Gerontological practice for the twenty-first century.* New York: Columbia University Press, 2006, 338–354.

Rix, S.E. Work in the new retirement. *Public Policy and Aging Report*, 2006, *16*, 9–15.

Schaie, K., Krause, N., and Booth, A. (Eds.). *Religious influences on health and well-being in the elderly.* New York: Springer, 2004.

Seeman, T., Dubin, L., and Seeman, M. Religiosity/spirituality and health: A critical review of the evidence for biological pathways. *American Psychologist,* 2003, *58,* 53–63.

Siegel, M., Muller, C., and Honig, M. *The incidence of job loss: The shift from younger to older workers, 1981–1996.* New York: International Longevity Center, working paper no. 2000–03, December 2000.

Sherraden, M., Morrow-Howell, N., Hinterlong, J., and Rozario, P. Productive aging: Theoretical choices and directions. In N. Morrow-Howell, J. Hinterlong, and M. Sherraden (Eds.), *Productive aging: Concepts and challenges.* Baltimore: Johns Hopkins University Press, 2001.

Shmotkin, D., Blumstein, T., and Modan, B. Beyond keeping active: Concomitants of being a volunteer in old-old age. *Psychology and Aging,* 2003, *18,* 602–607.

Smith, D., and Moen, P. Retirement satisfaction for retirees and their spouses: Do gender and the retirement decision-making process matter? *Journal of Family Issues,* 2004, *25,* 262.

Smith, T., McCullough, M., and Poll, J. Religiousness and depression: Evidence for a main effect and the moderating influence of stressful life events. *Psychological Bulletin,* 2003, *129,* 614–636.

Social Security Administration (SSA). *Income of the Population 55 or older, 2004.* Washington, DC: Social Security Administration. SSA Publication No. 13–11871, 2006.

Streib, G., and Schneider, C.J. *Retirement in American society. Impact and process.* Ithaca, NY: Cornell University Press, 1971.

Szinovacz, M.E., and Davey, A. Honeymoons and joint lunches: Effects of retirement and spouse's employment on depressive symptoms. *Journals of Gerontology,* 2004a, *59B,* P233–P245.

Szinovacz, M.E., and Davey, A. Predictors of perceptions of involuntary retirement. *The Gerontologist,* 2005, *45,* 36–47.

Szinovacz, M.E. and Davey, A. Retirement transitions and spouse disability: Effects on depressive symptoms. *Journals of Gerontology,* 2004b, *59B,* S333–S342.

Szinovacz, M.E., and DeViney, S. The retiree identity: Gender and race differences. *Journals of Gerontology,* 1999, *54B,* S207–S218.

Taylor, R., Chatters, L., and Levin, J. *Religion in the lives of African Americans.* Thousand Oaks, CA: Sage, 2004.

Theiss-Morse, E., and Hibbing, J. Citizenship and civic engagement. *Annual Review of Political Science,* 2004, *8,* 227–249.

Urban Institute. *Work and retirement: Facts and figures.* Washington, DC: Urban Institute, 2006.

U.S. Census Bureau. *Annual demographic supplement. Current Population Survey.* Washington, DC: U.S. Government Printing Office, March 2002.

U.S. Census Bureau. *Income, poverty and health insurance coverage in the United States: 2004.* Washington, DC, 2004.

U.S. Census Bureau. *The older population in the United States: March 2002.* Washington, DC: U.S. Government Printing Office, April 2003a.

U.S. Census Bureau. *Current Population Survey, 2005 Annual Social and Economic Supplement.* Washington, DC, 2005.

U.S. Census Bureau. *Current Population Survey, 2006 Annual Social and Economic Supplement.* Accessed February 2, 2007, from http://pubdb3.census.gov/macro/032006/pov/new01_100_01.htm.

U.S. Census Bureau. *Reported voting and registration by race, Hispanic origin, sex and age groups: November 1964 to 2004.* Accessed July 7, 2005, from http://www.census.gov/population/www/socdemo/voting.html.

U.S. Congressional Budget Office. *The retirement prospects of the baby boomers.* Washington, DC: Congressional Budget Office, 2004a.

U.S Congressional Budget Office. *Retirement age and the need for saving.* Washington, DC: Congressional Budget Office, 2004b.

Van Hook, M., Hugen, B., and Aguilar, M. *Spirituality within religious traditions in social work practice.* Pacific Grove, CA: Brooks/Cole.

Van Ness, P., and Larson, D. Religion, senescence and mental health. The end of life is not the end of hope. *American Journal of Geriatric Psychiatry,* 2002, *10,* 386–397.

Van Willigen, M. Differential benefits of volunteering across the life course. *Journals of Gerontology,* 2000, *55B,* S308–S319.

Verghese, J., Lipton, R., Katz, M., Hall C., Derby, C., et al., Leisure activities and the risk of dementia in the elderly. *New England Journal of Medicine,* 2003, *348,* 2508–2516.

Verma, S.K. *Retirement plan coverage of boomers. Analysis of 2003 SIPP data.* AARP, 2006. Accessed February 1, 2007, from http://assets/aarp.org/rgcenter/econ/sipp_cb_2006.pdf.

Wacker, R., Roberto, K., and Piper, L. *Community resources for older adults* (2nd ed.). Thousand Oaks, CA: Pine Forge Press. 2003.

Walker, A. Aging and politics: An international perspective. In R.H. Binstock and L.K. George (Eds.), *Handbook of aging and the social sciences* (6th ed.). San Diego: Academic Press, 2006.

Wan, H., Sengupta, M., Velkoff, V., and DeBarros, K. U.S. Census Bureau, *Current Population Reports, P23–209, 65+ in the United States: 2005.* Washington, DC: U.S. Government Printing Office, 2005.

Wilson, L., and Simpson, S. (Eds.) *Civic engagement and the baby boomer generation. Research, policy and practice perspectives:* Binghamton, NY: The Haworth Press, 2006.

Wink, P., and Dillon, M. Religious involvement and health outcomes in late adulthood: Findings from a longitudinal study of women and men. In T.G. Plante and A.C. Sherman (Eds.), *Faith and health: Psychological perspectives.* New York: Guilford Press, 2001.

Wu, K.B. *Poverty experience of older persons: A poverty study from a long-term perspective.* Washington, DC: AARP, 2003.

Wu, K.B. *Sources of income for older persons in 2004.* Accessed January 31, 2007, from http://assets.aarp.org/rgcenter/econ/dd148_income.pdf.

Yee, D. Insuring health and income needs of future generations. *Generations,* 2005, *29,* 13–20.

Zedlewski, S., and Schaner, S. Older adults engaged as volunteers. *Perspectives on productive aging.* Washington, DC: Urban Institute, The Retirement Project, 2006.

13

Death, Dying, Bereavement, and Widowhood

You have probably heard of people who "lost their will to live" or "died when they were ready." Such ideas are not simply superstitions. Similar to other topics addressed throughout this book, death involves an interaction of physiological, social, and psychological factors. The social context is illustrated by the fact that all cultures develop beliefs and practices regarding death in order to minimize its disruptive effects on the social structure. These cultural practices influence how members of a particular society react to their own death and that of others. Although measures of death are physical, such as the absence of a heartbeat or brain waves, psychosocial factors, such as the will to live, can influence the biological event. For instance, people with terminal illness may die shortly after an important event, such as a child's wedding, a family reunion, or a holiday, suggesting that their social support systems, enthusiasm for life, and "will to live" prolonged life to that point. How people approach their own death and that of others is also closely related to personality styles, sense of competence, coping skills, and social supports, as discussed in Chapter 6.

The Changing Context of Dying

In Western society, dying is associated primarily with old age. Although we all know that aging does not cause death and younger people also die, there are a number of reasons for this association. The major factors are medical advances and increased life expectancy. In preindustrial societies, death rates were high in childhood and youth, and parents could expect that one-third to one-half of their children would die before the age of 10. Most deaths now occur from chronic disease. This means that it is increasingly the old who die, making death predictable as a function of age. Death in old age has thus come to be viewed as a timely event, the completion of the life cycle.

Others view death not only as the province of the old, but also as an unnatural event that is to be fought off as long as medically possible. In this sense, death has become medicalized, distorted from a natural event into the end point of untreatable or inadequately treated disease or injury. Prior to the 1900s, the period of time spent dying was relatively short, due to infectious diseases and catastrophic events. With improved diagnostic techniques and early detection, individuals are living longer with terminal and chronic illnesses. At the end of a prolonged illness, when medicine may care for but not cure the patient, dying may seem more unnatural than if the person had been allowed to die earlier in the progression of the disease. With expanded technological mastery over the conditions of dying, chronically ill people have often been kept alive long beyond the point at which they might have died naturally in the past. Achieving a peaceful death is more difficult today because of the complexity of drawing a clear line between living and dying—which is a result of both technology and societal and professional ambivalence about whether to fight or accept death.

The surroundings in which death occurs have also changed with increased medical interventions. In preindustrial societies, most people died at home, with the entire community often involved in rituals surrounding the death. Approximately 90 percent of adults today indicate their wish to die at home, without pain, surrounded by friends and family. Yet 80 percent of all deaths occur in institutions where aggressive treatment is common, generally in hospitals (60 percent) and nursing homes (approximately 20 percent), and with only a few relatives and friends present. Older adults who are African American and less educated are even more likely to die in a hospital. Contrary to hopes for a peaceful death, the majority of dying patients, regardless of age, experience severe, undertreated pain, and spend a period of time in an intensive care unit (National Center for Health Statistics, 2003; Weitzen et al., 2003).

Attitudes toward Death

More insulated from death than in the past, many Americans are uncomfortable discussing it, especially the prospect of their own death. This discomfort is shown even in the euphemisms people use—"sleep," "pass away," "rest"—instead of the word "death" itself. Freud, in fact, recognized that although death was natural, undeniable, and unavoidable, people behaved as though it would occur only to others; that is, *they* will die, but not *me*. Fear and denial, even when facing a terminal illness, are natural responses to our inability to comprehend our own death and lack of physical existence. Such fear tends to make death a taboo topic in our society. Although in recent years death has become a more legitimate topic for scientific and social discussion, most people talk about it on a rational, intellectual level, rather than discuss and prepare for their own deaths or those of loved ones (Cicirelli, 2006). Both acceptance and denial

POINTS TO PONDER

Do you ever talk about death, your own or others, with someone else? If so, whom do you talk with? What kinds of concerns, fears, hopes, or questions do you express? How comfortable are you in talking about death? What might increase your feelings of comfort?

Spirituality is a source of strength for many older adults.

reflect the basic paradox surrounding death, in which we recognize its universality, but cannot comprehend or imagine our own dying. Dying is one of the few events in life certain to occur, but for which we do not plan.

Whether people's fear of death is natural or learned is unclear. When asked what they fear most about death, respondents mention suffering and pain, loss of their physical body and personality, loss of self-control, concern over an afterlife and the unknown, their spiritual or mental annihilation, loneliness, and the effects of their death on survivors. In general, people fear the inability to predict what the future might bring and the process of dying, particularly a painful death (Cicirelli, 2006). Older patients tend to choose *quality* of life in their end-of-life decision making, although this may vary both with the terminal illness and hopes and plans for the future. Older African Americans, however, are more likely to want lifesaving technology and to resist advanced directives, even though their belief in the afterlife may reduce their fear of death. While health professionals use the term *end-of-life,* African Americans tend to use the term *passed over,* because of their beliefs that the immortal soul carries on a journey of life after death (Crawley, 2001). It is essential that health care providers take account of such cultural differences in order to ensure both a good life and a good death.

Variation by Age and Gender

Multiple factors, particularly age, previous experience with the death of loved ones, and gender, influence socioemotional responses to death and dying. Younger women tend to express significantly greater fear than older women regarding death of others and themselves. Older women more often report anxiety and fear of dying, but less fear of the unknown than their male counterparts, although this may reflect gender differences in religiosity and socialization, and women's greater ability to express emotions such as fear. Findings are mixed regarding fear of death among older adults compared with younger persons (Wilkinson and Lynn, 2001). In general, the oldest-old think and talk more about death and appear to be less afraid of their own death than are midlife and young-old adults.

Aware of their limited survival, those age 75 and over may desire more time beyond what is expected (Cicirelli, 2002, 2006). Midlife and oldest-old adults who have "unfinished business" and goals they still want to accomplish appear to fear death more than the young-old. Regardless of age, a near-universal fear is the pain of dying, and concern over an afterlife—the possibility of either no afterlife or a threatening one (Cicirelli, 2006; Fortner, Neimeyer, and Rybarczyk, 2000).

A number of factors may explain this apparent paradox of elders' lessened fear of death in the face of its proximity. Having internalized society's views, the current cohort of elders may see their lives as having ever-decreasing social value, thereby lowering their own positive expectation of the future. If they have lived past the age they expected to, they may view themselves as living on "borrowed time." A painless death tends to be preferred over physical or mental deterioration, being socially useless or a burden on family. In addition, dealing with their friends' deaths, especially in age-segregated retirement communities or nursing homes, can help socialize older people toward an acceptance of their own. Experiencing "bereavement overload" through deaths of family and friends, they are more likely than younger people to think and talk in a matter-of-fact way about death on a regular basis and to develop realistic and effective means of coping, including humor (Lamberg, 2002; Thorson and Powell, 2000; Tomer and Eliason, 2000). On the other hand, having sustained contacts with younger family members and goals to accomplish creates a greater desire to prolong life (Cicirelli, 2006).

POINTS TO PONDER

We spend more time planning for a 2-week vacation than we will for our last 2 weeks of life. What factors might explain this?

Older adults facing death often turn inward to contemplation, reminiscence, reading, or spiritual activities. The awareness of one's mortality can stimulate a need for the "legitimization of biography," to find meaning in one's life and death through life review. Elders who engage in such review and achieve the developmental stage of ego integrity, as described in our discussion of Erikson in Chapter 6, are generally able to resolve conflicts and relieve anxiety, becoming more accepting of death. People who successfully achieve such legitimization experience a new freedom and relaxation about the future and tend to hold favorable attitudes toward death. Older people generally consider a sudden death to be more tragic than a slow one, since they desire time to see loved ones, say good-bye, settle their affairs, and reminisce. Older adults usually can accept the inevitability of their own death, even though they tend to be concerned about the impact of their death on relatives.

Religion may interact with age and cohort to affect attitudes toward death. For instance, in all age groups, the most religious persons who hold the strongest beliefs in an afterlife have less anxiety about dying. The religious have less fear of the unknown and view death as the doorway to a better state of being. Those most fearful about death are irregular participants in formal religious activities, or those intermediate in their religiosity whose belief systems may be confused and uncertain (Cicirelli, 2006). Religion can either comfort or create anxiety about an afterlife, but across cultures, it provides some individuals with one way to try to make sense of death. The age of the person who died is also a factor in how survivors react to death. Because the death of older people is often anticipated, it may be viewed as a "blessing" for someone whose "time has come" rather than as a tragic experience. Consider the different reactions you may have to the death of a child compared to that of a very old person.

POINTS TO PONDER

What thoughts, feelings, or images do you experience when you hear that a baby has died? What about the death of a young adult just graduating from college? A 50-year-old mother just starting her new career? An 80-year-old who has advanced domentia? A 79-year-old who is hit by a car while crossing the street? What varibles or factors might explain differences in your reactions?

The Dying Process

As noted earlier, most older people do not fear being dead as much as the painful process of dying. The stages of dying, one of the most widely known and classic frameworks for understanding the **dying process,** was advanced by Kübler-Ross (1969, 1981). Each stage represents a form of coping with the process of death.

The five stages of grief are a widely known and debated classic framework applied to both the dying and their survivors. Kübler-Ross (1969, 1981) identified the stages of:

1. shock and denial
2. anger ("why me?"), resentment, and guilt
3. bargaining, such as trying to make a deal with God
4. depression and withdrawal from others
5. adjustment/acceptance

Although Kübler-Ross cautioned that these stages were not invariant, immutable, or universal, she nevertheless implied that dying persons need to complete each stage before moving onto the next. She encouraged health care providers to help their patients advance through them to achieve the final stage. This widely debated perspective, sometimes misused with the dying and the bereaved, has been empirically rejected. Family members and health care providers must be cautious about implying that the dying person must move through these stages, and thus creating an illusion of control or what one "should do." Grief is more "messy" than sequential stages. Grieving does not proceed in a linear fashion, but reappears again and again to be reworked, and the emotional reactions to dying vary greatly (Neimeyer, 1998; Walter, 2003). In fact, sequencing may not occur at all; rather, feelings of guilt, protest, anger, fearfulness, and despair can intermesh with humor, hope, acceptance, and gratitude, with the dying person moving back and forth between them. Alternatively, some people remain at one of the earlier stages of denial or anger, while others move readily into acceptance (Weiss, 2001).

Although agreement now exists that there is no "typical," unidirectional way to die through progressive stages, Kübler-Ross's controversial work was a pioneering catalyst; it increased public and professional awareness of death and the needs of the dying and their caregivers. Her framework can be a helpful cognitive grid or guideline, not a fixed sequence that determines a "good death." Another contribution was her emphasis on dying as a time of growth and profound spirituality. By accepting death's inevitability, dying persons can live meaningfully and productively and come to terms with who they really are. Since the dying are "our best teachers," those who work with them can learn from them and emerge with fewer anxieties about their own death (Kübler-Ross, 1969, 1975, 2001).

Other models conceptualize dying and grief as *tasks* (Worden, 2002), *phases,* or *processes* (Parkes, 1972; Stroebe et al., 2001; Weiss, 2001). As C.S. Lewis wrote, "sorrow turns out to be not a state, but a process. It needs not a map but a history . . . there is something new to be chronicled everyday" (1961:38–39). A process perspective recognizes the alternating currents of emotion, thought, and behavior, which individuals move through at varying rates, oscillating through some emotions multiple

"Once you learn how to die, you learn how to live" (Moyers and Moyers, 2000).

times. Phases of the grieving process are conceptualized as:

1. *Avoidance:* shock, numbness, disbelief, and denial, all of which can function as buffers from the painful reality, especially when first learning that one is dying; fear, anxiety and dread; feelings of unreality, disorganization, and not being able to comprehend the situation; trying to gain some control and understanding by gathering facts of what happened. Some dying individuals surround themselves with as many people as possible, while others isolate themselves or may even reject loved ones' presence.
2. *Confrontation:* guilt; blaming self or others; rage; feelings of being overwhelmed and losing control; helplessness, panic, confusion, and powerlessness; the diffused energy of unfocused anger and despair, loss of faith, sense of injustice or disillusionment; intense sadness.
3. *Accommodation:* acceptance of the reality of death, saying good-byes, and gradually letting go of the physical world.

To summarize, consistent with the framework of dynamic interactions discussed throughout this book, the process of dying is shaped by:

- an individual's own personality, resilience, and philosophy of life
- the specific illness
- the social context (e.g., whether at home surrounded by family who encourage the expression of feelings, or isolated in a hospital)
- the cultural context: values, beliefs, shared meanings, and rituals

What is most important is that family and health care providers create choices and supports for the dying person, without making judgments about "the right way to die." In all instances, cross-cultural variations in how dying is experienced and grief expressed need to be attended to by health care and social service providers.

End-of-Life Care

The concept of the dying process highlights the importance of the ways in which end-of-life care is provided. As noted earlier, although most older people prefer to die at home, the common practice has been to hospitalize them, with most deaths occurring in hospital intensive care units or nursing homes. Rather than death as sudden from accident or infection, death is now most often the culmination of years with chronic illness, such as dementia, congestive heart failure, or cancer. The majority of older people die of chronic diseases, and often suffer debilitating symptoms such as nausea, delirium, or severe pain in the process. Since medicine focuses on treating the diseases, physicians and families may see death as a defeat, not an inevitable culmination. The traditional problem-oriented model of health care that emphasizes life-enhancing therapies falls short in guiding end-of-life care. Increasingly, adults express a preference for quality of life in the time they have remaining, and a "good death." According to the Institute of Medicine, a "good death" is characterized by:

- knowledge that death is coming, and an understanding of what to expect
- the ability to retain reasonable control over what happens and to experience dignity
- adequate control of pain and other symptoms
- choice about where death occurs

POINTS TO PONDER

If you have experienced the dying process of someone close to you or for whom you provided care, what phases did you observe? Did you observe the dying process as flowing, alternating between different stages, or unidirectional? Did the person reach the stage of acceptance? How did you know?

- access to information and expertise of whatever kind is needed
- supports to minimize spiritual and emotional suffering
- access to hospice or palliative care in any location
- adequate time to say good-bye (DeSpelder and Strickland, 2002; Dula and Wiliams, 2005; Richardson and Barusch, 2006).

Because of traditional medicine's emphasis on cure, many patients and families find that care provided at the end of life is inappropriate or unwanted. SUPPORT (Study to Understand Prognoses and Preferences for Outcomes and

DECIDING TO FORGO MEDICAL TREATMENTS

Some terminally ill patients, both young and old, decide to forgo extraordinary or special treatments in order to live their remaining months, or even years, in ways they choose. Some opt out because they feel that the burdens of treatment outweigh the benefits; others do so because they are concerned that another round of chemotherapy treatment or another transplant will only add to their suffering with no chance of a cure. In some cases, these patients outlive their doctors' predictions, but for most, the primary gain is control over one's remaining life. A prominent example of such a patient is the columnist Art Buchwald, who died in 2007 after refusing kidney dialysis a year earlier. He outlived his doctors' predictions, and made the most of his time remaining by visiting with family and friends across the country.

Risks of Treatment), funded by the Robert Wood Johnson Foundation, is the largest study ever to examine the care of seriously ill and dying patients. It found that patients and their physicians did not routinely make plans for end-of-life care or for how to address predictable complications, nor did they discuss the overall course of dying and aims of care. Patients most often died in pain and in intensive care units, with their families financially devastated by efforts to keep them alive. Even in illnesses with a predictable course, physicians considered an order to forgo resuscitation only in the patients' last few days (Christopher, 2003; Kaufmann, 2002; Schroepfer, 2006).

Medical experts agree that at least 90 percent of all serious pain can be effectively treated, yet at least 25 percent of dying patients receive inadequate pain medication (Dula and Williams, 2005). The pain of dying is intensified by the fact that terminal patients often experience depression, delirium, anxiety, despair, helplessness, hopelessness, anticipatory grief, and guilt. Both depression and delirium are underdiagnosed in older patients, yet they are treatable causes of suffering at the end of life. As discussed in Chapter 6, the prevalence of depression increases with the severity of the illness, pain, and limitations related to symptoms or treatment. Yet depression is often dismissed as a natural reaction of sadness and grief from knowing that one's life is ending. When left untreated, depression causes significant suffering, reduces patients' ability to fully participate in life and comply with medical treatments, and can contribute to other medical problems (Adamek, 2003; Surgeon General, 1999). The incidence of depression is perhaps not surprising, given findings that older patients with cancer, for example, have less symptom management than other age groups. One study found that 25 percent of nursing home cancer patients who reported daily pain received no analgesia; in addition, patients age 85 and over, and those of color were more likely to receive no analgesia (Bern-Klug, Gessert, and

Forbes, 2001). Although older patients have higher levels of untreated symptoms, there is limited information on pain and drug therapy; among this group, especially elders of color, additionally, older adults are often excluded from research trials and studies on pain management (Dula and Williams, 2005; Wilkinson and Lynn, 2001).

The **Dying Person's Bill of Rights,** developed nearly 35 years ago, states that individuals have the right to personal dignity and privacy; informed participation, including to have their end-of-life choices respected by health care professionals; and considerate, respectful service and competent care. As highlighted below, the **right to die** with dignity and without pain is currently supported by laws, public policies, and clinical practice more than it was at the time the Dying Person's Bill of Rights was introduced. Although controversy surrounds the use of life-sustaining technology, both sides agree that the dying person's self-determination and right to be free from physical pain are essential to humane care. As articulated by the American Geriatrics Society (1996), dying persons should be provided with opportunities to make the circumstances of their dying consistent with their preferences and lifestyles.

The U.S. Supreme Court ruled in 1997 that Americans have a constitutional right to palliative care. **Palliative care** focuses not on lifesaving measures, but on relief of pain and other physical symptoms by addressing the patient's emotional, social, and spiritual needs. Physicians, nurses, and social workers use both pharmacological and psychosocial approaches to cope with symptoms and needs. Palliative care is most effective when integrated into existing care settings, such as the hospital, nursing home, or private home (National Consensus Project for Quality Palliative Care, 2004). The box on this page differentiates pain management, hospice care, and formalized palliative care, with pain management as a major component of both types of care.

With palliative care, both the patient and health care providers recognize that, although the

---

TYPES OF PAIN AND PALLIATIVE CARE SERVICES AS DEFINED BY THE AMERICAN HOSPITAL ASSOCIATION

- **Pain management:** a formal program that educates staff about how to manage chronic and acute pain based on accepted academic and clinical guidelines.
- **Hospice:** a program providing palliative care and supportive services that use interdisciplinary teams to address the emotional, social, financial, and legal needs of terminally ill patients and their families.
- **Palliative care program:** a program providing specialized medical care, drugs, or therapies to manage acute or chronic pain and to control other symptoms. The program, run by specially trained physicians and other clinicians, also provides services such as counseling about advance directives, spiritual care, and social services to seriously ill patients and their families.

Although the number of palliative care programs in hospitals is increasing beyond the 14 percent identified in 2002, they still are far from the norm and do not easily fit into the coverage and payment policies of Medicare and other insurers. Funding for these programs often depends on piecing together resources from different funding streams, including short-term grants. This funding pattern jeopardizes existing formal palliative care programs (Kayser-Jones, 2006; Last Acts, 2002).

---

disease cannot be cured, quality of life can be enhanced. It does not treat the terminally ill patient as on the brink of death. It neither hastens nor postpones death. Instead, it simply recognizes that life can be meaningful and rewarding even with a diagnosis of a terminal illness (Richardson and Barusch, 2006). In many instances, psychosocial factors, such as loss of autonomy and control, lack of social support, and limited enjoyment and meaning in life are more important than pain in older adults' wishes for a speedy death. These findings underscore the importance of palliative care programs that have a holistic rather than a largely medical perspective (Jost, 2005;

Schroepfer, 2006). Such care is characterized by respect for the patient's values and choices about privacy and end-of-life care, candid and sensitive communication, encouragement to express feelings, and a multidisciplinary team approach. Music, art therapy, spiritual exploration, and reminiscence through photos and mementos may all be encouraged as a way to add pleasure and meaning at the end of life. The social support of friends and family can be a major source of strength and enhance the quality of the dying process. Medical professionals now are more open in talking about death with their patients and families than in the past. Most believe that dying persons have the right to know their prognosis and to have some control over their death. They now think of pain as the "fifth vital sign." Increasingly, the pursuit of a peaceful, pain-free death is viewed as the proper goal of medicine, even though less agreement exists on how this is to be achieved (e.g., how aggressively pain-killers should be used). This breaking of "professional silence" is in part a reaction to external pressures, including growing public support for physicians to provide aggressive pain control and palliative care along with patients who insist on having some control over their dying.

Some physicians still wrongly assume that they will be censured or prosecuted for giving controlled substances to the terminally ill, even when

the controlled drug is the approved treatment. In fact, the Supreme Court has cited two legal methods for more aggressive pain management:

1. the "morphine drip," a continuous administration of morphine at a dose that will abolish pain, and if that is not effective,
2. physician-prescribed "terminal sedation" with barbiturates and other drugs providing continuous anesthesia.

Despite the growth of Websites for "pain control" or "death and dying," many patients and their families are unaware that pain-killing narcotics are legally available. However, both professional and public awareness of these options is growing.

A 1997 report by the Institute of Medicine criticized health care providers for failing to provide competent palliative and supportive care and recommended ways to improve care, as summarized in the box on page 549 (Field and Cassel, 1997). Many of these principles are subsequently reflected in the 2004 Clinical Practice Guidelines for Quality Palliative Care. Although certification in palliative care is now available for physicians and nurses, few providers who offer this care have specialty training. For example, as of 2002, only 917 physicians nationwide had passed the certifying exam of the American Board of Hospice and Palliative Medicine. Although accreditation standards for medical schools now include the mandate to cover end-of-life care, the requirement contains no clear standards for teaching this topic (Last Acts, 2002). Nevertheless, there are many encouraging signs among the professional associations of medicine, nursing, and social work, including the following:

- American Medical Association and the American College of Physicians: guidelines for quality pain-management technologies
- American Medical Association: a profession-wide educational program on how to provide quality advance care planning and comprehensive palliative care

---

FACING DEATH ON YOUR OWN TERMS

Ruth, age 85, was diagnosed with incurable cancer. She told her family and doctor that she wanted to live long enough (5 months) to see her first granddaughter married. Her doctor arranged for low-dose chemotherapy that did not cause much discomfort, and she experienced a remission. After her granddaughter's wedding, the doctors found that the cancer had returned and spread. Her response was that she was now ready to die. She received excellent palliative care, lived three months without pain with the help of morphine, and was alert almost to the end, sharing memories and saying good-bye to her family.

AN INTEGRATED HOSPITAL-BASED PALLIATIVE CARE PROGRAM

One of the nation's premier hospital-based palliative care programs is the Lillian and Benjamin Hertzberg Palliative Care Institute at Mount Sinai Hospital in New York City. A consultation team is composed of a nurse, physicians, rotating fellows, and medical residents in training. This team advises hospital physicians who care for seriously ill patients on topics such as when to use comfort care, how to talk about treatment choices with patients and families, and pain and symptom management.

A four-bed inpatient unit is available for patients with complex emotional and physical symptoms and for those who need help in planning a course of care for their terminal illness. Nurses, social workers, interns, and residents staff this unit, working closely with the consultation team. Home care is available for seriously ill patients who are able to return home. All efforts are made to allow patients to go home, usually with hospice care, or to a nursing home, rather than die in a hospital.

To ensure that palliative care is available to all patients in the hospital, new physicians are trained in palliative care through bedside teaching, clinical rotations, and lectures. All oncology and geriatric fellows at Mt. Sinai Hospital are required to complete a one-month clinical palliative care rotation.

- American Geriatrics Society: fosters the development and study of instruments that measure quality of care at the end of life, including physical and emotional symptoms, advance care planning, and aggressive care near death
- American Board of Internal Medicine: educational resources to promote physician competency during internal medicine residency and subspecialty training
- American Association of Colleges of Nursing: national education program to improve training in end-of-life care in nursing curricula

- National Association of Social Workers: standards for social work practice in palliative and end-of-life care. The national association has established Standards for Social Work Practice in Palliative and End-of-Life Care
- Social Work Leaders in End-of-Life Care: Priority Agenda set at the Social Work Summit on End-of-Life and Palliative Care
- Institute for Health Care Improvement: breakthrough collaborative in quality improvement for end-of-life care, for advanced heart and lung disease, and for pain
- The Joint Commission for Accrediting Hospitals: requirement for hospitals to implement pain management plans for terminally ill patients
- Department of Veterans Affairs: innovations aimed at better care of advanced illnesses; pain as a fifth vital sign; quality measures in advance care planning and pain management, and faculty development
- National Consensus Project on Palliative Care sponsored by five national palliative care/hospice associations in 2004
- The Soros Foundation's Death in America Project: fellowships in end-of-life care awarded to physicians and social workers
- Last Acts: a coalition of 72 organizations launched by the Robert Wood Johnson Foundation, to enhance communication and decision making among health care providers, insurers, hospitals, nursing homes, and consumers

We turn next to discussing the primary delivery system for end-of-life care—hospice.

Hospice Care

Another trend toward being more responsive to dying patients and their families is the expansion of the **hospice** model of caring for the terminally ill. Hospice is not always a "place"

RECOMMENDATIONS OF THE INSTITUTE OF MEDICINE FOR IMPROVING END-OF-LIFE CARE

- People with advanced, potentially fatal illnesses and those close to them should be able to expect and receive reliable, skillful, and supportive care.

- Health care providers should commit themselves to improving care for dying patients and to use existing knowledge effectively to prevent and relieve pain and other symptoms.

- Policy makers, consumer groups, and purchasers of health care should work with health care practitioners, organizations, and researchers to:

  1. strengthen methods for measuring quality of life and other outcomes of care for dying patients and those close to them

  2. develop better tools and strategies for improving the quality of care and holding health care organizations accountable for care at the end of life

  3. modify mechanisms for funding care so that they encourage rather than impede good end-of-life care

  4. reform drug prescription laws, burdensome regulations, and state medical board policies and practices that impede effective use of opioids to relieve pain and suffering

- Educators should initiate changes in undergraduate, graduate, and continuing education to ensure that practitioners develop empathy, knowledge, and skills to care well for dying patients. Palliative care should become a defined area of expertise, education, and research.

- The nation's research establishment should define and implement priorities for strengthening the knowledge base for end-of-life care.

- Public discussion on end-of-life issues is needed to improve understanding of the experience of dying, the options available to patients and families, and the obligations of communities to those approaching death (Field and Cassel, 1997).

but a philosophy of, and approach to, care that is offered primarily in the home but also in hospital and nursing home settings. In fact, availability of hospice care along with caregiver support often determines whether an older person dies at home (Cantwell et al., 2000). Hospice is a central component of palliative care by providing integrated physical, medical, emotional, and spiritual care not only to the patient but also to his or her support system. As one type of end-of-life care, hospice is dedicated to helping individuals who are beyond medicine's curative power to remain in familiar surroundings where pain is reduced and personal dignity and control over the dying process maintained. Ensuring the patient's quality of life, and assessment and coordination of the physical, psychosocial, and spiritual needs of the patient and family, are fundamental to the hospice approach. More nursing homes and hospitals,

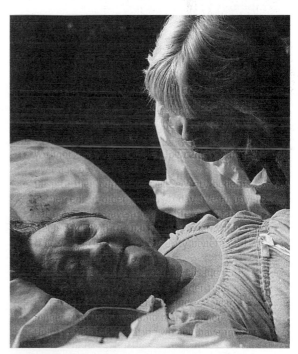

Hospice care can enhance quality of life for the dying person.

responsive to a changing market, are providing hospice care and pain management programs, although the percentage of nursing home residents or hospital patients who participate is only around 25 percent (Last Acts, 2002).

Most hospice programs share the following characteristics:

- focus on quality of life
- service availability 24 hours per day, 7 days per week, as needed
- respite care and support for the family
- management of physical symptoms, including managing pain through medications
- psychological, social, and spiritual counseling for patients and their families
- coordination of skilled and homemaker home care services and collaboration among providers (home health care, hospitals, nursing homes)
- physician direction of services by a multidisciplinary team
- use of volunteers as central to the team
- inpatient care when needed
- bereavement counseling for family and friends after the death

St. Christopher's Hospice, started in Great Britain in 1967, was the first formal hospice in the world, although TB asylums for younger people had informally performed similar functions. The first hospice in the United States was developed in 1974 in New Haven, Connecticut; today there are over 3500 hospices nationwide (Topics in Advanced Practice, 2007). The majority of these provide in-home services for cancer and HIV/AIDS patients with a prognosis of 6 months or less to live. In 1986, Congress passed legislation making hospice a permanent Medicare benefit, including reimbursement for prescriptions, and granting a modest increase in reimbursement rates. Medicare's hospice benefit includes services that are not generally covered under Medicare, such as home nursing care without homebound or

skilled service requirements, on-call availability of providers for crises 24 hours a day and 7 days a week, interdisciplinary team management for comprehensiveness and continuity, spiritual counseling, family support, treatment for pain/symptoms, medications, emergency acute medical care, bereavement care for survivors, and inpatient care when needed (e.g., for respite or symptom management). Medicare pays a capitated, all-inclusive, prospectively set per day rate for four categories of service; of these, routine home care accounts for almost 90 percent of all care delivered (Wilkinson and Lynn, 2001).

Hospice professionals and volunteers, working as an interdisciplinary team, advocate for giving dying persons full and accurate information about their condition. They also try to develop supportive environments in which people can tell their life stories (e.g., life review), resolve and reconcile relationships, and find meaning in their deaths. Listening to and touching the dying person, music and art, family involvement, and ritual celebration of special events such as birthdays and weddings are all encouraged. For those who value spirituality, staff supports them in their quest for meaning and dignity in the last stage of life. In addition, hospice staff work directly with family and friends to help them resolve their feelings, clarify expectations, relate effectively to the dying patient, and then provide bereavement counseling after the death. Hospice programs also offer counseling and support to staff members to help prevent "burnout."

Hospice care benefits the patient both financially and in terms of extending life. Some studies have documented that hospice care is associated with lower Medicare costs and financial savings to families, regardless of length of stay, compared to conventional care (Pyenson, et al., 2004). There is increasing evidence that hospice provides better quality of life for both end-of-life patients and their caregivers than hospitals (Last Acts, 2002). Most dramatically, a study of

8700 Medicare patients with 16 different terminal conditions found that for all conditions, patients age 65 and over in hospice lived longer than those in other settings (Brink, 2007). Despite these benefits, only about 30 percent of dying Americans of all ages participate in hospice, the majority of whom have cancer and are age 65 and older, even though it is estimated that twice as many probably should have received hospice (Abelson, 2007).

The reasons for this relatively low rate of participation are complex. One of the barriers to a "good death" is that doctors often refer patients to hospice too late. Approximately, 33 percent of all hospice patients (82 percent of whom are over age 65) die within a week of admission. The median length of stay in a hospice for Medicare patients is between 21 and 29 days, far less than the 180 days of care covered by Medicare (National Hospice and Palliative Care Organization, 2004). Despite technological advances, it is still difficult for doctors to predict length of survival of terminally ill patients. In addition, some physicians remain uncomfortable with telling a person that he or she is dying. Instead, physicians tend to convey an optimistic bias when discussing prognoses with each other and sharing them with patients and families. They are likely to overestimate survival and future quality of life, in part because they may fear that a short prognosis will be self-fulfilling.

As a result of late referrals, most patients come to hospice during a period of rapid physical decline and often in crisis. At such times, the immediate management of symptoms and relieving the family overshadows the need to address the emotional and spiritual issues of remembering, forgiving, and bringing closure to a person's life. When more time is available, the dying person can participate in the process of validating the past and planning for the future, and this gives the family the chance to enjoy or repair family relationships. As a result, some hospice professionals view this short-term use of

Medicare-covered services as a problem (Brickner et al., 2004). However, short periods of hospice utilization may actually represent an informed

THE COMFORT PROVIDED BY HOSPICE CARE

Three months of chemotherapy followed by 6 weeks of radiation was not working for Mr. Frank. His last hope was a stem cell transplant, but those prospects were dimming each day, as he became weaker and weaker. Mr. Frank decided that he did not want to spend his final days in a losing battle with his rapidly advancing and painful lymphoma. He preferred to be as comfortable as possible and to leave the hospital and return home.

Mr. Frank and his wife Jean contacted a local hospice that helped them set up a range of services that would assist both of them through the final months of his life. A nurse and physician were assigned to his care. The hospice staff also trained Jean, friends, and family in how to administer Mr. Frank's pain medications and to use tiny ice chips to help him deal with his extremely dry throat and mouth. The staff also taught Jean how to tell when Mr. Frank's pain was increasing, so that he could be given a high dose of morphine before it became unbearable.

Mr. Frank also received visits from the hospice team social worker who talked with him about how to resolve some issues with his daughter, who held considerable anger toward her father. When the hospice team estimated that Mr. Frank would probably die in 3 days, they encouraged Jean to contact family and friends who lived at a distance so that they would have time to visit and say good-bye. In those last 3 days, Mr. Frank was lucid and able to talk, laugh, and cry with those who loved him, including his daughter.

His family and friends all commented later that they felt Mr. Frank had a "good death." They appreciated being able to be part of his peaceful death in the comfort and familiar surroundings of his home. The hospice social worker kept in touch with Jean for a year after her husband's death, encouraging her to express her grief and learn new coping skills. Mr. Frank's daughter was especially grateful for the opportunity to reconcile with her father before he died.

preference for delaying formal end-of-life care for families and patients unlikely to use hospice earlier. For them, 2 to 3 weeks may be just the right amount of time (Waldop, 2006). And even short hospice stays in the last month of life can be less expensive than end-of-life care in other settings, depending on the acuity of needs at the end (Miller et al., 2004). Nevertheless, the National Hospice Organization tries to educate physicians on how to predict appropriate entry points to hospice for various conditions so that patients are fully aware of their options for palliative care.

Another barrier is that the oldest-old are more likely to die from chronic illnesses, such as heart or lung disease or dementia, rather than cancer. Unlike the treatment of cancer, where a more definable process of decline can be projected, most older adults die from the accumulation of conditions that actually may be more imminently terminal yet do not meet the hospice criterion of a prognosis of death in six months or less. In other instances, even patients with cancer do not receive an accurate diagnosis and are unlikely to be informed about or qualify for hospice benefits, including pain relief. Among those who do, a substantial percent resist hospice because it requires acknowledging that one is dying and abandoning hope of cure (Tilly and Wiener, 2003; Waldrop, 2006). In the past, hospice patients had to give up all treatment to qualify for hospice. Therefore, those who did not choose hospice often spent their last days in a hospital receiving expensive medical care. However, a few insurance companies, such as Aetna, have instituted an "open access" approach that continues to cover advanced medical treatment, such as radiation, chemo- therapy, and dialysis, for hospice patients. This means that patients are not forced to choose between treatment for the disease and palliative care from hospice. As a result of continued treatment and the supportive at-home approach of hospice, some patients have even been able to gain the weight and strength necessary to leave the program (Abelson, 2007). Another barrier is that patients enrolled in hospice no longer receive coverage if they show signs of getting better rather than worse, although patients can continue to receive hospice for more than six months if they are getting worse.

Low-income individuals and persons of color also appear to be underserved by hospice, even though, as described in Chapter 4, groups such as African Americans have a higher overall incidence of death from cancer, a greater likelihood of inadequate treatment of pain, and greater financial strain and difficulties of paying for care (Anderson, Mendoza, and Valero, 2000; Cone et al., 2003; Welch, Teno, and Mor, 2005). The reasons for this are complex and reflect historical, economic, cultural, and religious factors, suggesting that racial disparities persist into end-of-life care and death, particularly related to communication and family needs (Dula and Williams, 2005). African Americans and Latinos are less likely than other groups to complete advance directives, to see physicians who spend time talking with them about end-of-life care, or to participate in hospice. When death is inevitable and imminent, African American families are twice as likely as whites to request aggressive life-sustaining treatments, including dialysis, artificial nutrition, surgery and antibiotics, even if the the patient is in a coma or permanent vegetative state, has little chance of survival, and will lose their life savings (Crawley, 2001; Dula and Williams, 2005; Payne, Medina, and Hampton, 2003).

In some cases, this may occur because African Americans perceive advance directives and palliative care as "giving up hope," or not respecting their cultural and personal values. For example, African American elders are more likely than whites to believe that God is the ultimate decision maker regarding the time, manner, and place of death, and to have religious prohibitions against limiting life-sustaining treatment (Johnson, Elbert-Avila, and Tulsky, 2005). Some may fear that hospice or palliative care is being prescribed as a way to limit care or "trying to get rid of them" rather than a vehicle for increasing control or self-determination. The fear of not receiving needed medical care at end of life is indeed based on the reality that various cardiovascular, cerebrovascular, cancer, and kidney transplant procedures are less available to blacks than whites (Epstein et al., 2000; Kressin and Peterson, 2001; Mitchell, Ballard and Matchar, 2000). Perceptions of palliative care as a way to control African Americans' survival stem in part from unethical research conducted on blacks in the past, along with health care disparities across the life course (Berger et al., 2002; Dula and Williams, 2005; Institute of Medicine, 2002; Owen, Goode, and Haley, 2001; Washington, 2007).

Given African Americans' shorter life expectancy, it is also understandable that they would prefer treatments that may enable them to live as long as possible. In contrast to a peaceful death, aggressive medical treatment ("fighting while going down" as an expected part of life's ongoing struggle) is often viewed as a sign of respect among African Americans, even if it means feeding tubes, pain, and loss of life savings. Providers need to be sensitive to cultural differences in how patients choose to die and be able to discuss ways to give African Americans the gift of a "good death," while not giving up hope. On a larger scale, palliative and end-of-life care is unlikely to be successful without addressing disparities in access to prevention, risk assessment, diagnosis, and evidence-based curative treatment across the life course (Crawley, 2001).

Despite the different definitions of **death with dignity** among culturally diverse groups, underutilization of hospice may also stem from inadequate knowledge of this service and the lack of culturally competent providers who are trained to discuss end-of-life care with persons of color. Working through African American

PALLIATIVE CARE PROGRAMS DEVELOPED BY AFRICAN AMERICAN COMMUNITIES

The mission of the Seattle, Washington African American Comfort Program (SAACP) is advocating, creating, and coordinating culturally respectful end-of-life services for African Americans. The program provides education about access to medical, psychosocial, spiritual, and legal services to African Americans who are facing end-of-life issues and considering hospice. Services are provided at no charge to individuals in the community at convenient locations, by telephone and through the program's Website. The program also provides training to health care providers.

The Balm of Gilead Project in Alabama's largest county was created to meet the palliative care needs of low-income African Americans. It aims to be responsive to the economic and social realities of the community, where dying patients often lack appropriate caregivers to remain at home and where distrust of the medical system is pervasive. The Balm of Gilead itself is an umbrella organization, providing an infrastructure for an array of services to address the holistic needs associated with terminal illness in each of its stages and treatment settings:

- Hospital based services, with a 10-bed inpatient palliative care unit, palliative care consultation, and educational efforts with hospital staff and students, all focus on pain management
- Home care services
- Long term residential care through a palliative care program at a local nursing home, and
- Community outreach and education involving Care Teams, civic groups, faith communities, and community education.

The Harlem Palliative Care Network assumes that an effective palliative care program must come from, and be of, the community. Organizers first established a base of expertise in palliative medicine at a community hospital and networked with community organizations—churches, social groups, and nursing homes. These networks helped to identify patients and families with advanced illnesses, who could benefit from palliative interventions, including pain management, early in the course of a disease to prevent emergency room care for an acute health crisis. The network also provides a nonmedical services to support patients and families emotionally and spiritually.

ministers and community centers may be a way to provide hospice information to black communities (Kurent, 2000). Culturally specific end-of-life care programs that originate in the African American community, such as the Harlem Palliative Care Network or the African American Comfort Care Program in Seattle, are more likely to be trusted. In addition, medications for managing pain must be affordable and accessible in pharmacies in minority neighborhoods. Religious organizations in a range of culturally diverse communities may be the best locus for discussing death, dying, and end-of-life care (Braun, Pietsch, and Blanchette, 2000; Crawley, 2001).

Although most research on end-of-life care focuses on Medicare utilization, Medicaid also funds end-of-life care, including hospice care, in the last 6 months of life. While Medicaid funding for hospice varies widely by states, Medicaid accounts for about 5 percent of total hospice revenues. Most of Medicaid's funding for long-term care for the dually eligible (those eligible for both Medicaid and Medicare), however, goes to nursing home care at the end of life. Although the proportion of hospice enrollees in nursing homes has increased from 9.9 percent in 1990 to 21.5 percent in 2002, a substantial percentage—ranging from estimates of 45 to 85 percent of nursing home residents—are in constant pain because of inadequate pharmacologic and nonpharmacologic pain treatment or none at all (Miller, Teno, and Mor, 2004; National Hospice and Palliative Care Organization, 2004; Teno et al., 2001; Won et al., 2004). The lack of pain management in nursing homes, even those that have hospice care, is generally attributed to shortages of nursing home physicians and nurses with adequate time and training to provide analgesics when hospice staff are unavailable (Kayser-Jones et al., 2006). Given the projected growth in long-term care it is essential that nursing home staff receive training and resources for palliative care.

The Right to Die or Hastened Death

Along with increased attention to the ways in which people choose to die and the meanings they assign to their deaths, the right-to-die movement is growing; this has given rise to new ethical and legal debates regarding the right to a "good death." Advocates of the right to die increasingly use the term **hastened death** rather than **euthanasia,** because it speeds up the inevitable. Whether others have a right to help people die, and under what conditions, has been discussed throughout history (see the box on page 555 summarizing the history of major events in the right-to-die movement). But recent debates about the ethical, social, and legal issues raised by euthanasia or hastened death have intensified with increased medical advances used to prolong life and the legal recognition of patients' autonomy. These issues revolve around three different types of patients:

1. the terminally ill who are conscious
2. the irreversibly comatose
3. the brain-damaged or severely debilitated who have good chances for survival but have limited quality of life (e.g., patients with Alzheimer's or Lou Gehrig's disease)

Central to these debates is the doctrine of **informed consent,** which establishes a competent patient's right to accept or refuse medical treatment based on his or her understanding of the benefits and harms of that treatment. Standard informed-consent procedures work best in the acute-care setting, where they involve treatment choices that lead to cure, significant improvement, or death. Decision making for older people with chronic illness, often in long-term care settings, is much more ambiguous than in acute-care environments, and long-term care providers tend to disagree about patients' rights to end their lives. Findings are mixed regarding the

> "The good death: We only get one time to get it right."

acceptability of a range of end-of-life decision options among older people. While increased age is generally associated with preferring quality over quantity of life, health care providers cannot always assume that this is the case, especially among some ethnic minorities (Dula and Williams, 2005).

The value of autonomy, articulated in informed consent and advance directives, may conflict with cultures that are more collectivist than individualist in nature. For example, decisions about end-of-life care in Asian and Pacific Islander cultures are influenced by the value placed on shared or deferred decision-making within families; filial piety; silent communication, whereby it is improper to discuss issues of

death and dying with one's parents; and preservation of harmony, whereby families may be unwilling to share bad news if it disrupts the group's harmony. When patients have difficulty making independent health care decisions and defer to the family or doctor, they may unfortunately be labeled noncompliant by traditional Western medicine. To take account of such cultural variations, family centered, shared, or negotiated models of medical decision making recognize the legitimacy of multiple points of view (McLaughlin and Braun, 1998). Similarly, African American religious beliefs and historical experiences were discussed earlier as one of the factors reducing their willingness to utilize hospice services and advance directives.

HISTORY OF MAJOR EVENTS RELATED TO THE RIGHT TO DIE MOVEMENT IN THE UNITED STATES

1937   The Euthanasia Society of America is founded.

1967   The first living will is written.

1968   The first living will legislation is introduced in Florida.

1973   The American Hospital Association creates the Dying Persons' Bill of Rights, which includes informed consent and the right to refuse treatment.

1974   The first U.S. hospice opens in Connecticut.

1975   The New Jersey Supreme Court allows Karen Ann Quinlan's parents to disconnect the respirator that was keeping her alive.

The California Natural Death Act is passed, which is the first aid-in-dying statute, which gives legal standing to living wills and protects physicians from being sued for failing to treat incurable illnesses.

1980   The Hemlock Society is founded, distributing how-to-die information.

1987   The California State Bar Conference passes a resolution to become the first public body to approve of physician aid-in-dying.

1990   The American Medical Association adopts the position that, with informed consent, a physician can withhold or withdraw treatment from a patient who is close to death, and may also discontinue life support of a patient in a permanent coma.

The Supreme Court decision in the Nancy Cruzan case rules that competent adults have a constitutionally protected right to refuse medical treatment and allows a state to impose procedural safeguards.

Congress passes the Patient Self-Determination Act; hospitals that receive federal funds are required to tell patients about their state's legal options.

1991   Washington State voters reject Ballot Initiative 119 (54 to 46 percent), which would have legalized physician aid-in-dying.

(Continued)

MAJOR EVENTS RELATED TO RIGHT TO DIE (Continued)

The Federal Patient Self-Determination Act requires health care facilities that receive Medicare or Medicaid funds to inform patients of their right to refuse medical treatment and to sign advance directives.

1992 California voters defeated Proposition 161, a law similar to the Washington State initiative, and at a similar proportion, 54 to 46 percent.

1993 Compassion in Dying is founded in Washington State.

1994 The Death with Dignity Education Center is founded in California.

Compassion in Dying files a lawsuit challenging the constitutionality of laws banning assisted dying in Washington State and New York. They win in the District Court in Washington State, but not in New York.

Oregon voters approve (51 to 49 percent) Measure 16, the Oregon Death with Dignity Act, which permits terminally ill patients, under proper safeguards, to obtain a physician's prescription to end life in a humane and dignified manner.

1995 Both Washington State's Compassion ruling and Oregon's Death with Dignity Act are ruled unconstitutional at the district court level.

1996 The Ninth Circuit Court of Appeals issues a landmark decision in *Compassion v. Washington State,* which upholds that assisted dying is protected by the liberty and privacy provisions of the U.S. Constitution.

1997 The U.S. Supreme Court reverses the Circuit Court decisions in Washington State and rules that state laws against assisted suicide are not unconstitutional. The Court also finds that patients have a right to aggressive treatment of pain and other symptoms, even if the treatment hastens death.

1997 Oregon citizens vote by a margin of 60 to 40 percent to retain the Oregon Death with Dignity Act.

1998 Congressman Harry Hyde introduces the Lethal Drug Abuse Prevention Act of 1998 to prohibit the dispensing or distributing of drugs for the purpose of causing the suicide or euthanasia of any individual. His intent is to overturn the Oregon law.

Jack Kevorkian videotapes himself administering a lethal medication to a terminally ill man, which is broadcast on *60 Minutes.* He is charged with first-degree premeditated murder.

2001 U.S. Attorney General John Ashcroft reinterprets the federal Controlled Substance Act in a way to nullify Oregon's Death with Dignity law. A U.S. district judge rules against this interpretation.

2002 The Hawaii Senate narrowly fails to pass legislation legalizing physician-assisted suicide, even though the measure had overwhelming support of the House and the governor.

2003 Oregon issues its fifth year report on the implementation of the Death with Dignity Act: 58 people received legal prescriptions for lethal medications, and 38 of them used the medication.

2005 The Schiavo case dominates national headlines, pitting her parents and husband in federal and state courts, and disability rights versus right-to-die groups.

2005 Partially as a result of the highly visible Schiavo case, legislation is introduced before Congress to establish a stricter rule for withdrawing food and water for Medicare and Medicaid patients than for terminating other types of life support, but does not pass.

2005 Compassion and Choices is formed as a coalition of end-of-life organizations, including Compassion in Dying and the Hemlock Society.

Passive Euthanasia (Voluntary Elective Death)

Euthanasia, which originally referred to as a painless or peaceful death, can be passive (allowing death) or active (causing death). In **passive euthanasia,** treatment is withdrawn, and nothing is done to prolong the patient's life artificially, such as using a feeding tube or ventilator. Suspension of medical interventions or physician aid in dying allows the natural dying process to occur, but no active steps are taken to bring about death. In order to relieve pain, medications are sometimes given that may hasten death, but the object is to relieve suffering, not to bring about death. Withholding or withdrawing useless or unwanted medical treatments, or providing adequate pain relief, even if it hastens death, has been determined to be legal and ethical, and is generally accepted. For example, 84 percent of Americans in a Pew 2005 poll approved of laws that let terminally ill patients make decisions about whether to be kept alive through medical treatment, even though the majority of Americans would favor doctors doing everything possible to save their lives (DiCamillo and Field, 2006). The legal context for this is the 1990 U.S. Supreme Court case of *Cruzan v. Director, Missouri Department of Health,* which recognized the right of a competent patient to refuse unwanted medical care, including artificial nutrition and hydration, as a "liberty" interest, and therefore as constitutionally protected. The Supreme Court later delegated regulation of this constitutional right to the states.

Another indicator of changing legal interpretations is the position of the American Medical Association (AMA). Their 1984 statement on euthanasia presented two fundamental guidelines:

- The patient's role in decision making is paramount.
- A decrease in aggressive treatment of the hopelessly ill patient is advisable when treatment would only prolong a difficult and uncomfortable process of dying.

In 1989, the American Medical Association adopted the position that, with informed consent, physicians could withhold or withdraw treatment from patients who are close to death. Most physicians agree that withholding and withdrawing nutrition and hydration are permissible in certain circumstances and that it is the physician's duty to initiate discussion of these issues with patients and their families.

In contrast to passive euthanasia, where deliberate decisions are made about withholding or withdrawing treatment, there is also a form of hastened death whereby older people may voluntarily make decisions that are equivalent to choosing to die. For example, an older person may refuse extra help at home or insist on hospital discharge directly to the home, in spite of the need for skilled nursing care. When an older person commits suicide through the process of **self-neglect,** the effects of his or her decisions are subtle and gradual. If older people neglect their care needs or choose an inappropriate living situation because of impaired judgment, involuntary treatment laws can sometimes be used to move them to protected settings. If their "failure to care," however, is not immediately life-threatening, they usually have to be allowed to deteriorate to that point before being legally compelled to comply with treatment.

POINTS TO PONDER

DEFINING END OF LIFE

How the end of life is defined has implications for quality of care and quality of life, when decisions need to be made about life-sustaining care, and eligibility for hospice. One definition of the end of life is the beginning of an illness that is characterized by any of the three dimensions of severity:

- Diagnosis of a potentially fatal illness
- The beginning of a functional limitation in one's ability to perform any of the basic physical activities of daily living, or
- The advent of pain or physical symptoms that are either or both (a) a major distress to the patient and (b) precursors to and resulting in death (Lawton, 2001).

What would you consider to be end of life? What kind of care would you want? Would you want any measures taken to sustain life, even if you were in a coma or had dementia?

Active Euthanasia

Active euthanasia refers to deliberate steps taken to bring about someone else's death, by administering a lethal injection or by some other means. It can be voluntary (at the dying person's request) or involuntary (without consent as in the Netherlands). Sometimes called *mercy killing,* the legality of active euthanasia has been tested by several highly controversial court cases, voter initiatives, and state legislation. As noted above, a subject of intense controversy is **assisted suicide** or **physician-assisted suicide (PAS);** this occurs when someone else provides the means by which an individual ends his or her life. For example, a physician may prescribe medication, typically barbiturates, knowing that the individual intends to use it to commit suicide, but it is the individual who decides when and whether to take it.

Those who argue against the legalization of assisted suicide, such as the U.S. Conference of Catholic Bishops and the National Right to Life Committee, fear a "culture of death" or "slippery slope" is being created, to the detriment of the oldest-old and persons with disabilities who could be pressured to feel that it is "their duty to die" (Jost, 2005). They fear that a law made to convey permission could come to be seen as prescriptive, with assisted suicide viewed as a solution to solve societal problems faced by the poor, persons of color, or individuals with disabilities. The public is nearly equally divided over legalizing PAS (45 to 46 percent) (DiCamillo and Field, 2006). The strongest supporters of PAS are Japanese Americans, followed by Caucasians, with the least support among African Americans and Filipino Americans (33 percent) (Braun, Tanji, and Heck, 2001). The American Medical Association (AMA), based on the historical role of physicians as advocates for healing, officially opposes physicians' directly assisting their patients in committing suicide by prescribing lethal medications; however, about nearly 60 percent of rank-and-file doctors believe that it is ethical to assist an individual who has made a rational choice to die due to unbearable suffering, and support PAS. While supporting that right, 46 percent would not personally participate in assisting any patient, and 54 percent believe that this should be a decision between patient and doctor, without government involvement (O'Reilly, 2005). Accordingly, the AMA advocates compassionate, high-quality palliative care and assistance in addressing fears as a way to reduce the expressed need for PAS.

Citizen initiatives and recent legislation in several states reflect increasing public support for PAS. In fact, approximately 70 percent of adults in nationwide polls believe that doctors should be allowed to help terminally ill patients in severe pain take their own lives, even if this is not legalized (DiCamillo and Field, 2006). The degree of support, however, diminishes among those with conservative religious affiliations. Most believe that forcing people to endure prolonged suffering is inhumane and cruel. *Compassion et al. v. Washington State* was the first case to challenge in a federal court the constitutionality of a state law on assisted suicide insofar as it applies to mentally competent, terminally ill patients seeking prescribed medications with which to hasten

THE CONTROVERSIAL DR. KEVORKIAN

One of the states in which the legality of assisted suicide has been the focus of public attention is Michigan, where Dr. Jack Kevorkian assisted over 100 people to commit suicide. In the first case, involving a woman with Alzheimer's disease, the court dismissed the murder charges on the grounds that no law in Michigan prohibited assisting in a suicide. Subsequently, the legislature passed a bill to stop Dr. Kevorkian's activities. While prior cases were dismissed on the grounds that the law against physician-assisted suicide is unconstitutional, Kevorkian was charged with second-degree murder in 1999. He was sentenced to 10 to 25 years in prison because he directly administered a lethal injection to an adult in the final stages of amyotrophic lateral sclerosis (ALS) rather than the dying individual taking the final action. Although controversial, Kevorkian's crusade to legalize active euthanasia pushed the debate on physician-assisted suicide to the forefront of public awareness.

A GOOD DEATH

Anne was a 68-year-old retiree who had battled breast cancer for over 4 years. She had received radiation and chemotherapy, but the cancer had metastasized and spread to other organs in her body. She had lost more than 40 pounds, had no appetite, and had difficulty breathing, even with the aid of an oxygen tank. She had decided to end her suffering and wanted to die.

Her husband contacted the local office of Compassion and Choices. The case management staff arranged for a visit and included medical staff to verify the primary physician's diagnosis. Mentally alert, Anne assured the staff that she understood and met the requirements outlined in Compassion's Guidelines and Safeguards. She indicated that her physician had already prescribed half the necessary medications needed to hasten her death; the rest would be obtained within 2 weeks. The physician carefully reviewed with Anne the procedures for self-administering the required medications. She hoped for a hastened death within 6 weeks. Her husband, Ed, confirmed that he supported Anne's decision to choose when the end would come rather than watch her continue to suffer.

A month later, Ed phoned the Compassion staff and indicated that Anne was ready. Upon their arrival, the staff reminded Anne that she need only tell them if she had changed her mind. She was clear and adamant in her decision to proceed: "Today is the day." According to Compassion's protocol, she ate some food to be certain she had something in her stomach before taking the first dose of medications. Anne began to take the pills with a glass of orange juice, according to Compassion's guidelines that patients must be able to ingest all of the medications by themselves. As suggested in the protocol, Anne asked for some vodka to speed the effect of the drugs. She expressed her appreciation to the Compassion staff for their assistance, kissed her husband and two sons, laid her head back on the pillow, and looked as if she were going into a peaceful sleep. In about 15 minutes, she stopped breathing. She had died what Compassion calls "a good death."

death. An initiative in Washington State to permit physician aid in dying was only narrowly defeated in 1991. However, 4 months after the initiative's defeat at the polls, the legislature passed a bill giving comatose and dying people the right to have food and water withdrawn. In 1994, the federal district court ruled that the Washington State ban on physician-assisted suicide violates the patient's constitutional right to liberty, but this ruling did not protect physicians from prosecution if they assisted in a terminally ill patient's suicide. In 1996, a federal appeals court struck down both Washington and New York statutes banning PAS. The plaintiffs (near-death patients and physicians) argued that no public interest is served by prolonging pain in hopeless situations and that to do so is to subject patients to potential abuse. The courts linked the right to facilitate death with the right to refuse medical treatment. They argued that the Fourteenth Amendment protects the individual's decision to hasten death with physician-prescribed medication and that statutes prohibiting PAS deny equal protection guaranteed by this Amendment to competent terminally ill adults who are not on life supports.

These conflicting state rulings and pressure from advocacy organizations such as the Compassion in Dying Federation brought the issue of assisted suicide to the U.S. Supreme Court. In June 1997, the Court ruled that there is no constitutional or fundamental "right to die." They thus upheld the Washington and New York laws that make it a crime for doctors to help patients kill themselves. This ruling by the Supreme Court, however, did not preclude states from deciding on their own to pass laws allowing physician-assisted suicide. By returning the debate to the states, the justices apparently opened the way for other jurisdictions to follow Oregon, the only state to legalize the physician-assisted suicide choice for patients who are diagnosed by two doctors as having less than 6 months to live. Several other states—Maine, California, Alaska, and Hawaii—have considered legalization of PAS but these bills and initiatives have failed. The Supreme Court ruling also left open the possibility that the court might extend federal constitutional protection in the future.

Nor did the 1997 Supreme Court ruling stop patients from seeking physicians to prescribe lethal medications or stop doctors from providing them illegally. The court ruled that prescribing medication with the intent to relieve suffering is legal and acceptable, but presenting drugs with the intent to cause death is not. Since "intent" is difficult to determine, the Court gives significant discretion and latitude to physicians to use adequate pain medication and explicitly endorses "terminal

> **IS THIS PHYSICIAN-ASSISTED SUICIDE?**
>
> An 89-year-old man was in tremendous pain from the end stages of pancreatic cancer. He had been diagnosed only 6 weeks earlier, and nothing could be done to halt the spread of this deadly cancer. His daughter flew him cross-country to her home in order to provide daily care and to have his beloved grandsons nearby. The day before his 90th birthday, he cried out for relief from the pain. His daughter called the hospice doctor, who delivered a bottle of morphine to her home. He advised the daughter to start a heavy dosage right after dinner. In leaving, he gently said to her, "and if he does not wake up, that may be a blessing." The next morning, her father did awaken, but he was very disoriented, appeared to have suffered a mild stroke during the night, and was crying from the pain. Anxious to relieve the pain, his loving daughter gave him another dose of morphine. Within a few hours, he was dead. Did the morphine hasten his death? What was the doctor's role? The daughter's?

sedation." The Court concluded that a dying patient who is suffering and is in pain has no legal barriers to obtaining medication from qualified physicians to alleviate that suffering, even to the point of causing unconsciousness and hastening death. In many ways, this solution, known as the "double effect," is an old one. In the Supreme Court's definition, this occurs when a physician, intending to relieve pain or suffering, gives a terminally ill patient medication that has the unintended—but foreseeable—side effect of hastening death. Often, this medication is morphine. Nevertheless, many physicians still incorrectly assume that they can be censured or prosecuted for giving controlled substances to dying patients. To address this, the American Civil Liberties Union put forth the "End of Life Care Act of 1998," which would have removed legal liability from physicians who offer patients a full range of end-of-life care choices, including palliative sedation. But the Act did not pass.

> **POINTS TO PONDER**
>
> Have you and your loved ones ever discussed how to die, your preferences and fears? If not, how could you initiate such a discussion, either with your parents, your partner, or your adult children?

As noted above, Oregon, the only state that has legalized physician-assisted suicide, leads the nation in aggressive pain management. To use the law, a patient must make three requests—two oral and one written—and be diagnosed by two doctors as terminal and expected to die within six months. The prescribing physician must inform the patient of feasible alternatives to suicide and must refer the patient for a psychological examination if needed. Oregon's Intractable Pain Act set rules to ease doctors' fears about prescribing controlled substances for pain control. In fact, the state's medical board shocked professionals around the country by disciplining a doctor for not prescribing enough pain medication! Not surprisingly, Oregon leads the country in lowest rates of in-hospital deaths, better attention to advance planning, more referrals to hospice, fewer barriers to prescribing narcotics, and a smaller percentage of dying patients in pain. California now has a similar law in which physicians who undertreat pain can be charged with unprofessional conduct (see the box on this page).

It is also not surprising that Oregon's law has been under challenge almost constantly since it was approved by a 51 percent majority in 1994. Nevertheless, there are no documented incidents of abuse of the law. Since 2002, both the number of prescriptions written for PAS and the number of terminally ill patients taking lethal medication have remained relatively stable, with about 1 in 800 deaths among Oregonians in 2005 resulting from PAS. The vast majority of the estimated 210 people who have ended their lives since 1994 had cancer. Physicians consistently report that concerns about loss of autonomy and dignity and decreased ability to participate in activities that make life enjoyable are the primary motivating factors in patient requests for lethal medication, a finding corroborated by families. While it may be common for patients with a terminal illness to consider PAS, such a request can be an opportunity for a medical provider to explore with the patient their fears and hopes around end-of-life care, and to make patients aware of other options.

UNDERTREATMENT OF PAIN SPARKS LEGISLATIVE CHANGE

At age 85, Mr. B. was dying of lung cancer. He was admitted to a medical center in Northern California in 1998, complaining of intolerable pain. During a 5-day hospital stay, nurses charted Mr. B.'s pain level at 10—the worst rating on their pain-intensity scale. Despite his family's intention that his pain be addressed, Mr. B.'s internist sent him home—still in agony—with inadequate medication. Ultimately, his family contacted another physician who took a more aggressive approach, and Mr. B. died at home without pain soon afterward.

The case inspired the California legislature to pass Assembly Bill 487, signed into law in 2001. This law requires that physicians who fail to prescribe, administer, or dispense adequate pain medication be charged with unprofessional conduct and be investigated by the California Medical Board's Division of Licensing. Physicians found guilty of undertreating pain must complete a pain-management education program.

SOURCE: Last Acts, 2002.

In most cases, once the provider has addressed a patient's concerns, he or she chooses not to pursue PAS (Jost, 2005; Oregon Department of Human Services, 2006). Actions taken by former Attorney General John Ashcroft to reinterpret the federal Controlled Substances Act so as to nullify Oregon's Death with Dignity Act were another sign of ongoing legal debates regarding assisted suicide and pain management. This Act makes using a controlled substance to "assist suicide" per se "illegitimate," thereby subjecting physicians or pharmacists who assist the dying person under the Oregon act to the possibility of having their prescribing license revoked, as well as criminal penalties under drug laws. Ashcroft's action was widely viewed as an unwarranted expansion of federal authority over states' rights to self-determination. The U.S. District Court of Appeals for Oregon ruled against Ashcroft's reinterpretation, a ruling upheld by the U.S. Supreme Court in

January 2006. Oregon's law remains in effect (http://www.oregon.gov/DHS/ph/pas/faqs.shtml).

Legal Options Regarding End-of-Life Care

While active euthanasia continues to be debated in courtrooms and the ballot box, all 50 states have laws authorizing the use of some type of **advance directive** to avoid artificially prolonged death. This refers to patients' oral and written instructions about end-of-life care and someone to speak on their behalf if they become incompetent; it may include proxy directives. The most common type of advance directive is a **living will** (see Figure 13.1). An individual's wishes about medical treatment are put into writing in the case of irreversible terminal illness or the prognosis of a permanent vegetative (unconscious) state. Under such conditions, living wills can direct physicians to withhold life-sustaining procedures and can assist family members in making decisions when they are unable to consult a comatose, or medically incompetent, relative.

Both federal and state laws govern the use of advance directives. The federal law, the **Patient Self-Determination Act,** requires health care facilities (hospitals, skilled nursing facilities, hospice, home health care agencies, and health maintenance organizations) that receive Medicaid and Medicare funds to inform patients in writing of their rights to execute advance directives regarding how they want to live or die. However, state regulations vary widely. State-specific advance directives can be ordered from the national organization, Compassion and Choices, or downloaded from their Website. However, these facilities do not require the patient to make an advanced directive; the law specifies only that people must be informed of their right to do so.

This act assumes that increased awareness of advance directives will generate discussion between patients and their health care providers, and result in more completed advance directives. Despite this act, less than 30 percent of the general population, primarily white and middle to upper

ADVANCE DIRECTIVES

To what extent do patients participate in determining their care? Research conducted by the Agency for Healthcare Research and Quality (AHRQ) indicates:

- Less than 50 percent of the severely or terminally ill patients studied had an advance directive in their medical record.
- Only 12 percent of patients with an advance directive had received input from their physician in its development.
- Between 65 and 76 percent of physicians whose patients had an advance directive were not aware that it existed.
- Advance directives helped make end-of-life decision in less than 50 percent of those cases where a directive existed.
- Providers and patient surrogates had difficulty knowing when to stop treatment and often waited until the patient had crossed a threshold into an actively dying state before the advance directive was invoked.
- Physicians were only about 65 percent accurate in predicting patient preferences and tended to make errors of undertreatment, even after reviewing the patient's advance directive.
- Surrogates who were family members tended to make prediction errors of overtreatment, even if they had reviewed the advance directive with the patient or assisted in its development.
- Overall, care at the end of life appears to be inconsistent with patients' preferences to forgo life-sustaining treatment, and many dying patients receive life-sustaining care that they do not want.

SOURCE: Kass-Bartelmes and Hughes, 2003.

class, has a written document stating their preferences about end of life care (DiCamillo and Field, 2006). African Americans are the least likely to have advance directives, such as living wills, or to have discussed end-of-life care with their doctors (Dula and Williams, 2005; Kahana et al., 2004). As noted above under palliative care, African Americans often do not want to complete a written

Florida Living Will

Declaration made this _____ day of _____ , _____ ,
                        (day)   (month)   (year)

I, _____ , willfully and
voluntarily make known my desire that my dying not be artificially prolonged under the
circumstances set forth below, and I do hereby declare that:

If at any time I am incapacitated and

        _____ I have a terminal condition, or

        _____ I have an end-stage condition, or

        _____ I am in a persistent vegetative state

and if my attending or treating physician and another consulting physician have determined
that there is no reasonable medical probability of my recovery from such condition, I direct that
life-prolonging procedures be withheld or withdrawn when the application of such procedures
would serve only to prolong artificially the process of dying, and that I be permitted to die
naturally with only the administration of medication or the performance of any medical
procedure deemed necessary to provide me with comfort care or to alleviate pain.

It is my intention that this declaration be honored by my family and physician as the final
expression of my legal right to refuse medical or surgical treatment and to accept the
consequences for such refusal.

In the event that I have been determined to be unable to provide express and informed consent
regarding the withholding, withdrawal, or continuation of life-prolonging procedures, I wish to
designate, as my surrogate to carry out the provisions of this declaration:

Name: _____

Address: _____

_____ Zip Code: _____

Phone: _____

FIGURE 13.1 **Florida Living Will**   *(continued)*

Florida Living Will: Page 2 of 2

I wish to designate the following person as my alternate surrogate, to carry out the provisions of this declaration should my surrogate be unwilling or unable to act on my behalf:

Name: ____

Address: ____

______________________________ Zip Code: ______________

Phone: ____

Additional instructions (optional):

I understand the full import of this declaration, and I am emotionally and mentally competent to make this declaration.

Signed: ____

Witness 1:

Signed: ____

Address: ____

Witness 2:

Signed: ____

Address: ____

FIGURE 13.1 **continued**

document that could be used to justify inferior and inadequate treatment, limit their autonomy, and needlessly hasten death. Many would prefer to have their families rather than health care professionals, whom they often don't trust, make the decision (Borum, Lynn, and Zhong, 2000; Dula and Williams, 2005). Among nursing home residents, 63 percent of whites and 27 percent of African Americans have advance directives. The primary reason for this higher rate compared to the general population is because nursing home residents or their proxies are required to be informed of advance directives (Troyer and McAuley, 2006). The box on page 562 summarizes the relatively limited impact of advance directives on end-of-life decision making (Butler, 2000).

In an attempt to resolve some of the problems with implementing the Patient Self-Determination Act, the **Uniform Health Care Decision Act** was passed in 1993 to provide uniformity and a minimum level of standards in statutes across state lines. This act promotes decision making autonomy by acknowledging individuals' rights to make health care decisions in all circumstances, including the right to decline or discontinue health care. Providers, agents, surrogates, and guardians are mandated to comply with an individual's instructions. Even with such safeguards, compliance is not guaranteed, and, as noted above, a health care provider may decline to honor an advance directive: (1) for reasons of conscience if a directive conflicts with institution policy or values, and (2) if the instruction is contrary to accepted health care standards. However, according to the act, reasonable efforts must be made to transfer the patient to a facility that can honor the directive. In such situations, the act provides for court mechanisms to resolve disputes. A major limitation of this act is that each state may choose whether to replace its own advance directive mandates with the Uniform Health Care Decisions Act. Without federal mandates, the number of states that have done so is limited.

Although it is human nature to delay discussions about aging and dying, in many

> ### STEPS TO TAKE TO AVOID AN ARTIFICIALLY PROLONGED DEATH
>
> - Download state-specific, advance-directive documents from Compassion and Choice.
> - Issue an advance directive, witnessed or notarized according to state laws.
> - Give copies to your personal physician and family members.
> - While healthy, make sure that your family understands your wishes.
> - Be sure that your desires are also noted in your medical record.
> - Begin this process while you are still healthy, your thought processes are clear, you are not in crisis, and time is available.

cases, families and patients may be confused about both their prognosis and their choices. Communication difficulties with health care providers are another common barrier to quality end-of-life care. Ironically, 33 percent of dying patients in a national study said they would discuss advance care planning if the physician brought up the subject, but 25 percent thought that such planning was only for people who were very ill or very old. Contrary to family and health care providers' perceptions that older people do not want to discuss their dying, only 5 percent of older patients stated that they found the discussions about advance planning too difficult (Kass-Bartelmes and Hughes, 2003). In SUPPORT, a 2-year clinical intervention to improve doctor-patient communication and understanding, doctors still did not know what their patients wanted, often did not put preferences in the medical records or if they did, frequently got them wrong (Covinksy, Fuller, and Yaffe, 2000; Dula and Williams, 2005; Phillips et al., 2002). For these reasons, it is crucial to encourage culturally competent communication between health care providers, patients and their families about the process of end-of-life decision-making tools and advance directives.

Some research indicates that adults of all ages, but particularly elders, do not like the standardized approach of advance care planning whereby preferences for specific life-sustaining treatments are documented and strictly followed near death. Instead, they preferred opportunities for ongoing verbal discussion of their values and goals for care with their **surrogate decision maker** and flexibility in decision making (Hawkins et al., 2005). There is growing recognition of the value of appointing a health care proxy—someone known and trusted to make emotionally complex decisions, rather than depending only on a written document (Jost, 2005). A 2005 Pew poll shows that more Americans today are willing to discuss end-of-life issues with their loved ones and to let family members make decisions about continuing medical treatment (DiCamillo and Field, 2006). When advance care planning is discussed with family members (or health care proxy) and physicians, patients' satisfaction, perceived ability to influence and direct their care, and belief that their physicians understand their wishes increase, while their fear and anxiety about dying decrease. Such discussions also help families, other designated surrogate decision makers, physicians, and patients to reconcile their differences about end-of-life care. These findings support the importance of physicians and other decision makers conducting advance care planning discussions with patients during routine outpatient office visits and hospitalization, and, when there are written documents, reviewing them on a regular basis and updating them to reflect patients' preferences at that point in time. The AMA's Advanced Care Planning Process is an ongoing series of discussions among the patient, physician, social worker, and family to clarify values and goals, and to agree on principles to guide decisions (Gossert, Forbes, and Bern-Klug, 2001).

Even when advance directives exist, other problems with implementation may arise. Older adults may fail to tell their doctors about the directive, instead trusting that their families know what to do. Or the advance directive may be in a safe deposit box, unavailable to either family or health care providers. Additionally, those who are designated to make medical decisions if they are unable may be unaware of their selection. When faced with the impending death of their loved one, family members may later change their minds about adhering to an advance directive, especially if the document has not been updated for years. In such instances, physicians are more likely to comply with the family's preference than with the written directive. In addition, federal law does not require health care providers to follow such directives, only that they adhere to state laws or court decisions that deal with advance directives. This means that, in some instances, the physician's decision may override both patient and family preferences. In one study, 65 percent of physicians stated that they would not follow a living will under certain circumstances (Jost, 2005), which points to the importance of having a health care proxy as an advocate.

Patients and their families can access their state's particular law and forms through national organizations, such as Compassion and Choices, local hospitals, state attorney general offices, or the Internet. In situations where there is no living will, the family of an incompetent patient must go to court to obtain legal authority if they wish to refuse life support on the patient's behalf. This expensive and time-consuming process is viewed as necessary where doctors and health care facilities are unwilling to make decisions to remove life-sustaining treatment because of the perceived risk of liability. To obviate this court process, 24 states and the District of Columbia have passed statutes governing surrogate decision makers or health care proxies. Such laws support the concept that the people closest to the patient are in the best position to know his or her wishes or to act in the patient's best interest. The surrogate has a duty to act according to the patient's known wishes. If those are not known, the surrogate must act according to the patient's best interest. Each state's law includes a prioritized list of people connected to the patient. The doctor must approach these individuals, in order of priority, to find someone who is willing to make decisions about life support.

Durable power of attorney is another type of written advance directive, usually in addition to a living will. This authorizes someone to act on an individual's behalf with regard to property and financial matters. The individual does not relinquish control with a power of attorney since it is granted only for the financial matters specifically set forth in the relevant document. An advantage of durable power of attorney is that a living will cannot anticipate what might be wanted in all possible circumstances.

A **medical power of attorney** (or durable power of attorney for health care) specifically allows for a health care surrogate to make decisions about medical care if the patient is unable to make them for him- or herself. A durable power of attorney for healthcare may be used instead of, or in addition to, a living will because it is more broadly applicable to nearly any type of health care during periods of incapacitation. *Durable* means that the arrangement continues even when the person is incapacitated and unable to make his or her own medical decisions. A durable power of attorney agreement may be written to go into effect upon its signing or only when the disability occurs. At that point, bills can continue to be paid and revenues can be collected while other more permanent arrangements are being made, such as the appointment of a conservator or guardian.

Conservatorship generally relates to control of financial matters. In this instance, probate court appoints a person as a conservator to care for an individual's property and finances because that person is unable to do so due to advanced age, mental weakness, or physical incapacity. Such a condition must be attested to by a physician. Once appointed, the conservator will be required to file an inventory of all the assets and to report annually all income and expenses. The individual, however, loses control over his or her property and finances.

Guardianship is a legal tool that establishes control over a person's body as well as financial affairs. In a guardianship, a probate court appoints someone to care for the individual's person, property, and finances because of the individual's mental inability to care for him- or herself. The guardian has the responsibility to direct the individual's medical treatment, housing, personal needs, finances, and property. To establish guardianship, a medical certificate from a physician must state that the individual is mentally incapable of caring for him- or herself. As with conservatorships, the medical certificate by the physician must be made not more than 10 days before the probate court hearing; so in this sense, guardianship cannot be arranged in advance of need. However, through a medical power of attorney, an individual may nominate someone he or she would like to act as guardian if such a need develops. Since the guardian manages all the individual's affairs, guardianship is generally considered a last resort. This is because the process essentially eliminates an individual's legal rights, since consent is not required, and it is costly and rarely reversible.

Family members who are concerned about finances may move too quickly through these options. However, families and service providers should try, as long as possible, to respect the older person's wishes with regard to living arrangements, legal will, and other financial decisions. In other words, the older person should be encouraged to exercise as much control as possible, to the extent that his or her cognitive status allows. In general, less restrictive approaches than guardianship, which balance the need for protection with self-determination, are needed.

Some nursing homes include a statement with their admissions packet that, unless otherwise noted in writing, there will be "no code" for the patient. This type of advance directive means that if the patient quits breathing or his or her heart stops, the staff will not "call a code" to initiate cardiopulmonary resuscitation (CPR). In other nursing homes or hospitals, this type of statement must be written in the patient's chart and signed by the patient and witnesses.

Compassion and Choices is now the largest and most comprehensive end-of-life organization in the country, with over 60 chapters and 30,000 members. By consolidating several end-of-life organizations, some of which had existed since 1938, euthanasia supporters dramatically increased their numbers, gained influence and power, and attracted more donors. Compassion and Choices seeks to support, educate, and advocate for choice and care at the end of life, while pursuing legal reform to promote pain control, advance directives, and legalized physician aid in dying. Living wills for each state can be downloaded from their Website, which provides up-to-date information about right-to-die legal and ethical issues and options nationwide. An organization that has attempted to change laws in order to legalize assisted suicide for the terminally ill is the **Hemlock Society.** The society's popular publication, *Final Exit,* by its founder, Derek Humphry, is a manual on nonviolent methods to commit suicide with prescription barbiturates to assure a gentle, peaceful death. The Hemlock Society distinguishes between "rational or responsible suicide" (i.e., the option of ending one's life for good and valid reasons) and suicide that is caused by a rejection of life because of depression or other psychological disorders. In response to prohibitions against PAS, the society also advocates methods that do not require direct physician assistance, such as gas masks and paper bags. It views the right to request assistance in dying as merely an extension of the individual's right to control the kind of treatment he or she receives. Rejecting remote chances of recovery as a basis to justify prolonging life, the society also discards the notion of ethical distinctions between stopping treatment and assisting someone to die. The Hemlock Society recently partnered with Compassion and Choices as a way to expand their lobbying effectiveness.

Societal cost-benefit criteria inevitably come into play in discussions of active and passive euthanasia. Admittedly, a significant proportion of the money spent on medical care in a person's lifetime goes to services received during the last years and months of life; for example, the proportion of Medicare expenditures spent on elders in their last year of life fluctuates from 27 to 31 percent. In spite of that, even if such end-of-life care were eliminated, Medicare expenditures would be reduced by only a small percentage (Hoover et al., 2002). Additionally, Medicare costs for hospice care tend to be lower than for elders not receiving hospice (Pyenson, 2004). What is projected to increase is non-Medicare expenditures for long-term care for chronic illness in the last year of life. Nevertheless, the public and policy makers still misperceive the costs of medical technology to keep alive a comparatively small number of people to be prohibitively high.

Rapid improvements in medical technology are not matched by refinements in the law and the ethics of using those therapies. This is the case even though **bioethics** or medical ethics, which focuses

---

ETHICAL DILEMMAS

"With the use of our moral imagination, we can reshape the way we behave toward people with any kind of disability. It goes back to Aristotle's question, How does one live a good life? How does ethical thinking help older people live a good life? Ethics is part of what we do every day. It's so much more than making a decision about putting in a feeding tube. . . ." (Holstein, 1998, p. 4). On a personal and practical level, many dying people find that the medical technology that prolongs their lives may financially ruin their families. It is important that families discuss in advance who should assume medical care decision making on the patient's behalf, if necessary, or under what circumstances life support should be removed. Most families find it emotionally difficult to do such planning, especially if the older adult refuses to do so or cannot make a rational decision because of dementia.

on procedural approaches to questions about death, dying, and medical decision making, has grown in the past 35 years. Hastened death raises not only complex ethical and legal dilemmas, but also resource allocation issues. Both policy makers and service providers face the challenge of how to balance an individual client's needs for personal autonomy with the community's demand to conserve resources. A fundamental question is whether the doctrine of personal privacy under the U.S. Constitution and related state laws extends to individuals' decisions about their physical care, even when those decisions involve life or death choices for themselves or others. Alternatively, as aging baby boomers seek to remain at home to die, what are equitable ways to allocate community services such as home care in the face of a growing public distrust of public programs combined with shrinking federal resources? As noted by Holstein (1998), providers, policy makers and families are taking ethics beyond autonomy and decision making into the broader realm of how we treat the terminally ill—how we look at them, what we expect of them, and how we talk to them.

Bereavement, Grief, and Mourning Rituals

Death affects the social structure through survivors, especially spouses and partners, who have social and emotional needs resulting from that death. How these needs are expressed and met varies across place, time, groups, and culture. This is because grief is a highly individualized phenomenon with a complex and wide range of what is considered "normal" within different social and cultural environments.

Bereavement and the Grief Process

Bereavement is defined as the objective situation of having lost someone significant (e.g., being deprived) and the overall adaptation to loss

---

AN INNOVATIVE GRIEF COUNSELING PROGRAM

Family members of patients dying in the intensive care unit of hospitals often experience a grief process characterized by anxiety, depression, and even post-traumatic stress disorder (PTSD). The usual practice of most hospitals is for health professionals and trained grief counselors to hold a brief conference with families of patients in the ICU. The impact of a structured counseling session has been tested, using the guidelines of: *V*aluing what family members had to say, *A*cknowledging their emotions, *L*istening to their feelings, *U*nderstanding, and *E*liciting questions from participants ("VALUE"). These families were compared with others who were given the the typical brief end-of-life conference. A follow-up 90 days later found that the VALUE approach reduced symptoms of anxiety, depression, and PTSD. These results point to the benefits of a proactive communication strategy with longer conferences that allow family members of the dying to express their feelings and have them acknowledged (Lautrette et al., 2007).

(Stroebe et al., 2001). It usually refers to loss through death, although individuals can be bereaved through other types of losses such as divorce or relocation. The **grief process** is the complex emotional response to bereavement and can include shock and disbelief, guilt, psychological numbness, depression, loneliness, fatigue, loss of appetite, sleeplessness, and anxiety about one's ability to carry on with life. **Mourning** signifies culturally patterned expectations about the expression of grief. What is believed about the meaning of death, how it should be faced, and what happens after physical death varies widely by culture and its associated religions. Cultural variations are particularly marked with regard to beliefs about the meaning of loss through death, including the possibility of future reunion with the dead, the significance of various emotions, and what to say to oneself and others following a death (Rosenblatt, 2001). With the increasing diversity of American society and globalization, professionals must be

Visiting the grave of a loved one provides solace for many elders.

sensitive to the influences of multiple cultures on elders and to the dying patient's generation and acculturation level. Even within an ethnic minority group such as Asian Americans, there is considerable diversity around the expression of grief. For example, Japanese Americans tend to be reluctant to talk about death; grief is kept within the family rather than expressed publicly, and the body is not to be moved nor organs removed for donation until the soul has had time to travel from it. In contrast, crying among bereaved Filipinos is sometimes uncontrollable, especially when viewing the body (Rosenblatt, 2001).

Although there are clusters or phases of **grief reactions,** the progression is more like a roller coaster—with overlapping responses and wide individual variability—rather than orderly stages or a fixed or universal sequence. As noted in the earlier discussion of Kubler-Ross's work, to

expect grieving individuals to progress in some specified fashion is inappropriate, and can be harmful to them. The highs and lows within broad phases can occur within minutes, days, months, or years, with grieving individuals moving back and forth among them. There can even be mixed reactions within the same person, who may simultaneously experience within a matter of hours anger, guilt, helplessness, loneliness, and uncontrolled crying—along with personal strength and pride in their coping. Emotions change rapidly, beginning with shock, numbness, and disbelief, followed by an all-encompassing sorrow. Early months following the loss are the most difficult. However, even when a grieving person has tried to work through early phases and move toward integrating the loss into his or her life, a picture, a favorite song of the deceased, or a personal object may evoke more intense grief.

An intermediate phase of grief often involves an idealization and seeking the presence of the deceased person, as well as an obsessive review to find meaning for the death and to answer the inexplicable "why"? Anger toward the deceased, a supreme being, and caregivers may also be experienced, as well as guilt and regrets for what survivors did not do or say. When the permanence of the loss is acknowledged and yearning ceases, anguish, disorganization, and despair often result. The grieving person tends to experience a sense of confusion, feelings of aimlessness, loss of motivation, confidence, and interest, and inability to make decisions. Simply getting out of bed in the morning can require intense effort. These feelings may be exacerbated if the grieving person tries to live according to others' expectations, including those of the deceased. Instead, successful accommodation requires active coping strategies in which the bereaved individual finds his or her own best way to live with grief.

The final phase of grief—reorganization—is marked by a resumption of routine activities and social relationships while simultaneously recognizing that life will never be the same and still remembering and identifying with the deceased. The ability to communicate effectively one's thoughts and feelings to others, form new relationships, and learn new skills and competencies enhances this reorganization phase. Some older adults may also experience personal growth and meaning through multiple losses. *Integration of the loss into one's life* might be more appropriate than the term *recovery* to describe changes in the person's identity and emotional reorganization to ordinary levels of functioning. This concept also recognizes that for many elders, grief is never completely resolved and always is present (Niemeyer, 2001; Wortman, 2002; Wortman and Silver, 2001).

Process of Mourning

A "six-R process of mourning" integrates much of what has been written about grief stages, phases, and tasks, and can provide guidelines for family members and professionals:

- Recognize and accept the reality of the loss.
- React to, experience, and express the pain of separation or active confrontation with the loss, including deep weeping and articulating feelings of guilt.
- Reminisce: tell and retell memories, writing, and dreaming.
- Relinquish old attachments. More recently, grief theorists have identified the importance of maintaining connections with the person who has died, but in ways different than in the past, while allowing oneself to form new relationships. For many elders, however, it is not relinquishing attachments but redefining them.
- Readjust to an environment in which the dead person is missing, adapt to new roles, and form a new identity.
- Reinvest in new personal relationships and acts of meaning rather than remaining tied to the past, while recognizing that the pain of the loss may continue throughout life (Stroebe et al., 2001; Weiss, 2001; Wortman, 2002; Wortman and Silver, 2001).

The classical paradigm of grief, derived from Freud's psychoanalytical perspective, assumed that grieving individuals needed to let go of their relationship to the deceased in order to complete their "grief work." Individuals who did not engage in grief work were assumed to be at risk of pathological grief and increased risk of physical and mental illness. Later postmodern and

---

HOW PROFESSIONALS AND FAMILIES CAN SUPPORT THE GRIEVING PROCESS

- Listen, without judgment or giving advice, to the bereaved individual's expression of feelings including guilt, anger, and anxiety, rather than suggesting what he or she *should* feel or do.
- Realize that the grieving process can be a lengthy and emotional roller-coaster, not a fixed progression
- Be careful to avoid endless chatter or simplistic statements ("I know just how you feel." "She is happier now." "God loved him more than you did." "You should feel better in six months." "You can marry again/you'll meet someone else").
- Resist telling your own stories.
- Listen carefully to the silences, to what is not said as well as said.
- Encourage sharing of memories.
- Sometimes the most helpful response is simply "to be there" for the bereaved.
- Time itself does not heal. Healing often occurs through dealing with grief, which can be painful and exhausting. But some mourners never engage in "grief work."
- Recognize that most people never completely get over loss through death but can learn to live with grief.
- Do not tell the bereaved to stop crying or not be sad; provide time and space to cry; sometimes hugging or patting the crying person's hand actually shuts down crying.
- Identify concrete tasks by which to help, such as organizing meals, child care, and house cleaning, so the bereaved has time and space to grieve.
- Recognize gender and cultural differences in grieving.
- Encourage meditation, deep breathing, self-care, and exercise.

constructionist theoretical perspectives do not presume the universality of how individuals respond to death. Instead, they acknowledge the tremendous diversity of healthy grieving, and that the "grief work" model of actively confronting negative emotions is not always the best approach. For some elders, denial, distraction, and humor can also be effective ways to grieve. From the postmodern perspective, the process of vacillation between the dual goals of avoiding and engaging in grief work is fundamental to reconstructing meaning and a basic sense of self. Later theorists also emphasized that the goal of grieving is not to disengage completely from memories and bonds with the deceased. Instead, as noted above, bereaved individuals redefine their connection to the deceased. It is important to acknowledge that conflicting views about healthy grieving exist, and that we have too little knowledge to claim that we know the best way for older adults to grieve (Klass, Silverman, and Nickerson, 1996; Lindenstrom, 2002; Walter, 2003; Wortman and Silver, 2001).

Many people never fully resolve their loss or cease grieving, but learn to live with the pain of loss for a lifetime. Older adults' experiences with grief may be even more complex than other age groups' for several reasons. As noted in Chapter 6, they are more likely to experience unrelated, multiple losses over relatively brief periods, at a time when their coping capacities and environmental resources are often diminished. The cumulative effects of losses may be greater, especially if the older person has not resolved earlier losses, such as a child's death, or interprets current losses as evidence of an inevitable continuing decline. Health care providers must be careful not to misdiagnose grief symptoms as physical illness, dementia, or hypochondria. On the other hand, prior losses can facilitate accommodation to a loved one's death, especially for older adults who are resilient. Personal capacities of resilience include prior experiences with handling losses, spirituality and religiosity, and capacity to find

meaning in life. Whether other losses have been interpreted as positive (i.e., leading to personal growth) and the degree to which relationships seem complete also appear to be critical factors in the grief process (Moss, Moss, and Hansson, 2001; Ramsey and Bleiszner, 2000).

Whether grieving is more difficult when death is sudden or unexpected is unclear. In comparison to the young, older people may be less affected by a sudden death because they have rehearsed and planned for the death of a partner or spouse as natural, and widowhood as a life-stage task. They have also experienced it vicariously through the deaths of their friends or partners of friends. An expected death allows survivors to prepare for the changes through **anticipatory grief,** but it does not necessarily minimize the grief and emotional strain following the death. In fact, some studies indicate that a longer period of anticipatory grief, through caring for an individual with chronic illness, can actually create barriers to successful adaptation and increase the risk of depression and other psychiatric disorders. For example, if a dying partner suffered, such as being in pain, the bereaved caregiver will be more prone to depression, guilt, and feelings of helplessness, and will recover more slowly (Carr, 2003; Carr et al., 2000; Richardson and Balaswamy, 2001).

Some studies report more anxiety, feelings of isolation, and alienation in partners who have provided care during a long illness (Carr et al., 2001; Richardson, 2006; Richardson and Balswamy, 2001). Family members who experience a death as a relief from long-term demands of caregiving may feel premature detachment, ambivalent and hostile feelings, guilt, depression, and a reduced ability to mourn publicly. A central dynamic in caregiver bereavement is the support experienced while providing care, as well as the possibility of continued support through surviving confidants (Almberg, Grafstroem, and Winblad, 2000). For example, widowers typically experience short-term relief after protracted caregiving, but those who experienced social isolation while providing care often suffer long-term consequences from the lack of social interaction (Carr, 2004; Schulz et al., 2003). The location of a partner's death—whether in a nursing home or at home—also affects bereavement, with less distress if a partner dies at home, particularly if the bereaved elder was present at the moment of death (Bennett and Vidal-Hall, 2002; Richardson and Balswamy, 2001). However, bereaved persons in one study adjusted more quickly when their partners died in a nursing home, perhaps because they had grieved in anticipation when their partner was placed there (Carr et al., 2001; Richardson, 2006). Other researchers have concluded that the overall grief process is similar whether the loss is expected or unexpected, although suddenness (i.e., being unprepared for death) may make a difference early in the process of bereavement (Barry, Kasl, and Prigerson, 2002). This may occur because no matter when a partner dies or under what circumstances, the surviving partner has to shift from "we" to "I" (Carr, 2003). When death is anticipated, some psychosocial interventions before the death can help prevent complications following the death. These include facilitating communication with the ill partner, preparing the survivor for the practical aspects of life without the partner, and enabling the surviving partner to deal with his or her own illness-related chronic stressors and losses. Health care providers now recognize the importance of attending to the bereaved's grief process and view grieving, often expressed in diverse ways, as a natural healing process. Assistance in grieving, perhaps through life review and encouragement of new risk-taking, is especially important for older adults (Hooyman and Kramer, 2006).

Mourning involves cultural assumptions about appropriate behavior during bereavement. Mourning rituals develop in every culture as a way to channel the expression of grief, define the appropriate timing of bereavement, and encourage support for the bereaved among family and friends. Professionals need to be sensitive to cultural and ethnic minority differences regarding the form and meaning of death and the burial or cremation of the dead. Grief rituals, such as sorting and disposing of personal effects and visiting the grave site, are often important in working through the grief process.

The funeral or memorial service, for example, serves as a rite of passage for the deceased and a focal point for the expression of the survivors' grief. Funerals also allow the family to demonstrate cohesion through sharing rituals, food, and drink, and thus to minimize the disruptive effects of the death. Funerals and associated customs are more important in societies with high mortality rates throughout the life cycle than in societies where death is predominantly confined to the old. Money donations instead of flowers, memorial services and celebrations of the deceased person's life instead of funerals, and cremations instead of land burial signal the development of new kinds of death rituals. Traditional funeral ceremonies are criticized for being costly, for exploiting people at a time when they are vulnerable, and for elaborate cosmetic restorations of the body. Legislation has been enacted to control some of the excesses of the funeral industry; organizations such as the People's Memorial Association ensure lower funeral costs to its members. Despite criticisms of the funeral industry, however, most people approve of some type of ceremony to make the death more real to the survivors and to offer a meaningful way to cope with the initial grief.

Widowhood

A spouse's death (or that of a partner, in the case of GLBT couples or unmarried heterosexual couples) may be the most catastrophic and stressful event experienced by older adults, altering one's self-concept to an "uncoupled identity." Widowhood for both men and women not only represents the obvious physical loss, but numerous

THE EXPERIENCE OF WIDOWHOOD

Darlene became a widow at age 56. Although she was too young to qualify for her husband's Social Security, her dependent children received a monthly benefit of approximately $1000 per child. A successful career woman, Darlene sought refuge in her work, her friends, and her children. She learned new skills, such as home and car repairs, and appeared to be self-sufficient and "moving on" to her friends and children. During the day, she functioned well. It was only at the end of the day, when other family members were asleep, that she would be overcome by feelings of intense loneliness, hopelessness, and regret. At times, she felt overwhelmed at the thought of all the years ahead when she would bear both responsibilities and pleasure alone, without an intimate with whom to share. For more than two years, she cried every night before she fell asleep.

Older widows generally have more extensive peer support than widowers.

other changes in the survivor's life that are experienced as losses. These include the loss of:

- a shared past and a future
- the role or status of married partner
- a sexual partner
- companionship, social networks, and a confidant
- economic security, especially for women

Death of a partner tends to trigger "cascading effects," with one's grief interacting with or exacerbating other changes, such as chronic illness, disability, or involuntary relocation (Cicirelli, 2002; Hooyman and Kramer, 2006).

As discussed in Chapter 15, among women age 65 and older, up to 70 percent are widowed, more than three times the rate among their male peers (Federal Interagency Forum, 2006). Marital dissolution through widowhood is an example of an anticipated or normative life course transition for older women, who may be better prepared for a spousal death than older men are. Of all wives, 85 percent outlive their husbands,

since women generally marry men older than themselves, live longer than men, and experience widowhood earlier than men. They also spend more years as a widow and, in their later years, seldom remarry after the death of their husbands. Among the oldest-old, widows outnumber widowers 5 to 1; among people of color, the proportion of widows is twice that among whites. Women of color are also widowed earlier, which reflects the shorter life expectancy of men of color in our society (Kreider, 2005). Older widows and widowers are more likely than younger adults to become sick or die in the short term, often within the first 6 months. Their immune systems may weaken; their chronic conditions and functional disabilities become exacerbated. They visit physicians more often, and are more likely to be hospitalized or spend time in a nursing home. Their health care utilization and costs increase, and they experience more depressive symptoms. The rates of physical and mental problems along with mortality are higher for widowers than widows. Physical symptoms include dry mouth, changes in appetite, muscle weakness, tightness in the chest, headaches, dizziness, insomnia, and physical exhaustion. Similarly, rates of depression, anxiety, substance abuse, mood alterations, obsessive thoughts of the deceased, disorientation, memory problems, and difficulties concentrating are found to be nearly 9 times as high among the newly bereaved, especially men, as among married individuals. These high rates of illness may result from hormonal responses to the stress of loss, which can lead to suppression of the body's immune system. Over the long term (i.e., more than 2 years), the effects on physical and mental health are greatly diminished (Goodkin et al., 2001; Hall and Irwin, 2001; Laditka and Laditka, 2003). Despite the stress of widowhood, the course of spousal bereavement is often characterized by resilience and effective coping, which allows feelings of self-confidence, self-efficacy, and personal growth to follow short-term depression and illness. Nevertheless, the greatest problem faced by widows and widowers is loneliness—and being alone, since the social relationships inherent in being a couple are disrupted. In fact, the terms *widow* and *alone* are almost synonymous, at least during the early phases of widowhood (Utz et al., 2002; van den Hoonaard, 2001; Worden, 2002).

The negative effects of widowhood can be attenuated through a number of psychosocial variables. Quality of the prior relationship affects how partners experience the death of a spouse. Grief tends to be less for those whose relationship was marked by conflict (Carr et al., 2000). By contrast, short-term grieving is more difficult for those whose marriage was harmonious and characterized by warmth, strong bonds and emotional dependence, but over time, these qualities may bring solace and foster personal growth. In addition, harmonious marriages appear to have a protective effect in terms of the use and costs of health care when both partners are alive, but such costs are higher for widows and widowers from harmonious marriages than for survivors of discordant marriages (Prigerson et al., 2000; Richardson, 2006; Worden, 2002).

Other variables that affect the long-term effects of widowhood are the adequacy of social support networks, including professional support and closeness to children and intimate friends; the individual's characteristic ways of coping with stress; religious commitment and cultural values and beliefs. Although family plays an important role following widowhood, approximately 20 percent of widowed persons report not having a single living relative to whom they feel particularly close. Older widows are more likely to use social supports as a coping strategy when their social networks are reciprocal, but men generally do not. At the same time, friendships developed on the basis of marital relationships may not survive widowhood. In fact, the ability to make new friends is an indicator of how well an individual is coping with the loss of a spouse/partner. Age, gender, and health status of the widowed person also affect the degree of stress. Age by itself, however, is found to have little effect on bereavement outcomes. Differences between younger and older widows can be explained largely by the relationship of age to employment status and income. Age is associated, however, with a greater need to learn new life skills, such as an older widow's mastering financial-management tasks, or widowers' learning housekeeping skills and managing social activities (van den Hoonaard, 2001).

Whether the stress of bereavement through widowhood is greater for the young than for the old is unclear. As noted above, the intensity of psychological distress immediately postdeath tends to be greater for younger widows than older ones, because of the unanticipated nature of the death. Although younger spouses are found to manifest more intense grief initially, a reverse trend is noted after 18 months, with the emotional and physical distress associated with grief lasting longer for older partners. This may be because the loss of a lifelong relationship results in greater disorganization of roles, commitments and patterns of daily life (Moss et al., 2001). As noted earlier, older people are more likely to experience other losses simultaneously, or **bereavement overload** (Kastenbaum, 1991), which may intensify and prolong their grief. On the other hand, spousal bereavement in later life is an "on-time" or normative event, especially for older women, who typically have had other opportunities to develop appropriate coping strategies for a variety of losses. In such instances, widowhood may be less stressful, even among the oldest-old, and different death circumstances do not appear to have a significant impact on long-term accomodation (Van den Hoonaard, 2001; Vinokur, 2002).

Preventive psychoeducational interventions initiated predeath, such as through hospice, can minimize problems in mourning, as opposed to interventions postdeath, after problems have surfaced. Interventions postdeath focus on assisting the surviving spouse review and reflect on the loss, providing support for grieving, and redefining the emotional attachment to the dead partner. Reviewing, evaluating, and perhaps reinterpreting prior experiences in order to resolve earlier conflicts can facilitate attaining a sense of meaning in the grief process (Corr, Nabe, and Corr, 2003; Raveis, 1999). Since bereaved partners who have extensive contacts with friends and family and belong to religious institutions and other voluntary associations are less likely to die soon after the death of a spouse, interventions need to encourage informal network building and organizational

affiliations. Community mental health centers, primary care clinics, and senior centers are suitable venues for such cost-effective support interventions.

Gender Differences in Widowhood

Whether widowhood is more difficult for women or men is unclear. Certainly, coping or adaptation to widowhood is related to income for both men and women. Adequate financial resources are necessary to maintain a sense of self-sufficiency and to continue participation in meaningful activities. As detailed in Chapter 15, older widows are generally worse off than widowers in terms of finances, years of education, legal problems, and prospects for remarriage. Women who have been economically dependent on their husbands often find their incomes drastically reduced. Financial hardships may be especially great for women who have been caring for a spouse during a long chronic illness or who have depleted their joint resources during the spouse's relocation to a long-term care facility. Furthermore, older widows generally have few opportunities to augment their income through paid work. Insurance benefits, when they exist, tend to be exhausted within a few years of the husband's death. Not surprisingly, higher income is found to be associated with better bereavement outcomes, especially rates of depresson that are lower postdeath than immediately prior to death (Schulz et al., 2006).

Some women do not depend on a man for economic or social support. Among women over age 70, 66 percent of whom are widowed, the married woman is the unusual case. But she may still have an extensive social support network formed across the life course and now largely composed of other widows. Such social connectedness can buffer some of the adverse effects of widowhood for recently bereaved women, including the risk of hospitalization and health problems (Laditka and Laditka, 2003; Miller, Smerglia, and Bouche, 2004). Even when their

DEVELOPING NEW ROLES IN WIDOWHOOD

Martha had always seen her role as wife and mother and left the "business" aspects of family life to her husband. Her "job" was to keep the home a comfortable place for him and their daughter. Widowed at age 63, she felt ill-prepared to take on paying the bills and budgeting. She sought the advice of her banker on the best way to set up a bookkeeping system. After paying the bills, and taking care of the Medicare paperwork for the past few years, she now sees herself as being in the role of "manager" for herself, arranging home repairs and is pleased with what she has learned.

friends die, women generally establish new relationships, exchanging affection and material support outside their families, although they may not want to call on such relationships to care for them (Ajrouch, Blandon, and Antonucci, 2005). Friends may be more supportive than children, especially when friends accept the widow's emotional ambivalence, do not offer unwanted advice, and respond to what she defines as her needs. Adjusting to the loss of a spouse is likely to be most difficult for women who are in poor health, have had few economic and social resources throughout their lives, and perceive themselves as dependent. The extent to which widows have strong friendship networks appears to vary with socioeconomic class and ethnic minority status, whether they had a social network and satisfying roles before their husbands' deaths, and the prevalence of widowhood among a person's own age, sex, and class peers. Latina and Asian American widows are more likely to live with others and thus to have more active support systems than Caucasian widows or those from other ethnic minority groups (Moen, 2001). Coping with widowhood may be hardest for women whose identity as a wife is lost without the substitution of other viable roles and lifestyles. A closely related factor appears to be whether a gap exists between the extent to which a woman was socialized to be dependent on a man and how she must now live more independently as a widow (van den Hoonaard, 2001). These recent findings of widows' extensive informal networks differs markedly from Lopata's (1973) classic study, where widows who did not have their own friends or who had only couple-based friendships before the husband's death generally had difficulty forming new friendships and developing satisfying roles. Because more women have entered the workforce in the past 35 years, employment-associated social networks of future cohorts of older women may also enhance their capacity to live on their own, compared to the women in Lopata's early studies.

While older widowed men are seven times more likely than older widows to remarry, many widows have no interest in remarriage. For some women who have been restricted in their relationship or faced long-term caregiving responsibilities, widowhood can bring relief and opportunities to develop new interests. Although a husband's death is devastating, personal growth can be a positive result of the loss. Some widows recognize how they have changed and redefined themselves, calling themselves "new women" (van den Hoonaard, 2001; Walter, 2003). Recent research indicates that overall, women living alone, including widows, feel more positive about their autonomy than women did in the past (AARP, 2006; Cheng, 2006).

A woman's change in status inevitably affects her relationship with her children and other relatives. Although their children may view their widowed mother as "helpless" and urge her to move in with them, most widows do so only as a "last resort." Older widows often grow closer to their daughters through patterns of mutual assistance, but sons tend to provide instrumental support (e.g., home repairs, yard work) for mothers in their own homes. Nevertheless, although children provide both socioeconomic support and assistance with tasks, this may not necessarily reduce their widowed parent's loneliness. For example, interactions with an adult child are less reciprocal than with a partner, while friends and neighbors are better suited for sharing leisure activities and providing companionship. Such reciprocity tends to be associated with higher morale. What is clear is the importance of diverse social networks that include age-generational peers, whether family or nonfamily.

Less is known about the effects of widowhood on older men, for whom their wife's death tends to be unexpected (think about how many widowers will say "I always thought I was the one who would go first"). Men more often complain of loneliness and appear to make slower emotional recoveries than do women. As noted above, they are more likely to experience physical and mental health problems, particularly depression (Fry, 2001). Compared to women's emotive patterns of coping, men tend to be more instrumental, although this is not determined by gender per se (Martin and Doka, 2000). Other factors that affect men's grief process appear to be their lower degree of involvement in family and friendship roles across the life course, their lifelong patterns of restraining their emotions, their limited prior housekeeping and cooking experiences, and, among older cohorts, their greater likelihood of a double role loss as paid worker and spouse. In addition, older men in this current cohort have more difficulty in seeking informal support and in expressing their feelings. Although older widowers describe themselves as sad and thinking about their wives nearly constantly, they typically do not share these feelings with others (Martin and Doka, 2000; Miller and Golden, 1998). For men who focused largely on work, their wife's death may raise issues of self-identity and profoundly affect their social relationships. One reason is that men tend to have larger non-kin networks, perhaps as a result of employment, but are less resourceful in planning social get-togethers and building informal networks that substitute for the sociability they typically enjoyed in marriage (Ajrouch et al., 2005; Moen, 2001).

Given these factors, men may "need" remarriage more than women do, and perhaps have been socialized to move more quickly into restructuring their lives through remarriage. Although the death of their wives may significantly impair older men's well-being, it is less likely to place men at an economic disadvantage. And in some instances, men experience pride and enhanced self-esteem from mastering new housekeeping skills. More research is needed on how men cope with the loss of their wives/partners, as well as more professional sensitivity to men's problem-focused style of grieving (Doka, 2000; Miller and Golden, 1998; Walter, 2003). Even less is known about how older men's experience of widowhood varies by social class or ethnic minority status.

As described in Chapter 9, informal social support can reduce the risk of illness and mortality (Krause, 2006; Lyra and Heikkenen, 2006). In order to provide such support for persons coping with loneliness and isolation, mutual help groups and bereavement centers are widely available in most communities. Women are the most frequent participants. These widow-to-widow groups are based on the principle of bringing together people who have the common experience of widowhood and who can help each other identify solutions to shared concerns. They recognize that a widowed person generally accepts help from other widowed people more readily than from professionals or family members. Support groups thus can provide widows with effective role models, help integrate them into a social network, and enhance their sense of competence toward their environment. Similar groups also need to be developed for GLBT elders who are coping with the loss of a partner. Some studies, however, have suggested that a widowed person's sense of self-esteem, competence, and life satisfaction may be as important resources as the self-help intervention itself—or more so. One implication is that group interventions should focus on ways for the bereaved to draw on and enhance their internal resources, to increase their confidence, and to learn new skills, not just serve

---

MEN AND WIDOWHOOD

George's first wife died in childbirth; his second wife, who suffered a long bout of cancer, died when he was 79, and his third wife died when he was 85. After the deaths of his first two wives, he quickly sought out someone else who could help fill the void left by their deaths. Each time, he looked for someone who would attend to his needs, listen to his stories, and join him on short outings and trips. He was seeking a companion, not a lover. After the death of his third wife, he became socially isolated and depressed. She had been the one who had kept their social life going. Without her, friends seemed to drop away.

as a forum to address the disruptive effects of the loss. More research is needed on how support-group dynamics and structure relate to specific adjustment outcomes for women and men from diverse ethnic minority groups.

The Death of Siblings and Friends

Although the likelihood of siblings dying increases with age, research on the effects of sibling death is relatively limited. Sibling relationships represent the one family bond that can last a lifetime. Yet the older person's grief at losing siblings may be overlooked by other family members and health care professionals, and few social supports exist specifically for bereaved siblings (Connidis, 2001). In one study, bereaved siblings rated their own health lower than a bereaved husband or wife did (Hays, Gold, and Pieper, 1997). The death of a friend is also often overlooked or minimized. For many older people, especially women, a friend may be a closer confidante than a partner. Lifelong friends share a history of memories and experiences that no one else can fully understand. With a friend's death—similar to that with siblings—older adults lose a past that can never be recaptured with anyone else. Relatively little is known about the cumulative effects of numerous friends' deaths in old age (Hooyman and Kramer, 2006).

Implications for the Future

The right-to-die movement, death with dignity, palliative care, pain management, and use of advance directives all raise ethical dilemmas related to the prolongation and termination of life. These dilemmas are often framed within the context of escalating health care costs and use of expensive technology to prolong life. Many older adults are now saved, often at considerable cost, from diseases that previously would have killed them, only to be guaranteed death from another disease at equally high or even higher cost. Physicians have traditionally been taught to spare no effort in keeping a patient alive. Nevertheless, health professionals and laypersons are increasingly questioning whether dying should be prolonged when there is no possibility of recovery.

The timing, place, and conditions of death are increasingly under medical control. For almost any life-threatening condition, some interventions can now delay the moment of death, but not its inevitability. As a sign of the increasing medicalization of aging, adults age 80 and over are the most rapidly growing group of surgical patients. In fact, three groups of medical procedures are becoming almost routine for the oldest–old: cardiac bypass, angioplasty, stent and other cardiovascular procedures; renal hemodialysis; and kidney transplants (Kaufman, Shim, and Russ, 2004). Doctors and nurses have always dealt with dying, but not until current higher use of technical advances have they had so much power and responsibility to control the medicalization of end of life. Accordingly, adults of all ages are faced with greater challenges of saying "no" to life-extending interventions. These new medical capacities demand a new set of ethics and practices. The field of bioethics was born out of the dilemmas surrounding the introduction and withdrawal of invasive treatments, the patients' decision-making capacity to participate in treatment decisions, and the quality of the patient's life. Health care facilities are now required to have the capacity to address such bioethical issues, typically through ethics committees. With the medicalization of aging, bioethics will continue to grow in this century, encompassing a wider range of professionals in debates about end-of-life care. Three features of the new ethos of care are:

1. the ways in which routine medical care overshadows choice
2. the transformation of the technological imperative to a moral imperative (e.g., caregiving

and love are tied to clinical acts that either extend life in advanced old age or allow "letting go").

3. the coupling of hope for cure and of "growing old without aging" with the normalization and routinization of life-extending interventions (Kaufman et al., 2004).

Concerns about when and whether treatment should be withheld frame the debates regarding the right to die and to assisted suicide. Proponents of the right to die and active euthanasia maintain that prolonging excruciating pain and threatening a person's dignity in a hopeless situation serve no public interests. These decisions become even more complex when the elder is mentally incompetent or comatose. Cross-cultural differences also affect how life-sustaining treatment and palliative care are interpreted and the value and respect accorded elders' lives.

The increased visibility of right-to-die legislation, court rulings, and individual cases means that more people know about their legal rights and have thought about what they might choose for themselves or other family members when faced with a terminal illness. In most cases, there is agreement that individuals should have the right to control how they die. However, disagreement persists about what is meant by terminal and medical finality and under what circumstances decisions to cease life-sustaining treatment should be made. The 1997 Supreme Court decision put at the forefront the issue of aggressive pain management and how well health care providers are trained in end-of-life care. More and more professional organizations are seeking to ensure that providers are prepared to provide palliative care.

Public support is relatively widespread for individual determination regarding life-sustaining treatment through advance directives, including living wills. Baby boomers, who will be better educated and accustomed to having control over their lives, are more likely to complete advance directives and to be outspoken about their end-of-life preferences than the current cohort of

elders. Even though all 50 states have laws authorizing the use of advance directives, variability across states in their interpretation and implementation will probably continue. This also highlights the need for older adults, their surrogate decision makers, and their physicians to have opportunities to discuss end-of-life preferences rather than depend only on a standardized written document.

Divided votes on state legislation to legalize assisted suicide will probably persist in the future. Regardless of the laws, however, individuals and their families will continue to make decisions to hasten death, especially for terminal cancer patients with pain or for those with neurological disorders such as Lou Gehrig's disease. Internet resources on dying, including those that provide information on how to hasten death, foster the debates taking place at the grassroots level and allow families and patients to take matters into their own hands. For example, Death.net, founded by Derek Humphrey of the Hemlock Society, offers a large collection of "right to die" materials and services on the Internet. The Website of Compassion and Choices is a comprehensive resource for information, the right-to-die movement, and to download advance directive packages geared to the laws and regulations of a particular state. Such Internet resources, which once were unimaginable, will increase in number and detail in the future. Not surprisingly, the number of anti-euthanasia Websites is also growing, such as Life WEB of the International Anti-Euthanasia Task Force. Such Internet resources articulating the pros and cons of the right to die and assisted suicide will undoubtedly proliferate. These legal and ethical debates—whether in courtrooms, ethics committees, or cyberspace—translate into daily practice and hard choices for those who are caring for chronically ill and dying elders. The questions of who should control decisions about life and death will continue to be argued philosophically and legally, but doctors, nurses, social workers, and families will be faced with the hard clinical decisions for timely practical solutions. As noted throughout this chapter, the professional preparation of a wide range of health care providers in the future must address such legal and ethical issues, as well as how to deliver culturally competent end-of-life care.

Summary

Although death and dying have been taboo topics for many people in our society, they have become more legitimate issues for scientific and social discussion in recent years. At the same time, there is a growing emphasis on the preparation of professionals to work effectively with the dying and their families, as well as a movement to permit death with dignity. A major framework advanced for understanding the dying process is the concept of stages of dying. However, the stage model is only an inventory of possible sequences, not fixed steps.

Most people appear to accept and deny death simultaneously, better able to discuss others' deaths than their own, and fearing a painful dying process for themselves more than the event of death itself. Different attitudes toward dying exist among the old and the young. As a whole, older people are less fearful and anxious about their death than younger people and would prefer time to prepare for their death. Likewise, survivors tend to view an older person's death as less tragic than a younger individual's.

Professionals and family members can address the dying person's fears, minimize the pain of the dying process, and help the individual to attain a "good death." One of the major developments in this regard is hospice, a philosophy of caring that can be implemented in both home and institutional settings, and which provides people with more control over how they die and the quality of their remaining days. However, hospice and other palliative care initiatives need to take account of cultural differences regarding the use of life-extending technology and advance directives.

The movement for a right to a dignified death has prompted new debates about euthanasia. Both passive and active euthanasia raise complex moral and legal questions that have been only partially addressed by the passage of living will legislation and a growing number of judicial decisions, including the June 1997 Supreme Court decision that ruled that there is no constitutional "right to die." Economic issues are also at stake; as costs for health care escalate, questions about how much public money should be spent on maintaining chronically ill people are likely to intensify. Bioethics, with its emphasis on informed consent, patient rights, and autonomy, addresses the moral issues raised by the health care of older people.

Regardless of how individuals die, their survivors experience grief and mourning. The intensity and duration of grief appear to vary by age and sex, although more research is needed regarding gender differences in reaction to loss of spouse and adjustment to widowhood.

By age 70, the majority of older women are widows. A much smaller number of older men become widowers, generally not until after age 85. The status of widowhood has negative consequences for many women in terms of increased legal difficulties, reduced finances, and few remarriage prospects. Although men are less economically disadvantaged by widowhood, they may be lonelier and have more difficulty adjusting than women. For men and women, social supports, particularly close friends or confidants, are important to physical and mental well-being during widowhood. In addition to mourning rituals to help them cope with their grief, services such as widows' support groups are also needed. Comprehensive and diverse service formats are essential, given the variety of grief responses, and interventions should be available early in the bereavement process and continue over relatively long periods of time to ensure maximum effectiveness. Health and social service professionals can play a crucial role in developing services for the dying and their survivors that are sensitive to cultural, ethnic minority, sexual orientation, and gender differences.

GLOSSARY

active euthanasia   positive steps to hasten someone else's death, such as administering a lethal injection; assisted suicide, generally by a physician

advance directive   documents such as living wills, wills, and durable power of attorney for health care decisions that outline actions to be taken when an individual is no longer able to do so, often because of irreversible terminal illness

anticipatory grief   grief for a loved one prior to his or her death, usually occurring during the time that the loved one has a terminal illness that may allow survivors to prepare; may be a barrier to adaptation

assisted suicide/physician-assisted suicide (PAS)   considered active euthanasia when a physician actively aids with a person's death, typically through the use of drugs

bereavement   state of being deprived of a loved one by death

bereavement overload   an experience of older adults who are exposed to the increased frequency of family and friends' deaths and become desensitized to the impact of death

bioethics   discipline of medicine dealing with procedural approaches to questions about death, dying, and medical decision making

Compassion and Choices   formed in 2005 by combining several national end-of-life organizations; it is the largest and most comprehensive organization of its type

conservatorship   designation by a court to manage the affairs, either personal or fiscal or both, of persons unable to do so for themselves

death with dignity   dying when one still has some autonomy and control over decisions about life

durable power of attorney   legal document that conveys to another person designated by the person signing the document the right to make decisions regarding either health and personal care or assets and income, or both, of the person giving the power; it is a durable power that does not expire, as a power of attorney normally does, when a person becomes incompetent

Dying Person's Bill of Rights   affirms dying person's right to dignity, privacy, informed participation, and competent care

dying process   five stages that may be experienced by the dying person, as defined by Kübler-Ross: (1) denial and isolation, (2) anger and resentment, (3) bargaining and an attempt to postpone, (4) depression and sense of loss, and (5) acceptance

euthanasia   the act or practice of killing (active euthanasia) or permitting the death of (passive euthanasia) hopelessly sick or injured individuals in a relatively painless way; mercy killing

grief process   intense emotional suffering caused by loss, disaster, or misfortune; acute sorrow; deep sadness

grief reaction   emotional and cognitive process following the death of a loved one or other major loss

guardianship   establishes legal control over another person's body, finances, and all legal affairs

hastened death   viewed as a more socially acceptable term than *euthanasia* because it speeds up the inevitable

Hemlock Society   national organization that promotes the right to die for terminally ill persons, calls for legalizing assistance for those who decide to take their own lives, and publishes information on nonviolent, painless methods to commit suicide

hospice   a program of care for dying persons that gives emphasis to personal dignity of the dying person, reducing pain, and sources of anxiety, and family reconciliation when needed

informed consent   written or oral document that states indications/reasons for treatment, its benefits, risks, and alternatives

living will   legal document in which an individual's wishes about medical treatment are put in writing should he or she be unable to communicate at the end of life, directing physicians and hospitals to withhold life-sustaining procedures, take all measures to sustain life, or whatever seems appropriate to the person executing the document

medical power of attorney   similar to "durable power of attorney," but focuses on a health care surrogate to make decisions about *medical* care

mourning   culturally patterned expressions of grief at someone's death

palliative care   treatment designed to relieve pain provided to a person with a terminal illness for whom death is imminent

passive euthanasia   voluntary elective death through the withdrawal of life-sustaining treatments or failure to treat life-threatening conditions

Patient Self-Determination Act   federal law requiring that health care facilities inform their patients about their rights to decide how they want to live or die; for example, by providing them information on refusing treatment and on filing advance directives

right to die   the belief that persons have a right to take their own lives, especially if they experience untreatable pain, often accompanied by the belief that persons have a right to physician assistance in the dying process

self-neglect   a process by which a person voluntarily makes decisions that are equivalent to choosing to die (e.g., refusing help, not eating)

surrogate decision maker   person legally designated to act according to patient's known wishes or "best interest," also known as proxy

Uniform Health Care Decision Act   mandates compliance with patients' health care decisions

RESOURCES

Web Resources on Grief and Loss   Web pages dedicated to grief and loss are increasing in both quantity and quality. Sites offer information on the grief process and provide opportunities to share feelings, questions, and concerns with others. Below is a small sampling of some of these sites. Log on to MySocKit (www.mysockit.com) for information about the following:

- AARP Grief and Loss Programs
- American Academy of Hospice and Palliative Medicine
- American Hospice Foundation
- Center to Advance Palliative Care
- Compassion and Choices
- Death with Dignity National Center
- Hemlock Society (partnership with Compassion and Choices)
- Hospice Foundation of America
- Last Acts Coalition
- National Hospice and Palliative Care Organization

REFERENCES

AARP. Looking at act II of women's lives: Thriving and striving from 45 on. *The AARP Foundation Women's Leadership Circle Study.* 2006.

Abelson, R. A chance to pick hospice and still hope to live. *The New York Times,* February 10, 2007, A1, B4.

Adamek, M. Late life depression in nursing home residents: Social work opportunities to prevent, educate and alleviate. In B. Berkman and L. Harootyan (Eds.), *Social work and health care in an aging society.* New York: Springer, 2003.

Ajrouch, K., Blandon, A., and Antonucci, T. Social networks among men and women: The effects of age and socioeconomic status. *Journals of Gerontology,* 2005, *60B,* S311–S317.

Almberg, B.E., Grafstroem, M., and Winblad, B. Caregivers of relatives with dementia: Experiences encompassing social support and bereavement. *Aging and Mental Health,* 2000, *4,* 82–89.

American Geriatrics Society. *Measuring quality of care at the end of life.* Washington, DC: Author, 1996.

Anderson, K., Mendoza, T., Valero, V., Richman, S., Russell, C., et al. Minority cancer patients and their providers: Pain management attitudes and practice. *Cancer,* 2000, *88,* 1929–1938.

Arbuckle, N.W., and deVries, B. The long-term effects of later life spousal and parental bereavement on personal functioning. *The Gerontologist,* 1995, *35,* 637–645.

Barry, L., Kasl, S., and Prigerson, H. Psychiatric disorders among bereaved persons: The role of perceived circumstances of death and preparedness for death. *American Journal of Geriatric Psychiatry* 2002, *10,* 447–457.

Bennett, K.M., and Vidal-Hall, S. Narratives of death: A qualitative study of widowhood in women in later life. *Ageing and Society,* 2000, *20,* 413–428.

Berger, A., Pereira, D., Baker, K., and O'Mara, A. A commentary: Social and cultural determinants of end-of-life care for elderly persons. *The Gerontologist,* 2002, *42,* 49–53.

Bern-Klug, M., Gessert, C., and Forbes, S. The need to revise assumptions about the end of life: Implications for social work practice. *Health and Social Work,* 2001, *26,* 38–43.

Borum, M., Lynn, J., and Zhong, Z. The effects of patient race on outcomes in seriously ill patients in SUPPORT: An overview of economic impact, medical intervention and end-of-life decisions: Study to understand prognoses and preferences for outcomes and risks of treatments. *Journal of the American Geriatrics Society,* 2000, *48,* S194–S198.

Braun, K.L., Look, M., Yang, H., Onaka, A., and Horiuchi, B. Native Hawaiian mortality in 1980 and 1990 in the state of Hawaii. *American Journal of Public Health,* 1996, *86,* 888–889.

Braun, K.L., and Nichols, R. Death and dying in four Asian American cultures: A descriptive study. *Death Studies,* 1997, *21,* 327–359.

Braun, K.L., Pietsch, J.H., and Blanchette, P.L. (Eds.). An introduction to culture and its influence on end-of-life decision making. In *Cultural issues in end-of-life decision making.* Thousand Oaks, CA: Sage, 2000.

Braun, K.L., Tanji, V.M., and Heck, R. Support for physician-assisted suicide: Exploring the impact of ethnicity and attitudes toward planning for death. *The Gerontologist,* 2001, *41,* 51–60.

Bretscher, M., Rummans, T., Sloan, J., Kaur, J., Bartlett, A., et al. C. Quality of life in hospice patients: A pilot study. *Psychosomatics,* July–August 1999, *40,* 309–313.

Brickner, L., Scannell, K., Marquet, S., and Ackerson, L. Barriers to hospice care and referrals: Survey of physicians' knowledge, attitudes and perceptions in a health maintenance organization. *Journal of Palliative Medicine,* 2004, *7,* 411–418.

Brink, S. Saying no and moving on. *The Seattle Times,* February 8, 2007, A3.

Butler, R. *Keynote address.* Presented at the Open Society Institute, Project on Death in America, Lake Tahoe, CA: July 17–22, 2000.

Cantwell, P., Turoc, S., Brenneis, C., and Hanson, J. Predictors of home death in palliative care cancer patients. *Journal of Palliative Care,* 2000, *16,* 23–30.

Carr, D. A good death for whom? Quality of spouse's death and psychological distress among older widowed persons. *Journal of Health and Human Behavior,* 2003, *44,* 215–232.

Carr, D. Gender, preloss martial dependence and older adults' adjustment to widowhood. *Journal of Marriage and the Family,* 2004, *66,* 220–235.

Carr, D., House, J., Wortman, C., Nesse, R., and Kessler, R. Psychological adjustment to sudden and antici-

pated spousal loss among older widowed persons. *Journals of Gerontology,* 2001, *56B,* S237–S248.

Carr, D., House, J.S., Kessler, R.C., Nesse, R.M., Sonnega, J., and et al. Marital quality and psychological adjustment to widowhood among older adults: A longitudinal analysis. *Journals of Gerontology,* 2000, *55B,* S197–S205.

Caserta, M.S., Lund, D.A., and Rice, S.J. Pathfinders: A self-care and health education program for older widows and widowers. *The Gerontologist,* 1999, *39,* 615–620.

Cheng, C. Living alone: The choice and health of older women. *Journal of Gerontological Nursing,* 2006, *32,* 24–25.

Christopher, M.J. The new place of end-of-life issues on the policy agenda. *Public Policy and Aging Report,* 2003, *13,* 23–26.

Cicirelli, V.G. Fear of death in mid-old age. *Journals of Gerontology,* 2006, *61B,* P75–P81.

Cicirelli, V.G. *Older adults' views on death.* New York: Springer, 2002.

Cicirelli, V.G. Personality and demographic factors in older adults' fear of death. *The Gerontologist,* 1999, *39,* 569–579.

Compassion in Dying. Senate bill threatens Oregon's death with dignity act and pain care nationwide. *Compassion in Dying,* 2000, 13.

Cone, D., Richardson, L., Todd, D., and Betancourt, J. Health care disparities in emergency medicine. *Academic Emergency Medicine,* 2003, *10,* 1176.

Connidis, I.A. *Family ties and aging.* Thousand Oaks, CA: Sage, 2001.

Corr, C., Nabe, C., and Corr, D. *Death and dying: Life and living.* Belmont, CA: Wadsworth, 2003.

Crawley, L. Palliative care in African American communities. *Innovations in end-of life care,* 2001, 3. Accessed February 16, 2007, from http://www2.edc.org/lastacts/archives/archivesSept01/editorial.asp.

Death with Dignity. *Physicians: leave assisted suicide to doctors, patients.* Accessed 2001, from http://www.Deathwithdignity.org/fss/opinion/amn62001.

DeSpelder, L., and Stickland, A. *The last dance: Encountering death and dying* (6th ed.). Boston: McGraw Hill, 2002.

DiCamillo, M., and Field, M. *Continued support for doctor-assisted suicide. Most would want their physician to assist them if they were incurably ill and wanted to die.* San Francisco, CA: Field Research Corporation, 2006.

Doka, K.J. *Men don't cry, women do: Transcending gender stereotypes of grief.* Philadelphia: Brunner/Mazel, 2000.

Dula, A., and Williams, S. When race matters. *Clinical Geriatric Medicine,* 2005, *21,* 239–253.

Epstein, A., Ayanian, J., Keogh, J., and Noonan, S. Racial disparities in access to renal transplantation. *New England Journal of Medicine,* 2000, *343,* 1537–1544.

Federal Interagency Forum on Aging. *Aging-related statistics. Older Americans 2006: Key indicators of well-being.* Washington, DC: U.S. Government Printing Office, 2006.

Field, M.J., and Cassel, C.K. *Approaching death: Improving care at the end of life.* Washington, DC: National Academy Press, 1997.

Fortner, B., Neimeyer, R.A, and Rybarczk, B. Correlates of death anxiety in older adults: A comprehensive review. In A. Tomer (Ed.), *Death attitudes and the older adult: Theories, concepts and applications.* Philadelphia: Taylor and Francis, 2000.

Freeman, H., and Payne, R. Racial injustice in health care: An editorial. *The Washington Post,* March 2000, 1–2.

Fry, P.S. The unique contribution of key existential factors to the prediction of psychological well-being of older adults following spousal loss. *The Gerontologist,* 2001, *41,* 69.

Galambos, C.M. Preserving end-of-life autonomy. The Patient Self-Determination Act and the Uniform Health Care Decisions Act. *Health and Social Work,* 1998, *23,* 275–281.

Goodkin, K., Baldewicz, T.T., Blaney, N.T., Asthana D., Kumar, M., et al. Physiological effects of bereavement and bereavement support group interventions. In M.S. Stroebe, R.O. Hansson, W. Stroebe, and H. Schut (Eds.), *Handbook of bereavement research: Consequences, coping and care.* Washington, DC: American Psychological Association, 2001.

Gossert, C.E., Forbes, S., and Bern-Klug, M. Planning end-of-life care for patients with dementia: Roles of families and health professionals. *Omega,* 2001, *42,* 273–291.

Hall, M., and Irwin, M. Physiological indices of functioning in bereavement. In M.S. Stroebe, R.O. Hansson, W. Stroebe, and H. Schut (Eds.),

Handbook of bereavement: Consequences, coping and care. Washington, DC: American Psychological Association, 2001.

Hawkins, N., Ditto, P., Danks, J., and Smucker, W. Micromanaging death: Process preferences, values, and goals in end of life decision-making. *The Gerontologist,* 2005, *45,* 107–117.

Hayes, J., Gold, D., and Peiper, C. Sibling bereavement in late life. *Omega,* 1997, *35,* 25–42.

Holstein, M. Ethics and aging: Bringing the issues home. *Generations,* 1998, *22,* 4.

Hoover, D., Crystal, S., Kumar, R., Sambamoorthi, U., and Cantor, J. Medical expenditures during the last year of life: Findings from the 1992–1996 Medicare current beneficiary survey. *Health Services Research,* 2002, *37,* 1625–1642.

Hooyman, N., and Kramer, B. *Living through loss: Interventions across the lifespan.* New York: Columbia University Press, 2006.

Institute of Medicine. *Unequal treatment: Confronting racial and ethnic disparities in health care.* Washington, DC: National Academy Press, 2002.

Johnson, K., Elbert-Avila, K., and Tulsky, J. The influence of spiritual beliefs and practices on the treatment preferences of African Americans: A review of the literature. *Journal of the American Geriatrics Society,* 2005, *53,* 711–719.

Jost, K. Right to die. *The CQ Researcher,* May 13, 2005, 423–438.

Kahana, B., Dan, A., Kahana, E., and Kercher, K. The personal and social context of planning for end-of-life care. *Journal of the American Geriatrics Society,* 2004, *52,* 1163–1167.

Kass-Bartelmes, B., and Hughes, R. *Advance care planning: Preferences for care at the end of life. Research in action.* Washington, DC: Agency for Healthcare Research and Quality, 2003.

Kastenbaum, R. *Death, society and human experience* (4th ed.). New York: Macmillan/Merrill, 1991.

Kaufman, S.R. A commentary: Hospital experience and meaning at the end-of-life. *The Gerontologist,* 2002, *42,* 34–39.

Kaufman, S.R., Shim, J., and Russ, A. Revisiting the biomedicalization of aging: Clinical trends and ethical challenges. *The Gerontologist,* 2004, *44,* 731–738.

Kayser-Jones, J., Kris, A., Miaskowski, C., Lyons, W., et al. Hospice care in nursing homes: Does it contribute to higher quality pain management? *The Gerontologist,* 2006, *46,* 325–333.

Klass, D.S., Silverman, P.R., and Nickonson, S.L. (Eds.), *Continuing bonds: New understandings of grief*. Washington, DC: Taylor and Francis, 1996.

Klass, D., and T. Walter. Processes of grieving: How bonds are continued. In M.S. Stroebe, R.O. Hansson, W. Stroebe, and H. Schut (Eds.), *Handbook of bereavement*. Washington, DC: American Psychological Association, 2001.

Krause, N. Social relationships in late life. In R. Binstock and L. George (Eds.), *Handbook of aging and the social sciences* (6th ed.). San Diego: Academic Press, 2006.

Kressin, N., and Peterson, L. Racial differences in the use of invasive cardiovascular procedures: Review of the literature and prescription for future research. *Annals of Internal Medicine*, 2001, *135*, 352–366.

Krieder, R. *Number, timing and duration of marriages and divorces, 2001*. Washington, DC: US Census Bureau Current Population Reports, 2005.

Kübler-Ross, E. *Living with dying*. New York: Macmillan, 1981.

Kübler-Ross, E. *On death and dying*. New York: Macmillan, 1969.

Kübler-Ross, E. (Ed.). *Death: The final stage of growth*. Englewood Cliffs, NJ: Prentice-Hall, 1975.

Kübler-Ross, E., and Kessler, D. *Life's lessons: Two experts on death and dying tell us about the mysteries of life and living*. New York: Scribner, 2001.

Kurent, J.E. *The Institute for Community and Professional Education in End-of-Life Care*. Presented at the Open Society Institute, Project on Death in America, Lake Tahoe, CA: July 17–22, 2000.

Laditka, J., and Laditka, S. Increased hospitalization risk for recently widowed older women and protective effects of social contacts. *Journal of Women and Aging*, 2003, *15*, 7–28.

Lamberg, L. "Palliative care" means "active care": It aims to improve quality of life. *Journal of the American Medical Association*, 2002, *288*, 943–944.

Last Acts. *Means to a better end: A report on dying in America today*. Washington, DC: Author, 2002.

Lautrette, A., Darmon, M., Megarbane, B., Joly, L.M., Chevret, S., Adrie, C., et al. A communication strategy and brochure for relatives of patients dying in the ICU. *New England Journal of Medicine*, 2007, *356*, 469–478.

Lawton, M.P. Quality of life and the end of life. In J. Birren and K.W. Schaie (Eds.), *Handbook of the psychology of aging* (5th ed.). San Diego: Academic Press, 2001.

Lewis, C.S. *A Grief Observed* (1st ed.). New York: Seabury Press, 1961.

Lindenstrom, T. It ain't necessarily so: Challenging mainstream thinking about bereavement. *Family and Community Health*, 2002, *25*, 11–21.

Lopata, H.Z. The support systems of American urban widows. In M. Stroebe, W. Stroebe, and R. Hanson (Eds.), *Handbook of bereavement: Theory, research and intervention*. New York: Cambridge University Press, 1993.

Lopata, H.Z. *Widowhood in an American city*. Cambridge, MA: Schenkman, 1973.

Lund, D.A., Caserta, M., and Dimond, M. The course of spousal bereavement in later life. In M. Stroebe, W. Stroebe, and R. Hanson (Eds.), *Handbook of bereavement: Theory, research and intervention*. New York: Cambridge University Press, 1993.

Lyyra, T.M., and Heikkinen, R.L. Perceived social support and mortality in older people. *Journals of Gerontology*, 2006, *61B*, S147–S153.

Maro, R. Victory through the courts. *Compassion in Dying*, Spring 1996, 1.

Martin, T.L., and Doka, K.J. *Men don't cry, women do*. Philadelphia: Brunner/Mazel, 2000.

Martin-Matthews, A. Widowhood and widowerhood. *Encyclopedia of Gerontology*, 1996, *2*, 621–625.

McClain, V.R., Tindell, S., and Hall, S.H. Ethical dilemmas in right to die issues. *American Journal of Forensic Psychology*, 1999, *17*, 77–88.

McLaughlin, L.A., and Braun, K.L. Asian and Pacific Islander cultural values: Considerations for health care decision making. *Health and Social Work*, 1998, *23*, 116–126.

Miller, J., and Goldman, T. *When a man faces grief: A man you know is grieving*. Fort Wayne, IN: Willowgreen Press, 1998.

Miller, N., Smerglia, V., and Bouche, N. Women's adjustment to widowhood: Does social support matter? *Journal of Women and Aging*, 2004, *16*, 149–167.

Miller, S., Intrator, O., Gozalo, P., Roy, J., and Barger, J., et al. Government expenditures at the end of life for short and long-stay nursing home residents: Differences by hospice enrollment status. *Journal of the American Geriatrics Society*, 2004, *52*, 1284–1292.

Miller, S., and Mor, V. The role of hospice care in the nursing home setting. *Journal of Palliative Medicine*, 2002, *5*, 271–277.

Miller, S., Teno, J., and Mor, V. Hospice and palliative care in nursing homes. *Clinics in Geriatric Medicine,* 2004, *20,* 717–734.

Miller, S.C., and Mor, V. The emergence of Medicare hospice care in U.S. nursing homes. *Journal of Palliative Medicine,* 2001, *15,* 471–480.

Mitchell, B., Ballard, D., and Matchar, D. Racial variation in treatment for transient ischemic attacks: Impact of participation by neurologists. *Health Services Research,* 2000, *34,* 1413–1428.

Moen, P. The gendered life course. In R.H. Binstock and L.K. George (Eds.), *Handbook of aging and the social sciences* (5th ed.). San Diego, CA: Academic Press, 2001.

Morrison, R.S., and Siu, A.L. Survival in end-stage dementia following acute illness. *Journal of the American Medical Association,* 2000, *284,* 47–52.

Moss, M., Moss, S., and Hansson, R. Bereavement in old age. In M. Stroebe, R. Hansson, W. Stroebe, and H. Schut (Eds.), *Handbook of bereavement research.* Washington, DC: American Psychological Association, 2001.

Muir, J.C. No title. Presented at the Open Society Institute, Project on Death in America, Lake Tahoe, CA: July 17–22, 2000.

Mutran, E.J., Danis, M., Bratton, K., Sudha, S., and Hanson, L. Attitudes of the critically ill toward prolonging life: The role of social support. *The Gerontologist,* 1997, *37,* 192–199.

National Center for Health Statistics. *National Mortality Followback Survey,* Hyattsville, MD: author, 2003.

National Consensus Project for Quality Palliative Care. *Clinical practice guidelines for quality palliative care.* 2004. Accessed February 14, 2007, from http://www.nationalconsensusproject.org.

National Hospice and Palliative Care Organization Research Department. *Hospice facts and figures.* Accessed December 18, 2004, from http://www.hnpco.org/files/public/Hospice_Facts_110104.pdf.

Neimeyer, R. Can there be a psychology of loss? In J.H. Harvey (Ed.), *Perspectives on loss.* Philadelphia: Taylor and Francis, 1998.

Neimeyer, R.A. Meaning Reconstruction and loss. In R.A. Neimeyer (Ed.), *Meaning reconstruction and the experience of loss.* Washington, DC: American Psychological Association, 2001.

Nieboer, A.P., Lindenberg, S.M., and Siegwart-Ormel, J. Conjugal bereavement and well-being of elderly men and women: A preliminary study. *Journal of Death and Dying,* 1999, *38,* 113–141.

Nolen-Hoeksema, S., and Larson, J. *Coping with loss.* Mahwah, NJ: Erlbaum, 1999.

Northwest Geriatric Education Center, Dealing with grief and loss, *NWGEC Viewpoint,* Winter 2000, *9,* 1–3.

O'Bryant, S.L., and Hansson, R.O. Widowhood. In R. Blieszner and V.H. Bedford (Eds.), *Handbook of aging and the family.* Westport, CT: Greenwood Press, 1995.

Olson, E. Physician-assisted suicide and euthanasia's impact on the frail elderly: A physician's reply. *Journal of Long Term Home Health Care: The Pride Institute Journal,* Summer 1998, *17,* 28–33.

Oregon Department of Human Services. *Eighth Annual report on Oregon's Death with Dignity Act,* Portland, OR: Office of Disease Prevention and Epidemiology, March 9, 2006.

O'Reilly, K.B. *Doctors favor physician-assisted suicide less than patients do. AMedNews.com,* Accessed November. 21, 2005, from http://www.compassionandchoices.org/documents/20051121suicidepolls.pdf.

Ostrom, C. New focus on debate on assisted suicide. *The Seattle Times,* January 1998, *1,* A18.

Ostrom, C. The war on pain. *The Seattle Times,* May 14, 2000, 1, A15, A17.

Owen, J.E., Goode, K.T., and Haley, W.E. End-of-life care and reactions to death in African American and white family caregivers of relatives with Alzheimer's disease. *Omega,* 2001, *43,* 349–361.

Parkes, C.M. *Bereavement: Studies of grief in adult life.* New York: International University Press, 1972.

Payne, R. At the end of life: Color still divides. *The Washington Post,* February 15, 2000.

Payne, R., Medina, E., and Hampton, J. Quality of life concerns in patients with breast cancer, evidence of disparity outcomes and experiences in pain management and palliative care among African American women. *Cancer,* 2003, *97,* 311–317.

Phillips, R., Hamel, M., Covinsky, K., and Lynn J. Findings from SUPPORT and HELP: An introductory study to understand prognoses and preferences for outcomes and risks of treatment: Hospitalized elderly longitudinal project. *Journal of the American Geriatrics Society,* 2000, *48.*

Prigerson, H.G., Maciejewski, P.K., and Rosenheck, R.A. Preliminary explorations of the harmful interactive effects of widowhood and marital harmony on health, health service use, and health care costs. *The Gerontologist,* 2000, *40,* 349–357.

Pyenson, B., Conor, S., Fitch, K., and Kinzbrunner, B. Medicare cost in matched hospice and non-hospice cohorts. *Journal of Pain and Symptom Management,* 2004, *28,* 200–210.

Ramsey, J.L., and R. Blieszner. Transcending a lifetime of losses: The importance of spirituality in old age. In J.H. Harvey and E.D. Miller (Eds.), *Loss and trauma: General and close relationship perspectives.* Washington, DC: Taylor & Francis, 2000.

Rando, T.A. *Grieving: How to go on living when someone you love dies.* Lexington, MA: Lexington books, 1988.

Rando, T.A. *Treatment of complicated mourning.* Champaign, IL: Research Press, 1993.

Raveis, V.H. Facilitating older spouses' adjustment to widowhood: A preventive intervention program. *Social Work in Health Care,* 1999, *29,* 13–32.

Richardson, V., and Barusch, A. *Gerontological practice for the 21st century: A social work perspective.* New York: Columbia University Press, 2006.

Richardson, V.E. Bereavement in later life. In V.E. Richardson and A.S. Barusch (Eds.), *Social work practice with older adults.* New York: Columbia University Press, 2006.

Richardson, V.E., and Balaswamy, S. Coping with bereavement among elderly widowers. *Omega,* 2001, *43,* 129–144.

Rosenblatt, P.C. A social constructionist perspective on grief. Introduction to M. Stroebe, R. Hansson, W. Stroebe, and H. Schut (Eds.), *Handbook of bereavement research: Consequences, coping and care.* Washington, DC: American Psychological Association, 2001.

Rozenzweig, A., Prigerson, H., Miller, M.D., and Reynolds, C.F., 3rd. Bereavement and late-life depression: Grief and its complications in the elderly. *Annual Review of Medicine,* 1997, *48,* 421–428.

Schoepfer, T. Mind frames towards dying and factors motivating their adoption by terminally ill elders. *Journals of Gerontology,* 2006, *61B,* S129–S139.

Schulz, R., Boerner, K., Shear, K., Zhang, S., and Gitlin, L.N. Predictors of complicated grief among dementia caregivers: A prospective study of bereavement. *The American Journal of Geriatric Psychiatry,* 2006, *14,* 650.

Schulz, R., Mendelsohn, A.B., Haley, W.E., Mahoney, D., Allen, R.S., et al. End of life care and the effects of bereavement on family caregivers of persons with dementia. *New England Journal of Medicine,* 2003, *349,* 1936–1952.

Stroebe, M., Hanson, R., Stroebe, W., and Schut, H. Chapter title? In M. Stroebe, R. Hansson, W. Stroebe, and H. Schut (Eds.), *Handbook of bereavement research: Consequences, coping and care.* Washington, DC: American Psychological Association, 2001.

Stroebe, M., and Schut, H. *The social context of grief and grieving.* Proceedings of the Social Context of Death, Dying and Disposal. Glasgow: Glasgow Caledonian University, 1998.

Stroebe, M., Schut, H., and Stroebe, W. Trauma and grief: A comparative analysis. In J.H. Harvey (Ed.), *Perspectives on loss.* Philadelphia: Taylor and Francis, 1998.

Teno, J., Gruneir, A., Schwartz, Z., Nanda, A., and Wetle, T. Association between advance directives and quality of end of life care: A national study. *Journal of the American Geriatrics Society,* 2007, *55,* 189–194.

Teno, J., Weitzen, S., Wetle, R., and Mor, V. Persistent pain in nursing home residents. (Letter to the editor). *Journal of the American Geriatrics Society,* 2001, *285.*

Thompson, L.W., Gallagher-Thompson, D., Futterman, A., Gilewski, M.J., and Peterson, J. The effects of late-life spousal bereavement over a thirty-month interval. In M.P. Lawton and Salthouse et al. (Eds.), *Essential papers on the psychology of aging. Essential papers in psychoanalysis.* New York: New York University Press, 1998.

Thorson, J., and Powell, F.C. Death anxiety in younger and older adults. In A. Tomer (Ed.), *Death attitudes and the older adult: Theories, concepts and applications.* Philadelphia: Taylor and Francis, 2000.

Thorson, J.A., Powell, F.C., and Samuel, V.T. African and Euro-American samples differ little in scores on death anxiety. *Psychological Reports,* 1998, *83,* 623–626.

Tilly, J.A., and Wiener, J.M. End of life care for the Medicaid population. *Public Policy and Aging Report,* 2003, *13,* 17–22.

Tomer, A., and Ellison, G. Attitudes about life and death. Toward a comprehensive model of death anxiety. In Tomer, A. (Ed.), *Death attitudes and the older adult: Theories, concepts and applications.* Philadelphia: Taylor and Francis, 2000.

Topics in Advanced Practice. The Growth of Hospice. Nursing e-Journal, Accessed February 15, 2007, from www.medscape.com/viewarticle/549702_2.

Troyer, J., and McAuley, W. Environmental contexts of ultimate decisions: Why nursing home residents are twice as likely as African American residents to have an advance directive. *The Journals of Gerontology,* 2006, *61B,* S194–S202.

Turvey, C.L., Carney, C., Arndt, R.B., and Herzog, R. Conjugal loss and syndrome depression in a sample of elders aged 70 or older. *American Journal of Psychiatry,* 1999, *156,* 1596–1601.

Utz, R., Carr, D., Nesse, R., and Wortman, C. The effect of widowhood on older adults' social participation: An evaluation of activity, disengagement, and continuity theories. *The Gerontologist,* 2002, *42,* 522–533.

van den Hoonaard, D. *The widowed self: Older women's journey through widowhood.* Waterloo, Ontario: Wilfred Laurier University Press, 2001.

Waldrop, D.P. At the eleventh hour: Psychosocial dynamics in short hospice stays. *The Gerontologist,* 2006, *46,* 106–114.

Walter, T. *The loss of a life partner: Narratives of the bereaved.* New York: Columbia University Press, 2003.

Washington, H. *Medical apartheid: The dark history of medical experimentation on Black Americans from colonial times to the present.* New York: Doubleday, 2007.

Weiss, R.S. Grief, bonds and relationships. In M. Stroebe, R. Hansson, W. Stroebe, and H. Schut (Eds.), *Handbook of bereavement research: Consequences, coping and care.* Washington, DC: American Psychological Association, 2001.

Weitzen, S., Teno, J., Fennell, M., and Mor, V. Factors associated with site of death: A national study of where people die. *Medical Care,* 2003, *41,* 323–335.

Welch, L.C., Teno, J.M., Mor, V. End-of-life care in black and white: Race matters for medical care of dying patients, and their families. *Journal of the American Geriatrics Society,* 2005, *53,* 1145–1153.

Wilkinson, A.M., and Lynn, J. The end of life. In R.H. Binstock and L.K. George (Eds.), *Handbook of aging and the social sciences* (5th ed.). San Diego: Academic Press, 2001.

Williams, R., Baker, P., Allman, R., and Roseman, J. The feminization of bereavement among community-dwelling older adults. *Journal of Women and Aging,* 2006, *18,* 3018.

Won, A., Lapane, K., Vallow, S., Schein, J., Morris, J., et al. Persistent nonmalignant pain and analgesic prescribing patterns in elderly nursing home residents. *Journal of the American Geriatrics Society,* 2004, *52,* 867–874.

Worden J.W. *Grief counseling and grief therapy: A handbook for the mental health practitioner.* New York: Springer, 2002.

Wortman, C., and Silver, R.C. The myths of coping with loss revisited. In M. Stroebe, R. Hansson, W. Stroebe, and H. Schut (Eds.), *Handbook of bereavement research: Consequences, coping and caring.* Washington, DC: American Psychological Association, 2001.

Wortman, C.B. *Changing Lives of Older Couples Study.* Accessed January 15, 2002, from http://www.cloc.isr.umich.edu/ index.htm.

14

The Resilience of Elders of Color

When discussing the changes experienced by older adults, there is a tendency to speak about them as if they were a homogeneous group. Yet, as illustrated throughout this book, the older population is more heterogeneous than any other. Two primary variables in this heterogeneity are gender and ethnic minority status; both influence an individual's position in the social structure and experiences across the life course. To be an older person of color, or an older woman, is to experience environments substantially different from those of a white male across the life course. For example, both older women and African American elders are more likely to have a low income and live alone, which places them at greater risk of poorer health status and social isolation.

The interaction of gender, ethnic minority status, living arrangements, and social class (or socioeconomic status) is illustrated by the following examples of health and economic disparities:

- The poverty rate for African American women who live alone is four to five times greater than for their married counterparts.
- African American and Latino households headed by women are almost three times more likely than non-Hispanic whites to be poor in old age.
- Older women of color are more likely to obtain health care from hospital outpatient units, emergency rooms, and neighborhood centers than from private physicians, generally because they lack adequate insurance.
- Older women of color who live alone form the poorest group in our society (Angel and Hogan, 2004; AOA, 2005; Heinz, Lewis, and Hounsell, 2006; Herd, 2006).

Consistent with the *life course perspective* described in Chapter 8, such disparities in old age are typically related not only to current living arrangements, but also to early experiences in education, labor force participation, health status, access to health care, and cultural beliefs and practices. Many elders of color bring to old age the cumulative effects of a lifetime of disadvantage because of their race (Whitfield, 2004). As noted in Chapter 12, early life inequities are usually intensified in old age.

Relevant differences among older people arising from their gender and their ethnic minority status are noted throughout this text. However, this chapter and the next focus specifically on these factors because of their interactive effects with age and the resulting higher incidence of poverty, poor health, barriers to health care, and inadequate living arrangements. In this sense, both older women in general and men and women of color are affected by environmental changes that are incongruent with their needs as they age. Socioeconomic status (SES) is a primary factor, along with race and gender, that creates inequities across the life course. SES influences variation within groups, not only between groups. Despite the greater problems facing both women and people of color, both groups display strengths and resilience in old age.

The concept of resilience or "hardiness," which was introduced in Chapter 6, encompasses the behavioral patterns, functional competence, and cultural capacities that individuals, families, and communities utilize under adverse circumstances, and the ability to integrate adversity as a catalyst for growth and development (Fredriksen-Goldsen, in press). Populations of color, despite experiencing great adversity, often have extensive personal (e.g., spirituality, sense of mastery, faith), cultural (e.g., beliefs, values and traditions), and social (e.g., friends, extended family) resources that help them cope with negative life conditions and experience well-being (Zauszniewski et al., 2005). By emphasizing resilience, we do not intend to minimize the growing economic and health inequities faced by populations of color within our society. However, a focus on resilience among ethnic minorities recognizes their considerable strengths in the face of such adversity. As such, it moves beyond individual characteristics to include contextual or environmental factors, and contrasts with earlier research that emphasized deficits among minority populations.

Defining Ethnicity and Culture

Cultural diversity refers to people's national origin, their language, and other cultural heritage they bring with them (Angel and Angel, 2006). Ethnicity has three components:

1. a sense of peoplehood evolved from a group's common ancestry and history
2. social status that can determine how people eat, work, celebrate, care for each other, and die
3. informal social support systems

Based on a combination of race, religion, and cultural history, ethnicity is retained, whether or not members explicitly realize their commonalities with one another. Its values are transmitted over generations by the family and reinforced by the surrounding community. Ethnicity patterns people's thinking, feeling, and behavior in both obvious and subtle ways, although generally people are unaware of it. Accordingly, it can be a powerful influence on older people's roles and their adaptation to aging (McGoldrick, Giordano, and Garcia-Preto, 2005). Within the P–E model, ethnicity is central to the individual's sense of competence vis-à-vis environmental demands. Ethnicity may serve the following functions for elders:

- an integrating force when experiencing significant life changes and transitions
- a buffer to stresses of old age, especially when the surrounding community supports the expression of "peoplehood" and culture
- a filter to the aging process, influencing beliefs, behaviors, and interactions with informal and formal supports

Given these functions, social and health care providers need to understand ethnicity and how it influences behaviors such as help-seeking, family obligation, and mutual support.

With a common ancestry and history, people have evolved shared values and customs that are passed on across generations. Their resulting *culture* is a complex system and process of shared knowledge, beliefs, traditions, symbols, language, art, spiritual orientation, and social organization. Culture is a lens through which individuals define their identity, perceive and interpret the world, provide coherence and create meaning out of life events, including death (Helman, 2000; Lum, 2003). Of interest to gerontologists is how culture influences the definition and conceptualization of problems as well as the meaning, values, and

experiences of aging, health, and healing. Based on its unique history and culture, each ethnic group develops its own methods of managing the inevitable conflicts between traditional and dominant westernized ways of life, leading to both vulnerabilities and strengths.

For most immigrants to the United States from non-European countries, cultural values of cooperation and interdependence contrast with Western norms of competition, independence and efficiency. For example, many Chinese American elders emigrated as youth in the early part of the twentieth century from small farming villages where ancestor worship was practiced, reflecting the respect traditionally accorded the old. They have grown old in a country where youth and material success are more highly valued than age, and thus may experience conflicts between their views and those of their children and grandchildren. By identifying an elder's cultural values, gerontological practitioners and researchers can gain a better understanding of attitudes and behaviors that influence both their experience of aging and utilization of social and health services. A classic study of how three ethnic minority groups manage their chronic illnesses highlights the central role of cultural values. Filipino Americans, for example, felt a strong sense of responsibility for maintaining good health, but this was to their family and social group, rather than their own individual well-being. Similarly, the Western notion of individual responsibility for illness was foreign to Latino elders, who did not perceive themselves as responsible for making lifestyle changes, such as exercise and diet, nor for developing self-care practices. Instead, they believed that medication alone would control their illness, although some also used alternative healing (e.g., herbal teas and roots) (Becker et al., 1998). Since people's cultural lens profoundly affects their behavior, social and health care providers must understand how ethnic, cultural, and racial differences affect diverse elders' well-being, utilization of services, and interaction with health care providers.

Defining Minority and People of Color

For purposes of this text, *ethnic minority elders,* including older people of color belong to groups whose language or physical and cultural characteristics make them visible and identifiable, have experienced differential and unequal treatment, share a distinctive history and bonds among group members, and regard themselves as objects of collective discrimination and oppression *by reason of their race.* For people of color, race interacts with ethnicity to shape an individual's values, behaviors, distribution of resources, and interaction with social structural factors (such as SES) to affect the aging process. It is not only their ethnic and cultural traditions that influence this process, but also their experience of being a racial minority within a white majority culture. Accordingly, the quality of life of elders of color is inevitably affected by the experiences of a lifetime of racial discrimination and disadvantage (Angel and Hogan, 2004; Rook and Whitfield, 2004; Williams, 2004, 2005).

Specifically, this chapter examines the life course conditions and adaptation to aging among people of color who are defined by the federal government as protected groups—African Americans, Latinos* (including Mexican Americans/Chicanos, Puerto Ricans, Cubans, and Latin Americans), American Indians, and Asian/Pacific Islanders (API). Data are typically collected in terms of these designations, but this overlooks preferences, such as *First Nations People,* increasingly used by American Indians (Weaver 2005). We recognize how ethnicity or cultural homogeneity influences the aging process, and the importance of ethnic identity for white populations, such as Jewish Americans. Our focus, however, is on people of color who have experienced discrimination, inequities, and disadvantage because of their race, and thus often face greater problems.

Two distinct perspectives—one of strengths and resilience, the other of disadvantage—should be kept in mind in this discussion of ethnic minority elders:

1. the unique historical and cultural calendar of life events and their impact on aging, many of which are positive and provide sources of strength and resilience
2. the consequences of racism, ageism, discrimination, and prolonged poverty, most of which are negative and perpetuate socioeconomic and health inequities across the life course

The Dramatic Growth of Populations of Color

Among the current population age 65 and over, about 17 percent are ethnic minorities; this is projected to increase to more than 33 percent by 2050, as noted in Chapter 1 (Angel and Angel, 2006; U.S. Census Bureau, 2006.) Ethnic minorities include a smaller proportion of older adults and a larger percent of younger adults than the white population. This differential rate results primarily from patterns of immigration, higher fertility rates among the young, and higher mortality rates among ethnic minorities over age 65 compared with their white counterparts. The median age of each group compared

---

*Twenty-eight years after the federal government agreed on the use of the term *Hispanic* to identify persons with mixed Spanish heritage, debate regarding whether to use "Hispanic" or "Latino" continues. *Latino* refers to the Latin-based Romance languages of Spain, France, Italy, and Portugal. *Hispanic* is an American derivative from "Hispana," the Spanish-language term for the cultural diaspora created by Spain. People who are disturbed because the diaspora is the result of a bygone age of conquest prefer the term Latino. A recent survey found that a majority of Hispanics and Latinos—53 percent—have no preference for either term, instead identifying themselves by national origin (e.g., Cuban, Mexican, Puerto Rican). Students, intellectuals, and scholars tend to use the term Latino. Throughout this textbook, we are using the term Latino because of the negative association of Hispanic with colonialism and because it appears to be most widely used in scholarly circles. Nevertheless, we recognize that both terms have limitations (Fears, 2003).

to Caucasians captures their relative youthfulness (U.S. Census Bureau, 2007):

General population	36.5 years
White	37.6
African American	30.9
American Indian	29.6
Asian	34.5
Latino	27.2

However, this pattern will shift dramatically by 2030, as described below. Ethnic minority older populations will grow at an extraordinary rate, partially because of the large proportion of children who, unlike their parents and especially their grandparents, are expected to reach old age.

Populations of color are of increasing concern to gerontologists because:

- their disproportionately high rate of population increase compared with whites is a growth rate over 183 percent, versus 74 percent among older Caucasians, between 1999 and 2030. The older Latino population is projected to grow the fastest of any population (254 percent) from just over 2 million in 2003 to 15 million in 2050, and to be larger than the older African American population by 2030. As shown in Table 14.1, elders of color

are projected to comprise about 36 percent of the older population in 2050 (16.4 percent Latino, 12.2 percent African American, and 6.5 percent Asian American) (Federal Interagency Forum, 2006). In most instances, by the middle of the twenty-first century, groups that are currently numerical minorities will become the majority in many states. The greatest growth will occur in those age 85 and over: from 1 in 10 today to 1 in 5 by the year 2050, with the largest increase among Latino oldest-old (Angel and Hogan, 2004; AOA, 2005). Despite their numerical majority, however, they may continue to face oppression and discrimination. For example, Latinos are the numerical majority in California but continue to be poorer and less healthy than their Caucasian counterparts (Torres and Moga, 2001).

- the disproportionately higher number of inequities that they face relative to whites. For example, as noted in Figure 14.1, rates of poverty and near-poverty are highest among persons of color, which negatively affects their retirement, health status, living arrangements, and access to health care and social services.

For the past two decades, immigration from Asia and Latin America has altered the American

TABLE 14.1   **Ethnic Minority Distribution of the Older Population**

	% OF TOTAL POPULATION, 65+	% OF THE ETHNIC MINORITY POPULATION, 65+	PROJECTED % IN 2050
Whites	84.3*	—	
African Americans	8.1*	8.4	12.2
Asian/Pacific Islanders	2.4*	7.5	6.5
American Indians	0.4*	7.2	0.6
Latinos	5.6*	5.8	16.4

*The sum of the specific percentages reported here will never round off to approximately 100 percent if a Latino percentage is included. The reason for this anomaly is that the U.S. Census Bureau does not treat the Hispanic category (which includes Mexicans, Venezuelans, and Latinos who self-designate themselves as being white) as one that is mutually exclusive from the racial categories. Thus, the Hispanic data are also included within each of the racial categories. Persons of Hispanic origins may be of any race, and represent 3 percent of the older population.

SOURCE: AOA, 1999.

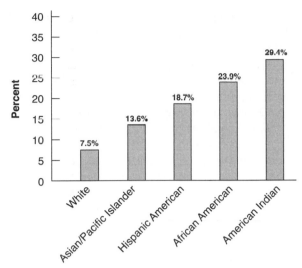

FIGURE 14.1   Poverty Rates across Elders of Color
SOURCE: AOA, 2005.

landscape, especially in major metropolitan areas. International immigration patterns (size, year of entry, and age and sex composition) have little effect on the white majority, or African American and Native American populations, but profoundly shape the characteristics of immigrant groups from Asia, Mexico and Central America. As described in Chapter 2, immigrants tend to be predominantly young, but since the 1980s, U.S. immigration laws have allowed these immigrants to bring their older parents and other relatives to the United States. In many cases, these elders are culturally and linguistically isolated. Depression among these displaced elders is a growing problem, as discussed in Chapter 2. On the other hand, given many immigrant groups' high fertility rate, the younger age strata nationwide will remain disproportionately minority, while older cohorts will remain non-Hispanic white, even in 2050. This is of societal concern because ethnic minority youth will still face lower educational levels and hold primarily low-wage jobs. Accordingly, such low-wage workers will not have the resources such as the taxes paid into Social Security to shoulder the burden of supporting a privileged non-Hispanic

white older population, thus weakening the social contract between young and old (Angel and Angel, 2006; Angel and Hogan, 2004).

There are recurring themes in analyses of ethnic minority status and aging, such as conflicts of cultural values with those of mainstream American society and barriers to use of social and health services. However, significant variations exist *within* as well as *among* these groups. Differences in immigration patterns, birthrates, region, social class, rural or urban location, gender, and acculturation level add to intragroup variations. Latinos, for example, who are defined by the Census Bureau as Spanish-speaking persons, include people from many different cultures and a high percentage of recent immigrants. Accordingly, no one term for persons of Spanish heritage is accepted by all. They can be from any of the following racial groups: Caucasians, Native American, and Indian/African. Mexican Americans are generally of Spanish-Caucasian/Indian descent, while

---

HURRICANE KATRINA: THE INTERSECTIONS OF RACE, CLASS, AND AGE

When Hurricane Katrina hit the Gulf Coast in August 2005, it exposed race and class disparities in the aftermath of the tragedy. What is often overlooked is that older people died in greater numbers. Of the 1400 people who died in Louisiana, 78 percent were age 51 and older, and 39 percent older than age 75. These were residents, some in nursing homes but others in their own homes, who could not crawl out on roofs or set off walking on highways. Many of them had special needs neglected by disaster workers, such as untreated chronic illnesses or higher rates of dehydration. Ageism contributed to their tragic deaths. A lesson learned from this tragic experience is that, as part of their disaster preparedness, city agencies need to compile lists by neighborhood of frail elders and those with disabilities, and develop plans for how to help them if needed. Even more important is that neighbors need to be responsible for their older neighbors (Gullette, 2006).

Cubans and Puerto Ricans are of Spanish-Caucasian/African descent. American Indian refers to the indigenous peoples of North America, including Indians, Eskimos, and Aleuts and over 500 recognized tribes, bands, or Alaskan Native villages. African Americans differ from one another in terms of cultural background, socioeconomic status, and geographic location—especially recent refugees from Ethiopia, Eritrea, Somalia, and immigrants from Haiti or the Caribbean Islands. Asian Americans will remain highly diverse because of immigration status. For example, recent immigrants from Laos, Cambodia, and Vietnam have a higher proportion of elders than do other Asian/Pacific Islander groups, and thus face different challenges than individuals of Chinese, Japanese, and Filipino origin, who remain the largest percent of Asian American elders. Given this within-group diversity, generalizations about ethnic minority elders' health, economic, and social status are limited, and numerous exceptions to the norm exist (Congress, 2004).

Research History

Ethnogerontology, a field of social gerontology, is the study of the causes, processes, and consequences of race, national origin, and culture on individual and population aging. From 1940 to 1970, when both scholarly and political concern with older adults grew, little was written about the circumstances of ethnic minority elders. In part, this was due to their relatively small size compared to Caucasian older adults (Markides and Black, 1996). In 1956, Tally and Kaplan first raised the **double jeopardy hypothesis:** Does being both minority and old result in a double disadvantage to health and well-being in old age? That is, do lifetime factors of economic and racial discrimination make the aging experience more difficult for African Americans (and other minorities) than for whites? Debates about double jeopardy—whether it exists and is related to

socioeconomic status or to race per se—have been central in research and policy discussions in ethnogerontology, although the growing empirical evidence on racial disparities in health status and health care indicates that racial inequities exist across the life course.

A second but related position asserts that patterns of racial inequality are changing, and that minorities' opportunities throughout their lives are related more to their socioeconomic class than to their race. Education and social class, not minority status, jeopardize them. The **multiple hierarchy stratification perspective** encompasses both views, defining race as one source of inequality along with class, gender, and age itself (Bengtson, 1979). A third widely tested hypothesis is that age is a leveler of differences in life expectancy. This mortality **crossover effect** refers to the fact that people of color experience poorer health and higher death rates than whites at all ages until very old age. From age 75 to 85, the death rates for African Americans, Asian/Pacific Islanders, and American Indians are actually lower than for whites. Accordingly, life expectancy after age 75 for these survivors is greater, due to a combination of biological vigor, psychological strength, and resources for coping with stress, such as religious and spiritual practices that link individuals to the community. Thus, the oldest-old segment of the ethnic minority population may represent selective survival of the biologically more robust or "hardy" individuals. In fact, although people of color may experience increasing income and health disparities with age, they nevertheless display considerable strengths and resilience that may mitigate the effects of cumulative adversity earlier in the life course. The apparent racial crossover may be partially due to enumerative errors, such as misreporting of age, and reliance on cross-sectional data to compare advantaged and disadvantaged populations (Beckett, 2000). Even if such errors do occur, however, there is increasing evidence of the reversal of health difference with advanced age (Alwin and Wray, 2005; Dannefer, 2003; House, Lantz, and Herd, 2005; Rook and Whitfield, 2004). The apparent racial crossover effect also raises questions about the usefulness of chronological age as a measure of aging. Functional age seems to be a better measure for elders who have faced racial and socioeconomic inequities affecting their well-being across the life course.

As noted in Chapter 4, the concept of **health disparities**—socioeconomic and racial/ethnic inequalities in health, mortality, and other adverse conditions across the life course—is a rapidly growing area of concern in health policy and gerontology. In the Healthy People 2000 Initiative, disparities in health remained or even increased for 7 health status indicators (NCHS, 2002). **Health care disparities** are defined as differences in access, quality, or use of health care services, where ethnic minorities have a substantively lower usage rate. Such differences in utilization rates appear to be a function of both a lack of trust due to failures within the health care system (e.g., overexposure to medical errors, missed diagnoses, and inappropriate treatments) and the patient's underutilization of existing services, often because of barriers to access, intended or unintended discrimination, and patient-physician communication problems (LaVeist, 2003; Yee-Melichar, 2004). The effects of social inequality and discrimination on health within ethnic minority populations appears to be compounded by age, leading to growing gaps in health status and access to health care (Angel and Hogan, 2004; Dunlop et al., 2002; Rooks

---

ISSUES COMMON ACROSS ELDERS OF COLOR

1. Cumulative structural disadvantages:
   - low-paying jobs limit their financial resources and use of health services across the life course
   - higher rates of poverty and near-poverty negatively impact health differences between peoples of color and whites
   - women outnumber men and are more likely to be widowed

2. Centrality of family/kin values affecting long-term care:
   - preference for in-home services
   - reluctance to use out-of-home services, especially nursing homes
   - more likely to turn to informal networks
   - expectations of adult children to provide care (filial responsibility)

3. Lower rates of insurance coverage and health care utilization, especially preventive services:
   - lower rates of Medicare and Medicaid coverage, especially among immigrants
   - sociocultural and political barriers to health care (e.g., different communication styles, history of racism, discrimination, segregation and language barriers)
   - preference for complementary medicine, such as non-Western methods of healing (especially among Asian/Pacific Islanders and American Indian elders)

4. Chronic illness:
   - higher rates of diabetes and heart disease
   - greater number of functional disabilities (e.g., restricted activity and bed-disability days); less so among APIs
   - social age may be older than chronological age
   - more likely to experience psychosocial distress and depression, especially among immigrants
   - misdiagnoses of mental health problems and culturally inappropriate treatment

and Whitfield, 2003; Smedley, 2003; Williams, 2004). The ultimate gauge of health disparities is health outcomes, with elders of color experiencing higher rates of mortality and morbidity and lower rates of self-assessed health and functional status compared to whites. The concept of health disparities is congruent with that of cumulative disadvantage/adversity, which was discussed in Chapter 8. Increasing policy concern about such disparities, captured in *Healthy People 2010,* led the National Institutes of Health (NIH) to fund research centers to address the reasons for and test interventions to reduce such disparities. The issue of health disparities has numerous policy implications for improving overall population health, compression of morbidity, and functional limitations (House et al., 2005).

Ethnic Minorities in Gerontology

The year 1971 marked a turning point in the recognition of ethnic minority elders as an area of gerontological study. In that year, the National Caucus on the Black Aged was formed (later becoming the National Center and Caucus on the Black Aged), and a session on "Aging and the Aged Black" was held at the White House Conference on Aging. This conference, especially important from a policy perspective, highlighted the need for income and health care supports. Since 1971, the National Association for Hispanic Elderly, National Indian Council on Aging, and National Asian Pacific Center on Aging have been established. These associations function as advocacy groups for elders of color, and as research and academic centers.

The census is the primary source of information on ethnic minority elders. Census data, however, are criticized for undercounting minority subgroups, misclassifying individuals, or merging data about various nonwhite groups. For example, the Census Bureau traditionally grouped people by race as "white," "black," or "other." However, the 2000 Census was the first to include

multiracial categories. Another problematic data source is the use of birth certificates and self-reports of age. Racial and ethnic classifications based on self-reports often fail to take account of the growing interracial/interethnic heterogeneity of individuals (Torres-Gil and Moga, 2001). In addition, the use of major racial and ethnic categories to define groups masks substantial within-group heterogeneity pertaining to cultural beliefs. Immigration dynamics (movements in and out of the country) and settlement patterns pose additional challenges for determining the morbidity and mortality experiences of diverse populations.

In addition to problems with census data, high-quality population-level mortality and disease data are limited. Studies in the 1970s and 1980s typically used small, nonrepresentative samples. Many national estimates have been limited to comparisons of blacks and whites and thus exclude other populations of color (Whitfield and Hayward, 2003). Research on ethnic minorities generally does not break down data by gender, and studies on older women do not cross-classify data by minority status. From the feminist perspective discussed in Chapter 8, it is difficult to determine how racism and sexism interact to produce gender-specific race effects and race-specific gender effects, which result in older women of color as the poorest group in our society. Fortunately, research methodology has improved, especially in the areas of cross-cultural measurement and sampling.

Because of census data limitations and the wide cultural variations, findings on one historically underserved group cannot be generalized to ethnic minority older populations as a whole. Using race per se as a variable may not lead to straightforward interpretations, because ethnicity, cultural values, education, patterns of immigration, and socioeconomic status are interdependent and difficult to separate. Within the overall context of these limitations, we next briefly review the life conditions of each of the four major ethnic minority groups that have been historically underserved in the United States.

Older African Americans

Although African Americans are the largest population of color, only about 8 percent of them are over 65 years of age, compared to 15 percent of the white population (AOA, 2005). The young outnumber the old, due primarily to the higher fertility of African American women and men's higher mortality in their younger years. The life expectancy for African Americans is 70.2 years, compared to 76.5 years for all population groups. The difference is particularly striking among African American men, who have a life expectancy of only 69.8 years compared to 75.3 years for their white counterparts (NCHS, 2006). Cohort effects and succession must be considered in studies of African Americans. To illustrate, the current cohort of elders grew up in a "Jim Crow" environment of racial segregation, discrimination, low socioeconomic status, and little access to physicians and hospitals within the dominant health systems available to whites. Although they have physically survived this

Older African American men can inspire their grandchildren.

disadvantaged social environment, its effects persist in terms of higher rates of mortality, morbidity, and poorer functional health. Additionally, this pattern is unlikely to change markedly in the future, because the gap in health status between African Americans and Caucasians has not narrowed in the past 50 years, and is now wider on some indicators such as infant mortality (Byrd and Clayton, 2002; Rooks and Whitfield, 2004).

While these disparities in life expectancy reflect differences in childhood and youth mortality rates and socioeconomic status, differences in life expectancy after age 75 are less dramatic. African Americans have a higher mortality than Caucasians up to age 75 to 85, but after this age range, have a longer life expectancy than their Caucasian counterparts (Rooks and Whitfield, 2004). This narrowing of differences in life expectancy after age 75 (the crossover effect discussed earlier) may be explained by the fact that African Americans who survive to this age tend to be the most robust of their cohort.

Although still a small percent of the African American population, adults over age 65 form its fastest-growing segment and are projected to grow by 45.6 percent by 2020. The young-old comprise nearly 60 percent of the African American older population. However, as with other groups, the oldest-old is the fastest-growing segment. The ratio of men to women age 65 to 75 is slightly lower than among whites because of the excess mortality that black men experience at every age. Oldest-old women are the most rapidly growing group of African American elders, and they have the longest average remaining life expectancy (Angel and Angel, 2006; Angel and Hogan, 2004; Rooks and Whitfield, 2004).

Economic Status

Three times as many older African Americans as whites live below the poverty line, 23.9 percent versus 7.5 percent, respectively (Holden and Hatcher, 2006). The poverty rate across groups is shown in Figure 14.1. The incidence of poverty increases dramatically among households composed of unrelated black individuals, especially females age 65 and over. The median income of African American men over 65 is approximately 60 percent of white men; that of black women about 66 percent that of white women. In fact, the proportion of older African American female-headed families in poverty has increased in the past 30 years. Poverty rates are highest among women living alone and the oldest-old, with the rate of poor African American women age 85 and older approximately 10 times that of young-old (age 65 to 74) white women (Hudson, 2002; Older Women's League, 2003).

The primary reasons for the lower socioeconomic status of older African Americans are tied to their history of segregation in our society, and include:

- limited access to educational opportunities in their younger years
- limited employment opportunities and long periods of unemployment or underemployment throughout their lives
- concentration in low-paying, sporadic service jobs, without benefits and the option of savings and private pensions
- greater likelihood of retirement or leaving the workforce earlier, frequently because of health problems
- greater likelihood of dependence on Social Security benefits as their only income source; as noted in Chapter 12, approximately 30 percent of older African Americans depend solely on Social Security for their income compared to 18 percent of non-Hispanic whites
- greater dependence on Supplemental Security Income (SSI) and Medicaid (Angel and Angel, 2006; Purcell and Whitman, 2006).

Differences in education do not explain the gaps in socioeconomic status, which have persisted since 1985. Instead, these inequities are increasing, due to greater unemployment and underemployment of blacks, the lack of growth in real wages, declines in pension coverage, and reductions in public supports such as SSI and Medicaid.

As noted in Chapter 12, African Americans often return to work after retirement because of economic necessity, creating the phenomenon of "unretired/retired." In such instances, blacks spend a greater proportion of their lives working in low-paid jobs, with fewer years in retirement compared to their white peers (Crystal and Shea, 2003; Schieman, Pearlin, and Nguyen, 2005). Other studies suggest that older African Americans face more difficulties in maintaining employment than whites and are often forced out of the labor market because of unemployment. This means that they are more likely to exit the labor market through pathways other than retirement and face difficulties in re-entry, because of lifetime patterns of unemployment and underemployment in low-skills jobs. Compared with whites, blacks not only have lower earnings at equivalent levels of education, but also less wealth at the same levels of income and less purchasing power due to higher costs in segregated urban communities. And if they are employed, they are less able to retire because of inadequate savings and pension benefits (Flippen, 2005; Hudson, 2002; Williams and Wilson, 2001).

Health

By most measures, the health of African American adults is worse than that of their white counterparts, again reflecting a lifetime of cumulative disadvantages from poverty and racism. As noted earlier, being either black or poor is a powerful predictor of higher rates of disability, illness, and mortality. A primary reason for continued health disparities among older African Americans is their lower socioeconomic status and greater exposure to segregated institutions at each stage of the life course. Fewer years of education, limited entry into high paying occupations, lower income, and less wealth accumulated over time compound health difficulties into old age (LaVeist, 2004; Rooks and Whitfield, 2004; Williams 2004). The socioeconomic disadvantages experienced by African Americans explain many of the black–white differences in health status, behaviors and self-reports of health, as follows:

- less access to health care services, often entering the health care system through public hospital emergency rooms
- lower utilization of health services
- greater delays in obtaining health care and medications, often due to cost
- lower likelihood of having private health insurance, such as Medigap insurance
- higher likelihood that life-threatening diseases are diagnosed later and treated less aggressively
- higher rates of mortality due to cancer, heart disease, diabetes, and strokes, as described in Chapter 4 (Anderson, 2002; Angel and Angel, 2006; Li, Malone, and Daling, 2003; Mikuls, 2003; National Center for Health Statistics, 2003)

The prevalence of chronic diseases is estimated to be twice as high among African Americans as among whites, and the former more often perceive themselves as being in poor health than do their white counterparts. While heart disease is decreasing among Caucasian men, it is increasing in African American males. Although heart disease, stroke, and cancer are the leading causes of death for both African Americans and whites at age 65 and older, rates for African Americans are higher for each of these conditions and occur at a younger age than for non-Hispanic whites. Blacks experience higher rates of heart disease and stroke at ages 45 to 54 than those reported for all other groups at ages 55 to 64. This pattern of premature or accelerated aging among African Americans means that other groups do not reach the level of mortality experienced by this group at ages 45 to 54 until many years later. Deaths from heart disease and stroke are associated with a clustering of risk factors, including obesity, high blood pressure, sedentary lifestyle, and diabetes (American Heart Association, 2005; Office of Minority Health Research, 2005, 2006).

As another example of the interactive effects of discrimination with health behavior, African Americans' higher rates of morbidity and mortality from certain cancers (e.g., stomach, prostate, and cervical) are an outcome of health practices, quality of health care, and greater risk factors, including higher occupational and residential exposure to cancer-causing substances, higher rates of obesity, higher prevalence of smoking, and less knowledge about cancer and its prevention. This greater vulnerability is compounded by disparities in access to health care and higher rates of undetected diseases, so that many cancers are not diagnosed early enough to prevent metastasis. Blacks receive curative surgery for early-stage lung, colon, and breast cancer less often than whites, and are generally inadequately treated for pain from cancer (Margolis et al., 2003; Mukamel, Weimer, and Mushlin, 2006; Office of Minority Health, 2005; Williams and Wilson, 2001).

As described in Chapter 4, African Americans also experience higher rates of Type 2 diabetes, typically associated with obesity, resulting in kidney failure, hypertension, diabetic retinopathy and other complications. African Americans are twice as likely as whites to die from diabetes (McDonald et al., 2004; Wen, Cagney, and Christakis, 2005; Whitfield and Hayward, 2003).

African Americans not only have a shorter life expectancy but also a protracted period of dependent life expectancy and managing chronic disabling conditions. They experience more rapid declines in functional ability, more days of functional bed disability (i.e., being confined to bed for at least half of the day), more use of assistive devices for walking and at earlier ages than whites. Compared to their white counterparts, nearly twice as many African American elders are completely incapacitated and unable to carry on any major activity (e.g., paid employment, keeping house), although still residing in the community (Angel and Angel, 2006; Kelley-Moore and Ferraro, 2004). These higher rates of disability have profound consequences for family caregivers.

African American elders also appear to have less access to quality health care than their white counterparts, and delayed access due to cost (Rooks and Whitfield, 2004; Williams, 2004). Unequal opportunities for good jobs limit access to health insurance and, in turn, medical care in the preretirement years, including preventive care and access to specialists. Across the life course and into old age, African Americans are more likely to use hospital emergency rooms for health care and to lack continuity in the health care they receive. Lower admission rates and untreated morbidity place African Americans at a higher risk than whites of being hospitalized for an extended stay and dying in hospitals (Ferraro et al., 2006; Kelley-Moore and Ferraro, 2004). Older blacks are more likely to depend on Medicaid and Medicare as their only health insurance and less likely to have private supplemental health insurance than their white counterparts (NCHS, 2001; Williams, 2004).

Most health disparities research has focused on physical health issues (Alwin and Wray, 2005). Racial disparities, including daily experiences with discrimination, may also affect mental health, although findings about depression among African Americans are mixed and reasons for differences are unclear. When standardized clinical measures are used, African Americans typically have lower rates of depression than whites, but this may be due to the use of culturally biased instruments that lead to misdiagnosis (Zhang and Snowden, 1999; Kessler et al., 2003). In contrast, when culturally appropriate measures are used, African Americans are found to have higher mean scores than whites on depression measures (Dwight-Johnson et al., 2001; Jackson-Triche et al., 2000). In one instance, 80 percent of the 47 associations examined in the literature between measures of discrimination and mental health found that higher levels of discrimination were associated with poorer mental health status, including major depression and generalized anxiety. Conversely, social support tends to be associated with lower rates of depressive symptoms, but is unable to mediate the stress associated with financial strain and traumatic events (Kessler, Mickelson, and Williams, 1999; George and Lynch, 2003; Skarupskii et al., 2005; Takeuchi, 2006; Williams, 2004; Williams, Neighbors, and Jackson, 2003). Yet other studies have found few differences in depression or depressive symptoms between whites and African Americans when researchers controlled for gender and income (Jackson-Triche et al., 2000). Clearly, more research is needed on depression and African Americans to disentangle the effects of discrimination, financial strain, gender, traumatic events, and social support.

Socioeconomic status is one of the strongest known determinants of variations in health, with persons of higher social status, regardless of ethnic minority group, enjoying better health than their lower SES counterparts (Alwin and Wray, 2005; Phelan and Link, 2005; Robert and Ruel, 2006; Williams, 2005). Gaps in mortality rates for blacks and whites are reduced to some extent when social class is controlled. In fact, marginal increases in income level and education generally have larger positive effects on the health of African Americans than on whites (Wen, Cagney, and Christakis, 2005). Similarly, high-income white and black men both live longer than their lower-income counterparts (Williams, 2004). The power of socioeconomic status to shape differences in health for both whites and blacks is vividly apparent when low-income whites are compared with high-income African Americans. High-income black men have a life expectancy at age 65 that is almost 3 years longer than that of white men in the lowest income groups (Williams and Wilson, 2001). Similarly, education can be protective against years of life lost. As noted in Chapter 4, African American women who have completed 0 to 8 years of school can expect 18.4 years of unhealthy life, while their counterparts with 13 or more years of education can anticipate just 12.9 years, two-thirds the length of disability experienced by less-educated elders (Crimmins and Saito, 2003). Although SES factors contribute to health status, they cannot fully explain health differences by race/ethnicity (Alwin and Wray, 2005). For example, the incidence of chronic disease is often higher or roughly equivalent for African Americans with 16 years of education than for whites with 8 years of education. As another example that race and SES are two related but not interchangeable systems of inequality, the highest SES group of African American women has equivalent or higher rates of hypertension and obesity than the lowest SES group of white women (Williams, 2004, 2005). This suggests that education and income do not fully overcome the disadvantages of being black in our society. These disadvantages include chronic everyday experiences of racism, discrimination, or unfair treatment based on race. Such experiences have been linked to poorer physical and mental health for Asian/Pacific Islanders and Latinos, as well as African Americans (Kessler et al., 1999; Williams, 2004; Williams and Wilson, 2001). In addition, some research suggests that ethnic minorities perceptions of discrimination, even among those in high status occupations, incrementally contribute to racial disparities in health beyond that of SES (Williams, Neighbors, and Jackson, 2003). In sum, a growing body of evidence shows race and ethnic differences probably result from patterns of institutional discrimination that produce differential social pathways contributing to varied health outcomes (Alwin and Wray, 2005).

African American elders also face a wide range of social and political barriers to physical and mental health care that affect their general well-being:

- Given a history of discrimination in health care systems, especially in the South, providers may be perceived as unwelcoming. This is not without basis, since some studies document that physicians view African American patients more negatively than white patients (Van Ryn, 2002; Van Ryn and Burke, 2000; Weisse et al., 2001).
- Residential segregation affects the health care facilities, providers, and pharmacists available to African Americans. They are more likely than whites to be treated at large inner-city hospitals, receive poorer quality medical care, and have less access to therapeutic medical procedures and physical and occupational therapy (Mukamel, Murthy, and Weimer, 2000; Smedley, Stitch, and Nelson, 2003).
- Providers may be unaware of how skin color can affect the presentation or manifestation of a disease.
- Potentially significant conditions may not be detected until advanced stages, or benign conditions may be misdiagnosed as more serious than they are.
- Indirect communication styles and mistrust of whites may interfere with the sharing of information, increasing the probability of misdiagnoses.

Social Supports and Living Situations

Living arrangements affect blacks' health and socioeconomic status. The proportion of married African Americans is lower than that of any other ethnic group. This is because of lower life expectancy for black men, resulting in high rates of widowhood among black women (48 percent are widowed compared to 19 percent of black men). Among African Americans over age 65, 56 percent of men and 24 percent of women are married. This compares with 75 percent and

42 percent, respectively, among whites. Widowhood, divorce, and separation account for the fact that over 40 percent of African American women live alone, a higher proportion than that of their white counterparts or older black males (19 percent). Those who live alone are more likely to be impoverished, marginally housed, and even homeless (AOA, 2006; Killon, 2000). In addition, rates of remarriage are lower than in other groups.

Even though most older African Americans do not live in extended families, approximately 32 percent, compared to 13 percent of their white counterparts, live with a family member other than their spouse (U.S. Census Bureau, 2007). Comparative studies have found that older African Americans have larger, more extended families than do whites, a higher frequency of family-based households with their adult children, and greater levels of social support from their extended families. Accordingly, older African American women are more likely than white women to live with their adult children, often because they do not have other options (Angel and Angel, 2006). These are often three- or four-generation households, with older women at the top of the family's power hierarchy, playing an active role in the management of the family. As noted in Chapter 9, older African American women often provide daily care for grandchildren, as well as children of other family members and friends. These cross-generational caregiving patterns are associated with higher rates of functional limitations and poverty (Hayslip and Kaminski, 2005; Minkler and Fuller-Thomson, 2005). Nevertheless, most African American grandmother caregivers exhibit considerable resilience, and know how to seek and utilize support services (Cox, 2002; Gibson, 2002).

Similar to whites, adult children are a primary source of assistance and support for older African Americans. For childless older adults, siblings are the most important kin tie. Intergenerational assistance, typically from older to younger, is a function not just of race, but of age, marital and socioeconomic status, and level of functional disability. In some instances, multigenerational households may be a way to cope with low socioeconomic status rather than an indicator of a supportive extended family. Some social supports may be characterized by negative social interactions, especially when financial hardship can adversely affect elders' well-being (Swindle, Heller, and Frank, 2000). Indeed, an increasing number of older blacks are affected by stressors influencing members of their social networks, such as crime and substance abuse by children and grandchildren, and face caregiving responsibilities as a result. On the other hand, intergenerational households that develop out of financial necessity illustrate the resourcefulness of African American families whose domestic networks expand and contract according to economic resources. Even though socioeconomic factors partially explain race differences in intergenerational exchanges, there is strong adherence to norms of filial support and attitudes of respect toward elders among African Americans across social classes. African Americans comprise 10 percent of all caregiving households, and are more likely to live with the care recipient than their white counterparts (AOA, 2005).

The African American family tends to have flexible definitions of membership and more elastic boundaries that can potentially expand to include **fictive kin.** Creation of fictive kin is another source of loving support. This includes foster parents or children who function in the absence of blood relatives or when family relationships are unsatisfactory. As an illustration, African American women active in church may turn to a variety of friends, fellow church members, and other nonrelative contacts in times of need, but these nonkin are considered part of an extended family network. Similarly, they are more likely than whites to have networks that include more distant family members among their pool of unpaid caregivers (Ajrouch, Antonucci, and Janevic, 2001; Chadiha et al., 2002). By redefining distant kin and friends as primary kin, they may increase the number of close relationships. The process of enlarging their extended family beyond lineal ties thus expands their pool of supportive resources.

Overall, African American elders appear to have a broader range of informal instrumental and emotional supports than is characteristic of Caucasian older people. Social support can enhance a sense of mastery or self-confidence, which has positive effects on mental health (Lincoln et al., 2003b, 2005). Norms of reciprocity are generally strong and have evolved from a cooperative lifestyle that served as a survival mechanism in earlier times and continues to be a source of both emotional and instrumental support. Such informal helpers often function as critical links to social services or meet immediate needs, such as providing housing or transportation (Dreeban, 2001; Lincoln, Taylor, and Chatters, 2003a; Lincoln, Chatters, and Taylor, 2005; Taylor, Chatters, and Celious, 2002). On the other hand, health and social service providers need to be cautious not to assume the existence of strong social supports, especially at the point of discharge to home care settings or in instances of chronic financial strain. In a study of home health service use among four ethnic minority groups, black elders were more likely than any other group to be left without any support for care, despite families' expression of the importance of filial support (Peng, Navaie-Waliser, and Feldman, 2003). Patterns of familial support vary within the African American population and are undoubtedly affected by economic pressures on younger family members. Such patterns need to be carefully assessed because of their implications for greater isolation, home confinement, stress on family caregivers, and need for additional health care services. It is also important to recognize that conflicts with members of support networks occur, which may reduce the level of emotional support and result in maladaptive mental health outcomes. In other words, not all social relationships provide unambiguous health protection (Lincoln, 2000; Lincoln et al., 2005; McDonald and Wykle, 2003; Mendes de Leon et al., 2001).

> **OUTREACH TO AFRICAN AMERICAN ELDERS**
>
> Scores of low-income African American older women live alone with chronic illness in substandard housing and apartments, often socially isolated and relatively invisible. The African American Elders program in Seattle, Washington, tries to find such isolated women. Many of these women moved from the Midwest as young adults, worked as poorly paid domestics and suffered from discrimination and poor-quality care during their lives. They have nevertheless managed to survive. Since most of the women are religious, the elders' program works through clergy and church members to make connections with them, offering rides, meals, or companionship. However, recent budget cuts at the county level threaten to eliminate this effective program (King, 2006).

African American elders' psychological well-being and life satisfaction are often explained in terms of their spiritual orientation and religious participation, including a belief in a higher power and the role of prayer in healing. In fact, prayer is found to have positive health-related outcomes for African American elders and families (Decoster and Cummings, 2004; Pinquort and Sorenson, 2005). As noted in Chapter 12, spirituality and religiosity, which are important in the lives of many black elders for adaptation and support, are related to feelings of well-being, self-esteem, and personal control (Jang et al., 2003; Taylor, Lincoln, and Chatters, 2005). The church also provides a support network of spiritual help, companionship, advice, encouragement, and financial aid. For these reasons, some have suggested that the church should implement spiritually based, community models of health promotion that are more likely to be accepted by African Americans than those through health care settings (Parker et al., 2002).

In the past, African Americans were less likely to enter a nursing home than whites, although they did so at higher rates than other ethnic minority groups. As noted in Chapter 11, their nursing home placement now exceeds that of non-Hispanic whites. African Americans residing in nursing homes are found to be more limited in their ability to carry out activities of daily living and less often receiving the appropriate level of care than are whites. They also are less likely to be discharged, largely because they are too impaired to live in the community and their informal resources have been exhausted (AARP, 2005; Angel and Hogan, 2004).

Older Latinos

As noted above, Latinos are the largest ethnic minority population and the fastest growing group in the United States, due to high rates of fertility and immigration. This ethnic group includes a diverse population, encompassing native-born, as well as legal and undocumented immigrants with varying lengths of residence in the United States. Although bonded by a common language, each group differs substantially by geographic location, income, education, cultural heritage, history, dialect, and their racial designation by the majority—all differences that pose challenges in providing culturally competent services to Latino elders. The predominant groups of Latino elders are illustrated in Figure 14.2.

Within each sub-population, those 65 and older comprise a relatively small proportion (Angel and Hogan, 2004):

Mexican Americans	4%
Central and South Americans	5%
Puerto Ricans	6%
Cuban Americans	21%

Latinos are also widely dispersed geographically, with Mexican Americans in the five primarily rural southwestern states, Puerto Ricans in the east, and Cubans in Florida. The largest proportion of Latinos—and also the poorest—are Mexican Americans. The history of some Mexican Americans predates colonial times and

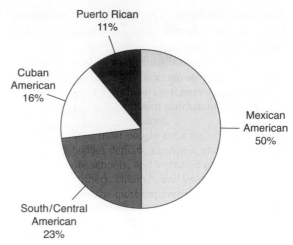

FIGURE 14.2 **Distribution of Latinos in the United States by Country of Origin**

settlement by English-speaking groups, while other Mexican Americans who have migrated since 1942 (the "bracero" period) were recruited primarily to fill the need for low-paid agricultural workers. More recent immigrants—both documented and undocumented—have dramatically increased the size of the Mexican population in the United States. In contrast to the early immigrants who are now the oldest-old, the

Family celebrations are an important part of Latino culture.

more recent Mexican immigrants are young. Their aging experiences will play a major role in the growth of the Latino older population in the future (Angel and Hogan, 2004). In contrast, Cubans who were political refugees created "Little Havana" in Miami, where they rapidly achieved economic success, and represent the wealthiest and most educated of Latinos. Puerto Rican elders are distinguished by their citizenship that provides full access to U.S. government services and their ability to travel freely between the mainland and Puerto Rico. Yet they have not achieved the degree of economic success that Cubans have. Elders among Central and South Americans face pressing needs for housing, assistance with the naturalization process, and help obtaining basic medical and social services. Latino elders' needs may be underestimated, since past studies typically included Latinos in either black or white categories. Furthermore, the Hispanic classification often fails to differentiate among the diverse subgroups.

Compared to other ethnic groups, the Spanish-speaking population is youthful, which is due to a number of factors. One variable is lower average life expectancy, which may be partially explained by poor economic and health status among Mexican Americans and Puerto Ricans. The most important contributing factor, however, is higher fertility rates among many Latino subgroups. The number of children born and the average family size among Latinos exceed the national average. High levels of net immigration and repatriation patterns are secondary factors, with the youngest (and often poorest) people most likely to move to a new country, and some middle-aged and older Mexican Americans moving back to Mexico. Despite its current relative youthfulness, the Latino population experienced the greatest increase in median age of all ethnic groups from 1960 to the late 1990s, with Latina women experiencing a great increase in life expectancy than non-Hispanic white women during that time period (Angel and Angel, 2006). As noted earlier, these changes will result in Latinos age 65 and

older growing from the current 6 percent to 18 percent of the Latino population in 2050 (Federal Interagency Forum, 2006). Accordingly, the parent support rate is expected to triple by 2030, with more middle-aged and young-old Latinos faced with family care responsibilities (Angel and Hogan, 2004; AOA, 2005).

Within the overall Latino population, the sex ratio varies because of the gender imbalance in previous immigration streams and women's greater survival rates. As a whole, there are proportionately more Latino men to women over age 65 than among the white older population:

- 76 men per 100 women age 65 to 74 among Puerto Ricans
- 78 men per 100 women among Cuban Americans
- 83 men per 100 women among Mexican Americans (Angel and Hogan, 2004)

This is due to the higher mortality rate of Latinas than white women at earlier ages, not to increases in longevity among Latino men. Nevertheless, the overall gender patterns of this population are similar to those of other older people. Women live longer and outnumber men. They more often remain widowed and live alone than men do. Older Latino men marry or remarry more often than men in other ethnic groups, with over 80 percent of older Latino males married, compared with 56 percent of older African Americans (AOA, 2005). Households headed by Latina women are the most likely to be poor.

Economic Status

Sociocultural conditions underlie Latinos' poor educational and economic status. More than any other group, they have retained their native language, because of geographic proximity to their home countries combined with the availability of mass communication. Approximately 33 percent of older Latinos speak only Spanish (NIH, 2000). Although this preserves their cultural identity, their inability to speak English is a major barrier to their education, employment, and utilization of health and social services. About 70 percent of older Latinos never completed high school, compared to 30 percent of the overall older population. Even when educational levels are the same, Latino elders often earn less than their non-Hispanic white counterparts (Munet-Vilaro, 2004).

A barrier encountered by those who entered the country illegally is the inability to apply for Social Security, SSI, Medicare, or Medicaid. Even those who entered legally require a sponsor for five years before they can apply for such benefits. Mexican Americans or Puerto Ricans who immigrated in middle or old age typically worked for low pay in physically exhausting jobs in their home country. They thus bring limited resources for finding better paying jobs in their old age. This work pattern combined with their inability to apply for public programs means that they are often dependent on their adult children, including their sponsor who must provide support for five years (Angel, 2003; Angel and Angel, 2006). Not surprisingly, they are least likely to receive Social Security, but when they do, it typically remains their sole source of income (Villa and Aranda, 2000). These employment and educational conditions contribute to the high rate of poverty among older Latinos. Approximately 19 percent live below the poverty level, compared to 7.5 percent of older whites. Another 31 percent, compared to 14.8 percent of older whites, hover just above the "near poverty" threshold at incomes below 125 percent of the poverty line (U.S. Bureau of the Census, 2005). The median personal income of Latino men age 65 and over is about 65 percent of white males; for Latinas, the median income is 68 percent of white females' income (Aranda, 2006).

Health

As noted in our discussion of African Americans, low socioeconomic status is typically associated with poorer health across the life course, which then reduces chances for employment, education, and accumulation of income. However, despite their high-risk profiles, including higher rates of poverty, Latinos in general have lower mortality rates from both acute and chronic diseases than whites. The primary exception to this profile of better health is that Latinos are 1.5 times as likely as whites to have diabetes. The discrepancy between their socioeconomic risk profile and their group's favorable health outcomes has been termed an "epidemiological paradox." The health status of Latinos in the southwest, for example, is more comparable to the health status of non-Hispanic whites than with that of African Americans, even though Latinos are socioeconomically similar to African Americans. The greatest mortality advantage is found among Mexican American men. This paradox of the Latino population (or the "Hispanic paradox") is not readily explained (Angel and Angel, 2006; Anderson, 2002; Markides and Eschbach, 2005). It may be partially due to personal health behaviors. For example, one study found the riskiest behaviors among Mexican American men in Texas, who smoked, engaged in acute alcohol drinking, and had poorer diets and higher obesity levels than other Latino men; this pattern resulted in higher rates of morbidity and mortality than other Latino groups (Ramirez et al., 2004). Other studies suggest a protective health factor associated with Latino culture, including strong traditional family norms and supports from large extended families and community mutual aid. Some research posits that the Hispanic paradox is a result of the return migration of midlife and older Mexicans with health problems to Mexico (Palloni and Arias, 2004). Last, there is probably a genetic component to these differences in mortality and morbidity. More research is needed to disentangle this complex, interactive set of biological, cultural, and SES variables (Angel and Angel, 2006; Hayward et al., 2000).

Immigration is a primary factor in the relatively good overall health profile of Latinos.

In fact, across all racial and ethnic groups in the United States, immigrants, even when they are lower in SES, tend to enjoy better health than the native-born. Recent immigrants appear to bring some protective aspects of their culture of origin with them, including a strong spiritual orientation, and experience better health throughout their lives. As they become more culturally and behaviorally American, their morbidity and mortality profiles more closely resemble those of native-born Americans (Angel and Angel, 2006). Studies of Mexican Americans, for example, find that disease rates increase progressively with acculturation to the United States. As length of stay increases, fiber consumption and breast feeding decline, but the use of cigarettes, alcohol, and illicit drugs increases. Rates of infant mortality, low birth weight, cancer, high blood pressure, adolescent pregnancy, and mental health disorders also increase with length of residence in the United States (Williams and Wilson, 2001). This suggests that increasing length of stay and greater acculturation of the Latino population to the dominant culture will lead to future trends in worsening health for those who came to the United States as youths and grew old here.

Despite their lower mortality rates, older Mexican Americans experience higher rates of adult onset (Type II) diabetes along with its resultant complications, including depression and diabetes mortality, even after controlling for demographic and SES factors. The fact that higher rates of diabetes cannot be fully explained by SES or obesity levels suggests that genetic factors may be involved (Otiniano et al., 2003). System-level factors are also salient, with later diagnoses and less aggressive treatment of diabetes occurring among older Mexican Americans who lack private health insurance (Angel and Angel, 2006). Mexican Americans, Puerto Ricans, and Dominicans, especially those who are female and living alone, suffer considerable chronic and disabling illness earlier in life, and experience more limitations in ADLs (Aranda,

2006). For these groups, physiological aging tends to precede chronological aging, with those in their early 50s experiencing health disabilities typical of a 65-year-old and "appearing older" than their chronological age. They are also more likely than the general population to require assistance with personal care and to have greater limitations in carrying out ADLs. Women are more likely than men to experience multiple chronic disorders. Compared with their white counterparts, Latinas have higher mortality rates from cervical cancer and cancer of the uterus. This may be due to inadequate access to health care and preventive services, resulting in cancer detection occurring too late for successful treatment (Angel and Angel, 2003; Munet-Vilaro, 2004).

Compared with older adults in general, Latinos are more likely to experience depression, which tends to be related to their low SES, chronic financial strains, and short-term financial crises (Angel et al., 2002; Chiriboga et al., 2002). Immigrant status and living alone also tend to be associated with depressive symptoms (Wilmoth and Chen, 2003). Latinos face an elevated risk not only for experiencing depression, but also for its underdiagnosis and undertreatment (Robison et al., 2002). They underutilize specialty mental health care, typically because of system level barriers such as lack of bilingual staff and inadequate insurance to cover medication costs. Delays in seeking treatment can worsen the depression and result in a sense of fatalism and longer-term health problems (Aranda, 2006; Lopez, 2002; Unutzer, 2003).

Early studies suggested that Latino elders were the least likely among all groups to utilize formal health services (Miranda, 1990). As with differences in mortality and morbidity, use of health care services varies within the Latino population. More recent research found that Puerto Ricans and Cuban Americans made more physician visits than whites, but this may be an outcome of better health insurance coverage (Angel and Angel, 2003). Immigrants, especially those who have not attained legal status, lack access to health insurance and thus to adequate health care, particularly preventive care. If they are dependent upon emergency room care, they typically deal with a new doctor on each visit and do not have the chance to build rapport and a trusting relationship. In addition, Latinos face communication difficulties, which can negatively influence their perceptions of physical and mental health care providers. Language and trust barriers combined with a greater reliance on home remedies, herbal medicine, and spiritual healing result in patterns of delayed diagnosis, which can impair their health status (Angel and Angel, 2006; Doty, 2003; Munet-Vilaro, 2004). These examples highlight the fact that the wide heterogeneity in immigration experiences and socioeconomic status profoundly affects how Latinos perceive their health and their service utilization.

Only about 3 percent of older Latinos are in nursing homes, rising only to 10 percent among those over age 85. Since families attempt to provide support as long as possible, when older Latinos do enter nursing homes, they tend to be more physically and functionally impaired than their Caucasian counterparts. Another reason for this higher level of impairment is that Latinos are less likely to use in-home health services compared to whites (Angel and Angel, 2006; Angel and Hogan, 2004).

Social Supports and Living Situations

Historically, the extended family has been a major source of emotional support to older Latinos. Living alone is less common among Latino males and females compared to other groups of older adults. Older Latinos are more likely than whites to turn to family than to friends, and to believe that elders should be cared for by family in the community (Williams and Wilson, 2001). They are more than four times as likely as Anglos between the ages of 65 and 74, and more than twice as likely as those 74 years of age and older, to live with their adult children. Widowed women

over 75 are the most likely to live in extended-family households. Latino older couples are more likely to head households containing relatives, and Latino older singles more likely to live as dependents in someone else's household than are other ethnic minority groups (Choi, 1999).

Co-residence increases the availability of social supports, including caregivers. Family caregiving among Latinos is influenced by the cultural values and beliefs of:

- *familism* (family as central to the life of the individual)
- *marianismo* (female superiority and the expectation that women are capable of enduring all suffering)
- *machismo* (socially learned and reinforced set of behaviors that guides male behavior)
- *respeto* (respect for people by virtue of age, experience, or service)

As a whole, Latinos highly value family relations and feel emotionally connected to relatives, believing that the needs of the family or its individual members should take precedence over one's own (Becker et al., 2003). Although patterns of intergenerational assistance are stronger than among whites, the percentage of Latinos living in multigenerational households has declined. With their urbanization and greater acculturation, some younger Latinos are unable to meet their older parents' expectations to support an extended family in one location. Those who live alone tend to live in substandard housing compared to whites (NIH, 2000). Nevertheless, despite cultural, economic, and lifestyle changes, the extended family continues to be the most important institution for Latinos regardless of their country of origin, length of residence, or social class (Beyene, Becker, and Mayen, 2002).

Even when Latino families live apart, elders often still perform parental roles; assist with child care, advising, and decision making; and serve as role models (Martinez, 2003). Although families remain the most important support for their older

EL PORTO LATINO ALZHEIMER'S PROJECT: A MODEL FOR CULTURALLY COMPETENT PRACTICE

El Porto Latino Alzheimer's Project in Los Angeles aims to increase the community's capacity to provide culturally and linguistically competent educational, medical, social, and supportive services for Latino elders with dementia, as well as to their caregivers. Services include outreach and education, support groups, day-care services, legal services, purchase of services, and case management. The program assumes that public awareness of the diseases and services is limited in the general Latino public. Emphasis is placed on outreach and access, beginning with the project name, meaning "the doorway" or entrance. Outreach efforts include the use of Spanish and English help lines, bilingual print and electronic media advertising (Spanish-language television and radio stations are the official project sponsors), community fairs, and informal referrals. Access is also enhanced through two agencies serving as points of entry for services; this also ensures a single fixed point of responsibility for assessing clients' needs. A full-time social work care advocate ("servidora") coordinates case management services, leads support groups, conducts family and community education, and provides informal services and referral (Aranda et al., 2003).

members, a division of labor is emerging. This takes place between the family, which provides emotional support and personal care, and public agencies, which give financial assistance and medical care, along with churches and mutual-aid, fraternal, and self-help groups. These community-based groups provide outreach, advocacy, and information about resources, socialization opportunities, financial credit for services, and folk medicine. The supportive social and cultural context of neighborhood and community is congruent with Latinos' strong sense of cultural identity. Being part of "La Raza" encompasses a shared experience, history, and sense of one's place in the world that can be a powerful base for community and political mobilization (Torres-Gil and Kuo, 1998).

Older American Indians

American Indian or First Nations refers to indigenous people of the United States, including Eskimos and Aleuts (i.e., Alaskan Natives).* Their median age is 29.6 years, compared to 36.5 for the general population. Only 7 percent of this population is 65 years of age and older and is projected to remain relatively small in the future. American Indians' life expectancy at birth is now around 74 years compared to 77.6 years for the white population (Indian Health Service, 2006). In fact, between 1940 and 1980, life expectancy for American Indians at birth increased by 20 years, from 51 to 71.1 years, compared to a 10-year increase for whites to 74.4 years during that same interval (John, 2004; AOA, 2005). This dramatic improvement is due, in large part, to efforts of the Indian Health Service (IHS) to eliminate infectious diseases and meet acute-care needs earlier in life. Accordingly, the greatest reductions have occurred in death rates due to tuberculosis, gastrointestinal disease, and maternal and infant mortality. Nevertheless, mortality rates for the major killers of older people—heart disease, cancer, and stroke—have not been reduced in the American Indian population. However, as noted for African Americans, there appears to be a mortality crossover effect. Up to age 75, American Indians have a higher mortality rate than the white population, but this shifts between 75 and 85, when their mortality rates are lower than whites (John, 2004). The rates of chronic and degenerative diseases are rising, creating needs for long-term care that are not addressed by the acute care focus of most Indian health care programs.

We know less about the health and well-being of American Indians than other populations. The two federal agencies responsible for collecting data, the Bureau of Indian Affairs

---

*Although the term First Nations is often preferred, American Indians is the category for data-gathering purposes (Weaver, 2005). Both terms are used in our discussion.

American Indian elders play a central role in their tribes' cultural activities.

(BIA) and the Census Bureau, frequently have different estimates, making it difficult to generalize about older American Indians. An additional complication in generalizing findings is that there are nearly 562 federally recognized tribes, an estimated 148 nonrecognized tribes, and approximately 300 federally recognized reservations. Between 60 to 70 percent live in urban areas rather than on reservations, and therefore their conditions and needs are less visible. Nevertheless, urban American Indians tend to have higher income and better health than those on reservations (Barusch, 2006). A further complication is that approximately 20 percent of American Indian elders who live in federally recognized areas are not enrolled in a tribe, and thus would not be seen by providers within the Bureau of Indian Affairs (BIA) or the Indian Health Service (IHS) (Baldridge, 2001). Among this highly diverse population, nearly 300 native languages are spoken, and cultural traditions vary widely. Despite the growing urbanization of this population, more American Indian elders live in rural areas than do other older ethnic minorities, with nearly 25 percent on reservations or in Alaskan Native villages. On the other hand, most urbanized American Indians do not

return to their reservations as they age, instead preferring to age in place. Relatively high levels of residential stability characterize the older First Nations population. Over 50 percent are concentrated in southwestern states, with the remainder mostly in states along the Canadian border (Williams and Wilson, 2001).

Economic Status

Nearly 30 percent of older American Indians are estimated to be poor, with per capita incomes approximately half that of whites. The median income is barely above the poverty threshold. Although about 50 percent of older urban American Indians live with family members, their families are also more likely to be poor than their white counterparts (AARP, 2000; Barusch, 2006; Redford, 2001). Similar to other ethnic minority populations, the poverty of First Nations elders tends to reflect lifelong patterns of unemployment, employment in jobs not covered by Social Security, especially on reservations, and poor working conditions. Of all populations, American Indian elders are the most likely to have never been employed. By age 45, incomes have usually peaked among men in this group, and decline thereafter. In addition, historical circumstances and federal policies toward tribes have intensified the pattern of economic underdevelopment and impoverishment in "Indian country," which has led to a steady net migration to urban areas (Baldridge, 2001).

First Nations women are generally less educated than their male counterparts, and seldom earn even half the income of the men, putting them in a severely disadvantaged position. Another factor that negatively affects their socioeconomic and living conditions is that nearly 50 percent of women age 60 and over are widowed. Compared with their male counterparts, older American Indian women are at greater risk of social isolation and economic hardship with health-related consequences as they age (Baldridge, 2001). High unemployment and low income levels tend to necessitate larger households of intergenerational living arrangements, with the elders often the sole provider of the family through their Social Security or SSI. A surprisingly high percent of American Indian elders do not receive Social Security and Medicare benefits, even though such public supports appear to be essential to their survival. A substantial percentage also does not receive Medicaid. The reasons for this lack of access to public programs are unclear, but probably rooted in their negative historical experiences with the federal government.

Health

American Indians may have the poorest health of all Americans, due largely to their high rates of poverty, inadequate housing conditions, and isolation of many of their communities. Older adults have a higher incidence than their white counterparts of diabetes, hypertension, arthritis, heart disease, liver and kidney disease, gallbladder problems, hearing and visual impairments, strokes, pneumonia, influenza, accidents, tuberculosis, and problems stemming from obesity. Nearly 50 percent of all adults have diabetes, which is more than three times the rate of the incidence among whites, and the third leading cause of death among American Indians. In fact, the Pima Indian reservation in Arizona has the highest rate of diabetes in the world. With diabetes at nearly epidemic proportions, families face heavy demands in managing their elders' diet, exercise, and insulin (Acton et al., 2002; John, 2004; Office of Minority Health, 2005; Roubideaux, 2002). American Indians have higher rates of obesity, smoking, and alcoholism. The death rate from chronic liver disease and cirrhosis is seven times higher than that of the United States generally. Alcoholism, however, usually takes its toll before old age. Alcohol-related deaths drop sharply among American Indians who have reached age 55. Automobile accidents also take a disproportionately heavy

toll on American Indian men across the life course. In addition, poverty has combined with the historical suppression of indigenous religions and medical practices to place American Indians at higher health risks due to environmental degradation. These risks result from living in poor-quality housing, which may lack electricity and running water; being exposed to local toxins; and lacking safe water supplies and sewage disposal systems. They also are less likely to engage in preventive behaviors, with American Indian women age 40 years and older the least likely of all women to get regular mammograms, colectoral screenings, or immunizations. Cancer survival rates are the lowest among all U.S. populations (NCHS, 2003). Health promotion efforts with American Indians need to address community and environmental factors, their low propensity to turn to Western health care providers for preventive health measures, and the need to combine native concepts of spirituality and wellness with Western medicine.

For First Nations people, medicine is holistic and wellness-oriented. It focuses on behaviors and lifestyles through which harmony can be achieved in the physical, mental, spiritual, and personal aspects of one's role in the family, community, and environment, as well as their connections with ancestors and multiple higher powers (Weaver, 2005). The loss of access to traditional environments and the suppression of religious and medicine men practices also threaten traditional knowledge derived from the use of plants and herbs. Fortunately, the IHS allows medicine men and other traditional healers to treat patients in some of their clinics. This may help

---

Characteristics of American Indians/Alaska Natives that influence their use of health services:

- strong values favoring tribal autonomy
- nonlinear thinking, especially about time
- use of indirect communication styles
- historical suspicion of authority

foster and preserve their heritage and enhance IHS professionals' learning of non-western healing practices. Unfortunately, most procedures that focus on treating specific diseases rather than the whole person have typically not incorporated healing elements, such as the medicine wheel and sweat lodges. This then reduces the effectiveness of such programs with American Indian elders.

As a result of differences in health practices and their living environments, described above, three times as many American Indian persons die before reaching the age of 45 than non-Indians (John 2004). American Indians have higher death rates than whites up through age 65. However, between the ages of 65 and 94, the rates are comparable, and after age 85, their death rates are lower than whites (i.e., mortality crossover). But there is no evidence of "disability crossover." Instead, about twice as many American Indians age 65 to 74 experience some type of functional impairment, particularly mobility limitations and fewer years of active life expectancy (i.e., more years of dependent life expectancy, in a state of disability) compared to whites. In other words, they experience an *expansion* rather than compression of morbidity. Over 30 percent of American Indians age 65 to 74 have lost all their natural teeth, the highest proportion of any group of elders. Not surprisingly, the lowest proportion among all ethnic groups who rate their health as excellent or very good is among older American Indians (Barusch, 2006; John, 2004). As a result of their higher incidence of multiple chronic conditions, the majority of First Nations elders experience high rates of functional disability, particularly mobility limitations.

Because of their higher rates of functional disability, many First Nations people look older than their chronological age, with adults on reservations appearing old by 45 years of age, and in urban areas, by age 55 (Barusch, 2006). As a result, American Indians often use social functioning and decline in physical activities

to define an elder. However, this presents barriers to using publicly funded health services, which base eligibility on chronological, not functional, age.

Given the importance of tribal sovereignty, First Nations elders generally believe that health and social services are owed to them as a result of the transfer of their lands and that these services derive from solemn agreements between sovereign nations. Despite such agreements, the majority of American Indian and Native Alaskan elders rarely see a physician, often because of living in isolated areas, poor transportation, and mistrust of non-Indian health professionals. Accordingly, the prevailing life circumstances for many elders—of poverty, unemployment, alcoholism, and substance abuse—may interfere with their ability to seek preventive health care. Language also remains a barrier. For example, some of the languages of indigenous elders contain no words for *cancer*.

SHARED CHARACTERISTICS AND EXPERIENCES AMONG HIGHLY DIVERSE FIRST NATIONS' ELDERS

Characteristics of American Indians/Alaska Natives that influence their use of health and social services:

- strong value of tribal autonomy
- nonlinear thought processes, especially related to time
- use of indirect communication and styles
- historical suspicion of government authority
- the rapid and forced change from a cooperative, clan-based society to a capitalistic and nuclear family–based system as a result of U.S. governmental policies and exploitation of land
- the outlawing by the government of language and spiritual practices
- the removal by government-funded boarding schools
- the death by generations to infectious disease or war
- the loss of the ability to use the land walked by their ancestors for thousands of years

Many feel that talking about the disease will bring it on; they may hold fatalistic views, or believe that their culture stigmatizes cancer survivors. In addition, many prefer traditional health care from their tribal medicine people and resist using non-Indian medical resources.

To understand their health care patterns, a life course perspective is necessary that considers their historical experiences with racism, especially the government's efforts to eradicate their culture through forced assimilation, boarding schools for youth, religious conversion, and eradication of native languages. The urbanization of the American Indian population during and after World War II created two worlds of aging. For American Indian elders who are dispersed among the general urban population, there is no tribal community or government concerned with their welfare. Nor do they have special government institutions, such as the Indian Health Service or the Bureau of Indian Affairs (BIA) that are responsible for the well-being of American Indians on reservations.

American Indians on reservations have access to the **Indian Health Service (IHS)** for health care, although IHS is severely underfunded and generally focuses on health care for children and young adults, resulting in shortages of personnel, training, and facilities to address elders' needs (John, 2004). As a result, the majority of American Indian elders receive social and medical services from the BIA and IHS only periodically. As noted earlier, the IHS is effective in controlling infectious diseases and providing acute care earlier in life, thereby extending life expectancy. The IHS generally does not address elders' long-term care needs, however (Barusch, 2006; John, 2004). For example, the IHS operates less than a dozen nursing homes on reservations, compared to approximately 50 hospitals. This means that older American Indians who need nursing home care may find themselves in geographically distant facilities that are not oriented to Indian peoples. Such cultural and geographic

barriers have resulted in a pattern of repeated short-term stays or revolving-door admissions for chronic conditions. Consequently, among those over age 65, only about 2 percent are in nursing homes (AARP, 2005). Recognizing the need for long-term care services, several tribes have established nursing homes and home health agencies on their reservations, which ensures that American Indian staff provide services that respect cultural values (Barusch, 2006). In urban areas, some intergenerational programs deliver home care as well as facilitate the passing on of cultural traditions and languages.

American Indian elders have the highest hospitalization rate and the lowest rate of outpatient visits (John, 2004). The sociocultural and political barriers to adequate health care among First Nations people encompass the following:

- They often ascribe ill health and disability to the normal aging process and are therefore less likely to seek care for treatable and curable conditions.
- Many distrust medical care that is not native.
- They encounter professionals' lack of sensitivity to ritual folk healing and cultural definitions of disease.
- They have experienced racism, discrimination, and stereotyping, and have been turned away from public clinics where staff insist that IHS is the sole agency responsible for their health care.
- They anticipate adverse contacts and being treated unfairly by non-Indian health professionals.
- They are unwilling to sit through long waits at non-native clinics.
- They perceive health care providers as rude because of such behaviors as shaking hands, getting right down to business, addressing strangers in a loud voice, confident tones, and frequent interruptions of the patient.
- There are too few American Indian health care providers.

First Nations elders perceive their mental health to be poorer than do white older adults. Depression is the most common mental health problem, often precipitated by external factors such as chronic unemployment and poverty-level income, but is difficult to diagnose because of cultural factors and alcohol use. In addition, American Indians tend to somaticize mental health problems and present them as physical health complaints. From their perspective, mind and body are one, so it is reasonable for the body to manifest physical symptoms whenever a person's life is not in balance. Some studies document a higher incidence of suicide, but findings are mixed, and suggest that suicide rates are highest for American Indians age 25 to 34 (John, 2004). American Indians' low utilization of mental health services is not necessarily a reflection of fewer emotional problems, but may represent barriers to treatment and lack of information about available services from their health care providers. It may also reflect the greater respect accorded elders for their wisdom and cultural heritage. To some extent, maintaining a tribal identity may serve to buffer various stresses. With age, American Indians appear to shift to a more passive relationship with their world, accepting age-related changes as a natural part of life and utilizing passive forbearance to cope. For example, in contrast with all other groups, American Indians are more accepting of dementia, sometimes viewing such elders as communicating with a supernatural "other side" (Henderson and Henderson, 2002). This movement from active mastery to passive accommodative styles is consistent with Gutmann's findings for diverse cultures, described in Chapter 6.

Mental health problems may be intensified by the degree to which older American Indians' lives are dictated by government bureaucratic policies. Unlike any other ethnic minority group, various tribes are sovereign nations that have a distinct relationship with the U.S. government, based largely, but not exclusively, on historical treaties. Congress and the BIA, not the individual states, largely determine daily practices on the reservations. Although the BIA's regulations are intended to ensure basic support, it is criticized for expending the majority of its budget on maintaining the bureaucracy, with only a small percentage actually going to services. It also has undermined some traditional cultural values. As an example, land-grazing privileges were historically extended to all tribal members for as long as they desired. Today, First Nations elders must transfer their grazing rights to their heirs before they qualify for supplemental financial assistance, such as SSI or Medicaid. This deprives the old of their traditional position of power and prestige within the tribal structure. In 2000, the head of the BIA apologized to tribal leaders for the agency's "legacy of racism and inhumanity," including attempts to eliminate Indian languages and cultures, but this apology was not made on behalf of the federal government as a whole (Kelly, 2000). The history of American Indian elders and the federal government's mistreatment of them must be considered in developing culturally competent social and health services that respect their distinctive values and history (Ferraro, 2001).

Social Supports and Living Situations

Historical and cultural factors also strongly influence family and community relationships. Family is the central institution; "honoring" and giving respect to elders and sharing family resources are an integral part of their ethos. The term *elder* in Native languages means "agent of God." First Nations' deep reverence for nature and belief in a supreme force, the importance of the clan, and a sense of individual autonomy as a key to noncompetitive group cohesion all underlie their practices toward their elders. Historically, as described in Chapter 2, the old were accorded respect and fulfilled specified useful tribal roles, including that of the "wise elder" who instructs the young and assists with child care, especially for foster children and grandchildren. They also maintained responsibility for remembering and relating tribal philosophies, myths, and traditions, and served as religious and political advisors to tribal leaders. These relationships have changed, however, with the restructuring of American Indian life by the BIA and by the increasing urbanization and assimilation of native populations fostered by federal policies.

Not surprisingly, with a gender ratio of approximately 64.5 men to every 100 women age 65 and over, women comprise almost 60 percent of American Indian elders. More than 75 percent of American Indian men, but less than 50 percent of their female counterparts, are married (Barusch, 2006). Approximately 66 percent of all American Indian elders live with family members (e.g., spouse, children, grandchildren, and foster children), and over 40 percent of these households are headed by an older woman. Some 25 percent of Indian elders, typically the grandmother, care for at least one grandchild, and over 66 percent live within 5 miles of relatives. Given cultural values and norms of intergenerational assistance, family caregivers may assume such care to reciprocate for the help they and their children have received from now-aging relatives, even though their care responsibilities adversely affect them. As noted above, this pattern of helping family members, combined with mistrust of government programs and the lack of long-term care services, may underlie American Indians' low utilization rates. In turn, these factors put undue pressure on families to keep their elders at home, even when they lack sufficient resources to do so (Baldridge, 2001). Despite the value of filial responsibilities, unintentional neglect may occur because of the caregiver's poverty, inadequate access to resources, and uncertainty about how to provide health care.

The grandparent role in Asian cultures is highly valued.

Older Asian/Pacific Islanders*

Asian/Pacific Islander (APIs) elders encompass at least 30 distinct cultural groups who speak more than 100 different languages:

1. Asian Americans include Burmese, Cambodian, Chinese, East Indian, Filipino, Indonesian, Japanese, Korean, Laotian, Malaysian, Thai, and Vietnamese.

*Although Asian/Pacific Islanders is the term used to describe Asian Americans *and* Pacific Islanders, most research has been conducted on Asian Americans. The fact that relatively little information is available about Pacific Islander elders is why our discussion largely focuses on Asian American elders' health, economic, and social status. Therefore, we refer primarily to Asian Americans in this chapter.

2. Pacific Islanders encompass Fijian, Guamanian, Hawaiian, Micronesian, Samoan, and Tongan populations.

Some classifications include Native Hawaiians and other Pacific Islanders under Native Americans. Each group represents a culture with its own history, religion, language, values, SES status, lifestyle, immigration patterns, and level of acculturation. They also differ widely in religious affiliation (Christian Filipinos and Koreans, Hindu East Indians, Muslim Indonesians and Malay, and Buddhist Cambodians and Laotians). The timing of immigration has resulted in two distinct groupings: (1) Japanese, Chinese, and Filipino elders who arrived during the late nineteenth and early twentieth century and their U.S.-born children, and (2) older immigrants, primarily from Southeast Asia, who entered the United States after the 1970s with their families. These two waves differ widely in terms of ethnicity and SES. Figure 14.3 illustrates the distribution of API elders by country of origin.

The first wave of immigrants shares the experience of discrimination and isolation that characterized the early part of the twentieth century. Laws discriminating against Asians were numerous:

- the Chinese Exclusion Act of 1882
- the Japanese Alien Land Law of 1913
- denial of citizenship to first-generation Asians in 1922
- the antimiscegenation statute of 1935
- the Executive Order of 1942 for the internment of 110,000 persons of Japanese ancestry during World War II
- more recently, Public Law 95–507 excluding Asians as a protected minority under the definition of "socially and economically disadvantaged"

Such legislation, combined with a history of racism, contributed to feelings of mistrust, injustice, powerlessness, and fear of government—and thus to a reluctance to utilize services among

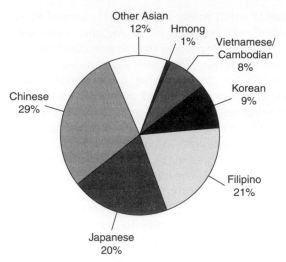

FIGURE 14.3 **Distribution of API by Country of Origin**

many API elders who came to the United States as young persons in the first half of the twentieth century.

In 1965, immigration quotas based on race and nationality were repealed. These changes resulted in a rapid growth of Southeast Asian immigrants, primarily after 1975, after the conflicts in Cambodia, Laos, and Vietnam. The majority of these more recent refugees were Vietnamese (60 percent), followed by Cambodians and Laotians (20 percent each). However, there is tremendous diversity by education, SES, language, and refugee experiences among Indochinese refugees, depending on the time of their immigration. The first wave, shortly after 1975, was largely the highly educated, wealthier Vietnamese, who had aided the American military during the Vietnam War. The second, more recent wave of Vietnamese, ethnic Chinese, Lao, Hmong, and Cambodian refugees included illiterate farmers and merchants from lower socioeconomic backgrounds who had experienced the ravages of war and revolution in their homeland. These conditions, combined with the trauma of dislocation and resettlement, adversely affected their health and economic status. For both waves, however, the normal aging process has been complicated by cultural, dietary, and language differences and difficulties with acculturation.

The diversity of the API population is also increased by the direct immigration in recent years of Asian American elders, often the parents or grandparents of younger immigrants, primarily from India, China, Korea, and Vietnam. Today, nearly 80 percent of Asian American elders in the United States are foreign-born and typically linguistically isolated, although their average length of residence in the United States is 23 years (Ruggles et al., 2004). Approximately 60 percent do not speak English, which is higher than the percent of Latino elders speaking only Spanish (Asian American Justice Center, 2006; U.S. Census Bureau, 2004), and most have deeply rooted Eastern traditional values that differ from the dominant culture, as described in Chapter 2. These differences intensify their difficulties in accessing services.

In addition, the 1996 welfare reform legislation posed new barriers, by restricting legal alien and immigrant older adults from receiving government assistance for their first 5 years in the United States. As described in Chapter 17, immigrants must also now provide proof of citizenship in order to receive Medicaid.

Approximately 8 percent of the Asian/Pacific Islander population is 65 and over (AOA, 2005). They are the third largest and the fastest-growing ethnic minority group, because of efforts to consolidate families through immigration and high birth rates among many API groups. Between 1990 and 2000, the population of elders among Asian Americans increased 78 percent (Min and Moon, 2006). Since 1970, Asians have comprised the largest percentage (43.5 percent) of the older immigrant population. As with other groups, the oldest-old are the most rapidly growing segment.

Economic Status

A widely held perception is that APIs are a "successful" minority because, as a whole, they are better educated and better off financially than other ethnic minority groups. However, this description as the model minority tends to trivialize the health problems of Asian Americans, suggesting that they can take care of these on their own and do not need services. It overlooks the socioeconomic and educational diversity among APIs and the problems faced by the newest refugees. In other words, the success of some masks the severe problems of others. Asians who immigrated prior to 1924, especially Japanese and Chinese, generally differ substantially in their occupational and educational backgrounds from those who came later. As a result of denial of property rights and discrimination against them for public jobs, most Asian elders who immigrated earlier are less educated and more economically deprived than their white counterparts, but this pattern has improved dramatically for their adult children and grandchildren. On the other hand, subgroups of poverty exist among recent immigrants, especially among Laotians, Hmong, and Cambodians, whose limited English proficiency reduces their ability to access public services and to find and maintain employment. Their social worlds may be limited to ethnic enclaves, such as Chinatown and Koreatown where they have developed small retail and service businesses, mutual-aid or benevolent societies, and recreational clubs, and have access to traditional health care. Although segregated from the larger society, these ethnic enclaves are nevertheless a center for social support and the delivery of services to elders.

These social functions, however, may not exist for future API generations, who will be more geographically and socially mobile and socioeconomically and linguistically diverse. Differences between foreign-born and American-born, urban residents and suburbanites, old timers and newcomers, Christians and Buddhists, professionals and laborers, and rich and poor frequently override a common ethnic identity, making unity at times an elusive goal.

Although U.S.-born Chinese American and Japanese American elders tend to be economically better off than other groups, over 13 percent of API elders are poor. As noted above, poverty rates increase dramatically among recent immigrants (AOA, 2005; Min and Moon, 2006):

Hmong	38%
Cambodian	29%
Laotian	24%
Vietnamese	21%

Poverty rates may be even higher than reflected in official statistics, since more API adults are self-employed as farmers or in small businesses than in other groups, thereby inflating reports of "family" income. Many older Chinese and Filipinos have experienced a lifetime of low-paying jobs, often in self-employment, garment factories, and service or farming work that is not covered by Social Security or other pensions. Filipino men, in particular, were concentrated in live-in domestic, migrant agricultural, or other transient work, often living in homogeneous male camps. This prevented them from gaining an insured work history as well as from developing close ties with family and neighbors.

As is the case with older Latinos, many API elders who qualify for public financial supports, such as SSI, Medicare, and Medicaid, do not apply. In some instances, they may be excluded from Medicare because they do not have the minimal work history and/or the payroll contributions to be eligible for enrollment or because they are recent immigrants. After years of living under discrimination and fear of deportation, many resist seeking help from a government bureaucracy that they may distrust. Their reluctance to seek nonfamilial assistance is also shaped by cultural and linguistic traditions emphasizing hierarchical relationships, personal social status, and self-reliance. When unsure of others' social status, some API elders avoid interacting with them. In the past, they turned to their families and the benevolent societies and clubs in their tightly knit communities. Now many are caught between their cultural traditions of group and familial honor and the values of their Western society that

stress independence and self-sufficiency, making them loath to seek financial or governmental support (Braun and Browne, 1998).

Health

Generalizing about older Asian Americans' health status as a whole is difficult because of the wide variability within population groupings. Immigrants are often healthier than native-born Americans, and some studies have defined the API population as a whole as healthier than the general U.S. population, especially in terms of health-promoting behaviors (e.g., healthy diets; lower rates of smoking and drinking) and reduced exposure to high risk factors (Min and Moon, 2006). For instance, the incidence of strokes in Chinese Americans and Japanese Americans is actually lower than among their counterparts in China and Japan. The relatively better health status of these two groups may be due to their diet, with lower fat and higher carbohydrate intakes compared with whites, and lower obesity rates compared with other groups. On the other hand, the rates of digestive system cancers, diabetes, and suicide are higher in Japanese

---

LONG-LIVED ASIAN AMERICAN ELDERS

In Bergen County, New Jersey, researchers discovered a surprising pocket of longevity. Asian American women here live longer than any other ethnic group in the United States. Their average lifespan is 91.1 years, compared with 77.5 for the general population, 86.7 for Asian women nationally, and about 80 years for Bergen County as a whole. To researchers, the exact causes of their longevity are unclear but the women have strong opinions about why they have lived so long. They attribute their longevity to a healthy diet, spirituality, religious participation, close-knit communities, access to quality health care, close families, and structured activities, including exercise, through a local Long Life Adult Day Care Center (Murray et al., 2006).

Americans than among their counterparts in Japan, in part because Japanese Americans in the United States tend to have a higher proportion of fatty tissue, probably a result of high-fat Western diets (Yee-Melichar, 2004).

Similar to socioeconomic status, there is a bimodal distribution in health status. Some APIs, such as Japanese and Chinese Americans who immigrated in the 1930s, fare quite well, while others have very low income and poor health status. As a whole, APIs face higher rates of hypertension, cholesterol, and cancer, especially among low-income subgroupings, and Asian American women have the highest rate of osteoporosis. As examples of within-group heterogeneity of health status, rates of diabetes are higher among Japanese Americans, cardiovascular disease among Korean Americans, hypertension among Chinese and Filipino immigrants than among whites, and native Hawaiian mortality rates for heart disease are generally higher than among other groups. Although Asian Americans tend to have the lowest rate of health services utilization, this does not necessarily mean that they are healthier (Braun et al., 2004; Min and Moon, 2006).

More API elders than whites suffer from psychiatric disorders. The rate of clinically diagnosable depression is slightly higher than that for whites, with the highest rate among Korean Americans, which may be attributed to their recent immigration status (i.e., shorter length of stay in the United States), and difficulties in adjusting to American society (Min, Moon, and Lubben, 2005; Tran, Ngo, and Conway, 2003). As discussed in Chapter 2, the discrepancy between Western culture and their native culture is a risk factor for depression for many immigrants, especially Asian American elders (Mui and Kang, 2006; Nandan, 2005). Data on mental disorders may be underestimates since cultural factors influence the diagnosis of mental health problems and utilization of services. Furthermore, available measures of depression may be culturally biased (Mui et al., 2003). The suicide rate

among API elders, especially Chinese women, is higher than for whites and African American women. Suicides are often explained by perceived incongruities between the elders' values and the reality of their relatively isolated lives in an alien culture, the stigma attached to mental health problems and reluctance to seek help. Another factor underlying higher rates of depression and suicide is that refugee and immigrant elders from Southeast Asia are likely to have suffered the trauma of war, torture, and loss of loved ones, and thus face mental health problems such as major depression and post-traumatic stress disorders. Yet, as noted in Chapter 2, they are unlikely to seek or use mental health services, and when they do, they tend to experience poor treatment outcomes (Chow, Jaffee, and Snowden, 2003; Davis, 2000; Kim, 2002; Min and Moon, 2006; Yee-Melichar, 2004; Ying, 2001).

Many API elders with mental health problems do not receive appropriate treatment, partially because mental illness is stigmatized, if not taboo in the API community. The perception that mental illness is caused by an unexplainable superpower, spiritual forces or one's predetermined fate and cannot be cured by Western or medical treatment is rooted in traditional Asian cultures. They also attempt to keep mental illness problems within the family. Seeking help for psychological distress is seen as a sign of weakness, resulting in loss of face. In addition, they may not trust service providers to keep matters confidential (Min and Moon, 2006). Some groups somaticize mental distress, in part because of the shame and stigma attached to mental illness and to seeking help from formal services. APIs' belief in the inseparability of affective and somatic systems and lack of experience in describing and communicating about psychological concerns are also barriers. For example, depression in Chinese culture is expressed by symptoms of fatigue, lower energy, sleep disturbance, and displaced homemaker syndrome. Korean American women refer to the illness of *Hya-Byung*—prolonged

SHARED EXERIENCES AMONG HIGHLY DIVERSE API ELDERS

1. **Health-Seeking Behaviors**
   - lack of knowledge of risk factors and preventive health promoting behaviors
   - lower likelihood than whites or African Americans to get checkups or blood pressure tests
   - lack of knowledge of what blood pressure is, and what can be done to prevent heart disease
   - low rates of breast self-exams or screening for breast or cervical cancer
   - limited familiarity with cancer risk factors
   - perceptions that illness always involves symptoms of pain, weakness, dizziness, or nausea; thus failure to seek treatment for diseases that cannot be seen (e.g., cancer, hypertension, diabetes mellitus)
   - difficulty in accepting their diagnoses or Western treatment regimens
   - holding themselves and their families responsible for their health rather than turning to providers

2. **Belief Systems**
   - belief in the supernatural powers of ancestral and natural spirits
   - perceptions of hospitals as places to die, not a place to get well
   - definitions of the use of public services as shameful and an indicator of dependency and inability to care for oneself
   - belief that cancer is inevitably fatal and carries a stigma

   - use of over-the-counter or traditional home remedies rather than going to physicians
   - discomfort with male physicians among women
   - reverence for authority may result in not questioning a physician's diagnosis and treatment, and indicating agreement when there is none
   - stigma associated with mental illness and the desire to "keep up appearances" result in low utilization of treatment for mental health and substance abuse

3. **Structural and Linguistic Barriers**
   - culturally accepted complementary alternative medicine (e.g., acupuncture and herbal medicines) that is not covered by insurance
   - high noncompliance rates with Western prescription medications
   - fear of communication problems
   - difficulties in translating English medical/health terminology into Southeast Asian languages and translating Asian health concerns to English (e.g., cancer is not mentioned as a disease in texts on Chinese medicine)
   - perception of health care providers as "impatient and disrespectful" of their culture
   - if residing in this country illegally, fear that seeking medical care will result in deportation

suppression of unbearable pain, suffering, loss, anger, or resentment, which develops into clinical depression, anxiety, and somatic symptoms. While a commonly accepted expression of one's psychological and physiological status, few Korean Americans seek any kind of professional help for dealing with *Hyu-Byung* (Min and Moon, 2006). Such culturally unique syndromes are less common in younger generations that have assimilated, suggesting that a clash of divergent cultures contributes to some of these syndromes.

Immigrant elders' use of mainstream health services is influenced by their status as a subordinate group and their degree of acculturation. The greater their acculturation, the more likely they are to use services. Overall, APIs tend to underutilize most social and health services.

Cultural values underlie their expectation to rely on family and friends and their reluctance to utilize services (Min and Moon, 2006). Filipino American elders, for example, are guided by values of both respect and shame. Respect includes listening to others, self-imposed restraints, loyalty to family, and unquestioning obedience to authority. Shame involves fear of being left exposed, unprotected, and unaccepted. Filipino American older adults are also concerned with good relations or the avoidance of disagreement and conflict. The high value they place on personal relationships may impede their accepting formal assistance, including nursing home care. For first-generation Japanese, or Issei, a value that transcends that of family is group conscience, characterized by cohesiveness, pride, and identity through devotion to and sense of mutuality among peer-group members. This value has been preserved through the residential and occupational isolation of older Japanese American cohorts from mainstream American culture. Even among the second generation (Nissei), the Japanese vision of Buddhism endures in the cherishing of filial devotion and the loving indulgence of the old toward young children. Such interdependence with and respect for elders who have greater life experience, knowledge, and wisdom are widely accepted values. Accordingly, Japanese American older people tend to value intergenerational interactions, hierarchical relationships, interdependency, and empathy—all values that may not characterize formal services. These situations illustrate a lack of person–environment fit between a group's cultural values and the service system's insensitivity to cultural differences. Those who do use home and community-based services are characterized by living alone, longer years since immigration, preference for service providers from their culture, and higher functional limitations (Kuo and Torres-Gil, 2001).

The health problems of API elders are thus exacerbated by this complex and wide set of cultural, familial, linguistic, structural, and financial barriers to care, which result in the underutilization of Western health services, as follows:

- lack of knowledge that the services exist, especially those that would support aging in place
- fewer chronic diseases compared with their white peers
- sociocultural, language, and structural barriers to health care
- lack of bilingual staff
- traditional values such as endurance and "looking the other way"
- a fatalistic worldview of the causes of illness and health
- reluctance to use formal Western health services and preference for herbal and acupuncture treatments
- greater likelihood of turning to traditional spiritual healers
- belief in the Yin-Yang equilibrium or balance
- collectivistic values regarding health care decision making (e.g., shared or deferred decision making, filial piety and silent communication), as opposed to individualistic decision making styles of Western culture
- perceptions that the Western concept of patient autonomy is burdensome

The spiritual values of being part of something greater than the individual, harmony with nature, and the importance of family in a quest to achieve a higher state of being (Van Hook, Hugan, and Aguilar, 2001). Cultural values also provide a source of mutual support and pride. For example, *Bayanihan* is the Filipino concept of a community working together, doing heroic deeds, and lending help for community betterment. As Filipino immigrants have adopted the individualistic spirit of the United States, the *Bayanihan* spirit has faded. The economic value placed on time has hampered volunteerism and devalued unpaid community work in this and other ethnic groups. However, in some communities, advocates are seeking to resurrect the spirit of *Bayanihan* to promote the health and well-being of Filipino elders. The concept of this spirit is also promoted as a culturally significant health advocacy tool (Bagtas, 2000). Similarly, traditional healers provide broader social benefits for native Hawaiian and Korean elders compared to Western medicine. For example, healers typically spend more time with older patients, discuss personal situations thoroughly, are more accessible after hours and on weekends, and have personal contact with family members and friends (Hurdle, 2002).

Social Supports and Living Situations

As discussed in Chapter 2, most Asian cultures are strongly influenced by Confucian teachings of filial piety and respect for older people. In traditional Asian families, age has been a symbol of authority and wisdom, with younger adults expected to obey, respect, and care for their older relatives. With younger generations of immigrants adopting Western values and lifestyles, APIs now face the erosion of filial piety, status and authority of older family members, and **law of primogeniture.** This refers to the relationship between aged parents and the oldest son who provides care for them (typically through his wife) and, in turn, inherits their wealth. Today all children, not just the oldest son, are expected to display filial piety and to repay their parents for sacrifices they made. Nevertheless, this value of filial piety is being eroded due to smaller family size, family mobility, increased employment of daughters and daughters-in-law, and acculturation of younger generations into the larger society. As a result, intergenerational living arrangements have declined, with increasing numbers of elders living by themselves or with a spouse, not with children (Chow, 2001; Pang et al., 2003). A strain faced by many families is the duality of cultures and the inevitable clashes when generations have different languages, values, and ethos. Erosion of the traditional family network

in some instances has resulted in intergenerational and family conflict. For example, Chinese American elders no longer can offer financial support, land, or other material goods as they would have in their homeland, and fear being a burden to their children. They generally live with their children only in cases of extreme poverty or poor health, or when dependent on them for language translation. In contrast, Korean American elders often accept separation from their upwardly mobile children as a way to promote their children's happiness and success. As noted in Chapter 2, they may prefer to live in urban areas in Asian enclaves. Nevertheless, compared with the majority culture, Asian Americans place a higher value on reciprocal exchanges between young and old, and the respect accorded the old. Accordingly, compared to other groups, higher proportions of APIs have extended-family arrangements and families serve as primary caregivers. Asian Americans are more likely to indicate old age or being old as the main problem of the person they care for (National Alliance for Caregiving and AARP, 2004). For these reasons, any discussion of family living arrangements and caregiving must consider differences in culture, social class, timing of immigration, and generations among APIs (Hikoyeda and Wallace, 2001; Min and Moon, 2006).

In contrast to other ethnic minorities and to white older persons, API men somewhat outnumber women until they reach age 75 and older; they also constitute a larger percent of elders living alone. This reflects the continuing influence of disproportionate male immigration in the early part of the twentieth century and past restrictions on female immigration, rather than a higher life expectancy for men. For example, in 1900, there were 14 men for every 1 woman among the Chinese in the United States. On the other hand, older women in this group are much more likely to be married (42 percent) than their white counterparts (15 percent), with a smaller proportion (21 percent) remaining single in their later years compared to non-Hispanic whites (Angel and Hogan, 2004; Yee-Melichar, 2004).

Although advancing age increases the probability of living alone, nursing home use among older Asian Americans is significantly lower than for their white counterparts. Only about 1.2 percent over age 65 are in nursing homes, compared to slightly fewer than 5 percent of whites (AARP, 2005; Yee-Melichar, 2004).

This chapter highlights only a few characteristics of API elders as a group, since large inter- and intragroup differences exist. Because of population and political pressures in Asia, the high rate of immigration is likely to continue, and the diversity under the label of API to increase. A major challenge for researchers and service providers is to recognize this diversity of history and cultural values when developing culturally competent research and practice models.

Implications for Services

Underutilization of social and health services is a common theme across ethnic minority groups. Although some service providers rationalize that elders of color do not use formal services because of their families' assistance, patterns of underutilization cannot be fully explained in this way. Barriers to service utilization can be conceptualized at the level of service recipients and the delivery system, as illustrated in the box on the next page. Gerontologists increasingly agree that services need to be designed to take account of inter- and intracultural and geographic differences within and across groups. From this perspective, preferential consideration is needed to reduce social inequities between the elders of dominant and minority groups, to respond to the diversity of needs, and to increase the participation of various groups. Accordingly, service providers need to be trained to be culturally competent, and the importance of cross-cultural care or **ethnogeriatrics** is increasingly recognized.

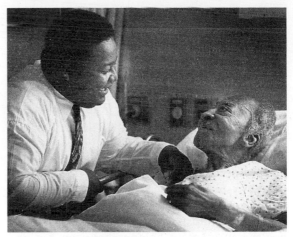

Shared cultural backgrounds can enhance communication between health care providers and older patients.

Additionally, there has been a shift from cultural sensitivity (awareness of cultural differences) to **cultural competence,** or specific knowledge, attitudes and skills to work effectively with ethnic minorities. In fact, when medical and psychosocial interventions are culturally competent, service utilization by ethnic minorities typically increases. The federal government has established standards for cultural competence in health care to promote respectful care compatible with the patient's cultural health beliefs, practices, and preferred language (USDHHS, 2001; Thobaben, 2002).

Fortunately, a growing number of health providers recognize and respect older ethnic minorities' adherence to traditional paradigms of health and illness, their spiritual orientation, and associated folk beliefs and behaviors that diverge from mainstream Western scientific medical concepts. Some elders combine these with orthodox or scientific treatments. Accordingly, current health promotion initiatives targeted to older whites may not be appropriate for populations of color. For example, social entities that play a key role in older African Americans' lives, such as the church and religious leaders, are more likely to influence health beliefs and behaviors than are traditional approaches to health promotion. The involvement of health-promotion experts from the same culture may also help bridge the gap between cultural values and scientific knowledge about the causes and treatment of disease. This is particularly true for American Indian and API cultures, where traditional ways of treating disease are still widely practiced among older cohorts. Health promotion efforts that ignore spirituality and traditional beliefs about harmony between the individual, nature, and the universe are unlikely to be effective in these cultures. To illustrate, the Chinese believe that health represents a balance between Yin and Yang energy forces; certain foods are assumed to bring about this balance. Believing that the aging process predisposes people to Yin (or cold

forces), Chinese elders avoid eating many cold foods such as leafy green vegetables. Health-promotion facilitators must recognize the basis for such avoidance if they are to encourage healthier diets among older Asians. Accordingly, many tools to assess psychological states may not be appropriate for elders of color unless they have been validated with these specific groups. For example, most research on caregiving among populations of color has described lower levels of burden. However, such caregivers may express their burden in different ways than Caucasian caregivers, and available measures of caregiver burden may not adequately measure the impact of caregiving on them. In fact, some qualitative studies have found that African American and Puerto Rican caregivers express anger, frustration, loneliness,

---

BARRIERS TO UTILIZATION OF SOCIAL AND HEALTH SERVICES SHARED BY ETHNIC MINORITY ELDERS

1. Cultural and Economic Barriers

- Cultural isolation, including language differences and inability to speak English.

- Perceived stigma of utilizing services, especially mental health, and embarrassment and fear in attempting to describe symptoms.

- Confusion, anger at, and fear of health care providers and hospitals, which may be related to present or historical acts of racism by medical providers or institutional segregation.

- Lack of trust and faith in the efficacy of service professionals within a Western biomedical health care system, which may be intensified by cohorts' experiences (e.g., segregated health care and explicit policies, such as the Tuskegee experiment with African Americans, and the internment of Japanese Americans in World War II underlie a distrust of the health care system).

- Lack of knowledge of services, including how to make appointments, negotiate a clinic visit, and describe symptoms.

- Interest in complementary alternative medicine

2. Structural Barriers within the Service System

- The 1996 Welfare Reform Bill that eliminated some public benefits to legal immigrants

- Lack of services that are oriented toward and operated by members of respective ethnic minority groups

- Real or perceived discrimination by service providers

- Assessment instruments whose meaning is altered in translation

- Geographic distance of services from ethnic minority neighborhoods

- Lack of low-cost, accessible transportation to services

- Staff with a different racial/ethnic background who are not bilingual and are insensitive to ethnic and cultural differences

and resignation similar to their white counterparts, despite their appearance of coping effectively through religion (Calderon et al., 2002; Dilworth-Anderson, Williams, and Gibson, 2002). Service use by ethnic minority elders is increased under the following conditions:

- Providers take account of the heterogeneity of ethnic minority populations.
- Assessment measures and instruments take account of cultural differences and their spiritual orientations.
- Providers attend to the way that elders describe their spiritual life and its relationship to their illness and health.
- Services are located in ethnic minority communities, easily accessible, and near complementary supports, such as acupuncture for Asian elders.
- Easily available transportation is free or at low cost
- Services adhere to the cultural integrity of the elders' lifestyles; for example, nutrition programs include favorite ethnic foods, and nursing homes offer culturally appropriate recreation and meals.
- The organizational climate is more informal, personalized, open and less bureaucratic than in mainstream agencies.
- Staff include bilingual, bicultural, and/or indigenous workers, or interpreters who are culturally competent, convey respect and use personalized outreach to establish trust and rapport. Medical and insurance forms, newsletters, and descriptions of services are bilingual.
- Ethnic minorities from the local community are involved in the planning and delivery of services.
- Services are advertised in ways to reach ethnic minorities, such as through minority-oriented television, radio programs and newspapers, and announcements made through religious institutions, neighborhood

organizations, civic and social clubs, natural support systems, and advocates.

- Given major differences in the epidemiology and risk factors of certain diseases (such as diabetes), screening, prevention, and education are essential.

GUIDELINES FOR CULTURALLY COMPETENT ASSESSMENT

- All staff assessing older adults' cognitive and functional status are trained to deal appropriately with the elder's cultural values and social structure (e.g, decision-making patterns) and how these affect behavior, including reactions to illness and services
- All staff develop ways to monitor their responses for any class, race, gender, or sexual identity biases that could interfere with the assessment.
- Issues of acculturation and language are considered when administering assessment measures and interpreting test results. Both the content of the test, as well as the language in which it is administered, affects a test's multicultural applicability.
- Test instructions written in simple, concise terminology to enable accurate translations.
- Use of "back translation" to obtain an equivalent fair battery for any language: Materials produced in one language are translated into another language by a bilingual translator, then translated back into English by a second individual, and then the original and back-translated English versions are compared.
- Bilingual staff, when available, are required to conduct assessments in the elder's native language.
- Culturally and sociopolitically relevant factors and events (e.g, refugees from war-torn nations) are documented.
- Religious and spiritual beliefs and values, including attributions and taboos, are considered since they affect world views and functioning.

SOURCE: Adapted from Bonder, Martin, and Miracle, 2001.

Overall, rather than a deficits model, in which interventions are developed to ameliorate personal or social problems, service providers should identify and build upon community strengths to supplement and augment existing services. This also suggests the value of utilizing existing organizational structures, such as religious institutions, to provide services and to link informal and formal sources of help. Underlying such strategies are assumptions that the needs of elders of color are best understood by members of their own communities, that these elders should be treated as distinct populations, and that research and professional training programs address issues of cultural competence. It is also important to employ ethnic minority practitioners, and to implement explicitly minority-specific statutes in federal regulations for aging programs. To advance research on populations of color and thus provide an empirical basis for service interventions, clear and consistent terminology is needed to define and target populations. Issues related to design, data collection, and measurement for and across different ethnic minority groups must also be addressed.

Implications for the Future

The recent trend of a faster growth of the older population among ethnic minorities than among whites is expected to continue. Nevertheless, white elders will continue to outnumber their ethnic minority peers. The socioeconomic status of ethnic minority elders is unlikely to improve greatly in the immediate future. This negative forecast is due largely to the growing income inequality in our society, with a worsening of economic conditions for a substantial portion of the population, many of whom are people of color. Accordingly, poor people of all ages face an increased risk of health problems and disabilities. Widening health disparities often parallel growing economic inequities. Since elders of color are overrepresented among

lower-income groups, declining health status linked to economic inequities is likely to affect ethnic minority elders disproportionately. In addition, increasing length of residence in the United States and greater acculturation of the Latino and Asian populations will lead to worsening health, as they adopt less-healthy Western diets and are exposed to unhealthy environments. The intractability of racism also suggests that the disparities in ethnic minority health, mortality, and well-being are likely to persist in the foreseeable future. These trends in health status point to increasing demands on ethnic minority caregivers, who report worse physical health, and among Asian American and Latino caregivers, higher rates of depression than their white counterparts (Pinquart and Sorensen, 2005). Service providers' assumptions of the strengths and extended nature of ethnic minority families may overlook these caregiving strains.

Growing rates of childhood poverty will profoundly affect the well-being of elders of color in the future. Among all children in the United States, about 20 percent are living in poverty; but this rate increases to 40 percent for African American and Latino children. The health status of adults is affected not only by their current SES but also by exposure to economic deprivation and unhealthy living situations over the life course. Early economic and health conditions appear to have long-term adverse consequences for adult health.

Although the likelihood of chronic illness increases with age, research increasingly shows that the origins of risk for chronic health conditions begin in early childhood or earlier (WHO, 2002; Takeuchi and Gage, 2003). Furthermore, risk continues to be impacted by factors such as SES and education across the life course. For example, childhood conditions explain a substantial portion of the difference in men's mortality by race, operating indirectly through adult socioeconomic achievement, not lifestyle factors (Warner and Hayward, 2002).

This pattern particularly affects African Americans, who have faced the greatest barriers to socioeconomic mobility (Williams, 2004). Increasingly, the importance of improving the economic and health status of groups earlier in life is being recognized as critical to well-being in old age. Fundamental changes in social policy that address nutrition, economic security, equitable educational opportunities, quality housing, and comprehensive community-based public health efforts are essential to reduce health disparities across the life course and especially in old age. New research paradigms are needed to capture the unique, cultural features of the aging process among ethnic minorities and to implement culturally competent interventions that effectively reduce racial and socioeconomic disparities in health status and health services utilization (Jackson, 2002). Future research also needs to give greater attention to characteristics presumably linked to race, such as SES, acculturation, and discrimination. Regardless of the nature of the research, recruiting and retaining older ethnic minorities as research participants presents complex challenges. Empirically tested strategies, participatory action research that builds trust and connection with the community, and involvement of minority researchers at all levels are vital (Curry and Jackson, 2003). In addition, as noted in the discussion of service implications, social and health providers must improve their cultural competence.

Summary

Although age is sometimes called the great equalizer, today's elders are highly diverse. As we have seen throughout this book, differences in income, health, and social supports significantly affect older adults' quality of life. An important source of this diversity is ethnic minority status. Ethnogerontology is the study of the causes, processes, and consequences of race, national origin, and culture on individual and population aging. An early debate was whether ethnic minorities experience double jeopardy because of their race or whether age is a leveler of differences in income and life expectancy. Recent studies indicate a narrowing of differences in health status and life expectancy after age 75, or a crossover effect, but health and socioeconomic disparities result in double, and even triple, jeopardy for ethnic minority women in particular.

This chapter reviewed the social, demographic, economic, and health status of African Americans, Latinos, American Indians, and Asian/Pacific Islander elders. Although we have seen great variability, several common themes also emerge. As a whole, ethnic minorities experience higher rates of mortality from diabetes, heart disease, and cancer, and higher rates of functional disability, although exceptions to this generalization can always be found. For most elders of color, their resources and status reflect social, economic, and educational discrimination experienced earlier in life. In particular, those who immigrated to the United States are more likely to experience cultural and language problems. As a whole, they face shorter life expectancy and increased risks of poverty, malnutrition, substandard housing, and poor health, although within-group variations exist, and life expectancy for Japanese Americans and Chinese Americans is longer than for whites. Nevertheless, many ethnic minority elders, especially among the oldest-old, display considerable strengths and resilience. Social and health care assistance is of particular concern. Cultural and language difficulties, physical isolation, and lower income, along with structural barriers to service accessibility, contribute to their underutilization of health and social services. Efforts must continue to modify services to be more responsive to the particular needs of ethnic minority older adults and to train social and health care providers to be culturally competent.

GLOSSARY

crossover effect the lower death rates among African Americans, APIs, and American Indians after age 75

cultural competence the knowledge and skills to take account of cultural meanings and work effectively with persons from different cultures

double jeopardy hypothesis the hypothesis that aging persons of color are in jeopardy in our society due to both growing old and their ethnic minority status

ethnogeriatrics cross-cultural geriatric care that recognizes cultural differences in response to health and disease

ethnogerontology study of causes, processes, and consequences of race, national origin, and culture on individual and population aging

fictive kin foster parents of children, close friends, or neighbors who function in the absence of blood relatives or when family relationships are unsatisfactory

health care disparities differences in access, quality, or rate of utilization of health care services, where ethnic minorities have substantially lower utilization rates

health disparities socioeconomic and racial/ethnic inequalities in health, mortality, and other adverse conditions across the life course

Indian Health Service (IHS) federal program that provides health care for Native Americans and Alaskans of all ages through hospitals and community clinics

law of primogeniture the exclusive right of the oldest son to inherit his father's estate that was traditional among Asian families

multiple hierarchy stratification the theory that both social class and ethnic minority status jeopardize older minorities

RESOURCES

Log on to MySocKit (www.mysockit.com) for information about the following:

- AARP Minority Initiative
- Administration on Aging Minority Initiatives
- National Asian Pacific Center on Aging
- National Association for Hispanic Elderly
- National Caucus and Center on Black Aged
- National Indian Council on Aging
- U.S. Public Health Service

REFERENCES

AARP. *Racial and ethnic differences among older adults in long term care service use. Fact Sheet Number 119.* 2005. Retrieved February 26, 2006, from http://assets.aarp.org/rgcenter/il/fs119_ltc.pdf

Acton, K., Burrows, N., Moore, K., Querec, L., Geiss, L., et al. Trends in diabetes prevalence among American Indian and Alaska Native children, adolescents and young adults. *American Journal of Public Health*, 2002, *92*, 1485–1490.

Administration on Aging (AOA). *Facts and figures: Statistics on minority aging in the U.S.* Washington, DC: Author, 2005.

Alwin, D., and Wray, L. A life-span developmental perspective on social status and health. *Journals of Gerontology*, 2005, *60B*, 7–14.

American Heart Association. *Heart disease and stroke statistics 2005 Update.* Dallas, TX: Author, 2005.

Anderson, R. Deaths: Leading causes for 2000. *National Vital Statistics Report.* Washington, DC: National Center for Health Statistics, 2002.

Angel, J. Devolution and the social welfare of elderly immigrants: Who will bear the burden? *Public Administration Review*, 2003, *63*, 79–89.

Angel, J., and Angel, R. Hispanic diversity and health care coverage. *Journal of Aging and Public Policy*, 2003, *13*, 8–12.

Angel, J., Angel, R., and Markides, K.S. Stability and change in health insurance among older Mexican Americans: Longitudinal evidence from the Hispanic Established Populations for Epidemiologic Study of the Elderly. *American Journal of Public Health*, 2002, *92*, 1264–1271.

Angel, J., Frisco, M., Angel, J., and Chiriboga, D. Financial strain and health among elderly Mexican-origin individuals. *Journal of Health and Social Behavior*, 2003, *44*, 536–551.

Angel, J., and Hogan, D. Population aging and diversity in a new era. In K.E. Whitfield (Ed.), *Closing the gap: Improving the health of minority elders in the new millennium.* Washington, DC: The Gerontological Society of America, 2004.

Angel, R., and Angel, J. Diversity and aging in the United States. In R. Binstock and L. George (Eds.), *Handbook of aging and the social sciences* (6th ed.). Academic Press, 2006.

Angel, R., Angel, J., Aranda, M., and Miles, T. Risk of nursing home use among elderly Mexican Americans. *Journal of Aging and Health,* 2004, *15,* 1–13.

Aranda, M.P. Older Latinos: A mental health perspective. In B. Berkman (Ed.), *Handbook of aging in health and social work.* New York: Oxford, 2006.

Aranda, M.P., Lee, P., and Wilson, S. Correlates of depression in older Latinos. *Home Health Care Services Quarterly,* 2001, *20,* 1–20.

Aranda, M.P., Villa, V.M., Trejo, L., Ramirez, R., and Ranney, M. The El Portal Latino Alzheimer's Project: A model program for Latino caregivers of Alzheimer's disease–affected persons. *Social Work,* 2003, *48,* 259–272.

Ajrouch, K., Antonucci, T., and Janevic, M. Social networks among blacks and whites: The interaction between race and age. *Journals of Gerontology,* 2001, *56B,* S112–S118.

Asian American Justice Center and Asian Pacific American Legal Center. *A community of contrasts: Asian and Pacific Islanders in the United States.* Washington, DC: Author, 2006.

Bagtas, A.P. Filipino elders community promotes health with dose of bayanihan. *Asian Pacific Affairs,* 2000, *8,* 1.

Baldridge, D. Indian elders: Family traditions in crisis. In D. Infeld (Ed.), *Disciplinary approaches to aging, Vol 4: Anthropology of aging.* New York: Rutledge, 2001.

Barusch, A. Native American elders: Unique histories and special needs. In B. Berkman (Ed.), *Handbook of aging in health and social work.* New York: Oxford, 2006.

Becker, G., Yewoubdar, B., Newsome, E.M., and Rodgers, V. Knowledge and care of chronic illness in three ethnic minority groups. *Family Medicine,* 1998, *30,* 173–178.

Beckett, M. Converging health inequalities in later life—An artifact of mortality selection? *Journal of Health and Social Behavior,* 2000, *41,* 106–119.

Bengtson, V.L. Ethnicity and aging: Problems and issues in current social science inquiry. In D.E. Gelfand

and A.J. Kutzik (Eds.), *Ethnicity and aging: Theory, research and policy.* New York: Springer, 1979.

Beyene, Y., Becker, G., and Mayen, N. Perception of aging and sense of well-being among Latino elderly. *Journal of Cross-Cultural Gerontology,* 2002, *17,* 155–172.

Bonder, B., Martin, L., and Miracle, A. Achieving cultural competence: The challenge for clients and healthcare workers in a multicultural society. *Generations,* 2001, *25,* 35–43.

Braun, K.L., and Browne, C. Cultural values and caregiving patterns among Asian and Pacific Islander Americans. In D.E. Redburn and L.P. McNamara (Eds.), *Social gerontology.* Westport, CT: Greenwood Press, 1998.

Braun, K.L., Yang, H., Onaka, A.T., and Horiuchi, B.Y. Asian and Pacific Islander mortality difference in Hawaii. In K. Braun, J. Pietsch, and P. Blanchette (Eds.), *Cultural issues in end-of-life decision making.* Thousand Oaks, CA: Sage Publications, 2000.

Braun, K.L., Yee, B., Browne, C., and Mokuau, N. Native Hawaiian and Pacific Islander elders. In K.E. Whitfield (Ed.), *Closing the gap: Improving the health of minority elders in the new millennium.* Washington, DC: The Gerontological Society of America, 2004.

Brown, A.S. Patterns of abuse among Native American elderly. In T. Tatara (Ed.), *Understanding elder abuse in minority populations.* philadelphia: Bruner and Mazel, 1999.

Burnette, D., and Mui, A.C. Physician utilization by Hispanic elderly persons: National perspective. *Medical Care,* 1999, *37,* 362–374.

Burton, L.M., and Whitfield, K.E. "Weathering" towards poorer health in later life: Comorbidity in urban low-income families. *Public Policy and Aging Report,* 2003, *13,* 13–18.

Byrd, W., and Clayton, L. *An American health dilemma: Race, medicine and health care in the United States 1900–2000 and the problem of race.* New York: Routledge, 2002.

Calderon, R.V., Morrill, A., Change, B.H., and Tennstedt, S. Service utilization among disabled Puerto Rican elders and their caregivers: Does acculturation play a role? *Journal of Aging and Health,* 2002, *1,* 3–23.

Cantero, P.J., Richardson, J.L., Baezconde-Garbanati, L., and Marks, G. The association between acculturation and health practices among middle-aged and elderly Latinas. *Ethnicity and Disease,* 1999, *9,* 166–180.

Chadidha, L., Adams, P., Phorano, O., Ong, S., and Byers, L. Stories told and lessons learned from African American female caregivers' vignettes for empowerment practice. *Journal of Gerontological Social Work,* 2002, *40,* 135–144.

Chiriboga, D., Black, S., Aranda, M., and Markides, K. Stress and depressive symptoms among Mexican American elderly. *Journals of Gerontology,* 2002, *57B,* P559–P568.

Choi, N.G. Frail older adults in nutrition supplement programs: A comparative study of African American, Asian American and Hispanic participants. *Journal of Gerontological Social Work,* 2001, *36,* 187–207.

Choi, N.G. Living arrangements and household compositions of elderly couples and singles: A comparison of Hispanics and Blacks. *Journal of Gerontological Social Work,* 1999, *31,* 41–61.

Chow, J., Jaffee, K., and Snowden, L. Racial/ethnic disparities in the use of mental health services in poverty areas. *American Journal of Public Health,* 2003, *93,* 792–797.

Chow, N. The practice of filial piety among the Chinese in Hong Kong. In I. Chi, N.L. Chappell, and J. Lubben (Eds.), *Elderly Chinese in Pacific Rim countries.* Hong Kong: Hong Kong University Press, 2001.

Chow, N., and Chi, J. *Assessment of Asian American/Pacific Islander organizations and communities.* London: Allyn and Bacon, 2001.

Chow, N., and Chi, I. *Twilight glory: Joy and sorrow of the elderly in Hong Kong.* Hong Kong: Cosmo Books, 2000.

Congress, E. Cultural and ethical issues in working with culturally diverse patients and their families. The use of the culturagram to promote cultural competent practice in health care settings. *Social Work in Health Care,* 2004, *39,* 249–262.

Cox, C. Empowering African American custodial grandparents. *Social Work,* 2002, *47,* 45–54.

Crimmins, E.M., and Sato, Y. Trends in healthy life expectancy in the United States: Gender, racial and educational differences. *Social Science and Medicine,* 2001, *52,* 1629–1641.

Crystal, S., and Shea, D. Prospects for retirement resources in an aging society. In S. Crystal and D. Shea (Eds.), *Focus on economic outcomes in later life: Public policy, health, and cumulative disadvantage.* New York: Springer, 2003.

Curry, L., and Jackson, J. The science of including older ethnic and racial group participants in health-related research. *The Gerontologist,* 2003, *43,* 15–17.

Dannefer, D. Cumulative advantage/disadvantage and the life course: Cross-fertilizing age and social science theory. *Journal of Gerontology,* 2003, *58B,* S327–S357.

Davis, R. Refugee experiences and Southeast Asian women's mental health. *Western Journal of Nursing Research,* 2000, *22,* 144–168.

Delgado, K.P., and Baker, D.W. Limited English proficiency and Latinos' use of physician services. *Medical Care Research and Review,* 1999, *57,* 76–91.

Department of Health and Human Services. *National standards for culturally and linguistically appropriate service in health care: Final report.* Washington, DC: Public Health Service, Office of Minority Health, 2001.

Dilworth-Anderson, P., Williams, I.C., and Gibson, R.E. Issues of race, ethnicity, and culture in caregiving research: A 20-year review. *The Gerontologist,* 2002, *42,* 237–272.

Doty, M. *Hispanic patients' double burden: Lack of health insurance and limited English.* New York: The Commonwealth Fund, 2003.

Dreeban, O. Health status of African Americans. *Journal of Health and Social Policy,* 2001, *14,* 1–17.

Dunlop, D., Manheim, L., Song, J., and Chang, R. Gender and ethnic/racial disparities in health care utilization among older adults. *Journals of Gerontology,* 2002, *57B,* S221–S233.

Dwight-Johnson, M., Unutzer, J., Sherbourne, C., Tang, L., and Wells, K. Can quality improvement programs for depression in primary care address patient preferences for treatment? *Medical Care,* 2001, *39,* 934–944.

Dwyer, K. Culturally appropriate consumer-directed care: The American Indian Choices Project. *Generations,* 2000, *24,* 91–93.

Fears, D. A defining moment for Hispanics. *Seattle Times,* October 19, 2003, p. A10.

Federal Interagency Forum on Aging and Related Statistics. *Older Americans 2006: Key indicators of well-being.* Hyattsville, MD: Federal

Interagency Forum on Aging and Related Statistics, 2006.

Ferraro, F.R. Assessment and evaluation issues regarding Native American elderly adults. *Journal of Clinical Geropsychology,* 2001, *7,* 311–318.

Ferraro, K., Thorpe, R., McCabe, G., Kelley-Moore, J., and Jiang, Z. The color of hospitalization over the adult life course: Cumulative disadvantage in black and white? *Journals of Gerontology,* 2006, *61B,* S299–S306.

Ferraro, K.F., and Farmer, M.M. Double jeopardy, aging as leveler or persistent health inequality? A longitudinal analysis of white and black Americans. *Journals of Gerontology,* 1996, *51B,* S319–S328.

Flippen, C., and Tienda, M. Workers of color and pathways to retirement. *Public Policy and Aging Report,* 2002, *12,* 3–8.

Flippen, M. Minority workers and pathways to retirement. In R. Hudson (Ed.), *The new politics of old age policy.* Baltimore: John Hopkins University Press, 2005.

Foley, K., Tung, J.S., and Mutran, E. Self-gain and self-loss among African American and white caregivers. *Journals of Gerontology,* 2002, *57B,* S14–S23.

Fredriksen-Goldsen, K. Caregiving and resiliency: Predictors of well-being. *Journal of Family Relations,* in press.

Freeman, H.T., and Payne, R. Racial injustice in health care. *New England Journal of Medicine,* March 2000, *11,* 17–20.

Garcia, J.L., Kosberg, J.I., Mangum, W.P., Henderson, J.N., and Henderson, C.C. Caregiving for and by Hispanic elders: Perceptions of four generations of women. *Journal of Sociology and Social Welfare,* 1999, *26,* 169–187.

George, L., and Lynch, S. Race differences in depressive symptoms: A dynamic perspective on stress exposure and vulnerability. *Journal of Health and Social Behavior,* 2003, *44,* 353–369.

Gibson, P. Barriers, lessons learned and helpful hints: Grandmother caregivers talk about service utilization. *Journal of Gerontological Social Work,* 2002, *39,* 55–74.

Gist, Y., and Hetzel, L. *We the people: Aging in the United States.* US Bureau of the Census, 2004.

Gullette, M. Tragic toll of age bias. *The Boston Globe,* August 27, 2006.

Hayslip, B., and Kaminski, P.L. Grandparents raising their grandchildren: A review of the literature and suggestions for practice. *The Gerontologist,* 2005, *45,* 262–269.

Hayword, M.D., Crimmins, E., Miles, T., and Yang, Y. The significance of socioeconomic status in explaining the racial gap in chronic health conditions. *American Sociological Review,* 2000, *65,* 910–930.

He, W. The older born foreign-born populations in the United States: 2000. *Current Population Reports,* P23–P211. Washington, DC: US Bureau of the Census, 2002.

Heinz, T., Lewis, J., and Hounsell, C. *Women and pensions: An overview.* Washington, DC: Women's Institute for a Secure Retirement (WISER), 2006.

Helman, C.G. *Culture, health and illness.* Oxford: Butterworth-Heinemann, 2000.

Henderson, J., and Henderson, L. Cultural construction of disease: A "supernormal" construct of dementia in an American Indian tribe. *Journal of Cross-Cultural Gerontology,* 2002, *17,* 197–212.

Herd, P. Crediting care or marriage: Reforming Social Security family benefits. *Journals of Gerontology,* 2006, *61B,* S24–S34.

Hikoyed, N., and Wallace, S. Do ethnic-specific long-term care facilities improve resident quality of life? Findings from the Japanese American community. *Journal of Gerontological Social Work,* 2001, *36,* 83–106.

Holden, K., and Hatcher, C. Economic status of the aged. In R. Binstock and L.K. George, (Eds.), *Handbook of aging and the social sciences* (6th ed.). New York: Academic Press, 2006.

House, J., Lantz, P., and Herd, P. Continuity and change in the social stratification of aging and health over the life course: Evidence from a nationally representative longitudinal study from 1986 to 2001/2002 (America's Changing Lives Study). *Journals of Gerontology,* 2005, *60B,* 15–26.

Hudson, R. Getting ready and getting credit: Populations of color and retirement security. *Public Policy and Aging Report,* 2002, *12,* 1–2.

Hurdle, D.E. Native Hawaiian traditional healing: Cultural based interventions for social work practice. *Social Work,* 2002, *47,* 183–192.

Indian Health Service. *Fact Sheet on Indian Health Disparities.* January 2006. Accessed February 26, 2007, from http:// info.ihs.gov/Files/DisparitiesFacts-Jan2006.pdf

Jackson, J.S. Conceptual and methodological linkages in cross-cultural groups and cross-national aging research. *Journal of Social Issues,* 2002, *58,* 825–835.

Jackson, P. Health inequalities among minority populations. *Journals of Gerontology,* 2005, *60B,* 63–67.

Jackson-Triche, M., Greer- Sullivan, J., Wells, K., Rogers, W., Camp, P., et al. Depression and health-related quality of life in ethnic minorities seeking care in a general medical setting. *Journal of Affective Disorders,* 2000, *58,* 89–97.

Jang, Y., Borenstein-Graves, A., Haley, W., Small, B., and Mortimer, J. Determinants of a sense of mastery in African American and white older adults. *Journals of Gerontology,* 2003, *58B,* S221–S224.

John, R. Health status and health disparities. In K. Whitfield, (Ed.), *Closing the gap: Improving the health of minority elders in the new millennium.* Washington, DC: Gerontological Society of America, 2004.

Jones, C. *The impacts of racism on health.* Keynote speaker for the Summer Public Health Research Videoconference on Minority Health. Chapel Hill, NC: The University of North Carolina, 2000.

Kelly, M. BIA head issues apology to Indians. *The Seattle Times,* September 9, 2000, 3A.

Kelley-Moore, J., and Ferraro, K. The black/white disability gap: Persistent inequality in later life. *Journals of Gerontology,* 2004, *59B,* S34–S43.

Kessler, R.C., Berglund, P., Demler, O., Koretz, D., Merikangas, K., et al., The epidemiology of major depressive disorders: Results from the National Comorbidity Survey Replication. *Journal of the American Medical Association,* 2003, *289,* 3095–3105.

Kessler, R.C., Mickelson, K.D., and Williams, D.R. The prevalence, distribution and mental health correlates of perceived discrimination in the United States. *Journal of Health and Social Behavior,* 1999, *40,* 208–230.

King, M. African American elders help forge connections. *The Seattle Times,* February 17, 2006, B1, B4.

Kim, W. *Ethnic variations in mental health symptoms and functioning among Asian Americans.* Doctoral Dissertation, University of Washington, 2002.

Kuo, T., and Torres-Gil, F. Factors affecting utilization of health services and home and community-based care programs by older Taiwanese in the United States. *Research on Aging,* 2001, *23,* 14–37.

LaVeist, T.A. Pathways to progress in eliminating racial disparities in health. *Public Policy and Aging Report,* 2003, *13,* 19–22.

Li, C., Malone, K., and Daling, J. Differences in breast cancer state, treatment and survival by race and ethnicity. *Archives of Internal Medicine,* 2003, *163,* 49–56.

Lincoln, K. Social support, negative social interactions and psychological well-being. *Social Service Review,* 2000, *74,* 231–252.

Lincoln, K.D., Chatters, L.M., and Taylor, R.J. Social support, traumatic events and depressive symptoms among African Americans. *Journal of Marriage and Family,* 2005, *67,* 754–766.

Lincoln, K.D., Taylor, R.J., and Chatters, L.M. Correlates of emotional support and negative interaction among older Black Americans. *Journals of Gerontology,* 2003, *58B,* S225–S233.

Lopez, S. Mental health care for Latinos: A research agenda to improve the accessibility and quality of mental health care for Latinos. *Psychiatric Services,* 2002, *53,* 1569–1573.

Lum, T. *Culturally competent practice: A framework for understanding diverse groups and justice issues.* Pacific Grove, CA: Brooks Cole, 2003.

Lum, Y.S., Chang, H.J., and Ozawa, M.N. The effects of race and ethnicity on use of health services by older Americans. *Journal of Social Service Research,* 1999, *25,* 15–42.

Lynch, J.W., Davey-Smith, G., Kaplan, G.A., and House, J.S. Income inequality and mortality: Importance to health of individual income, psychosocial environment, or material conditions. *British Medical Journal,* 2000, *320,* 1200–1204.

Ma, G.X. Between two worlds: The use of traditional and western health services by Chinese immigrants. *Journal of Community Health,* 1999, *24,* 421–437.

Margolis, M.L., Christie, J.D., Silvestri, G.A., Kaiser, L., Santiago, S., et al. Racial differences pertaining to a belief about lung cancer surgery: Results of a multicenter survey. *Annals of Internal Medicine,* 2003, *139,* 558–563.

Markides, K., and Eschbach, K. Aging, migration, and mortality: Current status of research on the Hispanic paradox. *Journals of Gerontology,* 2005, *60B,* S68–S75.

Markides, K.S., and Black, S.A. Race, ethnicity and aging. In R.H. Binstock and L.K. George (Eds.), *Handbook of aging and the social sciences* (4th ed.). San Diego, CA: Academic Press, 1996.

Markides, K.S., Liang, J., and Jackson, J. Race, ethnicity and aging: Conceptual and methodological issues. In R. Binstock and L.K. George (Eds.), *Handbook of aging and the social sciences* (3rd ed.). New York: Academic Press, 1990.

Martinez, I.L. The elder in the Cuban American family: Making sense of the real and ideal. *Journal of Comparative Family Studies*, 2003, *33*, 359–370.

McDonald, P., Brennan, P., and Wykle, M. Perceived health status and health-promoting behaviors of African American and white informal caregivers of impaired elders. *Journal of National Black Nurses Association*, 2005, *16*, 8–17.

McDonald, P., and Wykle, M. Predictors of health-promoting behavior of African American and white caregivers of impaired elders. *Journal of National Black Nurses Association*, 2003, *14*, 1–12.

McDonald, P., Wykle, M., Kiley, M., and Burant, C. Depressive symptoms in persons with Type 2 diabetes: A faith-based clinical trial, *The Gerontologist*, 2004, *44*, 417.

McGoldrick, M., Giordano, J., and Garcia-Preto, N. (Eds.), *Ethnicity and family therapy* (3rd ed.). New York: Guilford Press, 2005.

Mendes de Leon, C., Gold, D., Glass, T., Kaplan, L., and George, L.K. Disability as a function of social networks and support in elderly African Americans and Whites: The Duke EPESE 1986–1992. *Journals of Gerontology*, 2001, *56B*, S179–S190.

Mikuls, T.R., Mudano, A.S., Pulley L.V., and Saag, K.G. Association of race/ethnicity with the receipt of traditional and alternative arthritis-specific health care. *Medical Care*, 2003, *41*, 1233–1239.

Min, J. Preference for long-term care arrangement and its correlates for older Korean-Americans. *Journal of Aging and Mental health*, 2005, *17*, 363–395.

Min, J., and Moon, A. Older Asian Americans. In B. Berkman (Ed.), *Handbook of social work in health and aging*. New York: Oxford, 2006.

Min, J., Moon, A., and Lubben, J. Determinants of psychological distress over time among older Korean Americans and non-Hispanic white elders. Evidence from a two-wave panel study. *Aging and Mental Health*, 2005, *9*, 210–222.

Minkler, M., and Fuller-Thomson, E. African American grandparents raising grandchildren: A national study using the Census 2000 American Community Survey. *Journals of Gerontology*, 2005, *60B*, S82.

Miranda, M. Hispanic aging: An overview of issues and policy implications. In M.S. Harper (Ed.), *Minority aging*. DHHS Publication #HRS (P-DV-90–4). Washington, DC: U.S. Government Printing Office, 1990.

Mouton, C.P., and Esparza, Y.B. Ethnicity and geriatric assessment. In J.J. Gallo, T. Fulmer, G.J. Paveza, and W. Reichel (Eds.), *Handbook of geriatric assessment*. Gaithersburg, MD: Aspen, 2000.

Mui, A., and Kang, S.Y. Acculturation stress and depression among Asian immigrant elders. *Social Work*, 2006, *51*, 243–255.

Mui, A., Kang, S.Y., Chen, L.M., and Domanski, M. Reliability of the geriatric depression scale for use among elderly Asian immigrants in the USA. *International Psychogeriatrics*, 2003, *15*, 253–271.

Mukamel, D.B., Murthy, A., and Weimer, D.L. Racial differences in access to high quality cardiac surgeons. *American Journal of Public Health*, 2000, *90*, 1774–1777.

Mukamel, D.B., Weimer, D.L., and Mushlin, A.I. Referrals to high-quality cardiac surgeons: Patients' race and characteristics of their physicians. *Health Services Research*, 2006, *41*, 1276–1285.

Munet-Vilaro, F. *Health promotion for older adults: Latino elders*. Seattle: University of Washington, Northwest Geriatric Education Center, 2004.

Murray C., Kulkarni S., Michaud C., Tomijima N., and Bulzacchelli, M. et al. Eight Americas: Investigating causes of mortality disparities across races, counties and race-counties. *PLoS Medicine*, 2006, *3*, 260.

Nandan, M. Adaptation to American culture: Voices of Asian Indian immigrants. *Journal of Gerontological Social Work*, 2005, *44*, 175–203.

National Alliance for Caregiving and AARP. *Caregiving in the U.S.* Bethesda, MD: National Alliance for Caregiving, and Washington, DC: AARP, 2004.

National Center for Health Statistics (NCHS). *Health, United States, with urban and rural health chart book*, Washington, DC: Author, 2001.

National Center for Health Statistics (NCHS). *Health, United States, 2002. With chartbook on trends in the health of Americans.* Hyattsville, MD: Author, 2002.

National Center for Health Statistics (NCHS). *Health, United States, 2003.* Hyattsville, MD: Author, 2003.

National Center for Health Statistics (NCHS). *National vital statistics reports, 2006, 54* (http://www.cdc.gov/nchs).

National Women's Health Information Center. *Women of color health data book,* Washington, DC: U.S. Department of Health and Human Services, Office on Women's Health, 2003.

Office of Minority Health. *Minority health disparities at a glance.* Washington, DC: 2005. Accessed November 18, 2005, from http://omhrc.gov/.

Office of Minority Health Research (OMHRC). *HHS fact sheet: Minority health disparities at a glance.* Accessed December 1, 2006, from http://www.omhrc.gov/templates/content.aspx?ID=2139.

Older Women's League (OWL). *Retirement security and women of diverse communities.* Washington, DC: Older Women's League, 2003.

Otiniano, M.E., Du, X.L., Ottenbacher, K., and Markides, K.S. The effect of diabetes combined with stroke on disability, self-rated health and mortality in older Mexican Americans: Results from the Hispanic EPESE. *Archives of Physical Medical Rehabilitation,* 2003, *84,* 725–730.

Palloni, A., and Arias, E. Paradox lost: Explaining the Hispanic adult mortality advantage. *Demography,* 2004, *41,* 385–415.

Parker, M. et al. A multidisciplinary model of health promotion incorporating spirituality into a successful aging intervention with African American and White elderly groups. *The Gerontologist,* 2002, *42,* 406–415.

Peng, T., Navaie-Waliser, M., and Feldman, P. Social support, home health use and outcomes among four racial-ethnic groups. *The Gerontologist,* 2003, *43,* 503–513.

Phelan, J., and Link, B. Controlling disease and creating disparities: A fundamental cause perspective. *Journals of Gerontology,* 2005, *60B,* 27–33.

Pinquart, M., and Sorensen, S. Ethnic differences in stressors, resources, and psychological outcomes of family caregiving: A meta-analysis. *The Gerontologist,* 2005, *45,* 90–106.

Pourat, N., Lubben, J., Wallace, S., and Moon, A. Predictors of use of traditional Korean healers among elderly Koreans in Los Angeles. *The Gerontologist,* 1999, *39,* 711–719.

Purcell, P., and Whitman, D. Income of Americans age 65 and older, 1969 to 2004. *Journal of Deferred Compensation,* 2006, *12,* 1–41.

Ramirez, A.G., Suarez, L., Chalela, P., Talavera, G.A., Marti, J., Trapido, E.J., et al. Cancer risk factors among men of diverse Hispanic or Latino origins. *Preventative Medicine,* 2004, *39,* 263–269.

Redford, L.J. Long-term care in Indian country: Important considerations in developing long-term care services. Paper presented at the meeting of the American Indian and Alaska Native Round Table of Long-Term Care. Final report 2002. Accessed from http://www.his.gov/PublicAffairs/PressRelease/Long_Term_Care_Report.org.

Robert, S., and Ruel, E. Racial segregation and health disparities between black and white older adults. *Journals of Gerontology,* 2006, *61B,* 5203–5211.

Robison, J., Gruman, C., Gaztambide, S., and Blank, K. Screening for depression in middle-aged and older Puerto Rican primary care patients. *Journals of Gerontology,* 2002, *57A,* M308–M314.

Rooks, R., and Whitfield, K. Health disparities among older African Americans: Past, present and future perspectives. In K. Whitfield (Ed.), *Closing the gap: Improving the health of minority elders in the new millennium.* Washington, DC: Gerontological Society of America, 2004.

Roubideaux, Y. Perspectives on American Indian health. *American Journal of Public Health,* 2002, *92,* 1401–1403.

Ruggles, S., Sobek, M., Alexander, T., Fitch C., Goeken, R. et al. Integrated Public Use Microdata Series: Version 3.0. Available from the Minnesota Population Center, http://www.ipumis.org, 2004.

Salgado de Snyder, V., and Diaz-Guerrero, R. Enduring separation: The psychological consequences of Mexican migration to the United States. In L. Adler and U. Gielen (Eds.), *Migration: Immigration and emigration in international perspective.* Westport, CT: Praeger, 2003.

Schieman, S., Pearlin, L.I., and Nguyen, K.B. Status inequality and occupational regrets in late life. *Research on Aging,* 2005, *27,* 692–724.

Skarupski, K. et al. Black-White differences in depressive symptoms among older adults over time. *The Journals of Gernotology,* 2005, *60B,* P136–P142.

Smedley, B., Stith, A., and Helson, A. Unequal treatment: Confronting racial and ethnic disparities in health care. Washington, DC: National Academy Press, 2003.

Stokes, S.D., Thompson, L., Murphy, S., and Gallagher-Thompson, D. Screening for depression in immigrant Chinese American elders: Results of a pilot study. In N. Choi (Ed.), *Social work practice with the Asian American elderly.* New York: Haworth Press, 2002.

Swindle, R., Heller, K., and Frank, M. Differentiating the effects of positive and negative social transactions in HIV illness. *Journal of Community Psychology,* 2000, *28,* 35–50.

Tally, T., and Kaplan, J. The negro aged, *Newsletter of the Gerontological Society,* 111, 4, December 1956.

Takeuchi, D., and Gage, S. What to do with race? The changing conceptions of race in the social sciences. *Culture, Medicine and Psychiatry,* 2003, *27,* 435–445.

Taylor R., Chatters L., and Celious A. Extended family households among Black Americans. *African American Research Perspectives,* 2003, *1,* 133–151.

Taylor, R.J., Lincoln, K.D., and Chatters, L.M. Supportive relationships with church members among African Americans. *Family Relations,* 2005, *54,* 501–511.

Thobaben, M. Racial and ethnic disparities in health care. *Community-based Health Care Management and Practice,* 2002, *14,* 479–481.

Torres-Gil, F.M., and Kuo, T. Social policy and the politics of Hispanic aging. *Journal of Gerontological Social Work,* 1998, *30,* 143–158.

Torres-Gil, F., and Moga, K. Multiculturalism, social policy and the new aging. *Journal of Gerontological Social Work,* 2001, *6,* 12–32.

Tran, T., Ngo, D., and Conway, K. A cross cultural measure of depressive symptoms among Vietnamese Americans. *Social Work Research,* 2003, *27,* 56–65.

Unutzer, J., Katon, W., Callahan, C., Williams, J., Hunkeler, E., et al., 2003. Depression treatment in a sample of 1801 depressed older adults in primary care. *Journal of the American Geriatrics Society,* 2003, *51,* 505–514.

U.S. Bureau of the Census. Current Population Survey, Annual Social and Economic Supplements, 2005, Poverty and Health Statistics Branch/HHES Division. Accessed February 26, 2007, from http://www.census.gov/hhes/www/poverty/histpov/histpov12.html.

U.S. Census Bureau. Population Division, Interim Statistics. Population projections by age: 2005. Accessed October 1, 2006, from http://www.census.gov/population/projections/SummaryTabC1.pdf.

U.S. Census Bureau. *Statistical Abstract of the United States, 2007.* Table 14. Resident Population, by Race, Hispanic Origin, and Age: 2000 to 2005. Accessed February 26, 2007, from http://www.census.gov/compendia/statab/tables/07s0014.xls.

VanHook, M., Hugen, B., and Aguilar, M. *Spirituality within religious traditions in social work practice.* Pacific Grove, CA: Brooks/Cole, 2001.

Van Ryn, M. Research on the provider contribution to race/ethnicity disparities in medical care. *Medical Care,* 2002, *40,* 1140–1151.

Van Ryn, M., and Burke, J. The effect of patient race and socioeconomic status on physicians' perceptions of patients. *Social Science and Medicine,* 2000, *50,* 813–828.

Villa, V., and Aranda M. The demographic, economic, and health profile of older Latinos: Implications for health and long-term care policy and the Latino family. *Journal of Health and Human Services Administration,* 2000, *23,* 161–180.

Warner, D.F., and Hayward, M.D. *Race disparities in men's mortality: The role of childhood social conditions in a process of cumulative disadvantage.* Unpublished manuscript, Philadelphia: University of Pennsylvania, 2002.

Weaver, H. Cultural identity: Theories and implications. In. H. Weaver (Ed.), *Explorations in cultural competence: Journeys to the four directions.* Belmont, CA: Thomson/Brooks/Cole, 2005, 25–46.

Weisse, C., Sorum, P., Sanders, K., and Syat, B. Do gender and race affect decisions about pain management? *Journal of General Internal Medicine,* 2001, *16,* 211–217.

Wen, M., Cagney, K.A., and Christakis, N.A. Effect of Community Social Environment on the Mortality of Individuals Diagnosed with Serious Illness. *Social Science and Medicine*, 2005, *61*, 1119–1134.

Whitfield, K., (Ed.). *Closing the gap: Improving the health of minority elders in the new millennium.* Washington, DC: Gerontological Society of America, 2004.

Whitfield, K.E., and Hayward, M. The landscape of health disparities among older adults. *Public Policy and Aging Report*, 2003, *13*, 3–7.

Williams, A. Therapeutic landscapes in holistic medicine. *Social Science and Medicine*, 1998, *46*, 1193–1202.

Williams, D., Neighbors, H., and Jackson, J. Racial/ethnic discrimination and health: Findings from community studies. *American Journal of Public Health*, 2003, *93*, 200–208.

Williams, D.A. The health of men: Structured in equalities and opportunities. *American Journal of Public Health*, 2003, *93*, 724–731.

Williams, D.R. The health of U.S. racial and ethnic populations. *Journals of Gerontology*, 2005, *60B*, 53–62.

Williams, D.R. Race, stress, and mental health. In C. Hogue, M. Hargraves, and K. Scott-Collins (Eds.), *Minority health in America.* Baltimore: Johns Hopkins University Press, 2000.

Williams, D.R. Racism and health. In K.E. Whitfield (Ed.), *Closing the gap: Improving the health of minority elders in the new millennium.* Washington, DC: The Gerontological Society, 2004.

Williams, D.R., and Rucker, T.D. Understanding and addressing racial and ethnic disparities in health care. *Health Care Financing Review*, 2000, *21*, 75–90.

Williams, D.R., and Wilson, C.M. Race, ethnicity and aging. In R.A. Binstock, and L.K. George (Eds.), *Handbook of aging and the social sciences* (5th ed.). New York: Academic Press, 2001.

Wilmoth, J., and Chen, P. Immigrant status, living arrangements and depressive symptoms among middle-aged and older adults. *Journals of Gerontology*, 2003, *58B*, S305–S313.

Wong, P., and Ujimoto, V. The elderly: Their stress, coping and mental health. In C.L. Lu and N.W. Zane (Eds.), *Handbook of Asian American psychology.* Thousand Oaks, CA: Sage, 1998.

World Health Organization (WHO). *Active aging: A policy framework.* Paper presented at the Second United Nations World Assembly on Aging, Madrid, Spain, 2002.

Yee-Melichar, D. Aging Asian Americans and health disparities. In K. Whitfield (Ed.), *Closing the gap: Improving the health of minority elders in the new millennium.* Gerontological Society of America, 2004, 13–38.

Ying, Y.W. Psychotherapy with traumatized Southeast Asian refugees. *Clinical Social Work Journal*, 2001, *29*, 65–78.

Zauszniewski, J., Picot, S., Roberts, B., Debanne, S., and Wykle, M. Predictors of resourcefulness in African American women. *Journal of Aging and Health*, 2005, *17*, 609–633.

Zhang, R., and Snowden, L. Ethnic characteristics of mental disorders in five U.S. communities. *Cultural Diversity and Ethnic Minority Psychology*, 1999, *5*, 134–146.

15

The Resilience
of Older Women

Previous chapters have illustrated how women's experiences with aging differ from men's: in patterns of health and life expectancy, marital opportunities, social supports, employment, and retirement. This chapter elaborates on these gender differences, with attention to how personal and environmental factors interact vis-à-vis the particular problems facing women in old age. The impact of social factors, particularly economic ones, on physiological and psychological variables is vividly illustrated in terms of women's daily lives of caregiving for others. The concept of resilience, defined in Chapter 6, captures older women's personal, social, and cultural capacities, despite the financial and health adversities they often face.

Rationale for a Focus on Older Women's Needs

A major reason for this separate chapter on older women is that they are the majority of older adults and form the fastest-growing segment, especially among the oldest-old, both in the United States and globally. As noted in Chapter 1, the aging society is primarily a female one. Women represent 58 percent of the population age 65 to 74 and 77 percent of those over age 85 (Federal Interagency Forum, 2006). They outnumber men age 65 and over by a ratio of three to two; men age 85 and over by five to two; and centenarians by three

Older women serve as role models of strength for younger women.

to one. Ethnic minority variations are striking, as described in Chapter 14. Chapter 1 noted that these disproportionate ratios result from a 5- to 6-year difference in life expectancy at birth for women (NCHS, 2005). This is due to a combination of biological factors, such as the genetic theory that the female's two X chromosomes make her physiologically more robust, and to lifestyle factors, such as women's greater likelihood of preventive health behaviors and their lower rates of smoking, substance abuse, and other high-risk behaviors across the life course. At age 65, women can expect to live an additional 19 years compared to 16.4 more years for their male counterparts. Even at age 85, female life expectancy is 1.5 years more than that for males. However, men who survive beyond age 85 are likely to have fewer chronic illnesses or disabilities and to have a similar life expectancy to women (Older Women's League, 2006).

Another reason to focus on older women is that gender structures opportunities across the life course, making the processes of aging and the quality of life in old age markedly different for men and women. Consistent with the feminist perspective described in Chapter 8, research on women and aging recognizes that gender and age interact to affect the distribution of power, privilege, social capital, and social well-being for men and women throughout the life course. In other words, older women do not always become poor with old age, but their circumstances across the life course (e.g., patterns of underemployment, caregiving and low wages, pensions, and Social Security benefits) make them more vulnerable to poverty and chronic illness. As noted by feminist gerontologists, as more women reach old age in Western culture, age compounds a woman's already devalued status and may increase her feelings of powerlessness (Browne, 1998; Garner, 1999; Moen, 2001). Since gender and age are powerful systems for patterning inequities in roles, relationships, and resources across the life course, neither can be understood fully without reference to the other (Moen, 2001).

Given these inequities, it is not surprising that the problems of aging are increasingly women's problems. Older women are more likely than older men to be poor; to have inadequate retirement income; to be widowed, divorced, and alone; to live in assisted living or nursing homes; to have chronic illnesses; and to be caregivers to other relatives. Women are viewed as experiencing double jeopardy—they face obstacles both for being old and for being female. Ethnic minority women, who are poorer and face more health problems than their Caucasian counterparts, experience triple jeopardy. In addition, the emphasis on youth and beauty in our society, which traditionally values women for their physical appearance, sex appeal, and ability to bear children, is particularly difficult for older women. In fact, it is this cultural emphasis on physical appearance as a basis of social acceptance that underlies the growing popularity of expensive chemical skin peels, laser treatments, cosmetic surgery, and anti-wrinkle creams, available largely to upper-middle-class white women.

Given the numerical predominance of older women and their greater probability of problems in old age, it is even more surprising that older women were nearly invisible in social gerontological research until the mid-1970s. To illustrate, they were only added to the Baltimore Longitudinal Study (described in Chapter 1) in 1978, since it was previously assumed that women's hormonal cycles would affect the data. The first older women's caucus was not held until 1975 at the annual meetings of the Gerontological Society of America. And the 1981 White House Conference on Aging was the first to sponsor a special committee on older women's concerns. Research on issues specific to women, such as menopause, breast cancer, hormone replacement therapy, and osteoporosis, was relatively limited until the late 1980s. In 1991, Congress directed the National Institutes of Health to establish an Office of Research on Women's Health to redress the inadequate attention paid to women's health issues in the biomedical and behavioral research community. One positive result is the Women's Health Initiative; as described in Chapter 4, this is the first randomized controlled study of postmenopausal women and the impact of fat intake and hormone replacement therapy on breast cancer and heart disease. It is to be completed by the year 2008, but preliminary results, especially related to hormone replacement therapy, have already had an impact on women's health practices. Similarly, the Women's Health and Aging Study, funded since 1994 by the National Institutes of Health, focuses on the causes, prevention, management, and rehabilitation of disability among older women. As another indicator of greater recognition of the challenges facing older women, most professional associations on aging now include an older women's caucus or interest group.

Research on aging has thus moved from (1) ignoring gender, (2) merely controlling for gender, (3) describing gender-based contrasts, to (4) efforts to understand the sources of gender variations as well as their implications for individuals. As noted in Chapter 8, a feminist gerontological perspective analyzes the intersections among age, race, class, gender, and sexual orientation, and communities, with the long-term goal of gender equity that will benefit both women and men. Feminist and postmodern researchers emphasize how women's unpaid and undervalued work as family caregivers, along with their employment in low-status, low-paid jobs, results in economic hardship in old age, with consequent negative effects on their health status and long-term care options. Accordingly, the women's movement has tended to ignore issues specific to older women, although some younger feminists are now aligning themselves with older women around shared concerns, such as those related to caregiving across the life course. In recent years, older women's resilience and strengths, not only their greater vulnerability to societal inequities, have been recognized, primarily as a result of the educational and advocacy efforts of such activist groups as the Older Women's League (OWL). Despite the greater visibility of older women's issues, such advocacy organizations confront major challenges, since older women's economic status still lags behind their male counterparts. This remains a major concern, given the relationship between economic status and quality of life in old age (Weitz and Estes, 2001).

Older Women's Economic Status

Financial resources—including older women's concerns about their economic situation—are major determinants of their life satisfaction and perceived quality of life (Choi, 2001). This is not surprising, given that women over age 65 account for over 70 percent of the poor older population. From 1998 to 2002, 27.8 percent of older women experienced at least one year of poverty compared to 17.6 percent of men (Wu, 2003). They form one of the poorest groups in our society, with nearly 13 percent living in poverty at any one point in time, compared to 7 percent of men (WISER, 2004; U.S. Census Bureau, 2006). The intersections of age, gender, and ethnic minority status affect economic well-being, with approximately 43 percent of African American and 35 percent of Latina women age 85 and older living below the federal poverty level. A major reason for the higher rates of poverty among women of color is that they earn even less than white women (67 cents for African American women and 58 cents for Latinas for each dollar earned by Caucasian men, compared with 80 cents for white women) (Bureau of Labor Statistics, 2006). Marriage often protects women against experiencing poverty in old age. More specifically, less than 5 percent of older married women face poverty, compared with 17 percent of unmarried older women (Federal Interagency Forum, 2006). Overall, poverty rates among African American women are three times that of white women; unmarried women have 4 to 5 times higher poverty rates than their married

counterparts (Heinz, Lewis and Hounsell, 2006; Herd, 2006).

The difference in women's greater economic vulnerability in old age as compared to men's is largely a consequence of the domestic division of labor and women's position in the labor market, resulting in lower earnings across the life course and into old age. This exemplifies the feminization of poverty across the life course. With fewer older women than men who are employed, their median annual income is approximately $12,000 compared to over $21,000 among their male counterparts. When all sources of income are taken into account, the difference increases from $18,199 for women to $35,728 for men (AOA, 2005; U.S. Census Bureau, 2006). In 2005, the median incomes of men and women differed by almost 60 percent; such differences persist even among employed women (AARP 2006; Employee Benefit Research Institute, 2006a). Another study, which followed employed middle-aged men and women across 15 years, found a 62 percent gap between their total earnings for that time period (Rose and Hartmann, 2004). Because African American and Latino men earn less, as a whole, than their white counterparts, the gender differences for these two ethnic minority populations narrow. Regardless of race, however, the long-term effects of such gender-based earning differentials are large and can be devastating for women as they age.

Such income differentials are unlikely to be reduced in the near future, since median earnings of working-age women who worked full-time, year-round were $30,000, compared to $40,000 for men in 2004 (Social Security Administration, 2006a). In 2003, a gender-based comparison of fully-employed workers revealed that women earn, on average, 79 cents for every dollar earned by men, even though it is over 30 years after the passage of the Fair Pay and Equal Pay legislation (U.S. Census Bureau, 2004). In addition, slightly more than half (52 percent) of women had at least one calendar year without any earnings compared to just 16 percent of men. Similarly, women are more than twice as likely as men

> ## A CATCH-22 FOR WIDOWS
>
> A widow who enters or continues in the workforce past age 65 receives credit for her own retirement benefits for any month after age 65 that she does not receive Social Security. If her own benefits are greater than her widow's benefits, she will receive credit toward her own retirement. But if her widow's benefits are the greater amount, when she retires she will actually receive no delayed retirement credits whatsoever. Her benefits could be identical to those she would have received if she had never entered the workforce, or had retired at an earlier age.
>
> SOURCE: OWL, 2003a.

(25 versus 11 percent) to work part-time—that is, fewer than 25 hours per week (Lee, 2005). Women's wages peak on average in their 40s, while men's median earnings continue to climb until their mid-50s. The long-term earnings data underscore the pattern that women's time spent in performing family care often profoundly limits their economic resources in later life. In fact, women who are caring for older parents are more than twice as likely to live in poverty as noncaregivers (Wakabayashi and Donato, 2004). Finally, women's longer life expectancy means that they may need to stretch more limited financial resources over a greater number of years than men.

While women among this current cohort of elders have less education and employment experience than both men and younger women, these differences do not completely account for gender-based inequities in income, which persist even among those who have the same educational levels as their male peers. Structural reasons for these economic differences result from gender-based economic factors. These include:

- the methods used to calculate Social Security (women are disadvantaged by their years spent in caregiving and out of the workforce that calculate as zero earnings);
- length of employment: men typically are employed for the 35 years required for

maximum Social Security benefits, while women spend, on average, about 12 years out of the workforce
- women's reduced access to other retirement income, particularly private pensions, and to retirement planning and investment opportunities (OWL, 2006).

Women's marital status is directly tied to their income in old age (Herd, 2006). To some extent, long-lived marriages—irrespective of marital satisfaction—offer economic protection in old age. Poverty for women is either created or exacerbated by widowhood or divorce, with 60 percent of older women not married. Being widowed, divorced, or separated renders a woman much more vulnerable to poverty when compared with an older woman currently and continuously married to the same man, who receives more retirement income. Of all widows in poverty, 80 percent become poor only after their husband dies, and divorced older women have higher poverty rates than widows of the same age (Herd, 2006; OWL, 2004). In addition, the economic gaps between married and widowed women—and between widowed men and women—are increasing, especially among the oldest-old. For example, the median income of widowed women is approximately 75 percent that of widowed men, since men are more likely to retain pension incomes through current earnings after their wife dies (OWL, 2003a).

Given these structural inequities, it is not surprising that poverty rates are highest among women who:

- never married (20 percent)
- are divorced (21 percent)
- are widows (18 percent)
- are ethnic minorities (nearly 75 percent of African American women and 66 percent of Latinas)
- are age 75 and over (approximately 50 percent of Caucasian women, a rate that increases dramatically among women of color) (OWL, 2003c; SSA, 2006b).

These figures may not reveal the full extent of poverty among women, especially widows, who are not counted as poor, despite their low income, because they live in households headed by younger persons whose income is above the poverty line or in a nursing home. When these hidden poor are taken into account, as many as 55 percent of older women are estimated to be poor. In addition, older women form 60 percent of the "near poor," falling within 125 to 200 percent of the poverty line (OWL, 2004; U.S. Census Bureau, 2006). Older women whose income falls below the poverty level may turn to SSI, and comprise nearly 63 percent of older SSI recipients (U.S. Census Bureau, 2005). However, for women who value economic self-sufficiency, dependency on government support can be stigmatizing.

As noted above, the **gendered nature of the life course**—for example, women's family roles throughout their lives—is the primary factor affecting women's economic status in old age. Gender differences in employment history, child care, parent care, and other household responsibilities, career interruptions, types of occupations, earnings, and retirement circumstances all contribute to older women's higher rates of poverty and near-poverty (Calasanti and Slevin, 2001; Gonyea and Hooyman, 2005; Herd, 2006). Most women of this current cohort of older adults did not consistently work for pay, largely because they were expected to marry, raise children, and depend on their husbands for economic support. Their labor force participation rate was only 9.7 percent in 1950, rose slightly in the 1950s, and then dropped to 7.8 percent in 1983, when many would have been near retirement age. When they were employed, they tended to be concentrated in low-paying clerical or service positions without adequate pensions and other benefits (OWL, 2006). Although older African American women are more likely to have been employed throughout their lives than their Caucasian counterparts, they were concentrated in low-paying jobs without benefits. Overall, most of the current cohort

---

OLDER WOMEN WHO CANNOT AFFORD TO RETIRE

For many older women, retirement is not an option. Instead of counting the days until retirement, some count the number of days they have worked in a row. Consider Patsy Secrest, who at age 58 rises at 3 A.M. to open up a fast food restaurant at 4 A.M., ready to serve the first drive-through customers at 5:30. She has worked in this service job for 28 years, but is paid only $8.50 an hour. She is caught in a vicious circle; employment exacerbates numerous chronic conditions, including high cholesterol and blood pressure, back pain, depression, and insomnia; the resultant rising co-payments of her frequent doctor visits ($300 a month) and prescription drugs ($3600 a year) necessitate that she remain employed to be able to cover her medical expenses. Her job has provided the health care benefits for her husband of 38 years, whose job is threatened by plant layoffs and who last year earned only $11,000. Her life consists of long hours at a physically exhausting job, surrounded by teenagers and young adults. In order to rise early, she needs to be in bed each evening by 6 P.M. This leaves her little time for a social life or leisure activities; her one indulgence of the week is a $16 shampoo and styling. At a time when more affluent couples are anticipating retirement, Mrs. Secrest sees only a future of long exhausting days, dozens of medications to manage her chronic illnesses, and Social Security as her sole source of retirement income.

SOURCE: Finkel, 2003.

---

of older women lacked the opportunities to build up their economic security separate from their husbands' pensions and Social Security earnings for old age.

Social Security and Gender Inequities

Social Security is the primary source of income for older women, and women are more likely than men to rely on it as their sole source of income. Women represent 50 percent of all Social Security beneficiaries at age 62 and over, and 71 percent of those age 85 and older (SSA, 2006a). In 2004, the average annual Social Security income received by women 65 years and older was $9,408 (less than $800 per month), compared to $12,381 for men (WISER, 2004). In addition, 46 percent of all older unmarried women compared to 29 percent of men receiving Social Security benefits relied on it for 90 percent or more of their income (OWL, 2004; SSA, 2006b). Among women of color, 25 percent have no other sources of income. Without Social Security, it is estimated that over 50 percent of all older women would be poor (OWL, 2003a; Weir, Willis, and Sevak, 2002).

Marital status directly affects benefits received. For widows 65 and older, Social Security benefits comprise 58 percent of their total income compared to 41 percent of unmarried older men's income and 33 percent of older couples' (OWL, 2004; SSA, 2006b). Analysis by race further reveals that Social Security provides more than half the retirement income for over 80 percent of non-married older African American and Latina women, compared with 73 percent of older white women. Similarly, for over 50 percent of African American and Latina women, Social Security represents 90 percent or more of their retirement income as compared with 40 percent of white women (Hounsell and Humphlett, 2006; SSA, 2006a). Yet their monthly benefit is often less than for their Caucasian counterparts because, as noted above, African American and Latina women who are full-time workers earn far less than white men and women (OWL, 2003b, 2003c).

As is true of women's economic status generally, family roles negatively impact their access to Social Security, because benefit levels are tied to earnings and based on the earnings of their best 35 years of employment. Due to family care responsibilities across the life course, women are far more likely than men to have been employed fewer than 35 years, and thus have several years of zero earnings included in the calculations of benefits. Even if a wife worked outside the home, she often draws a higher Social Security benefit based on her husband's employment record, since he typically received a higher income for more years of employment. Although almost all men (95 percent) receive a benefit based fully on their own employment histories, only about 40 percent of women have garnered worker benefits from their own employment (SSA, 2005). Lower income is also associated with a greater risk for earlier onset of a number of chronic and disabling health conditions that might force earlier retirement decisions, especially among women of color in service and direct care roles (Kijakazi, 2002). African Americans, Latinos, and women experience more involuntary job separation in the years immediately prior to retirement, and these periods of joblessness often result in permanent labor force withdrawal (Flippen, 2005). The box below highlights some of the reasons why Social Security is so central to the economic well-being of Latina women.

Because women's economic security is so closely tied to their husband's work history, when they become widowed or divorced and

---

WHY IS SOCIAL SECURITY IMPORTANT TO LATINA WOMEN?

- In 2004, Latina women received an average monthly Social Security benefit of $633 based on their employment history.
- Without Social Security, 51 percent of Latinas over age 65 would be poor.
- Despite their current Social Security benefits, 22 percent of older Latinas today live in poverty.
- Latina women have a longer life expectancy when compared to that of all women; therefore they will receive Social Security benefits for a longer period of time.
- Latina women's life expectancy at age 65 is 22.8 years, that is 2.9 years longer than non-Hispanic white women, and 4.2 years longer than non-Hispanic black women.
- Only 33 percent of Latina women have income from savings or assets.

SOURCE: WISER, 2004.

turn to Social Security, their benefits may be less than anticipated. At age 65, widows can receive full Social Security benefits based on their husband's earnings or their own, whichever is larger. However, because most women age 60 and over are not employed full time, the majority opt for benefits that are substantially less than what they would have received if their husbands had lived to retire at age 65. On average, widowed women receive nearly 60 percent of their income from Social Security compared to 40 percent of widowed men (SSA, 2006b). If a widowed woman becomes disabled more than 7 years after her husband's death, she is not eligible for disability benefits based on his earnings.

Divorced women tend to fare even less well in terms of Social Security, with 60 times more divorced women than men depending on their former spouse's income (OWL, 2003a, 2003b). A divorced woman age 62 and older at the time of divorce can receive Social Security based on her former husband's earnings record if:

- she had been married at least 10 years prior to the date of divorce, and
- her former husband is age 62 or older, and
- he is drawing Social Security.

If her former husband is still in the workforce, she must wait until he retires. For women without other options, this waiting period can be a time of economic deprivation and can be experienced as penalizing women who are divorced. Women who have been divorced or widowed earlier in their lives tend to have lower retirement incomes than those who have been continuously married (Calasanti and Slevin, 2001).

Inequities for Women under Proposals to Privatize Social Security

Although there are no major proposals currently before Congress to privatize Social Security, the Administration's 2007 budget includes the cost of private accounts, and the trend toward privatization of government programs is likely to continue (OWL, 2007). If Social Security were privatized, as discussed in detail in Chapter 16, this would negatively affect women, especially women of color, more than men. Under privatization, the progressive benefit formula of Social Security, which replaces a higher percentage of earnings for lower-income workers than higher-income workers, would be lost. Instead, as low-income and part-time employees, many women would have smaller private accounts to invest. With more limited financial resources, women typically avoid higher-risk investments, which means that their accounts would yield lower-than-average returns. In fact, low- and moderate-income women might find a large share of their private accounts going to administrative costs associated with individual accounts (Diamond, 1998; Munnell, 1999). Ultimately, the burden for the management of the investment portfolio would fall squarely on an individual woman's shoulders. And, older women who have historically received little training in financial management may be at greater risk for poor investment decisions.

Because of generally limited private investments, women are less likely than men to have sufficient income to last until their death. Privatization means that there would no longer be a lifetime guarantee of a benefit; instead, when funds in the account are exhausted, the account ceases to exist. Given women's longer life expectancy than men's, coupled with their smaller accounts, women would face a greater prospect of outliving all of their savings and assets. Although women can purchase lifetime annuities, private annuities, unlike Social Security, are monthly payments based on gender-based life expectancies, resulting in women receiving a lower lifetime benefit even when their investments are equal to men's (Gonyea and Hooyman, 2005).

In addition, privatization would eliminate death and disability protection and the cost of living increases available through Social Security, all changes that would disadvantage women. Women are much more likely than men to be responsible for children and/or themselves after a spouse's disability or death. How privatization would affect divorced women is unclear. In a privatized system, the core benefit for divorced individuals might be reduced and division of the private account between husband and wife would fall under the jurisdiction of a divorce court. The primary beneficiaries of privatization will be higher income unmarried workers, largely Caucasian males, who will not be born until 2025. In the short term, women would bear the burden of transition and administrative costs, including the need to cut current Social Security benefits if funds were to be diverted into individual accounts. They would also be taxed twice, that is, paying for their own retirement through private accounts while continuing to pay for current beneficiaries (Cavanaugh, 2002; Favreault and Sammartino, 2002; Williamson, 2002).

Proposals to Reduce Gender Inequities in Social Security

Several other proposals for programmatic reforms to Social Security could eliminate some gender inequities and reduce older women's financial vulnerability. These include raising the minimum benefit, increasing the survivors benefit for widows, and providing dependent care credits. Raising the minimum Social Security benefit would be particularly valuable to women and persons of color, given their overrepresentation in low-paying jobs with few benefits. Moreover, many women and persons of color are employed in physically demanding or taxing jobs

---

GENDER INEQUITIES IN SOCIAL SECURITY: CARE CREDITS TO IMPROVE BENEFITS FOR OLDER WOMEN

Care credits that reward women's disproportionate caregiving responsibilities would:

- Move away from marital status as criteria for eligibility (e.g., eliminate spousal benefits),
- Shift women onto worker benefits that are contributory in nature,
- Reflect the societal value of women's unpaid care work by moving women onto the worker benefit, while buffering their low earnings by valuing their unpaid work,
- Improve the progressive nature of benefits, and
- Contrast with earnings-sharing proposals that divide total earnings of married couples between the Social Security accounts of both spouses.

Care credits that drop zero earning years from women's benefit calculations have limitations:

- Women most likely to have zero earnings years are those who can afford not to work outside the home, primarily white, upper-income women.
- Women's care labor is only rewarded when they do not participate in paid labor; but most women combine paid work and unpaid care work.

- Fewer women are going to have zero earnings years in their benefit calculations in future cohorts.
- Only 43 percent of women currently in the workforce would benefit from this proposal.

Care credits, which drop low earnings years (on top of 5 currently allowed) from the benefit calculation, benefit women with high earnings more than women with low earnings.

Care credits that place a value on caregiving would:

- Be a set amount of earnings, which would substitute for a certain number of years of earnings that are below this level. If a credit were set at $15,000, a woman, within her highest 35 years of earnings, who had two years where she earned only $7000, would be credited with an additional $8000 for those years.
- Reward those who suffer significant cuts in earnings because of caregiving work.
- Benefit low-income women and women of color (Herd, 2002).

(e.g., domestic, industrial, and farm labor) that lead to an earlier departure from the paid labor force. Increasing the minimum Social Security benefit would help poor working women who either never married or were married less than 10 years and thus receive a benefit based solely on their own employment histories (Gonyea and Hooyman, 2005). In fact, a special minimum Social Security benefit currently exists for low-wage workers with a history of steady employment that provides these retirees with a higher monthly benefit than they would receive under the regular formula. Few individuals, however, are currently eligible for the special minimum benefit due to its restrictive eligibility requirements (Anzick & Weaver, 2001).

As described above, women often experience significant declines in income with the death of their husband. For most widows, the loss of Social Security income greatly exceeds the reduction of their living expenses. For these reasons, increasing survivors benefits could benefit widows who did not have long-term employment histories, if the surviving spouse's benefit would not be reduced by more than 25 percent of the couple's combined benefit (Favreault and Sammartino, 2002).

Dependent care credits are a way to reward and recognize women's disproportionate responsibilities for raising children. In fact, all industrialized countries except the United States reward parenthood through their public pension systems (Thompson and Carasso, 2002). Some feminists argue that women's economic contributions to households should be recognized, while others advocate that women move out of the home and into employment. Regardless, dependent care credits would be a more progressive way to distribute benefits than spousal benefits, since women would move on to the worker benefit and their lower incomes would be buffered by the economic value assigned to their unpaid care work. With dependent care credits, marital status would not be an eligibility criterion. Instead, women would receive benefits based on their contribution to the economy through both their laborforce

participation and their unpaid work of child care. The most commonly debated care credit proposal is to remove zero earnings years—when women have been out of the paid workforce because of child care responsibilities—from women's benefit calculation. This approach may further exacerbate gender and racial inequities, however, since upper-income white married women, who can afford not to work for pay, are more likely to benefit than low-income married women of color who are employed out of economic necessity. This means that low-income women are unlikely to have zero earnings years in their benefit calculation.

Another option is **earnings sharing,** whereby each partner in a marriage is entitled to a separate Social Security account, regardless of which one is employed. Covered earnings would be divided between the two spouses, with one-half credited to each spouse's account. Alternatively, additional low-earnings years (9 years versus 5) could be dropped from the benefit calculations. Since the rewards for caregiving are directly tied to women's earnings histories, women with high earnings would again fare better than women with low earnings. Placing a value on dependent care is a third way to structure care credits; such credits would be a set amount of earnings, which would substitute for a certain number of years of low earnings. To illustrate, if the care credit were $15,000 and a woman within her highest 35 years of earnings had two years where she earned only $8,000, she would be credited with an additional $7,000 for those years. This approach would benefit lower-income women and women of color more than those with higher earnings (Herd, 2002, 2006). Generally, low-income women would be hurt most by a system that dropped more zero or low-earnings years and would benefit most if half of their median wage were substituted into low earnings years. None of these proposed dependent-care proposals would benefit all women, but more women would fare better than they do now under the current one breadwinner model (Gonyea and Hooyman, 2005; Herd, 2006).

Private Pensions and Gender Inequities

Women are also less likely than men to receive a private pension, either as a retired worker or a surviving spouse (28 percent of women compared to 45 percent of men). Of those who received pension benefits in 2004, about 39 percent were entitled solely to a retired worker benefit; 29 percent were dually entitled to a retired-worker benefit and a wife's or widow's benefit; and 32 percent were receiving wife's or widow's benefits only (SSA, 2005). One reason for these differences is that mandatory pension laws were not in effect when the relatively small proportion of women in the current oldest-old cohort was employed. Yet, even when an older woman does have pension income, it is, on average, 57 percent of an older man's due to women's relatively lower earnings because of salary differentials and shorter employment work histories (Employee Benefit Research Institute, 2006b). Most pension plans vest after 5 years; but women average a job change every 3.5 years (OWL, 2003b). Although pension coverage has increased somewhat for women of all ages, it is still less than for men. This inequity is exacerbated for women of color, with only 28 percent of African American and 12 percent of Latina women earning a pension (Hounsell and Humphlett, 2006; SSA, 2006b). As discussed in Chapter 12, pension plans reward the long-term steady worker with high earnings and job stability, a pattern more characteristic of men than women. Women are also more likely to be concentrated in low-wage, service, part-time, non-union and small firm jobs where pension coverage is not common, and to receive a reduced pension benefit because of retiring before the age of full eligibility.

For both genders, the most common reason for not participating in a pension plan is that their employer simply does not offer one. Almost equal percentages of men and women—39 and 35 percent, respectively—report the lack of an employer-sponsored plan as the primary reason for nonparticipation (Lee and Shaw, 2003).

However, significant gender differences in pension participation exist among employees working for companies that offer pension plans: Female employees (24 percent) were almost twice as likely as male employees (13 percent) to report that their nonparticipation was due to an insufficient number of hours to qualify for enrollment. This finding raises concern for women's future economic status, given the dramatic expansion of part-time and temporary employment. Nearly 25 percent of the U.S. workforce is engaged in part-time work with few employment-based benefits; these positions are disproportionately occupied by both women and men of color (Hudson, 2000; Heinz et al., 2006).

A woman whose family role resulted in economic dependence on her husband can benefit from his private pension only if the following conditions exist:

- He does not die before retirement age.
- He stays married to her.
- He is willing to reduce his monthly benefits in order to provide her with a survivors monthly annuity.

Federal Pension Law requires that an employer-provided defined benefit plan pay a joint benefit and 50 percent annuity, unless a spouse approves the choice of a single life or lump sum payment. Given the economic vicissitudes of aging, some older men choose higher monthly benefits rather than survivors benefits. Such a choice can be detrimental to their wives, who typically outlive their husbands. About 60 percent of the widows of men with pensions receive a pension benefit. The average amount is two-thirds of their deceased husbands' pensions (WISER, 2006). Fortunately, pension provisions enacted by Congress in 1984 (Retirement Equity Act) benefited older women by shortening the time it took to earn a pension and improving coverage for lower-income workers, for those who began work after age 60, and for those who continue to work after age 65. Most of these provisions, however, are not effective for years worked before 1988, and thus do not benefit the current cohort of older women. In addition, federal laws designed to provide protection to spouses of private pension recipients do not apply to state government plans. As a result, over half the states do not have a requirement that a wife must agree to her husband's waiving survivors benefits (i.e., **spousal consent requirement**). This means that a wife may discover only after her husband's death that she will no longer be entitled to pension benefits that were paid when he was alive. Another limitation is that policies to address women's vulnerability as unemployed or late-entry workers generally benefit women at risk of impoverishment as they age, not those who have been poor throughout life. Not surprisingly, never-married older women who have been employed throughout their lives are far more likely than their divorced or widowed counterparts to derive their income from pensions, annuities, interest, and dividends. These figures do not hold true, however, for never-married single mothers.

In summary, women's traditional family roles and limited job options tend to result in discontinuous employment histories. This pattern, combined with fewer pension opportunities and lower Social Security benefits, produces a double or triple jeopardy for economic status among older women, especially women of color. These structural barriers and the interaction of gender, age, and race/ethnicity mean that government policies (e.g., Social Security, SSI, and public pensions) are differentially effective in raising men and women of the majority and those of color out of poverty. Accordingly, women of color remain at the lowest income levels across the life course. Since most changes in Social Security and pension laws have improved the benefits of women as dependents rather than as employees, they do not address the growing numbers of divorced, single-parent, and never-married women who are likely to remain in poverty in the future (Avison and Davies, 2005).

Given these patterns, the economic outlook for women in the future remains bleak. Poverty and insecurity will continue to be a problem for older women in the middle of this century, especially since women still earn less than what men earn (WISER, 2006). The Social Security system was designed over 70 years ago at a time when women had limited employment prospects (and therefore depended on the marriage benefit), were widowed young, and divorce was unusual. These conditions are dramatically different today. Even though more middle-aged and older women are employed, they are more likely to hold part-time and poorly paid jobs, increasingly in the service sector. It is predicted that by the year 2020, poverty will remain widespread among older women of color and those living alone—those who are divorced, widowed, or never married—while Social Security and pension systems will have greatly reduced poverty among older men and couples (Smeeding, Estes, and Glass, 2000). Accordingly, fewer women will receive spousal or survivors benefits due to their increased earnings, declines in marriage rates, and increasing rates of divorce and single parenthood.

Despite the seeming intractability of these interconnections among gender, age, and class, a number of strategies could reduce the poverty rate among older women. These are in addition to strategies described above to reduce gender inequities in Social Security benefits.

- Increasing survivors benefits would improve the status of widowed women.
- Improving benefits for low earners would help many divorced and never-married women.
- Improving the SSI Program would assist the poorest older women (e.g., increase asset limits).
- Targeted benefits could be established within Social Security, such as an income-tested minimum benefit guarantee of $600 per month for beneficiaries taking home less than $400 a month.

- The number of years of marriage required for qualification for spousal benefit for divorced persons under Social Security could be lowered.
- Earnings sharing could be instituted by combining a couple's earnings and dividing the credits.
- Social Security plans could be developed to provide a better return on earnings and better survivors benefits.

From both a feminist and political economy perspective (discussed in Chapter 8), some of these strategies are incremental and fail to address gender inequities across the life course. For example, legislation such as the Family and Medical Leave Act of 1993, which supports women's "taking time off" for caregiving of dependents across the life course, does not promote women's long-term economic security. This is because such legislation fails to provide paid leave, credit toward Social Security, or access to private pensions. As long as women leave the paid workforce to provide unpaid work in the home, they remain dependent on a husband's retirement or Social Security, which is problematic for their future economic security (Weitz and Estes, 2001). Such feminist and political economy analyses recognize that women's economic status and retirement are conditioned by **gendered employment patterns** and by social and economic policies that link women's economic security to that of men's. An examination of the interconnections between women's family and employment roles requires solutions that provide benefits for women's unpaid caregiving in the home (such as care credits), ensure adequate access to pensions in positions typically held by women, and work toward increasing women's salaries and wages across all positions. Until those inequities are addressed, gender and racial inequities in economic status will remain in old age (Calasanti and Slevin, 2001).

Older Women's Health Status

Women's disadvantaged economic status increases their health risks. Although women in all industrialized countries and nearly all developing countries live longer than men, they have higher rates of illness, physician visits, and prescription drug use as a result of more acute illnesses and nonfatal chronic conditions (Gold et al., 2002; Moen and Chermack, 2005). As described in Chapter 4, older people who are poor, composed primarily of women and ethnic minorities, tend to be less healthy than higher-income older adults. Their living conditions generally are not conducive to good health. Compared to their wealthier peers, low-income elders as a whole are more likely to live alone, have inadequate diets, less access to health promotion information, and fewer dental visits and physician contacts per year. Since women, especially the divorced and widowed, predominate among the older poor, women's health status is more frequently harmed by the adverse conditions associated with poverty than is men's. Older women of color, for example, are more likely to obtain health care from hospital outpatient units, emergency rooms, and neighborhood clinics than from private physicians and specialists. In turn, poor health combined with inadequate insurance can deplete low-income women's limited resources.

Health Insurance and Gender Inequities

As is true of economic security in old age, previous family and employment patterns affect older women's access to adequate health care. For example, the workplace has traditionally determined such access through opportunities to enroll in group insurance plans, although less than 50 percent of American workers had health insurance through their own jobs in 2004, compared to 63 percent in 1994 (OWL, 2004). Most insurance systems exclude the occupation of homemaker, except as a dependent. As a result, more older women than men lack supplementary health insurance other than Medicare or Medicaid at a time when health care costs are soaring. This is often because women of this current cohort of older adults have never been, or have sporadically been, employed or in part-time service positions that did not provide health benefits. For example, only 22 percent of workers in the service sector in 2003 had employer-provided health insurance (OWL, 2004). Low-income divorced and/or widowed women, unable to rely on their husbands' insurance, are especially disadvantaged. Divorced women are about twice as likely to lack private supplemental health insurance as married women, and are more likely than widows to be uninsured. Women of color, especially Latinas, also have lower rates of insurance coverage, including Medicare and Medicaid, than their white counterparts. Some of this differential in publicly funded insurance may be due to immigration status and new restrictions regarding proof of citizenship (Christopher, 2006).

Women in their early 60s are the most likely group to lack health insurance, even more so than minor children (OWL, 2004). Some uninsured women gamble on staying healthy until qualifying for Medicare coverage at age 65. Because the incidence of chronic disease is higher among older women than among men, many women do not win this gamble. For example, if a divorced woman is diagnosed with cancer in her late 50s, she is too young to qualify for Medicare and too sick to obtain private insurance; yet she may fall just above the income limits for Medicaid; and, as a divorcee, she is unable to turn to her former husband's insurance. Similarly, a woman whose husband retires at age 65 is at risk of becoming uninsured if she is younger than he and has been insured through his job, since he is covered by Medicare, but she is not. Fortunately, groups such as **Older Women's League** have succeeded in advocating for **conversion laws** (Consolidated Omnibus Budget Reconciliation Act or COBRA) that require insurance companies to allow

women to remain in their spouse's group insurance for up to 3 years after divorce, separation, or widowhood, although 18 months is typically the limit. When their COBRA runs out, uninsured women typically have limited options to find or change jobs in order to get health insurance. And if they have a pre-existing health condition, the chances of their finding health insurance are reduced even more. After age 65, women comprise the vast majority of Medicare beneficiaries, with women age 85 and over forming 70 percent of beneficiaries. Even with health insurance, older women spend more of their annual income for out-of-pocket health care costs than on food (OWL, 2004). Since women have more chronic conditions than men, their prescription drug usage is also high. How Medicare Part D (described in Chapter 17) has affected women compared to men is not yet evident, although women are more likely than men to be Medicaid beneficiaries who have been shifted to private drug plans.

Because of their lower socioeconomic status, older women comprise the majority—70 percent—of Medicaid beneficiaries ages 65 to 84, and 80 percent of those age 85 and older (Kaiser Family Foundation, 2006). A negative effect of this dependency is that some health care providers, concerned about low reimbursement rates, are unwilling to accept Medicaid patients. This may make it difficult for older women to obtain adequate health and long-term care. Male–female differences in longevity, marital status, and income are central in assessing the impact of recent Medicaid cuts. Women outnumber men two to one among frail elders for whom health and long-term care use and costs are greatest. For example, white women living alone are most likely to use nursing homes and home health services and for longer periods of time than white males. As more Medicaid costs are shifted to the patient through higher copayments and deductibles, more low-income frail women may be unable to afford adequate health care.

Higher Incidence of Chronic Health Problems

Limited insurance options and greater dependence on Medicaid are especially problematic, since 85 percent of older women have a chronic disease or disability. A gender and health paradox is that while women are living longer than men, they have higher morbidity rates and in later years, diminished quality of life. Men experience more life-threatening chronic illness (e.g. heart disease, stroke, and cancer), but are more prone to die from them earlier in life. Women are more prone to experience the disabling effects of multiple chronic conditions as they age, including autoimmune diseases (e.g., thyroid, systemic lupus) and arthritis (55 percent vs. 43 percent among men 65 and older). Women also have more acute conditions such as upper respiratory infections (Federal Interagency Forum on Aging, 2006; Moen and Chermack, 2005; Rieker and Bird, 2005; Schoenborn, Vickerie, and Powell-Griner, 2006).

Heart disease is the number one killer for both men and women, although at every age, more men die of this condition. Women are more

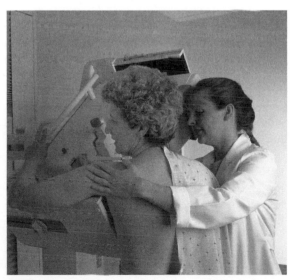

Mammograms are an important part of health promotion for older women.

likely to die from heart disease than all kinds of cancer combined. The primary causes of heart disease are unhealthy diets and sedentary lifestyles, which affect cholesterol levels and blood pressure. The likelihood of heart disease increases for women age 65 and over, so that rates are equal for men and women by age 85. This is because, as noted in Chapter 4, women lose the advantage of estrogen's protection against heart disease after menopause (Schoenborn et al., 2006; Wingert and Kantrowitz, 2006).

Women also face health problems specifically associated with their reproductive functions, such as breast, cervical, and uterine cancers—as well as high-risk complications from hysterectomies. Of women with breast cancer, 75 percent are over age 50. In the past 25 years, the chances of a woman developing breast cancer from birth to death have grown from 1 in 16 to 1 in 8 (National Cancer Institute, 2003), while prevention, diagnosis, and treatment have lagged. One improvement made by Congress in 1990 was to include **mammography** screening as a biennial Medicare benefit. In addition, the 1997 changes in Medicare provided for fuller reimbursement for mammograms. Yet, physicians frequently do not refer older women for mammography, even though yearly mammograms generally are recommended after age 40. Even when referred, some older women may not get a mammogram, mistakenly believing that they will not get breast cancer because of their age. In reality, the longer a woman lives, the more likely she is to develop breast cancer, although it may be slow-growing. A similar pattern is seen where women over age 60, who are most at risk of cancers of the reproductive system, are least likely to have annual pap smears (American Cancer Society, 2007).

Women also suffer from more depressive disorders than men, with women's rates 50 to 100 percent greater than men's (Kessler et al., 2003; Mirowsky and Ross, 2003). Women's higher rates reflect a real gender difference across the life course in health rather than an artifact of differences of help-seeking behavior or willingness to report symptoms. These high rates are of concern since major depression is associated with increased mortality in general and cardiovascular disease in particular. Depression is also associated with immune function and disease severity by magnifying pain and disability. Pain and depression can, in turn, amplify each other. Depressed women are more likely than men to have comorbid anxiety while men are more prone to comorbid substance abuse. While there are some psychosocial risk factors contributing to women's higher rates of depression, the determinants of these differences remain unclear. What is apparent, however, is that gender differences in mental health contribute in unknown ways to gendered patterns of physical health (Kessler et al., 2003; Rieker and Bird, 2005).

Such chronic health conditions, although not life-threatening, interfere with daily functioning (ADLs and IADLs) and require frequent physician contacts. Some studies find that older women also experience more injuries and more days of restricted activity and bed disability than older men. These measures are generally indicators of chronic disorders, such as high blood pressure and arthritis, although they may reflect women's greater readiness to take curative action and spend more time in bed recuperating when they are ill. Women are less likely than their male peers to engage in leisure-time physical activity and their levels of inactivity increase with age (Centers for Disease Control and Prevention, 2007). Nevertheless, they may be more likely to engage in walking, yard work, or household chores as a way to keep active. Women who begin an exercise program even in their 70s and 80s can improve their fitness and strength.

Among people age 85 and over, gender differences in patterns of illness become even more striking, with 65 percent of women age 85 and over likely to enter a nursing home compared to 50 percent of men. Women comprise about 75 percent of nursing home residents, and 66 percent of home care consumers. Among women over age 65, 52 percent will spend at least a day in a nursing home, compared to 33 percent of their male peers (OWL, 2003a). Several factors besides health status may account for such differences. Men who survive to age 75 and older are the healthiest and hardiest of their cohort. As discussed in Chapter 9, older men are more likely to be married, with wives to care for them at home instead of being placed in a nursing home. Women over age 75, on the other hand, have fewer available resources for home-based care, and are often unable to afford private home health services.

There is no clear explanation for the **paradox of gender differences in health.** Biological explanations of the health advantages from different hormones and physiological systems that facilitate pregnancy and childbirth have been challenged by recent clinical trials of hormone replacement therapy (See Chapter 4). Evolutionary selection also does not explain differences in men and women's longevity beyond prime reproductive age. Behavioral theories have focused on lifestyle, including men's higher rates of tobacco and alcohol use and differential use of health care. Sociocultural and environmental theories emphasize social position as mediating access to social and environmental factors, such as increased occupational hazards along with societal expectations for men to engage in more risk-taking behavior. A growing body of research indicates that the complexity of health differences between men and women extends beyond narrow concepts of the relative disadvantage or advantage of men's and women's biology or how their lives are socially constructed. A recent model of **constrained choice** draws on both biological and social factors; such choices influence biological processes. These in turn affect psychological and physiological responses to stress while gender differences in constraints contribute to health disparities by affecting men's and women's choices and cumulative biological risk (Rieker and Bird, 2005). A process of strategic selection—whereby the gendered nature of occupational and family-caregiving paths produces patterned disparities in a constellation of health-related resources, relationships, and risks as well as feelings of mastery and control—has also been proposed as a way to explain the paradoxes related to men and women's health (Moen and Chermack, 2005). Given the range of factors identified in various models, it can be concluded that gender disparities in health are more complicated and nuanced than suggested by biological or medical explanations alone.

Some studies have discovered a "new paradox." Women generally rate their health as better than men, especially among the oldest old, despite women's higher level of functional impairment (Gold et al., 2002). This suggests that associations between gender and health are not necessarily clear-cut, and may not be in the direction commonly assumed: that women experience more health and mental health difficulties as they age. This also suggests the limitations of trying to make "all things equal" in a social order where gender remains such a powerful influence on life chances. Proponents of this gender-based approach also recognize the importance of considering ethnic minority status, social class, and sexual orientation along with gender when examining health status (Calasanti and Slevin, 2001).

Osteoporosis

As noted in Chapter 4, the majority of older people with osteoporosis are women. In fact, 25 percent of women over age 65, and 70 percent of women in their 80s have osteoporosis in their hips or spine. One in two women will have an osteoporosis-related fracture in their lifetime (NIH, 2006). Osteoporosis is called a silent disease because a woman feels no pain as her bones gradually thin to the point where even a slight bump or fit of coughing can cause a fracture. The higher incidence of wrist, spinal, and hip fractures related to postmenopausal osteoporosis is one reason for the greater number of injuries and

> **LIFE COURSE RISK FACTORS FOR OSTEOPOROSIS**
> - being female
> - advanced age
> - family history of osteoporosis
> - smoker; moderate or heavy drinker
> - Caucasian or Asian descent
> - weighing less than 127 pounds; thin, small-boned
> - sedentary lifestyle with little exercise
> - cessation of menstrual periods from strenuous exercise or dieting
> - low estrogen after premature or surgically induced menopause
> - history of anorexia or bulimia
> - taking steroids, thyroid hormone, or other medicines that can cause osteoporosis
> - a history of fractures, especially from low-impact trauma

days of restricted activity among older women. Spinal fractures that are frequent and severe enough to cause dowager's hump (loss of up to 8 inches in height) occur in 5 to 7 percent of women. Over 50 percent of postmenopausal Caucasian women are estimated to have at least one fracture of the spine, wrist, hip, or other bones in their lifetime. Of concern is the fact that the incidence of hip fractures in older women doubles every 5 years after the age of 60 (Sedlak, Doheny, and Jones, 2000). The threat of hip fractures can create numerous fears and losses among older women—and circumscribe their social world, especially since half of those affected lose the ability to walk independently. Indeed, about 24 percent of older patients with hip fractures die within a year from fracture or surgery-related conditions (NIH, 2003).

Since women can lose up to 5 percent of bone mass a year, the case for and against hormone replacement therapy (HRT), as discussed in Chapter 4, is not clear-cut. HRT can increase bone mass in the spine and hip by 3 to 5 percent in the first year; this increase is maintained as long as the individual takes hormones. These

> ### WAYS TO PREVENT OSTEOPOROSIS AND RELATED INJURIES
>
> - Be physically active through weight-bearing and strength-training exercises (brisk walking, running, hiking, dancing, climbing stairs, dancing, lifting weights, and jumping rope).
> - Do not smoke, since smoking weakens bones.
> - Get enough calcium (1200–1500 mg) and vitamin D (400–800 mg) through supplements, but do not exceed recommended daily allowances for women.
> - Eat yogurt, milk, cheese, sardines, dry roasted soybeans, or leafy green vegetables, which are high in calcium and vitamin D.
> - Prevent falls:
>   - Avoid high-heeled or loose-fitting shoes, throw rugs, slippery bathtubs, and wet steps.
>   - Turn on lights when the room is dark; move things that one could trip on; use nonslip bathmats and bathroom grab bars.
>   - Talk to your health care provider about cutting down on drugs that make you more likely to fall and those that lead to bone loss (pain and sleep medications, steroids, epilepsy medicines, and thyroid hormones).

benefits decline, however, after age 75, when women are most at risk. Because of growing concern about the cancer risks of HRT, diet (increased calcium and vitamin D), calcium supplements, and exercise are now emphasized as the best ways to reduce bone loss (Cauley et al., 2003). Fortunately, increasing attention is directed toward both the prevention and treatment of osteoporosis. Bone density tests, including X-rays, CT scans, and ultrasound, are now covered by Medicare. The National Osteoporosis Foundation recommends testing all women age 65 and over, as well as younger postmenopausal women who are small-boned, have low estrogen levels, or a family history of the disease. Osteoporosis education is now more widely available, but the extent to which it has increased preventive health behaviors, such as exercise, is unclear (Howard, 2001).

Menopause

The physiological changes associated with menopause were discussed in Chapters 3 and 7. Menopausal symptoms provide another example of the interaction of normal physiological changes with psychological conditions and societal cultural expectations. For example, many of its associated discomforts result from Western society's tendency to view menopause as a disease rather than a normal biological process. Hence, many women assume that depression, loss of sexual desire and sexual attractiveness, and such signs of aging as wrinkled skin and weight gain, are inevitable with menopause. Contrary to such expectations, menopause is not an illness or a

> ### NONMEDICAL APPROACHES TO MENOPAUSE
>
> - Hypnosis, meditation, biofeedback, acupuncture, paced respiration, and muscle relaxation techniques
> - Exercise, aerobic and weight-bearing, with paced respiration
> - Support groups and use of humor
> - Vitamin E to alleviate hot flashes
> - Dietary changes to reduce fats, preservatives, caffeine, alcohol, and spicy food while increasing fiber, calcium, soy (through tofu, soymilk, tempeh, miso)
> - Layered lightweight clothing, portable fans, lightweight blankets for sleeping
> - Certain antidepressants and the antiseizure medication gabapentin
> - Herbal, remedies, such as black cohosh roots to reduce hot flashes; Kava to reduce mood swings, irritability, and stress; St. John's wort for depression and anxiety. Despite the growing popularity of herbal approaches, most herbs sold in health food stores (as capsules, teas, tinctures, extracts, or infusions) are not regulated by the Food and Drug Administration and have not been tested adequately for effectiveness. Caution also needs to be exercised in terms of possible interactions with prescription drugs.
>
> SOURCE: Manson and Bassuk, 2006.

deficiency, and major mood problems may never occur. With 30 to 50 percent of women having no symptoms as they pass into menopause, many find it to be a positive transition that brings a renewed sense of living and time for oneself or what the anthropologist Margaret Mead termed **postmenopausal zest** (Gonyea, 1998). For most women, menopause is a critical juncture, when their choices can shape their physical and emotional lives for years to come.

The culturally prevalent model of menopause as a disease attributes changes to loss of estrogen. When it is thus defined as a "deficiency disease," the implication for treating symptoms has been to replace estrogen. On the other hand, if menopause is viewed as a normative life transition, lower estrogen levels among postmenopausal women can be considered normal. Many women now use nonmedical approaches to minimize uncomfortable symptoms. However, as noted in earlier chapters, the safety and effectiveness of these alternative therapies have not been fully determined. For example, in a study of 351 women suffering from hot flashes and night sweats, those given the herbal treatment black cobash achieved approximately the same relief as those taking a placebo (Newton et al., 2006). Menopausal women may find that behavioral changes— dressing in layers of light clothing, sleeping in a cooler room, and avoiding triggers such as hot liquids and alcohol—are an effective way to deal with hot flashes. Larger lifestyle changes— increasing aerobic exercise and weight training, reducing stress, losing weight, pursuing a healthy diet of vegetables, fruit, whole grains, and low-fat dairy products, and stopping smoking—may be the most effective and safest approach to minimizing menopausal symptoms (Manson and Bassuk, 2006).

Although the disease model of menopause suggests that endocrine changes are responsible for depression, this condition in postmenopausal women appears to be more closely associated with psychosocial variables, particularly changes in women's roles and relationships, than with physiological factors. Those at highest risk are women who have had prior episodes of depression, especially during other periods of hormonal fluctuation (e.g. postpartum depression), those with poor social supports, and those who experience menopause at a younger age. However, menopause itself is *not* a risk factor for depression. Health care providers have often treated the symptoms of depression with drugs, or have assumed that women were "too old" to benefit from therapeutic interventions. More recently, efforts have been made to provide women with ways of exerting control over their lives, and to develop counseling and social support interventions as a means of combating depression. Support groups are found to reduce women's feelings of isolation and to enhance their self-esteem and self-efficacy (Arthur, 2006; Shearer and Fleury, 2006). Unfortunately, women do not always receive useful information for coping with menopause. Some doctors do not talk about the long-term health effects of decreased estrogen unless women are experiencing unpleasant menopausal reactions, such as hot flashes or mood swings. This puts women at a disadvantage in making informed decisions on how to reduce risks. In addition, nonmenopausal health conditions may be ignored because they are attributed to the "change of life." Increasingly, newer cohorts of middle-aged women are proactive in seeking accurate information, often from the Internet, about what to expect, what therapies work, and their risks and benefits. Regardless of age and marital or socioeconomic status, women can take steps that are conducive to active aging.

Older Women's Social Status

Approximately 40 percent of older women (compared to 19 percent of older men) live alone for nearly one-third of their adult lives, primarily because of widowhood or divorce; about 4 percent have never married. With

> **PLANNING PROACTIVELY FOR ACTIVE AGING**
>
> - Promote your health (diet, exercise, screening tests).
> - Improve your skills (e.g., computer literacy).
> - Maximize your workplace benefits (e.g., Simplified Employee Pension plan).
> - Learn as much as you can about your retirement income.
> - Take charge of your finances.
> - Determine if you are eligible for public benefits.
> - Research your housing options.
> - Learn about resources to assist with caregiving.
> - Be prepared for changes in your marital status.
> - Continue to build your informal support networks, including with younger members.
> - Protect yourself through safety strategies.

increased longevity, divorced or widowed women are living alone for longer periods of time than ever before. In fact, only about 40 percent of all women age 65 and over live with their spouses, compared to 72 percent of men. Only 17 percent live with other family members, generally a daughter. Among women age 75 and over, the proportion living with their spouse drops to less than 30 percent, compared with 70 percent of men; and those living alone increases to approximately 57 percent, a rate almost twice that of older men. Only about 3 percent of older women live with nonrelatives, although a growing number say they would consider asking a friend for assistance and view living with other women as a desirable option (AARP, 2006; U.S. Census Bureau, 2005).

Living alone in itself does not necessarily translate into low socioeconomic status and loneliness for women; nor does it cause deterioration in functional health. For example, never-married single women in old age have typically developed skills and resources earlier in life, such as autonomy and self reliance, which prepare them for a lifetime of singlehood. Because the never-married have not experienced marital

dissolution and its associated stressors, they may also feel less strain from living alone as they age than their widowed or divorced peers. Because of a higher ratio of women to men, African American women are more likely to never marry compared to whites, and less likely to perceive singlehood as source of strain. Women who were employed throughout their lives may enjoy more stable and secure financial circumstances, higher levels of education, and better health than do widowed, separated, and divorced women. In addition, single women, especially African Americans, often maintain extensive social networks of friends, neighbors, and siblings, and levels of social participation in old age that are comparable to those established earlier in life (Pudrovska, Schieman, and Carr, 2006). Such support systems prevent their relocation to a nursing home, although this social network advantage probably disappears among the oldest-old. The negative consequences of living alone are probably greatest for those who were previously married and unaccustomed to being alone (Connidis, 2001; Pudrovska et al., 2006).

Older women of color, especially African American and Latina women who are divorced and widowed, are more likely to live in extended family households, with children, grandchildren, other relatives and fictive kin. As described in Chapter 9, women of color often extend their households to include children and grandchildren, assuming child care and housekeeping responsibilities into old age. Such grandparenting and caregiving responsibilities generally have negative consequences for women's health and finances.

Widowhood

As discussed in Chapter 13, the average age of widowhood for women in a first marriage is 59 years (Kreider, 2005). Marital dissolution through widowhood is an example of an anticipated or normative life-course transition for older women, who may be better prepared for a spousal death than older men are. Of all wives, 85 percent outlive their husbands, since women generally marry men older than themselves, live longer than men, and, in their later years, seldom remarry after the death of their husbands. Some 43 percent of women age 65 and older are widowed, in contrast to 14 percent of men in this age group; this gap increases dramatically with age. The expected years of widowhood are far more than the 7-year difference in life expectancy between women and men at these ages, with some women living up to a third of their lives as widows. Not surprisingly, after age 85, 57 percent of women live alone compared to 30 percent of men (U.S. Census Bureau, 2005, 2006). Moreover, this increased time living alone is accompanied by shrinking family size, with fewer children available as potential caregivers (Moen, 2001). The probability of widowhood increases among older women of color; for example, 75 percent of African American women over age 75 are widows (Weir et al., 2002).

As noted previously, the primary negative consequence of widowhood is low socioeconomic status. Women who have been widowed longest have the highest poverty rate; within this grouping, women who were widowed in their 50s are among the poorest, often having depleted their assets by the time they reach old age (Weir et al., 2002). Economic status has numerous social implications. Low-income women have fewer options for social interactions, affordable and safe living situations, and resources to purchase in-home support services. The worst outcome of widowhood is that their economic situation may preclude women from continuing to live independently when health problems arise. In fact, widowhood is found to result in increased health service use and costs and, in some instances, higher rates of hospitalization (Laditka and Laditka, 2003; Prigerson, et al., 2000).

Despite these objective disadvantages of widowhood, the "lonely widow" appears to be a stereotype, and widowhood does not necessarily produce the major, enduring negative emotional effects typically reported. Instead, over the long term, widowhood may represent a positive shift into a new life phase, especially for women who may have felt constrained in their marriages. Recent research indicates that, overall, women living alone feel psychologically secure and positive about their lives (AARP, 2006; Carr, 2004a; Cheng, 2006).

Limited Opportunities to Remarry

Although remarriage may be viewed as a way to ensure economic security, older widowed and divorced women have fewer remarriage options than do their male peers. In addition, they may choose not to remarry, either because their marriage was not a positive experience, they now enjoy being on their own, or they do not want to care for an ill or disabled husband. Widowed and divorced men are more likely to remarry than women, especially men with the highest levels of resources (Pudrovska et al., 2006). The primary obstacles to remarriage for older women are their disproportionate numbers to men and the cultural stigma against women dating and marrying younger men. With the ratio of 80-year-old women to men being three to one, the chances for remarriage decline drastically with increasing age. Women who do remarry generally enjoy higher incomes and worry less about finances than those who do not (Moorman, Booth, and Fingerman, 2006). According to the Changing Lives of Older Couples study, men's interest in dating and remarriage is conditional on the amount of social support received from friends. Six months after spousal loss, only those men with low or average levels of social support from friends are more likely than women to report interest in remarrying someday. Similar patterns emerge for interest in dating 18 months after losing a spouse. Persons who both want and have a romantic relationship report significantly fewer depressive symptoms 18 months after loss, yet this low prevalence is attributable to their greater socioeconomic resources (Carr, 2004b). Such gender and class differences lead to differential needs for support in the face of failing health; most older men are cared for by their wives, whereas most older women rely on their children, usually daughters, for help. Increasingly, adult daughters who assist their widowed mothers are themselves in their 60s or even early 70s, and are faced with their own physical limitations. As a result, older women may have to depend more on public support services available through the Aging Network described in Chapter 16. As discussed in Chapter 10, women's work as invisible laborers is essential to their relatives' long-term care, but it is not adequately supported by public policies.

In the future, the proportion of old women living alone, including those unmarried throughout their adult lives, will rise more dramatically, because of more women living alone across the life course and the growing rates of divorce. As noted earlier, the absence of children and a partner also increases the chance of moving into a long-term care facility. This suggests that women may be in such settings for social rather than medical reasons, and may be inappropriately placed when alternative community supports might have permitted more autonomous lifestyles.

Informal Networks and Social Support

In general, older women have fewer economic but more social resources and richer, more intimate informal networks than do older men. Their social networks are larger and more diverse, including more people whom they consider very close. The mutuality and voluntary nature of friendships are highly valued, although the benefits of social support vary with the nature and size of women's networks. Social connectedness is found to buffer some of the adverse effects of widowhood for recently bereaved women, including the risk of hospitalization and health problems (Laditka and Laditka, 2003; Miller, Smerglia, and Bouche, 2004). Some research suggests that women respond to stressful life events by "tending and befriending" rather than men's tendency to "fight and flight" (Taylor et al., 2000). Differences in men and women's networks

> **FORMATION OF COMMUNITY AMONG OLDER WOMEN IN A BEAUTY SHOP**
>
> An unintentional community of older women formed at an old-fashioned beauty shop, based on a shared meaning as Jewish mothers, housewives, and caregivers in a society that expects women to be attractive, despite the realities of aging and physical decline. Women in a beauty shop are brought together around a common concern with appearance as a source of self-worth and with taking care of themselves. The face and the body are used to maintain self-respect and community status. Friendships formed in the beauty shop illustrate the diversity of women's connectedness and their varied expression of mutual supportiveness and caring. They talk about illness, aches, and pains, experiencing an outlet for topics that they feel they cannot discuss with family. Discursive personal stories permit exchange of lived experiences and strengthen social bonds. Shows of physical and verbal affection, humor about the inevitability of wrinkles, sags, and bags, and shared food further strengthen social ties. The beauty shop is a search for a good old age among women disadvantaged by age and gender. In the process of seeking beauty, the women gain a sense of belonging, affirmation, and being cared for. The beauty shop thus also acts as a community of resistance against being old and female in a gendered society.
>
> SOURCE: Adapted from Markson, 1999.

result from gendered experiences within various roles and resulting opportunities for establishing social networks (Ajrouch, Blandon, and Antonucci, 2005). Men tend to have larger nonkin networks, perhaps as a result of employment, but are less resourceful in planning social get-togethers and building networks that substitute for the sociability they typically enjoy in marriage (Erickson et al., 2000; Moen, 2001). Even when their friends die, women generally establish new relationships, exchanging affection and material support outside their families, although they may not want to call upon such relationships to care for them. Widowed women, in particular, and women in retirement communities generally have frequent and intimate contacts with friends. One reason for this is that retirement communities provide women with peers at the same stage of life and similar experiences. One study of female participants in senior center activities who live alone documented their ability to form late-life friendships, which then extended outside the center and had positive effects on their mental and physical well-being (Aday, Kehoe, and Farner, 2006). Similarly, support groups for widows and family caregivers build on such reciprocal exchange relations among peers to enhance self-efficacy and personal competence.

In general, social networks and self-efficacy are found to be associated with life satisfaction and improved health outcomes (Blazer, 2002; Ferreria and Sherman, 2006; Greaves and Farbus, 2006). A study of quilting groups among Amish, Appalachian, and Latter Day Saints women identified extensive horizontal and vertical connections and a sense of collectivity toward others. Specifically, quilting group members exhibited generativity by teaching their skills to others, building bonds with grandchildren through quilting, and leaving legacies through their quilts. Friendships developed with other quilters provided social support to deal with life challenges (Piercy and Cheek, 2004). Some programs specifically seek to enrich friendship and reduce loneliness among women in later life as a component of active aging (Cattan et al., 2005). One goal-setting intervention found that a combination of developing new friendships and improving existing ones significantly reduced loneliness within a year (Stevens, Martina, and Westerhof, 2006). Other interventions to reduce social isolation among women note greater self-efficacy, resulting in more health-promoting behaviors and better health outcomes (Greaves and Farbus, 2006; Shearer and Fleury, 2006). Increasingly, women across diverse cultural groups also rely on fictive or chosen kin for reciprocal support (Jordon-Marsh and Harden, 2005).

> ### OLDER WOMEN'S POSITIVE NETWORKS
>
> I have friends. I have organizational things that I join. I do belong to one senior group, which is very heavily female. You have to build a new network after being widowed. And that's really very important to do. It's helpful because within that network, there's always someone who has been down that road before you. (74-year-old respondent to 2006 AARP Survey, 19).
>
> I admire a lady down the block from me who's in her 80s. She's ramrod straight. I'm trying to be like her. She lives alone, with grandchildren coming and going. She's an interesting person to talk to. She'll talk about the neighborhood or politics or where she's going next on one of her trips. She drives all over the place. She has a friend out of state she goes and visits. And I thought, that's great. I hope when I'm 80-something, I can do that too. (77-year-old respondent to 2006 AARP Survey, p. 18)
>
> [In anticipation of a long life] I keep telling my friends that we all need to buy a big house with a common area downstairs and live together—not like a nursing home, but truly a place where we have communal living. . . . It just doesn't make sense having all these women living alone in these big houses. It would be nice to have some kind of pooled arrangements specifically built for people who want some sense of sharing but do not want to give up their privacy. (57-year-old respondent to 2006 AARP Survey, p. 68)

One function of the affirmation of women's competencies by the women's movement has been to encourage support for each other rather than depending primarily on men. This is evidenced by the growth of shared households, co-housing, older women's support and advocacy groups, groups for caregiving grandmothers, and intergenerational alliances between younger and older women. Increasingly, shared housing has both companionship and financial benefits (AARP, 2006). Furthermore, as noted in Chapter 9, some women first become comfortable with being open about their lesbianism and their strong emotional bonds with other women in old age. This includes women who earlier in their lives were married, had children, and later accepted their attraction to women, as well as those who lived with women all their lives and had well established social networks, but who hid their identity from co-workers and family. For many in this current cohort, to be "out" publicly was to risk discrimination and marginalization. "When I was in school and I was a teacher—you did not—you were not out. If you were, you were unemployed and not admitted in polite society" (Classen, 2005, p. 238). Coming out for this cohort of older lesbians was typically not about gay pride, but rather an individual process of increasing awareness of who they are, acknowledging their sexual orientation to themselves and becoming comfortable with it (Classen, 2005). Despite growing old in a society that criminalized homosexuality, they manage by finding "others of their kind" and display resilience, in part because of the obstacles they faced in the past (Clunis et al., 2005). Overall, lesbian and heterosexual older women share many of the same concerns about aging since, as we have seen throughout this chapter, all older women's lives are distinctly structured by gender (Thompson, 2006).

Consistent with feminist gerontology discussed in Chapter 8, a feminist analysis of older women's social status would articulate their strengths and resilience, as well as their vulnerabilities. To be old is defined by our society as being unable to function in some way; but most older women, despite economic and health obstacles are active, competent, surrounded by other long-living women, and find meaning and spiritual resilience in their lives (Latimer, 1997). Although cohort, period, and gender-based life circumstances mold older women, they are not passive. By studying gender and age power differentials, feminists seek to deepen our understanding of both women and men, their uniqueness, and their similarities in actively meeting life's challenges (Calasanti and Slevin, 2001).

Feminists are also developing an area of inquiry called "age studies" that is less concerned with biological markers than with identifying and critiquing the social meanings

CHANGING CONCEPTS OF BEAUTY AND AGE

The feminist Gloria Steinem, when told that she looked really good for her age, responded, "This is what 60 looks like on me." The model Lauren Hutton, who returned to modeling at age 44, remembers opening the *New York Times Magazine* and seeing a beautiful old face and realizing it was herself. She is now in her 60s and considering returning to modeling. One of her reasons: "It's good to show what beauty is—all ages, all sizes" (Sherill, 2003). Although these women have the financial and social resources to purchase numerous antiaging products and surgeries, both are conveying a more positive image of older women—celebrating their age rather than focusing on looking younger.

ascribed to age (Gullette, 1998; Woodward, 1998). A growing body of feminist research on the aging body or the "rejected body," with its subtext of inactivity, disability and incompetence, rejects the physical self and focuses on the "actual or inner self." From feminist and social constructionist perspectives, "old" is a label assigned by younger people on the basis of surface appearance and function. It does not accurately describe many women's subjective experience of aging, which often is not centered on the body and how they look (Morell, 2003). Think of women you may know who say, "I don't feel old, until I look in a mirror." A sense of personal power is achieved when a woman refuses to identify primarily with her body. Instead, women who define themselves in terms of an "able self" enjoy new experiences, learning and relationships. Even women with physical limitations derive meaning from the activities they can continue to do and the adversities that they have overcome (Ahern, 1996). The concept of an "able self" is also consistent with the theory of gerotranscendence that focuses on inner changes, as described in Chapter 8. While an empowerment approach emphasizes strengths and overcoming limitations, the frailty and inevitability of death also need to be acknowledged. Some feminists now argue for the destigmatization of disability and death, and the need to transform these into acceptable human experiences shared by all. A dialectical approach to empowerment openly acknowledges the physical changes associated with aging, but seeks to integrate power and powerlessness, strength and weakness, life energy and death, and power and vulnerability (Morell, 2003). This approach is also congruent with the postmodern perspective discussed in Chapter 8 that views the "aging body" as a social and cultural phenomenon that affects the social construction of the aging identity. Postmodernists maintain that, even though physical appearance changes with age, a person's essential identity does not (Longino and Powell, 2004; Powell, 2006). As noted on page 661, a survey of midlife and older women provides empirical evidence that many women are thriving, although women of color and those with limited retirement income less so. Even women living alone in this national sample considered their older years as a time to pursue activities that they have always wanted to do (AARP, 2006).

Implications for the Future

Since women's socioeconomic status compounds problems they face in old age, fundamental changes are needed to remove inequities in the workplace, Social Security, and pension systems. Most such changes, however, will benefit future generations of older women, rather than the current cohort, which was socialized for employment and family roles that no longer prevail. For example, efforts in some states to assure that women and men earn equal pay for jobs of comparable economic worth and to remove other salary inequities may mean that future generations of older women will have retirement benefits based on a lifetime of more adequate earnings, and will have more experience in handling finances. Some businesses and government agencies have initiated more flexible work arrangements with full benefits, which will allow men and women to share employment and family responsibilities more equitably. Recent national and state legislation to increase the minimum wage will have more economic repercussions for women across the life course than men, since women predominate in low wage positions.

When such options exist, women may have fewer years of zero earnings to be calculated into their Social Security benefits, and will be more likely to hold jobs covered by private pensions. Even so, it is predicted that 60 percent of women in the year 2030 will still have 5 or more years of zero earnings averaged into the calculation of their Social Security benefits. This will widen the current gap between older women living alone and all other groups (Herd, 2006). This is in large part due to the fact that despite three decades of legislation, women have not achieved equality in the workforce. Women remain disproportionately in the secondary service sector, marked by low wages, few benefits, part-time employment, and little job security. Even the entrance of more women into previously male-dominated positions has not resulted in a significant restructuring of the distribution of roles within families; women are still primarily responsible for the majority of child care, housework, and elder care (Moen, 2001).

As noted above, changes in Social Security to benefit women workers have been proposed by federal studies and commissions. The current Social Security system is based on an outmoded model of lifelong marriage, in which one spouse is the paid worker and the other is the homemaker. As the prior discussion of divorce and changing work patterns suggests, this model no longer accommodates the emerging diversity of employment and family roles. Nor, for that matter, has this model ever represented the diversity of American families. Credits for homemaking and dependent care across the life course, partial benefits for widows under age 62, full benefits for widows after age 65, and the option of collecting benefits as both worker and wife have been proposed by advocacy groups and some policy makers. The likelihood of any such changes being instituted in the future is small, given the current emphasis on privatized solutions, the record-high federal deficit, and escalating military expenditures.

More corporations and state and local governments in recent years have eliminated pensions for their employees. When pensions do exist, men benefit more than women. In the long run, more fundamental changes are needed in society's view of work throughout the life course, so that men and women may share more equitably in caregiving and employment responsibilities. At the same time, employers must value skills gained through homemaking and voluntary activity as transferable to the marketplace. As discussed in Chapters 9 and 12, the ways in which women contribute to society through their volunteerism, caregiving, housekeeping responsibilities, and informal helping of others need to be recognized under a broad concept of productivity, rather than equating productivity with only paid work.

Another positive direction is that, despite our societal emphasis on physical appearance, more women are comfortable with their aging and accept its visible signs, such as wrinkles and gray hair. They value exercise, nutrition, and meditation as pathways to better health and personal growth, not simply as means to avoid looking older. Freed from past roles as primarily a wife or mother, they discover the strength from learning who they are and sharing their feelings, insights, and fears about aging with each other. Some women collectively identify themselves as "Crones" or "Sages," rejecting past stereotypes and restoring images of wisdom, honor, and respect to being an old woman. Fortunately, some women who are highly visible, including actresses such as Sally Field and Helen Mirren, who have agreed not to use antiaging treatments, are also helping to change concepts of old age for women. Another positive trajectory is that older female baby boomers will probably be healthier than current cohorts. Nevertheless, the sheer number of female boomers means that many will still face chronic illness or disability, although perhaps later in life than current cohorts.

Because of lower rates of marriage, increasing divorce, and growing numbers of single mothers, more women will enter old age accustomed to living alone, even though they may bring fewer economic resources to old age because of being the sole earner. Perhaps because of more years on their own, women of all ages are increasingly supporting one another, as illustrated by the intergenerational advocacy efforts of the Older Women's League, cross-generational support groups, and co-housing for women. Groups of widows and women caregivers encourage members to meet their own needs and expand women's awareness of available formal support services. This function of educating and politicizing older women also helps many to see the societal or structural causes of the difficulties they have personally experienced. Awareness of external causes of their problems may serve to bring together for common action women of diverse ages, ethnic minority status, social class, and sexual orientation. Cross-cultural evidence shows that age permits women in a wide range of cultures to experience

Group exercise offers physical and social benefits.

increased freedom and to become more dominant and powerful, with fewer restrictions on their behavior and mobility, and increased opportunities to engage in roles outside the home. Growing numbers of older women are aiming to resist denigration and invisibility. As women unite to work for change, they can make further progress in reducing the disadvantages of their economic and social position.

Summary

Older women are the fastest growing segment of our population, making the aging society primarily female. In addition, the problems of aging are increasingly the problems of women. Threats to Social Security, inadequate health and long-term care, and insufficient pensions are issues for women of all ages. Increasingly, older women are not only the recipients of social and health services, but also are cared for by other women, who are unpaid daughters and daughters-in-law, or underpaid staff within public social services, nursing homes, and hospitals.

Women's family caregiving roles are interconnected with their economic, social, and health status. Women who devoted their lives to attending to the needs of children, spouses, partners, or older relatives often face years of living alone on low or poverty-level incomes, with inadequate health care, in substandard housing, and with little chance for employment to supplement their limited resources. Women face more problems in old age, not only because they live longer than their male peers, but also because, as unpaid or underpaid caregivers with discontinuous employment histories, they have not accrued adequate retirement or health care benefits. If they depended on their husbands for economic security, divorce or widowhood increases their risks of poverty. As one of the poorest groups in our society, women account for nearly 75 percent of the older poor. The incidence of problems associated with poverty increases dramatically for older women living alone, for ethnic minority women, and for those 75 and older. Frequently outliving their husbands and sometimes their children, they have no one to care for them and are more likely than their male counterparts to live in long-term care facilities.

On the other hand, many women show remarkable resilience in the face of adversity. Fortunately, the number of exceptions to patterns of economic deprivation and social isolation is growing. With their lifelong experiences of caring for others, for example, women tend to be skilled at forming and sustaining friendships, which provide them with social support and intimacy. Increasing attention is now given to older women's capacity for change and to their strengths, largely because of efforts of national advocacy groups such as the Older Women's League. Current efforts to expand employment and educational opportunities for younger women will undoubtedly mean improved economic, social, and health status for future generations of women.

GLOSSARY

constrained choice model structural factors affect health care choices and biological risk

conversion laws legal requirement for insurance companies to allow widowed, divorced, and separated women to remain on their spouses' group insurance for up to 3 years

dependent care credits proposed change to Social Security where women would receive benefits based on workforce and family care contributions

earnings sharing proposed change in Social Security whereby each partner in a marriage is entitled to a separate Social Security account, regardless of employment status

gendered nature of the life course ways in which gender, which is socially constructed, influences the nature, extent, and experience of caregiving for older relatives across the life course

mammography an X-ray technique for the detection of breast tumors before they can be seen or felt

Older Women's League   a national educational and advocacy organization on issues affecting older women

paradox of gender differences in health   women live longer than men but have higher morbidity rates

postmenopausal zest   renewed sense of life and time for oneself that many women experience at menopause

spousal consent requirement   federal law requiring that a spouse must agree to waiving survivors benefits from Social Security; not true of state government pension plans

RESOURCES

Log on to MySocKit (www.mysockit.com) for information about the following:

- AARP Women Leadership Circle (WLC)
- Institute for Women's Policy Research
- National Black Women's Health Project
- National Program on Women and Aging
- National Women's Health Network
- Older Women's League
- Women's Institute for a Secure Retirement

REFERENCES

AARP. *Looking at act II of women's lives: Thriving and striving from 45 on.* The AARP Foundation Women's Leadership Circle Study. 2006.

Aday, R., Kehoe, G., and Farner, L. Impact of senior center friendships on aging women who live alone. *Journal of Women and Aging,* 2006, *18,* 57–73.

Administration on Aging (AOA). *Profile of older Americans.* Washington, DC: Author, 2005.

Ahern, K. *The older woman: The able self.* New York: Garland, 1996.

Ajrouch, K., Blandon, A., and Antonucci, T. Social networks among men and women: The effects of age and socioeconomic status. *Journals of Gerontology,* 2005, 60B, S311–S317.

American Cancer Society. *Cancer Facts and Figures.* Atlanta: American Cancer Society, 2007.

Anzick, M.A., and Weaver, D.A. *Reducing poverty among elderly women.* ORES Working Paper Series Number 87, Washington, DC: Social Security Administration, Office of Research, Evaluation and Statistics, 2001.

Arthur, H. Depression, isolation, social support and cardiovascular disease in older adults. *Journal of Cardiovascular Nursing,* 2006, *21,* S2–S7.

Avison, W., and Davies, L. Family structure, gender and health in the context of the life course. *Journals of Gerontology, Special issue on Health Inequalities across the Life Course,* 2005, 60B, 113–116.

Blazer, D. Self-efficacy and depression in later life: A primary prevention proposal. *Aging and Mental Health,* 2002, 6, 315–324.

Browne, C.V. *Women, feminism, and aging.* New York: Springer, 1998.

Bureau of Labor Statistics. *Highlights of women's earnings in 2005.* U.S. Department of Labor, Report #995, September 2006.

Calasanti, T., and Slevin K. *Gender. Social inequalities and aging.* Walnut Creek, CA: Altima Press, 2001.

Carr, D. Gender, pre-loss marital dependence and older adults' adjustment to widowhood. *Journal of Marriage and the Family,* 2004a, *66,* 220–235.

Carr, D. The desire to date and remarry among older widows and widowers. *Journal of Marriage and Family,* 2004b, *66,* 1051–1068

Cattan, M., White, M., Bond, J., and Learmouth, C. Preventing social isolation among older people: A systematic review of health promotion interventions. *Ageing and Society,* 2005, *25,* 41–67.

Cauley, J.A., Robbins, J., Chen, Z., Cummings, S.R., Jackson, R.D., LaCroix, A.Z., LeBoff, M., et al. Effects of estrogen plus progestic on risk of fracture and bone mineral density. *Journal of the American Medical Association,* 2003, *290,* 1729–1738.

Cavanaugh, F. *Feasibility of Social Security individual accounts.* Washington, DC: Public Policy Institute, AARP, 2002.

Centers for Disease Control and Prevention (CDC). *Health characteristics of adults 55 years of age and over: United States, 2000–2003. Advance data from vital and health statistics; no 370.* Hyattsville, MD: National Center for Health Statistics. 2006.

Cheng, C. Living alone: The choice and health of older women. *Journal of Gerontological Nursing,* 2006, *32,* 24–25.

Choi, N.G. Relationship between life satisfaction and postretirement employment among older women. *International Journal of Aging and Human Development,* 2001, *52,* 45–70.

Christopher, G.C. Medicare Part D: A woman's issue. *Joint Center Focus Magazine, 34*(3), 2006. Accessed, February 17, 2007, from http://www.jointcenter.org/publications1/focus/.

Claassen, C. *Whistling women: A study of the lives of older lesbians.* Binghamton, NY: Haworth Press, 2005.

Clunis, D., Fredriksen-Goldsen, K., Freeman, P., and Nystrom, N. *Lives of lesbian elders: Looking back, looking forward.* Binghamton, NY: Haworth Press, 2005.

Connidis, I.A. *Family ties and aging.* Thousand Oaks, CA: Sage, 2001.

Diamond, P.A. The economics of Social Security reform. In R.D. Arnold, M.J. Graetz, and A.H. Munnell (Eds.), *Framing the Social Security debate: Values, politics, and economics,* Washington, DC: Brookings Institution Press, 1998.

Employee Benefit Research Institute (EBRI). *EBRI Data book on Employee Benefits, Chapter 6: Income Statistics of the Population 55 and older.* Employee Benefit Research Institute, 2006a.

Employee Benefit Research Institute (EBRI). *Retirement annuity and employment-based pension income among individuals aged 50 and over.* Employee Benefit Research Institute, 2006b.

Erickson, M.A., Dempster-McClain, D., Whitlaw, C., and Moen, P. Does moving to a continuing care retirement community reduce or enhance social integration? In K. Pillemer, P. Moen, E., Wethington, and N. Glasgow (Eds.), *Social integration in the second half of the life course.* Baltimore: Johns Hopkins University Press, 2000.

Favreault, M.M., and Sammartino, F.J. *Impact of Social Security reform on low-income and older women.* Washington, DC. Public Policy Institute, AARP, 2002.

Federal Interagency Forum on Aging. *Older Americans 2006: Key indicators of well-being.* Hyattsville, MD: Federal Interagency Forum on Aging and Related Statistics, 2006.

Ferreira, V., and Sherman, A. Understanding associations of control beliefs, social relations and well-being in older adults with osteoarthritis. *International Journal of Aging and Human Development,* 2006, 62, 255–274.

Finkel, D. Stuck behind the counter. Retirement is an elusive dream for women. *The Seattle Times,* October 7, 2003, A3.

Flippen, C. Minority workers and pathways to retirement. In R. Hudson (Ed.), *The new politics of old age policy.* Baltimore: John Hopkins, 2005.

Furman, F.K. *Facing the mirror: Older women and beauty shop culture.* New York: Rutledge Press, 1997.

Garner, J.D. *Fundamentals of feminist gerontology.* Binghamton, NY: Haworth Press, 1999.

Gold, C., Malmberg, B., McCleran, G., Pedersen, N., and Berg, S. Gender and health: A study of older unlike-sex twins. *Journals of Gerontology,* 2002, 57B, S168–S176.

Gonyea, J.G. Midlife and menopause: Uncharted territories for baby boomer women. *Generations,* Spring 1998, 87–89.

Gonyea, J., and Hooyman, N. Reducing poverty among older women: The importance of Social Security. *Families in Society,* 2005, 86, 338–346.

Greaves, C., and Farbus, L. Effects of creative and social activity on the health and well-being of socially isolated older people: Outcomes from a multi-method observational study. *Journal of Research on Social Health,* 2006, 126, 134–142.

Gullette, M. *Welcome to middle age! (and other cultural fictions).* Chicago: The John D. and Catharine T. McArthur Foundation Series on Mental Health and Development, 1998.

Heinz, T., Lewis, J., and Hounsell, C. *Women and pensions: An overview.* Washington, DC: Women's Institute for a Secure Retirement (WISER), 2006.

Herd, P., Crediting care or marriage: Reforming Social Security family benefits. *Journals of Gerontology,* 2006, 61B, S24–S34.

Herd, P. Care credits: Race, gender, class and Social Security reform. *Public Policy and Aging Report,* 2002, 12, 13–18.

Hounsell, C., and Humphlett, P. *Minority women and retirement income.* Washington, DC: Women's Institute for a Secure Retirement (WISER), 2006.

Howard, W.J. A critical review of the role of targeted education for osteoporosis prevention. *Journal of Orthopedic Nursing,* 2001, 5, 131–135.

Hudson, K. *No shortage of "nonstandard" jobs.* Washington, DC: Economic Policy Institute, 2000.

Jordan-Marsh, M., and Harden, J. Fictive kin: Friends as family supporting older adults as they age. *Journal of Gerontological Nursing,* 2005, 31, 24–31.

Kaiser Family Foundation. *Medicaid's Role for Women. Issue Brief: An Update on Women's Health Policy.* New York: Kaiser Family Foundation, 2006.

Kessler, R., Barker, P., Colpe, L., Epstein, J., Gfroerer, J., et al. Screening for serious mental illness in the general population. *Archives of General Psychiatry,* 2003, *60,* 184–189.

Kijakazi, K. Impact of unreported Social Security earnings on people of color and women. *Public Policy and Aging Report,* 2002, *12,* 9–12.

Krieder, R., *Number, timing and duration of marriages and divorces, 2001.* Washington, DC: U.S. Census Bureau. Current Population Reports, 2005.

Laditka, J., and Laditka, S. Increased hospitalization risk for recently widowed older women and protective effects of social contacts. *Journal of Women and Aging.* 2003. *15,* 7–28

Latimer, R. *You're not old until you're ninety . . . best to be prepared, however.* Nevada City, CA: Blue Dolphin, 1997.

Lee, S. *Women and Social Security: Benefit types and eligibility.* Washington, DC: Institute for Women's Policy Research, 2005.

Lee, S., and Shaw, L. *Gender and economic security in retirement.* Washington, DC: Institute for Women's Policy Research, 2003.

Longino, C.F., and Powell, J.L. Embodiment and the study of aging. In V. Berdayes (Ed.), *The Body in human inquiry: Interdisciplinary explorations of embodiment.* New York: Hampton Press, 2004.

Manson, J., and Bassuk, S. *Hot flashes, hormones and your health.* New York: McGraw Hill, 2006.

Markson, B. Communities of resistance: Older women in a gendered world. Review of Frida Furman, Facing the Mirror. *The Gerontologist,* 1999, *39,* 496–497.

Miller, N., Smerglia, V., and Bouche, N. Women's adjustment to widowhood: Does social support matter? *Journal of Women and Aging,* 2004, *16,* 149–167.

Mirowsky, J., and Ross C. *Social causes of psychological distress* (2nd ed.). New York: Aldine de Gruyter, 2003.

Moen, P. The gendered life course. In R.H. Binstock and L.K. George (Eds.), *Handbook of aging and the social sciences* (5th ed.). San Diego, CA: Academic Press, 2001.

Moen, P., and Chermack, K. Gender disparities in health: Strategic selection, careers and cycles of control. *Journals of Gerontology, Special Issue on Health Inequalities across the Life Course,* 2005, *60B,* S99–S108.

Moorman, S., Booth, A., Fingerman, K. Women's romantic relationships after widowhood. *Journal of Family Issues,* 2006, *27,* 1281–1304.

Morell, C. Empowerment and the long-living woman: Return to the rejected body. *Journal of Aging Studies,* 2003, *17,* 69–85.

Munnell, A. *Reforming Social Security: The case against individual accounts.* Boston, MA: Center for Retirement Research at Boston College, 1999.

National Cancer Institute. *Lifetime risk tables. SEER cancer statistics review 1975–2003.* Accessed January 15, 2007, from http://seer.cancer.gov/csr/1975_2003/results_merged/topic_lifetime_risk.pdf.

National Center for Health Statistics (NCHS). *Health, United States, 2003.* Accessed 2003, from http://www.cdc.gov/nchs/data/hus/hus03.pdf.

National Center for Health Statistics (NCHS). *National Vital Statistics Reports,* 2006, *54.* Accessed 2006, from www.cdc.gov/nchs.

National Center for Health Statistics. *Health characteristics of adults age 55 and over: United States 2000–2003. Advance data from vital and health statistics; no. 37.* Hyattsville, MD: National Center for Health Statistics. Accessed January 15, 2007, from http://www.cdc.gov/nchs/data/ad/ad370.pdf.

National Center for Health Statistics (NCHS). *Health, United States, 2005.* Accessed January 15, 2007, from http://www.cdc.gov/nchs/data/hus/hus05.pdf.

National Institutes of Health (NIH). Osteoporosis and Related Bone Diseases—National Resource Center. Fast facts on osteoporosis. Accessed 2003, from http://www.osteo.org/fast+facts+on+osteoporosis&docty.

Newton, K., Reed, S., LaCroix, A., Grothaus, L., Ehrlich, K., et al. Treatment of vasomotor symptoms of menopause with black cohosh, multibotanicals, soy, hormone therapy or placebo. *Annals of Internal Medicine,* 2006, *145,* 869–879.

Older Women's League (OWL). *A poor prognosis: Health care costs and aging women.* Washington, DC: Older Women's League, 2004.

Older Women's League (OWL). *The state of older women in America.* Washington, DC: Older Women's League, 2003a.

Older Women's League (OWL). *Women and retirement income.* Washington, DC: Older Women's League, 2003b.

Older Women's League (OWL). *Retirement security and women of diverse communities.* Washington, DC: Older Women's League, 2003c.

Older Women's League (OWL). *Social Security: Privatization is still a false promise for women.* Accessed January 21, 2007, from http://www.owlnational.org/index.htm. 2004.

Older Women's League (OWL). *Women and long-term care: Where will I live and who will take care of me?* Washington, DC: Older Women's League, 2006.

Piercy, K., and Cheek, C. Tending and befriending: The intertwined relationships of quilters. *Journal of Women and Aging,* 2004, *16,* 17–33.

Powell, J.L. *Social theory and aging.* Lanham, MD: Rowman and Littlefield, 2006.

Prigerson, H.G., Maciejewski, P.K., and Rosenbeck, R.A. Preliminary explorations of the harmful interactive effects of widowhood and marital harmony on health, health service use, and health care costs. *The Gerontologist,* 2000, *40,* 349–357.

Pudrovska, T., Schieman, S., and Carr, D. Strains of singlehood in later life: Do race and gender matter? *Journals of Gerontology,* 2006, *61B,* S315–S322.

Rieker, P., and Bird, C. Rethinking gender differences in health: Why we need to integrate social and biological perspectives. *Journals of Gerontology, Special Issue on Health Inequalities across the Life Course,* 2005, *60B,* 40–47.

Rose, S.J., and Hartmann, H.I. *Still a man's labor market: The long-term earnings gap.* Washington, DC: Institute for Women's Policy Research, 2004.

Schoenborn, C.A., Vickerie, J.L., and Powell-Griner, E. *Health characteristics of adults 55 years of age and over. United States, 2000–2003.* Advance Data from Vital and Health Statistics, No. 370. Hyattsville: MD: NCHS, 2006.

Sedlak, C.A., Doheny, M.O., and Jones, S.L. Osteoporosis education programs: Changing knowledge and behaviors. *Public Health Nursing,* 2000, *17,* 398–402.

Shearer, N., and Fleury, J. Social support promoting health in older women. *Journal of Women and Aging,* 2006, *16,* 3–17.

Sherill, M. Walk on the wild side. *AARP Magazine,* Nov.-Dec. 2003, 10–14.

Smeeding, T., Estes, C., and Glasse, L. *Social Security in the 21st century: More than deficits: Strengthening security for women.* Washington, DC: Gerontological Society of America, 2000.

Social Security Administration (SSA). *Annual Statistical to the Social Supplement Security Bulletin.* Washington, DC: Social Security Administration (SSA). SSA Publication no. 13–11700, 2005.

Social Security Administration (SSA). Benefits in Current Payment Status – 2004. http://www.ssa.gov/policy/docs/statcomps/supplement/2005/5f.html. Accessed 2004.

Social Security Administration (SSA). *Income of the Population 55 or older, 2004.* Washington, DC: Social Security Administration. SSA Publication No. 13–11871, 2006. Released May 2006a, http://www.ssa.gov/policy/docs/statcomps/income_pop5 5/2004/incpop04.pdf. Accessed January 15, 2007.

Social Security Administration (SSA). *Social Security is important to women.* Fact Sheets. Washington, DC: Social Security Administration, 2006b.

Stevens N., Martina C., and Westerhof, G. Meeting the need to belong: Predicting effects of a friendship enrichment program for older women. *The Gerontologist,* 2006, *46,* 495–502.

Taylor, S., Klein, L., Lewis, B., Gruenewald, T., Gurung, R., and Updegraff, J. Behavioral response to stress in females: Tend-and-befriend, not fight or flight. *Psychology Review,* 2000, *107,* 411–429.

Thompson, E. Being women, then lesbians, then old: Femininities, sexualities and aging. *The Gerontologist,* 2006, *46,* 300–305.

Thompson, L., and Carasso, A. *Social Security and the treatment of families: How does the U.S. compare to other developed countries.* In M. Favreault, F. Summartino and C. Eugenesteurle (Eds.), *Social Security and the family.* Washington, DC: Urban Institute Press, 2002.

U.S. Census Bureau. *Current Population Survey, 2005 Annual Social and Economic Supplement.* Washington, DC, 2005.

U.S. Census Bureau. *Current Population Survey, 2006 Annual Social and Economic Supplement.* Accessed January 15, 2007, from http://pubdb3.census.gov/macro/032006/pov/new01_100_01.htm.

U.S. Census Bureau. Current Population Survey, 2005 *Annual Social and Economic Supplement* Internet Release Date: September 21, 2006. Accessed January 15, 2007, from http://www.census.gov/population/socdemo/hh-fam/cps2005/tabA1-all.csv.

Wakabayashi, C., and Donato, K. *The consequences of caregiving for economic well-being in women's later life.* Presented at the annual meeting of the American Sociological Association, San Francisco, 2004.

Weir, D.R., Willis, R.J., and Sevak, P.A. The economic consequences of widowhood. Papers wp9905, University of Michigan, Michigan Retirement Research Center, 2002.

Weitz, T., and Estes, C.L. Adding aging and gender to the women's health agenda. *Journal of Women and Aging,* 2001, *13,* 3–20.

Williamson, J.B. What's next for Social Security: Partial privatization? *Generations,* 2002, *26,* 34–39.

Wingert, P., and Kantrowitz, B. *Is it hot in here or is it me? The complete guide to menopause.* New York: Workman Publishing, 2006.

Women's Institute for a Secure Retirement (WISER). *Rights of surviving spouses,* Washington, DC: WISER. 2006.

Women's Institute for a Secure Retirement (WISER). *Hispanics and Social Security.* Washington, DC: WISER 2004.

Woodward, K. (Ed.). *Figuring age: Women, bodies, generations.* University of Indiana Press, 1998.

Wu, K.B. *Poverty experience of older persons: A poverty study from a long-term perspective.* Washington, DC: AARP, 2003.

part five

The Societal Context of Aging

The final section of this book examines aging and older people from a broader context. The values and beliefs that policy makers and voters hold toward a particular group or issue are often the basis for developing policies and programs. To the extent that these policies also are grounded in empirically based knowledge, they can enhance the status and resources of that group. On the other hand, policies that are based on stereotypes or generalizations may be inadequate and even detrimental.

Throughout this book, the current state of knowledge about the physiological, psychological, and social aspects of aging has been reviewed. We have examined variations among older ethnic minority groups, between older men and women, and among other segments of older adults. The diversity in the aging process has been emphasized. Differences in lifestyle, health behaviors, employment, family caregiving patterns, and social networks in earlier periods of life can significantly impact functioning in old age, often reflecting health and socioeconomic disparities across the life course. As a result, older adults differ more from each other than any population group. As Chapter 16 points out, increasingly this diversity affects the development, implementation, and effectiveness of social policies and programs. Chapter 16 addresses social and income maintenance policies, while Chapter 17 focuses on health and long-term care policies.

Some age-based programs such as Social Security are directed toward all people who meet age criteria, whereas others, including Supplemental Security Income (SSI) and food stamps, are based on financial need. Eligibility criteria and services are often determined by the prevailing social values and by the political party and presidential administration in power. These values, in turn, reflect society's attitudes toward older people's vulnerabilities and responsibilities to society. For example, attitudes and values regarding older people's deservingness, whether chronological age should be a basis for services, and whether care of the aging population is a societal or individual responsibility all influence the development and funding of social, health, and long-term care policies. The historical development of aging policy and alterations in existing programs are also reviewed within the context of larger societal changes that influence such values. One societal change examined in this section is the growing economic well-being of some older adults. This change, in turn, has fueled an attitude that *all* elders are financially better off and unconcerned about the well-being of other age groups. As noted in Chapter 12, such an attitude stereotypes older adults as being "all alike"; it overlooks both their economic and racial/ethnic diversity, and the fact that younger and older generations engage in reciprocal exchanges of resources across the life course.

Health and long-term care policies toward older people have evolved incrementally in response to society's values and expectations of individual responsibility and need. Chapter 17 describes these policies; their rising expenditures; the growing need for a system of comprehensive long-term care coordinated with acute care; obstacles to their public funding; current cost-containment initiatives in Medicare and Medicaid, including the 2003 Prescription Drug Reform; and the growing emphasis on home-based management of chronic disease.

The following vignettes illustrate the impact of changing societal attitudes and policies regarding the older population on individuals who represent different cohorts. The historical, cultural, and societal context, in turn, influences the services and economic supports to older adults and the likelihood that they will be utilized.

AN OLDER PERSON BORN EARLY IN THE TWENTIETH CENTURY: MR. O'BRIEN

I was born in 1922 in New York City. My parents had migrated to the United States from Ireland 10 years earlier, in search of better employment opportunities for themselves and a better life for us children. One of my brothers died during a flu epidemic while still in Ireland; a sister and brother who were born in New York died of measles. My three surviving siblings and I worked from the age of 12 in our parents' small grocery store. I could not go to school beyond high school because my father's death from tuberculosis at age 45 left me in charge of the family store. I thought about signing up for the newly created Social Security program as a young adult, but I was confident that I would not need any help from the government when I got old. The family grocery was

supporting my wife and me quite well, and I planned to work until the day I died. Besides, my family had all died in their 40s and 50s so I couldn't imagine myself as old, especially since I was a heavy smoker all my life, just like my father had been. As I approach my 86th birthday, I've started having second thoughts about old age. My emphysema and arthritis make it difficult for me to manage the store. And I was scared by two heart attacks in the past 10 years, both of which could have been fatal if it had not been for the skills of the emergency medical team and their sophisticated equipment in our local hospital. My savings, which had seemed substantial a few years ago, now are dwindling as I pay for my wife's care in a nursing home and for my medications and doctor's care for my heart condition, emphysema, and arthritis. Despite these struggles, I still don't want any help from the government or from my children and grandchildren. I've done a pretty good job of appearing financially independent to others because I still manage to work part-time, and tell my family I don't need any help.

AN INDIVIDUAL BORN IN THE POSTWAR BABY BOOM: MS. SMITH

I was born in 1949, soon after WWII ended and my father returned from military duty. My dad took advantage of the GI bill to complete his college education and purchase a home in one of the newly emerging suburbs around Chicago. Growing up, my parents gave me all the advantages they had missed as children of the Depression: regular medical and dental check-ups, education in a private school, a weekly allowance, and a college trust fund. I completed college, obtained a master's degree in business, and now hold a middle-level management position in a bank. I'm already planning a "second career" by starting work on a master's degree in computer science. I have read numerous studies about the value of health promotion at all ages. So I've been a member of a health club for several years, participating in yoga classes and jogging every day. I've also convinced my parents, now in their early 80s, to take part in fitness activities in their assisted living facility. My parents both receive pensions, are enrolled in Medicare Parts A and B, and have planned for the possibility of catastrophic illness by enrolling in a supplemental health insurance program. I've also urged my parents to get on the waiting list of an excellent assisted living facility nearby, should they ever need it.

With the help of a financial planner, I am reviewing my investments and pension plan because I know that Social Security can't be my primary source of income after retirement. I recently purchased private long-term care insurance and have explored several new retirement complexes nearby. In this way, both my parents and I are planning for an independent and, to the extent that we can control it through prevention, a healthy old age.

These vignettes illustrate the changing social and economic status of older people today and in the future. The implications of these changes for the development, implementation, and funding of policies, programs, and services, as well as on individuals' planning for their own aging, are discussed in the remainder of this book.

Chapter

16

Social Policies to Address Social Problems

This chapter focuses on

- Definitions of policy
- Differentiation of types of public policies
- Factors that affect public policy development and should be considered in policy analyses
- The relatively slow development of aging policies prior to the 1960s, with the rapid expansion of programs in the 1960s and 1970s, and the federal budget cuts of the 1980s, 1990s, and today
- Social Security benefits, its fiscal challenges, and proposed reforms, including privatization
- Other policies that affect economic well-being, such as Supplemental Security Income (SSI), pensions, and tax benefits
- Direct social services funded through the Administration on Aging (AOA) and Title XX
- Policy dilemmas and implications for future directions

A wide range of policies, established within the past 75 years, aim to improve older people's social, physical, and economic environments. Approximately 50 major public programs are directed specifically toward older persons, with another 200 affecting them indirectly. Prior to the 1960s, however, the United States lagged behind most European countries in developing public policy for its older citizens. For example, Social Security benefits were not awarded to American retirees until 1935, publicized by posters such as the photo on the facing page. In contrast, Social Security systems were instituted in the nineteenth century in Western European countries. The United States slowly and cautiously accepted the concept of public responsibility, albeit only partial, for its older citizens. In the 1960s, federal spending for programs for older adults rapidly expanded, resulting in the "graying of the federal budget" and a dramatic change in the composition of expenditures. The growth in federal support for these services is vividly illustrated through budgetary figures (see Figure 16.1). About 40 percent of federal expenditures support general health, retirement, and disability programs for older adults, compared to 13 percent in 1960 (Cubanski et al., 2005).

Medicare, Medicaid, Social Security, and civil service and military pension expenditures comprise approximately 75 percent of federal spending on **entitlement programs**—those for which spending is determined by ongoing eligibility requirements and benefit levels rather than by annual Congressional appropriations.

Social Security poster, 1935.

Social Security represented 38 percent, Medicare 27 percent, and Medicaid 13 percent of the entitlement spending of the federal budget in 2006. Today these programs represent 37 percent of the budget, compared to 19 percent in 1970 (Cubanski et al., 2005; Gist, 2007) (see Figure 16.2). By 2030, growth in spending for Social Security, Medicare, and Medicaid is projected to outpace overall economic growth by two to three times. For example, growth in Medicare spending by 2030 will be 211 percent of the Gross Domestic Product (GDP), compared to a 69 percent growth in the GDP overall (Gist, 2007; Walker, 2007). This long-term increase in the share of the budget spent on older adults occurred primarily because of legislative improvements in income protection, health insurance, and social services enacted in the late 1960s. Concern about the long-term financial viability of these programs and whether older adults are benefiting at the expense of younger groups has intensified among baby boomers. This is reflected in contemporary debates about fundamental changes in Social Security and Medicare, including privatization, to reduce age-based public expenditures.

It is important to recognize, however, that when Social Security and Medicare are excluded from these federal allocations, only about 4 percent of the total federal budget is devoted to programs that benefit older adults. These growing expenditures also mask the fact that funded aging services are often fragmented, duplicated, and do not reach those with the greatest need, thus perpetuating health and income disparities described in Chapter 14. Despite growing expenses, the United States nevertheless lacks an integrated, comprehensive, and effective public policy to enhance the well-being of all older adults. The complex policy challenges and escalating federal deficit facing our country are largely due to tax cuts, the wars in Iraq and Afghanistan, and reallocation of funds to homeland security, not the growth of the older population per se.

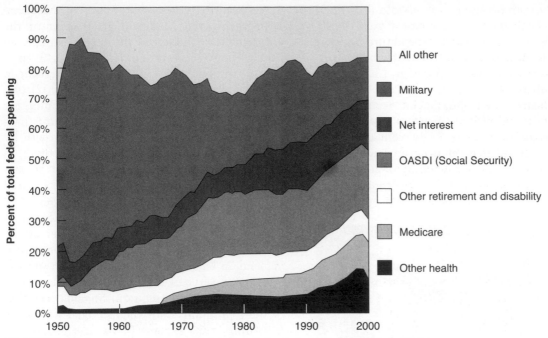

FIGURE 16.1   **Change in the Composition of the Federal Budget, 1950–2000**

Variations among Policies and Programs

The purview of **social policy** is not only to identify problems, but also to take action to ameliorate them. Public policy therefore must be responsive to changes in systems, practices, beliefs, or behaviors.

The procedures that governments develop for making such changes encompass planned interventions, bureaucratic structures for implementation, and regulations governing the distribution of public funds. Policy for the older population thus reflects society's definition of what choices to make in meeting their needs and the division of

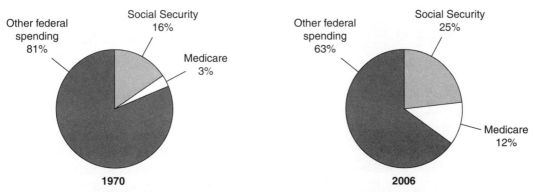

FIGURE 16.2   **Social Security Spending Is a Growing Part of the Federal Budget**
SOURCE: Gist, 2007.

responsibilities between the public and private sectors. As policies for older adults have developed since 1935, each has served to determine which older persons should receive what benefits, from which sources, and on what basis.

Social programs and regulations are the visible manifestations of public policies. The implementation of the 1965 **Older Americans Act,** for example, resulted in numerous programs—senior centers, nutrition sites, Meals-on-Wheels, homemaker and home health services, and adult day care. Some programs are designed specifically for older people, whereas others benefit them indirectly. Programs can be differentiated from each other by their **eligibility criteria;** these dimensions are presented in Table 16.1 and described next.

1. *Eligibility Criteria for Benefits:* When eligibility for benefits depends on age alone (i.e., a person is entitled to Medicare benefits at age 65), **age-based entitlement programs** are categorical and specifically for older adults. However, in **need-based programs,** eligibility depends on financial need. These include Medicaid, SSI, food stamps, and public housing. Most programs for older adults are **age entitlement programs,** with the government automatically paying benefits to anyone who meets the age criteria. In contrast, programs for children and for younger persons with disabilities are typically discretionary and means-based in order to limit numbers of participants.

2. *Form of Benefits:* Another variation is the form in which benefits are given, either **direct** or **indirect,** through a **cash transfer** or **cash substitute.** Social Security benefits are a *direct cash transfer,* and vouchers for the purchase of goods, such as food stamps and rent supplements, are a *direct cash substitute.* Tax policies that affect selected groups (e.g., personal income tax exemptions for older persons) are *indirect cash transfers* of funds from one segment of the population to another. Medicare payments to health care providers, rather than directly to beneficiaries, are *indirect cash substitutes.*

3. *Method of Financing:* Programs also vary in how they are financed. Social Security and Medicare are **contributory plans;** entitlement is

TABLE 16.1 Dimensions along Which Programs and Policies Vary

PROGRAM DIMENSIONS	EXAMPLES
Eligibility	
On basis of age	Medicare
On basis of financial need	Supplemental Security Income
	Medicaid
Form of benefits: Direct or indirect	
Cash	
Direct cash transfers	Social Security
Indirect cash transfers	Income tax exemption
Cash substitute	
Direct cash substitutes	Vouchers
Indirect cash substitutes	Medicare payments to service providers
Method of financing	
Contributory (earned rights)	Social Security
Noncontributory	Supplemental Security Income
Universal or selective benefits	
Universal—for all persons who belong to a particular category	Older Americans Act
Selective—determined on an individual basis	Food stamps

tied to a person's mandatory contributions to the system as a paid worker across the life course. In contrast, SSI is a **noncontributory program** available to older persons and adults with disabilities of all ages who meet financial need criteria, regardless of their prior contributions through payroll taxes.

4. *Universal or Selective Benefits:* Programs differ according to whether they benefit populations on a universal or selective basis. **Universal benefits** are available as a social right to all persons belonging to a designated group. Eligibility for Medicare, the Old Age Survivors Disability Insurance of Social Security (OASDI), and the Older Americans Act is established by virtue of belonging to the older population. In contrast, **selective benefits** are determined individually. These include SSI, Medicaid, food stamps, and housing subsidies, which use economic need as a criterion. Whether aging services should be targeted to low-income elders and subsidized by higher-income older adults is debated. Public consensus on the best approach to service delivery does not exist, as reflected in the following discussion of the factors that influence social policy for older adults.

Factors Affecting the Development of Public Policies

Despite the orderliness of these dimensions, the policy development process is not rational or strategic. Approaches to the financing and delivery of services for older adults evolved in a very different time period, when life expectancy was shorter and federal revenues and deficits were of less concern. A major characteristic of the United States public policy process is its shortsightedness—its general inability, because of annual budgetary cycles and the frequency of national partisan elections, to deal with long-term economic, demographic, and social trends, or to anticipate future consequences of current policies to meet needs or political imperatives. As the number and diversity of older adults has grown,

shortsightedness in public policy development has resulted in a fragmented array of services with separate entitlements and eligibility requirements (Teles, 2005). In fact, this complexity can be so confusing to older people and their families that it has spawned the growth of private case or care managers, Internet services, and toll-free phone services to locate, access, and coordinate services.

The complexity of the public policy formation process is also magnified by the variety of societal factors influencing it, including:

- individual and societal values and beliefs
- economic, social, and governmental structures
- the configuration of domestic and international problems
- powerful interest groups and their lobbyists

Values Affecting Social Policy

Because public policy reflects what and whom we value as a society, it is fundamentally a matter of values and social justice. Ultimately, it represents our collective definition of a just and caring society that will best promote the common good, as well as elders' health and income security. Public policy debates also raise issues of older adults' dignity. While dignity is important at all ages, it is particularly salient in old age because ageism, illness, and losses threaten elders' identity (Holstein, 2005; Neale, 2005). Two different sets of core values have been played out in American social welfare policies regarding older adults:

1. Individual welfare is essentially the *person's responsibility* within a free-market economy unfettered by government control. This belief in individualism, autonomy, self-determination, and privacy is deeply rooted in our history and culture, is widely embraced by many segments of our society, and underlies many public policies.

2. Individual welfare is a matter of the common stake and thus the responsibility *of both*

the individual and the community at large. Government intervention is necessary to protect its citizens and to compensate for the free market's failure to distribute resources equitably. Nevertheless, because our society values individual productivity and competitiveness, some degree of income disparity is accepted as inevitable.

Our society's emphasis on individual and family responsibility has resulted in government's *residual* or "back-up" role to informal support systems. Programs are developed to respond *incrementally* to needs, not to prevent problems or to address their underlying causes. This contrasts with the approach of many other countries, where national health and welfare polices represent a consensus that citizens are universally entitled to have certain needs met. Even when the U.S. government intervenes, it is generally justified because of the failure of the market economy, the family, or the individual to provide for themselves or their relatives. Accordingly, solutions tend to be patterned after private-sector initiatives, as illustrated by many of the changes proposed by the Republican Administration and legislators in both Social Security and Medicare (Hudson, 2005a; Olson, 2003).

Since the New Deal of the 1930s, policy has oscillated between these two core value orientations as public mood and national administrations have shifted. Public perceptions of older people as "deserving" converged to create universal **categorical** programs (e.g., the Administration on Aging, Medicare) available only to older persons, regardless of income. In contrast, policies that use income (e.g., means-testing of Medicaid) to determine if a person is "deserving" of services reflect our society's bias toward productivity and economic self-sufficiency. Although Social Security was the first federal initiative to address older adults' income needs, it succeeded largely because it was perceived as an insurance plan for "deserving" elders who had contributed through their prior employment and suffered devastating effects from the Great Depression, not as a means-tested income maintenance policy for all vulnerable citizens.

In the past, the American public tended to perceive older people as more deserving of assistance than other groups. Accordingly, Social Security and Medicare have, until recent years, been viewed as inviolate and not to be cut drastically. The passage of such otherwise unpopular programs as a national health insurance for older people (i.e., Medicare) and guaranteed income (i.e., SSI) can be partially explained by the fact that older persons in the past aroused public sympathy and support. In addition, older adults are often viewed as a powerful, organized constituency. As a result, they are more likely than low-income or homeless families, for example, to arouse a favorable political response. As noted in Chapter 12, the increasingly diverse older population is now less likely to act as a unified block to influence legislation than in the past. Nevertheless, most politicians do not want to lose older adults' votes.

Ongoing debate about the nature and extent of public provisions versus the responsibility of individuals, families, and private philanthropy often has moral overtones. Judgments about the relative worth of vulnerable populations that compete for a share of limited resources (e.g., older persons within the prison system) and about the proper divisions between public and private responsibilities are ultimately based on individual or group values. A major policy issue therefore revolves around the question of whose values shape policy.

Economic Context

Not surprisingly, current economic conditions significantly influence policy development. Adverse economic conditions can create a climate conducive to the passage of income-maintenance policies. For instance, Social Security was enacted in part because the Great Depression dislodged the middle class from financial security and from widely held beliefs that older adults who needed financial assistance were undeserving. A strategy to increase the number of persons retiring at age 65 was also congruent with economic pressures to reduce widespread unemployment in the 1930s. With economic constraints, program cost factors were also salient; Social Security as a public pension was assumed to cost less than reliance on local poorhouses, as had been the practice prior to the 1920s. Thus, a variety of economic and resource factors converged to create the necessary public and legislative support for a system of social insurance. In contrast, periods of economic growth can also be conducive to new social and health care programs. For example, Medicare and the Older Americans Act were passed in the 1960s and early 1970s. During this period of economic growth and increased social consciousness, government resources expanded under the War on Poverty on behalf of both the younger poor and older people. Funding for the National Institute on Aging (NIA) increased during the economic boom of the late 1990s but is now constrained, largely because of the federal deficit and cuts to domestic programs.

The influence of both economic resources and cultural values is also evident in the current federal government's emphasis on tax cuts, voluntarism and civic engagement, cost-effectiveness and containment, and targeting services to those most in need. Under the personal responsibility values of the Republican Congresses during the 1990s and until its 2006 takeover by the Democrats, the concept of states' rights and prerogatives was emphasized. Because of federal budget cuts and cost-shifting strategies, states have had to assume a greater role in the development and financing of social programs. This has resulted in increased variability of eligibility criteria and benefits for programs such as SSI and Medicaid among the states. Periods of scarcity tend to produce limited and often punitive legislative responses, as occurred in the 1980s and early 1990s. Illustrating the erosion of public support for universal age-based benefits in the 1980s and 1990s, Medicare co-payments, deductibles, and Part B premiums increased;

Social Security benefits for higher-income older people were taxed; and many legislators proposed cutting Medicare and Medicaid, or privatizing Social Security to reduce federal expenditures. Growing preoccupation since the 1990s with ways to limit public funding has placed priority on the most efficient and least expensive solutions, often by private or faith-based organizations, rather than ensuring equity and the common good by government.

In sum, these values, economic conditions, and the consequent resources available underlie a *categorical, residual, and incremental* policy approach toward older adults. One of the most vocal critics of this approach, Estes (1979, 1984, 1989, 2000; Estes, Linkins, and Binney, 1996) maintains that our conceptions of aging socially construct the major problems faced by older people, and thereby adversely influence age-based policies. These conceptions, discussed as the political economy perspective in Chapter 8, are shown in the box on page 681. According to Estes, our society's failure to develop a comprehensive, coordinated policy framework reinforces older persons' marginality and segregates them.

In contrast to Estes, others maintain that the older population benefits at the expense of other age groups and is "busting the budget." Age-based benefits are viewed as a cause of growing federal expenditures and the allocation of resources away from younger groups with higher rates of poverty. Spending for entitlement programs is perceived as "mortgaging the future" of succeeding generations. In reality, however, the actual contribution of Social Security and Medicare to the federal deficit has been nearly the same since 1980. In fact, the current reserves in the Social Security Trust Fund help fund other federal expenditures. Additionally, cuts to programs for older adults do not mean that more resources would necessarily be redistributed into programs that benefit younger generations (Hudson, 2005a). Within this context of the factors affecting policy development, we

A FRAMEWORK FOR CRITICALLY ANALYZING PUBLIC POLICIES

- Legislative and historical origins and context of the policy
- Its goal or purpose: Who is the policy intended to benefit?
- The issue or problem that the policy is intended to address, including ways in which the issue or problem is socially constructed:
  - How is the issue/problem defined by both those who support policy and those who do not?
  - Who was involved and who was excluded in defining the issue/problem and its underlying causes?
- Values underlying this policy (e.g., individualism, personal and family responsibility, common good)
- Competing perspectives on this policy:
  - Who supports the policy? Who opposes it?
  - Whose interests are reflected in the policy and whose are excluded?
  - Who benefits or loses, and in what ways?
- The implementation process and its impact on the intent/outcomes of the policy
- The extent to which the policy promotes social justice and reduces inequities
- Changes needed in the policy or in its implementation (e.g., programs and regulations) to promote social justice across the life course

POLITICAL ECONOMY OF AGING

This theory of aging suggests that structural variables affect services for elders:

1. Older individuals, not economic or social structural conditions, are defined as a "social problem."
2. Older people are seen as special and different, requiring separate programs.
3. Through categorical and age-segregated services, public policy has promoted an "aging enterprise" of bureaucracies and providers to serve older people.
4. The problems of older adults cannot be solved by national programs, but rather by state and local government initiatives, the private sector, or the individual.
5. The problems of older people are individually generated and best treated through direct medical services to the individual. This has resulted in the medicalization of aging and limited public funding for home- and community-based social services as alternatives to nursing home care.
6. The use of costly medical services is justified by characterizing old age as a period of inevitable physical decline and deficiency (Estes et al., 1996; Estes, 2002).

turn now to the formulation of public policy for older persons. The box above suggests factors for you to consider whenever you try to analyze a policy, especially in terms of its underlying values and who benefits.

The Development of Public Policies for Older People

1930 to 1950

As noted above, the United States had few social programs specifically for older adults prior to the 1930s. Family, community, charity organizations,

and local government (e.g., county work farms) were expected to be responsible. Factors such as the low percentage of older adults, a strong belief in individual responsibility, and the free-market economy partially explain why our government was slow to respond. Table 16.2 traces these historical policy developments. The Social Security Act of 1935, the first national public benefits program, grew out of the market failure of the Depression and established the federal government as a major player in the social welfare arena (Hudson, 2005a). The act legitimated the status of older adults as a governmental responsibility and is based on an implicit guarantee of social insurance—that the current younger

TABLE 16.2   Major Historical Developments of Policies That Benefit
Older People and Their Families

1935	Social Security Act
1950	Amendments to assist states with health care costs
1959	Section 202 Direct Loan Program of the Housing Act
1960	Extension of Social Security benefits
1960	Advisory commissions on aging
1961	Senate Special Committee on Aging
1961	First White House Conference on Aging
1965	Medicare and Medicaid, Older Americans Act, establishment of Administration on Aging
1971	Second White House Conference on Aging
1972 & 1977	Social Security amendments
1974	Title XX
1974	House Select Committee on Aging
1974	Change in mandatory retirement age
1974	Establishment of the National Institute on Aging
1980	Federal measures to control health care expenditures
1981	Third White House Conference on Aging
1981	Social Services Block Grant Program
1986	Elimination of mandatory retirement
1987	Nursing Home Reform Act
1989–90	Medicare Catastrophic Health Care Legislation passed, then repealed
1995	Fourth White House Conference on Aging
1996	Family and Medical Leave Act
1999	United Nations: International Year of Older Persons
2000	National Family Caregiver Support Program
2003	Medicare Prescription Drug Bill
2005	Fifth White House Conference on Aging

generation will provide for its older members through their Social Security contributions as employees. The original provisions of the act were intended to be only the beginning of a universal program covering all "major hazards" in life. However, this broader concept, including a nationwide program for preventing illness and ensuring security for children, was never realized.

After the passage of the Social Security Act, national interest in policies to benefit older persons subsided until the 1960s. One exception was President Truman's advocacy to expand Social Security benefits to include farmers, self-employed persons, and some state and local government employees. He also proposed a national health insurance plan, but was opposed by organizations such as the American Medical Association. However, President Truman succeeded in his push for a 1950 Social Security amendment to assist states that chose to pay partial health care costs for needy older persons. This amendment became the basis for establishing Medicare in 1965. Wilbur Cohen, the Secretary of Health Education and Welfare (the federal agency that is the predecessor to the current Department of Health and Human Services) under President Johnson, noted that major initiatives for older adults come in 30-year cycles (Achenbaum, 2006). The expansion of benefits for elders in the 1960s illustrates this cycle.

> ### FACTORS THAT HAVE AFFECTED THE DEVELOPMENT OF SOCIAL SECURITY
>
> #### Demographics
>
> Only 5 percent of the population was age 65 and older in 1935. As a result, reserves were projected for the system, and early retirees benefited significantly from the "pay as you go" system.
>
> #### Historical and Economic Context
>
> - the New Deal and federal response to the Great Depression
> - recognition that the private sector could not guarantee economic security for retirees
> - compassionate stereotype of older adults as "deserving"
> - incentive for and institutionalization of retirement within the labor market and federal government; the disengagement or exit of older workers from the workforce helped create more opportunities for younger workers
> - influence of other Western European countries that had funded social security systems

Program Expansion in the 1960s and 1970s

Since the 1960s, programs for older people rapidly evolved, including Medicare, Medicaid, the Older Americans Act, SSI, the Social Security Amendments of 1972 and 1977, Section 202 Housing, and Title XX social services legislation. The pervasiveness of "compassionate stereotypes"—which assumed that most older adults are deserving poor, frail, ill-housed, unable to keep up with inflation, and therefore in need of government assistance—created a "permissive consensus" for government action on age-based services. A negative consequence of "compassionate ageism," however, was the development of programs that did not take account of economic and racial diversity among the older population. A large constituency—including older adults who are not poor, frail, or inadequately housed—benefited from the policy consensus built on the "compassionate stereotype" of the 1960s and 1970s (Binstock and Day,

1996; Hudson, 2005a). Since old-age constituencies have been viewed as relatively homogeneous (white, English-speaking, and male), many older women, ethnic minorities, the oldest-old, those living alone, and GLBT elders have not always benefited from program improvements relative to their greater needs.

The first White House Conference on Aging and the establishment of the Senate Special Committee on Aging, both in 1961, addressed age-based needs. Four years later, Medicare and the Older Americans Act (OAA) were passed. Although OAA established the Administration on Aging (AOA) at the federal level, as well as statewide area agencies and advisory boards on aging services, funding to implement these provisions was low relative to need. Therefore, one of the primary objectives of the 1971 White House Conference on Aging was to strengthen the OAA. In 1972, Social Security benefits were expanded 20 percent, and the system of *indexing* benefits to take account of inflation (**cost-of-living adjustments** or **COLA**) was established. Additional funding was provided for the OAA in 1973.

The 1970s, with a prevailing liberal ethos, propelled more developments to improve older people's economic status:

- the creation of SSI
- protection of private pensions through the Employee Retirement Income Security Act (ERISA)
- formation of the House Select Committee on Aging
- increases in Social Security benefit levels and taxes
- the change in mandatory retirement from age 65 to 70 (as noted in Chapter 12, mandatory retirement was later abolished for most jobs in 1986)

As described by Hudson (2005a), public policy on aging resulted in more policies creating its own constituencies. During this period of federal expansion, more than 40 national committees and subcommittees were involved in legislative efforts affecting older adults. As a result of the expansion of age-related programs, along with more age-based interest groups, individuals grew to expect that they were automatically entitled to receive benefits based on age rather than income or need. Yet, many aging advocacy organizations appear to have been more influential in defending existing policy rather than affecting the development of new policies. Paradoxically, many older adults assume that they are entitled to continued political support and public benefits, even though their economic needs, along with their political impact, has declined.

Program Reductions in the 1980s and 1990s

Although compassionate stereotypes and a "permissive consensus" underlay the growth of age-entitlement programs in the 1960s and 1970s, fiscal pressures and increasing concern about the well-being of younger age groups in the 1980s and 1990s raised questions about the size and structure of age-based programs. In those years, a new stereotype of older people as relatively well-off resulted in their being scapegoated and blamed as "greedy geezers." In fact, older people were sometimes seen as responsible for increasing the poverty rates among younger age groups (Hudson, 2005a; Minkler, 2002).

The impact of tax cuts, reductions in federal programs, the huge federal deficit, and an overemphasis on economic growth prevented consideration of any large or bold programs for domestic spending in social and health services during the Reagan Administration (1980–1988). Instead, "Reaganomics" implemented policies to reduce or restrain public expenditures for welfare, pensions and services to older people (Walker, 2006). At the same time, public perceptions of and support for aging programs varied widely. Advocates urged more funding for older adults, particularly for social services, and

closely guarded Social Security. Concern over the future of Social Security was fueled by the near-term deficit facing the Social Security trust fund in the 1980s. As a result, Social Security was amended in 1983 to address short-term financing problems. As public scrutiny of the costs of Social Security, Medicare, and Medicaid grew, *cost-efficiency* measures were implemented, such as taxing Social Security benefits and providing less generous cost-of-living increases.

During the 1980s, the political reality of the economic, cultural, and social diversity of the aging population—that chronological age is not an accurate marker of financial status or functional ability—became more apparent. The variability in distribution of income is reflected among three different groups of older people:

- those ineligible for Social Security, including both the lifelong poor and working poor who have discontinuous employment histories, low hourly wages without benefits, and few assets, typically women and elders of color
- those who depend heavily on Social Security, with small or no private pensions and few assets except for their homes
- those with generous private pensions and personal savings investments, in addition to Social Security benefits

A number of policies passed in the 1980s recognized older adults' differential capabilities to help finance public programs, so that both age and economic status were considered for eligibility for old-age benefits (Binstock, 2002; Hudson, 2005a). For example, the Social Security Reform Act of 1983 taxed Social Security benefits for higher-income recipients. The Tax Reform Act of 1986 provided tax credits on a sliding scale to low-income older adults and eliminated a second or third exemption on federal tax income. In addition, programs funded under the OAA were gradually targeted toward low-income individuals. These policy changes, combined with public perceptions that older people are better off than younger ones, reflect a transition from the legacy of a modern aging period (1930–1990) of universal benefits to all who qualify because of age to a new period in which old age alone is not sufficient grounds for public benefits to ensure human dignity (Holstein, 2005; Hudson, 2005b).

The Politics of Diversity and Deficit Spending in the 1990s

Efforts to reduce the growing federal deficit profoundly affected public policy development in the 1990s. Two major options were available to reduce the deficit—reductions in spending through program cutbacks, or revenue enhancement through higher taxes. National groups that cut across the political spectrum, such as the Bipartisan Commission on Entitlement and Tax Reform and the Concord Coalition, maintained that entitlement programs for older people were growing so fast that they would consume nearly all the federal tax revenues by the year 2012, leaving government with little money for anything else. Increasingly, such groups argued that Social Security, Medicare, and Medicaid must be drastically curtailed to balance the federal budget early in the twenty-first century. Such a perspective is reflected in the Balanced Budget Act of 1997 where Medicare and Medicaid were cut, but not Social Security. In reality, since Social Security is financed by its own dedicated payroll tax, none of the federal deficit has ever been caused by Social Security spending, but this fact is typically not portrayed by the media (NCPSSM, 2003b).

The broader political arena reflected growing political conservatism, with President Clinton predicting that the federal deficit would be eliminated by 2015. In the 1996 Personal Responsibility Act, Clinton signed restrictive welfare legislation, but vetoed the bill containing changes to alter the nature of entitlements to Medicare and Medicaid. Resistance against dramatically changing these age-based entitlement programs remained strong in the Clinton Administration. However, such entitlements are now challenged by Republicans in the White House and Congress, who favor privatizating Social Security and other government programs. The fact that such age-based programs are "under attack" and that Medicare now uses a means test (see Chapter 17) reflects a societal shift in attitudes toward the older population. Elders are now less likely to be perceived as a "politically sympathetic" group compared to other segments (Binstock, 2002; Hudson, 2005b; Hudson and Quadagno, 2001). At the same time, disparities within the older population are more evident, with subgroups of poor, ethnic minorities, women, and persons living alone likely to join political alliances around class, race, or ethnicity that compete with groups of more affluent elders. The "politics of diversity" may thus fragment the political influence of established aging organizations and reduce support for universal programs. In fact, incremental changes in Social Security, the OAA, and Medicare to target benefits toward low-income older people reflect recognition of this diversity and a slight shift away from universality (Torres-Gil and Moga, 2001).

Such diversity among the older population, combined with a focus on reducing federal expenditures, has resulted in a greater emphasis on private sector initiatives that can be utilized by higher-income older adults (e.g., individual retirement accounts or IRAs instead of Social Security). Even in the 1990s under a Democratic administration, some members of Congress and the Social Security Advisory Council advocated private savings accounts. With more older adults able to self-finance or privately insure against the social and health costs of later life, the base of support for quality government programs further eroded in the 1990s. To avoid increasing inequality among the older population, a policy challenge in the

1990s was to target resources to those who had never had economic stability, while maintaining public support for the financing of quality universal programs. These complex issues set the framework for the 1995 White House Conference on Aging, where delegates voted to maintain Social Security, the basic features of Medicaid and Medicare, and some advocacy functions under the OAA. Reflecting the Democrats' intent to preserve age-based programs, these directions conflicted with the priority of the Republican Congress to reduce the federal deficit by cutting entitlement programs, reducing taxes, and allowing more individual control over Social Security investments. The fact that taxing Social Security was put forth in numerous Republican proposals reflects the shifting base of support compared to earlier time periods when even mentioning such taxes would have been political suicide (Hudson, 2005a).

Era of the Market and Personal Responsibility

Debates about universal entitlements for older adults are increasingly about political ideology rather than population dynamics. Cost and intergenerational inequity issues that surfaced in the 1980s are still salient, but are secondary to beliefs about the appropriate role of government, private sector, and individual responsibility for elders' economic well-being (Hudson, 2005a). Instead, the present emphasis on private sector competitiveness, tax cuts for upper income adults, and personal responsibility are reflected in a range of privatization proposals to: (1) privatize Social Security in full or in part with individuals responsible for making their own investments; (2) encourage enrollment of Medicare beneficiaries in managed care organizations as reflected by financial incentives for managed care in the 2003 Prescription Drug Bill; (3) provide partial federal tax credits and deductibility for premiums paid for private long-term care insurance; and

(4) promote individual health savings accounts. The politics of responsibility encourages private sector competition and voluntary enrollment in personal savings plans as a way to "save" Social Security and Medicare. These shifts are setting the framework for more policy approaches to combine public programs with private mechanisms of incentives for savings (Binstock, 2002; Hudson, 2005a, 2005b; White, 2003). They were also reflected in the agenda of the 2005 White House Conference on Aging. Its emphasis on baby boomers and personal responsibility and accountability for health and well-being was visible in pre-conference events focused on the Healthy Living Celebration and presentations on civic engagement and community service. It was also the first White House Conference on Aging where the U.S. President did not address the delegates. Despite the focus on individual responsibility, the top resolution was to reauthorize the OAA within the first 6 months following the conference. This occurred by the fall of 2006.

We next review specific programs that account for most age-based federal expenditures:

- Social Security (Old Age and Survivors Disability Insurance or OASDI) and SSI

Politicians, who seek the support of older voters, may be reluctant to alter Social Security.

- tax provisions and private pensions that provide indirect benefits
- social services through Title XX block grants and the Aging Network of the OAA

As noted earlier, OASDI, federal employee retirement, and Medicare and Medicaid combined represent the largest and most rapidly growing federal entitlements. However, many younger people also benefit from OASDI and Medicaid, as shown in Figure 16.3.

Income Security Programs: Social Security and Supplemental Security Income

Social Security

As noted earlier, the 1935 Social Security Act aimed to establish a system of income maintenance for older persons to protect against financial risk. A secondary purpose was to provide a basic level of protection for the most needy older adults, initially through state plans for OASDI and, since 1974, through the federally funded SSI program. A more recent objective is to provide compensatory income to persons, regardless of age, who experience a sudden loss of income, such as widows, surviving children, and persons with disabilities. The values underlying Social Security were captured in a 1938 radio address by President Franklin D. Roosevelt to mark the third anniversary of the Act. Noting that our individual strengths and wits were no longer enough to guarantee our security, President Roosevelt reminded the nation that each person's safety is bound to that of our friends and neighbors. His comments made clear that Social Security was a *social* insurance program that would give people a basic level of security (Neale, 2005). As such, Social Security aims to protect dignity as a social, not an individual value, and to foster social solidarity and human interdependence.

To meet these objectives, Social Security has four separate *trust funds:*

1. Old Age and Survivors Insurance (OASI)
2. Disability Insurance (DI)
3. Hospital Insurance (HI), which is funded through Medicare
4. revenues for the supplemental insurance portion of Medicare, as described in Chapter 17

Social Security is financed through separate trust funds; revenues raised equally from the mandatory participation and contributions of employees and employers through payroll taxes; and income based on current tax revenues. This reflects a fundamental concept of Social Security: Individuals pool their resources in order to spread economic risks. Social Security was never intended to be about wealth-building, but rather a shared sense of responsibility for the income security of all older people (Feder and Friedland, 2005; Neale, 2005). Figure 16.3 illustrates who benefits from three of the Social Security trust funds. This discussion focuses on the combined OASDI fund, while Medicare is addressed in Chapter 17.

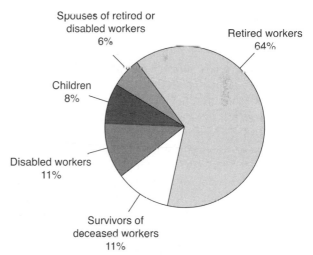

FIGURE 16.3   Recipients of Social Security Benefits

SOURCE: Social Security Administration, 2003.

As described in Chapter 12, Social Security is based first on the concept of earned rights. Initially, only 60 percent of the labor force was eligible to earn future benefits on the basis of the 1935 law. Coverage has since expanded to insure over 95 percent of workers (part time workers whose employers do not pay Social Security payroll taxes do not qualify), reflecting nearly universal protection across social classes. In addition, wage-price indexing protects recipients against economic changes over which they have no control. Although Social Security provides a pooled mechanism to share the risk, no one is excluded no matter how "bad" a risk he or she may be. This is a fundamental difference from private insurance or income maintenance programs for children and families (Hudson, 2005; Williamson, McNamara, and Howling, 2003; Williamson, Watts-Rey, and Kingson, 2002; Yee, 2005). Social Security is similar to fire or collision insurance. You may never need to collect on your policy, but that does not mean you do not need to pay the premiums!

Contrary to public perceptions, Social Security is not an investment program or the sole source of retirement income, but rather a minimum floor of protection. Yet, as described in Chapter 12, it is the major source of income (providing for at least 50 percent of total income) for 66 percent of total beneficiary units, and the only source for about 20 percent. Retirees typically need 70 to 80 percent of their preretirement income to continue living comfortably. Social Security's average older recipients are paid 42 percent of their income, a figure that is projected to remain stable through the year 2040 (SSA, 2006a, 2007a). This average percentage varies with income, however. Social Security provides 83 percent of the aggregate income of the lowest-income older households, 42 percent of income for those earning $30,000–$40,000, and only about 20 percent of the income of elders with the highest income (over $80,000 a year) (SSA, 2006b). While higher-income workers receive higher benefits in absolute dollars,

lower-income workers are assured a greater rate of return for what they have paid into the system (i.e., the *proportion* of preretirement earnings that is replaced after retirement is higher for lower-paid workers). Social Security benefits therefore are progressive or most helpful to those with low and moderate income who qualify. In fact, middle-income workers receive benefits roughly equal to their lifetime Social Security taxes (SSA, 2006b). Despite Social Security's progressive benefit formula and its greater relative importance as a source of income for low-income elders, it has not produced a convergence of economic well-being because the highest income quartile of older Americans still receive substantially higher benefits (Whitman and Purcell, 2004). This distribution of benefits reflects Social Security's dual goals of social adequacy and individual equity.

- *Social adequacy* refers to a shared societal responsibility to provide a basic standard of living for all potential beneficiaries, or a "safety net," regardless of the size of their economic contributions.
- *Individual equity* refers to an individual's receiving benefits that reflect that person's actual monetary contributions proportionate to what they have paid into the system.

Critics of Social Security, including those who advocate privatization, often overlook its cross-generational benefits, such as life and disability insurance for workers and their families. It is a myth that Social Security is a funded pension system in which retirees are merely paid back, with interest, the "contributions" made during their working years. Instead, it is a system whereby current workers support retired or disabled workers and thus is intergenerational in nature. This "pay-as-you-go" system is like a pipeline; payroll taxes from today's workers flow in, are invested in special U.S. government bonds, and simultaneously flow out to current beneficiaries. Today's retirees

The issue of privatizing Social Security generates activism among older adults.

CURRENT CONTEXT FRAMING SOCIAL SECURITY DEBATES

- era of the stock market and personal responsibility
- the longevity revolution; when Social Security was enacted, life expectancy was 61 years, compared with over 78 years today
- the changed age-dependency ratio:
  - 1935: 50 to 1 (passage of Social Security)
  - 1950: 16 to 1
  - 2003: 3.3 to 1
  - 2031: 2 to 1
- a shift from a focus on adequacy of benefits for older adults, persons with disabilities and survivors to a preoccupation with financing Social Security
- improved economic status of older adults, partly resulting from Social Security and Medicare
- older adults are healthier, better educated, and can continue to work, although increasing numbers are employed out of economic necessity
- economic pressures on young adults, many of whom are employed in the contingent service sector
- government preoccupation with terrorism, wars in Iraq and Afghanistan, national security, the federal deficit, and cuts in domestic spending

generally recoup their Social Security contributions within 7 years. Actuaries expect that today's young workers will recoup their contributions after 11 years of retirement (NCPSSM, 2003b). In short, Social Security's nearly universal coverage and predictability of income make it the foundation of economic security for most retirees.

Payroll taxes, however, have risen significantly, from a combined 3 percent on employers and employees in 1950 to 12.4 percent today. At the same time, the average return that a worker can expect has declined dramatically. An average (middle income) earner born in 1940 could expect to get back over a lifetime about the same amount that he/she paid into the system ($169,400, adjusted for inflation and interest), while retirees born in 2000 will get back about $249,800 compared to their contribution of $350,900 through payroll taxes. This contrasts with the average retiree born in 1915 who got back about $60,000 more than they paid into the system (SSA, 2006a; Wan et al., 2007). This pay-as-you-go method of financing partially underlay the fiscal crisis in the early 1980s, when the Social Security reserves were inadequate for projected benefits. Primary factors behind threats of bankruptcy in the 1980s were:

1. The economic recession: High unemployment and low productivity resulted in fewer taxes collected, so that less money was available in the Social Security trust funds.
2. Increased longevity and more retired workers in proportion to younger employees, with fewer workers paying into Social Security.

The box above summarizes the changing demographic, economic, and political context that now frames debates about the future of Social Security.

The Future of Social Security

Within this context, many policy makers and the media portray Social Security as being in crisis. They argue that "apocalyptic demography" will make it difficult for our nation to sustain all age-related benefits through the first half of this century. The "graying of the welfare state" is perceived as having catastrophic consequences for the after-tax living standards of most working-age Americans. This view is put forth by groups such as the Third Millennium, which points to a 1997 survey in which people under age 35 stated that they believed in UFOs more than in Social Security's future viability. Data such as these, however, are misrepresented as public support for "radical reform." In fact, many polls show that Americans, even younger adults, overwhelmingly support protecting Social Security, even though they lack confidence in its future and are confused about eligibility criteria (Blendon, et al., 2005). In fact, the majority of Americans do not perceive that older people gain at the cost of younger populations or that benefits are too costly. In one recent poll, 68 percent think that Social Security is the most important government program benefiting the population (53 percent of those age 21 to 34 and 78 percent of those 50 and older). And fewer Americans currently view Social Security in crisis compared to those who did in 1998, although the majority support incremental reform to ensure that the trust fund has enough money for benefits for the next 50 years (Harris Poll, 2007; Wright and Davis, 2007). Any future changes in Social Security must recognize that the majority of Americans support protecting this program. Such public support may reflect recognition of how Social Security currently benefits younger generations (Blendon et al., 2005; Generations United, 2005; Minkler, 2002; Williamson et al., 2002), as summarized in the box opposite. Cross-generational transfer programs may actually receive more public support than typically portrayed by the media and politicians, an issue discussed below vis-à-vis the intergenerational equity framework.

As noted above, the short-term danger of bankruptcy was averted through remedial legislation in 1983, which reduced benefits and increased the age of full Social Security eligibility from 65 years to age 67, beginning in 2003 (and to be fully

---

CROSS-GENERATIONAL NATURE OF SOCIAL SECURITY BENEFITS

Contrary to common perceptions, Social Security benefits individuals across the life course, not just older adults. The importance of Social Security to the economic well-being of younger families is well documented:

- It ensures basic protection for the neediest (SSI), regardless of age
- Every worker contributing to Social Security, regardless of age, has disability insurance worth over $350,000 for workers with major disabilities that prevent them from being employed, and life insurance equivalent to a $400,000 policy for children of deceased workers
- Social Security provides compensatory income, regardless of age, to those who experience sudden loss of income (e.g., widows, surviving children, persons with disabilities), as illustrated by the following facts:
  - 30 percent of the approximately 47 million Social Security beneficiaries are not retirees
  - 3.1 million children under age 18 receive Social Security checks as dependents of deceased, disabled or in a few cases, retired workers
  - another 2.2 million children, while not receiving benefits themselves, live with relatives who do
  - Social Security lifts one million children above the poverty threshold
  - Social Security is the largest source of cash benefits for custodial grandparents, who are often low-income. Such survivor or disability support for a grandchild or step-grandchild is based on the earnings record of a grandparent or step-grandparent
  - Social Security frees the middle generation from financial support to older relatives, and allows them to direct their resources toward their children

implemented in 2027). These reforms allowed the system to accumulate reserves, which currently exceed the benefits paid. It is also important to recognize that there are great risks of error in making long-range forecasts of 75 years, and dire projections are only speculations about the future, not fact. When and if Social Security expenditures (or the "outgo") will exceed funds collected through current taxes is unknown. The latest report of the Social Security actuaries predicts that a funding shortfall will not occur until at least 2040. If, however, the fund continues to grow well above actuarial projections, a shortfall could be smaller or even nonexistent. If a shortfall does occur, where the benefit payouts exceed taxes and interest, the reserves in the trust fund would be drawn down. The exhaustion of the trust fund, however, would not mean that Social Security benefits would stop; this would happen only if Congress passed legislation ending Social Security payroll taxes. Instead, benefits would have to be reduced by about 25 percent or the payroll tax would have to be sharply increased by about 50 percent. This means that Congress would still be able to pay around 75 percent of its obligations promised to future retirees (e.g., 75 cents for every dollar of benefits). On the other hand, the financial security of the trust fund would be lost, and benefits would be lower (Feder and Friedland, 2005; Herd and Kingson, 2005; Social Security and Medicare Boards of Trustees,

2006; Teles, 2005; Williamson, McNamara, and Howling, 2003; Wright and Davies, 2007).

In contrast to the warnings of crisis, a more optimistic view is that projected shortfalls are a warning that can be addressed with relatively minor adjustments (NCPSSM, 2000b). The National Committee to Preserve Social Security and Medicare (NCPSSM) maintains that full solvency can be extended beyond 2040 by expanding the number of workers participating in Social Security (e.g., requiring local and state workers to participate); raising the cap on taxable income; or allowing the government to invest the funds in equity markets. Such changes are likely to be incremental, and represent political compromises between those who favor privatization and those who view Social Security as a "sacred entitlement." But even changes as small as a 0.7 percent reduction in annual cost-of-living adjustments would, over time, result in enormous cost savings. Accordingly, future benefits to older people will not depend solely on the proportion of workers to retirees. It will also rely on whether the economy generates sufficient resources to be transferred and whether the political will to transfer them to older adults exists. Points of view thus vary widely about the magnitude of the Social Security crisis, along with proposed solutions. Variations in Social Security reform proposals can be attributed to

---

SHOULD A 30-YEAR-OLD WORRY ABOUT FUTURE SOCIAL SECURITY BENEFITS?

If no changes are made to Social Security, when a 30-year-old in 2008 reaches age 64 in the year 2042, benefits for all retirees could be cut by 27 percent and reduced every year thereafter. If this 30-year-old lived to age 100 (which will be more common by then), his or her scheduled benefits could be reduced by 35 percent from today's levels. But this future elder will still receive approximately 65 percent of scheduled benefits (SSA, 2006a).

POINTS TO PONDER

How much will *your* Social Security benefits be when you retire? Since 1988, the Social Security Administration has sent individual statements to every U.S. worker age 25 and older, listing their years of employment, earnings, and Social Security taxes paid each year. Best of all, it lists each person's estimated benefits if they retire at age 62, 67, or 70, based on past contributions to the system, current age, and income. Individual workers can also estimate their benefits by completing the benefits calculator on SSA's Website.

differing perspectives regarding program goals, whether as:

- *social insurance* (i.e. provide benefits upon disability or death), or
- *income redistribution* (transfer resources from the wealthier to those with fewer resources, both within and between generations).

Contemporary critics of Social Security prefer to view it as a savings program that maximizes the "rate of return" to beneficiaries and fosters economic growth by encouraging savings. They argue for the privatization of Social Security by greater reliance on individual savings, and predict higher rates of return on individual contributions through investments in the stock market. **Privatization** would divert payroll taxes (or general revenue income tax credits) to new systems of Social Security investment accounts. Proponents of privatization maintain that the fundamental goals of any reforms should be to:

- provide insurance to prevent retirees from outliving their resources
- promote consumer choice
- promote at least some redistribution of resources to lower-income households
- promote market efficiency
- substitute personal savings for tax-financed entitlement
- take advantage of economies of scale (Smalhout, 2002)

The most frequently discussed privatization models are:

- Workers invest a portion of their Social Security retirement funds in the stock market and set aside the remainder in individual retirement accounts (IRAs).
- Workers contribute to a "first-tier" minimum benefit account through Social Security; above that amount, however, con-

tributions would be deposited in a worker's own personal retirement account.
- Future benefits would be prefunded through direct investments of the trust funds into the stock market (Mitchell, 2002; Williamson, 2002).

These models assume a strong economy and stock market as well as individual knowledge and skills to make informed investment decisions. Yet these assumptions are undermined by the uncertainty of the stock market's performance since the crash in 2000 and the fact that most workers fail to adequately plan financially for retirement. Supporters of privatization are primarily Republican lobbyists (e.g., insurance and investment companies; corporations that would profit from privatization), and Washington, D.C. think tanks such as the conservative Concord Coalition and the libertarian CATO Institute. They maintain that personal investment

---

VALUES REFLECTED IN SOCIAL SECURITY DEBATES

Values Reflected in Current Social Security System

- universalism
- mutual responsibility: obligation of those who can work to provide for those who cannot
- federal government bears the risks, not individuals
- earned right as a result of a lifetime of paid work: benefits can be counted on regardless of inflation, business cycles, and market fluctuations
- maintain dignity of older adults and persons with disabilities, strengthen families and communities

Values Reflected in Privatization

- market as the most efficient way to distribute resources across generations; social insurance undermines free markets
- increase individual savings, reward individual effort and private initiative
- primacy of individual responsibility and freedom of choice (and risks)
- limited role of government in ensuring economic security of future elders

accounts, by allowing individual ownership and responsibility over retirement investments, would lead to higher benefits. Personal accounts would also allow participants to pass wealth to their survivors in the event of a premature death (i.e., before the age of Social Security eligibility). Proponents point to over 20 countries that have established versions of personal accounts. Nevertheless, supporters acknowledge that private accounts would not solve all of Social Security's financing problems, and initial returns will be low since workers are already committed to paying for the system's past debt (Hudson, 2005b).

In contrast, a wide range of negative outcomes of privatization have been identified by the Social Security Administration (SSA), Presidential commissions appointed to study privatization, economists and policy scholars, and even an organization of young adults, the "2030 Center," that aims to strengthen Social Security. The costs of privatization include:

- The transition costs of moving from the current system to a privatized plan, estimated to be more than $1 trillion over 10 years.
- Costs entailed by adding a new federal agency in addition to the Internal Revenue Service and the Social Security Administration.
- High administrative costs (13 to 20 percent of workers' annual contributions) of managing individual accounts. This would amount to $2 to $3 million in general revenue transfer and would dramatically accelerate the federal debt.
- Any money directed into individual retirement accounts must be replaced or Social Security benefits must be cut dramatically (approximately 45 percent for younger workers).
- Funds used to pay current retirement benefits would have to be replaced, whether by increased taxes or benefit costs.
- Current workers would be double taxed: They have to pay for their own retirement through their private accounts while continuing to pay for current beneficiaries through Social Security.

- There is no protection from inflation.
- The uncertainty and vicissitudes of the stock market mean that investment income may not be sufficient to last until a person dies.
- Individual investments are unpredictable compared to the guaranteed security of U.S. Treasury bonds. Even with optimistic assumptions of return rates, benefits could fall 20 percent for a single wage earner, and 38 percent for married couples. In fact, approximately 75 percent of adults age 55 to 70 who own investments reported losses during 2002–2004.
- Most workers are not knowledgeable about investment options and tend to invest too heavily in the companies that employ them, which can be lost if they unexpectedly lose their jobs (as many Enron employees discovered when that company collapsed in 2002).
- Death and disability protection and the cost of living (COLA) adjustments available through Social Security would be eliminated. This would disadvantage young workers who are disabled early in their careers before investments yield a profit.
- Privatization would not be cost-effective because of the large numbers of very small businesses and low-income employees.
- Privatization disproportionately negatively impacts low-income workers, especially women and ethnic minorities.
- Privatization represents a fundamental shift from government to individual responsibility, while not resolving Social Security's long-term financial problems. While proponents argue that privatization is a way to "save universal programs," it would probably destroy Social Security by shifting from its universal nature and value of social solidarity. For example, prefunding through individual accounts, which is largely pro-business, would actually worsen Social Security's financial problems (Blendon et al., 2005; Bosworth, Butler, and Keys, 2003; Cavanaugh, 2002; Favreault and Sammartino, 2002; Herd, 2005, 2006;

Herd and Kingson, 2005; Holstein, 2005; NCPSSM, 2003b).

One of privatization's major costs is how it would negatively impact low-income, historically underserved workers, by putting them at greater financial risk rather than guaranteeing a benefit based on their earnings history. The primary beneficiaries of privatization would be higher-income, unmarried workers who will not be born until 2025 and will be largely Caucasian males. Low-income women and ethnic minorities, who are the most vulnerable elders and benefit the most from Social Security, would be hurt the most, because of their limited resources to invest privately. In addition, low-income workers who lack skills and knowledge about investment decisions will be disadvantaged, and class inequities in retirement income will most likely increase (Herd and Kingson, 2005; NCPSSM, 2003b).

Most proposals for future funding of Social Security encompass variations on raising payroll taxes, increasing the age of eligibility, using means testing, increasing borrowing, reducing benefits, or relying on economic growth.

1. *Raising the retirement age for full benefits to age 69 or 70, and for partial benefits to age 65.* However, this could negatively impact ethnic minorities, who have lower life expectancies and face greater pressure to retire early from low-paying, physically demanding jobs.

2. *Increasing the number of years needed to compute Social Security benefits from 35 to 38 to 40 years.* This would negatively impact women and other low-wage workers who are less likely to have been employed that length of time.

3. *Increasing payroll taxes from the current rate of 12.4 percent to about 16 percent.* This would be regressive in its impact, because the increased tax would represent a greater share of workers' income, especially for women and ethnic minorities. On the other hand, more than 20 countries already have Social Security taxes that are higher than that of the United States.

4. *Reducing the cost-of-living adjustments (COLA) to the level equal to actual inflation.* This across-the-board reduction in benefits would create the greatest hardship for the poorest beneficiaries, primarily women and ethnic minorities.

5. *Reducing benefits across-the-board (3 to 5 percent).* This also is regressive, negatively affecting the lowest-income workers who depend on Social Security for a greater share of their retirement income than do higher-income retirees.

6. *Raising the cap on the amount of wages and salaries subject to payroll taxes.* This would be progressive in its impact, with higher-income workers facing the greater burden of closing the Social Security funding gap.

7. *Extending the coverage to state and local public employees.*

8. *Increasing the penalty for early retirement (before the age of full benefits); this would negatively impact elders who must retire due to poor health or unemployment.*

9. *Eliminating the "legacy debt"* (i.e., benefits received by early participants well in excess of their contributions plus interest) by

---

SOCIAL SECURITY BENEFITS FOR ETHNIC MINORITIES

African American women rely disproportionately more than whites on nonretirement aspects of the Social Security program, given their higher rates of disability and their greater likelihood of surviving their husbands. More than 33 percent of children receiving benefits as survivors and/or dependents of a person with a disability are African American or Latino (Generations United, 2005; Gonyea and Hooyman, 2005; Herd and Kingson, 2005; NCPSSM, 2004).

imposing a 3 percent tax on earnings above the maximum earnings base.

10. *Affluence testing by eliminating benefits for higher-income workers above an income threshold ($40,000 in 2003 dollars).* Such proposals alarm even liberal supporters of social insurance, because they are a shift away from Social Security's universal age-based nature and would allow higher-income workers to opt out of the system (Blendon et al., 2005; Breyer and Kifmann, 2002; Social Security and Medicare Board of Trustees, 2006; Diamond, 2004, 2005; Hudson, 2005a; Williamson et al., 2002).

Many of these proposals are contrary to the basic philosophy of a social insurance plan with universal eligibility. This moral basis of Social Security represents society's willingness to compensate as a group people whose income has been destroyed or lowered by marketplace forces, regardless of their actual contributions. These proposals then challenge the fundamental notion that the federal government should subsidize programs deemed to be in the common good. They may also undermine Social Security's role in preventing poverty in old age (Gorin, 2000; Herd, 2005; Herd and Kingson, 2005; Holstein, 2005). Although there are currently no credible plans to replace Social Security as the foundation for retirement, incremental modifications are likely in the near future. Even if Social Security remains solvent, another concern is that the federal deficit is turning the surplus into paper savings. This could occur because the Treasury Department borrows and then spends the Social Security reserves by investing them in Treasury bonds. In effect, it gives Social Security an IOU, so that the reserves accumulated now may be consumed by deficits in later years. In effect, this is akin to a family borrowing from their college trust fund to pay off their household debts (Moody, 2002c).

Supplemental Security Income (SSI)

As described in Chapter 12, about 5 percent of Social Security recipients receive SSI. This program is financed fully by the federal general revenues (not the Social Security Trust funds) and administered by the Social Security Administration (SSA). States may supplement federal payments through state revenues, which results in benefit variability among states. In most states, a person who receives SSI benefits is automatically eligible for Medicaid health benefits. SSI beneficiaries include older adults, persons with disabilities, and those who are visually impaired. Since its inception in 1972, the percent of older persons receiving SSI benefits has declined, while those who are blind or disabled have increased. This difference is partially due to Social Security's annual COLA benefits that decreased the number of older persons who fall into poverty (Beedon, 2000). On the other hand, SSI only reaches 40 to 60 percent of eligible low-income persons, often because they lack information about it, have had prior negative experiences with it, or do not want to be stigmatized by receiving "welfare" (Choi, 2006; Holstein, 2005). SSI's eligibility rules related to resource and income limits (i.e., $2000 for an individual, $3000 for a couple, and face value of life insurance policy and burial plot) also threaten the dignity of recipients. The monthly benefit is reduced by subtracting monthly *net income,* but in the case of an eligible individual with an eligible spouse, the amount payable is divided equally between the two spouses, further reducing benefits (SSA, 2007b).

While SSI is intended to be a protective system or "safety net," it has not eliminated poverty among vulnerable elders. The primary reason is that the federal benefit level equals only about 77 percent of the poverty level for single individuals and 82 percent for couples age 65 and over (SSA, 2007). When the program was designed, it was assumed that SSI recipients would also receive benefits such as food stamps and that states would provide revenues to bring their total benefit package up to the poverty threshold. Even with state supplements, however, SSI fails to raise needy older adults out of poverty. In addition, only about 17 percent of low-income older adults receive food stamps. One reason for this low participation rate is that eligible older adults think that their income or assets make them ineligible. Congress has attempted to facilitate elders' participation in the food stamp program by enacting provisions that make applications and certification of need easier. Even if outreach is intensified and the application process streamlined and made less intimidating to those with limited education and resources, the means-tested nature of SSI is likely to prevent applications by aging baby boomers (Kassner, 2001; Wu, 2006).

Private Pensions and Income Tax Provisions

Private Pensions

Some older persons receive public and/or private pensions to supplement Social Security. As described in Chapter 12, less than 50 percent of the current labor force, primarily middle- and high-income workers, is covered by an employer-sponsored pension plan. However, only about 10 percent of these receive in private pensions an amount equivalent to that of Social Security (Lee and Shaw, 2003). Overall, the rate of pension growth has slowed due to the changing nature of the workforce. Manufacturing jobs that historically provided pensions have declined, while service sector and part-time, temporary contingent and nonunion jobs have grown. In addition, with the bankruptcy of large corporations such as Enron, pension plans have disappeared or shrunk to levels too low to support retirees.

As noted in Chapter 12, the pension system tends to perpetuate systematic inequities across the life course by income level, ethnic minority status, and gender. Lower-income workers, often women

Older people who have multiple sources of income are generally financially secure.

and persons of color, are least likely to work in jobs covered by pensions and to have attained the vesting requirements (i.e., 5 years on the same job). Another inequity is that retired military veterans, civil service workers, and railroad employees also receive cash benefits in addition to Social Security. This means that cash benefits from government-supported private savings plans and favorable tax policies accrue to those who are already relatively well off, intensifying economic disparities over time. Although private pensions help upper- or middle-income workers to replace more of their income when they retire, they do not meet the principles of adequacy and shared risk inherent in Social Security, since lower-income workers generally do not participate (Purcell, 2002).

The Employee Retirement Income Security Act of 1974 (ERISA) established standards for participation, vesting, and minimum funding to protect workers. Since then, corporate contributions to pension plans have declined, and many businesses have instead used pension funds to pay for employee health care expenses and to increase their own profitability. Defined benefit plans that help employees have been reduced from covering 80 percent of workers in 1985 to only 33 percent in 2003, and replaced by voluntary contributory plans, such as 401(k)s and 403b plans that increase employees' uncertainty (Federal Interagency Forum, 2006). Similar to privatization within Social Security, the growth of voluntary plans represents a shift in pension responsibility from the company to the individual.

Income Tax Provisions

Pension plans are not the only "tax expenditures" related to aging. Some older individuals also enjoy extra tax deductions and pay on average a smaller percent of their income in taxes. For example, many older people who file tax returns benefit from not paying a tax on railroad retirement and other government pensions. Higher-income older persons enjoy property-tax reductions and preferential treatment when selling their home (exemption from capital gains taxation for the sale of a home after age 55). The 1997 Tax Reform Act also benefits wealthy older adults who own stocks and bonds. Capital gains realized from the sale of stocks and mutual funds now are taxed at lower rates for those in the highest income brackets. Nearly 80 percent of mortgage interest deductions and 90 percent of state and local tax deductions benefit the top 20 percent of households. Overall, tax benefits go to the older population with annual incomes of over $20,000, not to those with less than $10,000. Tax provisions are thus another way that public benefits are inequitably distributed within the older population (Gist, 2007).

Social Services

Federal and state policies and expenditures are primarily oriented toward medical care. Only about 1 percent of the older population's share of the federal budget is spent on social service programs. From a political economy perspective, social services are underfunded because they do not fit within the dominant medical model (Estes et al., 1996, 2000).

In addition to Medicare and Medicaid, funding for age-based social services derives from four federal amendments to the Social Security Act **(Title XX or Social Services Block Grants)**, and the Older Americans Act (OAA) of 1965. Title XX, established in 1975, provides social services to all age groups. Entitlements are means tested, with most services to older adults aimed at those receiving SSI. In terms of the program classification system discussed earlier, Title XX is a universal program aimed at redressing needs. Yet income is an eligibility criterion. This means that older people compete with a diverse group of Title XX recipients—primarily families with dependent children and persons who are visually impaired or mentally and/or physically disabled. Title XX encompasses basic life-sustaining, self-care services to compensate for losses in health and functional ability: homemaker and chore services, home-delivered meals, adult protective services, adult day care, foster care, and institutional or residential care services. These have generally ensured a minimum level of support for vulnerable older adults.

Under the federal Omnibus Budget Reconciliation Act of 1981, Title XX was converted to the Social Services Block Grant program, while federal funds allocated to the states were reduced on average by 30 percent. The Social Services Block Grant program was one of the initial decentralization efforts emerging from the new federalism era of President Reagan in the 1980s. Services had to be directed to one of its five goals:

1. Prevent, reduce, or eliminate dependency
2. Achieve or maintain self sufficiency
3. Prevent neglect, abuse, or exploitation of children and adults
4. Prevent or reduce inappropriate institutional care
5. Secure admission or referral for institutional care when other forms of care are not appropriate (Keigher, 2006)

Block grant funding increased the states' discretion in determining clients' needs and allocating Title XX funds among the diverse eligible groups. For example, national income-eligibility guidelines aimed at targeting programs to needy persons were eliminated. Accordingly, there was an increase in the competition for funds and greater variability in services between and within states. As a result, most states allocated a greater percentage of block grant funds to children than to older adults. Decentralization decreased revenues for social services under Title XX for older people, although the demand for services increased. Competition for limited funds has intensified under the Bush administration; cross-generational policy approaches may represent valuable ways to reduce such conflicts.

The **Older Americans Act (OAA)** was funded in 1965 to create a national network for the comprehensive planning, coordination, and delivery of aging services. President Lyndon Johnson, signing the law, concluded that the OAA "affirms our nation's sense of responsibility toward the well-being of all of our older citizens" (AOA, 2004, p. 1.). At the federal level, the act charges the Administration on Aging (AOA), through the Assistant Secretary on Aging, to oversee and support the **Aging Network** (i.e., the system of social services for older adults) and to advocate for them nationally. The establishment of AOA as a discrete unit in the Department of Health and Human Services took more than 27 years, from before the passage of the Act until 1992, and required 13 amendments. At that time, the Administration for Children and Families was also established. This decision to create parallel organizations rather than giving special status to the AOA made a significant statement regarding equity of responses to the needs of all age groups. The primary grant programs administered by AOA are:

1. Title III: community planning and services to meet older adults' needs
2. Title IV: research and development promotes evidence-based research on program design, including innovative models for service to individuals with Alzheimer's and their families
3. Title V: the Senior Community Service Employment Program (SCSEP) provides part-time employment and training opportunities for low-income adults age 55 and older who perform service type jobs
4. Title VI: provides grants to American Indians and native Hawaiians for supportive and nutrition services
5. Title VII: establishes protection systems for the prevention of elder abuse, neglect, and exploitation, including the long-term care ombudsman programs and state legal assistance development

Title III is the single federal social service statute designed specifically for all adults age 60 and over, regardless of income and need; it funds the services typically associated with AOA, such as senior centers, home delivered and congregate meals, information and referral, and, more

---

SERVICES PROVIDED UNDER THE OLDER AMERICANS ACT

Access Services: Information and referral; care management.

In-Home Services: Homemaker assistance, respite care, emergency response systems, friendly visiting, minor home repairs and telephone reassurance, and increasingly nonmedical home health care.

Senior Center Programs: Social, physical, educational, recreational, and cultural programs, with a growing emphasis on health enhancement and wellness.

Nutrition Programs: Meals at senior centers or nutrition sites; in-home meals (Meals on Wheels).

Legal Assistance Advocacy: For individual older adults and on behalf of programs and legislation. The OAA is the only major federal legislation that mandates advocacy on behalf of a constituency.

Additional services are provided based on local community needs and resources.

recently, respite and other services for caregivers. In terms of the policy criteria in Table 16.1 on page 677. Entitlement is universal, based on age. The Aging Network encompasses the federal, state, and local area agencies on aging, along with its advisory and advocacy groups. Of the 56 State Units on Aging (SUAs), each has an advisory council to engage in statewide planning and advocacy. The SUAs designate local **Area Agencies on Aging (AAAs)** to develop and administer service plans within regional and local areas. There are nearly 660 AAAs and 244 tribal organizations that fulfill these functions. Each one has an advisory board, which must include older adults in decision-making roles (Keigher, 2006).

In addition to federal, state, and local agencies that are responsible for planning and coordination, a fourth tier of the network is composed of about 30,000 direct service providers and 500,000 volunteers in local communities. Many of these OAA services, central to long-term care, overlap with the goals and provisions of the Social Services Block Grants. Within this wide range of programs, the relatively low level of

funding means that OAA must target services to low-income, ethnic minority, rural elders, and frail older adults at risk of nursing home placement, even though it still retains its original goal of universality.

Because participation rates in many OAA services are highest among middle-income elders, proposals for cost sharing of services have been introduced. Some OAA program staff and advocates fear that cost sharing would introduce means testing and stigmatize OAA programs as "welfare," thereby discouraging their use. However, by targeting services to those with the greatest social or economic need and functional disability, these programs are already implicitly means-tested. Another goal is to increase participation by elders of color through targeted outreach and increased recruitment of ethnic minority staff and board members of agencies receiving OAA funds. Such targeting, however, could result in reductions in prevention and wellness programs that could have long-range benefits for all elders. Cost-sharing, means testing, targeting, sliding fee schedules, private fundraising and partnerships are alternative approaches to provide more services than can be offered with limited OAA funds.

Many agencies funded by the OAA provide free or low-cost transportation services.

A CATCH-22 FOR MEALS ON WHEELS

The Meals on Wheels program, funded by OAA, has delivered food to older adults and persons with disabilities since 1954. Nationwide, approximately 2 million older adults are on waiting lists to receive Meals on Wheels. A factor underlying the growing waiting lists is a shortage of volunteer drivers, in part due to high gasoline prices and the growing numbers of elders who need to work for pay instead of volunteering. Some of the 4000 Meals on Wheels programs nationwide pay volunteers (as well as their mileage) to deliver the meals. But with flat funding for Meals on Wheels, it is not sustainable to provide such stipends over time. If you were director of a Meals on Wheels program, what strategies would you use to recruit and retain volunteers, given the growing demands for this service?

However, each of these revenue strategies challenges the OAA's basic premise of age-based entitlement and raises questions about its effect on the quality and quantity of services for the very poor. For example, senior centers that charge a fee for fitness activities may deter the very elders who would most benefit from these programs, even if there is a sliding scale. Alternatively, providing home care services to all who request or require them raises questions of fairness when well-off elders can afford to purchase such care. Advocates of aging services are concerned that the OAA may start to provide a two-tiered system, one for the poor and another for the well-to-do. The fundamental dilemma is whether the Act can meet increasing demand for services without major increases in funding. Other OAA advocates fear that, in the absence of a national long-term care policy, AOA activities have become the nation's de facto provider of many chronic care services targeted to frail homebound elders, but without the benefit of a national policy or adequate funding (Hudson, 2005a; Koff and Park, 1999). As examples of this shift to chronic disease management, the OAA increasingly provides home and community-based services (HCBS) with 33 SUAs as the operating agency for Medicaid HCBS waivers for older adults and younger persons with physical disabilities. As part of President Bush's New Freedom Initiative, aging and disability resource centers are now jointly funded by the AOA and Centers for Medicare and Medicaid to access long-term care services (Keigher 2006).

The OAA must be reauthorized for funding every 7 years. After years of inaction, Congress in fall 2006 passed the necessary reauthorization, with a new theme of "Choices for Independence," which is congruent with the era of individual responsibility. As has been true for the past 40 years, funding remained essentially flat, even though needs are growing. The nature of services available through the Aging Network will undoubtedly shift with the aging of the baby boomers, with greater emphasis on health and wellness enhancement and lifelong learning opportunities as well as fee-based services. Service providers will also seek to reach middle age caregivers willing to pay for assistance with their care tasks. Already, OAA includes several provisions with an intergenerational impact:

- Multigenerational disease prevention and health promotion services
- Supportive services and multipurpose senior centers, including services to facilitate regular interaction between school-aged children and older individuals
- The National Family Caregiver Support Act, which applies to caregivers across the life course
- Intergenerational Meals Programs
- Community service and employment programs that promote older adults working with younger generations (Generations United, 2001)

The number of cross-generational programs with the potential for other sources of funding is likely to grow in the future, especially with only modest funding projected for the OAA.

Policy Dilemmas

Age-Based versus Needs-Based Programs

The preceding discussion of Social Security, SSI, and the OAA highlights long-lasting debates about the need for age-based programs, choices about whom to serve, and how to restrict benefits eligibility. Advocates of age-based programs view them as an efficient way to set a minimum floor of protection, less stigmatizing than means-tested services, and promoting the values of dignity and autonomy. Efficiency is presumably enhanced by the fact that age-based policies exclusively or predominantly affect people above the age of 60 or 62. Similarly, universal programs based on age are assumed to be less administratively intrusive into elders' lives (Holstein, 1995, 2005). Neugarten (1982; Neugarten and Neugarten, 1986) was among the first gerontologists to argue strongly against age-based services. She maintained that they reinforce the perception of "the old" as a problem, thereby stigmatizing elders, and adding to age segregation. In her view, the OAA implicitly views anyone over age 60 as vulnerable. Yet, as we have seen, some aging network programs benefit growing numbers of young-old who are relatively healthy, have adequate incomes and do not need services. Because up to 25 percent of the population qualify for age-related benefits, a purely age-based approach is politically and economically not feasible (Torres-Gil, 1992). Rather than age, economic and health needs should be the basis for selectively targeting services. Proposals for income eligibility, such as means-testing for Social Security and Medicare, are congruent with a needs-based approach. Some advocates for targeting services to high-risk older persons favor a combination of categorical and group eligibility mechanisms. For example, a portion of OAA service funds could be allocated only to SSI and older Medicaid recipients, thereby reaching elders with the lowest incomes and presumably the most service needs. Given the increasing economic inequality within the older population, means-testing programs that comprise the "safety net" for the most vulnerable older adults (e.g., SSI and Medicaid) are viewed as priorities for improvement.

The Politics of Productivity versus the Politics of Entitlement

Closely related to the ongoing debate about age-based versus needs-based programs is the "politics of productivity versus entitlement" (Moody, 2002b). As implied throughout this chapter, the **politics of entitlement** is characterized as follows:

- In a "failure model of old age," older people are defined as needy, worthy, and deserving of public support, solely because of their age.

- Issues are defined in terms of needs and rights.
- The emphasis is on what older people deserve to receive as their right rather than what they can give to others.
- Resources are transferred to the older population as a categorical group.
- Other groups must pay for the benefits due the older population.

The **politics of productivity,** as discussed in Chapters 8 and 12, is characterized in contrasting ways:

- The older population is increasingly diverse.
- The implementation of new policies requires an expanding economy toward which older adults can contribute.
- Older people are defined as a resource in an interdependent society and can help younger populations. Old age is a time for cross-generational assistance to families and communities.
- "Investing in human resources" across the life course is essential to future economic growth that benefits all ages.

As noted earlier, political conservatives question entitlement programs for all age groups. While they point to the increased socioeconomic diversity of the older population as a rationale for means testing, they do not agree on how much to target resources to benefit those most at risk, such as women and elders of color. In other words, most advocates for changing entitlement programs appear to be motivated by fiscal goals, not by a desire for service adequacy to reduce status inequities within the older population. Similar macro-level patterns are occurring in many Western European countries, where policy makers have rejected the consensus on which social insurance programs were based—that is, older people as deserving poor. Instead, the cost of population aging is questioned and aging is defined as the problem, as noted in the discussion of the social construction of aging in

Chapter 8. Even in countries with a strong welfare state, pension systems have been reduced and the public interest privatized, undermining long-standing public pension and social protection systems (Walker, 2006).

Intergenerational Inequity Framework

Closely related to entitlement/productivity debate is the **intergenerational inequity** argument that measures the relative hard times of one generation (e.g., children) against the relative prosperity of another (elders). The intergenerational inequity debate began in 1984 with Samuel Preston's classic analysis of poverty rates among the young and old, and public expenditures on behalf of older people. The old were perceived to be thriving, at the expense of children, as a result of expanded Social Security benefits and inflationary increases in real estate and home equity (Preston, 1984). This generated a rather simplistic picture of generational conflict, expounded in a growing number of newspaper editorials and TV spots on the "crisis" in Social Security. It also resulted in the formation of groups such as Americans for Generational Equity (AGE), which later merged with the American Association of Boomers (AAB) and the National Taxpayers Union, although these organizations are no longer active. These organizations maintained that the baby boom generation will collectively face a disastrous retirement, and its children will, in turn, be disproportionately burdened with supporting their parents as no other generation has been historically. Likewise, the Third Millennium and PAC 20/20 emerged in the 1990s out of concerns about the future of Generation X, young adults in their 20s.

Underlying their arguments is the assumption that significant distribution choices must be made about how to pay the costs of an aging society. It was in this political climate that some of the long-standing features of old-age programs began to undergo major revisions in the 1980s and 1990s: Social Security benefits at higher-income levels were taxed for the first time; the Tax Reform Act

> **THEMES OF THE INTERGENERATIONAL INEQUITY ARGUMENT**
>
> - Older citizens, now better off financially than the population as a whole, are selfishly concerned only with personal pension and income benefits, and with maintaining their share of the federal budget.
> - Programs for older people are a major cause of current budget deficits, economic problems, inadequate schools, and increased poverty among mothers, children, and young adults.
> - Children are the most impoverished and vulnerable age group.
> - Younger people today will not receive a fair return for their Social Security and Medicare investments in the future.

of 1986 eliminated the extra personal exemption for all older adults, although tax credits continue for very low-income older persons on a sliding scale; and the OAA began targeting services to low-income older adults.

The intergenerational inequity debate is prominent again today, but within a broader concept of **generational justice** (Jecker, 2002). It is fueled primarily by issues of Social Security and the demographic challenges of low fertility and increased longevity. In all Western societies, older adults are the primary recipients of public income transfer programs while children are, to a large extent, financed privately by their parents. Issues of generational justice are thus primarily economic conflicts—not political or cultural ones—that focus on the distribution of limited resources. The generational justice perspective argues that differential treatment on the basis of age is morally justified because of sequential reciprocity across the life course. That is, as we age, our membership in age groups changes. The fact that so many Americans are successfully living through all the stages of life makes treating them differently in old age morally acceptable, since so many of us will

Positive experiences with grandparents reinforce our beliefs about intergenerational support.

eventually benefit as well. Intergenerational sharing of burdens and rewards is fair to the extent that each successive generation can expect to receive the same treatment as the preceding and following ones as it moves through each life stage. In such a system, financing older people during one's earnings years is fair because one can expect to reap the same benefits in one's retirement, funded by the next generation (Holstein, 2005; Kohli, 2006; Myles, 2005).

Critique of the Intergenerational Inequity Framework

The major criticisms of the intergenerational inequity framework are as follows:

- It overlooks subgroups of poverty and the fact that the United States has the highest level of old age inequality among developed nations (Meyer, 2005).

- Although older people's economic status has improved overall, not all older adults have adequate finances, as noted in our discussion of poverty among older women, ethnic minorities, and the oldest-old. Advocates for older adults acknowledge the growing poverty among children and young families; nevertheless they seek to ensure economic well-being for the oldest members of our society and to avoid elders' being scapegoated for larger societal problems.

- Evidence of significant intergenerational conflict is limited. Younger and older generations generally recognize their interdependence and support benefits for each other across the life course. For example, the Children's Defense Fund argues that funding for programs for the young should be increased at the cost of military spending, not at the expense of programs for the old. The AARP concurs, and maintains that older people's well-being contributes to the welfare of all other generations.

- The definition of fairness put forth by groups such as Americans for Generational Equity is narrow and misleading. When fairness is equated with numerical equality, this assumes that the relative needs of children and older adults for public funds are identical, and that equal expenditures represent social justice. Even if needs and expenditures for each group were equal, this would not result in equal outcomes or generational justice.

- There is no evidence that cutting Social Security expenditures would result in increased benefits for young families, given current federal priorities of homeland security and anti-terrorism, and the conservative trend toward more restrictive concepts of public welfare, as reflected in the Temporary Assistance for Needy Families (TANF) Program.

- By framing policy issues in terms of competition and conflict between generations, the intergenerational inequity perspective implies that public benefits to older individuals are a one-way flow from young to old, and that reciprocity between generations does not exist. As we have seen throughout this book, resources typically flow from old to young until the older generation needs care. The distribution of benefits extends far beyond the older population, with the majority of American families receiving at least one benefit from entitlements or other safety-net programs.

• The intergenerational debate is a convenient mechanism to justify shifting responsibility for all vulnerable groups from the federal level to individuals, the private sector, and local governments.

• It overlooks other ways to increase public resources through economic growth, increased tax revenues, or reduced defense spending, and that future generations' economic well-being will ultimately depend on growth rates of real wages. The economy of the future, barring unforeseen disasters, will be able to support a mix of programs for all age groups (Holstein, 2005; Kingson, Hirshorn, and Cornman, 1986; Kingson, Hirshorn, and Harootyan, 1994; Kingson and Williamson, 2001; Minkler, 2002; Williamson et al., 2003; Wisensale, 2003).

Nevertheless, advocates for older adults acknowledge that it is no longer realistic to proceed on the assumption that all age-based benefits are sacrosanct. They now recognize that it is counterproductive to oppose all measures imposed on financially better-off older persons, such as treating part of Social Security as taxable income.

The Interdependence of Generations Framework

Consistent with social exchange theory described in Chapter 8, a "contract between generations" exists through sharing of burdens and solidarity across generations. Typically, this is defined as parents to children and children to aging parents. The **interdependence of generations framework** recognizes the changing societal and political context: Never before have so many individuals

lived so long, and never have there been relatively so few members of the younger generation to support them. Within this larger context, public and private intergenerational transfers are viewed as central to social progress. As described in Chapters 9 and 10, generations assist one another primarily through the family. Most **generational investments** flow downwards from older to younger generations through care for children and dependent adults, financial support, gifts, trust funds and inheritances. Private intergenerational transfers are essential to meet families' needs across the life course and to transmit legacies of the past (e.g., culture, values, and

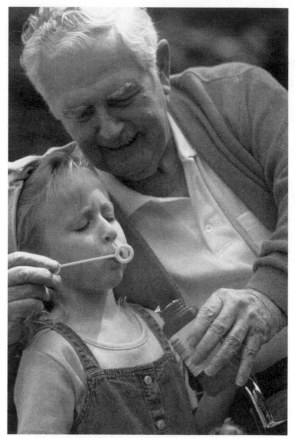

Most older adults are concerned about the welfare of younger generations.

knowledge). In addition, the growing number of intergenerational programs reflects how both generations gain from these social exchanges (Wisensale, 2003).

Transfers based on public policy (e.g., education, Social Security, and health care programs) also serve intergenerational goals. As noted above, Social Security benefits are distributed widely across all generations and protect against risks to families' economic well-being across the life course, such as when a younger worker becomes disabled or a middle-aged parent dies. Younger generations gain from age-based programs that support their older relatives' autonomy and relieve them from financial responsibilities. As another example of cross-generational benefits, long-term care serves all age groups—particularly younger adults with developmental disabilities or chronic mental illness. Likewise, it is erroneous to think of education as a one-way flow to children that is resisted by older people. Older adults' support for school levies reflects their recognition that they also benefit from education programs that increase workforce productivity (Caputo 2005; Moody, 2002a).

Within the framework of interdependence, other paradigms are proposed as ways to conceptualize how burdens and opportunities can be fairly shared among generations. One paradigm is the concept of generational investment, in which age-based services and other social programs, such as public education, play an integral part in the system of reciprocal contributions that generations make to one another. Social Security and Medicare are mechanisms through which generations invest in one another and publicly administer returns to older cohorts for the investments made in the human capital of younger groups. As such, old-age benefits represent claims based on merit and social contributions and should not be subject to means-testing.

Similarly, older people can be the vanguard of renewed efforts to ensure a decent standard of living for all Americans, perhaps by support-

> ## THE INTERGENERATIONAL COMPACT
>
> - Most intergenerational transfers of resources are from the old to the young.
> - More than 3 million children under the age of 18 receive Social Security benefits because their parents are disabled, retired, or deceased.
> - Temporary Assistance to Needy Families (TANF) assists children and their caretaker relatives (parents or grandparents).
> - More than 3 million children live in households where an adult, often a grandparent, receives Social Security.
> - A growing percentage of older adults volunteer to help children, adolescents, and young families.
> - Both old and young are more concerned about major societal issues, such as health care and strategies to reduce climate change, than they are about Social Security.

ing measures such as paid family leave that recognizes the societal contributions of child-rearing (Williamson et al., 2002). This assumes that enhancing opportunities earlier in people's lives can reduce intergenerational competition. A broadened welfare consensus also can be fostered through an understanding of life-course disparities that lead to problems in old age. This perspective of our common human vulnerability across the life course is not a new one. In fact, President Lyndon B. Johnson's charge to the 1968 Task Force Report on Older Americans was to determine the most important things to be done for the well-being of most older Americans. Since vulnerability in old age is the product of experiences throughout life, the task force concluded that providing social and economic opportunities for young and middle-aged persons is a high priority (Binstock, 1995).

Similar to the "politics of productivity" and the interdependence framework, Torres-Gil and Moga (2001) argue for a New Aging paradigm. The politics of the New Aging aims to identify how all generations can contribute to the common good. Our society must alter both our view of older adults as relatively homogeneous to acknowledge their growing diversity and how we respond to differential needs. With such increased heterogeneity, intergenerational conflict cannot be assumed. Although some tensions between young and old will remain, the politics of diversity will become the norm, whereby some older adults have more in common with younger age groups, perhaps based on race, ethnicity, sexual orientation or immigrant status, than with their chronological age peers. Differences of political opinions among older people and between age cohorts will increase, with more linkages based on political and ideological priorities, not on age per se. Additionally, the focus increasingly is on relationships between age groups in society rather than individuals within the family.

In the politics of the New Aging, advocacy should be rechanneled from special-interest issues toward policies to benefit all future generations. Groups of older adults should shift from the horizontal alliances that characterize interest-group politics to new vertical alliances, representing common needs across older and younger groups (Binstock, 1995). Previously underrepresented groups of older persons— ethnic minorities, women, and rural residents— must establish alliances with younger populations. In fact, this is already occurring through the founding of Generations United by the Child Welfare League of America, the National Council on the Aging, and the Children's Defense Fund. This coalition of 135 consumer, labor, children, and senior groups seeks to reframe policy agendas around our common stake in cross-generational approaches. AARP is also forming networks with national ethnic minority organizations and supports policies to benefit children cared for by grandparents. The United States Students Association and the Gray Panthers joined together to support policies to enhance quality of life for all. Not only should older adults be viewed as a resource that can contribute to the economy and their own income security, but the young should be educated to assume full adult responsibilities and prepare for their own aging. The real potential of cross-generational advocacy depends on whether the approach pioneered by Generations United is adopted by mainstream age-based social service organizations.

For the interdependence framework to address the problems of the underserved, an ideological consensus is required that government should help all people in need, regardless of age. Given that such consensus does not exist, some policy analysts argue that the real issue for the future is not intergenerational interdependence but rather redefining the role of the public sector in caring for its vulnerable citizens and the relationship between the public and private sectors.

Who Is Responsible?

These policy debates ultimately revolve around the role, size, and purpose of the federal government, and the division of responsibility between the public and private sectors. The current public–private debate is not new, but long-standing, reflected even in the passage of Social Security. Until recently, Social Security benefits, Medicare, Medicaid, SSI, and OAA services represented society's primary responsibility for older citizens. It was to be a collective responsibility, exercised through the national government, and a protection to which every older citizen was entitled, simply by virtue of age. Since the Reagan era, public officials and policy makers have asserted that the problems of older adults and other historically underserved groups cannot be solved with federal policies and programs alone. For former President Clinton to have stated in the 1990s that the "era of big government is over" indicates a major shift in how public policy and government intervention were viewed (Hudson, 2004). Individuals are assumed to be responsible for their own well-being, and federal government interventions are considered to be costly and often ineffective. Instead, it is argued that solutions must come from state and local governments, and from private-sector and individual initiatives, such as advocacy, self-help, family care, personal retirement planning and private investments, individual health care accounts, faith-based organizations, and civic engagement and community service. An antitax mentality of the past decade resulted in legislative changes to reduce federal funds and to rely increasingly on the states through block grants. Some categorical programs have been reconfigured into flexible but small state grants and greater local autonomy (Keigher, 2006).

The assumption that states can most efficiently and creatively respond to local needs is used to justify such federal cuts. This decentralized approach, however, is flawed by the fact that states have the fewest resources to provide services, especially during economic downturns. For example, states have been the least likely to respond to the needs of the most vulnerable. Historically, decentralization has not assured policy uniformity and equity for powerless groups across all states. Evidence for such inequality exists in state-funded education, Head Start, and nutrition programs for children and youth. Stable, uniformly administered federal policies are necessary to bring the states with the lowest expenditures up to a minimum standard, but are improbable in the near future. While past changes to Social Security and AOA services may seem modest, the growing emphasis on cost containment, privatization, and federal retrenchment has started to dismantle the priority on the common good established in the 1935 Social Security Act (Holstein, 2005; Meyer, 2005).

Reductions in Government Support

Closely related to debates about the extent of federal or state responsibility is the level of public fiscal support. Although public spending for older adults has increased in terms of total dollars, it has declined when measured as a percentage of the gross national product or as government expenditures per capita, corrected for inflation. Economically disadvantaged older persons have also been hurt by budget cuts, especially under the Republican "Contract with America," the 1996 "Personal Responsibility and Work Opportunity Legislation," and current reductions in Medicaid and Medicare. Even if Democrats continue to hold the majority in Congress, adequate federal funding for vulnerable citizens of all ages is unlikely in the near future, given the need to cut programs to reduce the skyrocketing federal deficit.

Public spending levels are being reduced at the same time that private and local spheres are being expected to help in managing chronic illness. Policy makers often assume that public programs reduce family involvement and that families should do more for their older relatives. However, as discussed in Chapter 10, most families provide all the support that they are able or willing to do and underutilize existing services. When resources become scarce, the family should not be viewed as simply a cost-effective alternative to nursing home placement and to publicly funded social services. Rather, as we have noted throughout this text, population aging affects families of all ages and therefore must be addressed by adequate government funding and national leadership (Achenbaum, 2006).

Not only are families unable to carry expanded responsibilities on their own, but the private non-profit service sector, especially faith-based organizations, lack the resources to fill the gaps created by federal cuts and changed priorities. In fact, federal tax laws have reduced tax incentives for corporate giving. In addition, private contributions traditionally have not been targeted to social services and programs for older adults. As a result, increased private giving would not automatically flow into areas most severely cut, nor would this benefit the age groups most in need. Chapters 6 and 12 also critiqued the individualistic ethos of successful aging and how civic engagement may not be an option for historically underserved groups. With the dramatic growth of baby boomers, it is critical to encourage strategic public and private funding innovations, including cross-generational policy and funding.

Implications for the Future

Our society is faced with complex, difficult policy choices. Social policies in the future will be shaped by the following macro-economic, demographic, and social factors, including the following:

- the demographic bulge of the aging baby boomers
- increasing economic and racial inequities across the life course and in old age
- budget cuts, or flat funding in federal and state programs, along with the escalating federal deficit, currently the largest in U.S. history
- the economic slowing nationally and globally, together with economic pressures for older adults to be employed longer, thereby gradually raising the average retirement age
- the national budgetary emphasis on homeland security and antiterrorism
- increased competition for limited public dollars, with greater emphasis on cost-effectiveness, fiscal responsibility, and devolution of federal authority to state and local levels
- privatization of public policies, such as the 2003 change in Medicare and the current administration's push toward individual savings accounts in lieu of Social Security
- growing expectations that the private sector, including faith-based organizations, civic engagement initiatives, and family and other informal caregivers will meet the needs of vulnerable populations
- the influential role of AARP in national policy debates, along with the need to advocate for cross-generational policies, programs, and funding as represented by Generations United
- deep partisan divisions at the federal level, with an intense focus on party positioning

- the globalization of aging issues and policies that affect societies and populations as a whole

Given this context of rapid demographic, social, and economic change, an expansion of public policies for older adults is unlikely, unless this expansion occurs through privatization. Instead, issues of income security will continue to be addressed in a piecemeal fashion, and deficit-driven budget pressures will collide with the needs of an aging population (Crystal, 2003). As suggested by Ornstein (2002) in his predictions of what type of reform can be expected in the current political context, the challenge of developing a comprehensive policy approach to the problems of an aging society is to adopt a framework larger than the current budget politics and partisan bickering. There is a critical need for compelling proposals for change. One such direction is to adopt an intergenerational or multigenerational approach to policy development, as represented by the strong support from both parties for national respite legislation that crosscuts all ages. Such life course initiatives move away from age-based categorical funding and pool resources across age groups. They also serve to move beyond the intergenerational competition debates that have framed policy discussions since the 1980s. Another way to frame a comprehensive policy approach would be to reconceptualize aging policy as family policy and the aging of the baby boomers as a crisis for families, rather than a crisis in Social Security (Binstock, 2002; Hudson, 2005b).

The challenge is even greater when we consider the fact that the older population is not one constituency but several, in which race, gender, socioeconomic class, sexual orientation, and rural/urban residence may be greater unifiers than age. A political agenda must be drafted that can unite different older constituencies—low-income, middle-class, and wealthy—as well as diverse populations with common needs that are not based on age. The probability of a comprehensive long-range policy approach that can bring together diverse actors in the near future is extremely low. Yet, limited public resources are not the primary barrier to action. For example, the cost of eliminating poverty among both older people and children is well within our societal resources, but our society lacks the public will, shared social values, and a political consensus to ensure a minimal level of economic security and health for all Americans. Progress in eliminating poverty at all ages could occur largely by improving the basic income support of SSI and expanding Medicaid eligibility. Unfortunately, such gains are unlikely to occur without major changes in our political structures and belief systems of democratic pluralism, states' rights, and individual freedom. Historically social issues have been addressed through partisan, piecemeal, incremental, and short-sighted government intervention; Social Security and Medicare are exceptions to this approach. Another barrier is the fragmentation of political power endemic to and increasing in our political system. And last remains the challenge of effective implementation that involves both private and public entities. The process of implementation often impedes fulfillment of the intent of policies. Social Security is an exception because it is a relatively self-implementing and therefore successful program (Binstock, 2002). On the other hand, the "crises" entailed by the aging of the baby boomers may force unified action, despite the lack of a forward-looking national policy. Until then, most Americans will continue to be personally generous, but reluctant to support expanding public income-maintenance programs for diverse groups of needy persons, or a national health care system that would threaten personal choice.

Gerontologists are needed to advocate for programs that benefit individuals across the life course and into old age. Translating gerontological research findings for policy makers and the public is inherent within effective advocacy. This means that gerontologists need to be visible at the local, state, and federal levels in presenting evidence-based testimony and offering comprehensive, creative, and cost-effective solutions. In fact, some aging advocates are even seeking ways to frame policies that benefit older adults within the current funding emphasis on national security! Given the nature of our political system and the critical policy and funding challenges created by aging boomers, gerontological policy, practice, and research need to be linked in the training and development of gerontological professionals who can influence policy making and implementation.

Summary

This chapter reviewed federal programs that assist primarily older persons, although many of these programs have cross-generational benefits. Since 1960, age-specific spending has increased significantly, mostly through Medicare and Social Security. In the past, such age-entitlement programs were based on public values and beliefs that older people are deserving. However, the rapid expansion of these programs, combined with the improved economic status of the majority of older adults, created a growing public and political sentiment that such age-based entitlement programs must be reduced, perhaps through privatization and means-testing to minimize the benefits received by higher-income older adults.

The United States developed age-based policies more slowly than European countries. The Social Security Act of 1935 was the first major policy benefit for older people. Social Security was expanded slightly in 1950 to support partial health care costs through individual states. These changes led to the enactment of Medicare in 1965. Since then, the number of programs aimed at improving older people's lives has grown significantly: the OAA and the Aging Network it created; SSI, the Social Security Amendments of 1972 and 1977; and Title XX social services legislation. National forums such as the 1961 and 1971 House Conferences on Aging strengthened these programs. During the 1980s, however, social service funding declined despite recommendations from the 1981 White House Conferences on Aging to increase funds for aging services. Federal allocations for homemaker, nutrition, chore services, adult day care, low-income energy assistance, respite, and volunteer programs for older adults all diminished during this period. These reductions were based on a national perception that the older population is financially better off than younger age groups. The fiscal crisis faced by the Social Security system in the early 1980s fueled this stereotype through speculations that the growing numbers of "Greedy Geezers" would drain the system before future generations could benefit. However, numerous structural factors, not the growth of older adults per se, are responsible for the problems. Changes that have subsequently been made in this system assure its future viability until approximately 2040.

The debate over age-based versus needs-based programs has also led to the emergence of organizations that argue that older people are benefiting at the expense of younger age groups. But evidence for such inequities is weak; numerous other organizations such as the Children's Defense Fund and Generations United recognize generational interdependence and the importance of seeking increased public support for all ages through other sources. This framework, known as the interdependence of generations, assumes that assistance from young to old and old to young benefits all ages and supports the role of families across the life course.

The policy agenda for older Americans early in the twenty-first century is full and complex. The current federal emphasis on fiscal austerity for domestic programs and decentralized government underlies all policy debates about how much the federal government should be expected to provide and for whom. Increasing public perceptions of older people as well off, combined with decreased government expenditures, will undoubtedly affect the types of future programs and policies developed to meet elders' needs.

Older adults are less likely to act as a unified bloc in support of age-based programs. Instead, their increased diversity suggests that alliances will be formed between at-risk elders and other age groups. Consistent with the frameworks of interdependence and generational investment, such alliances may foster policies that benefit both older people and future generations. Threatening such cross-age efforts, however, is the antitax mood of the public, and the Bush administration's other financial priorities. These pressures suggest that advocates for older adults will need to find new ways to address the complex needs created by elders' increased life expectancy and diversity. A major challenge is the development and funding of health care, especially home and community-based long-term care, the topic addressed next in Chapter 17.

GLOSSARY

age-based programs   programs only available to people of a certain age

Aging Network   the system of social services for older adults funded by the Older Americans Act

Area Agencies on Aging (AAA)   offices on aging at the regional and local levels that plan and administer services to meet the needs of older adults within that area; established and partially funded through the Older Americans Act

cash substitute   a benefit given in a form other than cash, such as a voucher, which may be exchanged for food, rent, medical care, etc.

cash transfer   a benefit paid by cash or its equivalent

categorical   in this context, a manner of dealing with social issues by addressing the problems of specific groups of persons rather than attempting solutions that are comprehensive to address problems affecting the entire population

contributory plans   programs providing benefits that require the beneficiary to contribute something toward the cost of the benefit

cost-of-living adjustments (COLA)   changes in benefits designed to maintain steady purchasing power of such benefits

direct benefit a benefit given directly, in the form of either a cash payment or of some commodity such as food or housing

eligibility criteria factors that determine the ability of programs to deliver benefits to people

entitlement programs government programs that do not require appropriations from a legislative body; rather, eligibility on the part of applicants triggers receipt of benefits regardless of the program's cost

generational investment investments made by one generation for the benefit of another, such as the payment of Social Security taxes by the working population for the benefit of retirees, the services provided by older persons for child care, and the payment of property taxes to benefit school children

generational justice older adults receiving benefits based on age is morally justifiable since all adults can eventually benefit from age-based programs

indirect benefit a benefit given through tax deductions or exemptions or other indirect means

interdependence of generations framework recognition of intergenerational transfers that occur across the life course

intergenerational inequity the view that one generation or age group receives benefits that are disproportional to those received by another

need-based (or **means-based**) **entitlement programs** social programs delivered to persons who meet defined criteria of eligibility based on economic need or ability to pay for the benefits

noncontributory programs programs providing benefits that do not require the beneficiary to contribute toward the cost of the benefit

Older Americans Act federal legislation for a network of social services specifically for older people

politics of entitlement political preferences, especially as applied to elders, for the allocation of resources based on the view of older persons as needy, worthy, and deserving of public support

politics of productivity political preferences for the allocation of resources based on the diversity of the aging population: well-off, poor, capable of continued productive work, or ill or disabled

privatization changes in Social Security that would divert payroll taxes to private investment accounts

selective benefits benefits available on an individually determined need or means basis

social policy government policy designed to address a social problem or issue

social programs the visible manifestations of policies

Title XX (or the **Social Services Block Grant**) funding for social services (e.g., homemaking chores, adult day care) based on need, not age

universal benefits benefits available as a social right to all persons belonging to a designated group.

RESOURCES

Log on to MySocKit (www.mysockit.com) for information about the following:

- The 2030 Center
- Administration on Aging (AOA)
- Cato Institute
- Generations United
- International Federation on Aging
- National Academy on Aging
- National Association of Area Agencies on Aging
- National Center for Policy Analysis
- National Committee to Preserve Social Security and Medicare
- Social Security Administration

REFERENCES

Achenbaum, W.A. Why did old-age policy making lose steam? *Innovations,* 2006, *1,* 3.

Administration on Aging (AOA). *Layman's guide to the Older Americans Act.* 2004 Accessed February 27, 2007, from http://www.aod.gov/about/legbudg/oaa/laymans_guide_pf.asp.

Beedon, L. *Supplemental Security Income (SSI): Yesterday, today and tomorrow.* Washington, DC: AARP, Public Policy Research Group, 2000.

Binstock, R.H. A new era in the politics of aging: How will the old-age interest groups respond? *Generations,* Fall 1995, *19,* 68–74.

Binstock, R.H. The politics of enacting reform. In S.H. Altman and D.I. Schatman, *Policies for an aging society.* Baltimore: Johns Hopkins University Press, 2002.

Binstock, R.H., and Day, C.L. Aging and politics. In R.H. Binstock and L.K. George (Eds.), *Handbook of aging and the social sciences* (4th ed.). San Diego, CA: Academic Press, 1996.

Blendon, R., Brodie, M., Benson, J., Neuman, T., Altman D. et al. Americans' agenda in aging for the new Congress. *Public Policy and Aging Report,* 2005, *15,* 20–25.

Bosworth, B., Butler, G.T., and Keys, B. *Implications of the Bush Commission pension reforms for married couples.* Chestnut Hill, MA: Center for Retirement Research at Boston College, 2003.

Breyer, F., and Kifmann M. Incentives to retire later—A solution to the Social Security crisis? *Journal of Pension Economics and Finance,* 2002, *1,* 111–130.

Caputo, R.K. Inheritance and intergenerational transmission of parental care. In R.K. Caputo (Ed.), *Challenges of aging on U.S. families: Policy and practice implications.* New York: The Haworth Press, 2005.

Cavanaugh, F.X. *Feasibility of Social Security individual accounts.* Washington, DC: Public Policy Institute, AARP, 2002.

Choi, N. Federal income maintenance policies and programs. In B. Berkman (Ed.), *Handbook of Social Work in Health and Aging.* New York: Oxford, 2006.

Cohen, E.S. Disability and aging: The quest for coherent public policy. *Public Policy and Aging Report,* 2004, *14,* 7–11.

Congressional Budget Office (CBO). *Economic and Budget Issue Brief. Is Social Security Progressive?* Accessed December 2006, from http://www.ssa.gov/OACT/TR/TR02/lrIndex.html.

Congressional Budget Office (CBO). *The Budget and Economic Outlook: Fiscal Years 2008 to 2017.* Accessed January 2007, from http://www.cbo.gov/ftpdocs/77xx/doc7731/01-24-BudgetOutlook.pdf.

Crystal, S. Groundhog day: The endless debate over Medicare "reform." *Public Policy and Aging Report,* 2003, *13,* 7–10.

Cubanski, J., Voris, M., Kitchman, M., Neuman, T., and Potetz, L. *Medicare chartbook.* New York: Henry J. Kaiser Family Foundation. 2005.

Diamond, P. *What are the best alternatives for meeting the impending crisis in Social Security financing?* Presented at the Conference on Public Policy and Responsibility across Generations. Newton, MA: Boston College, 2004.

Estes, C.L. *The aging enterprise.* San Francisco: Jossey-Bass, 1979.

Estes, C.L. Aging, health and social policy: Crisis and crossroads. *Journal of Aging and Social Policy,* 1989, *1,* 17–32.

Estes, C.L. Austerity and aging. 1980 and beyond. In M. Minkler and C.L. Estes (Eds.), *Readings in the political economy of aging.* Farmingdale, NY: Baywood, 1984.

Estes, C.L. From gender to the political economy of aging. *European Journal of Social Equality,* 2000, *2,* 28–45.

Estes, C.L., Linkins, K.W., and Binney, E.A. The political economy of aging. In R.H. Binstock and L.K. George (Eds.), *Handbook of aging and the social sciences* (4th ed.). San Diego, CA: Academic Press, 1996.

Favreault, M.M., and Sammartino, F.J. *Impact of Social Security reform on low-income and older women.* Washington, DC: Public Policy Institute, AARP, 2002.

Feder, J., and Friedland, R. The value of Social Security and Medicare to families. *Generations,* Spring, 2005, *29,* 78–85.

Friedland, R.B. *Investing in our future.* Washington, DC: National Academy on an Aging Society, 2000.

Generations United. *Intergenerational elements in the Older Americans Act. Fact Sheet.* Washington, DC: Generations United, 2001.

Generations United. *Social Security: A program that benefits all ages. Fact sheet.* Washington, DC: Generations United, 2005.

Gist, J.R. *population aging, entitlement growth, and the economy.* AARP. Accessed January 2007, from http://assets.aarp.org/rgcenter/econ/2007_01_security.pdf.

Gonyea, J., and Hooyman, N. Reducing poverty among older women: The importance of Social Security. *Families in Society,* 2005, *86,* 338–346.

Gorin, S.H. Generational equity and privatization: Myth and reality. *Health and Social Work,* 2000, *25,* 219–225.

The Harris Poll #1. January 3, 2007. *The American Public strongly supports Social Security reform.* Accessed March 18, 2007, from http://www.harrisinteractive.com/harris_poll/index.asp?PID=717.

Henkin, N., and Kingson, E. Advancing an intergenerational agenda for the twenty-first century. *Generations,* 1998/1999, *22,* 99–105.

Herd, P. Crediting care or marriage: Reforming Social Security family benefits. *Journals of Gerontology,* 2006, *61B,* S24–S34.

Herd, P. Universalism without targeting: Privatizing the old-age welfare state. *The Gerontologist,* 2005, *45,* 292–299.

Herd, P., and Kingson, E. Reframing Social Security: Cures worse than the disease. In R.H. Hudson (Ed.), *The new politics of old age policy.* Baltimore: Johns Hopkins Press, 2005.

Holstein, M. The normative case: Chronological age and public policy. *Generations,* Fall 1995, *19,* 11–14.

Holstein, M. A normative defense of universal age-based public policy. In R.H. Hudson (Ed.), *The new politics of old age policy.* Baltimore: Johns Hopkins Press, 2005.

Hudson, R.H. Contemporary challenges to age-based policy. In R.H. Hudson (Ed.), *The new politics of old age policy.* Baltimore: Johns Hopkins Press, 2005a.

Hudson, R.H. The contemporary politics of old age policies. In R.H. Hudson (Ed.), *The new politics of old age policy.* Baltimore: Johns Hopkins Press, 2005b.

Hudson, R.H., and Quadagno, J. Aging and politics. In R.H. Binstock and L.K. George (Eds.), *Handbook of aging and the social sciences* (5th ed.). San Diego: Academic Press, 2001.

Jecker, N. Intergenerational justice. In D. Ekerdt (Ed.), *The Encyclopedia of Aging.* New York: McMillan, 2002.

Kassner, E. *The food stamp program and older Americans.* Washington, DC: AARP, Policy Institute Research Group, 2001.

Keigher, S. Policies affecting community-based social services, housing and transportation. In B. Berkman (Ed.), *Handbook of social work in health and aging.* New York: Oxford, 2006.

Kingson, E.R., Hirshorn, B.A., and Cornman, J.C. *Ties that bind: The interdependence of generations.* Cabin John, MD: Seven Locks Press, 1986.

Kingson, E.R., Hirshorn, B.A., and Harootyan, L.K. *The common stake: The interdependence of generations (A policy framework for an aging society).* Washington, DC: The Gerontological Society of America. Reprinted in H.R. Moody, *Aging: Concepts and controversies.* Thousand Oaks, CA: Pine Forge Press, 1994.

Kingson, E.R., and Williamson, J. Economic security policies. In R.H. Binstock and L.K. George (Eds.), *Handbook of aging and the social sciences* (5th ed.). San Diego: Academic Press, 2001.

Koff, T., and Park, R. The Aging Network. In T. Koff and R. Park, *Aging public policy: Bonding the generations* (2nd ed.). Amityville, NY: Baywood Publishing, 1999.

Kohli, M. Aging and justice. In R.H. Binstock and L.K. George (Eds.), *Handbook of aging and the social sciences* (6th ed.). New York: Academic Press, 2006.

Lee, S., and Shaw, L. *Gender and economic security in retirement.* Washington, DC: Institute for Women's Policy Research, 2003.

Meyer, M.H. Decreasing welfare; increasing old age inequality: Whose responsibility is it? In R.H. Hudson (Ed.), *The new politics of old age policy.* Baltimore: Johns Hopkins Press, 2005.

Minkler, M. "Generational equity" and the new victim blaming. In H.R. Moody, *Aging: Concepts and controversies* (4th ed.). Thousand Oaks, CA: Sage, 2002.

Mitchell, O.S. *Personal retirement accounts and Social Security reform.* Philadelphia: Pension Research Council, The Wharton School, University of Pennsylvania, 2002.

Moody, H.R. Focus on practice: Intergenerational programs. In H.R. Moody, *Aging: Concepts and controversies* (4th ed.). Thousand Oaks, CA: Sage, 2002a.

Moody, H.R. Should age or need be the basis for entitlement? In H.R. Moody, *Aging: Concepts and controversies* (4th ed.). Thousand Oaks, CA: Sage, 2002b.

Moody, H.R. What is the future of Social Security? In H.R. Moody, *Aging: Concepts and controversies* (4th ed.). Thousand Oaks, Sage, 2002c.

Myles, J. What justice requires: A normative foundation for U.S. pension reform. In R. Hudson (Ed.), *The new politics of old age policy.* Baltimore: Johns Hopkins University Press, 2005.

National Committee to Preserve Social Security and Medicare (NCPSSM). *Disability insurance and survivors' benefits.* Washington, DC: Author, 2004. Accessed from http://www.ncpssm.org/news/archive/vp_surviorsbenefits.

National Committee to Preserve Social Security and Medicare (NCPSSM). *The many myths about Social Security privatization.* Washington, DC: Author, 2003a.

National Committee to Preserve Social Security and Medicare (NCPSSM). *The truth about privatization.* Washington, DC: Author, 2003b.

Neale, A. American values and social justice: Who should pay for elders' income and healthcare security? *Generations,* 2005, *29,* 88–90.

Neugarten, B. Policy in the 1980s: Age or need entitlement. In B. Neugarten (Ed.), *Age or need: Public policies for older people.* Beverly Hills, CA: Sage, 1982.

Neugarten, B., and Neugarten, D. Changing meanings of age in the aging society. In A. Pifer and L. Bronte (Eds.), *Our aging society: Paradox and promise.* New York: W.W. Norton, 1986.

Olson, L.K. *The not-so-golden years. Caregiving, the frail elderly and the long-term care establishment.* Lanham, UK: Rowman and Littlefield, 2003.

Ormstein, N.J. Enacting reform: What can we expect in the current political context? In S.H. Altman and D.I. Shactman, *Policies for an aging society.* Baltimore: Johns Hopkins Press, 2002.

Preston, S.H. Children and the elderly in the United States. *Scientific American,* 1984, *251,* 44–49.

Public Agenda Online. Accessed 2003, from http://www.publicagenda.org/issues/factfiles.cfm?issue_type=ss.

Purcell, P.J. Pension sponsorship and participation: Trends and policy issues. *Social Security Bulletin,* 2001–2002, *64,* 92–102.

Smalhout, J.H. Benefit design choices for personal Social Security accounts. *Benefits Quarterly,* 2002, *18,* 44–64.

Social Security Administration (SSA). *Fiscal Year 2006 Performance and accountability report. Overview of the Social Security Administration.* 2006a. Full report. Accessed March 16, 2007, from http://www.ssa.gov/finance/2006/FY06_PAR.pdf.

Social Security Administration (SSA). *Frequently asked questions about Social Security's future.* Washington, DC: Author, 2003.

Social Security Administration (SSA). *Income of the aged chart book, 2004.* SSA Publication No. 13–11727, Released September 2006b. Accessed http://www.ssa.gov/policy/docs/chartbooks/income_aged/2004/iac04.pdf.

Social Security Administration (SSA). *Social Security retirement benefits.* SSA Publication No. 05–10035, ICN 457500. January 2007a.

Accessed March 17, 2007, from http://www.ssa.gov/pubs/10035.pdf.

Social Security Administration (SSA). *SSI federal payment amounts.* Updated 2006c. Accessed March 1, 2007b, from http://www.ssa.gov/OACT/COLA/SSI.html.

Social Security Administration (SSA). *Updated long-term projections for Social Security.* June 2006d. Accessed March 17, 2007b, from http://www.cbo.gov/ftpdocs/72xx/doc7289/06–14-LongTermProjections.pdf.

Social Security and Medicare Boards of Trustees. *Status of the Social Security and Medicare Programs. A summary of the 2006 annual reports.* 2006. Accessed March 17, 2007c, from http://www.ssa.gov/OACT/TRSUM/trsummary.html.

Teles, S. Social Security and the paradoxes of welfare state conservatism. In R.H. Hudson (Ed.), *The new politics of old age policy.* Baltimore: Johns Hopkins Press, 2005.

Torres-Gill, F.M., and Moga, K. Multiculturalism, social policy and the new aging. *Journal of Gerontological Social Work,* 2001, *36,* 12–32.

Torres-Gil, F.M. *The new aging: Politics and change in America.* New York: Auburn House, 1992.

Walker, A. Aging and politics: An international perspective. In R. Binstock and L.K. George (Ed.), *Handbook of aging and the social sciences,* (6th ed.). New York: Academic Press, 2006.

Walker, D.M. Fiscal, Social Security, and health care challenges. Government Accountability Office (GAO). Accessed January 2007, from http://www.gao.gov/cghome/d07345cg.pdf.

Wan, H., Sengupta, M., Velkoff, V., and DeBarros, K., *65+ in the United States: 2005.* Washington, DC: U.S. Census Bureau, Current Population Reports, P23–P209, U.S. Government Printing Office, 2005.

White, J. The Social Security and Medicare debate three years after the 2000 election. *Public Policy and Aging Report,* 2003, *13,* 15–19.

Whitman, D., and Purcell, P. *Topics in aging: Income and poverty among older Americans.* Washington, DC: Congressional Research Service, 2004.

Williamson, J.B. What's next for Social Security? Partial privatization? *Generations,* 2002, *26,* 34–39.

Williamson, J.B., McNamara, T., and Howling, S. Generational equity, generational interdependence and the framing of the debate over Social Security reform. *Journal of Sociology and Social Welfare,* 2003, *30,* 3–14.

Williamson, J.B., Watts-Ray, D.M., and Kingson, E.R. The generational equity debate. In H.R. Moody, *Aging: Concepts and controversies* (4th ed.). Thousand Oaks, CA: Sage, 2002.

Wisensale, S.K. Global aging and intergenerational equity. *Journal of Intergenerational Relationships,* 2003, *1,* 29–46.

Wright, W., and Davies, C. *Retirement security survey report.* Washington, DC: AARP. February 19, 2007. Accessed March 1, 2007, from http://assets.aarp.org/rgcenter/econ/retirement_security.pdf.

Wu, K. *Income and Poverty of Older Americans in 2004.* AARP and Public Policy Institute, 2006.

Yee, D. Insuring health and income needs of future generations. *Generations,* 2005, *29,* 13–20.

Health and Long-Term Care Policy and Programs

This chapter covers

- Definitions, status, and expenditures for acute and long-term care
- Medicare, home care, cost-reductions, and the 2003 Medicare prescription drug bill
- The growing need for long-term care, especially home care
- Medicaid, community-based services, and nursing home care
- Private long-term care insurance, its costs and limitations
- Cost-containment initiatives, including Medicare managed care
- State innovations under Medicare and Medicaid

Throughout this book we have examined the interplay of social, physiological, and psychological factors in how older people relate to their environments, and how health status affects this interaction. Technological advances oriented toward cure have created the paradox that, while adults now live longer, they face serious, often debilitating or life-threatening disabilities that create the need for ongoing care. Although Chapter 4 notes that disability per se in old age does not create dependency, many older adults, especially among the oldest-old, are physically or mentally frail and depend on informal supports as well as medical and social services. This dependence is often intensified by the interaction of age, race, gender, poverty, and sexual orientation, as well as changes in family structure described in Chapter 9. And, as we have seen, the oldest-old, persons of color, women, and those who are low-income are most prone to have chronic disabilities that affect their ability to function.

As described in Chapter 11, *long-term care* (LTC) refers to a range of supportive services and assistance provided to persons who, as a result of chronic illness or disability, are unable to function autonomously on a daily basis. The need for LTC does not necessarily correspond to medical conditions, but rather to problems with performing *activities of daily living (ADL)*—bathing, dressing, toileting, eating, and transferring—and *instrumental activities of daily living (IADL)*—shopping, cooking, and cleaning. LTC services are oriented toward managing and living with chronic illness, not curing them, and aim to ensure continuity of care rather than episodic interventions. LTC currently is neither an integrated system of care nor comprehensive policy; instead, it is characterized by incremental, oftentimes fragmented services to minimize, rehabilitate, or compensate for the loss of functioning, and to enhance functional capabilities. As described in Chapter 10, LTC services, which are largely "low-tech" assistance with basic activities, are nevertheless increasingly complicated because individuals with complex medical needs are discharged shortly after hospitalization for an acute epidode. Since nursing homes are the major setting for long-term care, many older people and their families first think of them when they consider such care. However, as seen in Chapter 11, the boundaries between LTC in institutional and noninstitutional environments are becoming blurred, because such services are increasingly provided in home- and community-based care settings and alternatives to nursing homes, such as assisted living, board and care, adult family homes, and adult day centers. Services provided within *home and residential care settings* encompass personal assistance, assistive devices and technology as described in Chapter 11. Those delivered in *community-based settings* include services funded by the Older Americans Act (described in Chapter 16) as well as respite, hospice, and transportation.

Although LTC services also are provided to younger adults with chronic physical and

> ### CHARACTERISTICS OF LONG-TERM CARE
>
> - It is targeted at persons of all ages who have functional disabilities.
> - Disabilities may be physical or mental, transitory, or permanent.
> - Aim is to enhance autonomy in functional abilities and quality of life, including the right to die with dignity.
> - It encompasses a wide range of services, professions, and settings of care.
> - Care addresses physical, mental, social, and financial aspects of a person's life.
> - Care is intended to be organized around the distinctive needs of each individual and family.
> - Services change over time as the patient's and family's circumstances change.
> - Unlike hospital services, it is not widely insured.
> - Funding sources are a patchwork of federal, state, and local governments; private foundations; and out of pocket.

mental illness, developmental disabilities, HIV/AIDS, and increasingly service-connected disabilities specifically through the Veterans Administration (VA), the focus of this discussion is on the structural, funding, and regulatory aspects of LTC services for older people. Overall, nearly 60 percent of those who report using LTC are age 65 or older. As described in Chapter 4, the need for such services is rapidly growing, especially among the oldest-old, who are the most vulnerable in terms of mental and physical health. While 4.5 percent of adults age 65 and over are in nursing homes at any one time, more than 12 percent in the community have ADL or IADL restrictions. Among those age 85 and over, the corresponding rates increase to 21 and 51 percent, respectively. About 49 percent of all elders will reside in a nursing home, if only for a short time period (for over 50 percent of these, less than a year) before they are discharged to community settings. *Upon discharge*, 75 percent of those over age 65 require some degree of home health care or personal assistance (Schmieding, 2006; Seperson, 2002; Stone, 2006). Although the health care system has traditionally emphasized primary and acute care, the boundaries with LTC are becoming less clear. In fact, our "acute" health care system is increasingly devoted to chronic care by various providers in a range of settings (Stone, 2000). Given the high incidence of chronic health needs, it is not surprising that health and LTC costs are among the most critical and controversial policy issues facing our nation.

Chapter 10 documented that informal networks provide the majority of LTC. After informal supports, the next most common providers are paraprofessionals or direct care workers such as certified nursing assistants in nursing homes or home care workers who deliver low-tech personal care and assistance with daily life tasks. Women predominate among these groups, comprising 75 percent of family caregivers and 90 to 96 percent of direct care workers (DHHS, 2003). In contrast to physicians who play a key role in acute-care hospital settings, nurses and ancillary therapists, who also are primarily women, are the major care providers within nursing homes. We turn next to examining the problem of rising health and LTC costs, and the factors underlying these.

Health and Long-Term Care Expenditures

Policy makers, service providers, and the general public are all concerned about the "crisis in health care." This crisis refers to the costs, the growing numbers of uninsured individuals of all ages, and the status and future of health care systems. People over 65 account for over 30 percent of the nation's annual federal health care expenditures. In fact, the average expenditure for health services for adults age 65 and over is nearly four times the cost for those under age 65 and increases even

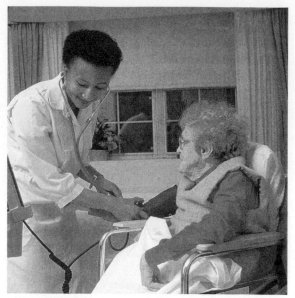

Preventive health services can reduce long-term care costs over time.

more among the oldest-old. Of all LTC expenditures in the United States (e.g., nursing home, home health care), nearly 70 percent are for people age 65 and over, or roughly $15,000 per person, with most costs paid out-of-pocket (Berkman, et al., 2005; Moon, 2006; Stone, 2006). Figure 17.1 shows dramatic spending increases by 2050, with families carrying the primary burden.

Although cost-containment changes in the private health care marketplace, such as managed care, are intended to slow the rate of acute health care costs, expenses are still rising faster than the cost of living. Spending on Medicare and Medicaid, which consumes approximately 26 percent of the federal budget, is expanding at several times the economic growth rate, adding to political demands for reform in order to reduce federal expenditures (Moon, 2006). Even though public expenditures for health and long-term care through Medicare, Medicaid, and the Veterans Administration are growing, older

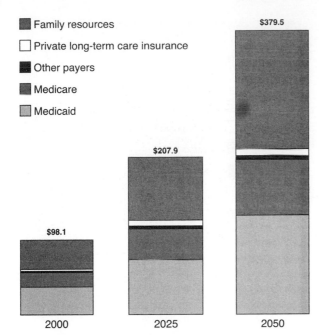

FIGURE 17.1 **Billions of 1999 Dollars Projected to Be Spent on Long-Term Care**
Note: The projected expenditure increases assume reductions in mortality of 0.6 percent a year and 0.6 percent a year in disability rates in the older population, current age- and sex-specific use rates for institutional and home care services, static public policies, and a real inflation rate of 1.2 percent for long-term care services.
SOURCE: *Urban Institute, 2001.*

the older population's ability to pay. At the same time, private health insurance costs are growing more rapidly than Medicare spending, and increases are greatest for home health and skilled nursing homes.

Factors Underlying Growing Costs

A number of structural factors underlie escalating health care costs.

- The success of modern medical care: Costs have grown in the overall number of visits to health care providers as well as the type and complexity of services. Although advances in medical science produce cost-saving break-throughs, they also make possible more sophisticated and expensive medical treat-ments. These tend to be used in addition to prior services rather than replacements for old technologies or procedures. For example, an older patient now may receive X-rays, CAT scans, and MRIs to diagnose a problem, whereas only X-rays would have been used in the past.
- Related to the success of medical technology in prolonging life is the conflict between the curative goals of medicine and the chronic-care needs of older adults. As a result, there is a poor fit between the long-term medical and social service needs of the older population and the funding mechanisms, regulations, and fragmented services of the health care system that is oriented toward acute care.
- Comprehensive, coordinated health and long-term care policy and programs that integrate acute and chronic care are limited, although demonstration projects at the state level provide some models of integrated care.

individuals and their families continue to pay more out of pocket for health care than do younger Americans. Older people now spend a higher proportion (and more in actual dollars) of their incomes on health care services than they did before Medicare and Medicaid were established in 1965 (28 versus 11 percent, respectively) (Federal Interagency Forum on Aging, 2006). Part of this increase is due to the rising costs of prescription drugs. In addition, long-term care costs have grown from less than 4 percent in 1960 to over 12 percent today (Stone, 2006). The distribution and sources of personal health care expenditures are illustrated in Figure 17.2. In sum, the financial burdens of health care are expected to expand faster than

As seen in Chapter 16, some powerful values and assumptions underlie these structural fac-tors. These include a distrust of government and its ability to fund health care, and a strong belief

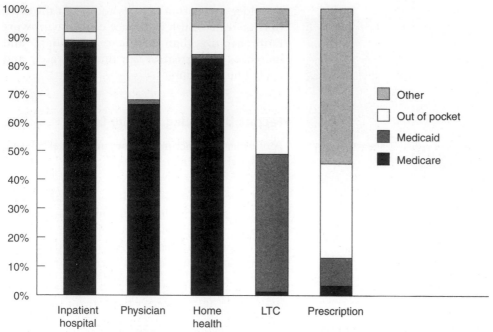

FIGURE 17.2   Estimated Personal Health Care Expenditures for Medicare Enrollees: 2003
SOURCE: Federal Interagency Forum on Aging, 2006

in the private sector. They combine to produce an approach to LTC and health care that is determined largely by the market or who provides the best services at lowest cost. In other words, the shape of health care is largely influenced by its method of payment. Health services are provided privately, without effective market control or uniform government regulation of expenditures. Patients have been largely free to choose the health care providers they prefer. In turn, physicians have been able to charge patients whatever they choose. Nevertheless, most health services are financed by a mix of public programs, private insurance, and direct patient payments. Federal and state efforts to limit health care expenditures are now the norm. Modifications to this fee-for-service system in order to control costs, such as Preferred Provider Plans (PPPs) and managed care, are described below.

A fundamental problem for older people is not funding per se but the fact that acute and long-term care remain two separate fragmented systems, with relatively distinct providers, treatment settings, financing structures, and goals, although some states have tried to integrate the two. Physicians are the primary care providers in hospitals and outpatient settings, covered mostly by Medicare. Nursing staff, direct care workers, and family members are the principal providers of LTC in nursing homes and private home settings. Medicaid pays for a large percentage of institutional care and, increasingly, home-based care. In the acute-care setting, intensity of services that are oriented toward cure determines costs, compared to duration of services in chronic care settings. The different purposes of Medicaid and Medicare are significant barriers to the integration of these two systems. Fortunately, there are a growing number of initiatives, primarily at the state level, to integrate systems of care, discussed on the next page.

EXAMPLES OF INTEGRATED CARE PLANS

The **National Chronic Care Consortium (NCCC)** is an alliance of over 30 nonprofit health systems that share a vision of integrated care. Member organizations serve as laboratories for establishing chronic-care networks. The Consortium advocates the creation of integrated administration, information, financing, and care management arrangements to help providers work together to minimize costs while maximizing the long-term health of the populations being served. It has developed the Self-Assessment for Systems Integration, funded by the John A. Hartford Foundation, that identifies nine key objectives for chronic care integration.

Innovations in Transitional Care

When older people must be moved between the acute care of hospital settings to long-term care settings—and perhaps back again—they often experience discontinuities of care (e.g., conflicting medical advice, medication errors, and inadequate follow-up care) and a lack of coordination that increases their vulnerability. Transitional care is the relatively brief time interval that begins with preparing a patient to leave one setting and concludes when the patient is received in the next. Transitions are often unplanned, result from unanticipated medical problems, occur on nights or weekends, involve clinicians who may not have an ongoing relationship with the older patient, and happen so quickly that formal and informal support systems cannot adequately respond. A Colorado medical center developed the Care Transitions Intervention where patients receive specific skills and tools that are reinforced by a "transition coach" who follows them across settings for the first 30 days after leaving the hospital. This "patient-centered care" encompasses four areas: medication self-management, creation of a personal health record maintained by the patient, timely follow-up care, and developing a plan to best seek care if particular symptoms arise. Patients who participated in this intervention were less likely to require re-hospitalization in the first 30 days, significantly cutting their health care costs, especially hospital costs. Positive effects continued up to six months later. Given its favorable impact on both costs and quality of care, this intervention has been implemented in 12 health care organizations nationwide, with funding from the John A. Hartford Foundation (Coleman and Berenson, 2004).

Medicare

As a social insurance system, **Medicare,** or Title XVIII of the Social Security Act of 1965, is intended to provide financial protection against the cost of hospital and physician care for people age 65 and over. It thus provides insurance to older people who are typically retired and lack access to employer-provided group insurance. Prior to the passage of Medicare, only about 50 percent of older adults had health insurance. A value underlying Medicare is that people are entitled to access to *acute medical care* on the basis of age, and society has an obligation to cover the costs associated with inpatient hospital care. Medicare's focus on the older population grew out of a compromise with the medical profession, which successfully opposed comprehensive health insurance for the general public. Yet Medicare was also viewed as the "first step" toward increasing access to health care for all age groups. Despite Medicare's goal of financial protection, it covers less than 50 percent of older adults' health expenditures (Moon, 2005, 2006). As noted earlier and illustrated in Figures 17.1 and 17.2, the remainder is paid by older people out-of-pocket by private supplemental insurance, by Medicaid, and by other public payers such as the Veterans Administration. Medicare accounts for about 17 percent of national LTC spending, including 13 percent of nursing home care and nearly 30 percent of home health care (Congressional Budget Office, 2004; CMS, 2005).

Contrary to many older adults' assumptions that their acute health care costs will be covered, Medicare pays only 80 percent of the allowable charges, not the actual amount charged by health providers. The patient must pay the difference between "allowable" and "actual" charges, unless the physician accepts "assignment" and agrees to charge only what Medicare pays. Beneficiaries whose doctors do not accept Medicare assignments are responsible for the amount that their doctor charges above the Medicare-approved rate, as illustrated by the vignette about

Medicare has been an important part of older adults'
health insurance since its inception in 1965.
SOURCE: Social Security Administration History Website
http://www.ssa.gov/history/history.html

Mr. Fox on page 728. Medicare beneficiaries must
also pay an annual deductible and copayments.

Medicare is composed of Part A (Hospital
Insurance) and Part B (Supplemental Medical
Insurance), both of which are funded through pay-
roll tax deductions for Social Security, although
not all people age 65 and over can afford Part B.
Services covered under Medicare are illustrated in

Figure 17.3. Medicare's major limitation for older
adults with chronic illness is its focus on acute care
(e.g., inpatient hospital and physicians). As shown
in this figure, Medicare provides limited coverage
for chronic-care expenses (e.g., only 100 days of
skilled nursing home care; lack of dental care and
social work services); and minimal coverage for
preventive care. The majority of Medicare dollars
pays for hospital care, typically for catastrophic illness and for home care only under restricted conditions. Nursing home care is limited to 100 days
of skilled care or rehabilitation services, with eligibility contingent on acute illness or injury after
hospitalization and requiring co-payments. This
automatically excludes ongoing care for chronic
conditions or disabilities. As a result, Medicare
covers 45 percent of all health care spending for
older people, but a smaller proportion for the
oldest-old who require more long-term care. In
fact, less than 29 percent of the total Medicare
budget covers nursing home expenditures. Accordingly, Medicare pays for the long-term care
expenses of only 3 to 5 percent of elders in residen-
tial-care settings. In a 2001 AARP survey, most
respondents underestimated nursing home care
costs, and over 33 percent mistakenly believed that

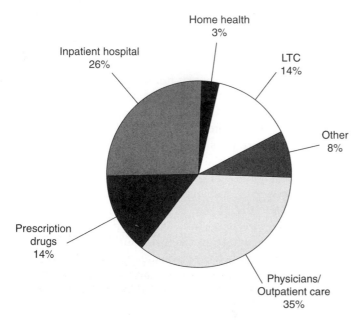

**FIGURE 17.3   Medicare Personal Health
Care Spending in 2003**
SOURCE: Federal Interagency Forum on Aging, 2006

Medicare covered LTC expenses (Barrett and Roper, 2001). In fact, some older adults become aware of Medicare's limited protection only upon their first hospitalization or admission to a nursing home (Berenson and Horvath, 2003).

Another limitation of Medicare is lack of **parity** of mental health services. This means that coverage for mental health is substantially limited compared to that for physical illness. For example, Medicare has a lifetime limit on inpatient psychiatric treatment, while there is no lifetime limit on general hospital care. For outpatient mental health services, Medicare requires beneficiaries to pay 50 percent, compared with only 20 percent for all other outpatient services. Providing less Medicare coverage for mental health services than for general health services is problematic; it financially discriminates against those seeking treatment for psychological disorders and perpetuates the stigma of mental health care as different from general health care (Sakauye et al., 2005).

Medicare coverage of mental health services has not changed since the program's inception in 1965, when many believed that mental illnesses resulted from moral defects or character flaws. Given the high rates of depression, dementia, and anxiety disorders among older people, mental

health parity under Medicare is a critical policy issue. There has been little public opposition to parity for mental health in Medicare, yet multiple bills in both the House and the Senate have been stuck in committee for at least the last 10 years. In June 2002, President Bush endorsed mental health parity and pushed for a compromise between both sides of the parity argument, but again, nothing has yet come from this endorsement.

Medicare-Funded Home Health Care

Of all health care expenditures, only about 2.4 percent is for home health care. A past gap in Medicare funding had been home- and community-based care, but now this is the most rapidly growing Medicare benefit and the fastest growing component of the overall health care sector (Caitlin et al., 2007). With over 20 percent of nursing home placements estimated to be incongruent with older persons' needs, home care is widely advocated as the lower-cost preferred alternative to inappropriate nursing home placement. Even elders in nursing homes or hospitals may require home care at some point, since 50 percent of elders who stay less than 3 months are able to return to the community. As described in Chapter 11, home care can cut costs through

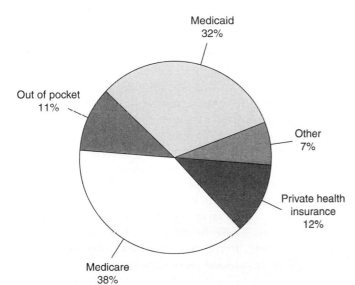

FIGURE 17.4   Spending for Home Health Care: 2004

SOURCE: Cynthia Smith, Cathy Cowan, Stephen Hettler, and Aaron Caitlin, "National Health Spending in 2004," *Health Affairs 25* (1) (2006) 186–196. Reprinted with permission.

earlier discharges and thus reduced days of hospital care. Not only do most older people require home care, but they also prefer it and tend to recover faster at home, when there is continuity of care (Kane and Kane, 2001). Over time, Medicare has responded to the need for home care, and can now provide unlimited home health care for accredited provider agencies, but only under specific restricted conditions, as noted in the box below. If these criteria are met, Medicare will fund the cost of other services, including home health aides and medical equipment and supplies. In addition, home health care services are available for as long as beneficiaries remain eligible, without any burden of co-payments or deductibles. But any personal assistance must be directly related to the medical treatment of an illness or injury, and social work services for non-medical conditions are not covered (Berenson and Horvath, 2003). Given elders' preference for home care, it is not surprising that the number of beneficiaries and the average number of visits per user have grown dramatically. Almost one in 10 Medicare beneficiaries have a home health visit during a given year. This translates into Medicare financing almost 38 percent of home care compared with funding by state and local sources, including Medicaid (32 percent) and out-of-pocket (11 percent), as shown in Figure 17.4 on page 723 (CMS, 2005).

> ### ELIGIBILITY FOR MEDICARE-REIMBURSED HOME CARE
>
> - Person must be homebound.
> - Person must be capable of improvement.
> - Person must require short-term intermittent nursing care, physical, occupational, or speech therapy, not long-term personal care.
> - All services and durable medical equipment must be prescribed by a physician, who presents a plan for recovery and certifies that skilled services are medically necessary.

Whether home care is cost-effective varies with the person's condition and the range and duration of services. In general, home health care is less expensive than hospital care, about 40 percent less than nursing homes, and comparable to adult foster care or adult family homes. However, costs become more comparable if 24-hour care is needed. In one study, home health agencies that were Medicare-certified recorded the actual costs of providing an array of services (e.g., skilled nursing care, physical therapy, home dialysis, and hospice). A U-shaped curve was found to be most cost-efficient; that is, a scope of 8 to 10 different services appears to be ideal for reducing the average cost of services provided by a home health agency. Those that provide either fewer or more services do so at a higher cost per visit; this suggests that home care agencies can function most economically if they provide an array of 8 to 10 services per client (Gonzales, 1997).

Another study examined hospital-use data among home health clients in a meta-analysis of 20 earlier studies. When home health was defined strictly as the delivery of nursing, medical, and support services in the home of a terminally or chronically ill older person, home health users had 2.5 to 6 fewer days of hospital use, compared to similar patient populations that did not use home health care. These results support the cost-effectiveness of home health care in curtailing the use of far more expensive acute care (Hughes et al., 1997). However, it is important to assess each elder's specific health care needs when initiating home care services. In one study of more than 7000 home care recipients age 75 and older, African American elders had few support services beyond home care. Asians and Latinos showed less improvement in their physical functioning than African Americans and whites, and white elders had more depressive symptoms than the other groups. These needs were not being addressed by their home care providers (Peng, Navaie-Waliser, and Feldman, 2003).

THE COST OF PRIVATE CARE

Mrs. R., age 87, suffers from severe osteoporosis and arthritis. Although she worries about falling, she wants to stay in her home as long as possible. Since she is not eligible for any publicly funded home care program, she must pay out of pocket for daily assistance with bathing, walking, and cooking. Her daughter is employed and has a family to care for, but tries to stay with her mother on weekends and assist her with household chores. Because the cost of home care is so much greater than her income, Mrs. R.'s savings are dwindling. She and her daughter worry that she will have to go into a nursing home as a Medicaid patient after her savings have been depleted.

A number of factors underlie the extraordinary growth in Medicare-funded *home health care services:*

1. Earlier hospital discharges as a result of the 1983 Prospective Payment Systems mean that patients require more technical care at home. Home care serves as the "safety net" for patients being discharged from acute and rehabilitation settings after shorter stays.

2. A 1989 class action lawsuit created a more flexible interpretation of definitions (homebound), scope of services (both management and evaluation), regulations (part-time or intermittent care) and skilled nursing assessments, not just skilled nursing care. In addition, some home health care remains a brief recovery "subacute" service, usually after a hospital stay. Medicare-funded home health benefits thus provide the short- and some long-term needs of beneficiaries.

3. The number of proprietary, or for-profit, home health agencies that are reimbursed under Medicare has increased dramatically. For-profit chains grew in response to the 1980 and 1981 Omnibus Budget Reconciliation Acts. These eliminated the requirement for state licensing as a basis for reimbursing proprietary agencies. These

regulatory changes served to stimulate competition for the provision and contracting out of services to new proprietary agencies, including managed care. Such agencies, however, are less likely to concentrate on the ambulatory care of older people after hospital discharge. The 1997 Federal Balanced Budget Amendment re-asserted that Medicare home care is only available for post-acute care patients and cut home care funding. This resulted in a 2-year temporary slowdown, which was later reversed by expanded funding in 1999–2000.

4. There are isolated instances of Medicare–certified home health agencies not complying with federal health and safety standards, overcharging, fraud and abuse, and providing substandard care.

5. High-tech home therapy, such as intravenous antibiotics, oncology therapy, and pain management, continues to grow. Such care involves expensive pharmaceuticals and equipment that require special staff expertise to use and monitor, and is costly to the patient or insurer.

Home health services are delivered by over 11,000 agencies nationwide, many of which are dually certified to serve the needs of both Medicare and Medicaid. The field, however, has shifted from primarily Visiting Nurses Associations and public agencies to hospital-based, including the Veterans Administration and private for-profit or nonprofit agencies. The data suggest that Medicare beneficiaries are using home health for longer periods and for less medically intensive services (e.g., more long-term, unskilled personal care by home health aides) for a recovery period after hospital discharge. This has translated into home health aide visits that are lucrative for the agencies, because less skilled and therefore less costly care is still highly compensated by Medicare. On the other hand, incentives for home health agencies to spend as little as possible could place patients who need the most skilled care at greatest risk.

The number of for-profit home health corporations that serve primarily private-pay and contract patients is also growing. They fill the demand for home care by patients who, because of age or type of need, do not qualify for Medicare or Medicaid. In general, they offer more services than Medicare-certified agencies. In contrast to the intermittent skilled visits of Medicare home care agencies, noncertified private agencies can provide 24-hour daily care for an indefinite period, as well as specialty services. They also offer homemaker/home health aide care services, typically on an on-call basis. As with all LTC, recruiting and retaining quality part-time contractual staff is problematic. A dilemma for families, however, is that many private agencies, especially those affiliated with large nationwide chains, require a minimum number of hours of care (typically 8-hour shifts), which can become prohibitively expensive.

Efforts to Reduce Medicare Costs

Medicare currently forms over 12 percent of the federal budget, the fourth largest expenditure following Social Security, defense, and interest on the national debt. Total Medicare spending is projected to grow by 10 percent per year over the next decade, just to provide the same level of services for a growing Medicare population. The Trustees of the Hospital Insurance Trust Fund continue to warn Congress of the need to restore the balance between income and spending in order to reduce insolvency, which is projected to occur in 2019 (Kaiser Family Foundation, 2004b). The threats to the Medicare trust fund are more immediate than those to Social Security, due largely to the rising cost of health care combined with the decreasing number of workers paying taxes relative to the number of beneficiaries (i.e., the age-dependency ratio discussed in Chapters 1 and 16).

Several measures over the past 20 years have attempted to reduce Medicare costs:

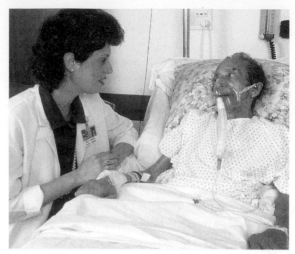

Medicare reform seeks to reduce the spiraling costs of hospitalization.

1. Diagnostic related groupings (DRGs), were instituted in 1983 to reduce incentives for physicians to provide more hospital-bed services under fee-for-service payment plans. Instead of reimbursing providers per service for each patient, Medicare payments were fixed prior to admission, based on the diagnostic category, medical condition, and expected length of stay for each patient. A hospital that keeps patients longer than needed or orders unnecessary tests must absorb the cost difference between the care provided and the amount reimbursed by Medicare. Alternatively, hospitals that provide care at a cost below the established DRG can keep the financial difference. This serves as an incentive for hospitals to release patients as soon as possible, putting pressure on nursing homes to provide sub-acute care and on families to assume more responsibility.

Although findings are mixed, DRGs appear to have reduced both lengths of stay per hospital admission and number of admissions. This is partially explained by the trend toward performing simple surgical and diagnostic procedures on an outpatient rather than an inpatient basis, usually in ambulatory settings and

SUMMARY OF COMPONENTS OF MEDICARE

Hospital Insurance (Part A)

- Covers 99 percent of the older population.
- Financed through the Social Security payroll tax of 2.9 percent.
- Available for all older persons who are eligible for Social Security.
- Pays up to 90 days of hospital care and for a restricted amount of skilled nursing care, rehabilitation, home health services (if skilled care is needed), and hospice care.
- Recipients are responsible for their first day's hospital stay and for copayments for hospital stays exceeding 60 days.
- When the 90 days of hospital care are used up, a patient has a "lifetime reserve" of 60 days.

Supplemental Medical Insurance (Part B)

- Covers 97 percent of the older population.
- Financed through a combination of monthly premiums and general tax revenues.
- Annual $100 deductible.
- Generally pays 80 percent of physician and hospital outpatient services; home health care limited to certain types of health conditions and specific time periods; diagnostic laboratory and X-ray services, and a variety of miscellaneous services, including 50 percent of the approved amount for outpatient mental health care.

doctors' offices. In addition, DRGs discourage the extra time required to make appropriate discharge plans and the use of ancillary personnel such as social workers, except to expedite hospital discharges (Olson, 2003). Early studies found patients being discharged on average 2 days earlier and sicker than before DRGs (Gaumer et al., 1989; Sager et al., 1989). Later studies suggest that findings of greater need for care and higher rates of mortality may be due, in part, to differences in risk factors (e.g., the inpatient population is now older and sicker than before DRGs were instituted), not because of shorter stays or declining quality of care. Nevertheless, quality of care may be affected by earlier

hospital discharge and restrictions on physician payment levels (Moon, 2006; Stone, 2006), as illustrated by the experience of Mr. Jones in the box below. While length of hospital stays has declined, DRGs have not reduced all the incentives for applying costly high-tech care. In fact, the use of specialists and improved procedures such as knee and cataract surgeries continue to increase, despite other efforts to reduce Medicare costs.

2. Congress passed the *Medicare Catastrophic Health Care Act* (MCHCA) in 1988 to reduce costs. Expanded benefits were to be financed by a mandatory supplemental premium, which meant that higher-income older adults would pay a surtax for benefits serving primarily low-income elders. This surtax affected approximately 40 percent of older adults, many of whom organized rapidly against changes in the basic premise of Medicare financing, which is its universal nature for all persons age 65 and older (Grogan, 2005). In 1989, Congress voted to repeal the legislation in response to this public outcry, leaving many legislators wary of making

THE COSTS OF EARLY DISCHARGE

Mr. Jones underwent major surgery—a radical prostatectomy for prostate cancer. Despite the pain that he was still experiencing, he was discharged after 3 days in the hospital and had to return home with a catheter in place that required careful monitoring by a physician or nurse. His wife was in her late 80s and unable to provide the skilled care that a catheter requires. He was extremely fatigued. With only his frail wife to care for him, he required the services of a visiting nurse. He continued to experience considerable pain for which his medication was inadequate; if he could have remained in the hospital, his pain could have been relieved by an anesthesiologist. Perhaps the most difficult issue was his uncertainty and anxiety about a variety of symptoms, such as loss of appetite, which could have been resolved with a somewhat longer hospital stay.

changes in Medicare until the 2003 prescription drug bill.

3. In 1992, reforms were implemented to limit Medicare spending on physician care. This established a physician fee schedule and a system of limiting payment increases when the total cost of physician services billed in a year exceeds estimated levels. It also limited the amount doctors can charge above the approved Medicare rate.

4. In an effort to maintain the solvency of Medicare, the 1997 Federal Balanced Budget Agreement cut $115 billion in Medicare payments to doctors, hospitals, and HMOs, the largest reduction in the program's history. It also aimed to limit escalating home health care costs and services. The **Centers for Medicare and Medicaid Services (CMS),** the federal agency that approves or denies Medicare claims, froze the licensing of new home health agencies. The **prospective payment system (PPS),** of which DRGs are one component, substantially reduced Medicare's payment for home health care by implementing new payment methods for post-acute (after hospitalization) services. Instead of separate payments for each visit, fixed payments were determined in advance for a general course of treatment. Similar to the DRG system limiting length of hospital stays, home care agencies and nursing homes are reimbursed with the **payments capitated** per patient per episode of service. This has resulted in reducing the number of visits and average cost per visit. Another iteration of PPS is the **Interim Payment System (IPS),** which sets more stringent caps on costs per home health visit and a cap per beneficiary. The IPS discouraged increases in number of visits per beneficiary but also reduced access for those with high-cost chronic care needs (Spector, Cohen, and Pesis-Katz, 2004).

As a result of these changes, many home health agencies, which had expanded with Medicare funding in the early 1990s, closed and patients were dropped from care. Reductions occurred in the proportion of Medicare beneficiaries who received the service; the number of

home health visits per beneficiary; the average length of home health care; the value of the services, and—as intended—overall Medicare expenditures (McCall and Korb, 2003). Despite the dramatic reductions in home care service use, IPS does not appear to have resulted in more adverse outcomes following hospital discharge (Spector et al., 2004).

5. The National Bipartisan Commission on the Future of Medicare was created by Congress in 1997 to study how Medicare can accommodate baby boomers. Some of the commission's recommendations were controversial, including giving beneficiaries a fixed amount of money to purchase private health insurance and to raise the age of Medicare eligibility from 65 to 67. Unable to achieve sufficient unity to forward official recommendations to Congress, the commission was disbanded in 1999. No bipartisan commissions on Medicare have been appointed since then.

6. Because of the 1997 cuts in funding, Medicare expenses declined in 1999. In response, a massive lobbying campaign to restore and expand funding was mounted by national associations of nurses, physicians, nursing home operators, hospitals, managed care organizations, and the home

---

MEDICARE PAYS ONLY PARTIAL HEALTH CARE COSTS

Mr. Fox went to his physician for a sigmoidoscopy, a procedure to examine the large colon for polyps or cancer. His physician charges $300 for his part of this procedure. Medicare determined that the typical fee for a sigmoidoscopy in Mr. Fox's community is $180, which means that Medicare pays the physician 80 percent of that amount, or $144. If Mr. Fox's physician accepts the assignment, then Mr. Fox owes his doctor the difference between $180 and $144, or $36. Fortunately, Mr. Fox has private "Medigap" insurance that covers this difference. If Mr. Fox's physician had not accepted assignment, then Mr. Fox would have been responsible for paying $300 less the amount paid by Medicare ($144) or a total of $156.

care industry; these providers threatened reduced access to services if Medicare funding was not restored to address the 1997 cuts. As a result of this intensive lobbying effort, Congress restored billions of dollars to various providers in 1999 and 2000.

7. Consistent with the current federal concern with accountability, Medicare is focusing on health outcomes and investing in information systems to target outcomes of specific high-cost diseases (Lee, 2006).

Initiatives to curb home health expenditures have lowered the number of users, average number of visits, and length of stay. Nevertheless, Medicare-funded home health care costs continue to grow, which suggests that more intensive and expensive services are being provided to high-cost participants (Spector et al., 2004). Ultimately, Medicare's fiscal problems are rooted in the overall increases in health care spending, predicted to grow from 15.3 percent of the Gross Domestic Product in 2004 to 25 percent in 2030 (MedPac, 2004). As noted by AARP (2005, p. 9), the "problem is not Medicare and Medicaid—the problem is health care."

The 2000 and 2004 presidential and congressional elections set the tone, temperament, and direction of budget, tax, and entitlement politics. Not surprisingly, Republicans and Democrats differ on the nature and size of cuts in Medicare, although both agree that changes are needed to address Medicare's long-term solvency. Republicans advocate increased application of competitive market principles to health care, privatization, such as individual health care accounts, and private insurance options. Proponents of privatization argue that more choices for consumers will lead to increased competition and, in turn, lower costs. But there is no evidence that increased competition would reduce Medicare costs, in part because more health plans will increase administrative costs and older adults would have to switch plans almost annually, which most are unlikely to do (Herd, 2005; Moon and Herd, 2002; Rice and Desmond,

2002). The shift to privatization, however, is reflected in the 2003 Medicare reform prescription drug bill implemented in 2006. It is discussed on page 730.

The New Medicare

The Federal Balanced Budget Act of 1997 also established the Medicare Plus Choice with dual goals of cost-savings and quality of care. This allows Medicare to pay for a wider range of preventive services, including mammograms, PAP smears, cervical exams, prostate screening, bone-density measurement procedures, diabetes screening and self-care, and vaccinations. The result, however, has been that some beneficiaries, typically those who are healthier and with higher incomes, have more choice in where and how they obtain health care. The choices available include:

1. Medicare **Health Maintenance Organizations/Preferred Provider Organizations (HMOs/PPOs):** Networks of independent hospitals, physicians, and other health care providers who contract with an insurance entity to provide care at discount rates. Medicare beneficiaries who join HMOs are given incentives to use HMO/PPO physicians in order to reduce costs. They may also use providers outside the network, but at higher out-of-pocket costs (See page 746 for more descriptions of Medicare HMOs).

2. Purchase of private insurance, including long-term care insurance (see page 743 for a discussion of such insurance).

3. Establishment of **medical savings accounts,** which allow beneficiaries to put what they would have paid in payroll taxes for Medicare into a tax-exempt account to pay for qualified medical expenses.

The medical savings account is combined with a high-deductible insurance policy to cover catastrophic injuries or illness. Advocates of these accounts believe that older adults will

> ### STRATEGIES PROPOSED TO REDUCE MEDICARE COSTS
>
> - Limit eligibility for the next cohort of Medicare recipients by increasing the age of eligibility to 67.
> - Bill enrollees $5 for home health visits.
> - Ration services by age.
> - Use an income test as a basis for eligibility.
> - Increase the combined payroll tax from 2.9 to 4.11 percent.
> - Increase coinsurance and deductibles to shift more financial risk onto the beneficiaries.
> - Increase Supplemental Medical Insurance premiums (Part B) for higher-income beneficiaries.
> - Reduce the coverage of services and the reimbursement given to providers.

become more cost-conscious because elders themselves, not their insurers, will decide where to seek care. Critics contend that only the wealthier and healthier older adults can afford such a plan. In general, most older adults have not benefited from the array of programs funded by Medicare Plus Choice. With all its options, this federal program begins to look more like a private health care system than a publicly funded base of services for all older adults.

Other strategies to reduce Medicare costs continue to be debated at the national level, as illustrated in the box above. Raising the age of eligibility from 65 to 67 is proposed most often, even though the cost savings would not be substantial (Moon, 2006). Contrary to these proposed changes, the majority of Americans agree that the federal government has a basic responsibility to guarantee adequate health care for older people and oppose cost-cutting. It is also noteworthy that while Medicare is the current focus of many cost-cutting debates, per capita costs remain below those of private insurers. One major reason for this is that Medicare is administratively far more efficient than most private insurers or HMOs (less than 3 percent vs. an average of 13 percent for overhead) (Davis, 2004). In addition, Medicare is more efficient at

controlling overall health care costs than the private sector (Herd, 2005; Moon, 2006).

Medicare Reform and Prescription Drug Coverage

The most dramatic and controversial change since Medicare's passage is **Medicare Part D,** the prescription drug bill passed by Congress in November 2003, after the longest roll call vote in the House chamber's history. What was not disputed is the need for prescription drug coverage for older adults. As noted in Chapter 4, over 90 percent of older people use at least one prescription medication. Adults age 65 and over account for over 40 percent of total spending by all age groups on medications, and have consistently spent more (approximately 50 percent of their out-of-pocket health expenditures) on prescription drugs than younger adults. In fact, Medicare beneficiaries in the past spent more, on average, out of pocket each year on prescription drugs than on physician care, vision services, and medical supplies combined. In addition, the price of the most commonly used drugs has increased by

The new prescription drug benefit of Medicare was intended to help elders manage the rising costs of their medications.

three times the rate of inflation and is expected to grow by 12 percent a year through 2011.

Of grave concern is the 40 percent of Medicare beneficiaries who have had no prescription drug coverage at some point each year. Medicare beneficiaries in 2001 who did not have drug coverage and who were in poor health averaged 27 prescriptions a year, while those with supplemental coverage and similar medical needs averaged 42 per year. Those without drug coverage tend to restrict their medications because of cost; they skip filling prescriptions, split drug amounts (e.g., breaking pills in half), eliminate doses, or rely on physician samples, all of which can result in adverse reactions and, over time, increase health care costs, especially for acute exacerbations of their chronic diseases (Federal Interagency Forum, 2006; Goulding, 2005; Kaiser Family Foundation, 2006; Safran et al., 2006; Sambamoorthi, Shea, and Crystal, 2003). The lack of prescription drug coverage under Medicare is a historical accident: When Medicare was enacted in 1965, drugs were less numerous and not a central part of medical treatment. Now, prescription drugs are often the primary means of treatment for elders with chronic illness, and account for 11 percent of every health care dollar spent (Schmieding, 2006).

Because of the lack of restrictions on drug prices in the United States, profit margins for drug companies surpass those of nearly every economic sector. Pharmaceutical lobbyists argue that such costs are necessary to cover research and testing of new, high-risk drugs. Admittedly, the research to produce new drugs is expensive and may yield only one or two FDA-approved drugs after years of testing. On the other hand, critics argue, what good are research and new drugs if no one can afford them? They maintain that too many dollars are spent on marketing and advertising drugs. Such costs and lack of coverage were hot issues in the 2000 presidential campaign, and the debate regarding ways to provide coverage has been long-running.

What was disputed in Congressional debates over the prescription drug bill was not the need

but rather the best way to solve the problem: the government taking more responsibility for controlling prices, better informing consumers, or market competition. Within this context, Congressional members argued whether this entitlement should be age based (i.e., universal) or needs based (i.e., means tested). The central issue being tested under Medicare Part D is whether private health care plans can deliver better care at lower cost than the traditional Medicare program. In addition to Democrat/Republican splits over the bill, a controversial and highly visible conflict revolved around AARP's support of it, which did not reflect the will of 65 percent of its members. Critics of the bill accused AARP, which sells insurance and prescription drugs and receives a commission from corporations for these sales, of selling out to pharmaceutical companies, HMOs, and Republican lawmakers. In response, 85 members of Congress canceled their AARP membership and thousands of AARP members burned their membership cards and jammed the association's phone lines protesting AARP's support of the bill. AARP justified its support by acknowledging that the bill was not perfect, but better than what existed. They also cited polls and focus groups with baby boomers, who are accustomed to employer-sponsored private health care and favored trying private competition with Medicare. Since the bill's passage, AARP has slightly modified its position by lobbying for changes to enable more older adults to qualify for financial assistance and for the government to negotiate drug prices directly as now occurs with the VA (AARP, 2005; Healthcare Financial Management, 2006).

The primary components of the prescription drug legislation implemented in 2006 are:

• The premium for the optional prescription benefit averages $35 a month, although some private plans cost as much as $100 monthly. The Medicare beneficiary is responsible for the first $250 of drug costs each year. After that, Part D covers 75 percent of drug costs up to the first

$2250 in purchases. Although payment of the monthly premium still continues, coverage then stops until the beneficiary has spent $3600 out-of-pocket, or about $5100 total annually. This difference between $2250 and $5100 is known as "the doughnut hole" and has raised concerns in the first year of Part D's implementation, as described below. Above $5100, catastrophic coverage covers 95 percent of the cost. This means that the standard plan covers one-third of the average drug bill of $3160. Medicare beneficiaries may choose to stay in traditional Medicare and obtain drug coverage by paying for a private stand-alone drug insurance policy rather than Part D. But if they decide to join Part D later, they pay an extra percent in premiums for every month since the deadline for enrollment has passed.

Who has benefited from prescription drug reform?

- Private insurance companies that are heavily subsidized by Medicare. In effect, Medicare reform offers an opportunity for free-market advocates to pilot a privatized version of a major entitlement program (Aaron, 2004; Antos and Gokhale, 2005).
- Elders with the resources to enroll in private plans can receive preventive health care through a comprehensive medical examination for new beneficiaries, screening exams for heart disease and diabetes, and coordinated care for those with chronic illnesses.
- Affluent elders are able to buy low-cost, high-deductible health insurance policies and then shelter income from taxes by putting money into private tax-free health savings accounts. The investment is tax deductible and earnings can be withdrawn tax-free as long as the money is used for health expenses, and can be passed on to a surviving spouse. Such health savings accounts are expected to cost the U.S. Treasury $6.4 billion over 10 years (Crenshaw, 2003).

- Although more affluent elders do not benefit in other ways from the prescription drug plan, they typically are able to absorb the additional costs. For the first time in Medicare's history, beneficiaries with annual incomes of more than $80,000 must now pay higher premiums for the part of Medicare that covers doctors' care. The size of their premium increases on a sliding scale, topping out at 80 percent for people with incomes greater than $200,000. In this instance, means testing is applied to the wealthy, not to low-income individuals, and reflects a shift from Medicare's universal nature (Antos and Gokhale, 2005).
- Drug companies are able to maximize profits, since the government cannot negotiate lower drug prices. This means that the problem of the high cost of medications continues under Part D.
- Private health care companies have received incentives of billions of dollars to return to the Medicare HMO market, which is called Medicare Advantage (Moon, 2006).
- Employers who offer health care plans with prescription coverage to their retirees are subsidized by Medicare to encourage them to continue such coverage. Nevertheless, many employers have dropped their prescription drug coverage, leaving some retirees to pay substantially more for prescriptions than before, as illustrated in the box on page 733.
- Low-income elders earning less than $12,123 a year and with less than $6000 in liquid assets benefit by having the premium, deductible, and coverage gap waived. In addition, individuals with income below 150 percent of the poverty level and with limited assets (less than $10,000) are also eligible for premium and cost-sharing subsidies. It is projected that beneficiaries who receive low-income assistance will spend 83 percent less for their drugs than they would have spent prior to Medicare Part D (Kaiser Family Foundation, 2005). On the down side, however, older Medicaid recipients were often unaware that they had been randomly assigned to a plan

and later discovered that some drugs were not covered by the new plan. Still others were unaware of the low-income subsidies available.

To date, Medicare Part D appears to have more negative outcomes and limitations than advantages for the majority of older adults. These include:

• Using income levels to determine access to Medicare benefits is counter to the idea that all beneficiaries earn access by virtue of paying Social Security and Medicare taxes throughout their employed years. This program thus begins to erode Medicare's universal nature. It also represents a shift from a defined benefit to a defined contributions program. With Medicare, one's payroll tax assures defined benefits at age 65, but with Medicare Part D, the nature of the benefit

varies widely, depending on the insurance chosen (Moffitt, 2006; NCOA, 2003).

• Privatization of Medicare's prescription drug coverage erodes its universal and entitlement nature. For example, private health plans through HMOs receive billions in subsidies over 10 years to encourage them to compete with Medicare. Private plans can change premiums and benefits after elders are enrolled, adversely affecting some enrollees.

• The "doughnut hole" in coverage between $2250 and $5100, plus the ongoing deductible and monthly payments make the plan costly for some older adults who can easily spend over $2250 on drugs in any given year. This gap, which was implemented to save the government money, means that some beneficiaries pay their $35 monthly premium while receiving no help until after they have incurred an additional $3600 in drug costs. But only a small proportion of older people require catastrophic care above $5100 on an annual basis. In addition, older adults who join Part D are no longer able to purchase **"Medi-gap" policies** to help cover drug costs created by the $3600 doughnut hole. Up to 24 percent of all Medicare beneficiaries belong to plans with the doughnut hole. Although older adults were informed of this gap in coverage, many elders are shocked at the costs incurred when they reach this gap. Fortunately, low-income elders are protected from this gap. Those whose incomes are below 150 percent of the federal poverty level can apply for subsidies through the Social Security Administration to close the gap (Levin-Epstein, 2006; Song, 2006).

• More than six million low-income elders lost the drug coverage they had under Medicaid, and have had to pay higher co-payments or lose access to particular drugs not covered under Medicare. As a result, some low-income older people actually have less drug coverage than they had through Medicaid.

• The law restricts the importing of less expensive, more readily available generic prescription

---

RISING DRUG COSTS AS A RESULT OF MEDICARE PART D

Under an employer-sponsored drug plan, a couple in their late 70s in Florida paid $40 a month for a powerful cancer medication that was keeping the husband alive. With the passage of Medicare Part D, the husband's former employer canceled their insurance which had paid a flat $40 fee for any medications through the plan's mail order program. This flat fee was replaced by a cost-sharing structure that caused the couple's out-of-pocket spending for drugs to skyrocket to $900 a month for the same medicine.

A 68-year old dialysis patient, who worked multiple low-paying jobs all her life, is struggling with the new co-payments for her medications. The medicines were previously covered by her state's Medicaid program, but now fall under Medicare Part D. Her income of $660 in Social Security benefits each month does not leave room for even the $3 to $5 co-pay she now faces (Shelton, 2006).

drugs from Canada and Mexico, which have been important sources for affordable medications.

• The government is prohibited from using the size of the Medicare program as leverage to negotiate lower drug prices or discounts from drug companies, as it has done effectively through the VA.

• The cost of implementation is higher than initially projected, at $400 billion for 8 years. This dramatically increases Medicare costs and poses additional threats to Medicare's long term solvency.

On January 1, 2006, 3.6 million older adults signed up for Medicare Part D. But its complexity has been a problem for both consumers and providers. In 2006, Medicare was subsidizing almost 3000 different plans with different premiums, co-payments, covered drugs, suppliers, rules for prescribing drugs and delivery schedules in 34 regions, creating a complex bureaucratic maze for older people to navigate. Older adults and their families often cannot determine whether to subscribe to a plan and if so, which one. Efforts to educate consumers, including phone help lines staffed by 4500 operators, were often confusing and, in some instances, conveyed inaccurate information. As a result, health and mental health provider organizations and senior advocacy groups have devoted considerable resources on educating their clients. Computer glitches and database errors often added to confusion and resulted in coverage gaps, especially for low-income elders who were automatically shifted from Medicaid to Part D. Drug expenses have actually increased for a significant portion of older adults. For example, some dually eligible consumers (i.e., those eligible for both Medicare and Medicaid), because of cost-sharing, are paying more than they did under Medicaid. The one day changeover from Medicaid to Medicare Part D also resulted in gaps in coverage, which necessitated that 20 state governments cover drug costs during this time period (Health Care Financial Management, 2006; Kaiser Family Foundation, 2006; Shelton, 2006). Mental health care providers attest to increased costs to them as well as their clients' frustration with the plan, especially since two commonly prescribed antipsychotic drugs are not covered by Part D and it is difficult to be reimbursed for increased dosages. In addition, some older people, especially those who had Medicaid drug coverage prior to Part D, discovered that prescriptions they had been taking were not covered by the new plan and were unaware of the process to appeal this. As a whole, more older adults have seen their out-of-pocket drug expenses rise than those who have seen a decline as a result of Medicare Part D. Overall, it appears that elders with complex illnesses and those requiring relatively expensive medicines, such as cancer drugs, are not benefiting from this program (Alonso-Zaldivar, 2006; Behavioral Healthcare, 2006; Levin-Epstein, 2006; Slaughter, 2006). Despite the numerous problems with implementation, individuals who did not have drug coverage in the past and who are eligible for the low-income subsidy can save money. In addition, the average monthly premium for some is lower than expected at $25 a month (Behavioral Health Care, 2006).

The long-range impact of Part D is unclear, but efforts are underway to modify some of the negative consequences for older adults. Grass-

NEGOTIATING LOWER DRUG PRICES FOR MEDICARE BENEFICIARIES

As an indication of their priority to reforming Medicare Part D, one of the first tasks of the new Democratic majority in 2007 was to propose legislation that would give Medicare the power to bargain with drug manufacturers for lower prescription drug prices. The AARP and the pharmaceutical industry placed full-page ads in the *Washington Post* during the first week of the 110th Congress in efforts to support or fight these efforts.

roots groups have mobilized to try to amend Part D to allow Medicare to negotiate drug discounts and to legalize the purchase of drugs from Canada. One of the first stated projects of the new Democratic-controlled Congress in 2007–2008 was to lower drug costs and closing of the "doughnut hole" under Medicare Part D. In fact, within the first two weeks of the new Congress, the House voted to lower drug costs.

Medicaid

In contrast to Medicare that is specifically for older adults, **Medicaid** is a federal and state means-tested welfare program of medical assistance for the poor, regardless of age (e.g., to recipients of Aid to Families with Dependent Children and SSI). Unlike Medicare, it covers LTC but only for the poor or those who become poor by paying for long-term or medical care, typically by using up their assets. Medicaid also differs from Medicare in that federal funds are administered by each state, which results in considerable variation in the quality and quantity of

services provided. Medicaid accounts for about 41 percent of the nation's $151 billion LTC expenditures (see Figure 17.5). Approximately 44 percent of that spending is on nursing home care, largely because of the nursing home industry's political strength (CMS, 2007; Congressional Budget Office, 2004). Ironically, when Medicaid was enacted, it was never intended to be a major payer of long-term care, especially nursing home care.

Medicaid plays three essential roles related to LTC for older adults:

1. It makes Medicare affordable for low-income beneficiaries by paying Medicare's premiums, deductibles, and other cost-sharing requirements. This is referred to as dual eligibility, and is described on page 737.
2. It pays for medical benefits that Medicare does not cover, such as prescription drugs and LTC.
3. It is the primary public source of financial assistance for LTC in both nursing homes and community-based settings.

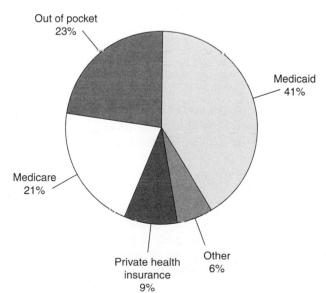

FIGURE 17.5   Spending for Long-Term Care: 2004

SOURCE: Cynthia Smith, Cathy Cowan, Stephen Hettler, and Aaron Caitlin, "National Health Spending in 2004," *Health Affairs 25* (1) (2006) 186–196. Reprinted with permission.

Older persons comprise a small percentage (about 10 percent) of the total users of Medicaid, yet they account for approximately 75 percent of the total expenditures nationally and, on average, 60 percent of state Medicaid budgets (Grogan, 2005). The primary cause of this disproportionate rate of expenditures is that Medicaid is the primary public funding source of LTC expenditures (Applebaum and Straker, 2005; Kitchener et al., 2006; Smith, et al., 2005, 2006). As with Medicare, the growth in expenditures is due primarily to price increases by health providers and fragmented funding mechanisms, not population growth per se or expansion of care. In fact, participation rates in Medicaid are relatively low because of many elders' reluctance to seek help from a "welfare program" or lack of awareness of potential eligibility. Medicaid, like Medicare, provides only 60 to 80 percent of daily care charges. Even though Medicaid is the primary funder of nursing home care, about 30 percent of such care is still paid by individuals out-of-pocket (Applebaum and Straker, 2005; Burwell, Sredle, and Eiken, 2004; Galambos, 2006; Moon, 2006; Schmieding, 2006).

Federal regulations require that all state Medicaid programs provide the following comprehensive services: hospital inpatient care, physician services, skilled nursing facility care, laboratory and X-ray services, home health services, hospital outpatient care, family planning, rural health clinics, and early and periodic screening. In contrast to Medicare, home health care services are a mandatory area of coverage for Medicaid, while personal-care services and home and community-based services are optional. Although Medicare covers skilled nursing care only for patients with rehabilitative potential in nursing homes, Medicaid can cover skilled care for both rehabilitation and intermediate nursing home care of a long-term custodial nature.

Although Medicaid is the second largest budget item for most states (approximately 15 percent of state budgets), states vary widely in their eligibility standards; the types, amount, scope, and duration of services; and reimbursement rates. For example, states may elect to provide coverage for personal care services but are not required to do so. States differ greatly in providing "optional" services, such as intermediate care, prescription drugs outside the hospital, dental services, eyeglasses, and physical therapy. Similar to Medicare, coverage for mental health and social services is limited. Medicaid is a highly visible target for federal and state cost-cutting, because it forms a growing proportion of state budgets while federal Medicaid funds to states have declined in the past decade (Smith et al., 2005). Ways that states have sought to reduce expenditures for both nursing home and home care are discussed below.

Older adults qualify for Medicaid in the following ways:

1. Participation in SSI, which encompasses the provision of Medicaid. Although Medicaid is the principal health insurance provided for the poor and is viewed as a "safety net program," only 33 percent of low-income elders meet these stringent categorical eligibility requirements. Those who do qualify for cash assistance under SSI are provided the broadest coverage under state Medicaid programs, including payment of Medicare cost sharing, premiums, and additional services such as prescription drugs, vision care, and dental care.

POINTS TO PONDER

What is your position on Medicaid "spend down"? Do you think that it unjustly impoverishes older people and their families needing nursing home care? Or do you think that those with assets can hire lawyers to find ways to protect them and still get Medicaid to cover the cost of nursing home care? Reflect on family members or others you know who have used the Medicaid spend down to access nursing home care. What were some of their experiences?

2. Designated as "medically needy" under state-specific rules (e.g., ineligible for cash assistance but in economic distress after paying medical expenses). Older adults who are "medically needy" can exclude their medical and long-term care expenses from income in determining whether they meet specific income limits, and may **spend down** by incurring medical bills that reduce their income and other resources to the necessary level. These income levels are established by each state and therefore differ.

3. Nursing home residents with income and assets below a state-designated cap of 300 percent of the SSI level. Depletion of almost all personal assets can occur prior to nursing home admission, and 33 to 40 percent of nursing home residents are eligible for Medicaid at admission. Of those who pay out of pocket at the time of admission, 66 percent spend down their savings to Medicaid levels, largely because of nursing home costs. Nursing home residents must contribute all of their income except a small personal-needs allowance toward the cost of their nursing home care. On any given day, up to 60 percent of nursing home residents have Medicaid as a payment source (Chen, 2006; Grogan, 2005).

4. Dual eligibility, which means being eligible for both Medicare and Medicaid; this applies to those whose income falls 100 percent below the poverty level and have limited financial assets. Dually eligible beneficiaries are the poorest and sickest elders, have significant ADL limitations, and are the highest users of health care services among Medicaid beneficiaries. They are also less likely to have a partner or any living children, and more likely to live in a nursing home. Known as qualified Medicaid beneficiaries (QMB) or specified low-income Medicaid beneficiaries (SLMB), Medicaid helps them cover Medicare's co-payments and deductibles (e.g., out-of-pocket expenses) and their monthly premium for physician and outpatient coverage. In other words, even though they have too many financial resources to be eligible for full Medicaid benefits, Medicaid pays for what Medicare does not cover, including

nursing home and home care. Not surprisingly, dual eligibles cost the federal government four times what each Medicare-only beneficiary costs (Fortinsky, Fenster, and Judge, 2004; Kaiser Family Foundation, 2004a; Lee, 2006).

Medicaid-Funded Nursing Home Care

As noted above, Medicaid is biased toward institutional care, covering over 44 percent of annual state expenditures on nursing homes (Bishop, 2003; Chen, 2006; Grogan and Patashnik, 2003). Since the federal government has reduced Medicaid funding to the states, states have focused on limiting their Medicaid expenditures, especially for LTC. Because states are required to pay for every Medicaid-eligible person residing in a nursing home, one of the earliest approaches was to control the supply of available openings. A majority of states in the late 1970s imposed certificate of need (CON) restrictions on additional Medicaid-certified beds and placed a moratorium on adding new nursing home beds or facilities. These CON restrictions then resulted in high occupancy rates, which inflated charges and bolstered nursing home profits. As another strategy to control the number of nursing home openings for Medicaid beneficiaries, states have also developed strict preadmission

---

LONG-TERM CARE OMBUDSMAN

The most successful approach to monitoring quality in nursing homes is the long-term care ombudsman. The Older Americans Act requires every state to have an Ombudsman Program, which develops nonregulatory approaches to monitoring care in nursing homes and, in most states, in other long-term care facilities as well. Ombudsmen advocate for residents' rights that are guaranteed under the 1987 federal Nursing Home Reform Act. Residents or their families can call on the ombudsman's office in their state to investigate and resolve complaints about resident rights in the LTC facility where they live. The ombudsman's influence is constrained, however, by limited funding and reliance on volunteers.

screening procedures and tightened the medical and functional eligibility requirements for nursing home admission, thereby limiting the number of Medicaid recipients entering nursing homes. Other approaches to reduce costs have been to:

- set nursing home reimbursement rates (e.g., managed care models of capitated payments), that result in lower payments for Medicaid nursing home residents
- restrict eligibility and utilization of benefits covered (e.g., eliminating prescription drug coverage)
- ration or limit services to those that proved most cost-effective (Gregory and Gibson, 2002).

Given such changes, Medicaid recipients, especially those requiring high levels of care, often have more difficulty finding a nursing home bed—and wait longer to do so—than higher-paying private-pay clients. In fact, some nursing homes do not even accept Medicaid patients and discharge them once their private funding runs out. In addition,

Medicaid is the primary source of public funding for nursing home care.

the mix of high occupancy rates and the comparatively low payment per bed tends to relegate Medicaid patients to substandard facilities; in fact, a relationship exists between residents' socioeconomic status and the quality of care received. Paradoxically, although many nursing homes need Medicaid residents to survive, they have decreased services, especially staffing, in order to maintain a profit, while offering fewer hours of direct care than nursing homes without Medicaid beds (Chen, 2006; GAO, 2002; Smith, 2006).

With the growth of the oldest-old who are most likely to use nursing homes, but lack the resources to pay for it, Medicaid is faced with how to provide coverage for low-income and vulnerable populations at a time of intense pressure to limit public spending. Overall, benefit reductions fail to address rising nursing home costs caused by provider price increases. In addition, efforts to control nursing home costs are difficult because of resistance by nursing home lobbyists. Another consequence of the nursing home industry's strength is Medicaid's limited funding for residential care options, such as assisted living and adult homes, which reduces the options available to low-income older people (Kitchener et al., 2006). On the other hand, as described in both Chapter 11 and more fully below, many states have begun to offer Medicaid waivers that allow qualified elders to use these less costly options.

Medicaid-Funded Home Health Care

As noted earlier, only about 30 percent of Medicaid expenditures go to community-based home health services, even though home health services are generally more cost-effective and preferred by elders and their families. Given elders' preference for home and community-based care, Medicaid's bias toward institutional care is slowly shifting, and spending on home and community-based services is growing more rapidly each year than for nursing homes (over 11 percent versus 6 percent in 2005) (CMS, 2005, 2007).

The *financing of home care services* under Medicaid occurs under three different coverage options:

1. Home health care, typically provided by a Medicaid-certified home health agency
2. Personal care, which are semiskilled or unskilled services provided to Medicaid beneficiaries who need assistance with basic activities of daily living in their own home (typically provided by nonlicensed individuals, these constitute the majority of total spending of home care services under Medicaid)
3. Home and community-based waiver services

Eligibility for Medicaid Home Health Care and Waiver Programs

To receive Medicaid-funded home care services, older adults must:

- meet strict income/asset eligibility criteria
- be medically eligible for nursing home placement
- require more services than just homemaker services

In addition, home care must not cost more than nursing home care (i.e., must be budget neutral). Although states are required to cover home *health* services under the Medicaid program, providing personal care at home is optional. Medicaid funds two options for non-medical home care coverage, the "personal care services" benefit and the Home and Community-based Waiver program. All states provide at least one of these options (Schmieding, 2006).

If a state provides the optional "personal care services" benefit, it must be made available to all Medicaid beneficiaries who meet the criteria for personal care. There cannot be a waiting list, but states can set coverage limits, regardless of need, and they are not required to pay for all of the personal care services that a Medicaid beneficiary might need.

The home and community-based waiver program was first authorized under the 1981 Omnibus Budget Reconciliation Act as a way to prevent or delay nursing home placement. This permits the waiver of Medicaid statutory requirements so that states can provide community-based options by targeting benefits to limited geographic areas and to specific groups and numbers of beneficiaries. The **Medicaid waiver program** specifies seven core services that have not been traditionally considered "medical," but which allow people to remain at home—case management, homemaker, home health aide, personal care, adult day care, rehabilitation, respite care—and other services approved by the federal government as "cost-effective." The primary criterion to qualify for a waiver is that states must demonstrate that the costs of such services are less than care in institutions, and that they serve to divert at-risk individuals from nursing home placement. Because recipients must be low income and qualify for nursing home care, the number of individuals who can use this option is limited (Applebaum and Straker, 2005). In addition, the program's cost-containment goals mean that most states restrict the scope of services and the number of recipients, resulting in waiting lists and continuing levels of unmet needs for low-income elders and adults with disabilities (Burke, Feder, and Van de Water, 2005). Nevertheless, waiver programs in 49 states have increased Medicaid spending for options in community-based long-term care, which have generally reduced unmet needs among participants (Galambos, 2006). Since findings on the cost savings of the waiver programs are mixed, states are focusing on increasing the cost-efficiency of implementing waivers (Mitchell et al., 2006; Wiener et al., 2004).

States vary greatly in implementation of the waiver program. In many states, there is a per diem cap on allowable services and long waiting lists, with children and young adults with developmental disabilities as the primary beneficiaries (Coleman, Fox-Grage, and Folkemer, 2002).

Some states, such as Oregon and Washington, have widely implemented waivers. They have deliberately reduced the number of nursing home beds and have chosen to support LTC options described in Chapter 11, such as in-home care, respite services, adult day care, and residential options such as assisted living, adult foster homes, and adult family homes. Several states have demonstration programs that improve the coordination of LTC with the acute care system, as described in the box on this page (Kitchener et al., 2006; Mollica, 2003). Other states use state funds to augment or create their own separate home care programs; a few fund community-based options through lottery revenues or county levies for long-term care. Aging and Disability Resource Centers are a recent initiative that integrate long term care services through a single coordinated system based on the traditional not-for-profit aging network, which is described in Chapter 16 (AOA, 2005). These centers have been implemented in 44 states. In general, states face the challenge of developing not-for-profit integrated long-term care systems that can compete with for-profit managed care organizations (Mitchell et al., 2006).

Consumer-directed care is a Medicaid waiver program, under the 2002 Independence Plus Initiative, that seeks to provide decision-making autonomy to elders and adults with disabilities. This model posits that consumers (in this case, frail adults and their families) have the right and ability to assess their own needs and determine how to meet them. Consumers take on all worker management tasks, including choosing their personal care attendant, with two exceptions: They do not get a cash allowance to pay the worker directly and they cannot pay their spouse. Within the consumer-directed care approach, **cash and counseling programs** provide consumers with a cash amount that they can use to hire and supervise their own caregivers; this can include family members who are paid for their services. Recipients of Medicaid personal care or home and community-based services receive a monthly cash allowance based on a professional assessment, which ranges from $400 to $1400. The cash allowances received are comparable to the value of services that would be provided through traditional agencies. Controlling their own budget, consumers become employers, choosing to hire (and fire) family or friends as workers; the states

---

INNOVATIONS TO MANAGE HCBS SERVICES EFFICIENTLY

Two states that have efficiently managed home- and community-based services (HCBS) are Arizona and Wisconsin. Arizona has contained LTC costs by consolidating budget control over both HCBS and nursing homes and by using a managed LTC approach with local government, for-profit, and on-profit providers. As a result, Arizona expanded HCBS and reduced nursing home care. Wisconsin's Family Care Program uses aging network-based services through a managed LTC system to provide a broad array of both HCBS and nursing home care in several areas of the state. Both these examples involve for-profit, government, and non-profit partnerships that would have seemed unlikely in the past, but reflect a shared goal of increasing the benefits and reducing the costs of LTC for both providers and older people and their families (Mitchell et al., 2006).

UNDERLYING VALUES AND ASSUMPTIONS OF CONSUMER-DIRECTED CARE

- Adults requiring LTC have a right and ability to make decisions about their care.
- Consumers are experts about their service needs and are capable of managing their own affairs; they have the right to "manage their own risk."
- The dignity of the consumer who needs personal assistance is preserved.
- Choice and control can be introduced into all service delivery systems, including the choice of hiring and firing personal care attendants.
- Consumer-directed care should be available to all persons needing long-term care, regardless of the payer (public or private).

provide bookkeepers to assist with the paper-work. For example, older consumers can decide whether to use funds to make their home more accessible, buy a pair of dentures, pay for over-the-counter medications, or hire a grandson to mow their lawn. Counselors or consultants are available to assist them with decision-making, but the consumer retains control of the final decision. Cash and counseling projects have been funded and implemented by the Kellogg Foundation in Florida, New Jersey, and Arkansas. Preliminary findings are:

- those who received a cash allowance were able to purchase more services to fit their needs than they could under traditional programs;
- nursing home costs were lower;
- Medicaid costs per recipient per month were identical for both the cash and counseling group and a control group;
- being able to hire their own caregivers was associated with satisfaction and quality of life for both the care recipient and caregivers (Cash and Counseling Demonstration and Evaluation Program, 2003; Simon-Rusinowitz et al., 2005; Stone, 2003).

Even when consumers cannot hire their families as caregivers, satisfaction with consumer-directed care was high and needs were met. These programs have also demonstrated better care for frail elders as indicated by fewer bed-sores and fewer emergency visits, as well as greater worker reliability and retention (Dale et al., 2005; Doty, 2004; Foster et al., 2003; Kane, et al., 2004; Kunkel and Nelson, 2005).

With Medicaid waivers and the growth of such alternatives to nursing home care, funding for home and community-based care has increased from 21 percent of LTC expenditures in 1990 to nearly 35 percent today (Burke, Feder, and Van de Water, 2005; Chen, 2006; Coronel, 2004; Eiken, Burwell and Walker, 2005). How-ever, older adults who have too many assets to qualify for Medicaid, but are unable to afford to

purchase private home care, typically lack access to these home-care alternatives (Kane and Kane, 2001; Olson, 2003). Nevertheless, with increas-ing recognition of the quality of care provided by these newer options and with the aging of baby boomers who are likely to reject nursing home care, this pattern of Medicaid and out-of-pocket expenditures may reverse in the future.

Medicaid Spend-Down

Another way to reduce Medicaid costs is to enforce current laws that make it more difficult to qualify. The 1993 Omnibus Budget Reconcilia-tion legislation prohibited the sheltering of assets through trusts during the 5 years prior to an application for Medicaid benefits, and the transfer of assets during the 3 years prior to a Medicaid application. It also mandated estate recovery, forcing states to reclaim Medicaid costs from the estate or property of beneficiaries age 55 and over who lived in nursing homes or received home and community services. States could consider jointly owned property, including homes and bank accounts, as part of the estate, recoverable after the death of the recipient or his or her spouse. Most states have not enforced these estate recov-ery laws and federal Medicaid officials have been reluctant to impose penalties for noncompliance.

This 1993 legislation, referred to as "Send Grandma to Jail," was extremely controversial and, in 1997, the legal burden was shifted to the Medicaid estate planning industry. Some lawyers practicing elder law recommend to relatively afflu-ent older people ways to shelter up to half of a nursing home resident's financial assets from the spend-down requirement, even within the 3-year time period. Elders with resources are able to establish trusts to preserve family estates without compromising their Medicaid eligibility. Congress also passed measures to protect against spousal impoverishment, raising the amount of income the "community spouse" could keep, and retreated from plans that would enforce adult children's financial responsibility for their parents. Through the Medicaid spend-down process, as well as the conversion and transfer of assets prior to a nursing home stay, only about 9 to 15 percent of Medicaid beneficiaries are from middle-class backgrounds (Lee, Kim, and Tanenbaum, 2006). The media, politicians, and senior organizations increasingly frame Medicaid for nursing home care as a social entitlement for all older adults. Yet, unlike Medicare and Social Security, Medicaid is not contributory. That is, program recipients do not have a legal or moral right to long-term care benefits on the basis of tax payments or a lifetime of employment. This extension of benefits to the middle class within the context of a means-tested program intended for low-income persons has been called "universalism without targeting"; i.e., Medicaid-funded benefits are increasingly available in nursing homes for elders based on age, not income. In fact, the difference between Medicare and Medicaid is often blurred by Medicaid extending its reach to the middle class while the universal Medicare program often provides extra benefits to low-income beneficiaries (Grogan, 2005; Grogan and Patashnik, 2003). Nevertheless, as long as the costs of home care, nursing homes, and long-term care insurance continue to rise, this tension between Medicaid as an entitlement program for low-income elders and strategies that middle- and upper-income elders use to qualify for Medicaid are likely to continue. Because the cost to Medicaid of assets transfer is relatively small, it is unlikely that most states will try to "crack down" on this issue, even though Congress in 2007 passed more regulations against sheltering assets (Lee et al., 2006; Quinn, 2007).

Private Supplemental and Long-Term Care Insurance

Although health and LTC systems are based on the assumption that individuals are first responsible for paying for their care, 5 million Americans under age 65 lack insurance for hospital and physician costs (AARP, 2005). A substantially greater number—over 200 million—have no insurance for LTC. Therefore, as noted earlier, about 30 percent of all LTC care expenditures are paid on an out-of-pocket basis (Cramer and Jensen, 2006). Older adults paying out of pocket use a combination of pension income, Social Security benefits, savings and investments, including reverse mortgages which allow them to tap the equity in their homes to pay for care.

Wide disparities exist among elders in their ability to purchase private supplemental and long-term care insurance. For those who can afford more extensive coverage than provided by Medicare Part A and B, private "Medi-gap" supplemental insurance is available to help with the catastrophic costs of intensive care, numerous tests, or extended hospitalization. Such policies also pay for services not covered by Medicare. These include deductibles and co-payments, services such as dental care, eye exams and hearing aids, and charges exceeding the amount approved by Medicare (in excess of Medicare's "allowable" or "reasonable" charges). However, the purchase of such private coverage is not a solution to health costs. Instead, it means that the average spending on health care has increased overall. Since the majority of older people pay fully for this insurance, they effectively still bear the burden of health care costs (AARP, 2005; Herd, 2005). Now, with the passage of Medicare Part D, the purchase of Medi-gap insurance to cover drug costs is no longer an option, although those who had Medi-gap policies may continue them for costs other than medications.

About 75 percent of the older population has purchased some private supplemental insurance, although less than 6 percent of the expenditures for nursing home or home care are paid by private insurance. Of these, about 30 percent were able to obtain coverage through their former place of employment. Higher-income retirees fortunate to have employer-sponsored plans have among the lowest out-of-pocket costs, even though they are heavy users of care

(Moon, 2006; NCPSSM, 2003). This translates into unequal access to private health insurance by higher-income elders or those who have access through employment or unions.

Eleven percent of Medicare's recipients have neither assistance from Medicaid (as dual eligibles) nor supplemental health coverage to help pay for Medicare's coinsurance, deductibles, and uncovered services. Those who have no supplemental coverage are less likely to see a doctor in any given year, less likely to have a usual source of care, and more prone to postpone getting care. For example, 21 percent of beneficiaries who rely on Medicare alone reported delaying care because of cost, but only 5 percent of those with private insurance did so (Gluck and Hanson, 2001). Not surprisingly, those without supplemental insurance are more likely to have low incomes and/or to be in poor health. Only 47 percent of poor or near-poor older persons, who suffer from more chronic illnesses and disability, have private insurance, compared to 87 percent of their higher-income and healthier peers. Less than 18 percent of older persons of color have private coverage, compared to 48 percent of poor older whites. Furthermore, older women, who have a higher incidence of chronic illness, are less likely than men to have access to group health insurance through employment (Chen, 2006). However, even higher income retirees may not have access to employer-sponsored plans, since cost-conscious employers are placing more controls on the use of health care, increasing premiums and co-deductibles, raising the age of eligibility, and changing benefit packages, particularly as a result of Medicare Part D (Moon, 2006).

Those who are able to purchase Medi-gap insurance do not necessarily see a reduction in out-of-pocket expenditures, since they must pay high premiums and the administrative costs of such policies are high. Few Medi-gap policies cover physician charges in excess of Medicare's allowable fees, nor do they ordinarily cover prescriptions in full, dental care, or nursing home care—all services essential to the long-term

well-being of the older population. In addition, most Medi-gap policies lack inflation protection and initial premiums may be raised later. Medi-gap is most useful for reducing potential catastrophic expenses for those who have high costs in a particular year (Moon, 2006). Elders with financial resources must carefully explore options before purchasing Medicare supplemental insurance to avoid scams, despite the 1990 passage of the Medi-gap Fraud and Abuse Prevention Act.

As older adults become more aware of the limits of public funding and pay increasing out-of-pocket costs, a growing number of insurance companies are selling private **long-term care insurance** plans. In 1991, 2.4 million people bought such insurance; by 2002 the number had jumped to 9.2 million (Coronel, 2004; Cramer and Jensen, 2006). Such insurance does not cover all long-term care costs, however. Some policies are written to exclude people with preexisting conditions or illnesses, and contain benefit restrictions that limit access to covered care. The period of coverage is usually only 4 or 5 years, since comprehensive policies for life are very costly. The majority of policies pay a fixed amount for each qualified day in a nursing home (at a range of $150 to $250 a day). Home health and adult day-care services are usually reimbursed at 50 to 80 percent of the selected nursing home benefit and for a set number of years, although coverage for home health has expanded in recent years (Coronel, 2004). The age when a long-term care policy is first purchased is important, because the premium paid rises sharply with the age when it is first purchased, although it remains level once the policy is purchased (Ali, 2005). For example, the average annual premium for a 50-year-old purchaser is approximately $1500, versus $2800 for a 65-year-old purchaser, and over $7000 for a 79-year-old. The high premiums and copayments mean that most LTC insurance policies are beyond the financial reach of up to 20 percent of Americans age 55 to 79 (America's Health Insurance Plans, 2004; Scanlon, 2001; Stone, 2006).

The policies are expensive for two reasons: Most are sold individually and therefore carry high administrative costs, and most are bought by older people whose risk of needing long-term care is great. Not surprisingly, women are less likely than men to be able to afford long-term care insurance, and they spend a higher proportion of their income when they do, reflecting both gaps in coverage and their lower median income. It can also be financially prohibitive for older couples, where each partner must purchase individual coverage (Chen, 2006; Stone, 2006).

The cost of purchasing some LTC services and insurance can be deducted from federal income taxes, but this benefits only those with higher-income levels who can take deductions. Not surprisingly, people who are most likely to purchase and benefit from LTC insurance are those:

- in relatively good health, that is, without serious preexisting chronic conditions
- in their 60s
- with higher income and assets
- with higher educational levels
- with a partner to protect
- without children living nearby, although informal networks have little overall effect on whether one purchases LTC insurance (Cohen, 2003)
- state employees in states that offer private LTC insurance to their workers
- federal employees, since the Office of Congressional Management offers access to such insurance to all federal employees and retirees as well as their parents (Stone, 2006)

Given the restrictions and costs of LTC insurance and widely held misperceptions that Medicare will cover LTC, it is not surprising that only about 4 percent of adult Americans have such insurance. Awareness of options, often more than cost, is a primary factor affecting the purchase of LTC insurance (Cramer and Jensen, 2006; Grogan and Patashnik, 2003; Stone, 2006). The number of LTC insurance

LONG-TERM CARE INSURANCE: TO BUY OR NOT TO BUY?

Even though long-term care insurance has been marketed since 1990, many adults are confused about whether to purchase such a policy. Two articles in the national press on the same day in March 2007 highlight reasons for the confusion. A *New York Times* article documented LTC insurance companies that had denied claims for trivial reasons, asked for information not specified in the insurance policy, sent written responses to outdated addresses, lost or destroyed documents, and set up numerous bureaucratic obstacles for policy holders. A daughter of an older woman who had moved to an assisted living facility after 24 hospitalizations and on physician's orders called an insurance company over 100 times in a two year time period to try to secure benefits for her mother. The insurance company claimed her mother "was not sick enough," even though her mother needed assistance with ADLs and insulin shots and suffered severe memory problems. Meanwhile, the family business had to be sold to pay for her mother's care, who eventually went onto Medicaid. While the *New York Times* documented numerous instances of unethical behavior, Jane Bryant Quinn, highly regarded financial writer for *Newsweek,* was encouraging adults to purchase LTC insurance and avoid "gaming the Medicaid system" by using lawyers to shelter assets. She concludes that LTC insurance is expensive, but it can "save your marriage and your peace of mind." With such conflicting information in two widely read publications, it is not surprising that individual sales of LTC insurance have fallen since 2000 (Duhigg, 2007; Quinn, 2007, p. 81).

beneficiaries will grow in the future with workplace education to encourage planning for LTC among employees, baby boomers' greater purchasing power, states' tax incentives for the purchase of such insurance, growing benefits for state employees, and younger policyholders who want to guarantee their lifestyle in old age by protecting their retirement assets. Nevertheless, private LTC insurance is likely to remain a relatively small market (Cohen, 2003; Cramer and Jensen, 2006; Yakoboski, 2002).

Resultant Inequities

Because public funding is biased toward nursing home and acute care, and private policies are beyond the financial reach of low-income elders, a *two-tier system of health and long-term care delivery* has resulted: one for those with private health insurance or the means to pay for expensive medical treatment, and another for those forced to rely on Medicaid or Veterans' Assistance, often times entailing long waits for services, or to do without health care insurance altogether.

Disparities exist even among Medicare recipients. Older people who have Medicare only, many of whom may be near-poor, tend to have fewer doctor visits and hospital stays, and buy fewer prescription medications than those who can afford cost-sharing provisions and other private insurance. In fact, low-income Medicare beneficiaries are nearly twice as likely to delay seeking health care as those with private or Medicaid coverage to supplement Medicare. Not surprisingly, the proportion of income spent on health care increases as income decreases (Lee, 2006). Out-of-pocket expenditures are highest for those in poor health, without Medicaid or supplemental insurance, and for low-income women who are not eligible for Medicaid (GAO, 2003). This pattern means that many moderate-income older adults who are admitted to nursing homes incur catastrophic financial expenses prior to admission.

Medicaid also perpetuates class inequities. In fact, less than 50 percent of all low-income Medicare beneficiaries benefit from Medicaid's financial protection. Inequities are intensified for elders of color who generally underutilize services that could enhance their health. Even in programs designed for the poor, such as Medicaid, elders of color are represented far less than their reported objective needs indicate. Such low participation levels are attributed to lack of awareness and understanding of Medicaid, complex enrollment processes, limited governmental outreach, and some elders' reluctance to apply for help from a welfare-linked program. A 2006 ruling that Medicaid applicants must be able to prove citizenship by means other than signing a declaration presents another barrier to immigrant and low-income populations, many of whom do not have a passport, certificate of naturalization, or birth certificate. While federal officials sought to reduce costs with this reform, most states contend that noncitizens are not a significant drain on the Medicaid program and that the new law will result in more uninsured elders using hospitals and clinics. Fortunately, some providers are recognizing the need for targeted outreach to underserved populations.

Another barrier is physicians who refuse to take Medicaid patients, especially those with a high level of need. This occurs because Medicaid reimbursement rates are generally below prevailing cost levels. Physicians who accept Medicaid patients typically limit them to a relatively small proportion of their patient load. As noted above, Medicaid patients also must wait longer for nursing home placement than do private-pay patients. These burdens fall disproportionately on older women and ethnic minorities. Another inequity is experienced by approximately 40 percent of the older population with incomes that are too high to be eligible for Medicaid, but insufficient to pay out of pocket for LTC. These middle- and lower-income individuals often receive inadequate care or must depend solely on families (Gardner and Zodikoff, 2003).

Health and Long-Term Care Reforms

Given these gaps, national reform in health and LTC is widely debated and is likely to be intensified under the Democratic majority in the 100th Congress (2007–2008). Such debates are often polarized between those advocating private-sector strategies and those who look to the public sector or some combination of public and private coverage. In some respects, the debates are not new, but rather more visible. In fact, since 1912, there have been several efforts to create a program of access to health care for all Americans. Yet the United States remains the only industrialized nation that does not provide some form of universal health coverage, regardless of ability to pay. Under the Clinton Administration (1993–2001), health care reform

---

HISTORY AND STATUS OF NATIONAL LONG-TERM CARE LEGISLATION

- **1988:** The first comprehensive LTC legislation was introduced by the late Florida Representative Claude Pepper, who linked an initiative to fund LTC in the home to the ill-fated catastrophic health care legislation.
- **1990:** The Pepper Commission recommended public funding of home, community, and nursing home care for seriously disabled Americans.
- **1992:** The Democratic leadership in the House and the Senate introduced bills for LTC known as the Long Term Care Family Security Act.
- **1992:** Bill Clinton was the first presidential candidate to call for expanded public funding for home care services provided on a non–means-tested basis.
- **1990–1994:** The National Committee to Preserve Social Security and Medicare and the Leadership Council of Aging Organizations proposed universal and comprehensive LTC plans for all people with disabilities; this encompassed institutional, home- and community-based care, and personal assistance.
- **1993:** President Clinton's National Health Security Act offered new LTC benefits and set forth the principles of universal access, comprehensive health care benefits, and high-quality care, but was not passed.
- **2000:** The Long-Term Care Security Act enables federal employees to purchase LTC insurance at group rates.
- **2007:** Older adults who purchase LTC insurance are able to use their payment premiums as tax deductions.

---

moved from academic debates to the legislative process, but ended in gridlock, without even modest changes in insurance industry practices. What ultimately killed national health care reform was the disproportionate influence of powerful special-interest lobbies, particularly insurance companies and small businesses that sought to protect their financial interests. In spite of escalating costs, growing numbers of uninsured citizens, and restrictive insurance policies, attempts to change the health care system are blocked by the federal government's goals of cost containment and the philosophy of individual choice versus guaranteeing access to all. Although the majority of Americans believe that government should guarantee adequate health care for all, they are generally satisfied with their own care. Public ambivalence is expressed further by people's overall unwillingness to accept government interference and any restriction of their own choice of doctors or hospitals, even if doing so would reduce health care costs or make universal coverage possible.

Health Maintenance Organizations (HMOs)

As noted earlier, the 1997 Balanced Budget Act created managed care options for older people under Medicare Plus Choice. Managed care refers to a health plan in which Medicare beneficiaries receive care from a network of providers employed by, or under contract to, an HMO. In this system, health care costs are covered and health care is provided through a prepaid premium. This means that a single payment per user covers all preapproved services, rather than fee for service. Because consumers pay on a capitated basis, HMOs offer a package of services intended to overcome the access barriers of fragmented funding. As private plans, Medicare HMOs are able to limit paperwork on claims forms and typically offer broader services such as prevention, education, eyeglasses, hearing aids, health promotion, and prescription drug coverage in addition to a traditional Medicare benefits package.

Most plans initially offer these benefits for no additional premiums and limit co-payments. However, enrollees have a limited choice of doctors, hospitals, and service providers. HMOs appear to be more effective at delivering preventive services, whereas traditional Medicare is better in other aspects of care related to access, responsiveness, and flexibility. On the other hand, findings are mixed whether HMOs have reduced racial disparities in accessing preventive care (Landon et al., 2004; Lin et al., 2005; Trivedi et al., 2005).

While HMOs have been able to negotiate lower prices from health providers, they assume the risk of providing the full range of Medicare-covered services in return for a fixed payment that approximates 95 percent of the costs for similar enrollees in fee-for-service systems. As a result, most HMOs try to avoid enrolling elders with illnesses that are ongoing and expensive to treat, and typically serve primarily younger, healthier populations (Olson, 2003; Rice et al., 2002). On the other hand, as these younger beneficiaries age, they may stay with the HMO so that their health status will not be a primary factor in choosing a health insurance plan, but their costs to the HMO will be higher (Jensen and Morrisey, 2004).

Although about 14 percent of Medicare beneficiaries initially enrolled in managed care plans, this number has declined (Barry and Kline, 2002). This is because an increasing number of managed care plans no longer accept Medicare coverage and have severely reduced their service areas, cut benefits, or avoided high-risk patients. To reduce costs, some HMOs have shortened hospital stays, set upper limits on the number of home care visits and rehabilitative services provided, steadily increased out-of-pocket beneficiary costs, and canceled or placed caps on special benefits that initially attracted beneficiaries (e.g., coverage of prescription drugs, eyeglasses, and hearing aids). This has resulted in a troubling pattern of declines in quality of care, reduced services, terminated plans, and dropped beneficiaries. In other cases, elders have chosen to withdraw (Barry and Kline, 2002; Montgomery et al., 2004). Those who are still enrolled are adversely affected by higher out-of-pocket costs (Cardin, 2003; Moon, 2005).

Because HMOs are a capitated system and thus charge a fixed fee per beneficiary, costs to Medicare are presumed to be more predictable. Yet findings are mixed on whether Medicare expenditures have decreased under HMOs. After controlling for factors such as health status, some studies find that the costs of HMO enrollment for Medicare are actually *higher* than through Medicare per se. This is because Medicare only "saves" 5 percent on each HMO participant, since the capitated rate is set at 95 percent of the

HMOs with a health promotion orientation offer exercise programs as a benefit.

expected expenditure level. HMO Medicare enrollment is associated with reduced health care utilization (e.g., hospital length of stay), but this may result from HMO beneficiaries being healthier than the average older adult. This means HMOs may selectively attract and contract with enrollees who are healthier than average, or have fewer propensities to use health services, and thus lower than expected costs. As a result, HMOs may skim off enrollees who would never have cost Medicare the estimated expenditure level even if they had remained in the regular fee-for-service part of Medicare. Furthermore, HMOs have healthier inpatients and shorter lengths of stay, but more costly per-day utilization. Therefore, HMOs do not represent a major Medicare savings, and managed care does not necessarily deliver promised cost savings nor reduce the regulatory burden on government (Revere, Large, and Langland-Orban, 2004). A greater concern is that chronically ill elders within HMOs may be denied benefits and access to care. While the effects on quality of care are unclear, critics fear that incentives to reduce costs are greater than incentives to improve quality (Berenson and Dowd, 2002). Consumers in HMOs are less satisfied with the quality of care and physicians' skills than those utilizing the fee-for-service system. But they are more satisfied with their out-of-pocket expenses being reduced because of their HMO membership (Pourat, Kaqawa-Singer, and Wallace, 2006). Regulatory procedures to ensure quality care in HMOs are needed, especially in light of the financial incentives for managed care plans under the 2003 prescription drug bill.

The 2003 Medicare Modernization Act (MMA) (also known as Prescription Drug Reform) funded **Medicare Advantage,** where enrollees agree to get all their coverage from a private insurance plan, typically an HMO, which receives a per capita payment from Medicare, rather than from a mix of Medicare reimbursement for services and private supplemental coverage. To increase the number of beneficiaries, the MMA increased federal payments to these private plans. This resulted in more older adults subscribing to Medicare Advantage. Medicare Part D promotes Medicare Advantage by offering additional monies to entice new insurers to participate and new beneficiaries to enroll in them. This is likely to allow private plans to provide more generous benefits, since private plan enrollees tend to be healthier than Medicare-only beneficiaries. The very sick, who are less likely to be accepted by private insurers, will not receive such expanded benefits through Medicare only. Overpaying private plans is justified as a way to generate savings for Medicare over time, but raises concern about the private sector's ability to offer cost-effective care (Moon, 2006).

Social Health Maintenance Organizations (SHMOs) and Other Innovative Programs

As noted throughout this chapter, there is increasing policy interest in bringing the acute-care and long-term care sectors together into a single integrated system. Some of the best known of these initiatives are **Social Health Maintenance Organizations (SHMOs),** On Lok, and the Program for All-inclusive Care for the Elderly (PACE). SHMOs were demonstration projects initiated by the federal government.

As prepaid health plans, SHMOs provided an extra payment to a Medicare HMO acute care plan to offer long-term services to voluntarily enrolled Medicare beneficiaries. They offered all Medicare benefits, as well as home and community-based care, prescription drugs, and case management to support beneficiaries' social needs. SHMOs tested whether comprehensive health services, with social services linking acute and chronic care under an integrated financing scheme within a managed care setting, could be provided at a cost that does not exceed Medicare and Medicaid expenditures; improve care; and reduce nursing home placement. In other words, they examined the relative cost-effectiveness of a capitated payment system that includes chronic and extended benefits and medical services.

SHMOs faced ongoing difficulties in controlling and coordinating acute and chronic care (Wallace et al., 2001). In fact, a 2001 CMS report identified few significant improvements in terms of utilization, health status, and functional ability. They recommended that the SHMO demonstration be phased out, which has occurred with the exception of one system in Nevada (Leutz et al., 2003).

Another model tested in a wide range of communities is the **On Lok** model of social care, which was first implemented in San Francisco's China Town, and means "peaceful happy abode" in Cantonese. On Lok aims to integrate a full continuum of acute and chronic care into one agency, thereby preventing nursing home placement of frail elders certified as needing a nursing home level of care. As a capitated system, On Lok is paid a flat amount for each person served, similar to the way that HMOs are paid. A comprehensive day health program is integrated with home care, including nursing, social work, meals, transportation, personal care, homemaker, and respite care. The On Lok model was shown to be effective at serving low-income and elders of color in their communities and has been replicated to varying degrees nationwide, often through the **Program for the All-inclusive Care for the Elderly (PACE).**

Similar to On Lok, PACE focuses on coordinating care for frail adults age 55 and older (120–300 per site) who are eligible for nursing home placement. Income is not an eligibility criterion. The average PACE participant is 80 years old, female, and has 7.9 medical conditions (Center for Medicare Education, 2001). In effect, PACE is built around the adult day health model described in Chapter 11, that combines primary care with long-term care. Now in over 70 sites nationwide, it has nearly 20 years of experience in integrating medical, home-based, and community-based care to keep enrollees in the community. "One-door access" is provided to a comprehensive care package of preventive, acute, and LTC services, and adults may keep their own doctor. PACE programs

must provide basic Medicare and Medicaid services, but have flexibility to use less typical interventions, including activities such as fishing trips and drama groups as well as educational or preventive activities. It also tries to address root causes of health care problems. For example, a Medicare beneficiary shows up at the emergency room on a monthly basis to be treated for skin infections due to flea bites. Rather than just treat the bites, the PACE team may decide to fumigate her home and provide a flea dip for her dog (Center for Medicare Education, 2001; Mui, 2001). Interdisciplinary teams of physicians, nurses, social workers, aides, therapists, and even van drivers are central to coordinating care through adult day health centers and case management at predetermined reimbursement rates. To date, evaluations of both On Lok and PACE reveal shorter and fewer days of hospitalizations, cost savings to Medicare and Medicaid, and success in integrating the delivery of acute and long-term care across both the Medicare and Medicaid programs. Despite its success, PACE has reached only a small proportion of Medicare beneficiaries (about 11,000), partially because of a low rate of referral and high start-up costs for the provider organization. Some of the early PACE demonstrations have achieved permanent provider status, but most elders, their families, and health care providers are unaware of the PACE model as a way to control costs and integrate quality services (Center for Medicare Education, 2001; Fortinsky et al., 2004; Robert, 2003).

States and providers are also attempting to integrate acute and LTC, especially for the population that is "dual eligible" for both Medicare and Medicaid. Some are experimenting with innovative financing and service delivery of acute and LTC for older people on Medicaid and younger people with disabilities. For example, the Minnesota Senior Health Options program offers acute and LTC services on a voluntary basis. Plans pay for community-based care, case management for high-risk patients, up to 180 days of nursing home costs, and financial incentives to minimize nursing home use and encourage early nursing home discharge. However, gaps in care are unlikely to be filled by the states' share of Medicaid and by programs funded entirely by states (Stone, 2006). In addition, some providers are creating integrated service systems, in part for altruistic reasons and in part for market incentives. Hospitals are integrating vertically—buying nursing homes, rehabilitation centers, and home health agencies—in an effort to become all-purpose providers in the community. Skilled nursing facilities and, to some extent, home health agencies are integrating horizontally—building alliances with hospitals, physicians groups, assisted-living developers, and other community-based providers. New models of managed care for nursing home residents are also emerging. Aiming to reduce hospitalization rates of nursing home residents, the Ever Care program enrolls residents in a risk-based HMO, with nursing home costs covered by Medicaid or private insurance. It is distinguished by a team of geriatricians and nurse practitioners who provide primary care services that are coordinated with LTC services provided by nurses and nurses' assistants. To date, savings from shorter hospital stays have been realized (Lynch, Estes, and Hernandez, 2003; Stone, 2006). While these and a range of other state managed programs attempt to integrate care and reduce costs, only a small proportion of older persons currently participate in such options (Applebaum and Straker, 2005; McGeehan, 2005).

Unfortunately, several barriers make service integration and quality care difficult to achieve:

- lack of a national long-term care policy or system
- fragmentation of financing systems of Medicare and Medicaid, with few incentives to integrate them
- inadequate risk adjustment methods to ensure that payments will cover the costs of the most disabled
- varying eligibility requirements and coverage rules that impede the development of a rational plan of care

- high start-up costs for the provider organization that aims to integrate services
- fear of financial risk on the part of providers involved in integrating acute and LTC
- lack of communication between acute and LTC providers, along with limited information and training to manage an array of services
- no recognized authority for managing care across time, place, and profession
- absence of management information systems and outcomes-based patient data bases that span time and place
- problems with quality in both nursing home and home and community-based care, where the emphasis is on structural and process indicators of quality (Applebaum et al., 2004; GAO, 2002, 2003; Stone, 2006).

Some agreement is emerging about the major components of an ideal long-term care system, but, as noted above, the national political will to achieve it does not exist. These components include:

- integrated administration and financing, such as flexible funding streams with incentives to integrate dollars and minimize cost-shifting
- adoption of mechanisms that can effectively integrate care (e.g., care planning protocols, easy access at a single point of entry, uniform client needs assessment, interdisciplinary care teams, and integrated information systems)
- broad and flexible benefits, including supports for caregivers
- far-reaching delivery systems that encompass home and community-based care, care management, social services, supportive housing and transportation, and overarching quality control systems with a single point of accountability (Stone, 2006).

A few states, such as Minnesota and Wisconsin, have developed a consumer-friendly single entry point approach to LTC that encompasses many of these components. Accessible information and assistance is at the core of this model to assure service coordination, efficient assessment and screening, consumer choice, support for informal caregivers, and a strong social infrastructure of nonmedical services such as accessible, affordable housing, transportation, and other home and community-based services. A designated "gatekeeper" or advocate is responsible for providing information, application assistance, and help navigating the maze of programs and services. Every region of the state must conduct a "service readiness assessment" to determine services gaps, and to implement innovative programs such as telemedicine, telehealth and telehomecare to reduce barriers (Healthcare Association of New York State, 2005).

Clearly, health care has shifted from a system oriented toward acute care, independent providers, and fee-for-service insurance to one that is focused on managing chronic care. Because of market changes and the growth of managed care and private insurance options, these patterns of consolidation and cost savings will continue at the local level. While the increased privatization of Medicare may not be reversible, a realistic approach is to implement and evaluate innovations in both private plans and traditional Medicare, with the latter remaining the primary insurance for older people (Moon, 2006). As noted throughout this chapter, the current dichotomy between LTC and acute care is not functional for either older persons or care providers, since LTC is a health crisis for which virtually every American is uninsured. From the perspective of older people, an ideal system would be a national health plan that integrates preventive, acute, hospital, ambulatory, community-based, and home care to ensure continuity of care across the life course regardless of income. In the short run, however, legislation at the federal level will be focused on ways to reduce Medicare and Medicaid

expenditures, delegating more financing responsibility to states, and funding demonstration projects that encompass care coordination, outcomes research, chronic disease management, and prevention.

Implications for the Future

Long-term care is characterized by the lack of a comprehensive policy, resulting in fragmentation, segmentation, and often bitter debates among advocates for various services. Past changes have focused on short-term fixes and responding to fiscal and regulatory concerns, particularly those of providers. Without dramatic changes in how LTC is delivered, costs will continue to escalate for the individual and for society as a whole.

Although concerns about LTC costs are widespread, there are many unresolved issues regarding potential solutions. Currently, the prospects for a comprehensive health and long-term care reform bill that guarantees universal access along with cost containment are low, even though 2008 presidential candidates are emphasizing the need for health care reform. As noted in Chapter 16, the economy and political factors profoundly shape public policy. The sluggish economy early in this century, the federal and state emphasis on cost containment, and the growing federal deficit due to tax cuts and the Iraq war suggest that cost-cutting of programs, especially Medicaid, and subsidies for private market solutions to address long-term care are likely to dominate the national agenda. The implementation of Medicare Part D represents a profound shift toward privatization and means testing of what had been a universal program based on age. Such reduced governmental responsibility and increasing reliance on private sector solutions could shift in the future as political parties and the economy change.

Although the future of long-term care is difficult to predict because of political and economic shifts and rapid changes in health care, we do know that the following factors will continue to shape the need for LTC:

- the growing numbers of older adults who rely on family caregivers for the majority of care
- the preference of elders for home and community-based care
- baby boomers' desires for choice and having more say about health care for themselves and their older relatives
- the increasing number of Iraqi war veterans with serious disabilities and need for long-term care
- the human tendency to avoid planning for potential disability or frailty, thus denying the need for LTC and the purchase of LTC insurance
- the importance of culturally competent LTC models that reduce racial and economic disparities across the life course
- the need for publicly funded, comprehensive, coordinated, and accessible in-home and community-based supportive services
- nursing homes taking on more rehabilitation and short-term skilled nursing responsibilities after hospitalization rather than LTC
- the emphasis on ambulatory care rather than hospitalization for acute conditions and the growth of managed care
- the use of technology as a way to provide information to consumers and to provide medical care to underserved areas
- the shortage of health care professionals trained in geriatrics
- the shortage of direct care staff, such as certified nursing assistants and home care aides
- the LTC industry as a major employer of low-income people, who increasingly are immigrants and often have cultural and language differences with the elders under their care.

As noted in Chapter 4, the growing number of older adults surviving with multiple chronic conditions requires health care providers trained in gerontology and clinical geriatrics. These specialists need the knowledge and skills to understand and manage the health needs of elders who live in long-term care facilities along with those who receive community-based LTC services. Geriatricians, nurses and nurse practitioners, pharmacists, social workers, dentists, physical therapists, and occupational therapists who can work with elders requiring LTC will be in even greater demand as baby boomers reach their 80s. The shortage of geriatric specialists in these health professions, estimated to be only 25 percent the number needed in 2030, will place significant demands on available providers. This projected shortage of geriatric specialists, especially those with long-term care experience, may also place frail elders at greatest risk if their chronic conditions are not effectively managed in the community, and hospitalization is required.

Given these contextual factors, the need for public/private partnerships for LTC insurance, service delivery, and accountability is critical. However, partisan debates about the role of government versus the marketplace and private sector; the modes of service delivery; and societal responsibility toward vulnerable low-income elders suggest that incremental compromises are the most we can expect in the near future.

Summary

The growing health and LTC expenditures by both federal and state governments and by older people and their families are a source of concern for most Americans. Escalating hospital and physician costs have placed enormous pressures on Medicare—the financing mechanism through which almost half of the funds for the older population's acute care flows. The government's primary response to these

Medicare costs has been cost-containment, especially through diagnostic-related groupings (DRGs), financial incentives for shortening the hospital stays of Medicare patients, greater deductibles and co-payments, and cuts in Medicare funding. Efforts have also been made to provide more choices for Medicare recipients, including managed care or HMO options. For most older adults, Medicare fails to provide adequate protection against the costs of home- and community-based care. In fact, changes in Medicare funding have affected the availability of nonprofit home care agencies. They have also meant that more older persons and their families have either had to pay privately for home care or do without. As a rapidly growing portion of the federal budget, Medicare is under intense scrutiny. The prescription drug bill that was fully implemented in January 2006 attempts to address the problem of rising prescription drug costs, but has already been fraught with problems.

Medicare is the major payment source of hospital and physician care for older adults, but it is almost absent from nursing home financing. The reverse applies to Medicaid, however. The largest portion of the Medicaid dollar goes to services needed by older persons, but not covered by Medicare—nursing home, home and personal care. However, as Medicaid has been increasingly subject to cost-cutting measures at the state level, benefits have been reduced. For example, copayments for health care services have increased as a way to reduce Medicaid spending, but this cost is borne disproportionately by low-income elders. Another disadvantage for Medicaid recipients is that most nursing homes and doctors limit the number of Medicaid recipients they will accept. Although waivers by the federal government have allowed state funding of some community-based alternatives, Medicaid remains biased toward nursing home care. Title XX and Older Americans Act home care programs have relatively flat funding levels and limited impact. Given the gaps in public funding for long-term care, private insurers are offering LTC insurance options, but these are beyond the financial reach of most older adults. These health and long-term care needs will be a major issue debated by the U.S. Congress in the coming years.

GLOSSARY

capitated payments   payments for services based on a predetermined amount per person per day rather than fees for services

cash and counseling programs   funded by the Robert Wood Johnson Foundation, older adults in three states receive a cash payment to purchase services and products they need to remain at home

Centers for Medicare and Medicaid Services (CMS)   the federal agency that administers the Medicare and Medicaid programs; prior to 2001, known as the Health Care Financing Administration (HCFA)

consumer-directed care   under Medicaid waiver system, older adults can hire personal care attendants, including family members (except for spouses)

diagnostic related groupings (DRGs)   Medicare payments are fixed prior to admission to hospital or home care, based on diagnostic category, medical condition, and expected length of stay

health maintenance organizations (HMOs)   health plans that combine coverage of health care costs and delivery of health care for a prepaid premium, with members typically receiving services from providers employed by or under contract to the HMO

Interim Payment System (IPS)   sets stringent caps on cost per home health visit and per beneficiary

long-term care insurance   private insurance designed to cover the costs of institutional and sometimes home-based service for people with chronic illness and disabilities

managed care   policies under which patients are provided health care services under the supervision of a single professional, usually a physician

Medicaid   a federal and state means-tested program of medical assistance for the categorically needy, regardless of age

Medicaid waiver program   allows states to provide home care services to elders at risk of nursing home placement "outside" of Medicaid regulations; must be budget neutral

medical savings accounts   proposed Medicare program that will allow beneficiaries to carry private "catastrophic" insurance for serious illness and pay routine costs from a special account

Medicare   the social insurance program, part of the Social Security Act of 1965, intended to provide financial protection against the cost of hospital and physician care for people age 65 and over

Medicare Advantage and **Medicare Plus Choice**   beneficiaries can choose between traditional Medicare and a Choice Plan that includes HMOs

Medicare Part D   prescription drug reform legislation; older adults pay for private insurance plan to cover medications; also known as the Medicare Modernization Act

"Medi-gap" policies   private supplemental insurance to help with the catastrophic costs of intensive care, numerous tests, or extended hospitalization

On Lok   a comprehensive program of health and social services provided to very frail older adults, first started in San Francisco, with the goal of preventing or delaying nursing home placement

Program for All-inclusive Care for the Elderly (PACE)   federal demonstration program that replicated On Lok's integrated services to attempt to prevent nursing home placement

parity   mental health services covered by Medicare at the same rate as health care services for physical disorders

preferred provider organizations (PPOs)   networks of independent physicians, hospitals, and other health care providers who contract with an insurance entity to provide care at discounted rates

prospective payment system (PPS)   a system of reimbursing hospitals and physicians based on the diagnostic category of the patient rather than fees for each service provided, as applied to inpatient services; includes DRGs

social health maintenance organizations (SHMOs)   prepaid health plans that provided both acute and long-term care to voluntarily enrolled Medicare beneficiaries; only one program is now funded

spend down   to use up assets for personal needs, especially health care, in order to become qualified for Medicaid

RESOURCES

Log on to MySocKit (www.mysockit.com) for information about the following:

- American Association for Home Care
- American Health Care Association
- American Medical Directors Association
- Centers for Disease Control and Prevention
- Center for Medicare and Medicaid Services (CMS) (formerly HCFA)
- Committee to Preserve Social Security and Medicare
- Families USA
- Henry J. Kaiser Family Foundation
- MetLife Foundation
- MetLife Mature Market Institute
- National Association of Directors of Nursing in Long Term Care
- National Association of Local Long-term Care Ombudsman Program
- National Association of Professional Geriatric Care Managers
- National Citizen's Coalition for Nursing Home Reform
- National Council on the Aging

REFERENCES

Aaron, H.J. Medicare: The good, the bad and the ugly. *The Washington Spectator*, 2004, 30.

Administration on Aging (AOA). CMS seek to expand network of one-stop resource centers. *Older Americans Report*, 2005, *29*, 137–138.

Ali, N.S. Long-term care insurance: Buy it or not! *Geriatric Nursing*, 2005, *26*, 237–240.

Alonso-Zaldivar, R. Medicare drug plan is scoring. *The Seattle Times*, March 7, 2006, p. 1.

American Association of Retired Persons (AARP). *Reimagining America: AARP's blueprint for the future.* Washington, DC: author, 2005.

America's Health Insurance Plan. *Research findings: Long-term care insurance in 2002*. Washington, DC: America's Health Insurance Plans, 2004.

Anonymous. Medicare Part D: Early experiences. *Behavioral Health Care,* June 2006, *26,* 43.

Antos, J., and Gokhale, J. Medicare prescription drugs: Medical necessity meets fiscal insanity. *Cato Institute Briefing Papers,* 2005, 91.

Applebaum, R., Schneider, B., Kunkel, S., and Davis, S. *A guide to quality in consumer-directed services.* Oxford, OH: Scripps Gerontology Center, Miami University, 2004.

Applebaum, R., and Straker, J. Long-term care challenges for an aging America. *Public Policy and Aging Report,* 2005, *15,* 1, 3.

Barrett, L.L., and Roper, A. *Costs of long-term care: Public perceptions vs. reality.* Washington, DC: AARP, 2001.

Barry, C.L., and Kline, J. *Medicare managed care: Medicare + choice at five years.* New York: Commonwealth Fund, 2002.

Berenson, R.A., and Dowd, R.E. *Future of private plan contracting in Medicare.* Washington, DC: Public Policy Institute, AARP, 2002.

Berenson, R.A., and Horvath, J. Confronting the barriers to chronic care management in Medicare. *Health Affairs,* 2003, *22,* W337–W353.

Berkman, B., Gardner, D., Zodikoff, B., and Harootyan, L. Social work in health care with older adults: Future challenges. *Families in Society,* 2005, *86,* 329 337.

Bishop, C. Long-term care needs of elders and persons with disability. In D. Bluementhal, M. Moon, M. Warshawksky, and C. Boccuti (Eds.), *Long-term care and Medicare policy: Can we improve the continuity of care?* Washington, DC: National Academy of Social Insurance, 2003.

Burke, S., Feder, J., and Van de Water, P.N. (Eds.). *Developing a better long-term care policy: A vision and strategy for America's future.* Washington, DC: National Academy of Social Insurance, 2005.

Burwell, B., Sredle, K., and Eiken, S. *Medicaid and long-term care expenditures in FY 2003.* Cambridge, MA: The METSTAT Group 2004.

Caitlin, A., Cowan, C., Heffler, S., and Washington, B. National health spending in 2005: The slowdown continues, *Health Affairs,* 2007, *26,* 142–153.

Cardin, B. National policy-makers on long-term care policy. In D. Bluementhal, M. Moon, M. Warshawksky, and C. Boccuti (Eds.), *Long-term care and Medicare policy: Can we improve the continuity of care?* Washington, DC: National Academy of Social Insurance, 2003.

Cash and Counseling Demonstration and Evaluation Program. Boston: Boston College Graduate School of Social Work, 2003.

Center for Medicare Education. The PACE model. *Issue Brief,* 2001, *3,* 1–8.

Centers for Medicaid and Medicare Services (CMS). *Medicare Program Rate Stats, 2006.* Accessed January 18, 2007, from http://www.cms.hhs.gov/MedicareProgramRatesStats/downloads/MedicareMedicaid Sumamries2006.pdf

Centers for Medicaid and Medicare Service (CMS). *National Health Expenditures Data, 2005,* accessed January 18, 2007, from http://www.cms.hhs.gove/NationalHealthExpendituresData/downloads/proj2005.pdf.

Chen, L.M. Policies affecting long-term care and long-term care institutions. In B. Berkman (Ed.). *Handbook of social work in health and aging.* New York: Oxford, 2006.

Cohen, M.A. Private long-term care insurance: A look ahead. *Journal of Aging and Health,* 2003, *15,* 74–98.

Coleman, B., Fox-Grage, W., and Folkemer, D. *State long-term care systems* (2nd. ed.). Washington, DC: AARP Public Policy Institute, 2002.

Coleman, E., and Berenson, R. Lost in transition: Challenges and opportunities for improving the quality of transitional care. *Annals of Internal Medicine,* 2004, *141,* 533–536.

Congressional Budget Office. *Financing long-term care for the elderly.* Washington, DC: Congressional Budget Office, 2004.

Coronel, S. 2004. *Long-term care insurance in 2002.* Washington, DC: America's Health Insurance Plans, 2004.

Cramer, A. and Jensen, G., Why don't people buy long-term care insurance? *The Journals of Gerontology,* 2006, *61B,* S185–S193.

Crenshaw, A.B. Medicare bill could spur changes in worker benefits. From the *Washington Post* and printed in *The Seattle Times,* November 28, 2003, D1.

Dale, S., Brown, R., Phillips, B., and Carlson, B. How do hired workers fare under consumer-directed personal care? *The Gerontologist*, 2005, 45, 583–592.

Davis, K. Making health care affordable for all Americans. Testimony before the Senate committee on Health, Education, Labor and Pensions, January 18, 2004. Accessed January 15, 2005, from http:// www .cmwf.org/usr/_doc/davis_senatehelptestimony_ 714.pdf.

Department of Health and Human Services (DHHS). *The future supply of long-term care workers in relation to the aging of the baby boom generation.* Report to Congress. Washington, DC: 2003.

Doty, P. *Consumer-directed home care: Effects on family caregivers. Policy brief.* San Francisco: Family Caregiver Alliance, 2004.

Duhigg, C. Aged, frail and denied care by their insurers. *The New York Times*, March 26, 2007.

Eiken, S., Burwell, B., and Walker, E. *Medicaid HCBS waiver expenditures FY 1999 through FY 2004.* Medstat, 2005.

Feder, J., Komisar, H.L., and Niefeld, M. The financing and organization of health care. In R. Binstock and L.K. George (Eds.), *Handbook of aging and the social sciences* (5th ed.). San Diego: Academic Press, 2001.

Federal Interagency Forum on Aging and Related Statistics. *Older Americans 2006: Key indicators of well-being.* Hyattsville, MD: Federal Interagency Forum on Aging and Related Statistics, 2006.

Fortinsky, R., Fenster, J., and Judge, J. Medicare and Medicaid home health and Medicaid waiver services for dually eligible older adults: Risk factors for use and correlates of expenditures. *The Gerontologist*, 2004, 44, 739–749.

Foster, L., Brown, R., Phillips, B., Schore, J., and Carlson, B. Improving the quality of Medicaid personal assistance through consumer direction. *Health Affairs*, 2003.

Galambos, C. Policies affecting health, mental health and caregiving: Medicaid. In B. Berkman, (Ed.), *Handbook of social work in health and aging.* New York: Oxford, 2006.

Gardner, D., and Zodikoff, B. Meeting the challenges of social work practice in health care and aging in the 21st century. In B. Berkman and L. Harootyan (Eds.), *Social work and health care in an aging society.* New York: Springer, 2003.

Gaumer, G.L., Poggio, E.L., Coelen, C.G., Sennett, C.S., and Schmitz, R.J. Effects of state prospective reimbursement programs on hospital mortality. *Medical Care*, 1989, 27, 724–736.

General Accounting Office (GAO). *Medicare home health agencies: Weaknesses in federal and state oversight mask potential quality issues.* Washington, DC: US Government Printing Office, 2002.

General Accounting Office (GAO). *Nursing home quality: Prevalence of serious problems, while declining, reinforces importance of enhanced oversight.* Washington, DC: US Government Printing Office, 2003.

Gluck, M., and Hanson, K. *Medicare chartbook.* Washington, DC: The Henry J. Kaiser Family Foundation, 2001.

Gonzales, T.I. An empirical study of economies of scope in home healthcare. *Health Services Research*, 1997, 32, 313–324.

Goulding, M. Trends in prescribed medicine use and spending by older Americans. U.S. Department of Health and Human Services, Centers for Disease Control and Prevention, *Trends in Health and Aging*, 2005, 5, 1–20.

Gregory, S.R., and Gibson, M.J. *Across the states: Profiles of long-term care* (5th ed.). Washington, DC: Public Policy Institute, 2002.

Grogan, C. M. The politics of aging within Medicaid. In R. Hudson, *The new politics of old age policy.* Baltimore: Johns Hopkins University Press, 2005.

Grogan, C.M., and Patashnik, E.M. Universalism within targeting: Nursing home care, the middle class and the politics of the Medicaid program. *Social Service Review*, 2003, 77, 51–71.

Healthcare Association of New York State. Point of entry. *Long-Term Care Reform Series*, Issues Brief #1, 2005.

Healthcare Financial Management. To address Medicare Part D confusion, states take matters into their own hands. *News Watch*, March 2006, 16–17.

Herd, P. Crediting care or marriage: Reforming Social Security family benefits. *Journals of Gerontology*, 2006, 61B, S24-S34

Herd, P. Universalism without the targeting: Privatizing the old-age welfare state. *The Gerontologist*, 2005, 45, 292–298.

Hughes, S.C., Ulasevich, A., Weaver, F., Henderson, W., Manheim, L., Kubal, J., and Bonango, F. Impact of home care on hospital days: A meta analysis. *Health Services Research*, 1997, *32*, 416–431.

Jensen, G., and Morrisey, M. Are healthier older adults choosing managed care? *The Gerontologist*, 2004, *44*, 85–94.

Kaiser Commission on Medicaid and the Uninsured. *The uninsured and their access to health care.* Washington, DC: author, 2003.

Kaiser Family Foundation. *Kaiser Commission on Medicaid Facts: Dual eligible. Medicaid's role for low income Medicare beneficiaries,* Washington, DC: author, 2004a.

Kaiser Family Foundation, *Medicare Chartbook: Financing Medicare,* Washington, DC: author, 2004b.

Kaiser Family Foundation. *Medicare: Low income assistance under the Medicare drug benefit. Fact Sheet,* Washington, DC: author, 2005.

Kaiser Family Foundation. *Medicare: Tracking prescription drug coverage under Medicare; Five ways to look at the new enrollment numbers.* Accessed February 2006, from http://kff.org/medicare/upload/7466.pdf.

Kane, R.L., Flood, S., Bershadsky, B., and Keckhafer, G. Effect of an innovative Medicare managed care program on the quality of care for nursing home residents. *The Gerontologist*, 2004, *44*, 95–103.

Kane, R.L., and Kane, R.A. Emerging issues in chronic care. In R. Binstock and L.K. George (Eds.), *Handbook of aging and the social sciences* (5th ed.). San Diego: Academic Press, 2001.

Kitchener, M., Hernandez, M. Ng, T., and Harrington, C. Residential care provisions in Medicaid home and community-based waivers: A national study of program trends. *The Gerontologist*, 2006, *46*, 165–172.

Kitchener, M., Ng, T., Miller, N., and Harrington, C. Medicaid home and community-based service waivers: A national survey of eligibility criteria, caps, and waiting lists. *Home Health Care Services Quarterly*, 2004, *23*, 55–69.

Kunkel, S., and Nelson, I., Consumer direction: Changing the landscape of long-term care. *Public Policy and Aging Report*, 2005, *15*, 13–16.

Landon, B., Zaslavsky, M., Bernard, S., Coffey, E., and Cleary, P. Comparison of performance of traditional Medicare vs. Medicare managed care. *Journal of the American Medical Association,* 2004, *291*, 1744–1752.

Lee, J. Policies affecting health, mental health and caregiving: Medicare. In B. Berkman (Ed.), *Handbook of social work in health and aging.* New York: Oxford, 2006.

Lee, J., Kim, H., and Tanenbaum, S. Medicaid and family wealth transfer. *The Gerontologist*, 2006, *46*, 6–13.

Leutz, W., Frod, T., Leung, M., Mueller, M., Nonnenkamp, L., et al. Medicare manged care and frail elders: Lessons from social HMOs. *Care Management Journals*, 2003, *4*, 161–169.

Levin-Epstein, M. A trouble beginning for Part D. *Behavioral Healthcare*, April 2006, *26*, 4.

Lin, C., Musa, D., Silverman, M., and Degenholtz, H. Do managed care plans reduce racial disparities in preventive care? *Journal of Health Care for the Poor and Underserved.* 2005, *16*, 139–151.

Lynch, M., Estes, C., and Hernandez, M. Chronic care initiatives: What we have learned and implications for the Medicare program. In D. Bluementhal, M. Moon, M. Warshawksky, and C. Boccuti (Eds.), *Long-term care and Medicare policy: Can we improve the continuity of care?* Washington, DC: National Academy of Social Insurance, 2003.

McCall, N., and Korb, J. *The impact of Medicare home health policy changes on Medicare beneficiaries.* Princeton, NJ: Robert Wood Johnson Foundation, Home Care Research Initiative, 2003.

McGeehan, S. *The role of case management in integrated models of care.* Oxford, Ohio: Miami University. Unpublished master's thesis, 2005.

Medicare Rights Center. *Medicare private plan overpayments: An anti-competitive practice that hurts Medicare.* Washington, DC: author, 2004.

MedPac. *A data book: Health care spending and the Medicare program.* Washington, DC: Medicare Payment Advisory Commission, 2004.

Mitchell, G., Salmon, J., Polivka, L., and Soberon-Ferrer, H., The relative benefits and cost of Medicaid home- and community-based services in Florida, *The Gerontologist*, 2006, *46*, 483–494.

Moffitt, R.E. *The President's modest Medicare budget proposal.* Accessed February 8, 2006, from http://www.heritage.org/Research/HealthCare.

Mollica, R. Coordinating services across the continuum of health, housing, and supportive services. *Journal of Aging and Health,* 2003, *15,* 165–188.

Montgomery, J., Irish, J., Wilson, I., Chang, H., Li, A., et al. Primary care experiences of Medicare beneficiaries, 1998 to 2000. *Journal of General Internal Medicine,* 2004, *19,* 991–998.

Moon, M. Organization and financing of health care. In R. Binstock and L. George (Ed.), *Handbook of aging and the social sciences* (6th ed.). New York: Academic Press, 2006.

Moon, M. Sustaining Medicare as an age-related program. In R. Hudson (Ed.), *The new politics of old age policy.* Baltimore: Johns Hopkins University Press, 2005.

Moon, M., and Herd, P. *A place at the table.* New York: The Century Foundation, 2002.

Mui, A. The Program of All-Inclusive Care for the Elderly (PACE): An innovative long-term care model in the United States. *Journal of Aging and Social Policy,* 2001, *13,* 533–567.

National Committee to Preserve Social Security and Medicare (NCPSSM). *Congress warned on changes needed to Medicare Rx Bill for support of key senior groups.* Letter submitted to the House and Senate, July 16, 2003.

National Council on Aging (NCOA). *NCOA supports Medicare bill with reservations.* Press release, November 21, 2003.

Olson, L.K. *The not so golden years: Caregiving, the frail elderly and the long-term care establishment.* Lantham, MD: Rowman and Littlefield, 2003.

Peng, T.R., Navaie-Waliser, M., and Feldman, P.H. Social support, home health service use, and outcomes among four racial-ethnic groups. *The Gerontologist,* 2003, *43,* 503–513.

Pourat, N., Kaqawa-Singer, M., and Wallace, S. Are managed care Medicare beneficiaries with chronic conditions satisfied with their care? *Journal of Aging and Health,* 2006, *18,* 70–90.

Quinn, J.B. How to pay for old-age care. *Newsweek,* March 26, 2007.

Revere, L., Large, J., and Langland-Orban, B. A comparison of inpatient severity, average length of stay and cost for traditional fee-for-service Medicare and Medicare HMOs in Florida.

Health Care Management Review, 2004, *29,* 320–329.

Rice, T., and Desmond, K. *An analysis of reforming Medicare through a premium support plan.* New York: Henry J. Kaiser Foundation, 2002.

Rice, T., Snyder, R.E., Kominski, G., and Pourat, N. Who switches from Medigap to Medicare HMOs? *Health Services Research,* 2002, *37,* 273–290.

Safran, D.G., Neuman, T., Schoen, C., Kitchman, M.S. et al. *Prescription drug coverage and seniors: Findings from a 2003 national survey.* Accessed November 26, 2006, from http://cmwf.org/publications/publication.

Sager, M.A., Easterling, D.U., Kindig, D.A., and Anderson, O.W. Changes in the location of death after passage of Medicare's prospective payment system. *New England Journal of Medicine,* 1989, *320,* 433–439.

Sakauye, K., Blank, K., Cohen, C., Cohen, G., Kennedey, G. et al. Medicare managed mental health care: A looming crisis. *Psychiatric Services,* 2005, *56,* 795–797.

Sambamoorthi, U., Shea, D., and Crystal, S. Total and out of pocket expenditures for prescription drugs among older persons. *The Gerontologist,* 2003, *43,* 345–359.

Scanlon, W. *Long-term care: Baby boom generation increases the challenge of financing needed services.* Testimony before the U.S. Senate Committee on Finance, Washington, DC, 2001.

Schmieding, L. *Caregiving in America.* New York: International Longevity Center and Schmeiding Center for Senior Health and Education of Northwest Arkansas, 2006.

Schoen, C., and Cooper, B.S. *Medicare's future: Current picture, trends, and prescription drug policy debate.* New York: The Commonwealth Fund, 2003.

Seperson, S. B. Demographics about aging. In S. B. Seperson and C. Hegeman (Eds.), *Elder care and service learning: A handbook.* Westport, CT: Auburn House, 2002.

Shelton, R. Florida faces shortage of physicians. *Orlando Sentinel,* October 3, 2006.

Shelton, R. Medicare drug plan benefits some; others fall through cracks. *The Seattle Times,* February 2, 2006, A3.

Simon-Rusinowitz, L., Mahoney, K., Loughlin, D., and Sadler, M.D. Paying family caregivers: An effective policy option in the Arkansas Cash and Counseling Demonstration and Evaluation. In R.K. Caputo (Ed.), *Challenges of aging on U.S. families: Policy and practice implications.* New York: Haworth, 2005.

Slaughter, L. Medicare Part D: The product of a broken process. *New England Journal of Medicine,* 2006, *354,* 2314–2315.

Smith, G. *In search of quality care: Low-income seniors left behind.* Seattle, WA: Northwest Federation of Community Organizations, 2006.

Smith, C., Cowan, C., Heffler, S., and Caitlin, A. National health spending in 2004. *Health Affairs,* 2006, *25,* 186–196.

Smith, G., Cowan, C., Sensenig, A., and Catlin, A. Health spending growth slows in 2003. *Health Affairs,* 2005, *24,* 185–194.

Smith, G., Cowan, C., Heffler, S., Catlin, A. National health spending in 2004. *Health Affairs,* 2006, *25,* 186–196.

Song, K.M Drug-plan gap trips up many older Americans. *The Seattle Times,* August 20, 2006, 1.

Spector, W. Cohen, J., and Pesis-Katzh, I. Home care before and after the balanced budget act of 1997: Shifts in financing and services. *The Gerontologist,* 2004, *44,* 39–47.

Stone, R. Emerging issues in long-term care. In R. Binstock and L. George (Ed.), *Handbook of aging and the social sciences* (6th ed.), New York: Academic Press, 2006.

Stone, R. *Long-term care for the elderly with disabilities: Current policy, emerging trends and implications for the twenty-first century.* New York: The Milbank Memorial Fund, 2000.

Stone, R.L., Dawson, S.L., and Harahan, S. *Why workforce development should be part of the long-term care quality debate.* Washington, DC: Institute for the Future of Aging Services, American Association of Homes and Services for the Aging, 2003.

Trivedi, A., Zaslavsky, A., Schneider, E., and Ayanian, J. Trends in the quality of care and racial disparities in Medicare managed care. *New England Journal of Medicine,* 2005, *353,* 692–700.

U.S. General Accounting Office (GAO). *Medicare: Cost-sharing policies problematic for beneficiaries and program.* Statement of W.J. Scanlon, Director of Health Care Issues. Washington, DC: U.S. Government Printing Office, 2001.

Wallace, S.P., Abel, E., Stefanowicz, P., and Pourat, N. Long-term care and the elderly population. In R. Anderson, T.H. Rice and G.F. Kominski (Eds.), *Changing the U.S. health care system: Key issues in-health services, policy and management.* New York: Jossey-Bass, 2001.

Weissert, W.G. Medicare Rx: Just a few of the reasons why it was so difficult to pass. *Public Policy and Aging Report,* 2003, *13,* 3–6.

Wiener, J., Brown, D., Gage, Bff. Khatusky, G. Moore, A. et al. *Home and community-based services: A synthesis of the literature.* Waltham, MA: RTI International, 2004.

Woolridge, J. *Social Health Maintenance Organizations: Transition into Medicare + Choice.* Contract 500-96-005 (2), submitted to the Health Care Financing Administration. Washington, DC: 2001.

Yakoboski, P.J Understanding the motivations of long-term care insurance owners: The importance of retirement planning. *Benefits Quarterly,* 2002, *18,* 16–21.

Photo Credits

INDEX

Note: *Italic* page numbers indicate where terms are defined.

761